WITHDRAWN BY THE
UNIVERSITY OF MICHIGAN

Programming Business Applications with

Microsoft® Visual Basic
Version 5.0

Programming Business Applications with

Microsoft® Visual Basic
Version 5.0

William E. Burrows
University of Washington

Joseph D. Langford
brilligware.com, inc.

Boston   Burr Ridge, IL   Dubuque, IA   Madison, WI   New York   San Francisco   St. Louis
Bangkok   Bogotá   Caracas   Lisbon   London   Madrid
Mexico City   Milan   New Delhi   Seoul   Singapore   Sydney   Taipei   Toronto

Irwin/McGraw-Hill
A Division of The **McGraw·Hill** Companies

Programming Business Applications with Microsoft Visual Basic: Version 5.0

Copyright © 1998 by The McGraw-Hill Companies, Inc. All rights reserved. Printed in the United States of America. Except as permitted under the United States Copyright Act of 1976, no part of this publication may be reproduced or distributed in any form or by any means, or stored in a database or retrieval system, without the prior written permission of the publisher.

This book is printed on acid-free paper.

1 2 3 4 5 6 7 8 9 0   VNH   VNH   9 0 9 8

ISBN 0–07–012143-5

Sponsoring editor: Rhonda Sands
Editorial coordinator: Carrie Berkshire
Production supervisor: Rich DeVitto
Project manager: Robert A. Preskill
Compositor: Cecelia G. Morales
Printer and binder: Von Hoffman Press, Inc.

Library of Congress Cataloging-in-Publication Data

Burrows, William E.
　　Programming business applications with Microsoft Visual Basic / William E. Burrows, Joseph D. Langford.
　　　　p.　cm.
　　Includes index.
　　ISBN 0-07-012143-5 (acid-free paper)
　　1. Microsoft Visual Basic for Windows.　2. BASIC (Computer program language)　3. Business—Computer programs.　I. Langford, Joseph D.　II. Title
HF5548.5.B3B86　1998
005.2'768—dc21　　　　　　　　　　　　　　　　　　　　　　　　97-50038
　　　　　　　　　　　　　　　　　　　　　　　　　　　　　　　　　　CIP

Information has been obtained by The McGraw-Hill Companies, Inc., from sources believed to be reliable. However, because of the possibility of human or mechanical error by our sources, The McGraw-Hill Companies, Inc., or others, The McGraw-Hill Companies, Inc., does not guarantee the accuracy, adequacy, or completeness of any information and is not responsible for any errors or omissions or the results obtained from use of such information.

http://www.mhhe.com

contents

Preface xi

CHAPTER ONE

Programs, Business Applications, and Visual Basic 1

1.1 Programs 2
1.2 Business Applications 3
1.3 What Is Visual Basic? 7
1.4 Creating Applications 11
1.5 How This Book Is Organized 14

CHAPTER TWO

Visual Basic Projects: Project Structure and VB's Programming Tools 17

2.1 From New Project to Finished Application 18
2.2 VB Project Structure 20
2.3 Overview of Controls 23
2.4 The Command Button Control 24
2.5 The Label Control 26
2.6 The Timer Control 27
2.7 The VB Environment 29
2.8 Project 1: How an Event-Driven Program Works 45
2.9 Files, Saving, and Printing 51
2.10 Project 2: Project Design Considerations 55
2.11 Project 3: A Business Simulation 63

Chapter Summary 69
Key Terms 70
End-of-Chapter Problems 71
Programming Problems 71

CHAPTER THREE

Representing Data: Constants and Variables 77

3.1 Two Kinds of Data 78
3.2 Constants 80
3.3 Variables 85
  Example 3.1: Simple Assignment Statements 94
  Example 3.2: Using Variables to Store Intermediate Results and to Reduce Redundant Data 103
  Example 3.3: Typographical Errors in Variable Names 107
3.4 The Form Control 110
3.5 Project 4: Using Multiple Forms 114

3.6 Variable Scope   119
Example 3.4: Local Variables   119
Example 3.5: Module-Level Variables   121
Example 3.6: Hidden Module-Level Variables   122
Example 3.7: Global Variables   125

3.7 Variable Lifetime   130
Example 3.8: Lifetime of Local Variables   130
Example 3.9: Lifetime of Module-Level Variables   132
Example 3.10: Static Variables   132

3.8 Constant Scope   133

3.9 Project 5: A Simple Payroll Application   133

Chapter Summary   139
Key Terms   141
End-of-Chapter Problems   141
Programming Problems   143

CHAPTER FOUR

Performing Calculations and Manipulating Data: Expressions   145

4.1 Using Expressions, Operators, and Functions in VB Statements   146

4.2 Simple Input and Output   152
Example 4.1: Using the InputBox() Function   153
Example 4.2: Using the MsgBox Statement   156

4.3 Arithmetic Expressions   158
Example 4.3: Using Cyclic Sequences   161
Example 4.4: Generating Random Numbers   163
Example 4.5: Overflow   164
Example 4.6: Roundoff   165
Example 4.7: Significant Digits   166
Example 4.8: Converting Strings to Numbers   167

4.4 String Expressions   169
Example 4.9: Using String Concatenation   169
Example 4.10: Using the Format$() Function   171
Example 4.11: Trimming Spaces   172
Example 4.12: Manipulating Names   174
Example 4.13: Using Carriage Return and Line Feed   176
Example 4.14: Using Multiple-Line Messages and vbCrLf   176
Example 4.15: Using Simple Encryption   177

4.5 The Text Box Control   179
Example 4.16: The Text Box's Text Property   180
Example 4.17: The Change Event   182

4.6 Project 6: A Present Value Calculator   183

4.7 Logical Expressions   187
Example 4.18: True and False   189
Example 4.19: Assignment versus Equality Comparison   189
Example 4.20: Type Mismatch   190
Example 4.21: Using Logical Operators   193
Example 4.22: Using the IIf() Function   196

4.8 Project 7: A Stock Trading Simulation   196

Chapter Summary 203
Key Terms 205
End-of-Chapter Problems 205
Programming Problems 206

CHAPTER FIVE — Specifying Alternate Courses of Action: Selection Statements 211

5.1 The Decision-Making Process 212

5.2 The If…Then…Else Statement 213
Example 5.1: Using the If…Then…Else Statement 214
Example 5.2: Using the If…Then Statement 219

5.3 Nested If Statements 222
Example 5.3: Using Shortcut Syntax for Embedded If Statements 224
Example 5.4: Using Embedded If Statements 226

5.4 The MsgBox() Function 227
Example 5.5: Using the MsgBox() Function 228

5.5 The Option Button Control 229
Example 5.6: Using Option Buttons 232

5.6 The Frame Control 234
Example 5.7: Using the Option Button's Click Event 236

5.7 The Check Box Control 238
Example 5.8: Using Check Boxes 239

5.8 Project 8: A Simple Expert System 240

5.9 The Select Case Statement 246
Example 5.9: Using the Select Case Statement 247

5.10 The Exit Sub Statement 251

5.11 Project 9: An Inventory Replenishment Simulation 254

Chapter Summary 260
Key Terms 261
End-of-Chapter Problems 261
Programming Problems 263

CHAPTER SIX — Reducing Program Complexity: General Sub Procedures and Programmer-Defined Functions 267

6.1 General Sub Procedures 269
Example 6.1: Public versus Private Procedures and Multiple Forms 278
Example 6.2: Using a Public General Sub Procedure 279

6.2 Procedures with Parameters 283

6.3 Programmer-Defined Functions 305
Example 6.3: Using a Programmer-Defined Function 307

6.4 Code Modules 309

6.5 The KeyPress Event 310
Example 6.4: Allowing Backspaces 313

6.6 The GotFocus and LostFocus Events 315
Example 6.5: Access Keys and Focus 316

6.7 Modal versus Modeless Forms 317
Example 6.6: Using Modeless Forms 317
Example 6.7: Using Modal Forms 318

6.8 Project 10: User Authorization   319

Chapter Summary   326
Key Terms   327
End-of-Chapter Problems   327
Programming Problems   328

CHAPTER SEVEN

Repeating Processing Tasks: Loop Structures   331

7.1 The Do…Loop Structure   332
  Example 7.1: Using a Do…Loop   333
  Example 7.2: Using a Do While…Loop   334
  Example 7.3: Order of Statements within a Loop   337
  Example 7.4: Using Immediate Termination   337
  Example 7.5: Using Do…Loop While   339
  Example 7.6: Initialization and Termination   342
  Example 7.7: Correcting Example 7.6   343

7.2 The For…Next Loop Structure   344
  Example 7.8: Using a For…Next Loop   345
  Example 7.9: Encryption   349
  Example 7.10: Using a Step Amount   350
  Example 7.11: Using Negative Step Amounts   351
  Example 7.12: For…Next Initializations   352
  Example 7.13: Changing the Counter Variable   353

7.3 Exit Do and Exit For   354
  Example 7.14: Using Exit For   354

7.4 Nested Loops   354
  Example 7.15: Using Nested Loops   356

7.5 The List Box and Combo Box Controls   357
  Example 7.16: Using Methods with the List Box Control   360
  Example 7.17: Using the DblClick Event   361
  Example 7.18: Entering List Box Items   362
  Example 7.19: Loops and List Boxes   363
  Example 7.20: Decryption   364
  Example 7.21: Multiple Selections   364
  Example 7.22: Using the Combo Box   368

7.6 Project 11: Monthly Payment Schedule Application   369

Chapter Summary   371
Key Terms   372
End-of-Chapter Problems   373
Programming Problems   374

CHAPTER EIGHT

Accessing Business Data: Processing Databases   379

8.1 A Database Primer   380

8.2 The Data Control   387
  Example 8.1: Bound Controls   389
  Example 8.2: Programming the Data Control   394
  Example 8.3: Finding Specific Records   403

8.3 VB's SQL Select Query   405

8.4 The FlexGrid Control   412
   Example 8.4: Using the FlexGrid Control   413
   Example 8.5: Using the FlexGrid's Click Event   415
   Example 8.6: Using the FlexGrid and Loops   416

8.5 The FlexGrid Control and Recordsets   419

8.6 The DBGrid Control   423
   Example 8.7: Using the DBGrid Control with a Single Table   425
   Example 8.8: Using the DBGrid Control with an SQL Query   427

8.7 Project 12: Real Estate Listings Database Application   427

Chapter Summary   433
Key Terms   435
End-of-Chapter Problems   435
Programming Problems   436

CHAPTER NINE

Handling Lists of Data: Arrays   443

9.1 Solving Problems with Arrays   444

9.2 Declaring Arrays   450

9.3 Applications of Arrays   453
   Example 9.1: Populating an Array via User Input   453
   Example 9.2: Populating an Array via Another Array   454
   Example 9.3: Populating an Array via Database Tables   455
   Example 9.4: Performing a Bubble Sort   468

9.4 Dynamic Arrays   472

9.5 Control Arrays   474
   Example 9.5: Creating Synchronized Control Arrays   477
   Example 9.6: Creating Controls at Run Time   479

9.6 Project 13: Order Entry Application Prototype   480

Chapter Summary   488
Key Terms   489
End-of-Chapter Problems   490
Programming Problems   491

CHAPTER TEN

Representing Entities with Data and Behavior: Programmer-Defined Types and Object Classes   495

10.1 Defining and Using Your Own Data Types   496
   Example 10.1: Using Programmer-Defined Types   498

10.2 Programmer-Defined Types and Arrays   501

10.3 Project 14: Student Grade Reporting   504

10.4 Programmer-Defined Classes and Object-Oriented Programming   508
   Example 10.2: Using Objects   521
   Example 10.3: Working with Similar Classes and Class Hierarchies   523
   Example 10.4: Using Collections   527

10.5 ActiveX Controls   531

Chapter Summary   547
Key Terms   549
End-of-Chapter Problems   549
Programming Problems   551

APPENDIX A	Debugging 555
APPENDIX B	The Menu Control 570
APPENDIX C	The Image and Picture Box Controls 579
APPENDIX D	Using Microsoft Access to Create a Database 586
APPENDIX E	File Processing 590
APPENDIX F	The Common Dialog Control and Error Handling 609
APPENDIX G	The Tabbed Dialog Control 623
APPENDIX H	Additional Projects 632
APPENDIX I	Answers to Selected Exercises 641

Index 663

preface

Business use of Microsoft Visual Basic (VB) has grown rapidly over the last few years, for reasons that we outline in Chapter 1. VB is also an excellent tool for learning to program, because

- its programming language is rigorously designed, and has the basic functionality of any serious programming language
- it provides tools to streamline the process of creating and maintaining applications
- it makes it easy to create powerful, attractive graphical user interfaces (GUIs)
- it's fun!

VB is a relative newcomer to the programming world, and much of its structure represents fundamentally new ways of programming. In particular, VB is based on an approach known as *event-driven programming*.

Most of the lessons which were important in traditional programming are still important in event-driven programming. However, the most effective ways of presenting these lessons are different. This text is designed to teach modern programming from the ground up.

Requirements for the Student

This book is founded on a few assumptions about the background of the student, and his or her access to hardware and software.

First, it assumes that the student has never programmed before. Students with previous programming experience can work through the first five chapters at an accelerated pace. Second, it assumes that the student is familiar with Microsoft Windows. Those who are not can probably learn Windows, while progressing through this text, by studying any of the many guides to Windows. Third, the student should have access to a microcomputer with Windows and VB 5.0.

Finally, access to the World Wide Web (WWW) is helpful, though not necessary. The student can browse the website for this book to

- download files which are useful throughout the text,
- pick up pointers on features of VB not covered in the text, and
- find answers to common questions about VB.

The content of this website and how to access it are discussed later in this preface.

Traditional Lessons Retained

Over the years the software development community has learned many lessons about good and bad programming practices. These lessons are difficult and costly to learn "on the job," so a good programming text should attempt to convey these lessons as well as a healthy respect for their implications.

The topics included in this text were chosen with a goal of providing thorough coverage of programming fundamentals and sound practices. We emphasize readability and maintainability at all times. For example, we introduce and employ:

- an application development process, with user requirements, design, and construction phases,
- programming conventions, such as naming, indenting, and requiring variable declarations,
- data types, variable scope, procedure scope, and so forth.

We provide numerous examples with accompanying discussions, to demonstrate and probe the issues underlying programming practices and strategies. The examples are provided in ready-to-use form as a set of VB project files, so that the student can easily run, modify, and experiment with them.

As a result of our emphasis on fundamentals, our coverage of features particular to VB is less broad than it might otherwise be. However, given a solid background in the fundamentals, the student can discover and master additional VB features relatively easily. One of the things for which we use this book's website is to introduce VB features not covered in the text.

The New Approach

Programming in VB differs from traditional programming in three major ways: the programs one creates with VB are event-driven; VB makes it easy to obtain data from relational databases; and VB has an object orientation, with significant support for object-oriented programming.

Event-Driven Programming

Events are signals generated within the computing environment that indicate something has happened to which the computer should respond. Some events are generated by actions of the user, such as clicking on a button or clicking on a menu item. The timing and sequence of these events is determined by the user. This contrasts with traditional, "procedural" programming, in which the programmer explicitly codes the sequence of processing steps.

Most user-generated events are easy to understand and the program's response to them is obvious. Some user-generated events are rather subtle, such as moving the mouse pointer over a certain area on the screen. Events can also be generated by the computer itself. An example of this is an error generated by the system when a program tries to access a database but encounters a problem.

Regardless of how an event is generated, the programmer has the option of writing program code (instructions) to respond to the event. For example, the programmer may write code which saves a file on disk when the user clicks on the Save command in the File menu.

To create an event-driven program, the programmer first designs the GUI and anticipates both user- and system-generated events. The programmer then creates the graphical objects (buttons, menus, etc.) and writes code that causes the system to respond appropriately to each event.

Use of Databases

We introduce database processing in Chapter 8. This chapter begins with a database overview designed to introduce the student to entities and relations and how these concepts are modeled using relational databases. The chapter then presents the details of using VB to access data from Microsoft Access databases, including how to compose SQL queries to combine data from several database tables.

We feel that it is important to expose students to database processing because of the way VB is used in organizations. VB is frequently used in the real-world to develop "front-ends" to databases.

In a closely related consideration, we chose to place the discussion of more traditional file processing (text, sequential, and random access files) in Appendix E. Instructors who choose to cover these concepts can assign reading of this appendix in addition to or in place of database concepts covered in Chapter 8.

We also delayed the presentation of arrays until near the end of the text (after databases). There were two reasons for this. First, it was hard to think of a way to motivate array processing unless we could get some interesting data into the arrays. The traditional approach in BASIC (the Data statement) is seldom used in practice and does not even exist in VB. Loading the data into an array from a database is the way it's done today. Second, and again we hated to admit this, the importance of arrays is not as high as it used to be (although arrays are still important). Controls such as List boxes and Grids now do much of the work the programmer used to have to perform with arrays. By simply creating a List box and setting its "Sorted" property to True, one produces an ordered list that can be searched just like a traditional array. So, we delayed the discussion of arrays until after we had introduced controls like List boxes and Grids and we could populate them with data from a database. In this way, it is easy to see how the algorithms that apply to arrays can also be applied to these controls.

Object-Oriented Programming

Object-oriented programming (OOP) is considered by many to be an important alternative to traditional procedural programming. In Chapter 10, we use VB's programmer-defined classes to introduce OOP. The presentation is intended to provide a sound introduction to OOP, its terminology, and its use. It is also designed to highlight the differences and potential advantages of OOP. Our coverage includes the creation of ActiveX controls.

Pedagogical Considerations

◆ ◆ ◆

We have chosen to present the material in an order based upon solving problems of gradually increasing complexity. We begin with fundamental concepts, then move through program control structures, and finally introduce realistic end-user applications (utilizing databases, arrays, and so forth).

We have chosen to introduce VB-specific controls as they are needed in our problem-solving efforts, rather than introduce all VB controls in one or two chapters. We have taught the course both ways, and have found that students can better understand a control by seeing it in a context where its function makes sense.

We have also chosen to link the topical material sequentially. That is, most chapters rely on an understanding of the preceding chapters. This allows us to go into greater depth and still retain our focus on fundamentals, because we need not wonder about the reader's background at any point in the text. For example, after databases are introduced in Chapter 8, they are used in Chapters 9 and 10 to provide data for examples, projects, and end-of-chapter programming problems.

The appendices stand somewhat apart from this sequential linking. Almost all of Appendix A, Debugging, can be studied at any time after completing Chapter 4. Appendix B, The Menu Control, and Appendix C, The Image and Picture Box Controls, can be covered any time after completing Chapter 5. Appendix D, Using Microsoft Access to Create a Database, goes nicely with Chapter 8. Material in Appendix F, The Common Dialog Control and Error Handling, as well as material in Appendix G, The Tabbed Dialog Control, can be covered after completing Chapter 7. Appendix H contains two additional projects that are more difficult than the projects in Chapters 1 through 10. These projects require databases (Chapter 8) as well as some material from various appendices.

What's New in the Second Edition

This edition incorporates a number of changes from the first edition. First, the text has been revised for version 5.0 of VB. The differences between VB 4.0 and 5.0 are primarily in the programming environment GUI, with few changes in the language; thus, most of these revisions are concentrated in Chapter 2.

Second, some new material has been added. Two new sections have been added to the body of the text: Section 8.6 discusses the data-bound grid (DBGrid), which allows database access with minimal effort, and Section 10.5 discusses the creation of ActiveX controls. There are also two new appendices: Appendix E discusses File Processing, and Appendix G discusses the Tabbed Dialog control.

The sections that were in the first edition's Chapter 11 (The Menu Control, The Common Dialog Control, The Picture Box Control, and Project 15) have been separated and placed in appendices. References to these appendices have been inserted at appropriate points throughout the text, to encourage the reader to explore this material as time allows rather than postponing it to the end.

Two more significant changes were made to the appendices. The first edition's Appendix A (Differences Between VB 4.0 and 3.0, and Windows 95 and 3.1) has been eliminated. The first edition's Appendix C discussed the Data Manager application as a means of creating databases; this appendix has been revised to use Microsoft Access instead of the Data Manager.

Finally, we have attempted to make a number of improvements in response to reviewer and student comments. We have increased the number of end-of-chapter problems in most chapters. We have rewritten a number of passages in the text in order to improve the clarity of discussion. And we have adopted a slightly modified style of source code indentation, which should help to improve the readability of printouts.

The Learning Edition of VB 5.0

The Learning Edition of Microsoft Visual Basic is available packaged with the text at substantial savings to students. The Learning Edition is compatible with all exercises, examples, and problems presented in the text.

Ancillaries

Supplemental materials for this book include an Instructor's Manual and a website.

Instructor's Manual

The Instructor's Manual contains answers to all exercises and end-of-chapter problems in the text, and sample exam questions. The Instructor's Manual includes a CD ROM, organized by chapter, that contains the following: complete VB solutions to all projects and end-of-chapter programming problems; PowerPoint presentations; and a code package. The code package contains VB project files for all the examples in the text. The student can use this code to run the examples on the computer, and conduct experiments by modifying the code and observing the results. The code package also contains databases that are required for some projects and end-of-chapter programming problems in Chapters 8 through 10.

The Website

Our home page can be accessed by browsing the Computer and Information Technology Website at www.mhhe.com/cit/program/burrows. It contains the downloadable code package (described under Instructor's Manual above), errata information, lab logistics (for example, how to avoid common mistakes when saving a VB project on a diskette to turn in for a grade), additional VB features, links to other VB-related websites, and a Meet-the-Authors section that includes information on the authors and what they do in their classes.

Acknowledgments

We would like to thank the students who took the course *Information Systems 320* at the University of Washington's School of Business for providing positive feedback and constructive criticism.

We would like to thank the reviewers of the text:

Lawrence Andrew	Upper Iowa University
David Cooper	New River Community College
Charles Dowling	Catonsville Community College
Marvin Harris	Lansing Community College
Pati Milligan	Baylor University
Diane Perreault	CSU Sacramento
Geoff Wennes	Highline Community College

We took their comments and suggestions very seriously, and found that they had a significant impact on the final outcome of the project.

We would also like to thank the McGraw-Hill team: Rhonda Sands, Carrie Berkshire, Steve Fahringer, Robert Preskill, Rich DeVitto, and Francis Owens. We would also like to acknowledge the contributions of Cecelia Morales. We are sure that there are many others that we have not had the pleasure of meeting who also contributed.

Of course we accept full responsibility for any errors that might have found their way into the text.

From Joe Langford

Many people have taught me to enjoy learning, creating, and teaching. Among those who influenced me most are the following. First, my brother Dave, who showed me enthusiasm and respect for all interesting things, and who also let me play with his programmable calculator back in the days when software still meant comfortable clothing. Second, John Daigle, who prompted me to go to graduate school, and who guided me through three graduate degrees and a fair amount of life besides. Third, William Burrows, who unwittingly served as my role model as I began to understand the value of learning to teach well.

I would also like to thank my partner Catherine for her continual encouragement and creative insights, and for keeping true to her promise of "never a dull moment," and our son Talyn, for providing a fresh perspective on, well, everything.

J. D. L.
December, 1997

From William Burrows

I would like to thank three former and present faculty members at the University of Washington, who over the years provided me with guidance, inspiration, and friendship. The first is Professor Emeritus Hellmut Golde. Professor Golde was my instructor for several computer science courses I took as an undergraduate and graduate student. He demonstrated by his example what it takes to be an excellent teacher and inspired me to try to be like him. I would also like to thank Professors George Prater (University of Washington) and George Diehr (now at the California State University San Marcos). The two "Georges" gave me my first opportunity to teach in the School of Business and provided constant support, friendship, and encouragement over many years. Without their help I am sure that I would not have stayed in higher education.

I would also like to thank Karen, my wife and best friend. She has provided unselfish support that has allowed me to spend the time and effort necessary to complete a project such as this.

W. E. B.
December, 1997

chapter ONE

Programs, Business Applications, and Visual Basic

Most businesses use computers to support their business operations. The capabilities of these computers depend on their programs. For example, a payroll program enables a computer to compute workers' salaries, determine withholding taxes, and print paychecks.

Microsoft's Visual Basic (VB) is a program that allows its user to create new programs. It is especially well suited to the creation of programs for supporting business operations, and it has gained considerable acceptance in companies around the world. In this text we introduce you to the task of designing and creating programs using VB.

We begin this chapter by examining general categories of programs and business applications in particular. We then discuss why VB is particularly suited to creating business applications. Next we describe the process of creating applications using VB and the "measures of quality" that underly this process. We conclude with an outline of the rest of the book.

Objectives

After studying this chapter you should be able to

- ✦ Evaluate alternative approaches for acquiring programs.
- ✦ Describe the characteristics of business applications.
- ✦ Explain what Visual Basic is and identify its strengths.
- ✦ Describe the process of creating programs using VB.
- ✦ Understand the "measures of quality" for business applications created in VB.

1.1 Programs

In order to perform any task, a computer requires instructions. **A** *program* **is a set of instructions that tell the computer how to perform a given task.** For example, if you want to use your computer to do word processing—create documents, store and retrieve form letters, prepare mailing lists, etc.—you must have a word processing program. Thus, the range of capabilities of a computer depends on the programs available to it.

In this section we briefly discuss three important categories of programs: how people acquire programs, and how people create and use programs.

Categories of Programs
◆ ◆ ◆

Programs can be classified as operating systems, utilities, and applications. **An** *operating system* **is the master control program for the computer, which performs such fundamental tasks as booting up (preparing the computer for operation when it is first turned on) and presenting other programs to the user.** Different computers may use different operating systems, but every computer uses one. Most PC-compatible microcomputers use the operating system created by Microsoft known as Windows, and others use the operating system created by IBM known as Warp. Apple Macintosh microcomputers use the operating system known as System 8. Many other computers use the UNIX operating system.

A *utility* **is a program that performs a task to help people manage the computer and its resources.** Some utilities that Microsoft provides with Windows include ScanDisk, which finds and fixes disk problems; Disk Defragmenter, which consolidates file fragments on disk to reduce the time consumed by File Open and Save operations; and the Add/Rename Program Utility, which helps the user add and rename programs on the computer.

An *application* **is a program that performs a particular task for the user.** Whereas operating systems and utilities make using the computer easier, applications make the user's life easier; applications are why the user wants to use the computer in the first place. Examples of applications that are used by millions of people every day are word processors and spreadsheets. We will see other examples shortly.

Acquiring Programs
◆ ◆ ◆

Since you need programs in order to use the computer, an important question is how to acquire programs. There are two possibilities: you buy them from someone else, or you create them yourself.

There are many tasks that are needed by all or nearly all computer users. For these tasks, programs can be readily purchased "off the shelf" from mail order and retail software distributors. Examples are operating systems, utilities for finding and fixing disk problems, and word processing applications. "*Shrink-wrap software*" is another term for such off-the-shelf programs.

Other tasks are more particular to the individual user or to the organization that needs them. An example of this might be an order entry application that a business uses to record data regarding customer orders. Exactly how such an application should operate depends on the activities performed by the business that uses it. For example, customer orders for a computer equipment retail outlet and a wholesale grocery distributor are likely to be vastly different. Thus, the order entry application must be tailored to (i.e., customized for) the business that needs it. For such custom tasks there is often no suitable program available for purchase, so the user or organization can **create the program itself,** called *inhouse development,* or **hire someone else to create the program,** called *outsourcing* the development.

Creating a new program is generally much more expensive than buying a shrink-wrap program. So when a business manager first recognizes the need for a program, he or she should check whether a shrink-wrap program exists that will fill the need before accepting the challenge of creating one. Fortunately, shrink-wrap programs exist which capably fill all users' needs for operating systems and most users' needs for utilities. When an individual or organization needs to create a program, it is almost always an application program.

Programmers and Users

A *user* is a person who uses a program. A *programmer* is a person who creates programs. Users may become expert in the use of programs but generally do not have the expertise and training to create their own. One of the programmer's goals is to create a program that satisfies the intended user. The user is the final judge of the product, not the programmer. Thus, in order to ensure that the program provides the capabilities the user needs, programmers and users must communicate with each other.

In addition, programmers often work in teams, especially when the application to be created is large. As a result, not only do programmers have to communicate with users, but they also have to communicate with each other.

If you are trained as a programmer, you can create a program for your own use. In this case, you play both the role of user and the role of programmer.

When an organization develops an application inhouse, it employs both the intended users and the programmers who create the application. When an organization outsources the creation of an application, it employs the intended users, but the company hired to create the program employs the programmers. In either case, the organization can schedule meetings between the programmers and users to facilitate the necessary communication.

Finally, in the case of shrink-wrap software, the communication between users and programmers is less direct. When you buy a copy of the software, you are in effect telling the programmers that the program does perform the tasks that you require, or at least that it is the most capable software you could find within your price range. Beyond that, as user all you can do is contact the company that produced the software and suggest features you would like to see in future versions of it.

1.2 Business Applications

Why do common business processes account for so many new application programs, and what characterizes a typical business application? We answer these questions in this section.

Applications, Users, and Programmers

Let us examine the users and programmers of four different applications to clarify what the term "business application" means.

1. A *word processing application* is used daily by millions of people—corporate executives, engineers, and students writing term papers. Its users do not require any special training beyond basic computer skills and a small amount of training on the use of the application itself. The application is foolproof and very efficient because it must meet the requirements of a large number of varied users. The programmers of these applications are trained in computer science techniques but need no other specialized training.

2. A *game application* that presents moving graphic images and sound effects is used by a large number of people with little training. The program must never (or seldom) fail unexpectedly, the graphics and sounds must be synchronized at all times, and the tempo of the game's action must be consistent. The programmers of these applications are trained in computer science techniques but need no other specialized training.

3. An *engineering application* is used by an aircraft manufacturer to perform the mathematical calculations necessary to design a new passenger jet. The users are engineers. That is, engineering training is required just to know what data to input into the program and how to interpret the output it produces. Similarly, the programmers are either engineers themselves or are directed by engineers who understand the mathematical calculations to be performed. The application is highly specialized to the aircraft design firm that uses it.

4. A *payroll program* is used by a business to compute employee salaries, determine withholding taxes, print paychecks, etc. The user needs to understand the payroll practices followed by the company but need not be an engineer or mathematician. Likewise, the programmer needs to understand the tasks the program must perform but need not be highly trained in computer science techniques.

The characteristics of these applications are summarized in Table 1.1. Let's compare these applications. First, word processor and game applications are available as shrink-wrap software, because a single application satisfies the needs of many users. However, they are expensive to produce; in the world today there are a relatively small number of teams of expert programmers creating these applications.

Second, specialized programs like the aircraft design application are very expensive to produce and the users must be highly trained. Consequently, the user population is very small. These applications are few in number.

TABLE 1.1 Some applications and their users and programmers

Application	Degree of Customization	Typical User	Size of User Population	Required Programmer Expertise
Word processor; game	None	Anyone	Large	Computer Science
Aircraft design	Very high	Engineer	Very small	Engineering
Payroll	Moderate	Payroll staff	Moderate	General programming

Third, programs like the payroll application require some customization to the particular individual or organization that uses it. Also, the user requires some background in the domain in which the application is to be used. The programmers require programming ability, but not specialized computer science or engineering expertise. For many businesses the benefits of creating such custom applications will outweigh the costs. As a result, there are many programmers creating such applications for large numbers of businesses, and these applications account for a large percentage of the new programs being created today.

Programmers need not have computer science or engineering expertise in order to create applications like the payroll application. After completing this text, which strives to impart sound programming techniques, you will be able to create useful business applications.

Characteristics of Business Applications

In this text we use the term "business application" to mean programs like the payroll program. They require some customization for the particular individual or organization that uses them, but do not rely heavily on sophisticated mathematical analyses, and speed of execution is not critical.

To be sure, businesses are not the only entities that use programs fitting this description; but businesses do account for the vast majority of them. Likewise, some businesses use applications that do not fit this description. The engineering application used by the aircraft design firm is one example. However, such specialized applications account for a relatively small fraction of applications used by businesses.

The key idea is that when a business decides whether to create an application, it is making an economic decision. Relatively few businesses find it economically viable to create highly specialized applications that require engineers and computer scientists to construct. But many do find it economically viable to create programs like the payroll application.

There are two additional characteristics of business applications. First, one reason why business applications require customization is that most businesses maintain all of their important data in databases. **A *database* is a carefully organized set of data stored on a computer and managed by a special application called a *database management system* (DBMS).** In order for an application to be able to obtain data from a database, the application must be customized to fit the organization of the database. Every business has its own databases; the data differ, and they are organized differently, from one business to the next.

Second, the environment in which any business operates—its customers, its suppliers, government regulations, technology, etc.—changes frequently. In order to be useful to the business, the applications it uses must reflect the realities of its environment. When the environment changes, the applications must be updated. As a result, most business applications must be modified frequently.

A Typical Business Application: Order Entry

Figure 1.1 shows the user interface for a portion of a simple order entry application used by a computer equipment retail outlet to record data regarding customer orders. This is a *graphical user interface (GUI),* **meaning it allows the user to use a mouse to click on boxes for entering text, to click on buttons to initiate processing steps, and so forth.** You can guess what this application

FIGURE 1.1

Example Order Entry Screen

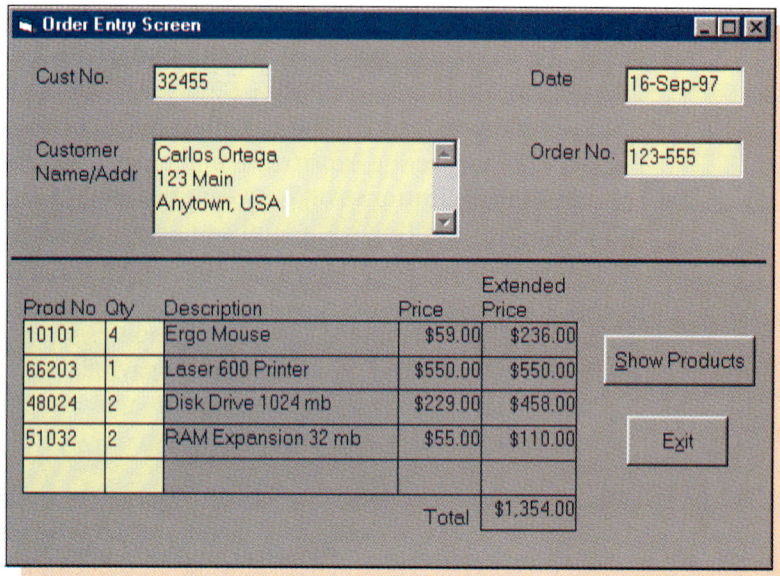

does just by looking at the screen. The user enters values in the yellow boxes: customer information in the upper half of the screen, and the products being purchased by the customer in the lower half of the screen.

When the user enters a product number (Prod No), the computer automatically looks up and displays the description and price of the product. Similarly, when the user enters the quantity (Qty), the computer automatically computes and displays the extended price (Price times Qty) and updates the total dollar amount of the order (Total).

There are two buttons on the screen, captioned "Exit" and "Show Products." The user clicks the Exit button to terminate the order entry process. The user clicks the Show Products button to see the list of products available for purchase, which is shown in Figure 1.2.

This screen helps the user who is not sure of a product number. When the user double-clicks on a given product number, the computer copies that product number plus the product description and price onto the Order Entry Screen. When the user clicks the Close button, the computer shows the Order Entry Screen again.

One advantage of a GUI like this is its ease of use. You could probably figure out how to use these two screens of the order entry application with little

FIGURE 1.2

Product List screen

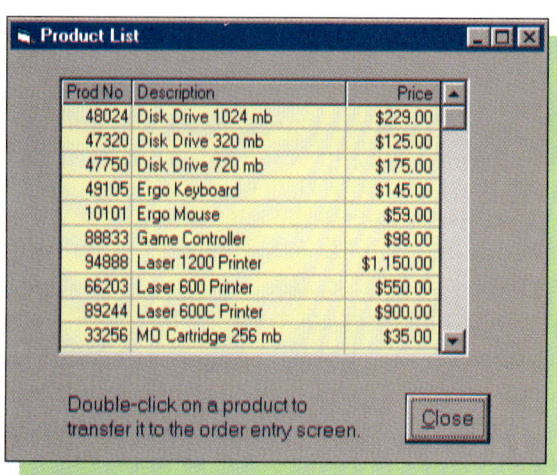

or no training. (If you want to give it a try, run the program named OE.Exe, located in the directory named C01 in the code package for this text—see the Preface.) Bear in mind, however, that the order entry application in its entirety may be much more complex and require some training to use.

Finally, observe that this order entry application was designed to be used by a computer equipment retail outlet, and it may not adequately fill the order entry requirements for other businesses. For example, imagine that a grocery wholesaler tried to use this application (with grocery items instead of computer equipment in the product list, of course). Two products available for purchase might be fresh tomatoes and canned tomatoes. But fresh tomatoes are probably sold by weight whereas canned tomatoes are sold by the can—and the size of the can has to be recorded. So the Qty field will have to be able to record units as well as numbers: for example, five pounds of fresh tomatoes, five 16-ounce cans, or five 28-ounce cans.

Such details may seem minor, but when you actually create a real order entry application for a real business you find that they are very important to the business. And each business has to keep track of many details which are particular to that business. This is a major reason why businesses often create their own custom business applications.

1.3 What Is Visual Basic?

Visual Basic (VB) is a *programming environment,* **that is, a program specifically designed to facilitate the creation of new programs**. A programmer uses a programming environment to construct, test, and refine new programs. Every programming environment provides two things to the programmer who uses it:

1. A set of *programming tools,* which enable the programmer to assemble and rearrange the components of the program under construction.
2. A *programming language,* which enables the programmer to compose the instructions that tell the computer how to perform the tasks required by the program under construction.

VB runs under the Windows operating system, and so do the new programs created using VB.

In this section we introduce VB's tools and language by looking at a typical business application created using VB. Then we discuss the strengths of VB, and why it is particularly suited to the creation of business applications.

An Order Entry Application Created in VB
◆ ◆ ◆

The order entry application presented in the previous section was created in VB. Let us examine the components of this application, introduce a few of VB's tools and its language, and briefly discuss how the programmer used them to create this application.

Some VB Tools

VB provides a large number of tools to the programmer, some as buttons, some as menu commands, and some as windows. There are several tools to help the programmer create GUIs, and these are among the first tools you will learn to use (starting in Chapter 2). They are conveniently arranged as two sets of buttons called the *Toolbar* and the *Toolbox*. Figure 1.3 shows the Toolbar and Toolbox and identifies some of the individual tools.

Recall that the order entry application contained two screens. In VB each screen is called a *form*. The programmer clicks on the toolbar's Add Form tool to cause VB to display a new, blank form, as shown in Figure 1.4.

The programmer can then use the tools in the toolbox to place labels, command buttons, and text boxes on the new form. For example, if the programmer double-clicks on the Command Button tool, VB will place a command button on the form, as shown in Figure 1.5.

The programmer can then use another of VB's tools, called the *Properties window*, to customize the command button. For example, the programmer may want the new command button to be captioned "Exit", as shown in Figure 1.6. The programmer can then use the mouse to select and drag the command button to any desired location on the form.

The programmer proceeds by placing more labels, command buttons, text boxes, etc., on the form, and customizing each as appropriate for the application. Figure 1.7 shows the completed order entry form, and identifies some of its labels, command buttons, and text boxes. The programmer follows the same procedures to create the Product List form shown in Figure 1.2.

FIGURE 1.3

Toolbar and Toolbox

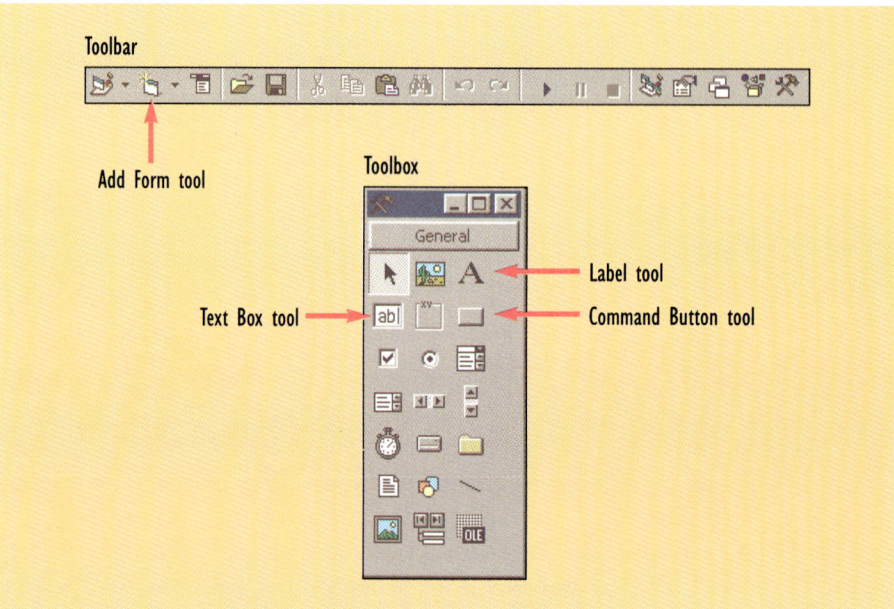

FIGURE 1.4

A new form

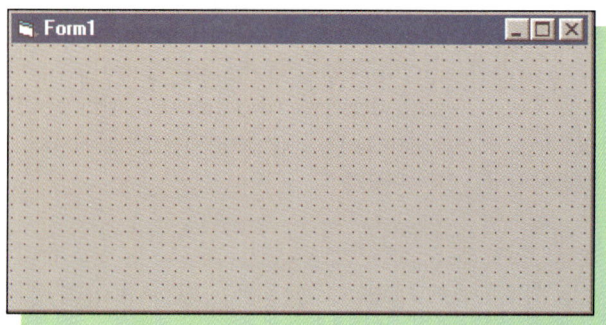

FIGURE 1.5

A command button on the new form

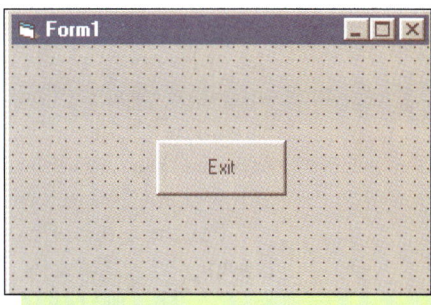

FIGURE 1.6

Command button after caption change to "Exit"

FIGURE 1.7

Completed Order Entry form

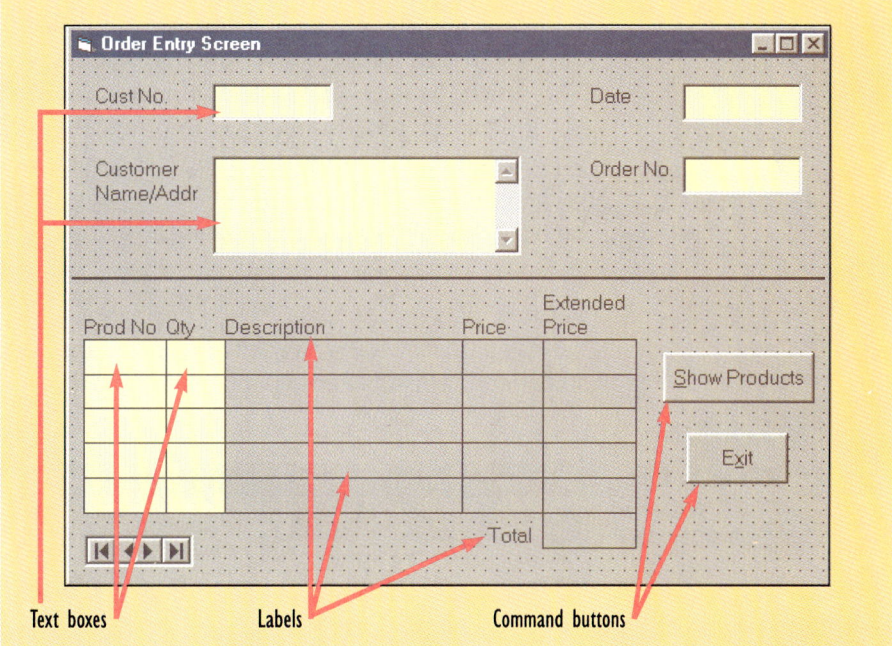

VB's Language

In our previous discussion of the order entry application, we said that if the user cannot remember a part number, he or she can click the "Show Products" button on the Order Entry form. In response to this user action, the computer should display the Product List form.

After the programmer has arranged all the labels, command buttons, text boxes, etc., on the form, he or she must provide explicit instructions that tell the computer how to respond to user actions. The programming language gives the programmer a way to provide these instructions to the computer. VB's programming language is a very powerful version of BASIC (Beginner's All-purpose Symbolic Instruction Code), the first widely used programming language devised for people without computer science or engineering training.

The programmer uses VB's language to compose a "processing script"[1] for each command button; **the *processing script* contains the instructions the**

---

[1] We use the descriptive term "processing script" in this chapter for the sake of clarity. In subsequent chapters we will introduce and use the (correct) technical terms of "event procedure," "general sub procedure," and so forth.

computer will follow when the user clicks the command button. In the case of the order entry application, the programmer composes a processing script for the Show Products button that tells the computer to display the Product List form. The completed processing script for this command button is shown in Figure 1.8. Don't be concerned if this processing script doesn't make sense to you at this point. It will look simple to you by the time you reach the end of this text.

For the order entry application the programmer also has to compose a processing script that tells the computer what to do when the user clicks on the Exit button. This processing script is also shown in Figure 1.8. As you might guess, the instruction "End" simply tells the computer to quit the application.

The programmer visualizes the GUI, the user's action of clicking a command button, and the processing script for the command button as shown in Figure 1.9. In contrast, most users are not aware that processing scripts even exist. While the user understands the net effect of clicking a given command button, only the programmer knows the actual instructions that the computer follows when the user clicks the command button.

In fact, the programmer has to provide such processing scripts for every user action that requires the computer to perform a task. Part of the process of learning to create applications is learning the programming language, and figuring out how to use it to make the computer perform desired tasks.

Strengths of VB

VB has gained wide acceptance in companies around the world. What are some of the reasons for its popularity? To understand this we must first realize

FIGURE 1.8

Computer instructions for the Show Products and Exit buttons

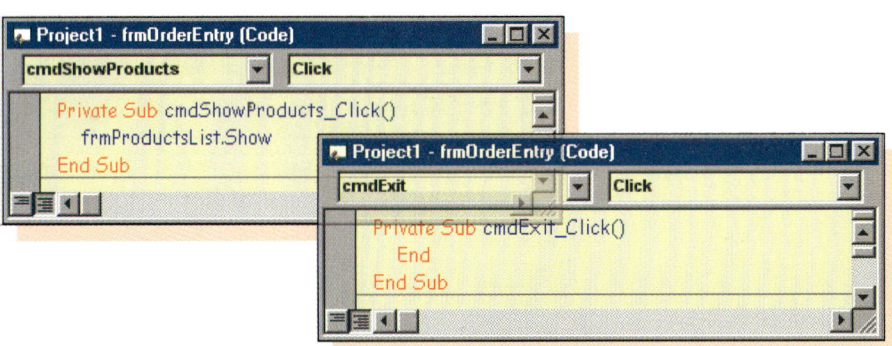

FIGURE 1.9

Clicking on the command button initiates the processing script for that button

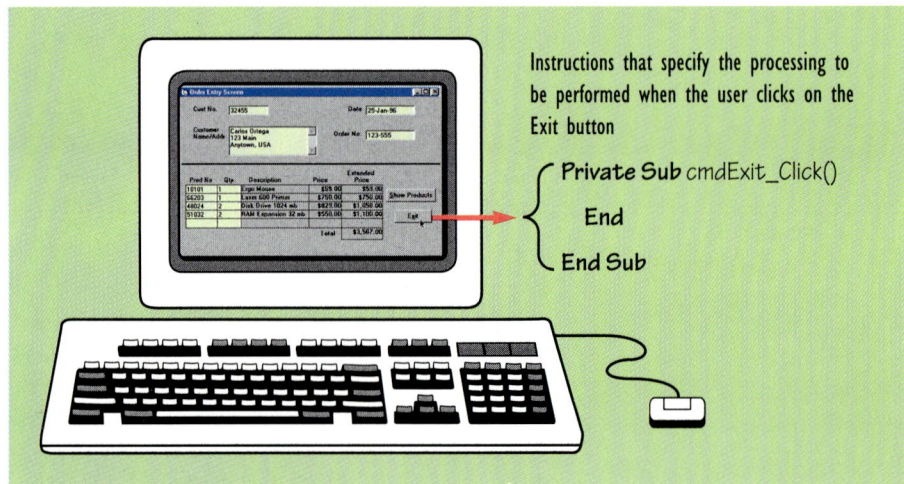

that the costs of creating an application arise from the time spent by users communicating their requirements to programmers and by programmers designing and constructing a program to meet those requirements. One strength of VB is that it provides tools that make it easier for the programmer to create good GUIs. As a result, the programmer can spend less time on this task and the users are more satisfied with the finished application.

VB also simplifies the programmer's job of writing the processing scripts that tell the computer what tasks to perform. Furthermore, a single application is likely to contain many such processing scripts, and VB makes it easy for the programmer to keep them organized. This is important, because otherwise the programmer may spend a lot of time trying to locate specific processing scripts and parts of processing scripts.

Furthermore, VB provides database tools that simplify the process of customizing an application to obtain data from a database. Since most business applications obtain data from databases, these tools can save a lot of time and money for most businesses.

The fact that most business applications require frequent modification amplifies the importance of these strengths of VB. The user interface and processing scripts can be changed quickly. If the organization of a database is changed, the application can be quickly modified to fit the new database organization.

Finally, because VB has gained wide acceptance by companies around the world, there are now many programmers who use VB, and it is easy to obtain assistance with technical problems. Moreover, VB's widespread popularity ensures that its creator (Microsoft) has continuing incentive to improve and expand it.

1.4 Creating Applications

Suppose that a business has decided it needs to create an application: the users think they know what the application must do, and the programmers are ready to begin work on it. The goal is to produce a good application without spending more time and money than necessary. What makes a business application "good," and how do the users and programmers proceed to create a good application?

Without the benefit of experience, a beginning programmer might imagine that the users can simply tell the programmers what they need and then the programmers can simply build it. Indeed, this approach has been tried many times, and the result is usually disappointing. More time and money is spent than necessary, and the resulting application is not as useful as it could be.

We begin this section by discussing the characteristics of good business applications. Then we present a formal procedure for creating applications. By following this procedure, programmers increase the quality of the resulting application.

Measures of Quality for Business Applications
◆ ◆ ◆

The objective of a business when it decides to create an application is to fulfill a business need effectively and at low cost. What characteristics can programmers build into applications they create that will help achieve this objective? That is, what are the defining characteristics of high-quality business applications? Here are four such measures of quality for business applications. The first two directly affect the users, and the last two affect only the programmers.

1. The application should fulfill the needs of its users. It must provide the required features, and it must perform them correctly.
2. The application should be easy to use. The less training the users will need to use the application effectively, the lower the cost will be. To achieve this goal, the programmer designs the application's user interface to be clear and simple.
3. The internal details of the application should be easy for programmers to understand. To achieve this goal, the programmer composes the processing scripts as clearly and simply as possible.
4. The application should have flexibility built into it—that is, the internal details of the application should be organized so that future changes can be made quickly. To achieve this goal, the programmer must anticipate which features are most likely to require changes in the future, and compose the associated processing scripts accordingly.

The first two items above are self-explanatory. But why do the internal details of the application—which users never encounter—have any bearing on the quality of the application? Won't the programmers have to spend more time in order to organize the internal details carefully?

Recall that business environments change over time, and that as a result, business applications have to be modified frequently. By carefully organizing the internal details of the application when he or she first creates it, the programmer can save much time and effort later when it needs to be modified. Not only does this save money, but it makes the users happier as well; when the users require new features in the application, the programmer will be able to get these features working and into the users' hands more quickly.

The *lifetime* of a typical business application spans several years; that is, it is used for several years after it is created. More often than not, the programmers who originally created it leave the company or are promoted during an application's lifetime. Then, when the application needs to be modified, the original programmers are not available to do the job, so different programmers are assigned the task. If the original programmers organized the internal details of the application carefully, the new programmers will be able to understand it easily and make the modifications quickly.

Surprising as it may seem, businesses commonly find that they spend two-to-five times more money maintaining an application (i.e., modifying and adapting it to changes in the environment) over its lifetime than they spent in its initial creation. Thus, organization of the application's internal details is a key factor in the total costs associated with it.

A Formal Procedure for Creating Applications

History has shown that the quality of applications is higher when the programmers follow a formal procedure for creating them. In fact, researchers have studied this problem for years, attempting to determine the best procedure. Entire textbooks are devoted to this subject. Many good formal procedures have been devised, used, and evaluated.

In this section we present one such procedure for creating applications, which we will employ throughout this book. This procedure is similar to many others. Some are more extensive, but this basic procedure serves as a good introduction to the topic and suffices for the applications we create in this text.

Our formal procedure is as follows:

1. Identify user requirements.
2. Design the application.
   + GUI
   + Functionality
3. Construct the application.
   + Build GUI.
   + Compose processing scripts.
   + Test.

In the first step, "Identify user requirements," the programmers[2] must communicate with the users to find out what the application is for, what features it must provide, and how it should operate. This step includes face-to-face meetings between the users and programmers. It is a very important step, and requires considerable skill and effort on the part of the programmer. Failure to correctly identify user requirements guarantees a poor finished application.

After the programmers understand the user requirements, they can begin to design the application. This is a planning stage. In effect, the programmers create a blueprint for the application. Their goal is to identify the components that will be part of the application and to carefully organize these components. The programmers also want to make sure that the application can actually be built, and at acceptable cost. Programmers accomplish much design work with paper and pencil, sketching the components of the application and determining how they fit together so that the finished product will work properly and be easy to use when it is assembled according to the blueprint.

After the programmers design the GUI, they then show the GUI design to the users to get their feedback and input on it. If necessary, the programmers then revise the GUI design and show it to the users again. This review of the GUI helps ensure that the application will be easy to use. When the GUI design is complete, the programmers proceed to design the internal details of the application—the processing scripts—which are of no interest to the users.

Finally, when the design is complete, the programmers use VB to actually construct the application. They construct the application a piece at a time by building some of its user interface, then adding some of the processing scripts for this part of the user interface, then testing this work. Usually minor adjustments are needed to get each new piece of the application working properly. As they proceed to construct the application, the programmers may periodically show it to the users to get feedback about the application's operation. This interaction with the users helps ensure that the finished application will operate correctly and be easy to use.

---

[2] In many organizations steps 1 and 2 are performed by people whose job titles are "Systems Analyst" or "Programmer Analyst."

1.5 How This Book Is Organized

The goal of this book is to help you develop the understanding and skills you will need to create good business applications using Visual Basic. In this brief section we outline the topics in the remaining chapters and describe the structure of each chapter.

The chapters are listed in Table 1.2. Each chapter begins with a discussion of a fundamental processing task and continues with sections on VB tools and programming language features that support that fundamental task. Beginning with Chapter 2, each chapter contains the following components.

- An introduction, with learning objectives.
- Examples that illustrate programming concepts. The examples are provided as VB projects in the code package for this text. While the presentation of these examples in the text itself is designed to convey the concepts, we recommend that you examine and experiment with the examples on the computer before proceeding to the next chapter.
- Numerous exercises. These are designed to reinforce key concepts, and we recommend you try them as you read the book. Answers to selected exercises appear in Appendix I.
- One or two projects. Most of these ask you to create small business applications. In Chapters 2 through 5 the projects include complete discussions of user requirements, design, and construction. Starting in Chapter 6, the projects include complete requirements, but begin to provide only outlines of the design and construction. Our expectation is that by Chapter 6 you should be comfortable with the VB environment and ready to begin developing your own skills for transforming requirements into working applications.
- Chapter summary.
- List of key terms.
- Approximately ten end-of-chapter problems. These are similar to the exercises.

TABLE 1.2 Sequence of topics

Chapter	Title: Subtitle
2	Visual Basic Projects: Project Structure and VB's Programming Tools
3	Representing Data: Constants and Variables
4	Performing Calculations and Manipulating Data: Expressions
5	Specifying Alternate Courses of Action: Selection Statements
6	Reducing Program Complexity: General Sub Procedures and Programmer-Defined Functions
7	Repeating Processing Tasks: Loop Structures
8	Accessing Business Data: Processing Databases
9	Handling Lists of Data: Arrays
10	Representing Entities with Data and Behavior: Programmer-Defined Types and Object Classes

TABLE 1.3 Appendixes

Appendix	Title
A	Debugging
B	The Menu Control
C	The Image and Picture Box Controls
D	Using Microsoft Access to Create a Database
E	File Processing
F	The Common Dialog Control and Error Handling
G	The Tabbed Dialog Control
H	Additional Projects
I	Answers to Selected Exercises

◆ Approximately five end-of-chapter programming problems. These include requirements for small business applications and just a few hints regarding design and construction.

Finally, appendixes are listed in Table 1.3. The text will suggest appropriate points at which you may want to consult Appendixes A through G. Appendix H contains two projects that are intended to provide additional challenge to the reader who has mastered most of the text. We suggest you attempt to answer the exercises as you read the text, and use Appendix I to check your understanding of the material.

chapter TWO

Visual Basic Projects

Project Structure and VB's Programming Tools

An application under construction in VB is called a *project*. Before you can begin to *design* applications, you must understand the structure of projects—their component parts and how the components can be arranged. And in order to *construct* applications, you must learn about the VB tools that enable you to build the project, make the computer execute the project, and save your work.

We begin this chapter with a brief overview of the application construction process—that is, how the programmer uses VB tools to complete a project after identifying the user requirements and designing the new application. This overview provides a framework for the remainder of the chapter.

Next we turn our attention to design issues. We start with the basic structure that all VB projects possess. We then present an overview of **VB controls**—**the objects that appear on the user interface**—and examine three controls in detail: the Command button, Label, and Timer controls. These three controls are sufficient to begin designing useful applications.

We then return to the construction process, and examine the elements of the VB environment that enable us to build and execute projects and save our work on disk.

Finally, we present three complete VB projects that use the preceding material. Each project includes a description of the user requirements, a complete design, and a step-by-step discussion of the process of creating the application in VB. These projects also illustrate basic issues of quality design.

Objectives

After studying this chapter you should be able to
- Design and construct simple complete applications from scratch.
- Explain the structure of VB projects.
- List the characteristics of several VB controls—the objects that appear on the user interface—and the uses for which each is appropriate.

- ✦ Identify the purpose of each major component of the VB environment.
- ✦ Explain basic programming practices that contribute to the readability of programs.

2.1 From New Project to Finished Application

We begin this section by examining the construction process from new VB project to finished application in the user's hands. We then introduce VB's modes of operation and discuss how the programmer uses them to build, execute, and test the project.

Overview of the Construction Process

Figure 2.1 illustrates the major steps in the application construction process. The programmer begins by starting VB, which initially presents a single blank form for a new project. The programmer then proceeds to build the project using the previously completed design as a blueprint. VB has three modes of operation for building the project—design, run, and break—which we will discuss later in this section.

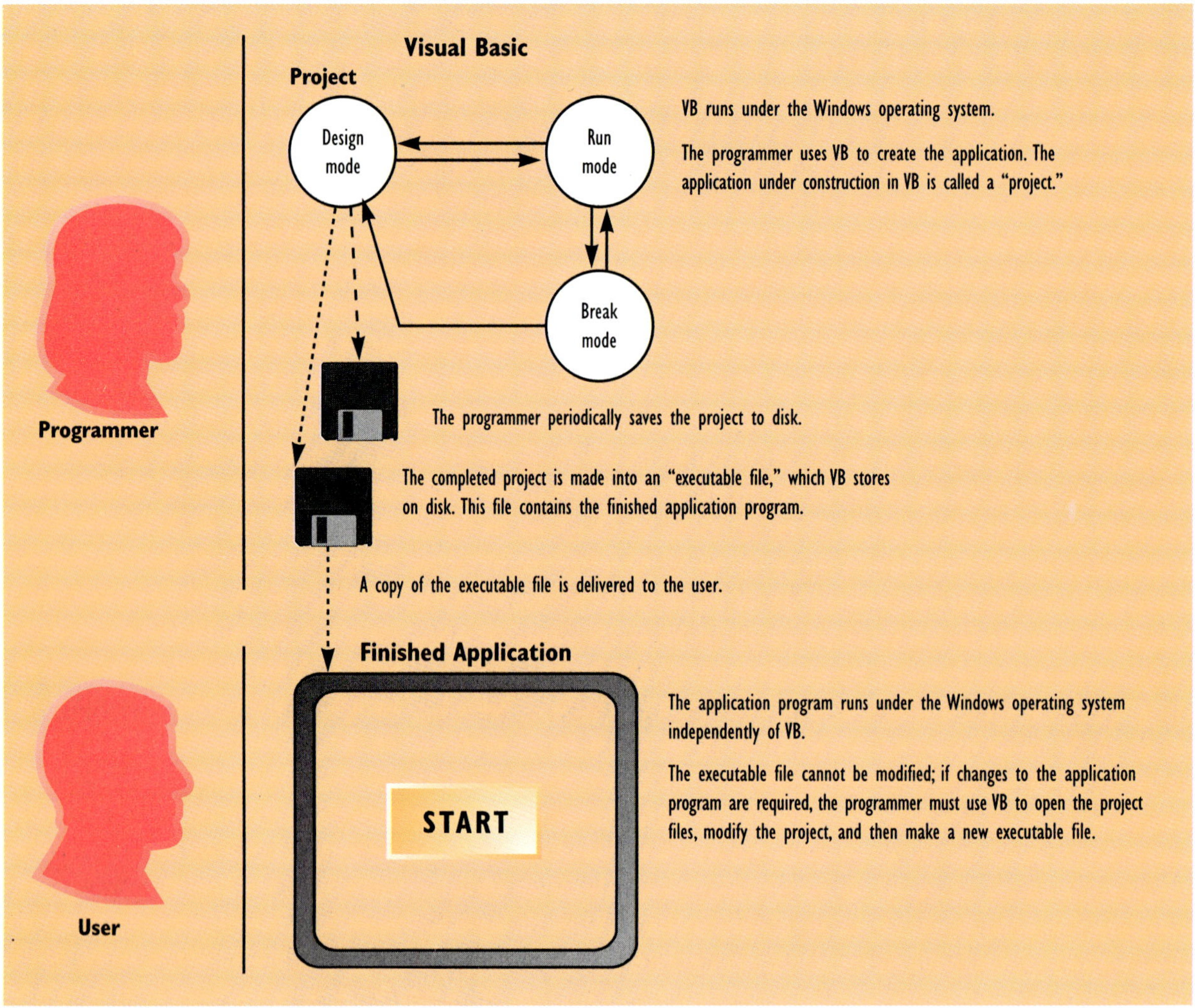

FIGURE 2.1 *VB project and finished application*

The time needed for the programmer to build the complete application depends on its complexity. A simple application can be constructed in a few minutes, while a complex application may take a team of programmers several months to build. In any case, the programmer periodically saves the project on disk while building it.

When finished building the project, the programmer saves it on disk one last time, then instructs VB to make an executable file. **An *executable file* is a file on disk that contains the finished application program, which the computer can execute independently of VB.** A copy of the executable file is delivered to the user, who can then run the application on another computer.

Two observations regarding this process are critical. First, the user need not know anything about VB. All the user knows is to expect a working program from the programmer. Second, the contents of the executable file are unintelligible to humans and cannot be modified.[1] If changes to the application are required, the programmer must use VB to open the project files, modify the project as required, save the project again, make a new executable file, and then give a copy of the new executable file to the user.

Because the executable file cannot be modified, the project files are the chief repository of the programmer's work. Typically, when you buy a software package you receive only an executable file. This enables you to run the application but prevents you from looking at its internal details to learn how it works or to modify it; only the programmers who have the project files are able to do this.

VB's Three Modes

As discussed in Chapter 1 the programmer typically constructs a project a piece at a time, by building some of its user interface and adding some of the processing scripts for this part of the user interface, then testing this work before going on. VB has three modes of operation to support this piece-at-a-time approach. As shown in Figure 2.1, the three modes are called design mode, run mode, and break mode. The programmer can switch between them as shown by the solid arrows in the figure.

Design Mode

Design mode **enables the programmer to build and modify the project.** Some of the tasks it allows the programmer to perform are

- Placing, arranging, and customizing the appearance of command buttons, labels, etc., on the form.
- Writing processing scripts.
- Saving the project.
- Making an executable file.

Run Mode

Run mode **enables the programmer to run the project and interact with it just as a user would.** That is, in run mode VB executes the project just as Windows would execute an executable file.

The project does not have to be complete for the programmer to use run mode. Typically, the programmer uses design mode to build a piece of the

---

[1] The computer instructions contained in the executable file are in machine language, which is the language of 0s and 1s that the computer operates with internally.

project, then switches to run mode to evaluate whether the new piece operates correctly. The programmer then switches back to design mode and either corrects problems discovered using run mode or starts building the next piece of the project.

The programmer may also use run mode to show the user how the (unfinished) project operates. This gives the user a chance to evaluate the project and provide suggestions for improvement, which the programmer may then be able to incorporate into the project.

Break Mode

Break mode **enables the programmer to temporarily suspend execution of the running project and examine the status of the project's processing scripts.** This capability helps the programmer with *debugging*, **which is the task of determining the cause of the problem when the project does not run as expected**. Debugging techniques are discussed in Appendix A.

After examining the status of the project's processing scripts, the programmer can switch back to run mode, which causes VB to resume executing the project where it left off (at the point when the programmer switched to break mode), or to design mode to make changes in the processing scripts or build the next piece of the project.

Design Time and Run Time

❖ ❖ ❖

When VB is in design mode the project is said to be at *design time*. **When VB is in run mode or break mode the project is said to be at** *run time*. These terms are useful because while building the project (at design time) the programmer must be able to visualize how it will appear and behave when the computer executes it (at run time).

The difference between design time and run time is important in locating and correcting errors. VB can detect some kinds of programming errors at design time, as the programmer types the processing script. VB immediately alerts the programmer when it finds such an error, and the programmer can correct the error on the spot. Other kinds of programming errors become apparent only at run time, when the computer executes the processing script. Here the programmer has to determine what circumstances arose at run time to cause the processing script to fail. As an example, suppose the processing script performs a calculation using a number entered by the user at run time. The processing script might work fine when the number is positive but fail when the number is negative. The programmer thus has to determine how to modify the processing script back at design time so that it won't fail at run time.

2.2 VB Project Structure

VB projects have a formal, hierarchical structure. Before we can begin to design applications we must understand this structure—its component parts and how the components can be arranged. VB project structure is depicted in Figure 2.2, where

❖ A *project* consists of one or more *forms*, zero or more *code modules*, zero or more *class modules*, and zero or one *resource file*.

- A *form* consists of one *general declarations section*, zero or more *general sub procedures*, and one or more *controls*.
- A *code module* has one *general declarations section* and zero or more *general sub procedures*.
- A *class module* has components similar to a code module.
- A *resource file* is self-contained.
- A *control* has one or more *properties*, zero or more *event procedures*, and one or more *methods*.

Also, in Figure 2.2 the entity at the lower end of a line "belongs to" the entity at the upper end of the line. For example, a property always belongs to a particular control, which in turn belongs to a particular form, which in turn belongs to a particular project.

As you work with VB you will see references to all of the entities in Figure 2.2. However, all of the projects in this chapter will have only one form with just a few controls. Figure 2.3 depicts the structure of such simple projects.[2] As we proceed through subsequent chapters our projects will grow in complexity, and when appropriate we will refer you to Figure 2.2.

The following descriptions of forms, controls, properties, and event procedures will give you a general idea of what each component is and what it does.

The Form

The *form* is the background of the GUI. In fact, the form is an ordinary "window" of the kind that you see when working with MS Windows.

Controls

Controls, as mentioned before, are the objects that appear on the GUI, sitting on top of the form. There are several different types. As a user of MS Windows you are familiar with some of these—such as command buttons, labels, and menus—although you may not be aware of their formal names. As a

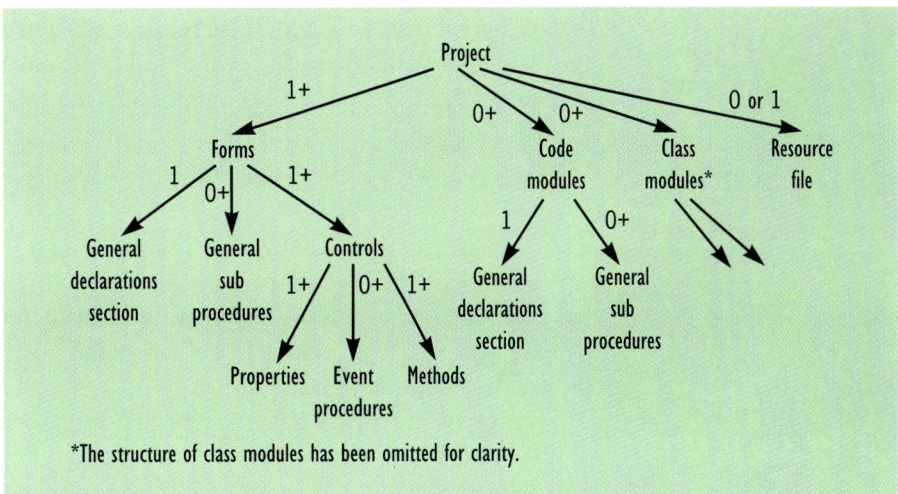

FIGURE 2.2

Structure of VB projects

---

[2] It is true that a form always has a general declarations section and a control always has at least one method, but in simple projects these are not used, so they are left out of Figure 2.3 for simplicity.

FIGURE 2.3

Structure of simple VB projects

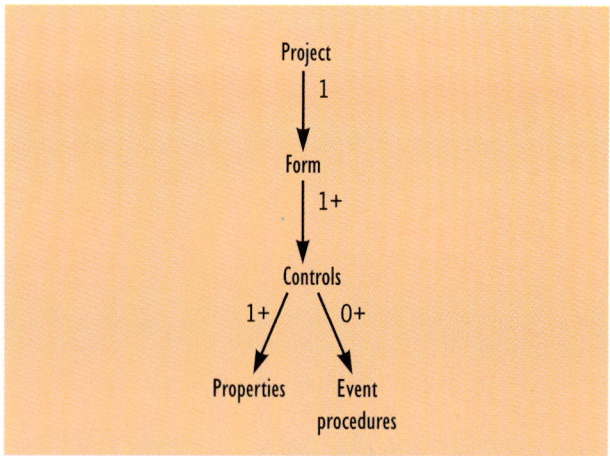

programmer, you will find that each new control you learn about allows you to create more flexible and useful applications.

Each type of control has a different visual appearance on the form, and each has a different purpose or category of tasks it is used for traditionally. For example, as a user of MS Windows you have probably encountered the "OK" button, and know that the user clicks on it to tell the computer to continue on to the next processing step. Similarly, you know that the E<u>x</u>it item under the <u>F</u>ile menu is used to end execution of the application.

Each type of control has a set of *properties* that define its characteristics and a set of *events* that it can respond to. Most users are unaware of properties and events. To know about them one must study programming.

Properties
◆ ◆ ◆

A *property* **is an attribute that defines some characteristic of the control.** Some properties establish the control's visual appearance, and others establish the control's behavior at run time. Each type of control has a prespecified set of properties.

As an example, among the properties possessed by all command buttons is the *Caption* **property, which enables the programmer to specify the descriptive text that appears on the command button.** At design time the programmer can, if desired, set the Caption property for one command button to "OK", and the Caption property for a second command button to "Cancel"; then, at run time, the user will see OK on the one button and Cancel on the other.

Event Procedures
◆ ◆ ◆

An *event* **is a signal, generated at run time, which indicates that something has happened to which the application must respond.** Most events are caused by user actions. As an example, a Click event occurs when the user clicks the mouse on a command button.

Each type of control has a prespecified set of events the control is capable of responding to. For example, the only event that menu controls can respond to is the Click event, while command buttons can respond to the Click event, the MouseMove event, and several others.

An *event procedure* **is a script containing the detailed instructions that the computer follows when the event occurs for a particular control.** Thus, an "OK" command button has an event procedure that specifies exactly what the computer should do when the user clicks on it. Up to this point we have used the descriptive term "processing script" instead of the formal term "event procedure"; from now on we will use the formal term.

2.3 Overview of Controls

In Chapter 1 we stated that good business applications should be easy to use. One of the ways VB helps programmers create user-friendly applications is by providing a standard set of controls that they can incorporate into their programs. Standard controls make it easier for users to learn and run new programs. Just by its appearance, a user knows roughly what a standard control's purpose is, how it behaves, and the kinds of actions to which it might respond.

Categories of Controls

VB controls fall into seven general categories of fundamental functions, listed in Table 2.1. For each category the table lists the controls that are most often appropriate in the "Primary Controls" column and other controls that can be used (but which are usually not the most appropriate) in the "Others" column.

TABLE 2.1 Categories of VB Controls

Category	Primary Controls	Others
Trigger: Initiate processing	Command button Menu Timer	Text box Image Picture box List box Form
Input: Get data from user	Text box Option button Check box List box Combo Box Scroll bar	Common dialog File list box Directory list box Drive list box
Output: Display results to user	Label FlexGrid Image Picture box	Text box List box Scroll bar Form
Organize: Group other controls	Form Frame SSTab	Picture box
Beautify: Simple Graphics	Line Shape	
Data Access: Interface with databases	Data DBList DBCombo DBGrid	
Integrate: Interface with other applications	OLE	

In some situations the programmer may want a single control to serve more than one purpose. For example, a text box can be used to get input data, display results, and trigger processing, and in a specific situation there could be practical reasons for using it for all three. However, when using a control for multiple purposes, the programmer must be careful that the result will not confuse the user.

The Correct Control for the Job

Part of designing a good GUI for an application is choosing controls to satisfy user requirements. In some situations selecting the correct control requires careful judgment, and experience is the best guide. New VB programmers, who lack experience, should abide by the conventional uses of controls and make exceptions only when there is good reason.

As an analogy, consider each type of control to be like a tool in a toolbox. Users and programmers alike recognize tools by their appearance and understand that different tools are good for different tasks. A carpenter knows that it's possible to drive a nail using a wrench, but it's generally much more difficult and you are more likely to bend nails and injure your hands than if you use a hammer. Similarly, a programmer can *make* a Text box control work in situations for which a Label control is really appropriate, but doing so is unwise. For example, consider the order entry application introduced in Chapter 1. The user enters a product number, and the application automatically looks up and displays the price of that product. The appropriate control for displaying the price is the Label; it displays text well, and, indeed, it can do nothing else. The text box, on the other hand, can display results, but its primary purpose is to accept user input. Thus, if the programmer chooses to use a text box instead of a label, the user, knowing that text boxes allow user input, might mistakenly infer that the displayed price could be changed. Using the proper control will avoid the possibility of this type of confusion.

In this chapter we introduce the Command button, Label, and Timer controls. You can see from Table 2.1 that with just these three controls we will not have any way of getting user input, but we will be able to trigger processing steps and display results in a well-organized fashion. Most of the other controls in Table 2.1 will be introduced at appropriate times as we proceed through the text.

2.4 The Command Button Control

The *Command button control* acts as a trigger with which the user can initiate execution of an event procedure.

Appearance and Use

The command button appears on the form as a rectangular button with a descriptive caption, a picture, or both a caption and a picture. Figure 2.4 shows a Command button control on a form at design time. In this figure the command button's caption is "Command1".

At run time, the user initiates execution of the event procedure by clicking on the command button with the mouse (i.e., by moving the mouse so that the mouse pointer is on top of the command button and then clicking the mouse button).

FIGURE 2.4

A Command button control

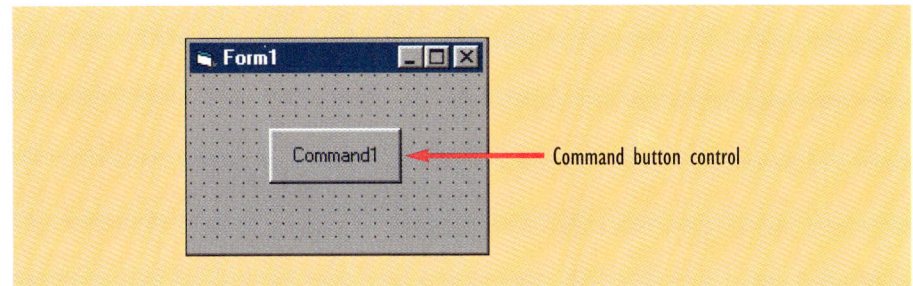

Properties

A control's property settings govern its appearance and behavior. Table 2.2 shows the properties of the command button that the programmer typically sets. Caption and Font simply establish the appearance of the text displayed on the button. As explained earlier, the Caption property determines the descriptive text. The *Font property* determines the typeface that will be used for that text. The *Picture property* determines the picture, if any, that the button will display.[3] The *Style property* determines whether the button will be able to display only a caption, or both a caption and a picture. The *Enabled property* determines whether or not the button will respond when the user clicks it. Similarly, the *Visible property* determines whether or not the button can be seen by the user. Finally, the *Name property* allows the programmer to assign a unique name to each control to distinguish it from other controls. Unique names make it possible to determine which command button the user clicked.

Events

The command button can respond to several different events, but by far the most important of these is the *Click event*, **caused by clicking on the command button with the mouse.** For each command button the programmer will write a Click event procedure specifying the detailed instructions the computer will follow when the user clicks on the button. As with the control's Name property, the user never sees the contents of the control's event procedure. The user will understand the result of clicking a particular command button but will not know the sequence of steps the computer followed to achieve the result.[4]

Another type of event the command button can respond to is the *MouseMove event*, **which occurs whenever the mouse pointer is over the command button and the user moves the mouse.** If the programmer wants to make the computer perform some processing step when the user does this, he or she must write a *MouseMove* event procedure for the command button.

Thus, the same control can have several different event procedures. For example, a single command button can have both a Click event procedure

---

[3] Microsoft provides a large number of icons with VB. However, to get them you must perform a custom install when running the VB setup program. (If you have already installed VB you do not have to reinstall it; you can run the setup program again and use its "Add" feature.) The "Icon Library" is under the Graphics option in the setup program. After you install the Icon Library, you should find a folder named "Graphics" in the VB folder. Then within the "Graphics" folder you will find an "Icons" folder.

[4] The functionality of the Menu control, discussed in Appendix B, is similar to that of the command button. However, the Click event is the only event to which the Menu control can respond.

TABLE 2.2 Properties of the Command button control

Property	Specifies
Caption	*The descriptive caption that the user sees on the button.* The caption should inform the user what the button does (i.e., what processing occurs when the button is clicked).
Font	*Characteristics of the font in which the caption is displayed.* In the Properties window (discussed in Section 2.7), clicking the ellipsis at the right of the setting causes VB to display a Font dialog window that is used to set the Font, the Font Style, and the Size. ✦ *Font* specifies the name of the font in which the caption is displayed. Possible values include MS Sans Serif, Courier, and Roman. ✦ *Font Style* specifies whether the caption will be displayed in italic, bold, or bold italic. ✦ *Size* specifies how large the displayed caption will be. Common values include 8, 9, 10, and 12, which refer to *points*, just as in word processors.
Picture	*The path and file name of a file containing a picture to be displayed.* The picture should be appropriate to the processing performed when the button is clicked. The Style property must be set to 1 - Graphical in order for the picture to be displayed. The valid file types are: ✦ Bitmaps (files with .bmp or .dib extensions) ✦ Icons (a 32 x 32 pixel image with a file extension of .ico) ✦ Metafiles (draw-type images of lines and shapes with a file extension of .wmf or .emf) ✦ GIF and JPEG (graphic image formats that are popular on the World Wide Web)
Style	*Whether the command button is able to display only a caption or both a caption and a picture.* The two possible settings are 0 - Standard and 1 - Graphical.
Enabled	*Whether or not the command button will respond when the user clicks it.* This property allows the programmer to "turn off" the command button. Possible values are True and False.
Visible	*Whether or not the command button will be visible to the user.* This property allows the programmer to hide the command button from the user. Possible values are True and False.
(Name)	*A unique name for the control that is used by the programmer.* The user is unaware of this property.

and a MouseMove event procedure, as illustrated in Figure 2.5. It is likely that the action to be performed in response to a Click event is different than the action to be performed in response to a MouseMove event, so the instructions inside the Click event procedure will be entirely different from the instructions inside the MouseMove event procedure.

2.5 The Label Control

The *Label control* displays information to the user.

FIGURE 2.5

Command button with two event procedures

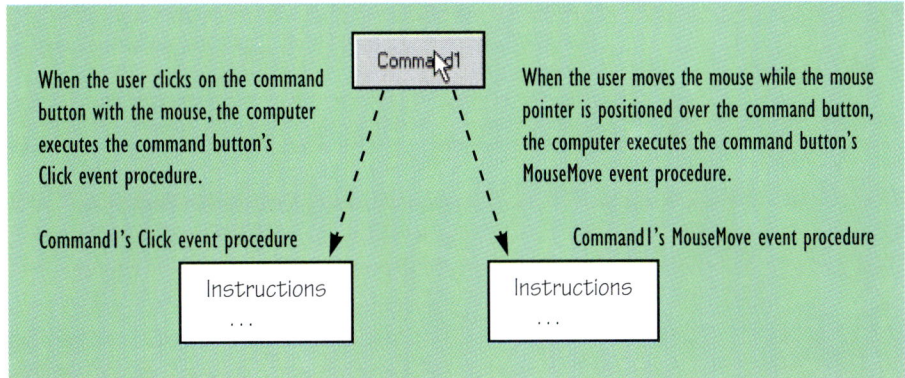

Appearance and Use

A label just appears as text on the form. Figure 2.6 shows a Label control on a form at design time. In this figure the label displays the text "Label1". Generally the user will not do anything with a Label control other than read the text it displays. However, in some applications, such as World Wide Web browsers, an underlined and colored phrase represents a *hypertext link*; the user clicks on this phrase to cause the application to display additional related information. Online help systems often display technical terms in underlined and colored fonts; when the user clicks on the term the system displays the definition of the term.

Properties

The properties of the Label control that the programmer typically sets are shown in Table 2.3. As you can see, several properties are common to both the command button and the label.

Events

The Label control can respond to several different events but is seldom made to do so. That is, in most cases all the user can do is read what the label displays. The programmer can use the Label control's Click event to implement the hypertext links described earlier.

2.6 The Timer Control

Like a command button, the **Timer control initiates execution of an event procedure**. However, instead of allowing the *user* to "pull the trigger," the

FIGURE 2.6

A Label control

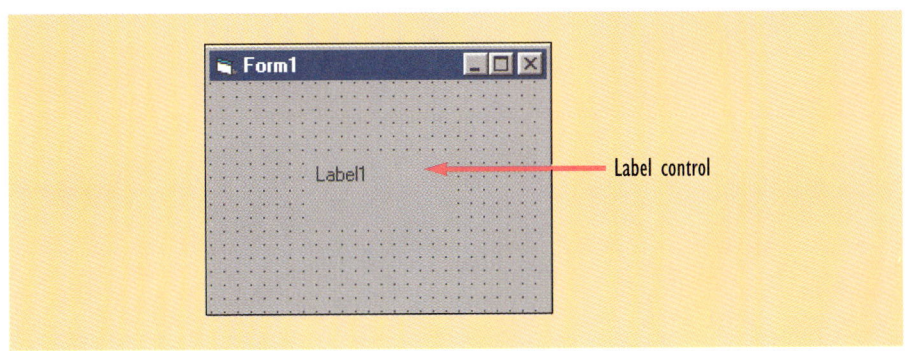

TABLE 2.3 Properties of the Label control

Property	Specifies
Caption	The text displayed by the label.
Font	Characteristics of the font in which the caption is displayed. In the Properties window (discussed in Section 2.7), clicking the ellipsis at the right of the setting causes VB to display a Font dialog window that is used to set the Font, the Font Style, and the Size. ♦ *Font* specifies the name of the font in which the caption is displayed. Possible values include MS Sans Serif, Courier, and Roman. ♦ *Font Style* specifies whether the caption will be displayed in italic, bold, or bold italic. ♦ *Size* specifies how large the displayed caption will be. Common values include 8, 9, 10, and 12, which refer to *points*, just as in word processors.
Alignment	How the caption text should be aligned (justified) within the boundary of the Label control. Possible values are 0 - Left Justify, 1 - Right Justify, and 2 - Center.
AutoSize	Whether or not VB should automatically resize the Label control to be large enough to display the entire caption. If not, then a caption too long to fit within the label will not be fully displayed. Possible values are True and False.
BorderStyle	The style of the Label control's border. Possible values are 0 - None and 1 - Fixed Single.
Visible	Whether or not the caption will be visible to the user. This property allows the programmer to hide the label from the user. Possible values are True and False.
(Name)	A unique name for the control that is used by the programmer. The user is unaware of this property.

Timer control does it *automatically*, and repeatedly, at a fixed interval of time. An example is the Autosave feature in many word processing applications. Autosave saves the user's document on disk periodically (say, every 10 minutes) without the user giving a command. This prevents the user from losing work in the event of a power outage, for example.

Appearance and Use

Figure 2.7 shows a Timer control on a form at design time. The Timer control is invisible at run time, so the user never actually sees or uses it.

FIGURE 2.7

A Timer control

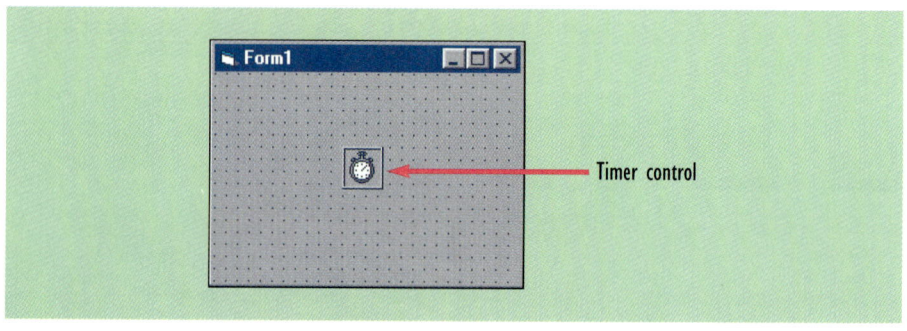

Properties

The properties of the Timer control that the programmer typically sets are shown in Table 2.4. Observe that Timer controls have no properties for establishing their appearance because they are invisible at run time. **The *Interval property* determines the length of time, in milliseconds, before the timer will initiate a processing step**. As an example, if the programmer sets a Timer control's Interval property to 10000, then the timer will initiate execution of its event procedure once every 10 seconds.

Events

The Timer control cannot respond to user actions. The only event it can respond to is the ***Timer event*, which is generated periodically by the Timer control itself**. If its Interval property is set to 10000, for example, then the Timer control will perform a "countdown," and when 10 seconds have elapsed it will generate a Timer event. The computer then follows the instructions in the Timer control's Timer event procedure, and when that is done the timer starts a new countdown, again for 10 seconds. Each time the countdown finishes, the Timer control generates a Timer event, which causes the computer to execute the instructions in the Timer event procedure. Then the timer starts a new countdown.

2.7 The VB Environment

The VB programming environment provides the tools needed to build, test, modify, and save projects, and to create executable files. In this section we discuss what to expect when you initially start VB, how you can arrange the tools to suit your tastes, and what the individual tools are for and how to use them.

Figure 2.8 identifies the major tools in the VB environment. When you initially start VB the tools may not be arranged exactly as shown in this figure, but you will be able to see and recognize at least some of them. If you haven't already done so, now is a good time to start VB and begin exploring. VB always starts in design mode.

Starting VB and Arranging Tools

VB allows the programmer to specify preferences for the layout of VB tools, including which tools should be visible initially. Thus, when you start VB what you will see depends on the preferences specified by the person who

TABLE 2.4 Properties of the Timer control

Property	Specifies
Interval	*The length of the countdown, in milliseconds (thousandths of a second). For example, if you want the timer to initiate a processing step every 2.5 seconds, then set its Interval property to 2500.*
Enabled	*Whether the Timer control is on or off. The timer does not initiate processing while off. Possible values are True and False.*
(Name)	*A unique name for the control that is used by the programmer. The user is unaware of this property.*

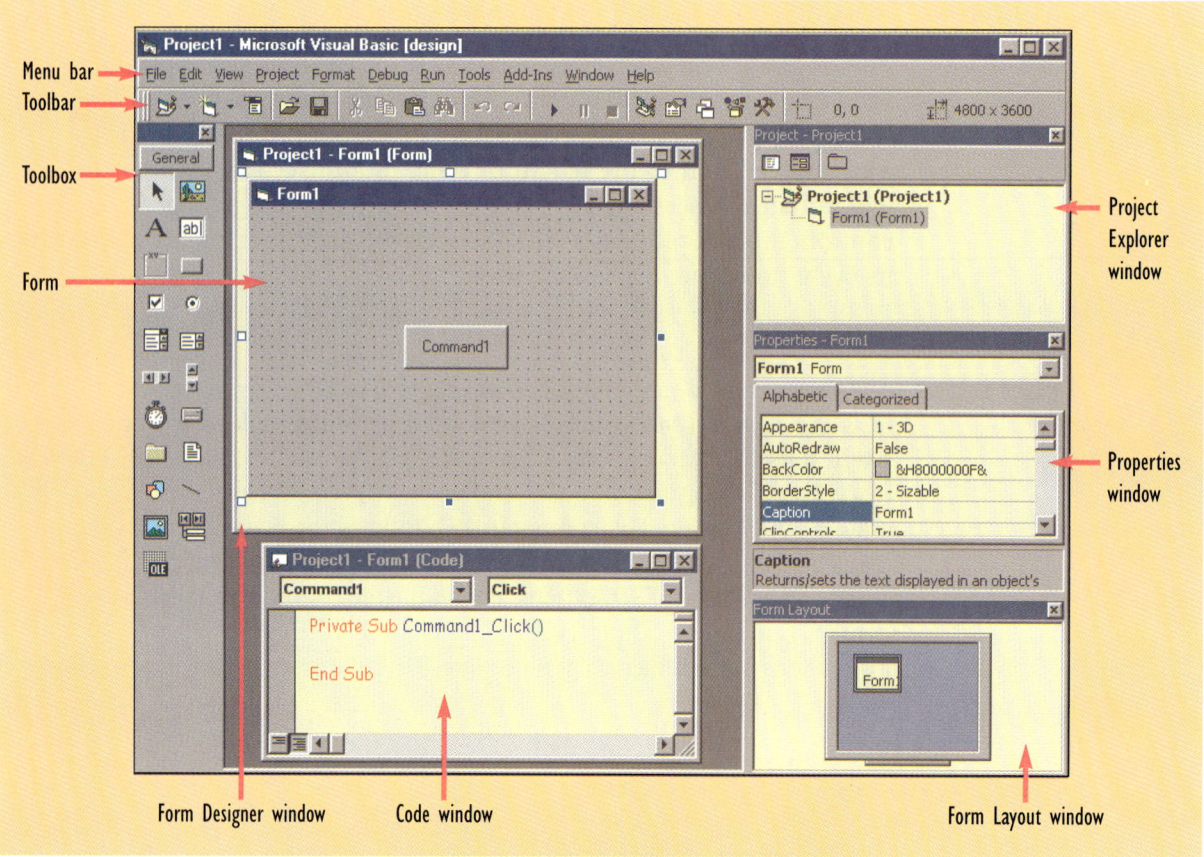

FIGURE 2.8 The VB environment

last used VB on your workstation. In this section, we explore the default tool layout after VB has been installed and explain how to specify your preferences.

The number of layout options may seem bewildering to the beginning VB programmer. You should not attempt to memorize them all; instead, read this section to get an idea of the possibilities, and to help you establish a layout that you like. As you gain experience your preferences may change, and you can return to this section for details then.

If you have just installed VB on your machine (that is, if you are the first one to use it) then when you start VB the first thing you will see is the New Project dialog shown in Figure 2.9. This dialog allows you to start work on a new project, or to open a previously created project; we'll discuss some of the features of this dialog at appropriate points in the text. Since our present objective is to explore the VB environment, we want to start work on a new project. To do this, click on the "Standard EXE" icon, then click the Open button.

Note that if you are not the first programmer to use VB on your workstation, you might not see the New Project dialog because the previous programmer may have checked the "Don't show this dialog in the future" box. In this case you can simply select New Project under the File menu in order to see it.

After clicking Open on the New Project dialog you will see a new project in design mode. If you are the first user, this will appear as shown in Figure 2.10. In this layout the major tools are *docked,* **which means that VB has placed them around the top and sides of the work area, and joined their borders together.** The advantage of this layout is that the work area is tidy, with no chance of one tool covering up another tool. The disadvantage is that it can be awkward

FIGURE 2.9

The New Project dialog

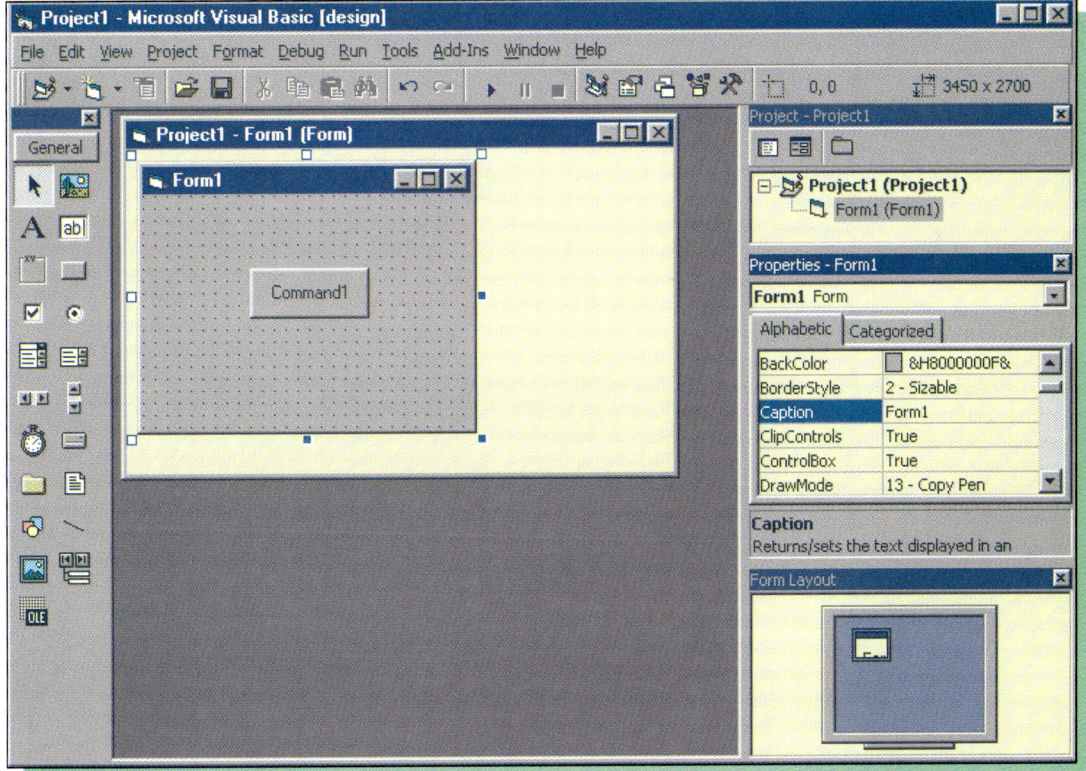

FIGURE 2.10 VB Tools in docked layout

to use; many programmers prefer to be able to resize and rearrange the individual tools.

You can resize a docked tool by clicking the mouse pointer on the tool's border and dragging. To help you see when the mouse pointer is positioned properly on the border, VB changes the mouse pointer from an arrow to a resize cursor, as shown in Figure 2.11. Here, the programmer can change the amount of vertical space devoted to the Project Explorer and Properties windows by dragging their common border up or down.

To see the full effect of docking, try moving the Form Designer window, which is not docked, around the screen by dragging its title bar (the title bar is the horizontal blue bar across the top of the Form Designer window). Then try moving the Project Explorer window, which is docked, toward the center of the screen and observe how it "detaches" from the right border. You can "redock" the Project Explorer window by dragging it back to its original docked location.

You can turn docking on or off by selecting Options… under the Tools menu, then selecting the Docking tab on the ensuing dialog. Figure 2.12a shows the default settings for docking. To "undock" a specific tool, uncheck its name. If you uncheck the tools as shown in Figure 2.12b and then click "OK," the environment will appear as shown in Figure 2.13.

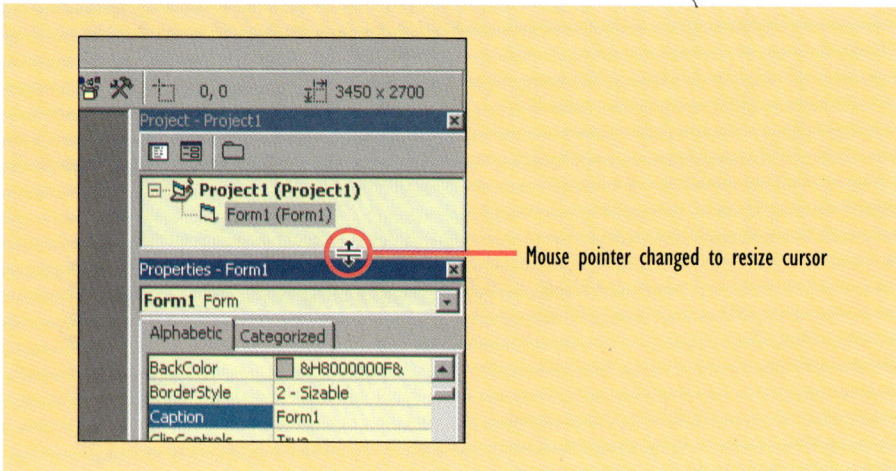

FIGURE 2.11

Resizing docked controls

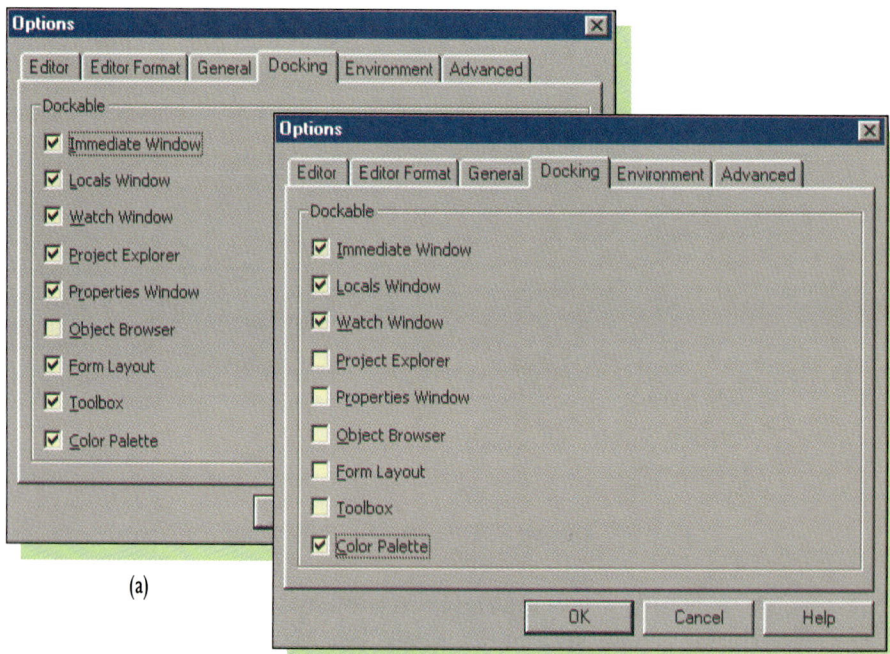

FIGURE 2.12

Turning docking on and off

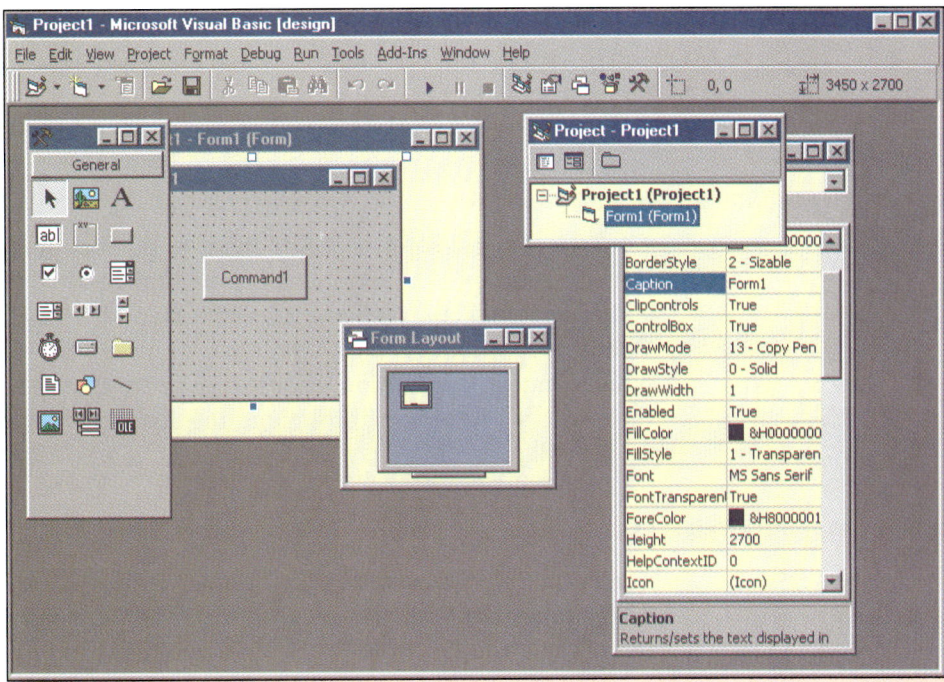

FIGURE 2.13 VB tools immediately after undocking

Figure 2.13 looks pretty messy, but you can easily resize (by dragging their borders) and rearrange (by dragging their Title bars) the individual tools. A good layout that you can create this way is shown in Figure 2.14. Indeed, if you are not the first person to use VB on your workstation, there's a good chance that Figure 2.14 looks a lot like what you see when you first start VB: the previous programmer may have chosen to turn off docking.

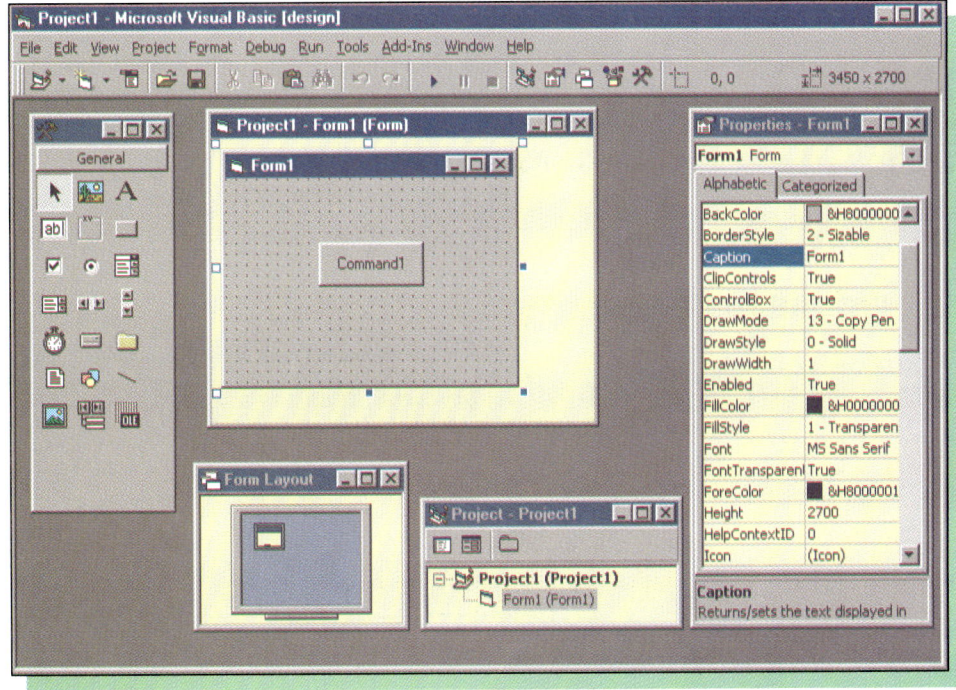

FIGURE 2.14 VB tools after undocking and rearranging

Whether the tools are docked or undocked, it is possible that not all of them will be visible. You can make a desired tool visible by selecting its name under the View menu.

Next, we discuss the purpose of the individual tools and how to use them.

The Menu Bar
◆ ◆ ◆

The *Menu bar* gives you access to many of the functions needed to create projects. For example, the File menu provides the commands for saving the project and for creating an executable file. VB's Menu bar is similar to those in other Windows applications. As one example, quitting VB is the same as quitting any other Windows application: choose Exit under the File menu. Menu bar functions will be introduced throughout the text as they are needed. In this chapter we will need only a few of them.

The Form Designer Window and Form Window
◆ ◆ ◆

The *Form Designer window* displays the Form window to the programmer at design time. The *Form window* comprises the form and the controls that sit on top of the form. Only the Form window is displayed to the user at run time.

When you first start VB you are presented with a Form Designer window that holds a blank form. A command button has already been placed on the form shown in Figure 2.8. You can position the Form Designer window anywhere on the computer screen by dragging its Title bar, and you can resize it by dragging its borders.

You can resize the form within its Form Designer window by clicking on one of the form's *resize handles* and dragging in the desired direction. The form's resize handles are shown in Figure 2.15. Note, however, that the form will always remain positioned in the upper left-hand corner of its Form Designer window. If you make the form larger than its Form Designer window, VB will automatically add scroll bars to the Form Designer window to let you view all parts of the form.

In Figure 2.8 the Form Designer window and the Form window were purposely made small in order to leave room for the other VB tools. In practice you will usually devote more of the screen's area to the form, which may contain many controls.

Finally, VB gives you the option of turning off the Form Designer window so that the Form window sits directly on the desktop as shown in Figure 2.16.

FIGURE 2.15

Resize handles on the form

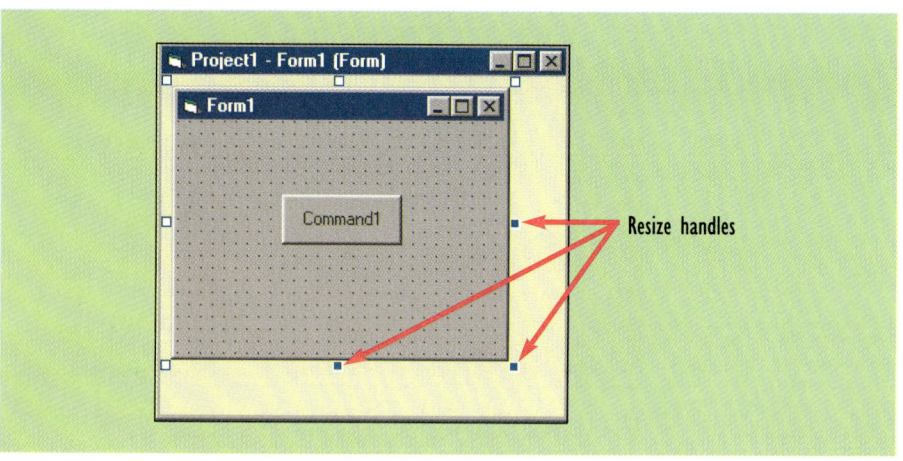

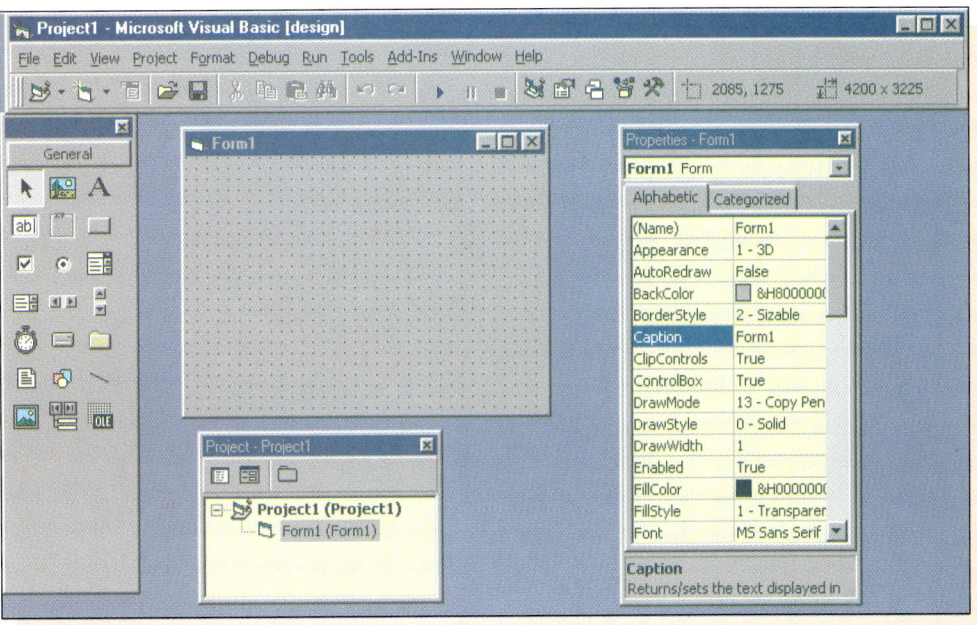

FIGURE 2.16 *The VB environment after turning off the Form Designer window*

To do this, select Options… from the Tools menu, then select the Advanced tab, then check the SDI Development Environment option, and finally quit and restart VB.[5] The screen images in the remainder of this text were produced using the SDI setting, and we will not use the Form Designer window again.

The Toolbox

The *Toolbox* is a collection of tools that you use at design time to place controls on the form. If the Toolbox is not visible, select Toolbox under the View menu to bring it up. You can reposition the Toolbox by dragging the thin horizontal bar at its top.

Figure 2.17 is an enlarged view of the Toolbox that identifies the tools for the Command button, Label, and Timer controls. To place a new control on the form, simply double-click on the tool for the type of control you want. If you want a new Command button control, double-click on the Command button tool. Double-clicking the tool places the new control at the center of the form; you can reposition the control by dragging it.

You can also "draw" a control directly at the desired location and in the desired size on the form. To do this, click once on the tool, then move the mouse pointer to the desired location on the form (it becomes a cross hair when it is over the form), then click-and-drag the cross hair. The control will appear when you release the mouse button.

When you place a new control on the form VB automatically provides *default settings*—*predefined initial settings*—for each of its properties. For example, if you create three Command button controls, VB will set their Name (and Caption) properties to Command1, Command2, and Command3. Similarly, Label controls are given the Name (and Caption) settings of Label1, Label2, etc.

[5] SDI stands for "Single Document Interface." VB's default installation setting is MDI, or "Multiple Document Interface." SDI and MDI are advanced topics, and you can use online help (discussed later in this section) to learn more about them.

FIGURE 2.17

The Toolbox

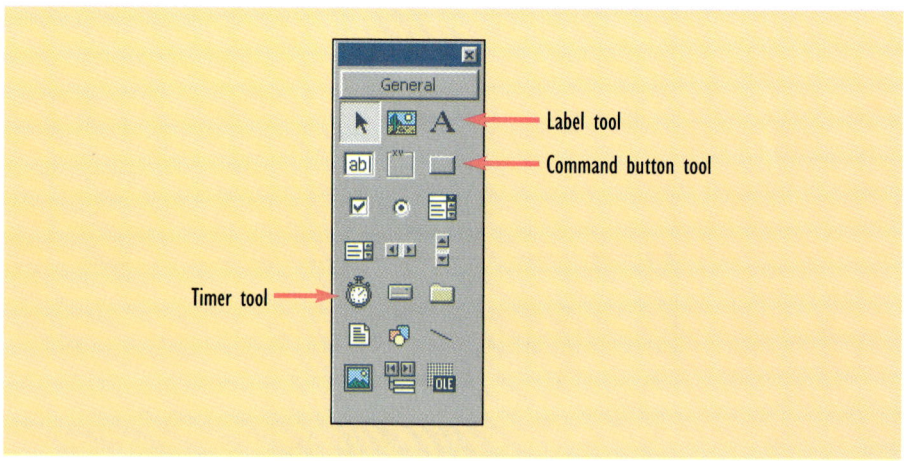

Suppose you place a control on the form, then later decide you do not want this control. How can you eliminate it? Click once on the control on the form to select it, then press the DELETE key. You can easily see when you have selected a control, because VB attaches resize handles to it (Figure 2.18). You can change the size of a control by selecting it, then clicking on one of its resize handles and dragging in the desired direction.

The Toolbox always shows tools for VB's standard controls. Microsoft provides with VB a large number of **additional types of controls,** called *custom controls,* and you can make the Toolbox show tools for these controls if you wish to use them in your projects. To do this, select Components... from the Project menu and then select the Controls tab on the ensuing dialog; you can then simply check the custom controls you wish to use.[6]

The Properties Window

The *Properties window* is used at design time to examine and change the settings for the properties of each control on the form. First select the control you wish to examine. If the Properties window is not visible, select Properties Window under the View menu to bring it up. You can reposition and resize the Properties window just as you repositioned and resized the Form Designer window.

If you select the command button as shown in Figure 2.18, the Properties window will appear as in Figure 2.19.

The Properties window has three parts: the Object box, the Property list, and the Description pane. The *Object box* shows the name of the selected control and

FIGURE 2.18

Resize handles on a selected command button

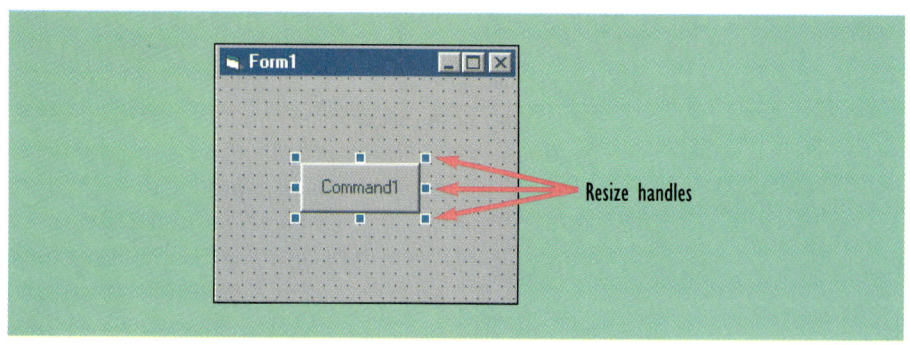

---

[6] You can purchase additional custom controls from third-party software developers.

FIGURE 2.19

The Properties window

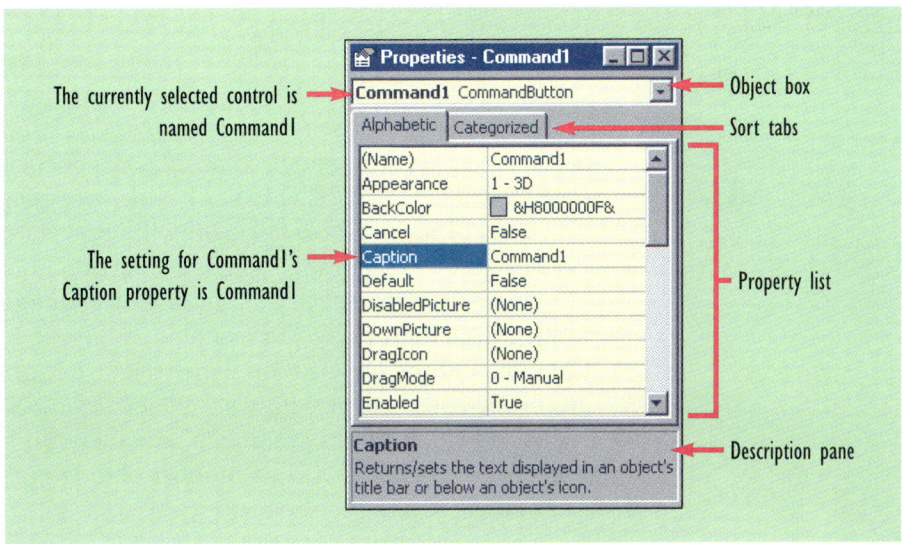

its type. In Figure 2.19, the selected control is named Command1, and it is a command button. You can change which control is selected using the Object box. Clicking the arrow at the right end of the Object box causes VB to display a list of all controls on the form, and clicking on a control in this list selects it.

The *Property list* shows the current property settings for the selected control (whose name appears in the Object box). It has two columns: the left column shows a property name and the right column shows its current setting. For example, in Figure 2.19 the current setting of the Caption property is Command1.

You can view the Property list in two ways: select the Alphabetic tab to see the properties in alphabetical order by property name; or select the Categorized tab to see the properties organized by function. In Figure 2.19 the Alphabetic tab has been selected. Observe that only some of the properties are visible; other properties can be viewed by resizing the Properties window to make it taller, or by scrolling downward. In Figure 2.20 the Categorized tab has been selected. Here, the category names appear in bold, next to a box containing either a

FIGURE 2.20

The Properties window with the Categorized tab selected

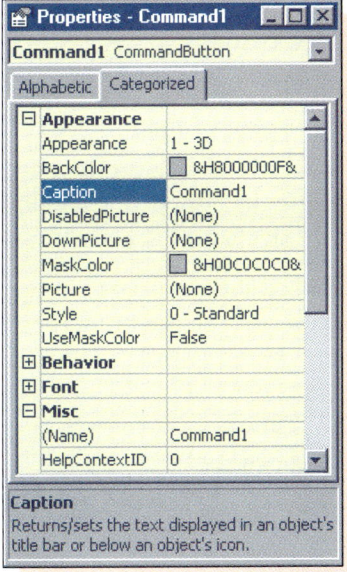

plus or a minus sign. Clicking a "plus box" causes the list of properties for that category to expand, and clicking a "minus box" causes the list of properties for that category to collapse so that you only see the category name.

For the beginner it may be easier to find a desired property using the Alphabetic tab. However, as you become more experienced with VB you may find the Categorized tab to be easier to work with, because you will be familiar with the functions of most properties, and will appreciate being able to shorten the Property list by collapsing categories that you know you can ignore.

Finally, the *Description pane* gives a brief reminder of the purpose of the currently selected property. For example, in Figure 2.19 the selected property is Caption, and the Description pane reads, "Returns/sets the text displayed in an object's title bar or below an object's icon." These reminders may seem vague to beginning programmers, but they can be helpful after you've had some experience with a large number of different properties. If you like, you can hide the Description pane.[7]

The way you modify property settings is the same for both the Alphabetic and Categorized tabs. First click on the name of the property in the Property list, then simply type the new setting, or edit the current setting by clicking the mouse at the desired point within the current setting and typing (you can use the BACKSPACE, DELETE, and arrow keys).

Sometimes a black "down arrow" will appear at the right side of the settings box; when this happens, clicking on the arrow will show a list of valid settings for you to choose from. Other times an ellipsis (three dots) will appear at the right side of the settings box; when this happens, clicking on the ellipsis will cause a dialog window to be displayed that will give you further information on selecting a valid setting.

If you haven't tried it yet, this would be a good time to try to reproduce the form in Figure 2.18. After you do, select the command button and explore its properties using the Properties window. Try changing some of its property settings. The following is a list of particularly interesting properties to experiment with; in each case, be sure to observe what happens on the form as you type the new setting.

- Change the command button's Caption property to your first name.
- Change its Height property to 1000.
- Change its Left property to 0.
- Change its Top property to about half of its current value.
- Change its Width property to about twice its current value.
- Change its Font properties (click on the Font property name, then click on the ellipsis, then use the Font dialog window that VB displays to change the Font, Font Style, Size, and Effects settings).

Note that the form itself has properties. You can select the form by clicking directly on it, and you can use the Properties window to change its property settings as with any other control. You may like to experiment with the form's property settings.

---

[7] To do this, right-mouse-click anywhere on the Properties window other than the Title bar and the tabs, then uncheck the Description option in the dialog that pops up.

The Code Window

Now that you know how to place new controls on the form and how to set their properties, the next task is to create event procedures. **The *Code window* allows you to view, write, and edit event procedures.** If it is not visible, you can bring it up by choosing Code under the View menu. Alternatively, you can simply double-click on any control on the form, or on the form itself. The Code window can be repositioned and resized just as the other windows can. Figure 2.21 shows the Code window that results from double-clicking on the command button in Figure 2.18.

The Code window displays event procedures. It has five parts: the Object box, the Procedures/Events box, the Code area, the Procedure View and Full Module View buttons, and the Margin Indicator bar.

The *Object box* shows the name of the control to which the displayed event procedure belongs. In Figure 2.21 this is Command1. Clicking the arrow at the right of the Object box causes VB to display a list of the names of all controls on the form; you can then select any one of these controls.

The *Procedures/Events box* shows the type of event the displayed event procedure corresponds to. In Figure 2.21 this is the Click event. The information in the Object and Procedures/Events boxes in Figure 2.21 tells us that the displayed event procedure contains the instructions that the computer will follow when the user clicks on Command1.

Clicking the arrow at the right of the Procedures/Events box causes VB to display a list of all valid events for the type of control currently shown in the Object box; you can then select any one of these events.

The *Code area* displays and allows you to edit the actual event procedure. Initially, it shows an empty template for the event procedure. The top line of the template begins with the words "Private Sub" and the bottom line is "End Sub". As programmer, you will enter the instructions of the event procedure between these lines.

The *Procedure View* and *Full Module View buttons* have an effect only when there are multiple event procedures. Clicking the Procedure View button causes VB to display only one event procedure at a time. Clicking the Full Module View button causes VB to display all the event procedures for the form, and allows you to scroll up and down through them. In the latter case, when you move the cursor around in the Code area the Object box automatically adjusts to correspond to the event procedure that contains the cursor.

FIGURE 2.21

The Code window

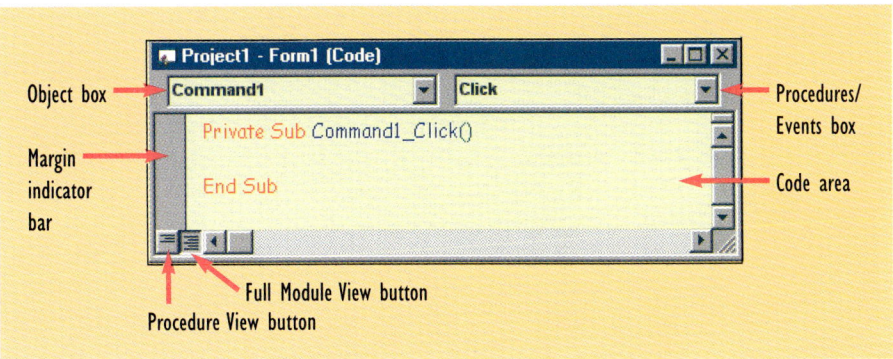

Finally, the *Margin Indicator bar* is useful for debugging (the topic of Appendix A). You can remove it by choosing Options… under the Tools menu, selecting the Editor Format tab, and unchecking the Margin Indicator Bar option.

Experiment by bringing up the Code window for the command button as shown in Figure 2.21. Try changing the event in the Procedures/Events box from Click to MouseMove, and observe the change in the Code area. Then change the event back to Click.

Next, edit the event procedure by adding a single line to it, so that the Code area reads as follows.

Private Sub Command1_Click()
    MsgBox "Hello"
End Sub

To edit the event procedure, you simply place the mouse pointer over the Code area (it will become an I-beam), click, then start typing. As you type the line above, you may notice a yellow *Quick Info* box appear as shown in Figure 2.22. VB's Quick Info boxes provide useful reminders to experienced programmers, but for beginning programmers they often provide too much information. You should ignore them and keep typing, or else turn off the Quick Info feature.[8]

Finally, if you type the new line correctly, you will create a valid event procedure. In a moment you can run the application and see its effect.

The Toolbar

The *Toolbar* provides easy access to some of VB's most frequently used functions. All of the Toolbar functions are also available via the Menu bar. Right now we will look only at the three Toolbar functions identified in Figure 2.23; we'll postpone the others until we need them.

Clicking the Start button at design time causes the computer to start executing your project. That is, clicking this button switches VB from design

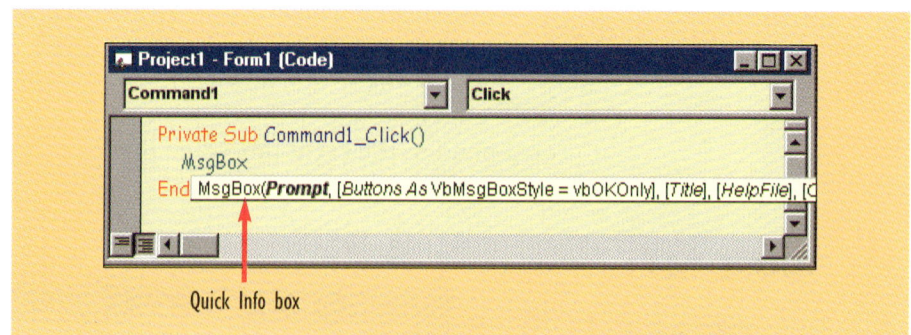

FIGURE 2.22
A Quick Info box

FIGURE 2.23
Three Toolbar functions

[8] To turn off the Quick Info feature, select Options under the Tools menu, then select the Editor tab, and then uncheck Auto Quick Info.

mode to run mode. This lets you test your event procedure. The Start button is disabled at run time (it turns gray as a visual cue).

Clicking the End button at run time causes the computer to stop executing your project. That is, clicking this button switches VB back to design mode. The End button is disabled at design time.

Clicking the Break button at run time causes the computer to temporarily suspend execution of your project and switches VB to break mode. Break mode is useful for debugging your project. The Break button is disabled at design time.

The actions of these three Toolbar buttons are summarized in Figure 2.24. If you've ever used a cassette tape player it should be easy to remember the purposes of these buttons. The icons on the Start, Break, and End buttons are the same as those on a tape player's "play", "pause", and "stop" buttons, respectively, and their purposes are analogous.

Before you start execution of your first project, it's good to know an absolutely foolproof way of ending execution. The End button is easy to use, but it is not foolproof, because the Toolbar can get covered by the running program's form. You can *always* end execution using the following steps:

1. Press CTRL+BREAK (the CONTROL key in conjunction with the BREAK key). This causes the computer to enter break mode.

2. Press ALT+R (the ALT key in conjunction with the R key). This activates the Run menu on VB's Menu bar.

3. Press E. This selects the End item under the Run menu.

Now execute the project. Simply click the Start button. VB then enters run mode: it displays the form, and hides the Toolbox and Properties window.

Now click the command button. If you modified its Click event procedure by adding the statement

    MsgBox "Hello"

as suggested earlier, you should see a simple message box displaying "Hello" and an OK button. Click the OK button. Click the command button again, if you like. End execution when you are satisfied. (Note that you cannot click the Toolbar's End button while the message box is displayed; you must click OK first.)

Notice that you cannot use the Toolbox or the Properties window at run time. These windows allow you to modify the project, and for that you have

FIGURE 2.24

Toolbar buttons for switching VB's mode

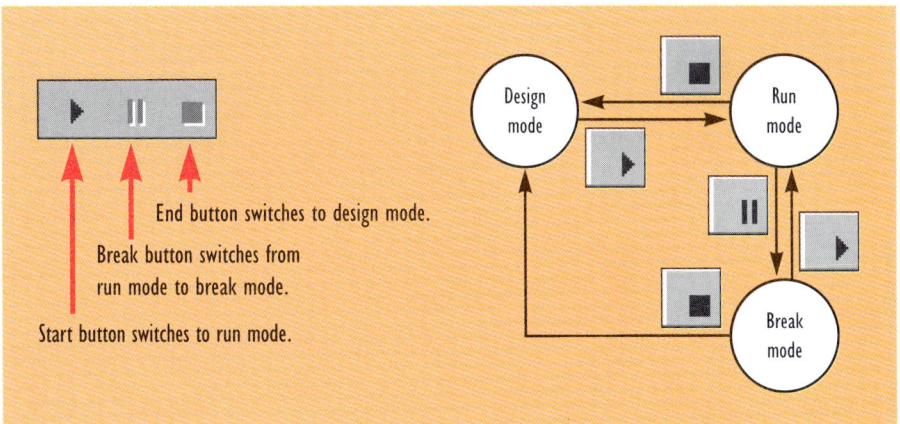

to switch back to design mode. After you've made the modifications, you can then switch back to run mode to test your changes.

The Form Layout Window

◆ ◆ ◆ The *Form Layout window* **allows you to specify where the form will appear on the screen at run time.** It can be used only at design time. As shown in Figure 2.25, the Form Layout window depicts a miniature monitor with a form icon sitting on it. To change the run time location of the form, use the mouse to drag the form icon to the desired location on the monitor. Experiment by dragging the form icon to the lower right-hand corner of the miniature monitor. Then run the program again, and observe the new location of the form at run time.

The Form Layout window is particularly useful in projects that have more than one form. It shows the location of all the forms, and allows you to position them as you wish; for example, you may want two forms to appear side by side at run time.

The Project Explorer Window

◆ ◆ ◆ The *Project Explorer window* **lists the project's forms, code modules, class modules, and resource file.** Figure 2.2, which diagrams the structure of VB projects, shows that projects may contain these items (code modules, class modules, and a resource file) in addition to forms; but, as indicated in Figure 2.3, they are not included in simple projects.

The Project Explorer window from Figure 2.14 is enlarged in Figure 2.26. It shows that this project currently consists of just one form. To see how the Project Explorer window works, try adding a few new forms to the project. To do this, you can choose Add <u>F</u>orm from the <u>P</u>roject menu, or simply click the Add Form button on the Toolbar, shown in Figure 2.27.

Each time you add a new form, you will see a new, blank form appear on the screen, and you will see a new entry appear in the Project Explorer window. Figure 2.28 shows the Project Explorer window after two new forms have been added. Note that you can resize the Project Explorer window, and you can scroll through the list it displays (which is useful when the list is long).

The Project Explorer window has three buttons (identified in Figure 2.26). When a form is not visible, you can click on the form's entry in the Project

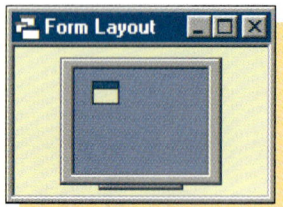

FIGURE 2.25

The Form Layout window

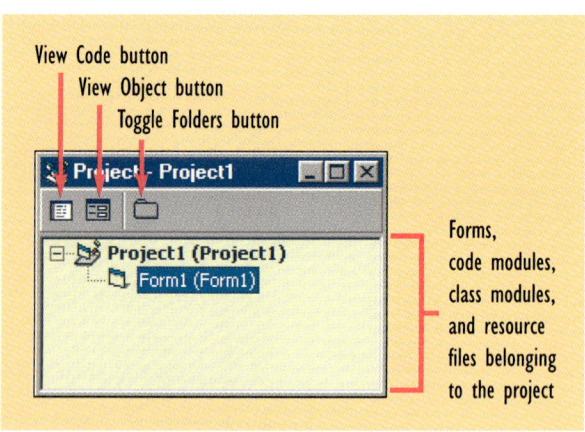

FIGURE 2.26

The Project Explorer window

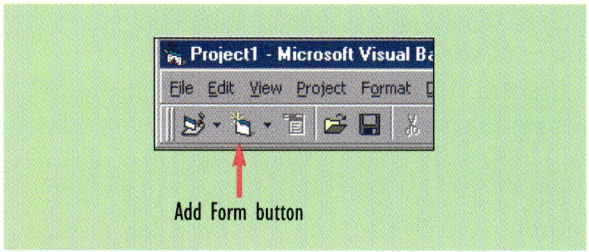

FIGURE 2.27

The Toolbar's Add Form button

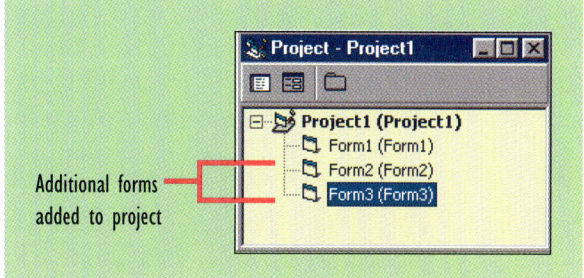

FIGURE 2.28

The Project Explorer window after adding two new forms

Explorer window, then click the View Object button. Similarly, clicking the View Code button brings up a code window for the form. You can see the purpose of the Toggle Folders button by clicking it a few times; it is particularly useful in projects that have code modules and class modules in addition to forms.

You can remove forms, code modules, class modules, and the resource file from the project. To do this, first click on the entry in the Project Explorer window; VB responds by highlighting it. Then choose Remove Form under the Project menu. Now remove the forms you just added to the project. Observe that when you remove a form, VB deletes its entry from the Project Explorer window and removes the form from the screen.

Online Help

Finally, you should take advantage of VB's online help. If you find you've forgotten some key detail while working on a project, online help is a quick way to look it up. Online help is also useful for probing further; there is much to know about VB, and so far we have examined only its most fundamental tools.

To bring up online help's main screen, choose Microsoft Visual Basic Help Topics from the Help menu. VB responds by displaying the window shown in Figure 2.29. The Contents tab in this window presents an overview of the available information, organized by topic. The book icons represent topics;

FIGURE 2.29

Online help's Contents tab

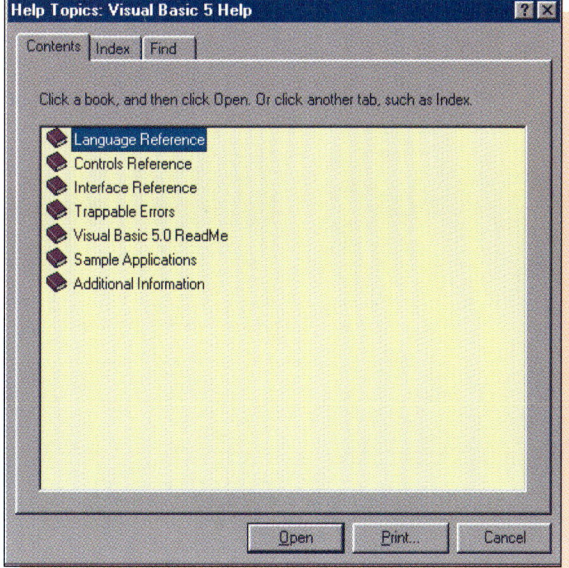

to see subtopics and useful information you must "open" a book of interest by clicking the book and then clicking the Open button.

To leave online help and return to your VB project, click on the Close button (the "⊠") at the upper right of the Help window.

The most frequent use of online help is to find answers to specific questions that arise while creating a project. For example, you might have a question about the Command button control. Clicking the Index tab in Figure 2.29 causes online help to display the Index window shown in Figure 2.30.

To find a topic quickly, begin typing the *search phrase*—**a word or words that describe the topic you wish to see information about**—in box 1 of the Index window. Usually you need only type the first few characters of the search phrase, because online help performs an incremental search through the index in box 2. That is, as you type each character in box 1, online help automatically jumps downward through the index in box 2 to the first topic that begins with the characters you've typed so far.

For example, to quickly find help about command buttons, begin typing the search phrase "command buttons" in box 1. Figure 2.31 shows how the index appears after the programmer has typed "comm". Note that in this case, by the time the programmer has typed the fourth character, online help has narrowed the search sufficiently. Now that "command buttons" is visible in box 2, the programmer can click directly on the term "described" right below it. Then clicking on the Display button at the bottom of the Index window causes online help to display the window shown in Figure 2.32, which contains online help's information about command buttons.

From this point on in the text, as we introduce new programming tools and language elements, we indicate search phrases you can use to find additional information quickly.

In the three projects that follow, we use the VB tools covered in this section. If you've been working with VB and wish to quit now, do so, and do not worry about saving your work.

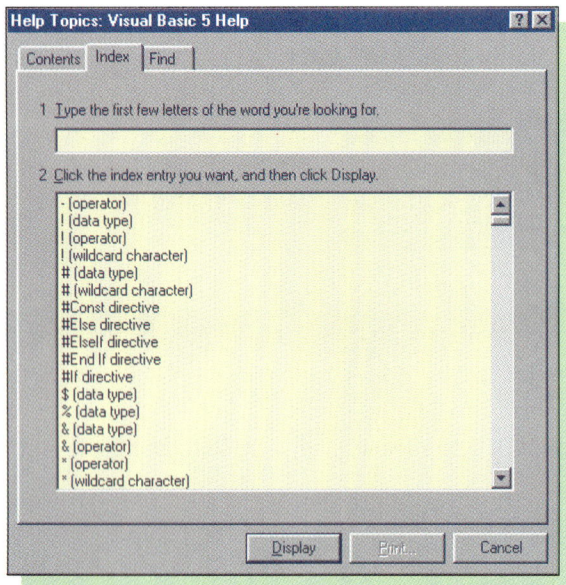

FIGURE 2.30

Online help's Index tab

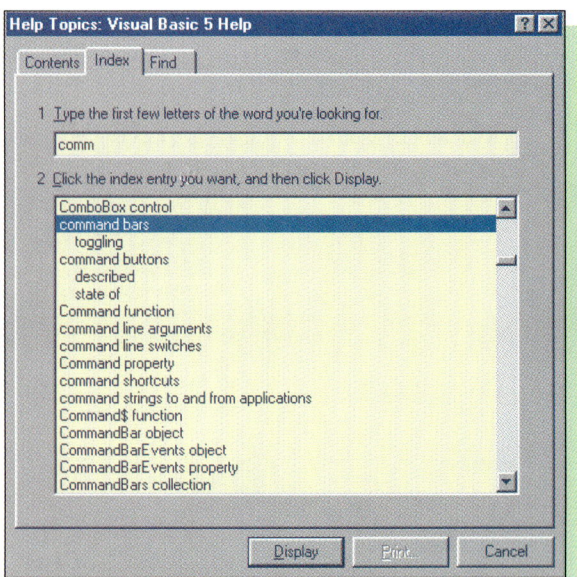

FIGURE 2.31

Online help's Index tab after typing "comm"

FIGURE 2.32

Online help's information about command buttons

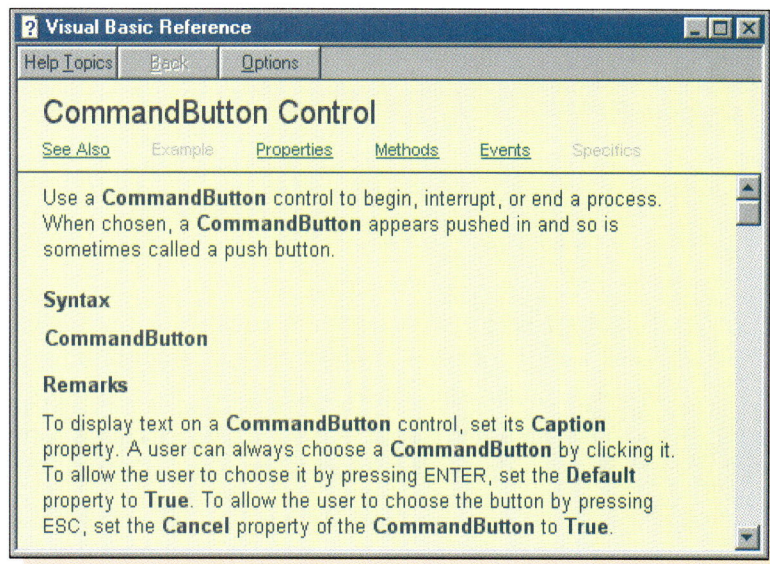

2.8 Project 1: How an Event-Driven Program Works

In this project we work through the steps of creating a finished application from scratch. Our goal is to integrate the information we have presented about VB's programming tools: the project includes all three of the control types, and we carefully examine how the project works at run time.

Rather than building a business application, this project takes the form of a tutorial. This is appropriate because you still do not know enough about VB's programming language to write event procedures. However, all subsequent projects use the concepts and skills developed in this project.

Before beginning work on a new project you should use Windows to create a new folder (also called a *directory*) on the disk where you will save the project. This practice helps keep your disk storage organized.

1. Create a new folder named Proj01 on the disk where you will save this project. To do this, first open the folder where you want to locate the new folder (using Windows Explorer or the "My Computer" icon on the Windows desktop). Then select New under the File menu, then select Folder, then type Proj01 and press ENTER.

   Now start VB, if you haven't already done so, and begin building the GUI.

2. Open a new "Standard EXE" project using the New Project dialog. When you first start VB this dialog may be displayed automatically. You can bring it up at any time by selecting New Project from VB's File menu.

3. Place one Label control and two Command button controls on the form as shown in Figure 2.33.

4. Use the Properties window to look at the Name and Caption settings of these three controls. These are the default settings provided by VB when you created the controls. Note that the Name property is always parenthesized in the Properties window, and if you are viewing the Alphabetic tab, (Name) always appears at the top of the list.

FIGURE 2.33

User interface for Project 1

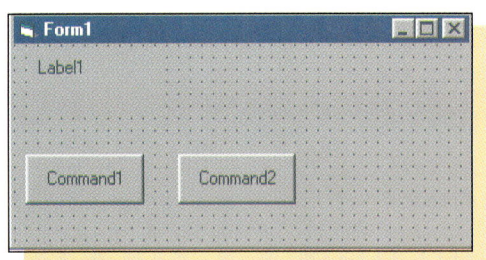

5. Execute the program by clicking on the Toolbar's Start button, or by pressing function key [F5]. Observe that nothing happens when you click on either command button. Why?

6. Return to design mode (i.e., end execution of the program). To do this, click on the Toolbar's End button, or select End from the Run menu.

At run time, nothing happens when you click on the command buttons because the event procedures that tell the computer what to do when the user clicks the command buttons are empty. Let us create an event procedure for one of the command buttons so that when the button is clicked at run time, it will change the text displayed by the Label control.

7. Double-click on the Command1 button. This will bring up the Code window as was shown in Figure 2.21. (Remember that you must be in design mode to get the Code window.)

This is a template for the event procedure that tells the computer what to do when the user clicks on the command button named Command1. Event procedures are sometimes called *sub procedures*, which is why you see the word "Sub" at the top of this template.

To create an event procedure, you type one or more **statements—instructions to the computer to perform particular actions**—inside the event procedure. VB's programming language defines what constitutes a valid statement.

8. Edit the event procedure by typing in a statement so that the event procedure appears as in Figure 2.34. You may observe a list box automatically pop up when you type the period following "Label1"; this is VB's "Auto List Members" feature, which lists all the valid properties for the Label control. You can ignore this list and keep typing, or you can click on Caption in the list and press [TAB] to cause VB to type Caption for you.[9]

The first line of an event procedure is called the *heading*. Here the heading begins with the words "Private Sub." It continues with the *event procedure name*, which is Command1_Click in this case, and ends with parentheses. All

FIGURE 2.34

Click event procedure for Command1

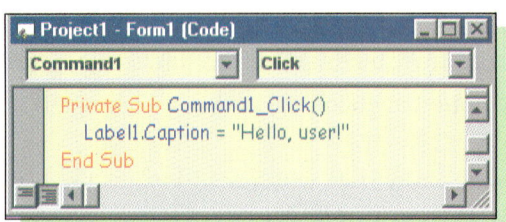

[9] You can turn this feature on or off. Select Options... under the Tools menu, then check or uncheck "Auto List Members" on the Editor tab.

event procedure names consist of two parts, separated by an underbar (_) character. The first part indicates which control the event procedure belongs to, and the second part indicates which event (for that control) causes the event procedure to execute. Thus, the name Command1_Click tells you that this event procedure will execute when the user *clicks* on the command button named *Command1*.

What happens when the computer executes an event procedure? It executes the statements inside the event procedure, one at a time, from top to bottom. The statement

```
Label1.Caption = "Hello, user!"
```

instructs the computer to change the setting of Label1's Caption property to "Hello, user!" Recall that the Caption property of a Label control specifies what the label displays on the form. Can you visualize how the application will behave when you run it?

9. Run the program, and observe what happens when you click on the buttons Command1 and Command2. Were you able to predict this? You won't cause any harm by clicking these buttons multiple times.

10. Return to design mode.

Next, create an event procedure for the Command2 button that changes the setting of Label1's Caption property to a different value.

11. Bring up the Code window for Command2's click event procedure by double-clicking on the Command2 button. Alternatively, if the Code window is already visible but showing a different event procedure, you can click on the arrow at the right of the Code window's Object box (see Figure 2.34), then select Command2.

12. Using the pattern of the statement you added to Command1_Click, modify the Click event procedure for Command2 to change the setting of Label1's Caption property to a different value. Use a value other than "Hello, user!" (The quotes are necessary here; just change the text between them.)

A good setting to try is **two double-quotes with nothing between them (i.e., "")**, **which is called the *zero-length string*.** This setting simply clears the caption.

13. Click the Code window's Procedure View button, then click its Full Module View button, and observe the change in the Code area. Since we now have two event procedures, these buttons have a useful effect. You may prefer Full Module View because it enables you to use the Code window's vertical scroll bar to move between event procedures in the Code area, instead of having to use the Object box.

14. Run the program again. Click alternately on Command1 and Command2, and observe how the label changes with each click.

15. Return to design mode.

At run time nothing happens until an event occurs for which the programmer has supplied an event procedure. The computer just "idles" between such events; that is, the computer simply waits for the next event to occur, or for the user to end execution. Programs that operate this way are called *event-driven programs*. VB is designed specifically to allow you to create event-driven programs.

Next change the design-time setting for the Label control's Caption property.

16. Use the Properties window to change the Caption property of Label1 to "Get Ready, Get Set". To do this, bring up the Properties window, click the arrow at the right end of its Object box, and select Label1 in the list that is displayed. Then click on the Caption property in its Property list, and edit its setting to read "Get Ready, Get Set" (do not include the quotes). Figure 2.35 shows the Properties window.

17. While you're still at the Properties window, change Label1's font size to 10. To do this, click on the Font property, then click on the ellipsis, then set the font size to 10 in the ensuing dialog.

18. Run the program again and observe how Label1's appearance on the form differs.

19. Return to design mode.

Setting properties at design time, using the Properties window, gives them *initial* values. When the program starts running, it uses these initial settings for every property of every control. At run time, a property can be changed only by the execution of a statement in an event procedure.

Thus, in our project, control Label1 starts out displaying "Get Ready, Get Set", which it continues to display until the user clicks, for example, Command1, which causes the statement Label1.Caption = "Hello, user!" to be executed.

Now let's experiment with Timer controls.

20. Add two Timer controls to the form, as shown in Figure 2.36. Note that it's not too important where you place Timer controls on the form because they will be invisible when the program runs. Just place them somewhere off to the side where they won't obscure the other controls at design time.

21. Use the Properties window to set Timer1's Interval property to 1000.

22. Add a statement to Timer1's Timer event procedure so that it appears as shown in Figure 2.37.

FIGURE 2.35

Changing Label1's Caption property at design time

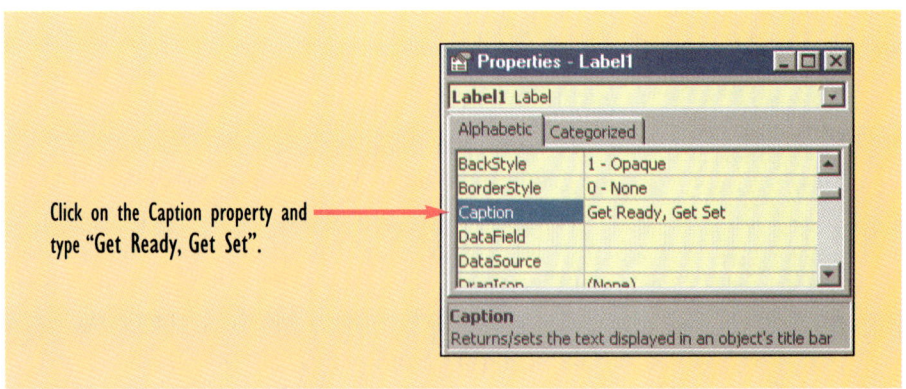

Click on the Caption property and type "Get Ready, Get Set".

FIGURE 2.36

Project 1's form after adding two Timer controls

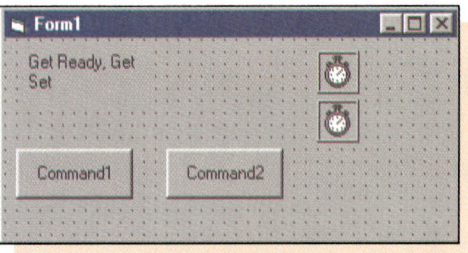

FIGURE 2.37

Timer event procedure for Timer1

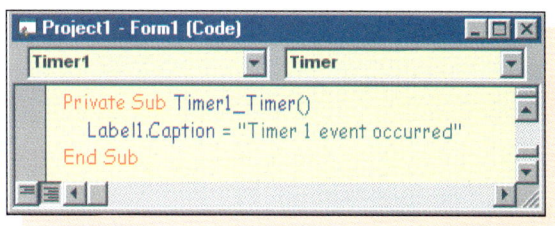

23. Similarly, set the Interval property for Timer2 to 1600 and add the statement

Label1.Caption = "Timer 2 event occurred"

to the Timer2_Timer event procedure.

Recall that Timer controls are used to make the computer automatically perform some action at a specified time interval. The interval is specified in milliseconds (thousandths of a second).

Thus, when we run our modified program, the Timer event for the control named Timer1 will occur (and the statement in the Timer1_Timer event procedure will be executed) every 1.0 seconds. Similarly, the Timer event for the control named Timer2 will occur (and the statement in the Timer2_Timer event procedure will be executed) every 1.6 seconds. Can you visualize how the running program will behave?

24. Run the program and see how the Label's caption changes automatically as a result of the Timer1 and Timer2 events. Observe that the Timer controls are invisible at run time. Click on Command1 and Command2 a few times to see their effect.

25. Return to design mode.

Note that the time needed for the computer to execute a single statement is very small. It is much less than a second, and much less than the time between clicks of a command button—even if the user clicks twice in rapid succession. This fact is sometimes important in applications that use Timer controls.

Now let's experiment with the Command button control's Picture property.

26. Add another Command button control to the form, and position it to the right of the two existing command buttons. Using the Properties window, first clear the new Command button's Caption property (i.e., delete the current Caption setting, and leave it blank). Then set its Style property to 1 - Graphical. Finally, select its Picture property and click on the ellipsis button (the three dots) that appears to the right of its setting as shown in Figure 2.38.

FIGURE 2.38

Setting the Picture property for Command3

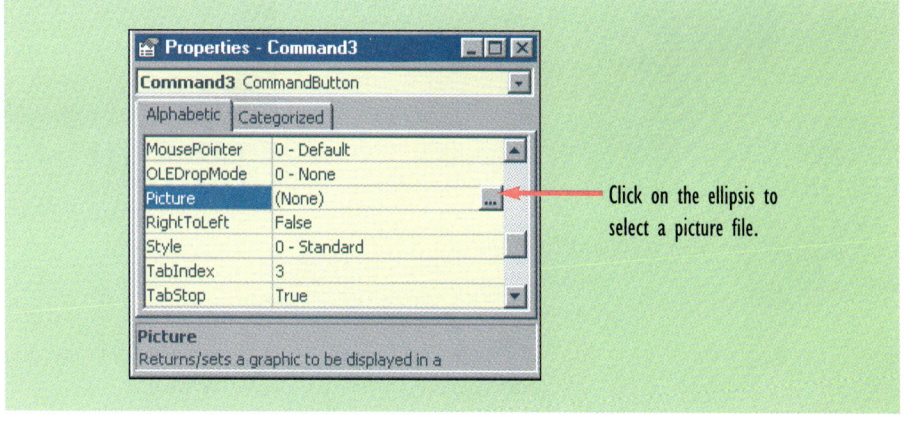

27. Clicking on the ellipsis button causes VB to display a Load Picture dialog window. In this dialog window, double-click on the following file folders (in sequence):[10]

   Graphics
   Icons
   Traffic

   At this point, the Load Picture window should appear as in Figure 2.39.

28. Click on the Trffc14 file and then click the Open button. Resize the command button to make your form appear as shown in Figure 2.40.

29. Add a statement to Command3's Click event procedure so that it appears as shown in Figure 2.41.

30. Run the program. Let it run for a few seconds, then click on the stop sign. Observe that executing Command3's Click event procedure, which contains the End statement, causes program execution to stop exactly as if you had clicked on the End button on VB's Toolbar.

   Now save the project on disk.

31. Select Save Project under the File menu. In the ensuing Save File As window, use the "Save in" dropdown list box to specify the folder named

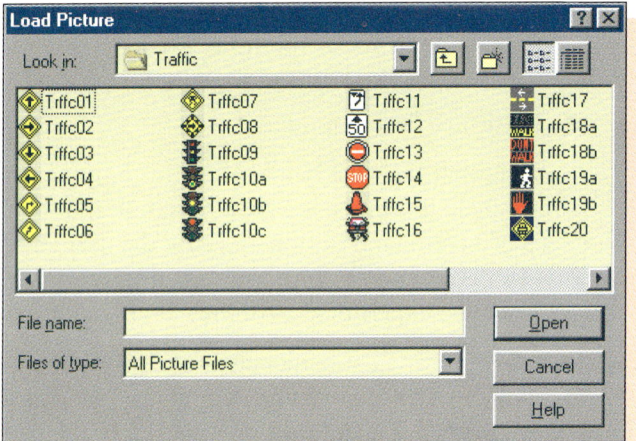

FIGURE 2.39
The Load Picture dialog window

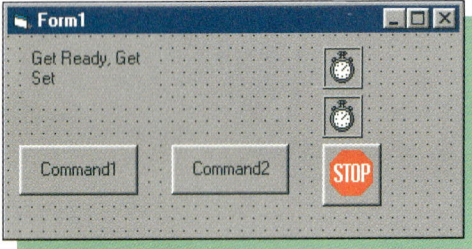

FIGURE 2.40
Project 1's form after adding a command button with a picture

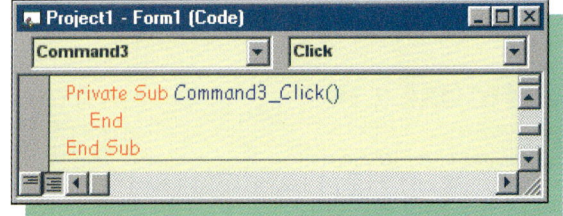

FIGURE 2.41
Click event procedure for Command3

---

10 As discussed in Section 2.4, Microsoft provides these graphics with VB, but you must perform a custom install in order to use them.

Proj01 that you created earlier, then click Save. (Note that if you forgot to create the folder Proj01, you can create it from the Save File As window by clicking the Create New Folder icon.) VB then displays another window titled Save Project As, which should show the same folder; click Save.

Finally, let us create and run an executable file.

32. Select Ma<u>k</u>e Project1.exe… under the <u>F</u>ile menu. VB displays a dialog window titled Make Project. Use the "Save in" dropdown list box to navigate to the folder named Proj01, then change the file name to App1, and then click OK. VB then creates the executable file containing the finished application.

33. Quit VB by selecting E<u>x</u>it under the <u>F</u>ile menu. If VB displays a final dialog that asks whether to save changes to the file Project1.vbp, click Yes.

34. Run the executable application. Do this in Windows by simply double-clicking on the App1 icon in the Proj01 folder.

You can distribute copies of the executable file to other Windows users, who can copy it onto their computers and run it even if they don't have VB.[11] However, the user's computer must have the file MSVBVM50.DLL in the WINDOWS\SYSTEM folder. Microsoft provides this file with VB, and allows you to distribute it free of charge. For more information, use online help with the search phrase, "MSVBVM50.DLL".

EXERCISE 2.1 Modify Project 1 so that the text displayed by Label1 is in italic font.

EXERCISE 2.2 Modify Project 1 so that the Timer1 and Timer2 events alternate evenly: one at 1.0, 3.0, 5.0, etc., seconds and the other at 2.0, 4.0, 6.0, etc., seconds.

Hints: (1) Set the initial settings for the Interval properties of both Timer1 and Timer2 to 1000; (2) set the initial setting for the Enabled property of Timer2 to False; (3) modify the Timer1_Timer event procedure to disable itself and enable Timer2 by adding the statements

```
Timer1.Enabled = False
Timer2.Enabled = True
```

and, similarly, modify the Timer2_Timer event procedure to disable itself and enable Timer1.

EXERCISE 2.3 Describe in words the user action that will cause the event procedure with the following name to be executed: Command9_Click.

EXERCISE 2.4 For a Timer control named Timer1, is it possible to have an event procedure named Timer1_Click? Explain.

2.9 Files, Saving, and Printing

Not only will you save your project on disk when you have completed it, but you should also save it periodically as you construct it. You may also want to print it out. There are many reasons for saving and printing your work.

---

[11] Executable files produced by VB5 will run only on 32-bit Windows platforms. In particular, they will not run on Windows 3.1 machines.

Electrical power failures cause the computer to lose the contents of its main memory. Any work you performed after your last save operation will be lost in this event. Experienced programmers therefore save the project under construction frequently, so that they will not lose much work if a power failure occurs.

Programmers also occasionally experience failures associated with disk storage. When a disk fails, everything on it is irretrievably lost. A less drastic failure occurs when the programmer mistakenly deletes a file from disk. Experienced programmers make *backup copies*, **which are copies of files on completely separate disks,** to avoid losing work due to disk failures and inadvertent file deletions. Paper printouts can also be used to help recover from such failures; the printout is a record of the content of the project (which the programmer can refer to instead of having to figure out the design details again).

In order to save and print VB projects you must first understand how VB organizes projects for storage in files.

Files

For storage, a single VB project is organized as a collection of files. These files correspond to the highest two levels of the hierarchical VB project structure, as illustrated in Figure 2.42.

A project may have several forms, code modules,[12] and class modules, and one resource file. Each form, code module, class module, and resource file occupies its own file on disk. In addition, each project has **one *project file*, which VB uses to keep track of the paths and names of all files belonging to the project.** You can think of the project file as storing on disk the contents of the Project Explorer window: they both list all files associated with the project.

File Types and Extensions

As a VB programmer, you will routinely create and choose names for form files, code module files, class module files, and project files. Generally, the computer doesn't care what names you choose, but with several files comprising a project you will find it much easier to remember which is which if you use descriptive file names.

Programmers have developed standard file-naming conventions to help out: use the file name to describe the specific purpose or action of what the file contains, and use the file name extension to indicate the general type of the file. Table 2.5 shows the commonly accepted extensions for several types of files.

FIGURE 2.42

Organization of files for VB projects

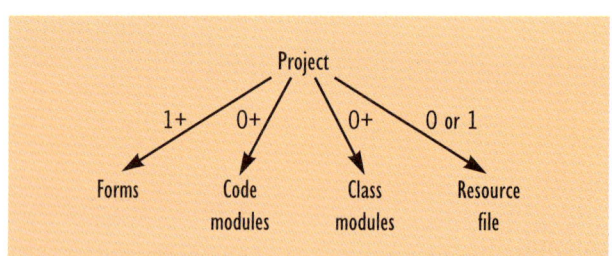

[12] The VB environment uses the term "module" instead of "code module." We discuss code modules in Chapter 6.

2.9 Files, Saving, and Printing

TABLE 2.5 Extensions for common file types

Application	Type of File	Extension
VB	Project	.vbp
	Form	.frm
	Code module	.bas
	Class module	.cls
MS Access	Database	.mdb
MS Excel	Spreadsheet	.xls
MS Word	Document	.doc
Generic	Text	.txt
	Executable	.exe

Saving Your Work

Recall that the simplest VB project consists of one form, no code modules, no class modules, and no resource file. Such a project will be saved as two files: a project file (defined earlier) and a *form file,* **which contains the form and all of its contents (controls, properties, event procedures, and so forth).**

When you save a project for the first time using Sa<u>v</u>e Project under the <u>F</u>ile menu, VB first displays a Save File As window, which you use to provide a path and name for the form file, then a Save Project As window, which you use to provide a path and name for the project file.[13] These dialog windows are shown in Figure 2.43.

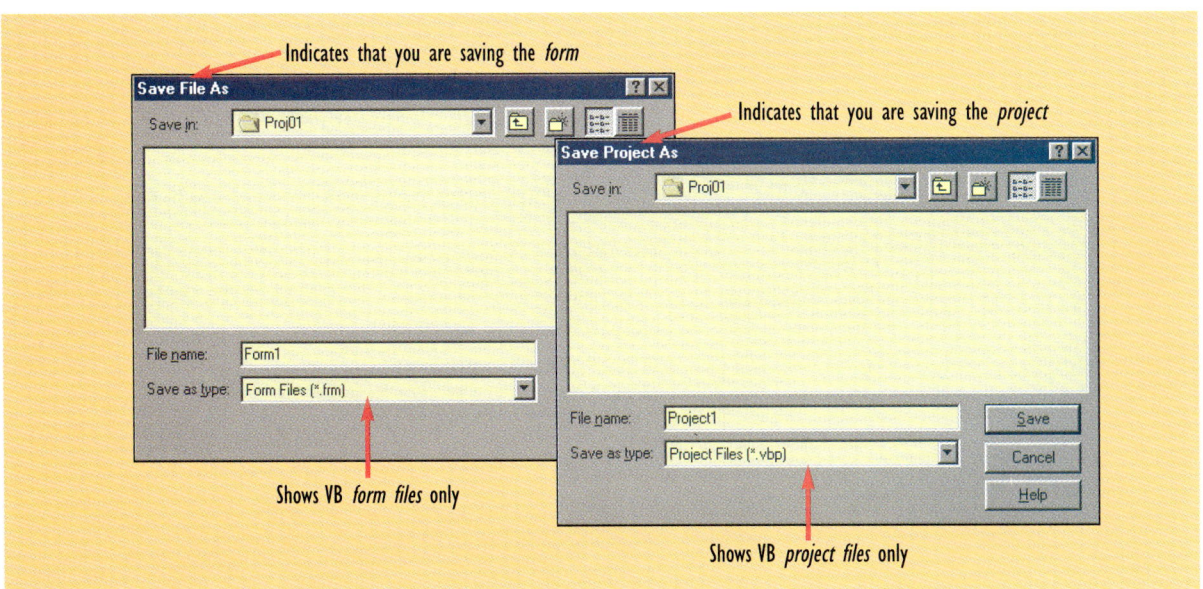

FIGURE 2.43   Save File As and Save Project As dialog windows

---

[13] A *path* specifies the location of a folder or file on disk. It consists of a drive designation letter followed by the sequence of folders in which the desired folder or file resides. For example, if a file resides in a folder named Samples, which is inside a folder named VB, which is on the C drive, then the path for this file would be C:\VB\Samples. In the Save File As and Save Project As windows, you don't have to type the path—just use the Save In drop-down list box.

When you save a project subsequently (i.e., after you've already saved it once, but have made changes you wish to save) you again use Sa<u>v</u>e Project under the <u>F</u>ile menu. This time VB displays neither the Save File As window nor the Save Project As window; it simply saves the files under the same path and file names you supplied the first time you saved the project. (Each new version you save replaces the previous version of the files.)

The following simple rules for the Save operation will serve you well.

1. Always use Sa<u>v</u>e Project to save your work.
2. Save your work periodically.

In most cases you will want to save the project file and all the form and code module files associated with a project in the same folder on disk. Since you will create many projects, you will find working with VB files much easier if you create a new folder before beginning each new project. Not only will this keep your disk organized, but it will also make it much easier to copy entire projects (for example, for backup purposes).

VB's <u>F</u>ile menu provides three other Save commands that are sometimes useful for special purposes. These menu items are shown in Table 2.6. Be careful when using these commands! They differ from Sa<u>v</u>e Project in an important way. Sa<u>v</u>e Project saves *every* file in the project, but each of the commands in Table 2.6 saves only *one* file. The danger is that you may think you are saving your entire project when in fact you are saving only one of its files.

Copying Projects from Hard Drive to Diskette

You will probably want to copy your work from your computer's hard drive to a diskette from time to time. Saving on the hard drive is faster than saving on diskette; thus, you will probably want to perform saves to the hard drive frequently, and make backup copies on diskette less frequently. When you copy a project, you must be sure to copy *all* of the project's files.

TABLE 2.6 Other Save commands under VB's File menu

Command	Action	Typically Used For
Sa<u>v</u>e Project As…	Provides a dialog window for you to specify the path and file name for the project file, then saves the project file.	Changing the location or name of the project file.
<u>S</u>ave File	Saves the selected form, code module, or class module file. The selected file is the one that is highlighted in the Project Explorer window.	Saving changes to a single form, code module, or class module.
Save File <u>A</u>s…	Provides a dialog window for you to specify the path and file name for the selected form, code module, or class module file, then saves the selected form, code module, or class module file.	Changing the location or name of the selected form, code module, or class module file.

Copying your work to diskette is easily done outside VB, using Windows Explorer or the "My Computer" icon on the Windows desktop. Just copy the entire folder containing the project. This approach is guaranteed to work as long as you keep all of the files for a project in the same folder.

You can also make copies from within VB, but this requires some care: you must first use Save File As..., once for each form file, then use Save Project As... (in this order). This approach is a bit risky because each Save File As and Save Project As operation saves only one file, and so it is possible to miss a file. If you attempt to exit VB with unsaved changes in any file, VB will notify you by providing a dialog identifying the file and asking whether to save it. In most cases the safe response is to save the file.

If you use Windows regularly, you should become competent with its file management operations. You will frequently need to create folders, copy files for backup purposes, rename files, and delete unwanted files and folders.

Printing Your Work
◆ ◆ ◆

To print your project, select Print under the File menu. VB will display the Print dialog box shown in Figure 2.44. To print all event procedures in your project, select the Current Project option and the Code box, as shown in that figure.

You may wish to select Current Module instead of Current Project if your project consists of multiple forms. The Current Module option prints only one form, whereas Current Project prints all of them. (The "current" form, i.e., the one that will be printed, is the one that is selected in the Project Explorer window.)

To print images of your forms (the user interface), choose the Form Image box. To print out additional information about your forms, such as the property settings for all controls, choose the Form As Text box.

2.10 Project 2: Project Design Considerations

Let us build a simple project to explore some of the design choices that you will frequently make as a programmer and to get a little more experience working with the VB environment. The project is a simple invoice application that computes the total charge for a customer who purchases a computer system consisting of a CPU, a monitor, and a keyboard.

This project and subsequent projects use the formal procedure for creating applications introduced in Chapter 1. Recall that this procedure consists of three steps: identifying user requirements; designing the application; and

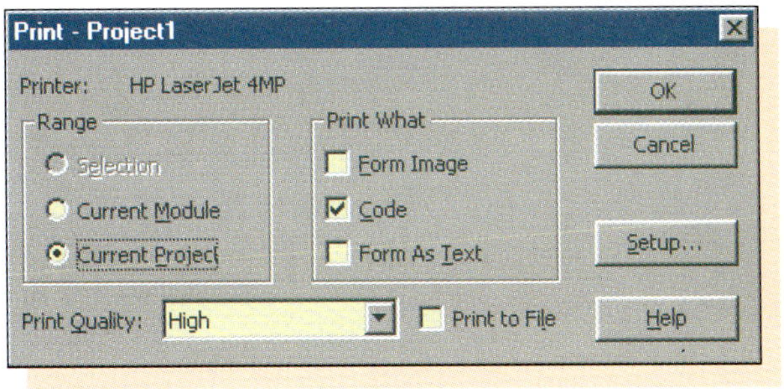

FIGURE 2.44
• • • • • • • • • • • • • • •
The Print dialog box

constructing the application. We begin each project by presenting the user requirements under the heading "Description of the Application."

Description of the Application

The invoice form appears in Figure 2.45. When the user clicks the Compute Invoice button, the program displays the customer's name and the prices of the CPU, monitor, and keyboard in the Label controls Label1 through Label4, respectively. Then it computes and displays the following values in Label5 through Label7:

- The subtotal is the sum of the CPU, monitor, and keyboard prices.
- The tax is the product of the subtotal and the tax rate.
- The total is the sum of the subtotal and the tax.

The program uses the customer name, component prices, and sales tax rate shown in Table 2.7.

Design of the Application

The design step of the application creation process is a planning stage. Its goal is to identify the components that will be part of the application and carefully organize them. Figure 2.45 shows most of the components of this project: there are several Label controls and a Command button control. Apart from the arrangement of these controls on the form, what else is there to "carefully organize" about these components? The answer has to do with the event procedure for the command button, which we cannot see in Figure 2.45.

In order to learn its importance firsthand, let us delay the remainder of the design step and proceed directly with the construction step (in this project only). As we construct the project we will encounter various difficulties as a result of our lack of planning. This will demonstrate the kinds of design problems that should be solved *before* beginning to create an application. We will learn from our mistakes in this project, and use this knowledge in future projects.

Construction of the Application

1. Create a new folder named Proj02 on the disk where you will save this project.

    Now start VB, if you haven't already done so. Then open a new project (if necessary) and begin building the GUI.

2. Place seven labels and a command button on the form, as shown in Figure 2.46.

TABLE 2.7 Data used by the invoice application

Item	Value
Customer name	Joe Govis
Price of CPU	$ 1450
Price of monitor	$ 715
Price of keyboard	$ 330
Tax rate	0.081

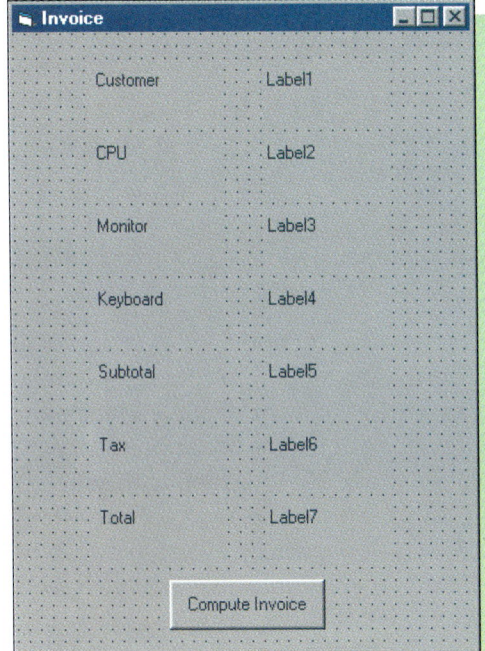

FIGURE 2.45

Invoice form user interface

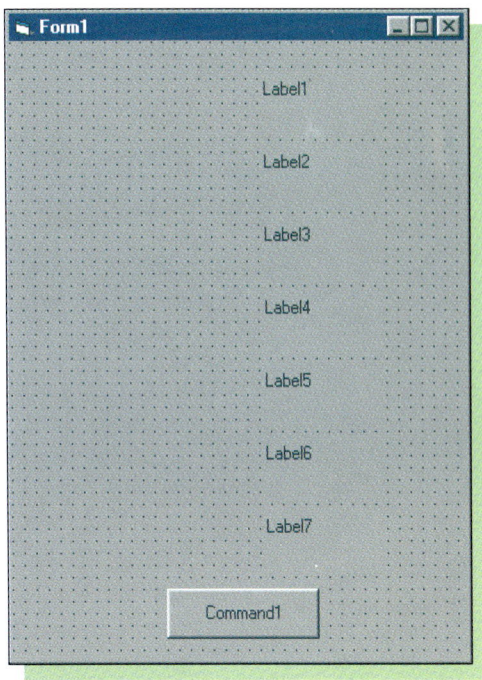

FIGURE 2.46

Initial user interface for Project 2

VB's Format menu provides a number of commands that you can use to quickly and neatly arrange controls on the form. You may wish to experiment with some of these commands. To arrange the seven labels in a column, for example, you can: create the labels on the form without too much concern for their alignment; select all of the labels; use the Format menu's Align submenu to align their left edges; use the Format menu's Vertical Spacing submenu to equalize the vertical spacing between the labels; and then use the Format menu's Vertical Spacing submenu to increase or decrease the vertical spacing between the labels.

3. In the Code window, create the Click event procedure for Command1 as shown in Figure 2.47.

Recall that when the computer executes an event procedure it executes the statements (the lines between Private Sub and End Sub) one at a time, from top to bottom. Try to predict what the program will do when you run it.

FIGURE 2.47

Click event procedure for Command1

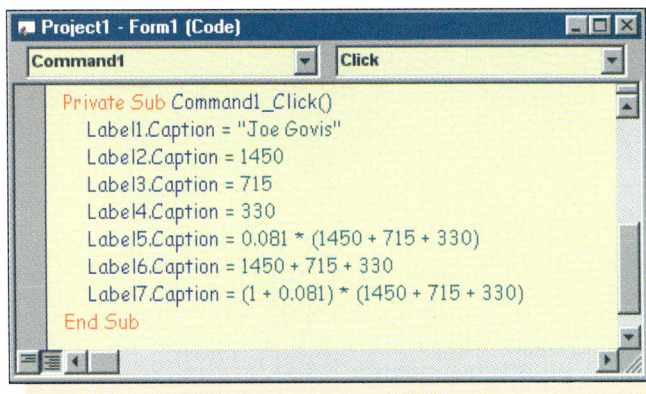

4. Before going further, save the project in folder Proj02 using Save Project under the File menu.

As you proceed to refine the project, you should periodically save it (using Save Project), so that if something like a power outage should happen, you will at least be able to recover a copy of your project up to the time of your last save before the outage.

5. Run the program, and observe what happens when you click the command button. Were you able to predict this? Return to design mode.

The project in its current form has very little descriptive information built into it. A programmer looking at the form and reading the event procedure can see that some arithmetic calculations are performed, the results of which are displayed on the form. By studying these calculations, the programmer may be able to guess roughly what each calculation is for. But interpreting this project takes time, and the programmer cannot always guess correctly. As much as possible, therefore, an application should be self-explanatory as to what its purpose is and how it works. Our application in its current form is *very* poor. Let's make some improvements to the project so that it will be easier to understand.

6. Add seven more labels to the form, and position them and set their captions as shown in Figure 2.48. Also, change the caption of the command button to "Compute Invoice", and the caption of the form to "Invoice".

These changes make it clear that the form is an invoice for the sale of computer hardware.

7. Run the program again and see how it works.

If you are observant, you should notice an error when you run the modified program. Actually, if you have been diligently trying to figure out how the application works, you may have noticed this error while you were typing in the Command1_Click event procedure. If so, congratulations are in order.

FIGURE 2.48

Improved user interface for Project 2

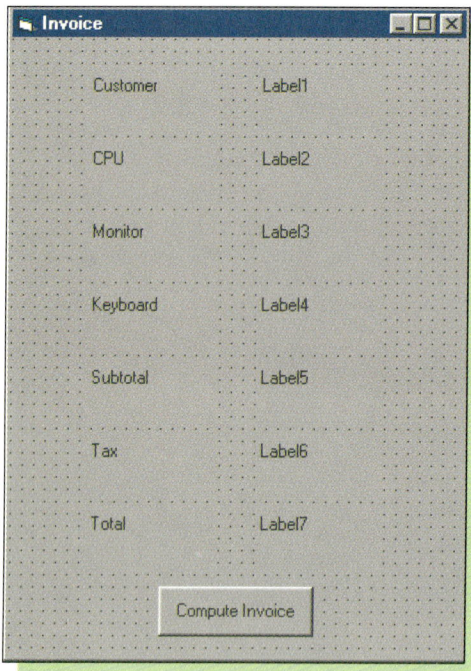

The error is that the program displays the tax where it should display the subtotal, and vice versa. Perhaps you are trying to figure out how to correct this error even as you read this.

Suppose we modify the Command1_Click event procedure by moving the sixth statement before the fifth statement, as in Figure 2.49. Will this correct the problem? If you are unsure of the answer, make the change and run the program again to find out.

To figure out how to correct the error, you have to cross-reference the labels as they appear on the form with the statements in the event procedure that refer to the labels. In a small project such as this one, this is not hard. But any realistic project is going to be larger than this one, and beginning programmers quickly learn that having to cross-reference objects on the form with statements in event procedures is extremely difficult, *unless* they use descriptive names for the objects involved in the statements.

Let us rename the important controls—those whose names appear in statements—in this project.

8. Use the Properties window to change the Name property settings of controls Label1 through Label7 as shown in Table 2.8.

Note that the names suggested in Table 2.8 for the Label controls all begin with the three-letter prefix "lbl". This **"lbl" *prefix* is used for all controls that are labels**. Likewise, we will use the **"cmd" *prefix* for all Command button controls, and the "tmr" *prefix* for all Timer controls**. This practice further reduces the necessity of cross-referencing and is commonly employed by VB programmers.

FIGURE 2.49

Proposed modification to Click event procedure for Command1

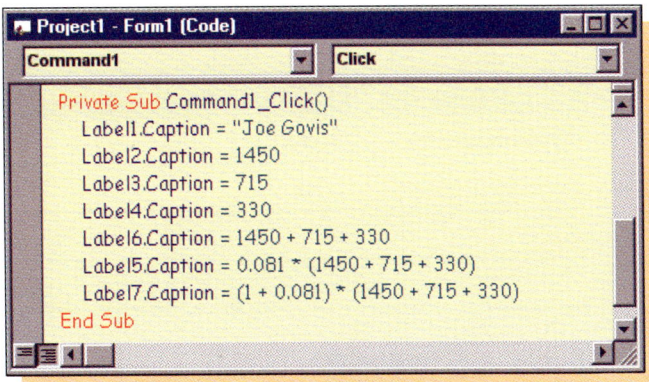

TABLE 2.8 Descriptive names for important controls in Project 2

Old Name	New Name
Label1	lblCustomer
Label2	lblCPUPrice
Label3	lblMonitorPrice
Label4	lblKeyboardPrice
Label5	lblSubtotal
Label6	lblTax
Label7	lblTotal

These prefixes, which are generally agreed upon by VB programmers, are summarized in Table 2.9. We will state the prefixes for other types of controls as we introduce them. Throughout this text we consistently employ three-letter prefixes in control names.

> **Convention** When choosing the name for a control, begin the name with the appropriate three-letter prefix for that type of control. Make the remainder of the name descriptive.

9. Now modify the event procedure so that it appears as shown in Figure 2.50.

Looking only at the event procedure statements, you can see that the computations for the tax and the subtotal are reversed. With descriptive names it is not necessary to cross-reference the layout of the labels on the form with the statements in the event procedure to figure this out, which makes the operation of this event procedure much easier to understand.

10. Modify the event procedure to correct the "reversed" tax and subtotal computations.

11. Now run the program. What happens? If you followed the preceding instructions exactly, VB should give you one of two error messages: "Object required" or "Variable not defined."[14] The source of this error is that the name of the Label control is lblCPUPrice, but the statement lblCPU.Caption = 1450 (see Figure 2.50) refers to a control named lblCPU. There is no control named lblCPU.

TABLE 2.9 Standard three-letter prefixes for control names

Type of Control	Prefix
Command button	cmd
Label	lbl
Timer	tmr

FIGURE 2.50

Click event procedure after changing control names

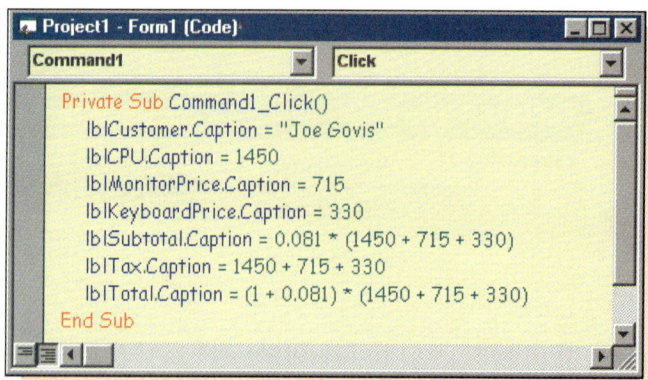

[14] Which of the two error messages you see depends on whether the Code window contains the statement "Option Explicit", which in turn depends on a programmer-specified preference. We discuss this statement in Chapter 3.

This error illustrates how the computer takes things literally. It may be easy enough for you and me to see the mistake, but the computer will not fix it for us. We need to fix the error. Do so now.

12. Click either End or OK on the message box, then change the statement lblCPU.Caption = 1450 to say lblCPUPrice instead of lblCPU. Then run the program again.

The Properties window is used at design time to specify initial settings for a control's properties, and these settings can be changed at run time by executing a statement in an event procedure. It's interesting to note, however, that VB does not allow the Name property of any control to be changed at run time. In light of the error we just encountered, changing a control's name at run time could be like "pulling the rug out from under" a statement that tried to refer to the control's original (design time) name.

There is still one important control that has an unsatisfactory name: the command button. In a sense, its name is more important than the names of the Label controls because it appears in the first line of the event procedure—the heading—which is the first thing a person sees when looking at the code. The term *code* **refers to the statements that, collectively, make up the event procedures belonging to a project.** Thus, you use the Code window to view, write, and modify the project's code.

What would be a good descriptive name for the command button? Recall that the standard three-letter prefix is "cmd". Since a command button initiates a processing step, a descriptive name should describe the action of the processing step; it is also helpful if it describes what the action is performed on or what it produces. How about cmdComputeInvoice? As a rough guide, good command button names often include a verb (the action) and a direct object (what the action is performed on).

13. Use the Properties window to change the Name property of the command button to cmdComputeInvoice.

14. Run the program again. Notice anything different? Now nothing happens when you click the command button.

To see why the program no longer works, return to design mode, then double-click on the command button to bring up the Code window. The event procedure appears as in Figure 2.51; it is empty.

Where did our earlier event procedure go? It still exists, and it is still named Command1_Click; however, there is no longer any control named Command1.

FIGURE 2.51

Click event procedure after changing command button's Name property

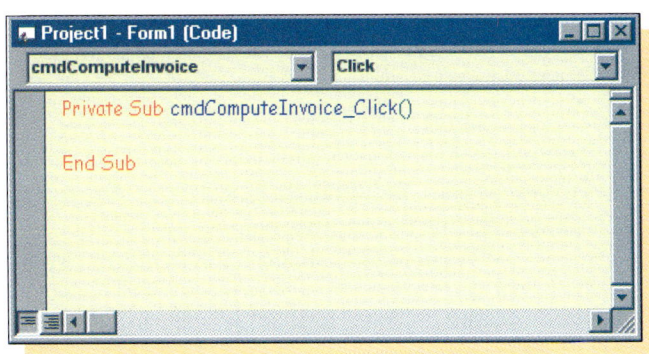

If the Procedure View button is depressed in your Code window, then your Code window will look just like Figure 2.51—you will not see the Command1_Click event procedure. In this case, to switch between the two event procedures you must use the Code window's Object box to select the name of the control whose event procedure you wish to work with. Since there is no longer any control named Command1, you will not find Command1 in the Object box. However, the Object box does contain the entry "(General)", which VB uses as a place to put sub procedures that are not associated with any control.[15] For now, we'll be content just to recover our event procedure, which is easiest to do when the Full Module View button is depressed.

15. Click the Code window's Full Module View button, if it is not already depressed. You should then see two event procedures: one named Command1_Click, and one named cmdComputeInvoice_Click. Delete cmdComputeInvoice_Click by highlighting it (all of its lines, beginning with Private Sub and ending with End Sub) and then pressing DELETE.

16. Edit the line

Private Sub Command1_Click()

to read

Private Sub cmdComputeInvoice_Click()

then press the ↓ key (to move the cursor off of this line in the Code window). This causes VB to recognize that this event procedure now belongs to the control named cmdComputeInvoice. You should now see cmdComputeInvoice appear in the Code window's Object box.

17. Have you been saving the project periodically? Save it now.

18. Run the program again to see that it works properly.

This project illustrates that the names of important controls—controls whose names appear in event procedure statements—are critical to making the program easy to understand. Naming these controls is part of the work you do to organize the project. You should decide on these names during the design step of the application creation process. These names will help you avoid errors during construction, such as reversing the calculations of subtotal and tax, and make it easier to locate such errors when you do make them.

Note that the computer runs any program just the same whether or not it is organized well. Humans are the ones who will suffer if it is organized poorly.

Project 2 is now much better organized than it was initially. However, some aspects of its organization are still quite poor; we will return to this project as an example and solve some of these problems in Chapter 3. One glaring deficiency is the way it displays numbers on the user interface: it would be nice if they were formatted as dollar amounts. We will see how to do this in Chapter 4.

In Project 2 there are seven labels, whose captions are Customer, CPU, Monitor, Keyboard, Subtotal, Tax, and Total. Do you think it is worthwhile to give these controls descriptive names, or is it just as well to leave them with the names VB provided (Label8, Label9, etc.)? Explain.

---

[15] Such sub procedures are called *general sub procedures,* and are the topic of Chapter 6.

EXERCISE 2.6

In Project 2 the Caption property setting for lblCustomer is Label1. The caption for lblCPUPrice is Label2, and so on. These settings are probably confusing to the user.

Using the Properties window, modify the project by deleting these Caption property settings (i.e., clear the Caption property for each of these controls using the DELETE key). Observe that these Label controls seem to "disappear" from the form. This may also be disconcerting to the user. Modify the project again by changing the setting of the BackColor property of these Label controls to some color other than the color of the form, and observe the effect on the user interface.

2.11 Project 3: A Business Simulation

For our last project in this chapter, let us construct a program that simulates a business operation. This project introduces you to the process of translating user requirements—presented in the form of a narrative description of a business operation—into a program design. By building the project you will gain more experience with the VB environment. And by running the program, you will see how computer programs can be used to experiment with and learn about complex real-world situations.

The scenario is as follows. I have created a database that contains information of interest to a large number of people, and I'm thinking of a starting a business to sell access to this database over a network (say, the Internet). I know roughly how the business will operate, but before I get too far along I want to determine whether the business will turn a profit and, if so, how profitable it might be. To help with this, I want a VB project that simulates the business operations that affect costs and revenues.

Description of Business Operations
◆ ◆ ◆

My plan is to connect a computer containing the database to a computer network. Via the network, prospective customers will send me "electronic orders," which are requests for particular pieces of information from the database. To process an order, my computer will retrieve the requested data from the database, then send it to the customer via the network.

As part of each order the customer always specifies an "offer," which is the amount they will pay for the particular information being requested. My computer can accurately estimate the amount of time it will require to process an order before beginning work on it.

The network is very fast, so I ignore the time it takes for the order to travel from the customer to my computer, and the time it takes for the retrieved data to travel from my computer back to the customer.

My computer can process only one order at a time. Also, for simplicity, I have made no provisions for a waiting line of customers. This means that I never accept a new order while my computer is already busy processing an order.

When my computer is idle (i.e., not busy processing an order) I can choose to accept or ignore any new order that arrives.

New orders arrive at the rate of one every 2 seconds. Order-processing times are randomly scattered in the range of 1 to 5 seconds, and the dollar amounts of offers are randomly scattered in the range of $.01 to $.12. The business has a fixed operating cost (overhead) of $.02 per second. It's a high-volume, low-margin business.

Design of the Application

How do we design a VB project to simulate these operations? A reasonable way to begin is to put yourself in the role of "operator" and sketch a computer screen that displays the information necessary for you to operate the business. What data should the screen display at run time, and how should it be arranged? One possibility is the Electronic Desktop depicted in Figure 2.52.

The next questions to consider might reasonably be "What events occur during operation of the real business?" and "How do these events relate to the controls on our Electronic Desktop?" An event occurs whenever something changes. Let us consider the following possible events in the real business:

1. A new order arrives.
2. We choose to accept an order and begin processing it.
3. We finish processing an order.

As we consider each event, let us summarize the actions we decide must be performed when the event occurs. This is best done by writing *pseudocode*, **which is the description, in English, of the actions to be performed by the event procedure, written in the structure of VB's event procedures.** It is more formal than a narrative listing of the programmer's thoughts, but not as precise as the actual VB program. Pseudocode is a very useful tool for the design stage of application development.

A New Order Arrives

A new order arriving to the real business corresponds to the "Processing Time" and the "Offer To Pay" labels on the Electronic Desktop changing to reflect the processing time and offer of the new order. In VB we can make this event occur automatically every 2 seconds using a Timer control. Every time the Timer event occurs, we generate and display a new random processing time and offer. In effect, we use a Timer control to simulate our customers. No Timer control appears on the Electronic Desktop in Figure 2.52 because Timer

FIGURE 2.52

User interface for Project 3

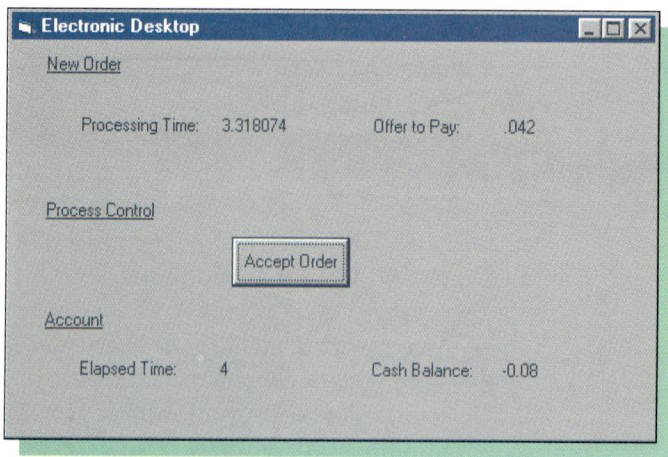

controls are invisible at run time. Following is pseudocode for the "new order arrives" event:

> *Private Sub tmrNewOrder_Timer*
>   *generate and display new processing time*
>   *generate and display new offer*
> *End Sub*

Notice that we have chosen a name for the Timer control, and have specified the full name of the event procedure, tmrNewOrder_Timer.

We Accept a New Order and Begin Processing It

This event in the real business corresponds to the user clicking the command button captioned Accept Order on the Electronic Desktop. The processing step initiated by the click should cause two things to happen: our cash balance should increase by the amount of the offer, and the command button should become disabled. While the command button is disabled, it will not respond when the user clicks it. This is one simple way to enforce the business rule that the computer should process only one order at a time.

> *Private Sub cmdAcceptOrder_Click*
>   *increase cash balance by amount of offer*
>   *disable cmdAcceptOrder*
> *End Sub*

When should the Accept Order button be enabled again? When the processing of the order is completed, since this will mean that the business's computer is available to process the next order.

We Finish Processing an Order

How can this event be made to occur in the simulation? We don't want to add a second command button and force the user to click it in order to re-enable the Accept Order button. It makes sense that, from the user's point of view, the Accept Order button should be re-enabled automatically.

When does this "processing finished" event occur? If we imagine starting a stopwatch when the user clicks the Accept Order button, then when an amount of time equal to the processing time of the order elapses, that's when the Accept Order button should be re-enabled. Timer controls are well suited for causing an event to occur automatically (from the user's point of view) after a specified delay. So, let's use a second Timer control. Following is pseudocode for the "processing finished" event procedure.

> *Private Sub tmrProcessingFinished_Timer*
>   *enable cmdAcceptOrder*
>   *disable tmrProcessingFinished*
> *End Sub*

But when did the Interval property of this timer (tmrProcessingFinished) get set equal to the processing time of the order being processed, and when did this timer get enabled? Surely that should be done when the user clicks on the Accept Order button. In other words, our pseudocode for cmdAcceptOrder_Click is incomplete. A revised version is shown on the next page.

```
Private Sub cmdAcceptOrder_Click
    increase cash balance by amount of offer
    disable cmdAcceptOrder
    set tmrProcessingFinished's interval equal to order's processing time
    enable tmrProcessingFinished
End Sub
```

Elapsed Time and Overhead Costs

The Electronic Desktop illustration has a label for Elapsed Time, which is a simple clock that shows how long the simulation has been running. How often should this label be updated? It is easiest to update it at the same time a new order arrives, every 2 seconds. Alternatively, we could use a third timer, with an interval of 1 second, for updating the label.

How do we implement the overhead cost of running the business, $.02 per second? This can be handled by decreasing the Cash Balance label by 0.02 every second or, equivalently, 0.04 every 2 seconds.

Suppose we let event procedure tmrNewOrder_Timer take care of the elapsed time and overhead cost operations. We need to revise its pseudocode this way:

```
Private Sub tmrNewOrder_Timer
    generate and display new processing time
    generate and display new offer
    increase elapsed time by 2 seconds
    decrease cash balance by 0.04
End Sub
```

The design process to this point has demonstrated the utility of pseudocode. As we make design decisions, we know that it's important to record them, but at the same time, we know that there are gaps in our proposed solution. We will fill in these gaps later in the process, after we've made more decisions. Paper-and-pencil procedures are wholly appropriate for this. Many programmers draw lines through ideas they reject, draw arrows to indicate reordering of actions, and so forth.

In any case, there is no sense trying to write actual VB statements early on in the process because you will probably make significant changes to them at a later point. Most programmers develop their own style of pseudocode, but they retain the essential idea of recording preliminary ideas informally and quickly, but with structure.

Property Settings for the Important Controls

Before diving into VB and creating the actual application, we need to catalog the important controls (those that are involved in event procedures) and their initial property settings. This helps solidify our plan and identify details we may have overlooked.

Table 2.10 lists the important controls and property settings for this project. Note that two of the controls have blank Caption settings (simply delete the setting for this property in the Properties window).

Construction of the Application

1. Create a new folder, named Proj03, on the disk where you will save this project.

2.11 Project 3: A Business Simulation

TABLE 2.10 Important controls and property settings for Project 3

Type	Property	Setting
Label	Name Caption	lblProcessingTime
Label	Name Caption	lblOffer
Label	Name Caption	lblElapsedTime 0
Label	Name Caption	lblCash 0.00
Command button	Name Caption	cmdAcceptOrder Accept Order
Timer	Name Interval Enabled	tmrNewOrder 2000 True
Timer	Name Enabled	tmrProcessingFinished False

Now start VB if you haven't already done so. Then open a new project (if necessary) and build the GUI.

2. Create the important controls. Position them on the form as in Figure 2.53, and set their properties as in Table 2.10.

3. Complete the GUI by creating the remaining labels and setting their captions as shown in Figure 2.53. Also, change the form's caption to "Electronic Desktop."

4. Save the project in folder Proj03.

Next, create the event procedures. Since the actual statements that make up event procedures are explored in later chapters, the pseudocode is translated

FIGURE 2.53

Project 3 controls

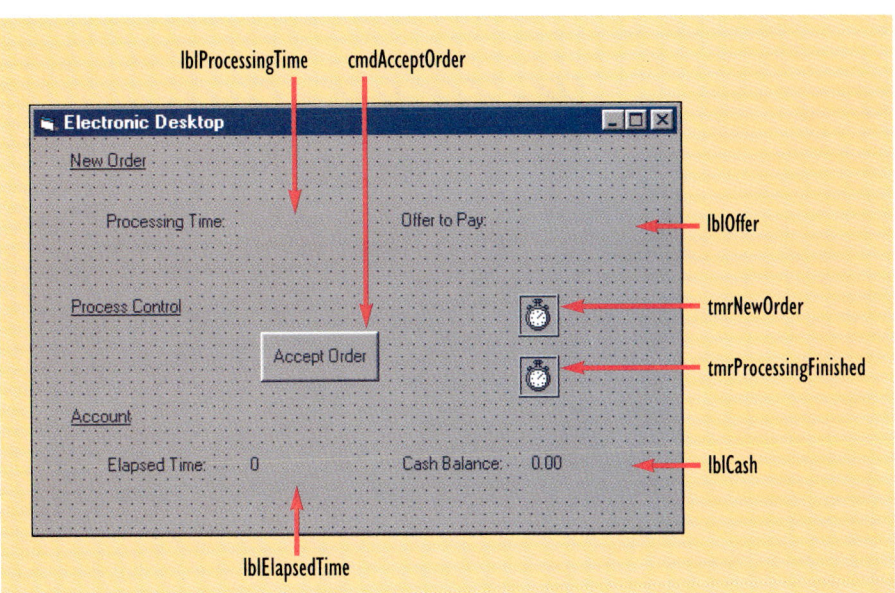

into complete event procedures for you in Figure 2.54. By comparing them to the pseudocode, you can probably guess roughly what each statement does.

5. Create event procedure tmrNewOrder_Timer as shown in Figure 2.54.
6. Run the program. Observe how the labels for Processing Time, Offer, Elapsed Time, and Cash change every 2 seconds. Return to design mode.
7. Create event procedure cmdAcceptOrder_Click as shown in Figure 2.54.
8. Run the program. Observe how the label for Cash changes when you click the command button. Also observe that this only happens the first time you click the command button, because its event procedure disables itself. Return to design mode.
9. Create event procedure tmrProcessingFinished_Timer as shown in Figure 2.54.
10. Run the program. Observe that the command button becomes disabled when you click it, and is re-enabled when the order's processing time elapses. Thus, when you choose to accept the current order you cannot accept another order until processing of the current order is finished.
11. Save the project.

Experiment with the simulation. See if you can get the business to turn a profit, by accepting orders wisely, over the course of about two minutes.

EXERCISE 2.7

In this business, what is the opportunity cost[16] of accepting an order? What is the opportunity cost of ignoring an order? Did you understand this before you experimented with the running simulation?

EXERCISE 2.8

As "operator" of this business, what rule do you use to decide whether or not to accept an order?

FIGURE 2.54

Event procedures for Project 3

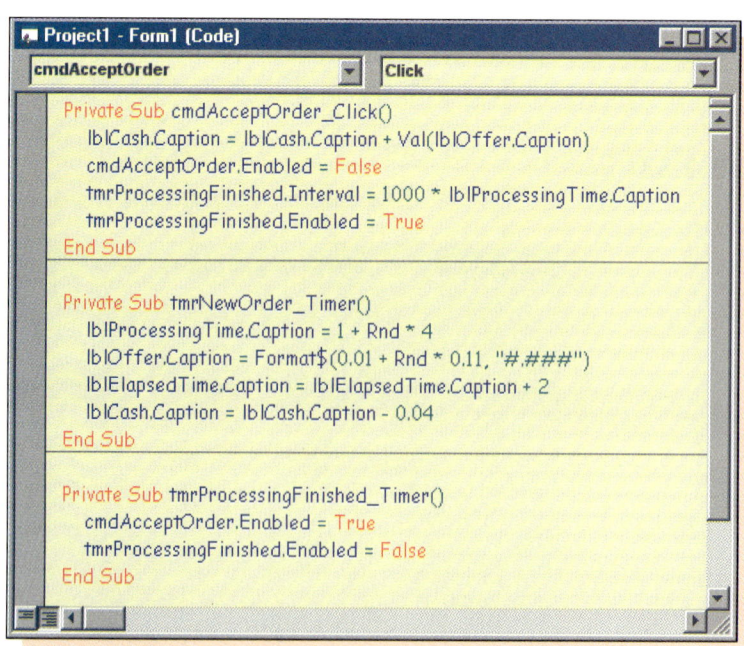

[16] In economics, the *opportunity cost* of an action is defined as wealth foregone as a consequence of that action.

EXERCISE 2.9 As user of this application, do you like the layout of the Electronic Desktop? If not, why not? Suggest ways to improve it.

EXERCISE 2.10 Do you think it is possible to automate the decision to accept or ignore an order? What would this require?

EXERCISE 2.11 The description of the business operation suggests that it does not make sense to process the same order twice: it is unlikely a customer would be willing to pay you twice for the same information. Suppose, however, that in the simulation an order arrives with a processing time of 1.1 seconds. As user of the simulation, is it possible for you to make the mistake of processing this order twice? If so, as programmer can you modify the application to prevent this? Explain.

EXERCISE 2.12 Many aspects of the description of this business's operations are highly simplified. Can you think of ways the description can be made more realistic, and also how the application could be modified to reflect this higher degree of realism?

Chapter Summary

1. An application under construction in VB is called a project. When the project is complete, the programmer creates an executable file that contains the finished application. A copy of the executable file is given to the user, who can run the application without knowing anything about VB.
   The executable file cannot be modified. When changes are required, the programmer must make the changes in VB using the project files, then create a new executable file for the user.

2. VB has three modes of operation. Design mode allows the programmer to build or modify the project. Run mode allows the programmer to execute the project in order to see whether it works correctly. Break mode allows the programmer to examine the status of the project's event procedures, which helps in the process of debugging. When VB is in design mode, the project is at design time; and when VB is in run or break mode, the project is at run time.

3. All VB projects have a hierarchical structure. A simple project consists of one form containing one or more controls. Each control, in turn, has many properties and may have one or more event procedures.

4. The form is the background of the GUI. A control is an object that sits on top of the form. A property is an attribute that defines some characteristic of the control. Each type of control can respond to a number of different kinds of events. An event is a signal, generated at run time, that indicates something has happened to which the program must respond. An event procedure is a script containing instructions the computer will follow when an event occurs for the control.

5. The Command button control allows the user to trigger a processing step. The Label control displays text. The Timer control is used to automatically trigger a processing step at regular intervals.

6. VB provides many programming tools that allow the programmer to assemble and rearrange the components that make up the project. VB presents its tools in the following groups for easy access: the Menu bar, the Form

Designer and Form windows, the Toolbox, the Properties window, the Code window, the Toolbar, the Form Layout window, the Project Explorer window, and online help.

The Menu bar provides access to most of VB's tools. Its View menu allows you to bring up the other groups of tools when they are not visible. The Form Designer window displays the Form window to the programmer at design time; the Form window comprises the form and the controls that sit on top of the form. The Toolbox contains the tools you use to place controls on the form. The Properties window allows you to change the property settings for each control. The Code window allows you to write event procedures. The Toolbar allows you to switch between VB's operating modes (design, run, and break). The Form Layout window allows you to specify where the form will appear on the screen at run time. The Project Explorer window lists the forms that belong to the project. And finally, online help allows you to find additional information about VB, and provides answers to questions you may encounter while working with VB.

7. During the design phase of the application creation process, you should choose descriptive names for every important control—defined as any control whose name appears in an event procedure—and you should write pseudocode for every event procedure.

A good descriptive name for a control always begins with the standard three-letter prefix for the type of control. This naming practice makes event procedures easier to read because the name of the control indicates what type of control it is.

8. For storage on disk, VB organizes projects as collections of files. Each project has one project file as well as one file for each form belonging to the project. Thus, simple VB projects are saved as two files. When choosing file names, programmers use standard file extensions to indicate the type of each file.

Store each project in its own folder on disk and save the project frequently. You may also wish to print out the project—you can print the code (the event procedures), the user interface, and the property settings.

Key Terms

backup copy
break mode
Caption property
Click event
"cmd" prefix
code
Code window
Command button control
control
custom controls
docked
debugging
default settings
design mode

design time
Enabled property
event
event procedure
executable file
Font property
form
Form Designer window
form file
Form Layout window
Form window
Interval property
Label control
"lbl" prefix
Menu bar

MouseMove event
Name property
Picture property
project
Project Explorer window
project file
Properties window
property
pseudocode
run mode
run time
search phrase
statement
Style property

Timer control   Toolbar   Visible property
Timer event   Toolbox   zero-length string
"tmr" prefix

End-of-Chapter Problems

1. Can a form have more than one general declarations section? Can a project have more than one general declarations section? Explain.
2. Explain the general function of a control's event procedures.
3. Explain the major differences between a Text box control and a Label control.
4. In general, what function does the Caption property serve?
5. What are control properties? What general function do they perform?
6. According to the information in Table 2.1, a text box can be used as a trigger, to get input, and to provide output. Which one of these three functions is its primary function? Explain how the text box works in this case.
7. Explain the difference between design time and run time as they relate to creating and using VB projects.
8. What is the primary purpose of the VB form?
9. What is the difference between the VB Toolbar and the Toolbox?
10. How do you cause the Code window showing an event procedure for a particular control to be displayed on the screen?
11. What is an event-driven program?
12. Assume that you want a VB project to react to the user's mouse click. What control are you most likely to use in this case? Where do you put the instructions that tell the computer what to do when the user clicks this control?
13. What is the difference between a VB project file and a form file?
14. What is pseudocode? Why is it used in designing programs?

Programming Problems

1. Create a VB project that produces a countdown as shown below.
   Initially, all of the label captions should be blank. When execution begins, the project should display Three, Two, One, and GO! at consecutive intervals of 1 second.

For your design, begin with the form shown at the top of page 72.

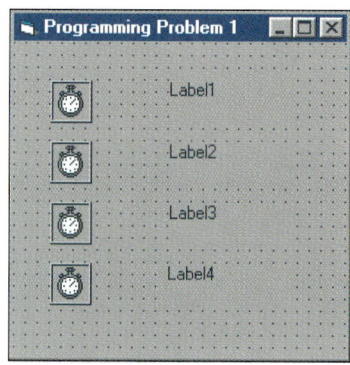

You'll need to program the timers to activate at the proper times (see the Interval property); and when they activate, they should change the label caption settings to the proper words.

2. Create the VB form shown here.

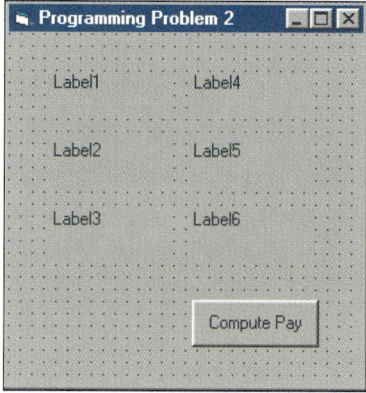

Next, change the captions for the labels and the command button as shown here.

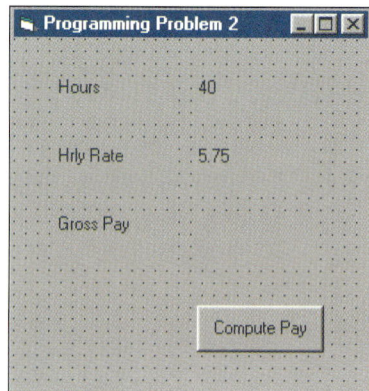

Finally, program the command button so that when it is clicked, the gross pay is computed and displayed. This event procedure requires only one statement. This statement should multiply the value of the label caption displaying the hours by the value of the label caption displaying the hourly rate, and set the label caption for the gross pay equal to the resulting value. See Project 2 for an example of multiplication.

When your project executes, it should produce the output shown at the top of page 73 after the command button is clicked.

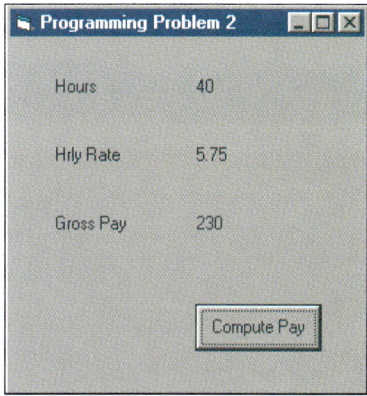

3. In this problem you will build a simple timer project. The final product will appear as shown here.

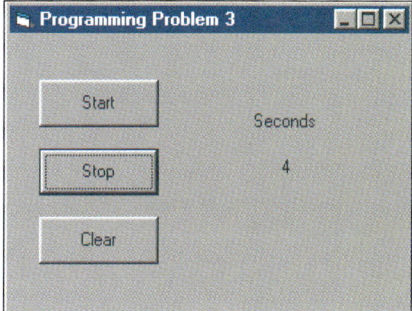

In the above example, the user has clicked the Start button, which caused the timer to begin counting by 1 each second, and then after 4 seconds the user clicked the Stop button.

Start by creating a form as shown here.

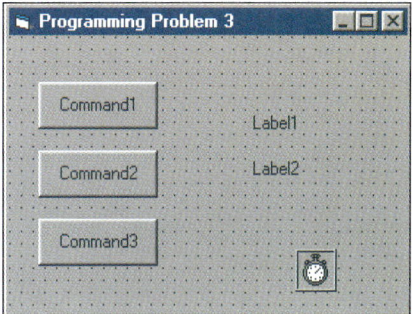

Next, change the captions for the various controls as shown.

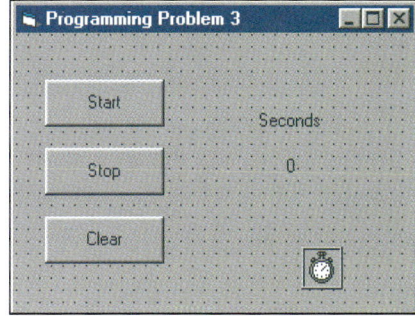

In the event procedures for the Start and Stop buttons you will need to set the timer's Enabled property appropriately. Make the initial setting of the timer's Interval property equal to 1 second. Program the Timer event procedure to add 1 to Label2's caption each time it is executed. To do this cumulative addition, use the following statement:

Label2.Caption = Label2.Caption + 1

The Clear button should reset Label2's caption to zero.

Finally, be sure that the timer does not start counting when you start execution of the project. It should wait for the user to click on the Start button.

4. Modify Project 3 by creating additional labels as shown.

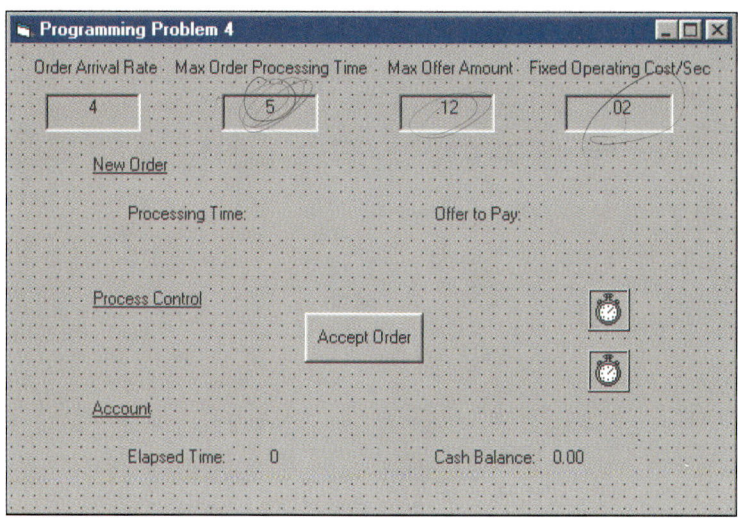

The four labels at the top of the form displaying the numbers 4, 5, .12, and .02 have had their BorderStyle properties set to 1 - Fixed Single.

Modify the code provided in Project 3 to use the label captions instead of the corresponding literal numbers. For example, in Project 3 the statement

lblProcessingTime.Caption = 1 + Rnd * 4

should be replaced with

lblProcessingTime.Caption = 1 + Rnd * (lblMaxProcTime.Caption - 1)

assuming that the label lblMaxProcTime displays the upper limit of the processing time range.

You will also need to add a new event procedure, Form_Load, that enables the tmrNewOrder control and sets its interval equal to the caption of the label that displays the Order Arrival Rate. See online help (search phrase "Load event") or Section 3.4 for details of the Form_Load event. The tmrNewOrder control should be disabled at design time and have its Interval property set to zero.

In the original code for Project 3 you will find the following statement in the cmdAcceptOrder_Click event procedure:

lblCash.Caption = lblCash.Caption + Val(lblOffer.Caption)

The Val() function (discussed in more detail in Section 4.3) converts the value in lblOffer's caption to a number, so that the addition operation works properly. If we did not use the Val() function in this case, the value in lblOffer.Caption would be concatenated (joined end-to-end) to lblCash.Caption rather than added to it. You may need to use this function in your modified code.

5. Create a timer project that you can use to time events to the nearest tenth of a second. Use command buttons with pictures (as shown below) to control starting and stopping the timer.

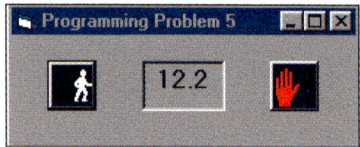

You should be able to find the icons for the command buttons in the traffic folder inside VB's icons folder (see footnote 3 in Section 2.4).

chapter THREE

Representing Data

Constants and Variables

The projects we introduced in Chapter 2 had limited processing capabilities. Their purpose was to introduce the VB environment and the structure of VB programs, and to demonstrate how VB's controls operate. Beginning with this chapter, we turn our focus to the job of composing event procedures that perform more sophisticated processing tasks. In this chapter we focus specifically on *data items*—**facts or quantities that describe things and that are processed by our programs**. Examples would be an employee name, a tax rate, or a product price.

We must specify the characteristics of each data item in our programs for VB to correctly input, process, and output the item. For example, we want VB to handle a product price differently than a customer name, because the price is a number and is likely to be needed in arithmetic calculations, whereas the customer name is not. We begin this chapter by examining how data items are defined in VB programs and how to specify the characteristics of data items.

In addition to studying data items, we continue our work with VB project structure. The projects we create in this chapter have more than one form, and they build on the simple structure of the projects presented in Chapter 2.

In Chapter 2 we stated that a VB project can have many forms, and each form can have many controls and associated event procedures. Can a data item defined in one event procedure be accessed by statements in a second event procedure? The answer to this question is determined by the data item's *scope*—**the domain of event procedures that are allowed to access the data item**.

Objectives

After studying this chapter you should be able to
- Differentiate between numeric and string data.
- Determine whether a data item should be a constant or variable.
- Code constants and variables in event procedures.
- Describe the characteristics and uses of standard data types.

- Create projects that consist of several forms.
- Explain scope and describe the domain of variables in event procedures and forms.

3.1 Two Kinds of Data

The data manipulated by a VB program fall into two broad categories: numeric and string. They differ both in form and use.

1. *Numeric data* must contain only numbers, whereas *string data* can contain any symbol.
2. Numeric values can be used in arithmetic calculations, but string values cannot.

When you analyze a problem to be solved by a computer program, one of the first things you must do is decide which facts and quantities will be represented as data items. Then you must determine whether each data item should be numeric or string. The computer will not manipulate data items correctly if you do not identify them correctly. Therefore, we begin our discussion of data by explaining how you can determine which data items should be numeric and which should be string.

If the value of a real-world quantity contains letters, it must be represented as string data. For such cases the numeric-versus-string decision is easy.

Real-World Quantity	Example Value
A person's name	Jane Arbor
A person's address	321 Alder Ave.

However, many real-world quantities look like numbers, and you could represent them as either numeric or string.

Real-World Quantity	Example Value
The weight of a shipping container to be loaded on a truck, in tons	9.35
The population of a city or town in a state	85783
The dollar amount of an item in an invoice	109.95
A ZIP code (U.S. postal code)	98765
A Social Security number	123456789
A phone number	12065551212

If you use a data item in arithmetic calculations, you should make it numeric. If the data item is never used in arithmetic, you should make it string.[1] Thus, you must evaluate how each data item will be used in the program.

[1] Actually, there are other reasons for selecting numeric rather than string. A programmer might make a data item numeric instead of string, even if it will never be used in arithmetic, if doing so saves a significant amount of storage space. We leave such considerations for experienced programmers to debate.

The operators of a trucking company will want to know the total weight carried by a truck. To do this, a program would have to add the weights of the shipping containers loaded on the truck. A program used by a marketing department to track demographics would want to accumulate the population totals for various cities. A company using a computer billing program would expect dollar amounts for items sold to be added on an invoice. All of these quantities should be numeric data.

How about a ZIP code? This real-world quantity looks like a number—it contains only digits—but we seldom think of adding up ZIP codes.

Suppose you are writing a program for your mail order company, and you decide to represent your customers' ZIP codes as numeric data. This will work as long as all your customers reside in the United States. But postal codes in some other countries contain letters and therefore cannot be represented as numeric data. Your program may work perfectly until the day when you get your first international customer, at which time the program fails. Unless you are on your toes, you may not immediately see the cause of the failure.

String data are more flexible than numeric data in the values they can represent, as long as arithmetic is not required. For example, Social Security numbers and phone numbers, like ZIP codes, are never used in arithmetic. An added benefit of choosing to make these strings is that we can insert hyphens, parentheses, spaces, and other characters, to format them so that they are easier for humans to read. **Formatting is the process of adding characters (such as dollar signs or commas) to a data item to make it easier for humans to read**.

Real-World Quantity	Example Formatted Value
A Social Security number	123-45-6789
A phone number	1 (206) 555-1212

Although string data cannot be manipulated mathematically, they can still be processed. For example, a list of names and addresses could be sorted by ZIP code in a program being used by an advertising company.

After deciding whether a data item should be numeric or string, the VB programmer must identify the data item as a constant or a variable. Figure 3.1 depicts this decision-making process. We discuss constants in Section 3.2 and variables in Section 3.3.

FIGURE 3.1

Decisions required to specify a data item in VB

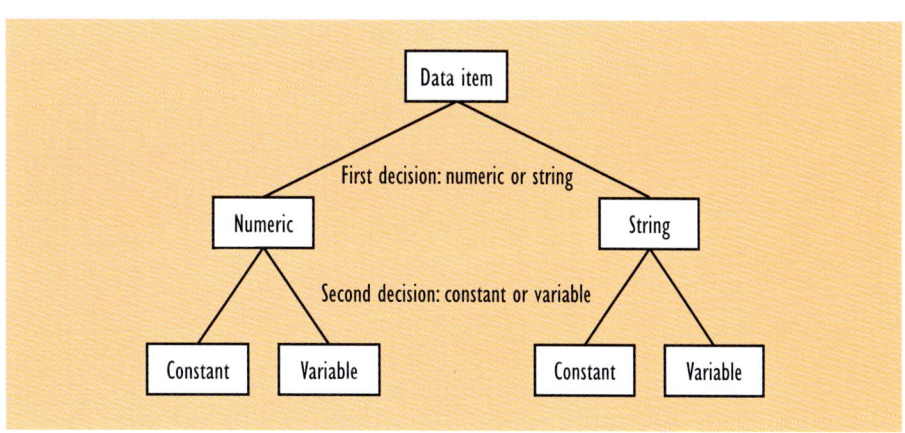

3.2 Constants

In a program, a *constant* is a data item whose value is specified at design time and cannot change at run time. A program can manipulate both numeric constants and string constants. Figure 3.2 shows that a constant is either literal or symbolic. A *literal constant* is simply a value. A *symbolic constant* is a descriptive name that the programmer substitutes for a literal constant. Using symbolic constants improves program readability because the programmer reading the program code attaches the real-world meaning to his or her interpretation of the code.

As you can see from Figures 3.1 and 3.2, there are actually four different kinds of constants:

- Numeric literal constants.
- String literal constants.
- Numeric symbolic constants.
- String symbolic constants.

We discuss each of these next.

Literal Constants

An example of a numeric literal constant is 123, and an example of a string literal constant is "John Doe". A numeric literal constant can be used in arithmetic calculations but can contain only certain symbols (digits). A string literal constant cannot be used in arithmetic but can contain any symbol.

Writing Numeric Literal Constants

You must follow a few rules to specify valid numeric literal constants in your programs.[2] For the most part, VB's rules conform to ordinary usage in writing numbers. The following are valid numeric literal constants in VB:

    1.23   +123   .1   –6   8.9E–6   0.0000089   8.9E+3

The first four of these are straightforward. A numeric constant that begins with a digit, a plus sign, or a decimal point is a positive number. A numeric constant

FIGURE 3.2

Classification of constants in VB

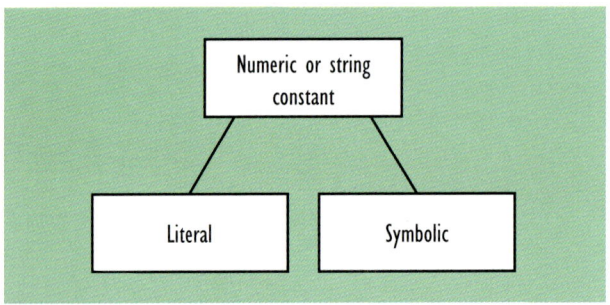

[2] Windows allows you to specify the country format, which affects, among other things, the way numbers appear. In this text we have chosen to use the U.S. format, for which the "decimal point" is the period. If you choose the German format, for example, the "decimal point" will be a comma.

that begins with a minus sign (this is the same as the hyphen key on your keyboard) is a negative number. VB treats the constant .1 the same as 0.1 (it ignores the leading 0).

The constant 8.9E–6 illustrates scientific notation in VB: the E– is read as "times 10 to the minus." This is the same as 8.9×10^{-6}. The notation $\times 10^{-6}$ means "move the decimal point six places to the left." Thus, the constants 8.9E–6 and 0.0000089 are treated identically by VB. The last example, 8.9E+3, is equivalent to 8.9×10^3, which is the same as 8900.

Scientific notation is convenient shorthand for representing very large and very small numbers. By using it, the programmer eliminates the likelihood of miscounting the number of leading or trailing zeros. The difference between .0000089 and .000089 is not as readily apparent to a human as the difference between 8.9E–6 and 8.9E–5. Note that computers seldom err when counting 0s but humans frequently do, and an error of a factor of 10 can have disastrous effects in many applications.

The familiar practice of using commas in large numbers is disallowed in VB; 2,123,234 is *not* a valid numeric constant in VB. Nor are other characters, such as spaces or dollar signs, allowed in numeric constants.

Writing String Literal Constants

A string literal constant begins with a quote mark and ends with a quote mark. Whenever you see quote marks in a program statement, you have found a string literal constant. Quote marks always occur in pairs. The symbols between the quote marks specify the value of the string constant. VB accepts any symbol (digit, letter, space, punctuation mark, etc.) you put between the quotes.

The quote marks merely serve to mark the beginning and end of the string constant and are not themselves part of the value. Thus, a person's name might be represented in a program as the string literal constant "Jane Arbor" and a person's address as "321 Alder Ave."

Symbolic Constants
◆ ◆ ◆

A symbolic constant is a descriptive name that the programmer associates with a literal constant, allowing the programmer to use the descriptive name instead of the literal constant. To demonstrate the purpose of symbolic constants, suppose the program requires a data item equal to 0.081, to be used in arithmetic calculations. The programmer could simply use the numeric literal constant 0.081 everywhere it is needed in the program, but this is a poor idea. For one thing, it is not clear what real-world quantity is represented by 0.081. The computer doesn't mind this, but it makes the program difficult for humans to understand and, as we discussed in Chapter 1, this can make the program more difficult to maintain.

Suppose the number 0.081 represents a sales tax rate. Then the programmer could make the program more readable by associating the descriptive name SALESTAXRATE with the value 0.081, and subsequently using this descriptive name instead of the cryptic value 0.081.

Writing Symbolic Constant Names

As programmer, you choose the symbolic constant name, but the name you choose must conform to certain rules. The first rule is that symbolic constant names can be no longer than 255 characters. These can include both letters and digits, but the first character must be a letter. Spaces, commas, and other punctuation marks are not allowed in constant names. In addition, **certain combinations of characters, called reserved words, are not allowed as constant names because they form parts of the VB language itself.** Reserved words, also called **keywords**, include Sub, If, End, and Print. VB ordinarily displays keywords in a different color than nonkeywords.[3]

> **Convention** Avoid digits and use all capital letters in symbolic constant names. Capitalizing all letters makes it easier to recognize symbolic constants in your code.

You now know enough about string and numeric constants to see how they differ and why you would choose one or the other for a particular data item. We now turn our attention to the *constant definition statement,* which is the vehicle for specifying the symbolic constants you use in a program and identifying whether they are numeric or string.

The Constant Definition Statement

To create a symbolic constant in an event procedure, at the top of the event procedure you write a *constant definition statement* (also called a *Const statement*), which begins with the keyword Const, followed by the symbolic name, then an equal sign, and finally the literal value. Each of the two constant definition statements that follow defines a symbolic constant.

```
Const SALESTAXRATE = 0.081
Const DRIVEEMPTY = "Please insert disk in drive A."
```

Following these statements in an event procedure, you can use the name SALESTAXRATE in place of the numeric constant 0.081, and the name DRIVEEMPTY in place of the string constant "Please insert disk in drive A."

The type (numeric or string) of a symbolic constant is determined by the type of the literal constant on the right-hand side of the equal sign. If the literal constant is numeric, then the symbolic constant is also numeric. If the literal constant is string, then the symbolic constant is also string.

Run Time: How the Computer Uses Symbolic Constants

Whenever VB first begins executing an event procedure, it creates an empty table of symbolic constants. Then, when VB executes a constant definition statement, it adds a row to the table showing the name and the value of the new symbolic constant. For example, suppose VB is executing an event procedure that contains the two constant definition statements presented earlier. After it has executed both of these, its table of symbolic constants will appear as follows.

Constant Name	Value
SALESTAXRATE	0.081
DRIVEEMPTY	"Please insert disk in drive A."

[3] You can specify the color VB uses for keywords by selecting Options… under the Tools menu. The Editor Format tab has a "Code Colors" feature you can use to change colors.

What happens when the computer subsequently executes a statement that contains a symbolic constant name? It first goes to its table of symbolic constants to look up the value that corresponds to the symbolic constant name. It substitutes this value for the name, then executes the statement just as if the statement had originally contained the literal value.

Advantages of Using Symbolic Constants

Symbolic constants have two advantages over literal constants:

1. They can make the program easier for humans to understand.
2. They reduce the chance of inconsistencies in the program.

To see these advantages in action, consider again Project 2, which produced an invoice for the sale of microcomputer components. Figure 3.3 illustrates the content of Project 2 as we left it, with a brief reminder of how it operates.

By studying this short event procedure, you can figure out that the numeric constant 0.081 represents a sales tax rate of 8.1 percent. Still, it would be more natural to humans if the programmer had just used the name SALESTAXRATE instead of 0.081; then you wouldn't have had to figure this out at all.

Now suppose the sales tax rate has just changed to 8.6 percent. To modify the program to use this new value, the programmer scans the event procedure, looking for 0.081, and changes it to 0.086, as shown in Figure 3.4a.

It is not so easy to see that the programmer missed the second occurrence of the sales tax rate and thereby introduced an inconsistency into the program. The program will still run, of course, but now it produces incorrect results. This is a very bad situation for the business that uses this program. Who will be the first to find the error? A customer? It is actually preferable that the program not run at all than that it run with incorrect results.

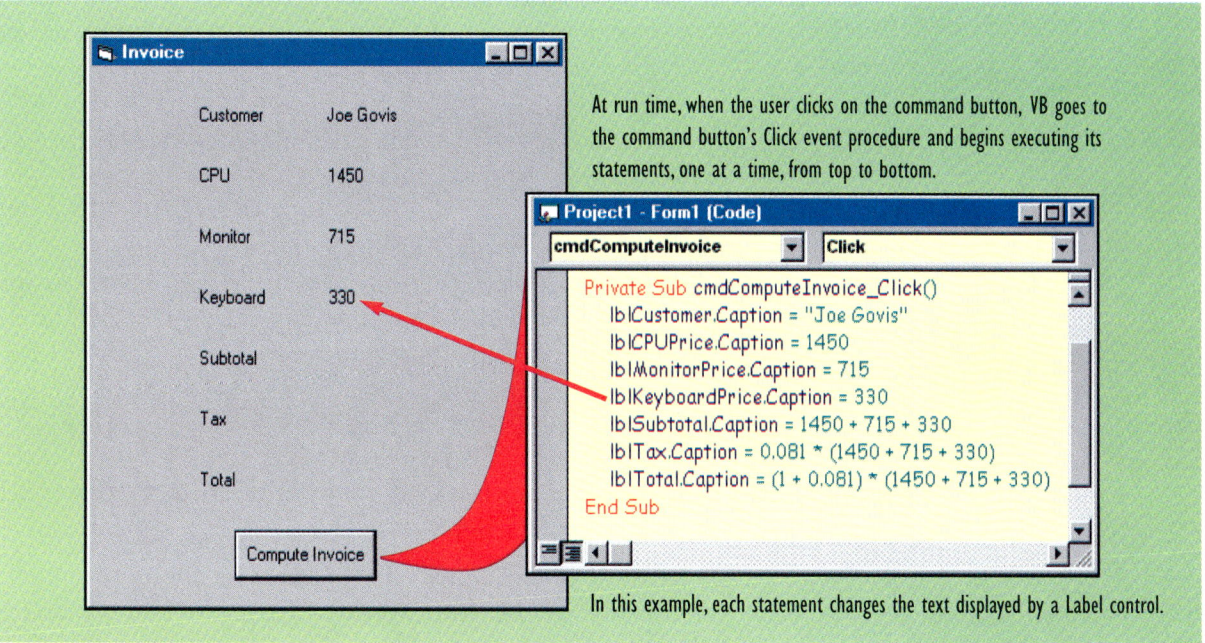

FIGURE 3.3 *Project 2's user interface and event procedure*

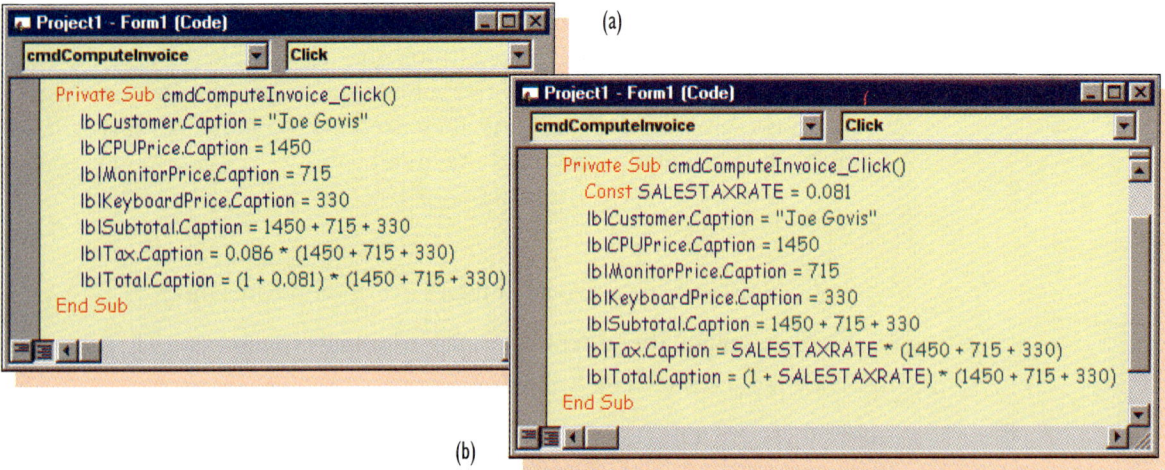

FIGURE 3.4 (a) Programmer's attempt to change the sales tax rate; (b) Using a symbolic constant for the sales tax rate

Using a symbolic constant for the sales tax rate, as shown in Figure 3.4b, improves the code for the invoice computation. Now the literal constant 0.081 appears in only one place—the constant definition statement—so there is no chance of inconsistency, and the programmer need not scan the code looking for occurrences of the number 0.081 in order to change the sales tax rate. This not only improves readability, but it also improves the maintainability of the code.

> **Convention** Place constant definition statements right after the event procedure's Private Sub statement so that they are easy to find.

Literal versus Symbolic Constants

When should you use literal constants, and when should you use symbolic constants? The following is a good rule of thumb.

> **Convention** A program should contain no literal constants, except the zero-length string ("") and the numbers 0 and 1.

For the time being we will ignore this convention in our examples; until we discuss ways of obtaining data from the user (or anywhere else), all data in our examples will necessarily be coded as constants. But starting in Chapter 4, our use of literal constants will drop off dramatically.

Typical Uses of Symbolic Constants

Constants are good for representing facts and quantities that do not change during program execution. Typical examples are

- Mathematical quantities like pi, physical quantities like the speed of light, and historical facts like the date the astronauts first set foot on the moon.
- The number of days in each month or the names of the days of the week.
- The number of lines per page a particular printer produces.

Predefined Symbolic Constants

VB provides a large set of predefined symbolic constants. For example, there is a symbolic constant called *vbRed* that VB uses to represent the color red. Many predefined symbolic constants are associated with the allowable property settings for certain controls; for example, *vbLeftJustify*, *vbRightJustify*, and *vbCenter* correspond to the allowed settings for the Label control's Alignment property. See online help (use the search phrase "constants, Visual Basic") for a list and description of the predefined symbolic constants.

EXERCISE 3.1 Write a statement that defines a symbolic constant representing the number of days in the month of January.

EXERCISE 3.2 Which of the following are not valid constant definition statements? Explain how they could be modified to make them valid.

    Const OURNAMES = "Joe, Bill"
    Const T1RATE = 1,544,000
    Const ANNSOFFICEPHONE = 555-1234
    Const MAX SPEED = 55
    Const COMPOSER = Ludwig Van Beethoven
    Const STARTINGCHECKNUMBER = 100

3.3 Variables

***Variables* are used in a program to store data items and to retrieve the data during processing.** That is, variables allow us to represent data items whose values change at run time.

Variables can be either numeric or string. For example, in an insurance application, you could create a numeric variable called *Age* that would hold the age of the person applying for insurance coverage. Similarly, you could create a string variable called *ApplicantName* that would hold the applicant's first and last names. Although you would know at design time what type of data each variable would store, you would not be able to predict the value those variables would hold at run time. Therefore, you could not use constants for these data items.

In this section we discuss how to work with variables. The first step is to give the variable a symbolic name and to inform VB of the characteristics of the data the variable will store. The *variable declaration statement*—the counterpart to the constant definition statement—is the vehicle for doing this. We will also discuss how to use variables in event procedures.

Variable Names
◆ ◆ ◆

As with symbolic constant names, you choose the names for the variables you create. VB places the same restrictions on variable names that it does on constant names: they can be no longer than 255 characters; and although they may contain both letters and digits, the first character must be a letter. Again, keywords are not allowed, nor are spaces, commas, and other punctuation marks.

You should choose descriptive names for your variables, that is, names that convey the real-world meanings of the values to be stored in the variables.

Using descriptive names makes your program much easier for other programmers to understand. (VB does not attempt to interpret the meaning of variable names.)

Choosing descriptive variable names is simple. A variable to store the user's first name, for example, might be called FirstName.

> **Convention** Use descriptive variable names. Use only letters, and capitalize the first letter of each word within the variable name.

All of the following are valid variable names:

FleetSize	NumberOfSeminarParticipants	EmployeeNumber
WageRate	EmployeeName	ExtendedPrice
AverageAge	NumBidUnits	Depreciation
MaximumCapacity	YTDEarnings	X

The variable name X, of course, usually cannot be considered descriptive and should not be used unless the value being stored has no real-world meaning. Mathematical programs sometimes require variables like this (which mathematicians often call *dummy variables*), but they are rare in business programs. Also, instructors sometimes use variable names like X when they teach to reduce the amount they (and their students) have to write.

Observe that the convention for symbolic constant names is to use all capital letters, but the convention for variable names is to capitalize only the first letter of each word in the name. Following these conventions in the code you write makes it easier to distinguish symbolic constants from variables.

EXERCISE 3.3

The following are not valid variable names:

Minimum#	Item Price	Sub	3rdAlternate

How does each of these violate the variable-naming rules?

Standard Data Types

When deciding what variables are needed for a program, you must also decide whether they should contain numeric or string data. Remember, a value stored in a numeric variable can be used in arithmetic calculations, whereas a value stored in a string variable cannot.

As you may be aware, internally the computer uses a binary language of ones and zeros (1s and 0s). Thus, by necessity, computer scientists have devised many different schemes for representing data as sequences of 1s and 0s. Each such scheme is called a *data type*. When you create a variable in a program you have to specify a data type for it. VB provides six different **predefined types, which are often called** *standard data types*.[4]

A variable's data type determines its characteristics, which include the kind of value it can store. Table 3.1 summarizes the characteristics of each type. There is only one string type, appropriately called String. However, there are five numeric types, called Integer, Long, Currency, Single, and Double. The programmer must specify one of these types for each variable.

[4] Actually, VB provides more than six standard data types, but we discuss only six of them here. For additional information, see online help (use search phrase "data types, variables", then select "Data Type Summary" in the ensuing Topics Found list).

TABLE 3.1 Characteristics of standard data types

Data Type	# Bytes	Range	Precision
String	1 per character	Up to approximately 2 billion characters	Not applicable
Integer	2	+32,767 to −32,768	Whole numbers only
Long	4	+2,147,483,647 to −2,147,483,648	Whole numbers only
Currency	8	922,337,203,685,477.5807 to −922,337,203,685,477.5808	Four places to the right of the decimal point
Single	4	3.4E38 to 1.4E−45, and −1.4E−45 to −3.4E38	Seven significant digits
Double	8	1.7E308 to 4.9E−324, and −4.9E−324 to −1.7E308	Fifteen significant digits

Number of Bytes

The "# Bytes" column of Table 3.1 shows the number of bytes of main memory that a variable of each type occupies. The numeric types each have a fixed size, but the size of a string variable depends on the value stored in it. For example, a variable of type Currency occupies eight bytes, regardless of the value stored in it, but a variable of type String occupies five bytes if the value stored in it is "board" and fifteen bytes if the value is "QWERTY keyboard" (one byte per character, counting *every* character, including spaces, commas, and other symbols).

Range

Range **refers to the largest and smallest values that can be stored in a numeric variable of the given type.** For string variables the range is the maximum length (number of characters) that can be stored.

Precision

Precision **indicates how close together two numeric values can be before VB cannot tell them apart.** Different numeric data types have different degrees of precision. For example, suppose we have two variables named TestInt and TestLong, of types Integer and Long, respectively. Further, suppose we try to store the number 1.2 in TestInt and the number 1.3 in TestLong. Variables of type Integer and Long can store only integer values (whole numbers), so both variables TestInt and TestLong will *actually* store the number 1. We say that types Integer and Long are *exact* for integer values but that they *round off* fractional values; equivalently, we say that the precision is limited to whole numbers for variables of type Integer and Long.

Currency, Single, and Double all store fractional values, but with varying degrees of precision. Suppose we try to store the value 654321.123456 in three variables named TestCurr, TestSing, and TestDoub, of types Currency, Single, and Double, respectively. The values that actually get stored in these variables are shown below.

Variable	Type	Actual Value Stored	Explanation
TestCurr	Currency	654,321.1235	Four digits to the right of the decimal point (VB "rounded up" the 456 to 500).
TestSing	Single	654,321.1	Maximum of seven significant digits is reached.
TestDoub	Double	654,321.123456	Full precision, because 12 significant digits is less than the maximum of 15.

Single and Double are called *floating-point types* **because they store numbers using a scheme based on scientific notation.** They are able to store very large and very small numbers. Suppose we try to store the number 0.0000123456789 in TestSing and TestDoub. The values that actually get stored in these variables are as follows.

Variable	Type	Actual Value Stored	Explanation
TestSing	Single	1.234568E-5	Maximum of seven significant digits is reached (VB rounded up the 789 to 800).
TestDoub	Double	1.23456789E-5	Full precision, because 9 significant digits is less than the maximum of 15.

Of course, such small numbers, as well as very large numbers like 6.02×10^{23}, are more common in engineering and scientific applications than in business applications, we don't normally think of using scientific notation to express numbers in business applications.

Speed of Arithmetic Calculation

Finally, note that the speed of arithmetic calculation differs for the different numeric types. As you would expect, the larger and more precise the number that can be stored, the more memory is required and the slower the arithmetic operations are.[5]

Choosing the Best Data Type for a Variable

Suppose that you know the characteristics of a real-world value you need to store in a variable and you have chosen a descriptive name for it. Which one of the six data types should you choose? Table 3.2 contains a set of decision rules to help you select the best type for the variable. To use this table, scan the left-hand column until you find the first description that matches the characteristics of the real-world value to be stored.

As an example, suppose we need a variable to store a city's population. We reject type String because we may want to use a city population in arithmetic.

---

[5] It takes the computer very little time to perform any simple arithmetic calculation. You will notice the speed difference for the different types only if your program performs thousands, or perhaps millions, of arithmetic operations.

TABLE 3.2 Decision rules for choosing a variable's data type

Nature of Value to Be Stored	Best Type	Reasons
Sequence of characters; not involved in arithmetic; may include letters and special characters	String	Only choice if value contains letters; more flexible if not involved in arithmetic.
Dollar amount	Currency	Can store $ and ¢; no round-off error with arithmetic; arithmetic reasonably fast.
Whole number:		
Always < 32767	Integer	Less memory required; faster arithmetic than other numeric types.
May be > 32767	Long	
Number with fractional part:		
Seven digits sufficient, and $<10^{38}$	Single	Slower arithmetic and round-off error, but guaranteed number of significant digits regardless of size of value.
Seven digits insufficient, or $>10^{38}$	Double	

It is not a dollar amount, so we reject type Currency. A city population is a whole number, and it is possible for a city's population to exceed 32767, so we choose type Long.

EXERCISE 3.4 What value is *actually* stored in a variable of type Currency if we *try* to store the value 0.0000123456789 in it?

EXERCISE 3.5 Suppose you need a variable to store the user's height, in centimeters. Which type would you choose for this variable? Explain your answer.

EXERCISE 3.6 Suppose you need a variable to store a five-digit ZIP code. Will type Integer work? Suppose you need a variable to store a nine-digit ZIP code. Will type Long work? Explain.

Declaring Variables: The Dim Statement

◆ ◆ ◆

To create a variable in an event procedure, at the top of the event procedure you write a *variable declaration statement* (also called a *Dim statement*), which begins with the keyword Dim, followed by the name of the variable to be declared, then the keyword As, and finally the data type for the variable.[6] The following are valid variable declaration statements:

    Dim ContainerWeight **As Long**
    Dim CityPopulation **As Long**
    Dim InvoiceAmount **As Currency**
    Dim EmployeeName **As String**
    Dim ZIPCode **As String** * 5

---

[6] The keyword "Dim" is short for "Dimension." In some sense, the type of a variable does indicate its dimensions (e.g., its size).

> **Convention** Place Dim statements right after the event procedure's Private Sub statement and after the constant definition statements (if any). This makes them easy to find and helps programmers understand your program more quickly.

Fixed-Length versus Variable-Length String Variables

The last Dim statement in the preceding list declares a variable named *ZIPCode* of type String * 5. This variation of the String type allows you to declare a *fixed-length string* **variable, one with a length that will not change.** The "* 5" specifies that this string variable always holds five characters, and therefore always occupies 5 bytes of main memory. If you try to store a value comprising more than five characters in *ZIPCode*, VB will *truncate* it—that is, it will store only the first five characters and will discard the rest. If you try to store a value comprising fewer than five characters in *ZIPCode*, VB will "pad" the value with spaces at its end to make a total of five characters before storing it.

In contrast, an ordinary string variable, such as *EmployeeName*, is called a *variable-length string* **variable, meaning VB adjusts its length automatically.** VB never pads or truncates the value stored in a variable-length string variable; instead, each time a new value is stored in the variable, VB adjusts the number of bytes of main memory allocated to the variable to be equal to the number of characters in the value.

Suppose we try to store the value "payment amount" in two variables, named *TestVarString* and *TestFixString*, of types String and String * 5, respectively. The values that actually get stored in these variables are as follows.

Variable	Type	Actual Value Stored	Explanation
TestVarString	String	`payment amount`	Size of variable is adjusted to fit size of value stored.
TestFixString	String * 5	`payme`	Variable stores only first five characters.

Next, suppose we try to store the value "pay" in the same two variables, named *TestVarString* and *TestFixString*. The values that actually get stored are as follows.

Variable	Type	Actual Value Stored	Explanation
TestVarString	String	`pay`	Size of variable is adjusted to fit size of value stored.
TestFixString	String * 5	`pay  `	Value is "padded" with spaces at end to make it five characters long.

Declaring Multiple Variables in One Dim Statement

It is possible to declare multiple variables in a single Dim statement. For example, the five Dim statements in the preceding example could be replaced by these three Dim statements:

```
Dim ContainerWeight As Long, CityPopulation As Long
Dim InvoiceAmount As Currency, EmployeeName As String
Dim ZIPCode As String * 5
```

This is a somewhat risky practice because you may inadvertently omit one of the types, as in the statement below. (Note that we have placed a "don't do this" icon next to this statement. Throughout the text we will use this icon whenever we show a statement that is incorrect or represents poor programming practice.)

> **Dim** ContainerWeight, CityPopulation **As Long**

VB will not object to this omission.[7] In simple programs this omission will not cause any problems; the program will run no differently because of it. However, in programs using general sub procedures (the subject of Chapter 6) this omission *can* cause trouble, and the source of the trouble will be difficult to locate. Therefore, in this text we generally adhere to the practice of declaring only one variable in each Dim statement.

Run Time: The Effect of the Dim Statement

How does the Dim statement work? Whenever the computer first begins executing an event procedure, right after it creates an empty symbolic constant table, it creates an empty table of variables. This table has two columns: one for recording the name of each variable and one for recording the value stored in each variable. An empty variable table appears as follows:

Variable Name	Value

When the computer executes a Dim statement, it performs three steps.

1. It adds a row to the variable table for the new variable.
2. It enters the variable's name in the left column of the new row.
3. It stores an initial value in the variable by entering the value in the right column of the new row.

For numeric variables the initial value will be zero. For string variables the initial value will be the zero-length string.[8] As an example, after the computer executes the five Dim statements

> **Dim** ContainerWeight **As Long**
> **Dim** CityPopulation **As Long**
> **Dim** InvoiceAmount **As Currency**
> **Dim** EmployeeName **As String**
> **Dim** ZIPCode **As String** * 5

its variable table will appear as shown at the top of the next page.

---

[7] Because no type was specified for variable ContainerWeight, VB will use type Variant for it. This means that VB will adjust the variable's type according to the context in which it appears. In this text we avoid type Variant because of subtle problems that sometimes arise when it is used.

[8] This is not precisely true for fixed-length String variables, but this fact is seldom important. To be precise, the initial value for a fixed-length string variable will be a sequence of *null characters* (equal in length to the length of the string variable). We will meet the null character in Chapter 4.

Variable Name	Value
ContainerWeight	0
CityPopulation	0
InvoiceAmount	0
EmployeeName	" "
ZIPCode	" "

EXERCISE 3.7 The following are not valid variable names:

    Minimum#   Item Price   Sub   3rdAlternate

In VB, edit any event procedure and add a Dim statement declaring a variable named Minimum# of type Integer. What is the exact error message that VB displays when you try this?

Try to declare variables having the other three names shown here. What error message does VB display for each?

EXERCISE 3.8 In VB, edit any event procedure and add the following Dim statement, which contains the misspelled word "Curency".

    Dim MySalary **As Curency**

Then run the program and execute the event procedure. What error message does VB display?

EXERCISE 3.9 What problem do you think some U.S. businesses had with their programs when they changed from five-digit to nine-digit ZIP codes?

Using Variables: The Assignment Statement

To change the value stored in a variable you use an assignment statement. It is called an "assignment" statement because storing a value in a variable is sometimes described as "assigning" a value to a variable. Our program examples have included assignment statements. Now we will see what constitutes a valid assignment statement and how it causes the computer to act at run time.

Syntax of the Assignment Statement

The term *syntax* means the correct form of a component of a programming language. The syntax of the assignment statement is

    variablename = *expression*

The italicized words represent positions at which the programmer provides specific details to customize the statement. Thus, a valid *assignment statement* consists of a variable name, followed by an equal sign, followed by an expression. You must create the variable using a variable declaration statement before you can use the variable in an assignment statement. The equal sign is called the *assignment operator.* **The *expression* may be a constant or a variable, or it may combine constants and variables using such operations as addition and**

subtraction. As you will see in Chapter 4, you can compose quite complicated expressions. In this chapter we work with simple expressions.

The following is an example of a valid assignment statement:

ContainerWeightA = 1000

Run Time: The Effect of the Assignment Statement

To execute an assignment statement, the computer performs two steps.

1. It *evaluates* the expression on the right-hand side of the equal sign to determine its value. That is, it determines the value of the expression.
2. It *stores* the value of the expression in the variable named on the left-hand side of the equal sign. That is, it changes this variable's value in the variable table.

To demonstrate how this process works, let us examine the actions of the computer as it executes the following two statements:

Dim ContainerWeightA **As Long**
ContainerWeightA = 1000

When it executes this Dim statement, the computer adds a row to its variable table and initializes the variable ContainerWeightA.

Variable Name	Value
ContainerWeightA	0

Next, the computer executes the assignment statement. To do this, it performs the sequence of steps depicted below.

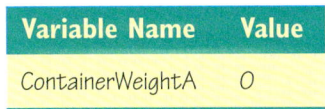

1. Computer determines value of expression to be 1000.
2. Computer stores 1000 in variable on left-hand side (changes its value in the variable table).

The net effect of executing this assignment statement is to change the value stored in the variable ContainerWeightA to 1000.

Variable Name	Value
ContainerWeightA	1000

The action of the assignment statement may seem trivial, but you should study it carefully. It is easy to confuse assignment statements with algebraic expressions, and the action of the assignment statement is completely different. You will have difficulty understanding even the simplest programs if you do not interpret assignment statements correctly.

Run Time: How the Computer Evaluates Expressions

When the expression in an assignment statement is just a literal constant, as in our example, the value of the expression is just the value of the constant. But what is the value of the expression when the expression is a variable? What is it when the expression combines constants and variables using addition and subtraction? In such cases, evaluating the expresssion is a two-step process.

In the first step, the computer carefully determines the identity of each component of the expression: it identifies the literal constants, the symbolic constants, and the variables, as well as any addition and subtraction symbols. In performing this step, it replaces each symbolic constant and variable with its value. To determine the value of a symbolic constant, the computer looks in its symbolic constant table. And to determine the value of a variable, it looks in its variable table.

In the second step, the computer performs any specified operations (e.g., addition and subtraction) to arrive at the expression's value. The following example includes figures to help you visualize how the computer evaluates expressions.

Example 3.1

Simple Assignment Statements

The purpose of this example is to observe the action of a variety of simple assignment statements. Since this is the first formal example in the text, we will begin with a brief discussion about using the examples.

All examples are provided as VB projects in the code package for this text (see Preface). You may wish to examine and experiment with them on the computer. All the examples in Chapter 3 are in the folder named "C03"; the examples in Chapter 4 are in the folder named "C04"; and so on.

Each example has its own project file and form file, and the name of the project file indicates the example it contains. For example, the project file for Example 3.1 is named "Ex0301.Vbp", and the project file for Example 3.2 is named "Ex0302.Vbp"; both of these files are located in the "C03" folder. Likewise, the project file for Example 4.1 (Chapter 4) is named "Ex0401.Vbp", and is located in the "C04" folder.

To open Example 3.1 in VB, select Open Project… under the File menu. In the ensuing "Open Project" dialog window, first change drives, if necessary, then select the "C03" folder and the "Ex0301.Vbp" file and click Open. You can then run the project, examine and make changes to the code, run the project again, and so forth, as you please.

Now let us examine Example 3.1. The form used in this example is shown in Figure 3.5. The form has just two important controls: a command button (cmdAssignmentTest) and a label (lblTotal). The Click event procedure for cmdAssignmentTest is shown in Figure 3.6. At run time, when the user clicks on cmdAssignmentTest, the computer begins executing cmdAssignmentTest_Click; it executes one statement at a time, from top to bottom. Initially, the symbolic constant table and the variable table are both empty.

FIGURE 3.5

Form and controls for Example 3.1

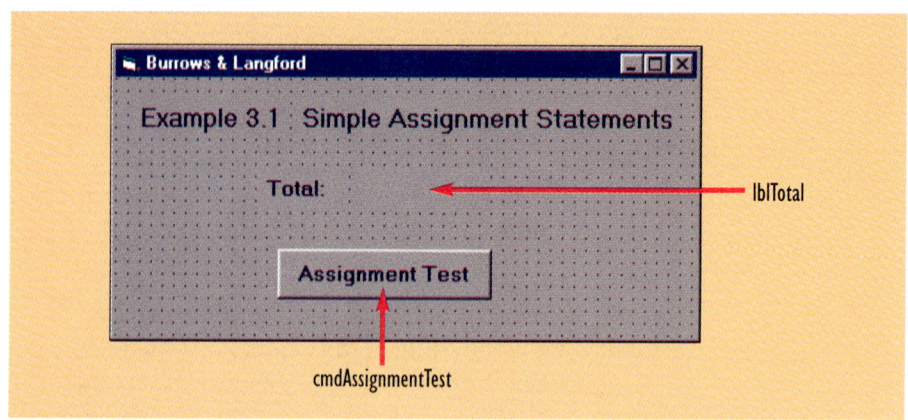

FIGURE 3.6

Code for Example 3.1

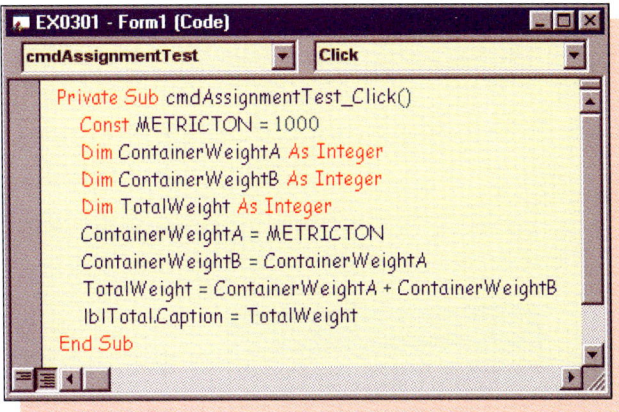

When the computer executes the constant definition statement, it adds a row to its symbolic constant table.

Constant Name	Value
METRICTON	1000

Then it executes the three Dim statements. These statements cause the computer to add three rows to its variable table.

Variable Name	Value
ContainerWeightA	0
ContainerWeightB	0
TotalWeight	0

Next, the computer executes the first assignment statement. To do this, it performs this sequence of steps:

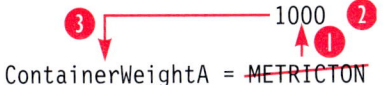

1. Computer replaces constant name by its value (from the symbolic constant table).
2. Computer determines value of expression to be 1000.
3. Computer stores 1000 in variable on left-hand side (changes its value in the variable table).

The net effect of executing this assignment statement is to change the variable table.

Variable Name	Value
ContainerWeightA	1000
ContainerWeightB	0
TotalWeight	0

Next, the computer executes the second assignment statement. To do this, it performs the steps shown on the next page.

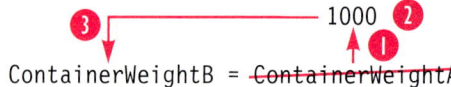

1. Computer replaces variable name by its value (from the variable table).
2. Computer determines value of expression to be 1000.
3. Computer stores 1000 in variable on left-hand side (changes its value in the variable table).

The net effect of executing this assignment statement is to again change the variable table.

Variable Name	Value
ContainerWeightA	1000
ContainerWeightB	1000
TotalWeight	0

Next, the computer executes the third assignment statement. To do this, it performs these steps:

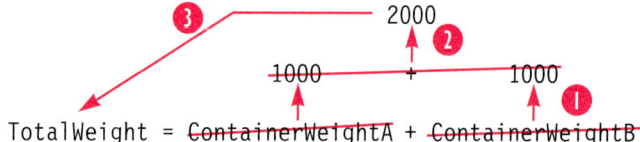

1. Computer replaces the variable names by their values (from the variable table).
2. Computer adds 1000 and 1000, determines value of expression to be 2000.
3. Computer stores 2000 in variable on left-hand side (changes its value in the variable table).

Once again the variable table is changed.

Variable Name	Value
ContainerWeightA	1000
ContainerWeightB	1000
TotalWeight	2000

The final assignment statement is a little different than the others: it has a control property, instead of a variable, on the left-hand side. You may recall seeing statements like this in examples in Chapter 2. The net effect of this statement is to display the value of TotalWeight on the user interface in the Caption property of the label named lblTotal. When the computer executes this statement, it performs the steps depicted next.

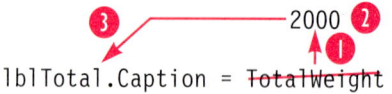

1. Computer replaces variable name by its value (from the variable table).
2. Computer determines value of expression to be 2000.
3. Computer stores 2000 in Caption property of label control, which displays it on the user interface.

Changing Variable Values during Execution

As you have seen, you can instruct the computer to do two things with a variable:

1. Store a value in the variable—the previous value in the variable will be *overwritten* (irretrievably lost) by this operation. To store a value in a variable, place the variable on the left-hand side of an assignment statement.
2. Retrieve the value from the variable—this operation will not change the value in the variable. It is done either to use this value in a calculation or processing step or to display it to the user. To retrieve the value from a variable, place the variable in an expression on the right-hand side of an assignment statement.

These are the only two things that you can do with a variable. You must understand these two ideas in order to be able to write correct assignment statements. For example, consider the following statement:

X = X + 1

Statements like this, where the same variable name appears both in the expression and on the left-hand side, are used very frequently in programs.

What does this statement do? Suppose that the variable table before this statement is executed is as follows.

Variable Name	Value
X	5

To execute the assignment statement the computer performs the sequence of steps depicted next.

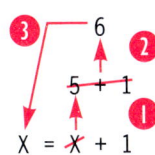

1. Computer replaces variable name by its value (from the variable table).
2. Computer performs addition, determines value of expression to be 6.
3. Computer stores 6 in the variable on left-hand side (changes its value in the variable table).

The net effect of executing the assignment statement is to change the variable table as shown below. Regardless of the value in X when the statement is executed, the statement's net effect is to increase the value stored in X by 1.

Variable Name	Value
X	6

To test your understanding of the assignment statement's action, let's work through a complete event procedure. This event procedure, which is associated with a command button named cmdAssignmentQuiz on a hypothetical form, is shown below.

```
Private Sub cmdAssignmentQuiz_Click()
    Dim A As Integer
    Dim B As Integer
    Dim C As Integer
    A = 5
    A = A + A
    B = A - 6
    C = A + B
    B = B + C
```

continues

```
            B = B - A
            B = B + 1
            lblQuiz.Caption = B
End Sub
```

Before reading further, see if you can figure out what value will be displayed in the Label control (lblQuiz) when the event procedure is finished executing. That is, what value will the variable B hold at the end of the procedure?

How did you do? Let's go through the procedure one statement at a time and see what happens. After executing the three Dim statements, the computer's variable table is

Variable Name	Value
A	0
B	0
C	0

Executing the statement A = 5 changes the variable table to

Variable Name	Value
A	5
B	0
C	0

Next, the computer executes the statement A = A + A. To do this, it performs these steps:

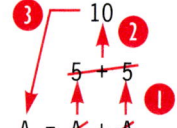

1. Computer replaces variable name by its value (from the variable table).
2. Computer performs addition and determines value of expression to be 10.
3. Computer stores 10 in variable on left-hand side (changes its value in the variable table).

The net effect of executing this statement is to change the variable table.

Variable Name	Value
A	10
B	0
C	0

After executing the statement B = A - 6, the variable table is

Variable Name	Value
A	10
B	4
C	0

After executing the statement C = A + B, the variable table is

Variable Name	Value
A	10
B	4
C	14

After executing the statement B = B + C, the variable table is

Variable Name	Value
A	10
B	18
C	14

After executing the statement B = B - A, the variable table is

Variable Name	Value
A	10
B	8
C	14

Finally, after executing the statement B = B + 1, the variable table is

Variable Name	Value
A	10
B	9
C	14

The final statement in the event procedure, lblQuiz.Caption = B, stores the value of the variable B in the Caption property of lblQuiz. Thus, the value 9 is displayed on the user interface.

You can see how tedious operations like this are for humans to perform. It is very easy to make a mistake. However, the computer never tires of performing these operations and gets them right every time.

Assignment Statements with Strings

You can use the assignment statement to store the result of string manipulations in string variables just as you store the result of arithmetic calculations in numeric variables. The main difference is that string expressions tend to be simpler than numeric expressions. To illustrate, the Click event procedure for a hypothetical command button named cmdStringAssignment is shown next.

```
Private Sub cmdStringAssignment_Click()
    Dim FirstName As String
    Dim LastName As String
    Dim FullName As String
    FirstName = "Benjamin"
    LastName = "Franklin"
    FullName = FirstName & LastName
    lblName.Caption = FullName
End Sub
```

This event procedure manipulates strings using statements similar to those we have seen that manipulate numbers. The & symbol[9] in the expression of the third assignment statement is called the *concatenation operator:* **it joins two string values together, end-to-end, to form a single string value**.

After executing the three Dim statements, the computer's variable table is as follows. (Recall that string variables are initialized to the zero-length string.)

Variable Name	Value
FirstName	""
LastName	""
FullName	""

Executing the statement FirstName = "Benjamin" changes the variable table to

Variable Name	Value
FirstName	"Benjamin"
LastName	""
FullName	""

After executing the statement LastName = "Franklin", the variable table is

Variable Name	Value
FirstName	"Benjamin"
LastName	"Franklin"
FullName	""

To execute the statement FullName = FirstName & LastName, the computer performs the following steps:

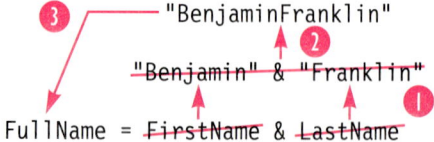

1. Computer replaces variable names by their values (from the variable table).
2. Computer performs string concatenation and determines value of expression to be "BenjaminFranklin".
3. Computer stores "BenjaminFranklin" in variable on left-hand side (changes its value in the variable table).

[9] The & symbol is often read as "ampersand."

The net effect of executing this statement is to change the variable table to

Variable Name	Value
FirstName	"Benjamin"
LastName	"Franklin"
FullName	"BenjaminFranklin"

The final assignment statement in the event procedure, lblName.Caption = FullName, displays the value "BenjaminFranklin" on the user interface.

The Type Mismatch Error

Numeric variables can store numeric values but cannot store string values. So what happens when the computer tries to execute the following event procedure?

Private Sub cmdTypeMismatchA_Click()
    Dim X **As Integer**
    X = "12a"   This assignment statement instructs the computer to store the string value
    lblX.Caption = X   "12a" in the numeric variable X.
End Sub

When the computer tries to execute the statement X = "12a", it fails. Because "12a" does not have the correct form for a number, it cannot be stored in a numeric variable. This mistake—**trying to store string data in a numeric variable**—is known as a *type mismatch error.* The computer stops executing the project and displays the error message shown in Figure 3.7.

In order to fix the problem, the programmer must modify the code, either by changing the Dim statement so that X is declared to be type String, or by changing the assignment statement so that the expression is numeric instead of string (e.g., 12 instead of "12a").

A type mismatch error also occurs when the computer tries to execute the statement X = Y in the following event procedure. The reason is the same as in the previous event procedure.

Private Sub cmdTypeMismatchB_Click()
    Dim X **As Integer**
    Dim Y **As String**
    Y = "12a"
    X = Y   This assignment statement instructs the computer to store the value retrieved
    lblX.Caption = X   from the string variable Y in the numeric variable X.
End Sub

FIGURE 3.7

Type mismatch error message

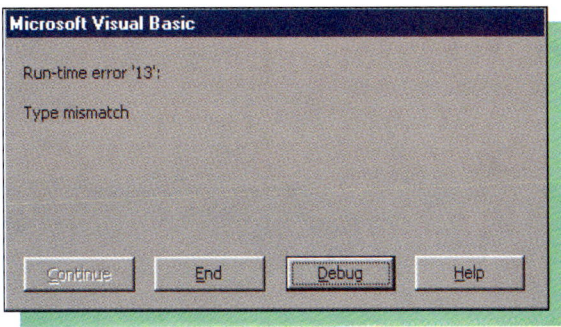

The type mismatch error is an example of a *run time error*—a condition arising during execution of a statement that prevents the computer from successfully executing the statement. Note that while VB can detect some errors at design time (e.g., when you try to type a variable name containing a space), it *cannot* detect the type mismatch error at design time.

Control Properties in Assignment Statements

Most control properties can be used just like variables in assignment statements. Thus, if *control.property* appears on the left-hand side of an assignment statement, then the computer stores the result of the expression in the specified property of the specified control. For example, the assignment statement

```
lblCPUPrice.Caption = 1450
```

causes the value 1450 to be stored in the Caption property of the control named lblCPUPrice.

If *control.property* appears in the expression of an assignment statement, then the computer will retrieve the value from the specified property of the specified control to use in evaluating the expression.

There are only two differences between a *control.property* and a variable:

1. To create a variable you must write a variable declaration statement; in contrast, you don't declare controls or their properties. VB automatically gives you a whole set of control properties when you draw the control on the form.

2. VB automatically links a *control.property* to some aspect of the control's behavior; for example, the value stored in a label's Caption property is automatically displayed on the user interface. Variables are just symbolic names for storage locations in memory and have no direct connection to the user interface.

Note in particular that, like variables, every property has a type. For example, the Caption property of labels is type String and therefore can store values containing any character.

A few control properties, such as Name, cannot be used in assignment statements (or any other statements, for that matter). A few others are "read only at run time," which means that you can retrieve their value at run time but you cannot change their value at run time; these control properties can appear in an assignment statement's expression, but cannot appear on the left-hand side of an assignment statement. We will point out control properties that have these restrictions as we introduce new controls.

Finally, the first of the two differences noted earlier between variables and *control.properties* deserves emphasis. As a beginning programmer you may be tempted to declare a control, or a property of a control, using a Dim statement. But the Dim statement creates variables, not controls. Suppose you draw a Label control on the form and set its Name property to lblPrice. If you also write the variable declaration statement

> **Dim** lblPrice **As Currency**

then your project will have both a control named lblPrice and a variable named lblPrice. This causes great confusion, because if you use lblPrice in a subsequent statement, it will be unclear whether the statement refers to the variable or the control.

> **Rule** Do not use the name of an existing control in a variable declaration statement. Likewise, never use a variable name beginning with one of the conventional three-letter prefixes for control names (e.g., cmd, lbl, tmr, and so forth).

Why Use Variables?

Since control properties can be used like variables in a program, why do you need variables? For example, Projects 1 through 3 in Chapter 2 contained no variables. But these were simplified, unrefined applications. When you try to write a useful, user-friendly program, you find that variables are essential. Sometimes a program needs to perform intermediate calculations that should not be displayed to the user. Since control properties are automatically linked to the user interface, you do not want to use them to store the results of intermediate calculations. Variables are ideal for storing such results because they have no direct connection to the user interface.

Similarly, in a well-designed application, values displayed on the user interface will be nicely formatted. But quite often, formatting a value for display requires introducing symbols (such as dollar signs), which VB does not allow in arithmetic calculations. Thus, it is typical to use variables to hold unformatted values for calculation, and then, when it is time to display a result, retrieve the value from its variable, format it, and store it in a control property. We discuss formatting values for display in Chapter 4.

Example 3.2

Using Variables to Store Intermediate Results and to Reduce Redundant Data

In this example we rewrite the event procedure from Project 2 using what we have learned about variables and constants to make the program more readable and reduce the chances that errors will occur in the code. Figure 3.8 repeats the code for the event procedure cmdComputeInvoice_Click in Figure 3.4b, which was our most recent version of this event procedure. However, to illustrate a point we have introduced a *typographical error* in the code—that is, the common kind of error that occurs when the programmer makes a simple typing mistake.

Except for the constant definition, every statement in cmdComputeInvoice _Click is an assignment statement with a *control.property* on the left-hand

FIGURE 3.8

Event procedure cmdComputeInvoice _Click

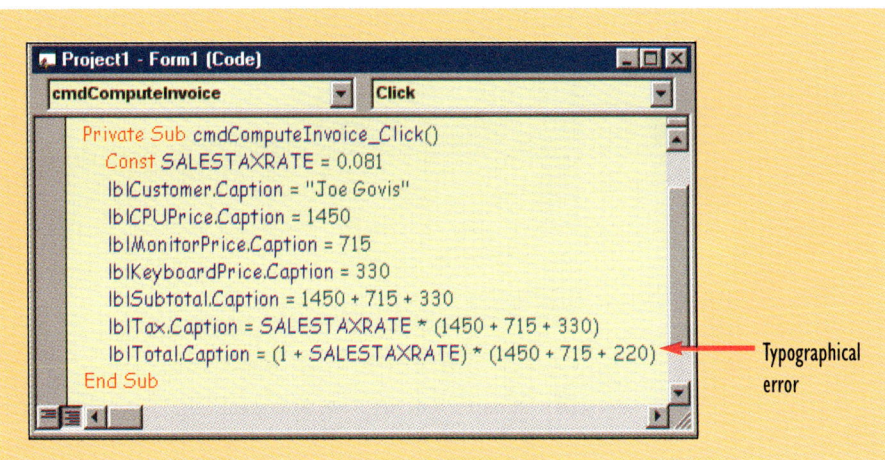

side. What calculations can reasonably be saved in variables? What types should these variables be, and what are good names for them?

The calculation 1450 + 715 + 330 is performed three times in this event procedure (is it?). This is a little inefficient, because as an alternative we can perform the calculation *once* and store the result in a variable, then retrieve this value when it is subsequently needed. Much worse is the possibility of making an error when we specify redundant calculations.[10] Figure 3.8 illustrates such an error. The programmer meant to specify the same calculation three times but made an error in typing one of them.

Let us create a variable in which to store the result of the calculation 1450 + 715 + 330. This variable should be type Currency, and a descriptive name for it is TotalPurchaseAmount. The revised code is in Figure 3.9.

Using a variable with a descriptive name has the same advantages as using a symbolic constant. The program is easier to read, since it uses the meaningful name TotalPurchaseAmount instead of the arithmetic expression 1450 + 715 + 330. Since the arithmetic expression now appears only once, there is no chance of inconsistency. The event procedure in Figure 3.9 will produce a different result than the version in Figure 3.8, which has an inconsistency.

There is still some data redundancy in the code of cmdComputeInvoice_Click, since the literal numeric constants 1450, 715, and 330 each occur twice. We can improve this situation with additional symbolic constants, as in Figure 3.10. This event procedure is easy to understand and avoids the pitfalls of redundant data. Still, it would be more useful if the sales tax rate and prices could change from one execution of the program to the next. Ideally, they would be obtained from a database, but they also might be input by the user via the keyboard. Both approaches require that we use variables instead of constants for these quantities. We discuss user input in Chapter 4 and database access in Chapter 8.

EXERCISE Describe, using everyday words, the net effect of the assignment statement X = X + 1.

FIGURE 3.9

Revised event procedure with variable TotalPurchaseAmount replacing two redundant calculations

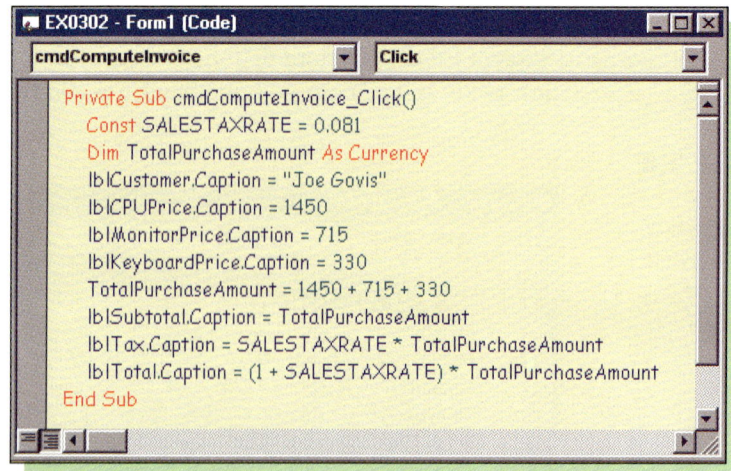

[10] Modern computers are so fast that the user will not notice the additional time consumed performing the same simple calculation three times instead of once. In contrast, an error caused by inconsistent data can have disastrous effects in a business application.

FIGURE 3.10

Event procedure after eliminating redundant data

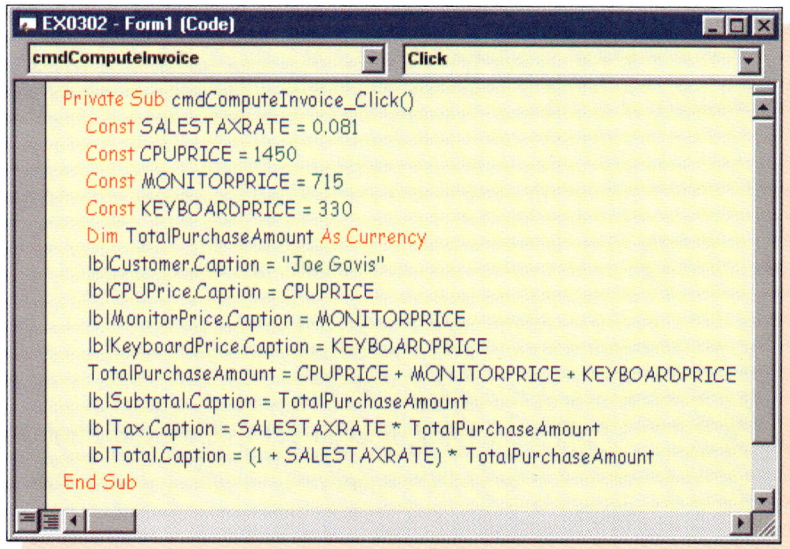

EXERCISE 3.11

Show the computer's variable table after it has executed the following two statements.

Dim X **As Integer**
X = X

What is the net effect of the statement X = X?

EXERCISE 3.12

The event procedure below contains the same statements as the event procedure cmdAssignmentQuiz_Click, discussed in the text, but the statements have been rearranged. What value is displayed in lblQuiz when cmdRearranged Assignments_Click is executed?

Private Sub cmdRearrangedAssignments_Click()
    Dim A **As Integer**
    Dim B **As Integer**
    Dim C **As Integer**
    C = A + B
    B = B + 1
    A = 5
    B = A - 6
    A = A + A
    B = B + C
    B = B - A
    lblQuiz.Caption = B
End Sub

EXERCISE 3.13

What value will be displayed in lblLetters when the following event procedure is executed?

Private Sub cmdStringAssignments_Click()
    Dim A **As String**
    Dim B **As String**
    Dim C **As String** * 3
    A = "X"
    B = "O"

continues

```
            A = A & B
            B = A & B
            A = B & A
            C = "00000"
            lblLetters.Caption = C & A
End Sub
```

EXERCISE 3.14 An event procedure contains the following three variable declaration statements:

Dim FirstName **As String**
Dim LastName **As String**
Dim FullName **As String**

The same event procedure also contains the following assignment statements:

FirstName = "William"
LastName = "Gates"
FullName = "FirstName" & LastName

What value is stored in the variable FullName after these three assignment statements are executed?

EXERCISE 3.15 Immediately after the following three assignment statements are executed, the variable FullName holds the value "BenjaminFranklin".

FirstName = "Benjamin"
LastName = "Franklin"
FullName = FirstName & LastName

How can you modify the third assignment statement above so that a space appears between the first and last names in the value stored in FullName?

EXERCISE 3.16 What value is stored in the variable TestDifference after the following statements are executed?

Dim TestNumberA **As Single**
Dim TestNumberB **As Single**
Dim TestDifference **As Single**

TestNumberA = 2.3456789
TestNumberB = 1.2345678
TestDifference = TestNumberA - TestNumberB

What value would be stored in TestDifference if the three variables were all type Currency instead of Single? Type Long? Type Double?

EXERCISE 3.17 Complete the following event procedure by writing a sequence of statements which, when used in place of *statementblock*, will cause the last two statements to display 2 in lblX and 1 in lblY. The statements you write should contain no constants. Do not modify or move any other statements in the event procedure.

Hint: Draw the computer's variable table immediately after it executes the statement Y = 2. Then consider what it needs to look like before the final two assignment statements can be executed. Be sure to check that your solution works correctly!

```
Private Sub cmdExchange_Click()
    Dim X As Integer
    Dim Y As Integer
    Dim Z As Integer
    X = 1
    Y = 2
    statementblock
    lblX.Caption = X
    lblY.Caption = Y
End Sub
```

Option Explicit

The computer makes no attempt to understand the human meaning of a variable name. As a result, if you make a typographical error in a variable name, the program will operate differently than you intended.

In the next example we demonstrate the potentially serious consequences of typographical errors. The cause of the difficulty is that VB considers variable names with different spellings to be different variables. After the example, we will show how you can let VB help you find typographical errors in your variable names.

Example 3.3 Typographical Errors in Variable Names

The variable name TotalPurchaseAmount occurs in five places in cmdComputeInvoice_Click (Figure 3.9). Suppose that the programmer mistakenly types TotalPurchasAmount in one of those places, as in Figure 3.11. A human reading the program is likely to overlook the missing "e" and, as a result, believe TotalPurchasAmount and TotalPurchaseAmount identify the same variable. In sharp contrast, it is *absolutely certain* that the computer will identify TotalPurchasAmount and TotalPurchaseAmount as two different sequences of characters, and will therefore treat them as different variables.

Such a simple error can baffle the programmer: the program will run, but not as the programmer had intended, and the source of the problem will be very

FIGURE 3.11

Event procedure with a typo in variable name

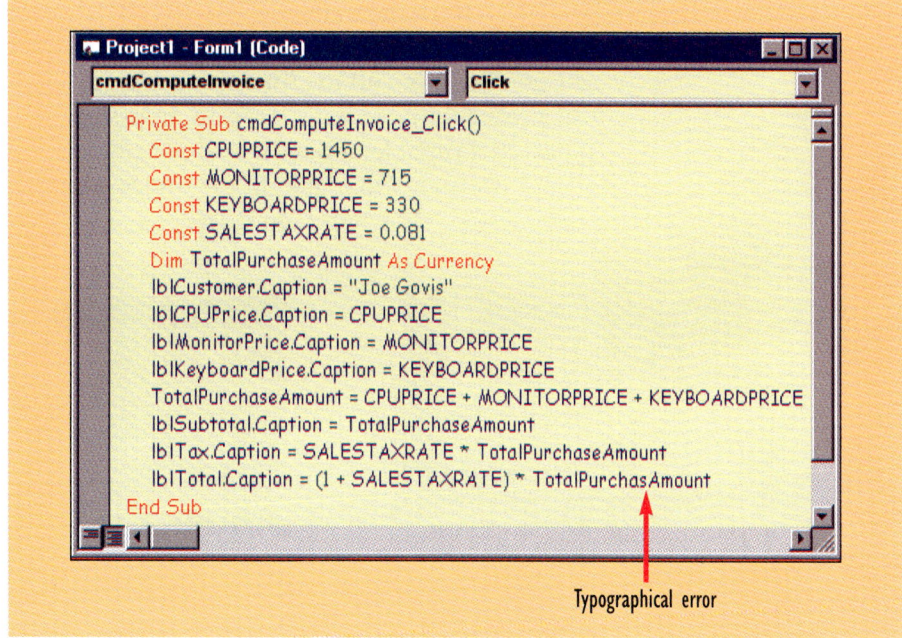

difficult to identify because it is caused by a single mistyped character. If you run Example 3.3, you will see that the Total value it displays is zero.

The following practices can both reduce your effort when typing statements and help you avoid typographical errors.

◆ First, be sure to create and name the important controls before working on event procedures.

◆ Second, type constant definition and variable declaration statements before any other statements, being sure to follow the conventions for capitalization of symbolic constant and variable names.

◆ Third, type the remaining statements using all lowercase letters.

The reason for the third recommendation is that, as you move the cursor off of each new statement you type, VB will automatically adjust the capitalization of every item (keyword, control name, symbolic constant name, variable name, etc.) it recognizes in the new statement. VB adjusts the capitalization of a control name to match the capitalization of its Name property setting, and adjusts the capitalization of a symbolic constant or variable name to match its capitalization in the corresponding Const or Dim statement. If the name remains in all lowercase, then you know that VB was unable to find a control, Const statement, or Dim statement with that name, and that you must have made a typographical error.

Even if you do follow the above practices, you should expect errors to escape your attention from time to time. To remedy this, you can make VB explicitly point out your misspelled variable names by including the Option Explicit statement in the Code window's general declarations section, as shown in Figure 3.12.

> **Convention** Always include the Option Explicit statement in the general declarations section.

Run Time: The Effect of the Option Explicit Statement

When you run a program, the first thing VB does is check whether the general declarations section contains the *Option Explicit statement,* **which, if present, causes VB to scan all the form's event procedures for undeclared variables.** If it finds a variable name (say, in an assignment statement) that does not appear in a variable declaration statement, then VB will not execute the program; instead, it will highlight the undeclared variable name and display the error message shown in Figure 3.13.

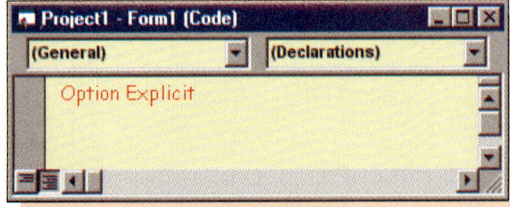

FIGURE 3.12

Option Explicit statement in general declarations section

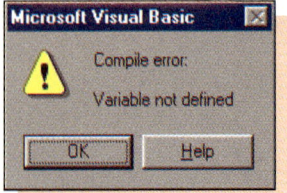

FIGURE 3.13

Error message resulting from misspelled variable name when Option Explicit statement is included

What effect would Option Explicit have on Example 3.3? The program would not run until the programmer either declared an additional variable, TotalPurchasAmount, or else corrected TotalPurchasAmount to TotalPurchaseAmount (which is already declared). The programmer would quickly rule out the first of these actions, since only one variable is needed to store the total purchase amount.

Essentially, then, Option Explicit causes VB to check for misspelled variable names, which is straightforward for the computer but extremely tedious for humans.

Edit the code for Example 3.3 to add the Option Explicit statement. To do this,

1. View the form for Example 3.3 by double-clicking on the EX0303.Frm entry in the Project window.
2. Double-click on the form to bring up its Code window.
3. Go to the general declarations section by selecting (General) in the Object box and (Declarations) in the Procedures/Events box, then type in the Option Explicit statement.

Now run the program and see the effect of this change.

Inserting the Option Explicit Statement Automatically

You can make VB automatically insert the Option Explicit statement in the general declarations section. To do this, select Options… under VB's Tools menu. VB will respond with the dialog window shown in Figure 3.14. On the Editor tab, turn on the check mark for the "Require Variable Declaration" option and click OK.

However, you must be aware of the following facts when using Option Explicit:

◆ Each form in a project has its own general declarations section.
◆ Each form's general declarations section must have its own Option Explicit statement—that is, Option Explicit applies only to variables in event procedures associated with that form.
◆ VB will *not* insert the Option Explicit statement into preexisting forms—it only inserts the statement in forms that are created *after* you check the Require Variable Declaration option.

FIGURE 3.14

VB's Options dialog window

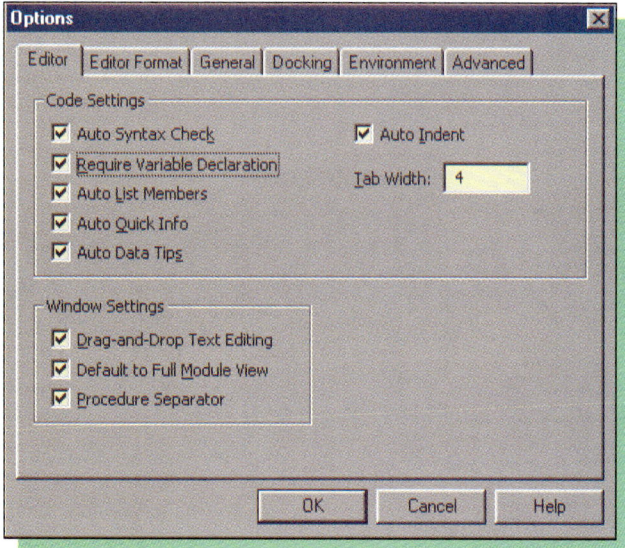

The first two facts apply to projects with more than one form. Our projects so far have had only one form, but business applications typically have more. We now turn to the Form control and examine the structure of more complex programs.

3.4 The Form Control

Up to this point we have seen the form only as the background of our user interface. While the form always plays this role, it can do much more. In fact, the *Form control* **is what organizes a project in terms of the appearance and functionality of its user interface, its constants and variables, and its storage on disk.**

Appearance and Use

What happens if a project is large? In particular, suppose there are more controls than can comfortably fit on a single form. Making the controls smaller and packing them more closely together is a bad idea because it makes the program hard to use. The solution is to use multiple forms in the design and construction of the project. Each form should have an objective, or theme, which the user easily comprehends. Each form should contain all the controls necessary to that objective, and the form should have a clear and attractive layout. Because of their ability to contain other controls, forms are often referred to as "container controls."[11]

During program execution each form is a user interface window. These are ordinary windows that are familiar to Microsoft Windows users. By establishing the number, content, and appearance of forms in a project, and also the timing with which forms are presented to the user at run time, the programmer controls the overall organization and behavior of the project as experienced by the user.

All forms have the same basic components, which are labeled in Figure 3.15. The Reduce and Enlarge buttons allow the user to change the size of the form. At run time, if the user clicks on a form's Reduce button, the form "collapses" into an icon on the Taskbar. In order to see the form again, the user can click on this icon. If the user clicks on a form's Enlarge button, the form will expand

FIGURE 3.15

Anatomy of a form

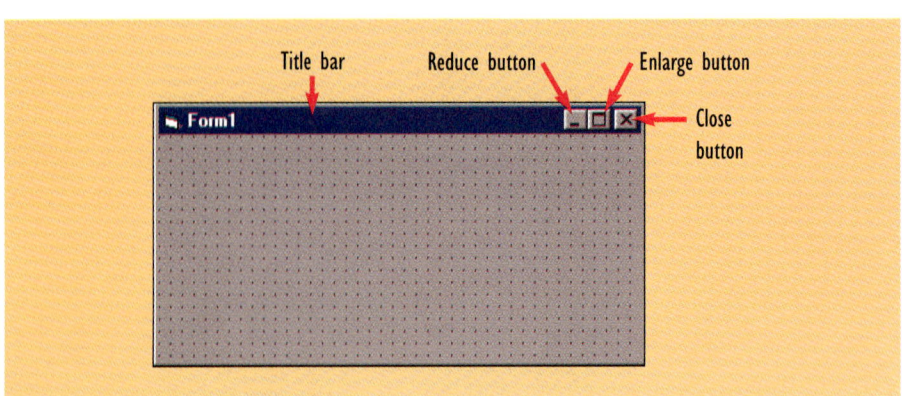

[11] Other types of container controls in VB include the Frame control (discussed in Chapter 5), the Picture box control (Appendix C), and the Tabbed dialog control (Appendix G).

to fill the entire screen. The user can change the form back to its original size and location by clicking the Enlarge button a second time. If the user clicks on the Close button, the form is removed from the screen (and execution of the application ends if this was the only form on the screen).

Properties

The properties of the Form control that the programmer typically sets are listed in Table 3.3. There are additional properties that allow the programmer to refine the form; for example, the programmer can suppress the Title bar and the Reduce and Enlarge buttons. You can easily learn about all the Form properties by experimenting or via online help (search phrase "form object").

> **Convention** Use the prefix "frm" for the Name property of Form controls. As with all other important controls, use a descriptive name for the Form control. Descriptive Form names are particularly useful in projects having multiple forms to help you recall the purpose and function of each.

Events

While the form's primary purpose is to help organize a project, it is also capable of responding to certain events. The simplest of these is the Click event; you can write a Click event procedure for a form just as you would write one for a command button. The event procedure will be executed when the user clicks directly on the form (i.e., not on a control that sits on top of the form). However, programmers rarely use the form's Click event. Be aware that if the user clicks on a form and no Click event procedure has been defined for the form, then nothing happens.

More useful are the Activate and Load events for a form. At run time only one form is active at any given time. The *active form* **is the form that the user**

TABLE 3.3 Properties of the Form control

Property	Specifies
Caption	*The descriptive caption that is displayed at the left end of the form's Title bar.* Use the caption to describe the objective or theme of the form.
BackColor	*The background color of the form.* To change the BackColor setting, in the Properties window select BackColor, then click on the down arrow button at the right end of its settings box. This will bring up a dialog with two tabs: Palette and System. On the Palette tab, simply click on the color you wish to use.

WindowState	*How the form is initially presented to the user at run time.* The three possible values and their effects are
	    0 - Normal; at run time the form will have the same size and location on the screen as it does at design time.
	    1 - Minimized; at run time only an icon for the form is displayed on the Taskbar (the user can click the icon to see the form).
	    2 - Maximized; at run time the form will fill the entire screen.

(Name)	*A unique name for the Form control.* As programmer, you use this property to distinguish forms from one another in a multiple-form project. The form's Name property is distinct from the name of the form file that saves the form on disk. As with the Name property for other controls, the user is completely unaware of the form's Name property.

can interact with. The user can click on a control on the active form and the control's event procedure will be executed. The active form always has its Title bar highlighted to indicate its active status.

When a user switches from using one form to another, an *Activate event* occurs for the form that becomes active. Thus, you can write an Activate event procedure that performs a particular processing task every time the form becomes active. As an example of this, some forms are always cleared each time they are presented to the user; to accomplish this, the programmer places the code that clears the form in the form's Activate event procedure.

The Load event enables the programmer to control how much of the computer's memory the project occupies at run time. Doing this may affect the program's speed of execution. Let us now briefly examine these issues.

Forms and Main Memory

In a large project with many forms it is possible to use up all the computer's main memory (RAM) at run time. To mitigate this problem, VB allows you to design a project such that at run time only one or just a few forms are in main memory at any given time. The remaining forms are stored on the computer's disk.

To make such a project work, the programmer writes code that loads a form when it is needed. To load a form means to transfer it from disk storage to main memory. The programmer also writes code that unloads the form when the user is finished working with it. Unloading a form makes the main memory that it occupied available for other forms.

You will learn about the statements that perform the load and unload actions later. In a project with only one form, VB automatically loads the form when program execution first begins.

Each time a form is loaded, a *Load event* occurs for the form. Thus, you can write a Load event procedure that performs a particular processing task every time the form is loaded. The term *initialization* **refers to tasks that are performed when an activity first starts**. Thus, we say that the Load event procedure is commonly used to initialize various aspects of the form.

Run Time Speed

The process of transferring data or code between disk storage and main memory is very slow compared with the speed of processes occurring in main memory. Thus, programmers generally try to minimize the amount of loading and unloading of forms. This is also why users and programmers alike prefer to have computers with large main memories.

Forms and Disk Storage

◆ ◆ ◆

Forms are also VB's primary way of organizing the storage of a project on disk. When you save the project, VB creates one file for each form. For each of these form files VB asks you to specify a file name, to which VB appends the extension ".Frm". Note that the name of the form file is different from the form's Name property. This difference is illustrated in Figure 3.16.

A form file contains information about the form, including the form's properties, all the controls (and their properties) that reside on the form, and all the event procedures associated with all the controls on the form.

3.4 The Form Control   113

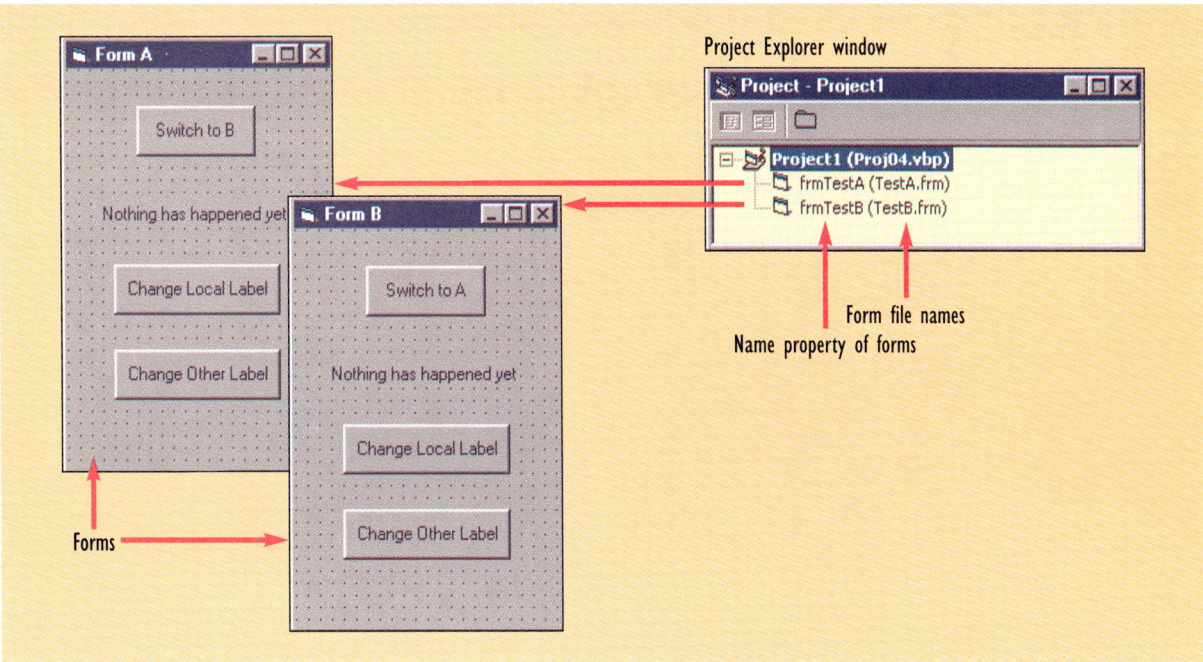

FIGURE 3.16   A project with two forms

Forms and Code Windows

Each form in a project has its own Code window. The Code window's Title bar shows the Name property of the form to which it belongs. It will show only the event procedures for the controls that reside on that form. Figure 3.17 shows the Code windows for the forms frmTestA and frmTestB depicted in Figure 3.16.

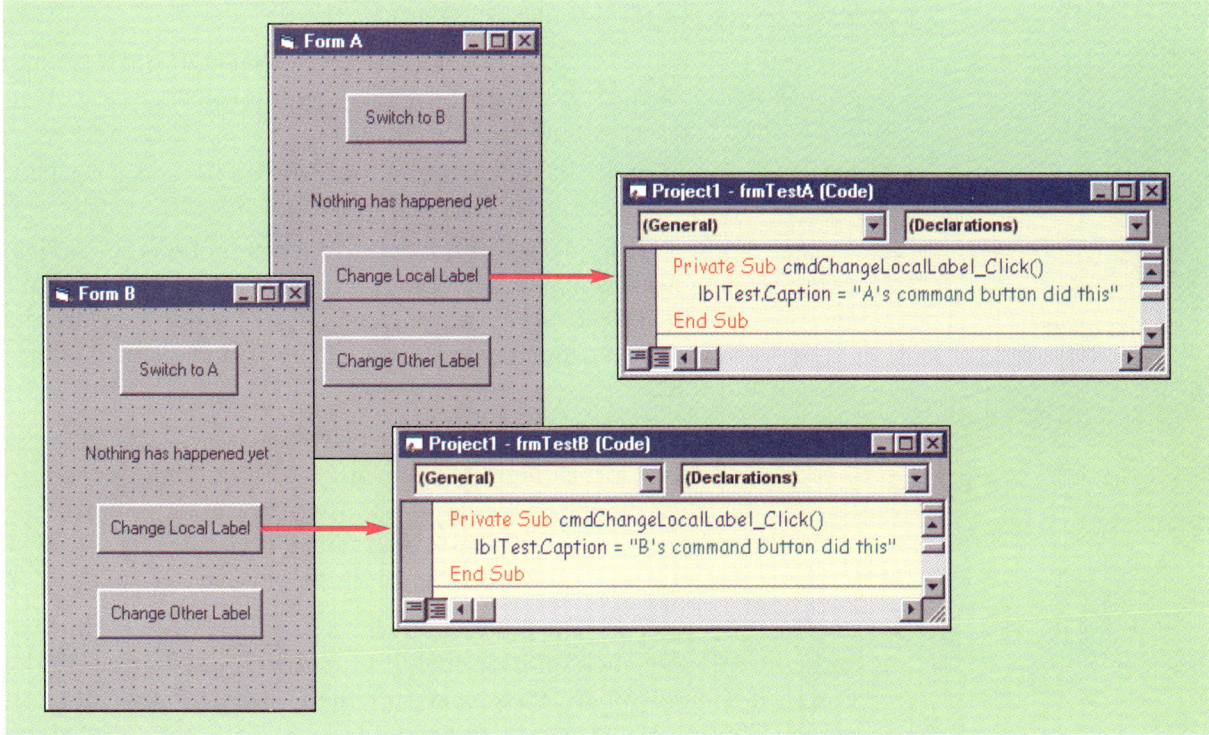

FIGURE 3.17   Code windows for a project with two forms

Interestingly, VB does not list the form's Name property in the Code window's Object box, as it does for all other controls on the form. Instead, it provides the entry "Form". Thus, if you want to write a Load event procedure for the form, you select Form in the Object box and Load in the Procedures/Events box. Accordingly, the event procedure will be named Form_Load, regardless of the form's Name property. This makes sense because each form has its own Code window.

3.5 Project 4: Using Multiple Forms

The following concepts are introduced in this project: methods, the Show method, syntax, the startup form, and qualified control names.

In this project we examine how forms establish the structure of a project. We also demonstrate the mechanics of building and managing a project with more than one form.

This project is not a business application; rather, it is a tutorial that lays the foundation for multiform applications and introduces the concepts needed to work with forms. Project 5 builds on this foundation to construct a simplified payroll application.

This project consists of the two forms shown in Figures 3.16 and 3.17. The user can switch between the two forms and also modify a control property on one form by clicking a command button on the other. When you complete this project, you should understand how to use multiple forms and how forms can communicate with each other.

Begin by creating a project and two forms.

1. Create a file folder in which to save this project before beginning work on it. This is particularly important for projects with multiple forms, because the number of files belonging to the project can be large.

2. Launch VB. As usual, VB automatically gives you one form to start with, to which it gives the default name Form1.

3. Using the Properties window, change the form's Name to frmTestA and change its Caption to "Form A". Observe how these changes appear in the Project Explorer window and on the form.

4. Select Options… under the Tools menu, then turn on the check mark for "Require Variable Declaration" on the Editor tab. Click OK.

5. Create a second form by clicking on the Add Form tool on the Toolbar, or by selecting Add Form under the Project menu. Observe that VB makes an entry for the new form in the Project Explorer window. Using the Properties window, rename the new form frmTestB, and change its caption to "Form B".

At design time you can use the Project Explorer window to switch back and forth between the two forms: highlight the entry for the form you want to work with, then click the View Object button. Alternatively, move one of the forms (by dragging its Title bar) so that it does not entirely cover up the other form. Then you can switch to the other form by simply clicking on it.

6. Look at the general declarations section of frmTestB (make frmTestB active and either double-click on it or click on the View Code button on the Project Explorer window; then make sure the Code window's Full Module View button is depressed). You should see the Option Explicit statement. This statement appears because you checked the Require Variable

Declaration box (step 4) before you created the form (step 5). Now look at the general declarations section of frmTestA. You will not see Option Explicit there (unless Require Variable Declaration was already checked before you started this project). Rectify this situation if necessary by typing Option Explicit in frmTestA's general declarations section (that is, at the very top of frmTestA's Code window).

7. On frmTestA, place a command button with Name cmdShowOtherForm and Caption "Switch To B". On frmTestB, place a command button with Name cmdShowOtherForm and Caption "Switch To A". After doing this, your forms should appear as shown in Figure 3.18.

Note that in a single project you cannot have two forms with the same Name. On a single form you cannot have two controls with the same Name. But you can have two controls with the same Name if they are on *different* forms. The ability to reuse control names is useful in large projects created by teams of programmers. For example, if you create one form and I create another, we don't have to bother to make sure we choose different names for controls that may perform similar functions. In fact, it may even help us understand each other's work if we do use the same names for controls that perform similar tasks.

8. View frmTestA and look at the list of objects in the Object box of the Properties window. Then view frmTestB and look at the list of objects in the Object box of the Properties window. Note that the Properties window displays only objects belonging to the selected form.

9. Run the project. Which form is displayed? VB automatically loaded frmTestA and made it active because it was the first form that was created in the project. Also note that nothing happens when you click its command button because its Click event procedure is empty.

10. End execution.

In any project VB will only automatically load and make active *one* form. This is called the *startup form*.

FIGURE 3.18

Project 4 forms with command buttons

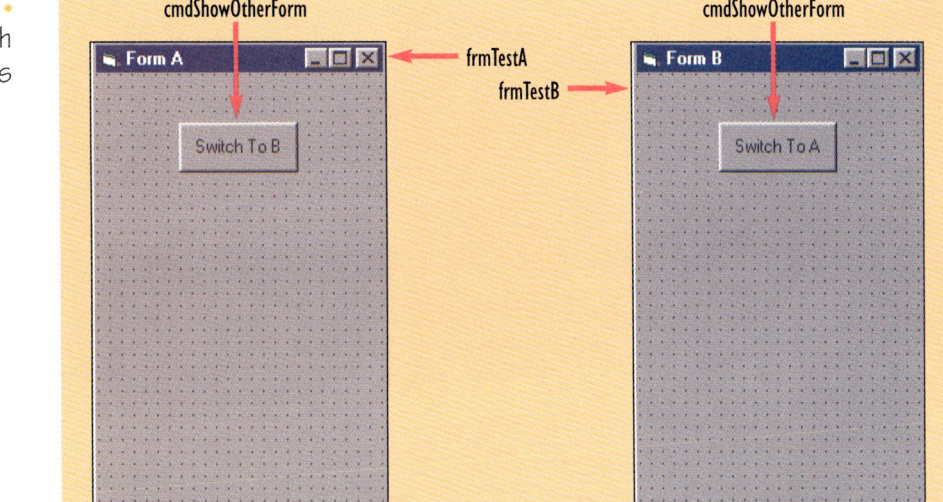

11. Under the Project menu select Project1 Properties… In the dialog window that ensues (see Figure 3.19), select the General tab and change the Startup Object dropdown list entry from frmTestA to frmTestB, then click OK.

12. Run the program again. Now which form is displayed? Again, clicking on its command button has no effect.

13. End execution.

The startup form entry allows you to specify which form will be the startup form.

14. Next, create Click event procedures for the command buttons as shown in Figure 3.20. Recall that the Code window's Title bar indicates the form.

Each form has its own Code window. Thus, after creating the event procedure for the command button on frmTestA, you have to change to the Code window for frmTestB before you can create the event procedure for the command button on frmTestB. If you like, you can resize and reposition the two Code windows so they are side by side on your computer screen.

15. After creating the event procedures, run the program and click the command buttons to see their effect.

16. End execution.

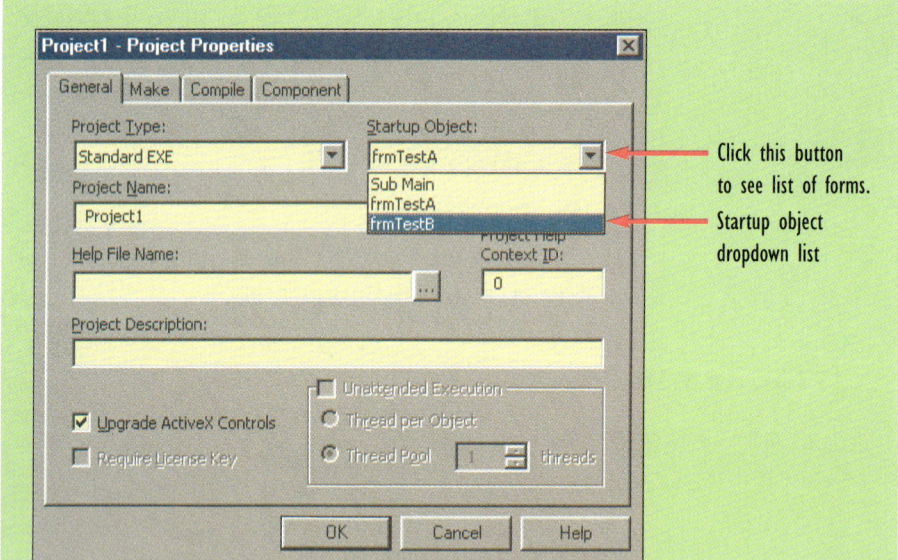

FIGURE 3.19

Setting the startup form

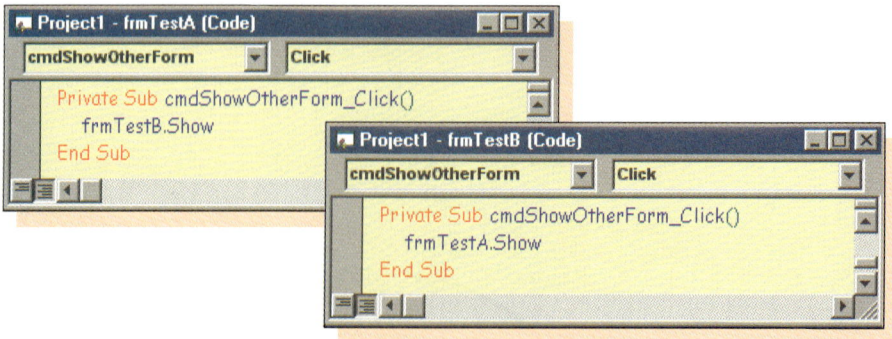

FIGURE 3.20

Click event procedures that change the active form

If frmTestA is your startup form, then the first time you click on the Switch to B command button, VB will load frmTestB and make it active. When you click on the Switch to A button, VB simply makes frmTestA active; it does not need to load frmTestA again because it was never unloaded.

You probably agree that the action of the statement frmTestB.Show is clear. At this point in your study of VB, this statement should look a little strange, because frmTestB is the name of a control but Show is *not* a property. So far, whenever we've seen a control name followed by a period followed by something else, that something else has been a property. However, this same sequence—control name followed by a period followed by something else—is also used for *methods,* **which are actions that apply to controls.** In this case, the **Show method** applies to a Form control, and it tells VB to display the form.[12] Programmers rephrase this idea concisely by saying that the syntax

xxx.yyy

has more than one possible meaning in VB. There are a few cases in VB where different components of the language share similar syntax, and it is important to be able to tell the components apart. In these cases meaning is determined by context.

We have seen *xxx.yyy* used as

- *filename.extension*. Example: Form1.Frm. Context: the Project Explorer window.
- *control.property*. Example: the statement lblCPU.Caption = 1450. Context: event procedure cmdComputeInvoice_Click.

Now we have a third meaning:

- *control.method*. Example: the statement frmTestB.Show. Context: event procedure cmdShowOtherForm_Click.

In this book we introduce additional methods as we need them. Until you see several different uses of methods, you can expect it to take you a while to recognize one when you see one. However, you can rely on the following differences between methods and properties to help you distinguish them:

- Properties are like variables; each stores a value. Methods are not like variables; a method *specifies an action* instead of storing a value.
- *Control.property* can appear on either side of an assignment statement, like a variable. *Control.method* cannot appear in an assignment statement.
- *Control.method* always appears on a line by itself. *Control.property* can never appear on a line by itself.

17. Now save the project by selecting Save Project under the File menu. VB presents you with *two* Save File As windows (one for each form file) and a Save Project As window. Use the names TestA and TestB for the form files, and the name Proj04 for the project file. Observe the change in the Project Explorer window.

At this point, you should know (a) how to specify the startup form, (b) that there can only be one active form at a time, and (c) that an event procedure

---

[12] There are other methods that apply to forms (e.g., Hide, Print, and Cls), as well as methods that apply to other types of controls. You can explore them using online help, or wait and learn about them as they arise in the text.

can cause another form to become active. We now turn our attention to making an event procedure on one form manipulate a control on another form.

1. Add one label and two command buttons to frmTestA, and set their properties as shown in Figure 3.21.[13] Set their captions to the text you see in the figure. You may have to resize the command buttons.

2. Add one label and two command buttons to frmTestB, using the same names and property settings as in step 1. The two forms should have the same visual appearance except for the form captions, and the captions of the Switch To command buttons (one is A and the other is B).

3. On frmTestA create the event procedure cmdChangeLocalLabel_Click so that it displays the value "A's command button did this" in the lblTest control of frmTestA. Similarly, on frmTestB create the event procedure cmdChangeLocalLabel_Click so that it displays the value "B's command button did this" in the lblTest control on frmTestB. These are straightforward event procedures (shown in Figure 3.17). After creating them, run the program again to verify that they work properly.

4. On frmTestA, create the event procedure cmdChangeOtherLabel_Click as follows.

Private Sub cmdChangeOtherLabel_Click()
    frmTestB!lblTest.Caption = "A's command button did this!"
End Sub

The left-hand side of this assignment statement shows how to refer to a property of a control on one form, from a statement in an event procedure on another form. The syntax for this is

formname!control.property

This is called *qualifying the control name* with the name of the form on which the control resides.

FIGURE 3.21

Controls for frmTestA

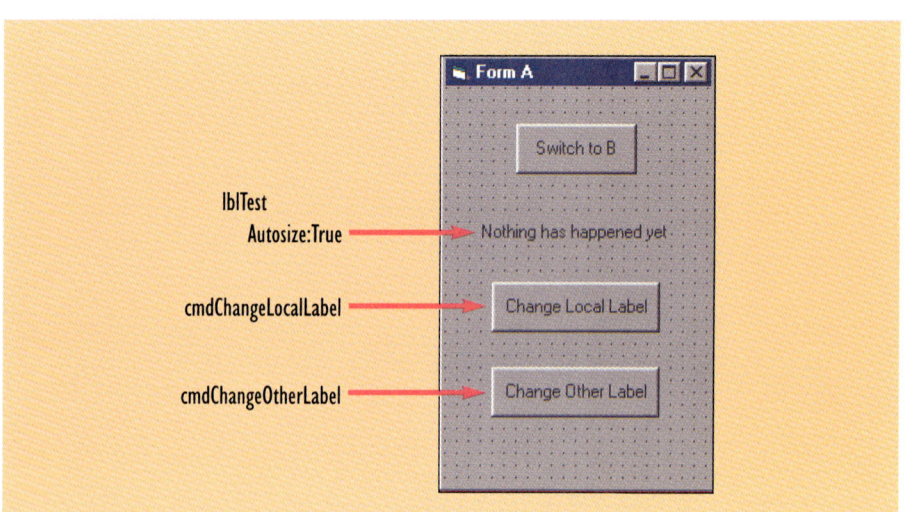

[13] Recall that we are following the control-naming conventions strictly, so you can tell the type of the control from the first three letters of its name. So far, our prefixes and control types are "cmd" for command button, "frm" for form, "lbl" for label, and "tmr" for timer.

Whenever you use a *control.property* in a statement without qualifying it (with a Form name), VB assumes the specified control resides on the same form that the statement belongs to. Since our previous projects each had only one form, we never had to qualify control names.

5. On frmTestB, create the event procedure cmdChangeOtherLabel_Click that will display "B's command button did this!" in the Label control on frmTestA.
6. Run the program, and verify that it works as you expect.
7. End execution, then save the project.
8. Change the WindowState properties of the forms (say, make one minimized and the other maximized), and run the program again to see the effect.
9. End execution.
10. Finally, create a third form, and observe the new entry that appears in the Project Explorer window. Now suppose you change your mind and you no longer want this form. How can you eliminate it from the project? Highlight the entry for this form in the Project Explorer window, then select Remove Form under the Project menu. Observe the change in the Project Explorer window.

EXERCISE 3.18 Make the two forms in Project 4 appear side by side when the program runs. What happens at run time when you alternately click on frmTestA and frmTestB without clicking on the Switch to A and Switch to B buttons?

3.6 Variable Scope

Can a variable that is declared inside one event procedure be accessed by statements inside a different event procedure? What if one of these event procedures belongs to one form, and the other belongs to a different form? These are important questions, especially when we contemplate trying to construct and maintain large projects. The answers are determined by VB's rules for *a variable's scope,* **the domain within which a variable can be accessed**. There are three levels of variable scope. In increasing size of domain these are called local scope, module-level scope, and global scope.

Local Variables

Any variable that is declared inside an event procedure has *local scope*. It is described as being "local to" the event procedure in which it is declared, and it can be accessed only by statements within that event procedure. All the variables we have used so far have been local.

Example 3.4

Local Variables

In this example we explore the scope of two variables, each defined in a different event procedure and therefore local to that procedure (local scope).

Consider the VB project consisting of one form with a label (lblName) and two command buttons (cmdGetMyName and cmdShowMyName) as shown in Figure 3.22.

The Click event procedures for the two command buttons are shown in Figure 3.23. Both have a variable named *MyName*. If you run the application, click

FIGURE 3.22

Form and controls for Example 3.4

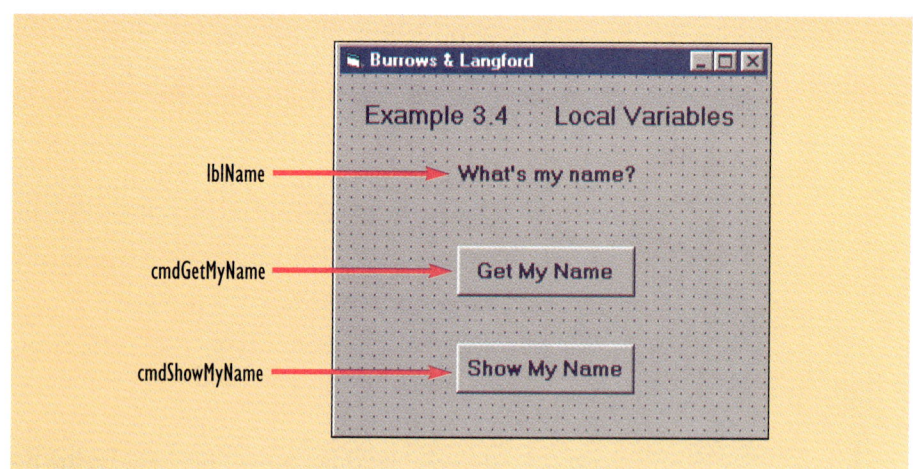

FIGURE 3.23

Code for Example 3.4

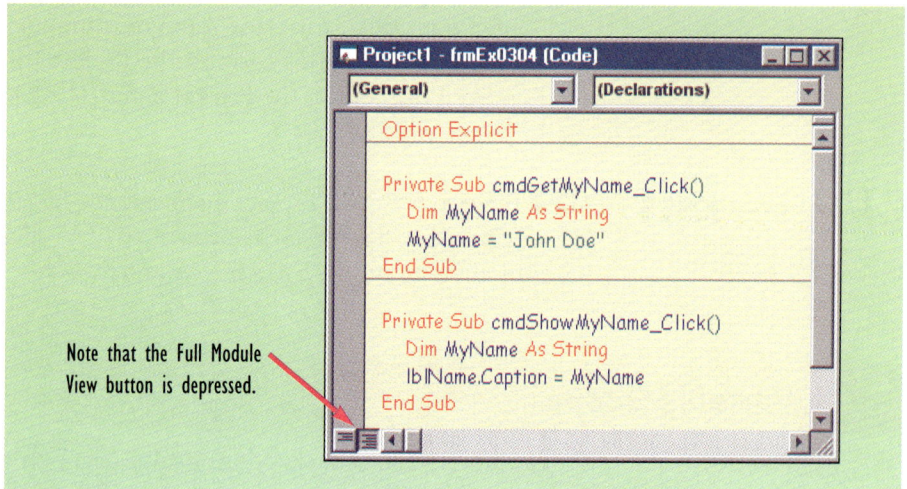

on cmdGetMyName (which causes "John Doe" to be stored in MyName), and then click on cmdShowMyName, will "John Doe" appear in the label caption? The answer is no. The variable MyName in event procedure cmdGetMyName_Click has no relationship to the variable MyName in event procedure cmdShowMyName_Click. Although they have the same name, they are actually two different variables, representing two different locations in main memory. We explain this in the next section.

Variable Tables for Local Variables

The reason the variables MyName in cmdGetMyName_Click and MyName in cmdShowMyName_Click represent different memory locations is that VB creates a different variable table for each event procedure. The variable tables for different event procedures are completely separate. The variables in an event procedure's variable table can be accessed only by statements in the same event procedure.

The variable tables for the two event procedures in Figure 3.23 are illustrated in Figure 3.24. These tables are shown alongside the event procedures to which they belong.

FIGURE 3.24

Local variables

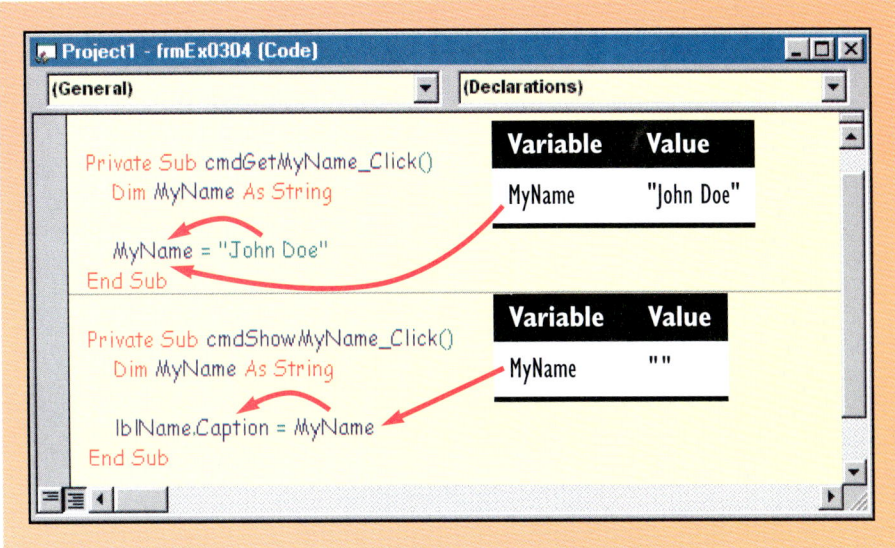

Although the separate variable tables may seem a little annoying at first, they make life much easier, especially when programmers work as a team to build a large program. I am free to choose whatever variable names I want in *my* event procedures, without having to worry whether they might conflict with variable names in *your* event procedures.

Module-Level Variables

Just as two employees in an office sometimes agree to share files, we sometimes want two event procedures on a form to share a variable. In this case we create a variable of *module-level scope* by using an ordinary Dim statement **placed in the form's general declarations section** instead of inside an event procedure. The scope of a module-level variable is the set of all event procedures associated with controls on the form. That is, a module-level variable can be accessed by any statement in any event procedure belonging to the form.

At last you can see the reason for the name "general declarations section." Variables declared there do not belong to any specific event procedure; rather, they belong, collectively, to all the event procedures on that form.

Example 3.5 Module-Level Variables

Let us modify the previous example by deleting the two local variable declarations and making MyName a module-level variable. The objective is to see how the program behavior differs with module-level scope compared with local scope. The modified code is shown in Figure 3.25.

If you run this program, click on cmdGetMyName, and then click on cmdShowMyName, "John Doe" will appear in the label caption because both event procedures share the variable. The first event procedure stores a value in the string variable MyName, and the second event procedure retrieves that value from MyName.

FIGURE 3.25

Code for Example 3.5

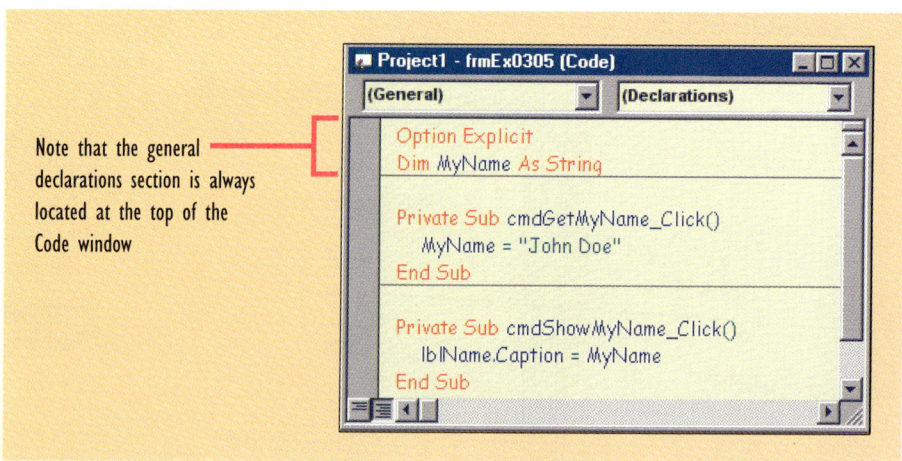

Variable Tables for Module-Level Variables

The variable tables that VB creates when Example 3.5 is executed are depicted in Figure 3.26. The general declarations section has its own variable table. The variable in this table is shared by both of the event procedures. Both local variable tables are empty, because neither event procedure has any Dim statements.

Note that if you run Example 3.5 again, but click on cmdShowMyName first, and *then* click on cmdGetMyName, the result will be different! Since string variables are initially set to the zero-length string when they are declared, clicking first on cmdShowMyName results in the zero-length string being displayed.

Example 3.6

Hidden Module-Level Variables

Often a given event procedure accesses both local variables and module-level variables. This example demonstrates what happens if the programmer uses the same variable name (same spelling) for both a local variable and a module-level

FIGURE 3.26

Module-level variable

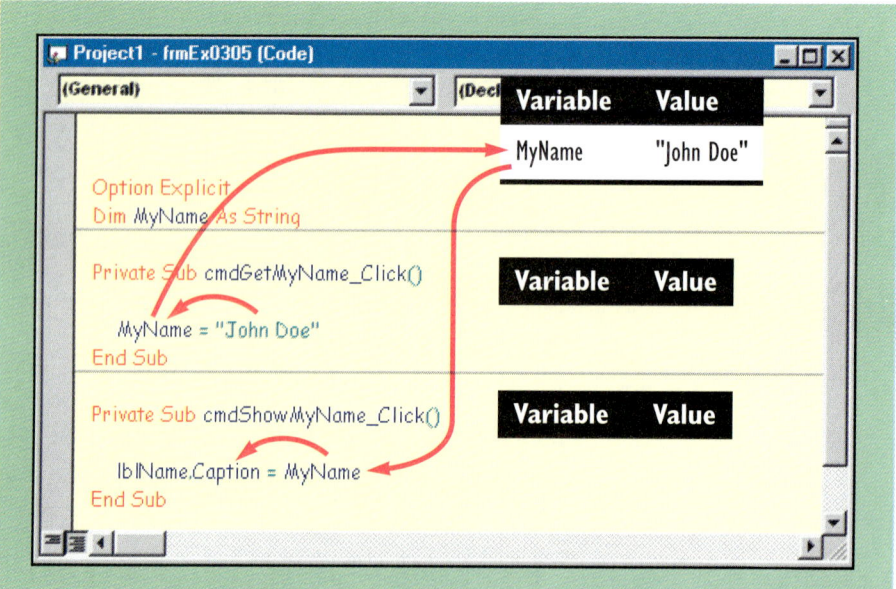

variable. In Example 3.6 the form has two labels (lblMyName and lblYourName) and two command buttons. This form and its controls are shown in Figure 3.27. The code is shown in Figure 3.28.

Note carefully that cmdGetNames_Click has no local variables, but cmdShowNames_Click has a local variable with the *same* name as one of the module-level variables. If you run this program, click on cmdGetNames, and then click on cmdShowNames, will "John Doe" appear in lblMyName and "Mary Smith" in lblYourName? The answer is no. The reason has to do with how VB handles the situation where the same variable name occurs in both a local variable table and a module-level variable table. We focus on this issue in the next section.

Variable Tables for Projects with Local and Module-Level Variables

In Example 3.6, the local variable YourName in cmdShowNames_Click is a *different* variable than the module-level variable YourName. Because they are in different variable tables, they have no relationship to each other even though they have the same name. The question, then, is which variable will the assignment statement lblYourName.Caption = YourName use: the local variable or the module-level variable?

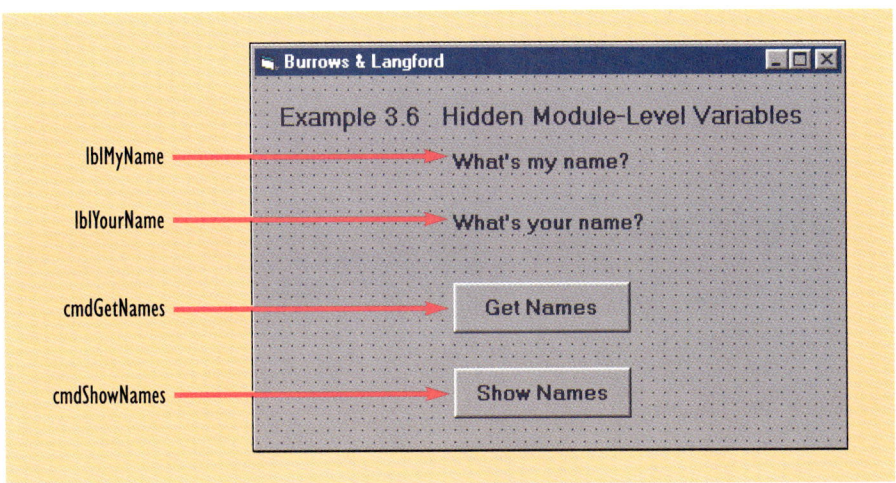

FIGURE 3.27

Form and controls for Example 3.6

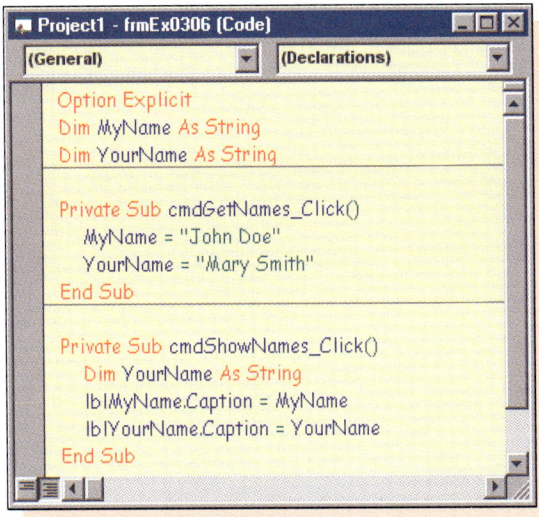

FIGURE 3.28

Code for Example 3.6

VB's rule for this is that an event procedure will always use the local variable if it exists. This is sometimes stated as "A local variable hides a module-level variable with the same name." Thus, event procedure cmdShowNames_Click is "unaware" that the module-level variable YourName even exists.

Figure 3.29 shows the variable tables that VB creates when Example 3.6 is executed. This figure assumes that the user clicks on cmdGetNames first, and then on cmdShowNames.

Global Variables

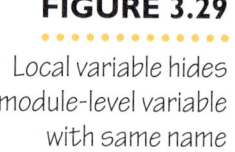

Suppose we have two event procedures that belong to different forms. Can they share a local variable? It should be clear that they cannot. Since they are on different forms, they cannot share module-level variables either. Each form has its own general declarations section, and variables declared in a form's general declarations section belong *only* to that form.

Of course there is a way for event procedures on different forms to share a variable. Variables that can be shared across forms have *global scope*. To create a variable with global scope, declare it using a Public statement in the general declarations section of a Code module.

The Public Statement

The Public statement is identical to the Dim statement except it uses the keyword Public instead of Dim. The **Public statement is used to create a global variable.**

Note that you must create a Code module to hold the declaration statements for global variables.

FIGURE 3.29

Local variable hides module-level variable with same name

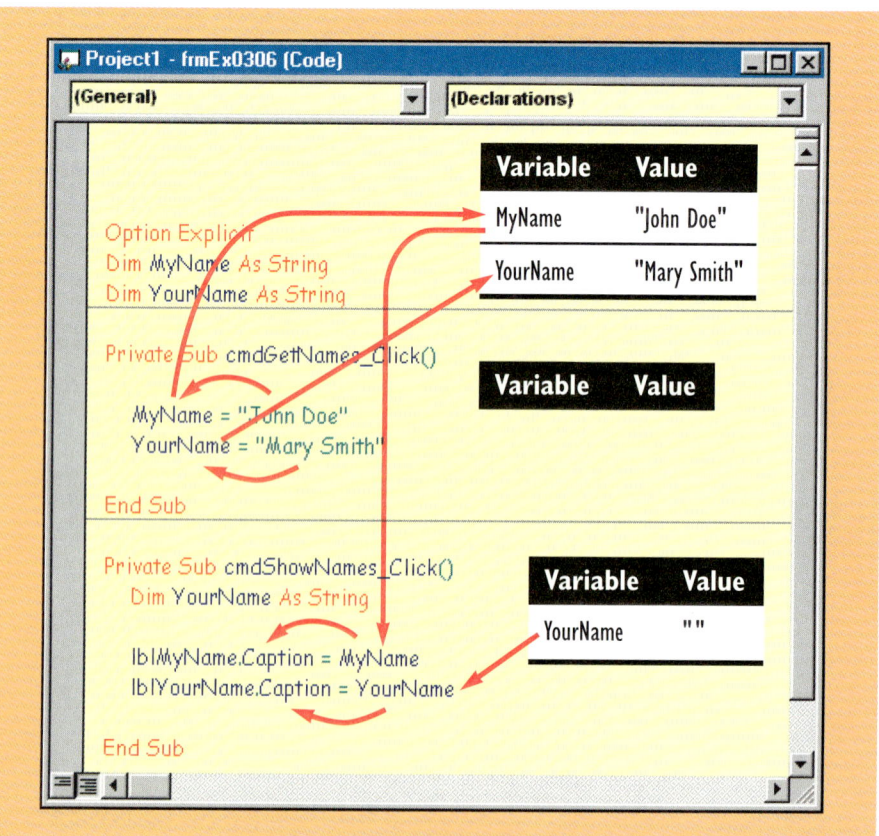

Code Modules

A *Code module*, also called simply a *module*, is identical to a form except that it has no user interface window, and therefore, no controls and no event procedures. What does that leave? A general declarations section.[14] You can think of a Code module as a repository for data that need to be shared by forms; that is, a repository for global variables.

To create a Code module select Add Module under the Project menu (alternatively, click the down arrow next to the Add Form button on the Toolbar, then in the list that drops down, click the Module button). VB makes an entry for the module in the Project Explorer window. When you save the project, VB creates a file for the module; VB asks you to specify a name for this file, to which it appends the extension .Bas. You can remove an unwanted Code module from the project the same way you remove a form from the project. And, like forms, each Code module has its own Code window. Each Code module also has a Name property, which appears at the top of its Code window.

Example 3.7 Global Variables

In this example, which uses two forms, we create a global variable and see how this variable can be accessed in two event procedures. Figure 3.30 shows the two forms and the Project Explorer window. The code is shown in Figure 3.31.

Note that the Code module has its own Option Explicit statement, just as each form has its own Option Explicit statement. There is one global variable, named OurName. Because OurName is global, it can be used by any event procedure in the project, regardless of which form the event procedure is on.

If you run this program, click on cmdGetOurName on form A, and then click on cmdShowOurName on form B, "John Doe" will appear in the label caption on form B because the event procedures share the global variable. The first event procedure stores a value in OurName, and the second event procedure retrieves that value from OurName.

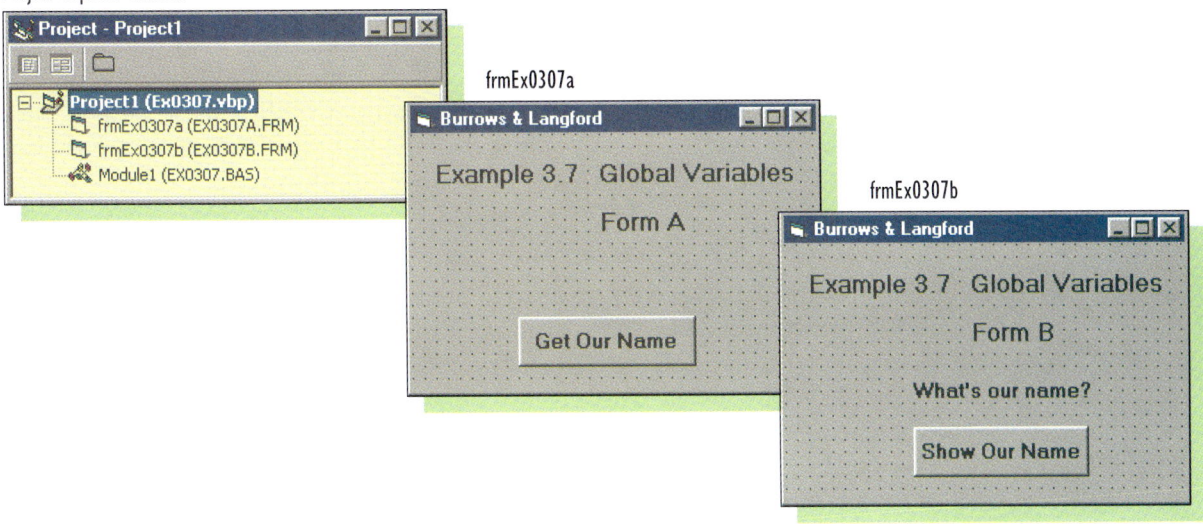

FIGURE 3.30   Forms and Project Explorer window for Example 3.7

---

14 In Chapter 6 we will see that Code modules and forms can (and usually do) also have general sub procedures.

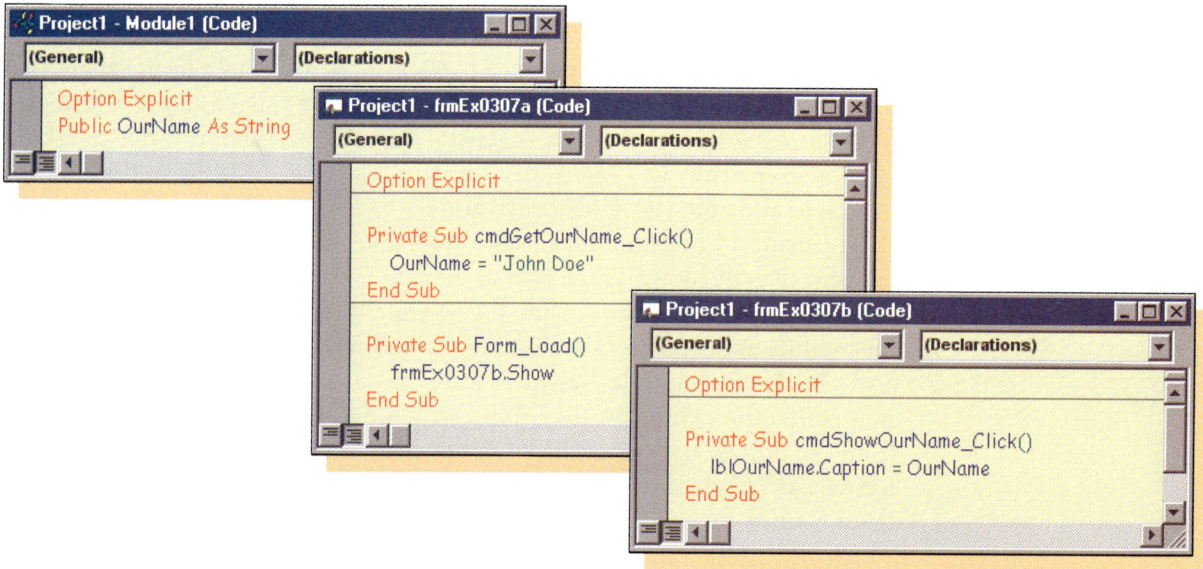

FIGURE 3.31 Code for Example 3.7

Variable Tables for Global Variables

The variable tables that VB creates when Example 3.7 is executed are depicted in Figure 3.32. The general declarations section in the Code module has its own variable table, which is created when execution begins. The variable in this table is shared by all event procedures in the project.

In this example the module-level and local variable tables are empty, because there are no Dim statements in the general declarations sections of either form, and there are no Dim statements in any of the event procedures.

Hiding Global Variables

As with module-level variables, a local variable in an event procedure "hides" a global variable with the same name; that is, the event procedure will always use the local variable if it exists. Similarly, a module-level variable declared in a form's general declarations section will "hide" (from all the event procedures on the form) a global variable with the same name. This behavior can be described thus: "An event procedure always uses the closest variable with the specified name." Local is closer than module-level, which in turn is closer than global.

Variable Scope versus Qualification of Control Properties

In Project 4 we observed that an event procedure on one form can access a property of a control that belongs to another form simply by qualifying *control.property* with the name of the form: *form!control.property*. In this sense, all control properties are global. There is no analogous way to qualify a variable name. Rather, a variable's scope is determined by where it is declared: inside an event procedure, in a form's general declarations section, or in a Code module's general declarations section (using a Public statement).

There is one exception to the rule that variable names cannot be qualified. If you use the Public statement to declare a variable in a form's general declarations section, then the variable will be global in the sense that event procedures on other forms will be able to access it by qualifying its name with the

FIGURE 3.32

A global variable

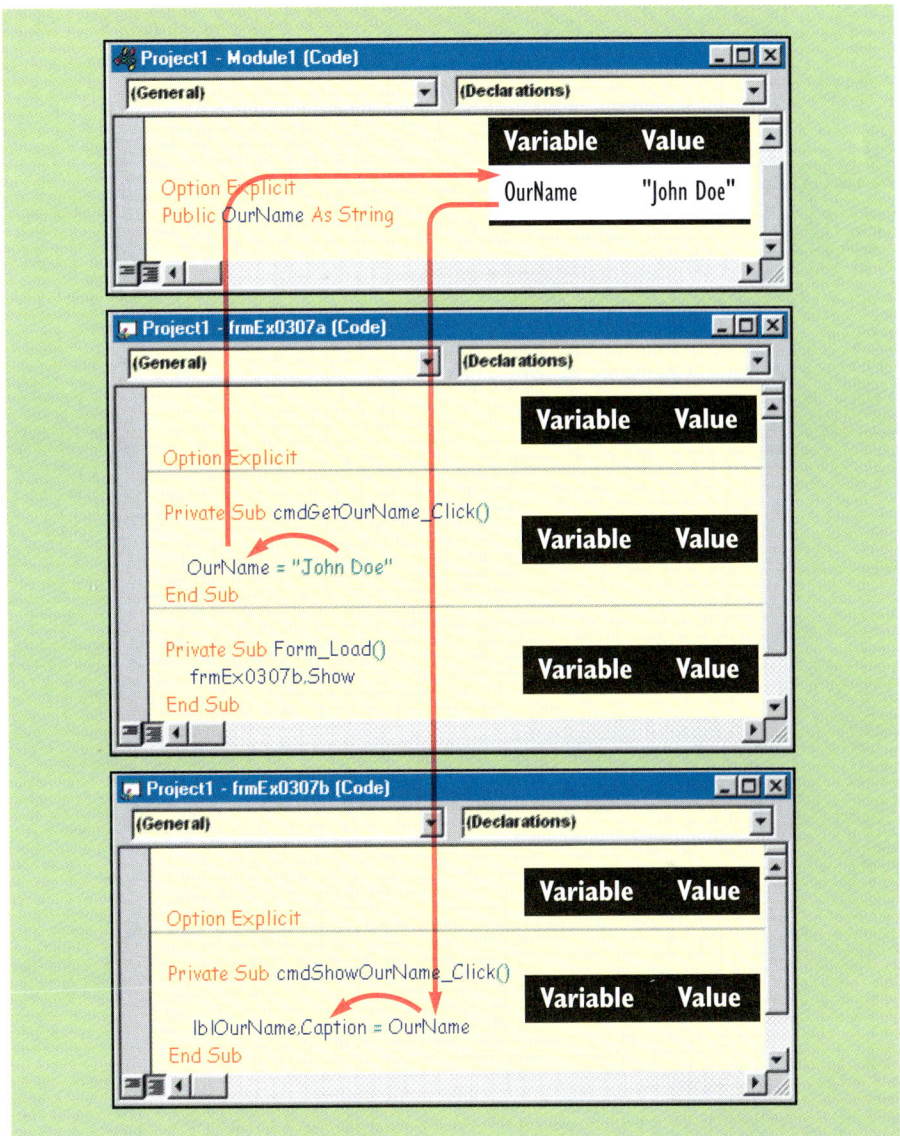

name of the form: *form.variable*. Note that the form name is separated from the variable name by a period, not by an exclamation point. Also note that the Public statement cannot be used inside an event procedure.

Local, Module-Level, and Global Scope

It may take you a while to digest these scoping rules. Rest assured, they do make development of large applications much easier. It may help you to experiment with Project 4, adding a few local, module-level, and global variables as in the preceding examples.[15]

Figure 3.33 consolidates the relationships between event procedures, forms, Code modules, and variable scope. In this figure, the project boundary is indicated by the red border; form and Code module boundaries are indicated by the green borders; and event procedure boundaries are indicated by the orange borders. A project consists of one or more forms and Code modules.

---

[15] It may also help you to associate the word "regional" with module-level scope. Then you can think of the three levels of scope as being local, regional, and global.

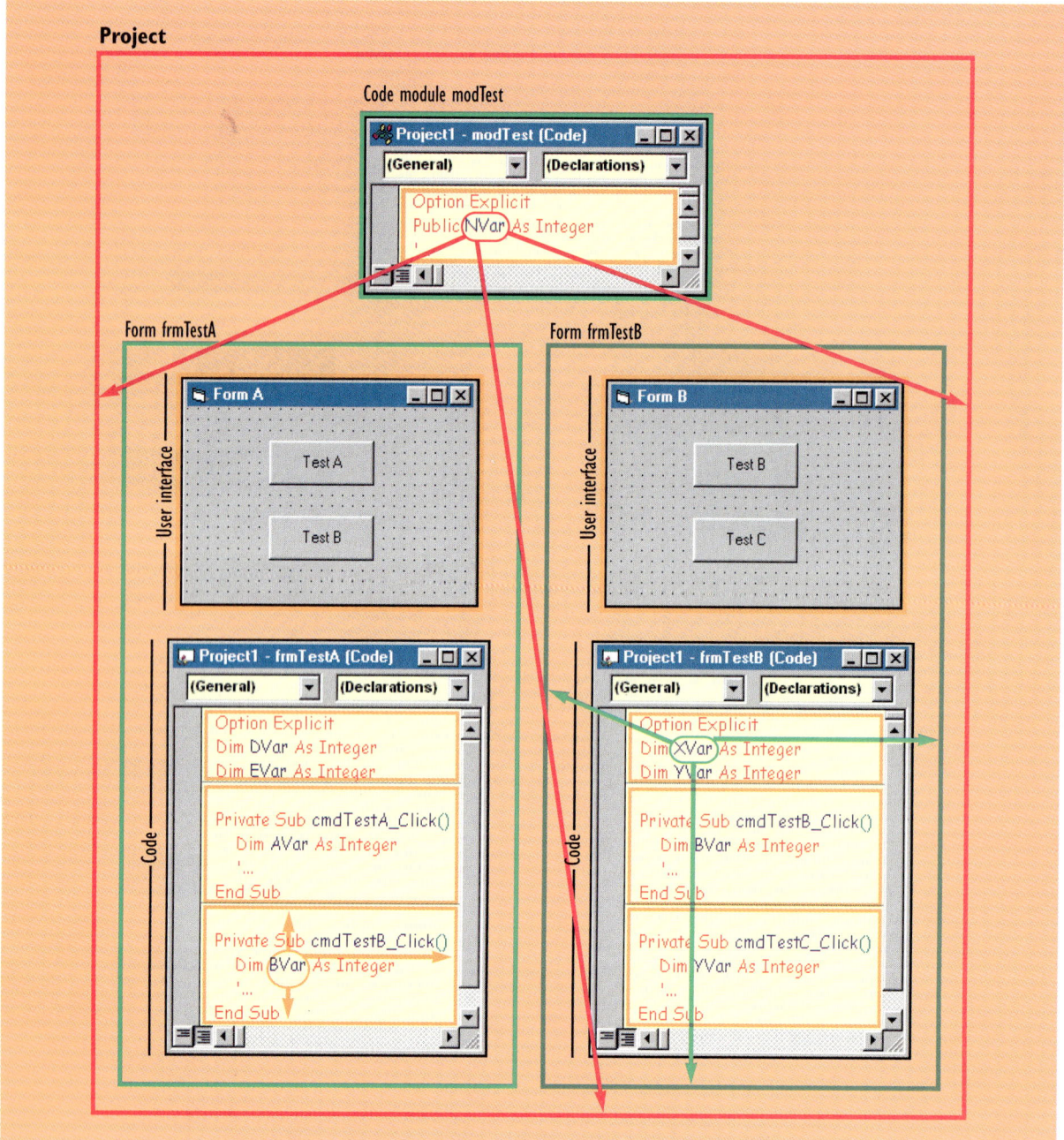

FIGURE 3.33 The three levels of variable scope

Each form and Code module is stored on disk in its own file. A form comprises a user interface window, a general declarations section, and a number of event procedures. A Code module comprises a general declarations section.

Global variables are declared in the general declarations section of a Code module using the Public statement. A global variable can be accessed by the code in any event procedure anywhere in the project. In Figure 3.33 this is depicted by the red arrows emanating from variable NVar, which extend to the project boundary in all directions.

A module-level variable is declared in the general declarations section of a form using a Dim statement. It can be accessed by any event procedure on the same form as the general declarations section containing the Dim statement.

FIGURE 3.34

Structure of VB projects

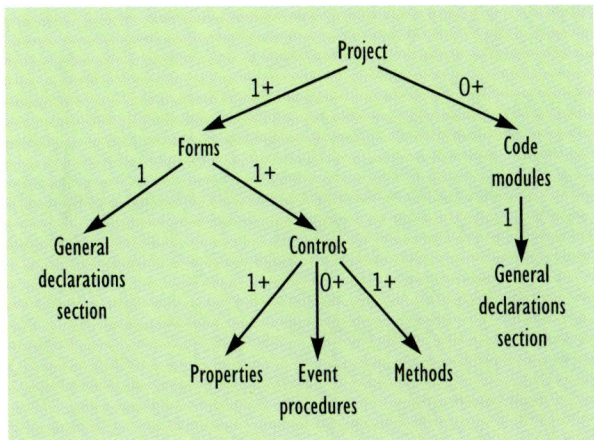

The scope of a module-level variable is depicted by the green arrows emanating from variable XVar, which extend only to the boundary of frmTestB.

A local variable is declared in an event procedure using a Dim statement. It can be accessed only in the event procedure in which it is declared. The scope of a local variable is depicted by the orange arrows emanating from variable BVar in cmdTestB_Click, which extend only to the boundary of cmdTestB_Click.

There is no conflict between control cmdTestB on frmTestA and cmdTestB on frmTestB. Similarly, there is no conflict between the two variables BVar in the two corresponding event procedures. The module-level variable YVar in frmTestB will not be accessible in event procedure cmdTestC, because of the local variable with the same name.

Finally, properties of controls are global. They can be accessed in any event procedure in any form by qualifying the control name with the name of the form, (i.e., *form!control.property*).

Project Structure Revisited

Now that you've been introduced to projects with multiple forms and Code modules, this is a good time to look again at VB project structure. Figure 3.34 includes the components we've discussed in this chapter. Observe that each form has one general declarations section and one or more controls. Each Code module has only a general declarations section. A Code module is necessary only if the project requires global variables, which can only be the case if the project has more than one form.

EXERCISE 3.19

A hypothetical form has two command buttons named cmdA and cmdB, and three labels named lblC, lblD, and lblE. The code for the general declarations section and all event procedures on the form is as follows.

```
Option Explicit
Dim W As Integer
Dim X As Integer

Private Sub cmdA_Click()
    Dim Y As Integer
    Dim Z As Integer
    W = 3
```

continues

```
        X = 6
        Y = W + X
        Z = 4
        lblC.Caption = X
        lblD.Caption = Y
        lblE.Caption = Z
End Sub

Private Sub cmdB_Click()
    Dim X As Integer
    Dim Y As Integer
    Y = W + X
    lblC.Caption = W
    lblD.Caption = X
    lblE.Caption = Y
End Sub
```

When the program runs, the user first clicks on cmdA, and then clicks on cmdB. What values do lblC, lblD, and lblE display immediately after the user clicks on cmdA? What values do they display immediately after the user clicks on cmdB?

EXERCISE 3.20 Modify Project 4 as follows. Place a command button named cmdGetMyName on frmTestA and a command button named cmdShowMyName on frmTestB. Then declare a variable named MyName, write a Click event procedure for cmdGetMyName that stores your name in MyName, and write a Click event procedure for cmdShowMyName that retrieves the value from MyName and displays it on frmTestB in lblTest's caption.

3.7 Variable Lifetime

When a project stops executing, the values of all variables are lost. But what happens to an event procedure's local variables when the event procedure is finished? Remember that after the event procedure finishes (that is, after the End Sub statement is executed), the project may still be executing. To answer this question, we must investigate *variable lifetime*, **which is the period of time a variable exists.**

Example 3.8 ### Lifetime of Local Variables

This example demonstrates what happens to the value of a local variable when an event procedure finishes. Consider the form with a label and a command button in Figure 3.35.

The Click event procedure for the command button is shown in Figure 3.36. At run time, what does the label display after you click on cmdLocalLifetimeTest once? What does the label display after you click on cmdLocalLifetimeTest a second time?

Let us consider the first time this event procedure is executed. VB creates a local variable table for the event procedure, and the Dim statement creates the variable named X in this table and initializes X to 0. The next statement

FIGURE 3.35

Form and controls for Example 3.8

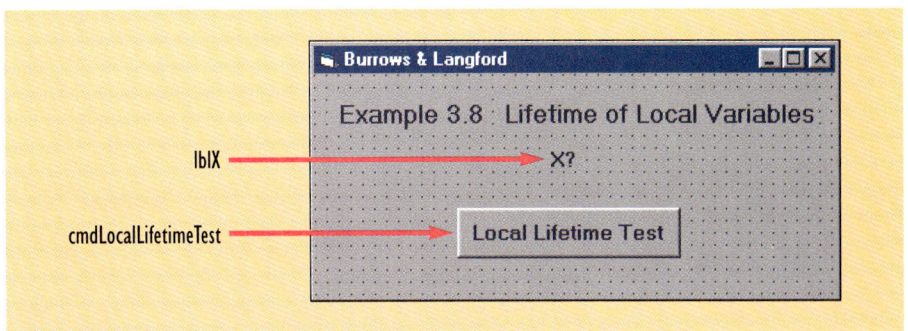

FIGURE 3.36

Code for Example 3.8

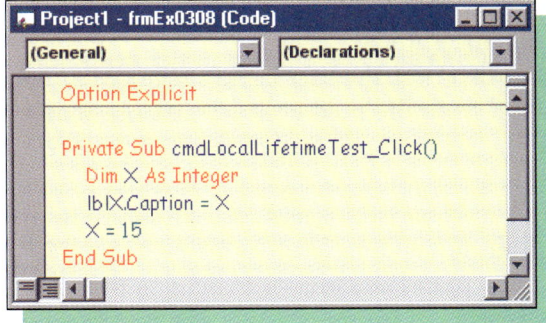

retrieves the value stored in X, which is 0, and stores it in the Caption property of the Label control. Hence the label will display the value 0. The next statement stores the value 15 in the variable X and then the event procedure ends (but the project remains running, waiting for the user to act again).

What happens when this event procedure is executed the second time? You might expect that the assignment statement lblX.Caption = X causes the value 15 to be displayed in the label, because the value 15 was stored in X at the end of the first execution of the event procedure. But what actually happens is that the label displays the value 0 again. Why?

Local Variable Tables
◆ ◆ ◆

Every time an event procedure is executed, VB creates a new, empty variable table for it. As Dim statements are executed, variables are added to the table and initialized. Subsequent statements in the event procedure may change the values stored in the variables. Then, when the end of the event procedure is reached, VB destroys the event procedure's local variable table.

This behavior is sometimes described thus: "Local variables live only while their event procedure is executing." In effect, a local variable cannot "remember" anything prior to the start of its event procedure's execution. Each time the event occurs, the event procedure's local variables are created from scratch and initialized, with no memory of prior values.

Module-Level and Global Variable Tables
◆ ◆ ◆

In contrast to local variables, module-level and global variables "live" for the entire duration of the project's execution. Here is how VB treats module-level and global variables. When program execution begins, before the startup form is even displayed to the user, VB examines the general declarations section of each form and Code module in order to create their variable tables. When it examines a general declarations section, VB creates a variable table for it, then creates and initializes variables in this table according to the Dim (or Public) statements. These variable tables are destroyed only when program execution ends.

Example 3.9

Lifetime of Module-Level Variables

In this example, we modify the code from Example 3.8 to demonstrate how the lifetime of module-level variables differs from that of local variables. The code for this example is shown in Figure 3.37. In this code X is module-level instead of local.

When program execution begins, VB creates the variable table for the form's general declarations section, then creates the variable X in this table and initializes it to 0.

The first time the user clicks on cmdModuleLevelLifetime, the value 0 is retrieved from the module-level variable X, and 0 is displayed in the label. Next, the value 15 is stored in the module-level variable X. The next time the user clicks on cmdModuleLevelLifetime, the value 15 is retrieved from the module-level variable X, and 15 is displayed in the label. Next, the value 15 is stored in the module-level variable X (again). And the same thing happens each subsequent time the user clicks cmdModuleLevelLifetime. The module-level variable is destroyed when program execution ends.

Static Variables

Sometimes as programmer you want a variable to have the scope of a local variable so that it can be accessed only by its own event procedure, yet to have the lifetime of a module-level variable, so that it can retain its value from one execution of the event procedure to the next. To achieve this behavior you declare a *static variable,* **inside the event procedure, using the keyword Static instead of the keyword Dim.**

VB gives special treatment to static variables. It stores them separately from the local variable table so that they are not destroyed when the end of the event procedure is reached. In addition, VB allows only the event procedure in which the static variable is declared to access it.

Example 3.10

Static Variables

In this example we see how to make the lifetime of a local variable extend beyond the termination of the procedure in which the variable is declared. The code for this example is shown in Figure 3.38. The variable X is declared as static. Describing the behavior of this event procedure is left as an exercise.

FIGURE 3.37

Code for Example 3.9

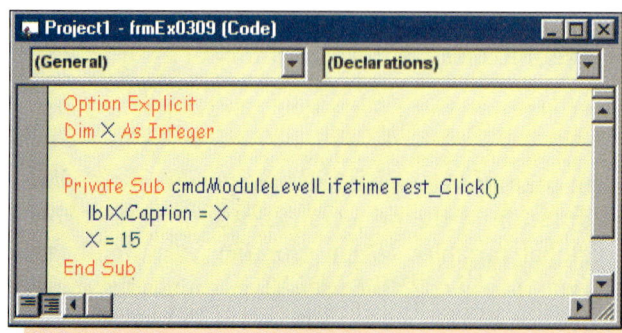

FIGURE 3.38

Code for Example 3.10

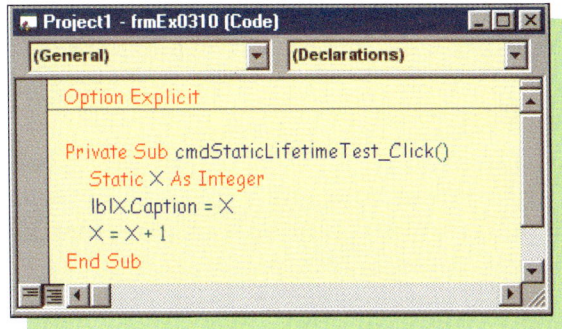

EXERCISE 3.21 In Example 3.10, what will be displayed in the caption of lblX the first time cmdStaticLifetimeTest is clicked? The second time? The third? Explain.

EXERCISE 3.22 Create a project that "counts," using one Timer control and one Label control. When program execution begins, the label should display the number 0, and every second thereafter it should increase the number displayed by 1.

EXERCISE 3.23 Create a variation of the "counting" project in Exercise 3.22 that still counts by 1s, but make the time between increments random (between 0.5 and 3.0 seconds) instead of fixed (always 1.0 seconds).

3.8 Constant Scope

Like variables, symbolic constants also have three levels of scope. A symbolic constant is *local* if it is defined inside an event procedure; it can be used only by statements inside that event procedure. It is *module-level* if it is defined in a form's general declarations section; it can be used by statements inside any event procedure belonging to that form. And it is *global* if it is defined inside a Code module's general declarations section using the **Public Const statement, which has the same syntax as the Const statement, except that the keyword is Public Const instead of just Const.** For example, if the following statement is placed in a Code module's general declarations section, then MINUTESPERDAY can be used by any statement in any event procedure in the entire project.

Public Const MINUTESPERDAY = 1440

EXERCISE 3.24 Generally, it is a good idea to *minimize* the scope of variables in a project. Why? On the other hand, it is a good idea to *maximize* the scope of symbolic constants in a project. Why?

3.9 Project 5: A Simple Payroll Application

The following concepts are introduced in this project: the BorderStyle property, the Line control, using copy-and-paste to copy controls, using Save Form As... to copy forms, and using Add File... to add forms to a project.

To create this project you'll combine what you've learned about constants, variables, data types, project structure, and scope.

The project is a simple payroll application with one form for each employee and a single summary form for all employees. This is not a good design for an actual payroll application, because if the company had 100 employees, the project would have 100 form files. Further, the payroll data are embedded in the program code as constants; in practice, these data would be retrieved from a database (the subject of Chapter 8). We will refine the design features developed here in more sophisticated applications in later chapters.

Description of the Application

This application uses the hours worked and the hourly pay rate for two employees to compute each employee's gross pay, employment tax, and net pay. In addition, the application computes summary information that aggregates the three calculated values for both employees.

The form for an employee appears in Figure 3.39. When the user clicks the Compute button, the program fills in the top three boxes with the employee's name, hours worked, and hourly rate (which are known at design time), then computes and displays the following values in the lower three boxes:

◆ Gross Pay is the product of hours worked and hourly rate.

◆ Tax Due is the product of gross pay and the tax rate.

◆ Net Pay is gross pay minus tax due.

When the user clicks the Show Emp2 button, the program displays the form for the second employee, which has the same components as this form. When the user clicks the Show Summary button, the program displays the summary form shown in Figure 3.40.

When the user clicks the Show Emp1 or Show Emp2 button, the program displays the corresponding employee form. When the user clicks the Update button, the program totals the gross pay for the two employees using the gross

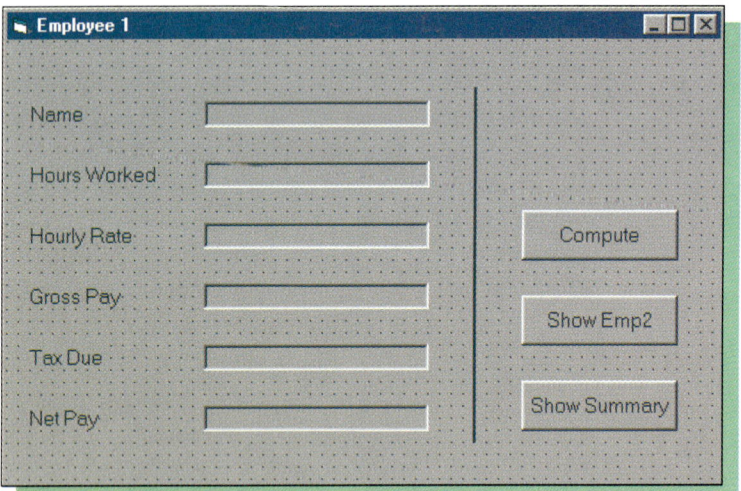

FIGURE 3.39

Employee form user interface

FIGURE 3.40

Summary form user interface

pay values previously computed on the employee forms, and displays this result in the top box. It similarly computes and displays the total tax due and total net pay for the two employees.

The data known at design time are the tax rate, which is 21 percent, and the employee data shown in Table 3.4. Each value should occur only once in the program; that is, there should be no redundant data.

Design of the Application

To successfully construct any project, you have to make some decisions regarding controls, properties, constants, variables, and scope. You should make these decisions before beginning to construct the project.

We have already made some design decisions by sketching out the forms and controls in Figures 3.39 and 3.40. We now need to give these controls names and note property values that are not obvious. Figure 3.41 shows property settings for the controls on the employee and summary forms.

What constants are needed in the project? The data provided in Table 3.4 do not change, so you can create symbolic constants for them. What should

TABLE 3.4 Employee data for Project 5

	Name	Hours Worked	Hourly Rate
Employee 1	Bram Stoker	40.0	7.50
Employee 2	Mary Shelley	46.5	8.25

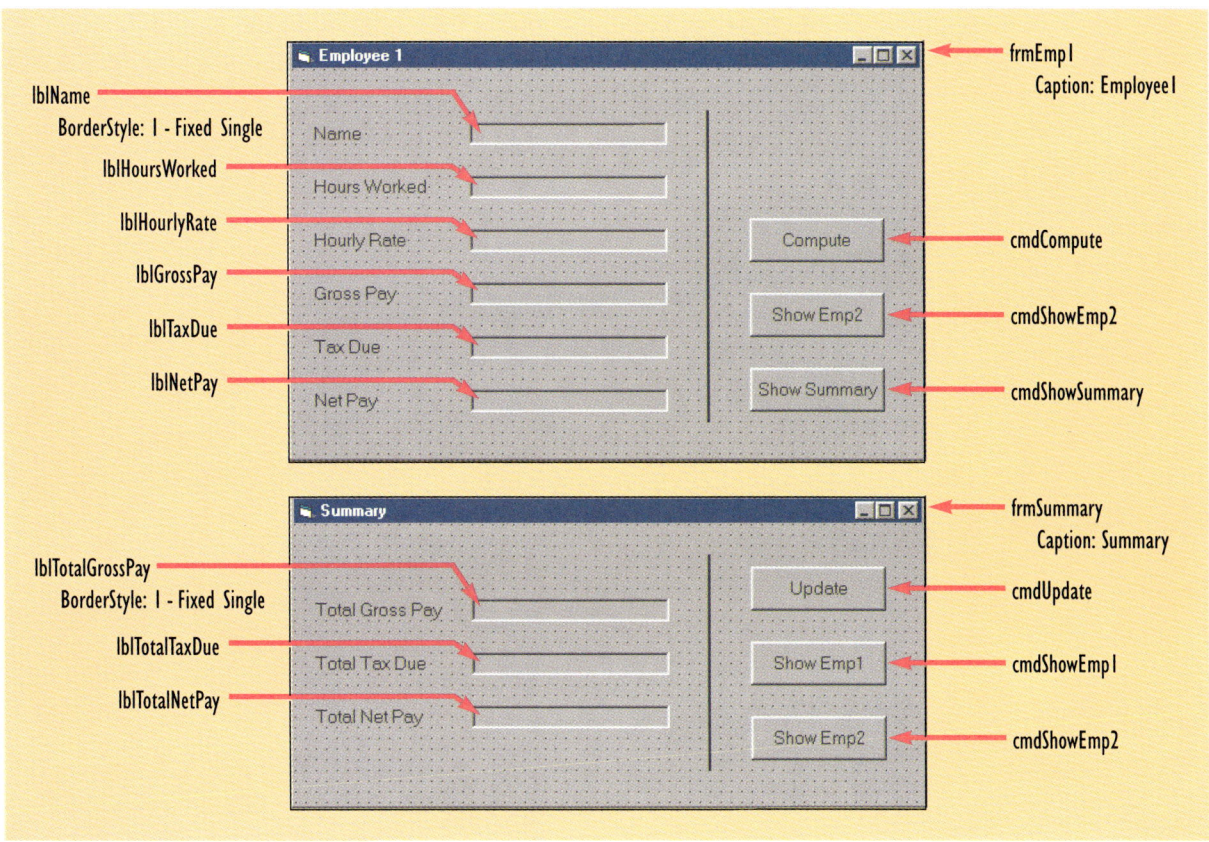

FIGURE 3.41 Employee and summary form controls

their scope be? The data for Employee 1 are used only in the Compute event procedure on the form for Employee 1, so they should be local to that procedure. Similarly, the data for Employee 2 should be local to the Compute event procedure on the form for Employee 2. The tax rate is the same for all employees, so it should be a global constant.

What variables are needed in the project, and what should their scope be? In the Compute event procedure on the Employee 1 form, gross pay, tax due, and net pay must be computed. Since these quantities are also needed on the summary form (which displays totals), these variables must be global. The same is true for the corresponding variables in the Compute event procedure on the Employee 2 form.

Since the project requires a global constant and several global variables, you will have to create a Code module. A good name for the Code module file is Global.Bas. Figure 3.42 depicts the constants and variables in the project.

Construction of the Application

When you're ready, open a new project. Begin by creating a Code module and declaring the global constant and global variables. It makes sense to do this before working on forms since all of the forms have code that uses these constants and variables.

When you initially opened the new project, VB automatically created a form, to which it gave the default name Form1. Change the form's Name property to "frmEmp1" and its Caption to "Employee 1" (do not include the quotes). On this form you will now create and place the controls as they appear in Figure 3.41.

First create the six labels you see on the far left-hand side of the form. To speed up your work, use copy-and-paste as described in the following steps:

1. Create the first label, then set its AutoSize property to True, its Caption property to "Name", and its font size to 10.

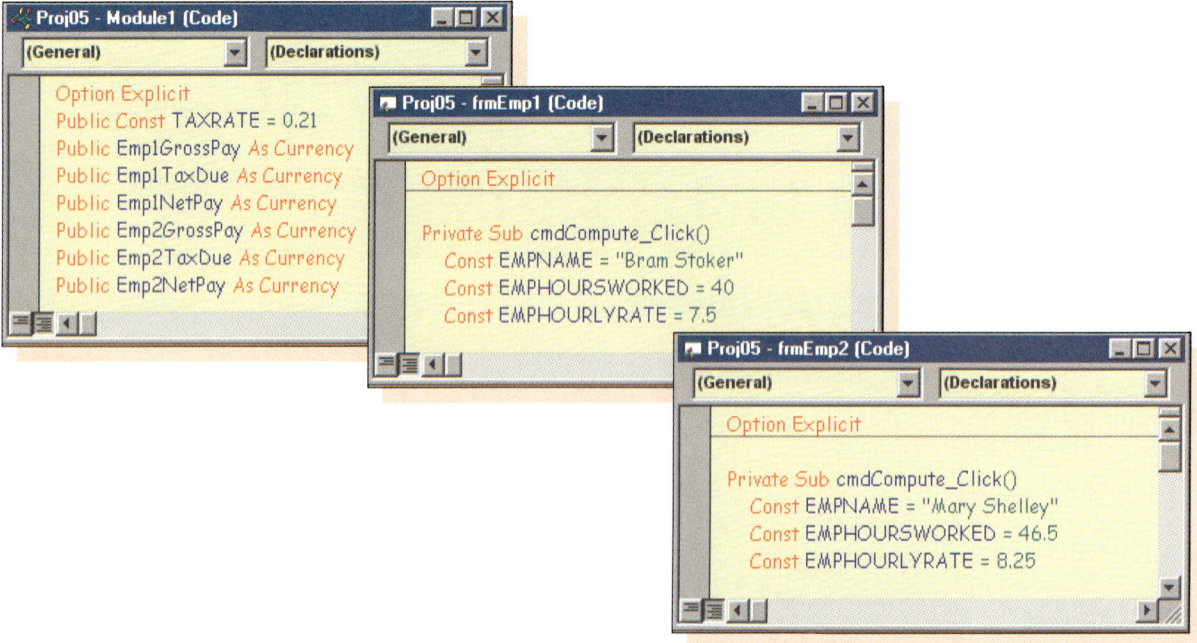

FIGURE 3.42 Constants and variables in Project 5

2. Select the control and copy it using Copy under the Edit menu.
3. Paste using Paste under the Edit menu. VB will respond with the question "Do you want to create a control array?" Click No.[16] VB then places a new Label control on the form whose properties (except for Name) are the same as the original control. This relieves you of having to set the Auto-Size and Font properties of the new control.
4. Drag the new control to where you want it on the form.
5. Continue pasting and repositioning Label controls on the form (you do not have to repeat the copy operation) until you have all six labels on the form.
6. Change the captions of each control as shown in Figure 3.41.

The boxes on the form in Figure 3.41 are Label controls with BorderStyle property set to "1 - Fixed Single". These labels, lblName through lblNetPay, will display the output. Create lblName and set its BorderStyle to "1 - Fixed Single" and its Caption to null (i.e., delete the Caption property's current setting in the Properties window). Then use copy-and-paste to create the remaining five labels. You will need to set the Name property for each one as shown in Figure 3.41.

The vertical line on the form is a *Line control* with BorderWidth property set to 2. A Line control does not respond to events, and is used only to improve the appearance of the GUI. Create the Line control (i.e., click the line tool in the Toolbox, then draw the line on the form), and set its BorderWidth property to 2.

Create the three command buttons, position them, and set their properties as shown in Figure 3.41. Construction of the GUI for this form is complete. We now turn our attention to writing the code for the event procedures.

First create the cmdCompute_Click event procedure, which computes the employee's gross pay, tax due, and net pay, and displays these quantities along with the employee's name, hours worked, and hourly rate. Figure 3.43 shows the code for this procedure. After you've completed this event procedure, run the program and verify that it works properly. If you haven't already done so, save the project.

FIGURE 3.43

Code for cmdCompute_Click for first employee

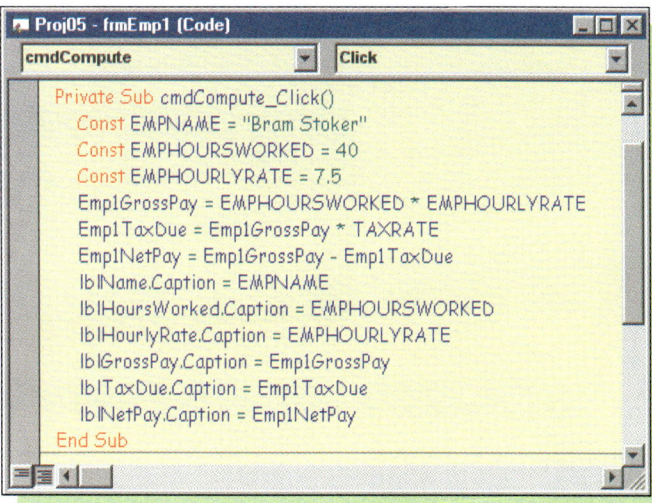

[16] Control arrays will be discussed in Chapter 9. If you inadvertently create a control array, you will see two (or more) controls that have the same Name property but different values in their Index property. The best thing to do at this point is delete them.

Now create the summary form. (You'll create the other Employee form later using a shortcut.) Change the form's name to frmSummary and its caption to "Summary". Create and name the controls for this form as shown in Figure 3.41. Then create the Click event procedures for the command buttons Show Emp1 (on the summary form) and Show Summary (on the employee form) to allow the user to switch back and forth between the two forms. The code for these procedures is in Figure 3.44. Run the program and verify that it works properly.

Now create the Click event procedure for the Update button on the summary form. When the user clicks this button, it should display the same values as the employee form does, since at this point there is only one employee form. (If the user clicks the Update button before clicking the Compute button on the employee form, your summary form will display zeros; this is fine.) The code for this event procedure is shown in Figure 3.45. Run the program and verify that it works properly. Save the project.

We now focus on the second employee form. Since it is nearly identical to the first employee form, you can avoid a considerable amount of work by copying the existing form file. You can do this directly in VB.

1. View the employee form.
2. Under the File menu select Save Form As... (VB substitutes the actual name of your form file for the word "Form" in this command). VB presents a Save File As dialog window; enter a name for the new file and click OK.

There are now two identical employee form files on magnetic disk. Observe the change in the Project Explorer window: VB has retained the new file in the project and removed the original file from the project. You need to add the original file back to the project.

3. Select Add File... from the Project menu.
4. Select the original employee form file in the ensuing dialog window, and click Open.

FIGURE 3.44

Event procedures to switch between employee and summary forms

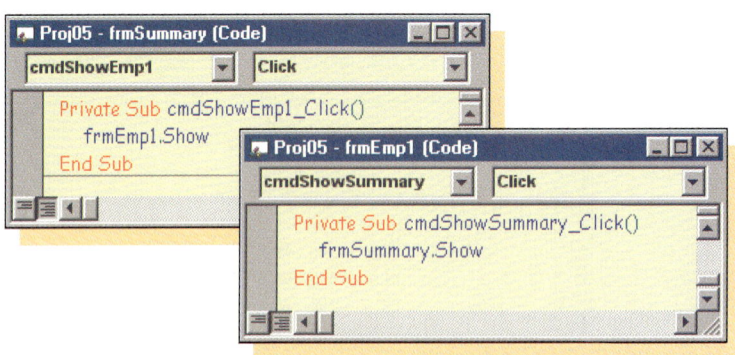

FIGURE 3.45

Code for cmdUpdate_Click procedure

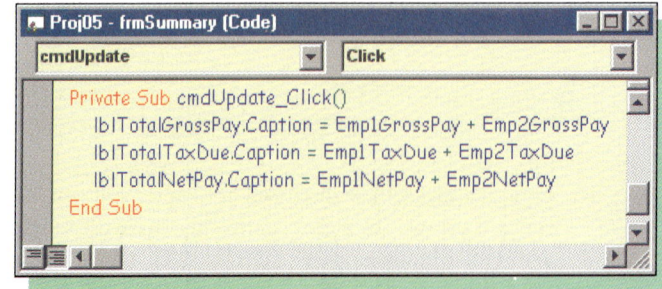

VB responds with the message "Errors during load. Refer to . . . for details." VB did not add the file to the project. The error message is VB's way of reminding you that a project cannot contain two forms with the same Name property setting.

5. Eliminate this problem by changing the Name property of the current employee form to frmEmp2. While you're at it, change the form's caption to "Employee 2"; the Show Emp2 button's name to "cmdShowEmp1"; and the Show Emp2 button's caption to "Show Emp1".

6. Now use Add File... to add the other form file (whose Name property is still frmEmp1) to the project. Look at the Project Explorer window to verify the result.

Note that this process of adding a file illustrates how a team of programmers can cooperate to construct a project. Each programmer might, for example, be responsible for creating a different set of forms. Upon finishing a form, the programmer adds it to the project under construction and runs the project to test the interaction of the new form with the other available forms.

7. Modify the Click event procedure for the Compute button on frmEmp2 to use the data for the second employee (in Table 3.4) and the global variables for the second employee.

8. Create the Click event procedures for the Show Emp1 and Show Emp2 command buttons on the two employee forms, and the Show Emp2 command button on the summary form. These are almost identical to procedures you have already created.

9. Run the project to verify these changes. Which form is now the startup form? You may wish to change this.

10. Save the project.

This project demonstrates how an application can use multiple forms and illustrates the use of global variables and constants to share data between forms. The construction steps also demonstrate shortcuts that are useful when a form has many similar controls or when two or more forms are very similar.

EXERCISE 3.25 In Project 5, how can you verify that the results displayed by your summary form are correct?

EXERCISE 3.26 It is better to construct and test an application a little at a time than to create the entire project before attempting to run it the first time. Why?

EXERCISE 3.27 Suppose you are part of a team of programmers who will cooperate to construct a large project. Is it important for the team to decide in advance on the module-level and global variables and constants that will be part of the project? Explain.

Chapter Summary

1. There are two basic kinds of data items: numeric data items that can be used in arithmetic, and string data items that cannot be used in arithmetic. Data items are represented in a program as either constants or variables.

2. Constants are data items that cannot change while the program is executing. Constants can be represented literally (the constant value itself),

or symbolically (a descriptive name that represents the value). Symbolic constants must be defined using the Const statement. Using symbolic constants makes a program easier to read and maintain, and reduces the likelihood of inconsistent values for the same constant in a program.

3. Variables are symbolic names for memory locations. Unlike constants, the values of variables can and often do change during program execution. Variables can be string or numeric. Numeric variables are further classified into specific types, which include Integer, Long, Currency, Single, and Double. Variables must be declared with a variable declaration statement, which specifies the name of the variable and its type. The Dim statement is one kind of variable declaration statement.

4. Expressions are combinations of variables, constants, and operators that produce a value. The + operator adds two numeric values, and the * operator multiplies two numeric values. The & operator concatenates (joins end-to-end) two string values.

5. An assignment statement is used to store the value of an expression into a variable or a control property. The syntax of the assignment statement is

    variablename = expression

    or

    control.property = expression

    The expression on the right-hand side of the equal sign is evaluated and reduced to a single value. This value is then stored in the variable or control property on the left-hand side of the equal sign. Both sides of the equal sign must be the same type; that is, they must both be string or they must both be numeric.

6. A project can have more than one form, but VB allows only one form to be active at a time. The active form is the form that the user can interact with and is visually identified by the color of the Title bar. Forms can also be loaded into main memory (from disk) and unloaded from main memory. The process of loading and unloading forms can be used to conserve main memory at run time. One form can access a control on another form. This is done by qualifying the reference to a control by adding the form name to the name of the control. The syntax is

    formname!control.property

7. A method specifies an action that is applied to a control. The Show method causes a form to become the active form. If the form is not already loaded, the Show method also causes the form to be loaded. Its syntax is

    formname.Show

8. A variable's scope is the domain within which the variable can be accessed. There are three levels of scope—local, module-level, and global. A variable with local scope is only known and accessible within a single procedure. Local variables are declared using a Dim statement placed in the procedure.

    A variable with module-level scope is known and accessible to any procedure of a given form or Code module. The Dim statement is used to declare the variable but it is placed in the general declarations section of the form or Code module.

A variable with global scope is known and accessible to any procedure of the project. To declare a global variable, a Public statement must be placed in the general declarations section of a Code module. The Public statement is just like the Dim statement except the word Dim is replaced with the word Public.

If a procedure has a local variable whose name is the same as a module-level variable, the event procedure uses the local variable and ignores the module-level variable. The general rule is that an event procedure always uses the closest variable with the specified name (where local is closer than module-level, which in turn is closer than global).

9. Variable lifetime refers to how long a variable exists. Module-level and global variables exist during the entire execution of the program. When the program starts, these variables are created, and when the program stops, the variable values are destroyed. In contrast, local variables exist only during the execution of the procedure in which they are declared. When the procedure starts to execute, its local variables are created and initialized. When the procedure terminates, the local variables are destroyed (their values are lost). To make local variables retain their values from one execution of the procedure to the next, declare the variable within the procedure using the Static statement instead of the Dim statement.

Key Terms

Activate event
active form
assignment statement
Code module
concatenation operator
Const statement
constant
constant definition
   statement
data item
Dim statement
expression
fixed-length string
floating-point types
Form control
formatting
global scope

initialization
keywords
literal constant
Load event
local scope
method
module-level scope
numeric data
Option Explicit
   statement
precision
Public Const statement
Public statement
qualified control name
range
reserved words
run time error

scope
Show method
standard data types
Standard module
static variable
string data
symbolic constant
syntax
type mismatch error
variable
variable declaration
   statement
variable lifetime
variable scope
variable-length string

End-of-Chapter Problems

1. For each of the following real-world quantities, write a Dim statement that declares an appropriate variable. State any assumptions you make.

    a. A part number that consists of four digits followed by two letters (e.g., 4745XY).
    b. The number of units sold for an item on an invoice.
    c. The comments entered into an employee's job evaluation form.
    d. The asking price of a home listed for sale.

e. The number of acres purchased for a commercial building site, which is the result of a geometrical calculation using the site's corner points.

2. Write the VB statement that increases by 5 the value stored in the integer variable N.

3. Assume that you want a variable that is declared in a Click event procedure to retain its value each time the procedure is executed. What is the correct way to accomplish this?

4. Explain the difference between module-level scope and global scope for a variable.

5. The following VB statement calculates the final balance of a $100 investment at the end of three years, assuming an 8 percent interest rate and annual compounding.

    FinalBalance = 100 * (1 + 0.08) ^ 3

    In the statement, * means multiply and ^ means "raised to the power of." Suppose we want to modify this statement to use in a real program. Of the values on the right side of the equal sign, which should be represented as variables, which as symbolic constants, and which as literal constants? Explain.

6. Suppose that the event procedures associated with two controls on the same form need to access the same variable. Explain how you would make this possible.

7. Suppose that you are in the process of choosing the type for a variable, and you have narrowed the choices to Currency and Double. Identify the important factors that you should consider when deciding whether the variable should be typed as Currency or as Double.

8. What value will be stored in the variable N at the end of the third time the following Click event procedure is executed?

    Private Sub cmdExample_Click()
        Dim N As Integer
        N = N + 1
    End Sub

9. What does the Option Explicit statement do? Why is it a good idea to always use this statement? Where is it placed in a VB program?

10. Do variables declared with global scope need to be declared as static variables if you want their values to be retained as the program executes? Explain.

11. Which of the following declares three Currency and two String variables?
    a. Dim X, Y, Z As Currency, A, B As String
    b. Dim X, Y, Z As Currency
       Dim A, B As String
    c. Dim X As Currency
       Dim Y As Currency
       Dim Z As Currency
       Dim A As String
       Dim B As String
    d. both b and c
    e. a, b, and c

Programming Problems

1. Create a form with one command button and four Label controls. Program the command button's Click event procedure to store the numeric value 875426.4796752 in four variables, one each of type Long, Currency, Single, and Double. Then have the Click event procedure display the values of the four variables in the four labels. Run the program and observe the result. Now, change the declaration of the variable of type Long to type Integer and run the program again. What happens? Explain.

2. Create a form that has three command buttons and one Label control. The first command button should set an Integer variable named FirstVar to the value 105. The second command button should set an Integer variable named SecondVar to the value 200. The third button should compute the sum of the two variables and display the result in the Label control.

3. Create a project with two forms. Then declare a global variable; this global variable should be the only variable in the project. On the first form, create four command buttons. The first command button should store the value 11 in the global variable. The second command button should change the value of the global variable to 22. The third button should display the value of the global variable in a Label control. The fourth button should show the other form.

    The second form should be identical to the first form, except that its first two command buttons should set the global variable to 33 and 44, instead of 11 and 22. Run the program and experiment by clicking its command buttons in various orders.

4. For this problem, you will create a multiform application with a main "control" form and a second "stop watch" form. The main form, which is shown below, provides three functions: displaying the stop watch form; displaying the current value of the stop watch's elapsed time (regardless of whether the stop watch form is visible); and terminating the application.

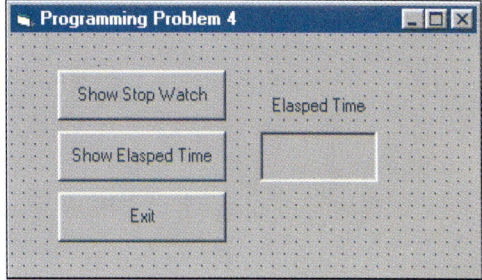

   The stop watch form (shown below) has a timer as well as: a button to start the timer; a button to pause the timer (start should resume the timing process); and a button to stop and reset the timer to zero.

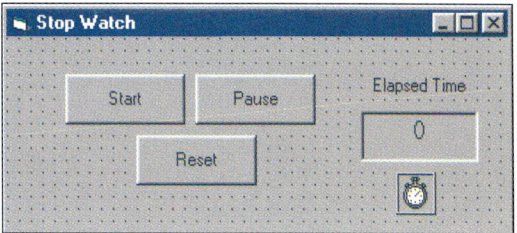

The timer should count in whole seconds.

The Show Elapsed Time button on the main form must access a variable to find the current elapsed time. That is, it should not access the Elapsed Time label on the stop watch form to find this information.

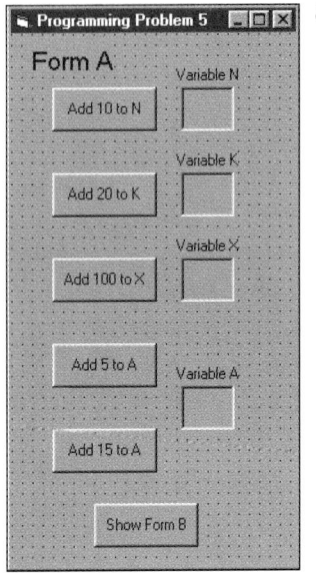

5. For this problem you are to create a multiform application that manipulates and displays the values of several variables. The form at left (Form A) has command buttons that manipulate variables named N, K, X, and A, and labels that display the values of these variables. Clicking on "Add 10 to N" should increase the value of the variable N by 10, and then display the value of N in its label. Thus, if you click this button repeatedly, the label should display 10, 20, 30, etc. Similarly, clicking on "Add 20 to K" should increase the value of the variable K by 20 (20, 40, 60, etc.). Clicking on "Add 100 to X" should add the constant 100 to the variable X, and then display the value of X in its label; however, instead of showing 100, 200, 300, etc., this label should show 100, 100, 100, etc. Finally, clicking on "Add 5 to A" and "Add 15 to A", should add 5 and 15, respectively, to the variable A. This action should be cumulative: for example, clicking on "Add 5 to A" first should change A to 5; then clicking on "Add 15 to A" should change A to 20, etc.

The Show Form B button should display the following form (Form B).

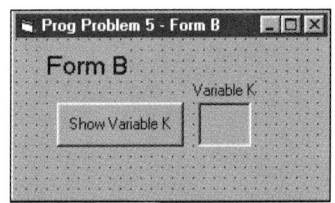

Clicking the Show Variable K button should cause the value of the variable K (as seen on Form A) to be displayed (the two values should be the same).

Your solution should use minimal scope for each variable. That is, if local scope works, it should be used instead of module-level or global scope. If local scope will not work but module-level scope will, then you should use module-level scope, not global. Use global scope only if it is the only scope that works.

Do not allow any controls on Form A to refer to controls on Form B or vice versa—use only variables to store and access values.

chapter FOUR

Performing Calculations and Manipulating Data

Expressions

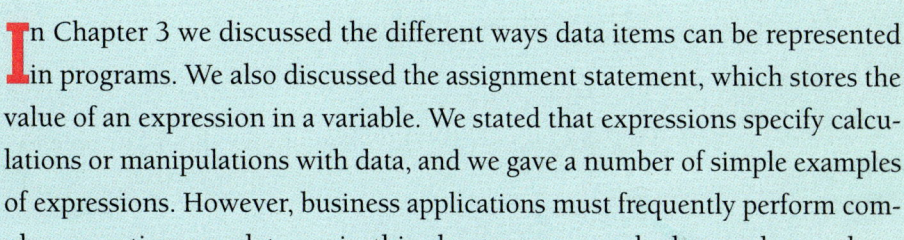

In Chapter 3 we discussed the different ways data items can be represented in programs. We also discussed the assignment statement, which stores the value of an expression in a variable. We stated that expressions specify calculations or manipulations with data, and we gave a number of simple examples of expressions. However, business applications must frequently perform complex operations on data, so in this chapter we extend what we know about expressions.

Expressions are made up of constants, variables, operators, and functions. The *operators* and *functions* specify how the data is to be manipulated, and the *constants* and *variables* provide the data. Operators and functions are part of the programming language. Thus, in order to write powerful expressions, you must become familiar with the operators and functions provided by the VB language.

Three kinds of expressions are typically used by business applications:
- *Arithmetic expressions* are used to perform arithmetic calculations.
- *String expressions* are used to manipulate string data.
- *Logical expressions* are used to select an appropriate action from a set of possible actions.

An arithmetic expression is made up of numeric constants and variables and arithmetic operators and functions. Arithmetic operators include addition, subtraction, multiplication, and division. An example of an arithmetic function is the square root function; if you give the number 4 to the square root function, the function returns the value 2.

A string expression is made up of string constants and variables and string operators and functions. We briefly discussed the string concatenation operator, &, in Chapter 3. The format function, which is used to format values for display, is an example of a string function.

A logical expression is made up of numeric and string constants and variables, comparison operators, logical operators, and logical functions. A logical expression "evaluates to" (a phrase discussed later in this chapter) either True or False. As an example, you can use a logical expression in a program to determine whether an invoice total exceeds $100.

We begin this chapter by introducing operators and functions, showing how they can be used to construct expressions, and giving examples of how they are used. We also introduce the InputBox() function and the MsgBox statement, which allow your programs to accept values from and display information to the user. Next, we discuss arithmetic and string expressions, and introduce the commonly used operators and functions for each. Then we introduce the Text box control and use it in a project that computes the present value of an investment. We then discuss logical expressions. The chapter concludes with a project that combines many of the topics in this and previous chapters to create a stock trading simulation.

Objectives

After studying this chapter you should be able to

- ✦ Describe the operators and functions used to create arithmetic, string, and logical expressions.
- ✦ Use InputBox() and MsgBox to accept input from and display information to the user.
- ✦ Describe how the Text box control can improve the interactivity of programs, and use it to create simple interfaces.
- ✦ Explain why errors such as overflow and roundoff occur and how to avoid them.
- ✦ Write logical expressions using comparison operators and logical operators to enable your programs to make simple choices while executing.

4.1 Using Expressions, Operators, and Functions in VB Statements

Each line of an event procedure is one statement,[1] and an expression is often part of a statement. An *expression* **instructs the computer to manipulate specific data in a specific way**, and the result of this manipulation is a single value. The *statement* **then tells the computer what to do with the value that results from the expression**—for example, store it in a particular variable or display it on the user interface.

We construct expressions from values, operators, and functions. **A *value* is a constant, a variable, or a control property.** An *operator* **is a symbol that specifies a common operation**, such as addition or multiplication. A *function*

---

[1] This is not entirely true. It is possible to split a long statement across several lines. However, in that case you would see a line-coninuation character (the underscore symbol, _) and know that you were looking at one statement.

is a descriptive name that specifies a less familiar or more complex operation than those performed by operators, such as computation of the square root of a number. Figure 4.1 shows the relationship between statements, expressions, values, operators, and functions.

We now describe statements, expressions, and the components of expressions to help you learn to use them in event procedures that manipulate data.

Statements

Statements differ in the kinds of actions they specify, and in their syntax. For example, we can easily distinguish a Dim statement, which is used to declare a variable, from an assignment statement, which is used to store a value in a variable or a control property.

Some statements, such as Dim, have no expressions. Others, like the assignment statement, require exactly one expression. Still other statements allow multiple expressions.

At run time, when an event occurs, the computer executes the statements inside the corresponding event procedure one at a time, from top to bottom. To execute a statement containing one or more expressions, the computer performs the following two steps, in order:

1. It evaluates the expressions, one at a time, arriving at a single value for each expression.
2. It performs the action specified by the statement, which entails doing something with the value(s) obtained in step 1.

Figure 4.2 illustrates these steps for the assignment statement.

Expressions

An expression is either a single value or a combination of values, operators, and/or functions that reduce to a single value. For example, 2 is an expression, and 2 + 3 is also an expression. When the computer encounters the expression

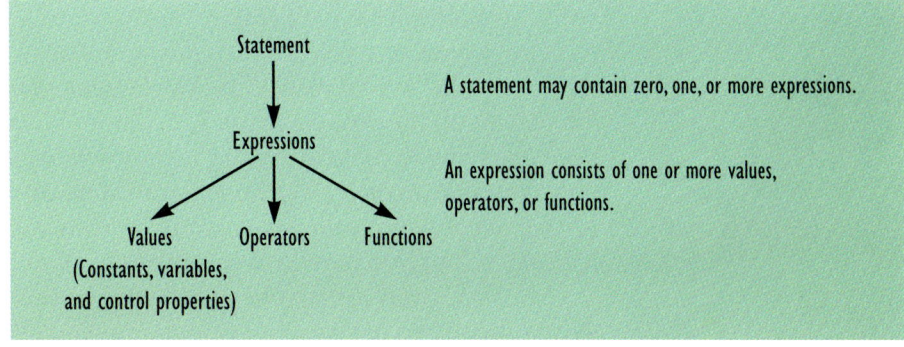

FIGURE 4.1
Statements, expressions, and the components of expressions

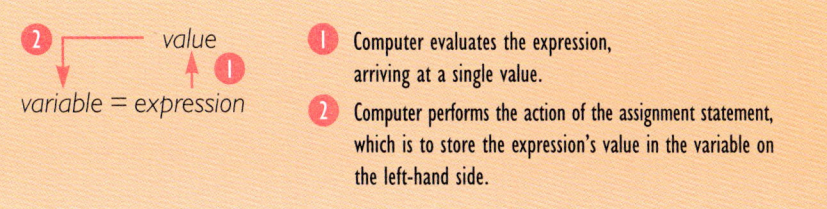

FIGURE 4.2
Steps in execution of the assignment statement

2 in a statement, it understands it to be the number 2. When the computer encounters the expression 2 + 3 in a statement, it performs the addition to arrive at the number 5. **Performing the calculation or manipulation specified by an expression is called** *evaluating the expression.* For example, we say that 2 + 3 *evaluates to* the value 5.

Evaluating expressions is step 1 in the execution of a statement. To evaluate an expression, the computer

1. Obtains the data to be manipulated by identifying the value of each constant in the expression and retrieving the value from each variable and control property in the expression.
2. Performs the specified manipulations, one at a time, using the values obtained in step 1.

The resulting value is always either numeric or string.

As mentioned before, there are three kinds of expressions:

- Arithmetic expressions, which specify ordinary arithmetic calculations. The result of an arithmetic expression is always a numeric value. An example is 2 + 3, which evaluates to 5.
- String expressions, which manipulate or combine string values. The result of a string expression is always a string value. An example is "A" & "B", which evaluates to "AB".
- Logical expressions, which represent True/False questions. The result of a logical expression is always numeric. More specifically, the result is always either the number –1, which represents the True outcome, or the number 0, which represents the False outcome. An example is 2 < 3, which evaluates to –1 because it is true that 2 is less than 3.

We form complex expressions by combining variables and constants with operators and functions. We describe operators and functions next.

Operators

An operator is a symbol that specifies a common operation such as addition or multiplication. The plus sign (+) is the addition operator and the asterisk (*) is the multiplication operator.

Most operators are **binary operators, so called because they combine the** *two* **values on either side of them into a single value.**[2] The addition operator is a binary operator. In the expression 2 + 3, the addition operator adds the value on its left to the value on its right, arriving at the single value of 5. A few operators **affect only the value on their right, and are called** *unary operators.*[3] In the expression –2 the minus sign is called the *negation operator*; since there is no value on its left side, it simply makes the 2 negative. The negation operator is unary.

Most operators are easy to understand because their use in VB is equivalent to their everyday use. For example, everyone is familiar with the binary subtraction operator, as in 3 – 2.

Functions

A function is a descriptive name that specifies a more complex operation than that performed by an operator. In VB, function names are always followed by

---

[2] The *bi* in binary means "two."

[3] The prefix *uni* means "one."

parentheses. Examples of functions are Sqr(), which computes the square root of a number, and Abs(), which computes the absolute value of a number.

To make the Sqr() function compute the square root of a number, place the number between its parentheses. For example, if an event procedure contains the statements

Dim X **As Single**
X = Sqr(4)

then after the assignment statement is executed, the variable X will store the value 2.

The value between the parentheses is called the *argument* of the function. A function manipulates or performs a calculation with its argument, then *returns* the result.[4] The phrase "returns the result" means that the function becomes the result; that is, the computer replaces the function with the result just as the computer replaces a variable name with its value from the variable table. **We also call the resulting value of the function the *return value*.** In the preceding example, the Sqr() function computes square roots, and its argument is 4; thus, Sqr(4) becomes the value 2. We use the phrases "Sqr(4) returns the value 2," "Sqr(4) becomes the value 2," and "Sqr(4) takes on the value 2" interchangeably.

The argument of a function is itself an expression. The computer first evaluates the argument—the expression between the parentheses—to arrive at a single value, then performs the action of the function upon this value. Suppose an event procedure contains the following statements:

Dim X **As Single**
Dim Y **As Single**
Y = 7
X = Sqr(2 + Y)

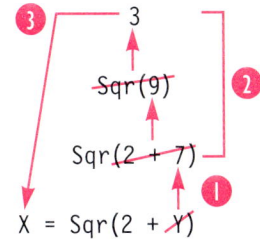

What value will X hold after the second assignment statement executes? When the computer executes this statement, it performs the steps depicted here.

1. Computer replaces variable name by its value (from the variable table).
2. Computer performs the specified manipulations: it adds 2 + 7 to get 9; then the function computes the square root.
3. Computer stores 3 in the variable X.

More Complicated Expressions

Operators and functions can be combined to compose complicated expressions, as illustrated by the following statements:

Dim X **As Single**
Dim Y **As Single**
Y = 7
X = Y - Sqr(Y + 9) + 5 + Sqr(2 + Y)

---

[4] At this point, think of a function as a *black box*, meaning a device that accepts an input and produces an output. We need to understand the input and the output, but we don't need to know how the black box transforms the input into the output. The square root function accepts a number as the input and produces the square root of the number as its output. We don't need to know how the output value was actually computed.

What value does X store after the second assignment statement executes? When the computer executes this statement, it performs the steps depicted here.

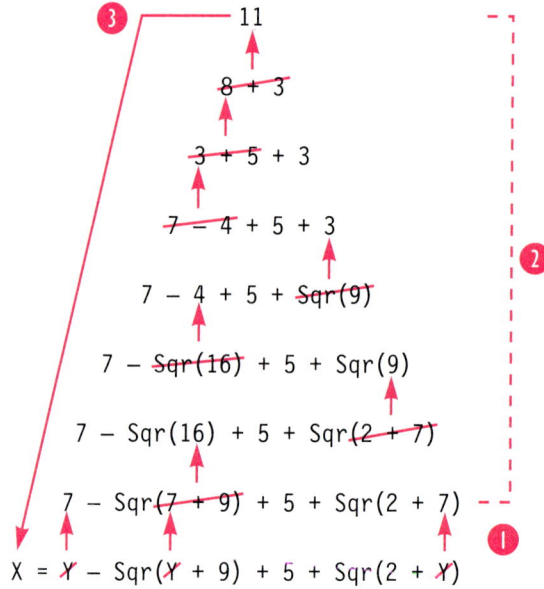

Because the argument of a function is itself an expression, a function's argument can also be complex. It may include another function, for example, as illustrated by the following statements:

Dim X As Single
Dim Y As Single
Y = 7
X = Sqr(10 + Sqr(Y + 29))

What value does X store after the second assignment statement executes? To execute this statement, the computer performs these steps:

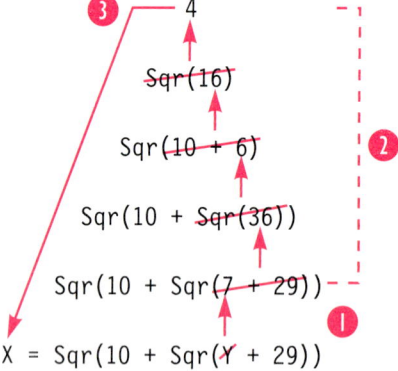

Let's look at a complete event procedure that illustrates the use of operators and functions to perform a moderately complex calculation. This event procedure is executed when the user clicks on a command button named cmdCalculateHypotenuseLength. The procedure calculates the length of a right triangle's hypotenuse given the lengths of the other two sides. The calculation uses the Pythagorean theorem from geometry, which states that if the sides of the right triangle have lengths A and B, then the length of the hypotenuse, C, is equal to the square root of $A^2 + B^2$.

The program has five variables. Variables A and B store the lengths of the two sides. Variables ASquared and BSquared store the results of computing the squares of the sides. Variable C stores the length of the hypotenuse, which is computed using the Pythagorean formula. The results are presented to the user using the Caption properties of three labels on the form. The code for the procedure is as follows:

```
Private Sub cmdCalculateHypotenuseLength_Click()
    Dim A As Single
    Dim ASquared As Single
    Dim B As Single
    Dim BSquared As Single
    Dim C As Single
    A = 3
    B = 4
    ASquared = A * A
    BSquared = B * B
    C = Sqr(ASquared + BSquared)
    lblA.Caption = A
    lblB.Caption = B
    lblC.Caption = C
End Sub
```

Expressions as a Part of Statements

An expression can never appear on a line by itself in an event procedure. That is, an expression by itself is never valid; an expression is always part of a larger statement. You will never see the following sequence of statements in a working VB program.

```
Dim X As Single
Dim Y As Single
7
Sqr(Y)
```

Intuitively, we know that 7 by itself is a simple enough expression for the computer to evaluate, but a valid statement will, in addition, always tell the computer what to do with the result. For example, an assignment statement can have an arbitrarily complicated expression on the right-hand side of the equal sign, and after the computer evaluates the expression, it knows what to do with the result: store it in the variable specified on the left-hand side of the equal sign.

EXERCISE 4.1

What values are stored in the variables X, Y, and Z after the following statements execute?

```
Dim X As Single
Dim Y As Single
Dim Z As Single
X = Sqr(5 + 20)
Y = 5 + Sqr(X + 11)
Z = Sqr(X + 2 + Y) + Sqr(4)
```

4.2 Simple Input and Output

In all the programs introduced so far, data have been embedded in the program code in the form of constants. But many programs accept data from the user. These programs, then, manipulate different data each time they execute and are more versatile than programs that use constants. For example, consider the procedure in Section 4.1 that computes the hypotenuse of a right triangle. As it is constructed, it can find the hypotenuse of only one specific right triangle. The program will be more useful if we modify it to accept the user's input for the lengths of the two sides.

Most interactive programs use dialog boxes to ask the user for specific information and to display information to the user. A *dialog box* **is a separate window displayed on the user interface that either informs the user of some special condition** (like an error message) **or provides a means for the user to enter data.** It is called a dialog box because it is a means of communicating (carrying on a dialog) between the program and the user.

In VB, the *InputBox() function* **provides a very simple way to obtain data from the user via a dialog box**, and the *MsgBox* **statement displays data to the user via a dialog box.** Beginning programmers can take advantage of these features to accept input and display output data without placing additional controls on the form. They can be used to quickly create bare-bones programs to experiment with new statements and expressions.

The InputBox() Function

To see how the InputBox() function works, consider the following statements:

Dim YourAge **As Integer**
YourAge = InputBox("How old are you?")

When the computer executes the assignment statement, it first evaluates the expression on the right-hand side of the equal sign, which consists of an InputBox() function with a string argument. To execute this InputBox() function, the computer displays the dialog box shown in Figure 4.3, then waits for the user to respond. Observe that the argument of the function is displayed in the dialog box. This argument, which must be type String, is called the *prompt* because it asks the user to enter certain information.

To input a data value, the user types the value into the text box at the bottom of the dialog box, then clicks the OK button. The computer removes the dialog box from the screen, then resumes execution, and the value typed by the user becomes the value of the InputBox() function. So, if the user types the value 20, then clicks OK, the value 20 will be the return value of the InputBox()

FIGURE 4.3

Dialog box displayed when InputBox() function executes

function and will be stored in the variable YourAge. Or the user can decide not to enter a value, and just click the Cancel button instead of OK.

The OK and Cancel Buttons

As you have seen, an input box has two buttons: OK and Cancel. The OK button causes the information in the text box to be used as the value that the function returns. The user can select the OK button by either clicking on it or by pressing the [ENTER] key.

The Cancel button causes the dialog box to be removed from the screen, and any information in the text box is ignored. This means that the function takes on the value of the zero-length string (""). The user can select the Cancel button by either clicking on it or by pressing the [ESC] key.

The [ENTER] and [ESC] keyboard alternatives to clicking with the mouse allow an experienced user to interact with the computer more quickly. The user can enter a value via an input box—without taking his or her hands off the keyboard—by simply typing the value and pressing [ENTER].

Example 4.1 Using the InputBox() Function

The objective of this example is to improve the code for the hypotenuse calculation discussed in the previous section. We use the InputBox() function to allow the user to input any two values for *A* and *B*. Every time the procedure is executed, the user can enter two different numbers and see a different result. The form and its controls are shown in Figure 4.4.

The main difference between the original version of this event procedure and the modified version is that we have replaced the two assignment statements

```
A = 3
B = 4
```

with two assignment statements that use the InputBox() function. The modified event procedure is shown in Figure 4.5.

Execute this event procedure a few times, entering different numbers in response to the input boxes. Be sure to try pressing [ENTER] instead of using the mouse. Also, try clicking OK without entering any value in the text box, and try clicking Cancel. What happens? We address this issue next.

FIGURE 4.4

User interface for Example 4.1

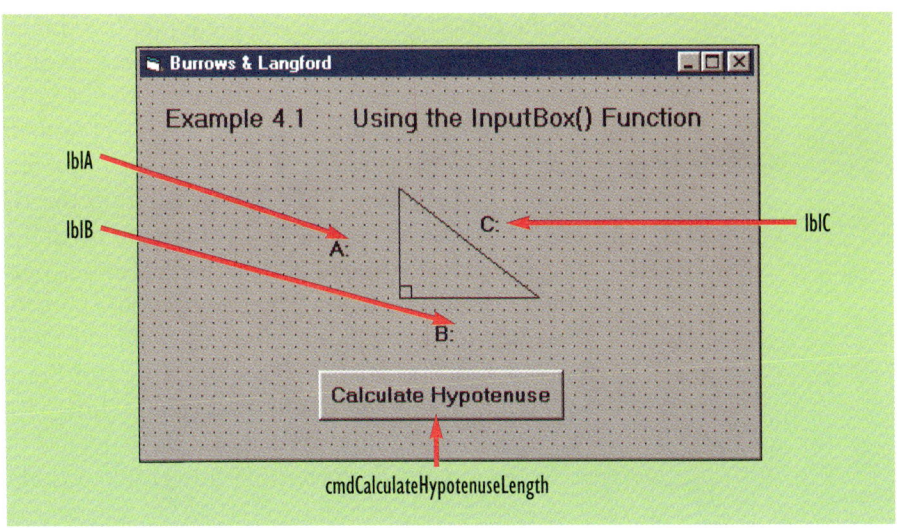

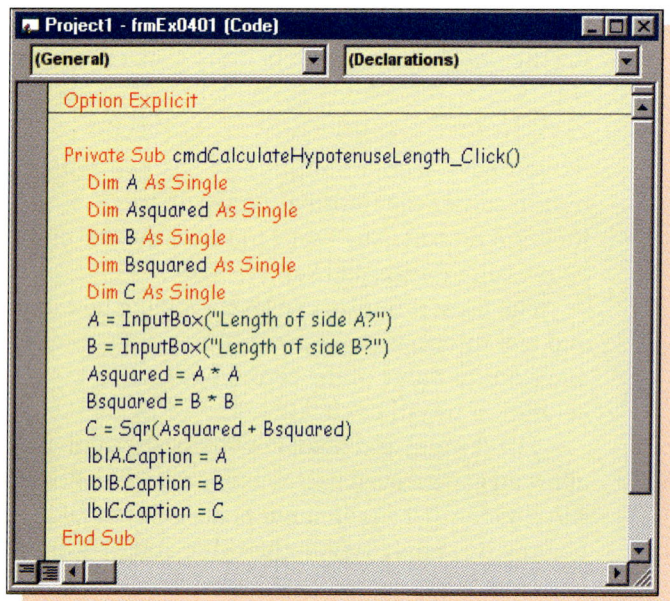

FIGURE 4.5

Interactive version of hypotenuse calculation program

The Type of the Value Returned by InputBox()

There is another reason the InputBox() function is useful for writing barebones code: its return value is type Variant. You may recall from Chapter 3 that a variant data type is automatically converted to whatever type is appropriate for the context of the statement. Consider these statements:

    Dim YourName **As String**
    Dim YourAge **As Integer**
    YourName = InputBox("Please enter your name")
    YourAge = InputBox("Please enter your age")

In the first assignment statement, the InputBox() function returns a string value because the variable on the left-hand side is type String (and therefore the expression on the right-hand side must yield a string). Similarly, the InputBox() function in the second assignment statement returns a numeric value. Thus, you can use the InputBox() function in an assignment statement regardless of the data type of the variable on the left-hand side.

What happens if the user clicks on OK without entering a value, or clicks on the Cancel button? VB sets the InputBox() function to the zero-length string. When the variable on the left-hand side is type String, as in the first assignment statement shown above, the zero-length string is stored in the variable. But when the variable on the left-hand side is numeric, as in the second assignment statement, a run time error occurs: type mismatch. **The *type mismatch* means that the type of the expression on the right side of the assignment operator and the type of the variable on the left side are not compatible.**

The variable YourAge is type Integer, so it is numeric. Accordingly, VB must convert the value returned by the InputBox() function to a number before it can be stored in YourAge. But what number should VB produce when the user either does not enter a value or clicks Cancel? Zero? Presumably, the user would have entered zero if it was the desired value. Thus, VB refuses to convert the zero-length string to a number and instead generates the type mismatch error.

One way of circumventing this problem is to use the Val() function:

    YourAge = Val(InputBox("Please enter your age"))

The Val() function, which we will discuss in greater detail later on, converts a string into a number. When its argument is the zero-length string, it returns the number zero, which eliminates the type mismatch problem.

There are other ways of handling this situation, and we will revisit this problem later in the text.

Additional Capabilities of the InputBox() Function

The InputBox() function has additional capabilities that allow you to improve the appearance of the dialog box displayed to the user. The syntax of the function allows five arguments:

InputBox(*prompt, title, default, xpos, ypos*)

Only the *prompt* is required. Like prompt, *title* and *default* must be type String. If provided, the value of *title* will be displayed on the dialog box's Title bar, and the value of *default* will be placed in its text box. The default argument is used to place the most likely response in the text box for the user. The user can accept the default value by not entering any text and just clicking OK.

The *xpos* and *ypos* arguments must be numeric. These allow you to specify the position of the dialog box on the screen. If you're interested in this, see online help (search phrase "InputBox function") for details.

As an example, the statement

YourAge = InputBox("What is your age?", _
    "Student Registration System", "20")

produces the dialog box shown in Figure 4.6. This statement illustrates how **the line-continuation character is used to split a long statement across two or more lines in the Code window**. The line-continuation character is actually a combination of two characters: a space followed by an underscore. To split a statement, when you near the right edge of the Code window you type a space followed by an underscore, then continue typing the statement on the next line in the Code window. The single statement will appear on two (or more) lines, but it will work the same as if you had entered it as one long line.

Note that you cannot use the line-continuation character in the middle of a string literal constant (VB will take the underscore to be part of the string value itself). If you want to split a statement in the middle of a string literal constant, terminate the string constant (with a quote mark), then type an & (the string concatenation operator), then the line-continuation character, and then continue the string constant (beginning with a quote mark) on the next line. For example, the statement

YourAge = InputBox("What is your age?", "Student Registration " & _
    "System", "20")

produces the same dialog box shown in Figure 4.6.

FIGURE 4.6

Example of Input-Box()'s title and default arguments

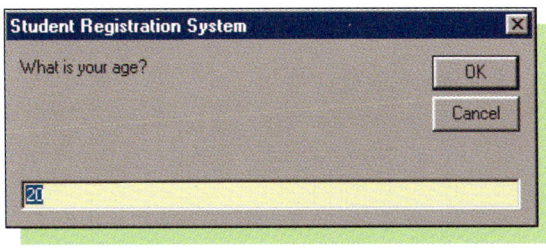

Finally, if you wish to include a default value but no title, you must include a comma where the title argument belongs, as a place holder. This is illustrated by the following statement:

YourAge = InputBox("What is your age?", , "20")

Note that if you do not provide a title, VB uses the name of the project as the caption of the dialog box.

The MsgBox Statement

The MsgBox statement displays information (a "message") to the user. As an example, the statement

MsgBox "Interest rate must be greater than zero."

displays the dialog box shown in Figure 4.7 and waits for the user to respond.

The MsgBox statement requires an expression, and it displays the result of this expression in the dialog box. After reading this message, the user responds by clicking the OK button or pressing [ENTER], which causes the computer to remove the dialog box from the screen and completes execution of the Msg-Box statement.

Although the MsgBox statement and the Label control both display data to the user, there are differences in their mode of operation. The MsgBox statement clearly draws attention to the data it displays; the user can't miss it, because program execution is halted until the user clicks OK. The Label control does not require any user action. Another difference is that the message box disappears when the user clicks OK, whereas the data displayed by a Label control persist until another statement changes the label's caption.

Because of the message box's behavior, it is typically used only when it is necessary to notify the user of an event right when the event occurs. For example, a message box alerts the user to an error.

In many examples in this text we use the message box to display the results of new statements and expressions.

Example 4.2 Using the MsgBox Statement

In this example, we show how the message box can be used to replace a label for displaying the results of a calculation. We use the MsgBox statement to rewrite Example 4.1, which computes the length of a right triangle's hypotenuse, so that the form has no Label controls. The revised event procedure is shown in Figure 4.8.

The user interface for this example is less attractive than the one for the previous example. However, this is not a drawback if our goal is simply to write a program that provides the answer—the length of the hypotenuse. Although the code is not much shorter than the previous versions, we can create this example much more quickly because there is no need to create controls on the form, position them carefully, and give them descriptive names.

FIGURE 4.7

A simple message box

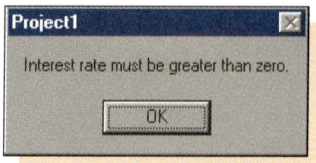

FIGURE 4.8

Code for Example 4.2

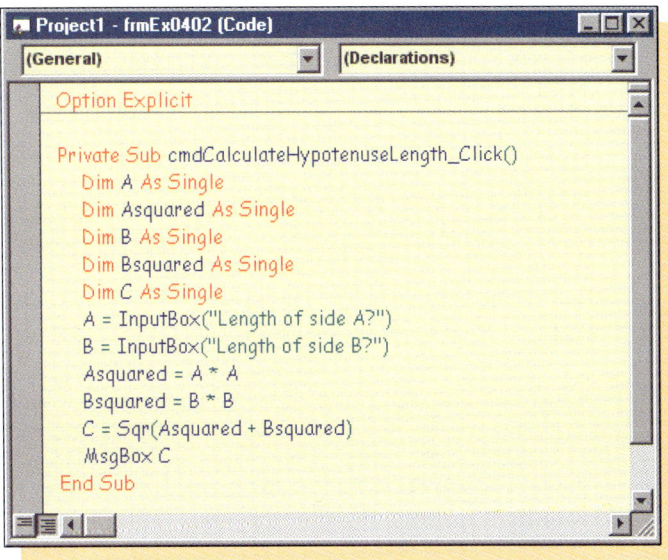

Additional Capabilities of the MsgBox Statement

The MsgBox statement has additional capabilities that allow you to improve its appearance. The MsgBox statement is, in fact, our first example of a statement having more than one expression. Its syntax allows three expressions:

MsgBox *message, mbtype, title*

The first expression, *message*, is required, and the other two are optional. If provided, *mbtype* must be numeric; its value specifies whether you want to include additional buttons or an icon for the message box. (VB's online help calls this parameter *buttons* instead of *mbtype*.) The *title*, if provided, specifies the value to be displayed on the message box's Title bar. As an example, the statement

MsgBox "Pleased to meet you", 64, "Greetings"

produces the message box in Figure 4.9.

VB provides four different icons for the message box, corresponding to the values 16, 32, 48, and 64 for *mbtype*. These icons and associated *mbtype* values appear in Table 4.1. Obviously, it is difficult to remember which number

FIGURE 4.9

Message box with icon and title

TABLE 4.1 Message box icons

Message Box Icon	Mbtype	Symbolic Constant
❌	16	vbCritical
❓	32	vbQuestion
⚠️	48	vbExclamation
ℹ️	64	vbInformation

produces which icon, so VB provides predefined symbolic constants (also shown in the table) for these numbers.

Using a symbolic constant instead of a literal constant, the statement

MsgBox "Pleased to meet you", 64, "Greetings"

becomes

MsgBox "Pleased to meet you", vbInformation, "Greetings"

Consult online help (search phrase "constants, message box") if you are interested in further capabilities of *mbtype* such as alignment of the message.

In the next two sections we will use InputBox() and MsgBox to create programs for exploring VB's arithmetic and string operators and functions.

EXERCISE 4.2 Write a complete Click event procedure for a command button named cmdSum that prompts the user to enter two numbers, then adds the numbers and displays the result. Assume that the command button is the form's only control.

EXERCISE 4.3 Write the VB statement that displays a message box titled "Uh oh!", containing the message "Watch out!", and including an exclamation icon.

4.3 Arithmetic Expressions

For the most part, arithmetic operators and functions are similar to their counterparts in ordinary arithmetic, but to write arithmetic expressions skillfully you must learn precisely how they are used in VB. In this section we describe arithmetic operators and functions and demonstrate their use.

Arithmetic Operators and Operator Precedence

Of the arithmetic operators listed in Table 4.2, only one requires explanation. **The *exponentiation operator* raises the first number to the power of the second number.** Thus, 3 ^ 2 means 3^2, and 2 ^ 5 means 2^5, etc. The numbers can have fractional parts, so, for example, 2.25 ^ 0.5 ($2.25^{1/2}$ or $\sqrt{2.25}$) will compute the square root of 2.25.

Although arithmetic operators are used in VB expressions pretty much the same as in ordinary algebra, you must compose complicated expressions

TABLE 4.2 The arithmetic operators

Symbol	Operator Name	Example Expression	Result
+	Addition	3 + 1	4
−	Subtraction	3 − 1	2
*	Multiplication	3 * 2	6
/	Division	3 / 2	1.5
^	Exponentiation	3 ^ 2	9

with care, since the order in which the operations are performed will affect the result. For example, for the expression

```
-1+2*4-4/2*3^2+3
```

is the result 3, 6.9835, –8, or something else?

As in ordinary algebra, you can use parentheses to force the order in which operations are performed: the operations in the innermost parentheses are evaluated first, then the operations in the next innermost parentheses, and so on. In the absence of parentheses VB follows an *operator precedence rule* that **specifies arithmetic operations to be performed in the following order:**

1. Unary negations
2. Exponentiations
3. Multiplications and divisions
4. Additions and subtractions

If two or more operators at the same precedence level occur in an expression, they are evaluated from left to right. For example, if an expression contains both a multiplication and a division operator, the left-most one is performed first.

The expression presented earlier has no parentheses, so VB follows the operator precedence rule and performs operations in the following order:

Unary negations	The –1 is identified as negative 1.
Exponentiations	3 ^ 2 yields the intermediate result of 9.

$$-1 + 2 * 4 - 4 / 2 * \overset{9}{\cancel{3\char`\^2}} + 3$$

Multiplications and divisions, left to right	2 * 4 yields the intermediate result of 8.
	4 / 2 yields the intermediate result of 2.
	2 * 9 yields the intermediate result of 18.

$$-1 + \overset{8}{\cancel{2*4}} - \overset{\overset{18}{\cancel{2}*9}}{\cancel{4/2}} * 9 + 3$$

Additions and subtractions, left to right	–1 + 8 yields the intermediate result of 7.
	7 – 18 yields the intermediate result of –11.
	–11 + 3 yields the final result of –8.

$$\overset{\overset{\overset{-8}{\cancel{-11}+3}}{\cancel{7}-18}}{\cancel{-1+8}} - 18 + 3$$

Of course, when you create an application, your goal is to make the computer perform a calculation that you need to have performed. One way to proceed is to study the operator precedence rule and arrange your arithmetic expression accordingly so that all operations are performed in the correct order. However, a better way to proceed is to write your expression in the clearest, most natural order you can, based on your experience with ordinary arithmetic, and use parentheses for added clarity and to override the operator precedence rules when necessary. This makes the expression easier to read, which in turn adds to the readability and maintainability of the program.

For example, a human can understand the expression we have been using as an example much more readily if it is written in the following form:

$$(3 - 1) + (2 * 4) - ((4 / 2) * (3 \wedge 2))$$

EXERCISE 4.4 What value results when the computer evaluates this numeric expression?

3 + 5 * 10

EXERCISE 4.5 Write a modified version of the expression in Exercise 4.4 to yield the value of 80.

EXERCISE 4.6 What values are displayed by the following event procedure?

```
Private Sub cmdSimpleArithmetic_Click()
    Dim X As Single
    Dim Y As Single
    Dim Z As Single
    X = 2 + 3
    MsgBox X
    Y = 7 * X
    MsgBox Y
    Z = X + Y / 10 + 2 ^ 3
    MsgBox Z
    X = X + 1
    MsgBox X
    MsgBox X + 1
    MsgBox X
End Sub
```

Integer Division

VB provides two operators for performing division with integers. The *Integer Division operator* calculates how many times one integer goes into another, ignoring the remainder. The *Mod operator* calculates the remainder produced when one integer is divided by another. These operators are shown in Table 4.3.

To see how they work, look at an ordinary pencil-and-paper example of integer division.

```
            2  ←  33 \ 12
        12 ⌐33
            24
            ─
             9  ←  33 Mod 12
```

TABLE 4.3 Integer arithmetic operators

Operator Symbol	Name	Example Expression	Result
\	Integer Division	33 \ 12	2
Mod	Mod (*remainder or modulo*)	33 Mod 12	9

If we divide 33 by 12, the answer is 2 with a remainder of 9. The VB expression 33 \ 12 evaluates to 2; it ignores the remainder. The VB expression 33 Mod 12 evaluates to 9; it generates only the remainder.

Be sure to note the difference between the integer divide symbol, \, which is sometimes called a *backslash,* and the ordinary division symbol, /, which is sometimes called a *slash.* The result of integer division is always an integer, while the result of ordinary division may have a fractional part.

Also, note that in the operator precedence rule, the \ and Mod operators come after multiply and divide but before add and subtract.

EXERCISE 4.7

What values will the following event procedure display?

    Private Sub cmdIntegerDiv_Click()
        MsgBox 18 / 4
        MsgBox 18 \ 4
        MsgBox 18 **Mod** 4
    End Sub

Example 4.3

Using Cyclic Sequences

Many programs simulate cyclical events such as changes in the seasons of the year, the schedule of a sales representative visiting clients, or the dividing of a group of students into teams. To solve such problems with the computer, programs use the Mod operator to generate a sequence of numbers matching the real-world event. As an example of this kind of calculation, the event procedure in Figure 4.10 generates the sequence 1, 2, 3, 0, 1, 2, 3, 0, 1, 2, 3, ... As the user clicks cmdCycleTest successively, the program counts and computes the remainder. This program is said to "count modulo 4".

Notice that the variable C is declared as static in the procedure. This is necessary to insure that it does not get reset to zero each time the command button is clicked.

The code in Figure 4.10 also illustrates the use of comments. **A *comment* is an explanatory remark placed in the code for the benefit of programmers.** The computer ignores comments. To place a comment in code, simply type an apostrophe followed by the explanatory text; the computer ignores everything to the right of and on the same line as the apostrophe. VB displays comments in a different color than other code to bring them to the programmer's attention.

The code in Figure 4.10 illustrates two common uses for comments. The first use is to record information such as the name of the programmer who wrote the code and the date it was written. A good place for these comments is in the

FIGURE 4.10

Code for Example 4.3

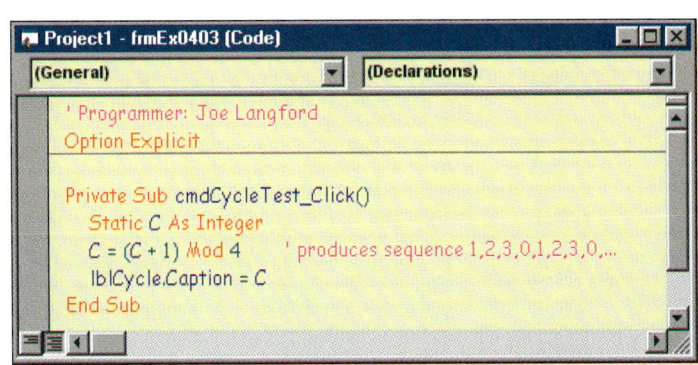

general declarations section, at the very top, because the code in the general declarations section appears at the top of printouts produced by VB.

The second use of comments is to help explain how the program works. Such comments should explain something that is not otherwise obvious to a knowledgeable programmer. For example, the comment in the line of code

MsgBox Y + Z   'display the sum of Y and Z

is poor, since it is obvious that this statement will display the sum of Y and Z. The comment is unnecessary. However, a complex processing step may involve some subtlety that even the best programmer cannot quickly understand. In this situation good comments are very valuable. Not only will they reduce the amount of time needed for another programmer to understand the code, but they will also reduce the likelihood of overlooking key details. The worst case is when a programmer *thinks* he or she understands the program but really does not!

EXERCISE 4.8 Modify cmdCycleTest_Click in Example 4.3, without changing the assignment statement lblCycle.Caption = C, so that it produces the sequence 1, 2, 3, 4, 1, 2, 3, 4, . . ., instead of the sequence 1, 2, 3, 0, 1, 2, 3, 0, ...

Arithmetic Functions

VB's built-in arithmetic functions make it easy to perform common mathematical calculations such as square roots or logarithms. To perform a calculation using a function, include the function in an expression. Some common arithmetic functions are listed in Table 4.4. In this section we describe these functions, starting with Abs(). We've already seen how Sqr() works in Section 4.1. You can learn about other VB arithmetic functions from online help (search phrase "math functions").

Abs() and Sgn()

The Abs() function returns the absolute value of its argument (i.e., it removes the sign and makes the value positive). The Sgn() function is the opposite of Abs(); it is useful when you can ignore the value of a number but need to know its sign. Sgn() takes on the value −1 if its argument is negative, 0 if its argument is 0, and 1 if its argument is positive. This function might be used, for example, to determine whether a customer's credit balance has gone negative.

TABLE 4.4 Common arithmetic functions

Name	Function Description	Example Expression	Result
Sqr()	Square root	Sqr(4)	2
Abs()	Absolute value	Abs(-4)	4
Sgn()	Sign	Sgn(-3.5)	−1
Fix()	Integer part	Fix(4.28745)	4
Exp()	Exponential (natural)	Exp(1)	2.718282
Log()	Natural logarithm	Log(2.71828)	0.9999993
Rnd()	Random number (0 to 1)	Rnd()	0.3845683

Fix()

The Fix() function truncates a number with a fractional part; that is, it throws away the fractional part and returns just the integer part. Several functions are variations on Fix(), including Int() and CInt(). Int() returns the largest integer less than or equal to its argument. The values returned by Fix() and Int() are the same except when the argument is negative: Fix(–4.3) takes on the value –4 and Int(–4.3) takes on the value –5. CInt() rounds its argument up or down to the nearest integer. If the fractional part of its argument is exactly .5, then CInt() rounds it to the nearest *even* integer; for example, CInt(3.5) returns 4 and CInt(2.5) returns 2.

Exp() and Log()

Exp() and Log() compute natural exponents and logarithms. That is, they perform the operations with e, sometimes called *Euler's number*, as the base. Exp() computes e raised to the power of its argument: Exp(X) returns the value e^X. The Log() function is the inverse of Exp(): Log(Y) returns the value X for which e^X is equal to Y.

The quantity e (approximately equal to 2.718282) occurs very frequently in mathematics and science, and less frequently in business applications. Nonetheless, business applications do sometimes need to be able to compute exponentials and logarithms. For example, they can be used to project growth trends for sales or stock prices. You can use Log() to compute logarithms to any base by using a simple formula; for further information see online help (search phrase "Log function").

Rnd()

The Rnd() function generates random numbers, which are often necessary for business simulations. For example, we might want to simulate the arrival of customers to a bank, and we can use random numbers to produce random arrival times for the customers. The Rnd() function takes no argument, and every time Rnd() is evaluated, it returns a different random fraction (greater than or equal to 0 and less than 1).

Example 4.4

Generating Random Numbers

In this example, we look at a procedure that generates random numbers ranging from 0 to 10. The event procedure is shown in Figure 4.11. Each time you click on cmdRandomTest, a new random number is computed and displayed. If you end execution and run the program again, you will see that it produces the same sequence each time the program is executed.

The repeated sequence is useful in some business simulations because repeatability allows you to check, and recheck, the result. But the repeated sequence is inappropriate in other situations. To make the computer produce a different sequence of random numbers each time the program runs, use the following statement:

> Randomize

This statement needs to be executed only once, before the first time Rnd() is executed. A good place for it is in the Load event procedure for the form.

FIGURE 4.11

Code for Example 4.4

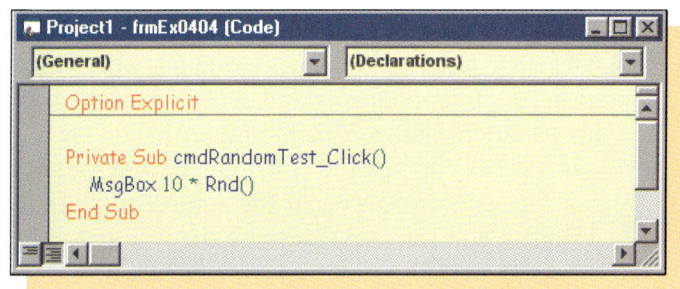

You might need to generate random integers that range between specific lower and upper limits. For example, you might need to generate random integers between 1 and 52 in a card game program. You can use the following expression for this:

Int((UpperBound − LowerBound + 1) * Rnd() + LowerBound)

As an example, the following statement stores a random integer in the range 1 to 52 (inclusive) in the variable RndCard.

RndCard = Int(52 * Rnd() + 1)

Avoiding Arithmetic Errors

Because of the inherent limitations of computer data types, your programs can produce mathematical errors if you do not write arithmetic expressions carefully. In this section we describe those limitations and note pitfalls you may encounter if you do not predict the results of your arithmetic expressions when designing your programs. We also describe programming practices that help you avoid these errors.

Overflow Errors

Recall that every numeric type has a largest possible value; for example, the largest value that can be stored in a variable of type Integer is 32767. **Overflow occurs when the computer attempts to store a number that is larger than the variable can hold.** Most commonly, it occurs because the result of an expression at run time is larger than the programmer anticipated when the type of the variable was chosen at design time. Every programmer encounters the overflow error from time to time, and it's best to get your initial experience with it in a small, simple program. It can occur with any type of numeric variable.

Example 4.5

Overflow

The objective of this example is to show an overflow error and how the computer reacts to it. In the event procedure shown in Figure 4.12, the user is asked to enter an integer, and the entered value is stored in the variable X. The variable X is then multiplied by 1000, and the result is stored in the variable Y.

What happens if the user enters the number 40 in the input box? The computer will store 40 in X and then evaluate the expression 1000 * X, which results in 40000. Because 40000 is greater than 32767 (the largest value that can be stored in a variable of type Integer), an overflow error occurs when this result is stored in the variable Y. The error message VB displays for overflow is shown in Figure 4.13.

FIGURE 4.12

Code for Example 4.5

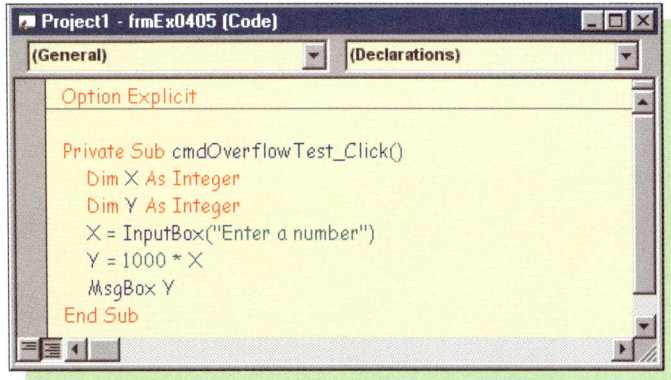

FIGURE 4.13

Overflow error message

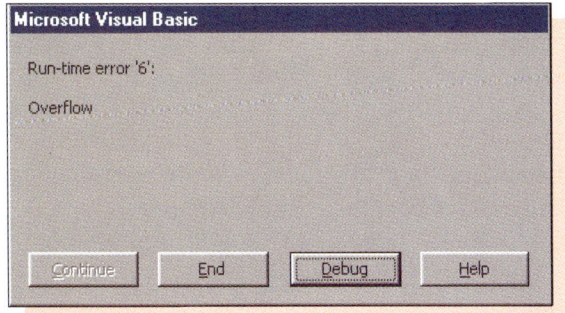

If you click the End button, execution terminates. If you click on Help, VB displays additional information to help you understand the nature of the problem. If you click on Debug, VB will switch to break mode, and you will see the Code window with the offending statement outlined. For more information on debugging, see Appendix A.

Roundoff Errors

Roundoff occurs when floating-point values or variables (types Single and Double) are used in a program, because the computer cannot represent certain base-10 fractions exactly in base-2 using a finite number of bits. Roundoff also occurs in manual computations. If you try to write the fraction 1/3 in base-10, the repeating fraction .3333333 . . . results. At some point you decide to stop writing 3s, and so the number you write is not exactly equal to 1/3.

Because the computer rounds off fractional amounts, sometimes a program produces results that are inaccurate.

Example 4.6

Roundoff

This example demonstrates how VB can produce an incorrect answer due to roundoff. Consider the event procedure in Figure 4.14. This Timer event procedure increases the value stored in the variable X by 0.01 and then displays the result in a Label control. This is analogous to counting pennies: as the Timer event occurs repeatedly the label *should* display the numbers 0.01, 0.02, 0.03, and so forth. However, by the tenth execution of the procedure, the label actually displays 0.09999999, and by the ninetieth execution it displays 0.8999994. This type of error might not be a problem in an application that estimates future sales, for example. However, most business programs that

FIGURE 4.14

Code for Example 4.6

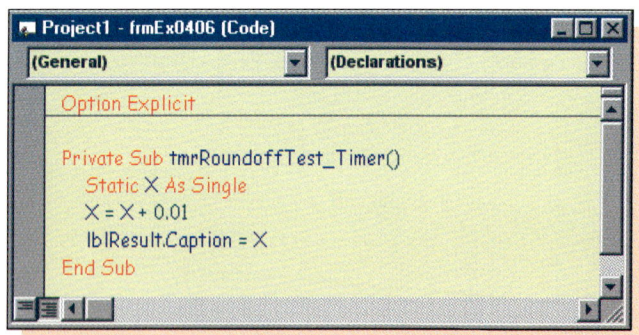

manipulate dollar amounts cannot tolerate errors like this. To correct the problem, VB provides the Currency data type. If you change the variable in this example to type Currency the roundoff error will not occur.

Problems Caused by Limited Significant Digits

In Chapter 3, Table 3.1 identified the *precision* of numeric data types and listed the number of *significant digits* for each type. The table also listed the range of each type. When performing arithmetic, the computer can process very large and very small numbers (range) but may not be able to keep all the digits due to limitations on the number of significant digits. For example, suppose that the U.S. national debt in 1993 was $4,407,351,498,474.15. This number can be stored exactly in a variable of type Currency. However, in a variable of type Single, it will be stored as 4.407351×10^{12}, which is equal to 4,407,351,000,000. This represents an error of $498,474.15!

We now look at an example that illustrates the loss of digits at run time.

Example 4.7

Significant Digits

This example adds two numbers and displays the result to ten digits. Figure 4.15 shows the code. Format$(), which is discussed later in this chapter, ensures that the exact value of Z, up to ten digits, will be displayed. The first message box produces the correct answer, 10,000,002. This is a little surprising,

FIGURE 4.15

Code for Example 4.7

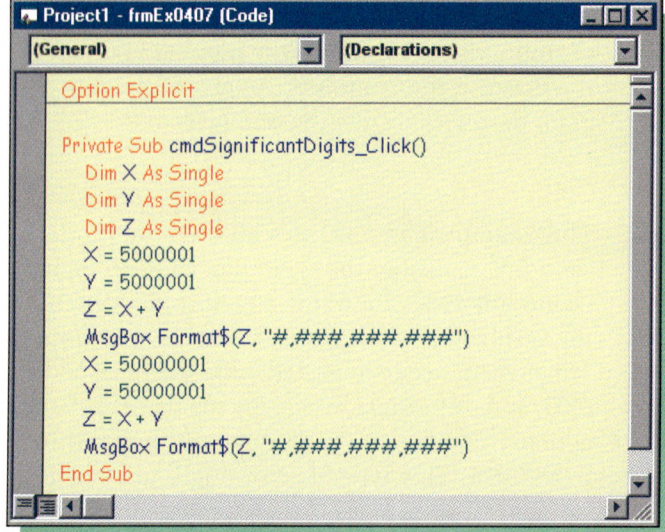

since the value 10,000,002 has eight significant digits while the variable Z, being type Single, generally represents at most seven significant digits. However, the second message box produces the answer 100,000,000—not the correct answer of 100,000,002. The value 100,000,002 has nine significant digits, which is too much for the variable Z. The digits that cannot be represented are replaced with zeros. No overflow error occurs because the range of type Single allows values up to 3.4×10^{38} and our answer is well below that limit.

If you are writing an accounting application that has to keep track of dollar amounts exactly (to the penny), and the amounts may be greater than 99999.99, then type Single will not work. Type Currency *will* work.

What is clearly a shortcoming of floating-point types in most business applications is actually a strength in many scientific applications and business simulations; the floating-point types automatically make a tradeoff between the size and the precision of the numbers they store. Type Single can store numbers much larger and much smaller than type Currency can. This is important when calculating physical quantities like the mass of the earth, 5.98×10^{24} kg. If a huge number like this is rounded off by a small amount, the result isn't going to cause geologists much of a problem. However, when you need extreme precision, you should be aware of the significant digits problem.

Converting Strings to Numbers: Val()

Occasionally a program will have a string data item that contains only digits and in fact represents a number. This happens, for example, if you display a number using a Label control: the label's Caption property is type String. As another example, you may prompt the user to enter a number via an input box: we have seen that when the user clicks on an input box's Cancel button, the InputBox() function returns the zero-length string. In order to avoid errors when performing arithmetic with these items, you should first convert them to numbers using the Val() function. As an example, Val("25") returns the numeric value 25. Similarly, if X is a variable of type String, and X holds the value "16", then Val(X) returns the numeric value 16.

The argument you provide to Val() must be string. However, if this string does not look like a number, Val() will still attempt to convert it to a number by proceeding from left to right until it encounters the first character that cannot possibly be part of a number. For example, Val("hello") returns the number 0, and Val("hello12.3") returns the number 0, but Val("12.3hello") returns the number 12.3. Also note that the Val() function returns the number 0 when its argument is the zero-length string.

Example 4.8 Converting Strings to Numbers

This example shows a procedure that fails because it tries to do arithmetic with string values. We then correct the problem using the Val() function.

The event procedure shown in Figure 4.16 computes the total number of customers by summing the number of customers in sales region A and sales region B. The user enters the two customer populations in response to the input boxes, and these values are displayed in Label controls. The values are then summed, and the result is displayed in another Label control. However, the program does not work correctly. If the user enters the value 10 for the number of customers in region A and 20 for the number of customers in region B,

FIGURE 4.16

Code for Example 4.8, which does not work correctly

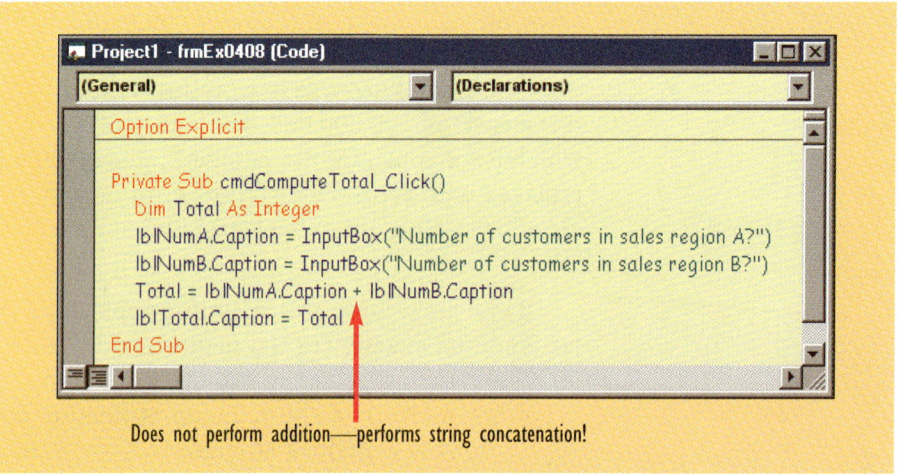

the total that is calculated and displayed in lblTotal.Caption is 1020—not the correct value of 30. Remember, the Caption property of Label controls is type String. The error is that when the values on both sides of the + operator are strings, VB concatenates the values instead of adding them.[5] The problem can be corrected using the Val() function as follows:

Total = Val(lblNumA.Caption) + Val(lblNumB.Caption)

If you modify the statement in the event procedure as above and execute it again it will work properly.

The failure of the code in Example 4.8 gives rise to the following programming convention:

> **Convention** Avoid using control properties in arithmetic expressions. In particular, use a label's Caption property only to display a value, not to hold a value that is needed in a calculation. Store numbers in numeric variables, and use these variables in arithmetic calculations as needed.

If we revise the event procedure in Example 4.8 using this convention, we obtain the following event procedure. Note that this revised event procedure does not require the Val() function.

```
Private Sub cmdComputeTotal_Click()
    Dim PopulationA As Integer
    Dim PopulationB As Integer
    Dim Total As Integer
    PopulationA = InputBox("Number of customers in sales region A?")
    PopulationB = InputBox("Number of customers in sales region B?")
    Total = PopulationA + PopulationB
    lblNumA.Caption = PopulationA
    lblNumB.Caption = PopulationB
    lblTotal.Caption = Total
End Sub
```

[5] VB does this to maintain consistency with older versions of the BASIC programming language. If one of the values (i.e., the value to the left or to the right of +) is numeric and one is string, then VB converts the string to a number and performs addition.

4.4 String Expressions

If you've worked with a word processing program to write letters or reports, you've experienced the manipulation of string data firsthand. For example, you've probably rearranged text by cutting and pasting and used commands to format the characters in your documents. In this section we describe how to manipulate strings using VB's string operators and functions. These operators and functions allow you to program a variety of tasks, such as displaying messages to users in an attractive manner or searching text for a given sequence of characters.

String Operators

The only string operator in VB is the & symbol, called the *string concatenation operator*. **To *concatenate* two values means to join them end-to-end, creating a single string.**

Operator Symbol	Name	Example Expression	Result
&	String concatenation	"ABC" & "123"	"ABC123"

The values to be concatenated can be any type (numeric or string), but the result of the concatenation operation will be a string. For example, if variable Num is type Integer and holds the number 123, then the result of the expression Num & " Elm St" will be the string value "123 Elm St".

The + operator actually does the same thing as & when used with strings, but you should avoid using + for this purpose because you can confuse it with the addition operator.

Example 4.9 Using String Concatenation

This example demonstrates string concatenation. It asks the user to enter his or her first name and then last name. The procedure uses the InputBox() function to obtain these values and stores them in string variables. The procedure then concatenates the strings, creating a new string in the form *LastName, FirstName,* and displays this result to the user in a message box. The code for this example is shown in Figure 4.17.

FIGURE 4.17

Code for Example 4.9

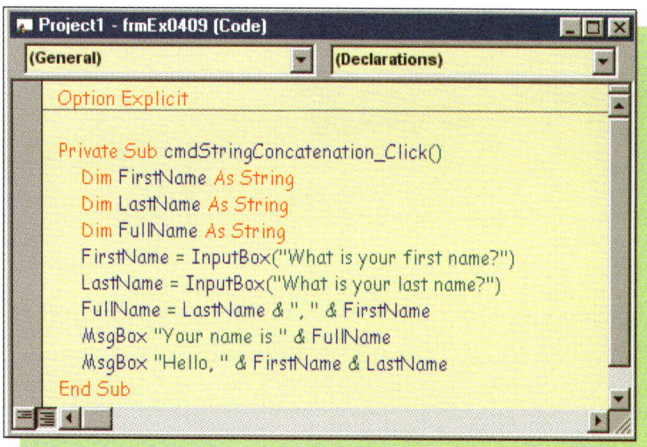

The example shows two MsgBox statements, both of which use string concatenation. This illustrates a common practice: programmers frequently want to display more than one data item in the message box, but the MsgBox statement allows only one expression for the message. Concatenating the data items produces a single value that can be displayed as the message.

EXERCISE 4.9

The message displayed by the second message box in Example 4.9 is unsatisfactory. Why is it unsatisfactory, and how can you fix it?

String Functions

The most frequently used string functions are listed in Table 4.5. Notice that some function names end with a $ symbol and others do not. This symbol is meaningful in VB: if a function name ends with $, then the function returns a string; if it does not end in $, then the function returns a number.

Some functions take more than one argument. The arguments must be placed in the correct order, separated by commas. For example, Left$("Theodolite", 4) works properly, but Left$(4, "Theodolite") does not, because the Left$() function requires its first argument to be string and its second argument to be numeric. Also, note that while many of our examples use constants as arguments, any expression of the correct type can be used as an argument.

TABLE 4.5 Common string functions

Function Name	Description	Example Expression	Result*
Val()	Convert string to number	Val("12a")	12
Str$()	Convert number to string	Str$(123.5)	"123.5"
Format$()	Convert with formatting	Format$(3.5, "$#.00")	"$3.50"
Left$()	Substring from left end	Left$("Theodolite", 4)	"Theo"
Right$()	Substring from right end	Right$("Theodolite", 4)	"lite"
Mid$()	Substring from interior	Mid$("Theodolite", 3, 4)	"eodo"
		Mid$("Theodolite", 4)	"odolite"
LCase$()	Convert to lowercase	LCase$("Phil Durt, Inc.")	"phil durt, inc."
UCase$()	Convert to uppercase	UCase$("Phil Durt, Inc.")	"PHIL DURT, INC."
LTrim$()	Trim spaces off left	LTrim$(" Hello ")	"Hello "
RTrim$()	Trim spaces off right	RTrim$(" Hello ")	" Hello"
Trim$()	Trim spaces off both	Trim$(" Hello ")	"Hello"
Len()	Length of string	Len("Theodolite")	10
String$()	Repeat character	String$(4, "A")	"AAAA"
InStr()	Substring search	InStr("arrows", "row")	3
Asc()	Convert char. to ANSI code	Asc("A")	65
Chr$()	Convert ANSI code to char.	Chr$(65)	"A"

*Note: All string results are shown enclosed in quotes. However, the quotes are not part of the result value.

Val() and Str$()

We discussed Val() in the preceding section. The Str$() function converts a numeric value to string. Thus, its action is the opposite of the Val() function. The Str$() function is needed only in a few relatively subtle situations, which we will not meet until later in the text. We include it here for completeness.

Format$()

In many programs, the programmer wants to control the appearance of values that are displayed on the user interface. For example, dollar amounts should appear as $1,234.50 (the usual format in the United States) instead of 1234.5. The Format$() function makes this easy. In its typical use, Format$() converts a numeric value to string and formats it. It takes two arguments: the first is the numeric value and the second is the format specification, which is type String. **The *format specification* specifies exactly how the result should appear.**

VB provides a number of predefined formats for common situations, including General Number, Currency, and Percent. Many business applications use the Currency format specification to format dollar amounts. (Note, however, that this format specification has no relationship to the standard data type of the same name.)

VB also provides *format characters* that you can use to construct your own custom specifications when none of the predefined formats is appropriate. These characters include the decimal separator (.), the thousands separator (,), and the digit place holders (# and 0). The # and 0 differ in how they treat leading and trailing zeros. See online help for more details (use search phrase "format function", then click on See Also on the ensuing help page for useful subtopics).

Now let's look at the use of format specifications in an example.

Example 4.10   **Using the Format$() Function**

This example asks the user to provide a numeric value and then displays a series of message boxes with this number formatted in different ways. If you execute the event procedure in Figure 4.18 several times, enter a different number (positive, negative, with and without fractional parts, large and small) each time and note the results.

Format$() can also be used to format strings, dates, and times. Again, use online help to learn about its full capabilities.

FIGURE 4.18

Code for Example 4.10

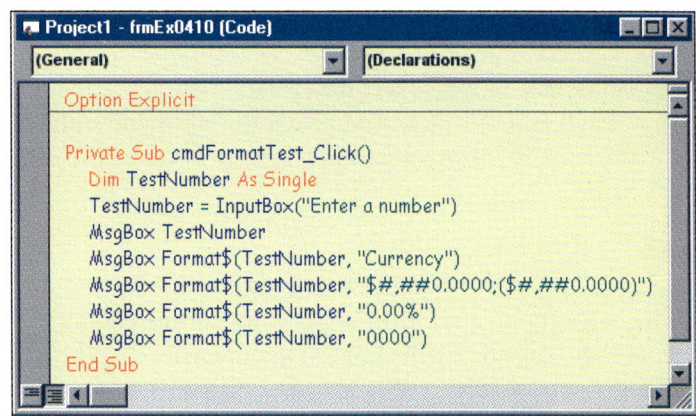

Left$(), Right$(), and Mid$()

In addition to joining strings, we often want to select portions of a string. In word processing, when you highlight a portion of a sentence or word for cutting or copying, you are selecting a substring. **A *substring* is a contiguous set of characters taken from another string.** To manipulate substrings in VB, you use the Left$(), Right$(), and Mid$() functions.

If the desired substring is located at an end of the given string, use Left$() or Right$(). These functions each require two arguments: the first argument is the given string, and the second argument is the number of characters in the desired substring. So Left$("Theodolite", 4) returns the left-most four characters from the string "Theodolite", that is, "Theo", and Right$("Theodolite", 4) returns the right-most four characters, "lite".

If the desired substring is somewhere in the middle of the string, use Mid$(). In its typical use, this function takes three arguments: the first is the given string, the second is the character position of the start of the desired substring, and the third is the number of characters in the desired substring. Thus, Mid$("Theodolite", 3, 4) says to start at character position 3 (the first "e") and extract four characters, "eodo".

When you want to extract a substring from the right end of the given string and you know the *starting character position* of the desired substring (instead of the *number of characters* in the desired substring) you can use Mid$() with just two arguments. Thus, Mid$("Theodolite", 4) returns the substring that starts at character position 4 (the "o") and extends to the right end: "odolite".

LCase$() and UCase$()

The LCase$() and UCase$() functions are useful for controlling the case of letters in string data items. Both of these functions require only one argument, which must be type String. As an example of their use, an application may require that a corporation's name be entered in all uppercase letters. Suppose that the user has already entered the corporation's name using a mix of lowercase and uppercase letters, and that this value has been stored in the variable CorpName. Then UCase$(CorpName) will return the name in all uppercase letters.

The LCase$() and UCase$() functions change only the letters in their argument. Other symbols such as punctuation, spaces, and digits remain unchanged in the return value.

LTrim$(), RTrim$(), and Trim$()

If you want to remove spaces from one or both ends of a string use the functions LTrim$(), RTrim$(), and Trim$(). LTrim$() removes spaces from the left end only, RTrim$() from the right end only, and Trim$() from both ends. Each of these functions takes only one argument, which must be type String.

Example 4.11

Trimming Spaces

The event procedure in Figure 4.19 demonstrates the effect of LTrim$(), RTrim$(), and Trim$(). If you run this example, the composer name in each message box will clearly illustrate what each function does (you should see the spaces before and after the composer's name get trimmed).

FIGURE 4.19

Code for Example 4.11

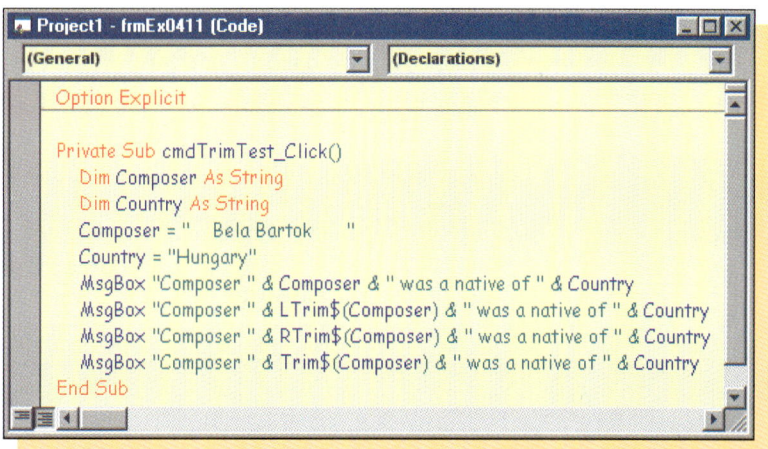

Len()

The Len() function takes as an argument a string and returns the number of characters in the string. Note that this count includes every character, including letters, digits, spaces, punctuation, and special characters. For example, Len("Quick, jump!") is 12.

String$()

The String$() function takes two arguments, a number and a single-character string, and returns a string consisting of the specified character repeated the specified number of times. For example, String$(80,"*") returns a string consisting of 80 asterisks.

InStr()

The InStr() function performs a string search operation. It takes two arguments: a *base string,* and a substring that we want to try to find within the base string. InStr() searches through the base string, proceeding from left to right, and stops when it encounters a match or reaches the end of the base string. If the search is successful, InStr() returns the character position at which the match was found; if unsuccessful, it returns the number 0.

For example, InStr("Eventful adventure","advent") returns the number 10, since the string "advent" occurs starting at position 10 in the first string (the base string); but InStr("Eventful adventure","venturi") returns the number 0.

Sometimes the second string occurs more than once in the base string. Using InStr() as described above you can find only the first occurrence. There is, however, a second form of InStr() that enables you to find all occurrences. This form takes three arguments: the first is the character position at which to start the search, the second is the base string, and the third is the substring to locate within the base. The search again proceeds through the base string from left to right, and stops when InStr() encounters a match or encounters the end of the base string.

For example, InStr(1, "Eventful adventure", "vent") returns the number 2, which is the first occurrence of "vent" that the search encounters when it begins the search at position 1. But InStr(3, "Eventful adventure", "vent") returns the value 12, which is the first occurrence of "vent" that the search encounters when it begins the search at position 3 (which is past the start of the first "vent" in

"Eventful"). Finally, InStr(13, "Eventful adventure", "vent") returns 0. Code similar to the following could be used to perform this multiple search:

```
FirstPos = InStr(1, "Eventful adventure", "vent")
SecondPos = InStr(FirstPos + 1, "Eventful adventure", "vent")
ThirdPos = InStr(SecondPos + 1, "Eventful adventure", "vent")
```

When this code is executed, FirstPos equals 2, SecondPos equals 12, and ThirdPos equals 0. Although this code works, it is not general; that is, it only works when trying to find the substring "vent" in the string "Eventful adventure" three times. A better solution uses string variables instead of string constants as the arguments. An even better solution would also search for the substring as many times as it might occur and not be limited to just three searches.

The searches are *case sensitive,* **meaning that they consider lowercase and uppercase letters to be different.** Thus, InStr("BAH!", "ah") returns 0 because "ah" is different from "AH". When using the three-argument form of InStr() you can make the search case insensitive by including the numeric constant 1 as a fourth argument. For example, InStr(1, "BAH!", "ah", 1) returns 2.

Example 4.12

Manipulating Names

The event procedure in Figure 4.20 uses the string functions Left$(), Mid$(), Trim$(), and InStr(). Its manipulation of first and last names is similar to, but more sophisticated than, what we saw in Example 4.9. The following diagram illustrates the situation when the user enters the name "Beethoven, Ludwig Van" in response to the input box. The InStr() function will find the comma at position 10.

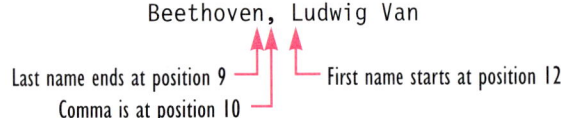

It then uses the position of the comma (CommaPos) to split the name into first name and last name.

Asc() and Chr$()

Internally, the computer represents string data as a sequence of numeric codes, with one code for each character in the string. The coding scheme used by VB,

FIGURE 4.20

Code for Example 4.12

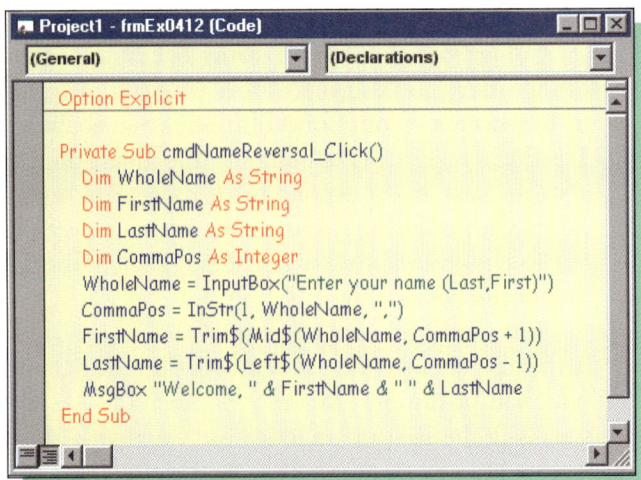

called ANSI, is shown in Table 4.6. **ANSI** stands for American National Standards Institute, the organization that devised this numeric coding scheme for string characters. The ANSI code has 256 different characters, numbered from 0 to 255. Why 0 to 255? Because that's as high as you can count in binary

TABLE 4.6 ANSI Code

0	null	32	space	64	@	96	`	128		160		192	À	224	à
1	soh	33	!	65	A	97	a	129		161	¡	193	Á	225	á
2	stx	34	"	66	B	98	b	130	,	162	¢	194	Â	226	â
3	etx	35	#	67	C	99	c	131	ƒ	163	£	195	Ã	227	ã
4	eot	36	$	68	D	100	d	132	,,	164	¤	196	Ä	228	ä
5	enq	37	%	69	E	101	e	133	…	165	¥	197	Å	229	å
6	ack	38	&	70	F	102	f	134	†	166	¦	198	Æ	230	æ
7	bell	39	'	71	G	103	g	135	‡	167	§	199	Ç	231	ç
8	backspace	40	(	72	H	104	h	136	ˆ	168	¨	200	È	232	è
9	tab	41	)	73	I	105	i	137	‰	169	©	201	É	233	é
10	lf	42	*	74	J	106	j	138	Š	170	ª	202	Ê	234	ê
11	vt	43	+	75	K	107	k	139	‹	171	«	203	Ë	235	ë
12	ff	44	,	76	L	108	l	140	Œ	172	¬	204	Ì	236	ì
13	cr	45	-	77	M	109	m	141		173	-	205	Í	237	í
14	so	46	.	78	N	110	n	142		174	®	206	Î	238	î
15	sI	47	/	79	O	111	o	143		175	¯	207	Ï	239	ï
16	dle	48	0	80	P	112	p	144		176	°	208	Ð	240	ð
17	dc1	49	1	81	Q	113	q	145	'	177	±	209	Ñ	241	ñ
18	dc2	50	2	82	R	114	r	146	'	178	²	210	Ò	242	ò
19	dc3	51	3	83	S	115	s	147	"	179	³	211	Ó	243	ó
20	dc4	52	4	84	T	116	t	148	"	180	´	212	Ô	244	ô
21	nak	53	5	85	U	117	u	149	•	181	µ	213	Õ	245	õ
22	syn	54	6	86	V	118	v	150	–	182	¶	214	Ö	246	ö
23	etb	55	7	87	W	119	w	151	—	183	·	215	×	247	÷
24	can	56	8	88	X	120	x	152	˜	184	¸	216	Ø	248	ø
25	em	57	9	89	Y	121	y	153	™	185	¹	217	Ù	249	ù
26	sub	58	:	90	Z	122	z	154	š	186	º	218	Ú	250	ú
27	escape	59	;	91	[	123	{	155	›	187	»	219	Û	251	û
28	fs	60	<	92	\	124	|	156	œ	188	¼	220	Ü	252	ü
29	gs	61	=	93	]	125	}	157		189	½	221	Ý	253	ý
30	rs	62	>	94	^	126	~	158		190	¾	222	Þ	254	þ
31	us	63	?	95	_	127	delete	159	Ÿ	191	¿	223	ß	255	ÿ

using only eight bits. The ANSI code uses one byte (eight bits) to represent each character.

The characters in positions 0 through 31 of the ANSI table are *nonprintable characters,* **which, as their name implies, cannot be printed or displayed** (for example, in a label) **but which control certain computer operations.** Table 4.6 shows short descriptive names (blue) for each of the nonprintable characters. For example, the character at position 7, *bell,* makes your computer emit a beep.

The Asc() function takes as its argument a single-character string, and returns the character's numeric code using the ANSI table. For example, Asc("a") returns the number 97. Why is this function named Asc()? Because the predecessor to the ANSI code was ASCII (American Standard Code for Information Interchange). The ASCII code uses only seven bits, and can therefore represent only 128 characters. In fact, the first half of the ANSI code is identical to the ASCII code.[6]

The Chr$() function does the opposite of Asc(): it takes a number as its argument and returns the character that resides at that position in the ANSI table. For example, Chr$(65) returns the string "A".

Now let's look at three examples that demonstrate how the Chr$() and Asc() functions help us manipulate strings in our programs.

Example 4.13 Using Carriage Return and Line Feed

In the early days of computing, people used teletype machines to interact with the computer. These devices were much like typewriters in that they had a printing mechanism—called the *carriage*—that moved across the paper from left to right. When the user pressed the key labeled RETURN, the carriage would return to the left edge of the paper and the paper would be advanced one line. The terms used to describe these actions were *carriage return* and *line feed.* Although your computer screen does not have a carriage, these terms are still used. **Carriage return means move the screen cursor to the left of the text field, and** *line feed* **means move down one row in the text field.**

Carriage return and line feed are supported by two nonprintable ANSI characters. The carriage return, abbreviated *cr,* has numeric code 13, and the line feed, *lf,* has numeric code 10. Together, these characters make it possible to display multiple lines in a message box or label caption, as illustrated by the event procedure in Figure 4.21.

Because the carriage return and line feed characters are nonprintable, the only way of specifying them in expressions is to use the Chr$() function. The message box displayed by this example is shown in Figure 4.22.

Example 4.14 Using Multiple-Line Messages and vbCrLf

Because programmers frequently need to use the carriage return/line feed combination, VB provides a predefined constant named vbCrLf whose value is equal to Chr$(13) & Chr$(10). This example demonstrates the use of this constant. It embellishes the two-line message in Example 4.13 using the String$() function, as shown in Figure 4.23. The function String$(25,"*") generates a string

---

[6] This is not the end of the character code evolution. There is a 16-bit international code, called Unicode, which represents 65,536 different characters. Unicode is useful for languages whose alphabets contain far more than 26 letters.

FIGURE 4.21

Code for Example 4.13

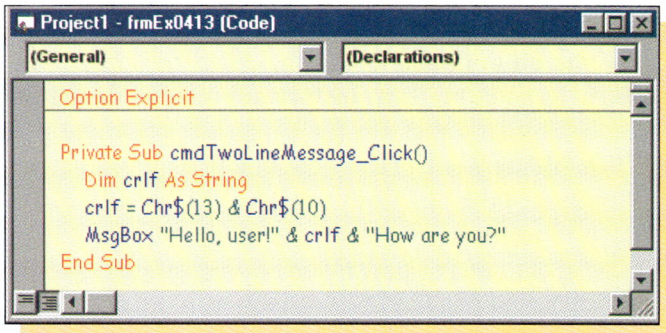

FIGURE 4.22

Message box with two lines created using carriage return and line feed

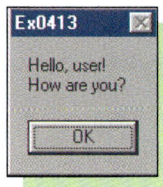

FIGURE 4.23

Code for Example 4.14

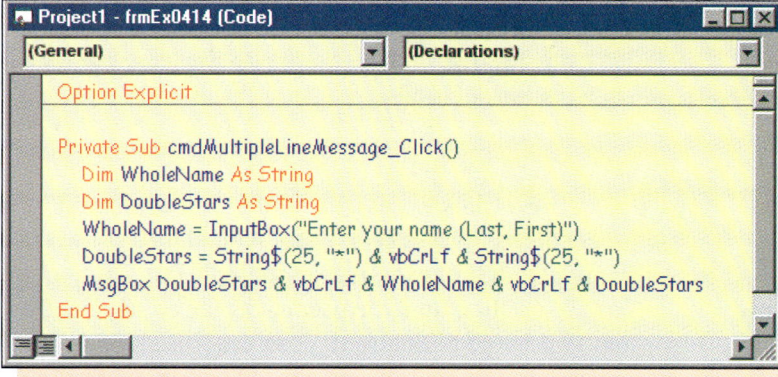

FIGURE 4.24

Example 4.14 message box

consisting of 25 asterisks. The message box displayed by this example when the user enters "Beethoven, Ludwig Van" is shown in Figure 4.24.

Example 4.15 Using Simple Encryption

As an example of the power of the Asc() and Chr$() functions, consider the problem of encrypting messages. An *encrypted message* **is a message that has been encoded into a different set of characters**. One reason for encryption is to protect the privacy of a message during transmission. The encrypted message will be unintelligible to anyone who gains access to it but does not know the coding scheme. Businesses use encryption when sending sensitive data such as financial transactions over a network.

The encryption procedure transforms the original message, called *plaintext*, into an unintelligible form, called *ciphertext*. The sender and receiver agree in advance on the transformation method, and the recipient must, of course, be able to transform the ciphertext back into plaintext. The transformation method must be clever enough that a third party, who isn't told the details of the method, can't easily *decipher* the cipher (i.e., transform the ciphertext back into plaintext).

One of the first encryption methods ever devised is called the *Caesar cipher*. In this method each letter in the plaintext is shifted by three positions in the alphabet; i.e., "A" is changed to "D", "B" to "E", etc. This is easily accomplished using the Asc() and Chr$() functions along with a simple addition operation as illustrated in Figure 4.25.

Each time procedure cmdCaesarCipher_Click is executed, the user is asked to enter a letter. This letter is concatenated to the Caption property of the label lblPlaintext. Then the letter is converted to its ANSI code, which is then increased by 3 and converted back into an ANSI character, and this converted character is concatenated to the Caption property of the label lblCiphertext.

There is nothing special about the number 3; as long as both the sender and receiver agree in advance on the number, any shift amount will work. Knowing the shift amount, the receiver can easily transform the ciphertext back into plaintext.

EXERCISE 4.10 Write a Click event procedure for a command button that shortens the value displayed by a Label control named lblTest by removing one character from its right end. For example, suppose lblTest.Caption initially holds the value "visual". The first time the user clicks the command button, the value in lblTest.Caption should be changed to "visua"; the second time the user clicks the command button, lblTest.Caption should be changed to "visu"; the third time "vis"; and so on.

Your event procedure should work regardless of the value initially displayed by lblTest. You can assume the user will not click the command button if the value in lblTest.Caption is the zero-length string.

EXERCISE 4.11 Repeat Exercise 4.10, but make your event procedure remove the character from the left end instead of the right end. For example, if lblTest.Caption holds the value "visual" before the user clicks the command button, then it should hold the value "isual" after the user clicks the command button.

FIGURE 4.25

Code for Example 4.15

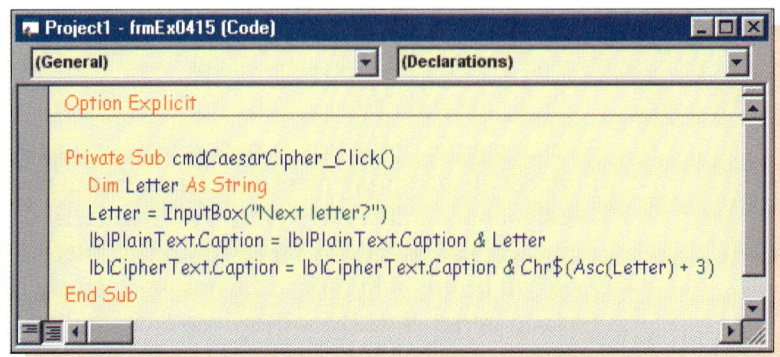

EXERCISE 4.12 What is the length of the zero-length string, Len("")?

EXERCISE 4.13 In cmdCaesarCipher_Click in Example 4.15, what happens if the user enters more than one letter in response to the input box? Run the example to find out.

EXERCISE 4.14 Write an event procedure that performs the inverse operation of cmdCaesarCipher_Click in Example 4.15. That is, the user should enter the letters in ciphertext, and your event procedure should display the corresponding plaintext letters.

EXERCISE 4.15 In cmdCaesarCipher_Click (Example 4.15), what characters are the letters X, Y, and Z transformed into?

EXERCISE 4.16 Modify cmdCaesarCipher_Click (Example 4.15) so it performs a cyclic shift. That is, it should transform X into A, Y into B, and Z into C, and all other letters should still be shifted up by three characters.

EXERCISE 4.17 Modify your solution to Exercise 4.16 so that it still performs a cyclic shift, but the amount of the shift is given by a symbolic constant named SHIFTAMOUNT. For example, if SHIFTAMOUNT is equal to 4, then W, X, Y, and Z should be transformed into A, B, C, and D, respectively, and all other letters should be shifted up by four characters. Your event procedure should work properly for any value of SHIFTAMOUNT between 1 and 25.

EXERCISE 4.18 Suppose we wanted to modify the cmdCaesarCipher_Click event procedure (Example 4.15) to allow the user to enter the whole plaintext string in response to the input box instead of entering a single letter at a time. We have not seen all the VB statements to make this possible. Write down instructions you would give to an assistant to perform this task manually using the ANSI table and pencil and paper. Be specific—assume the assistant can follow directions precisely but doesn't have the ability to fill in any missing information in your instructions.

4.5 The Text Box Control

We now turn our attention away from expressions and focus on a new VB control. You have probably filled out forms (financial aid forms, scholarship forms, tax forms, college admissions forms) that required you to fill in information in specific boxes on the form. The *Text box control* allows the user to type a value in the text box. Unlike an input box, the control does not "disappear" after the user enters the value. It stays visible so the user can see what is entered and change it if necessary.

Appearance and Use

Visually, a text box appears as a rectangle. Figure 4.26 identifies the Text box tool and shows a Text box control on the form at design time. At run time, the user selects a text box either by tabbing to it or by positioning the mouse pointer over the rectangle, then clicking the mouse. VB acknowledges this action by placing a text cursor (a flashing vertical line) in the rectangle. Called

FIGURE 4.26

Text box tool and control

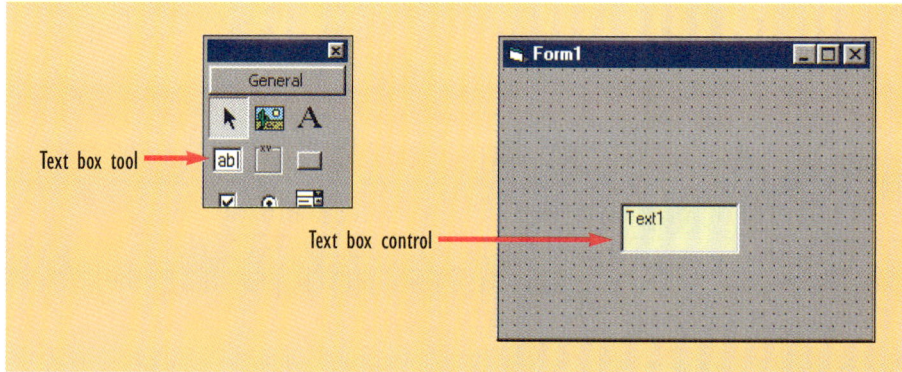

the *insertion point,* this flashing cursor indicates where the next character typed by the user will be displayed.

Focus

The flashing text cursor is a visual cue to the user that the text box has the *focus,* **meaning it has been selected and will now accept characters from the keyboard**. A form may have several text boxes, but only one text box can have the focus at any given time. The user can give the focus to a specific text box by clicking on it with the mouse or pressing the TAB key. Program statements can also give the focus to a specific text box.

Understanding the concept of focus is critical for writing code in an event-driven environment like VB. You can think of focus as specifying the currently active control, that is, the control that the user can interact with using the mouse or the keyboard. In fact, several types of controls other than the Text box control are capable of receiving the focus, but only one control on the form can have the focus at any given time.

Properties

Table 4.7 lists some of the properties of the Text box control. We will discuss other Text box properties later in the text.

Convention Use the prefix "txt" for the names of Text box controls.

Example 4.16 The Text Box's Text Property

This example demonstrates how the user can enter data using a text box. The user interface for this example is shown in Figure 4.27. The Text property of the text box is similar to the Caption property of a label—it stores the value the user sees on the user interface. The difference is that the user can change the value in a text box but not the value displayed by a label. Every time the user changes the value in the text box, VB automatically saves this value in the text box's Text property.

The Text property can also be set by statements in code. Event procedure cmdClearTextBox_Click in Figure 4.28 demonstrates code that changes a text box's Text property. If you run the example, type your name in the text box, and then click the Copy to Label button. Your name should now be in both the text box and the label. Enter a different name in the text box, then click the Clear Text Box button. When the zero-length string is assigned to the Text property, it appears to the user as if the contents of the text box are erased.

TABLE 4.7 Properties of the Text box control

Property	Setting
Text	*The text that is displayed in the text box.* Characters are displayed in the text box as the user types them, and they are also saved in the text box's Text property.
BorderStyle	*Whether or not a rectangle appears as the border of the text box.* The two possible settings are 0 - None and 1 - Fixed Single.
Enabled	*Whether or not the text box can receive the focus* (that is, whether or not it can accept user input).
MaxLength	*The maximum number of characters the text box will accept.* If MaxLength is set to 0, the limit will be about 32,000.
MultiLine	*Whether or not the text will be "wrapped" onto multiple lines if the amount of typed text exceeds the width of the text box.*
Alignment	*Whether the text will be displayed left justified, right justified, or centered in the text box.* MultiLine must be set to True in order for the alignment setting to take effect.
ScrollBars	*Whether the text box will have horizontal scroll bars, vertical scroll bars, or both.* This is useful if MultiLine is True and the Text property is likely to hold more characters than the text box can display given its width and height.
TabStop	*Whether or not the user can tab to the text box* (i.e., whether or not the text box can receive the focus as the result of the user pressing the TAB key).
TabIndex	*The position of the text box in the "tab cycle."* When a form becomes active, VB automatically gives the focus to the control with the lowest TabIndex. When the user presses the TAB key, the focus jumps to the control with the next highest TabIndex (if there is no control with a higher TabIndex setting, the focus jumps back to the control with the lowest TabIndex setting).

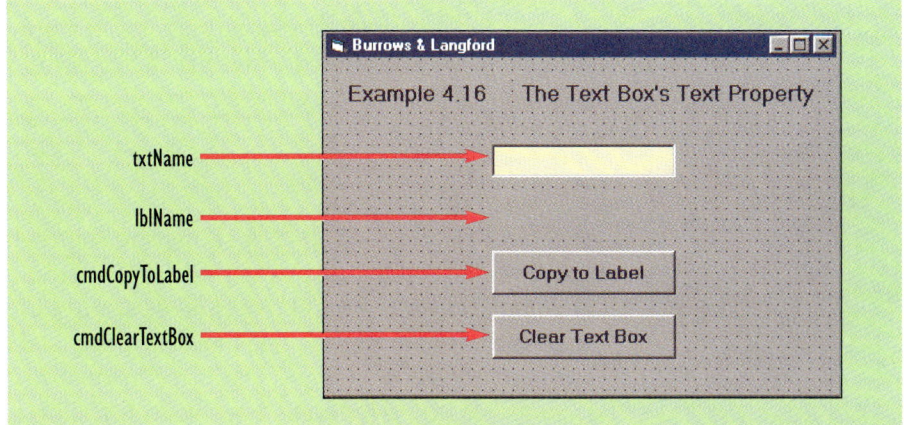

FIGURE 4.27

Form and controls for Example 4.16

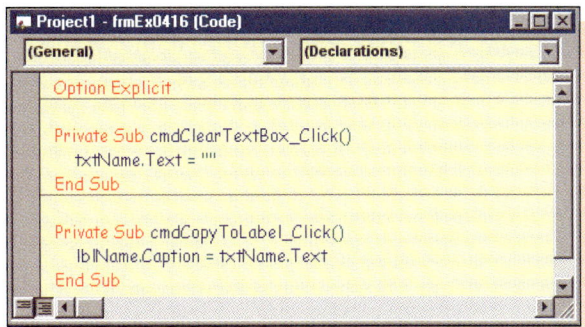

FIGURE 4.28

Code for Example 4.16

You can also use this program without using the mouse as follows.

1. Press [TAB], if necessary, to move the focus to the text box. Type your name.
2. Press [TAB] once to move the focus to the Copy to Label command button. Then press [ENTER] instead of clicking the mouse.
3. Press [TAB] once to move the focus to the Clear Text Box command button. Then press [ENTER] instead of clicking the mouse.
4. Press [TAB] once to move the focus back to the text box, then type a value, then repeat steps 2 through 4!

Also try pressing [SHIFT]+[TAB] instead of [TAB], and note that the tab direction reverses.

This example shows how the text box can be used for obtaining user input without writing any event procedures for it. The user can enter values, make changes, and, when satisfied, click a command button to initiate processing of the data.

Events

The text box is capable of responding to several events. In this section we discuss only one of these, the Change event. We examine others when we revisit the text box in Chapter 6.

The *Change event* occurs whenever the value of the text box's Text property changes. This happens every time the user types a character into the text box. For example, assume a text box currently has the word "computer" stored in it, and the insertion point is just to the right of the "r". If the user presses [BACKSPACE], the "r" is erased. This generates a Change event because the text box now stores the word "compute", which is different from "computer". The Change event is useful in situations, for example, where a value should be automatically recomputed whenever the content of the text box changes. This is demonstrated in Example 4.17.

Example 4.17 — The Change Event

The form for this example is shown in Figure 4.29. It has two text boxes (txtPrice and txtQuantity) and one Label control (lblCost). The user enters a price into one of the text boxes and a quantity into the other, and the cost is automatically computed (price times quantity) and displayed in the label. If the user subsequently changes the price or quantity, the cost is automatically recomputed and displayed. The event procedures are shown in Figure 4.30.

If you run the example, entering various values in the text boxes and changing them, you may notice a behavior that you regard as undesirable. For example, suppose that txtPrice contains the text 12, and txtQuantity contains the text 100. The label lblCost shows a cost of $1,200.00. Assume you want to change the price from 12 to 130. If you press [BACKSPACE], the Price text box will change to 1, and the Cost label will change to $100. If you then type a 3 in the Price text box, the cost will show $1,300.00. When you enter the final 0 in the Price text box, the cost will show $13,000.00. While the final cost value is accurate, it might be alarming for the user to see the cost value change with every keystroke. We'll see a way of avoiding this type of behavior in Chapter 6 when we study the Text box control in greater depth.

FIGURE 4.29

Form and controls for Example 4.17

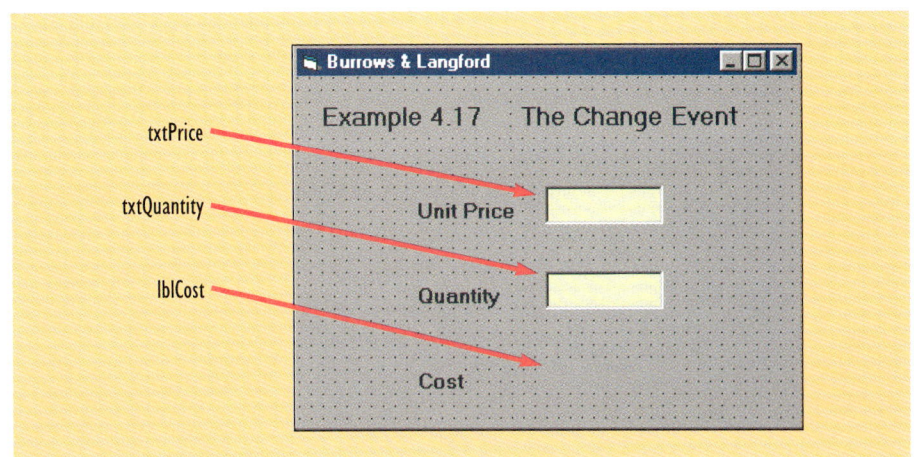

FIGURE 4.30

Code for Example 4.17

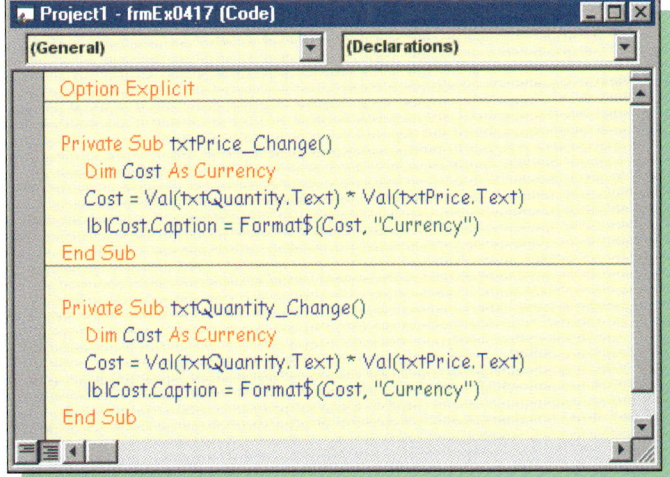

EXERCISE 4.19 In Example 4.17, what happens if you enter $4.55 (with the dollar sign) in the Price text box? Explain why this happens.

EXERCISE 4.20 Example 4.17 described the undesirable behavior of the cost value changing every time the user presses a key. This happens because the Change event occurs every time the value in the text box changes. Describe in words a new event that you could use to correct this behavior. That is, describe the user action that should cause the cost value to be recomputed. This new event should occur for the Text box control, so that you do not have to add another control (e.g., a command button) for the user to initiate the calculation.

4.6 Project 6: A Present Value Calculator

This project uses arithmetic expressions, string expressions, and text boxes to create a present value calculator. It also addresses the issue of testing, that is, verifying that the project works correctly before giving the finished application to the user.

Present value **is a measure of the value of a future cash flow in today's dollars.** To see why this measure is useful, consider the choice you'd make if someone offered you $1,000 today or $1,000 a year from now. If you accept the

$1,000 today, you can deposit it in an interest-bearing account or invest it—and a year from now you'll have more than $1,000. The difference in the value of money over time is measured by present value. Financial analysts often use present value to compare investments offering different payments over time to determine which is the most profitable.

The present value calculator we develop in this section answers the question, "What amount would you have to invest today in order to accumulate a given amount in the future?" The user has to input the time period of the investment, the interest rate, and **the amount of money to be accumulated, called the** *future value*.

Description of the Application

The form for this application appears in Figure 4.31. The user first enters values into the text boxes for Future Value, Annual Interest Rate, and Number of Years, then clicks the Compute PV button. The computer uses the input values to calculate the present value (PV) using the following formula:

$$PV = \frac{FV}{(1 + r)^n}$$

where: *FV* is the future value.
 r is the periodic interest rate.
 n is the number of compounding periods.

For this project, we assume that interest is compounded monthly. This assumption means that the periodic interest rate (*r*) is one-twelfth the annual interest rate, and the number of compounding periods (*n*) is twelve times the number of years. When finished using the application, the user clicks the Exit button to end execution.

Design of the Application

As always, before beginning construction of the project you have to make some decisions regarding controls, properties, constants, variables, and scope. Figure 4.32 shows property settings for the controls on the form.

Since all calculations are performed in a single event procedure (Compute PV) all constants and variables in the project can be local to that event procedure. Are any constants needed? Most data are input by the user. Because interest is compounded monthly, some of the calculations will involve a factor of 12. We can represent this factor by a symbolic constant, and a good name for it is NUMBEROFPERIODSPERYEAR.

FIGURE 4.31

User interface for Project 6

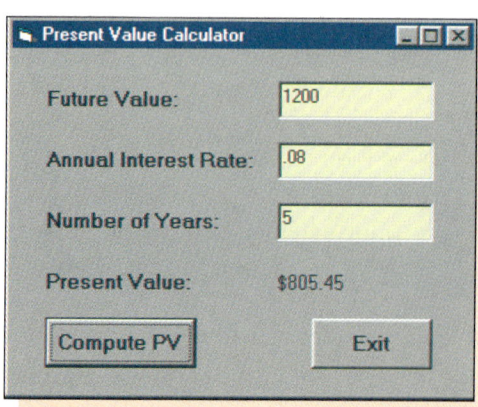

FIGURE 4.32

Present value calculator controls

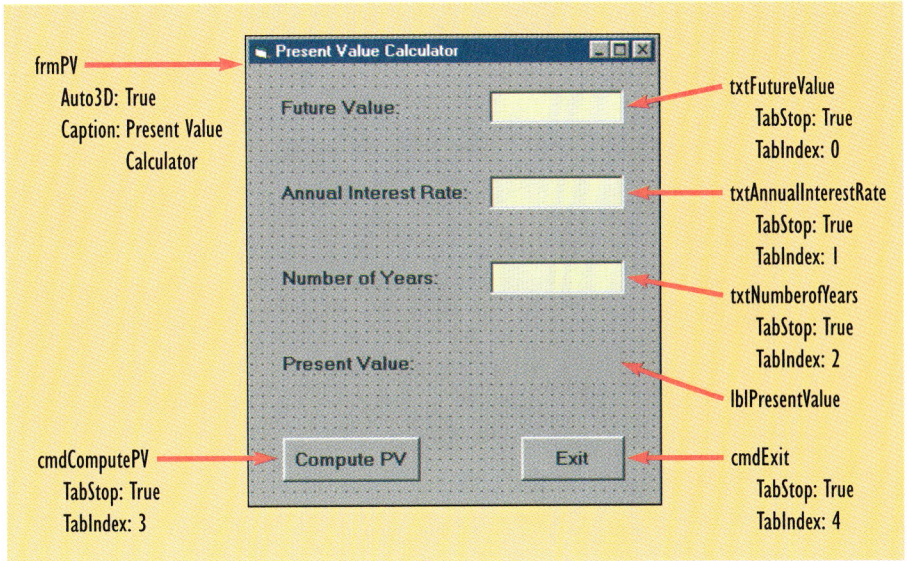

What variables are needed? Use a variable for each quantity involved in the calculation (i.e., for each quantity in the present value formula). Table 4.8 shows good names and types for these variables. Why does the table recommend type Single for the interest rate variable? It must allow for a fractional part; for example, if the annual interest rate is 8 percent, then the periodic interest rate would be 0.08 / 12, or 0.006666. . . . If we store this quantity in a variable of type Currency, it will be stored as 0.0067, which in turn corresponds to an annual interest rate of 12 * 0.0067, or 8.04 percent. Using type Single will reduce this discrepancy.

Construction of the Application

As always, start the project by creating a new folder in which to save it. As you proceed, be sure to save periodically.

Open a new project and place the controls on the form. Arrange the controls and set their properties as in Figure 4.32. Next, create the Click event procedure for the Exit button. This event procedure should contain the single statement, End, which simply causes execution to terminate.

Run the program and verify that the TAB key moves the focus from control to control and that clicking the Exit button causes the program to terminate. You can change the TabIndex property of a control if you want to change its position in the tab cycle.

Next, create the Click event procedure for the Compute PV button (see Figure 4.33). This procedure calculates the interest rate and the number of periods, then stores the future value in its variable, and then calculates the present

TABLE 4.8 Variables in the present value calculator

Variable Name	Type
PresentValue	Currency
FutureValue	Currency
InterestRate	Single
NumberOfPeriods	Integer

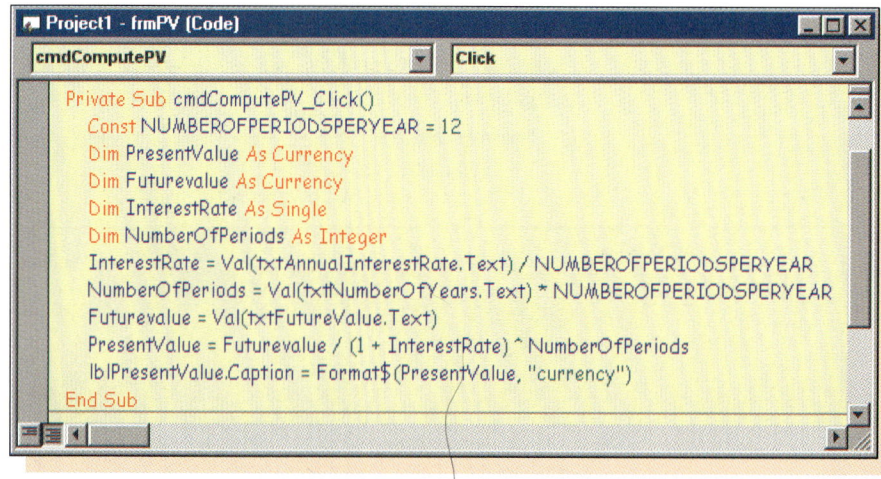

FIGURE 4.33

Click event procedure for the Compute PV button

value using the present value formula. Finally, it displays the present value formatted as a dollar amount. After you've completed this event procedure, run the program and verify that it works properly.

Testing the Application

It is always important to test a program thoroughly before users start to rely on it. How can you be sure the present value displayed by your program is correct? The calculations are complicated enough that you shouldn't take this for granted.

One way to test this program is to compare the results it produces with results produced by another program that is known to be correct. You might, for example, have a spreadsheet or calculator that performs the same calculation. For simple problems like this, you can also compute some answers by hand.

If you don't have another program to use as a check, you should at least perform some commonsense checks. You can usually develop checks like this by examining the formulas used in the calculations. Table 4.9 shows some simple checks that were derived from the present value formula. For example, the last check simply means that if the interest rate is high and the number of compounding periods is high, then the present value will be low.

A final comment regarding testing and user-friendliness is in order. Users commonly expect to see interest rates in two different forms: as decimal numbers (0.12) or as percentages (12 percent). The user interface shown in Figure 4.31 does not tell the user which form to use. If the expressions in your event procedure assume one form and the user employs the other form, the computed result will be incorrect.

TABLE 4.9 Tests for verifying present value calculations

	Input Values		Result
Future Value	Annual Interest Rate	Number of Years	Present Value
1	0	1	1
1	1	0	1
1	12	.08333	Approximately 0.5
1	1	100	Almost 0

A well-designed user interface accepts all reasonable input, or else informs the user of the required format of values. It also displays error messages when the user fails to provide data in a format that the program can accept. We will see how to program these checks in later chapters.

EXERCISE 4.21 Modify Project 6 so that the number of compounding periods per year (assumed to be 12) is an additional value supplied by the user. That is, allow the user to specify the number of compounding periods in a year.

4.7 Logical Expressions

Almost all computer programs have to perform tasks that involve selecting an action from several alternative actions. For example, depending on the value of an account balance, a billing program might have to select an action that would cause an overdue-payment notice to be sent. And depending on the number of hours worked, a payroll program might have to pay a higher rate for some of the hours (overtime hours). Logical expressions, as mentioned earlier, are used in programs to evaluate the conditions (account balance overdue or hours greater than 40) that dictate the correct action to select. In this section we examine logic operations, and we will see their full utility in Chapter 5.

A logical expression has the form of a True/False question, and its result is numeric; specifically, the result is always either the number –1, which represents the True outcome, or the number 0, which represents the False outcome. The simplest logical expressions use *comparison operators* **to compare one value to another.** More powerful logical expressions can be formed by using *logical operators* **to combine results from comparisons.**

Comparison Operators

The comparison operators, which compare two expressions, are shown in Table 4.10. The result of a comparison is always either –1 or 0, but for readability, VB allows you to use the keyword True in place of the constant –1 and the keyword False in place of the constant 0.

Most often programmers use comparison operators to compare two variables or a variable and a constant. It's unlikely that you would see the comparison 2 < 3 in an actual program, because the programmer knows in advance that this expression is True, so there's no reason to make the computer evaluate it.

As an example of a useful comparison, consider the following: Price < 10. As with any expression containing variables, to evaluate this expression the computer will first retrieve the value stored in the variable Price. If this value is less than 10, the result of the expression is True; otherwise it is False.

If you compare one numeric value to another numeric value, the result is the same as in algebra; for example, the expression 2 < 3 is True. You can compare a string value to a numeric value if the string value has the form of a number; in this case, VB converts the string value to numeric before performing the comparison. Thus, the expression "2" < 3 is True. However, if you attempt to compare a string value to a numeric value and the string value does not have the form of a number, VB generates the *type mismatch* run time error. For example, the expression "2a" < 3 is a type mismatch.

Comparing two string values is a little more complicated than comparing two numeric values.

TABLE 4.10 Comparison operators

Operator Symbol	Name	Example* Expression	Result
<	Less than	A < B B < B	True False
<=	Less than or equal to	B <= B B <= -4	True False
>	Greater than	-2 > B C > A	False True
>=	Greater than or equal to	A >= A A >= 5	True False
=	Equal to	B = B B = C	True False
<>	Not equal to	B <> B B <> C	False True

*Assume numeric variables A, B, and C have been declared and contain the values 2, 3, and 4, respectively.

Comparison of Strings

Strings are ranked alphabetically, much as words are arranged in a dictionary. There are, however, some differences between VB's dictionary order and what you might think of as dictionary order. These differences are a result of the way VB interprets uppercase and lowercase letters and nonletter symbols. These are treated according to the ANSI table. In technical language, we say that the ANSI code defines VB's *collating sequence*—the idea of an alphabetical order extended to include all 256 symbols of the ANSI table.

To compare two string values, VB first compares the first character of one to the first character of the other. If they are not equal, then the smaller string value is the one whose first character has the lower ANSI value. If they are equal, then VB compares the second character from one string to the second character of the other string. If these characters are not equal, then the smaller string value is the one whose second character has the lower ANSI value. If they are equal, then VB compares the third character from one string to the third character of the other string, and so on.

This process can end in three ways. In the first case, VB finds the first instance (from the left) where corresponding characters in the two strings are different, and identifies the smaller of the two strings accordingly. This case would arise in the comparison of "VISIBLE" to "VISUAL"; the first three characters are identical, but the fourth characters differ, and since "I" comes before "U" in the ANSI table, "VISIBLE" is less than "VISUAL".

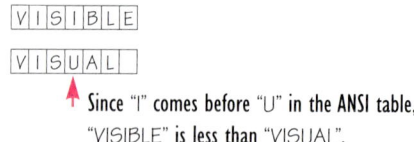

↑ Since "I" comes before "U" in the ANSI table, "VISIBLE" is less than "VISUAL".

In the second case, VB reaches the end of one string (no more characters) before identifying any different characters and before reaching the end of the other string. This would arise in the comparison of "VISUAL" to "VISUALLY"; the first string is six characters long, the first six characters of the two strings are identical, and the second string is longer than six characters. In this case, the shorter string is the lesser of the two.

```
V I S U A L
V I S U A L L Y
```
↑ Since all characters of the first string match the second string, the shorter one is the lesser of the two: "VISUAL" is less than "VISUALLY".

In the third case, VB reaches the end of both strings at the same time without identifying any different characters. An example of this case is the comparison of "HELLO, USER" to "HELLO, USER". In this case the strings are equal.

```
H E L L O ,   U S E R
H E L L O ,   U S E R
```
↑ The ends of both strings are encountered at the same time with no difference in characters. These strings are equal.

Finally, note that *every* character, including spaces, digits, punctuation marks, and other special symbols, is used in string comparisons, and the case of the letters (lowercase versus uppercase) counts. For example, the string "lex icon" is less than the string "lexi con" because the space character (position 32 in the ANSI table) comes before the "i" (position 105) in the ANSI table. Note also that all uppercase letters appear before all lowercase letters in the ANSI table. Thus, for example, "SMALL" is less than "small".

The Boolean Data Type

◆ ◆ ◆

To help clarify code involving logical expressions VB provides the Boolean standard data type.[7] The only two values that can be stored in variables of type Boolean are –1 and 0 or, equivalently, True and False. Variables of type Boolean are useful for storing the results of logical expressions.

Example 4.18

True and False

You can make a logical expression easier to interpret by storing its result in a descriptively named variable of type Boolean. Figure 4.34 shows an event procedure that illustrates this point. The variable Price is set equal to a random number ranging from 5 to 14.9999. Remember that the Rnd() function returns a value less than 1 and greater than or equal to 0. The logical expression Price < 10 will be True if the value stored in Price is less than 10. Otherwise the logical expression will be False. The result is stored in the variable GoodPrice, so GoodPrice will be True if Price is less than 10. That is, Price < 10 means that you got a good price.

Example 4.19

Assignment versus Equality Comparison

Assignment statements with comparison operators can sometimes look a little confusing, because in VB the equal sign plays two roles: *assignment* operator and *equality comparison* operator. Consider the event procedure in Figure 4.35, which is entirely valid.

---

[7] The Boolean data type was omitted from the discussion of standard data types in Section 3.3 for simplicity.

FIGURE 4.34

Code for Example 4.18

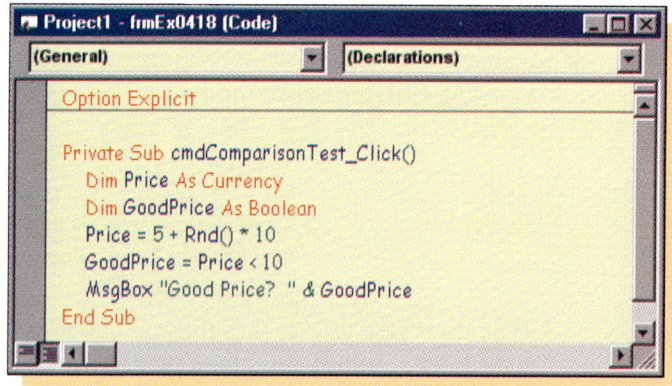

Any statement that begins with a variable (or control property) followed by an equal sign is an assignment statement, and the first (i.e., left-most) equal sign in an assignment statement is always the assignment operator. Everything to the right of the assignment operator is the expression, and any equal sign in an expression is a comparison operator. So the assignment statement in Figure 4.35 is perfectly valid. However, you can write it more clearly by using parentheses:

ExactlyTwenty = (Age = 20)

Example 4.20

Type Mismatch

You can compare numbers and strings if the string has the form of a valid number. In this case, VB converts the string to a number—similar to the way the Val() function works—and does a numeric comparison. However, if the string does not contain a valid number, VB will report the type mismatch error. Look at the procedure in Figure 4.36. If you enter a valid number in response to the input box, then the logical expression Age < 20 works just fine even though the variable Age is type String. However, if you enter a response such as "twenty one" in the input box, then a type mismatch occurs.

EXERCISE 4.22

What does the message box display?

```
Private Sub cmdZeroLengthStringTest_Click()
    Dim X As String
    Dim Y As Boolean
    Y = (X = "")
    MsgBox Y
End Sub
```

FIGURE 4.35

Code for Example 4.19

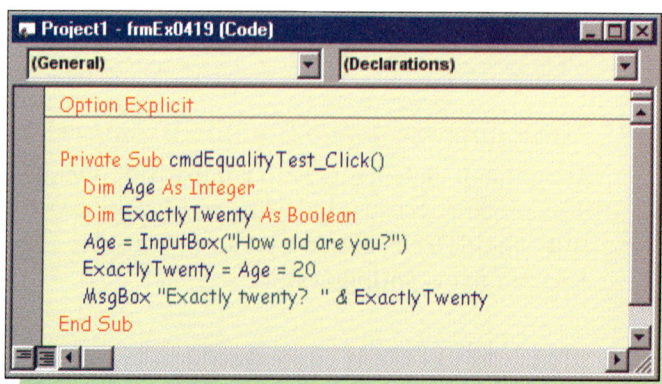

FIGURE 4.36

Code for Example 4.20

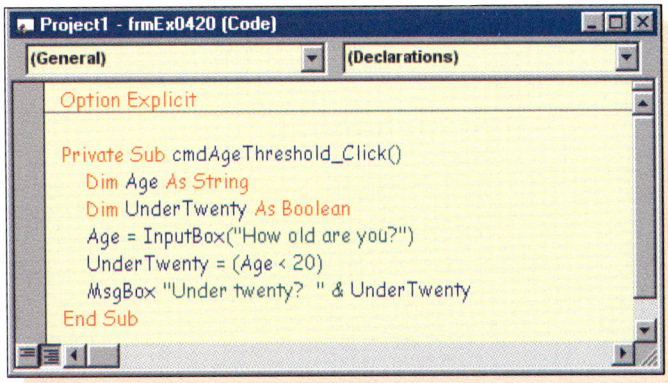

EXERCISE 4.23

Consider the code fragment below. (Remember that the keyword True is synonymous with the constant −1.)

Dim X **As Integer**
Dim Y **As Boolean**
X = InputBox("Enter 0 or -1")
Y = (X = True)

Replace the assignment statement Y = (X = True) with a simpler assignment statement that accomplishes exactly the same thing.

EXERCISE 4.24

Consider the following event procedure.

Private Sub cmdAgeThreshold_Click()
    Dim Age **As String**
    Dim UnderTwenty **As Boolean**
    Age = InputBox("How old are you")
    UnderTwenty = (Age < "20")
    MsgBox "Under twenty? " & UnderTwenty
End Sub

There is no type mismatch error, since the variable Age is type String and is compared to the string value "20". However, does this event procedure perform as it should? What happens if the user is less than 10 years old? What happens if the user is older than 99 years old? Explain.

EXERCISE 4.25

What will the message box display?

Private Sub cmdComparisons_Click()
    Dim A **As String**
    Dim X **As Boolean**
    Dim Y **As Boolean**
    Dim Z **As Integer**
    A = "study"
    Z = 10
    X = (5 < Z)
    Y = (A >= "stupefy")
    Z = X < Y
    MsgBox X & Y & Z
End Sub

EXERCISE 4.26

What will the message box display?

```
Private Sub cmdComparisons_Click()
    Dim A As String
    Dim B As String
    Dim C As Single
    Dim D As Integer
    Dim X As Boolean
    A = "cran"
    B = "crankshaft"
    C = -0.5
    D = 2
    X = ((A & "berry") < B) * (-3^3) + (((D / 2) = 1) + 3)
    MsgBox X
End Sub
```

Logical Operators

Logical operators, as mentioned earlier, combine simple logical expressions to create more complex logical expressions. Suppose a multinational firm wants to identify job candidates who have more than five years of business experience. To do this, a program might have the statement

Qualified = (YearsExperience > 5)

What if this firm wants to identify job applicants who speak at least three languages? To do this, a program might have the statement

Qualified = (NumberOfLanguages >= 3)

But what if the firm wants a candidate who has both qualifications? This is where a logical operator helps. In a program that evaluates candidates who satisfy both requirements we might see the statement

Qualified = (YearsExperience > 5) And (NumberOfLanguages >= 3)

This expression uses the binary And operator to join the simple comparisons YearsExperience > 5 and NumberOfLanguages >= 3. The entire expression evaluates to True if both comparisons evaluate to True, and it evaluates to False if either one or both of the comparisons are False.

The most common logical operators are shown in Table 4.11. There are other logical operators (Xor, Eqv, and Imp) which are less commonly employed; for information consult online help (search phrase "Logical Operators").

The unary Not operator takes the value of the expression to its right and negates it; Not True evaluates to False, and Not False evaluates to True.

Result of Not A

A	Not A
True	False
False	True

The And and Or operators are both binary. The result of And'ing two expressions is True if both of the expressions are True, and False if either one or both of them are False (see the results on the next page).

4.7 Logical Expressions

TABLE 4.11 Common logical operators

Operator Symbol	Name	Example* Expression	Result
Not	Not (*negation*)	Not (A < B)	False
		Not (A >= B)	True
And	And (*conjunction*)	(A < B) And (B < C)	True
		(-2 < B) And (4 = B)	False
		(A > B) And (B <= B)	False
		(-2 >= B) And (C < B)	False
Or	Or (*disjunction*)	(A < B) Or (B < C)	True
		(-2 < B) Or (C = B)	True
		(A > B) Or (B <= B)	True
		(-2 >= B) Or (C < B)	False

*Assume numeric variables A, B, and C have been declared and contain the values 2, 3, and 4, respectively.

Result of A And B

	B True	B False
A True	True	False
A False	False	False

The result of Or'ing two expressions is True if either one or both of them is True, and False if they are both False.

Result of A Or B

	B True	B False
A True	True	True
A False	True	False

Example 4.21 — Using Logical Operators

The event procedure in Figure 4.37 evaluates whether the user is between 10 and 20 years old, inclusive. To evaluate the expression (10 <= Age) And (Age <= 20), the computer first evaluates the left-most comparison, 10 <= Age, to arrive at True or False, then evaluates the right-most comparison, Age <= 20, to arrive at True or False, then And's these two truth values. If they are both True then the final result is True; otherwise the final result is False.

Observe that there is more than one way to write the logical expression in Example 4.21 and still get the same result: (20 >= Age) And (10 <= Age), for example. However, one expression that *will not* yield the same result is 10 <= Age <= 20. To evaluate this expression, VB will first compare 10 <= Age, arriving at True (–1) or False (0), and then compare the result of this comparison to 20.

FIGURE 4.37

Code for Example 4.21

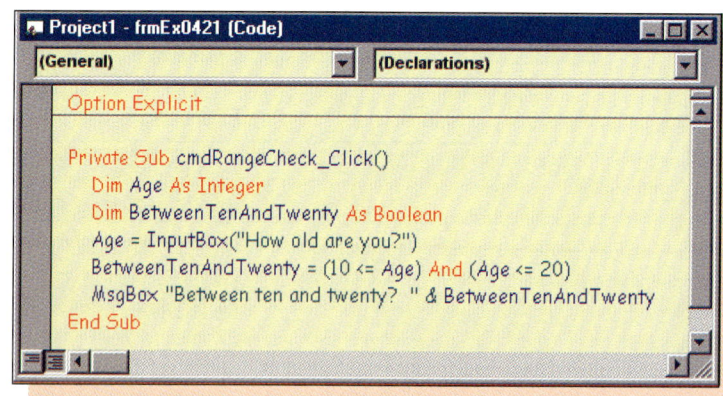

In either case the result is True, since −1 is less than 20 and so is 0. In other words, this expression is worthless because it always gives the result True.

This is an easy trap for beginning VB programmers to fall into, because from algebra we are used to writing expressions like

$$10 \leq X \leq 20$$

In fact, the computer will not notify you of this error because it is syntactically correct. As a programmer you have to be careful to remember to write out one comparison at a time, then use the logical operators And or Or to join the comparisons appropriately.

Logical expressions can be constructed that are quite large and complex, and may be time-consuming to understand. Also, the values on either side of the comparison operators can be large arithmetic expressions. In such expressions VB will perform all the arithmetic operations first, then the comparison operations, and then the logical operations (first Nots, then Ands, and finally Ors). As with arithmetic expressions, it makes sense to use parentheses to keep the expression easy to read.

EXERCISE 4.27

Is the following expression True or False?

(Not (3 < 2) And (5 < 7 - Sqr(16))) Or (Not (2 * 5 + 1 > 3))

EXERCISE 4.28

In Example 4.21, what happens if the programmer mistakenly types Or instead of And in cmdRangeCheck_Click? Explain.

EXERCISE 4.29

Change the statement

Qualified = (YearsExperience > 5) And (NumberOfLanguages >= 3)

so that a candidate is still considered to be qualified if he or she meets the specified requirements, but now any candidate who speaks six or more languages (regardless of years of experience) is *also* considered to be qualified.

EXERCISE 4.30

What will the message box display?

```
Private Sub cmdLogicalOperators_Click()
    Dim A As Integer
    Dim B As Integer
    Dim C As Integer
    Dim D As Integer
```

```
Dim X As Boolean
Dim Y As Boolean
Dim Z As Boolean
A = 2
B = 3
C = 4
D = 5
X = Not (A < B)
Y = (A < B) And (C > D)
Z = (A < B) Or (C > D)
MsgBox X & Y & Z
    End Sub
```

Logical Functions

The two most frequently used logical functions are listed in Table 4.12.

IsNumeric()

The IsNumeric() function takes one argument, and returns True or False according to whether the argument has the form of a valid number. Thus, IsNumeric("12a") returns False, while IsNumeric("12") returns True. The argument can be any type, although in practice it will usually be type String.

IsNumeric() is useful for avoiding the type mismatch run time error. Suppose that an application requires the user to enter a number. Directly storing the user's input into a numeric variable will result in a type mismatch if the user makes a mistake. As an alternative, the program can first store the user's input in a string variable (so there will be no chance of a type mismatch), and then use IsNumeric() to evaluate whether the value is a valid number. If it is, the value can be safely stored in the numeric variable, and if not, the user can be notified of the mistake. We will see examples of this kind of user input validation in Chapter 5.

IIf()

The Immediate If function, IIf(), provides a way for your program to make simple decisions. Given two expressions, the function chooses which one to evaluate. As we will see in Chapter 5, most programs have to make decisions, and VB provides sophisticated statements for handling more complex decisions.

The IIf() function takes three arguments: the first is a logical expression, and the second and third can be string or numeric expressions. The action of IIf() is as follows. It first evaluates the logical expression (its first argument) to arrive at True or False. If the outcome is True, it then evaluates and returns

TABLE 4.12 Common logical functions

| Function | | Example* | |
Name	Description	Expression	Result
IsNumeric()	Check for valid number	IsNumeric("12a")	False
IIf()	Immediate If	IIf(B < A, A + B, A * B)	6

*Assume numeric variables A and B have been declared and contain the values 2 and 3, respectively.

the result of the second argument; otherwise it evaluates and returns the result of the third argument. An illustration of this action follows:

IIf(LogicalExpression, Expression1, Expression2)
First evaluate LogicalExpression:
  If True, IIf() takes on the value of ──────┐
  If False, IIf() takes on the value of ─────────┘

In the example IIf(B < A, A + B, A * B) in Table 4.12, the logical expression B < A is False, so the third argument, A * B, is evaluated, and its result, 6, is returned.

Example 4.22 Using the IIf() Function

The event procedure in Figure 4.38 illustrates the use of the IIf() function. In this example, the user enters two string values in response to the input boxes. The IIf() function compares the first string (A) to the second string (B). If A is less than B, then string A is displayed. If A is not less than B, then string B is displayed.

Simply put, this procedure displays via a message box the lesser of two strings that are input via input boxes.

Exercise 4.31

In Example 4.21, modify cmdRangeCheck_Click so its message box displays

> Between ten and twenty? Yes

if the user's age is between ten and twenty, and

> Between ten and twenty? No

if the user's age is not between ten and twenty.

4.8 Project 7: A Stock Trading Simulation

The following concepts are introduced in this project: access keys, and imprecision of timer intervals.

The idea behind making a killing on the stock market is simple: buy low, sell high. Putting this strategy into practice isn't so simple. To train finance students about the workings of the market and to give them experience buying and selling, many instructors use games that simulate the behavior of the stock market. In this section, we create such a simulation.

In a typical game of this sort students shout out prices at which they are willing to buy or sell a hypothetical security, and take up other students on their

FIGURE 4.38
Code for Example 4.22

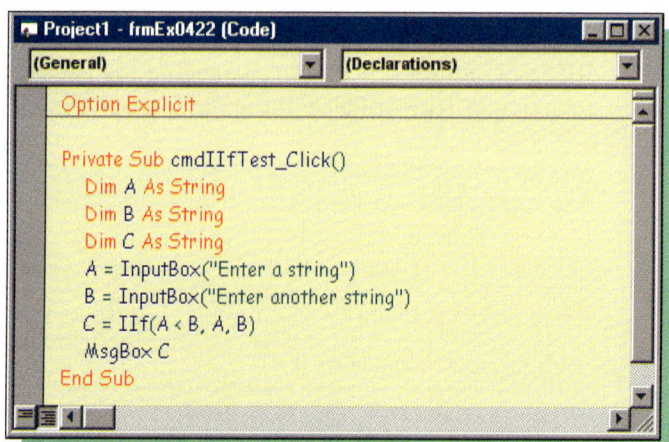

offers. Student A will buy from Student B, for example, when Student B offers to sell the security at a price that is less than what Student A estimates its true value to be. The primary trick in such games, as in real-world markets, is being able to accurately estimate the "true" value of the security.

Description of the Application

Figure 4.39 shows the user interface for this application. This screen is updated periodically with two kinds of *quotes*:

1. An *ask quote* indicates that someone in the market is willing to *sell* the trader a specified number of shares at a specified price (the "asking" price); the trader can choose to buy or not.

2. A *bid quote* indicates that someone in the market is willing to *buy* from the trader a specified number of shares at a specified price (the "bidding" price), and the trader can choose to sell or not.

Every 2.5 seconds the program displays a new ask quote. The number of shares and the asking price are both random numbers between 5 and 15. By clicking the Buy button the trader can buy shares at that price.

Similarly, every 3.0 seconds the program displays a new bid quote. The number of shares and the bidding price are both random numbers between 5 and 15. By clicking the Sell button the trader can sell shares at that price.

In this simulation, the user plays against the computer and tries to maximize his or her cash balance at the end of the game. Three details add a little challenge to the game.

1. The user is charged a fixed transaction fee of $10 for every click on Buy or Sell.

2. The game ends after 65 seconds.

3. The user starts out with no inventory of shares and no cash, and is allowed to have a negative inventory and negative cash during the game. However,

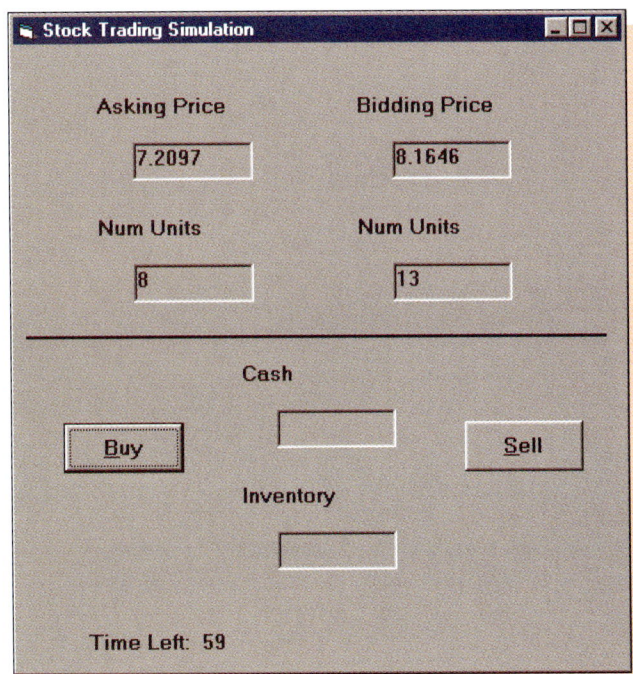

FIGURE 4.39

User interface for Project 7

at the end of the game the user's cash balance is reduced $20 for every unit of inventory below zero (this is called a "penalty for being short"). Since the goal is to maximize the cash balance at the end of the game, the user must try to avoid having a negative inventory as time runs out.

Design of the Application

This project has one form. The controls and their property settings are shown in Figure 4.40. Note that the controls that look like text boxes are actually Label controls with BorderStyle property set to "1 - Fixed Single" and Caption property set to the zero-length string.

The ampersand (&) preceding the "B" in cmdBuy's Caption property specifies an access key for the command button. **An *access key* is a combination of keys that the user can type to produce a Click event for a control.** Thus, at run time the user can use the key combination ALT+B (i.e., press and hold the ALT key, then press B) as a shortcut for clicking the command button with the mouse. VB will visually indicate the presence of the access key by underlining the "B" in the command button's caption.

Note that this is a second meaning of the ampersand symbol in VB. In a string expression, & is the concatenation operator. In a Caption property it specifies an access key. All good Windows applications employ access keys.

With practice, the user can be much quicker with access keys than with the mouse, and with experience the user will begin to look for underlined characters on command button captions. The caption for cmdSell specifies ALT+S as its access key.

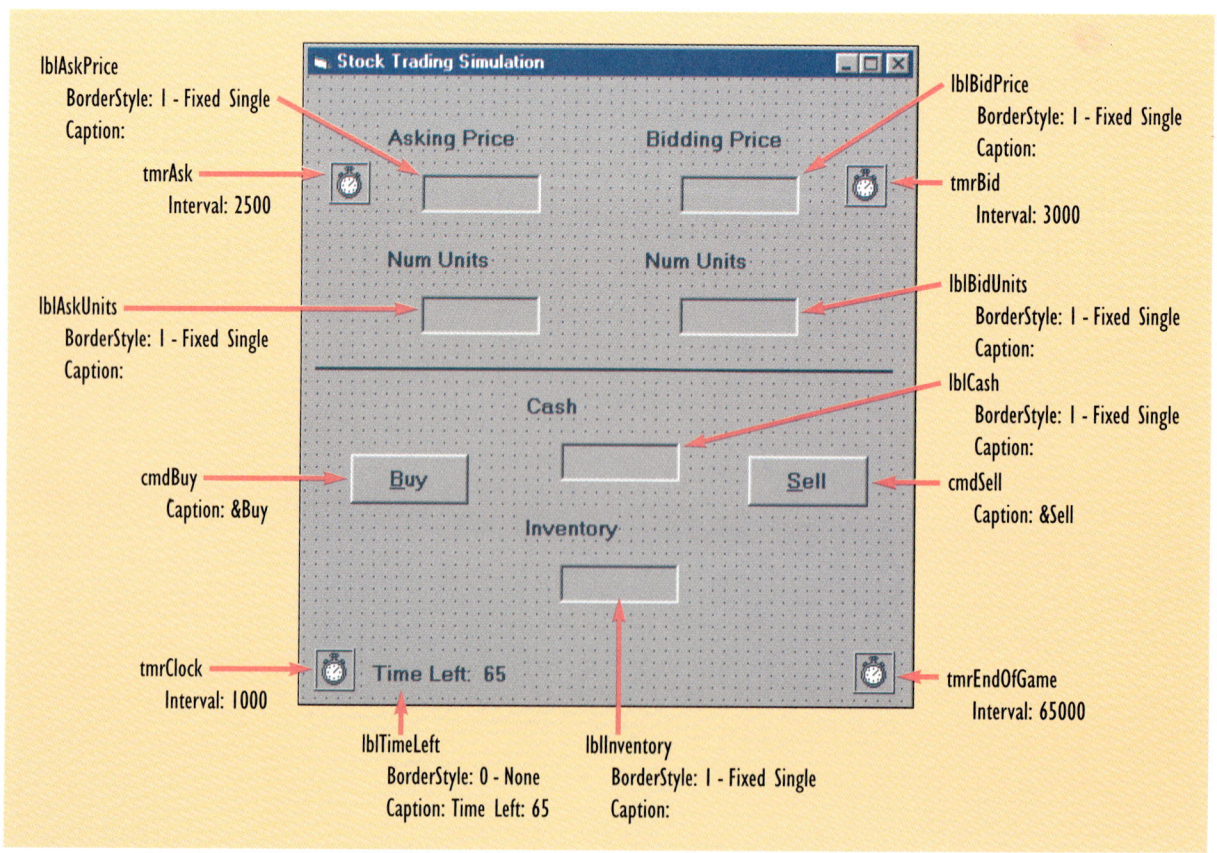

FIGURE 4.40 Controls and property settings for Project 7

Six events occur during the game:

1. A new ask quote is generated (when the interval for tmrAsk expires).
2. A new bid quote is generated (when the interval for tmrBid expires).
3. The user clicks on cmdBuy.
4. The user clicks on cmdSell.
5. A second elapses (when the interval for tmrClock expires).
6. The game ends (when the interval for tmrEndOfGame expires).

You need one event procedure for each of these events. Let us examine each of these in turn.

The tmrAsk_Timer Event

When this event occurs the following tasks must be performed:

- A new random AskPrice should be generated, then displayed in the corresponding label.
- A new random AskUnits should be generated, then displayed in the corresponding label.

Note that it is necessary to store the AskPrice and AskUnits in numeric variables because these are needed in arithmetic calculations if the user subsequently clicks the Buy button. Since they are used by two event procedures, the scope of these variables must be module-level.

The tmrBid_Timer Event

This event is handled identically to the way the tmrAsk_Timer event is handled, except that new random BidPrice and BidUnits are generated and stored in numeric variables, then displayed in corresponding labels.

The cmdBuy_Click Event

When this event occurs, the following tasks are performed:

- The user's Cash is *reduced* by the transaction fee (equal to 10) and by AskPrice * AskUnits, and the new value of Cash is displayed in its label.
- The user's Inventory is *increased* by AskUnits, and the new value of Inventory is displayed in its label.
- The AskPrice and AskUnits variables are set to zero (so that the user can't click Buy again to get the same price).
- The labels corresponding to AskPrice and AskUnits are cleared as a visual cue to the user that the transaction has been processed.

Note that it is necessary to store Cash and Inventory in numeric variables because these values are needed in arithmetic calculations the next time the user clicks the Buy button or the Sell button (and also at the end of the game). These variables must have module-level scope.

The transaction fee should be a symbolic constant. It is also used in the event procedure for the Sell button, so its scope must be module-level.

The cmdSell_Click Event

This event is handled similarly to the cmdBuy_Click event. The user's Cash is reduced by the transaction fee and *increased* by BidPrice * BidUnits; the user's

Inventory is *decreased* by BidUnits; the BidPrice and BidUnits variables are set to zero (so that the user can't click Sell again to get the same price); and the corresponding labels are cleared.

The tmrClock_Timer Event

When this event occurs, the number displayed in the Time Left label is reduced by 1. Since this requires an arithmetic calculation, you should use a variable to hold the number of seconds remaining in the game. The value in this variable starts out at 65; a convenient way to get the value 65 into this variable at the beginning of the game is to place an assignment statement in the Form_Load event procedure. It follows that this variable must have module-level scope. It is also a good idea to use a symbolic constant for the length of the game (65).

The tmrEndOfGame_Timer Event

When this event occurs, the following tasks are performed:

- The user's Cash is recomputed, to reduce it by the penalty for being short. The penalty is zero if the Inventory is zero or more, and 20 times the absolute value of Inventory if Inventory is negative.
- The final Cash value is displayed, formatted as a dollar amount, in a message box.
- Program execution is terminated.

The unit penalty for being short (20) should be a symbolic constant. It is only used in this event procedure, so its scope can be local. However, code maintainability is improved by making it module-level so that all symbolic constants are located in the same place.

Table 4.13 summarizes the symbolic constants and variables in the project.

Construction of the Application

Begin by creating and placing controls on the user interface and setting their properties as shown in Figure 4.40. Then create the statements for the module-level symbolic constants and variables. These statements belong in the general declarations section of the form and are shown in Figure 4.41.

TABLE 4.13 Symbolic constants and variables in Project 7

Constant Name	Value	Scope	Variable Name	Type	Scope
LOWQUOTE	5	Module-Level	AskPrice	Currency	Module-Level
HIGHQUOTE	15	Module-Level	AskUnits	Integer	Module-Level
TRANSACTIONFEE	10	Module-Level	BidPrice	Currency	Module-Level
UNITSHORTPENALTY	20	Module-Level	BidUnits	Integer	Module-Level
GAMELENGTH	65	Module-Level	Cash	Currency	Module-Level
			Inventory	Integer	Module-Level
			TimeRemaining	Integer	Module-Level

FIGURE 4.41

General declarations section with module-level symbolic constants and variables

FIGURE 4.42

Code for tmrAsk_Timer event procedure

Figure 4.42 shows the code for the tmrAsk_Timer event procedure. In this procedure, we assume that the ask price has a fractional part and that the number of units is a whole number. The expression

LOWQUOTE + (HIGHQUOTE - LOWQUOTE) * Rnd()

generates a random number between 5 and 15; and the expression

LOWQUOTE + Int((1 + HIGHQUOTE - LOWQUOTE) * Rnd())

generates a random integer between 5 and 15, inclusive.

Figure 4.43 shows the code for the tmrBid_Timer event procedure. Note that the two expressions that generate the random bid price and number of units are the same as those in the tmrAsk_Timer event procedure. Event procedures cmdBuy_Click and cmdSell_Click are straightforward to code. They are in Figures 4.44 and 4.45. Notice that the displayed cash value is formatted as a dollar amount.

FIGURE 4.43

Code for tmrBid_Timer event procedure

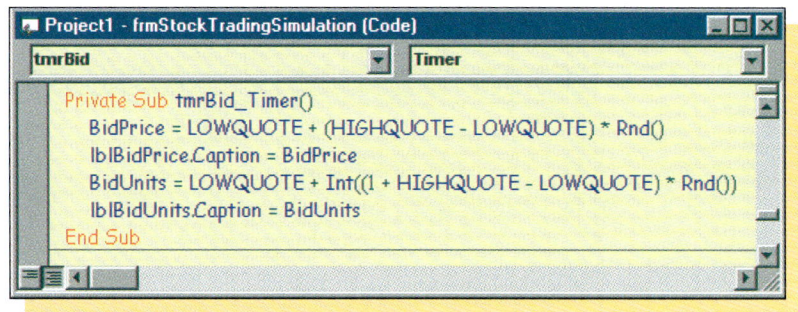

FIGURE 4.44

Code for cmdBuy_Click event procedure

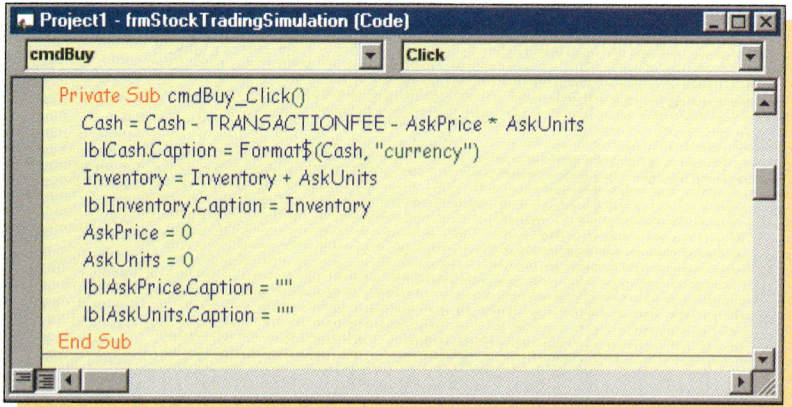

FIGURE 4.45

Code for cmdSell_Click event procedure

Event procedure tmrClock_Timer (Figure 4.46) is also straightforward to code. However, for it to operate properly, the variable TimeRemaining has to hold the length of the game, in seconds, at the start of the game. Therefore, you need to place an assignment statement in the Form_Load event procedure to perform this initialization (Figure 4.47).

FIGURE 4.46

Code for tmrClock_Timer event procedure

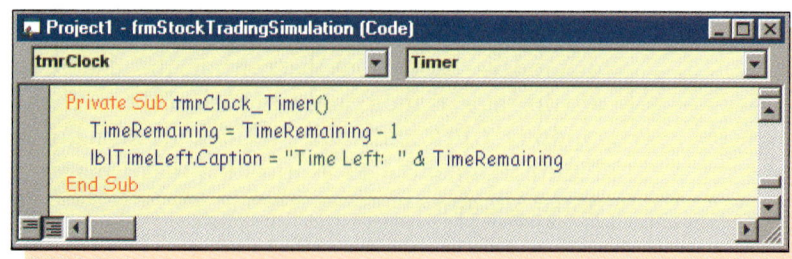

FIGURE 4.47

Code for Form_Load event procedure

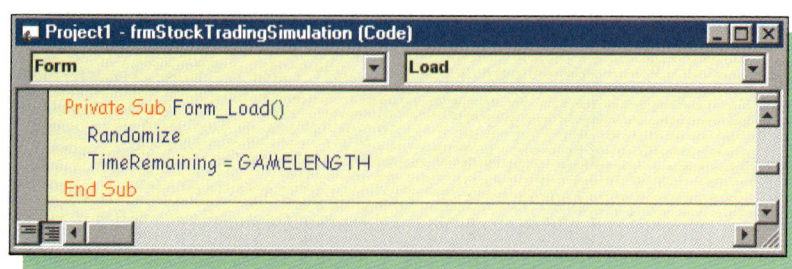

FIGURE 4.48

Code for tmrEnd-OfGame_Timer event procedure

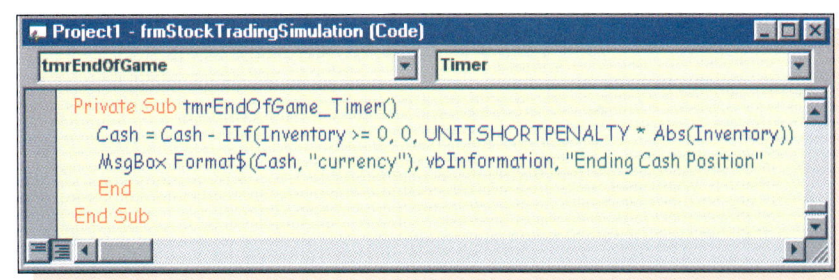

Event procedure tmrEndOfGame_Timer (Figure 4.48) has one tricky point. There is a penalty for being short only if the Inventory is negative. The following expression computes the penalty.

IIf(Inventory >= 0, 0, UNITSHORTPENALTY * Abs(Inventory))

Note that we choose to display the final cash amount in a message box and not in the Label caption. The message box interrupts program execution so that the user can view it, whereas the Label control is cleared immediately upon program termination.

You will probably observe a timing discrepancy at the end of the game. This is because the time between events for a Timer control is only approximately equal to the value specified by its Interval property. There are two different timers counting down to 0: one updates the Time Remaining label, and the other controls the actual end of the game. And 65 events approximately 1 second apart do not add up exactly to 1 event approximately 65 seconds in the future.

After you have the game up and running, see if you can develop a good strategy for when to buy and sell!

EXERCISE 4.32 In Project 7, event procedure cmdBuy_Click sets the AskPrice and AskUnits variables to zero and clears their corresponding labels "so that the user can't click Buy again to get the same price." Event procedure cmdSell_Click performs the analogous operations with BidPrice and BidUnits. How would the game change if cmdBuy_Click and cmdSell_Click did not perform these operations? Would the user's final cash amount generally be lower or higher? Explain.

EXERCISE 4.33 In Project 7, can you think of a way to use the Enabled property of command buttons to prevent the user from buying or selling twice at the same price? In terms of its effect on the user, do you think this approach is better or worse than setting the AskPrice and AskUnits variables to zero and clearing their labels? Explain.

EXERCISE 4.34 In Project 7, will a skilled user generally score higher by using the access keys or by using the mouse to click on the Buy and Sell buttons? Explain.

Chapter Summary

1. Expressions are used as part of a statement—they are not statements themselves. For example, the assignment statement uses an expression on the right-hand side of the equal sign.

   Expressions can be either numeric, string, or logical. When evaluated, a numeric expression produces a single number as its value, a string expression produces a single string value, and a logical expression produces either True (–1) or False (0).

2. Expressions consist of constants, variables, operators, and functions. An operator is a symbol that specifies a simple operation, such as addition. A function is a descriptive name that specifies a more complex operation, such as the square root calculation.

   Function names always end in parentheses; for example, the name of the square root function is Sqr(). Functions take arguments and return values. Arguments are expressions that specify the values to be used by the function, and are placed between the parentheses. For example, in Sqr(4), the argument is 4 and the returned value is 2.

3. The InputBox() function presents a dialog box to the user and prompts for a response. The user's response becomes the value that the InputBox() function returns to the program. The type of the value returned by the InputBox() function can be string or numeric, depending on how the function is used.

4. The MsgBox statement presents a dialog box that displays a message to the user. The user must respond by clicking a button to remove the dialog box from the screen. In addition to displaying a message, you can make the box display an informative icon and a title.

5. Arithmetic expressions are composed of numeric constants and variables and arithmetic operators and functions. Arithmetic expressions are evaluated using an operator precedence rule, which specifies a particular order in which operations are to be performed. You can override the operator precedence rule by using parentheses, since parenthesized parts of the expression are always evaluated first.

   When the computer evaluates arithmetic expressions, it is possible for arithmetic errors to occur. An overflow error occurs when the computer attempts to store the result of an expression in a variable that does not have the capacity to hold the result. Roundoff errors occur with variables of type Single and Double. The impact of roundoff errors must be evaluated in the context of the problem being solved by the program.

6. String expressions are composed of string constants and variables and string operators and functions. VB's string concatenation operator & (the ampersand), joins (concatenates) two values end-to-end. String functions are very frequently used in creating applications with VB. Any function whose name includes a dollar sign, $, returns a string value.

   Two functions used with strings provide access to the ANSI table. Chr$() takes a numeric argument and returns its equivalent ANSI character. This function is needed to specify nonprintable characters in a string. Asc() takes a single character (string) as the argument and returns its equivalent ANSI number.

7. Logical expressions consist of variables, constants, comparison operators, logical operators, and logical functions. A logical expression has the form of a True/False question. That is, a logical expression evaluates to either True or False. VB provides the Boolean standard data type for storing the result of a logical expression.

8. Comparison of numeric values is straightforward, but comparison of string values is more complex. String values are compared character-by-character beginning at the left-most character, using the ANSI table to determine

which character is smaller. Two strings are equal if they are the same length and contain identical characters.

The logical operators Not, And, and Or can be used to combine logical expressions to form a more complex logical expression.

9. The logical function IIf() is used to select one of two expressions depending on the value of a logical expression. The function's first argument is the logical expression. If this logical expression evaluates to True, then the function takes on the value of the expression defined by the second argument. If the logical expression evaluates to False, then the function takes on the value of the expression defined by the third argument.

10. The Text box control allows the user to enter text into the control at run time. The text entered in the control is available to the program through the text box's Text property. The Text box control can respond to a number of events. The Change event is used to cause processing to be performed whenever the value in the text box changes.

11. Finally, an access key is a combination of keys that the user can type to produce a Click event for a control. This provides the user with a keyboard alternative to using the mouse.

Key Terms

access key
ANSI
argument
arithmetic expression
binary operator
carriage return
case sensitivity
Change event
collating sequence
comment
comparison operator
concatenation
dialog box
encrypted message
evaluating the expression
exponentiation operator
expression
focus
format specification
function
future value
InputBox() function
Integer division operator
line-continuation character
line feed
logical expression
logical operator
Mod operator
MsgBox statement
nonprintable character
operator
operator precedence rule
overflow
present value
return value
roundoff
statement
string expression
substring
Text box control
type mismatch
unary operator
value

End-of-Chapter Problems

1. Convert the following algebraic expressions into valid VB expressions.

   a. $\dfrac{A + B}{C}$

   b. $\sqrt{A^2 + B^2}$

   c. $\dfrac{A + B \times C}{X - Y}$

   d. $\dfrac{[A + B]^2}{\sqrt{X \times Y - Z}}$

   e. $A + [B \times C - D] \times E$

2. Evaluate each of the following VB expressions. That is, determine the result of the computation that will be performed by the computer. Assume that all the variables are declared as type Single, and that A = 10, B = 2, C = 5, D = 25, and E = 3.
   a. A + B * C + D
   b. A ^ B + (D / C) ^ E
   c. A / B * C / D / E
   d. A ^ 2 + B ^ 2 / C
   e. D / (A + C + E - B) ^ B

3. Evaluate each of the following string expressions. That is, determine the result of the manipulation that will be performed by the computer. Be aware that there may be syntax or runtime errors in one or more of the expressions. Assume that all the variables are declared as type String and that A = "Apple", B = "Banana", C = "Apply", and D = "banana".
   a. A & Chr$(115)
   b. Left$(B, 2) & Right$(C, 4)
   c. Mid$(C, 2, 3)
   d. String$(5, Mid$(C, 4, 1))
   e. InStr(D, "ana", 3)

4. Evaluate each of the following logical expressions. That is, determine whether they evaluate to True or False. Assume that all the variables are declared as type Integer and that A = 10, B = 50, C = 0, and D = 100.
   a. (A < B) And (C = 0)
   b. B >= D Or B <= A
   c. 10 <= B <= D
   d. B > A And (A = 0 Or B <= 50)
   e. Not C And (D >= B) Or A = 100

5. Evaluate each of the following logical expressions. That is, determine whether they evaluate to True or False. Assume that all the variables are declared as type String and that A = "Apple", B = "Banana", C = "Apply", and D = "banana".
   a. A > B
   b. B = D
   c. A < C And B > D
   d. A > "annual" Or B <> "Fruit"
   e. "Apricot" <= B <= "Kumquat"

Programming Problems

1. Create a VB form that has two text boxes, each identified by a label. The captions of the labels should read "ANSI Character" and "ANSI Code." Then create two command buttons with captions "Convert Code to Character" and "Convert Character to Code."

    Program the Click event procedures of these two buttons to perform the appropriate conversions. When the user clicks the Convert Code to Character button, the code value in the ANSI Code text box should be used to determine the corresponding ANSI character, and this character should be placed in the ANSI Character text box. The reverse operation should be performed when the user clicks the Convert Character to Code button.

2. Create a VB project that computes the *economic order quantity* (EOQ) using the *fixed order quantity lot size* decision rule. This rule helps retailers, manufacturing managers, etc., determine the number of units to order each time a particular item must be ordered because of low stock. The EOQ is the most economical quantity possible under a certain set of conditions. The equation for computing the economic order quantity is

$$EOQ = \sqrt{\frac{2RS}{kC}}$$

where S is the cost to prepare an order.
R is the annual demand.
C is the cost per unit.
k is the cost rate of carrying $1 of inventory per year.

Your project should let the user enter values for S, R, C, and k, and it should have a button that the user clicks to compute and display the EOQ.

3. Create a VB project that compares two string values entered by the user. The form should have two text boxes with corresponding labels captioned "String 1" and "String 2", and a command button captioned "Compare Strings". At run time, the user should first enter values into the text boxes, and then click the command button. The button's event procedure should then compare the two values in the text boxes and accordingly display either the message "String 1 is less" or the message "String 2 is less".

4. Create a VB project that searches for a substring within a larger string. Create a form with a Label control, and set the label's caption to "How now brown cow? The fox jumped over the fence." Add a command button with the caption "Find Word". When this button is clicked, have the system display an input box that asks the user to enter any word. Then search the label caption to see if the user's word is in the caption. Use a message box to display the result. Make the message box look like the following (which assumes that the user entered the word "cow" in the input box).

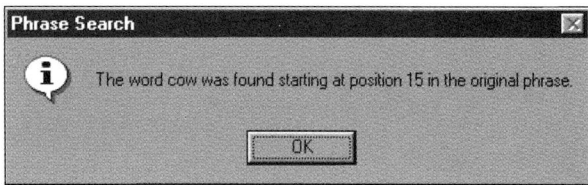

5. Create a VB project that implements Find and Find Next operations similar to those found in word processors. The form should have a Text box control and two command buttons. The figure at the top of page 208 shows the user interface after the user has typed a memo in the text box and then initiated a search for the word "look".

When program execution begins, the Find button should be visible but the Find Next button should not be visible. The user first enters text into the text box. After the text has been entered, clicking on the Find button causes the following actions to occur:

a. An input box is displayed, which prompts the user to enter the text to find; this text is stored in a variable named Target.
b. A search is performed to find the location of the first occurrence of Target in the text box, and the result of the search is stored in a variable named FoundPos.

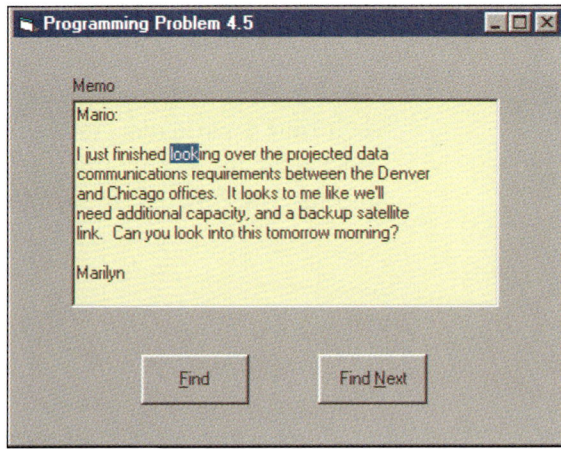

c. If the search is successful (FoundPos > 0), then the occurrence of Target in the text box is highlighted.
d. The Find Next button is made visible if the search is successful and invisible if the search is unsuccessful.

The preceding figure shows an example of how the form might appear after the user types text in the text box, clicks Find, and enters the word "look" as the target. Subsequently clicking the Find Next button should cause the same actions as clicking the Find button, except for the following: the input box is not displayed (the same Target is used); and the search finds the *next* occurrence of Target (instead of the first occurrence). For example, if the user clicks the Find Next button on the form shown above, the appearance of the text box should change as shown below.

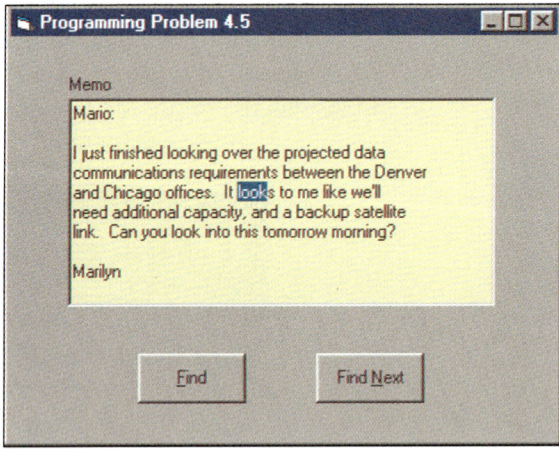

Hint 1: The following sequence of statements accomplishes the action of step c given earlier, assuming the Text box control is named txtMemo. (See online help for more information on these properties and methods of the Text box control.)

```
txtMemo.SelStart = IIf(FoundPos > 0, FoundPos - 1, 0)
txtMemo.SelLength = IIf(FoundPos > 0, Len(Target), 0)
txtMemo.SetFocus
```

Hint 2: What scope should variables Target and FoundPos have?
Hint 3: See the discussion in the text on using InStr() for multiple searches.

6. Create a VB project that computes the future value of a given dollar amount. An example user interface is shown below.

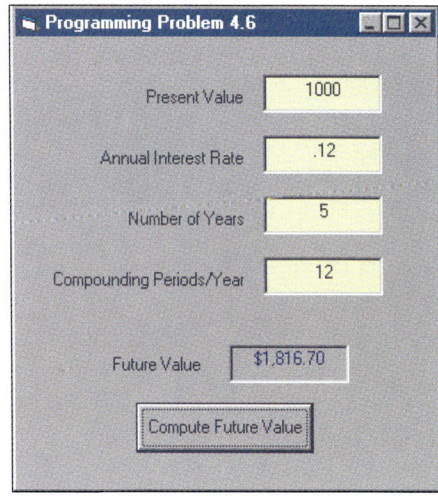

The formula for computing the future value is:

$$FV = PV \times (1 + AnnualRate/PerPerYr)^{Years \times PerPerYr}$$

where AnnualRate is the annual interest rate and PerPerYr is the number of compounding periods per year.

The annual rate must be a fraction. For example, for a 10 percent rate the number .10 should be used in the formula. If the user enters a number greater than 1 (as shown above), the program should divide the value by 100 to locate the decimal point at the correct place (the value 12 in the example was divided by 100 and the resulting value .12 was used in the calculation).

7. Create a VB project that computes the monthly payment amount for a loan. An example solution is shown below.

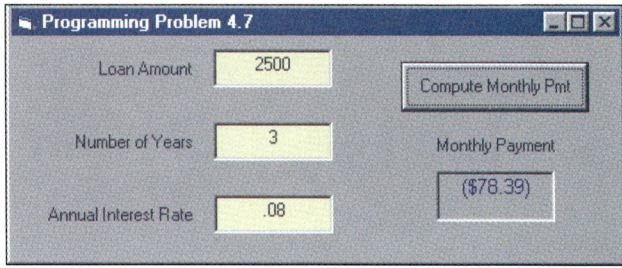

Use VB's built-in payment function, Pmt(). The syntax of the Pmt() function is

Pmt(PeriodicRate, NumberOfPeriods, LoanAmount)

where PeriodicRate is the rate per period (per month in this case), NumberOfPeriods is the number of months over which the loan will be payed off, and LoanAmount is the amount borrowed. Since the user enters the number of years and annual rate, you will need to adjust the entered values to be consistent with the parameters of the function. You can consult online help (search phrase "Pmt") for additional information on this function.

The user should be able to enter the interest rate either as a fraction or as a whole number (as shown above). However, the function requires the rate to be a fraction. Thus, your program will have to convert any values that are greater than 1 into fractions. Do this by dividing the value by 100.

chapter FIVE

Specifying Alternate Courses Of Action

Selection Statements

◆ ◆ ◆ ◆

Most business applications need to be able to select an appropriate action from several alternatives, depending on certain conditions that occur in the data. For example, an accounts receivable program must be able to handle overpayments, when they occur, by producing refund checks.

In the programs we wrote in previous chapters each event procedure always performed the same actions, regardless of the data it processed. For example, in the sample order entry application discussed in Chapter 1, the user enters a product number and quantity, and the program computes the extended price and updates the order total. The actions the program performs to accomplish these calculations are the same regardless of which product and what quantity the user enters. This is because, up to this point in our use of VB, statements within an event procedure have been executed one at a time, from top to bottom, and no statements have ever been skipped.

But suppose we wanted to include sales tax, varying from city to city and from state to state, in the sample order entry application? We would need the program to examine the customer's address and select the appropriate tax rate for that address. For this, we need new VB statements that allow us to ask a question (where does the customer live?) and, based on the answer, choose the appropriate course of action. Under these circumstances, statements are still executed one at a time and in top-to-bottom order, but some statements are skipped (at least sometimes). This makes sense because the answer to the question can be different each time the event procedure is executed.

In this chapter we show how a program can select alternate courses of action depending on the data to be processed. Two statements make this possible: the If…Then…Else statement and the Select Case statement. In addition, we introduce VB controls that make it easy to design GUIs that allow the user to indicate choices such as whether an employee wants optional life insurance.

Typically, the program responds to this kind of input by selecting an action that corresponds to the user's choice.

If…Then…Else and Select Case statements are composed of multiple lines of code. They can be complex and hard to understand. Therefore, we also discuss how to format these statements so they are as easy to read as possible.

Objectives

After studying this chapter you should be able to

- Construct programs that select alternative actions using the If…Then…Else and Select Case statements.
- Compare the Select Case statement with the If…Then…Else statement and describe situations for which each is appropriate.
- Create GUIs using the MsgBox() function and three new controls—Option button, Frame, and Check box—which present a set of options to the user and allow the user to input choices.

5.1 The Decision-Making Process

We make so many decisions each day that it is easy to overlook the process we go through to choose one option instead of another. But when writing a program that must select one action from several alternatives, we must be very precise in how we construct the decision criterion and write the alternative actions. Therefore, we begin our investigation of programs that make choices by looking carefully at the structure of decisions.

If you look closely at the decision-making process, you will see that the action you take depends upon the *conditions* of the situation. As represented by Figure 5.1, each condition has two or more possible *outcomes,* and for each possible outcome there is an appropriate *action*.

To demonstrate how these steps work, consider a program that checks to see whether a student is eligible to register for a course. For example, assume that a student must take Intro to Business Computing before taking Intro to Programming. The condition is, has the student passed Intro to Business Computing? If the outcome is yes, then the appropriate action is to allow the student to enroll in Intro to Programming. If the outcome is no, then the appropriate action is to deny the student permission to enroll.

In a program,

- A *condition* is represented as an expression.

FIGURE 5.1

Elements of a decision in a program

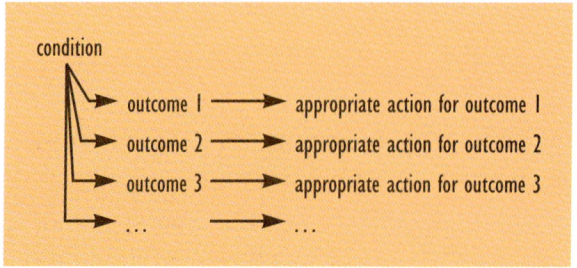

- An *outcome* corresponds to a value produced when the computer evaluates the expression.
- An *appropriate action* is specified as a group of statements.

At design time the programmer has to specify the condition, its possible outcomes, and the appropriate action for each outcome. At run time, the computer evaluates the condition (an expression), identifies the outcome, then executes the group of statements for that outcome.

5.2 The If…Then…Else Statement

The *If…Then…Else statement* allows a program to handle situations having two outcomes. Accordingly, the statement has three parts:

1. The condition.
2. The statements to perform for the first outcome.
3. The statements to perform for the second outcome.

We begin this section by examining the syntax and action of the If…Then…Else statement, and looking at an illustrative example. We then discuss the task of reading and writing If…Then…Else statements, and briefly discuss logical expressions in the context of If…Then…Else statements. Finally, we look at a variation of the If…Then…Else statement.

Syntax and Action of If…Then…Else

The If…Then…Else statement has the following syntax:

```
If condition Then
    statementblock1
Else
    statementblock2
End If
```

The italics indicate positions at which you, as programmer, provide specific details to customize the statement. The reserved word If marks the top of the If…Then…Else statement, and the reserved word End If marks its bottom. The reserved word Then separates the *condition* from *statementblock1*, and the reserved word Else separates *statementblock1* from *statementblock2*.

The condition is a logical expression that you provide. Recall that a logical expression always evaluates to either True or False. Hence, the If statement's condition allows only two outcomes.

A *statement block* is any sequence of zero or more statements. If…Then…Else requires you to provide two statement blocks. *Statementblock1* is used for outcome True, and *statementblock2* is used for outcome False.

Run Time: The Effect of the If…Then…Else Statement

The action of the If…Then…Else statement is as follows. When the computer executes the If statement, it first evaluates the condition and determines whether its outcome is True or False. If the outcome is

- True: the computer executes the statements in *statementblock1*, one at a time, in top-to-bottom order, then skips to the statement following End If.

♦ False: the computer skips immediately to Else, executes the statements in *statementblock2*, one at a time, in top-to-bottom order, then resumes at the statement following End If.

Example 5.1

Using the If...Then...Else Statement

The event procedure in Figure 5.2 uses an If...Then...Else statement to implement a simple guessing game. The variable Target is set to a random integer ranging from 1 to 6. Then the user responds to the input box by entering an integer between 1 and 6, and this response is stored in the variable Guess.

The If...Then...Else statement evaluates the condition, which determines whether the user's guess and the random target are equal. If they are equal, the computer beeps and displays a message box offering congratulations. If not, it displays a message box indicating that the guess did not match the random target.

Figure 5.3 shows the components of the If...Then...Else statement in cmdGuessMe_Click. Figure 5.4 shows the action of the statement when the condition evaluates to True and when it evaluates to False; in each case the statements that are executed are shaded. Note that the reserved words Then, Else, and End If don't cause the computer to perform any action; they merely serve to *delimit*—mark the beginning and end of—the two statement blocks.

Figure 5.4 shows a color bar after the End If statement. This indicates that when the If...Then...Else statement finishes executing either *statementblock1* or *statementblock2,* the program continues executing at the first statement after the End If statement.

FIGURE 5.2

Code for Example 5.1

```
Option Explicit

Private Sub cmdGuessMe_Click()
    Dim Target As Integer
    Dim Guess As Integer
    Target = 1 + Int(6 * Rnd())
    Guess = InputBox("Enter a guess between 1 and 6, inclusive.")
    If Guess = Target Then
        Beep
        MsgBox "Correct -- congratulations!"
    Else
        MsgBox "Incorrect -- bummer!"
    End If
End Sub
```

FIGURE 5.3

Components of If...Then...Else statement in Example 5.1

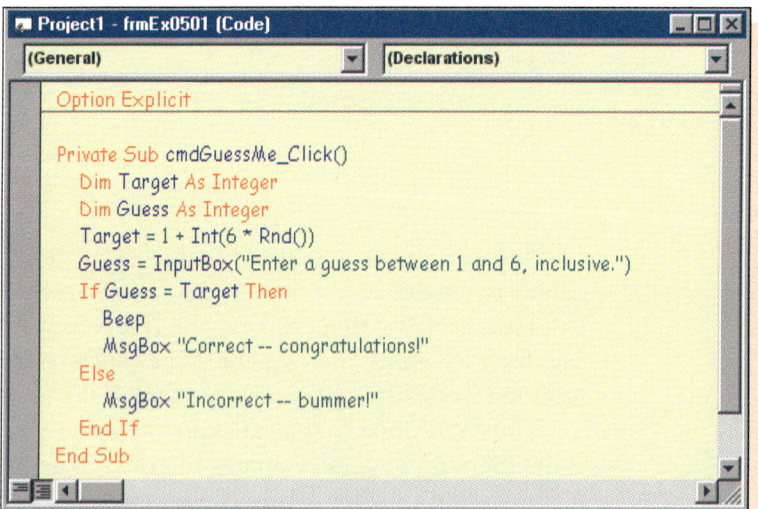

FIGURE 5.4

Action of If…Then…Else statement in Example 5.1

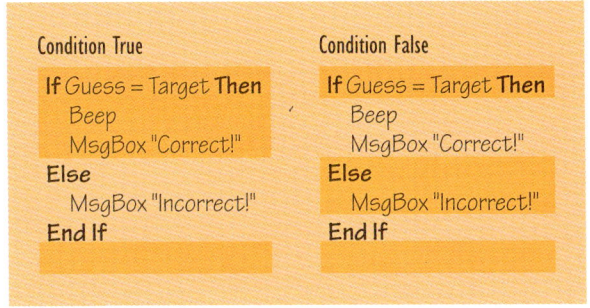

Note that in Example 5.1 it is impossible to say whether the condition will be True or False until the user enters a guess. It will be True only if the number entered by the user just happens to be equal to the number stored in the variable Target.

As programmers, we want our code to be easy to understand, so we should emphasize the presence of If…Then…Else statements. Programmers do this by *indenting* the statement blocks in the interior of If…Then…Else.

EXERCISE 5.1 Suppose the user of the program in Example 5.1 wants to make a correct guess in as few tries as possible. The user clicks on cmdGuessMe and enters a guess between 1 and 6, and repeats this until the guess is correct. Consider the following two guessing strategies:

Strategy A: Guess the same number every time.

Strategy B: Guess a different number each time.

Which strategy is better? That is, which strategy will help the user make a correct guess in fewer tries? Explain.

EXERCISE 5.2 Suppose we modify Example 5.1 by making the variable Target module-level instead of local to cmdGuessMe_Click, and moving the statement Target = 1 + Int(6 * Rnd()) from cmdGuessMe_Click to Form_Load. Now answer Exercise 5.1's question again, assuming the code has been modified as suggested.

Meta Statements

The If…Then…Else statement is our first example of a *compound statement*, meaning that a single If…Then…Else statement may contain many individual statements. That is, there are two statement blocks, and each statement block can contain one or more statements.

Compound statements can be harder to understand than simple statements. For example, the simple statement

```
GrossPay = HoursWorked * HourlyRate
```

is easy to understand—it has a single action. The compound If…Then…Else statement

```
If Guess = Target Then
    Beep
    MsgBox "Correct -- congratulations!"
Else
    MsgBox "Incorrect -- bummer!"
End If
```

is harder to understand because it specifies multiple alternative actions. However, you might describe this If…Then…Else statement with a phrase like "Process user's guess and display result." This phrase captures the essence of the compound statement. **When we describe a compound statement with a single phrase, we say that the phrase is a** *meta statement.* "Meta" means to "go beyond or transcend." A meta statement goes beyond the individual statements and describes the concept represented by those statements.

In the design phase, while developing the logic of our code, using the meta statement lets us understand *what* the code accomplishes without having to constantly keep in mind the details of *how* the code accomplishes it. In the current example, what the code does is "process the user's guess and display the result." We need to examine how the code accomplishes this only when we write the code and when we modify what it does.

Problem Solving and Pseudocode

A major part of designing any project is writing the code that performs the tasks needed to satisfy the user requirements. Programmers often use the term ***problem solving* for the process of writing code that performs a required task.** Problem solving can be quite challenging.

Meta statements can facilitate the problem-solving process. To illustrate this, consider the following narrative description of the user requirements for a computerized guessing game.

> *When the user clicks on a command button, the computer generates a random integer between 1 and 6, inclusive, then prompts the user to enter a guess. If the guess is correct, the computer beeps, then displays the message "Correct -- congratulations!" If the guess is incorrect, the computer displays the message "Incorrect -- bummer!"*

Pretend for a moment that you have not already seen the code for Example 5.1 and that you need to write the code that implements this guessing game. How do you proceed?

By reading the above narrative you can get a firm understanding of *what* the application should do without concern for exactly *how* the program code will accomplish the tasks. It is critical that you reach this level of understanding before trying to write the code. You may find this hard to believe, but programmers often cannot resist the temptation to start writing code before they have this understanding.

It is not always easy to translate user requirements directly into VB code. As an intermediate step, programmers sometimes use pseudocode—or "false" code. It's not real code because it does not follow any strict rules of syntax. **Pseudocode is an English-like outline that is easy to write and easy to translate into real code.**

Let's look at some pseudocode for the guessing-game problem.

> *generate random integer between 1 and 6*
> *obtain user's guess via input box*
> *determine whether guess is correct and respond accordingly*

The first two lines of this pseudocode are easy to translate into actual VB statements because we've used similar statements many times, and because they are simple (not compound) statements. The third line represents a meta statement. That is, it describes what will eventually become a compound statement (If…Then…Else).

5.2 The If...Then...Else Statement

Often we expand a meta statement in pseudocode after we have written our first draft. The idea is to start with a very broad overview of what needs to be done, and then refine this with more and more detail until finally we write the actual VB code. The advantage of this approach is that it enables us to think about the problem-solving steps without worrying about rules of syntax.

Let's revise our pseudocode to expand the meta statement into more detail.

generate random integer between 1 and 6
obtain user's guess via input box
If user's guess = random integer Then
    beep
    display congratulations
Else
    display condolences
End If

Now we can easily translate this pseudocode into a working event procedure like the code in Figure 5.2.

This example is typical of the process that programmers follow to translate the user requirements for an application into working code. In the first pass, the pseudocode may be a simple list of fairly vague actions. In each subsequent pass the pseudocode is refined a little, and it begins to look more and more like actual program statements. The translation from pseudocode to VB statements is smoother if you include VB reserved words (such as If, Then, Else, and End If) in your pseudocode.

Most problems have more than one solution, and different programmers may think about the same problem in different ways. For example, one programmer might create the following pseudocode when translating the guessing-game description into working code.

obtain user's guess via input box
generate random integer between 1 and 6
If user's guess <> random integer Then
    display condolences
Else
    beep
    display congratulations
End If

The user will not be able to tell the difference between the two solutions. However, the fact that different programmers think about the same problem in different ways contributes to the difficulty of understanding someone else's code. This, in turn, increases the cost of maintaining business applications in the real world.

To make it easy for someone else to read your programs, use common sense in designing and coding problem solutions. For example, humans usually compare two quantities for equality rather than comparing them for inequality, so unless there are other reasons for using an inequality, the equality comparison will seem simpler.

EXERCISE 5.3

Modify cmdGuessMe_Click in Example 5.1 so that each time the button is clicked, the user enters a guess and the computer displays the total number of guesses the user has taken and the number of guesses that were correct.

EXERCISE 5.4 Modify cmdGuessMe_Click in Example 5.1 so that the user still enters a guess each time the button is clicked, but now when the user guesses correctly, it displays its congratulations, displays the number of guesses taken, and ends execution of the program (using the End statement). When the user's guess is incorrect, the event procedure should merely display condolences.

EXERCISE 5.5 An automobile insurance company allows customers to pay the amount of the insurance, called the *premium*, in one of two ways: twice a year or monthly. Each month the insurance company sends the customer a bill showing the balance (equal to the premium minus the total amount paid to date) and the minimum amount due. The minimum amount due is equal to the lesser of the following two quantities: (1) the balance and (2) the premium divided by 6.

The company is creating a VB form to process customer payments. Assume the form has module-level variables named Premium and Balance, and that these have been initialized to the correct amount for a given customer. Also assume that the form has Label controls named lblBalance and lblAmountDue, and their captions have also been initialized appropriately. The initializations might be performed in the Form_Load event procedure as shown below. (In a real application the premium and balance would be obtained from a database.)

```
Private Sub Form_Load()
    Premium = 435.00
    Balance = Premium
    lblBalance.Caption = Format$(Balance, "currency")
    lblAmountDue.Caption = Format$(Premium / 6, "currency")
End Sub
```

Write a Click event procedure for a command button named cmdProcessPayment that does the following:

1. Asks the user to enter the amount paid, then updates the balance by subtracting the amount paid from it.
2. If the balance is now greater than or equal to 0, makes lblBalance display the balance, and lblAmountDue display the minimum of the following two quantities: (a) the balance and (b) the premium divided by 6.
3. If the balance is now negative, makes lblBalance display the absolute value of the balance followed by "CR" (to indicate credit), and makes lblAmountDue display $0.00.

Be sure to format all dollar amounts. Use the IIf() function to compute the minimum of two quantities.

Using Logical Expressions in If...Then...Else Statements

Since the condition of the If...Then...Else statement is a logical expression, you can apply what you learned about logical expressions in Chapter 4. Recall the example used in that chapter of a multinational firm that wants to identify job candidates who have more than five years of business experience and who also speak at least three languages. To evaluate whether or not a candidate satisfies these requirements, we wrote the following logical expression:

(YearsExperience > 5) **And** (NumberOfLanguages >= 3)

We can use this expression as the condition of an If…Then…Else statement.

If (YearsExperience > 5) **And** (NumberOfLanguages >= 3) **Then**
   'statementblock to set up interview with candidate
Else
   'statementblock to display message that candidate does not meet requirements
End If

Alternatively, we can store the result of the logical expression in a Boolean variable, then use the variable in the condition of the If…Then…Else statement.

Qualified = ((YearsExperience > 5) **And** (NumberOfLanguages >= 3))
If Qualified = True **Then**
   'statementblock to set up interview with candidate
Else
   'statementblock to display message that candidate does not meet requirements
End If

Using a descriptive name for the variable makes the program easier to read. And if the result of the logical expression is needed in more than one place in the program, then evaluating it once and storing it in a variable can eliminate potential inconsistencies as well as shorten the program.

EXERCISE 5.6 It is possible to write event procedure cmdGuessMe_Click in Example 5.1 without any variables. Rewrite the If…Then…Else statement to accomplish this. Is the resulting code easier or harder to understand than when variables are used?

If…Then

Some decisions have two outcomes, only one of which requires processing. Consider, for example, a payroll program that computes overtime. If the condition determines whether a worker has put in extra hours, then a True outcome requires the calculation of the worker's extra pay, and a False outcome does not. In such situations we use VB's If…Then statement.

The syntax of the If…Then statement is

If condition **Then**
   statementblock
End If

Its action is as follows. When the computer executes the If statement, it first evaluates the condition and determines whether its outcome is True or False. If the outcome is

♦ True: the computer executes the statements in the statementblock, one at a time, from top-to-bottom, then resumes at the statement following End If.

♦ False: the computer skips immediately to the statement following End If.

Example 5.2

Using the If…Then Statement

As an example of the If…Then statement, suppose you want to use a Timer control to initiate a processing step after a delay of 100 seconds. Unfortunately, the maximum allowable value for the Timer control's Interval property is 65535, which corresponds to a delay of only about 65 seconds. One way to get around this constraint is to set the timer's Interval to 1000 (corresponding to a delay of 1 second), and have its event procedure count. When the count reaches 100, the event procedure can take the desired action. The event procedure in Figure 5.5 illustrates this idea.

The variable ElapsedTime is declared as a static variable—it retains its value from one execution of the procedure to the next. Every second the procedure is called and the value of the variable ElapsedTime is increased by 1. If the value is not equal to 100, the procedure does nothing—it just ends. However, if the value is equal to 100, the procedure displays the message "End of game" in a message box and terminates execution.

The If…Then statement is a simplified version of the If…Then…Else statement. If…Then…Else is useful when the two outcomes dictate either action A or action B. If…Then is useful when the two outcomes dictate either action A or no action. Because they are otherwise identical, in the remainder of the text we will refer to If…Then…Else and If…Then collectively as If statements.

EXERCISE 5.1

Complete the following event procedure by providing the statement block that will ensure that the message displayed in the message box is always correct. For example, if the user enters 3 followed by 5, then the message should read "3 <= 5", and if the user enters 7 followed by 4, then the message should read "4 <= 7".

Recall that a statement block is any sequence of zero or more statements. It may include If statements.

Do not modify, move, or add any statements before or after *statementblock*.

```
Private Sub cmdSort_Click()
    Dim X As Integer
    Dim Y As Integer
    Dim Z As Integer
        X = InputBox("Please enter an integer")
        Y = InputBox("Please enter another integer")
        'statementblock
        MsgBox X & " <= " & Y
End Sub
```

FIGURE 5.5

Code for Example 5.2

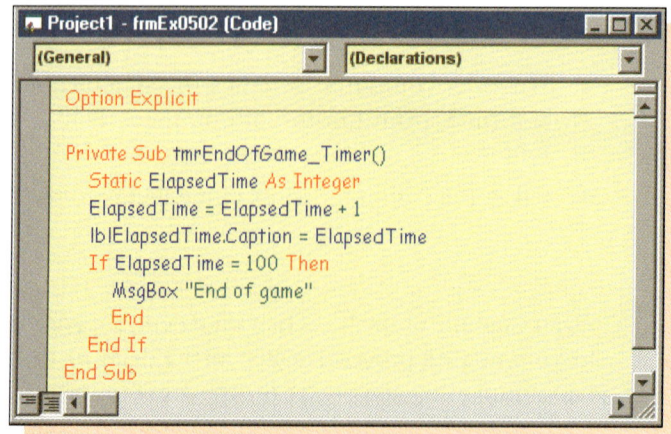

5.2 The If...Then...Else Statement

EXERCISE 5.8

Complete the following event procedure by providing the statement block that will ensure that the message displayed in the message box is always correct. For example, if the user enters the numbers 3, 5, and 6 in response to the input boxes, the message should read "Sequence 3, 5, 6 is in ascending order", but if the user enters 7, 4, 2 the message should read "Sequence 7, 4, 2 is not in ascending order".

Recall that a statement block is any sequence of zero or more statements. It may include If statements.

Do not modify, move, or add any statements before or after *statementblock*.

```
Private Sub cmdVerifyAscending_Click()
    Dim X As Integer
    Dim Y As Integer
    Dim Z As Integer
    Dim Sequence As String
    Dim BlankOrNot As String
    X = InputBox("Please enter an integer")
    Y = InputBox("Please enter a second integer")
    Z = InputBox("Please enter a third and final integer")
    'statementblock
    Sequence = "Sequence " & X & ", " & Y & ", " & Z
    MsgBox Sequence & " is " & BlankOrNot & " in ascending order"
End Sub
```

EXERCISE 5.9

Suppose that a user of the Caesar cipher encryption scheme (discussed in Example 4.15) needs to encrypt an entire sentence. A user employing the event procedure below would be wise to omit the spaces between words. Explain why.

```
Private Sub cmdCaesarCipher_Click()
    Dim Letter As String
    Letter = InputBox("Next letter?")
    lblPlaintext.Caption = lblPlaintext.Caption & Letter
    lblCiphertext.Caption = lblCiphertext.Caption & Chr$(Asc(Letter) + 3)
End Sub
```

Now modify cmdCaesarCipher_Click so that the user can include spaces without "giving the code away." That is, modify it so that it shifts only the alphabetic characters "A" through "Z" and "a" through "z". All nonalphabetic characters in the plaintext should appear unchanged in the ciphertext.

EXERCISE 5.10

Modify Project 7 (the stock trading simulation) to make the duration of the game equal to 100 seconds instead of 65 seconds. Eliminate either tmrClock or tmrEndOfGame by consolidating their actions. (This will eliminate the timing discrepancy that the user observes at the end of the game.)

EXERCISE 5.11

Modify Project 7 by automating the Buy and Sell operations. That is, have the program automatically buy whenever the asking price is less than the constant value THRESHOLDBUYPRICE and have the program automatically sell whenever the bidding price is more than the constant value THRESHOLDSELLPRICE.

To do this, create a Timer control with a small Interval (say 0.5 seconds) that compares the current asking and bidding prices to their respective thresholds.

Experiment with your program and see if you can determine the best values for THRESHOLDBUYPRICE and THRESHOLDSELLPRICE.

EXERCISE 5.12 In Exercise 5.11 the rule for when to buy (sell) considered only the asking price (bidding price). Should it also consider the number of units? Explain. Modify your solution to Exercise 5.11 to use both the asking price and the number of units in the rule for when to buy, and both the bidding price and the number of units in the rule for when to sell. Then experiment with the program to see if you can determine the best rules.

5.3 Nested If Statements

Frequently a statement block in the interior of an If statement contains another If statement. In fact, the "inner" If statement may have yet another If in its interior, and on and on. **If statements that are arranged in this way, with one containing another, are called** *nested* **or** *embedded.*

As an example, consider the problem of determining whether a sequence of three numbers is in ascending or descending order. The event procedure in Figure 5.6 provides a partial solution to this problem. Looking at the event procedure you can see that the comment must be replaced by a statement block whose action is to store an appropriate value ("ascending" or "descending") in the string variable AscOrDesc.

The statement block has to make a choice, because we do not know in advance what sequence of numbers the user will enter. The problem description identifies only two possible outcomes: the sequence is either in ascending or descending order. If you think about it, you will see that there is another possibility: the user might enter 5, 8, 1, for example, which is neither in ascending nor descending order. In this third case we would probably like the program to display the message "Sequence 5, 8, 1, is in neither ascending nor descending order."

How do we handle this decision, which has three outcomes? A common way of proceeding when faced with a new problem is to focus on only a part

FIGURE 5.6

Partial solution to ascending/descending problem

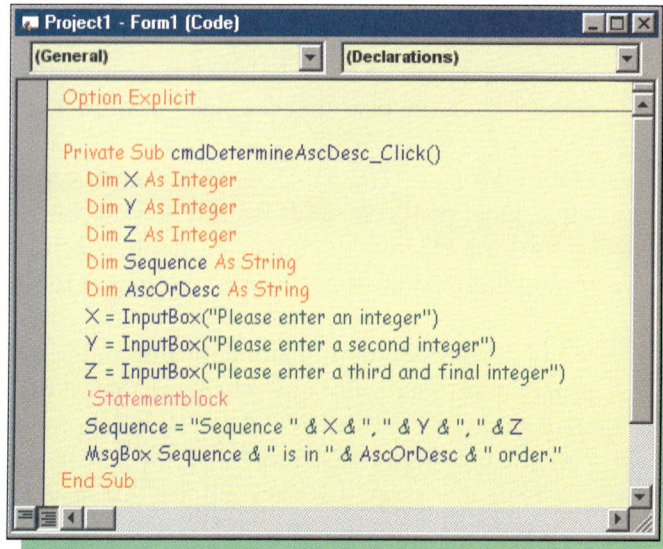

of the problem first, write out its solution in pseudocode, then assess whether it is possible to build on the partial solution. Consider the following pseudocode:

```
If (X < Y) And (Y < Z) Then
    AscOrDesc = "ascending"
Else
    what now? we know it's not ascending
End If
```

This pseudocode is actual VB code except for the second interior statement block "what now? we know it's not ascending." Can we translate this statement block into working VB statements?

Given that the sequence is not ascending, it must be either descending or neither. That is, at the position of "what now? we know it's not ascending," we still have a decision, but now there are only two possible outcomes: either the sequence is descending, or it is neither ascending nor descending. We know how to handle a two-outcome decision with an If…Then…Else statement, so we can write our If statement as

```
If (X < Y) And (Y < Z) Then
    AscOrDesc = "ascending"
Else
    If (X > Y) And (Y > Z) Then
        AscOrDesc = "descending"
    Else
        AscOrDesc = "neither ascending nor descending"
    End If
End If
```

This is a solution to the problem.

As you can see, indentation is even more important when using embedded If statements. Each If statement has its own Else and its own End If. To keep clear which Elses and End Ifs belong to which Ifs, the "I" in If should line up vertically with both the "E" in its Else (if it has one) and the "E" in its End If, and the statement blocks in the interior should be indented.

Embedded If statements are frequently used this way to handle decisions with more than two outcomes. They are used so frequently that VB provides a shortcut syntax that you should use when the statement block following Else begins with an If. The code in our example can be written more clearly using this shortcut as follows.

```
If (X < Y) And (Y < Z) Then
    AscOrDesc = "ascending"
ElseIf (X > Y) And (Y > Z) Then
    AscOrDesc = "descending"
Else
    AscOrDesc = "neither ascending nor descending"
End If
```

Note carefully that there is now only one If, one Else, and one End If. The ElseIf belongs to the If above it in the same way that the Else belongs to the If above it. When it can be used, this syntax is preferable to a nested If because it is easier to see the conditions and outcomes.

The shortcut syntax can be extended to handle any number of outcomes. There are only two restrictions: (1) there can be only one Else, and (2) no ElseIfs can follow the Else; that is, the Else must represent the last (bottom) outcome.

The syntax for a decision with five outcomes follows:

If *condition1* **Then**
    statementblock1
ElseIf *condition2* **Then**
    statementblock2
ElseIf *condition3* **Then**
    statementblock3
ElseIf *condition4* **Then**
    statementblock4
Else
    statementblock5
End If

As before, exactly one of the statement blocks in this structure will be executed. VB evaluates the conditions in order (starting at the top and proceeding through subsequent ElseIfs) and stops at the first one that evaluates to True. VB then executes the corresponding statement block and resumes at the statement following End If. If none of the conditions evaluate to True, then VB executes the statement block following Else.

Example 5.3 — Using Shortcut Syntax for Embedded If Statements

A labor union bases its wage rate for a particular job class on number of months of service.

Wage Rate Categories Based on Months of Service	Wage Rate
< 3	$ 9.75
≥ 3 and < 6	10.25
≥ 6 and < 12	11.00
≥ 12 and < 24	12.50
≥ 24	14.75

We need a Click event procedure that asks the user to input the number of months of service, then determines the corresponding wage rate from the table, stores it in a module-level variable named *WageRate*, and displays it in a message box. The solution is shown in Figure 5.7.

After the value for *MonthsOfService* is entered by the user, it is tested to see which wage rate category it belongs to. For example, if the user enters 10, the first condition (*MonthsOfService* < 3) is False, so the first ElseIf condition is evaluated. Its condition (*MonthsOfService* < 6) is also False, so the next ElseIf condition is evaluated. Its condition (*MonthsOfService* < 12) is True, so *WageRate* is set equal to 11. This completes execution of the If statement, so the MsgBox statement is executed next.

Figure 5.8 shows a very poor solution to the same problem. It produces the same result as the solution in Figure 5.7, but is much longer than necessary. Also, it is redundant in two ways. As always, these redundancies create potential for the program to behave inconsistently, which may annoy the user or cause the program to produce incorrect results. Try to spot the redundancies.

FIGURE 5.7

Code for Example 5.3

FIGURE 5.8

Poor solution to wage rate problem

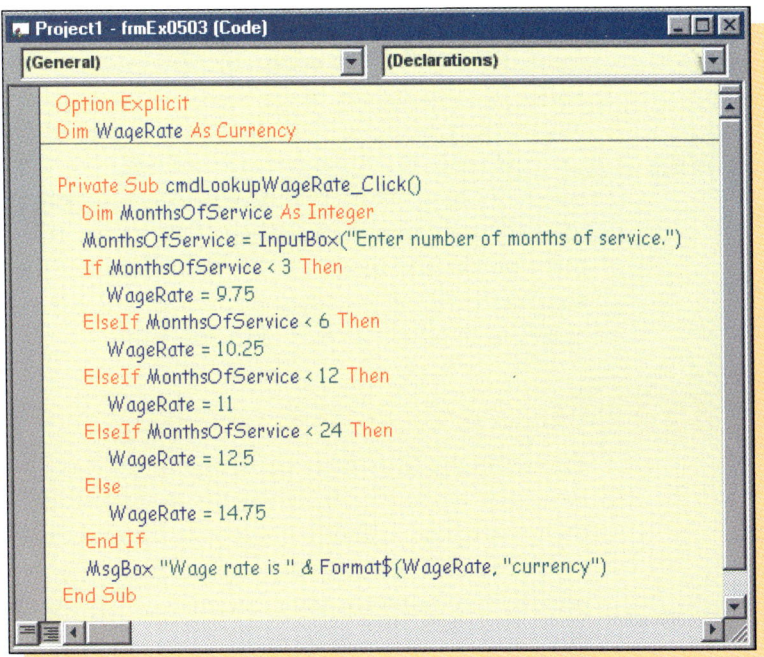

One redundancy is the repetition in the conditions. The constant 3, for example, occurs in *condition1*,

MonthsOfService < 3

and in *condition2*,

(MonthsOfService >= 3) **And** (MonthsOfService < 6)

In *condition2*, it is not necessary to check whether the months of service is greater than or equal to 3. Why? The computer evaluates *condition1* first, and if *condition1* is True, it executes *statementblock1*, then jumps to the statement following End If. The computer will evaluate *condition2* only if *condition1* is False; but this means that MonthsOfService must be greater than or equal to 3, and so there is no need to check this as part of *condition2*.

The other redundancy is the message box statement, which occurs in the statement block of every outcome. Any time you see the same statement occur in every statement block of an If structure, try to remove it from the statement blocks and place it either before or after the If structure. After all, if the statement will be executed regardless of the outcome, it is probably not necessary to handle it as part of the decision.

Example 5.4

Using Embedded If Statements

This example illustrates that sometimes it is better not to use the shortcut syntax for embedded If statements. You must use common sense to determine the most readable and maintainable form of the If statements.

An automobile insurance company uses a customer's risk factors to compute the premium for the customer's policy. As an intermediate step, it computes a "risk rate" based on the customer's age and sex.

Age	Risk Rate Male	Risk Rate Female
≤ 18	.34	.26
>18 and <21	.28	.22
≥ 21	.22	.18

We need an event procedure that asks the user to enter a customer's sex and age, then determines the risk rate for the customer, stores the risk rate in a module-level variable named RiskRate, and displays it. The event procedure in Figure 5.9 is one solution to this problem.

An alternative solution uses ElseIfs as follows. This solution contains more redundancy than the solution in Figure 5.9.

```
If (Sex = "Male") And (Age <= 18) Then
    RiskRate = 0.34
ElseIf (Sex = "Male") And (Age < 21) Then
    RiskRate = 0.28
ElseIf (Sex = "Male") Then
    RiskRate = 0.22
ElseIf (Sex = "Female") And (Age <= 18) Then
    RiskRate = 0.26
ElseIf (Sex = "Female") And (Age < 21) Then
    RiskRate = 0.22
Else
    RiskRate = 0.18
End If
```

Exercise 5.13

In Example 5.4, what happens if the user enters "male" instead of "Male" in response to the first input box? Explain. Suggest a way to modify the code so this doesn't happen. *Hint:* Use the UCase$() function.

FIGURE 5.9

Code for Example 5.4

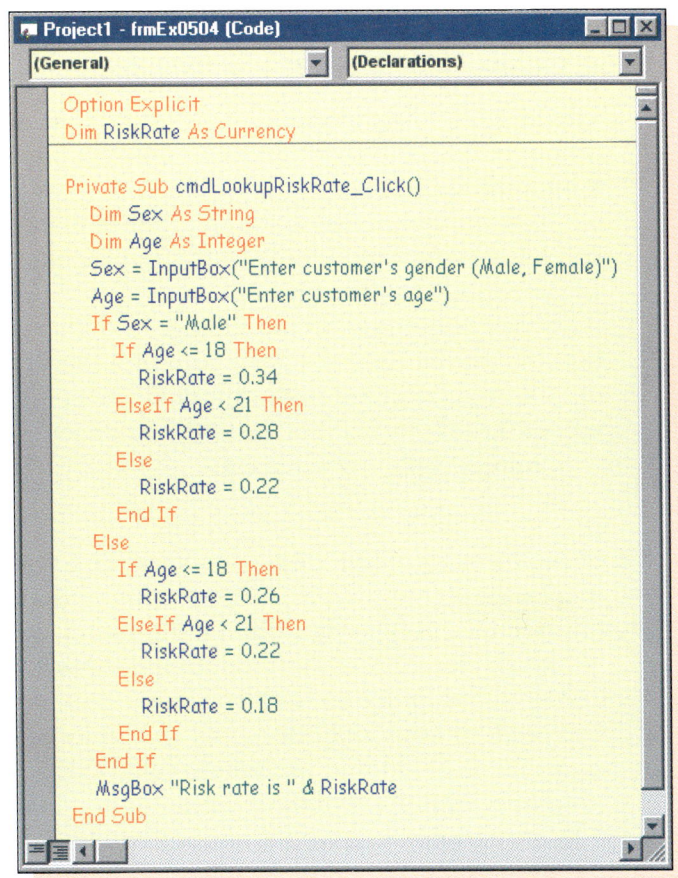

EXERCISE 5.14 What happens in Example 5.4 if the user makes any typographical errors when attempting to enter "Male" or "Female" in response to the first input box? Explain. Suggest a way to modify the code so this doesn't happen.

EXERCISE 5.15 A credit card company sends monthly bills to its customers. The bill shows the customer's balance (amount owed) and minimum amount due. The minimum amount due is computed from the balance as follows. If the balance is less than $0 (meaning the customer has overpaid), then the minimum amount due is $0. If the balance is between $0 and $20, inclusive, the minimum amount due is equal to the balance. If the balance is greater than $20, the minimum amount due is equal to the larger of the following two quantities: $20, or 2 percent of the balance.

Write a Click event procedure for a command button that asks the user to enter a customer's balance, then computes and displays the corresponding minimum amount due.

5.4 The MsgBox() Function

Applications frequently display dialog boxes containing combinations of buttons like OK and Cancel, or Yes and No, to allow the user to make simple choices. **The *MsgBox() function* displays a message box on the screen and waits for the user to click one of the buttons; then it returns a value that indicates which button the user clicked.** This value can then be used by decision-making code to select an action that corresponds to the user's choice.

The syntax of the MsgBox() function is

MsgBox*(message, mbtype, title)*

This looks a lot like the syntax of the MsgBox statement. The difference in their actions is that the MsgBox statement does not provide any indication of which button the user clicked.

Now let's look at the *mbtype* argument in more detail (VB's online help calls this argument *buttons* instead of *mbtype*). In addition to specifying an icon style for the message box, the (numeric) value of *mbtype* specifies the combination of buttons to be displayed in the message box. The six different button combinations are listed in Table 5.1 along with the value of *mbtype* that produces them.

The value returned by the MsgBox() function indicates which button the user clicked. Table 5.2 lists the return value for each button.

As an example, the statement

Response = MsgBox("You've taken 10 guesses. Quit now?", 4)

causes the computer to display the message box shown in Figure 5.10, then wait for the user to click one of the buttons. If the user clicks Yes, the MsgBox() function returns the value 6, and if the user clicks No, it returns the value 7.

Recall that to specify an icon for the message box, we use one of the values 16, 32, 48, or 64 for the *mbtype* argument (see Table 4.1 for the association between icons and constants). To specify both an icon and a particular combination of buttons, use *mbtype* equal to the sum of the constant for the icon (from Table 4.1) and the constant for the button combination (from Table 5.1). For example, to make the message box show both a question icon (*vbQuestion* = 32) and the Yes and No button combination (*vbYesNo* = 4), use *mbtype* equal to 36. Thus, the statement

Response = MsgBox("You've taken 7 guesses. Quit now?", 36)

displays the message box in Figure 5.11.

Using VB's predefined symbolic constants for the MsgBox() function makes your code easier to read. This is illustrated in the next example.

Example 5.5 — Using the MsgBox() Function

The event procedure in Figure 5.12 modifies the guessing game from Example 5.1. When the user guesses correctly, it displays congratulations and then terminates execution. It also counts the number of guesses the user has made,

TABLE 5.1 MsgBox() button combinations

Button Combination	Mbtype	Symbolic Constant
OK only	0	vbOKOnly
OK and Cancel	1	vbOKCancel
Abort, Retry, and Ignore	2	vbAbortRetryIgnore
Yes, No, and Cancel	3	vbYesNoCancel
Yes and No	4	vbYesNo
Retry and Cancel	5	vbRetryCancel

TABLE 5.2 MsgBox() return values

Button Clicked	Return Value	Symbolic Constant
OK	1	vbOK
Cancel	2	vbCancel
Abort	3	vbAbort
Retry	4	vbRetry
Ignore	5	vbIgnore
Yes	6	vbYes
No	7	vbNo

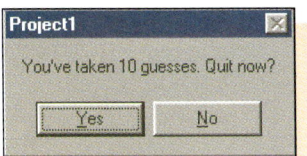

FIGURE 5.10

Message box showing Yes and No buttons

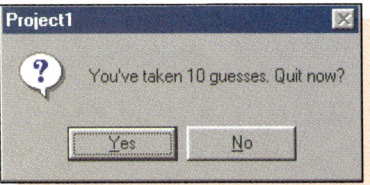

FIGURE 5.11

Message box with Yes and No buttons and an icon

FIGURE 5.12

Code for Example 5.5

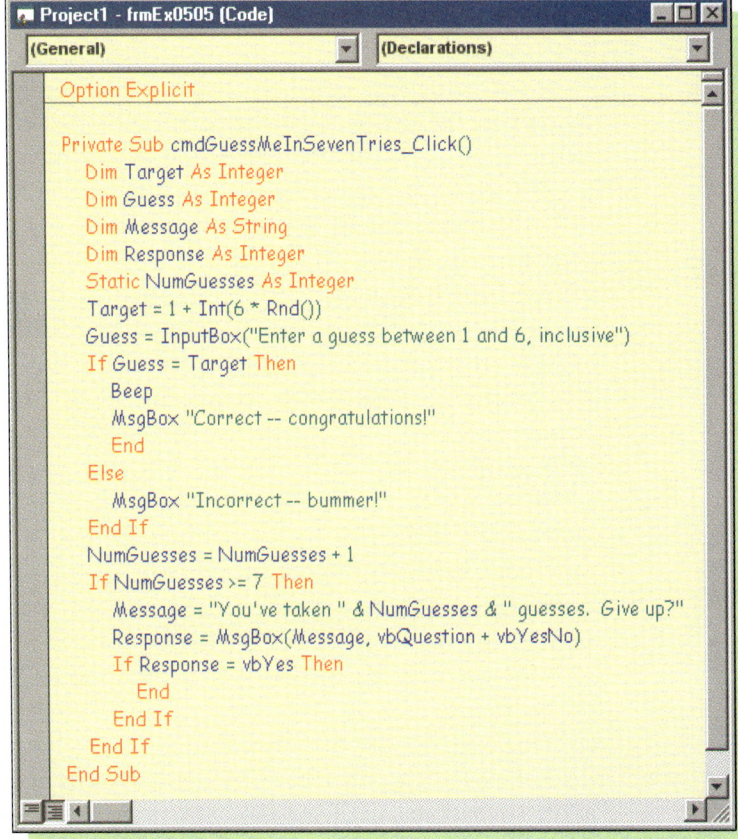

using the static variable NumGuesses; if this count reaches 7, it displays a message and gives the user the option of quitting. If the user chooses to quit, program execution terminates.

5.5 The Option Button Control

Many programs have options from which the user must select exactly one. For example, in a medical records system the user needs to specify the sex (male or female) of the patient. VB's *Option button control*, **which ensures that the user will select only one option**, is simple and very effective in such situations.

Appearance and Use

Figure 5.13 identifies the option button tool and shows an Option button control on the form at design time. Visually, an option button appears as descriptive text next to a circle. At run time, the user selects an option button

FIGURE 5.13

Option button tool and control

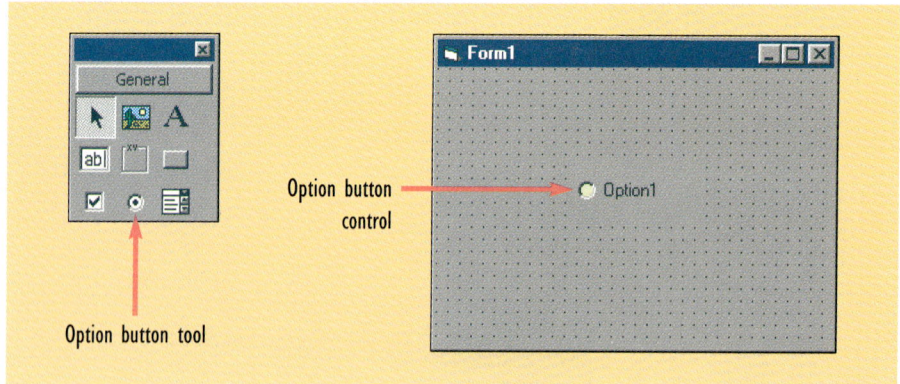

by moving the cursor atop either the text or the circle, then clicking the mouse. VB acknowledges the user's selection by placing a black dot in the circle.

If the user subsequently selects a different option button, VB automatically erases the black dot from the previously selected option button and moves it to the newly chosen option button. Thus, the user is able to select *only one* option from a group of option buttons.[1] The programmer often provides a command button to let the user initiate processing after making a choice.

Like the Text box control and Command button control, the Option button control is capable of receiving the focus. The user can move the focus among controls using the mouse or the [TAB] key. In addition, the user can change the selected option button using the [↑] and [↓] keys.

To demonstrate the use of option buttons, let us work with a computerized replica of the U.S. Individual Income Tax Return (Form 1040). The Filing Status section of this form presents the taxpayer with five options. The taxpayer is required to specify exactly one of them. If option buttons are used, this section might appear as in Figure 5.14.

When you design an application with option buttons, be sure to keep the number of options the user has to choose from small, no more than seven or so. This is an important rule of thumb for designing GUIs. Researchers in the field of psychology have long known that most people cannot keep more than about seven items in their short-term memory and, as a result, it is difficult for them to make a selection if the list of options is longer than that.

FIGURE 5.14

User interface for filing status section of income tax form

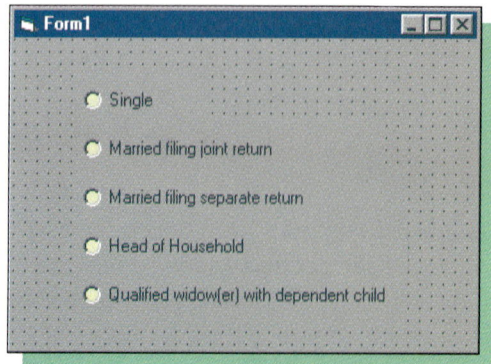

[1] Option buttons are also called *radio buttons* because they act like the channel selector buttons on a car radio. You can push only one at a time and when you push another, the prior button is deselected.

Properties

Table 5.3 lists some properties of the Option button control.

> **Convention** Use the prefix "opt" for the names of Option button controls.

TABLE 5.3 Properties of the Option button Control

Property	Specifies
Caption	*The descriptive text that is displayed next to the circle.* As with command buttons, you can specify an access key (a keyboard alternative to clicking the mouse) by including an ampersand (&) in the caption immediately preceding the letter that is to be the access key. VB visually informs the user that the access key exists by underlining its letter in the caption, and the user employs the access key by pressing that letter in combination with the ALT key.
Alignment	*Whether the caption should be displayed to the left or to the right of the circle.*
Value	*Whether or not the option button is the selected one.* When VB places the black dot in the circle, it also sets the option button's Value property to True; similarly, when VB "clears" the circle (because the user selects a different option button), it sets the option button's Value property to False. At run time the program can determine which option button the user selected by accessing this property.
Picture	*The path and file name of a file containing a picture to be displayed.* When this property is specified the option button's appearance changes from a "circle with a black dot" to a button that is "pushed in" when selected and "raised" when not selected. The picture should be appropriate to the function of the option button. The Style property must be set to 1 - Graphical in order for the picture to be displayed. The valid file types are bitmap (.bmp or .dib), icon (.ico), metafile (.wmf or .emf), GIF (.gif), and JPEG (.jpg).
DownPicture	*The path and file name of a file containing a picture to be displayed when the option button is selected.* The option button will show the picture specified by Picture when it is not selected, and the picture specified by DownPicture when it is selected.
Style	*Whether the option button is able to display only a caption or both a caption and a picture.* The two possible settings are 0 - Standard and 1 - Graphical.
TabStop	*Whether or not the user can tab to the option button* (i.e., whether or not the option button can receive the focus as the result of the user pressing the TAB key).
TabIndex	*The position of the option button in the tab cycle.* When a form becomes active, the focus is given to the control with the lowest TabIndex. When the user presses the TAB key, the focus jumps to the control with the next highest TabIndex (if there is no control with a higher TabIndex setting, the focus jumps back to the control with the lowest TabIndex setting).
MousePointer	*What the mouse pointer should look like when the user moves it atop the option button* (at run time). For example, if the MousePointer property is set to 0 - Default, then when the user moves the mouse pointer over the option button, it will retain the same shape it had when it was over the form. But if the MousePointer property is set to 2 - Cross, then when the user moves the mouse pointer over the option button, it will change to a crosshair shape, regardless of what shape it had when it was over the form.* This can provide a useful visual cue: when the user sees the mouse pointer change, it is obvious that the pointer is over the option button.

*The Form control also has a MousePointer property, so that programmers can specify the shape the mouse pointer should "ordinarily" have (i.e., when it is over the form but not over the option button).

In terms of its role in a program's operation, the Value property is the option button's most used property. This property is binary: it has two allowable settings, True and False. As a result, the Option button control is a natural partner of the If statement. The event procedure that processes the user's selections can use an option button's Value property as the condition of an If statement.

Events

The Option button control is capable of responding to the Click event. Often, however, the option button's Click event procedure is not used to perform major processing tasks. Instead, the Option button control is used just as a means of getting input from the user, and the user initiates processing by clicking on a command button.

Example 5.6 Using Option Buttons

An automobile insurance company uses a computer program to compute a driver's premium. The premium is based on the risk rate, which in turn depends on the driver's age and sex. The user must specify either male or female, and option buttons are a good way to accomplish this. Figure 5.15 shows the user interface.

The user first selects the appropriate option button, then clicks the command button. The Click event procedure for cmdComputeRiskFactor is shown in Figure 5.16. The condition *optMale.Value = True* will be True if the user selected the Male option; otherwise it will be False.

An equivalent way of writing the logical expression in

If *optMale.Value* = **True Then**

is as

If *optMale.Value* **Then**

You may think that this syntax is not valid because it is not comparing optMale.Value to another value. However, these two alternatives are identical as far as VB is concerned. In the first alternative, optMale's Value property is retrieved and then compared to the logical constant True. If they are equal, VB executes the "True action" of the If statement. The second one looks at the current contents of optMale's Value property and if it is True, executes the "True action" of the If statement.

FIGURE 5.15

User interface for insurance risk rate program

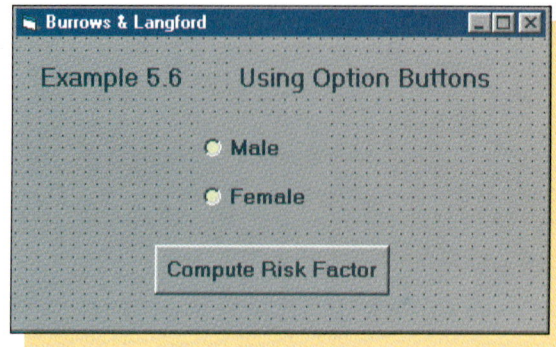

FIGURE 5.16

Code for Example 5.6

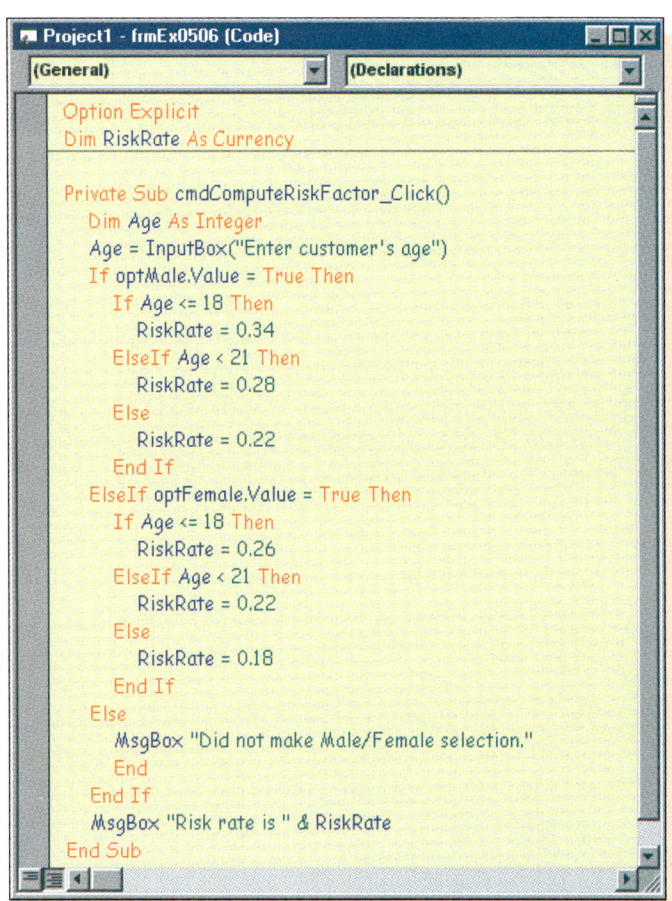

Note that we include a condition for the case in which neither option button is selected. Why do we do this? Suppose we did not provide it; then what would happen if neither option button was selected when the user clicked the command button? Since the Value property of both option buttons would be False, none of the actions in the If statement would be executed. Thus, the module-level variable RiskRate would not be modified, and its value would be whatever value was left over from the previous execution of the procedure. This would be a very serious error in the code because the program would produce an incorrect risk rate and the user would be unaware of the error. To be safe, you should always include an outcome in decision-making code for the user's failure to make a selection.

EXERCISE 5.16 Suppose you have a project consisting of a single form with several option buttons, and the Value properties of all of the option buttons have been initialized to False. When program execution begins, how many of the option buttons will be selected (i.e., how many will have a black dot)? Which one(s)? Create a simple VB project to find out.

EXERCISE 5.17 Suppose that you have just finished an application and given it to a user to try out. Your application requires the user to answer a Yes/No question, and you have provided option buttons for this purpose. The user complains that a text box is preferable because typing is quicker than positioning the mouse. How do you respond to this criticism?

5.6 The Frame Control

Some programs require the user to answer more than one question. For example, on the U.S. Income Tax form, taxpayers are asked two Yes/No questions:

- Do you want $3 to go to this fund?
- If a joint return, does your spouse want $3 to go to this fund?

The answers to these questions are easily processed using four option buttons. The interface for this part of the tax form might appear as in Figure 5.17. However, VB allows only one option button to be selected at any given time. If we put these four option buttons on the same form as the Filing Status option buttons, then there will be a total of nine option buttons on the form, only one of which can be selected. But there are really three separate questions. What we need is a way to inform VB of this fact, so that VB will allow one option button to be selected for each question. **The *Frame control* allows you to group option buttons to correspond to categories of items, so that the user can select exactly one item in each category.**[2]

Appearance and Use

Visually, the Frame control appears as a rectangle surrounding the controls it groups together. Descriptive text appears at the top left corner of the rectangle. Figure 5.18 identifies the Frame tool and shows a Frame control on the form at design time.

To group option buttons, you first must draw the Frame control on the form, and then draw the option buttons in the frame. Double-clicking the Option button tool always places a new option button directly on the form

FIGURE 5.17

User interface for campaign fund section of income tax form

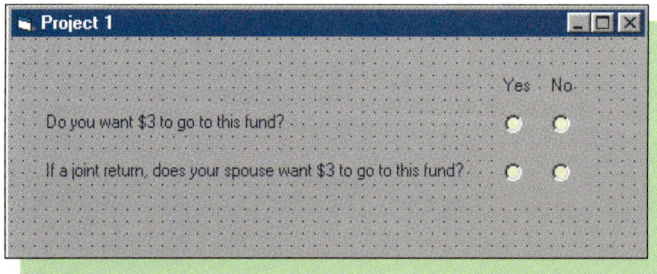

FIGURE 5.18

Frame tool and control

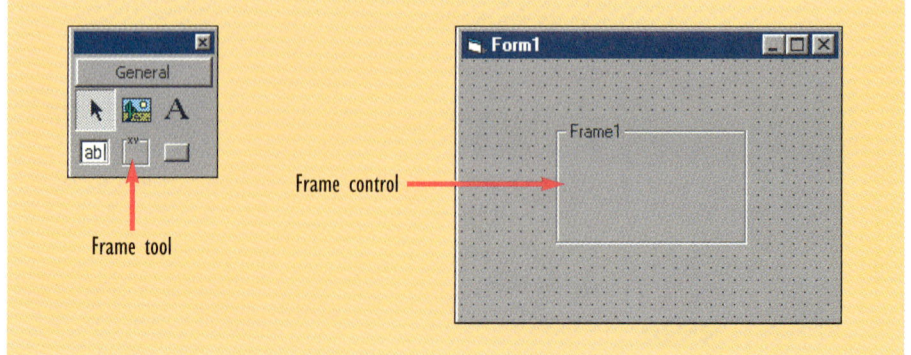

[2] The Frame control can contain other types of controls besides option buttons, and is often referred to as a "container control." Other examples of container controls include the form and the picture box (discussed in Appendix C).

(hence, not in a frame), and an option button that resides directly on the form cannot be dragged into a frame. To move an option button from the form to a frame (or from frame to frame), use a cut-and-paste procedure: select the option button, cut it (Cu_t under the _Edit menu), select the destination frame, and then paste (_Paste under the _Edit menu).

If you attempt to drag option buttons from a form to a frame, then you are likely to be misled by the resulting visual appearance because it may be the same as when the frame really does group the option buttons. To verify that the frame does indeed group the option buttons, try dragging the frame (at design time); the option buttons should move with it.

Properties

Table 5.4 lists some important properties of the Frame control.

> **Convention** Use the prefix "fra" for names of Frame controls.

Events

The Frame control is capable of responding to Click events. However, the frame's Click event procedure is seldom used to perform major processing tasks. The Frame control's fundamental purpose is to organize the controls on a form.

With the Frame control we can add the questions about Presidential Election Campaign contributions to the U.S. Individual Income Tax Return form. The form shown in Figure 5.19 contains three Frame controls. The rectangle surrounding the label displaying "Presidential Election Campaign" is not a frame, but is rather just a *Shape control* with its Shape property set to 0 - Rectangle. The filing status frame has its Caption property set to "Filing Status", and the other two frames have empty captions.

The names of the frames and option buttons on this form are shown in Table 5.5. If you look carefully at the option button names you can discern a common naming convention. All of them begin with *opt*. But the next few letters of these names are an abbreviation that suggests the name of the frame in which the option button resides. This is a simple trick to help the programmer keep track of which option buttons reside in which frame.

We know that when the user selects an option button at run time, VB sets its Value property to True, places a black dot in the button, and generates a Click event. But the option button can also be selected in code by executing an assignment statement such as the following:

optPECYouYes.Value = **True**

TABLE 5.4 Properties of the Frame control

Property	Specifies
Caption	*The text to be displayed at the top left corner of the frame.*
Enabled	*Whether or not the frame, and the controls it groups, can respond to events. When a Frame control is disabled, all of the controls it groups together are also disabled.*
MousePointer	*What the mouse pointer should look like when the user moves it over the frame.*

FIGURE 5.19

Expanded user interface for income tax return application

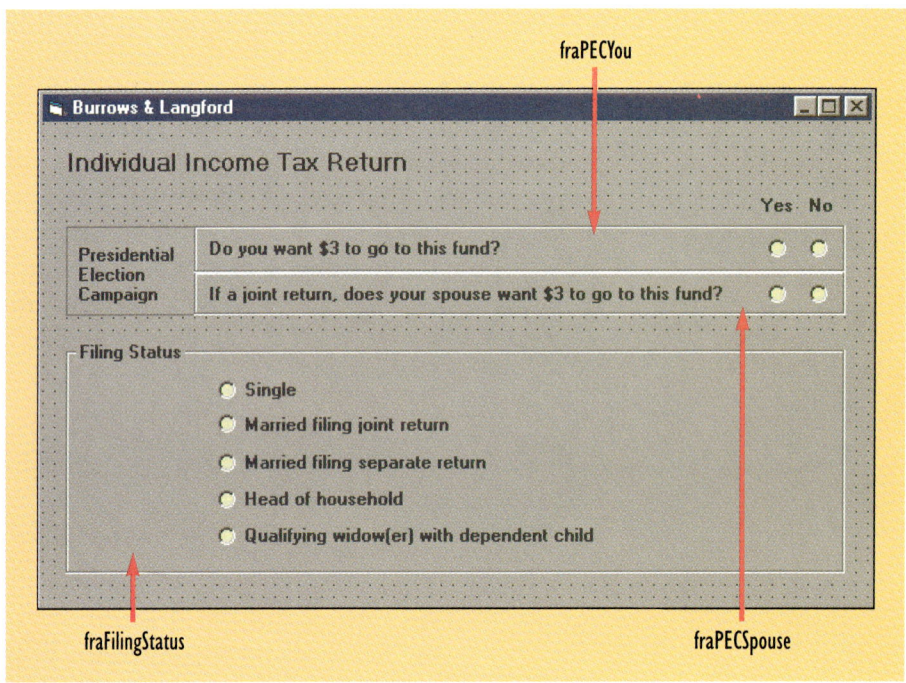

TABLE 5.5 Main controls for user interface of Figure 5.19	
Frame	Option Buttons
fraPECYou	optPECYouYes
	optPECYouNo
fraPECSpouse	optPECSpouseYes
	optPECSpouseNo
fraFilingStatus	optFSSingle
	optFSMarriedJoint
	optFSMarriedSeparate
	optFSHeadOfHousehold
	optFSWidower

When this statement executes, VB places a black dot in the option button and generates a Click event.

Setting an option button's Value property in code can often be used to good effect, as our next example illustrates.

Example 5.7 Using the Option Button's Click Event

The three separate questions on the income tax form in Figure 5.19 are not entirely independent of one another. The event procedures in Figure 5.20 make the user aware of this. Event procedure optFSSingle_Click disables the Election Campaign question that a single taxpayer cannot answer, and event procedure optFSMarriedJoint_Click enables it again for a married taxpayer.

Event procedure optFSSingle_Click is executed when the user selects filing status Single. It performs the following actions:

✦ It deselects the two option buttons optPECSpouseYes and optPECSpouseNo, by setting their Value properties to False.

FIGURE 5.20

Code for Example 5.7

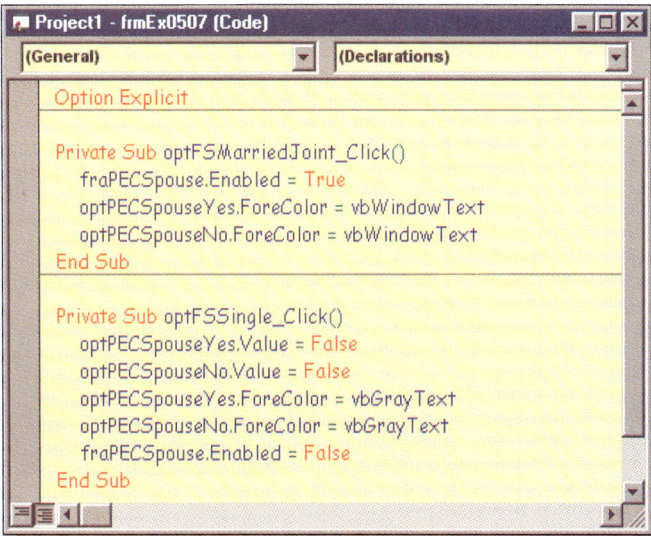

- It changes the color of the two option buttons and their captions to light gray, which provides a visual cue to the user that this question does not apply.
- It disables the Frame control (by setting its Enabled property to False). This has the effect of disabling the controls in the frame (optPECSpouseYes and optPECSpouseNo) so that the user cannot select either of them.

Figure 5.21 shows the effect, at run time, when the user selects filing status Single.

Event procedure optFSMarriedJoint_Click is executed when the user selects filing status Married filing joint return. This event procedure undoes the effect of optFSSingle_Click, which is necessary because the question "If a joint return, does your spouse want $3 to go to this fund?" is again applicable. The user can switch back and forth between the two filing statuses, each time observing the applicability or nonapplicability of the choice regarding his or her spouse's $3.

In the code in Figure 5.20, *vbWindowText* and *vbGrayText* are predefined symbolic constants. VB provides a number of predefined symbolic constants for representing colors. See online help (search phrase "color constants") for further information.

FIGURE 5.21

User interface when user selects filing status Single

Changing the color of controls on a form to provide a visual cue to the user is a common technique in GUI applications. Most Windows users are accustomed to seeing certain controls (notably command buttons and menu items) turn light gray when they are disabled.

5.7 The Check Box Control

Users sometimes have to make decisions that require selecting a combination of options from a set of alternatives. For example, in a real estate application the user may be asked to specify whether the houses to be viewed should have a garden, a garage, and/or a view. Any combination of these options is valid. For such situations, **where a combination of options may be selected,** VB **provides the** *Check box control.*

Appearance and Use

Figure 5.22 identifies the Check box tool and shows a Check box control on the form at design time. A check box appears as descriptive text next to a square. At run time, the user selects a check box by moving the cursor atop either the text or the square, then clicking the mouse. VB acknowledges the user's selection by placing a checkmark in the square. The user can remove the checkmark by clicking on it again; this action is called *deselection*.[3]

Functionally, the essential difference between option buttons and check boxes is that option buttons impose the restriction that the user selects only one option, whereas check boxes do not. This is an important difference. Experienced users rely on the visually different appearance of option buttons and check boxes to quickly infer whether they are allowed to select only one option or several. Thus, a programmer who uses check boxes when option buttons are appropriate will construct programs that users find confusing.

Properties and Events

The commonly used properties of the Check box control are the same as those of the Option button control. However, instead of True and False, the allowed values of the check box's Value property are 0 - Unchecked, 1 - Checked, and 2 - Grayed.

Like the option button, the check box can respond to a Click event.

FIGURE 5.22

Check box tool and control

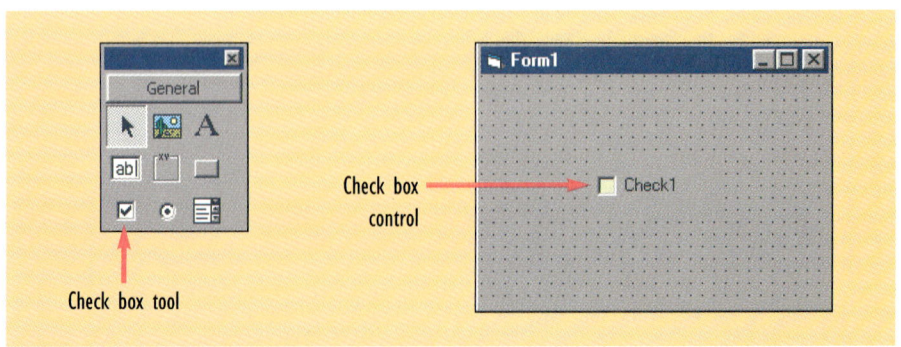

---

[3] Any type of action that alternately turns something on and off is called a *toggle*.

Convention Use the prefix "chk" for the names of Check box controls.

Example 5.8   Using Check Boxes

The U.S. Individual Income Tax Return (Form 1040) contains an Exemptions section. In our computerized application, this section might appear as shown in Figure 5.23. The taxpayer may check neither, one of, or both of the boxes for Yourself and Spouse.

A subsequent step in the income tax form requires counting the number of exemptions claimed by the filer. The event procedure in Figure 5.24 performs this task; it stores the result in a module-level variable named *NumberOfExemptions* and displays it. Observe that the code works correctly for every possible combination of checkmarks in the two boxes. Also observe the use of the pre-defined symbolic constant *vbChecked*. Two other predefined constants that are useful with the Check box control are *vbUnchecked* and *vbGrayed*.

EXERCISE 5.18

Is it ever necessary to group check boxes using a Frame control? If so, why? If not, would it hurt to group them anyway, or might it help? Explain.

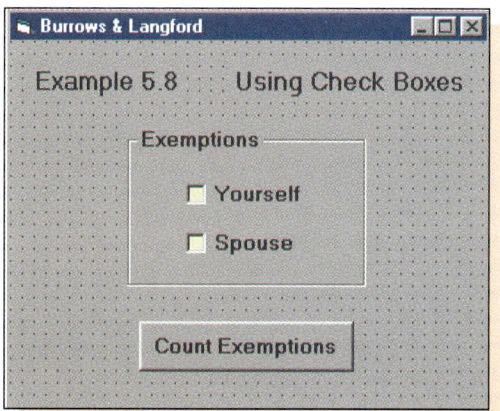

FIGURE 5.23

User interface for Example 5.8

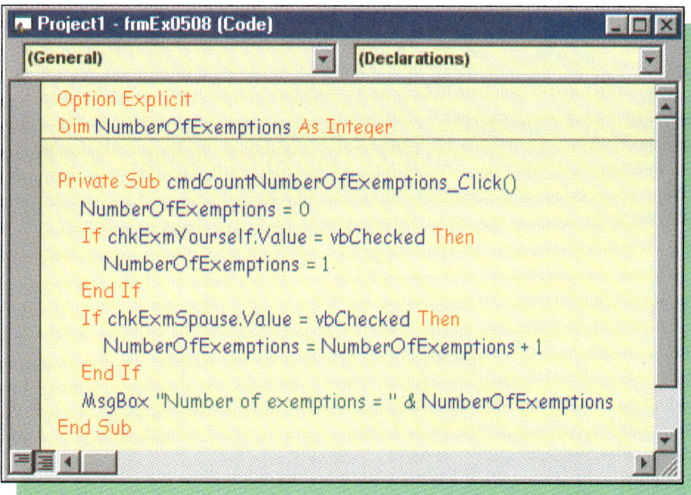

FIGURE 5.24

Code for Example 5.8

EXERCISE 5.19 A form contains two check boxes (chkA and chkB), two option buttons (optA and optB), and a command button (cmdShowTotals). The code for this form is shown below. Note that two of the controls, chkB and optY, do not have event procedures (which means that nothing happens when the user clicks on them). When program execution begins, both of the check boxes are clear (they don't have checkmarks in them). The user then clicks on the controls in the following order:

chkA, chkB, chkA, optX, optY, optX, cmdShowTotals

Show the values that are displayed by the message boxes in cmdShowTotals_Click.

```
Option Explicit
Dim TotalA As Integer
Dim TotalX As Integer

Private Sub chkA_Click()
    If chkA.Value = vbChecked Then
        TotalA = TotalA + 10
    Else
        TotalA = TotalA - 5
    End If
End Sub

Private Sub optX_Click()
    If optX.Value = True Then
        TotalX = TotalX + 10
    Else
        TotalX = TotalX - 5
    End If
End Sub

Private Sub cmdShowTotals_Click()
    MsgBox "Total A = " & TotalA
    MsgBox "Total X = " & TotalX
End Sub
```

5.8 Project 8: A Simple Expert System

An expert is a person who possesses special knowledge or ability in a particular area. Accordingly, an *expert system* **is an application program that embodies some of the knowledge or ability of a human expert.** The goal of developing an expert system is to reduce the cost of providing expertise by embedding it in a program which can be copied and distributed inexpensively.

As an example of an expert system, consider the problem faced by banks when presented with a loan request. Given information about the applicant, how does the bank decide whether to grant or refuse the loan? The bank wants to predict the likelihood that the applicant will repay the loan. If the likelihood is high, the bank grants the loan; if it is low, the bank refuses the loan.

The job of predicting the likelihood that an applicant will repay a loan has traditionally been assigned to loan managers, who, over time, gain experience and develop expertise assessing a borrower's creditworthiness. By interviewing experienced loan managers, we can discover at least some of the rules that guide their decision-making process, and we can then embed these rules in a computer program. Perhaps it would be unwise to entirely supplant human judgment with this program, but it seems reasonable to expect the program to identify and handle the clear-cut cases, and pass the difficult cases on to the human loan manager.

Complex expert systems today are usually created using specialized development environments called expert system shells. Using a shell, the developer usually only enters the rules, and the shell software decides how to translate the rules into a working expert system. VB is a general-purpose programming environment (i.e., it is not specifically tailored for creating expert systems), but in this example we use it to create a greatly simplified expert system and illustrate the creation of interfaces that allow program users to make choices that cause the program to select alternative actions.

Description of the Application

From our interviews of loan managers, we have found that they concur with the following description of their decision processes. First, categorize the applicant's Income as High, Medium, or Low.

- If Income is High, *grant* the loan.

- If Income is Medium, categorize the applicant's Employment and level of Education. If the applicant is Employed and has High Education, *grant* the loan. If the applicant is Employed and has Low Education, or is Unemployed and has High Education, *investigate further*. If the applicant is Unemployed and has Low Education, *refuse* the loan.

- If Income is Low, categorize the applicant's References as Good or Bad. If the References are Good, *investigate further*. If the References are Bad, *refuse* the loan.

The expert system will apply these rules[4] to the input data for a customer's loan request to arrive at one of three possible recommendations: grant the loan, refuse the loan, or investigate further. The last recommendation means that the loan request should be turned over to a human loan manager.

We can neatly summarize these rules using a *decision tree*—a diagram that shows the conditions, outcomes, and appropriate actions involved in making a decision. Read the decision tree in Figure 5.25 by starting at the left, answering the question, and following the corresponding line rightward

FIGURE 5.25

Decision tree for loan manager expert system

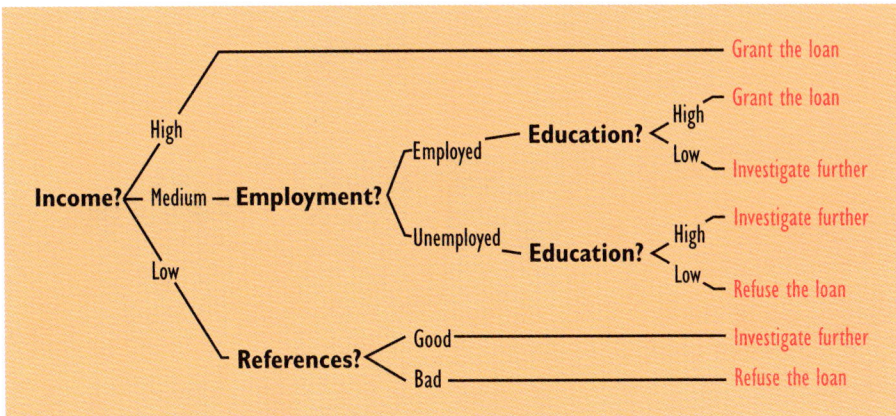

[4] This type of expert system is called *rule-based* because the decision-making process here can be specified as a set of rules expressed in the form of If statements. There are other types of expert systems, for example, those based on neural networks.

to the next question. (Regular text terms are outcomes and bold terms with a question mark are conditions.) The right-most column (in color) shows the final decision.

The input data are provided by the user, who will, as necessary, indicate the applicant's Income level (High, Medium, or Low), Employment (Employed or Unemployed), Education level (High or Low), and References (Good or Bad). For simplicity, we will have the user categorize the applicant's Income, Employment, Education, and References using option buttons. In a real-world version of this expert system the user would input detailed raw data about the applicant (e.g., educational institutions attended, degrees earned, and so forth) and the program would process the raw data to categorize it (e.g., Education level High or Low).

Design of the Application

One way to organize this application is to place the Income, Employment, Education, and Reference option buttons, suitably grouped by frames, together with a command button on a single form. The user selects one option in each group and then clicks the command button, whose Click event procedure contains the If statements necessary to decide on the loan action.

However, this is not the most convenient organization, because it sometimes causes the user to enter data not used in the decision process. If the applicant's Income is High, the user must enter Employment, Education, and References even though high income alone is sufficient for the borrower to get the loan.

There are better ways to organize this application. Let us proceed with the following approach. Use five forms: a startup form and one form each for Income, Employment, Education, and References. Each of these forms should contain a command button captioned "Evaluate", which the user will click after inputting the data required by the form. In response, the application will either show the next form (to get more input data) or else display the recommended loan action (Grant, Refuse, or Investigate further).

Figure 5.26 shows the sequence in which forms are presented to the user. Note the close resemblance to the decision tree of Figure 5.25. The startup form is the one that is displayed first when program execution begins. It should

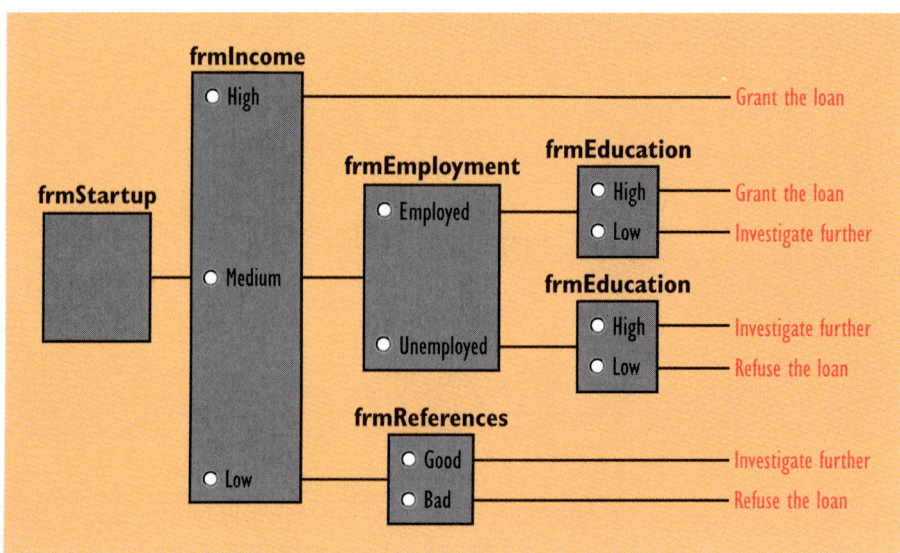

FIGURE 5.26

Order of form presentation

contain labels which explain to the user that a sequence of input forms will be presented, and to click "Proceed" to begin. When the user clicks this command button, the application should show the Income form.

The Income form should have three option buttons, for income levels High, Medium, and Low, and the Evaluate command button. After the user selects an income level, he or she clicks the command button, whose event procedure follows the loan experts' decision rule to determine what to do next:

- If the income level is High, then the application should display a message box titled "Recommendation", with the message "Grant Loan" and the information icon. It should then terminate execution.
- If the income level is Medium, then the application should show the Employment form.
- If the income level is Low, then the application should show the References form.

Whichever form is displayed next, the user selects one option on the form and clicks its Evaluate command button; the application responds by following the loan experts' decision rule to determine what to do next.

Construction of the Application

Begin by creating a folder for this project and starting VB. Construction of this project involves creating multiple forms, each with a few controls. The actual code is not very complex.

Use the form that VB creates (when it starts) as the initial form, which instructs the user on how to proceed. Figure 5.27 shows this form and the code for the Proceed button, which simply shows the next form.

Next create a new form and name it frmIncome. Figure 5.28 shows this form and the code for its Evaluate button. The code first checks to see if Income is High. If it is, a recommendation is made. Otherwise it shows either the Employment or the Reference form.

Create another form and name it frmReferences. Figure 5.29 shows this form and the code for the Evaluate button, which tests the optGood control. If optGood has been selected, it recommends that further investigation be done. Otherwise the loan is refused.

The Employment form is next. Create a new form, name it frmEmployment, and add the controls as shown in Figure 5.30. The code for this form's Evaluate

FIGURE 5.27

Initial form and code for the expert system

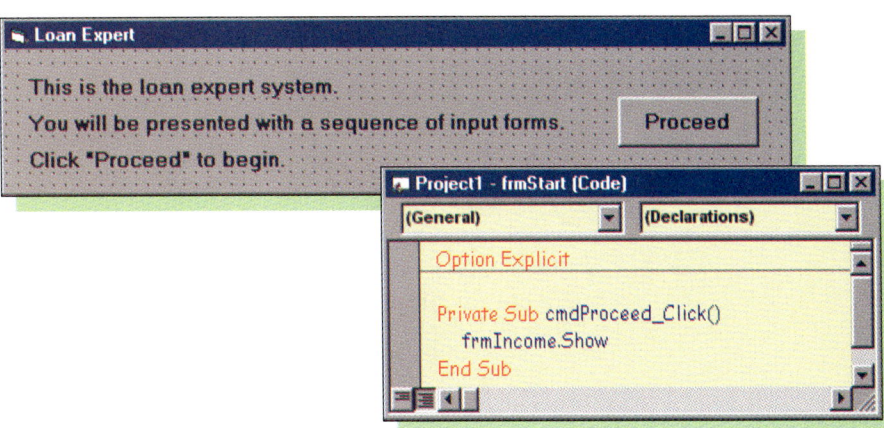

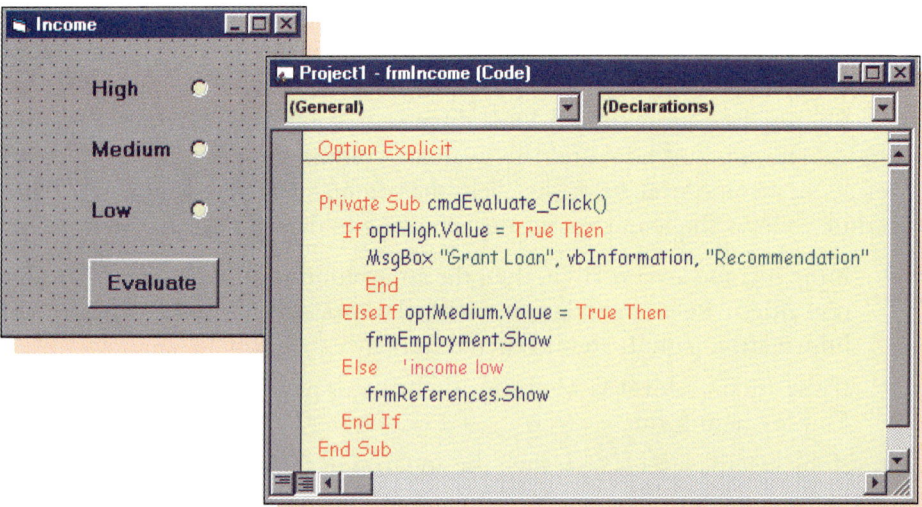

FIGURE 5.28 Income form and code for the expert system

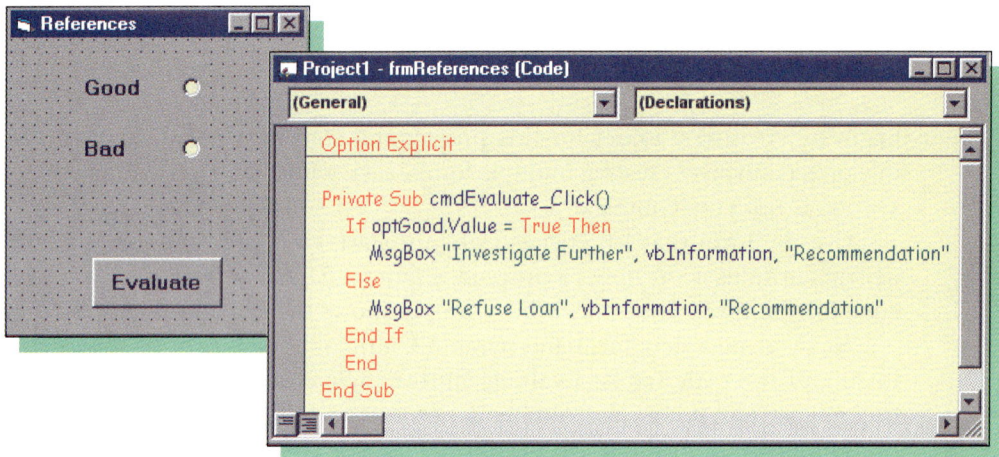

FIGURE 5.29 References form and code for the expert system

FIGURE 5.30 Employment form for the expert system

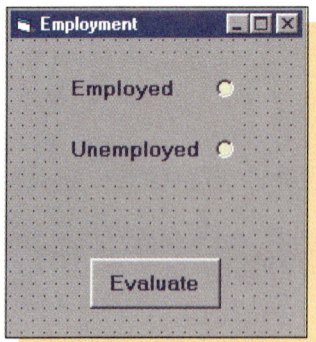

button is very simple. Regardless of which option button is clicked, the Evaluate button simply shows the Education form using the statement

frmEducation.Show

The final form is for Education. Create this form, name it frmEducation, and add the controls as shown in Figure 5.31. The code for this form's Evaluate

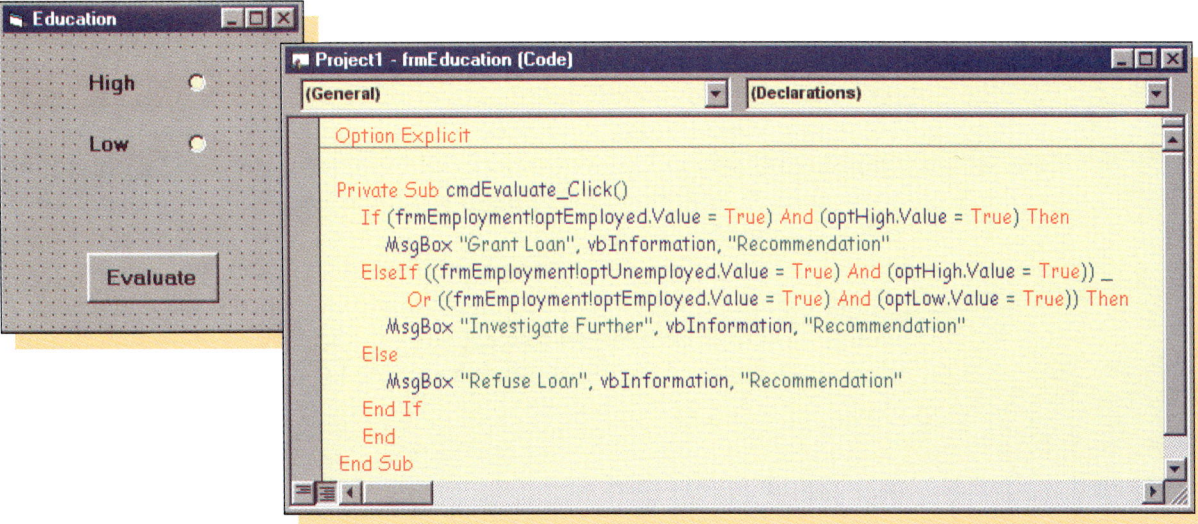

FIGURE 5.31   Education form and code for the expert system

button needs to look back to the values of the option buttons on the Employment form. Recall that to do this, you need to qualify the control name with the form name. Figure 5.31 also shows the code for this procedure.

After creating the forms, run and test your application to be sure it works.

It is interesting to experiment with the arrangement of forms on the screen. For example, you can set their sizes and locations so that they appear to fit together like tiles. Or you can make them "pop up" and "disappear" (when the user clicks Evaluate) like input boxes.

EXERCISE 5.20   Suppose that the application in Project 8 was actually used by a bank. What would happen if a hasty user failed to select an option before clicking Evaluate on one of the forms? By initializing one (only one) option button's Value property to True on each form, you may be able to affect the consequences of this kind of user error. Which option button would you choose for each form, and why?

EXERCISE 5.21   Modify Project 8 so that the user cannot "depart" from a form without first clicking one of the option buttons on it. To be user-friendly, when a form is first displayed none of its option buttons should be selected (you can ensure this by writing an Activate event procedure for the form that sets each option button's Value property to False). Also, if the user clicks on Evaluate before selecting an option, a message should be displayed indicating that an option must be selected before proceeding.

EXERCISE 5.22   Modify Project 8 so that the user's selections are recorded, as they are made, on the startup form. This will give the user a visual reminder of the input data provided so far.

EXERCISE 5.23   Modify Project 8 by adding buttons that let the user go back to the previous form. This would be useful if the user decided to change selections in the middle of a session.

5.9 The Select Case Statement

As we have seen, a single If statement can only handle a condition having two outcomes. We can handle conditions having more than two outcomes with embedded If statements. VB's **Select Case statement can handle conditions with multiple outcomes**, and in many situations is easier to read than embedded If statements.

Like the If...Then...Else statement, the Select Case statement is a compound statement, meaning it can contain many individual statements. Also, as with If...Then...Else, you can conceptualize the Select Case statement as a single meta statement to help you think about the logic used to solve a problem.

Syntax and Action of Select Case
♦ ♦ ♦

The Select Case statement spans more than one line in an event procedure. The statement itself has several parts and multiple statement blocks. Its syntax is as follows:

>   **Select Case** *testexpression*
>   **Case** *expressionlist1*
>   *statementblock1*
>   **Case** *expressionlist2*
>   *statementblock2*
>   . . .
>   **Case** *expressionlistN*
>   *statementblockN*
>   **Case Else**
>   *statementblock*
>   **End Select**

An example Select Case statement is:

>   **Select Case** MonthAbbr
>   **Case** "JAN", "MAR", "MAY", "JUL", "AUG", "OCT", "DEC"
>   DaysInMonth = 31
>   **Case** "APR", "JUN", "SEP", "NOV"
>   DaysInMonth = 30
>   **Case** "FEB"
>   DaysInMonth = 28
>   **Case Else**
>   MsgBox MonthAbbr & " is not a valid month abbreviation."
>   **End Select**

The *test expression* (the string variable MonthAbbr in the example) may be any numeric or string expression. An *expression list* ("APR", "JUN", "SEP", "NOV" in the example) is simply a list of expressions separated by commas. If the test expression is numeric, then the expressions in each list must also be numeric; and if the test expression is string, then the expressions in each list must also be string.

Note that the test expression in Select Case is different from the condition in If...Then...Else. The test expression in Select Case can be any numeric or string expression, whereas the condition in If...Then...Else must be a logical expression.

Run Time: The Effect of the Select Case Statement

When the computer executes the Select Case statement, it first evaluates the test expression, and then attempts to match the resulting value with one of the expression lists. That is, it starts searching at the top expression list and proceeds through subsequent expression lists, stopping at the first match. VB then executes the corresponding statement block and resumes at the statement following End Select. If none of the expression lists match the test expression result, VB executes the *Case Else* statement block, then resumes at the statement following End Select.

As with the If statement, you improve the readability of your code by indenting the statement blocks (and only the statement blocks) in a Select Case statement.

Example 5.9 — **Using the Select Case Statement**

This example shows how the Select Case statement presented earlier works. The complete event procedure containing this statement is shown in Figure 5.32. Although it is very simple, it demonstrates how Select Case is useful for decisions that can be described as "classifications" or "groupings." In this example, the user enters a month abbreviation, which is stored in variable MonthAbbr. This variable is then used as the test expression in the Select Case statement. The variable DaysInMonth is set according to which expression list contains the value stored in MonthAbbr.

EXERCISE 5.24 — In Example 5.9, what happens when the user enters "Mar" or "mar" instead of "MAR"? How can you modify the code so that it treats these three inputs identically?

EXERCISE 5.25 — In Example 5.9, if the user enters "ARG" in response to the input box, the message "ARG is not a valid month abbreviation" is displayed, and then the message "ARG has 0 days" is displayed. Modify cmdMonthDays_Click so that

FIGURE 5.32

Code for Example 5.9

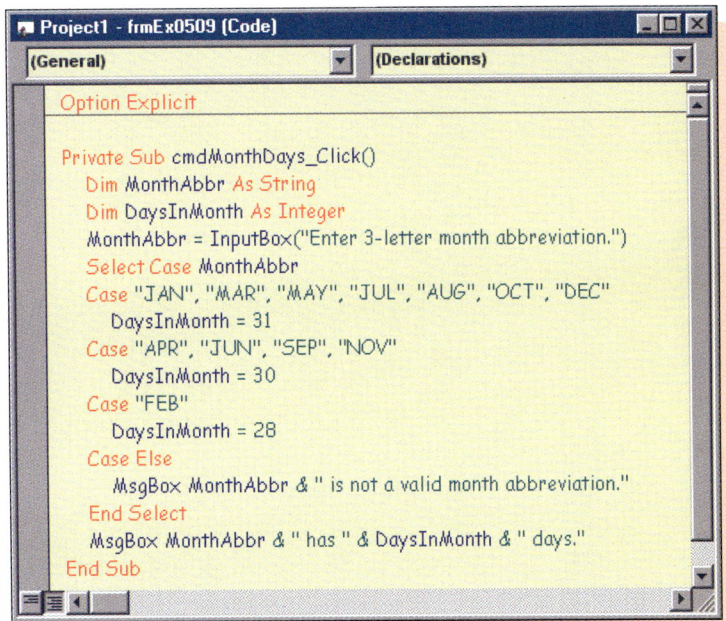

it does not display the latter (meaningless) message when the user enters an invalid month abbreviation.

Ranges

In the previous example, the expression lists were simply lists of distinct values. But Select Case also allows you to specify *ranges* of values in your expression lists. There are two variations:

1. Two expressions separated by the keyword *To*. For example, the range

   8 **To** 10

   will match the test expression value if it is between 8 and 10, inclusive.

2. The keyword *Is*, followed by a comparison operator, followed by an expression. For example, the range

   Is <= 10

   will match the test expression value if it is less than or equal to 10.

Ranges are illustrated by the event procedure in Figure 5.33, which is a version of our simple guessing game that uses a "loaded die." In our previous version each integer from 1 through 6 had an equal chance of coming up, because the random integer was generated by the statement Target = 1 + Int(6 * Rnd()). This statement has been replaced by a Select Case statement. Recall that the Rnd() function returns a random fraction between 0 and 1. In this example there is a 20 percent chance of Target equaling 1, a 10 percent chance of Target equaling 2, and so on. This is why we called the die "loaded."

VB will not complain if the ranges in two or more expression lists overlap; it will simply execute the statement block for the first case it matches. This can

FIGURE 5.33

Event procedure for "loaded die" guessing game

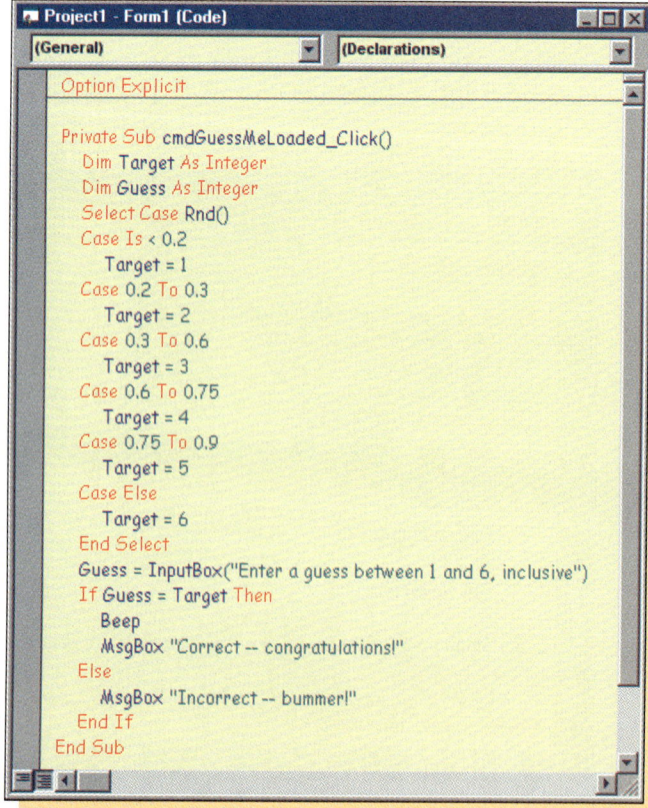

be important. For example, the number 0.6 appears in two consecutive ranges in Figure 5.33. If we had used

Case 0.61 **To** 0.75

instead of

Case 0.6 **To** 0.75

so that there was no overlap, then there would have been a "gap" between 0.6 (the upper bound of the one range) and 0.61 (the lower bound of the next range). Consequently, if the random number happened to be 0.605, it would fall into this gap. Since it would not be covered by either Case, it would be handled by the Case Else, which is probably not what we would have intended.

Working with numeric expressions as in the previous code is straightforward. It is clear what values lie in the "To" range. But what about string expressions? Consider the following Select Case statement:

Select Case Letter
Case "A" **To** "H"
   MsgBox "First Group"
Case "I" **To** "P"
   MsgBox "Second Group"
Case Else
   MsgBox "Third Group"
End Select

What does the range "A" to "H" include? It includes any string that begins with a capital letter between "A" and "H", inclusive; examples are "Apple", "BANANA", "Dawg House", and "Hello". VB uses the ANSI table to define the values included in the range with string expressions.

Another interesting version of our guessing game is shown in Figure 5.34. It uses the "Is" variation for specifying ranges. This version generates a random target when the form is loaded. The user is then asked to guess the number.

FIGURE 5.34

Event procedure for modified guessing game

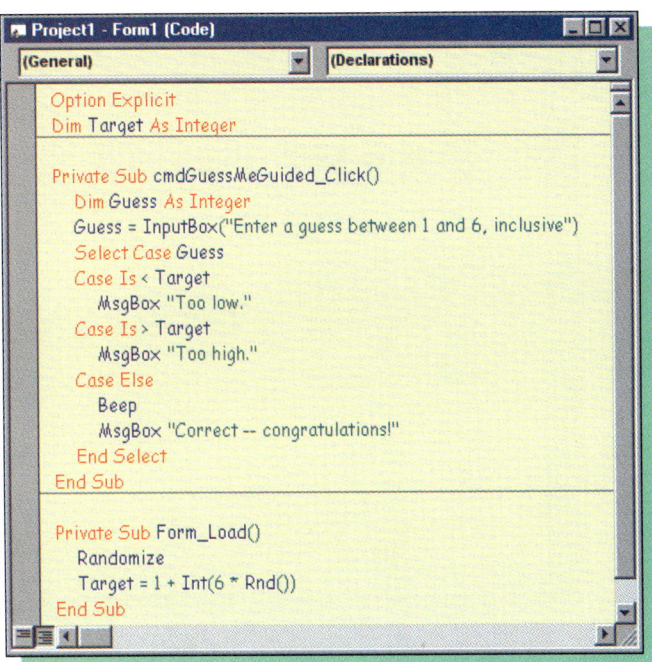

If the guess is wrong, the message says whether it was too high or too low. This additional information should help the user with the next guess because it eliminates some possible numbers.

A single expression list can contain both ranges and individual expressions, separated by commas. Expression lists of this type are useful in situations where a single outcome corresponds to a collection of "scattered" items. As an example of this, suppose the letters of the alphabet (capital letters only) are divided into four categories as shown in Figure 5.35. Observe that each letter belongs to exactly one of the categories. The event procedure in Figure 5.36 takes a letter as input and displays the category to which the letter belongs.

The Select Case syntax does not require the Case Else; it is optional. However, even when the expression lists prior to Case Else cover all possible outcomes, as in Figure 5.36, it is still a good idea to have a Case Else. This practice helps to identify problems that may arise due to unanticipated outcomes, which even experienced programmers encounter in complicated programs.

Even if a programmer successfully handles all possible outcomes when originally creating the program, at some point in the future the program may need to be modified and new outcomes added. If the programmer overlooks one of the cases at that time, he or she will be thankful for including the Case Else at the outset.

FIGURE 5.35

Letter categories

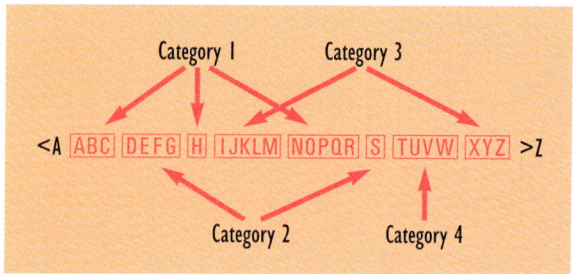

FIGURE 5.36

Event procedure that determines a letter's category

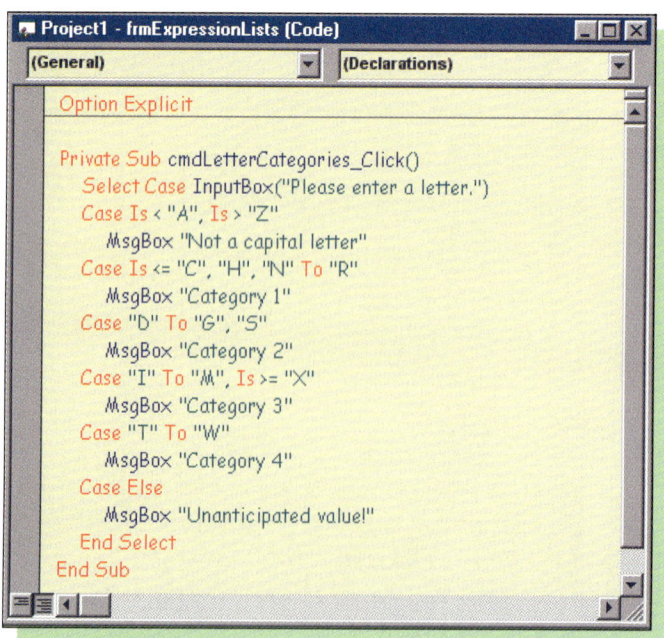

EXERCISE 5.26 In the code in Figure 5.33, which is the most likely value of Target? The most unlikely?

EXERCISE 5.27 The ranges in the Select Case statement in Figure 5.33 contain redundant data. Rewrite the ranges in this Select Case statement using Is instead of To in order to eliminate this redundancy. Which form is more readable? Explain.

Hint: The second expression list, 0.2 To 0.3, can be written as Is <= 0.3. Remember that VB does not mind if ranges overlap.

EXERCISE 5.28 In the guessing-game example in Figure 5.34, what is the largest number of guesses an intelligent user of cmdGuessMeGuided_Click might reasonably take to guess correctly? Explain.

EXERCISE 5.29 Modify Project 8 so that the user enters the loan applicant's income as a dollar amount instead of selecting an option button. Then have your code categorize the income level as follows: Low if it is less than $15,000; Medium if it is at least $15,000 but less than $40,000; and High if it is $40,000 or more.

If versus Select Case

◆ ◆ ◆

Select Case is similar to embedded If statements, except that the outcome of the decision is determined by a single expression at the top. In contrast, an embedded If has one condition at the top and one for each ElseIf, and each of these conditions is a separate expression. Thus, embedded If structures allow for much greater complexity than Select Case.

As a programmer, when should you use embedded Ifs and when should you use Select Case? The following decision rules may help you choose:

+ If a decision has only two outcomes, and the condition can be expressed as a single logical expression, then the If statement is easier to read than a Select Case. The programmer has only to understand the condition, and the two statement blocks are readily apparent because of indentation.

+ If a decision has multiple outcomes, which depend only on a single expression, Select Case is usually easier to read than nested If statements.

+ If the outcomes depend on a number of conditions that may be independent of one another, then the flexibility of embedded If statements makes them the better choice.

EXERCISE 5.30 Solve Exercise 5.15 using Select Case instead of embedded If statements. Which approach is better? Explain.

5.10 The Exit Sub Statement

Suppose you are designing an application in which the user is supposed to enter some data and then click a command button to invoke an event procedure to process the data in some way. What should the event procedure do if it discovers that one or more of the input values are not valid and therefore the processing cannot be carried out? Most likely the procedure should notify the user via a message box and then stop and wait for the user to correct the data. How would you write the code to implement this behavior?

VB provides the *Exit Sub statement* **for decisions where one of the appropriate actions is to perform no further processing.** When executed, this statement causes execution to skip all subsequent statements and jump directly to End Sub.

The Exit Sub statement is not limited to If…Then…Else and Select Case statements, but it is most often used within these statements.

As an example, consider again procedure cmdMonthDays_Click, repeated in Figure 5.37. This event procedure responds poorly if the user enters an invalid month abbreviation. For example, if the user enters the month abbreviation "GEB", it will display the message "GEB has 0 days" in the final message box.

The problem is that the message box statement at the end of the procedure is always executed, but it makes no sense to display its message if the entered value is invalid. We would like to modify the event procedure so that this statement is executed only if the entered value is valid. How?

The following sounds like a possibility. We can put the message box statement inside an If statement whose condition determines whether the entered value was valid. Here's some code that uses this approach.

```
Select Case MonthAbbr
Case "JAN", "MAR", "MAY", "JUL", "AUG", "OCT", "DEC"
    DaysInMonth = 31
Case "APR", "JUN", "SEP", "NOV"
    DaysInMonth = 30
Case "FEB"
    DaysInMonth = 28
Case Else
    MsgBox MonthAbbr & " is not a valid month abbreviation."
End Select
If DaysInMonth > 0 Then
    MsgBox MonthAbbr & " has " & DaysInMonth & " days."
End If
End Sub
```

FIGURE 5.37

Poorly handled Case Else

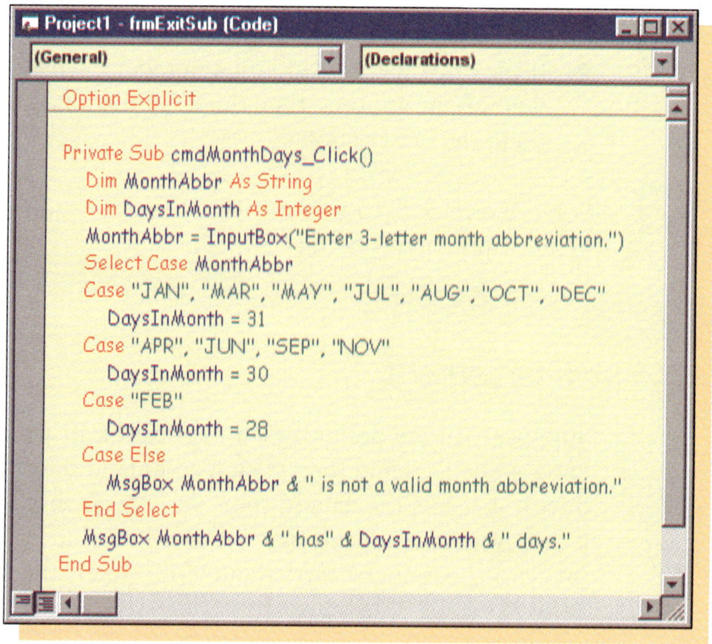

```
Option Explicit

Private Sub cmdMonthDays_Click()
    Dim MonthAbbr As String
    Dim DaysInMonth As Integer
    MonthAbbr = InputBox("Enter 3-letter month abbreviation.")
    Select Case MonthAbbr
    Case "JAN", "MAR", "MAY", "JUL", "AUG", "OCT", "DEC"
        DaysInMonth = 31
    Case "APR", "JUN", "SEP", "NOV"
        DaysInMonth = 30
    Case "FEB"
        DaysInMonth = 28
    Case Else
        MsgBox MonthAbbr & " is not a valid month abbreviation."
    End Select
    MsgBox MonthAbbr & " has" & DaysInMonth & " days."
End Sub
```

Right after the End Select statement, the variable DaysInMonth will hold zero if the entered value is invalid—because the Dim statement initializes DaysInMonth to zero—and we can test for this value in the If statement.

This strategy yields a poor solution to the problem. Its obvious weakness is that the condition of the If statement fails to say what it means. However, even if you can infer that DaysInMonth > 0 *really* means that the entered value is invalid, you have to read the entire Select Case statement and all of its statement blocks to make sure this will work. That is, you have to be sure that all of the valid cases set DaysInMonth to some value greater than 0, and that the Case Else does not.

Figure 5.38 shows an alternative solution that uses Exit Sub. This solution is much easier to understand. The Case Else handles the invalid entry by displaying an appropriate message and then skipping the rest of the procedure by using Exit Sub.

The Exit Sub statement is frequently used in connection with the InputBox() and MsgBox() functions to skip further processing when the user clicks Cancel.

EXERCISE 5.31 The following event procedure, cmdSquareRoots_Click, fails if the user clicks the Cancel button on the input box. The reason is that the InputBox() function returns the zero-length string when the user clicks Cancel, and attempting to store the zero-length string in a numeric variable causes a type mismatch run time error.

```
Private Sub cmdSquareRoots_Click()
    Dim X As Single
    Dim Y As Single
    X = InputBox("Enter a number.")
    Y = Sqr(X)
    MsgBox "The square root of " & X & " is " & Y
End Sub
```

FIGURE 5.38

Exit Sub statement

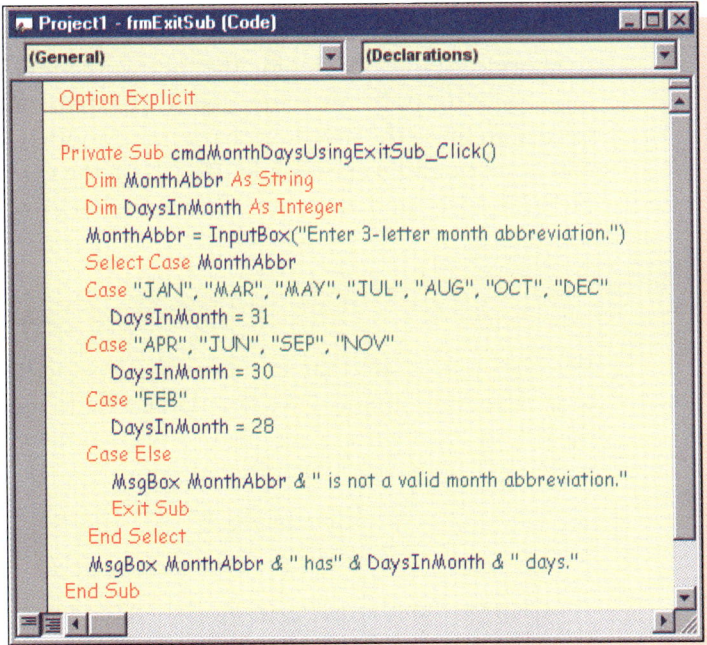

Modify cmdSquareRoots_Click so that the run time error does not occur when the user clicks Cancel. Of course, if the user clicks Cancel, the square root should not be computed; the rest of the procedure should be skipped.

Hints: (1) Declare a new variable of type String named EnteredValue, and store the result of the input box in EnteredValue instead of in X. (2) Check to see whether EnteredValue holds the zero-length string; if it does, exit the procedure. (3) Store EnteredValue in X, and then compute the square root as before.

5.11 Project 9: An Inventory Replenishment Simulation

Companies that produce and distribute goods monitor their inventory closely. For each item they have to decide

- When to order more units (that is, how low should the item's inventory be allowed to fall before an order is placed to replenish it).
- What quantity to order.

We can describe the flow of inventory in a retail store as follows: The store manager orders an initial quantity of some good and puts it on the shelves. As customers buy small quantities of it over time, the manager monitors the number of units remaining in stock (its *inventory* of the good). Several factors affect the manager's decision of when and how much to order.

The manager places an order to the store's suppliers before the inventory hits zero because it typically takes some time (called *lead time*) for the ordered goods to be delivered. If the inventory actually falls to zero, the store may lose sales and create customer dissatisfaction.

The store wants to avoid large inventories because it has to pay its supplier at the time of delivery but does not earn any revenue until its own customers buy the goods off the shelf. This time lag between paying and getting paid represents an actual cost (called *holding cost*) to the store. On the other hand, the store tries not to order too frequently, because deliveries are not free (there is an *ordering cost*).

Businesses facing the tradeoff between inventory costs and lost sales due to shortages typically employ the following kind of policy: Let the inventory fall until it drops below some quantity, *L*; then order however many units are needed to bring the inventory back up to another quantity, *H*. The numbers *L* and *H* are carefully chosen and depend on the customer demand, holding and ordering costs, and lead time. Of course, they are always chosen so that *L* is less than *H*.

Description of the Application

We want a program that simulates the interaction between a store, its customers, and its supplier. We should be able to use the program to learn how this interaction works, and also to find good values of *L* and *H* by experimenting. Let us make the following simplifying assumptions:

- The store sells only one good.
- Customers pay $6 for each unit of the good they buy.
- Each period of time, customers demand between 0 and 5 (random) units of the good.

- The store cannot sell more units than it has in stock; thus, the number of units actually sold in any period of time is equal to the lesser of the demand and the inventory.
- Each period of time, the store incurs a holding cost of $0.50 for each unit of the good in stock.
- The ordering cost is $20 and the unit cost is $2; that is, the cost for the store to order N units from its supplier is $(20 + 2 * N).
- The lead time for an order is a minimum of two periods and may be as long as six periods. It is randomly distributed in this range.

The simulation should (1) generate customer sales, (2) employ the (L, H) inventory policy just described to replenish inventory, (3) generate the delivery lead times, and (4) keep track of and display the store's cash and inventory. To highlight the ordering process, the simulation should beep every time an order is placed. At the start of the simulation, the store should have $100 cash and zero inventory, and the simulation should end after 50 time periods elapse.

Design of the Application

The application requires only one form. The user interface should display the quantities cash, inventory, and current period number. It should also have two text boxes for the user to enter the values for L and H, and a command button for the user to start the simulation. Figure 5.39 shows a sample form with its controls.

The three timers control the events of the simulation. Let's look at each one and decide what should happen when its Timer event occurs.

Event procedure tmrPeriod_Timer is executed once every second and represents one period in the simulation. This procedure is responsible for keeping

FIGURE 5.39

User interface for Project 9

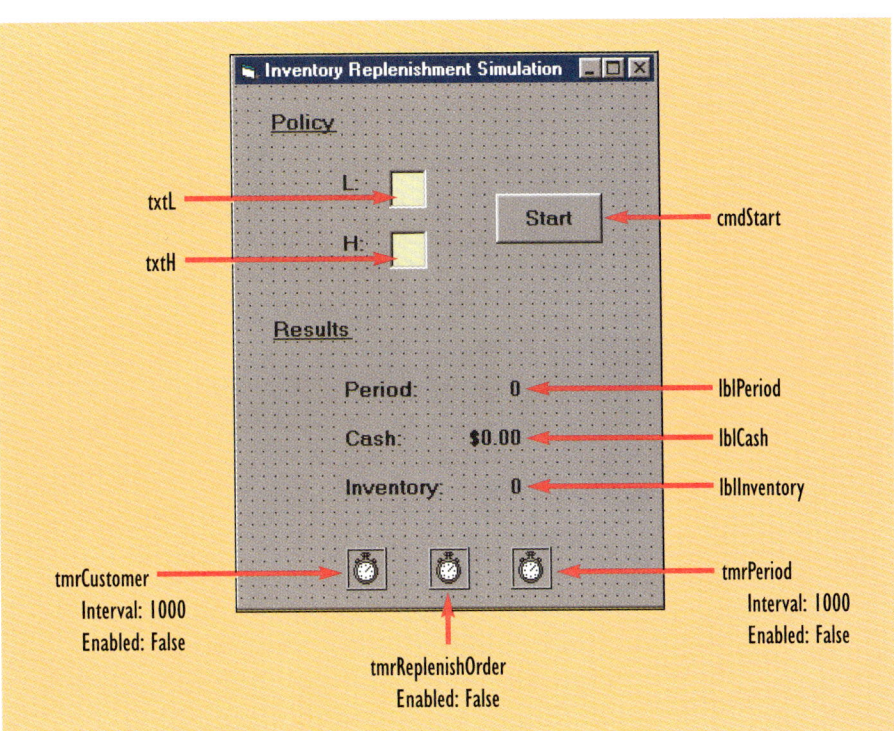

track of the current period number, stopping the simulation after 50 periods, applying holding costs, and checking the level of inventory to see if a new order needs to be placed. Let's write some pseudocode to better understand the logic involved.

> *If period number = 50 then end the simulation*
> *Add one to the current period number*
> *Decrease cash by subtracting unit holding cost times current inventory*
> *Update the labels displaying the period number and the cash*
> *Place a new order if necessary*

This pseudocode is complete except for the last step, which is a meta statement. "Place a new order if necessary" can be expanded as follows:

> *If current inventory < lower limit (L) and a new order has not already been*
>   *placed Then*
>   *Set order quantity = upper limit (H) – current inventory*
>   *Set lead time = minimum lead time plus a random interval*
>   *Set the Interval property of tmrReplenishOrder to the lead time*
>   *Enable tmrReplenishOrder*
>   *Beep*
> *End If*

Event procedure tmrCustomer_Timer is executed once every second (once every period) and represents the customer demand for the good. This event procedure is responsible for generating a random demand, processing the amount sold based on this demand, adjusting cash and inventory levels to reflect the sale, and updating the cash and inventory displays on the form. Again, pseudocode may be helpful.

> *Set demand = random integer between 0 and max demand defined for the*
>   *simulation*
> *Set sale amount = minimum of demand and current inventory*
> *Increase cash by adding sale amount times price*
> *Decrease current inventory by sale amount*
> *Update labels displaying cash and current inventory*

The final Timer event procedure, tmrReplenishOrder_Timer, simulates the arrival of a replenishment order. This timer's Interval property was set by tmrPeriod when that event procedure detected that the inventory level had dropped below the minimum amount (L).

Pseudocode for the tmrReplenishOrder procedure is as follows:

> *Reduce cash by subtracting the fixed order cost and the unit cost times the*
>   *number of units in the order (defined by tmrPeriod)*
> *Increase current inventory by the number of units in the order*
> *Update labels displaying cash and current inventory*
> *Disable this timer (wait for the tmrPeriod procedure to enable it again)*

The last step may need some explanation. We place an order in the tmrPeriod procedure by setting the Interval and Enabled properties of tmrReplenishOrder. When the Timer event for tmrReplenishOrder occurs (the order arrives), we disable tmrReplenishOrder because we don't want another order to be placed until the tmrPeriod procedure detects the circumstances that justify a new order.

There are two other event procedures that need to be coded. One is for the command button that starts the simulation (cmdStart). This procedure reads the values of L and H from the two text boxes txtL and txtH and stores them in variables. It then disables the two text boxes and enables both the period and customer timers (tmrPeriod and tmrCustomer) to start the simulation.

Finally, there are two initialization steps that need to take place when the simulation first starts. The cash balance and current inventory level must be set to 100 and 0, respectively, and the labels that display these values must also be initialized. We'll use the Form_Load event procedure to perform these steps.

We conclude the design section with a discussion of the data and variables used in the simulation. There will be five variables with module-level scope. These are

Variable	Type
Cash	Currency
Inventory	Integer
OrderQuantity	Integer
Low	Integer
High	Integer

These variables have module-level scope because they are used in several procedures. For example, Cash and Inventory are used by the tmrCustomer, tmrPeriod, tmrReplenishOrder, and Form_Load procedures. The variable OrderQuantity is set by tmrPeriod and used later by tmrReplenishOrder. Low and High are set by cmdStart and used later by tmrPeriod.

Symbolic constants implement the assumed numeric values. These symbolic constants are

Symbolic Constant	Numeric Value
MAXDEMAND	5
PRICETOCUSTOMER	6
ORDERFIXEDCOST	20
ORDERMARGINALCOST	2
HOLDINGCOSTPERUNIT	0.5
MINLEADTIME	2
MAXLEADTIME	6
INITIALCASH	100
INITIALINVENTORY	0
SIMULATIONLENGTH	50

Construction of the Application

Begin by creating a folder for the project. Start VB, place the controls on the form, and set the properties of the controls as indicated in Figure 5.39.

Begin coding by declaring the module-level variables and constants. Figure 5.40 shows the general declarations section of the form. Figure 5.41 shows the code for the cmdStart_Click and Form_Load procedures, which are straightforward.

Next we code the Timer events. Procedure tmrPeriod_Timer is in Figure 5.42. If you compare this code to the pseudocode given earlier, you'll see a great deal of similarity. Let's compare some of the pseudocode and actual code. The pseudocode for placing a new order was:

If current inventory < lower limit (L) and a new order has not already been
　placed Then
　　Set order quantity = upper limit (H) − current inventory
　　Set lead time = minimum lead time plus a random interval
　　Set the Interval property of tmrReplenishOrder to the lead time
　　Enable tmrReplenishOrder
　　Beep
End If

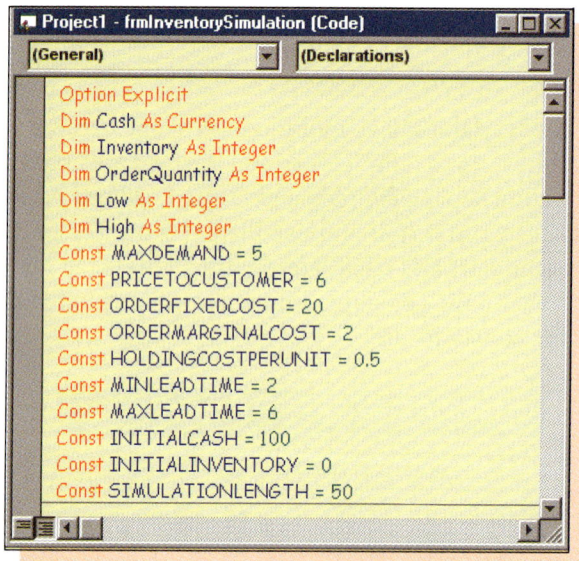

FIGURE 5.40

General declarations section of form

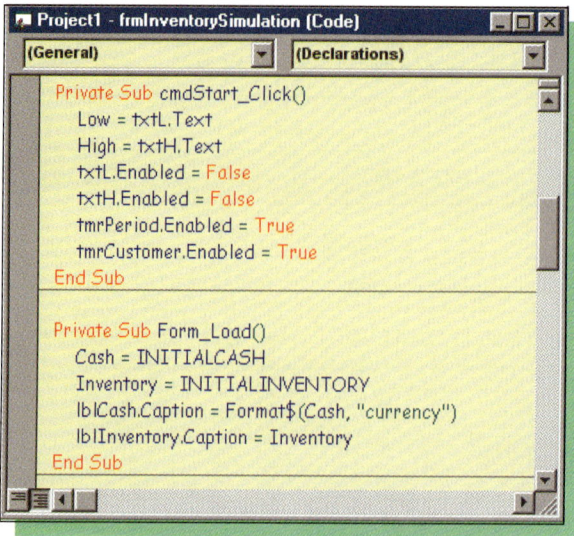

FIGURE 5.41

cmdStart_Click and Form_Load event procedures

The actual code for the If statement is

```
If (Inventory < Low) And (tmrReplenishOrder.Enabled = False) Then
    OrderQuantity = High - Inventory
    LeadTime = MINLEADTIME + Int((MAXLEADTIME - MINLEADTIME + 1) * Rnd())
    tmrReplenishOrder.Interval = 1000 * LeadTime
    tmrReplenishOrder.Enabled = True
    Beep
End If
```

The logical expression tmrReplenishOrder.Enabled = False tests to see if no order is pending. If this timer's Enabled property is True, then an order has already been placed and the simulation is waiting for the order to arrive. The expression MINLEADTIME + Int((MAXLEADTIME - MINLEADTIME + 1) * Rnd()) generates a random integer ranging between MINLEADTIME and MAXLEADTIME.

The next two statements enable tmrReplenishOrder and set its interval equal to the lead time (recall that the Interval property must be in milliseconds). The effect of this is to place an order that will arrive at some random time in the future.

Now code the tmrCustomer_Timer event procedure (Figure 5.43). Compare this code to the pseudocode.

Set demand = random integer between 0 and max demand defined for the simulation
Set sale amount = minimum of demand and current inventory
Increase cash by adding sale amount times price
Decrease current inventory by sale amount
Update labels displaying cash and current inventory

There is a very close correlation between the two.

The final timer event is tmrReplenishOrder_Timer (see Figure 5.43). Notice that the last statement of this procedure disables the timer. This prevents the timer from activating again (since otherwise the event occurs repeatedly) unless it is re-enabled by the tmrPeriod procedure.

FIGURE 5.42

Code for tmrPeriod_Timer event procedure

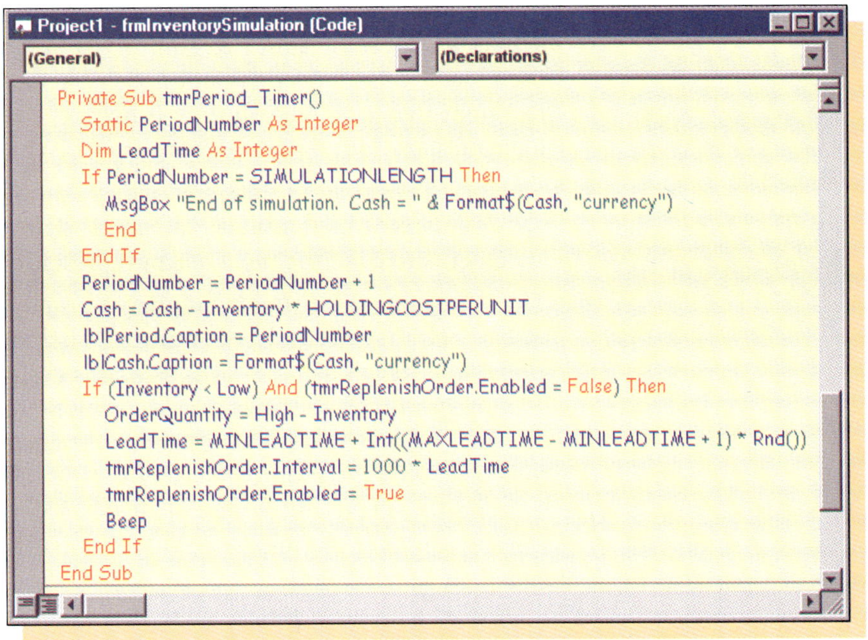

```
Private Sub tmrPeriod_Timer()
    Static PeriodNumber As Integer
    Dim LeadTime As Integer
    If PeriodNumber = SIMULATIONLENGTH Then
        MsgBox "End of simulation.  Cash = " & Format$(Cash, "currency")
        End
    End If
    PeriodNumber = PeriodNumber + 1
    Cash = Cash - Inventory * HOLDINGCOSTPERUNIT
    lblPeriod.Caption = PeriodNumber
    lblCash.Caption = Format$(Cash, "currency")
    If (Inventory < Low) And (tmrReplenishOrder.Enabled = False) Then
        OrderQuantity = High - Inventory
        LeadTime = MINLEADTIME + Int((MAXLEADTIME - MINLEADTIME + 1) * Rnd())
        tmrReplenishOrder.Interval = 1000 * LeadTime
        tmrReplenishOrder.Enabled = True
        Beep
    End If
End Sub
```

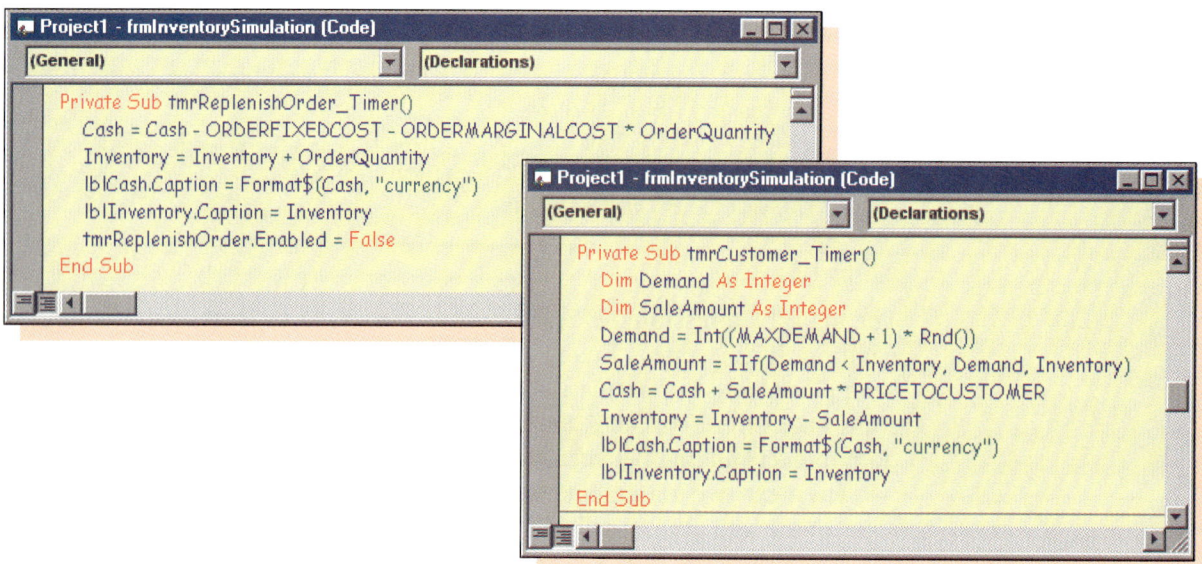

FIGURE 5.43 Code for tmrCustomer_Timer and tmrReplenishOrder_Timer event procedures

After coding the procedures, run the simulation to be sure that it works. After verifying that it works, experiment with different values of *L* and *H* to see if you can maximize the cash position at the end of the simulation. Watch the inventory level as time goes by and you'll get a better feel for how to adjust the values of *L* and *H*.

Chapter Summary

1. To make a decision, we first evaluate a condition and determine its outcome. The correct action to perform depends upon that outcome. This basic decision-making process needs to be mimicked in programs that select alternative courses of actions.

2. The logic used in procedures that specify alternative courses of action can be complex. It is difficult to get the logic correct and worry about statement syntax at the same time. To simplify their thinking, programmers use pseudocode. Pseudocode is an English-like outline that describes the logical steps in a problem solution. It helps the programmer to focus on the logic of the solution without concern for syntax rules.

3. A complex compound statement may be more easily understood as a single statement, called a meta statement, that goes beyond the individual statements to describe the concept represented by those statements.

4. The If…Then…Else statement gives a program the ability to choose one of two actions based on a condition. The condition can be any logical expression (recall that logical expressions evaluate to either True or False). The programmer specifies one or more statements, called a statement block, to be executed if the outcome is True, and another statement block to be executed if the outcome is False.

    The If…Then…Else statement has a variation that uses the ElseIf clause to extend the number of conditions that a single If…Then…Else statement can support.

    Either statement block of the If…Then…Else statement can include another If…Then…Else statement, creating nested If statements.

5. Three VB controls are associated with the GUI and the user's ability to make choices. The Option button control presents the user with a set of options from which to select exactly one. The option button that is chosen has its Value property set to True.

    The Frame control allows the programmer to group option buttons to correspond to different categories of items. This allows the user to select exactly one option from each category.

    The Check box control allows the user to select multiple options from a set of options—any combination of zero, one, or more check boxes at the same time.

6. The Select Case statement is designed to handle the situation where a single condition can have more than two outcomes. It can be used to identify a set of categories and specify the processing associated with each category.

7. Finally, the Exit Sub statement makes it possible to stop executing a procedure before it is completed. This might be necessary because some condition has been detected for which the appropriate action is to skip the rest of the procedure.

Key Terms

appropriate action
Check box control
condition
decision tree
embedded If statement
Exit Sub statement
expert system

Frame control
If...Then...Else statement
meta statement
MsgBox() function
nested If statement
Option button control

outcome
problem solving
pseudocode
Select Case statement
statement block

End-of-Chapter Problems

1. What function do the keywords Then, Else, and End If perform in the context of the If...Then...Else statement?

2. What is a meta statement? What is its value to a programmer/problem solver? How are meta statements and pseudocode similar? How are they different?

3. A university uses the following tuition table to determine a student's quarterly tuition:

	Residence Status	
	In-State	Out-of-State
Undergraduate	$ 450	$ 780
Graduate	1,250	3,275
Professional	2,300	5,200

    Assume that you have a variable called ResStatus that holds the value 1 for in-state students and the value 2 for out-of-state students. Also assume that you have a variable ClassStanding that holds 1 for undergraduates, 2 for graduates, and 3 for professional students. Given this information, write an If...Then...Else statement that sets the variable Tuition equal to the appropriate value based on the current values of ResStatus and ClassStanding. Now do the same thing using a Select Case statement. Comment on the two alternative approaches.

4. Explain when you would use option buttons for user input and when you would use check boxes.

5. What important function does the Frame control serve? How does the Frame control relate to both option buttons and check boxes?

6. Both the option button and the check box have a Value property. Assume that you have several option buttons in one frame and several check boxes in another frame. How would the Value properties of the set of option buttons potentially differ from the Value properties of the set of check boxes?

7. Using the Select Case statement and ranges, construct the correct VB statement to implement this table.

Age	Risk Factor
≤ 2	.03
> 2 and < 10	.07
≥ 10 and ≤ 30	.15
> 30	.12

The statement should set the variable RiskFactor to its proper value depending on the current value of the variable Age. Assume that the value stored in variable Age is a whole number.

8. In question 7, does it make any difference if you assume that the variable Age is declared as type Integer versus one of the floating-point types (either Single or Double)? Explain.

9. Assume you have the segment of VB code shown here.

Dim Letter **As String**

Select Case Letter
Case "A" **To** "H"
 MsgBox "In the first third"
Case "I" **To** "P"
 MsgBox "In the middle third"
Case "Q" **To** "Z"
 MsgBox "In the final third"
Case Else
 MsgBox "Not in any group"
End Select

Given this code, assume that the Letter variable holds the value "B". What message would be printed? Explain why VB makes this decision. (*Hint:* Think about ANSI codes.) Now assume that the Letter variable holds the value "b". What message would be printed? Explain.

10. Assume you are given the following event procedure:

```
Private Sub optTest_Click()
    Dim Choice As Boolean
    Choice = optTest.Value
    If Choice = True Then
        ' do something
    Else
        ' do something else
    End If
End Sub
```

There is a serious conceptual problem with this code. What is it? How would you rewrite this procedure correctly?

Programming Problems

1. Assume that you own a small deli that sells bagels. You want a simple program that computes the price of a purchase based on what the customer orders. A sample user interface is shown below.

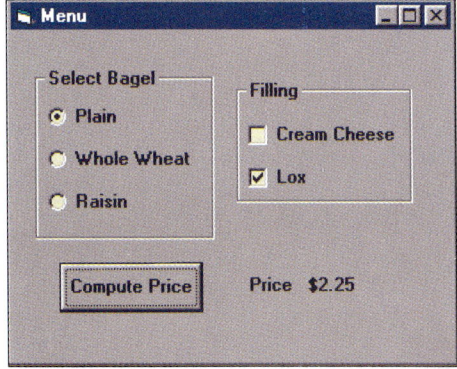

You charge $1.75 for a plain bagel, $1.95 for a whole wheat bagel, and $2.15 for a raisin bagel. In addition, you add $.50 if customers want lox on the bagel and $.75 for cream cheese (they might want both). Write the code so that after the customer's preferences are input, clicking on the Compute Price button will cause the price to be computed and displayed as shown above.

2. Construct a menu calculator as shown below. Bagels cost $2.25. Selecting lox adds $1.20 to the price, and cream cheese adds $1.00. A spinach salad costs $2.75 and a chef salad costs $3.25. Sodas are $1.25 regardless of type (see the two forms at the top of page 264).

The form should not show the options if the main selection has not been made. In the right-hand figure, salad has not been selected, so the Spinach and Chef options are not displayed.

The price should be cleared whenever a main selection is "deselected." In the two figures shown, the deselection of Salad caused the "3.25" to be cleared from the price column. However, the total price does not have to be updated automatically—you can assume that the user will click on the Compute Total button to recalculate the total.

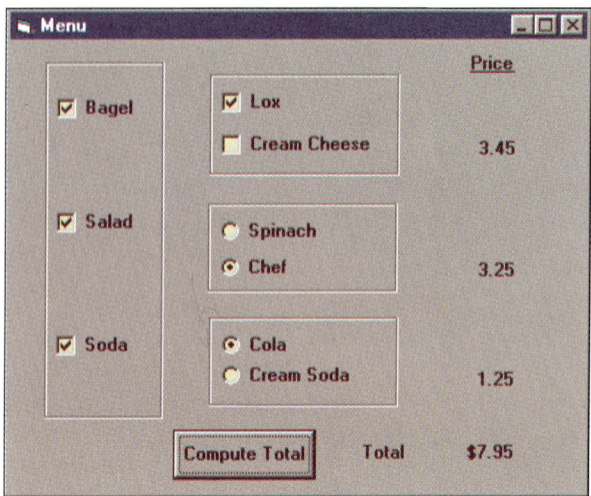
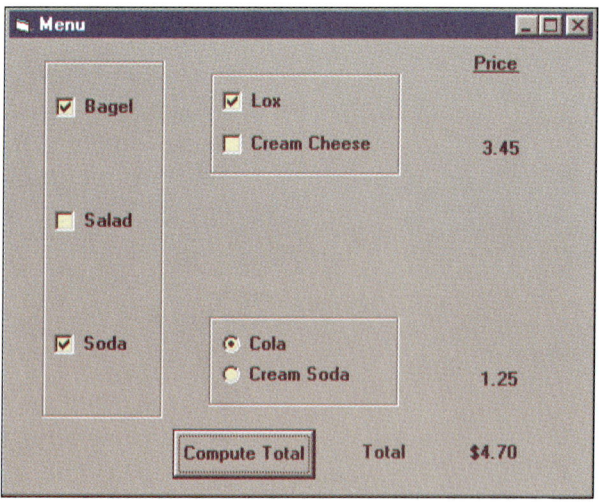

When a main selection has been deselected and then selected again, the project should clear the options. In the figure below, the Bagel selection was deselected and then reselected. As you can see, the Lox option has been cleared and the price is correct for just a Bagel.

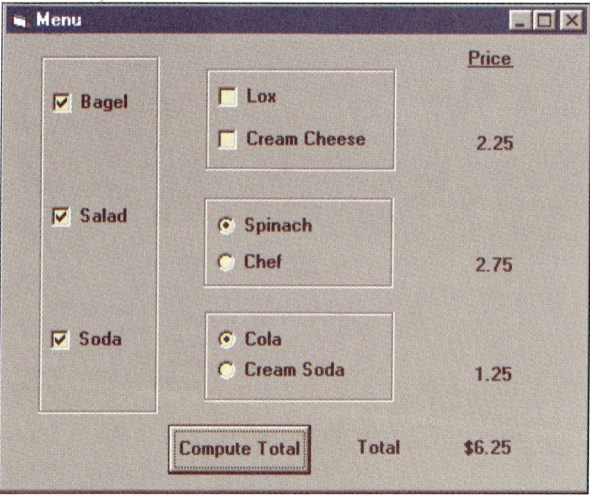

Finally, be aware that the Bagel options behave differently than the Salad options. The Bagel options are cumulative; that is, you can select both, and the price should reflect this. In contrast, the Salad options are mutually exclusive; you will only have one or the other (and there will be no price until the user selects one). See Exercise 5.19 for a hint as to one way to implement the Bagel options.

3. Complete the requirements of problem 2, but have the total price update automatically. That is, remove the Compute Total button and have the project update the total price as the individual selection prices change.

    Hint: Think about using a Change event.

4. A company needs a program to help calculate the yearly bonus for each employee. The bonus is determined by considering several different factors. The first factor is the number of years a person has been employed by the firm. Being employed for 1 to 5 years adds $100 to the bonus, being employed for 6 to 10 years adds $200 to the bonus, and being employed

for 11 or more years adds $350 to the bonus. Assume that years of experience are always rounded up to the nearest whole number.

In addition to years of experience, an employee's job grade is considered. For job grade Level I, $75 is added to the bonus; for Level II, $100 is added to the bonus; and for Level III, $125 is added to the bonus. Also, if an employee has participated in community service then an additional $100 is added to the bonus. And finally, 5 percent of the employee's current salary is computed and added to the bonus. The sum of all these values represents the yearly bonus.

Create a VB project to solve this problem. Use check boxes, option buttons, Frame controls, and the InputBox() function as appropriate. Try to use controls that make it difficult for the user to make typographical errors when inputting data.

5. Validating data input is an important part of many applications. In this problem you will implement some simple data validation operations. Use the InputBox() function to get the name, the salary, the years of experience, the department code, and the job title of a hypothetical employee. As each field is input, it should be displayed on the form followed by either the word "Valid" or the words "Not valid".

Names should be less than 18 characters long. A valid salary must be between $10,000 and $150,000, inclusive. Valid years of experience must be greater than or equal to zero and less than or equal to 75.

There are three valid department codes: PROD, ACCTG, and MKTG. Your project should ensure that only these three codes are marked as valid. However, the user should be able to enter the codes using either uppercase or lowercase (review string functions to get an idea of how to do this). If an invalid code is detected, have the project notify the user (via a message box), then terminate execution (using the End statement).

Assuming that the department code is valid, the title needs to be validated. Valid titles for the PROD department are MGR, SUPERVISOR, and STAFF. Valid titles for the ACCTG department are MGR, AUDITOR, and STAFF. Valid titles for the MKTG department are ACCT REP and SALES REP (note that there is a single blank between SALES and REP). Again, allow the user to enter titles using either uppercase or lowercase.

Place the code to input and validate the data in the Form_Load event procedure so that it starts to execute as soon as the project starts to run. You can use the form Show method as the first statement in the code to ensure that the form is displayed during execution.

chapter SIX

Reducing Program Complexity

General Sub Procedures and Programmer-Defined Functions

◆ ◆ ◆ ◆

A project can contain many event procedures, and the processing tasks performed by each of them can be complicated. Three important considerations help us design, construct, and maintain complex programs:

1. We can understand complex tasks more readily by breaking them into smaller "subtasks."
2. We can make the meaning of each subtask clear by giving it a descriptive name.
3. We can avoid duplication of effort, as well as potential inconsistencies, by finding processing tasks that have subtasks in common. For example, the subtask "print a check" may be involved in both payroll processing and accounts payable processing.

The following event procedure illustrates points 1 and 2:

```
Private Sub cmdPayEmployee_Click()
    GetEmployeeData
    ComputeGross
    ComputeDeductions
    ComputeNet
    PrintCheck
End Sub
```

The processing task performed by cmdPayEmployee_Click consists of five subtasks. Each of the five statements in the event procedure refers to a different general sub procedure. A **general sub procedure contains the statements necessary to perform a single subtask** (such as printing a check), **and is given a descriptive name** (PrintCheck). Since the descriptive name stands for several actual statements, it is like a *meta statement* in pseudocode. That is, the descriptive name goes beyond the individual statements of the general sub procedure to describe the concept represented by those statements.

If more than one event procedure needs to perform the same subtask, they can share the general sub procedure. The following event procedure and cmdPayEmployee_Click together illustrate point 3. Both event procedures refer to the same general sub procedure named PrintCheck.

Private Sub cmdPayInvoice()
    GetInvoiceData
    PrintCheck
End Sub

General sub procedures allow us to create *reusable code*—that is, **code that can be used by more than one procedure.** One programmer figures out the statements necessary to accomplish a given subtask, and records them as a descriptively named general sub procedure. Subsequently, other programmers can use that general sub procedure whenever they create a procedure that requires the subtask. This way we avoid constantly "reinventing the wheel."

In this chapter we examine general sub procedures in detail: how they work and how to create them. We also examine *programmer-defined functions*: you can write your own functions, which you can then use just as you use VB's predefined functions, such as the square root function Sqr(). Our study of general sub procedures and functions includes an important mechanism for sharing data known as *parameter passing*.

We then discuss how code modules help in organizing projects by acting as containers for general sub procedures and programmer-defined functions.

Finally, we use our understanding of general sub procedures and parameter passing to extend our mastery of the user interface. We examine the KeyPress event, whose event procedure uses parameter passing to determine which key the user pressed. We then discuss the GotFocus and LostFocus events, which are natural partners of the KeyPress event because applications commonly allow the user to press certain keys (e.g., ENTER) to move the focus from one control to another. Finally, we examine the topic of *form modality*, in which the user can be forced to respond to a request on one form before being allowed to move to another form. The statement that achieves this (a variation of the Show method) works much as general sub procedures work.

Objectives

After studying this chapter you should be able to

- Share code by creating general sub procedures and functions.
- Use parameters to share data between procedures and functions.
- Use code modules to organize code for reusability.
- Use three new events—KeyPress, GotFocus, and LostFocus—that are useful for data editing and for causing the user interface to respond when the user activates or deactivates a control.
- Use the concept of form modality to decide the best way to display forms to the user.

6.1 General Sub Procedures

As mentioned in the introduction, a general sub procedure contains the statements necessary to perform a single subtask. Each event procedure that requires the subtask "calls" or "invokes" the general sub procedure by its name. To illustrate how general sub procedures can improve the organization of a program and to demonstrate how procedures are used in projects, we begin this section by rewriting the U.S. Individual Income Tax Return application from Chapter 5. We then examine precisely how general sub procedures work and how to create them.

Using General Sub Procedures in a Project

We can improve the design of the computerized income tax application by placing statements that are common to multiple processing steps in a general sub procedure. Figure 6.1 shows the user interface we developed for this application in Chapter 5. Recall that the three separate questions appearing on this form are not independent of one another: in particular, the question "If a joint return, does your spouse want $3 to go to this fund?" applies to users who select "Married filing joint return" but not to those who select "Single".

The program we created in Chapter 5 has two Click event procedures, shown in Figure 6.2, which implement a visual cue to show the user when the

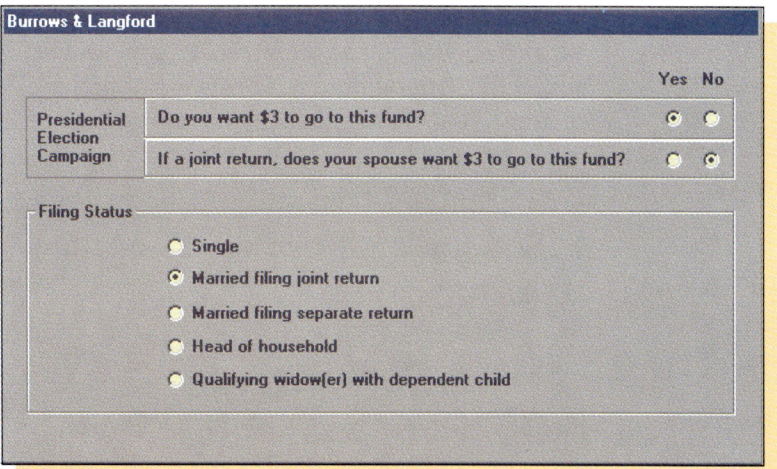

FIGURE 6.1

User interface for income tax return application

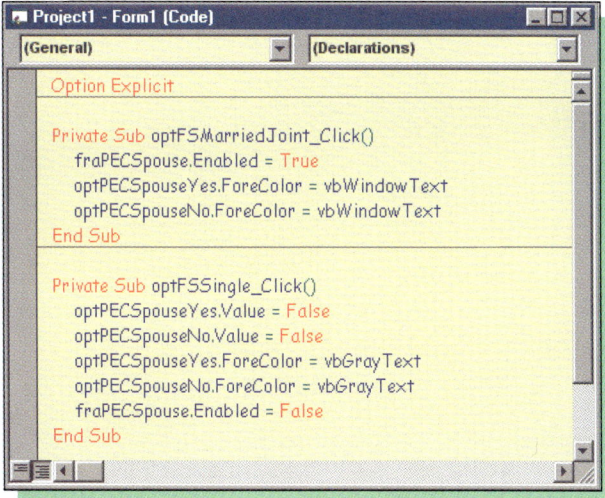

FIGURE 6.2

Event procedures for income tax return application

second question is not applicable. They work by appropriately setting the Value and ForeColor properties of the Yes/No option buttons, and the Enabled property of the frame that holds them. When the user selects filing status "Single", the second Presidential Election Campaign question changes to gray (see Figure 5.21). If the user selects filing status "Married filing joint return", the appearance of the user interface reverts to Figure 6.1.

When we turn to the user requirements for linking the Presidential Election Campaign question to the three remaining filing status categories, we find that they are like the "Single" filing status category: the question "If a joint return, does your spouse want $3 to go to this fund?" does not apply. Thus, we should create Click event procedures for optFSMarriedSeparate, optFSHeadOfHousehold, and optFSWidower, that are *identical* to optFSSingle_Click.

Adding these new Click event procedures makes the code substantially longer, increasing the number of statements from 13 (in Figure 6.2) to 34. In addition, when you retype the lines again and again, you might make a typographical error or omit a line, introducing an inconsistency that causes one event procedure to execute differently from the others.

We can shorten the program and eliminate the chance of inconsistencies by placing the common statements in a general sub procedure. The sub procedure will have a descriptive name that will appear in each event procedure that requires its subtask. In Figure 6.3 the general sub procedure is named WithdrawPECSpouseQuestion.

The descriptive name WithdrawPECSpouseQuestion is easy to interpret. Now when we want to know what happens when the user clicks the "Head of household" option button, the answer is immediately apparent; the event procedure contains only one statement, and it is descriptive.

FIGURE 6.3

Income tax program with general sub procedure

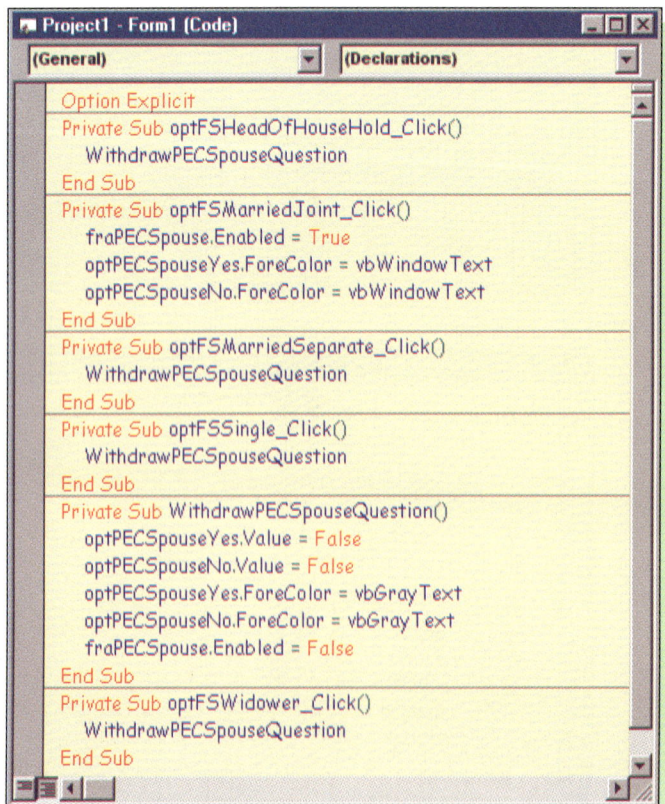

This example illustrates how a program can be simplified with a general sub procedure. In order to write your own general sub procedures, you must understand how execution flows from an event procedure to the general sub procedure and back to the event procedure. We turn to this topic next.

EXERCISE 6.1

In the revised income tax application (Figure 6.3), would it make sense to create a general sub procedure containing the statements that are currently in event procedure optFSMarriedJoint_Click? If so, explain why and suggest a name for it.

Execution of General Sub Procedures

Even if you agree that the code in Figure 6.3 looks good, it may not be obvious to you exactly how it executes at run time. By looking at the code alone, how can you tell which are event procedures and which are general sub procedures? Does it matter? Which statement is executed when?

You can determine whether a procedure is an event procedure or a general sub procedure from its name. The names of event procedures always end with an underscore followed by the type of event, whereas the names of general sub procedures do not. Because of our convention for naming controls, the names of event procedures begin with a three-letter prefix for the type of control to which the event procedure belongs. Since general sub procedures are not associated with controls, their names do not begin with a prefix for a control type.

From now on we will often use only the term *procedure,* trusting that you can tell from the procedure's name whether it is an event procedure or a general sub procedure. Note that a printout of the code in a VB project does not explicitly distinguish between event procedures and general sub procedures. Programmers have to be able to recognize which are event procedures and which are general sub procedures in order to understand how the processing steps are performed.

We know that to execute an event procedure, the computer executes its statements one at a time, from top to bottom. How does the computer execute a statement that is just the name of a general sub procedure? It performs the following steps:

1. Transfers execution from the event procedure to the named general sub procedure.

2. Executes the statements in the general sub procedure.

3. Returns execution to the event procedure and resumes with the event procedure's next statement.

Figure 6.4 illustrates this process. When the user clicks the option button named optFSSingleModified, the computer begins executing the statements in event procedure optFSSingleModified_Click. The numbers in Figure 6.4 indicate the order in which statements are executed. The arrows show the flow of execution between the procedures.

The statement numbered 2 in Figure 6.4 is sometimes referred to as a ***procedure call* because it calls, or invokes, the specified procedure**—in this case, WithdrawPECSpouseQuestion. In the example shown, optFSSingleModified_Click is the *calling procedure,* and WithdrawPECSpouseQuestion is the *called procedure.*

FIGURE 6.4

Flow of execution in programs with general sub procedures

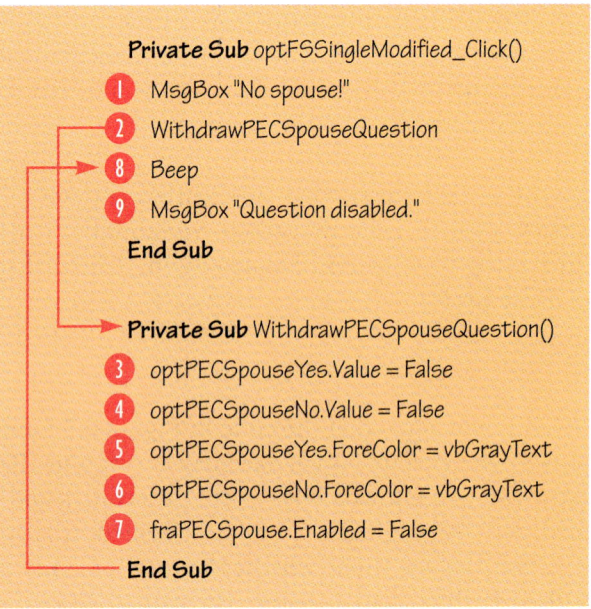

 EXERCISE 6.2   Analyze the following code (i.e., explain what it does) and sketch the flow of execution as in Figure 6.4.

```
Private Sub cmdCallsQuiz_Click()
    lblConcat.Caption = ""
    DisplaySomething
    lblConcat.Caption = lblConcat.Caption & "E"
    DisplayAnotherThing
    lblConcat.Caption = lblConcat.Caption & "HING"
End Sub

Private Sub DisplayAnotherThing()
    lblConcat.Caption = lblConcat.Caption & "T"
End Sub

Private Sub DisplaySomething()
    lblConcat.Caption = lblConcat.Caption & "S"
    lblConcat.Caption = lblConcat.Caption & "OM"
End Sub
```

Local Variables in General Sub Procedures

General sub procedures can access module-level and global variables just like event procedures. They also have their own local variable tables, and, for general sub procedures and event procedures alike, local variables in one procedure have *no relationship whatsoever* to local variables in any other procedures, regardless of their names. We now illustrate this rule with examples, because the flow of execution between the *calling* and the *called* procedure can make local variables seem confusing at first.

Recall that a procedure's local variable table is created when the procedure begins executing and is destroyed when its End Sub statement is encountered. A local variable exists until the procedure's End Sub statement is encountered, even if the flow of execution moves to another procedure because of a procedure call. That is, transferring execution to another procedure has no effect on the calling procedure's local variables. An example of this behavior is illustrated by the code in Figure 6.5. Before reading further, try to number the statements in Figure 6.5 in the order in which they execute (as in Figure 6.4) when the user clicks the command button named cmdTestCall.

When the user clicks on cmdTestCall, the computer starts executing cmdTestCall_Click. It first creates the local variable X, then stores the value 100 in X, and then calls the general sub procedure named TestProcedure. This call transfers execution to TestProcedure. The computer beeps, displays a message box, and then encounters the End Sub in TestProcedure, which returns execution to cmdTestCall_Click. It then executes the statement

```
MsgBox "X = " & X
```

Will X still hold the value 100?

The answer is yes. TestProcedure has no effect on the variable X because X is local to cmdTestCall_Click. Therefore, X continues to exist until the End Sub statement in *its* procedure, cmdTestCall_Click, is encountered.

A procedure can call another procedure, which in turn can call a third procedure, which in turn can call a fourth procedure, and so on. Each procedure can have its own local variables, as illustrated by the code in Figure 6.6. Before reading further, try to predict what values will be displayed and in what order when the user clicks on cmdTestMultipleCalls. Note that TestProcedureB is called twice, once by TestProcedureA and once by cmdTestMultipleCalls_Click.

When cmdTestMultipleCalls_Click starts to execute, it creates a local variable X and sets it equal to 100. It then transfers execution to procedure TestProcedureA. This procedure creates its own local variable X and sets its value

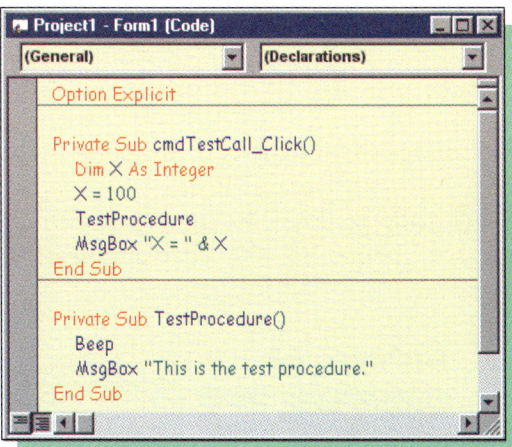

FIGURE 6.5

Code demonstrating local variable's lifetime

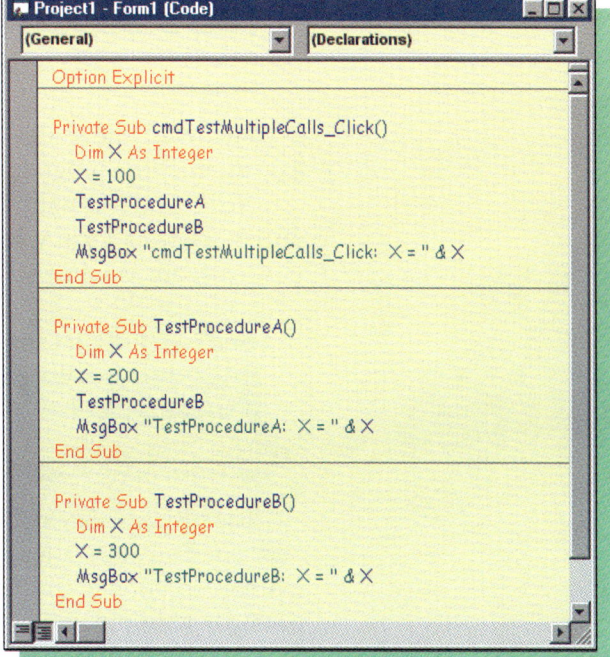

FIGURE 6.6

Code showing multiple local variables with the same name

to 200. At this point in the execution of the program there are two local variable tables, as depicted below.

cmdTestMultipleCalls_Click

Variable	Value
X	100

TestProcedureA

Variable	Value
X	200

TestProcedureA now transfers execution to TestProcedureB. TestProcedureB creates a variable named X in its own local variable table, and sets it equal to 300. Now there are three local variable tables:

cmdTestMultipleCalls_Click

Variable	Value
X	100

TestProcedureA

Variable	Value
X	200

TestProcedureB

Variable	Value
X	300

The MsgBox statement in TestProcedureB is executed, displaying the value 300. The End Sub statement destroys TestProcedureB's local variable table, and returns execution to TestProcedureA (the procedure that called TestProcedureB). Now the MsgBox statement in TestProcedureA is executed, displaying the value 200. This procedure's End Sub statement is then encountered, which destroys TestProcedureA's local variable table and returns execution to procedure cmdTestMultipleCalls_Click (the procedure that called TestProcedureA). Now only one local variable table exists.

cmdTestMultipleCalls_Click

Variable	Value
X	100

Figure 6.7 shows the flow of execution that brought us to this point in the execution of the program.

Next, cmdTestMultipleCalls_Click calls TestProcedureB, and TestProcedureB creates a local variable X and sets it equal to 300. The variables that now exist are as follows:

cmdTestMultipleCalls_Click

Variable	Value
X	100

TestProcedureB

Variable	Value
X	300

The MsgBox statement in TestProcedureB is executed, displaying the value 300. The End Sub statement destroys TestProcedureB's local variable table and returns execution to cmdTestMultipleCalls_Click. Finally, the MsgBox statement in cmdTestMultipleCalls_Click is executed, displaying the value 100. Then its End Sub statement is encountered, which destroys its local variable table.

The variable X in TestProcedureA is a different variable from X in TestProcedureB, even though both variables have the same name. We could rewrite this code, using Y instead of X in TestProcedureA, and Z instead of X in TestProcedureB, but the program would operate identically.

FIGURE 6.7

Flow of execution for code in Figure 6.6

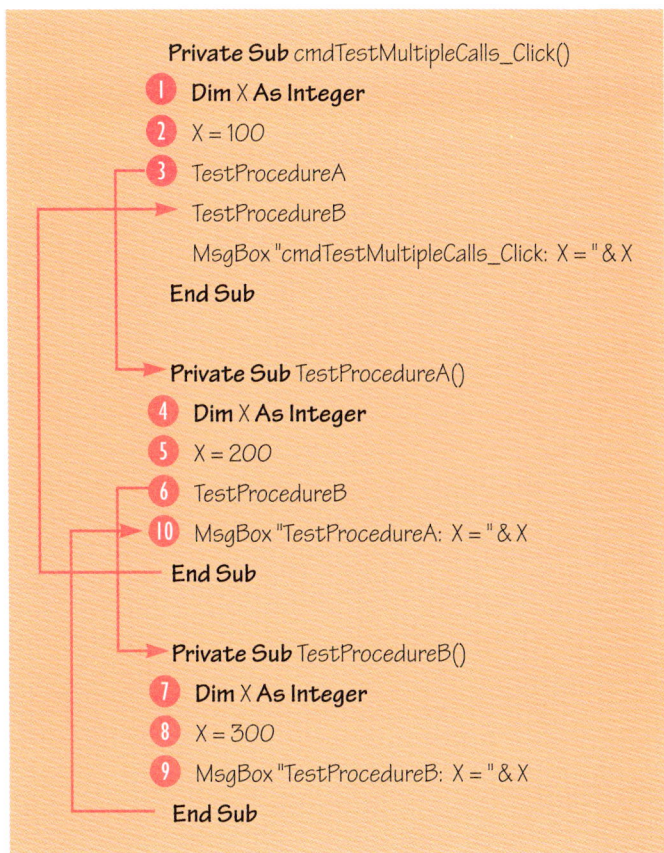

EXERCISE 6.3

Predict what values the following code displays, and in what order, when the user clicks on cmdScopeQuiz. Note the module-level variable named X.

```
Dim X As Integer

Private Sub cmdScopeQuiz_Click()
    Dim Y As Integer
    Dim Z As Integer
    Y = 2
    Z = 5
    X = Y + Z
    MsgBox X & Y & Z
    SQuizProcedureA
    SQuizProcedureB
    MsgBox X & Y & Z
End Sub

Private Sub SQuizProcedureA()
    Dim X As Integer
    Dim Y As Integer
    Y = Y + 4
    X = X + Y
    MsgBox X & Y
End Sub
```

continues

```
Private Sub SQuizProcedureB()
    Dim Y As Integer
    Dim Z As Integer
    Y = Y - 1
    Z = 3
    X = X + Y + Z
    MsgBox X & Y & Z
End Sub
```

General Sub Procedures and Project Structure

In this section we discuss how general sub procedures are handled by the VB programming environment and examine their position in the hierarchical structure of projects. We start by showing how to locate a general sub procedure in the Code window, and then discuss the scope of a procedure (i.e., which procedures are able to call it). Finally, we discuss code modules, which act as containers for general sub procedures and can be used in more than one project.

Locating a General Sub Procedure in the Code Window

In the VB programming environment, the Code window is where we enter and view event procedures—but it is also where we enter and view general sub procedures. A general sub procedure is called *general* because, unlike an event procedure, it is not associated with any control.

When the Code window's Full Module View button is depressed we can find any desired procedure simply by scrolling up and down until we see its heading. However, when the Code window contains many procedures, it can be difficult to find the desired one using this method. In that case, we use the Code window's Object and Procedures/Events boxes.

Suppose we are working with our computerized income tax application. The project has one form, and the form has several controls. Five of its option buttons have Click event procedures, and there is one general sub procedure named WithdrawPECSpouseQuestion.

Recall that to view an *event* procedure—say, optFSMarriedJoint_Click—we

1. Select the name of the control, optFSMarriedJoint, in the Code window's Object box.
2. Select the event, Click, in the Procedures/Events box.

This is depicted in Figure 6.8.

FIGURE 6.8

Selecting an event procedure in the Code window

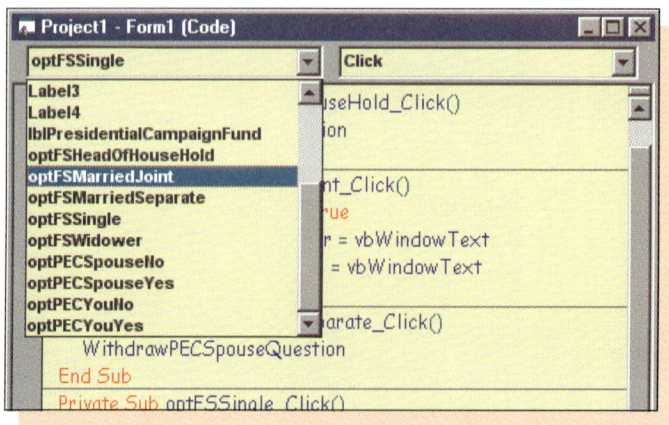

However, the name of a general sub procedure will never appear in the Code window's Object box, because the Object box lists only control names. To view a general sub procedure—say, WithdrawPECSpouseQuestion—we

1. Select (General) in the Code window's Object box.
2. Use the Procedures/Events box to select the name of the general sub procedure, WithdrawPECSpouseQuestion.

This is depicted in Figure 6.9.

The Code window's *General object* is where VB places program components that do not belong to any particular control.

Procedure Scope

Like variables and constants, procedures—both event procedures and general sub procedures—have scope. A procedure's *scope* determines which procedures are able to invoke it. A procedure is *private* if it begins with the keywords Private Sub. **A *Private procedure* is module-level, which means that it can be invoked by all procedures in the same form but cannot be invoked by any procedure in a different form.** A procedure is *public* if it begins with the keywords Public Sub. **A *Public procedure* is global, which means that it can be invoked by all procedures in all forms of the project.**

As with variables, it is a good idea to limit the scope of procedures that you create. That is, every procedure should be private unless it is intended to be invoked by procedures in other forms.

Procedure scope applies to event procedures as well as general sub procedures. (Note that all the event procedures we have seen so far have begun with the keywords Private Sub.) In fact, as long as scope allows it, any procedure can invoke any other procedure regardless of whether they are event procedures or general sub procedures.

You may wonder why we even need general sub procedures if event procedures can call other event procedures. Why not just use event procedures? Remember that an event procedure is associated with a specific event for a specific control, e.g., a command button's Click event. General sub procedures are not directly related to any single control and often perform processing that is independent of the concept of controls, such as alphabetizing a set of names.

The code in Figure 6.10 demonstrates one event procedure calling another event procedure. It contains two event procedures that are both private, and no general sub procedures. Both event procedures belong to the same form. Event procedure cmdBeepMessage_Click invokes event procedure cmdBeep_Click by simply including its name as a statement. Executing this

FIGURE 6.9

Selecting a general sub procedure in the Code window

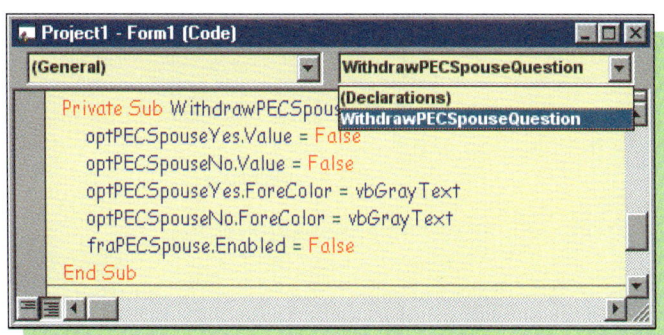

FIGURE 6.10

Code showing one event procedure that calls another event procedure

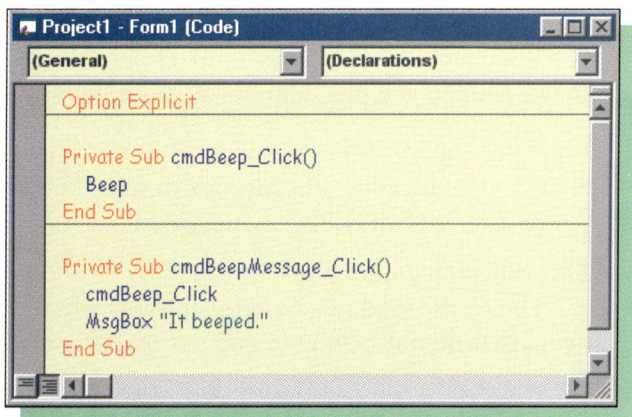

statement will cause exactly the same processing step to be performed as if the user had clicked on cmdBeep.

Example 6.1 Public versus Private Procedures and Multiple Forms

This example shows how an event procedure on one form can invoke an event procedure on another form. This example has two forms, A and B, which are shown in Figure 6.11. The code is shown in Figure 6.12. The Click event procedure for the command button on form A exchanges the captions of the two labels on form A. The Click event procedure for the command button on form B invokes the Click event procedure for the command button on form A. Thus, both buttons cause the same thing to happen.

Note that event procedure cmdExchange_Click (on form A) is public, which is why the event procedure on form B is able to invoke it. If you modify cmdExchange_Click to make it private instead of public, then event procedure cmdExchangeFormALabels_Click will no longer work (it cannot access a private procedure on another form).

The statement in cmdExchangeFormALabels_Click (on form B) that invokes cmdExchange_Click (on form A) is frmEx0601A.cmdExchange_Click. This

FIGURE 6.11

Forms and controls for Example 6.1

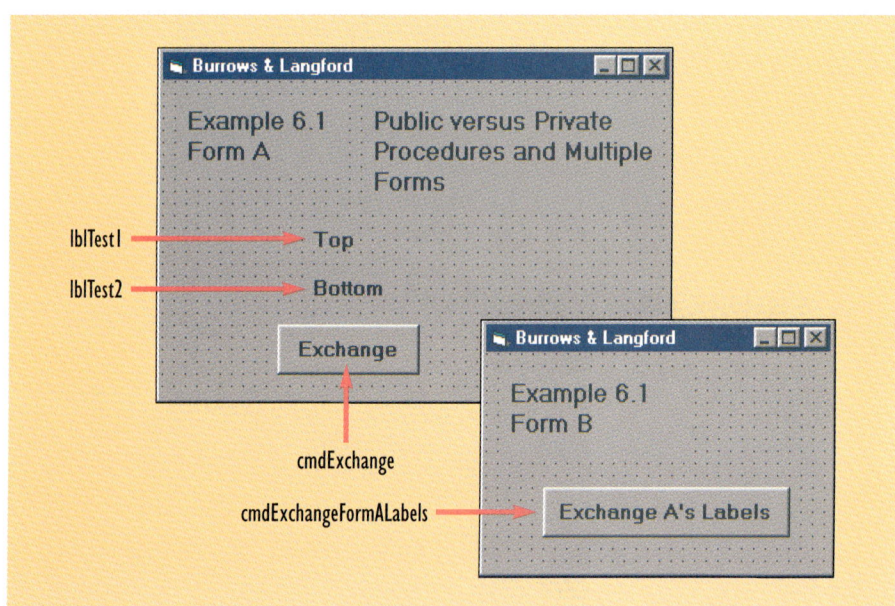

FIGURE 6.12

Code for Example 6.1

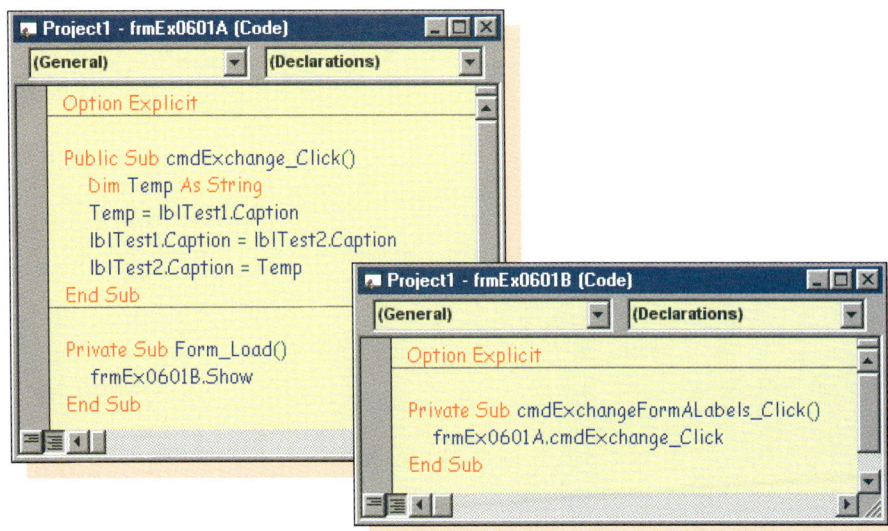

statement illustrates the syntax for invoking a procedure that belongs to a different form. The procedure name must be *qualified* by the name of the form.

formname.procedurename

This is similar to the syntax for accessing a control property on a different form.

formname!control.property

Note that the call uses a period (.) instead of an exclamation point (!) to separate the form name from the procedure name.

Example 6.2

Using a Public General Sub Procedure

This example illustrates a public general sub procedure. It has two forms, shown in Figure 6.13. The code is shown in Figure 6.14. Form A has two procedures: a private event procedure named cmdBeepTime_Click and a public general sub procedure named DisplayTime. Form B has a private event procedure named cmdQuietTime_Click. Both event procedures invoke the public general sub procedure that resides in form A.

Observe that cmdBeepTime_Click (on form A) does not have to qualify the procedure name to invoke DisplayTime because it too resides on form A.

FIGURE 6.13

Forms and controls for Example 6.2

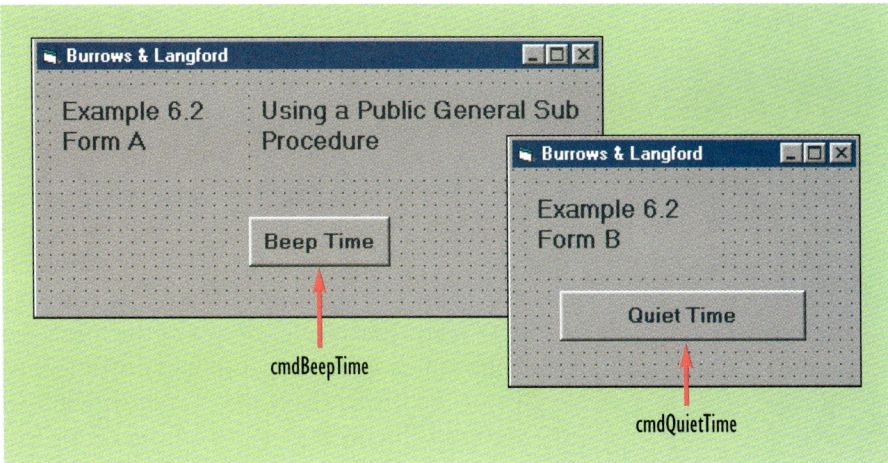

FIGURE 6.14

Code for Example 6.2

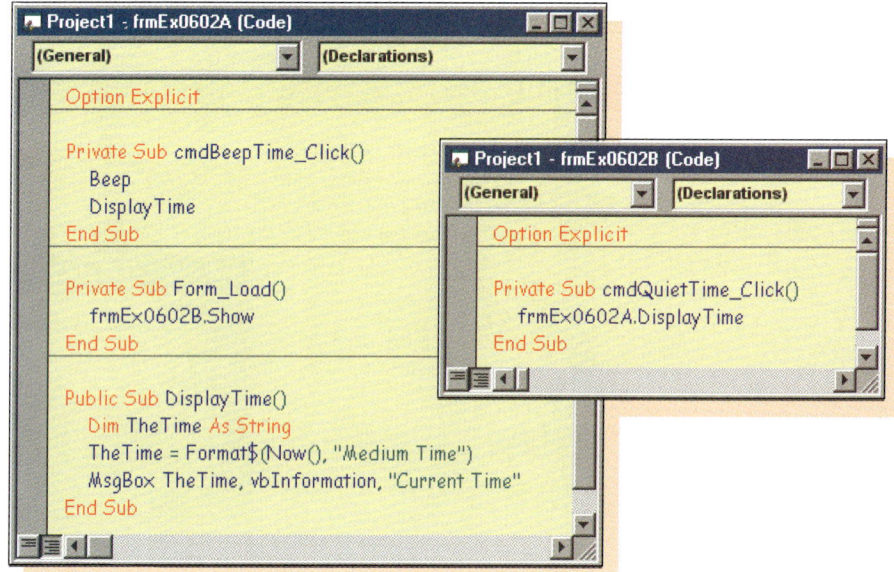

However, cmdQuietTime_Click (on form B) does have to qualify the procedure name to invoke DisplayTime because DisplayTime resides on a different form.

Procedure DisplayTime uses VB's built-in Now() function to determine the current time, and the Format$() function with the predefined format specification Medium Time to format the current time. If you are interested in the details of how these work, see online help. (Use search phrases "Now" and "Format Function"; on the "Format Function" help page, click the See Also link and select the "Named Date/Time Formats" topic.)

Code Modules

In Chapter 3 we saw how to use a code module as a place to declare global variables and symbolic constants. The code module has another purpose: it can contain general sub procedures. Even though forms can contain general sub procedures, we often use code modules to improve the project's organization.

Forms and code modules both serve to help organize a project, and they behave similarly in most respects (in fact, VB's online help often uses the term "Module" for both). However, a code module cannot contain event procedures because it has no user interface window to hold the associated controls.

Many processing tasks are generic in the sense that they are not associated with any particular control and can be used by more than one form. Specifically, event procedures on many different forms—possibly forms in many different projects—may require the same processing task. To allow these event procedures to share code, a programmer creates a general sub procedure that performs the processing task and places it in a descriptively named code module. This code module can then be included in many different projects.

Example 6.2 contains a general sub procedure named DisplayTime that displays the current time, nicely formatted, in a message box. In Example 6.2, procedure DisplayTime resides in one of the forms. However, the task performed by DisplayTime could be useful in many different applications.

By moving DisplayTime into a code module, we make it easy to include in other projects. Figure 6.15 shows the code for Example 6.2 after making this change. The user interface for this example is the same as in Example 6.2 (see

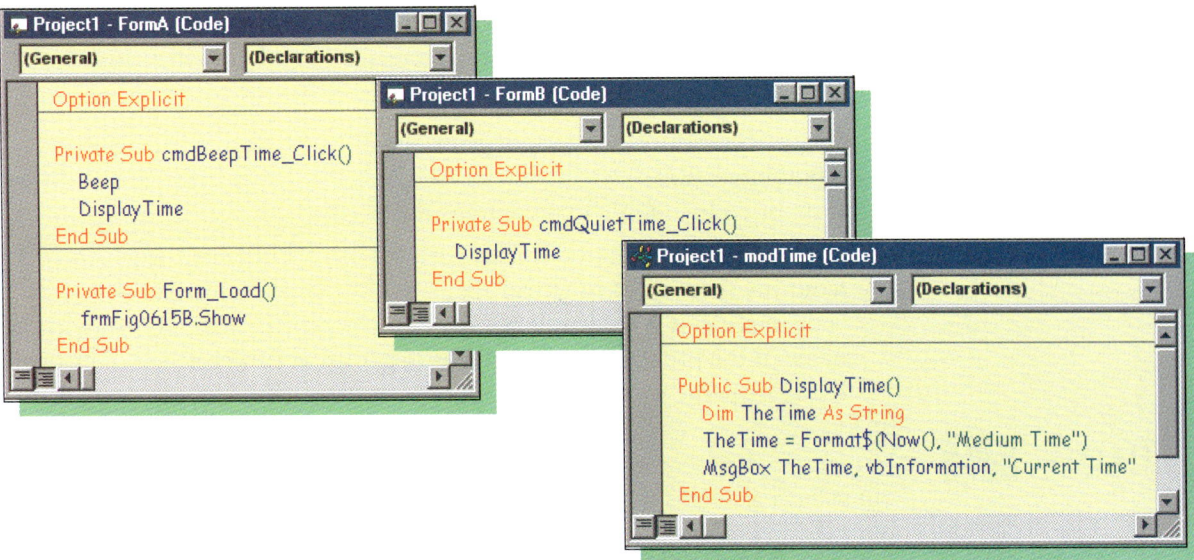

FIGURE 6.15   Code for modified version of Example 6.2 with code module

Figure 6.13). The user cannot tell any difference between the two examples. The only difference is in the organization of the code.

The code module's Name property appears in its Code window's Title bar. In Figure 6.15, the code module is named modTime. Note carefully that the event procedures in the forms do not have to qualify the general sub procedure name with the name of the code module in which it resides. A public general sub procedure in a code module can be invoked by any procedure in any form or code module of the project simply by using its name.

Project Structure

Now is a good time to incorporate our understanding of general sub procedures into our view of project structure. Figure 6.16 is an expanded version of Figure 2.2 that includes the scope of variables, procedures, and properties.

FIGURE 6.16

Structure of VB projects

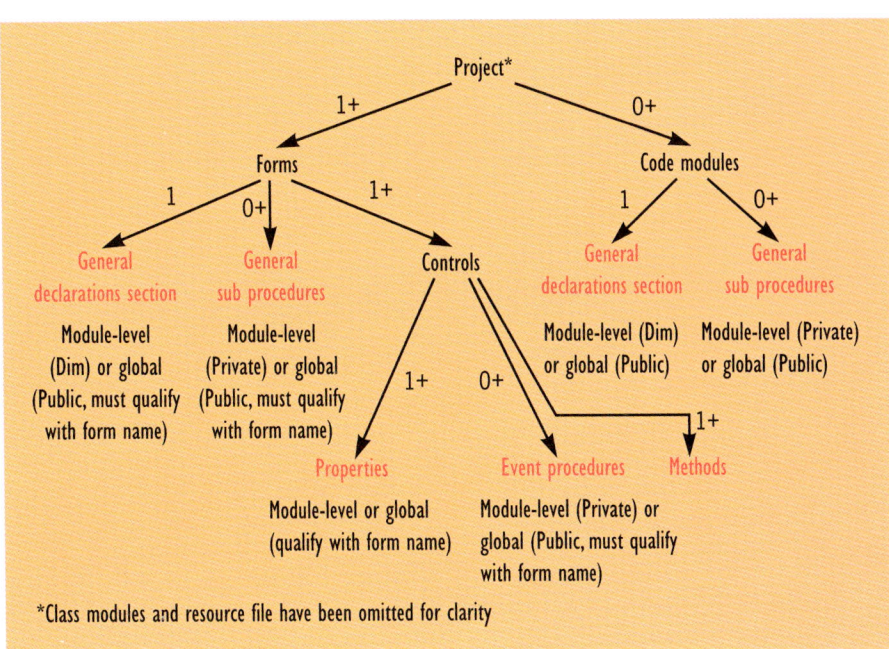

The key terms Public, Private, and Dim in this figure are intended to highlight the close analogy between procedure scope and variable scope in VB. The analogy can be summarized as follows:

- Private procedures, like variables declared using Dim in the general declarations section, have module-level scope: they are accessible only in the form or code module that contains them.

- Public procedures, like variables declared using Public in the general declarations section, have global scope. If the procedure or variable is in a code module, it is accessible anywhere in the project without qualifying its name. If the procedure or variable is in a form, it can be accessed by qualifying its name with the name of the form that contains it.

EXERCISE 6.4 In Figure 6.3, we could have eliminated the possibility of inconsistencies without using a general sub procedure by leaving optFSSingle_Click alone, and having the Click event procedures for the other option buttons invoke it. Would this have been a good idea? Explain.

Creating General Sub Procedures

To create a general sub procedure, first bring up the Code window for the form or code module in which you wish to place the procedure. Then select Add Procedure… under the Tools menu. VB presents you with the dialog box shown in Figure 6.17. Select type Sub, select either Public or Private scope, then enter the name you wish to give the sub procedure in the Name text box and click OK. VB will return you to the Code window, showing (General) in the Object box, the name you specified in the Procedures/Events box, and a procedure template in the Code window. If you enter WithdrawPECSpouseQuestion as the name, for example, the Code window will show the template in Figure 6.18.

To complete the general sub procedure you need only enter its statements, just as you would for an event procedure.

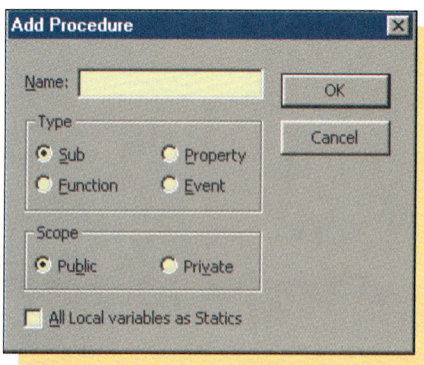

FIGURE 6.17

VB's Add Procedure dialog box

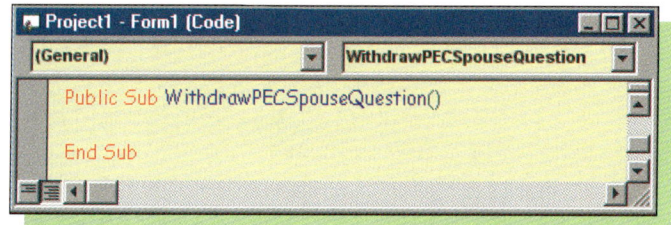

FIGURE 6.18

New general sub procedure in the Code window

> **Convention** Choose descriptive procedure names. Good procedure names often include a verb indicating the action performed by the procedure and a direct object indicating the entity on which the action is performed.

EXERCISE 6.5 Modify the project for Example 5.7, which contains the income tax application before introducing general sub procedures, as follows: First, modify the code by creating general sub procedure WithdrawPECSpouseQuestion, so that the code appears as in Figure 6.3. Then run the project to verify that it works properly. Next, create a general sub procedure containing the statements that are currently in event procedure optFSMarriedJoint_Click, and have optFSMarriedJoint_Click invoke this new procedure. Again, run the project to verify that it works properly.

EXERCISE 6.6 Modify the code for Example 5.3 (see Figure 5.7), which computes and displays an employee's wage rate based on number of months of service, as follows: First, move the entire If statement from event procedure cmdLookUpWageRate_Click into a new general sub procedure named ComputeWageRate. Then, at the If statement's original location, place the name of the new general sub procedure. Finally, make the variable MonthsOfService module-level instead of local, so that both procedures cmdLookUpWageRate_Click and ComputeWageRate can access it. Run the project to verify that it works properly.

EXERCISE 6.7 Modify the code for Example 5.9 (see Figure 5.32), which computes and displays the number of days in any desired month, as follows: First, make the variables MonthAbbr and DaysInMonth module-level instead of local. Then create a general sub procedure named FindNumDaysInMonth which performs the task of looking in variable MonthAbbr to find a month abbreviation, then determining the number of days in that month and storing this result in variable DaysInMonth. Finally, modify event procedure cmdMonthDays_Click to invoke the new general sub procedure instead of using the Select Case statement directly. Run the project to verify that it works properly.

6.2 Procedures with Parameters

Suppose that you wanted to write a general sub procedure that prints a check. Suppose the calling procedure possesses the data for the dollar amount and the name of the payee to appear on the check. How can the calling procedure communicate this data to the general sub procedure? We have already worked with one approach: module-level or global variables. However, there is a better approach, called *parameter passing*, **in which we pass data between the calling procedure and the called procedure.**

Parameter passing offers more flexibility than using module-level or global variables. To set the stage for our work with parameters, we discuss the drawbacks of sharing data using module-level and global variables, and then observe how using parameters corrects these problems.

Drawbacks of Module-Level and Global Variables

Although module-level and global variables allow procedures to share data, this process has two serious drawbacks. To illustrate, suppose that two or more procedures in a project need to share data, and we create a global variable for this purpose. The first drawback is that *every* procedure in the project has access to this variable, even if only two or three *should* have access to it. Thus, the possibility exists that a procedure that really should not have access to the data item will modify it, causing trouble for those procedures that legitimately rely on the data item. The inadvertent change of a variable is very common and very troublesome in large projects with many procedures. When a data item gets corrupted, it is difficult to discover the procedure that is corrupting it.

The second drawback is that the procedures wanting to share data using the global variable have to "know" its name. That is, the exact name of this variable must appear in the code of these procedures. As a result, the procedures will be able to share data *only* through this particular variable. This approach is inflexible, particularly when the programmer has identified a processing subtask that is generic. Lack of flexibility is an obstacle to the goal of reusable code.

Consider the following code:

```
Dim MyInitials As String

Private Sub ReverseTwoCharString()
    MyInitials = Right$(MyInitials, 1) & Left$(MyInitials, 1)
End Sub

Private Sub cmdReverseMyInitials_Click()
    MyInitials = InputBox("Enter your first and last initials.")
    ReverseTwoCharString
    MsgBox "Your reversed initials are: " & MyInitials
End Sub
```

This code uses the module-level variable MyInitials to facilitate the sharing of data between the event procedure cmdReverseMyInitials_Click and the general sub procedure ReverseTwoCharString. The event procedure uses the InputBox() function to get the user's initials and stores them in MyInitials. It then calls procedure ReverseTwoCharString. Procedure ReverseTwoCharString retrieves the value from MyInitials, performs the reversal (putting the original left character on the right of the new string and the original right character on the left of the new string), and stores the result back in MyInitials. Execution then returns to the event procedure, where the reversed initials are displayed using the MsgBox statement.

The code is clear and concise, but the variable name MyInitials makes no sense inside procedure ReverseTwoCharString. Imagine we wanted a new event procedure to obtain and then reverse the two digits of a person's age. Since the procedure ReverseTwoCharString uses the module-level variable MyInitials, this new event procedure would be

```
Private Sub cmdReverseMyAge_Click()
    MyInitials = InputBox("Enter your age.")
    ReverseTwoCharString
    MsgBox "Your reversed age is: " & MyInitials
End Sub
```

While this works, it is confusing. Storing the user's age in a variable named MyInitials makes no sense.

EXERCISE 6.8 What happens if the user enters three or more letters, instead of two, in response to the input box in cmdReverseMyInitials_Click? What can you say about this use of procedure ReverseTwoCharString? What can you say about the name of procedure ReverseTwoCharString? Explain.

Parameter Passing

If we can somehow "send" the two characters to be reversed directly to the general sub procedure, then we can make the general sub procedure truly generic. By *generic,* we mean that the procedure will work and will be easy to understand when it is used to reverse *any* string consisting of two characters. *Parameter passing* allows us to do this. The calling procedure hands the called procedure a variable, and the called procedure then uses the variable as if it were one of its own local variables. When the called procedure is finished executing, it hands the variable back to the calling procedure. This sharing lasts only while the called procedure is executing.

Figure 6.19 shows the program that reverses two initials (or two digits of an age), modified to use parameter passing. In the next few sections we describe how parameter passing works.

Parameter Lists

Procedure headings contain important information, and they are about to become even more important to us because they identify the parameters being passed. In every procedure heading, the parentheses following the procedure's name surround a *parameter list,* **a list of data items that the procedure expects any calling procedure to send it.** Prior to this point in our study of VB, these parentheses were always empty, meaning that no parameters were used. But note that procedure ReverseTwoCharString in Figure 6.19 does specify a parameter.

Private Sub ReverseTwoCharString(TwoChars **As String**)

                                        Parameter list

FIGURE 6.19

Code for reversing two characters using a parameter

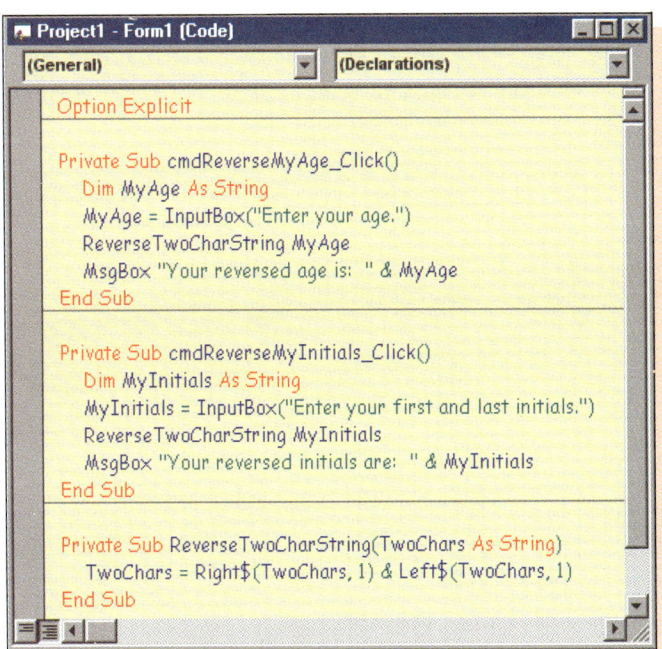

This parameter list specifies the following:

1. Any procedure calling ReverseTwoCharString must provide a variable of type String. This variable is called an *argument*, and we say that the argument is *passed* from the calling procedure to the called procedure.

2. Inside procedure ReverseTwoCharString, this variable is referred to as TwoChars, regardless of what its name is in the calling procedure.

Anything that procedure ReverseTwoCharString does with the parameter it refers to as TwoChars *actually* happens with the argument passed to it by the calling procedure. That is, TwoChars is not a separate variable; it is just another name for the variable passed to procedure ReverseTwoCharString.

The variable in the procedure call is referred to as an *argument*, and the corresponding variable in the procedure heading is called a *parameter*. In Figure 6.19, the variable MyInitials in the statement ReverseTwoCharString MyInitials is an argument. The variable TwoChars in the heading Private Sub ReverseTwoCharString(TwoChars As String) is a parameter. Using the terms argument and parameter helps to clarify discussions of parameter passing.

Procedure Calls with Parameters

Programmers sometimes draw arrows on source code printouts to highlight parameter passing. This is illustrated in Figure 6.20. In procedure cmdReverseMyInitials_Click, the statement

    ReverseTwoCharString MyInitials

invokes procedure ReverseTwoCharString and provides it with the string variable MyInitials (MyInitials is the argument). Procedure ReverseTwoCharString then begins executing, and it uses the variable MyInitials, but refers to it as TwoChars instead of MyInitials.

Similarly, in procedure cmdReverseMyAge_Click in Figure 6.20, the call

    ReverseTwoCharString MyAge

invokes procedure ReverseTwoCharString and provides it with the string variable MyAge. Procedure ReverseTwoCharString then begins executing, and it uses the variable MyAge, but refers to it as TwoChars instead of MyAge.

FIGURE 6.20

Parameter passing

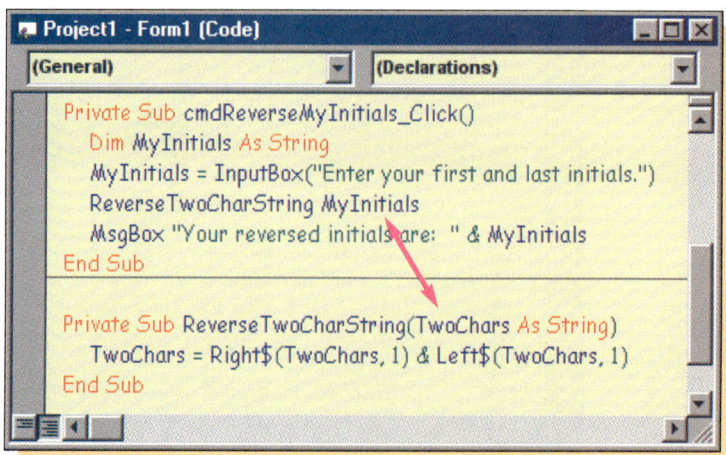

Analyzing Procedures That Use Parameters

In order to fully understand parameter passing, we need to "hand-check"—that is, simulate execution of the code by hand—a few examples. When you hand-check code you should heed the following practices to help you keep track of the details:

♦ Execute statements one at a time, in the same order the computer does.

♦ Place a number next to each statement as you execute it so that later you can review the order in which statements were executed.

♦ Create variable tables to keep track of the value stored in each variable. Be sure to create a different table for each procedure's local variables, for each form or code module's module-level variables, and for the global variables.

♦ Add the new variable to the appropriate table and initialize it when a variable declaration statement is executed.

♦ Draw a line through a variable's old value and write the new value below it when a variable's value changes. This way, the current value in the variable is always obvious. This also enables you to review your work when you're finished and contemplate the effect of individual statements.

Let's hand-check the program in Figure 6.20. Suppose the user has just clicked on cmdReverseMyInitials, causing the Click event procedure to begin executing. We simulate the action of the computer executing the Dim statement by creating the variable MyInitials and initializing it to the zero-length string. Next, we visualize an input box being displayed and a value being entered by the user. Suppose that the user enters "A1"; we cross out the old value in MyInitials and record the value "A1" just below it. The next statement to execute is the procedure call. At this point our hand-check work should look something like Figure 6.21. The variable MyInitials is the argument being passed to procedure ReverseTwoCharString, and the variable table for procedure cmdReverseMyInitials_Click shows its current value.

Figure 6.22 shows the hand-check after the flow of execution has been transferred to procedure ReverseTwoCharString and the computer has executed the assignment statement reversing the two letters. Note that in the variable table for procedure cmdReverseMyInitials_Click, the variable names MyInitials and TwoChars are actually the same variable. Also note that the variable table for the called procedure is empty. This is because procedure ReverseTwoCharString has no variables of its own—it just has access to the argument that was passed to it.

FIGURE 6.21

Hand-check as sub procedure is being called

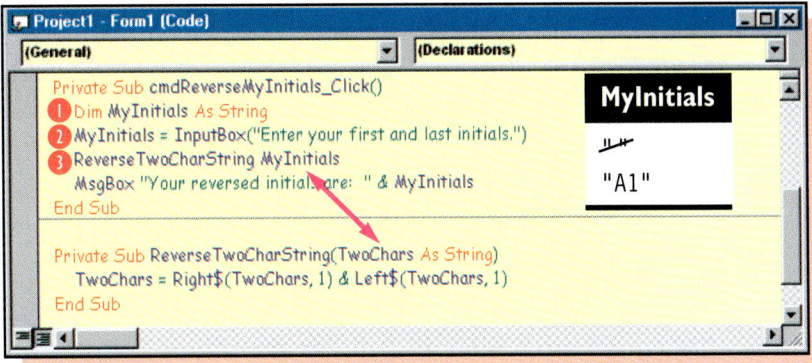

FIGURE 6.22

Hand-check as called procedure executes

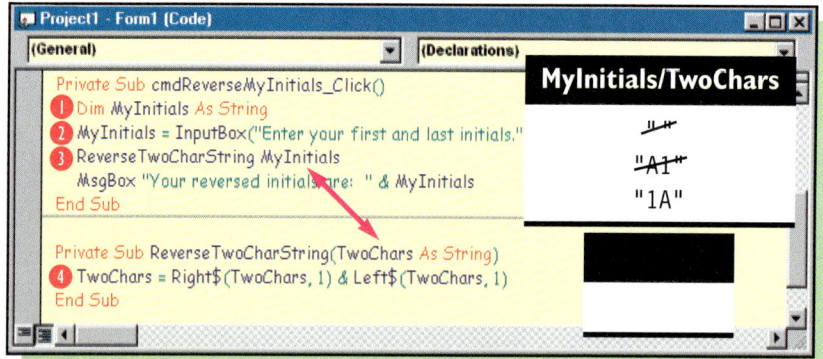

FIGURE 6.23

Hand-check with execution back in calling procedure

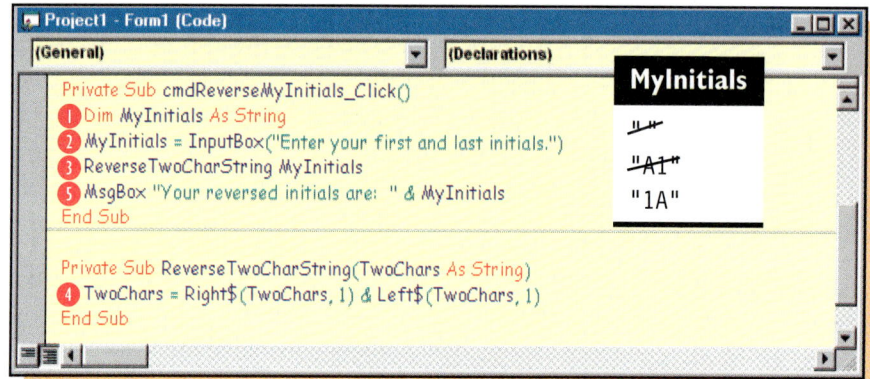

When the End Sub is encountered in the called procedure, execution returns to cmdReverseMyInitials_Click. Figure 6.23 shows the hand-check as the MsgBox statement is being executed. Look carefully at the variable table. The parameter name TwoChars is now gone because the called procedure has finished executing. Also note that the change in the value of the argument MyInitials, which took place in the called procedure, remains. The message box will display the message "Your reversed initials are: 1A".

Parameter passing does not involve either of the drawbacks of module-level and global variables. We have arrived at the following very important rule.

> **Rule** Unless a large percentage of the procedures in the form (or project) require access to a data item, don't use a module-level (or global) variable for that data item. Instead, make it a local variable, and use parameter passing when it is necessary to share the data item with another procedure.

EXERCISE 6.9

Hand-check procedure cmdParameterQuiz1_Click and show its output.

```
Private Sub cmdParameterQuiz1_Click()
    Dim BuildUp As String
    BuildUp = "From "
    QuizProcedureA BuildUp
    QuizProcedureB BuildUp
    BuildUp = BuildUp & "sentence."
    MsgBox BuildUp
End Sub
```

```
Private Sub QuizProcedureA(Message As String)
    Message = Message & "short "
End Sub

Private Sub QuizProcedureB(Phrase As String)
    Phrase = Phrase & "words emerges a "
    QuizProcedureA Phrase
End Sub
```

EXERCISE 6.10 Hand-check procedure cmdParameterQuiz2_Click and show its output.

```
Private Sub cmdParameterQuiz2_Click()
    Dim X As Integer
    X = 1
    QuizProcedureC X
    X = X + 1
    QuizProcedureD X
    X = X + 1
    MsgBox X
End Sub

Private Sub QuizProcedureC(Y As Integer)
    QuizProcedureD Y
    Y = Y + 10
End Sub

Private Sub QuizProcedureD(Z As Integer)
    Z = Z + 100
End Sub
```

Multiple Parameters

♦ ♦ ♦

You can write procedures that receive and process more than one parameter. The parameter list is the key to this. Every parameter list specifies four important pieces of information:

1. The *number* of arguments that the calling procedure must provide.
2. The *types* of the arguments that the calling procedure must provide.
3. The *sequence* of the arguments that the calling procedure must provide.
4. The *names* the arguments are referred to as *inside* the called procedure.

To demonstrate how to work with multiple parameters, let's hand-check an example that passes two arguments to a procedure.

Procedure Rotate, which has two parameters, performs the Caesar cipher operation of shifting a letter in the alphabet (see Figure 6.24). If the letter is D and the shift amount is 3, then Rotate changes the letter to G (i.e., three positions past D in the alphabet). This is a cyclic shift—it implements *wrap around* at the end of the alphabet—which is why the procedure is named Rotate. If the letter is X and the shift amount is 3, then Rotate changes the letter to A.

FIGURE 6.24

Code for Caesar cipher example

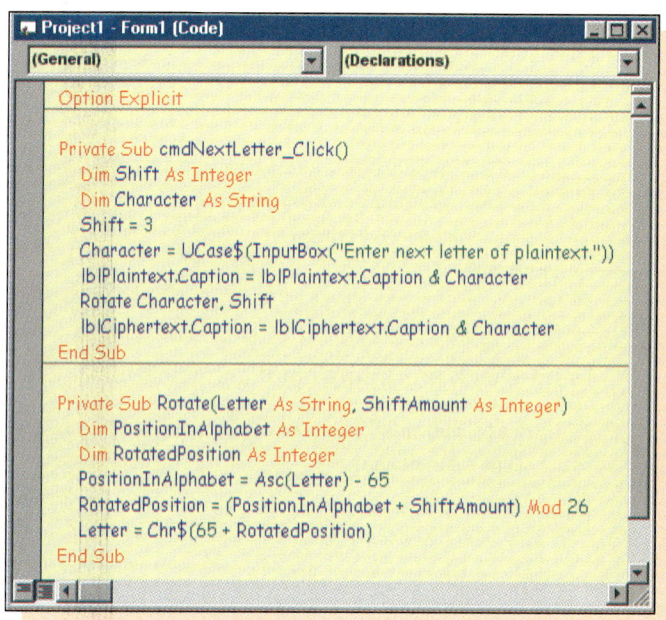

Rotate's heading specifies the parameter list

Letter **As String**, ShiftAmount **As Integer**

This parameter list tells us the following:

1. Any procedure calling Rotate must provide Rotate with *two* arguments.
2. The first argument must be type String, and the second must be type Integer.
3. The first argument represents the letter to be shifted, and the second argument represents the amount the letter should be shifted.
4. Inside procedure Rotate, the first argument is referred to by the name Letter, and the second argument is referred to by the name ShiftAmount.

Accordingly, in cmdNextLetter_Click we find a local variable named Character of type String, a local variable named Shift of type Integer, and the call

Rotate Character, Shift

Let us hand-check this program to see how it executes. When the user clicks on cmdNextLetter, the event procedure cmdNextLetter_ Click begins executing. First, we create the variables Shift and Character, and initialize them to 0 and the zero-length string, to mirror the action of the Dim statements. Next, we store the value 3 in Shift. When the input box is displayed, the user enters a letter. Suppose that the user enters "p". We cross out the old value in Character and record the value "P" below it. (Note that the string function UCase$() converts lowercase letters into uppercase.) The next statement causes the letter "P" to be appended to the value displayed by lblPlaintext. At this point, our hand-check appears as in Figure 6.25.

The next statement to execute is the procedure call. The arguments are passed in the order in which they appear in the procedure call, as illustrated by the double arrows and shading in Figure 6.26.

Now we execute procedure Rotate. The parameters Letter and ShiftAmount are associated with the corresponding arguments Character and Shift in the calling procedure's variable table. Next, the Dim statements in procedure Rotate

FIGURE 6.25

Caesar cipher example as it begins to execute

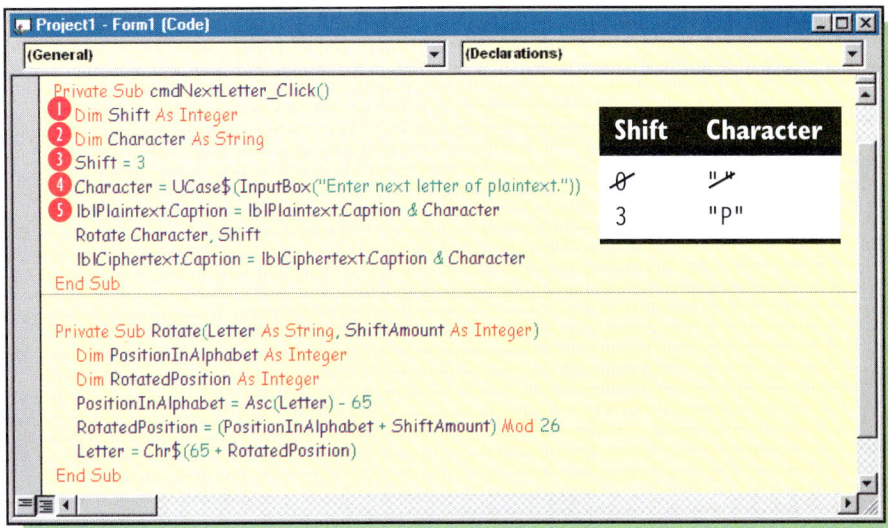

FIGURE 6.26

Caesar cipher example as called procedure executes

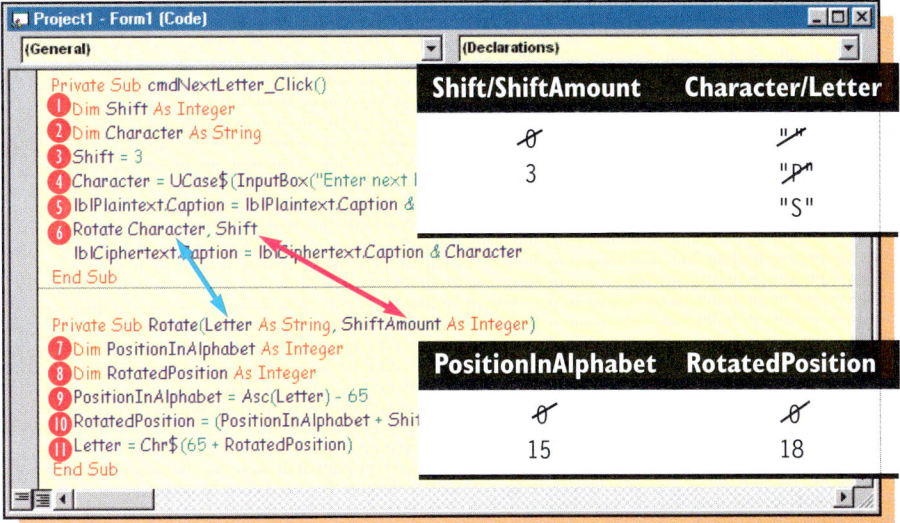

are executed; this creates a local variable table for procedure Rotate, with variables PositionInAlphabet and RotatedPosition, both initialized to zero.

Since "P" is at position 80 in the ANSI table, the next statement stores the number 15 in variable PositionInAlphabet (80 − 65 = 15). The statement after that stores the number 18 in variable RotatedPosition. The final assignment statement of procedure Rotate stores the value "S" in variable Letter (which is the same variable as Character in cmdNextLetter_Click).

When the End Sub is encountered, procedure Rotate stops executing, its local variable table is destroyed, and execution returns to the calling procedure (see Figure 6.27). The final statement retrieves the value from variable Character and appends it to lblCiphertext's Caption property.

The net effect of executing procedure Rotate was to change the value stored in variable Character from P to S. Procedure Rotate changes the value stored in its first parameter, but it does not change the value stored in its second parameter. That is, it "rotates" the letter, but only "examines" the shift amount to determine how much to rotate the letter.

FIGURE 6.27

Caesar cipher example as execution returns to calling procedure

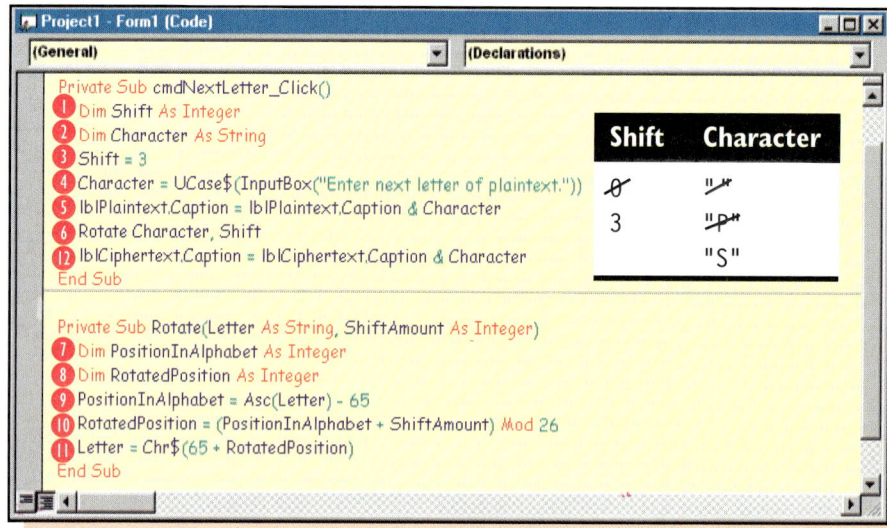

What were the roles of local variables PositionInAlphabet and RotatedPosition in procedure Rotate? They were used to hold the results of the intermediate calculations that procedure Rotate performed along the way to arriving at the new value of Letter. No other procedure in the project would ever be interested in the existence of this sort of intermediate calculation; that is, there is no need for procedure Rotate to ever share these data items with any other procedure. This is why these variables were made local variables and not parameters.

In our next example the procedures do not accomplish useful tasks, and the variable names are not descriptive. In fact, we have purposely chosen the variable names to obscure the parameter passing operation (we call this the "obscure parameter name" example). The objective of this example is to reinforce the argument-parameter relationship.

Figure 6.28 shows the code for this example. You might want to hand-check this code before reading further to test your understanding of parameters.

FIGURE 6.28

Code for "obscure parameter name" example

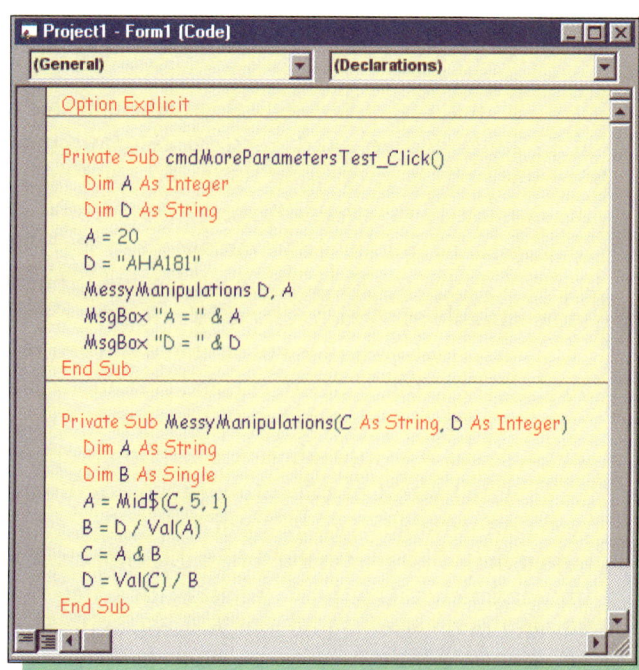

When the user clicks the cmdMoreParametersTest button, execution of cmdMoreParametersTest_Click begins. Figure 6.29 shows the code after execution has begun. In accordance with the Dim statements, we create the variables A and D and initialize them to 0 and the zero-length string. Next, we store the value 20 in A and the value "AHA181" in D.

The next statement to execute is the procedure call. The parameter list specifies that the calling procedure must provide two arguments, that the first must be type String, and that the second must be type Integer. Accordingly, the procedure call provides variable D of type String as the first argument and variable A of type Integer as the second argument. Also, while the flow of execution is in procedure MessyManipulations, variables D and A in the calling procedure are referred to as C and D, respectively. In Figure 6.30, the variable table for procedure cmdMoreParametersTest_Click shows this association.

Now we begin executing procedure MessyManipulations. We start out with parameters C and D containing the values "AHA181" and 20, respectively. The only thing we need to remember is that if we change the value stored in C in procedure MessyManipulations, then the same change occurs to D in

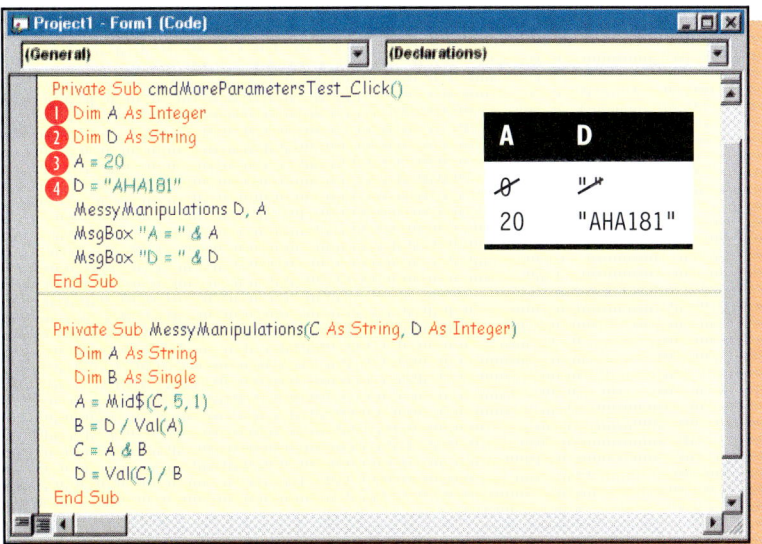

FIGURE 6.29

"Obscure parameter name" example just before procedure call

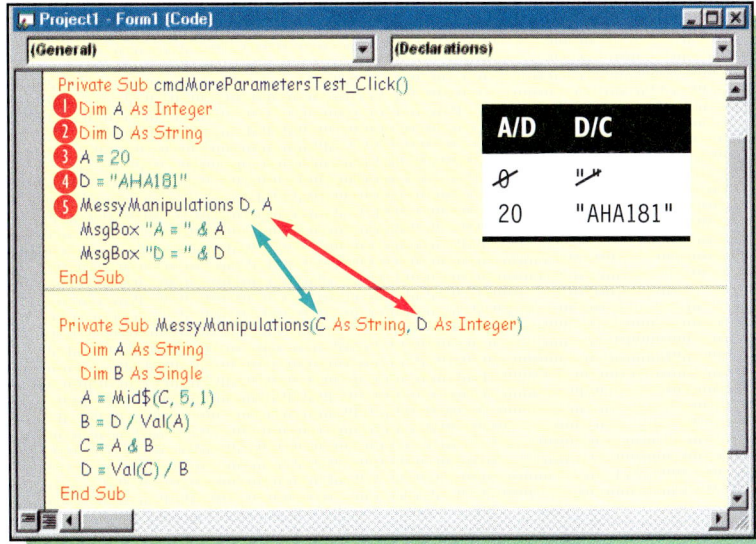

FIGURE 6.30

Procedure call in "obscure parameter name" example

procedure cmdMoreParametersTest_Click, because they are actually the same. Similarly, if we change the value stored in D in MessyManipulations, then the same change occurs to A in cmdMoreParametersTest_Click.

In accordance with the Dim statements, we create variables A and B, and initialize them to the zero-length string and 0, respectively. Since these are local to MessyManipulations, they have no connection to any other variables anywhere in the project. Executing the next two statements, we change A to "8", then B to 2.5. The next statement causes us to change C to "82.5", and the final statement causes us to change D to 33. See Figure 6.31.

When the End Sub is encountered, flow of execution returns to the calling procedure and the called procedure's local variable table is destroyed (see Figure 6.32). When the message box statements are executed, the value of A is 33 and the value of D is "82.5".

This example demonstrates how variables in the parameter list represent the corresponding arguments in the procedure call, and that this association is independent of the names of the parameters. Figure 6.31 is particularly important.

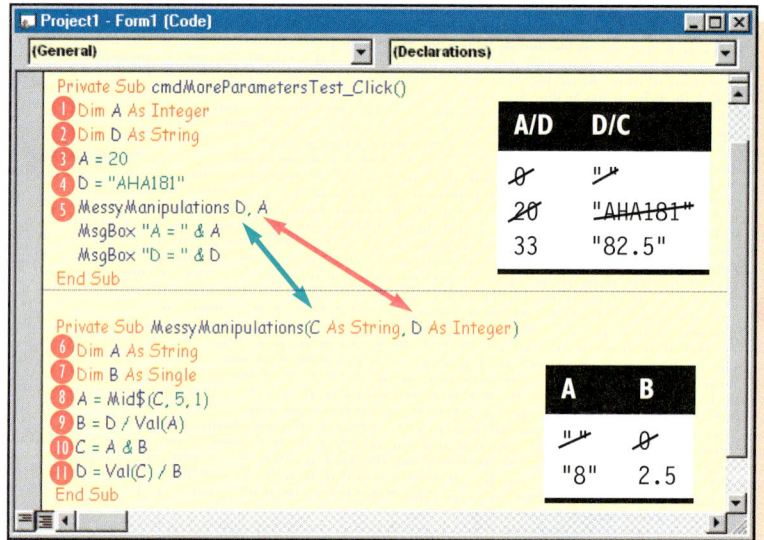

FIGURE 6.31

Execution of called procedure in "obscure parameter name" example

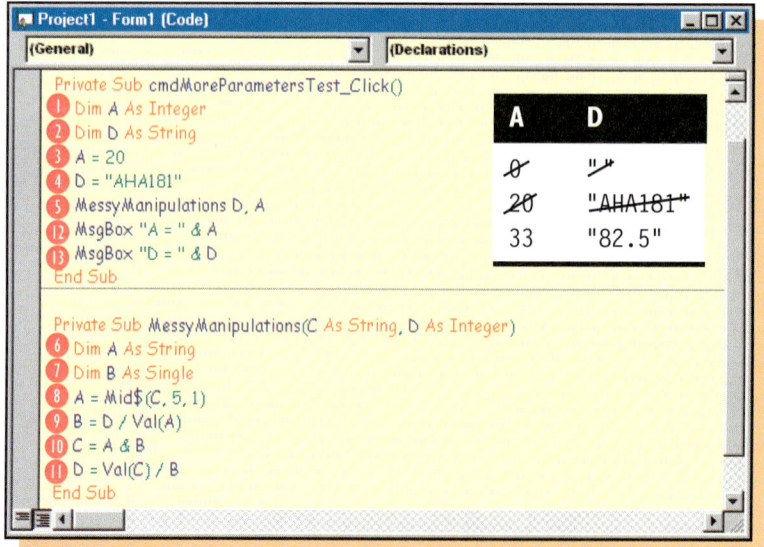

FIGURE 6.32

"Obscure parameter name" example as flow of execution returns to calling procedure

It shows that the parameter D in the called procedure is the same as the local variable A in the calling procedure, and that the local variable A in the called procedure is *not* the same as the local variable A in the calling procedure.

EXERCISE 6.11

In Figure 6.24, procedure cmdNextLetter_Click uses the function UCase$() to convert the letter entered by the user to uppercase. Suppose we remove this function. What effect will procedure Rotate have if the user enters a lowercase letter?

EXERCISE 6.12

Hand-check procedure cmdMultipleParametersTest_Click and show its output.

```
Private Sub cmdMultipleParametersTest_Click()
    Dim A As Integer
    Dim B As Integer
    Dim C As Single
    A = 2
    B = 4
    SimpleCalculations A, B, C
    MsgBox "A = " & A
    MsgBox "B = " & B
    MsgBox "C = " & C
End Sub

Private Sub SimpleCalculations(X As Integer, Y As Integer, Z As Single)
    Dim W As Single
    W = X + Y
    X = X + 1
    Y = Y * 2
    Z = (X + Y) / W
End Sub
```

EXERCISE 6.13

Suppose we modify Exercise 6.12 by changing the statement

    SimpleCalculations A, B, C

in procedure cmdMultipleParametersTest_Click to

    SimpleCalculations B, A, C

What values will the message boxes display? Can you figure this out without having to work through the code by hand?

EXERCISE 6.14

Write a procedure named Swap that performs the task of exchanging the values stored in two variables of type Single. If your procedure is correctly written, the message boxes in the event procedure below should display the same two numbers that the user enters in response to the input boxes, but in reverse order.

```
Private Sub cmdSwapTest_Click()
    Dim A As Single
    Dim B As Single
    A = InputBox("Enter a number")
    B = InputBox("Enter another number")
    Swap A, B
    MsgBox A
    MsgBox B
End Sub
```

EXERCISE 6.15 Given the following code, predict what values will be displayed, and in what order, when the user clicks on cmdParmQuiz.

```
Private Sub cmdParmQuiz_Click()
    Dim A As String
    Dim B As String
    Dim C As String
    Dim D As String
    A = "maga"
    B = "zine"
    C = "busi"
    D = "ness"
    Rearrange C, D
    MsgBox A
    MsgBox B
    MsgBox C
    MsgBox D
End Sub

Private Sub Rearrange(A As String, B As String)
    Dim C As String
    Dim D As String
    C = Mid$(A, 2, 2)
    D = Mid$(B, 2, 2)
    A = Left$(A, 1) & Right$(A, 1) & Left$(B, 1) & Right$(B, 1)
    B = C & D
End Sub
```

EXERCISE 6.16 Suppose we modify Exercise 6.15 by changing the statement

Rearrange C, D

in procedure cmdParmQuiz_Click to

Rearrange A, B

What values will the message boxes display? Can you figure this out without having to work through the code by hand?

Passing by Reference and Passing by Value

We know that the called procedure can change the value stored in variables passed to it. We have also seen that sometimes the called procedure need not change the value passed to it. In Figure 6.24, the argument Shift was unchanged after the called procedure executed.

VB provides the *ByVal keyword* to specify explicitly in the parameter list that the called procedure cannot change the value stored in a variable passed to it. To do this, simply place the keyword ByVal before the parameter name.

Consider the following revised heading for procedure Rotate. A programmer reading this procedure need only look at its parameter list to determine that it may modify the value stored in the first argument but *cannot* modify the value stored in the second argument.

Private Sub Rotate(Letter **As String**, ByVal ShiftAmount **As Integer**)

When you create a procedure's parameter list, it is important that you specify ByVal for those parameters that you know the procedure will not modify. This makes it much easier for you and other programmers to understand your procedure quickly and with confidence.

When a parameter is *not* preceded by ByVal, we say that the parameter is *passed by reference*. **This means that the argument in the calling procedure and the corresponding parameter in the parameter list are the same**; that is, they refer to the same storage location in memory.

When a parameter *is* preceded by ByVal, we say that the parameter is *passed by value*. **In this case, the argument in the call and the corresponding parameter in the parameter list are *different* variables.** In the called procedure, the ByVal parameter is a local copy of the variable that was passed by the calling procedure. That is, the ByVal parameter in the parameter list is

1. Created when the called procedure begins executing, and placed in the called procedure's local variable table.
2. Initialized to the value of the corresponding argument in the call.

Subsequently, this variable is just like any other local variable in the called procedure. It has no connection with any other variables in the project, and it goes away like other local variables when the procedure's End Sub is encountered.

If you work through the code shown in Figure 6.33 by hand, you will observe the difference between passing by reference and passing by value.

Suppose that the user has just clicked on cmdPassByValueTest. We begin executing the statements in the Click event procedure. Stopping just short of the procedure call, we place values for variables A, B, and C in the variable table (Figure 6.34).

The next statement to execute is the procedure call. As always, the variables in the call are associated with the variables in the called procedure's parameter list by position. Thus, A is associated with X, B with Y, and C with Z. However, we must also note that X and Z are ByVal parameters, and Y is not.

FIGURE 6.33

Code that demonstrates passing by value

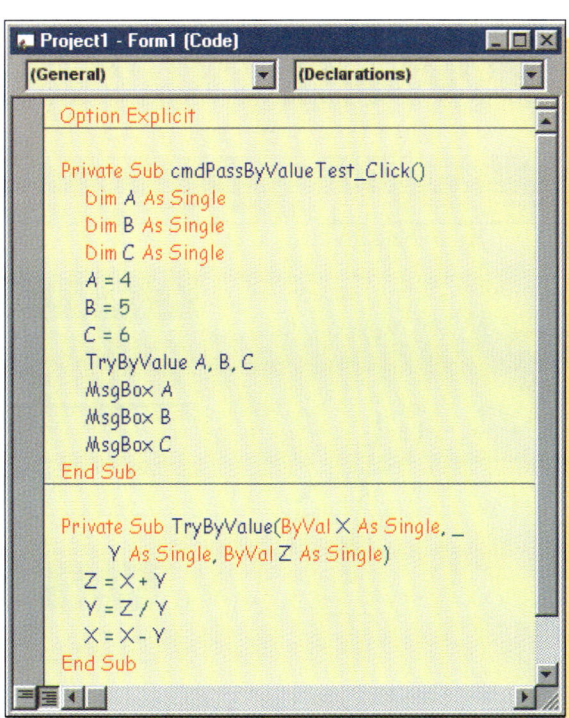

FIGURE 6.34

Hand-check of passing by value example

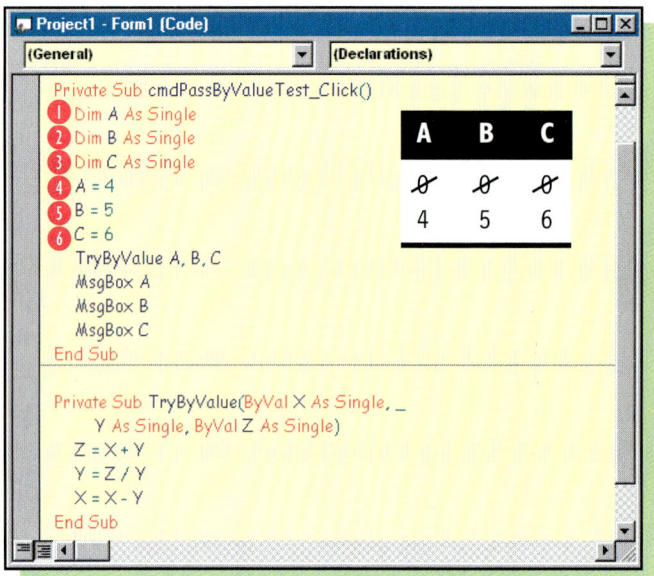

In Figure 6.35, the arrows from A to X and from C to Z are one-way, from calling procedure to called procedure. This is intended to signify that

1. X and Z will be initialized with the values in A and C, respectively. Thus, data are copied from the calling procedure to the called procedure through these variables.

2. X and Z are different variables from A and C, so any subsequent changes to X and Z will not affect the values in A and C. Thus, data *cannot* be transferred from the called procedure back to the calling procedure through these variables.

Since Y is not ByVal, it and B are the same. Thus, data can be transferred in both directions through this variable. Accordingly, this arrow in Figure 6.35 is two-way.

From the variable tables, we see that the variables X, Y, and Z contain the values 4, 5, and 6, respectively, as the called procedure begins to execute. The only thing we need to remember is that if we change the value stored in Y in

FIGURE 6.35

The procedure call

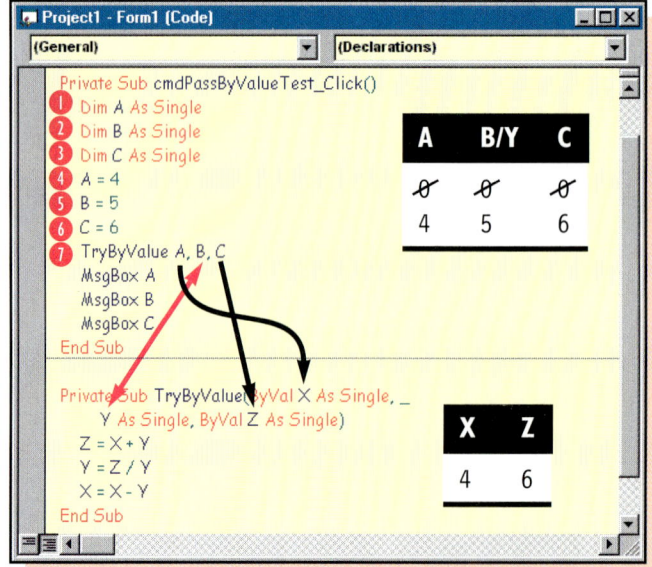

procedure TryByValue, then the same change occurs to B in procedure cmdPassByValueTest_Click, since these are the same memory locations. Variables X and Z, however, no longer have any connection to any other variables anywhere in the project.

In accordance with the three assignment statements (Figure 6.36), we change Z to 9, then Y to 1.8, then X to 2.2.

When the End Sub is encountered, flow of execution returns to the calling procedure, and the variable table for procedure TryByValue (which contains the ByVal parameters) is destroyed. Figure 6.37 shows the code and variable table after execution returns to the calling procedure. The remaining statements in cmdPassByValueTest_Click are straightforward.

If we compare Figures 6.34 and 6.37, we see that the net effect of executing the statement TryByValue A, B, C was to change B to the sum of the original A and B values divided by the original B value. Since the parameter list's first and third parameters were ByVal, the values of A and C were unchanged.

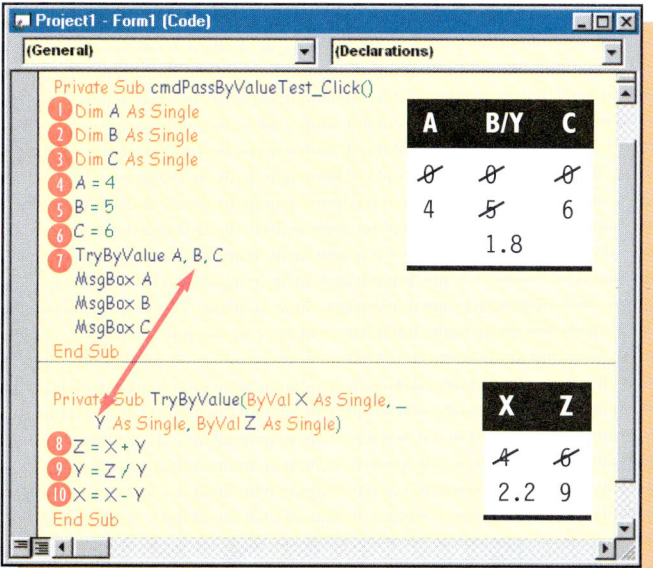

FIGURE 6.36

Execution of called procedure

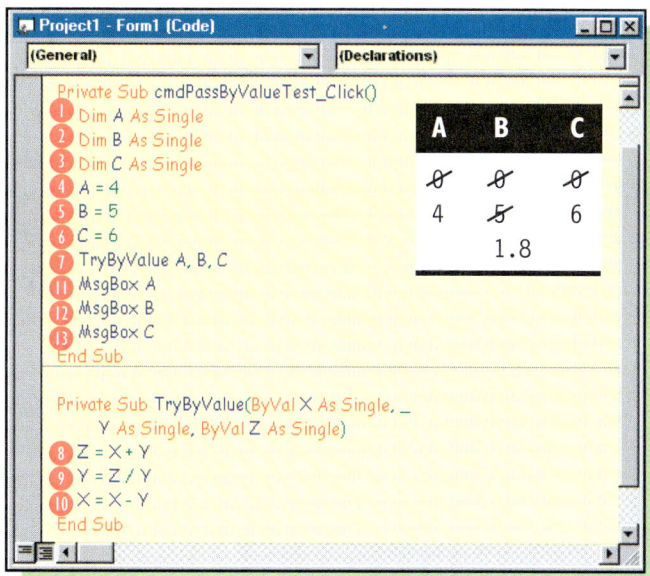

FIGURE 6.37

Code after flow of execution returns to calling procedure

EXERCISE 6.17 Suppose we modify the code in Figure 6.33 by changing the statement

   TryByValue A, B, C

in procedure cmdPassByValueTest_Click to

   TryByValue B, A, C

What values will the message boxes display? Can you figure this out without having to work through the code by hand?

Passing Expressions

The calling procedure can pass an expression instead of a variable to the called procedure. That is, the argument can be an expression. The following modified version of procedure Rotate illustrates passing expressions. Instead of passing a variable that holds the shift amount, procedure cmdFixedShift_Click passes the symbolic constant SHIFT as the argument.

```
Private Sub cmdFixedShift_Click()
   Const SHIFT = 3
   Dim Character As String
   Character = UCase$(InputBox("Enter next letter of plaintext."))
   lblPlaintext.Caption = lblPlaintext.Caption & Character
   Rotate Character, SHIFT
   lblCiphertext.Caption = lblCiphertext.Caption & Character
End Sub

Private Sub Rotate(Letter As String, ByVal ShiftAmount As Integer)
   Dim PositionInAlphabet As Integer
   Dim RotatedPosition As Integer
   PositionInAlphabet = Asc(Letter) - 65
   RotatedPosition = (PositionInAlphabet + ShiftAmount) Mod 26
   Letter = Chr$(65 + RotatedPosition)
End Sub
```

Since ShiftAmount is specified as ByVal in Rotate's parameter list, the operation of the modified code is virtually identical to the operation of the original version of Rotate. The variable ShiftAmount is created when Rotate begins executing, is initialized to 3, then behaves like an ordinary local variable in procedure Rotate.
   If we change the call to

   Rotate Character, 3

the procedure again works identically. If it were necessary to the task at hand, we could also pass a more complicated expression, such as

   Rotate Character, SHIFT * 4 Mod 9

Correcting Common Mistakes in Parameter Passing

Beginning programmers often make mistakes when using parameter passing.[1] In this section, we describe the most common errors and how to correct them.

---

[1] VB's Auto Quick Info feature can help you type procedure calls correctly. To turn on Auto Quick Info, use the Editor tab on VB's Options dialog (under the Tools menu). Create a general sub procedure before typing any statements that call it. Then, as you type a procedure call, VB will display a Quick Info box showing the called procedure's parameter list.

We organize the discussion by the error messages VB will display if you make these errors.

Argument Not Optional

When the number of arguments provided by a procedure call does not match the number of parameters in the called procedure's parameter list, an *argument not optional error* occurs. The code in Figure 6.38 illustrates this error. The procedure call has only one argument, but Rotate's parameter list specifies two parameters. If you try to execute the program, the computer stops and displays the error message shown.

When you see this error message, count the number of parameters in the called procedure's parameter list, then count the number of arguments in the call and determine which must be corrected.

Argument Type Mismatch

When the types of the arguments in the procedure call do not match the types specified in the called procedure's parameter list, an *argument type mismatch error* occurs. The code in Figure 6.39 illustrates this error. Rotate's parameter list specifies two parameters. The procedure call in cmdNextLetter_Click,

   Rotate Character, Shift

provides the correct number of arguments. This is not the source of the error.

Rotate's parameter list specifies that the first parameter should be type String and the second should be type Integer. Checking the Dim statements in cmdNextLetter_Click, we find that Character is type String—correct—and Shift is type Currency—incorrect. In this case, when the computer tries to execute the procedure call it stops and displays the error message shown in the figure.[2]

FIGURE 6.38

Argument not optional error

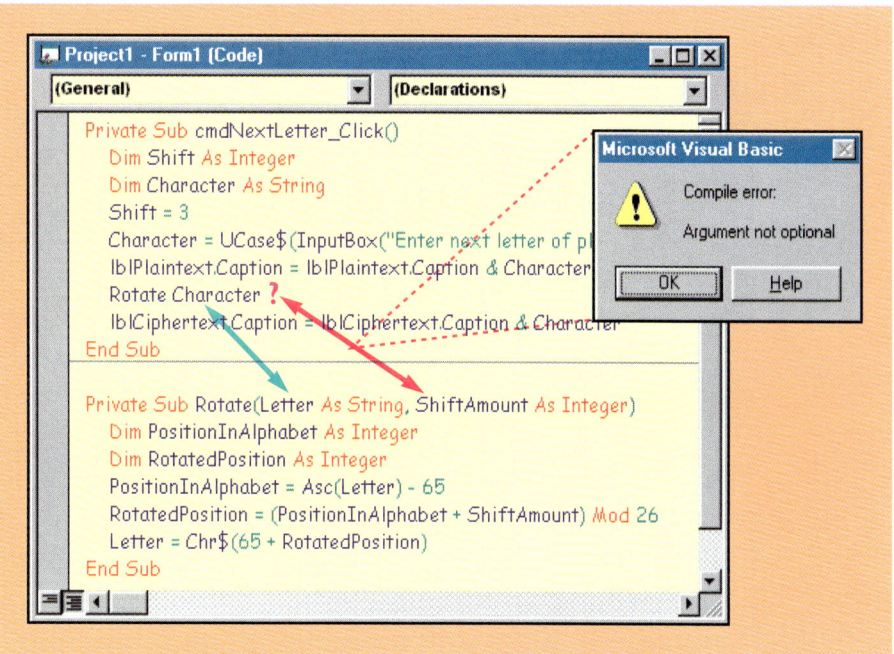

[2] If you change the parameter list in this example by making ShiftAmount ByVal, VB will not report an error. For ByVal parameters VB automatically performs a type conversion when the call is executed.

When you see this error message, compare—one by one and from left to right—the types specified in the parameter list with the types of the arguments provided by the call. If the arguments are variables, you must find their Dim statements to determine their types. To help you identify the problem, you can sketch lines on a printout of the source code that go from the parameter list, through the call, to the Dim statements.

When you receive a type mismatch error message, you must eliminate the mismatch. Change the type of either the argument in the call or the parameter in the parameter list, whichever is appropriate. Also check to see that the arguments are not out of order.

Arguments Out of Order

The arguments in a call are associated with the parameters in the parameter list by position, not by name. The programmer who wrote the code in Figure 6.40 made a mistake in writing the procedure call. VB displays the "argument type mismatch" error message.

To fix the type mismatch problem, you might first try to change the Dim statements in the calling procedure, making Shift type String and Character type Integer. This would eliminate the type mismatch, but would cause worse problems because the variables would have the incorrect data types. The real problem lies in the fact that the arguments in the procedure call are in the wrong order.

Another problem can result if a programmer orders the arguments in a call incorrectly and the arguments are the same data type. In this case, the program executes incorrectly and there is no error message to warn of the problem. This situation is illustrated by the code in Figure 6.41. Here an investor who purchased a stock predicted that its price in one year would be $3.33. After the year elapsed, the stock price was actually $2.22. The procedure is supposed to compute and display the percentage error in the predicted price. Does it?

FIGURE 6.39

Argument type mismatch error

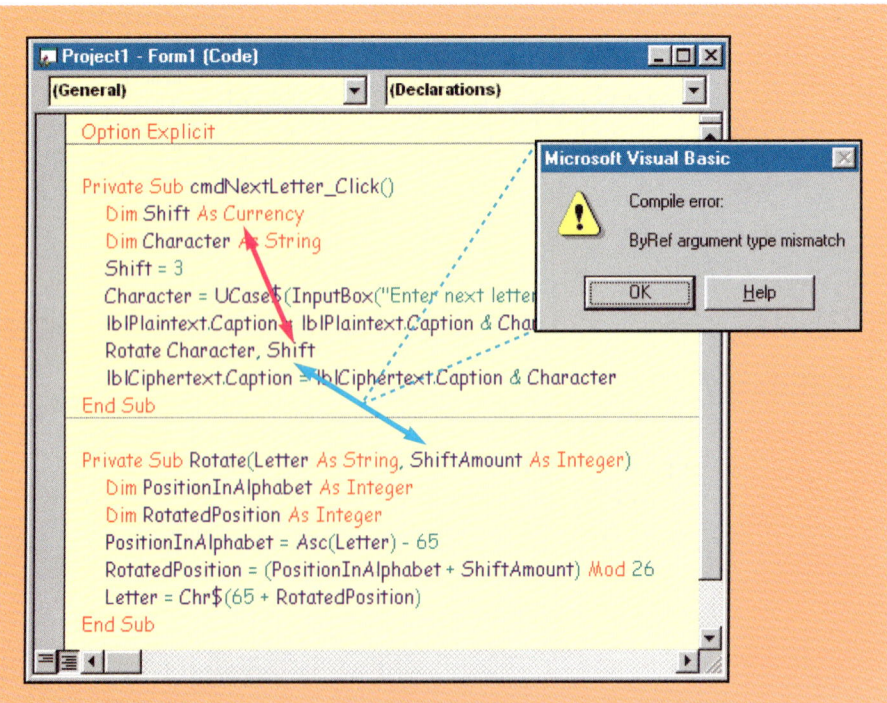

FIGURE 6.40

Code with error in procedure call in cmdNextLetter_Click

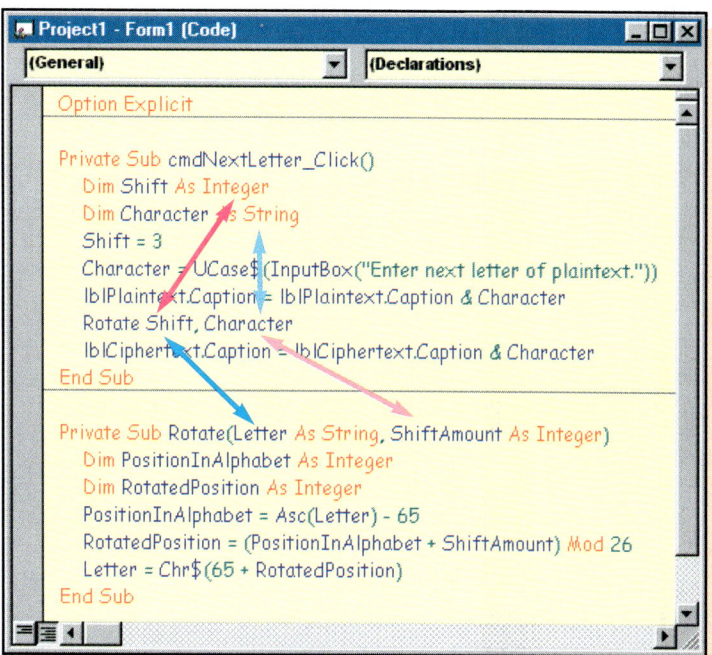

FIGURE 6.41

Arguments in wrong order but of same type

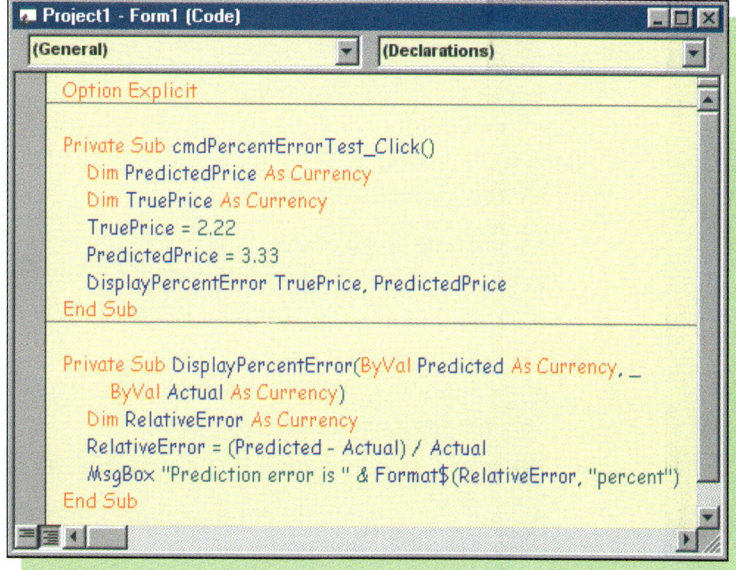

It is easy to make an error in this simple calculation, even using a hand calculator. The correct answer is that the prediction was 50 percent high, because the predicted price is equal to 1.5 times the true price. The code here runs and does not give an error message, but the result it displays is "Prediction error is −33%".

To keep errors like this from going undetected, it is important to thoroughly test the code by entering values with known answers and verifying that the code produces the correct answers. The fact that a program produces no error messages does not necessarily mean it works correctly.

Conflict between Parameter Name and Local Variable Name

VB does not allow you to declare a local variable in the called procedure that has the same name as a parameter in the procedure's parameter list. Suppose,

FIGURE 6.42

Local variable conflicting with parameter

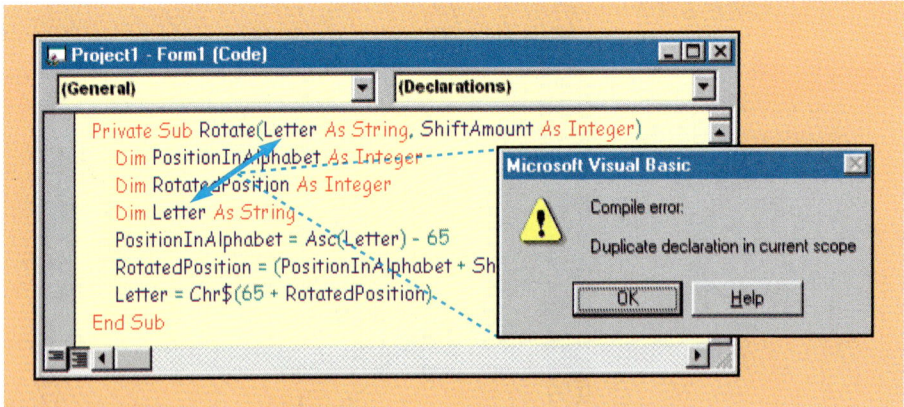

for example, that in procedure Rotate we try to add a Dim statement that declares a local variable named Letter, as shown in Figure 6.42.

When we try to run the program after adding this Dim statement, VB displays the error message shown in the figure. In effect, this Dim statement would cause Rotate to have two variables with the same name, which VB will not allow. To proceed, we must either delete the Dim statement altogether, change the name of the local variable, or change the name of the parameter.

General Sub Procedures versus Event Procedures

♦ ♦ ♦

Although general sub procedures and event procedures have many similarities, there are two important differences. First, an event procedure is always associated with a control. We have discussed this fact already, but now is a good time to review its implications.

- ♦ The naming conventions differ. Event procedure names begin with the name of the associated control, followed by an underscore character, and ending with the type of event. General sub procedure names do not have this form.
- ♦ The way we get at them through the Code window is different. General sub procedures are grouped together under the General object and event procedures are listed as separate objects.
- ♦ Event procedures cannot be located in code modules.

Second, for a general sub procedure the programmer creates the procedure heading, including the parameter list; whereas for an event procedure, VB creates the procedure heading. The programmer is allowed to modify the parameter list for a general sub procedure. However, VB *does not allow* the programmer to modify the parameter list for an event procedure.

We will see event procedures that use parameters. For these event procedures VB creates the procedure heading, complete with the parameter list. As programmer, you may be tempted to modify the parameter list in order to add or delete a parameter, or change the name of a parameter, but VB does not allow this.

EXERCISE 6.18

Modify your solution to Exercise 6.6 as follows: First, make both variables WageRate and MonthsOfService local to event procedure cmdLookUpWageRate_Click instead of module-level. Then modify the heading for general sub procedure ComputeWageRate by adding parameters for the wage rate and months of service (be sure to specify ByVal where appropriate). Finally, modify the procedure call by adding WageRate and MonthsOfService as arguments. Run the project to verify that it works properly.

EXERCISE 6.19 Modify your solution to Exercise 6.7 as follows: First, make both variables MonthAbbr and DaysInMonth local to event procedure cmdMonthDays_Click instead of module-level. Then modify the heading for general sub procedure FindNumDaysInMonth by adding parameters for the month abbreviation and the number of days in the month (be sure to specify ByVal where appropriate). Finally, modify the procedure call by adding MonthAbbr and DaysInMonth as arguments. Run the project to verify that it works properly.

6.3 Programmer-Defined Functions

In Chapter 4 we discussed VB's built-in functions. These functions, such as Sqr() and Chr$(), perform some manipulation on an argument and return a result. Recall that these built-in functions are always used in expressions. For example, we saw the statement

lblHypotenuse.Caption = Sqr(ASquared + BSquared)

In VB, the **programmer can create custom functions—called** *programmer-defined functions*—**to perform calculations or string manipulations**. In this section we show how to write and use programmer-defined functions.

Almost everything we know about general sub procedures also applies to functions. Specifically,

- Functions are not associated with any control, so they appear in the Code window under the General object just like general sub procedures.
- Functions have parameter lists just like general sub procedures.
- A variable declared inside the function is local to the function.

The main difference between a general sub procedure and a programmer-defined function is that, like VB's built-in functions, the programmer-defined function returns a value.

Let's look at an example of a programmer-defined function. The code in Figure 6.43 shows a function named Rotate() that performs the same processing task as the general sub procedure named Rotate used in previous examples.

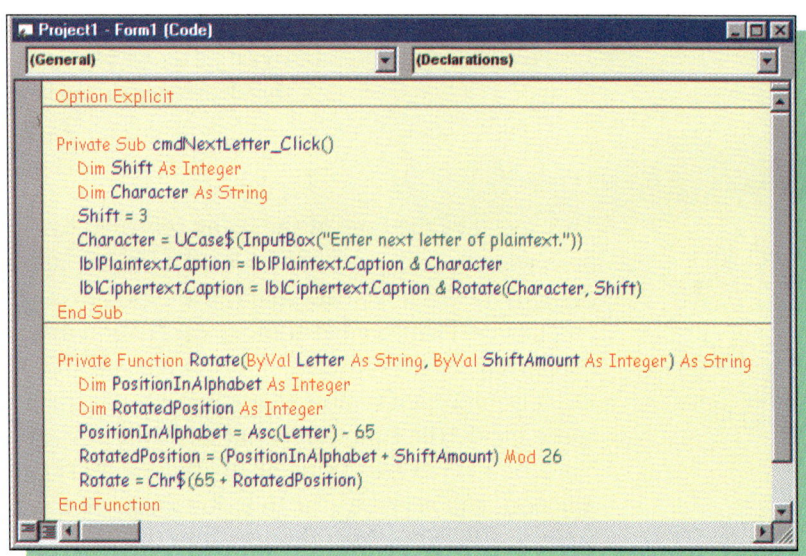

FIGURE 6.43

Programmer-defined function

Notice how event procedure cmdNextLetter_Click invokes the function: the name of the function appears on the right-hand side of an assignment statement (i.e., in the expression), just like one of VB's built-in functions:

lblCiphertext.Caption = lblCiphertext.Caption & Rotate(Character, Shift)

When the computer executes this assignment statement, it first goes to the right-hand side (as always) to evaluate the expression. It needs to obtain two values and then concatenate them. It retrieves the value in the Caption property of lblCiphertext, which is easy. Then it encounters the name of the function, Rotate().

When the computer encounters the name of a function in an expression, it transfers execution from the current procedure to the named function (passing it any specified arguments). We describe this operation as *invoking* the function.

When the function is finished executing, it returns its result, and the flow of execution returns to the calling procedure where it left off. In this example, when function Rotate() is finished executing, execution resumes in the assignment statement in cmdNextLetter_Click. The letter returned by function Rotate() is concatenated to the value retrieved from lblCiphertext.Caption, and the result of the concatenation is stored in lblCiphertext.Caption.

You may wonder how the function returns its result to the calling procedure. Let us look at the function in Figure 6.43 and answer that question.

Unlike a procedure, in a programmer-defined function there *must* be a statement that assigns a value to the *name* of the function. In function Rotate(), this statement is

Rotate = Chr$(65 + RotatedPosition)

Think of the function name as a "store-only local variable" inside the function. When executed, the assignment statement shown here stores a value in Rotate. The value that the function name contains when End Function is encountered is the value the function takes on when execution returns to the calling procedure.

Programmer-defined functions differ from general sub procedures in several ways. An obvious difference is that programmer-defined functions begin with the keyword Function and end with the keyword End Function.

Another difference is in the function heading: a type specification follows the parameter list.

Private Function Rotate(**ByVal** Letter **As String,** _
    ByVal ShiftAmount **As Integer**) **As String**

This specifies the type of the return value

This specifies the type of the value returned by the function. Since the job of procedure Rotate() is to take a letter as input and return a "shifted version" of the letter, which is string data, the type of its return value is String. If our function performed an arithmetic calculation instead, we would have specified As Currency, or As Integer, or As Single, etc., as appropriate.

It is important to note that you cannot retrieve the value from the function name inside the function. That is, while it is necessary to see the function name on the left-hand side of an assignment statement somewhere inside the function, you *never* see the function name on the right-hand side of an assignment statement inside the function.

If you put the function name in an expression inside the function, when the computer tries to evaluate the expression it will invoke the function again instead of retrieving a value. That is, the function will invoke itself.

Finally, **the *Exit Function* statement** plays the same role for functions that the Exit Sub statement plays for procedures: **it causes function execution to end, and whatever value is stored in the function name at that time is the value returned by the function.** Exit Function is often used in functions that make decisions. Certain outcomes may dictate that no further processing is necessary to obtain the return value, and the appropriate action is to simply return execution to the calling procedure.

Example 6.3

Using a Programmer-Defined Function

The code in Figure 6.44 contains a simple arithmetic function. The function computes the handling charge for orders processed by a mail-order company. The amount of the charge depends on the amount of the order; thus, the function contains a Select Case statement. The function examines the order amount, determines the appropriate charge, and stores this value in the function name, which becomes the value returned by the function.

Observe in Figure 6.44 that the function name occurs in multiple statements within the function, but always on the left-hand side of assignment statements. Note also that the type of the function's return value is Currency. Because the function does not modify the value stored in the argument passed to it, `OrderAmount` is specified as a ByVal parameter.

Creating Functions

To create a function, first bring up the Code window for the form or code module in which you wish to place the function. Then select Add Procedure… under the Tools menu. VB will present you with the dialog box shown in Figure 6.45. Select type Function, select the scope you wish the function to have,

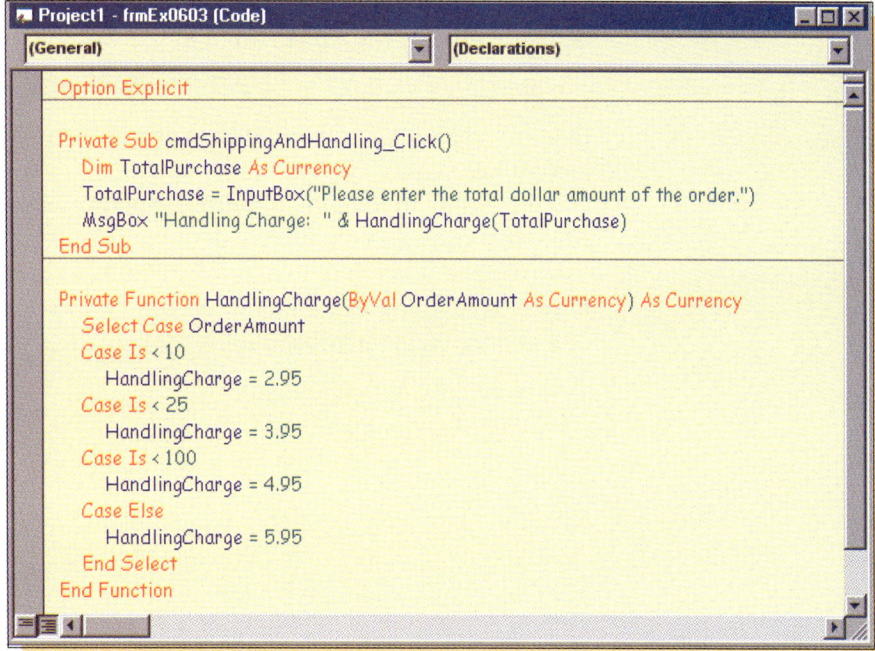

FIGURE 6.44

Code for Example 6.3

FIGURE 6.45

VB's Add Procedure dialog box

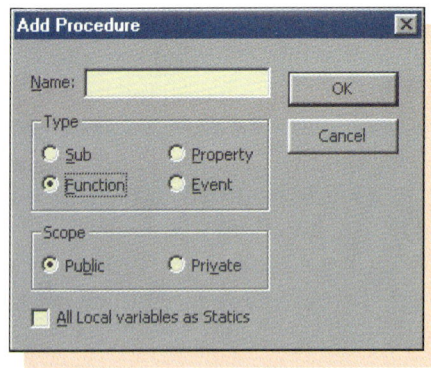

then enter the name you wish to give the function in the Name text box and click OK. VB will return you to the Code window, showing (General) in the Object box, the name you specified in the Procedures/Events box, and a function template in the Code window. To complete the function, modify the template by adding the parameter list, the type of the function's return value, and the function's statements.

Functions versus General Sub Procedures

When is it appropriate to create a general sub procedure, and when a function? A simple rule of thumb is to use a function when the end result of the processing task is a single value, and use a general sub procedure otherwise. If the processing task results in two or more new values, or if it results in changes to the user interface, a general sub procedure is probably more appropriate.

If the result of the processing step is a single value, then we can make this the value returned by the function, and we can make all of the function's parameters ByVal. This is advantageous because functions are very easy to understand when all of their parameters are ByVal. For example, all the parameters are ByVal for all of VB's built-in functions. The statement

```
X = Sqr(Y)
```

does not change the value stored in the variable Y, and the statement

```
ShortText = Mid$(BigText, StartCharPos, EndCharPos)
```

does not change the value stored in any of the variables BigText, StartCharPos, or EndCharPos.

According to this rule of thumb, Rotate() is better implemented as a function than as a general sub procedure. Let us go back to our examples and compare the procedure that invoked "the procedure Rotate" with the procedure that invoked "the function Rotate()" to see which is simpler. Here's the one that invokes the procedure:

```
Private Sub cmdNextLetter_Click()
    Dim Shift As Integer
    Dim Character As String
    Shift = 3
    Character = UCase$(InputBox("Enter next letter of plaintext."))
    lblPlaintext.Caption = lblPlaintext.Caption & Character
    Rotate Character, Shift
    lblCiphertext.Caption = lblCiphertext.Caption & Character
End Sub
```

And here's the one that invokes the function:

```
Private Sub cmdNextLetter_Click()
    Dim ShiftAmount As Integer
    Dim Character As String
    Shift = 3
    Character = UCase$(InputBox("Enter next letter of plaintext."))
    lblPlaintext.Caption = lblPlaintext.Caption & Character
    lblCiphertext.Caption = lblCiphertext.Caption & Rotate(Character, Shift)
End Sub
```

The example that invokes the procedure is one statement longer. The call statement

```
Rotate Character, Shift
```

causes the value stored in variable Character to be changed to the value we need. However, to discover this fact we had to look at the parameter list for procedure Rotate. In contrast, the statement that invokes the function

```
lblCiphertext.Caption = lblCiphertext.Caption & Rotate(Character, Shift)
```

is clear in the sense that we don't have to look at the function heading to understand that the value we need is returned by the function. That is what functions do: they return the needed value.

6.4 Code Modules

So far we have seen code modules used to declare module-level and global variables and to store general sub procedures. They can also store programmer-defined functions. We now examine two additional uses of code modules.

Sub Main

Recall that VB allows you to specify a startup form, which is the form that VB automatically displays when program execution begins. As an alternative, you can use **Sub Main to specify that VB begin execution of the program by executing a general sub procedure.** To use Sub Main, choose Project Properties… under the Project menu, and in the Project Properties window that VB displays, select the General tab. Then, in the Startup Object box, select Sub Main, as shown in Figure 6.46.

After specifying Sub Main as the startup form, you must create a public general sub procedure named Main *in a code module*. It can be in any code module, but you must not have more than one procedure named Main, even if they are in different code modules. Then, when program execution begins, VB will not load any form but instead will find the procedure named Main and begin executing it.

What might you use procedure Main for? You could use it to initialize global variables or properties of controls on different forms before showing one of the forms using the Show method. If the project has multiple forms, you might want the program to decide which form to display first. That is, you can have decision-making statements in procedure Main that determine the order in which to present the various forms to the user. This provides more flexibility than specifying a startup form at design time.

FIGURE 6.46

Specifying Sub Main in VB's Project Properties window

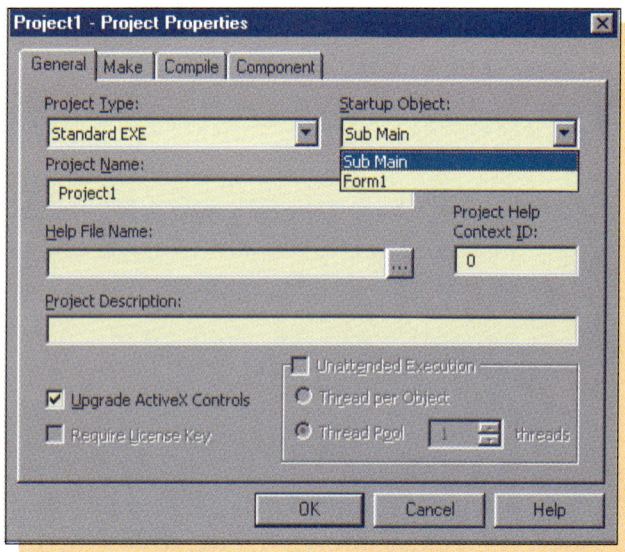

Libraries

◆ ◆ ◆

General sub procedures and programmer-defined functions make it possible to create *reusable code*. One programmer writes a procedure or function to perform a given task, and subsequently other programmers can use this procedure or function whenever they require the task it performs. In practice, programmers have found that such reusable code is essential for successfully building maintainable, large systems.

Programmers try to organize reusable code for easy access. To do this, they identify categories of processing tasks, create one code module for each category, and arrange the reusable procedures and functions in the code modules appropriately. Processing tasks might be broken into categories such as financial calculations, database processing, graphic image processing, user interface operations, statistical calculations, etc. **A collection of code modules organized this way, according to categories, is called a** *library*.

The code module for financial calculations, for example, contains all the previously written general sub procedures and functions having to do with financial calculations. If a programmer has to create a new application that involves financial operations, then he or she should become familiar with the content of this code module to take advantage of code that has already been written.

Using libraries tends to reduce the amount of detail a programmer needs to keep track of. The procedures and functions in the library act as meta statements that the programmer can use directly instead of having to craft all of the individual statements that perform the larger task.

6.5 The KeyPress Event

We now turn our attention to VB controls and some additional events. Unlike previous event procedures we have seen, for some events VB uses parameters to pass data values to the event procedure. Having studied parameters, we can now fully understand these event procedures.

In this section we examine the *KeyPress event,* **which enables your programs to respond to keystrokes made by the user.** This capability might be useful, for example, in determining whether the user is entering valid characters.

Any control that can have the focus is capable of responding to the KeyPress event, which occurs when the control has the focus and the user presses an ANSI key. (Non-ANSI keys, such as SHIFT, CTRL, ALT, and the arrow keys, will not cause the KeyPress event.) Typically, you will write decision-making statements in the KeyPress event procedure to determine which key the user pressed and to perform appropriate processing steps.

The empty template for a KeyPress event procedure for a Text box control named txtSSN follows. Recall that VB creates the entire procedure heading for event procedures, including the parameter list.

Private Sub txtSSN_KeyPress(KeyAscii **As Integer**)

End Sub

Every KeyPress event procedure specifies a parameter named KeyAscii of type Integer. At run time, when the KeyPress event occurs, VB first stores the ANSI code of the key the user pressed in the parameter KeyAscii, and then begins executing the statements inside the KeyPress event procedure.

The KeyPress Event for Text Box Controls

Programmers frequently write KeyPress event procedures for Text box controls. As mentioned previously, one use of KeyPress is to validate user input. For example, if the user is supposed to enter a numeric value in the text box, we can use the KeyPress event to prevent the user from entering letters.

Ordinarily, when a Text box control has the focus and the user presses a key, the character is immediately appended to the text box's Text property. However, when the text box has a KeyPress event procedure, the sequence of events includes execution of the event procedure, as follows:

1. The user presses a key.
2. VB stores the ANSI code of the key in the KeyAscii parameter.
3. VB begins executing the KeyPress event procedure.
4. When the End Sub statement is encountered, VB retrieves the value from KeyAscii, converts it from an ANSI code into a character, and appends the character to the text box's Text property.

Using KeyPress you can include statements in the event procedure that will modify the value stored in KeyAscii, which will in turn modify the value that VB appends to the Text property of the text box. Thus, the character that appears in the text box need not be the same as the key the user pressed.

Finally, setting KeyAscii to zero in the KeyPress event procedure will cause the Text property to remain unchanged. That is, this nullifies (cancels) the user's keystroke.

The code in Figure 6.47 shows a KeyPress event procedure for a text box that allows the user to enter a Social Security number (SSN). An SSN consists of nine digits (ignoring the dashes). From the ANSI table we see that if KeyAscii is between 48 and 57, inclusive, then the user pressed one of the digit keys (0 through 9); otherwise the key was not a digit. Since a Social Security number consists of digits only, the user should not be allowed to enter other characters, such as letters, punctuation, etc. Setting KeyAscii to 0 in those cases nullifies the user's keystroke. The Beep alerts the user that he or she pressed an invalid key.

FIGURE 6.47

Using KeyPress to restrict SSN input to digits only

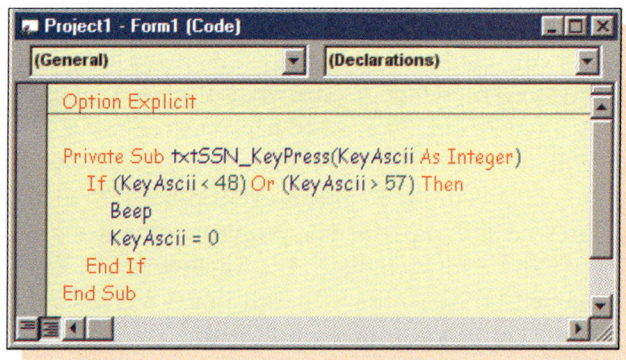

While the action of the KeyPress event is straightforward, KeyPress event procedures that use literal numeric constants for ANSI codes are not so easy to read. For example, the statement KeyAscii = 0 really means "nullify the keystroke." To improve the readability of such statements, VB provides predefined symbolic constants for the numeric codes of many symbols in the ANSI table. Table 6.1 lists some of these; see online help (search phrase "keycode constants") for others.

Using the information in Table 6.1 we can write the If statement in Figure 6.47

> **If** (KeyAscii < 48) **Or** (KeyAscii > 57) **Then**
>   Beep
>   KeyAscii = 0
> **End If**

more clearly as

> **If** (KeyAscii < vbKey0) **Or** (KeyAscii > vbKey9) **Then**
>   Beep
>   KeyAscii = vbEmpty
> **End If**

TABLE 6.1 ANSI Code Symbolic Constants

Character	ANSI Code	Symbolic Constant
null	0	vbEmpty
backspace	8	vbKeyBack
cr	13	vbKeyReturn
0	48	vbKey0
1	49	vbKey1
2	50	vkKey2
...	...	...
9	57	kbKey9
A	65	vbKeyA
B	66	vbKeyB
C	67	vbKeyC
...	...	...
Z	90	vbKeyZ

Note that VB does not provide symbolic constants that correspond to the lowercase letters. Programmers often use the fact that the ANSI code for each lowercase letter is 32 greater than the ANSI code for its uppercase equivalent. Thus, for example, the ANSI code for lowercase "a" can be written as *vbKeyA + 32*.

Example 6.4

Allowing Backspaces

The procedure in Figure 6.47 has a significant flaw: the [BACKSPACE] key is nullified, preventing the user from correcting typographical errors in the text box. The code in Figure 6.48 corrects the problem. In the Select Case statement, a separate case is defined for the backspace key. The statement block for this case contains only a comment, so this Case does nothing; that is, it just lets the character that was typed pass on to the text box (as does the case for valid digits).

The SetFocus Method

Many applications allow the user to move the focus from one text box to another using either the [ENTER] key or the [TAB] key. VB provides the TabStop and TabIndex properties so that you can easily enable the user to switch between controls using the [TAB] key, but you have to do a little coding to enable the user to switch between controls using the [ENTER] key.

You can write code that causes the focus to move to a specific control using the *SetFocus method*. Recall that a *method* specifies an action to be performed on a control, and that the syntax is *control.method*. Thus, for example, the statement

   txtName.SetFocus

causes the focus to move to the control named txtName.

The code in Figure 6.49 illustrates how the SetFocus method can be used in a KeyPress event procedure to allow the user to press [ENTER] to move the focus between controls. The ANSI code for the [ENTER] key is 13, which is the carriage return (*cr*) symbol in the ANSI table (see Table 6.1). Observe that the code in Figure 6.49 allows the user to enter digits, but not letters, in txtSSN, and letters, but not digits, in txtName.

FIGURE 6.48

Code that lets user enter backspaces to correct typing errors

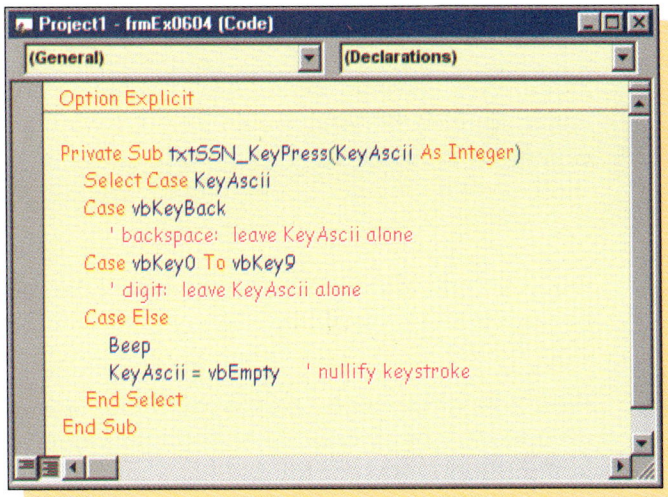

FIGURE 6.49

KeyPress event procedures that make pressing ENTER move the focus between two text boxes

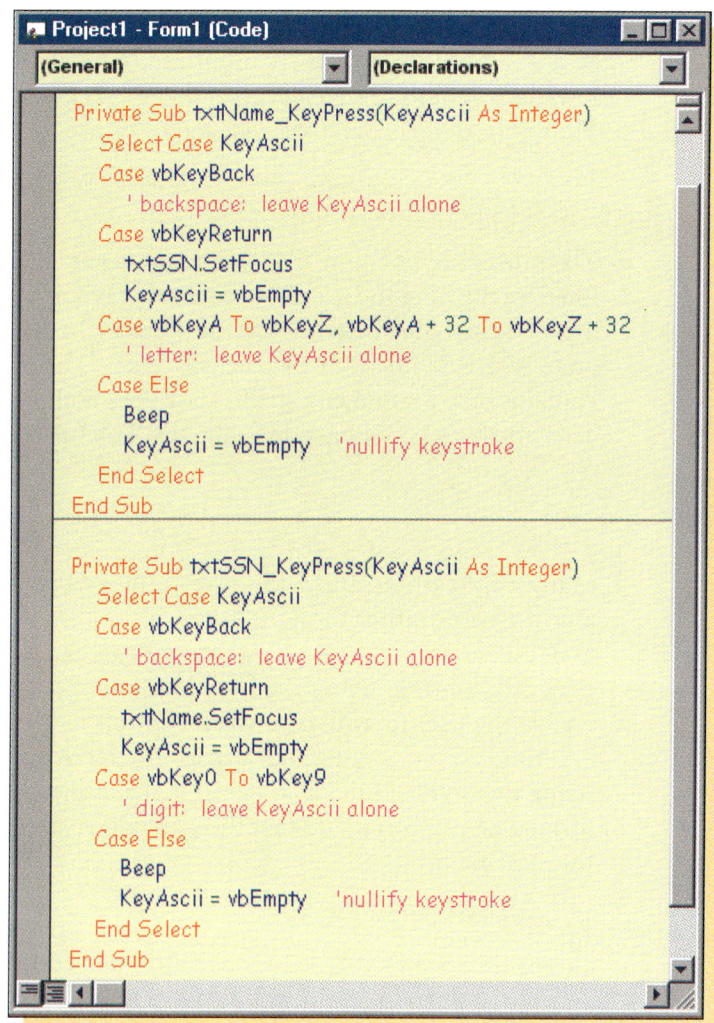

One subtlety for which we did not give a comment in this code is the statement KeyAscii = vbEmpty in Case vbKeyReturn. If you remove this statement you will find that VB beeps at you when you press ENTER; this is because VB ordinarily does not allow the user to press ENTER when a text box has the focus. By setting KeyAscii to 0 in this case, we prevent VB from "objecting" when the user presses ENTER, because the text box never "sees" the character.

EXERCISE 6.20 Suppose you entered your full name, including middle initial, in the Name text box in Figure 6.49. What would happen? What are some of the general shortcomings of txtName_KeyPress? Modify txtName_KeyPress to eliminate these shortcomings.

EXERCISE 6.21 Can you think of a way, without modifying the code in Figure 6.49, to prevent the user from entering more than nine digits in txtSSN?

EXERCISE 6.22 Write a KeyPress event procedure for a text box that automatically performs the operation of procedure Rotate on the characters that the user types. That is, if the user types "A", the text box should display "D", and if the user types "B", the text box should display "E", and so on.

6.6 The GotFocus and LostFocus Events

Any control that can have the focus is capable of responding to the GotFocus and LostFocus events. **The *GotFocus event* occurs for a control when the control receives the focus.** The *LostFocus event* occurs for a control when the control loses the focus (because the focus is moved to another control). Both events can be caused by user actions (clicking the mouse on a control, pressing TAB, or pressing an access key) or by execution of a statement containing the SetFocus method.

The programmer can use the GotFocus and LostFocus events to make an application behave more intuitively for the user. For example, the user might enter a customer number in a text box and then click or tab to another text box. This action causes the LostFocus event to occur for the Customer Number text box. As a result, the programmer can write a LostFocus event procedure that uses the customer number to look up the customer's name and address and then fills this information into text boxes on the form. From the user's perspective, the user enters a customer number, then moves to another text box, and the application automatically fills in the customer's name and address.

The code in Figure 6.50 illustrates a technique for conveying information about program execution to the user. The form contains two text boxes (one for a Name and another for an SSN), a label, and a command button. When the user clicks on the Name text box (txtName), event procedure txtName_GotFocus is executed. This causes the phrase "Please enter your full name (Last, First, Middle Initial)." to be displayed in the label (lblExplanation). If the user clicks on the SSN text box (txtSSN), then the explanation changes to "Please enter your Social Security Number." This technique informs the user of what type of entry is expected in the currently active text box.

FIGURE 6.50

Code that tells user what to enter

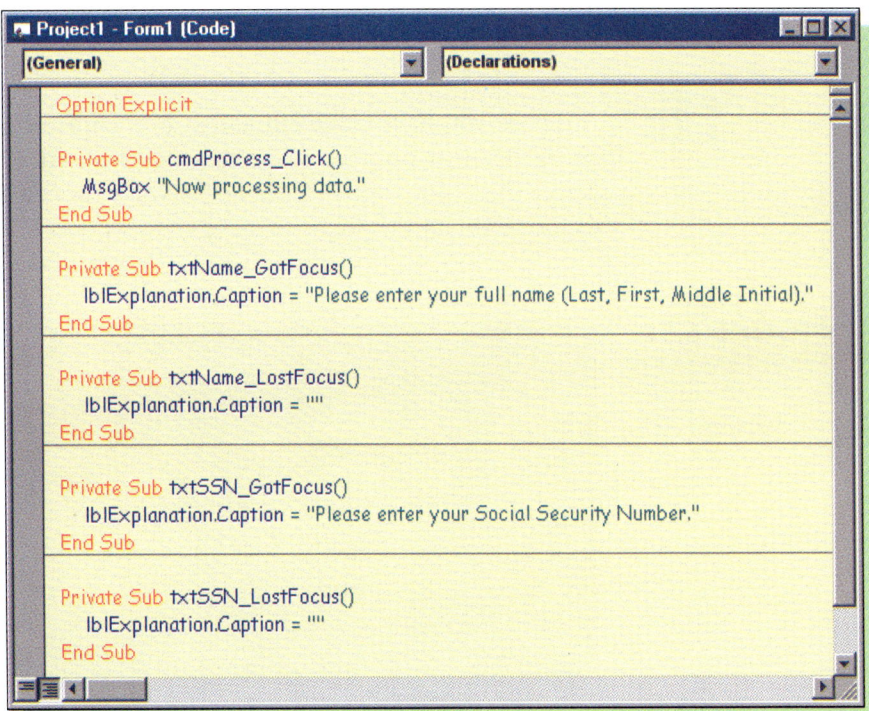

Each time a text box loses the focus, the explanation label is cleared. This ensures that a message will not linger after the user moves on to another control (perhaps the command button).

Access Keys and Text Boxes

Recall that at run time an underlined character in a caption is VB's cue that an access key exists, and the user can press ALT in conjunction with the underlined character to select the control. Selecting the control moves the focus to it. How can we provide an access key for a Text box when the text box control does not have a Caption property?

To do this, we place a Label control next to the text box, specify an access key for the Label control, and set the value of the TabIndex property of the Label control to be one less than the TabIndex property of the Text box control. When the user employs the label's access key, the label is unable to receive the focus, so VB moves the focus to the control having the next higher TabIndex value.

Example 6.5

Access Keys and Focus

Figure 6.51 shows the form for Example 6.5. This form has three text boxes (txtName, txtAddress, and txtSSN), two option buttons (optGenderMale and optGenderFemale), two command buttons (cmdProcess and cmdMoveFocus), and a label (lblControlWithFocus).

Each Text box, Option button, and Command button control has a GotFocus event procedure that causes its own name to be displayed by lblControlWithFocus. In addition, the Click event procedure for command button cmdMoveFocus uses the SetFocus method to move the focus to an Option button control. Figure 6.52 shows the code that supports these actions. When the user clicks on cmdMoveFocus the event procedure displays a message box and then gives the focus to the option button named optGenderFemale, which causes the optGenderFemale option button to be selected.

EXERCISE 6.23

Suppose you have provided a Text box control to allow the user to enter a Social Security number. Write the code that will ensure that the entry has no fewer than nine digits (since an SSN always consists of exactly nine digits) before allowing the focus to leave the text box.

FIGURE 6.51

Form and controls for Example 6.5

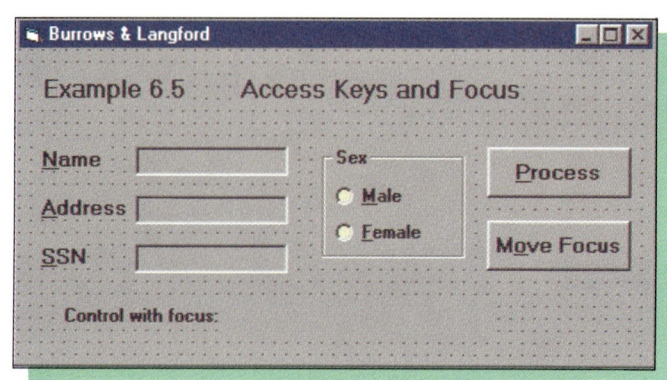

FIGURE 6.52

Code for Example 6.5

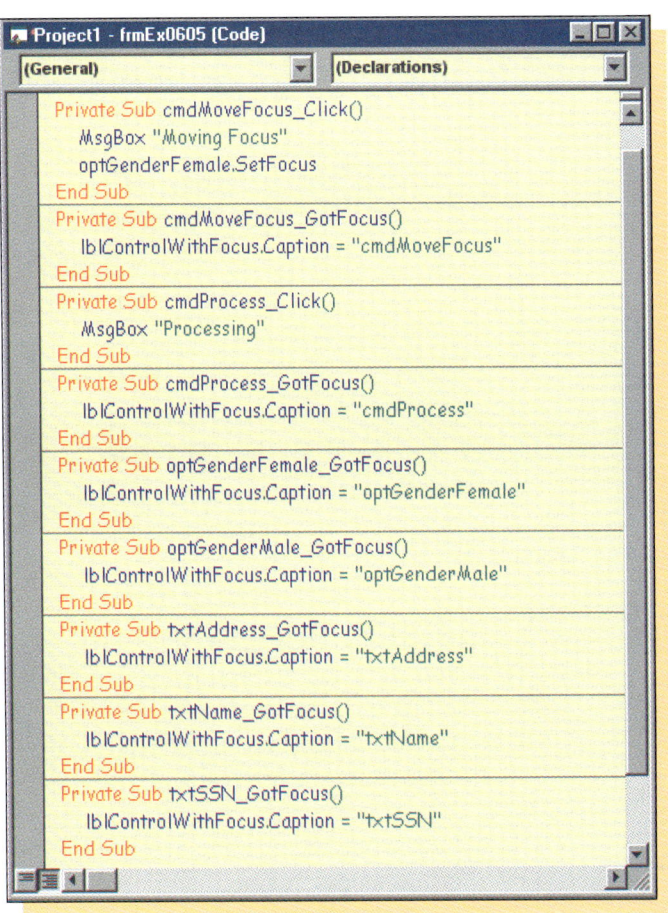

6.7 Modal versus Modeless Forms

As we know, most real-world applications have multiple forms, with each form having a particular objective or theme. In most such applications the programmer must carefully design and control the order in which forms are presented to the user. Otherwise, if the user is allowed to navigate through the forms at random, the application looks confusing, is unnecessarily complicated, and is difficult to use. One approach for controlling how a form is displayed is *form modality*.

When a *modal form* is shown, **controls on other forms do not react to user actions**; the user must respond to the modal form. A modal form must be hidden before the controls on other forms can be used. **When a *modeless form* is displayed, both its controls and the controls on other forms can react.** When you work through Examples 6.6 and 6.7, you will observe the differences.

Example 6.6 Using Modeless Forms

This example has three forms. The startup form contains a Label control named lblStep and a command button named cmdShowForms. The other two forms each contain a command button named cmdDone. Given the code in Figure 6.53, can you predict what will happen when the user clicks on

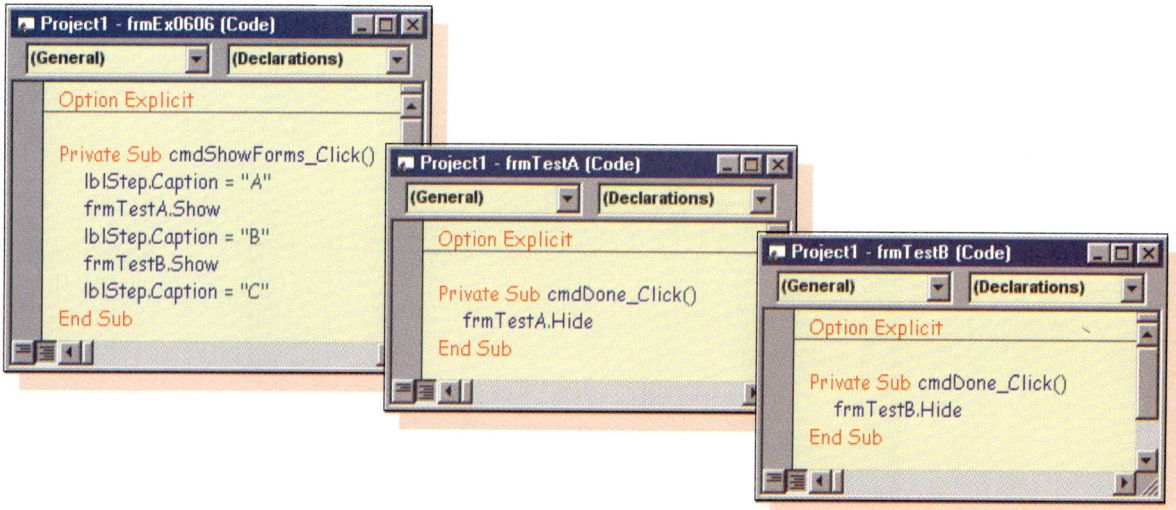

FIGURE 6.53   Code for Example 6.6

cmdShowForms? (Recall that the Show method is used to display a form on the screen, and the Hide method is used to remove a form from the screen.)

After clicking on cmdShowForms, the user will see frmTestB (it will cover up frmTestA), and lblStep on the startup form will display "C". If the user then clicks cmdDone on frmTestB, it will disappear, and the user will see frmTestA.

This behavior may seem a bit surprising. It occurs because the computer executes the statements in cmdShowForms_Click one after another without pause. The most recently "shown" form is on top.

Example 6.7   Using Modal Forms

Example 6.7 also has three forms. The only difference between it and Example 6.6 is in cmdShowForms_Click: the predefined symbolic constant *vbModal* is an argument to the Show method. Figure 6.54 shows this code. Now after clicking on cmdShowForms, the user will see frmTestA, and lblStep on the startup form will display "A".

To execute the statement

frmTestA.Show vbModal

the computer shows frmTestA, then suspends further execution of the event procedure cmdShowForms_Click until frmTestA is hidden (using the Hide method) or unloaded (using the Unload statement). Clicking cmdDone on frmTestA executes the Hide method for the form, and execution of cmdShowForms_Click resumes.

While frmTestA is shown, the computer can execute procedures on frmTestA, but no user input is allowed on any form other than frmTestA until after frmTestA is hidden or unloaded (at which time control returns to cmdShowForms_Click).

The forms frmTestA and frmTestB are said to be *modeless* in Example 6.6 and *modal* in Example 6.7. Note that frmTestA and frmTestB are identical in the two examples; what differs is the Show method and its argument.

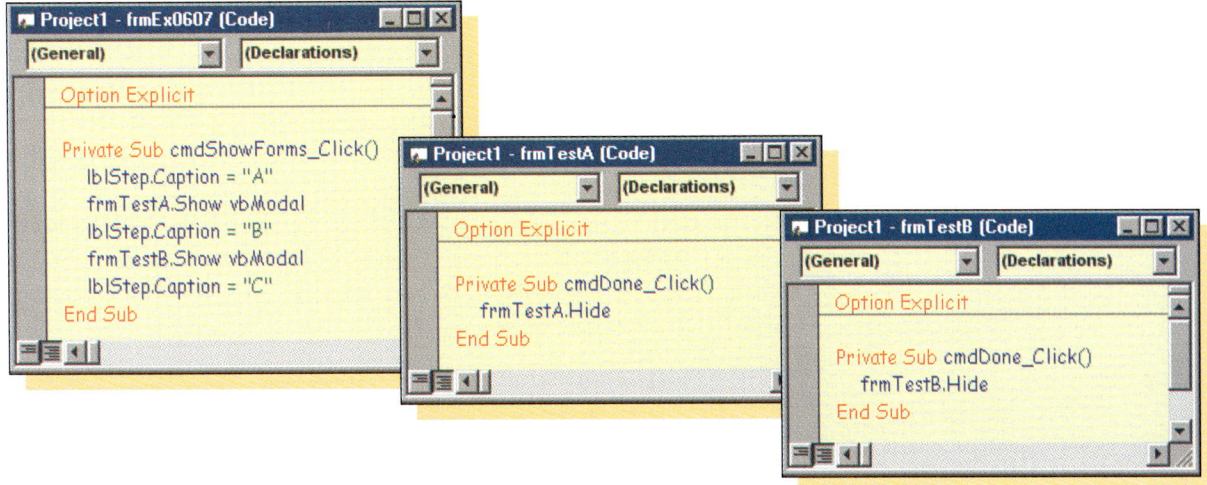

FIGURE 6.54   Code for Example 6.7

Modal Forms

A message box is the simplest example of a modal form. It displays a message and an OK button, and control does not return to the procedure containing the MsgBox statement until the user clicks the OK button (which hides the message box).

The File dialog window is also modal. When the user selects Open from the File menu of any Windows application, the application displays the File Open window. The user is expected to select a file and then click either the Open or the Cancel button. If the user tries to move to a different form without first clicking either Open or Cancel, the application just beeps. This is an important feature, because the user could not be certain whether the file opened if he or she could switch to a different form before completing the file operation.

Presenting a Sequence of Forms

Suppose you want the program to present a sequence of forms to the user. This is common, and it often happens that the appropriate sequence depends on one or more choices the user makes. To do this using modeless forms, the first form has to have the code to show the second form, the second form has to have the code to show the third form, which in turn has to have the code to show the fourth form, and so on. Using modal forms, all the code that controls the sequence of presentation of forms can be conveniently located in a single procedure.

6.8 Project 10: User Authorization

The following concepts are introduced in this project: the Text box control's PasswordChar property, and the Command button control's Default and Cancel properties.

Many business applications allow access to authorized users only. To do this, the application requires the user to identify himself or herself and also provide proof of identification. An obvious example is the program executed by a bank's automatic teller machine. Another example is a computerized registration application that enables students to enroll in classes for the upcoming term. Such an application would be worthless if I could easily fool it into thinking that I am you, because I could then enroll you in classes you don't want to take or drop you from classes you do want to take (which I might do in order to make room for me, if the class is full when I want to enroll in it).

A simple and common way to prevent unauthorized users from accessing a system is to assign each legitimate user a *username* and a *password*. The computer maintains a table that stores the username/password combination for each user.

To access the system, the user must provide both username and password. The username identifies the user to the system, and is usually treated as public information. However, each user's password is secret; thus, the password serves as proof that the user is in fact the person identified by the corresponding username.

Such systems are familiar and present the user with a login window similar to that in Figure 6.55.

Description of the Application

We want to create reusable code to check user authorization. We can then include this code in any application we wish to restrict to selected users. When an application with this code begins executing, it should behave as follows.

First, the Login form should be displayed. The Login form's caption should read "Log in to the " followed by the name of the application that is using the user authorization code. In Figure 6.55, the application name is Student Registration System. The user then types in his or her username and password and clicks either OK or Cancel.

The characters that the user types in the Password text box are not displayed. Instead, the text box displays asterisks. This prevents other people from seeing a password by simply looking over the user's shoulder.

If the user clicks the Cancel button, then program execution ends. If the user clicks the OK button, the computer checks whether the username/password combination entered in the text boxes is valid. If it is valid, then the program displays the first form of the application (i.e., the user is allowed access to the application). If the username/password combination is not valid, the program displays a brief error message, then clears the text boxes on the login form and allows the user to try again.

The user is allowed up to three attempts to provide a valid username/password combination. If the combination entered on the third try is invalid, program execution ends.

Finally, if the user succeeds in providing a valid username/password combination, then the application will want to know the username. In the case of a student registration system, for example, the application needs the username so it can record *who* is registering for the classes.

FIGURE 6.55

Sample login form

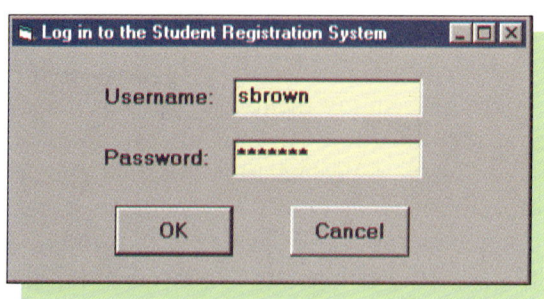

Design of the Application

We want the user authorization code to be easy to integrate into any application that needs it, and we want to structure it so that it can be "plugged into" any application without modification. Which form should be the startup form? Since the Login form is the first thing the user sees, we might consider making it the startup form for the application that uses it. However, if we do this, we'll have to write a statement somewhere in the Login form (or associated code) that loads the first form of the application when the user logs in successfully. Since this "first form" will have a different name for each application, this approach would require modifying our user authorization code for each application.

An alternative approach is to create a Sub Main in the application that needs to use our user authorization code, and have Sub Main invoke this code. This way our user authorization code will not require any modification to work with any application.

Our reusable code will be easiest to use if Sub Main needs to invoke only a single procedure or function in order to use it. Assuming this is possible, which should it be, a procedure or a function?

The net effect of our user authorization code will be either to end execution (if the user fails to provide a valid username/password combination) or to return control to the application, along with the valid username. If the user fails, execution can be ended by either a procedure or a function. If the user succeeds, there is only one value (the username) to be returned to the application, so a function appears to be appropriate. What is a good name for the user authorization function? How about AuthorizeUser()?

The proposed structure of the project as we have described it so far is illustrated in Figure 6.56. Because we want the user authorization code to work with any application, we must design it to operate independently of the details of the application. The vertical bar signifies this independence.

We can develop our ideas further by building on this figure. Sub Main must be in a code module, and its scope is Public. Since Sub Main invokes function AuthorizeUser(), the scope of AuthorizeUser() must be Public.

What is the type of the value returned by AuthorizeUser()? The value to be returned is a username, which commonly contains letters, digits, and other symbols, so let us use type String. Does function AuthorizeUser() have any parameters? AuthorizeUser() should receive the name of the application that invokes it, so it can set the Login form's caption. The user will enter the username and password into the text boxes on the Login form, so these should not be passed as parameters. Figure 6.57 is a refinement of Figure 6.56 that incorporates these ideas. The rectangles represent code modules and forms.

We need to examine the sequence of tasks to be performed by the user authorization code. Here is a list of the major tasks.

◆ Display a Login form similar in appearance to Figure 6.55. The user can either click the Cancel button or enter username and password in the text boxes, then click OK.

FIGURE 6.56

Application code and user authorization code

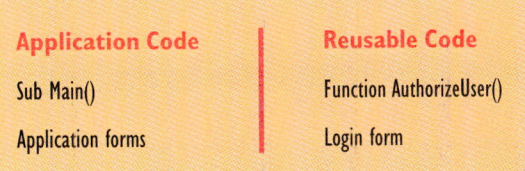

FIGURE 6.57

Refined application code and user authorization code

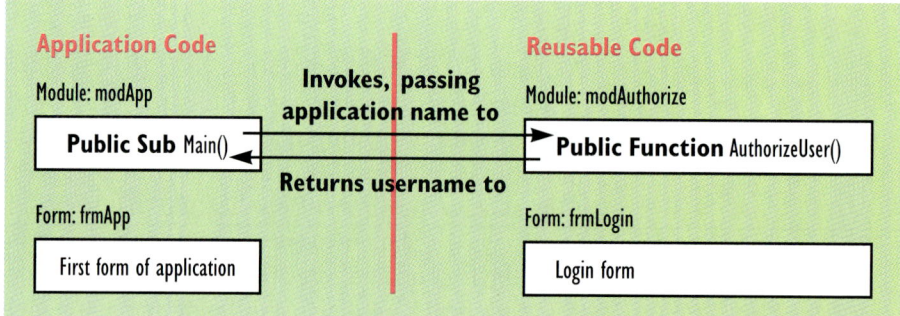

- If the user clicks the Cancel button, then execution should end.
- If the user clicks the OK button, the username/password combination entered by the user should be checked to see whether it is valid. If it is valid, return the username. If it is not, display a message saying it is invalid, and display the login form again with cleared text boxes. (Remember to give the user at most three chances.)

Figure 6.58 shows another refinement of our figure, depicting these tasks and indicating the sequence in which they must be performed. Note that there are two tasks labeled 4, since the user may click either OK or Cancel, and there are two tasks labeled 5, since the username/password combination may or may not be valid. Let us use the information in this figure to write pseudocode for function AuthorizeUser().

Public Function AuthorizeUser (ByVal ApplicationName As String) As String
set Login form's caption to show application name
show Login form   ' step 2
' if this comment is reached user must have clicked OK at step 3
If username/password is valid Then   ' step 4
*   AuthorizeUser = username   ' step 5*
*   Exit Function*
End If

FIGURE 6.58

Sequence of tasks in user authorization

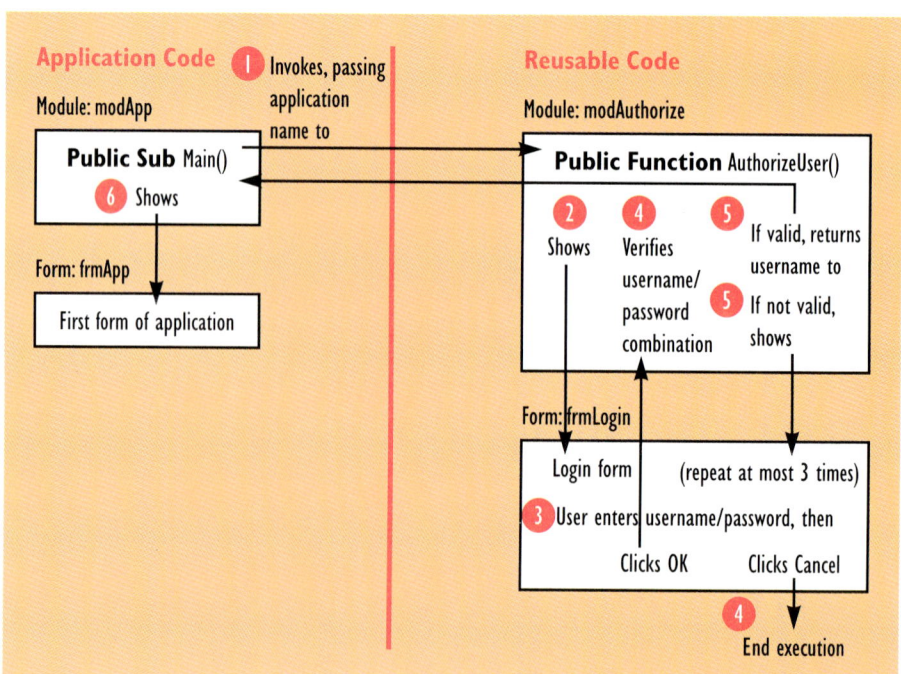

```
' if this comment is reached username/password must have been invalid
display message indicating invalid username/password
show Login form, with clear text boxes    ' step 5, user gets to try again
If username/password is valid Then
      AuthorizeUser = username
      Exit Function
End If
display message indicating invalid username/password
show Login form, with clear text boxes
If username/password is valid Then
      AuthorizeUser = username
      Exit Function
End If
display message indicating invalid username/password
End    ' user failed in all three attempts
End Function
```

Let's refine this pseudocode. Try to answer the following questions before reading further:

- Should the Login form be modeless or modal?
- In function AuthorizeUser(), how can we obtain the username/password entered by the user on the Login form?
- Given the username/password combination, how can we determine whether it is valid?

A good name for the Login form is frmLogin. It should be a modal form, because when the form is shown we need the values entered by the user before the next statement in function AuthorizeUser() can be executed. (Do you see now what the Click event procedure for frmLogin's OK button should do?)

The username/password entered by the user can be accessed (globally) by qualifying the names of the username and password Text box controls by the name of the form they reside on: frmLogin!txtUsername.Text and frmLogin!txtPassword.Text.

The description of the application says that the computer maintains a table of valid username/password combinations. In a real application such a table would be maintained in a database. For the sake of this project, let us keep the valid username/password combinations as symbolic constants in a general sub procedure or function. The task for this procedure or function will be to take the values frmLogin!txtUsername.Text and frmLogin!txtPassword.Text, then compare them to the symbolic constants and report whether or not they constitute a valid combination.

Should this task be implemented as a procedure or a function? It should probably be a function, since it only has to return one value: True if the user entered a valid combination, False otherwise. What is a good name for this function? How about ValidUserPassCombination()? What is the type of its return value? Boolean. Does it require any parameters? No, not if we have it access frmLogin!txtUsername.Text and frmLogin!txtPassword.Text directly.

Now we can complete the coding of function AuthorizeUser().

Public Function AuthorizeUser(**ByVal** ApplicationName **As String**) **As String**
    frmLogin.Caption = "Log in to the " & ApplicationName
    frmLogin.Show vbModal

continues

```
        If ValidUserPassCombination() = True Then
            AuthorizeUser = frmLogin!txtUsername.Text
          Exit Function
        End If
        MsgBox "Invalid username/password combination", vbExclamation
        frmLogin!txtUsername.Text = ""
        frmLogin!txtPassword.Text = ""
        frmLogin.Show vbModal
        If ValidUserPassCombination() = True Then
            AuthorizeUser = frmLogin!txtUsername.Text
          Exit Function
        End If
        MsgBox "Invalid username/password combination", vbExclamation
        frmLogin!txtUsername.Text = ""
        frmLogin!txtPassword.Text = ""
        frmLogin.Show vbModal
        If ValidUserPassCombination() = True Then
            AuthorizeUser = frmLogin!txtUsername.Text
          Exit Function
        End If
        MsgBox "Invalid username/password combination", vbExclamation
        End
      End Function
```

We leave the coding of function ValidUserPassCombination() to you as an exercise. For this project, assume that there are two authorized users, with usernames and passwords given in the symbolic constant definitions below.

```
Const USERNAME1 = "JSmith"
Const PASSWORD1 = "7yWA8"
Const USERNAME2 = "EPoe"
Const PASSWORD2 = "nSe9T"
```

Note that if "JSmith" and "nSe9T" are the username and password, function ValidUserPassCombination() should return False. The only valid password corresponding to username "JSmith" is "7yWA8".

Remember that the function ValidUserPassCombination() requires no parameters so its parameter list is empty. Also, since the function returns True or False, the type of its return value should be Boolean.

Construction of the Application

Let us create the reusable user authorization code and a mock-up of a student registration application that uses it. Before beginning work on the project, create two folders, named Authoriz and Register. You will save the reusable code (one form and one code module) in the Authoriz file folder and the application code (one form and one code module) in the Register file folder. Be sure to use descriptive names for the reusable form and code module files, since they are intended to be part of a useful library. Figure 6.59 shows this recommended organization of forms and code modules on disk. Figure 6.60 shows how the forms and code modules will appear in the Project Explorer window for the finished VB project.

Create frmLogin, with an appearance similar to that shown in Figure 6.55, and write the Click event procedures for the two command buttons. Make the Password text box display asterisks instead of the characters that the user types by setting its PasswordChar property to an asterisk (*).

FIGURE 6.59

Organization of files on disk

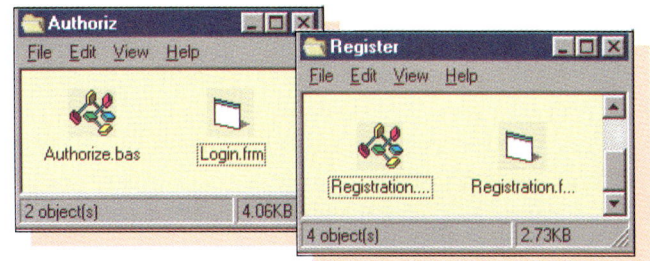

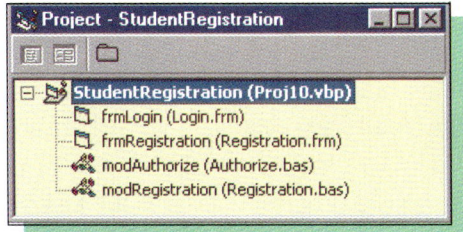

FIGURE 6.60

Project Explorer window for finished project

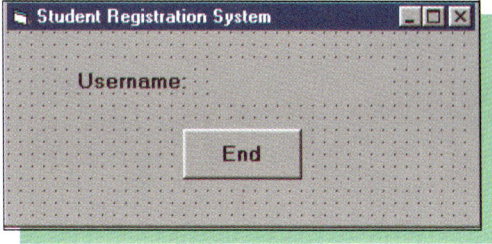

FIGURE 6.61

Form for student registration system mockup

Make the OK button frmLogin's *Default button* by setting its Default property to True. This allows the user to press ENTER as an alternative to clicking on the OK button. Note that a form can have only one Default button.

Make the Cancel button frmLogin's *Cancel button* by setting its Cancel property to True. This allows the user to press the ESC key as an alternative to using the mouse to click on the Cancel button. Note that a form can have only one Cancel button.

Run the project with frmLogin as the startup form, and verify that the password text box displays asterisks, that you can press ENTER instead of clicking OK, and that you can press ESC instead of clicking Cancel.

Now, save frmLogin in the file folder named Authoriz. Next, create functions AuthorizeUser() and ValidUserPassCombination() in a code module. Save this code module in the file folder named Authoriz.

Create a mock-up of a student registration application. This should consist of a form and a code module. A good name for this form is frmRegistration, and it should appear as shown in Figure 6.61. It has a Label control to display the username if the user logs in successfully. Save the form in the file folder named Register.

The code module should contain procedure Main. When program execution begins, sub Main should invoke AuthorizeUser(), passing to it the string "Student Registration System". If the user logs on successfully, execution returns to Main, which should then store the username returned by AuthorizeUser() in frmRegistration!lblUser.Caption and then show frmRegistration.

Save this code module in the file folder named Register. Then make Sub Main the startup object and run the application. If all goes well, the first thing you should see is the Login form. Click Cancel and verify that execution ends. Run the program again and enter "JSmith" and "7yWA8" in the Login form, then click OK. The application should respond by displaying the form in Figure 6.61, with lblUser showing "JSmith".

Run the program again, entering invalid username/password combinations and clicking OK, and verify that the application ends execution after three attempts.

EXERCISE 6.24 Would it make sense to unload frmLogin in function AuthorizeUser()? Explain. If so, where should the Unload statement be placed?

EXERCISE 6.25 If the user enters an invalid username/password combination, which control will have the focus when the Login form is redisplayed? To be user-friendly, which control should have the focus? Modify the code to automatically give the focus to your chosen control the second and third times the Login form is displayed.

Chapter Summary

1. General sub procedures and programmer-defined functions provide a way to break a programming solution into small parts that facilitate sharing of code (code reuse) and also facilitate the problem-solving process itself.

2. A general sub procedure performs a specific processing task. If the task is applicable in more than one program, then the same general sub procedure can be used in each program that needs it. In this way, a library of procedures performing common tasks can be used by programmers in building projects.

3. Unlike event procedures, general sub procedures are not linked to any control on a form. Accordingly, VB places them in the General object section of their form or code module. They can be called (or invoked) from other general sub procedures or from event procedures by using the name of the procedure to be invoked as a statement. When they are called, the flow of execution passes from the calling procedure to the sub procedure. When the end of the called procedure is reached, the flow of execution returns to the calling procedure at the statement immediately following the call.

4. A programmer-defined function returns a single value when it executes. As with built-in functions, this value may be string or numeric. Also, as with built-in functions, programmer-defined functions can be invoked only in expressions. This is consistent with the fact that they take on a value when they execute.

5. Both procedures and functions can use parameters to facilitate sharing of data between the calling and the called procedure or function. An argument is a variable in the calling procedure that is made available to the called procedure or function. Inside the called procedure or function this variable is referred to as a parameter. Corresponding arguments and parameters must be the same type. For example, if the first parameter in a sub procedure is type Integer, then the variable used as the first argument in the call must also be type Integer.

6. An argument can be passed to a procedure or function either by reference or by value. Passing by reference means that the parameter in the called procedure or function refers to the same variable as the argument—the parameter and the argument are the same variable. In contrast, passing by value causes the called procedure or function to make a local copy of the argument passed to it. Since the parameter is a copy of the argument—not the same variable—changing the value of the parameter does not affect the value of the argument. Passing by value is specified by placing the ByVal keyword before the parameter in the function or sub heading.

7. The KeyPress event procedure has a parameter (KeyAscii) in which VB passes the ANSI value of the key that the user pressed. The programmer can

write code to test the value of the KeyAscii parameter and, depending on its value, perform appropriate actions.

If the KeyPress event procedure changes the value of the KeyAscii parameter, the net effect is to change the character that the user typed. Setting the KeyAscii parameter to zero in the event procedure has the effect of canceling the character that the user typed.

8. The GotFocus event occurs when the user gives the focus to a control by clicking on it, tabbing to it, or using an access key for the control. One use of the GotFocus event is to display an informative message when the user clicks on a control. The LostFocus event is just the opposite—it occurs when the focus leaves a control.

9. Finally, form modality (modal or modeless) refers to the way forms behave when two or more are displayed at one time. When a modal form is shown, controls on other forms do not react to user actions; the user must respond to the modal form. A modal form must be hidden before the controls on other forms can be used. When a modeless form is displayed, both its controls and the controls on other forms can react.

Form modality is specified by the Show method. If the Show method passes argument vbModal, the form will be modal. If there is no argument (or the argument is vbModeless), then the form will be modeless.

Key Terms

argument
argument not optional error
argument type mismatch error
ByVal keyword
Exit Function statement
General object
general sub procedure
GotFocus event
KeyPress event
library
LostFocus event
modal form
modeless form
parameter
parameter list
parameter passing
passing by reference
passing by value
Private procedure
procedure call
programmer-defined function
Public procedure
reusable code
SetFocus method
Sub Main

End-of-Chapter Problems

1. Explain why using parameters to communicate data between a procedure or function and the associated calling procedure is superior to using global or module-level variables.

2. Write a function that computes and returns the present value of a given future amount of money. The function should be passed the future value (Currency), the number of years (Integer), the number of times the interest is compounded each year (Integer), and the annual interest rate (Single).

    The formula for present value (PV) is

    $$PV = \frac{FV}{\left(1 + \frac{r}{m}\right)^{(n \times m)}}$$

    where: FV is the future value.
    n is the number of years.
    m is the number of times interest is compounded per year.
    r is the annual interest rate.

Be sure to specify that the function cannot modify the arguments passed to it.

3. Explain the difference between a parameter that is passed by value and one that is passed by reference.

4. Does it make sense to "pass by reference" a constant as an argument to a procedure?

5. Is it possible to define a function that has no parameters? Would you even want to do so? Explain.

6. Write a KeyPress event procedure for a text box named txtName that beeps and rejects all keystrokes that are not capital letters (A–Z) or dashes.

7. Explain the difference between modal and modeless forms. Give an example of when it would make sense to use each type.

8. You have a text box named txtPartNumber. You want to make sure that when the user finishes typing in the box (as indicated by clicking on another control), the text box has at least three characters in it. Write the appropriate event procedure to accomplish this.

9. What is a code module? How is the "code library" concept related to the concept of a code module?

10. What is the difference between a procedure and a function? Explain when it is appropriate to use each one.

Programming Problems

1. Create a VB code module that includes a function that computes the future value of a given present amount. The formula for future value (FV) is

$$FV = PV \times [1 + (i / m)]^{m \times y}$$

where PV is the present amount.
               i is the annual interest rate.
               m is the number of compounding periods per year.
               y is the number of years.

Create a form that allows the user to input the four parameter values. After typing in the values, the user should click a command button to cause the future value to be computed and displayed on the form. The calculation should be performed using your function. An example form is shown here.

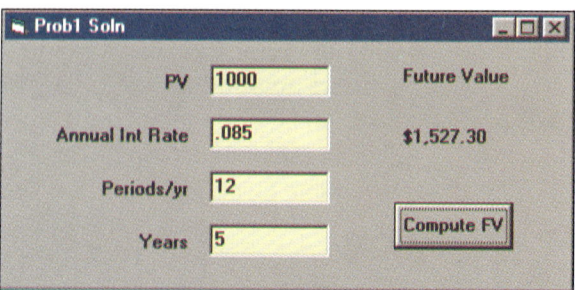

Use labels and text boxes as appropriate. Be aware that the names PV and FV are reserved words and cannot be used as variable names.

Extra credit: If the user clicks on the Compute FV command button and has not supplied values for all four parameters, have the system display a message box informing the user that all four values must be supplied. (*Hint*: See the Exit Sub command.)

2. Create a VB project that allows the user to provide the price of an item and the quantity sold. At the direction of the user, the project should then compute and display the gross sales amount (price time quantity), the discount, and the net sales amount. The discount should be computed using the table shown here.

Quantity	Discount
0–10	0%
11–25	5
26–100	8
101 +	10

Use a programmer-defined function to determine the percentage discount figure.

3. You have a simple form with a text box for input as shown here.

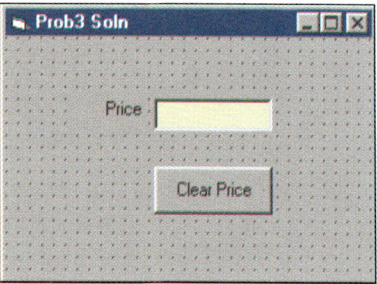

Write code that checks the user input in the Price text box and enforces all of the following rules:

a. Any digit is legal.
b. A maximum of one decimal point is legal.
c. A maximum of one dollar sign is legal as long as it is the first character.
d. Commas are legal (don't worry about where they are located).

If any illegal character is detected, have the system beep and reject it.

When the user clicks the Clear Price button, the Price text box should be cleared so that another test can be performed. Be sure that the mechanism you use to detect errors is also reset so that, for example, the new input can begin with another dollar sign.

4. Create a form as shown here.

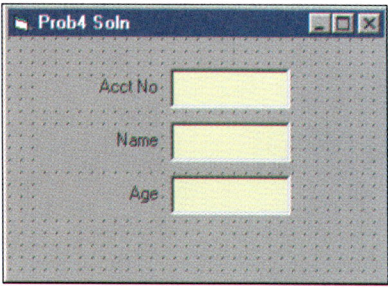

When the user enters data into the Account Number and Age text boxes, the system should automatically test for valid input, as prescribed by the table provided here.

Quantity	Valid Range
Account Number	1000 to 99999, inclusive
Age	0 to 99, inclusive

The test should be made as soon as the user clicks on the next text box. If an invalid value is detected, the system should display a message indicating the nature of the error, clear the text box, and then place the focus back on that text box (the user will not be able to leave a text box unless a valid value is entered). (*Hint*: See the SetFocus method.)

5. Create a VB project that reorders three string values input by the user into sequence from the largest to the smallest. The form shown below uses text boxes for user input.

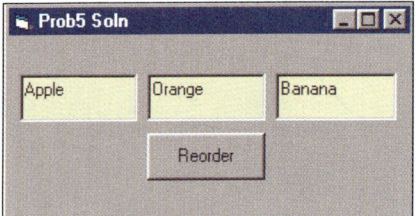 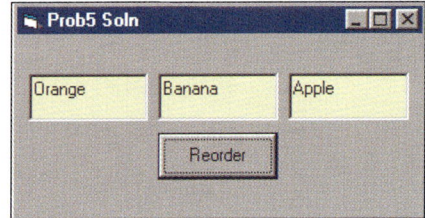

Use a general sub procedure to perform the reordering. Remember that you can compare two string variables, and VB will determine which one is larger based on the ANSI collating sequence. Be aware, though, that this reordering scheme is not a good, general-purpose solution for sorting. You will see a general solution later (in Chapter 9).

6. A university charges tuition based on the table shown here.

	Resident	Nonresident
Undergraduate	$35/credit	$65/credit
Graduate	$70/credit	$135/credit

Create a VB project that allows the user to indicate resident or nonresident status, class standing, and number of credits. Then provide a way for the user to request that tuition be computed and displayed.

Provide appropriate controls for user input (text boxes, option buttons, check boxes, etc.). Use a programmer-defined function that determines the cost per credit given the student's residency status and class standing.

chapter SEVEN

Repeating Processing Tasks

Loop Structures

Most business applications have processing steps that must be performed repeatedly. An example is an order entry application that accepts and processes a list of items a customer wants to order. The program must process many items, and the steps required to process one item are identical to the steps required to process any other item. Indeed, the real power of the computer is not unleashed until it is put to work on repetitive tasks.

In a program, **the structure used to execute a group of statements repeatedly is called a** *loop.* The loop structure controls how many times the statements are executed. In the order entry example, the programmer determines the statements necessary to process one item and places those statements inside a loop. The programmer composes the loop so that the statements are executed once for each item on the order form.

As we know, statements in a procedure always execute one at a time. To this point in our study of VB, all statements have been executed in order, from top to bottom, with, technically, two exceptions: the If and the Select…Case statements can cause certain statements to be skipped, depending on the value of a specified condition. Of course, we can view If and Select…Case as meta statements, and from this perspective they are not exceptions to the "top-to-bottom" rule at all. Like the If and Select…Case statements, a loop

✦ Has a top and a bottom that are clearly indicated by reserved words.
✦ Has a statement block in its interior.
✦ Technically, introduces an exception to the rule that statements are executed from top to bottom.
✦ When viewed as a meta statement, is not seen as an exception to the "top-to-bottom" rule.

In VB there are two kinds of loops. The *Do…Loop structure* executes the statement block in its interior repeatedly until a specified condition occurs.

331

The *For...Next structure* **executes the statement block in its interior a specified number of times.** It is important to use the appropriate loop for each given situation.

As we shall see, many programs must process lists of data items. VB provides two controls, the list box and combo box, for maintaining and displaying lists of text data. Loops and these controls are natural partners.

Objectives

After studying this chapter you should be able to

- Use the Do...Loop and For...Next structures and know when each structure is appropriate.
- Understand how nested loops operate.
- Construct user interfaces with the List box control and its close relative, the Combo box control.

7.1 The Do...Loop Structure

Programmers use the Do...Loop structure when they do not know how many times the statements inside the loop will be executed. For example, suppose you are writing a program that examines a list of credit card transactions in order to make sure there are no duplicate transactions. That is, your program looks for pairs of identical transactions (having the same date, time and total charge amount for a customer). When the loop begins executing, you do not know when—or even if—a duplicate transaction will be found.

The Do...Loop structure has a number of variations in how it determines when to stop repeating the statements inside the loop. We will look at each of these variations in turn, then examine initialization and termination conditions.

Syntax and Action of the Do...Loop

Loops, like decision-making statements, consist of multiple statements. The Do...Loop consists of a minimum of three statements. The simplest has the following syntax:

> **Do**
>   *statementblock*
> **Loop**

The reserved word Do marks the top of the loop, and the reserved word Loop marks its bottom. Recall that a statement block is any sequence of zero or more statements.

To make loops more readable and understandable, programmers indent the statement block (in the interior of the loop).

Run Time: The Effect of the Do...Loop Structure

The reserved word Do does not cause the computer to take any action; it simply marks the top of the loop. The statements in the loop's interior are executed one at a time, in order, from top to bottom. The reserved word Loop causes execution to go back up to the top of the loop—that is, back to the Do statement.

Figure 7.1 illustrates this action. The net effect is that the statements inside the loop are executed repeatedly.

Example 7.1

Using a Do...Loop

The event procedure in Figure 7.2 illustrates the use of Do...Loop. This event procedure executes, but it has the disadvantage of executing forever. **A loop that executes forever is called an *infinite loop*.** Nearly all programmers have inadvertently created an infinite loop or two. How do you make it stop? Read on.

Infinite Loops and CTRL+BREAK

When execution enters an infinite loop, you will find that the End button on VB's Toolbar does not respond, nor do any of the menu items. The reason is that the computer is too busy executing statements to pay attention to the user.[1] **To terminate the infinite loop, you must press CTRL+BREAK** (i.e., press and hold the CTRL key, then press the BREAK key); **this causes VB to enter break mode.** From break mode you can

♦ Click the End button, or choose End from the Run menu, to stop execution of the program.

♦ Click the Run button, or press F5, to resume execution of the program.

♦ Use VB's debugging tools to locate and correct the problem. See Appendix A for an introduction to debugging.

You need to use CTRL+BREAK to end execution of Example 7.1.

FIGURE 7.1

Action of the Do...Loop

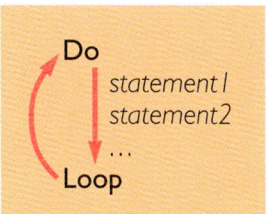

FIGURE 7.2

An infinite loop

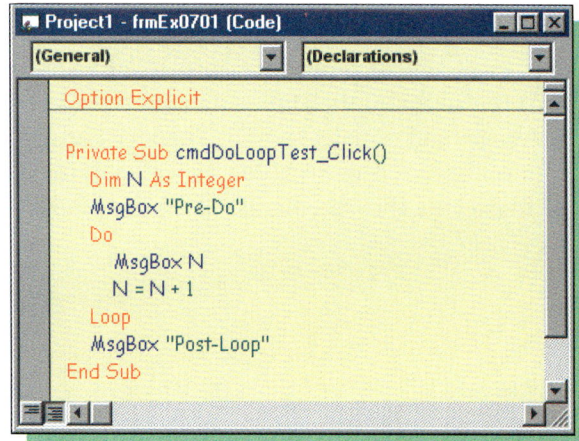

[1] What happens when you run Example 7.1? When a message box is displayed, you must click OK before you can interact with VB's Toolbar or menu. This is because the message box is a modal form. But when you click OK, VB resumes executing statements in the event procedure, and almost immediately another message box is displayed.

Do While...Loop

Infinite loops are rarely desirable. Therefore, VB provides variations of the Do...Loop that allow you to specify a condition—called the *termination condition*—that terminates execution of the loop. The first variation is the *Do While...Loop*, which places the termination condition at the top of the loop. It has the following syntax:

Do While *condition*
    statementblock
Loop

The reserved words Do While mark the top of the loop, and the reserved word Loop marks its bottom. The *condition* is a logical expression that the programmer provides.

Run Time: The Effect of the Do While...Loop Structure

Each time the computer encounters Do While, it evaluates the condition.

- If the condition is False, **execution skips to the statement following the reserved word Loop, which we call** *exiting the loop,* or, equivalently, *terminating* it.
- If the condition is True, the computer executes the statements in the loop's interior one at a time and in order, from top to bottom. The reserved word Loop then causes execution to go back up to the top of the loop—that is, back to the Do While statement.

Each time the Loop statement sends execution back up to Do While, the computer executes the Do While statement again, by evaluating the condition, and then either exiting the loop or executing the statement block. The loop continues to execute "while the condition is true." Figure 7.3 depicts the action of the Do While...Loop.

Example 7.2 Using a Do While...Loop

The code in Figure 7.4 illustrates the Do While...Loop. Let us hand-check this code to make sure you understand the action of the Do While...Loop. When the user clicks the command button named cmdDoWhileTest, the statements inside event procedure cmdDoWhileTest_Click begin to execute. To mirror the action of the Dim statement, we create a local variable named X of type Integer and initialize it to 0. Then we execute the Do While statement. Its condition is X < 3. Since X holds the value 0, the condition is True, so we proceed to execute the statements inside the loop.

FIGURE 7.3

Action of Do While...Loop

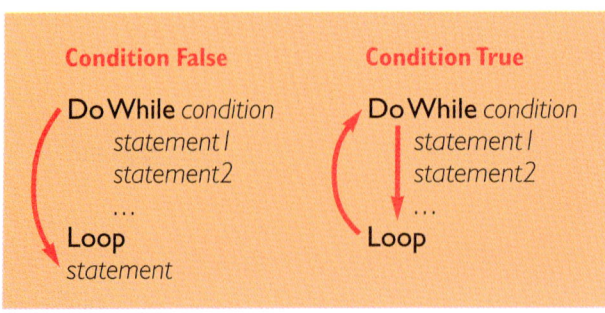

FIGURE 7.4

Code for Example 7.2

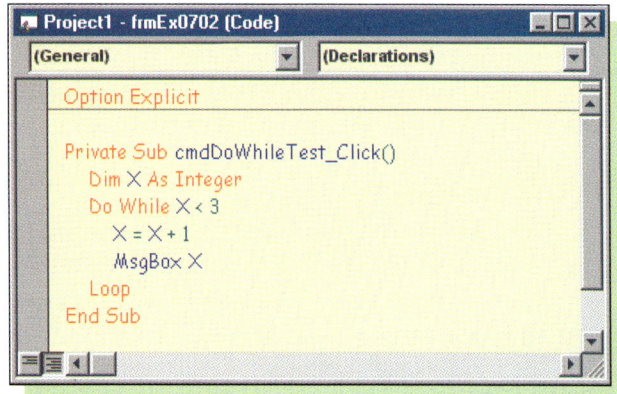

We simulate the action of the assignment statement X = X + 1 by changing the value stored in X to 1. The message box then displays the value 1. At this point our hand-check appears as shown in Figure 7.5a.

Next, we execute the Loop statement. **When the Loop statement sends execution back up to the Do While statement, we say that we have completed one** *iteration* **of the loop.** We execute the Do While statement by evaluating

FIGURE 7.5

Iterations of the loop

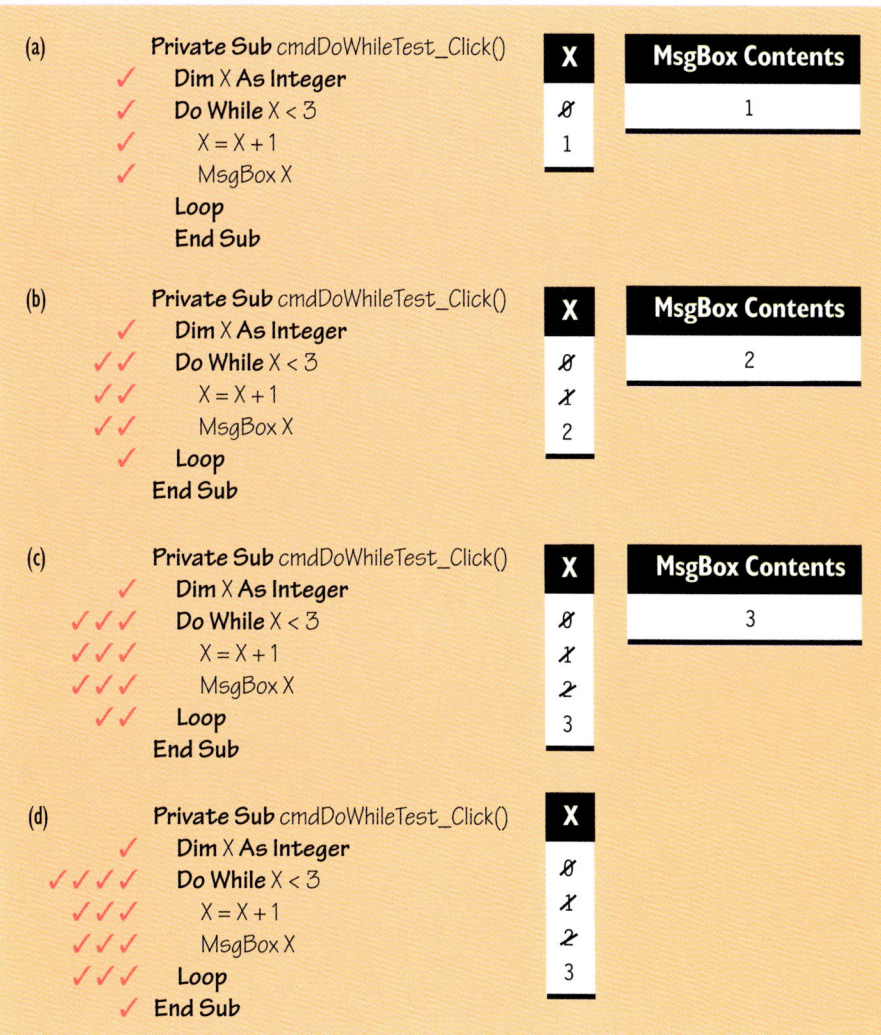

its condition. Since X holds the value 1, the condition (X < 3) is True, so we execute the statements inside the loop.

The assignment statement X = X + 1 changes the value stored in X to 2. Then the message box displays the value 2 as shown in Figure 7.5b. Note that our hand-check shows additional check marks that show the second iteration through the loop.

Next, we execute the Loop statement, which sends execution back up to the Do While statement. We execute the Do While statement by evaluating its condition. Since X holds the value 2, the condition (X < 3) is True, so we execute the statements inside the loop.

The assignment statement X = X + 1 changes the value stored in X to 3. Then the message box displays the value 3 as shown in Figure 7.5c.

Next, we execute the Loop statement, which sends execution back up to the Do While statement. We execute the Do While statement by evaluating its condition. Since X holds the value 3, the condition (X < 3) is False, so we exit the loop. The next statement to be executed is the statement following Loop, which is the End Sub. The completed hand-check is shown in Figure 7.5d. We see that the net effect of the event procedure was to display three message boxes, containing the values 1, 2, and 3.

Use the hand-checking procedure illustrated in the preceding example to verify the action of loops you write or study. It takes practice to be able to quickly determine the net effect of a loop, and performing hand-checks will help you gain the necessary expertise. Also, VB's debugging tools (Appendix A) make it easy to view the values of variables at any point during execution of a program. Using these tools to watch values change during iterations of a loop can help solidify your understanding of loops as well as aid you in identifying and fixing problems when they arise.

Coding the Loop Body

When coding the statements in the interior of the loop—sometimes called the *loop body*—keep the following factors in mind.

First, one or more statements in the loop body must eventually cause the condition to become False. Otherwise, the loop will execute forever. In Example 7.2, the statement X = X + 1, executed repeatedly, eventually caused the value of X to be 3, so that the loop's condition (X < 3) became False.

Second, the order of statements inside the loop affects the result of the loop. After a programmer has decided on the loop's condition and the statements inside the loop, he or she must make sure that the statements in the interior of the loop are arranged in the correct order, and that the loop condition will cause the computer to exit the loop at the right time. To do this, the programmer typically hand-checks the loop for a few iterations.

Third, it is possible for the loop to terminate immediately. That is, the condition can be False the first time the Do While statement is executed, so that the statements inside the loop are executed zero times. This behavior is sometimes appropriate.

Finally, a loop can be viewed as a meta statement. This is true because the computer begins executing the loop at its top (the Do While statement), and when it exits the loop, the next statement to be executed is the one right below the bottom of the loop (the Loop statement). As an example, the meta statement for the loop in Example 7.2 might be worded as "display the numbers

FIGURE 7.6

Code for Example 7.3

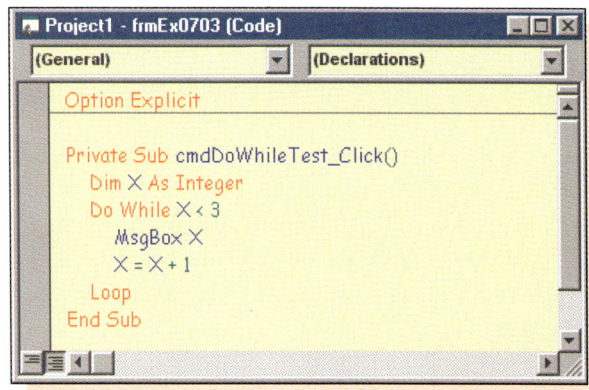

1, 2, and 3 in message boxes." The following examples strengthen some of these observations.

Example 7.3

Order of Statements within a Loop

The loop in Figure 7.6 differs from Example 7.2 only in that the order of the two statements inside the loop has been reversed. In this example, the message box statement executes before the variable X is incremented by 1. Therefore, during the first iteration of the loop, the value of X is still zero when the message box displays its value (recall that Example 7.2 incremented X before it was displayed).

Since this loop displays X before it is incremented, the values displayed by the message boxes will be 0, 1, and 2—*not* 1, 2, and 3 as was the case in Example 7.2.

Example 7.4

Using Immediate Termination

The code in Figure 7.7 simulates a coin-tossing game. Each time a coin is tossed, it is equally likely to come up heads or tails. The event procedure keeps tossing the coin until it comes up tails, then displays the number of heads that appeared before the first occurrence of tails.

FIGURE 7.7

Code for Example 7.4

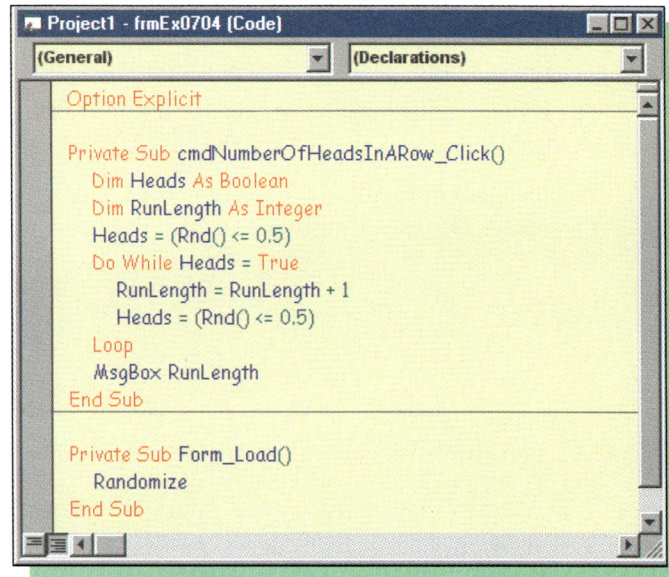

The assignment statement

Heads = (Rnd() <= 0.5)

stores True in the Boolean variable Heads if the random fraction returned by Rnd() is less than or equal to 0.5, and False otherwise. When this statement is executed the first time, Heads may be False; if so, when Do While is executed its condition will be False, and the loop will be exited immediately.

The meta statement for this loop might be worded as "generate random numbers until you encounter one greater than 0.5, and count how many you generated."

EXERCISE 7.1 Modify Example 7.2 to display the numbers 1 through 10. Also modify Example 7.2 to display the even numbers from 2 to 20 (i.e., 2, 4, 6, 8, . . . , 20).

Do…Loop While

The *Do…Loop While structure* works like the Do While…Loop structure except that the termination condition is at the bottom of the loop instead of at the top. This guarantees that the statements inside the loop are executed at least once, unlike the Do While…Loop which may terminate immediately. Do…Loop While has the following syntax:

Do
  statementblock
Loop While *condition*

The reserved word Do marks the top of the loop, and the reserved words Loop While mark its bottom. The *condition* is a logical expression that the programmer provides.

Run Time: The Effect of the Do…Loop While Structure

The reserved word Do does not cause the computer to take any action; it simply marks the top of the loop. The statements inside the loop are executed one at a time and in order, from top to bottom. Each time the computer encounters Loop While, it evaluates the condition.

✦ If the condition is False, execution resumes at the statement following Loop While. That is, the computer exits the loop.

✦ If the condition is True, execution jumps back up to the top of the loop—that is, back to the Do statement.

As illustrated in Figure 7.8, each time the Loop While statement sends execution back up to Do, the computer executes the statements inside the loop again. It

FIGURE 7.8

Action of Do…Loop While structure

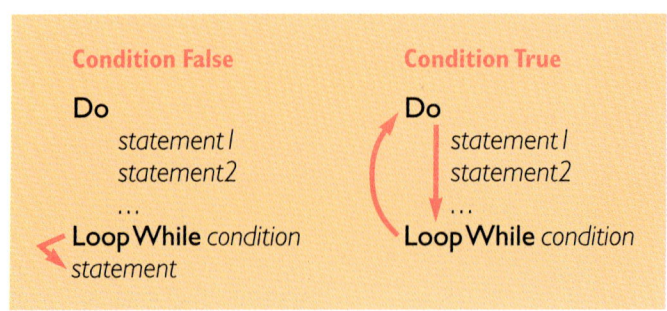

then encounters the Loop While statement again, which it executes by evaluating the condition and either exiting the loop or jumping back up to Do. The loop repeats "while the condition is true."

Example 7.5

Using Do...Loop While

The code in Figure 7.9 is a simple guessing game in which the computer generates a random integer between 1 and 6 and the user is asked to guess what the integer is. Do...Loop While is appropriate in this instance because in a guessing game the user should certainly be allowed to make at least one guess.

In contrast, the code in Example 7.4 simulates the number of times in a row a tossed coin comes up heads. We use Do While...Loop there because if the first coin toss turns out to be tails, then we don't want the statements inside the loop to be executed (which would cause RunLength to be incremented to 1).

EXERCISE 7.2

Rewrite the event procedure in Example 7.5 using Do While...Loop instead of Do...Loop While. Your new event procedure should behave identically to that in Example 7.5. In particular, it should allow the user to make at least one guess. Which event procedure is easier to understand? Explain.

EXERCISE 7.3

Suppose we modify Example 7.5 by moving the statement

    Target = 1 + Int(6 * Rnd())

from just after Do to just before Do. How will the game change? Explain.

Do Until...Loop and Do...Loop Until

The two final variations of the Do...Loop are the *Do Until...Loop structure,* which has the termination condition at the top of the loop, and the *Do...Loop Until structure,* which has the termination condition at the bottom of the loop.

FIGURE 7.9

Code for Example 7.5

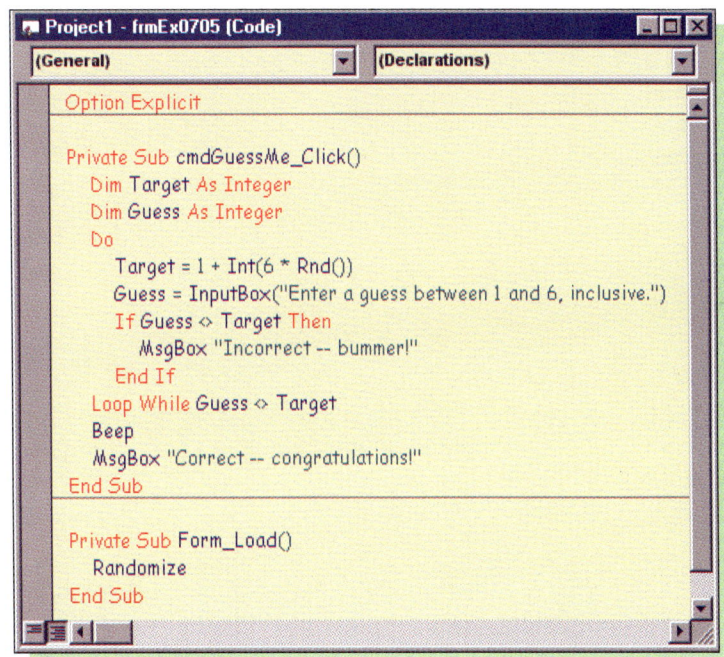

The syntax and action of the Do Until...Loop are the same as the syntax and action of the Do While...Loop, with two exceptions:

1. There is an obvious difference in the keywords: Do Until instead of Do While.
2. The loop statements inside Do Until...Loop are executed when the condition is False, and the loop is exited when the condition is True, which is just the opposite of Do While...Loop.

The action of Do Until...Loop is illustrated in Figure 7.10. This structure can be interpreted as "execute the statements inside the loop *until* the condition becomes *True*." In contrast, the Do While...Loop statement means "execute the statements inside the loop *while* the condition is *True*," or, equivalently, "execute the statements inside the loop *until* the condition becomes *False*."

Any loop you create using Do While...Loop can also be written using Do Until...Loop, and vice versa. It is necessary only to negate the condition. For example, if the original condition was X = 3, the negated condition will be X <> 3. Or if the original condition was X > 3, then the negated condition will be X <= 3. As an example of this, consider the event procedure in Example 7.2, which used Do While...Loop. Figure 7.11 shows this event procedure written using Do While...Loop and Do Until...Loop. The two procedures behave identically.

Does it matter which you use? Since the two versions behave identically, the only issue is which one is easier to read. Quite often, as in the code in Figure 7.11, the difference is not significant.

Suppose, however, that you are writing pseudocode for a procedure to print employee paychecks. Which of the following do you prefer?

Do While there are more employees
    get current pay data for an employee
    print the employee's paycheck
Loop

FIGURE 7.10

Action of Do Until...Loop structure

Condition False
Do Until condition
    statement1
    statement2
    ...
Loop

Condition True
Do Until condition
    statement1
    statement2
    ...
Loop
    statement

FIGURE 7.11

Equivalent Do While and Do Until loops

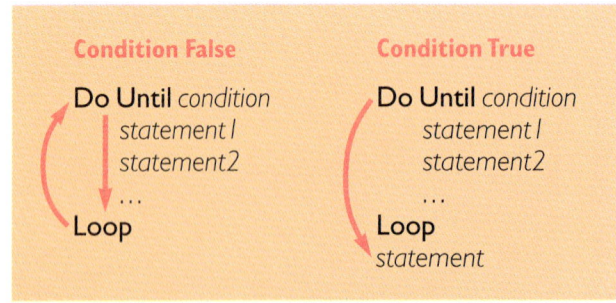

```
Private Sub cmdDoWhileTest_Click()
    Dim X As Integer
    Do While X < 3
        X = X + 1
        MsgBox X
    Loop
End Sub
```

```
Private Sub cmdDoUntilTest_Click()
    Dim X As Integer
    Do Until X >= 3
        X = X + 1
        MsgBox X
    Loop
End Sub
```

or

> *Do Until there are no more employees*
>   *get current pay data for an employee*
>   *print the employee's paycheck*
> *Loop*

Both seem reasonable so far. But as you refine the pseudocode, you will eventually have to figure out how to express the condition as a logical expression. As we will see in Chapter 8, if you obtain the employee data from a database, you will want to use the database property EOF (end of file). VB sets the EOF property to True when the end of the database has been reached (no more employees to be processed), and to False when the end of the database has not been reached (still more employees to be processed).

So the two versions of pseudocode become

> *Do While database.EOF = False*
>   *get current pay data for an employee*
>   *print the employee's paycheck*
> *Loop*

or

> *Do Until database.EOF = True*
>   *get current pay data for an employee*
>   *print the employee's paycheck*
> *Loop*

While the difference is not earth-shattering, in this case Do Until...Loop is a little more straightforward because this loop's condition becomes True when database.EOF becomes True.

The same similarities and differences apply to the Do...Loop Until and the Do...Loop While structures. The action of Do...Loop Until is illustrated in Figure 7.12.

EXERCISE 7.4 Complete the event procedure below by providing the statement block that performs the following tasks: First, ask the user to input a guess between 1 and 127. If the user's guess is less than the value stored in Target, display the message "Too low" and ask the user to input another guess between 1 and 127. If the user's guess is greater than the value stored in Target, display the message "Too high" and ask the user to input another guess between 1 and 127. Repeat this until the user's guess is equal to the value stored in Target. Store the number of guesses entered by the user in the variable named Count. These actions occur after the user clicks a single time on cmdGuidedGuessMe.

FIGURE 7.12

Action of Do...Loop Until structure

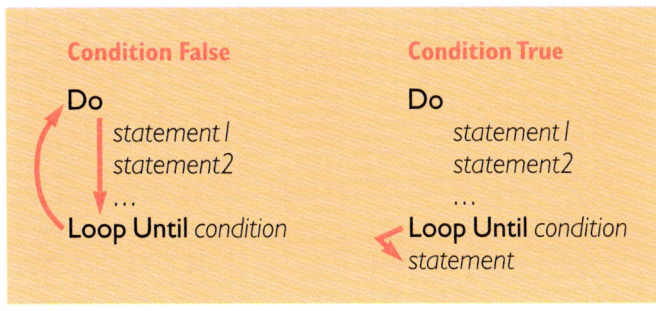

Do not modify, move, or add any statements before or after *statementblock*. Recall that a statement block consists of any sequence of zero or more statements. It may include decision-making statements and loops.

```
Private Sub cmdGuidedGuessMe_Click()
    Dim Target As Integer
    Dim Guess As Integer
    Dim Count As Integer
    Target = 1 + Int(127 * Rnd())
    'statementblock
    MsgBox "It took you " & Count & " guesses."
End Sub
```

EXERCISE 7.5 Write a complete Click event procedure for a command button named cmdRunningSum that performs the following tasks: Ask the user to input numbers, and compute the sum of the numbers as they are entered, until the sum becomes either less than −10 or greater than +10. Then display how many numbers the user entered and their final sum. Display only the final count and sum. Do not display the results of intermediate calculations. For example, if the user entered the numbers 3, 5, 1, and 7, your event procedure should display only the messages "You entered 4 numbers" and "The sum is 16".

Initialization and Termination

A common error is for the loop to perform one iteration more or one iteration less than desired. The error often stems from the initial value of a variable involved in the loop condition, or from the loop condition itself. In Examples 7.2 and 7.3, the initial value of the variable X was 0 (as defined by the Dim statement). The following examples demonstrate the problem and show how to correct it.

Example 7.6  ### Initialization and Termination

The programmer who wrote the event procedure in Figure 7.13 intended to first ask the user to input a number, and then to display that many letters of the alphabet (starting at A). The code uses the Chr$() function to convert an integer into a letter. The first letter of the alphabet, A, appears at position 65 in the ANSI table, and VB's predefined symbolic constant vbKeyA is equal to 65.

FIGURE 7.13

Code for Example 7.6

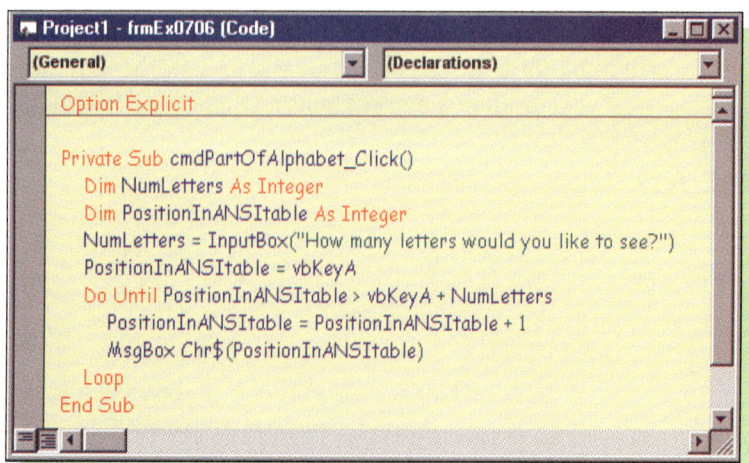

If the user enters the number 3 in response to the input box, the program should display the letters A, B, and C in separate message boxes. Unfortunately, it displays B, C, D, and E instead. This error is common when composing a loop. Actually there are *two* errors:

- The first value displayed is incorrect (B instead of A).
- The number of values displayed is incorrect (4 instead of 3).

What are the causes of these errors?

The statement

```
PositionInANSItable = vbKeyA
```

just before the loop is said to *initialize* the variable PositionInANSItable, **meaning it defines the value that the variable initially holds when the loop begins executing**. Initialization statements are common before loops, because statements inside the loop often manipulate one or more variables and the correct operation of the loop often requires that a variable hold a particular value when the loop is first entered.

In this procedure we want to initialize the variable PositionInANSItable to 65. This way, the first letter displayed by the MsgBox statement will be A. However, since the statement

```
PositionInANSItable = PositionInANSItable + 1
```

occurs *before* the MsgBox statement, the letter B is the first letter displayed. This causes the loop to "start in the wrong place." One way to fix this problem is to change the initialization statement to

```
PositionInANSItable = vbKeyA - 1
```

After this change, the event procedure will display A, B, C, and D when the user enters 3 in response to the input box.

The remaining problem is that the loop displays one too many letters. It is quite common for a newly composed loop to iterate one too many or one too few times. In the code above, we can correct this problem by changing the loop condition to

```
PositionInANSItable >= vbKeyA - 1 + NumLetters
```

Example 7.7 Correcting Example 7.6

The code in Figure 7.14 incorporates the suggested changes to the event procedure in Example 7.6, and operates correctly.

There is, however, a "cleaner" solution to the problems of Example 7.6, as Figure 7.15 illustrates. Here the initialization statement is the same as that of Example 7.6, and the loop condition is only slightly modified (> was changed to >=). The substantial change was to swap the order of the statements inside the loop.

From time to time you may create a loop that starts in the wrong place and has a termination condition that is off by one iteration. Likely sources of the problem are

- An initialization statement that is off by one.
- A loop condition, in which > may need to be changed to >=, or vice versa (or < may need to be changed to <=, or vice versa).

FIGURE 7.14

Loop now executes correct number of times with correct values

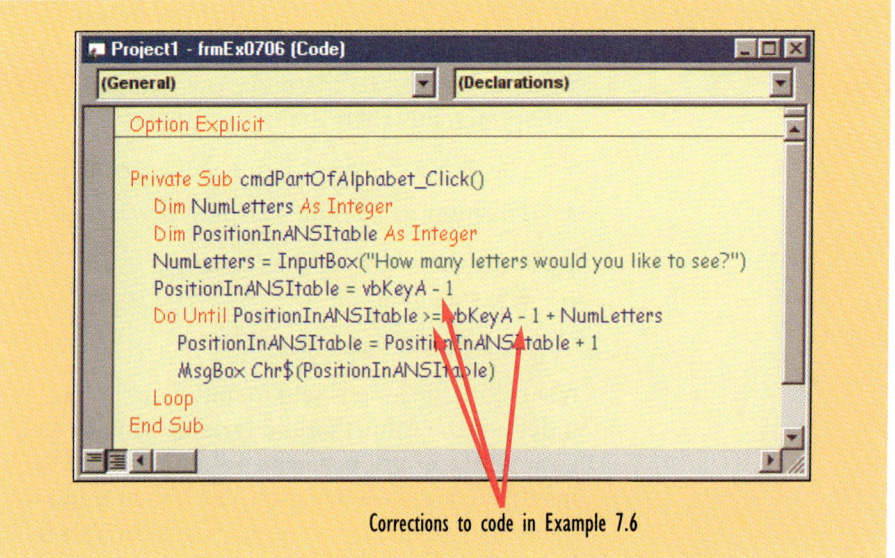

Corrections to code in Example 7.6

FIGURE 7.15

Code for Example 7.7

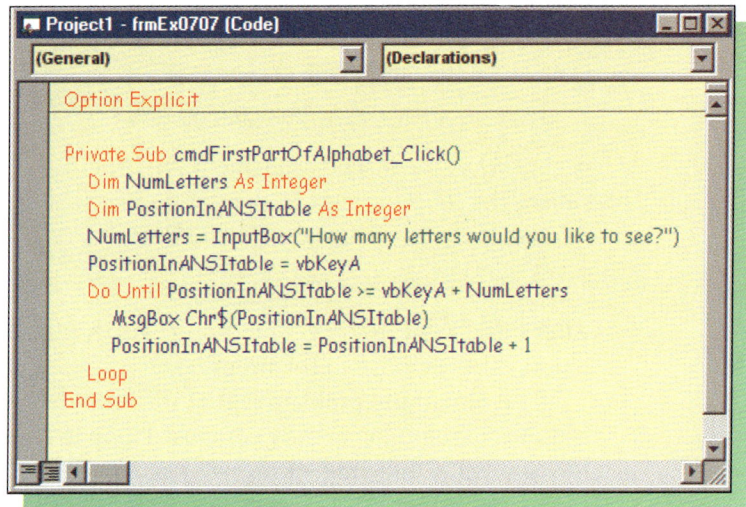

◆ The statements inside the loop, which may need to be reordered.

Don't try to change all three at once when fixing loop errors. Instead, hand-check a few iterations of the loop first, and try to identify the source of the error. Then make one modification and test it. If this doesn't improve (or completely correct) the situation, undo the modification and try another.

EXERCISE 7.6 In Example 7.7, describe the output if the user enters –1 in response to the input box.

EXERCISE 7.7 Modify Example 7.2 to display the numbers 50 through 60, inclusive.

7.2 The For...Next Loop Structure

In contrast to Do...Loops, in which the number of repetitions of the loop body is unknown prior to processing, the For...Next loop is used when the programmer can write an expression that specifies how many iterations the loop will perform. For example, suppose that we want a loop that computes the average grade for a class of 33 students. Each iteration of the loop processes a different student. Since there are 33 students in the class, we know that the loop will need to be executed 33 times.

Syntax and Action of For...Next

◆ ◆ ◆

Like Do...Loop and its variations, the For...Next loop consists of multiple statements that can be viewed as a single meta statement. The syntax of the For...Next loop is

> **For** counter = start **To** end
>   statementblock
> **Next** counter

The reserved word For marks the top of the loop, and the reserved word Next marks its bottom. **The *counter* is a numeric variable that the programmer provides and that the loop uses to count iterations.** Note carefully that this variable must appear after both For and Next. Both *start* and *end* are numeric expressions that the programmer provides.

Run Time: The Effect of the For...Next Structure

When the computer executes the For statement the first time (that is, right after it finishes executing the statement above For), it

1. Evaluates the expression *start* and stores the result in the variable *counter*.
2. Evaluates the expression *end* to arrive at the *ending value*.
3. Compares the value stored in *counter* to the *ending value*, and
   a. If the value stored in *counter* is greater than the *ending value*, then the computer exits the loop, and execution resumes at the statement following Next.
   b. If the value stored in *counter* is less than or equal to the *ending value*, it executes the statements inside the loop one at a time, top to bottom.

When the computer executes the Next statement, it:

4. Increases the value stored in *counter* by 1.
5. Causes execution to go back up to the For statement.

After "jumping up" from Next to For, the computer executes the For statement by performing only step 3.

To fully understand the action of the For...Next loop, you must keep in mind that operations 1 and 2 are performed only once, when the computer enters the loop from above. These operations are the *initialization* operations of the For...Next loop.

The action of the For...Next loop, after the initialization operations have been completed, is depicted in Figure 7.16. This action may seem complicated, but if you work through the following examples, you will see that it is not difficult.

Example 7.8

Using a For...Next Loop

The code in Figure 7.17 illustrates the For...Next loop. Let us hand-check this example. The statements inside event procedure cmdForNextTest_Click begin to execute after the user clicks on cmdForNextTest. To mimic the action

FIGURE 7.16

Action of the For...Next structure

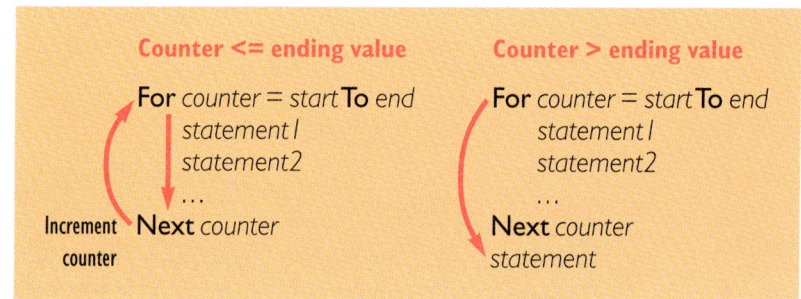

of the Dim statement, we create a local variable named X of type Integer and initialize it to 0. Then we execute the For statement. Since we've just entered the loop, we have to perform its initialization operations. Operation 1 stores the start value 1 in the counter variable X, and operation 2 determines the ending value to be 3.

To finish execution of the For statement, we compare the value stored in the counter X to the ending value. Since 1 is less than or equal to 3, we execute the loop body.

The only statement inside the loop is the message box statement, which displays the value 1 as shown in Figure 7.18a.

Next, we execute the Next statement, which does two things: it increases the value stored in the counter X by 1, and it sends execution back up to the For statement. This time, we do not initialize the counter and end values when we execute the For statement; we simply perform operation 3, which compares the value stored in the counter X to the ending value. Since 2 is less than or equal to 3, we proceed to execute the statement inside the loop. As shown in Figure 7.18b, the message box displays the value 2.

We then execute the Next statement, which increases the value stored in X by 1, then sends execution back up to the For statement. To execute the For statement we compare the value stored in X to the ending value. Since 3 is less than or equal to 3, we execute the statement inside the loop. The message box displays the value 3 as shown in Figure 7.18c.

We execute the Next statement, which increases the value stored in X by 1, then sends execution back up to the For statement. To execute the For statement we compare the value stored in X to the ending value. Since 4 is greater than 3, we exit the loop. The next statement to be executed is the statement following Next. Since this is the End Sub statement, we are finished executing the event procedure (see Figure 7.18d). We see that the net effect of the event procedure is to display the values 1, 2, and 3 in message boxes.

FIGURE 7.17

Code for Example 7.8

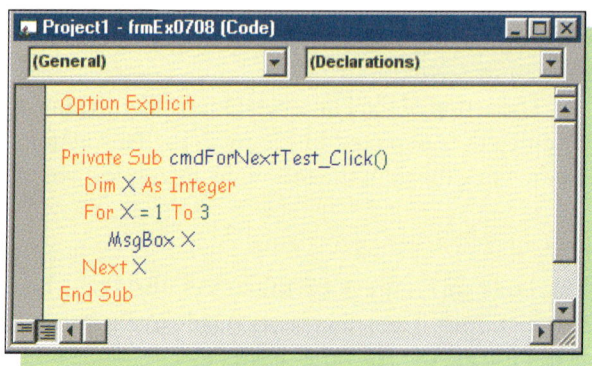

FIGURE 7.18

Iterations of a For...Next loop

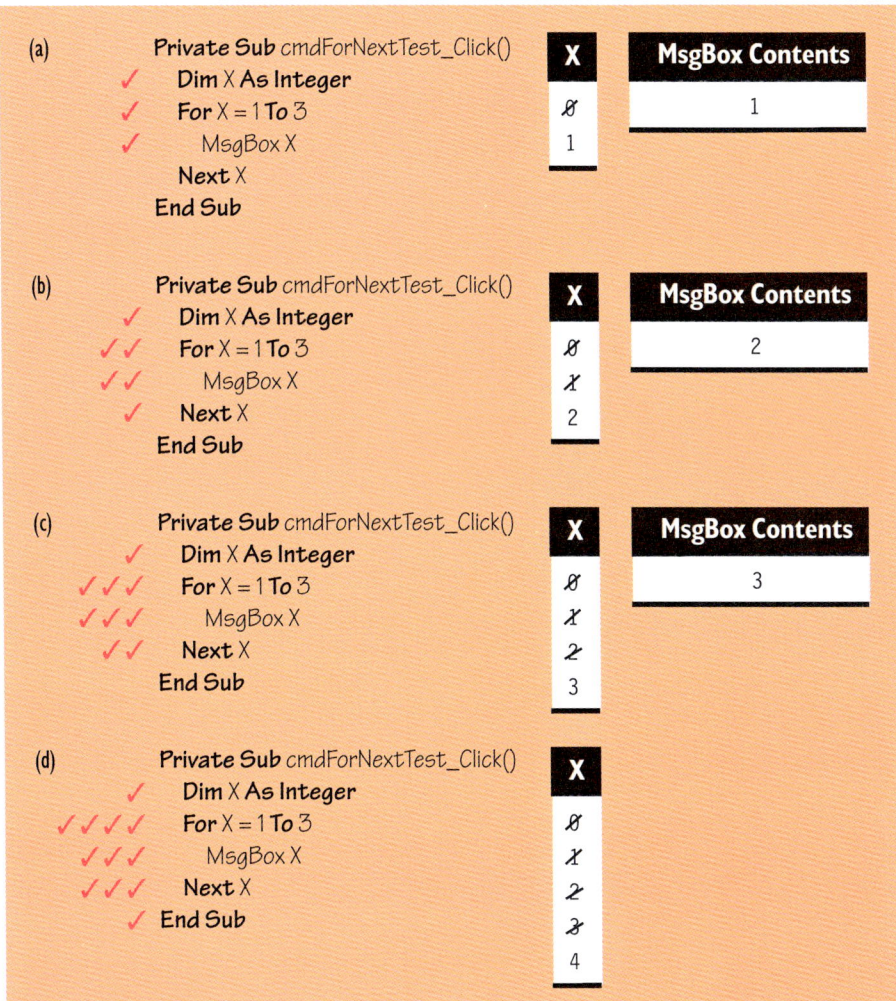

For...Next versus Do...Loop Variations

It is interesting to compare Example 7.8 with Example 7.2, which produced the same net effect but was written with a Do While...Loop structure instead of a For...Next structure. After working with a few examples using For...Next, you will discover that loops using For...Next are actually simpler than loops using Do...Loop.

When you see

For X = 1 To 3

at the top of a loop, you know immediately that

♦ The statements inside the loop will be executed three times.[2]
♦ The first time the statements inside the loop are executed, counter X will hold the value 1.
♦ The second time the statements inside the loop are executed, counter X will hold the value 2.

---

[2] Actually, it is possible for the loop to terminate early as a result of executing an Exit Sub statement or an Exit For statement (see Section 7.3) inside the loop.

✦ The third time the statements inside the loop are executed, counter X will hold the value 3.

In contrast, when you see

Do While X < 3

at the top of a loop, you can only conclude that the statements inside the loop will be executed as long as X is less than 3. You'll have to look at statements above the loop to see what value X holds going into the loop (perhaps the loop statements will be executed 0 times), and you'll have to study the statements in the loop's interior to figure out how the value in X changes each time they are executed.

In some situations Do...Loop is appropriate and in others For...Next is appropriate. Choosing the correct one for each given situation will make your programs easier to understand and modify.

> **Convention** Use For...Next when the number of iterations the loop will perform can be determined at the time the loop is entered. Use a variation of Do...Loop only when the number of iterations the loop will perform depends on the results of executing the statements inside the loop.

As a more practical example of the use of For...Next, consider the following function, which we designed in Project 10. The function gives the user up to three chances to successfully log into an application. Accordingly, you will find a statement block (color) that occurs three times.

```
Public Function AuthorizeUser(ByVal ApplicationName As String) As String
    frmLogin.Caption = "Log in to the " & ApplicationName
    frmLogin.Show vbModal
    If ValidUserPassCombination() = True Then
        AuthorizeUser = frmLogin!txtUsername.Text
        Exit Function
    End If
    MsgBox "Invalid username/password combination", vbExclamation
    frmLogin!txtUsername.Text = ""
    frmLogin!txtPassword.Text = ""
    frmLogin.Show vbModal
    If ValidUserPassCombination() = True Then
        AuthorizeUser = frmLogin!txtUsername.Text
        Exit Function
    End If
    MsgBox "Invalid username/password combination", vbExclamation
    frmLogin!txtUsername.Text = ""
    frmLogin!txtPassword.Text = ""
    frmLogin.Show vbModal
    If ValidUserPassCombination() = True Then
        AuthorizeUser = frmLogin!txtUsername.Text
        Exit Function
    End If
    MsgBox "Invalid username/password combination", vbExclamation
    End
End Function
```

The function can be improved by using a loop, as follows:

```
Public Function AuthorizeUser(ByVal ApplicationName As String) As String
    Const MAXNUMBEROFATTEMPTS = 3
    Dim Attempt As Integer
    frmLogin.Caption = "Log in to the " & ApplicationName
    For Attempt = 1 To MAXNUMBEROFATTEMPTS
        frmLogin!txtUsername.Text = ""
        frmLogin!txtPassword.Text = ""
        frmLogin.Show vbModal
        If ValidUserPassCombination() = True Then
            AuthorizeUser = frmLogin!txtUsername.Text
            Exit Function
        End If
        MsgBox "Invalid username/password combination", vbExclamation
    Next Attempt
    End
End Function
```

The code is shorter and reduces the possibility of inconsistency. It is also easier to understand, because it clearly shows that the identical statement block is being performed three times; to be certain that this is true in the version without the loop you have to compare statements carefully.

If you look closely, you'll notice that in this modified version the text boxes on frmLogin are cleared before frmLogin is shown the first time. While not necessary, this doesn't hurt anything, either.

Example 7.9 Encryption

As another example of using loops, consider the problem of encrypting an entire string of characters. The form for this example has one text box (txtPlaintext), one command button (cmdEncryptMessage), and one Label control (lblCiphertext). The user enters a message in the text box and then clicks the command button, which encrypts the message and displays the result in the label.

Previously we created a function named Rotate() that "rotates" a capital letter by a specified number of positions in the alphabet. Function CaesarCipher() in Figure 7.19 takes a message as an argument, encrypts the entire message, and returns the ciphertext. It works by invoking function Rotate() repeatedly, one time for each letter in the message.

The For statement

```
For C = 1 To Len(Plaintext)
```

sets up the counter variable C to start at 1 and stop at the last character in the variable Plaintext. For example, if Plaintext stored "VISUAL BASIC", then the counter C would start at 1 and end at 12. Inside the For...Next loop, the Mid$() function is used to identify a single character. Thus, Mid$(Plaintext, C, 1) returns the single character at location "C" in the variable Plaintext.

EXERCISE 7.8

Modify Example 7.8 to display the numbers 1 through 10.

EXERCISE 7.9

Should the solution to Exercise 7.5 use For...Next or one of the variations of Do...Loop? Explain.

FIGURE 7.19

Code for Example 7.9

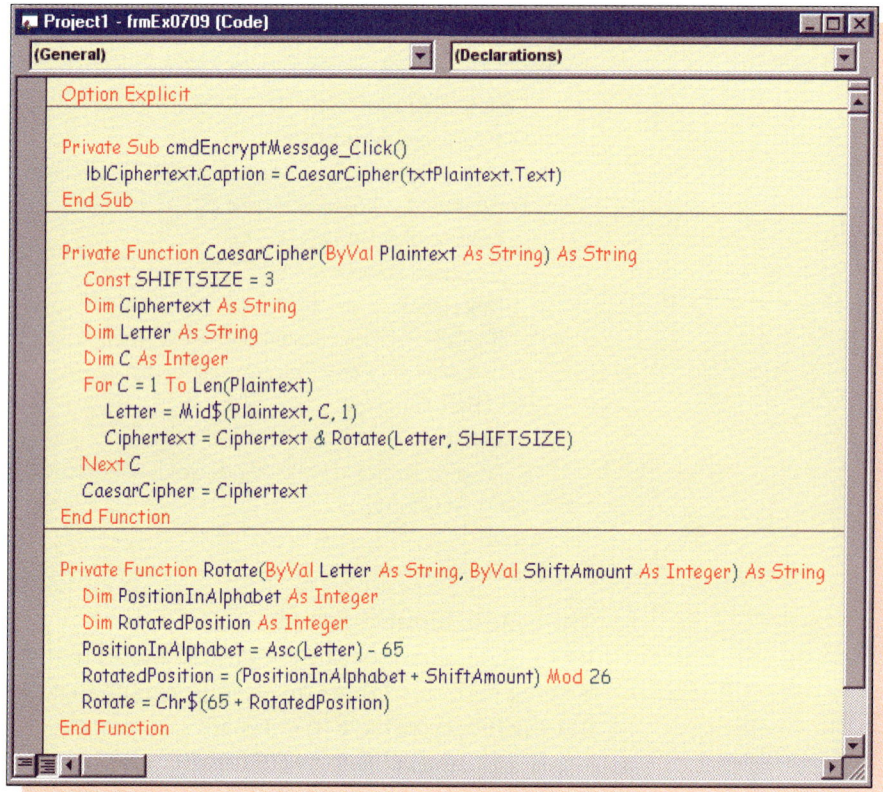

EXERCISE 7.10 Write a complete event procedure that simulates a coin-tossing experiment by performing the following tasks: First, ask the user to input the number of tosses. Then "toss a coin" that many times, counting the number that turn up heads. Finally, display a message box showing the fraction of tosses that turned up heads.

The Step Amount

The For…Next statement has a variation that allows you to specify the amount by which the Next statement increases the counter variable. Its syntax is

> **For** counter = start **To** end **Step** increment
>   statementblock
> **Next** counter

The action of this variation is the same as the For…Next loop described earlier, with the following exceptions:

◆ When the loop is first entered, the numeric expression *increment* is evaluated to arrive at the *step amount*.

◆ Each time the Next statement is executed, the computer increases the value stored in *counter* by the *step amount*, instead of by 1.

Thus, **by specifying a** *step amount,* **you can make the loop "count by 2s,"** or by 3s, by 1.5s, or by any other number.

Example 7.10

Using a Step Amount

Figure 7.20 shows an event procedure that displays the numbers 50, 60, and 70 in message boxes. The step amount is 10.

FIGURE 7.20

Code for Example 7.10

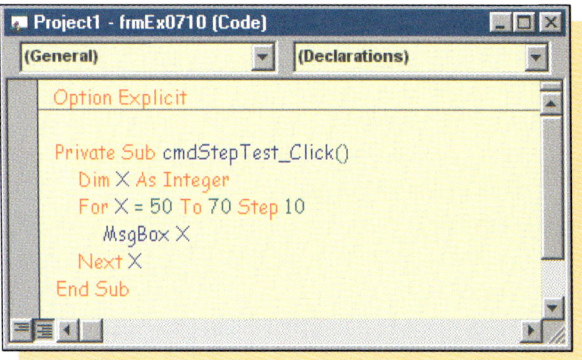

Negative Step Amounts

You can make the For…Next loop count backward by specifying a negative step amount. When the step amount is negative, For…Next changes its rule for deciding when to exit the loop. As before, when the For statement is executed, the computer compares the value stored in *counter* to the *ending value*. But when the step amount is negative,

- If *counter is greater than or equal to the ending value,* the computer executes the statements inside the loop.
- If *counter is less than the ending value,* the computer exits the loop.

That is, when the step amount is negative, the computer counts down from the starting value to the ending value. If the starting value is less than the ending value when the loop is first entered, the statements inside the loop will be executed 0 times.

Example 7.11 **Using Negative Step Amounts**

As an example of negative step amounts, Figure 7.21 shows an event procedure that counts backward from 30 to 0 by 5s.

EXERCISE 7.11 Modify Example 7.8 to display the even numbers from 2 to 20 (i.e., 2, 4, 6, 8, . . ., 20). Then modify Example 7.8 to display the even numbers from 20 down to 2 (i.e., 20, 18, 16, . . ., 2).

FIGURE 7.21

Code for Example 7.11

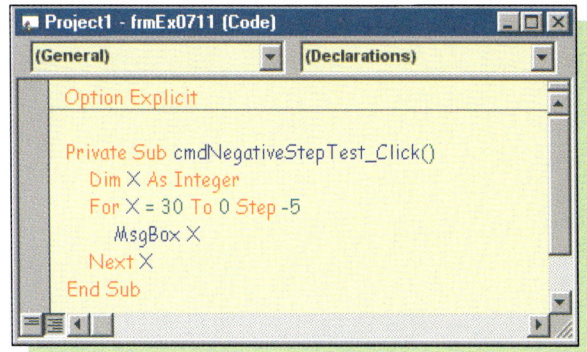

EXERCISE 7.12 What values are displayed by the following event procedure? Explain.

```
Private Sub cmdAnnoyingLoop_Click()
    Dim N As Integer
    Dim StartVal As Integer
    Dim EndVal As Integer
    Dim StepAmount As Integer
    StartVal = 1
    EndVal = 10
    For N = StartVal To EndVal Step StepAmount
        MsgBox N
    Next N
End Sub
```

Avoiding For…Next Errors

A programmer must understand exactly how the For…Next loop executes to code a loop that will execute properly. It is possible to add statements to the loop body that will alter the loop's execution and produce unintended results. We discuss these pitfalls here.

Programmers who forget that the *start*, *end*, and *increment* expressions are evaluated only when the loop is first entered might try to modify one or more of these values in the loop body. For example, the programmer might try to change the end value in order to stop the loop. However, this will not work.

Example 7.12 ### For…Next Initializations

This example, shown in Figure 7.22, demonstrates the action of the For…Next loop and its initialization operation. It looks as if the assignment statements inside the loop will make the loop counter, N, run through the values from 100 to 200 by 10s. However, this is not what happens when the loop executes. The loop will display the values 1, 2, and 3, because its initialization operation is performed only once, when the loop is first entered. At the time this loop is

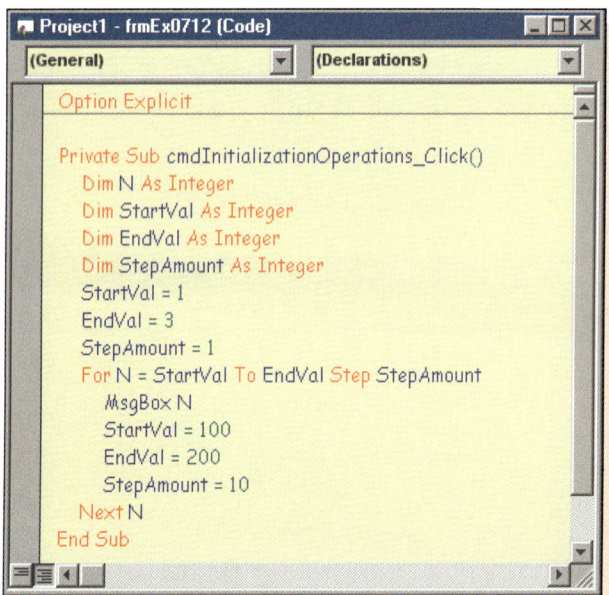

FIGURE 7.22
Code for Example 7.12

first entered, the *start* expression evaluates to 1, the *end* expression evaluates to 3, and the *increment* expression evaluates to 1.

It is true that the assignment statements inside the loop will change the values stored in the variables `StartVal`, `EndVal`, and `StepAmount`, but by the time these statements are executed the loop's initialization operation has already been performed; the *starting value*, *ending value*, and *step amount* used by the loop no longer have any connection to these variables.

To avoid confusion, do not place statements inside the loop that change the values stored in variables appearing in the *start*, *end*, and *increment* expressions.

Another potential problem arises from the fact that it is possible to include statements inside the loop that change the value stored in the *counter* variable. Unlike Example 7.12, where the *starting value*, *ending value*, and *step amount* cannot be changed within the loop, the value of the counter variable can be changed (but you should not do it).

Example 7.13 — Changing the Counter Variable

The code in Figure 7.23 illustrates the confusion that can result when a statement that changes the value stored in the *counter* variable is included inside the loop. Can you predict what values this code will display?

Upon seeing the following statement:

For N = 1 **To** 10

the programmer wants to believe that the loop will be executed 10 times, with the loop variable starting at 1 and increasing by 1 each time the loop is executed. But the statement

N = N + 3

inside the loop increases N by 3 each time the loop is executed. The loop itself increases N by 1 each iteration, so the net effect is to increase N by 4 each iteration. The loop displays the values 1, 5, and 9. This is very deceptive and probably not what the programmer intended.

> **Rule** Never include a statement in the interior of a For…Next loop that changes the value stored in the loop's *counter* variable.

FIGURE 7.23

Code for Example 7.13

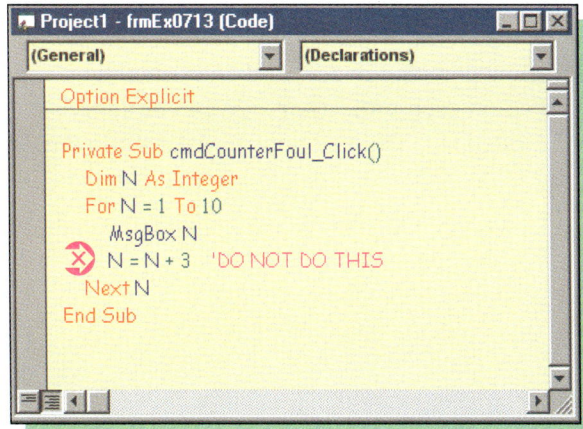

If you want to do something tricky like this, you should use one of the variations of Do…Loop instead of For…Next. Since the Do…Loop structure does not automatically initialize or increment any variables, you don't have to worry about "deceiving" yourself or other programmers who read your Do…Loop code.

7.3 Exit Do and Exit For

Occasionally the statements in the interior of a loop make a decision for which the appropriate action is to exit the loop immediately. For such situations VB provides the Exit Do and Exit For statements.

The *Exit Do statement* **is used inside a Do…Loop structure to cause execution to jump to the statement following the Loop statement.** Similarly, the *Exit For statement* **is used inside a For…Next loop to cause execution to jump to the statement following the Next statement.** The Exit For statement is illustrated in Example 7.14.

Example 7.14 Using Exit For

Let us modify the guessing game so that it generates a random integer between 1 and 127, then gives the user up to seven tries to guess it. After each guess the procedure should inform the user whether the guess was correct, too high, or too low. With this modification, the user should be able to arrive at the right value fairly quickly. Figure 7.24 shows one solution to this problem using a For…Next loop and Exit For.

If the guess matches the target, a congratulatory message is displayed. Then the Exit For statement is executed, causing the loop to terminate, and the If statement following the loop is executed. Note that this If statement is executed regardless of whether the loop terminated normally (after seven iterations) or early via the Exit For. That is why the If statement checks whether Guess <> Target. If this condition is True, then the loop must have terminated normally after seven iterations, which means that the user did not guess correctly in seven tries.

7.4 Nested Loops

Often the statements in the interior of one loop include another loop. **Loops embedded inside other loops are called *nested loops*.** We might use nested loops in payroll processing. The outer loop would process employees (one iteration per employee), and the inner loop would accumulate the hours worked on each project for a given employee.

Nested Do While…Loops have the following structure (the nested loop is color):

    Do While *condition1*
        statementblock1a
        Do While *condition2*
            statementblock2
        Loop
        statementblock1b
    Loop

FIGURE 7.24

Code for Example 7.14

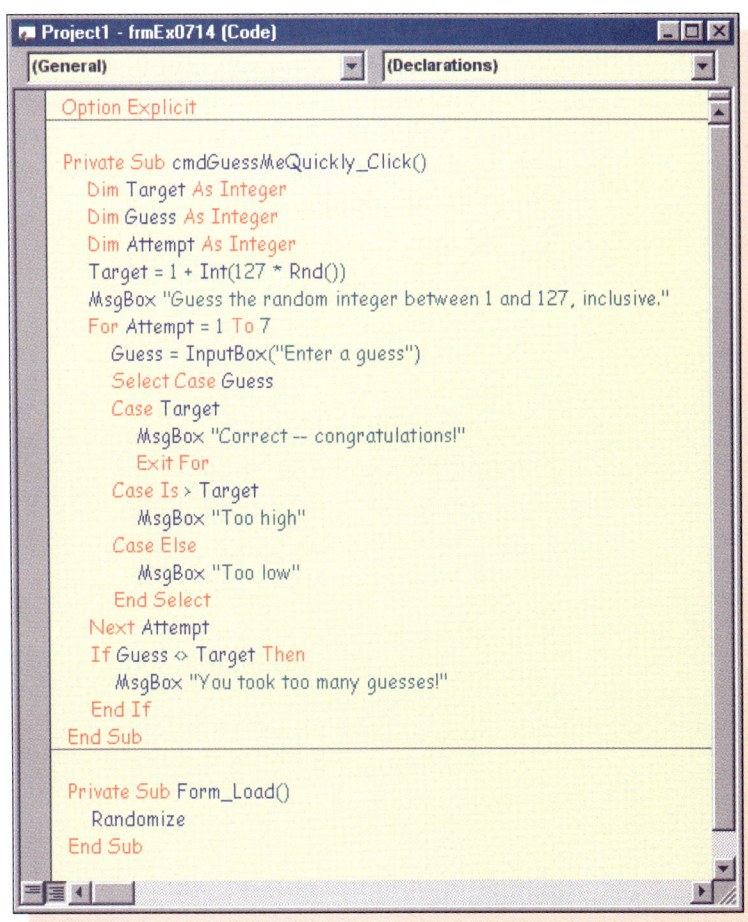

Note that the Do statements and the Loop statements occur in matched pairs. The inner Loop statement belongs to the inner Do statement, and the outer Loop belongs to the outer Do. Therefore,

◆ When the inner Loop statement is executed, it causes execution to jump up to the inner Do statement (its partner). When the outer Loop statement is executed, it causes execution to jump up to the outer Do statement (its partner).

◆ When the inner Do While's condition causes the computer to exit the inner loop, execution jumps to the statement following the inner Loop statement. Similar behavior holds for the outer Do While.

As with embedded Ifs, indentation is very important to the readability of your code. The "L" in Loop should line up vertically with the "D" in the Do it belongs to, and the statements in the interior of the loop should be indented.

A procedure may have two loops, one of which entirely precedes the other. In this case, the loops are not nested. This is shown below.

Do While *condition1*
    statementblock1
Loop
. . .
Do While *condition2*
    statementblock2
Loop

In nested For...Next loops, as in nested Do...Loop statements, the For statements and Next statements occur in matched pairs. This is readily apparent in For...Next loops because the same counter variable name appears in both the For and its partner Next. You cannot use the same counter variable for both the outer and inner loop. Nested For...Next loops have the following structure (the nested loop is color):

For *counter1* = *start1* **To** *end1*
   statementblock1a
     For *counter2* = *start2* **To** *end2*
       statementblock2
   Next *counter2*
   statementblock1b
Next *counter1*

Note that whenever loops are nested, one of the loops is inside the other. It is not possible for the loops to "cross" each other. That is, the following is not valid:

For *counter1* = *start1* **To** *end1*
   statementblock1a
     For *counter2* = *start2* **To** *end2*
       statementblock2
   Next *counter1*
     statementblock1b
Next *counter2*

Example 7.15 Using Nested Loops

The procedure in Figure 7.25 shows an example of a nested For...Next loop. Remember that each loop behaves just like the previous examples. Try to predict what the event procedure will display.

The outer loop starts to execute with X equal to 1. While this loop is executing, the inner loop starts to execute. Since X equals 1, the inner For loop is actually

For Y = 1 **To** 1   'because X = 1 at this point

The inner loop performs one iteration.

FIGURE 7.25

Code for Example 7.15

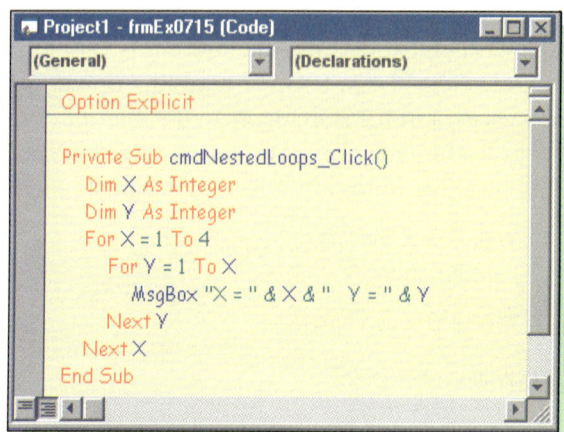

When the inner loop terminates, the Next X statement is executed. This changes X to 2 and the outer loop repeats. The inner loop now starts over. Since X equals 2, the inner For statement is now actually

For Y = 1 To 2   'because X = 2 at this point

This time the inner loop performs two iterations, with values of 1 and 2.

This process continues for X equal to 3 and X equal to 4. It is important to note that the inner loop always starts over for each iteration of the outer loop.

7.5 The List Box and Combo Box Controls

We now turn our attention to the GUI and two VB controls that are often associated with loops. We first present a basic description of each control, and then describe how they can be combined with loops for processing.

So far, all the controls we have encountered have displayed at most one value at a time. For example, the text box has a single property (the Text property) for storing and displaying information. Even if the text box has multiple lines, all these lines are associated with the single Text property. Labels are similar. The List and Combo box controls are different in that they can reference multiple text values.

You see this type of list when you open a file in any Windows application: the File Open dialog box presents you with a list of files and a list of directories that you can scroll through and use to select a file and directory.

The List Box

To design a user-friendly GUI you might want to **display a list of items from which the user makes a selection, and the** *List box control* **makes this easy.** For example, you might present the user with a list of state abbreviations. After the user selects a state, the program then uses it in further processing.

Appearance and Use

A list box appears as a rectangle that displays rows of text. Each row is an item that the user may select. If the number of rows is too large to fit within the rectangle, VB automatically provides a vertical scroll bar on the right side of the list box. Figure 7.26 identifies the List box tool and shows a List box control on the form at design time. At run time, the user selects an item by clicking on it with the mouse or by pressing an arrow key when the list box has the

FIGURE 7.26

List box tool and control

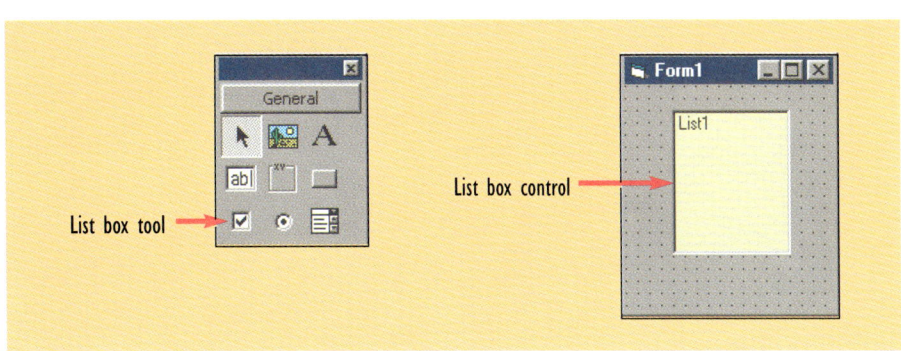

FIGURE 7.27

List box with item selected

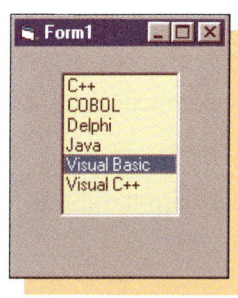

focus. VB automatically highlights the currently selected item. An example of a list box at run time is shown in Figure 7.27.

List boxes can be used both as a means of obtaining input from the user and as a means of providing output to the user. For example, the list box in Figure 7.27 may be presenting the user with the names of programming languages being researched.

Properties

Some properties of the List box control are shown in Table 7.1. As you scan this table you may find that some of the descriptions are difficult to understand. Some of the list box's properties are moderately complex, and we will illustrate them with examples.

> **Convention** Use the prefix "lst" for the names of List box controls.

Events

A user typically interacts with a list box as follows: The user first gives the list box the focus by tabbing to it or clicking the mouse on an item in it. Then the user presses arrow keys or uses the mouse to move the highlight to—that is, to select—a desired item. Finally, the user initiates some processing step involving the selected item.

Typically, the DblClick event, which occurs when the user double-clicks on an item in the list box, initiates processing of the selected item. The Click event cannot be used effectively for this purpose because it occurs every time the selected item changes; that is, pressing an arrow key as well as clicking the mouse causes the Click event to occur.

While the most common event used for a list box is the DblClick event, the List box control is also capable of responding to other events, such as KeyPress, GotFocus, and LostFocus.

Methods

Three methods—AddItem, RemoveItem, and Clear—are often used with the List box control. **The *AddItem* method adds a new item to the end of a list box.** The syntax is

lstboxname.**AddItem** *TextOfItem*

where *TextOfItem* is a string expression. **The *RemoveItem* method deletes a specific item from the list box.** The syntax is

lstboxname.**RemoveItem** *Index*

TABLE 7.1 Properties of the List box control

Property	Specifies
ListCount	*The number of items currently in the list box.* This property is not available at design time. At run time, VB automatically updates the value of this property whenever an item is added to or removed from the list.
ListIndex	*The number (position in the list) of the currently selected item, if any.* This property is not available at design time. At run time, VB automatically updates the value of this property whenever the user changes the selected item. If a program statement changes the value of this property, then VB moves the highlight to the corresponding item in the list. The positions of items in the list are numbered in increasing order, from 0 (at the top) to ListCount−1 (at the bottom). If no item is selected, then VB sets ListIndex to −1. Similarly, if a program statement changes the value of ListIndex to −1, then VB removes the highlight (as a visual cue that no item is selected).
Text	*The text of the selected item, if there is a selected item.* This property is automatically updated by VB at run time. If no item has been selected, this property is the zero-length string. Read-only at run time.
Sorted	*Whether or not VB will automatically maintain the list in sorted order.* If so, the sort is according to the ANSI collating sequence, but case of letters is ignored. This property cannot be changed at run time.

MultiSelect	*Whether only one item can be selected at a time, or multiple items can be selected.* All selected items will be highlighted. Possible values of MultiSelect are
	
	    0 - None. Only one item can be selected at a time.
	
	    1 - Simple. Multiple items can be selected. The items can be scattered throughout the list box. The user toggles an item between selected and deselected by clicking on it or by pressing the space bar.
	
	    2 - Extended. Multiple items can be selected. The items may form a contiguous range (no gaps). The user selects the range by dragging the mouse from the item at one end of the desired range to the item at the other end of the desired range. Alternatively, the user can click on the first item of the range and then [SHIFT]+click on the last item. All items between and including the first and last of the range will be selected. To select noncontiguous items, the user can [CTRL]+click to select/deselect an item.

List	*The individual values in each row of the list box.* The List property is VB's internal data representation of the items the user can see in the list box. Each row in the list box is a separate item in the List property. Can be read or written to (changed). To enter values at design time, select the List property and click on the down arrow in the settings box; then type a line and press [CTRL]+[ENTER] to prepare for entering the next line. If you just press [ENTER] at the end of the line, the list of items will close and you will have to open it again by clicking on the down arrow.
Selected	*Whether an individual item in the list box has been selected.* The Selected property has one entry for each item. The entry has a value of either True or False. The entry is True if the corresponding item has been selected and False if it has not been selected. This is useful when the MultiSelect property is set to 1 or 2 (the ListIndex property suffices if MultiSelect is 0). Available only at run time.

Style	Whether each item has a checkbox next to it. Possible values of Style are
	
	    0 - Standard. The items in the list box are shown without checkboxes next to them.
	
	    1 - CheckBox. A checkbox is shown to the left of each item in the list box. MultiSelect must be set to 0 - None in order to use the checkbox style. When the user clicks on a checkbox, the ItemCheck event procedure executes. This procedure includes a parameter (Item) that indicates which item was clicked (with the first item numbered as item 0). The checkmark toggles off and on as the user clicks on the same item multiple times.

where *Index* is a numeric expression indicating the number of the item to be removed. Items are numbered beginning with zero. Thus, to remove the first item, you would say

lstboxname.**RemoveItem** 0

The *Clear method* removes all items from the list box. The syntax is

lstboxname.**Clear**

Example 7.16 Using Methods with the List Box Control

This example illustrates the use of the list box's methods. Figure 7.28 shows the form at run time, just after the user has clicked the Add Items to List button. The code for this example is also shown in Figure 7.28.

Here are some things to try when you execute this example.

1. Click on Add Items to List. Then put the focus in the list box.

2. Change the item that is selected by pressing the ↑ and ↓ keys; then try pressing the A, B, C, and D keys (the first letters of items in the list box). The latter is a shortcut method of selecting items in the list based on the first letter of each item. What happens if you press B several times?

3. Click on Add Items to List several times, and observe the scroll bar that appears. VB automatically places the scroll bar on the list box when it is needed. Click on Clear List.

4. Click on Add Items to List, select an item, then click on Remove Selected Item. Try clicking on Remove Selected Item when nothing is highlighted; were it not for the If statement in cmdRemoveSelectedItem_Click, this would cause a run time error. As shown in Table 7.1, when no item is selected, the ListIndex property is set to –1.

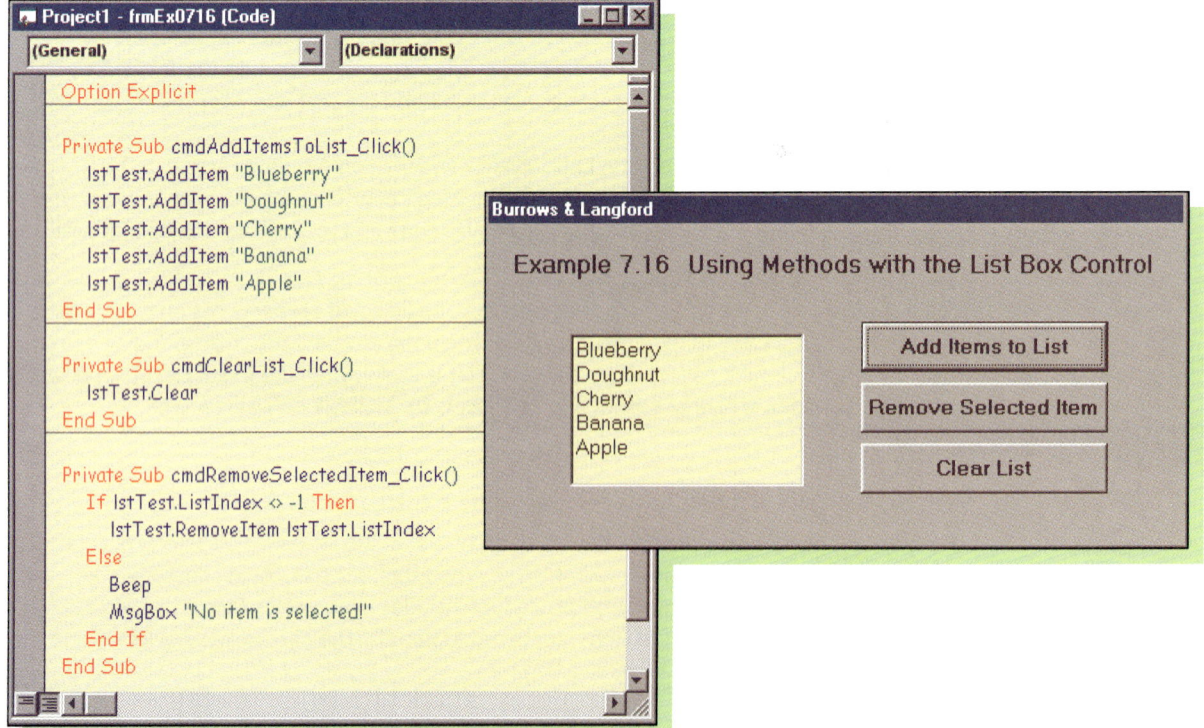

FIGURE 7.28 *Code for Example 7.16 and form at run time*

5. End execution, and at design time change the list box's Sorted property to True. Then run the example again. Click Add Items to List two or three times to see the effect. The order of the items in the list is determined by ANSI code sequence.

Example 7.17 Using the DblClick Event

This example illustrates how the DblClick event can be used to initiate processing of the selected item. It also shows how the KeyPress event can be used to allow the user to press [ENTER] as an alternative to double-clicking the mouse.

The example employs two list boxes. Figure 7.29 shows the application at run time. In this figure, the user has double-clicked on Cherry in List A and it has been copied to List B. The code for this example is also shown in the figure.

Here are some things to try when you execute this example.

1. Click on Add Items to List A. Then double-click on an item in List A and observe the effect. Then select an item in List A, press [ENTER], and observe the effect.

    The lstTestA_DblClick event procedure causes the selected item in List A to be added to List B. The lstTestA_KeyPress event looks for the [ENTER] key (*vbKeyReturn* is equal to 13, the ANSI code for *cr*), and if it finds it, calls the lstTestA_DblClick event procedure.

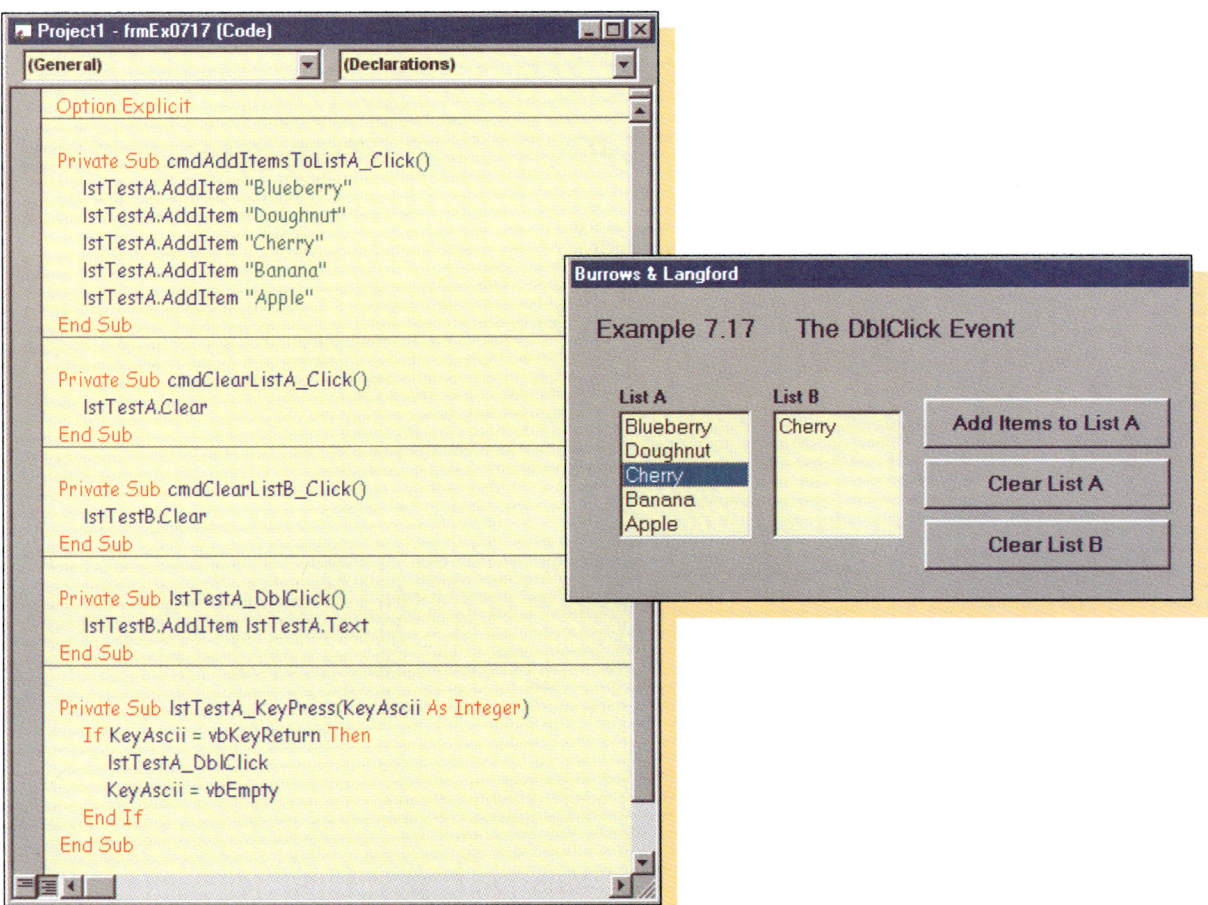

FIGURE 7.29 *Code for Example 7.17 and form at run time*

362 CHAPTER 7 Repeating Processing Tasks

2. Press either the ↑ or ↓ key to change which item is selected in List A. Then press the TAB key to move the focus to List B.
3. Press either the ↑ or ↓ key to change which item is selected in List B. Then press TAB to move the focus back to List A.

Observe that both list boxes can have a selected item at the same time, but only one list box can have the focus at any given time.

Example 7.18 Entering List Box Items

This example demonstrates one way of allowing the user to enter items into a list box. First the user enters values in two text boxes: txtName and txtAddress. Then the user clicks on Add to List, which concatenates the entered values and adds the result to the list box. Figure 7.30 shows the application at run time, just after a name and address have been placed in the text boxes and the Add to List button has been clicked. The code for this example is also shown in the figure.

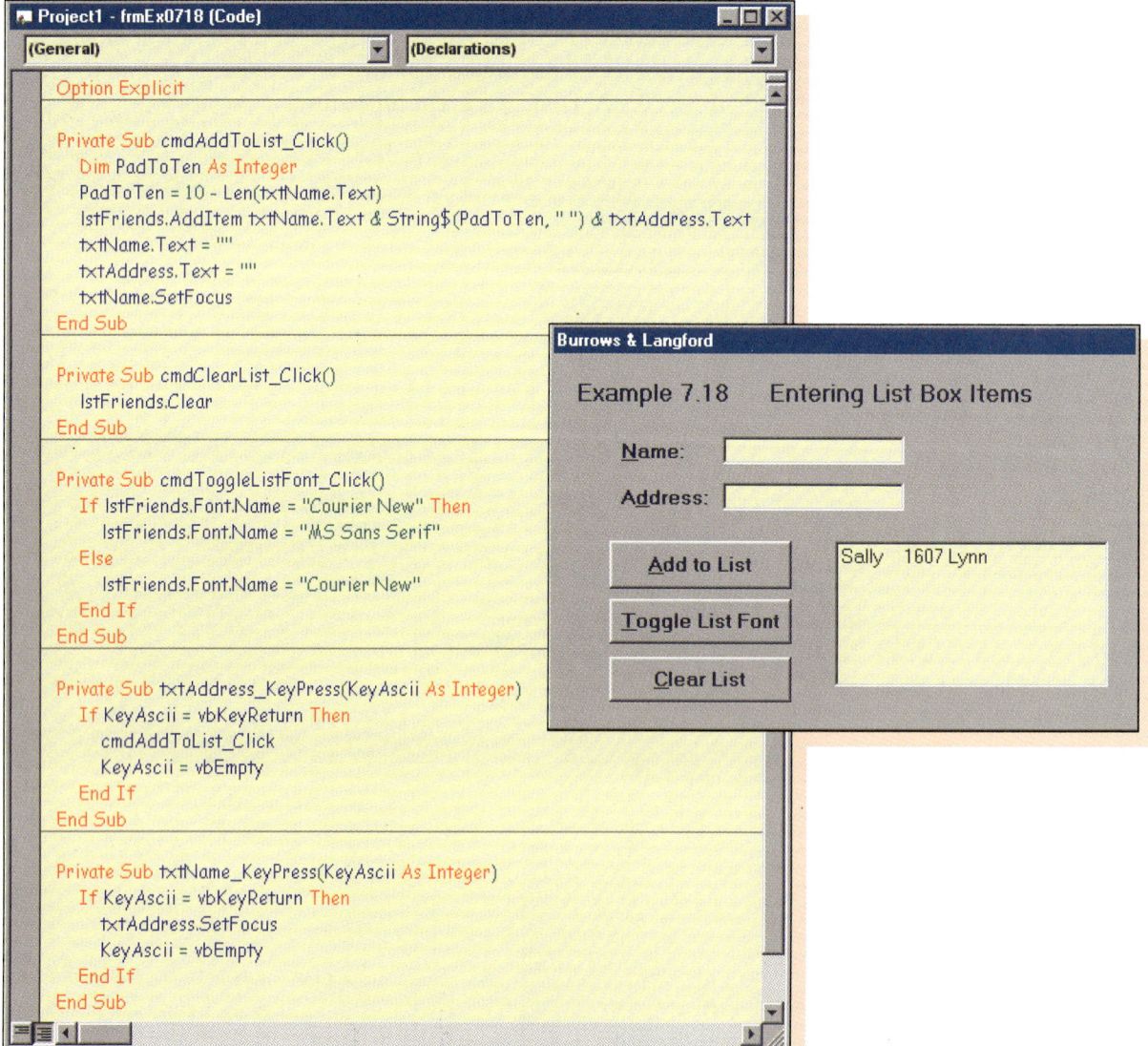

FIGURE 7.30 Code for Example 7.18 and form at run time

Although you cannot tell from the code, the MaxLength property of the two text boxes is set to 10 so that the user cannot enter a name or address longer than 10 characters. Note that cmdAddToList_Click "pads" the name value with spaces (i.e., adds space characters to its end) to make it exactly 10 characters long before it concatenates it with the address value. This is done here to demonstrate proportional versus fixed-width fonts.

To observe how cmdAddToList_Click works

1. Enter the following short names and addresses into the list box:

Raul   123 Elm St
Cassandra   5100 Main
Ed   18 N 53 St
Janet   53 NW 35th

2. Click the Toggle List Font button two or three times, and observe the effect.

Event procedure cmdToggleListFont_Click toggles the font used by the list box between Courier New and MS Sans Serif.[3] The results are shown in Figure 7.31. As you can see in the figure, one of the fonts causes the text to line up neatly and the other does not. The difference is caused by the width of the letters in the fonts. Some fonts (notably Courier) are *fixed-width,* **which means that every character is the same width:** an "i" is as wide as an "m" in such a font. Other fonts (such as MS Sans Serif) are called *proportional,* **which means that each character is only as wide as it needs to be:** an "i" is much narrower than an "m" in such a font. You can sometimes use fixed-width fonts together with padding to improve the alignment of characters in a list box.

Example 7.19

Loops and List Boxes

This example illustrates one way in which loops are sometimes used in connection with list boxes. The program displays two list boxes. Figure 7.32 shows the application at run time, just after the user has clicked the Add Items to List A and the Copy List A to List B buttons. The code for this example is also shown in the figure.

Event procedure cmdCopyAToB_Click uses a For...Next loop to copy all items from List A to List B. This procedure deserves some explanation. Individual items in a list box are numbered beginning at zero. If there were five items in the list box, then its ListCount property would be 5, and the items would be numbered 0, 1, 2, 3, 4. This is

FIGURE 7.31

Fixed-width versus proportional fonts

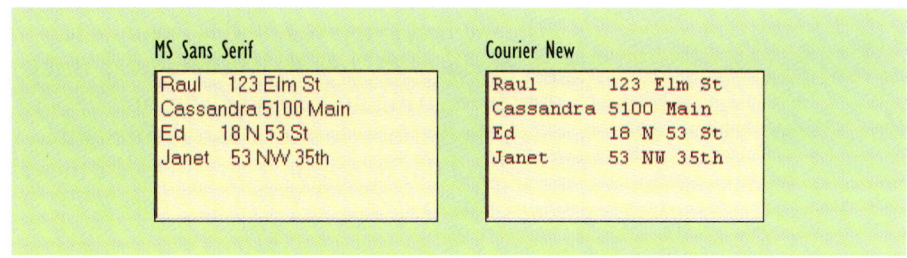

[3] In the code for cmdToggleListFont_Click, you will see the reference lstFriends.Font.Name; this syntax refers to the Name property of the Font object belonging to the list box. The Font object has additional properties, such as Bold and Size, that can also be manipulated in code. Objects, including the Font object, other predefined objects provided by VB, and programmer-defined objects are discussed in Chapter 10.

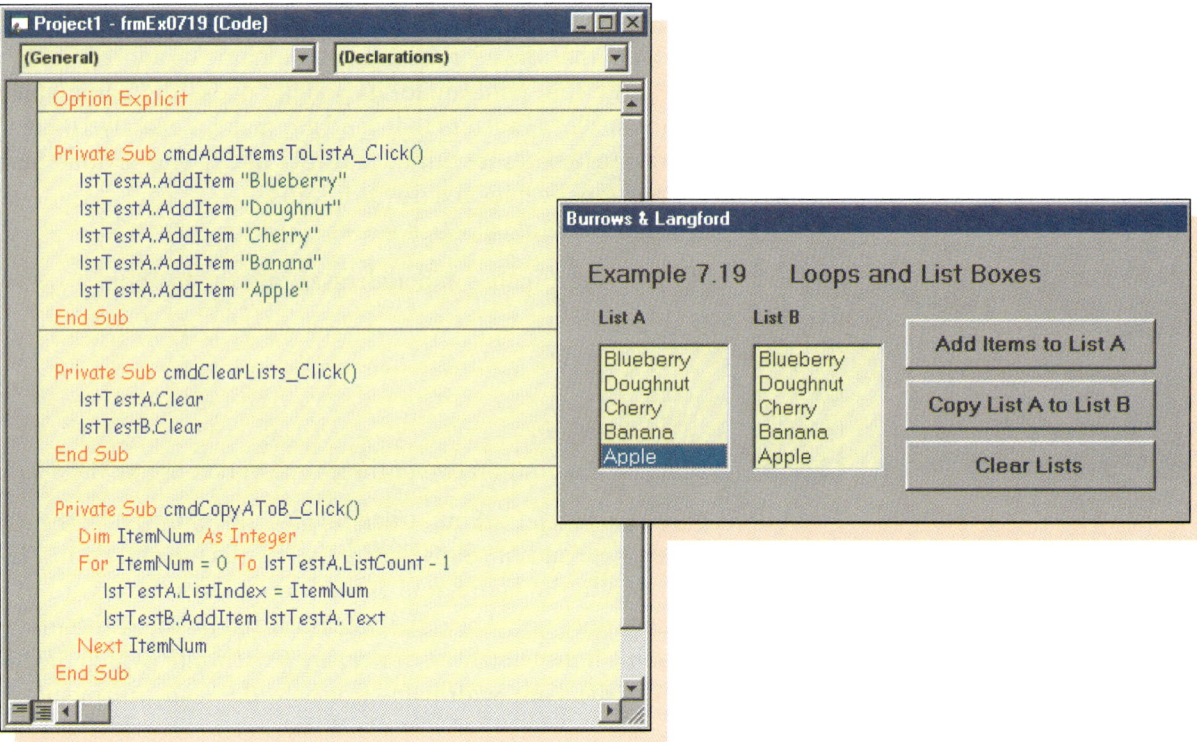

FIGURE 7.32 Code for Example 7.19 and form at run time

why the For statement goes from 0 to ListCount − 1. The first statement inside the For loop (lstTestA.ListIndex=ItemNum) selects the item specified by the value of ItemNum. (If ItemNum equals 2, then the third item in List A would be selected.) Selecting an item, in turn, causes VB to set the Text property of lstTestA equal to the text of the selected item. The second statement in the For loop takes this Text property and adds it to the other list.

Example 7.20 Decryption

This example is another illustration of using loops in conjunction with list boxes. Assume that someone has given us the string "PHWTHPHWTHIWT-NPAAUPAASDLC", which was produced by event procedure cmdEncryptMessage_Click (Example 7.9) with an unknown shift amount and with the spaces removed. If you were a code breaker, how could you recover the original message?

The method employed by this example uses the "brute force" method: it simply produces 25 "rotated" versions (all possible shift amounts from 1 to 25) of the given string and places them in a list box. Then the user can scroll through the list box to find the one intelligible version. Figure 7.33 shows the results of this operation. Can you locate the valid decrypted message? The code for this example is shown in Figure 7.34.

Example 7.21 Multiple Selections

This example demonstrates multiple selections and the List and Selected properties. As Table 7.1 shows, there are two settings of the MultiSelect property that allow for multiple selections. When multiple selections are made by the user, the program must determine which items the user has selected.

FIGURE 7.33

Result of executing Example 7.20

FIGURE 7.34

Code for Example 7.20

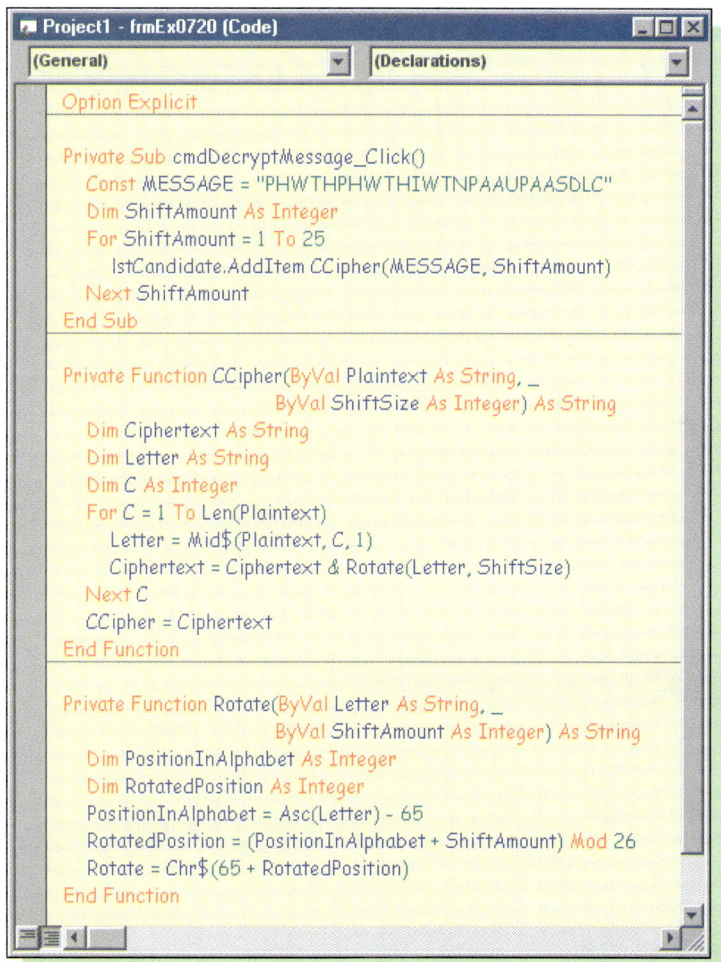

Suppose you are given the list box (lstStates) in Figure 7.35. This figure depicts the list box, its List property, and its Selected property. As you can see, the List property is actually five properties—one for each item in the list. This makes it possible to write code that manipulates (tests, changes, etc.) the individual items.

The Selected property also has one value for each item in the list box. A value of False means that the specific item has not been selected. Figure 7.36 shows the same list box with Washington and Hawaii selected. By scanning the Selected properties (0 through 4) and seeing whether they are True or False, the program can identify the selected items.

FIGURE 7.35

List box and associated properties for Example 7.21

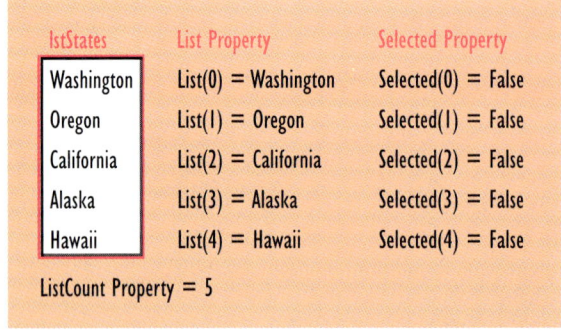

FIGURE 7.36

List box with two items selected

Figure 7.37 shows this example at run time. You can see that Washington, California, and Hawaii were selected in the list box on the left. When the user clicked the Copy Selected Items button, the selected items were copied to the list box on the right. The code for this example is also shown in the figure. The important procedure is cmdCopySelectedItems_Click. Its For loop controls the systematic scanning of the Selected property. The For loop is the appropriate type of loop because you know what the first value should be (0), what the last value should be (ListCount − 1), and the increment (1).

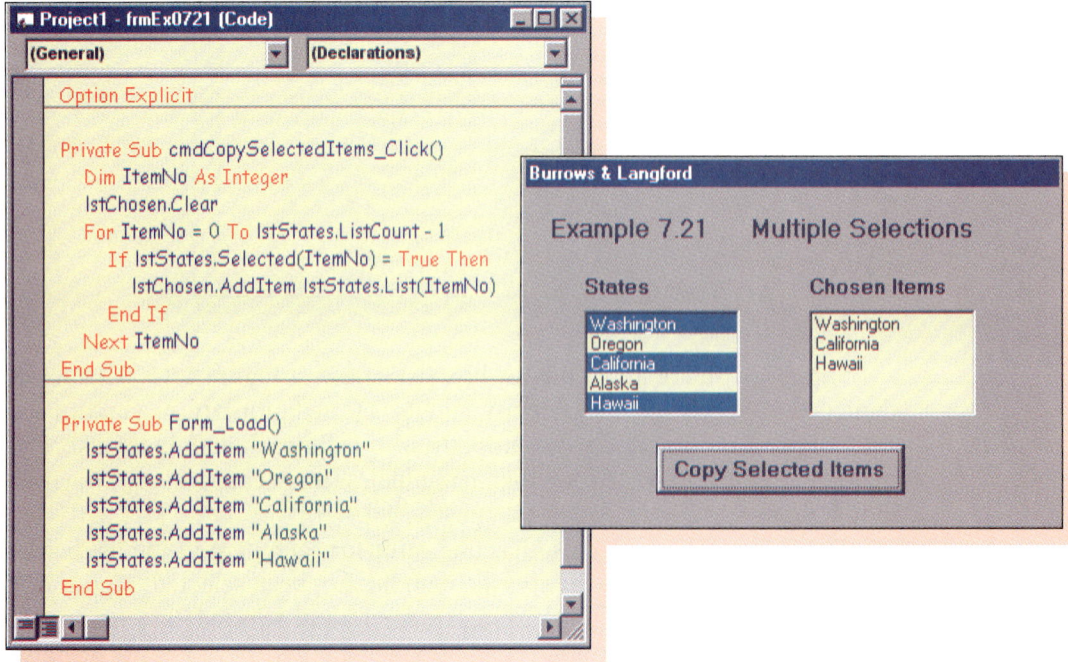

FIGURE 7.37 Code for Example 7.21 and form at run time

7.5 The List Box and Combo Box Controls

EXERCISE   Write GotFocus and/or LostFocus event procedures for the list boxes in Example 7.17 so that only the list box with the focus has a highlighted item. (That is, make it so that at most one of the list boxes has a highlighted item at any given time.)

EXERCISE   In Example 7.19 one of the items in lstTestA remains selected after the event procedure cmdCopyAToB_Click is executed. Which one? Modify Example 7.19 so that no item remains selected in lstTestA after cmdCopyAToB_Click is executed.

The Combo Box
◆ ◆ ◆

Many situations require the user to input a value that usually, but not always, comes from a predefined list of values. If the value does come from the predefined list of values, then we can save the user time and effort by providing a list box from which to select the value. If not, then we can provide a text box in which to type the value. **The *combo box* is a combination text box/list box that provides both a text box for entering the value and a list box of predefined values.**

Appearance and Use

Visually, a combo box appears as a thin text box next to a down arrow button. Figure 7.38 identifies the Combo box tool and shows a combo box on the form at design time. At run time, the user can click on the down arrow at the right of the control, which causes a list box to drop down (i.e., appear below the text box). The user can then select an item in this list. When the user makes a selection, by clicking the mouse or pressing [ENTER], the list box disappears and the value of the selected item is displayed in the text box. The user can edit the value in the text box if so desired. Alternatively, the user can simply type a value directly in the text box.

Properties

The Combo box control has many of the properties of the List box control, but it does *not* have a MultiSelect property. It also has some of the properties of the Text box control. The combo box's Text property holds the value displayed in its text box.

The **Combo box control's *Style property*** is described in Table 7.2. The three styles are shown in Figure 7.39.

> **Convention** Use the prefix "cbo" for the names of Combo box controls.

FIGURE 7.38

Combo box tool and control

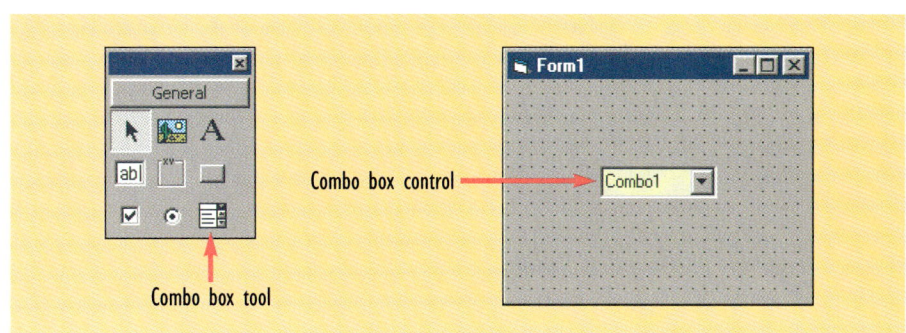

TABLE 7.2 The combo box's Style property

Property	Specifies
Style	*The style of the combo box.* Possible values are
	0 - Dropdown Combo. This style has a text box next to a down arrow. Clicking on the down arrow at run time causes a list box to drop down.
	1 - Simple Combo. The list box is always displayed below the text box at run time. For this style you must resize the combo box in order to see the list below the text box.
	2 - Dropdown List. This style is like the dropdown combo style except that the user cannot type in the text box; that is, the user can only select from the list box.

FIGURE 7.39

Examples of the dropdown Style properties

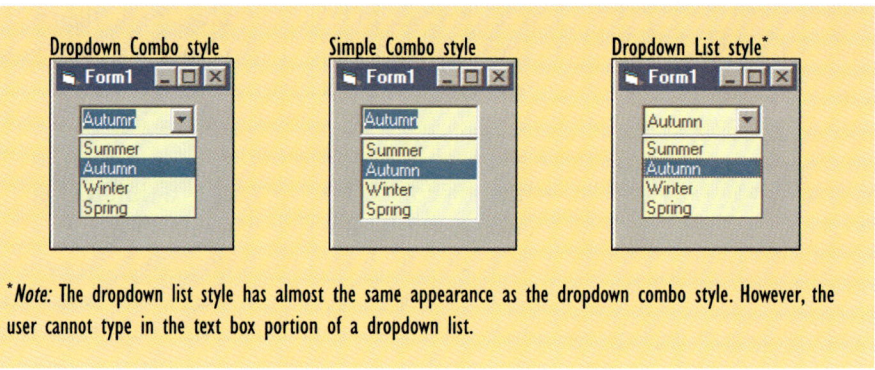

Note: The dropdown list style has almost the same appearance as the dropdown combo style. However, the user cannot type in the text box portion of a dropdown list.

Events

The Combo box control responds to the same events as the list box.

Example 7.22

Using the Combo Box

This example shows how you might use a combo box to supply the interest rate to a simple loan payment calculator. Figure 7.40 shows the application while it is executing. Notice that the combo box that shows the interest rate is dropped down for the user to make a selection. The code for this application is also shown in the figure. The Form_Load procedure uses a For...Next loop and the AddItem method to generate the interest rates and fill the combo box. Again, this is an ideal place to use For...Next loops.

The cmdComputePayment_Click procedure uses VB's built-in Pmt() function to compute the monthly payment. You may want to use online help (search phrase "Pmt") to get more information on this function.

The statement

    IntRate = Format(cboRate.Text, "general number")

takes the value from the text box portion of the combo box and stores it in the numeric variable IntRate. The Format() function with the "general number" format specification removes the "%" character from the text box value and makes it a legal number.

7.6 Project 11: Monthly Payment Schedule Application

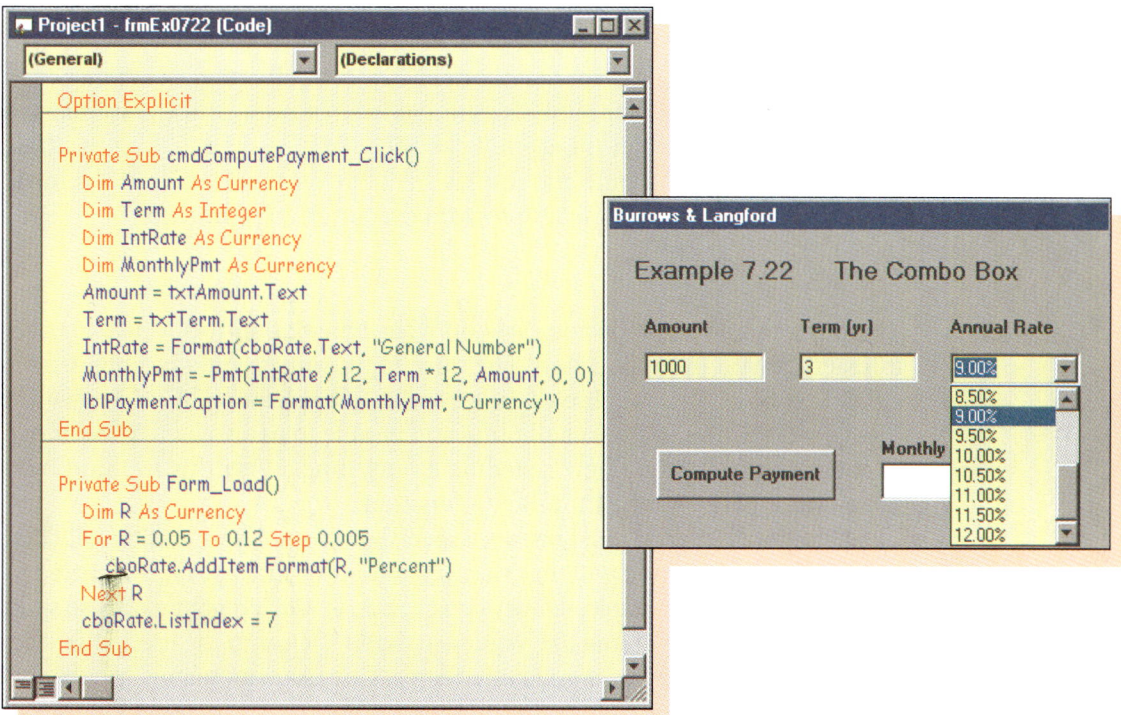

FIGURE 7.40 Code for Example 7.22 and form at run time

7.6 Project 11: Monthly Payment Schedule Application

When a customer borrows money from a lender, part of the contract includes a loan repayment schedule. The schedule shows the following: the monthly payment amount; the contribution of each payment to the principal (which reduces the loan balance) and to the interest; and the remaining loan balance at the end of the month. Many commercial financial software packages perform this type of calculation. However, the calculations are straightforward, so we can easily create our own. The user interface for our application is shown in Figure 7.41.

FIGURE 7.41

User interface for Monthly Payment Schedule application

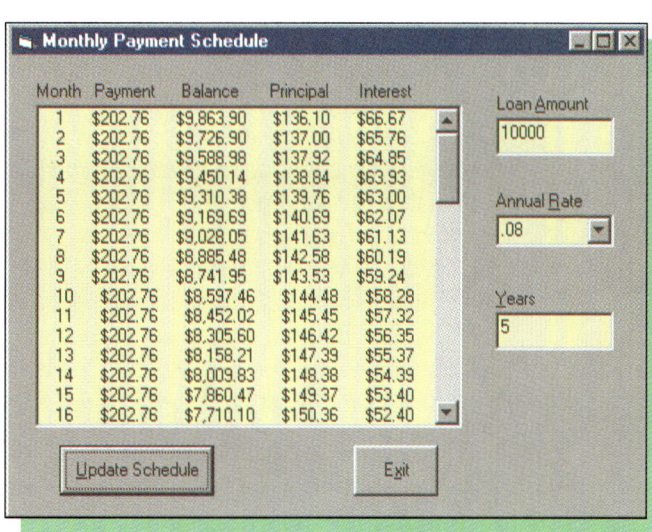

Description of the Application

From Figure 7.41 you can see that the application requires the user to first enter three values: the loan amount, the annual interest rate, and the number of years of the loan. When the user clicks the Update Schedule button, these values are used to compute and display the table on the left side of the form. Clicking the Exit button causes program execution to terminate.

Design of the Application

The programmer must decide early on what type of controls to use for user interaction with the application. The three input values could be obtained via either text boxes or input boxes. However, in an application like this we want the user to see these values at all times and be able to easily change one or two of them and generate a new schedule at any time. With this in mind, text boxes are superior to the InputBox() function.

The annual interest rate presents a special problem. Users traditionally find it difficult to determine whether they should enter interest rates as percentages or as rates. For example, do they enter 8, 8%, or .08? Programmers also seem to have a hard time wording the request so that it is clear to the user. These factors make the combo box a good alternative. The user can plainly see the format of the values. Our application, shown in Figure 7.41, expects the user to enter rates (e.g., .08). Another benefit of the combo box is that it provides a list of common rates, so the user may not need to type a number at all.

The payment schedule requires one line for each month. Thus we need a control that readily shows more than one line. The list box fulfills this requirement perfectly. The only additional effort required is the formatting of each line. As you can see from Figure 7.41, the alignment needs adjustment. You can fix this by using a fixed-width font and padding as shown in Example 7.18.

The only other user-interface consideration is the decision to place the column labels outside the list box. An alternative would be to place them in the first line of the list box, but if we do that they will not be visible to the user when scrolling down. This would make interpreting the columns difficult.

The main piece of coding required by the application is the event procedure for the Update Schedule button. Good names for some of the variables needed by the procedure are Years, LoanAmount, Rate, Payment, Balance, Month, MonthlyInterest, and MonthlyPrincipal. Pseudocode for the procedure follows.

1. Obtain values for Years, LoanAmount, and Rate from the appropriate controls on the form
2. Clear the list box
3. Compute Payment using VB's Pmt() function (discussed below)
4. Set Balance = LoanAmount
5. For Month = 1 To Years * 12
    5.1 Compute MonthlyInterest = Balance * Rate / 12
    5.2 Compute MonthlyPrincipal = Payment – MonthlyInterest
    5.3 Compute Balance = Balance – MonthlyPrincipal
    5.4 Add the month number (Month), the Payment, and the three computed amounts to the list box

VB has many built-in financial functions in addition to the payment function, Pmt(). You should take some time to become familiar with them. The Pmt() function has the following syntax:

Pmt(rate, nper, pv)

Rate is the periodic rate. Since our user specifies the rate as an annual rate, you need to divide this input value by 12 to get the monthly rate. *Nper* is the number of periods. Our user specifies the number of years, so you need to multiply this input value by 12 to get the number of months. *PV* is the present value, which in our case is the loan amount. You should enter this into the function as a negative number so that your payments will have a positive sign. Payments and PV always have opposite signs because they represent cash flowing in opposite directions.

Construction of the Application

The application is straightforward. Start by placing all the controls on the form and giving them appropriate names. Next, create the event procedure for the Exit button. Then compose the Form_Load event procedure to add the interest rate items to the combo box. Use a loop to generate the values (.05 to .15 in steps of .01). When the loop is done, set the ListIndex property to the interest rate you want displayed as the default.

Run the program and verify that the Annual Rate combo box contains the interest rate values, that your chosen default rate is selected, and that the combo box functions correctly. Next, create the event procedure for the Update Schedule button using the pseudocode presented earlier as a guide. Since this procedure does not share any data with other procedures, all variables should be local to the procedure. Your application should now be ready to run and test.

EXERCISE 7.15

As you can see from Figure 7.41, the vertical alignment of the values in the payment schedule needs adjustment (the alignment is particularly bad near the bottom of the schedule, which is not visible in the figure). Correct this by using a fixed-width font and either padding (as demonstrated in Example 7.18) or using the "@" format character (see online help using search phrase "user-defined formats" then select "User-Defined String Formats", from the See Also hyperlink). To keep your code clear, write a programmer-defined function that takes as input the five values to appear on one line of the schedule, and returns a single string value consisting of the five values, separated with padding spaces as necessary.

Chapter Summary

1. Loop structures are used to execute a group of statements repeatedly. Without loops, many types of problems could not be solved effectively.

2. There are two fundamental types of loops. In the first type, the number of iterations performed by the loop is unknown at the time the loop starts to execute. For this type of loop VB provides the Do…Loop structure and its variations. In the second type of loop, the number of iterations performed by the loop is known at the time the loop starts to execute. For this type of loop VB provides the For…Next structure.

3. Two variations of the Do…Loop structure are Do While…Loop and Do…Loop While. These structures continue to iterate "while a condition is true." The condition is any logical expression.

    The Do While…Loop and the Do…Loop While structures differ in where the condition is evaluated. In the Do While…Loop, the condition is evaluated at the beginning of the loop. If the condition is False initially, then the loop is terminated immediately—thus, it is possible for the loop to iterate zero times. In the Do...Loop While structure, the condition is evaluated at the end of the loop. Thus, the statements inside the loop will be executed at least one time.

4. Two other variations of the Do...Loop structure are Do Until...Loop and Do...Loop Until. These are identical to the While variations except that the condition used to control the loop is negated. For example, Do While X > 0 is equivalent to Do Until X <= 0. Whereas the Do While loop repeats "*while* a condition is true," the Do Until loop repeats "*until* a condition is true."

5. An important consideration of the Do...Loop variations is that the statements inside the loop must somehow change the values of the variables involved in the condition. For example, if the condition of a Do While loop is initially True, the loop starts to execute, and there must be a statement somewhere in the loop that can cause the condition to become False. Otherwise the loop will never stop iterating—it will be an infinite loop.

6. The For...Next loop structure uses a counter variable to control the number of iterations. When the For...Next loop begins to execute, it first sets its counter variable to a specified initial value. Before beginning each iteration, the loop compares the counter variable to an ending value. If the counter variable is greater than the ending value, the loop terminates. Otherwise, the body of the loop is executed. The loop then increments the counter variable by a specified step value, and the loop repeats as long as the value of the counter variable is less than or equal to the ending value.

7. Variations of the Do...Loop can be terminated early using the Exit Do statement. When this statement is executed, the loop is immediately terminated and execution continues with the first statement following the loop. Similarly, a For...Next loop can be terminated early using an Exit For statement.

8. The body of a loop can include another loop. In this case, the inner loop is called a nested loop. The nested loop operates independently of the outer loop and executes completely for each iteration of the outer loop.

9. The List box control provides a means of presenting the user with a list of items that can be selected. The selected item can then be used by the program in further processing. The programmer can use the MultiSelect property to specify whether the user can select only one item or several items from the list box. If multiple selections are to be allowed, the programmer can use the Selected and List properties to determine which items were selected and the values of those selected items. To do this, the ListCount property and a loop are used to systematically check the Selected and List properties one item at a time.

10. The Combo box control is a combination of a list box and a text box. Thus, it combines the capabilities of a list box—providing a list of items for the user to select—with a text box in which the user can type a value if the list of items does not include what the user wants.

Key Terms

AddItem method	combo box	CTRL+BREAK
Clear method	counter	Do...Loop structure

Do...Loop Until structure
Do...Loop While structure
Do Until...Loop structure
Do While...Loop structure
Exit Do statement
Exit For statement
exiting the loop
fixed-width font
For...Next structure
infinite loop
initialization
iteration
List box control
loop
loop body
nested loops
proportional font
RemoveItem method
step amount
Style property
termination condition

End-of-Chapter Problems

1. Study the following code segment (assume the variables have been declared appropriately).

   ```
   Sum = 0
   Count = 0
   Do While X < 100
      Sum = Sum + X
      Count = Count + 1
   Loop
   Average = Sum / Count
   ```

   What is wrong with this code? What needs to be done to fix it?

2. Explain the major difference between Do While...Loop and Do...Loop While. Can they be used interchangeably?

3. How are For...Next and Do While...Loop similar? How are they different?

4. Classify each of the following code segments as either "legal," "legal but not recommended," or "not legal." In all cases assume the variables have been declared appropriately.

   a.
   ```
   For I = 1 To 10
      I = I + 1
   Next I
   ```

   b.
   ```
   For J = 1 To N
      X = InputBox("Enter a value")
      S = S + X
   Next J
   ```

   c.
   ```
   For K = 1 To N
      For J = 1 To N
         MsgBox K & J
      Next K
   Next J
   ```

   d.
   ```
   For J = 1 To 10
      Do Until J > 5
         MsgBox J
      Loop
   Next J
   ```

5. How many times will the MsgBox statement in the following code be executed? Specify your answer as a formula if necessary.

   ```
   For J = 1 To N
     For K = 1 To M
       MsgBox "Count me"
     Next K
   Next J
   ```

6. Write a code segment that performs the following tasks: It should first ask the user to enter the number of items in a sales transaction. The code should then ask the user to enter the price and quantity sold for each item in the transaction set. It should sum the extended price (price times quantity) during this process. When all the items have been processed, the total price (the sum of extended prices) should be displayed to the user.

7. Consider the following code segment:

   ```
   For I = 1 To N Step X
     MsgBox I
   Next I
   ```

   Explain how the loop will behave if
   a. X is greater than 0.
   b. X is less than 0.
   c. X is equal to 0.

8. Assume you are presented with a situation for which Do While…Loop is appropriate. Could one use Do Until…Loop equivalently in this situation, without any qualifications? Explain.

9. Suppose you are given the list box depicted here, in which the name Ann is the currently selected item.

   a. What does lstNames.ListCount equal?
   b. What does lstNames.ListIndex equal?
   c. What does lstNames.Text equal?
   d. What does lstNames.List(2) equal?
   e. What does lstNames.Selected(3) equal?

10. What is the main difference between a combo box and a list box?

11. Explain how a list box typically reacts to a click and how it typically reacts to a double-click.

Programming Problems

1. A *check digit* is a value associated with an identifier such as a bank account number. The purpose of the check digit is to help detect errors in data entry, such as transposing two digits of the account number or entering the wrong digits.

The check digit is derived from the account number using a specific procedure, and is then appended to the account number. Subsequently, data entry personnel are required to enter both the account number and the check digit whenever the account number is needed. To check whether the account number was entered correctly, the check-digit calculation is recomputed using the entered account number, and the result is compared to the entered check digit. If they do not match, it is assumed that an error has been made in entering the account number.

For example, suppose that the account number is 436518, and the check digit calculation applied to it yields 6. Subsequently, data entry personnel enter the account number and check digit in the form 436518-6. If the account were entered incorrectly as 436618-6, the check digit calculation applied to 436618 would yield 2. Since the calculated check digit (2) is not equal to the entered check digit (6), the error would be detected.

There are several procedures used to derive check digits. The procedure just described is called the modulus-11 check-digit procedure. It works as follows:

a. Associate weights with each digit of the original number. The weights are the integers 2, 3, 4, ..., with the 2 being associated with the rightmost digit. For the account number 436518, the weights and their association with the digits are shown here.

Account No.	Weight
4	7
3	6
6	5
5	4
1	3
8	2

b. Multiply each digit times its weight. Sum these products.

Account No.	Weight	Digit × Weight	Sum
4	7	28	
3	6	18	
6	5	30	
5	4	20	
1	3	3	
8	2	16	115

c. Divide the sum by 11 and find the remainder. In this case, the remainder after dividing 115 by 11 is 5.

d. Subtract the remainder from 11. In this case, 11 − 5 = 6. This is the check digit. In the case where the result is 10, make the check digit an X; and in the case where the result is 11, make the check digit a 0 (zero).

Using this information, compose a programmer-defined function that takes an account number as a parameter, then computes and returns the check digit. To test your function, create a form that contains a text box, a command button, and a label. The user enters an account number in the text box and then clicks the button, which should invoke your check-digit function and display the check digit in the label.

2. Write a programmer-defined function that computes the factorial of a whole number. The factorial of a number, N, is defined as the product of the numbers from 1 to N. For example, 4 factorial (written as 4!) is defined as $1 \times 2 \times 3 \times 4 = 24$. Create a test form that allows the user to enter a number in a text box and click a button to request that the factorial be calculated. Display the answer in a label. Be aware that factorials get large quickly. Use data types that support large numbers, but be prepared for possible overflow errors.

3. Create an application that computes the future value of an investment at the end of each year. The user should be able to specify the initial amount, the interest rate, and the number of compounding periods per year. The interest rate should use a drop-down combo box with values ranging from 5 percent to 12 percent in 1 percent increments. Periods per year should use a simple combo box with 1, 4, 12, and 365 as the valid values. The user should also be able to specify the first and last year to be displayed. Use a list box to display the yearly values. A sample solution is shown here.

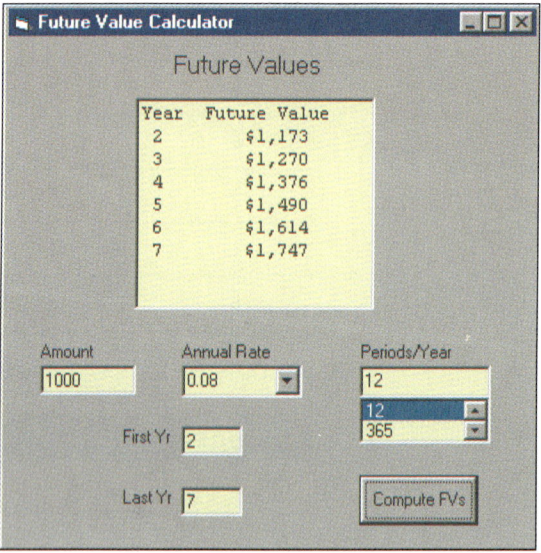

Use VB's built-in FV() function to perform the calculations. See online help for details on the use of this function. Note that in this application, the payment argument for the FV() function will be zero.

4. Create a depreciation calculator. Your calculator should be able to compute both straight-line depreciation and sum-of-the-years' digits depreciation (SYD). Use VB's built-in SLN() and SYD() functions to perform the actual calculations. Use option buttons to specify the depreciation method, a combo box to specify useful life, and text boxes for the remainder of the input parameters. Display your depreciation schedule in a list box. A sample user interface is shown at the top of page 377.

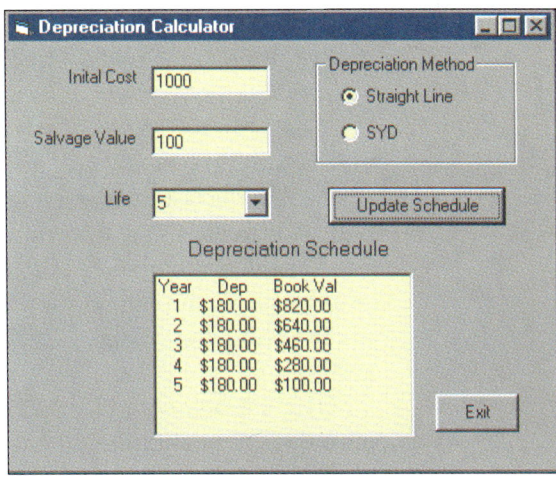

This year's *book value* is defined as last year's book value minus this year's depreciation. For year 1, use the initial cost as last year's book value.

5. Write a programmer-defined function that determines how long it will take for an investment amount to double in value. For example, if you invest $1000 today at a given interest rate, how many years will it take for the investment to equal $2000?

   The value at time period *t* can be calculated using the following formula:

   $$\text{Value}_t = \text{Value}_{(t-1)} * (1 + \text{InterestRate})$$

   Assume that compounding is performed annually. Therefore, the value returned by your function will be the first year in which the investment is at least twice as large as the initial amount.

   Create a test form that allows the user to enter an investment amount and an annual interest rate. Provide a command button that, when clicked, invokes your function to determine the answer, then displays the answer in a message box.

   Extra Credit: Write your solution so that it is not restricted to annual compounding. That is, let the user specify the number of compounding periods per year in addition to the other parameters.

6. Create a payment calculator. Your calculator should compute monthly payments for a loan calculated with a variety of different interest rates. A sample solution is shown here.

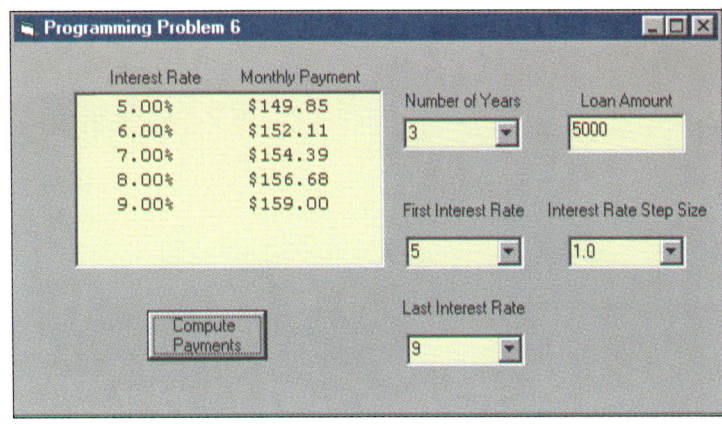

Your solution should use VB's Pmt() function. See online help (search phrase "Pmt() function") for help on using this function. Be aware that the Pmt() function requires decimal interest rates (e.g., 0.10 for 10%).

Your solution should also check to be sure that a loan amount is provided (the text box is not blank) and that the first interest rate is less than or equal to the last interest rate. If either of these conditions is not met, display an error message informing the user of the problem.

For the combo boxes, load the numbers 2 through 10 in the Number of Years list, 1 through 10 in the First Interest Rate list, and 2 through 12 in the Last Interest Rate list. Include Interest Rate Step Sizes of 0.1, 0.5, 1.0, and 2.0.

The list box should be cleared before a new set of payments is displayed. That is, do not add a new set of payment calculations to the end of the current set.

chapter

EIGHT

Accessing Business Data

Processing Databases

♦ ♦ ♦ ♦

The programs we have written so far have demonstrated VB's controls and programming language, as well as application design considerations and good programming techniques. But as business application programs they fall short because of their limited ability to access data. To get data into these programs we either included the data as part of the program itself, or we designed the program so that users could key in information. But the data that even a small business must process into reports, customer invoices, or employee paychecks are far too extensive to be coded into a program or to be rekeyed by a human every time the program is run.

The way to efficiently manage data is to store it in files on disk. The data files and program are separate. When the program is executed, the user provides the name of a file that contains data to be processed, and the program reads and uses these data. Since data files are not part of any program, they never appear in a VB project window. A data file simply exists on disk, ready to be used by any program that can correctly interpret its contents.

This practice is superior to making data part of the program for two reasons. First, the program need not be modified when the data change—only the data file needs to be modified. Second, different programs can share the same data files; this eliminates the need to replicate the data, and hence reduces data redundancy. Data redundancy has several negative effects, including excessive storage, the need to update data in more than one place, and the possibility that not all duplicate data items will get updated, resulting in inconsistent values for the same data item.

Managing large amounts of related data that are processed by different programs can be difficult unless the data and relationships are organized carefully. Most businesses achieve this by placing their data in a database. A *database* **is an organized collection of data describing entities (things) and relationships that exist between entities.** (Relationships and entities will be defined and discussed in detail in this chapter.) You can think of a database as a large data file on disk that contains related data organized in a particular way. An example of a noncomputer "database" is the phone book, which stores names, addresses, and phone numbers in a structured manner for many individuals; if you imagine such a list on a computer disk, you will begin to understand the arrangement and order of data in a database.

A business typically uses a program called a *database management system (DBMS)* to create and maintain a database, which contains the company's data. After the database has been created, many different programs can access the data it contains. Commercially available DBMSs include Microsoft Access and Oracle Corporation's Oracle.

Because databases are so widely used, VB provides tools for programmers to build database-access capability into their programs. In this chapter we explore some of these tools. To give you the background needed to understand how programs can work with databases, we begin with a discussion of database structure and use. We then turn to VB's Data control, which links a VB program and a database. Often programs require selective parts of a database, and VB's SQL Select query allows the programmer to specify the required data. Finally, we examine VB's FlexGrid and DBGrid controls, which allow programmers to display and modify data in a tabular form on the GUI.

We address two related topics in appendixes: Appendix D discusses how to create databases using Microsoft Access, and Appendix E discusses how to create and process nondatabase files using VB.

Objectives

After studying this chapter you should be able to

- Understand and use relational databases.
- Use the Data control to link a VB application to a database.
- Use bound controls to display and modify specific fields within a database.
- Use methods of the Data control's recordset to code sophisticated processing tasks.
- Write SQL Select queries to extract data from a database.
- Use the FlexGrid control to display information (including recordsets) in tabular form on the GUI.
- Use the DBGrid control to both display the contents of a database table and allow the user to edit the data in the database.

8.1 A Database Primer

The first step in writing programs that access data in a database is to understand how the database is arranged, and this section discusses these fundamentals. Since most databases in current use share a common structure, once you master the general principles you can quickly surmise what you need to know about any database in order to write programs that work with it.

Entities and Relationships

Every database contains two kinds of information:

1. *Entities*, which are any of the things of interest to a business and about which the business collects data, such as products, employees, suppliers, customers, purchases, and sales.

2. *Relationships*, which express real-world associations between entities. Examples of relationships among entities are products purchased by customers, and employees responsible for particular sales.

Because a database can include a large number of entities and relationships, database designers often use an *entity-relationship diagram (ERD)* to document a database's structure.

The simple ERD in Figure 8.1 shows three entities: Publisher, Title, and Author. The data stored about a Publisher might include a publisher identifier, name, and address. The data stored about a Title might include the International Standard Book Number (ISBN), title, and publisher. The data stored about an Author might include an author identifier, name, and year born.

A relationship is represented in an ERD by a line joining two entities. The symbols at the ends of the line show an important fact about the relationship: "how many" of the entity at one end can be related to "how many" of the entity at the other end. The term *cardinality* is used to describe **the number of one entity that can be related to another entity.** Figure 8.2 shows the cardinality symbols and their meanings.

To interpret a relationship appearing in an ERD, you must read it in both directions: once from left to right, and once from right to left. When you read from left to right, ignore the symbol at the left end of the line, and when you read from right to left, ignore the symbol at the right end of the line.

Let's interpret the relationship between Publisher and Title in Figure 8.1. When read from left to right, it means "a publisher can be related to zero or more titles." When read from right to left, it means "a title can be related to one publisher." Combining the interpretations from reading in both directions, we say that this is a *one-to-many* relationship. In the abstract language of the

FIGURE 8.1

Entity-relationship diagram

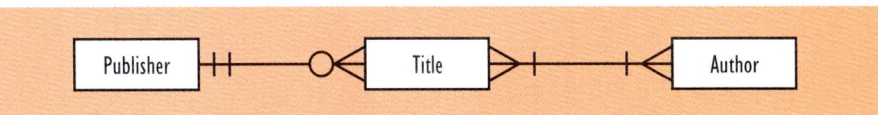

FIGURE 8.2

ERD symbols used to show cardinality

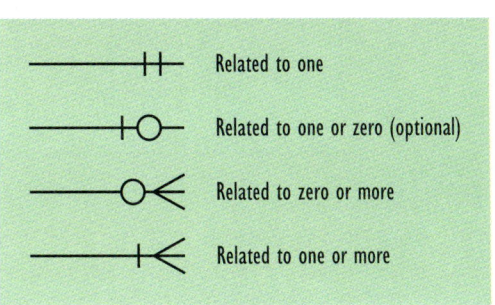

ERD, it says "one publisher is related to many titles and a title is related to one publisher." Common sense tells us that it expresses the real-world fact that any given publisher may publish many different titles, but any given title is published by a single publisher.

How about the relationship between Title and Author in Figure 8.1? When read from left to right it means "a title can be related to one or more authors." When read from right to left it means "an author can be related to one or more titles." This is a *many-to-many* relationship. The diagram indicates that any given title has at least one author (maybe more) and that any given author has written at least one title (maybe more).

Relational Database Tables

A database stores both the data describing the entities and the relationships that exist between the entities. Several approaches are used to store this information but the most common is the relational database. **A *relational database* stores the data for each entity in a table with rows and columns.** We use the relational database approach in this chapter because of its popularity and because it is compatible with Visual Basic.

Figure 8.3 shows an example table that stores data about the Author entity. Note the alternative terms for the parts of relational database tables. The columns in the table are called either *fields* or *attributes*. The rows are referred to as either *rows* or *records*.

Each table in a relational database can have **a *key field*, which consists of a specific field or combination of fields guaranteed to be unique from one row to another.** In the Author table in Figure 8.3, Au_ID is the key field. Thus, you would not see two rows in this table that have the same value of Au_ID. A key field that is a combination of two or more fields is called a *compound key*.

FIGURE 8.3

Author table in a relational database

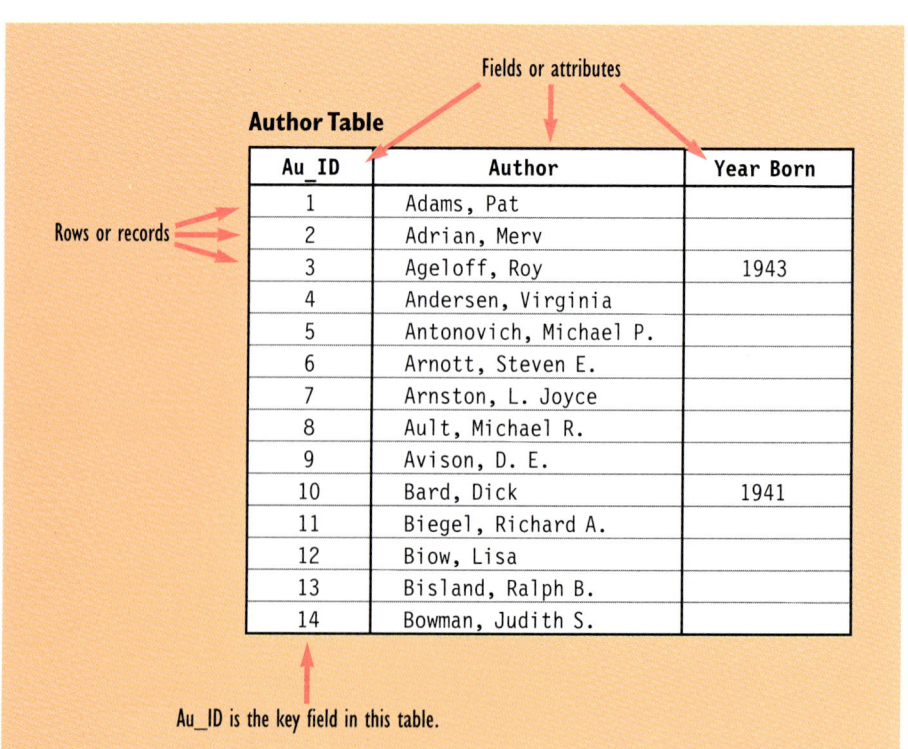

From the ERD in Figure 8.1 we know that the Author entity and the Title entity are related to each other. Observe in Figure 8.3 that the Author table contains only data about authors; specifically, it does not contain any data that establish the relationship between "authors" and their "titles." The way we store data about a relationship depends on the cardinality of the relationship. We will return to this issue shortly.

Figure 8.4 shows example data from the Publisher and Title tables.

Notice that the field PubId exists in both of these tables. In the Publisher table this field uniquely identifies the records; that is, each publisher has a different PubId. Therefore, PubId is the Publisher table's key field. In contrast, in the Title table you can see more than one title with the same PubId. The PubId field is a nonkey field in the Title table.

(a) Publisher Table

PubId	Name	Address	City	State	Zip
1	ACM	11 W. 42nd St., 3rd flr.	New York	NY	10036
2	Addison-Wesley	Rte 128	Reading	MA	01867
3	Bantam Books	666 Fifth Ave	New York	NY	10103
4	Benjamin/Cummings	390 Bridge Pkwy.	Redwood City	CA	94065
5	Brady Pub.	15 Columbus Cir.	New York	NY	10023
6	Computer Science Press	41 Madison Ave	New York	NY	10010
7	ETN Corporation	RD 4, Box 659	Montoursville	PA	17754-9433
8	Gale	835 Penobscot Bldg	Detroit	MI	48226-4094
9	IEEE	10662 Los Vaqueros Circle	Los Alamitos	CA	90720
10	Intertext	2633 E. 17th Ave.	Anchorage	AK	99508
11	M&T Books	501 Galveston Dr	Redwood City	CA	94063-4728
12	Macmillan Education	175 Fifth Ave	New York	NY	10010
13	McGraw-Hill	1221 Ave of the Americas	New York	NY	10020
14	Microsoft Press	One Microsoft Way	Redmond	WA	98052-6399
15	Morgan Kaufmann	2929 Campus Dr, Suite 260	San Mateo	CA	94403

(b) Title Table

Title	Year Published	ISBN	PubId
Guide to ORACLE	1990	0-0702063-1-7	13
The database experts' guide to SQL	1988	0-0703900-6-1	10
Oracle/SQL; a professional programmer's guide	1992	0-0704077-5-4	13
SQL 400: A Professional Programmer's Guide	1994	0-0704079-9-1	52
Database system concepts	1986	0-0704475-2-7	13
Microsoft FoxPro 2.5 applications programming	1993	0-0705015-3-X	61
First look at-dBASE IV, version 1.5/2.0 for DOS	1994	0-0705107-5-X	80
Applying SQL in Business	1992	0-0705184-2-4	13
Database design	1977	0-0707013-0-X	13
Introduction to Oracle	1989	0-0770716-4-6	13
SQL—the standard handbook; based on the new SQL standard	1993	0-0770766-4-8	52
Paradox; the complete reference	1988	0-0788139-0-5	13
Paradox	1988	0-0788140-4-9	13
Paradox made easy	1988	0-0788141-3-8	16
Using dBASE IV	1988	0-0788147-5-8	16

FIGURE 8.4 Some records from the Publisher and Title tables

One-to-Many Relationships

When one table's key field appears in a second table and is not the key field in the second table, it is called a *foreign key* in the second table. Foreign keys link, or associate, the rows in the two tables. Specifically, foreign keys implement one-to-many relationships. The relationship is established by placing the key field of the "one" entity's table into the "many" entity's table as a foreign key.

Study the placement of the key and nonkey fields in the Publisher and Title tables. The first row of the Title table shows a book titled *Guide to ORACLE* published in 1990 by PubId 13. Using this value for PubId, we search the Publisher table to find a match. We find the match at row 13 and discover that the publisher is McGraw-Hill. The common field (PubId) allows us to link the two rows of the two tables; we can then use the combined fields of both rows to produce reports or to answer user questions about books and publishers.

Since PubId is unique in the Publisher table, we would expect to find only one match when we search this table for PubId = 13. This agrees with the ERD, which showed that a title can be related to one publisher. But if we search the Title table for PubId = 13, we find many matches. This also agrees with the ERD, which showed that a publisher can be related to many titles.

Many-to-Many Relationships

We can also link tables to establish many-to-many relationships. If you scan the Author table (Figure 8.3), you'll see that it contains no information to associate it with the Title table. Similarly, the Title table (Figure 8.4b) contains no information to associate it with the Author table. Many-to-many relationships are *not* established by foreign keys. So how do we implement a many-to-many relationship? The answer is by constructing an entirely **new table, called a *correlation table*, or *intersection table*, which contains the key fields from both tables for the entities in the many-to-many relationship.**[1] Figure 8.5 shows such a table, named Title/Author.

FIGURE 8.5

Title/Author table used to support a many-to-many relationship.

Title/Author Table

ISBN	Au_ID
0-0131985-2-1	13
0-0238669-4-2	113
0-0280042-4-8	11
0-0280042-4-8	120
0-0280095-2-5	171
0-0702063-1-7	26
0-0702063-1-7	65
0-0702063-1-7	104
0-0703900-6-1	96
0-0704077-5-4	59
0-0704077-5-4	99
0-0704079-9-1	59
0-0704079-9-1	74
0-0704079-9-1	99

[1] Correlation tables are described in Sally Shlaer and Stephen J. Mellor, *Object-Oriented Systems Analysis: Modeling the World in Data* (Yourdon Press, 1988).

Verify the many-to-many relationship by looking down the ISBN column of the correlation table in Figure 8.5. Note that book 0-0702063-1-7 is associated with three authors (26, 65, and 104). Similarly, looking down the Au_ID column you can see that author 59 is associated with two titles (0-0704077-5-4 and 0-0704079-9-1).

Some correlation tables include additional data fields. These additional fields contain facts related to both entities. For example, in the Title/Author table we might want to store the royalties paid to each author for a specific book. In this way we could record different royalty amounts for each author/book combination. **A correlation table that includes additional fields beyond the two key fields is called an** *associative object.*

Normalized Databases

This text will not teach you to design databases. You will, however, have to write code to access data from databases, so you will encounter foreign keys, correlation tables, and associative objects. You may be curious as to how database designers decide where to place information. **The process of deciding what data goes into each table is based on the desire to eliminate or reduce potential problems, and is called** *normalization.*[2]

One problem that normalization solves is excess *data redundancy,* that is, storing the same information more than once in a database. For example, suppose you are storing employee addresses. Without proper planning, you might store this information once in a payroll table and again in a human resources table. Obviously this redundancy requires extra storage space, but more importantly, it can lead to data inconsistencies. If an employee moves and notifies the payroll office, payroll will correct the address. However, unless the payroll department notifies the human resources department, the old address may remain in the human resources table. Now there are two different addresses for the same person.

The precise process associated with normalization is beyond the scope of this text. However, a simple rule can be used to judge whether a table is in satisfactory form, known as *third normal form:* **a table is in** *third normal form* **if the nonkey fields depend on the key field, the whole key field, and nothing but the key field.**[3]

In a normalized database each nonkey field must be determined only by the key field. A table with Employee Number (key field), Employee Name, Department Code, and Department Name is not in third normal form because Department Name can be determined by the Department Code (which is not the key field). That is, if you know what the Department Code is, you can tell what department you are talking about, so you know the Department Name.

---

[2] The inventor of relational databases, Edgar F. Codd, coined the term *normalization.* "We all have trouble organizing even our personal information. Businesses have those problems in spades. It seems to me essential that some discipline be introduced into database design. I called it normalization because then-President Nixon was talking a lot about normalizing relations with China. I figured that if he could normalize relations, so could I." [Matthew H. Rapaport, "A 'Fireside' Chat," DBMS 6, no. 13 (1993): 54–60.]

[3] Data are said to be unnormalized (bad), in first normal form (1NF—better), in second normal form (2NF—better yet), or third normal form (3NF—reasonably good). There are forms beyond 3NF but they generally solve relatively rare problems within the data.

We would normalize this table by splitting it into two tables: one table with Employee Number (key field), Employee Name, and Department Code, and a second table with Department Code (key field) and Department Name.

In addition, if you have a compound key (two or more fields), then each non-key field should be determined by all the fields that make up the compound key, not just some of them. For example, a table with Student Number *and* Course Identifier as the compound key, and Student Name and Grade as nonkey fields, is not in third normal form. The problem is that the Student Name can be determined by just part of the compound key, the Student Number. Again, we would normalize this table by splitting it into two tables. The first would include the original compound key Student Number and Course Identifier, plus the Grade (which needs both fields to determine its value). The second table would include the Student Number (key field) and Student Name.

Database Queries

A relational database is made up of tables, each focusing on a single entity. But what happens when we want to use the database to answer questions, called *queries* in database terminology? Often the data needed to answer the query comes from more than one table. Thus, with a relational database, one must be able to "combine" data from several tables in order to provide useful information to the user.

Most relational database systems use a query language called **structured query language (SQL) to specify how to combine data in related tables and how to select only the desired data.** Visual Basic uses SQL, which we discuss in greater detail in Section 8.3. Let's look at a simple query now, to complete our introduction to relational databases.

Suppose that you have a database with the three tables shown in Figure 8.6. Suppose, too, that the user of this database wants to query the database by asking for a list of all students who completed BA 420. The user wants the list to include the student number (StNo), student name (StName), course identifier (CourseId), course name (CourseName), and grade (Grade). The data needed to answer this query come from all three tables. The common fields in the three tables make it possible to determine which rows are appropriate to answer the query.

FIGURE 8.6

Sample database with three tables

Student Table

StNo	StName
123	Jim
543	Sue
333	Joe

Course Table

CourseId	CourseName
BA 310	Programming
BA 420	Database Design
BA 430	Systems Analysis

Transcript Table

StNo	CourseId	Grade
123	BA 310	A
123	BA 420	B
543	BA 420	A-
333	BA 420	B
333	BA 430	B-

The computer answers the query by searching the tables for the data it needs. In this case, it starts out in the Course table and finds a match for BA 420 in row 2. The computer now has access to the correct course name. Then the computer searches the Transcript table row by row looking at the CourseId field. Each time it finds a match with BA 420 (rows 2, 3, and 4), it uses the value of the student number to search the Student table. For example, the first match, found in row 2 of the Transcript table, yields student number 123. This student number is found in row 1 of the Student table and the name Jim is extracted. The computer now has all the information it needs to produce one line of output (the first student it found who took BA 420). This process continues with the second match for BA 420 in the Transcript table (row 3), and then again for the next match (row 4).

The process of searching tables and matching common fields is the general solution employed by the computer to answer relational database queries. There are additional options and types of queries, but the basic idea is the same.

8.2 The Data Control

The *Data control* enables a VB project to access databases by providing the project with the information it needs to locate the database on disk and to interpret its contents. VB is able to use databases created by the Microsoft Access DBMS as well as several others.[4]

Appearance and Use

Figure 8.7 identifies the data tool and shows a Data control on the form at design time. In its simplest use, at run time the Data control has access to a single table of a specified database. For example, if the database consisted of the Author, Publisher, and Title tables, we could specify that the Data control have access to the Publisher table. We could access additional tables by using more than one Data control—one Data control for each table we want to access.

The Data control accesses records in a table one at a time. (Recall from Figure 8.3 that the terms "record" and "row" are synonyms.) **The record that is currently being accessed is called the *current record*.** The Data control has an

FIGURE 8.7

Data tool and control

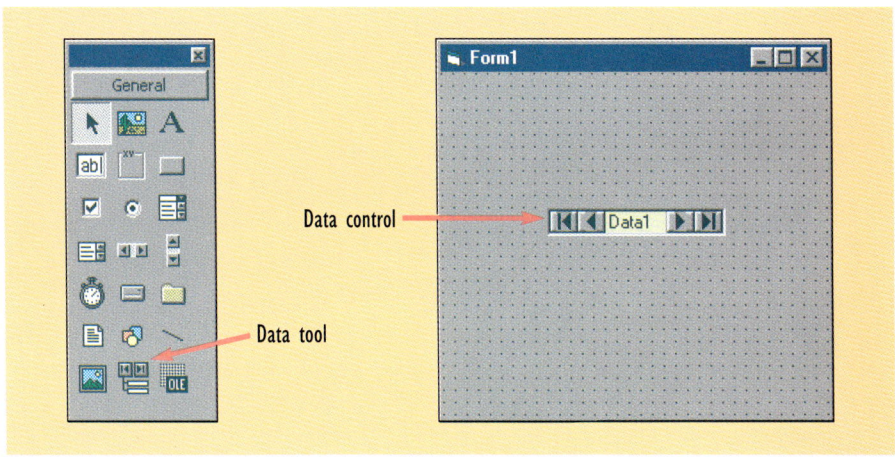

[4] Appendix D discusses how to create databases using MS Access.

internal value called the *record pointer* that keeps track of which record in the table is the current record. Users need not know that the record pointer even exists, but programmers sometimes have to write statements that manipulate it.

The Data control has **buttons that the user clicks to move through the records in the database table, which is called** *navigating* or *browsing* **the table.** These buttons and their functions are shown in Figure 8.8. Each button actually repositions the record pointer, which changes which record in the table is the current record. For example, clicking the Get First Record button moves the record pointer to the top of the table so that the first record in the table becomes the current record.

Properties

Some important properties of the Data control are listed in Table 8.1. We will discuss each of these properties in examples.

> **Convention** Use the prefix "dat" for the names of Data controls.

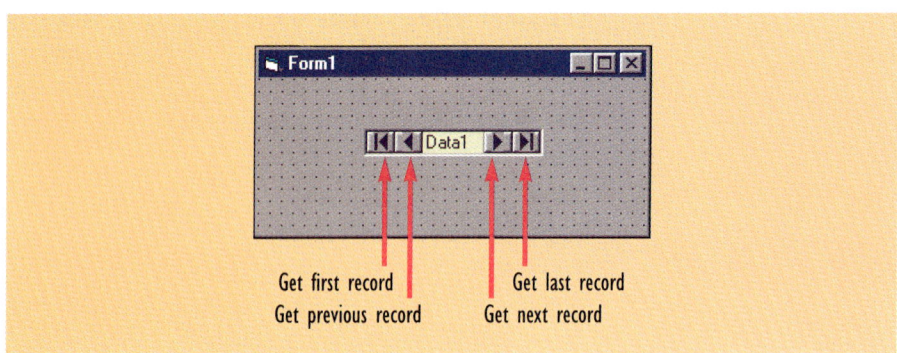

FIGURE 8.8

Data control navigation buttons

TABLE 8.1 Important properties of the Data control

Property	Specifies
Caption	The descriptive text that is displayed in the middle of the Data control.
DatabaseName	The location and name of the database on disk. The setting must specify both the path and the name of the database. For example, to use the Access bibliography database that Microsoft provides with VB, the setting would be C:\Program Files\DevStudio\VB\Biblio.mdb (assuming VB was installed on the C drive).
RecordSource	The name of the desired table within the database specified by DatabaseName. Alternatively, this can be text that stores an SQL query (discussed in Section 8.3).
Recordset	The current set of records that are the result of the Data control's RecordSource property. If the RecordSource property contains the name of a table, then the Recordset property refers to this table. If the RecordSource property contains an SQL query, then the Recordset property refers to the table that is the result of the query. This property is available only at run time.

Bound Controls

◆ ◆ ◆

The Data control provides your VB project with a connection to a database table but does not itself display the table's data. To display the data, we can use familiar controls such as text boxes or labels, or two new controls we will examine in Sections 8.4, 8.5, and 8.6 (the FlexGrid and DBGrid controls). A *bound control* **is a control like a text box or label that has been associated with (bound to) a Data control.** A bound control accesses and displays data from the table associated with the Data control.

For example, suppose we have set a Data control's properties so that it is connected to the Publisher table in the example bibliographic database. In this case, we can bind a Label control to this Data control so that the label displays the value of the Name field in the Publisher table. To display the values of additional fields in the Publisher table, we would bind additional Label controls to the Data control.

Only certain types of controls can be bound. These include the Label, Text box, Check box, List box, Combo box, FlexGrid, Image, and Picture controls. In addition, VB provides three controls that are specifically intended to be bound to a Data control: the Data-Bound Combo control (DBCombo) and the Data-Bound List box control (DBList), plus the Data-Bound Grid control (DBGrid). This text does not cover the DBCombo or DBList controls (you can use VB's online help to learn more about them). The DBGrid is discussed in Section 8.6.

Bound controls have properties that specify the Data control (to which the control is bound), the field in the database table, and whether the value displayed by the control differs from the corresponding value in the current record. These properties, shown in Table 8.2, make the bound control "data-aware"—that is, aware of a field within a database table.

Example 8.1 Bound Controls

This example demonstrates the use of a Data control and a bound Label control to access and display the records from a single table in a database. The example has no coding, but it does require a number of steps to correctly set up the

TABLE 8.2 Properties that make bound controls "data aware"

Property	Specifies
DataSource	*The Data control that the control is bound to.* This is necessary since a VB project may have more than one Data control; a label, for example, could be bound to any one of them. Since the Data control is in turn associated with a specific database, this property indirectly associates a bound control with a specific database.
DataField	*The field in the Data control's Recordset that the bound control has access to.* This property allows the bound control to be associated with a specific field in the database.
DataChanged	*Whether the data in the bound control has changed since it was last set by the Data control.* If the data currently in the bound control are not the same as the corresponding field in the Data control's current record, VB sets this property to True. If the data in the bound control are the same as the corresponding field in the Data control's current record, VB sets this property to False.

Data control and the bound control. Thus, we describe the creation of the project from start to finish.

For this example we use the Access bibliographic database, Biblio.mdb, that Microsoft provides with VB. This database is similar (but not identical) to the examples shown earlier in Figures 8.1, 8.3, 8.4, and 8.5.

We create a project that accesses the Publisher table from the database and displays publisher names. A Data control (datPubName) is connected to the database, and a label (lblName) is bound to the Data control. The project allows the user to move through the records in this table, one record at a time, and continuously displays the contents of the Name field of the current record.

Figure 8.9 depicts how the Data control and the bound Label control interact to specify the part of the database to be accessed. The Data control's DatabaseName property specifies the name of the database that contains the desired data. The Data control's RecordSource property indicates which specific table within that database the Data control will access. Together, the DatabaseName and RecordSource properties specify the data that will comprise the Data control's *recordset*—the collection of records available to the Data control at run time. The Label control's DataSource property binds it to the Data control. This property is necessary because a VB project may have more than one Data control, and it is necessary to indicate which one of the Data controls the label is to be bound to. You can think of DataSource as specifying the Data control that is the source of data for the bound Label control. The bound Label control's DataField property specifies which field from the Data control's recordset the label should display.

To begin the project, we first place a Data control and a Label control on the form, setting the name of the Data control to datPubName and the name of the Label control to lblName. Construction of the project proceeds in four steps:

1. Specify the database by setting the Data control's DatabaseName property. Figure 8.10 shows the Data control's DatabaseName property set to D:\Pro-

FIGURE 8.9

The binding of a Label control to a database through a Data control

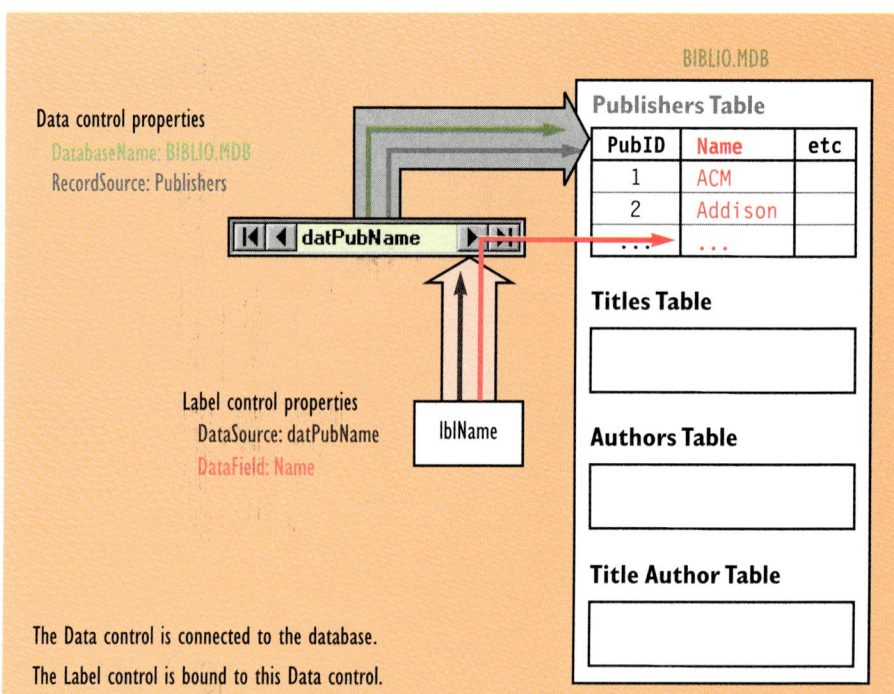

FIGURE 8.10

DatabaseName property

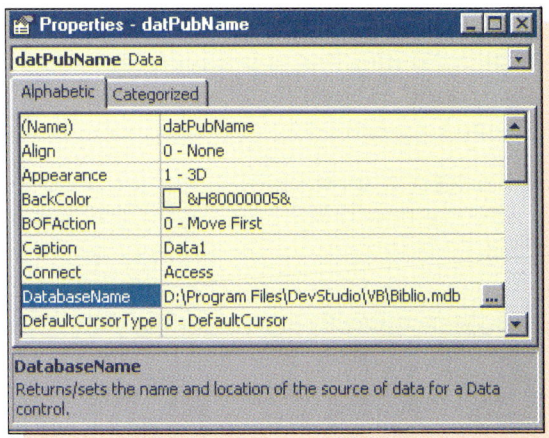

gram Files\DevStudio\VB\Biblio.mdb. We can either type this into the DatabaseName property box or click on the ellipses at its right end and locate the database using the Open dialog window that will appear on the screen.

2. Specify the database table by setting the Data control's RecordSource property. Once we've set the DatabaseName property, VB can access the names of the tables in the database. We can now set the RecordSource property by clicking on the dropdown list in its setting box and selecting one of the table names. Figure 8.11 shows the list of tables in the Biblio.mdb database.

   In this example, we select the Publisher table. We have now associated the Data control with the database Biblio.mdb and selected the Publisher table as the source for its Recordset.

3. Bind the label to the Data control by setting the label's DataSource property. Figure 8.12 shows this. In our case we only have one Data control (named datPubName), so it is the only choice appearing in the setting box's dropdown list. We select it.

4. Select the field to display in the label by setting the label's DataField property. Since the Data control's Recordset has been established (steps 1 and

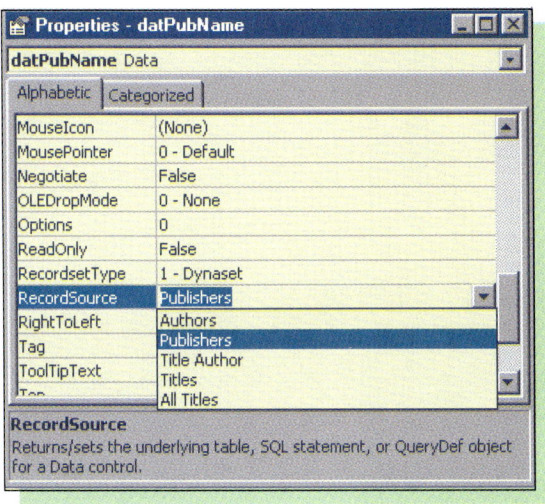

FIGURE 8.11

Tables that can be used as a source for the records

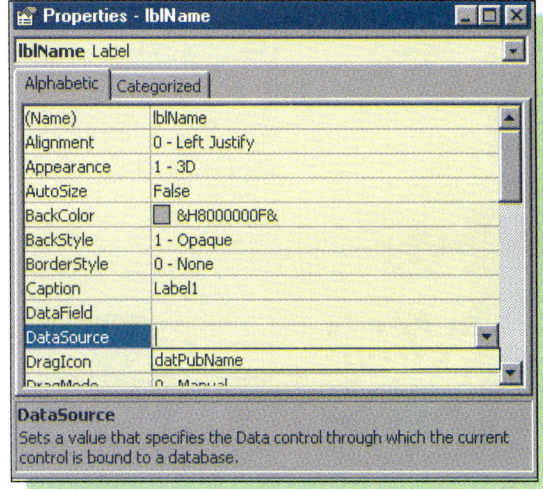

FIGURE 8.12

Selecting the Data control to be used as the label's DataSource

2), and since the label is bound to the Data control (step 3), the label's DataField setting box now has access to the list of fields belonging to the Recordset. Figure 8.13 shows the choices appearing in the DataField setting box's dropdown list. For this example we choose the Name field.

The project is now ready to run. Figure 8.14 shows the project at run time, with the bound label displaying the Name field from a record of the Publisher table. If you run the project and click on the Data control's four navigation buttons, you will observe how they move through the records of the database. As mentioned before, viewing records in a database like this is often called *browsing* the data. Note that the processing of records in this example is limited to displaying the contents of one field.

No programming was required to create this project. All we did was to first set the DatabaseName and RecordSource properties of the Data control, and then set the DataSource and DataField properties of the bound Label control.

In addition to displaying data from a database, bound controls can be used to modify the data in a database. Suppose we had bound a text box instead of a label to the Data control in Example 8.1. Like the Label control, at run time the text box will display the value of the Name field in the current record. However, the user can modify the data in the text box, which modifies the Name field in the current record, and this change will be stored in the database. We will see examples of this shortly.

FIGURE 8.13

Data fields in the Recordset

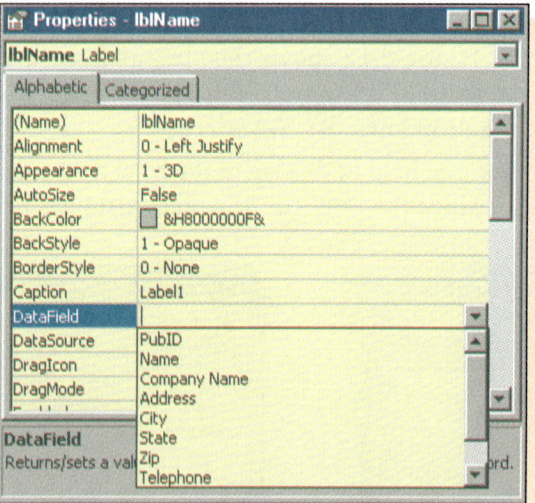

FIGURE 8.14

The form at run time showing a record from the Publisher's table

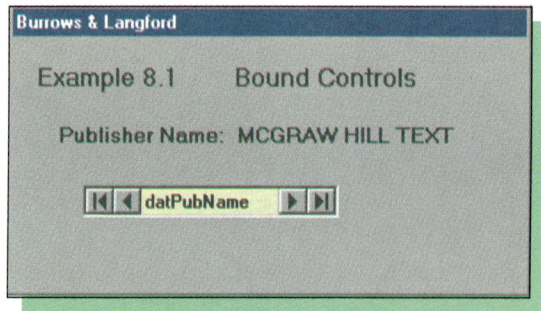

EXERCISE 8.1 Add bound Label controls to Example 8.1 so that in addition to the Name field, the Address, City, State, and Zip fields are also displayed on the form when you browse the Publisher table.

EXERCISE 8.2 Create a new project that browses the Authors table and displays the Author field in a label.

Programming the Data Control

♦ ♦ ♦

When your program connects to a database at run time, VB makes **a set of records available to the Data control in accordance with its DatabaseName and RecordSource properties. This set of records is called the Data control's** *recordset*. In fact, the Data control has **a method, called** *Refresh,* **which allows you to change the Data control's recordset at run time.** To do this, just change the DatabaseName or RecordSource properties as desired, then use the Refresh method. Executing the Refresh method causes the computer to reconstruct the recordset using the new values of DatabaseName and RecordSource.

Every recordset has an order; that is, it has a first record, a second record, . . . , and a last record. This order is the same as the order of the records in the database table that the records come from.

In addition, the Data control has a record pointer that always points to a specific record in the recordset. **The record pointer also can point beyond the last record—a condition called** *End Of File,* **or** *EOF*—**or before the first record**—a condition called *Beginning Of File,* or *BOF*.

There are several ways to cause the record pointer to move to a new record. One way is for the user to click on the Data control's navigation buttons. However, these buttons only allow the user to move the record pointer ahead or back one position or to the first or last record in the recordset. As programmer, you can write code to manipulate the record pointer and thereby move through the database. In addition, program statements can modify, delete, and add records in the recordset (and hence, in the underlying database). VB provides these capabilities as properties and methods of the recordset. Table 8.3 shows some useful properties for working with recordsets, and Table 8.4 lists several useful methods for managing recordsets.

The MoveFirst, MoveNext, MoveLast, and MovePrevious methods can collectively be described as simply the Move methods. Their function is straightforward: **the Move methods reposition the record pointer in exactly the same ways as when the user clicks on the Data control's navigation buttons.** The other methods in Table 8.4 are moderately complex and are best illustrated by an example.

TABLE 8.3 Important recordset properties

Property	Specifies
BOF	Whether the current position of the record pointer is before the first record of the recordset. True or False.
EOF	Whether the current position of the record pointer is after the last record of the recordset. True or False.
RecordCount	The number of records in the recordset.

TABLE 8.4 Important methods for managing recordsets

Method	Action
MoveFirst	*Moves the record pointer to point at the first record in the recordset. The first record in the recordset becomes the current record.*
MoveNext	*Moves the record pointer down one position in the recordset. The next record in the recordset becomes the current record. If the MoveNext operation moves the record pointer past the last record in the recordset, VB sets the EOF property to True and there is no current record.*
MoveLast	*Moves the record pointer to point at the last record in the recordset. The last record in the recordset becomes the current record.*
MovePrevious	*Moves the record pointer up one position in the recordset. The previous record in the recordset becomes the current record. If the MovePrevious operation moves the record pointer above the first record in the recordset, VB sets the BOF property to True and there is no current record.*
Delete	*Deletes the current record from the recordset.*
AddNew	*Clears the copy buffer and makes it the current record. The copy buffer is a storage area where you collect the values of the fields for a new record or modify the fields of an existing record.* *Use the AddNew method in preparation for adding a new record to a recordset. Then fill the copy buffer with values for the new record (see Example 8.2 for instruction on how to do this). Finally, use the Update method to actually add the new record to the recordset.*
Edit	*Prepares the current record for editing by copying its contents to the copy buffer. Use this method when you want to change the contents of the current record. After using the Edit method, modify the copy buffer's contents as desired, then use the Update method to actually save the new values to the recordset.*
Update	*Copies the contents of the copy buffer into the recordset.*
Close	*Informs VB that the program is finished using the recordset. If the current record has been changed (or it is a new record), then VB will automatically update it (save it in the recordset) as part of the process of closing the recordset. If you want to access the recordset after it has been closed, you must first reconstruct it using the Refresh method.*

Example 8.2

Programming the Data Control

In this example we build a simple data manager that allows us to look at records in a database table one at a time, add new records, delete existing records, and modify existing records. Figure 8.15 shows this project's form at run time. Figure 8.16 shows the form at design time with the names of its controls. Compare these two figures. The Data control (datPeople) shown in Figure 8.16 does not appear in Figure 8.15; this is because we want the controls on the lower left of the form, not the Data control's buttons, to be the navigation controls. Thus, we set the Data control's Visible property to False. Also note that we use the Picture property of the Previous and Next command

FIGURE 8.15

Simple data manager application at run time

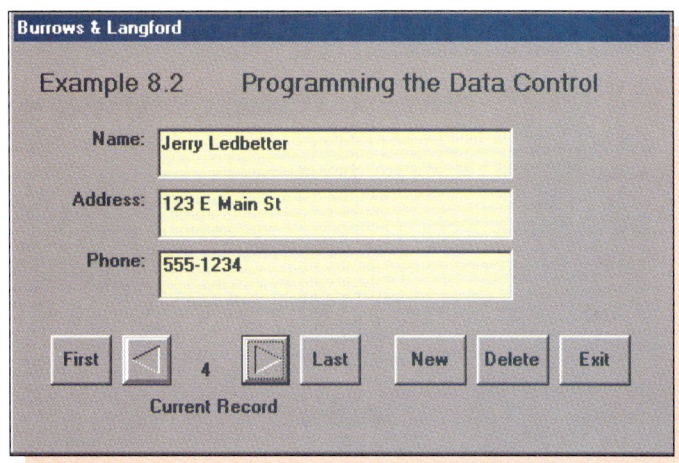

FIGURE 8.16

Controls for the simple data manager application

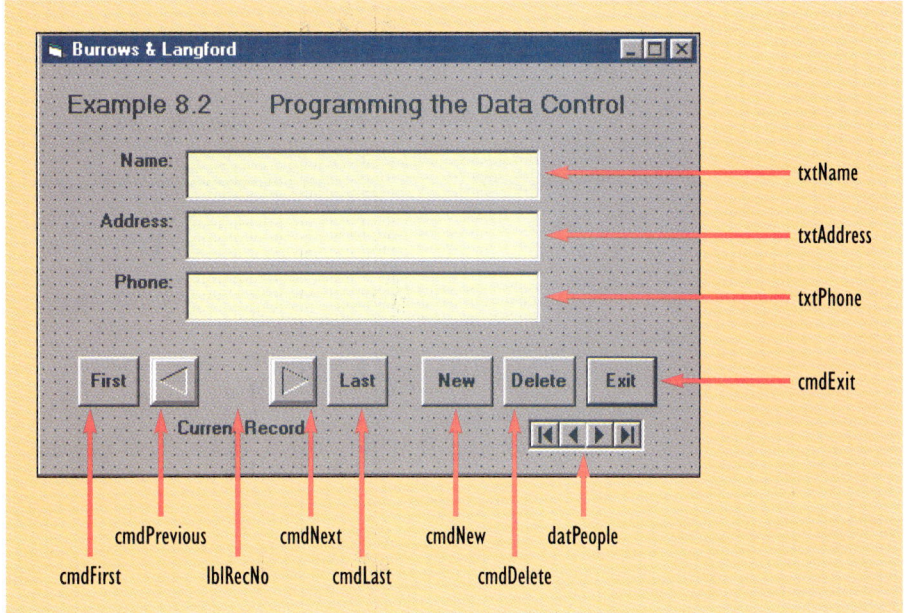

buttons. The icons used for these pictures mimic the controls on a VCR or audio CD player.

The database that we use is called People.mdb (stored in the subdirectory C08 in the code package for this text). This database consists of a single table called Info. The fields in this table are shown in Figure 8.17. All three fields are text-type fields.

Several controls have properties that need to be set at design time. Table 8.5 lists these controls and their property settings. Note that the Name properties are the same as those in Figure 8.16.

FIGURE 8.17

People.mdb database

PEOPLE.MDB
Info Table

Name	Address	PhoneNo
xxxx	xxx	xxx
xxxx	xxx	xxx

TABLE 8.5 Design time property settings for simple data manager application controls

Control	Property	Setting
datPeople	Visible	False
cmdNext	Style Picture	1 - Graphical D:\DevStudio\Vb\Graphics\Icons\Arrows\arw01rt.ico
cmdPrevious	Style Picture	1 - Graphical D:\DevStudio\Vb\Graphics\Icons\Arrows\arw01lt.ico
lblRecNo	Caption	empty
txtAddress	DataSource DataField Text	datPeople Address empty
txtName	DataSource DataField Text	datPeople Name empty
txtPhone	DataSource DataField Text	datPeople PhoneNo empty

Let us now look at the code for the application. We compose event procedures for the form's Load event and for the seven command buttons.

The Form_Load Event

Note that in Table 8.5 we did not specify DatabaseName and RecordSource settings for the Data control. We set these properties in the Form_Load event procedure. Setting these properties at run time is useful for two reasons. First, it makes it possible for the user to specify the database and table to be used by the program.[5] Second, it allows us to specify more reliably the location of the database.

VB provides a special object named *App* that it uses at run time to make information about the application available to the application itself. For example, VB stores the application's path (location on disk) in the Path property of the App object (i.e., in App.Path). Properties of the App object are available only at run time.

We want to avoid specifying the location of the database using the Properties window (at design time) because we may eventually want to copy the entire application, including the database, to a different location on disk. Doing this would change the path, which would mean that we'd have to change the DatabaseName setting in the Properties window. As long as we keep the database in the same directory as our application, then at run time App.Path will always specify the correct location of the database on disk, even if we relocate the directory.

The current record label (lblRecNo) contains the record number of the current record. When program execution begins, the Data control automatically starts with its record pointer pointing at the first record, so lblRecNo

---

[5] This is illustrated in Appendix F, "The Common Dialog Control and Error Handling."

should display 1 initially. Our Form_Load event procedure appears as follows. The database, People.mdb, is stored in the same directory as the application.

```
Private Sub Form_Load()
    datPeople.DatabaseName = App.Path & "\People.mdb"
    datPeople.RecordSource = "Info"
    datPeople.Refresh
    lblRecNo.Caption = 1
End Sub
```

The cmdFirst_Click Event

This is one of the navigation controls. It sets the record pointer to point at the first record using the recordset's MoveFirst method. It also updates the current record label to reflect this change:

```
Private Sub cmdFirst_Click()
    datPeople.Recordset.MoveFirst
    lblRecNo.Caption = 1
End Sub
```

Note the syntax of the statement that uses the MoveFirst method: you first specify the Data control, then its recordset property, and finally the method. This statement means "move the record pointer for the recordset of datPeople to its first record."

The cmdLast_Click Event

This button sets the record pointer to point at the last record. Its code is very similar to the code for cmdFirst_Click.

```
Private Sub cmdLast_Click()
    datPeople.Recordset.MoveLast
    lblRecNo.Caption = datPeople.Recordset.RecordCount
End Sub
```

The *RecordCount property* determines the record number of the last record. We update the current record label (lblRecNo) with this value.

The cmdNext_Click Event

This control uses the recordset's MoveNext method to advance the record pointer one position in the recordset. This operation may cause the record pointer to go beyond the end of the recordset (EOF). Thus, it is necessary to include an If statement that uses the EOF property to detect this situation and then takes corrective action if it occurs (which includes moving the record pointer back to the last record).

```
Private Sub cmdNext_Click()
    datPeople.Recordset.MoveNext
    If datPeople.Recordset.EOF = False Then
        lblRecNo.Caption = Val(lblRecNo.Caption) + 1
    Else
        MsgBox "Already at end of table", vbInformation
        datPeople.Recordset.MoveLast
    End If
End Sub
```

The cmdPrevious_Click Event

The code for this control is similar to cmdNext_Click. The primary differences are the recordset's method (MovePrevious) and the test for moving above the beginning of the file (BOF).

```
Private Sub cmdPrevious_Click()
    datPeople.Recordset.MovePrevious
    If datPeople.Recordset.BOF = False Then
        lblRecNo.Caption = Val(lblRecNo.Caption) - 1
    Else
        MsgBox "Already at beginning of table", vbInformation
        datPeople.Recordset.MoveFirst
    End If
End Sub
```

This takes care of the four navigation controls at the lower left of the form.

The cmdExit_Click Event

The obvious thing this button should do is end program execution. However, since the user is allowed to change the values of the current record in the three text boxes, it is wise to warn the user that any changes will be lost (if any have been made).

To determine whether a value in a bound control has been changed since it was obtained from the database, use the control's DataChanged property. Since we have three bound text boxes, we need to check all three to see whether any of them have been changed. If so, then we need to include a warning and then have the user decide how to proceed.

```
Private Sub cmdExit_Click()
    Const WARNUNSAVEDCHANGE = _
        "Data have been changed, do you want to Exit without saving?"
    Dim UnsavedChange As Boolean
    Dim BoxType As Integer
    Dim Response As Integer
    ' See whether any of the DataChanged properties are true
    UnsavedChange = txtName.DataChanged Or txtAddress.DataChanged Or _
        txtPhone.DataChanged
    If UnsavedChange = False Then
        End          'end execution because no changes detected
    End If
    'changes detected; ask user how to proceed
    BoxType = vbYesNoCancel + vbCritical + vbDefaultButton2
    Response = MsgBox(WARNUNSAVEDCHANGE, BoxType)
    If Response = vbYes Then
        End          'end execution, discarding changes
    Else
        Exit Sub     'leave the procedure and don't end execution
    End If
End Sub
```

The warning that we give the user should be phrased carefully. The warning for our application is shown in Figure 8.18. Note that the default button (No) is the one that causes minimal damage if the user inadvertently selects it. If the

FIGURE 8.18

Warning displayed when user clicks Exit when a record has been changed and not updated

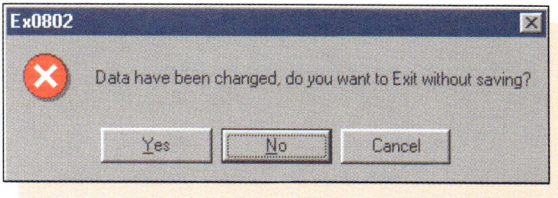

user clicks No, execution does not end. This behavior may seem a little awkward to the user who wants to save the changes and quit execution. Modifying the code to improve this behavior is left as an exercise.

The cmdNew_Click Event

This control employs the *copy buffer*, described in Table 8.4, to add a new record to the database. **The *copy buffer* has the same fields as the recordset and is a temporary place to collect values of fields in preparation for adding a new record to the database or modifying an existing record in the database.** As programmer, you don't have to do anything to create the copy buffer—VB creates and manages it.

The first step is to execute the recordset's ***AddNew* method, which clears the copy buffer.** Then we can place values in the appropriate fields of the copy buffer. The syntax for this is fairly simple. For example, the statement

   datPeople.Recordset("Name") = "Smith"

stores the text "Smith" in the Name field of the copy buffer for datPeople's Recordset.

After placing values for all three fields in the copy buffer, we execute the recordset's ***Update* method to place the contents of the copy buffer in a new record in the recordset.** If the recordset is based on a table that does not have an index[6] (as in this example), the new record will be placed at the end of the table. If the recordset is based on a table that does have an index, VB will position the new record according to the index's order.

```
Private Sub cmdNew_Click()
    datPeople.Recordset.AddNew
    datPeople.Recordset("Name") = InputBox("Enter Name")
    datPeople.Recordset("Address") = InputBox("Enter Address")
    datPeople.Recordset("PhoneNo") = InputBox("Enter Phone")
    datPeople.Recordset.Update
End Sub
```

We use input boxes to obtain field values for the new record from the user. Figure 8.19 shows the input box for obtaining the Name information. As an alternative to input boxes we could have let the user just enter new values into the three text boxes. The AddNew method clears the bound controls, displaying the form with empty text boxes. We use AddNew in this manner in Project 12.

The cmdDelete_Click Event

This is the final control to be programmed. The behavior of this button is potentially ambiguous. After you delete the current record, which record

---

[6] A database table can have an index defined for it. Just as a reader uses a book's index, the database management system uses the table's index to locate a record quickly without having to search the entire table. When a field is defined as an index, the order of the records in the table is maintained according to this field's values.

FIGURE 8.19

Input box used to obtain person's name

should become the new current record? For example, suppose you delete record number 5 in a table with 10 records. Since record 5 is gone, the record that previously was record 6 is now considered record 5 (out of 9 total). Which record do you display next? Should you display the former record 6 and label it record 5? Or should you move to the top of the recordset and display record 1? Or maybe you should do something else.

Design questions like these should be answered by the user, not the programmer. But even the user may have a difficult time deciding if you pose the question in words. The user will have a much easier time deciding if you provide prototypes and allow experimentation with the alternatives.

For this example, we assume that immediately after deleting a record the user wants the record following it to be displayed. So if we delete record 5 (of 10), the form then shows the prior record 6 but now calls it record 5 (of 9). The only complication in this scheme arises when the user deletes the last record. If record 10 (of 10) is deleted, there is no prior record 11 to become the new record 10. Thus, when the last record is deleted, the prior second-to-last record (the new last record) becomes the record to display on the form.

```
Private Sub cmdDelete_Click()
    Const WARNDELETE = "Are you sure you want to delete this record?"
    Dim BoxType As Integer
    Dim Response As Integer
    BoxType = vbYesNo + vbCritical + vbDefaultButton2
    Response = MsgBox(WARNDELETE, BoxType)
    If Response = vbYes Then
        datPeople.Recordset.Delete
        If lblRecNo.Caption > datPeople.Recordset.RecordCount Then
            cmdLast_Click           'move to last record (resets lblRecNo)
        Else
            datPeople.Recordset.MoveNext        'lblRecNo unchanged
        End If
    End If
End Sub
```

Note that before a delete operation is allowed to be completed, the user is given a warning to confirm the decision to delete. This warning is shown in Figure 8.20. Again notice that the default button is the button that causes no harm when the user inadvertently selects it.

FIGURE 8.20

Warning message issued before delete operation

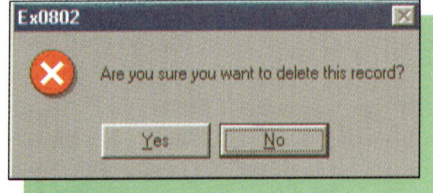

Finally, when one of the values displayed in the bound text boxes has been modified by the user, executing any of the Move methods automatically causes the current record to be updated—saved in the database—before the move takes place. As programmer, you do not need to do anything special to make this happen. Thus, if the user displays record 2, edits the phone number, and then clicks on cmdNext (causing the MoveNext method to be executed), the new phone number for record 2 will automatically be saved in the database before the system moves to record 3.

EXERCISE 8.3

Suppose that the user of the application in Example 8.2 has just changed the value in one of the text boxes, then clicked the Exit button. The application responds by asking the user whether or not to exit without saving. Suppose the user clicks No in response. How does the user save the changes? Explain.

Modify cmdExit_Click so that it gives the user the option of saving changes and ending execution.

Finding Specific Records

Example 8.2 uses the Move methods to reposition the record pointer to the top or the bottom of the recordset, or up one or down one position in the recordset. The user has no control over the content of the record that is displayed as a result—whatever the record contains is what the user gets. Often the user wants to retrieve a record based on the *value of a field* as opposed to the position of the record pointer.

As an example, suppose you have a recordset that includes information on parts and that these parts are identified by unique part numbers. You might want to find a record whose part number equals a specific value, say, 1088. You could accomplish this by starting at the first record (MoveFirst) and then using a loop to go through the records one at a time (MoveNext), searching for part number 1088. However, VB provides a concise alternative that allows you to specify "find the record whose part number equals 1088" in a single statement. In fact, VB provides four methods—FindFirst, FindLast, FindNext, and FindPrevious—**that allow you to find a record in a recordset. We call these methods the** *Find methods.*

All of the Find methods require that you specify a *criterion,* in the form of a string expression, to identify the record to find. For example, suppose you want a record with a part number of 1088. Assuming that the Data control is named datParts, and the part number field is named PartNo and is numeric, the following statement will find this record and make it the current record:

```
datParts.Recordset.FindFirst "PartNo = 1088"
```

What if there is no record whose PartNo field equals 1088? Then the FindFirst operation will fail. **The recordset has a property called *NoMatch* that VB sets to True if the Find operation fails and False if it succeeds.** Therefore, the value of this property should always be checked after the Find to see what happened. Extending our previous example, this might appear as follows:

```
datParts.Recordset.FindFirst "PartNo = 1088"
If datParts.RecordSet.NoMatch = True Then
   ' Find failed - handle this situation
Else
   ' Find succeeded - process the record
End If
```

You can also use the other comparison operators in criteria you compose for Find methods. Why might you want to use a comparison other than equality? Consider what the following statement does:

```
datParts.Recordset.FindFirst "PartNo >= 1088"
```

This statement finds the first record whose PartNo field is greater than or equal to 1088, if there is one. Specifically,

- If a record exists with part number 1088, then that record becomes the current record.
- If no record with part number 1088 exists, then the first record having a part number greater than 1088 becomes the current record.
- If all the records have part numbers less than 1088, then the record at the beginning of the recordset becomes the current record.

For this kind of search the NoMatch property will always be False.

To execute a Find method, the computer searches through the recordset to find a record matching the specified criterion. Often, multiple records in the recordset match the search criterion. In such cases, which one of the matching records will the Find method find? The answer depends on where (in the recordset) the search begins and the direction of the search. Table 8.6 shows where the search starts and the direction of the search for each of the Find methods.

Thus, of the records that match the criterion, the FindFirst method finds the one closest to the top of the recordset, and the FindLast method finds the one closest to the bottom of the recordset. Likewise, of the records that match the criterion, the FindPrevious method finds the one closest to and above the current record, and the FindNext method finds the one closest to and below the current record.

To illustrate the FindNext operation, suppose that you want to process all records whose publisher identifier is equal to 13 in the Title table shown in Figure 8.4. You can see from the figure that the Title table contains many records that match this criterion. To perform the search, you might use code like the following (which suggests placing selected fields from the records in a list box).

```
datTitles.Recordset.FindFirst "PubId = 13"
If datTitles.Recordset.NoMatch = True Then
    MsgBox "No records found"
Else
    Do Until datTitles.Recordset.NoMatch = True
        ' add current record to list box
        datTitles.Recordset.FindNext "PubId = 13"
    Loop
End If
```

TABLE 8.6 Search start and direction for Find methods

Find Method	Search Starts At	Search Direction
FindFirst	Beginning of recordset	Toward end of recordset
FindLast	End of recordset	Toward beginning of recordset
FindNext	Current record	Toward end of recordset
FindPrevious	Current record	Toward beginning of recordset

Finally, the Find methods automatically update the current record if it has been modified, just as the Move methods do.

Example 8.3

Finding Specific Records

Let us create a project that allows the user to specify a publisher identifier, then searches the Titles table for all matches and places the value of the Title field of each matching record in a list box. That is, after the search, the list box displays all the titles published by the specified publisher. The application and its controls are shown in Figures 8.21 and 8.22.

FIGURE 8.21

User interface for Example 8.3 at run time

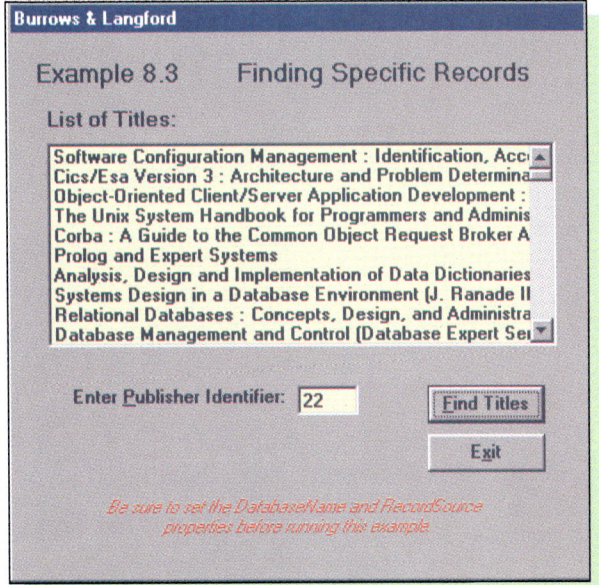

FIGURE 8.22

Controls and important properties for Example 8.3

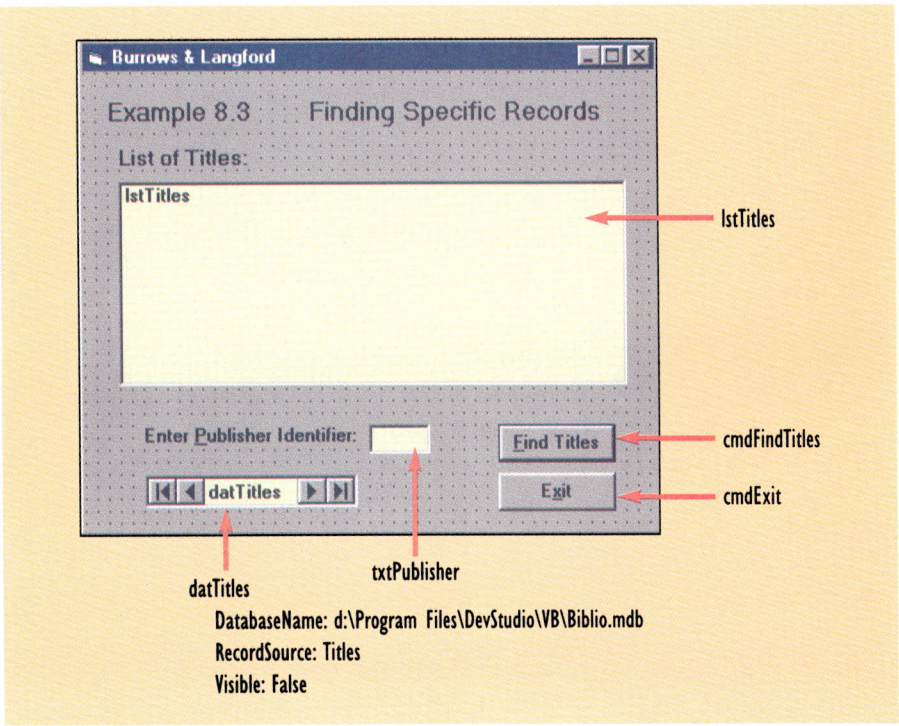

Before we look at the code for the Find Titles button, let us review how to refer to a specific field of the recordset's current record. The following expression identifies the Title field from the current record of a recordset:

```
datTitles.Recordset("Title")
```

You can place the name of any valid field in the recordset between the parentheses.

Unlike the previous examples, this example has no bound controls. The list box, in particular, is not bound; it is just a simple list box like those we have seen in the past. We use the statement

```
lstTitles.AddItem datTitles.Recordset("Title")
```

to add the value of the current record's Title field to the list box.

The code used to find the required records is straightforward. The essence of this code is shown here (with the user input error checking removed).

```
Target = "PubId = " & txtPublisher.Text
datTitles.Recordset.FindFirst Target          'Get the first record
If datTitles.Recordset.NoMatch = True Then
    MsgBox "No records found"
Else
    Do Until datTitles.Recordset.NoMatch = True    'Get the rest
        lstTitles.AddItem datTitles.Recordset("Title")
        datTitles.Recordset.FindNext Target
    Loop
End If
```

Figure 8.23 shows the complete code for this project. Note that much of it performs tasks associated with validating the user input. This is typical of real applications.

The Like Operator

Users sometimes need to find records based on incomplete information for the search criterion. For example, a user who is unsure of the exact spelling of an employee's name may want to browse all records for employees whose names begin with "Bur". VB provides the *Like operator* to handle such cases.

The following statement is an example of a find using the Like operator. Observe that the value 'Bur*' is enclosed in single quotes. This is necessary when the field specified in the criterion is type String[7]; ordinarily, we would use double quotes for this, but the criterion itself is enclosed in double quotes.

```
datFoo.Recordset.FindFirst "Name Like 'Bur*'"
```

This statement will find the first record whose Name field begins with "Bur". The asterisk is called a *wild card* character, and it means that any sequence of characters (after "Bur", in this case) will match. The following code shows how the above criterion is constructed when the value to match is input by the user and stored in a variable. Look carefully for the single quotes.

```
Dim PartialName As String
PartialName = InputBox("Enter first part of name to find")
datFoo.Recordset.FindFirst "Name Like '" & PartialName & "*'"
```

---

[7] It is the type of the field as specified in the database that matters here. For example, suppose you have a database table that contains a field for Social Security Number (SSN). Did the creator of this table specify the SSN field to be numeric or text? If the answer is text, then the value in the Find criterion must be enclosed in single quotes.

FIGURE 8.23

Code for Example 8.3

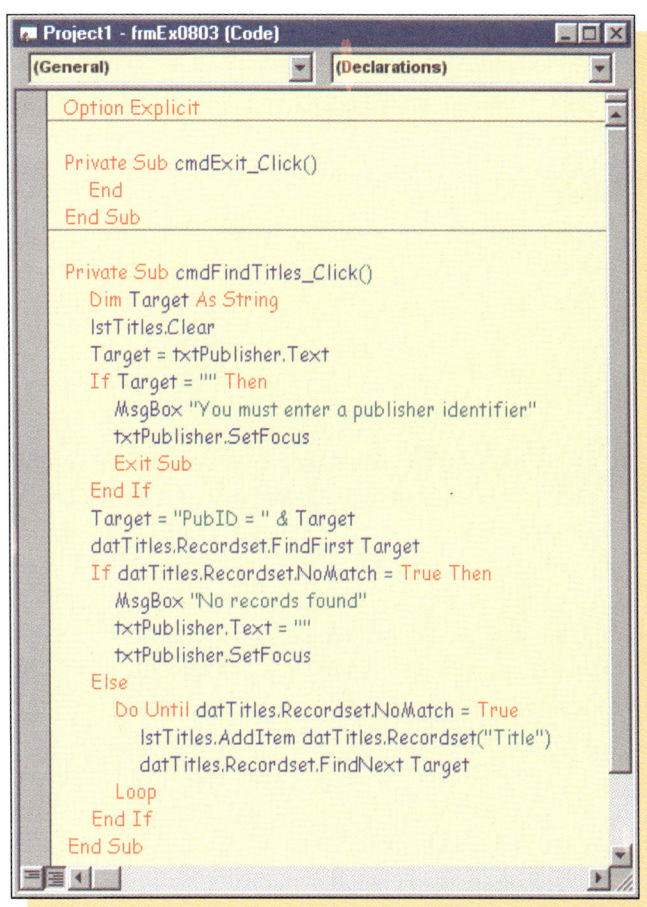

Two other wild card characters that are useful with the Like operator are the question mark (?), which means any single character will match, and the pound symbol (#), which means any single digit will match. For more detail, see online help (search phrase "Like Operator").

EXERCISE 8.4 In Example 8.3, suppose you would like to include the publisher name on the form along with the publisher identifier. That is, if the user enters publisher identifier 13, you want the project to look up and display the publisher name. How would you do this? (*Hint:* See Figure 8.4(a) and remember that you can have more than one Data control on a form.)

8.3 VB's SQL Select Query

Structured Query Language (SQL) is the standard language for manipulating databases in relational database management systems. Microsoft's Access, for example, supports a version of SQL for defining queries. VB, in turn, allows you to compose SQL queries when your project is working with an Access database. The results of a query are stored by VB as a recordset.

To specify database queries in VB, one composes an SQL *Select query* — not to be confused with VB's *Select Case statement*.[8] This section introduces the basic Select query syntax and presents an example to illustrate how you can

---

[8] The creators of SQL called it the Select query because it selects specified data from a database.

FIGURE 8.24

Tables used in demonstration of SQL Select query

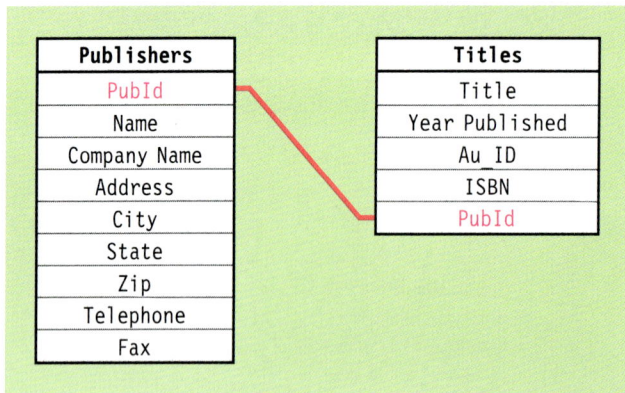

use it to combine the data from two related tables. We do not cover the complete syntax of the SQL Select query, but the concepts discussed here will give you a firm foundation for future studies in database management and design.

We begin with a set of data that we would like to query. Figure 8.24 shows two tables from the Biblio.mdb database that Microsoft supplies with VB. This figure shows you one of the ways Microsoft Access displays tables. Notice that this display is similar to an ERD except that it includes the field names. You can see that there is a common field (PubId) in both tables. As described in Section 8.1, PubId in the Titles table is a foreign key.

We want to create a VB form that displays the book title from the Titles table and the corresponding publisher name from the Publisher table. As always, we must create a Data control, and we must set its DatabaseName and RecordSource properties. We specify Biblio.mdb for the DatabaseName property. What should we specify for the RecordSource property?

When you specify the RecordSource, you must specify a single table. Since the required data comes from two tables, Titles and Publishers, how do we do this? We compose an SQL Select query to form a new set of data. This new set of data is not a new table in the database because it will not exist when program execution ends. It is a temporary set of data used by the application only while it is running.

We have already used this "new set of data" concept—we called it a recordset. Now you see the true definition of a *recordset: a collection (set) of data available to a VB project while the project is executing.* In the previous section, our recordset was the same as a single table. In that case we did not need to distinguish between the table in the database and the recordset. Even though we were working with a table, we always used the term *recordset*—not the term *table*.

Now let's look at the query. The basic syntax of the SQL Select query is

Select *fields* **From** *tables* **Where** *condition*

The italicized words are supplied by the programmer. *Fields* specifies which fields should be placed in the recordset. For our example, we want the Title field from the Titles table and the Name field from the Publisher table. Because two tables can have fields with the same name (which may or may not have the same contents), we must qualify the field names by indicating their table source. In SQL we do this by specifying the table name, followed by a period, and then the field name. So for our example the SQL Select query begins with the following:

Table name   Field name

Select Titles.Title, Publishers.Name

Tables lists the names of the tables (separated by commas) that must be combined to obtain the desired data. Our example uses the Titles and Publishers tables. Thus, the SQL Select query continues as follows:

Table names

Select Titles.Title, Publishers.Name From Titles, Publishers

Condition specifies how to combine the records of the two tables. It is similar to the target expression in the Find method. In our example, we want to combine the rows of the two tables that have matching publisher identifiers (PubID). Therefore, our complete SQL Select query is as follows:

Select Titles.Title, Publishers.Name From Titles, Publishers
   Where Titles.PubID = Publishers.PubID

Condition

The interpretation of this query is straightforward: using the Titles and Publishers tables, select the Title field from the Titles table and the Name field from the Publishers table where the publisher identifiers match in the two tables. To execute this query, the computer matches each record in the Titles table with the record in the Publishers table that have the same PubId, temporarily combines the two records, and then extracts the Title and Name fields for the recordset.

The result of this query will become the recordset for a Data control in the VB project. Each record of this recordset will have a Title field and a Name field. There is one record in this recordset for each record in the original Titles table.

Our example form and its important controls and properties are shown in Figure 8.25. Notice that in this example we bind the two text boxes to the Data control (datSQLExample). However, we do not set these bound controls' DataField properties at design time, and we do not set the Data control's RecordSource property at design time.

FIGURE 8.25

Form and controls used to create Publisher-Title report

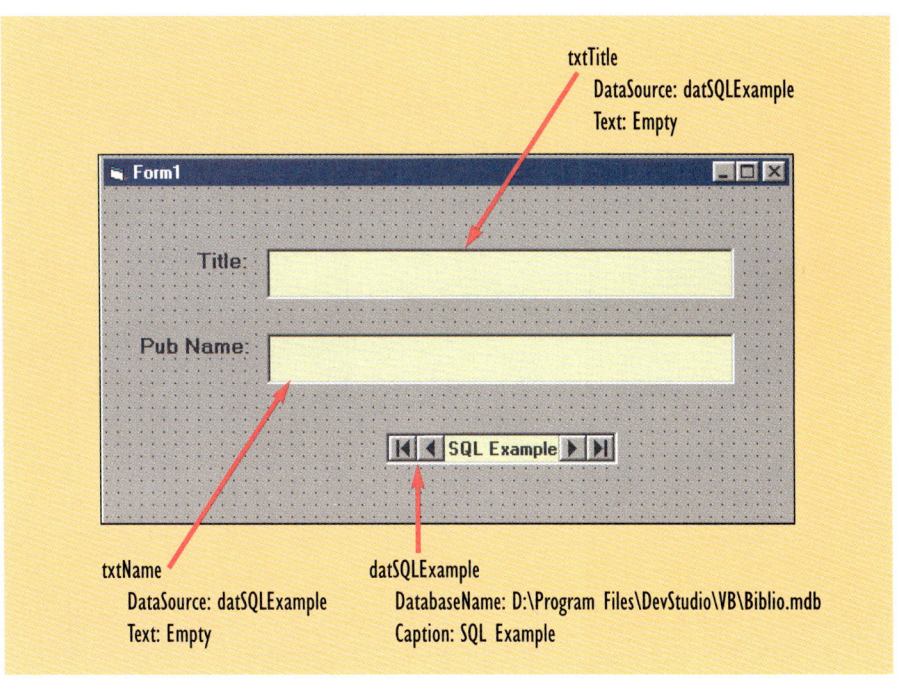

We could set the record source at design time by entering our SQL Select query into the RecordSource setting box. However, this often results in syntax errors because the SQL query is long and difficult to view in the Properties window. So we will set the record source in our program code.

We place code to define the SQL Select query, the Data control's RecordSource property, and the DataField properties for the text boxes in the form's Load event procedure. This code is shown in Figure 8.26. We use simple string concatenation to construct the Select query and store it in a string variable. We then use the string variable to set the Data control's RecordSource property, and then execute the Refresh method. **The *Refresh method* causes VB to construct the recordset by executing the SQL query to obtain the specified data from the database.**

The last two statements set the DataField properties of the two text boxes to the two fields that exist in our recordset.

Refreshing The Recordset

Suppose we modify our Publisher-Title report application to allow the user to add new records to the Titles table. In particular, suppose we add another data control and a command button to the form in Figure 8.25. We connect the new data control to the Titles table, and write code for the command button so that when it is clicked, it prompts the user to enter the fields for a new title and then stores them as a new record in the Titles table.

If the user adds a new title and then continues browsing the Publisher-Title recordset, will he or she see the new title with its publisher name? Note that in this application the Publisher-Title recordset, which contains fields from both the Titles and the Publisher tables, is created in the Form_Load event procedure. Form_Load is executed before the user enters the new record into the Titles table. So the question is, if we add a new record to the Titles table *after*

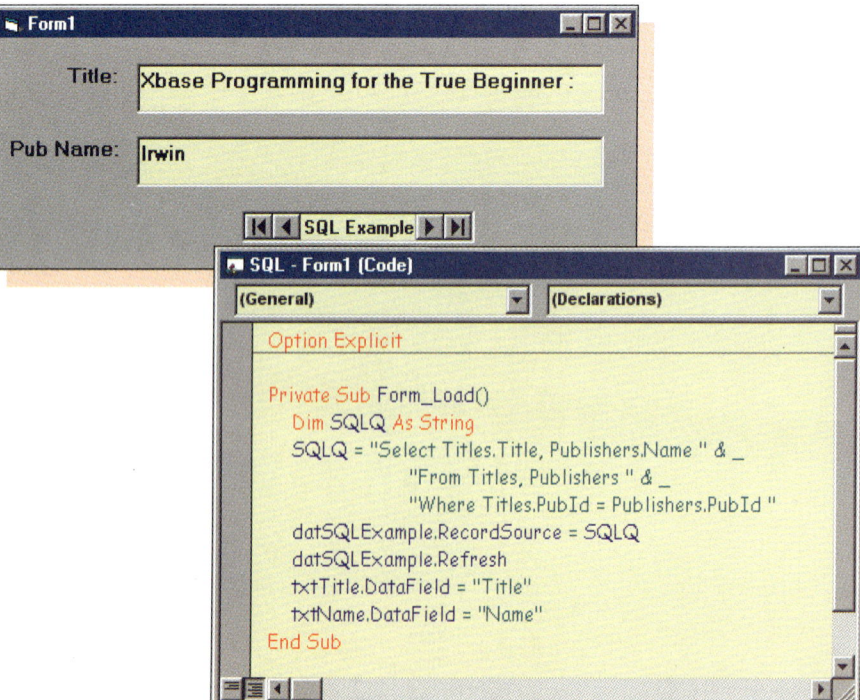

FIGURE 8.26

Code for SQL Select query example and form at run time

the (multitable) recordset is created, will the recordset automatically be updated to include an entry for the new Titles record? The answer is no; this updating is not automatic.

As programmer, if you want to bring a (multitable) recordset "up to date" after changes have been made (edits, added records, or deleted records) to its underlying tables, you must include a statement to execute the Refresh method. This is called "refreshing the recordset." To bring the new title record into the Publisher-Title recordset in our example, we simply add the following statement to the bottom of the command button's event procedure (using the Update method for the Titles table).

datSQLExample.Refresh

Note that it is not necessary to set the data control's DatabaseName and RecordSource properties again.

EXERCISE 8.5

Modify the example to include each book's ISBN number and year published in addition to the title and publisher name.

SQL Errors

When using SQL Select queries to create recordsets, you may encounter run time errors that are difficult to understand. Part of the difficulty stems from the fact that the error is not actually detected by VB, but rather by the Microsoft Access subsystem that VB uses to process the query. The Microsoft Access subsystem processes the Select query when the VB code executes the Refresh method. Any problems detected by the Access subsystem are communicated to VB, and VB then reports the error as being associated with the Refresh method. At times, the information VB provides in the error message is not very helpful to the programmer. The following examples discuss the most common mistakes and the corresponding error messages that VB displays.

Missing Spaces in the SQL Query

When you construct the SQL query, you often have to use string concatenation because of the length of the query string. When you do this, be careful to include spaces between keywords and field names. Be particularly careful at the beginning and end of each concatenated part of the Select query.

Figure 8.27 shows the Form_Load procedure that attempts to create an SQL Select query. The figure also shows the error message generated because of an error in the query.

The error message reproduces part of the query: 'Publishers.NameFrom Titles'. Notice that there is no space between "Name" and "From". Now look carefully at the original query and notice that a space is missing after the word "Name" in the first line of the query. The concatenation process combines the lines exactly as coded, and it is up to the programmer to make sure that necessary blank spaces are provided.

Figure 8.28 shows the code window after the programmer has clicked on the Debug button in the Error dialog box. Notice that VB has highlighted the Data control's Refresh method to indicate that this is the statement that produced the error. This will always be the case because the Refresh method causes the SQL query to be processed by the Microsoft Access subsystem, which is where the problem is detected.

FIGURE 8.27

SQL Select Query with missing blank space and resulting error message

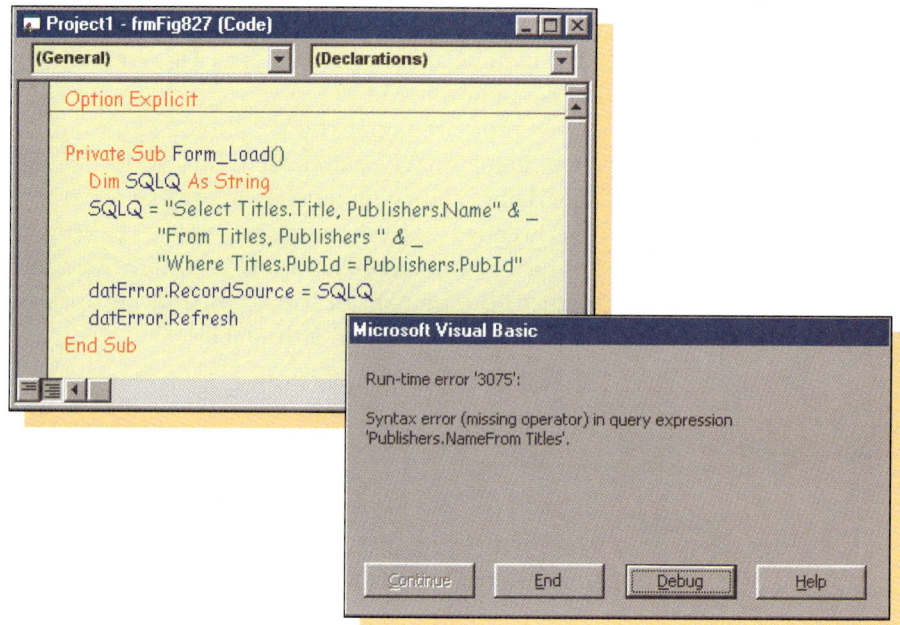

FIGURE 8.28

Code window with the statement causing the error highlighted

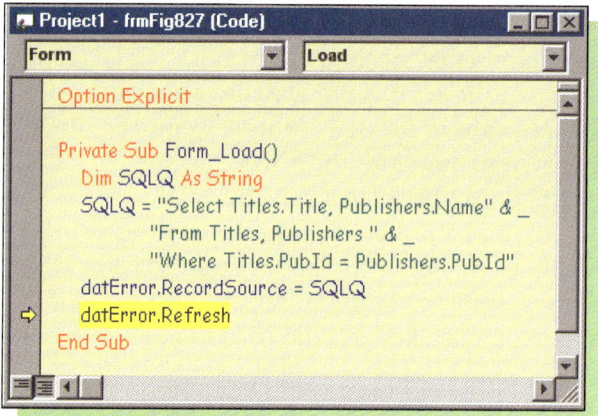

Ambiguous Field

When you create a Select Query, you must be careful to fully qualify field names that appear in more than one of the tables in your query. That is, be sure to precede the field with the name of the table (e.g., Titles.PubId). In the example in Figure 8.29, the PubId field in the Select clause is not qualified with the table name, and both the Titles and the Publishers tables have fields named PubId. As a result, the system does not know which table to use as the source for the PubId field. Instead of making an arbitrary choice, the system halts and displays an error message.

To correct the error, you should qualify the field name by adding the table name. The correct query is

```
SQLQ = "Select Titles.Pubid, Name, ISBN From Titles, Publishers " & _
       "Where Titles.PubId = Publishers.PubId"
```

Note that you do not have to qualify field names that occur in only one table. Since the Name field exists only in the Publishers table and the ISBN field exists only in the Titles table, the above query is not ambiguous and works.

FIGURE 8.29

Code and resulting error message caused by an ambiguous field name

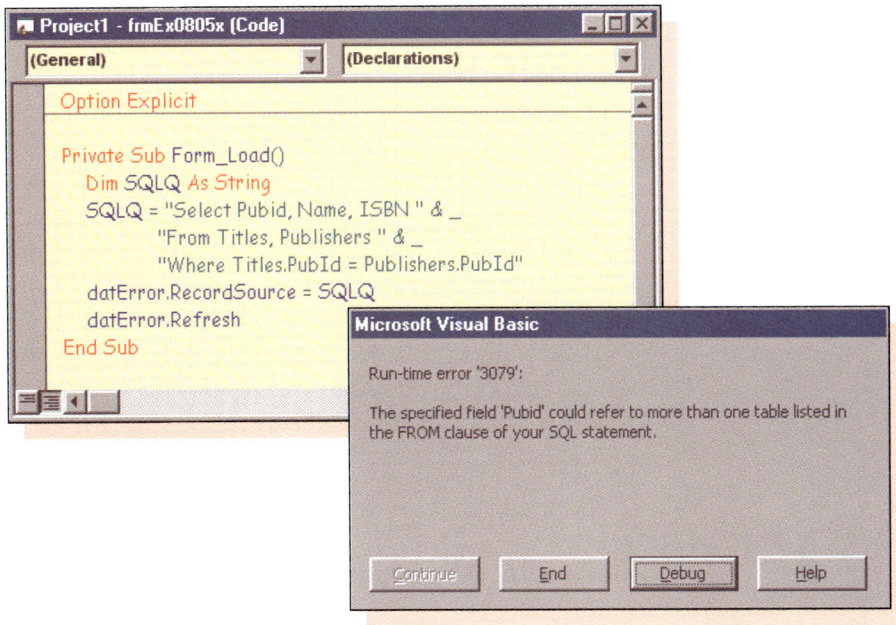

Invalid Field Names

If you misspell the name of a field in your Select Query, the error message shown in Figure 8.30 is displayed. Notice that in the code in Figure 8.30 the PubId field name in the "Where" clause has been misspelled (PubNo instead of PubId).

The error message in this situation is not very helpful at all. It is certainly not as helpful as the error messages in the previous two examples. This is unfortunate, but just remember that an error generated by the Data control's Refresh method usually means that there is a problem in your Select query. Carefully analyze the query for missing spaces and misspellings.

FIGURE 8.30

Code and resulting error message caused by a misspelled field name

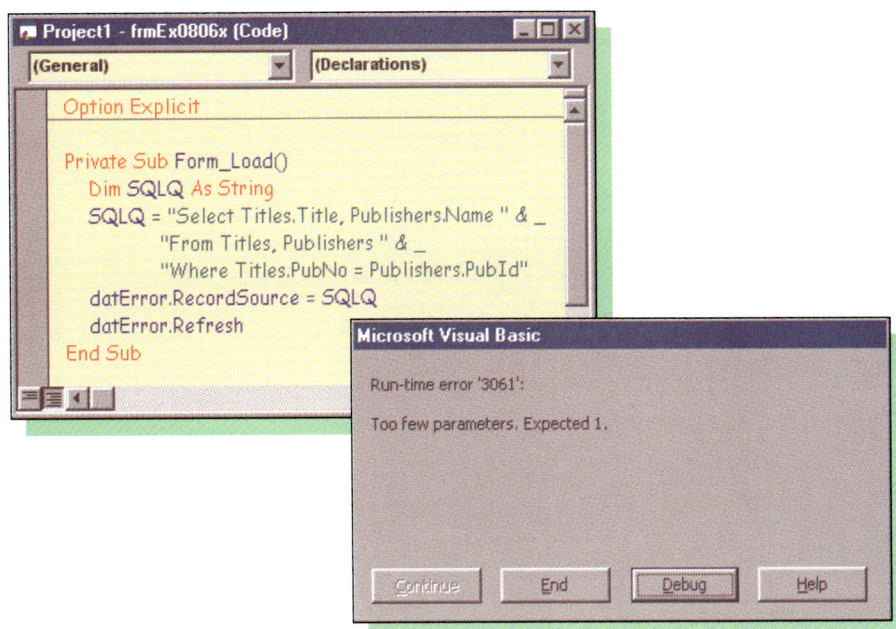

8.4 The FlexGrid Control

The recordset is a table with rows and columns, and we may want to display it on a form as a table. A bound Text box or Label control displays only one field of one record. A List box control can easily be used to display a single field for several records, but neatly displaying several fields within the same list box requires complex string manipulation. VB provides the *FlexGrid control* **to make it easy to display information to the user in a two-dimensional, table-like format.** In this section we examine the FlexGrid control and how to display data on the GUI using the grid. In Section 8.5 we demonstrate how to use the FlexGrid control to display a recordset from a database. In Section 8.6 we look at a different control, the DBGrid (data-bound grid), that is used exclusively with databases and allows the user to edit the data in the database.

Appearance and Use

Visually, a grid appears as a set of rows and columns on the form. The programmer has full control over the number of rows and columns, the column width and row height, and the ability of the user to scroll both horizontally and vertically. **The intersection of a specific row and column is called a *cell*.** If a grid has 10 rows and 5 columns, then it has a total of 50 cells. Figure 8.31 identifies the FlexGrid tool and shows a FlexGrid control on the form at design time.

For any project that uses a FlexGrid control you must include the FlexGrid tool by selecting Components... from the Project menu.[9] The FlexGrid tool is called the Microsoft FlexGrid Control 5.0 in the Components dialog box.

As shown in Figure 8.32, grids are made up of fixed and nonfixed rows and columns. Also note that rows and columns are numbered, beginning with row 0 and column 0. Fixed rows are always at the top of the grid, and fixed columns are always on the left of the grid. Fixed rows and columns will not scroll even if scrolling is enabled. That is, the user can scroll only through the nonfixed rows and columns.

The FlexGrid control is fairly complicated, with almost 50 different properties. In this section we present some of its major properties and demonstrate the use of the control via examples.

FIGURE 8.31

FlexGrid tool and control

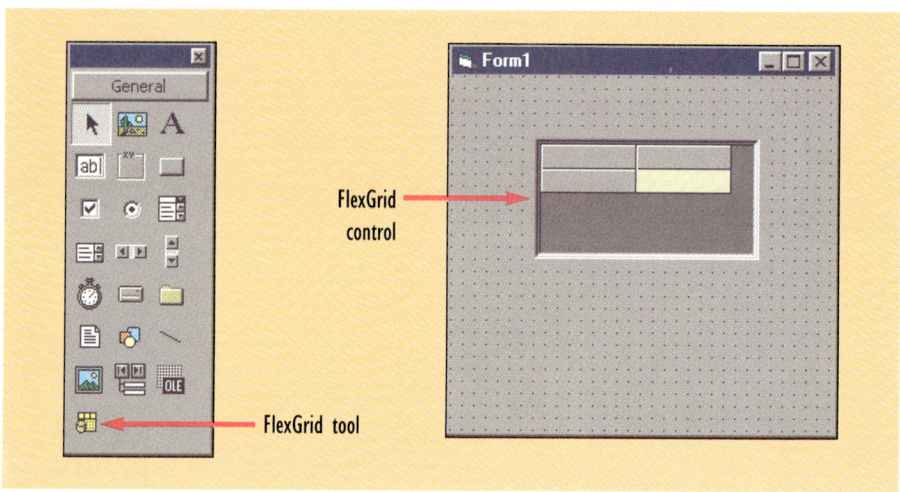

[9] The FlexGrid tool will not appear in the Toolbox until you do this.

FIGURE 8.32

Fixed and nonfixed rows and columns in a grid

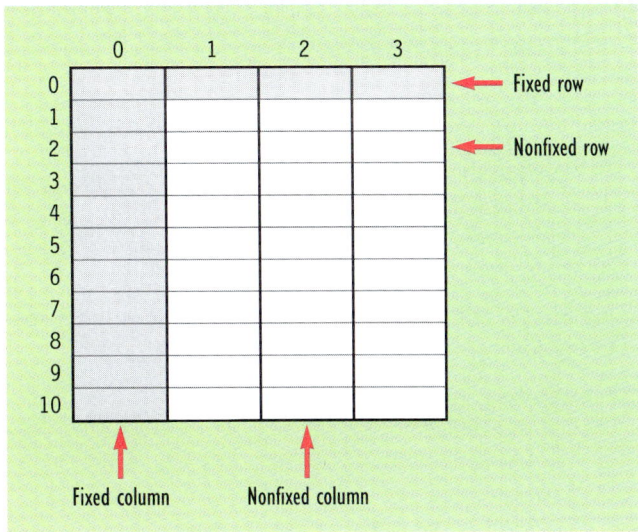

Properties

Table 8.7 summarizes some common properties of the FlexGrid control. Note that some of the properties are restricted to being changed at design time only or at run time only. The Row, Col, Text, and TextMatrix properties are the most frequently used properties of the FlexGrid control. Their use will be illustrated in the examples that follow. Note carefully in Table 8.7 (on pages 414 and 415) that the Row and Col properties are not the same as the Rows and Cols properties.

> **Convention** Use the prefix "grd" for the names of FlexGrid controls.

Events

The FlexGrid control can respond to Click, DblClick, GotFocus, LostFocus, KeyPress, and other events. However, the user cannot type values directly into the grid's cells; that is, cells are not like text boxes. Fundamentally, the FlexGrid control just displays values to the user. If you want to enable the user to input values into the grid, you have to write the code to provide this functionality.

Example 8.4 Using the FlexGrid Control

This example illustrates the fundamentals of programming the FlexGrid control. The program asks the user to enter words and displays them in the cells of a FlexGrid control with two rows and two columns. None of the rows or columns is fixed. Figure 8.33 shows the project as it is executing.

When the user clicks the Enter Words command button, procedure cmdFillInGrid_Click is executed (see Figure 8.33). This procedure uses the InputBox() function to prompt the user to enter four words, and stores each word in a different cell of the grid.

You will note in the procedure that accessing a specific cell requires that you first select the cell by setting the grid's Row and Col properties. After setting Row and Col, you use the grid's Text property to store text in the cell. Also, once the Row or Col property is set, that row or column remains set until you change it. Thus, you can set Row to 1 and then change Col from 1 to 2 to 3, etc., and you will stay in row 1. Observe that the top row corresponds to Row = 0 and the left-most column corresponds to Col = 0.

TABLE 8.7 Properties of the FlexGrid control, Part 1

Property	Specifies

AllowUserResizing	Whether the user can resize a row or column at run time. Possible settings are
	
	    0 - flexResizeNone
	    1 - flexResizeColumns
	    2 - flexResizeRows
	    3 - flexResizeBoth

CellAlignment	The alignment of text in the currently selected cell (i.e., the cell specified by the current Row and Col property settings). Possible settings are
	
	    0 - flexAlignLeftTop
	    1 - flexAlignLeftCenter
	    2 - flexAlignLeftBottom
	    3 - flexAlignCenterTop
	    4 - flexAlignCenterCenter
	    5 - flexAlignCenterBottom
	    6 - flexAlignRightTop
	    7 - flexAlignRightCenter
	    8 - flexAlignRightBottom
	    9 - flexAlignGeneral
	
	The alignment can be adjusted both vertically within a cell (Top, Center, Bottom) as well as horizontally (Left, Center, Right). The "General" alignment causes strings to be left-justified and numbers to be right-justified (both with Center vertical alignment). Not available at design time.

ColAlignment()	The alignment of text in a nonfixed column. Requires the specific column number to be supplied in the parentheses, and applies to the entire column. Possible settings are the same as the CellAlignment property. Not available at design time.
Col	The column containing the selected cell. The intersection of Row and Col specifies the currently selected cell. Not available at design time.

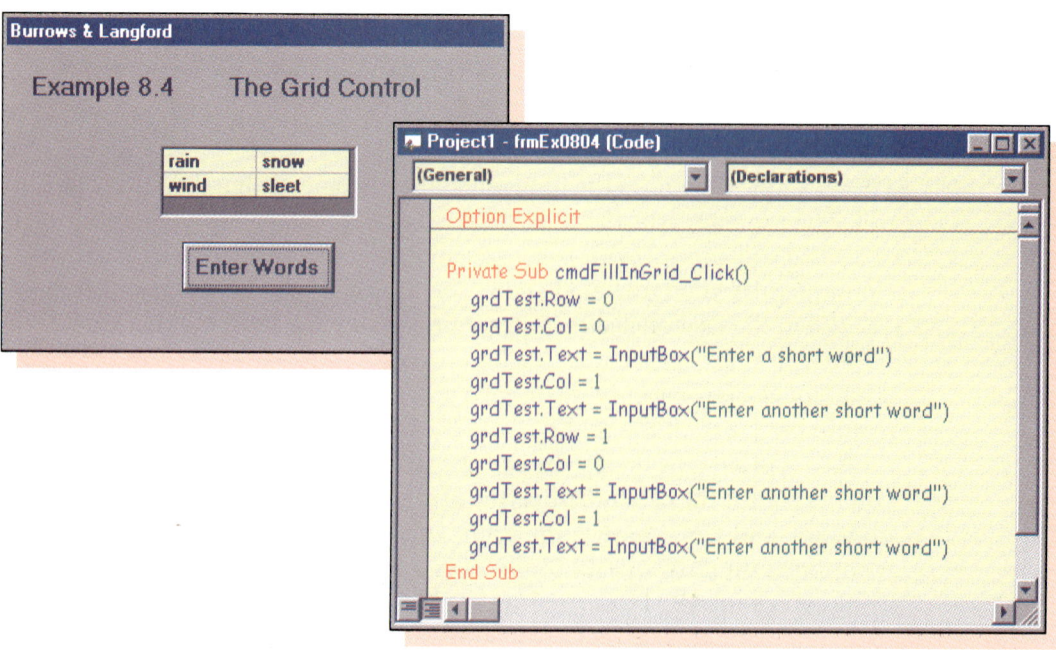

FIGURE 8.33 Form displaying user entry at run time and code for Example 8.4

TABLE 8.7 Properties of the FlexGrid control, Part 2

Property	Specifies
Cols	*The total number of columns in the grid,* including both fixed and nonfixed columns.
ColWidth()	*The width of a column.* Requires the specific column number to be supplied in the parentheses. Width is in twips (one *twip* equals 1/1,440 of an inch). Not available at design time.
FixedAlignment()	*The alignment of text in a fixed column.* Requires the specific column number to be supplied in the parentheses, and applies to the entire column. Possible settings are the same as the CellAlignment property. Not available at design time.
FixedCols	*The number of fixed columns in the grid.*
FixedRows	*The number of fixed rows in the grid.*
GridLines	*Whether or not gridlines are shown in the grid.* True or False.
Row	*The row containing the selected cell.* The intersection of Row and Col specifies the currently selected cell. Not available at design time.
Rows	*The total number of rows in the grid,* including both fixed and nonfixed rows.
RowHeight()	*The height of a row.* Requires the specific row number to be supplied in the parentheses. Height is in twips (one *twip* equals 1/1,440 of an inch). Not available at design time.
ScrollBars	*The type of scrolling enabled.* Possible settings are 0 - flexScrollBarNone (default), 1 - flexScrollBarHorizontal, 2 - flexScrollBarVertical, or 3 - flexScrollBarBoth. Can be set only at design time (read-only at run time).
Text	*The text displayed in the currently selected cell* (i.e., the cell specified by the current Row and Col property settings). Available only at run time. It is not possible to store values in grid cells at design time.
TextMatrix()	*The text displayed in a desired cell.* Requires the cell's row and column numbers to be supplied in the parentheses. This property allows you to set or retrieve the text in the specified cell without setting the Row or Col properties. Available only at run time.

Example 8.5 Using the FlexGrid's Click Event

The user can select a cell by clicking on it. That is, when the user clicks on a cell in a grid, VB automatically sets the grid's Row and Col properties to correspond to the clicked cell. Thus, it is easy to code the grid's Click event procedure to process the data in the clicked cell.

This example is similar to Example 8.4, except that there is no command button, and the user chooses which cell to enter a value into instead of the application prompting the user to enter data into all four cells in a particular order. The form has two grids, grdTestA and grdTestB, each with two rows and two columns.

When the user clicks on a cell in grdTestA, an input box is shown for entering a word. That word is then placed in the selected cell. When the user clicks on a cell in grdTestB, a similar input box is shown; in this case, however, the cell's row and column numbers are also displayed in the input box prompt. The user's input is placed in the selected cell, just as with the other grid. The two Click event procedures are shown in Figure 8.34.

FIGURE 8.34

Code for Example 8.5

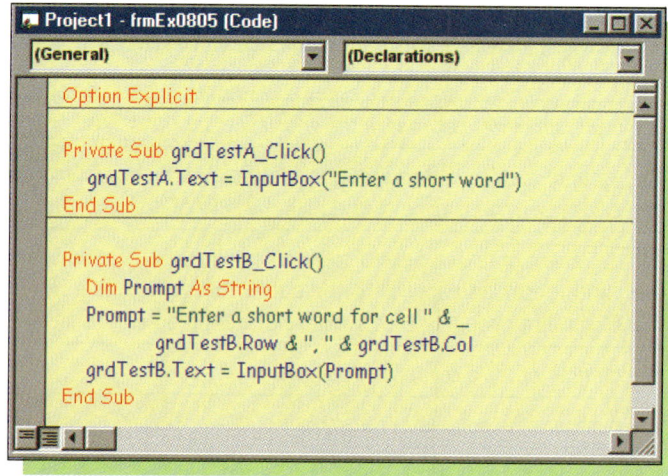

Example 8.6 Using the FlexGrid and Loops

This example illustrates additional properties of the FlexGrid control and shows how loops can be used with FlexGrid controls. It displays a table showing the future value (FV) factor for a number of years and different interest rates. The formula for the FV factor is

$$\text{FV Factor} = (1 + r)^n$$

where r is the annual interest rate and n is the number of years. Our code computes and displays the FV factors for interest rates of 3 percent, 4 percent, . . . , 10 percent, and for two, three, four, and five years.

Figure 8.35 shows the layout of headings within the grid as well as the row and column indexes. To create this application we first place a FlexGrid control and a command button on the form as shown in Figure 8.36. We make the FlexGrid control fairly large. After running the program we'll get a better idea of how large it should really be; we can then return to design mode and resize it. Alternatively, we could write code to compute its appropriate size and set it at run time.

FIGURE 8.35

Grid layout for Example 8.6's FV table

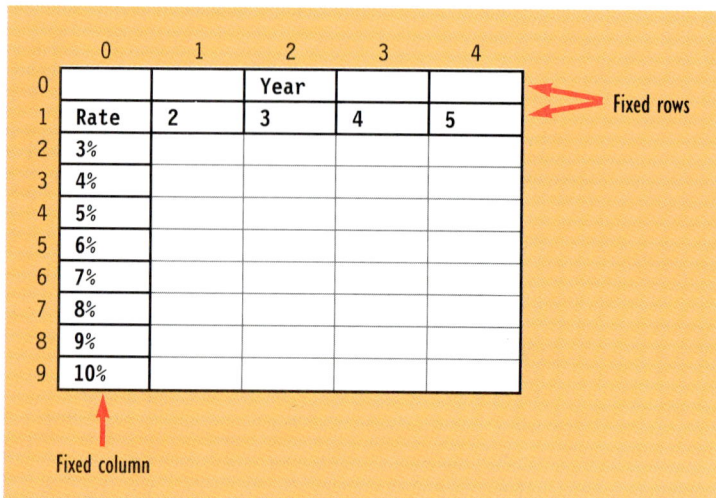

FIGURE 8.36

User interface for FV table

The property settings for the FlexGrid control are as follows:

Property	Setting
Name	grdFV
Rows	10
Cols	5
FixedCols	1
FixedRows	2
GridLines	0 - flexGridNone
GridLinesFixed	0 - flexGridNone
ScrollBars	0 - flexScrollBarNone

To place the column headings on the grid we use the form's Load event procedure. This procedure will place the text "Year" in row 0, column 2, the text "Rate" in row 1, column 0, and the year numbers 2, 3, 4, and 5 in row 1, columns 1 through 4.

We also use the Load event procedure to adjust the widths of all the columns so that they are wide enough to hold the numbers. Here we use a trick. Instead of figuring out the width in twips (1/1,440 of an inch), we use the VB function *TextWidth()*, **which takes a string value as its argument and returns the horizontal width required to display it.** The string value that we pass this function is somewhat arbitrary; we use "999.999". This allows a little extra space for the FV factors, which are typically numbers like 1.43.

The form's Load event procedure is

Private Sub Form_Load()
    Dim C **As Integer**
    grdFV.Row = 0
    grdFV.Col = 2

continues

```
        grdFV.Text = "Year"
        grdFV.Row = 1
        grdFV.Col = 0
        grdFV.Text = "Rate"
        For C = 1 To 4       'Note we are still in row 1
            grdFV.Col = C
            grdFV.Text = C + 1
        Next C
        For C = 0 To 4
            grdFV.ColWidth(C) = TextWidth("999.999")
        Next C
    End Sub
```

Running the program at this point produces the result shown in Figure 8.37.

What remains to be completed is the Click event procedure for cmdComputeFV. This procedure places the rate labels (3%, 4%, etc.) in the first column (column 0) and then computes and displays the future value factors. We use the Format$() function to format the text in the cells. For the interest rate figures we use the format "##%" and for the FV factors we use the format "###.00".

The procedure uses nested loops. The outer loop generates the interest rates. The inner loop computes the future value factors for the four years. In addition to computing the values, the loops also manage row and column numbers so that the values are placed in the proper cells. The Click event procedure is

```
    Private Sub cmdComputeFV_Click()
        Dim N As Integer, R As Currency
        Dim FVal As Currency
        Dim CurRow As Integer, CurCol As Integer
        CurRow = 1
        For R = 0.03 To 0.1 Step 0.01
            CurRow = CurRow + 1
            grdFV.Row = CurRow
            CurCol = 0
            grdFV.Col = CurCol
            grdFV.Text = Format$(R, "##%")
            For N = 2 To 5
                FVal = (1 + R) ^ N
                CurCol = CurCol + 1
                grdFV.Col = CurCol
                grdFV.Text = Format$(FVal, "###.00")
            Next N
        Next R
    End Sub
```

Running the project and clicking the Compute FV button produces the output shown in Figure 8.38.

The code shown above that computes and displays the future value factors sets the Row and Col properties to specify the cell into which the future value factor is placed. Alternatively, we could have used the TextMatrix property to specify the cell. The code below shows a segment of the cmdComputeFV_Click

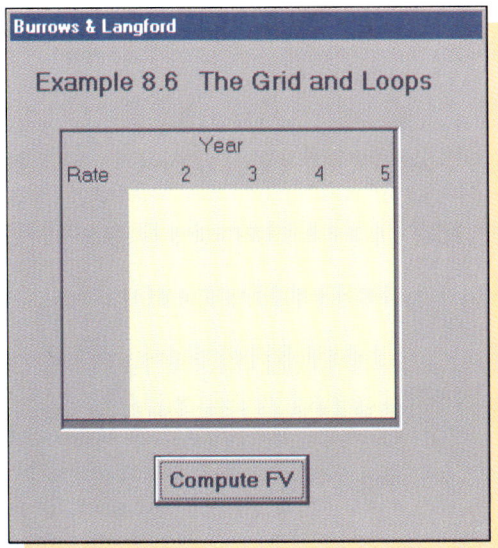

FIGURE 8.37

Column headings at run time

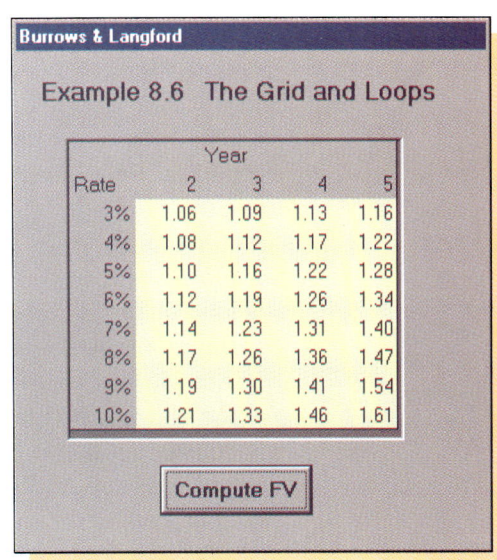

FIGURE 8.38

Output produced by the FV table example

procedure modified to use the TextMatrix property instead of the Row and Col properties.

```
CurRow = 1
For R = 0.03 To 0.1 Step 0.01
    CurRow = CurRow + 1
    CurCol = 0
    grdFV.TextMatrix(CurRow, CurCol) = Format$(R, "##%")
    For N = 2 To 5
        FVal = (1 + R) ^ N
        CurCol = CurCol + 1
        grdFV.TextMatrix(CurRow, CurCol) = Format$(FVal, "###.00")
    Next N
Next R
```

EXERCISE 8.6 Modify Example 8.4 so that it uses loops.

EXERCISE 8.7 Modify Example 8.6 so that vertical and horizontal scroll bars are included in the grid. Then modify the code so that interest rates range from 3 percent to 15 percent and years range from 2 to 10 years. Run the modified example to verify your changes.

8.5 The FlexGrid Control and Recordsets

Now that you have seen examples of how the grid can be used, you can understand why the grid is a good control to use for displaying the contents of a recordset. We can place each record in its own row of the grid, with each field of the record occupying its own cell in the row. Thus, the mapping from a recordset to a grid is simple and intuitive.

VB also provides the DBGrid control, which is quite easy to use with recordsets. The two controls are not equivalent—each has its own advantages and disadvantages. The FlexGrid is "read-only" from the user's point of view (that is, the user cannot directly edit the contents of a FlexGrid cell), whereas the DBGrid allows direct in-cell editing, with the changes automatically updating the underlying recordset. The programmer has more control over the appearance of the FlexGrid (for example, the DBGrid does not have the CellAlignment property), while the DBGrid has a large set of database transaction-oriented methods and properties (which are beyond the scope of this text).

It's important to be able to use both the FlexGrid and the DBGrid in the context of databases. In this section we use an example to illustrate how to manage the grid yourself; we explore the DBGrid control in Section 8.6.

Before looking at our example, let us examine the FlexGrid's AddItem method. Like the AddItem method for List box and Combo box controls, **the AddItem method for the FlexGrid control adds a new row to the grid**. This makes it simple to place a record in its own row in the grid. The syntax is

>   *grdName*.**AddItem** *item*

where *item* is a string expression consisting of the values to be placed in each cell of the new row, separated by tab characters (ANSI character 9). When the computer executes this statement, it first creates a new row at the bottom of the grid, then increments the grid's Rows property, and then places the values specified by the string expression *item* into this new row. As an example, suppose we had a FlexGrid control named grdTest with three columns. Executing the statements

>   **Dim** NewRow **As String**
>   NewRow = "rain" & vbTab & "snow" & vbTab & "sun"
>   grdTest.AddItem NewRow

would add a new row to the bottom of the grid, and place the word "rain" in this row's first (left-most) cell, "snow" in its second cell, and "sun" in its third cell.

Now let's look at an example application that displays a recordset from the Biblio.mdb database. The recordset combines the data in the Titles and Authors tables using the Title Author correlation table, shown in Figure 8.39. To combine these tables we compose an SQL query. For our example, we want the Title and ISBN fields from the Titles table and the Author field from the Authors table. The correct SQL query to extract these fields is

>   Select Authors.Author, Titles.Title, Titles.ISBN
>   From Authors, [Title Author], Titles
>   Where (Authors.Au_ID = [Title Author].Au_ID)
>   And ([Title Author].ISBN = Titles.ISBN)

Notice the square brackets in the above query. These are necessitated by the space in the table name "Title Author". MS Access, like many other DBMSs, allows spaces in table and field names, whereas VB, like most programming

FIGURE 8.39

Tables to be combined in recordset

languages, does not allow spaces in names chosen by the programmer. The square brackets tell VB that "Title Author" is a single table name in the database.

Our application has a single FlexGrid control and a single Data control on the form. These two controls, as well as the properties that differ from the default settings, are shown in Figure 8.40. The user of this project will not use the Data control to navigate through the recordset. Rather, when the application executes, the recordset will be processed and the records placed in the grid, where the user can scroll through them as desired. Thus, the Data control's Visible property is set to False. The executing application is shown in Figure 8.41.

The code for this application resides in the form's Load event procedure and in some general sub procedures. The form's Load event procedure is

```
Private Sub Form_Load()
    Dim SQLQuery As String
    SQLQuery = "Select Authors.Author, Titles.Title, " & _
    "Titles.ISBN From Authors, [Title Author], Titles Where (Authors.Au_ID = " & _
        "[Title Author].Au_ID) And ([Title Author].ISBN = Titles.ISBN)"
    SetupRecordset SQLQuery
    SetupGrid
    FillGrid
End Sub
```

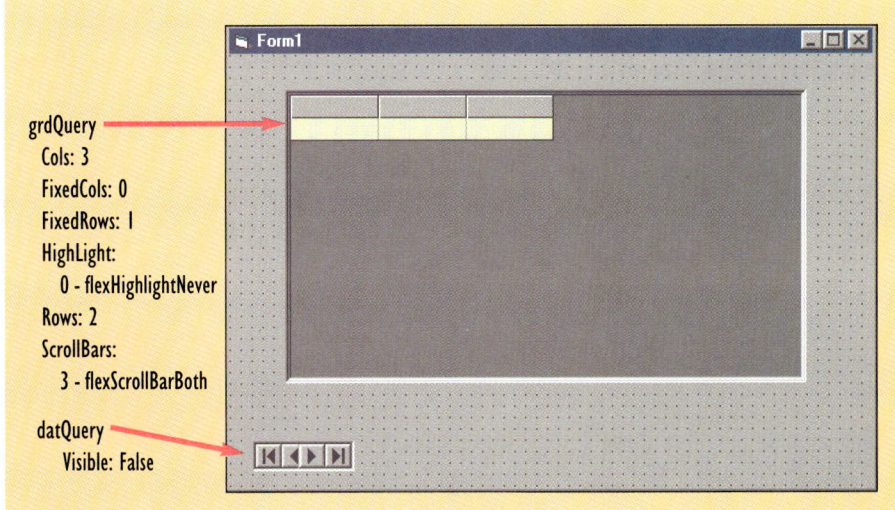

FIGURE 8.40

Controls used for Recordset/FlexGrid application

FIGURE 8.41

Recordset/FlexGrid application at run time

As you can see, the form Load procedure defines the SQL query in a string variable and then passes it to the SetupRecordset procedure. This procedure opens the database and creates the recordset. Once SetupRecordset is finished executing, the SetupGrid procedure is called to generate grid headings. Finally, the FillGrid procedure is executed, which actually places the contents of the recordset into the cells of the grid.

The SetupRecordset procedure is straightforward. It sets the DatabaseName and RecordSource properties for the Data control (datQuery) and then executes the Refresh method.

```
Private Sub SetupRecordset(ByVal QueryString As String)
    datQuery.DatabaseName = "C:\Program Files\DevStudio\Vb\Biblio.mdb"
    datQuery.RecordSource = QueryString
    datQuery.Refresh
End Sub
```

The SetupGrid procedure sets the column widths, the grid's width (by summing the column widths), and the headings in the fixed row (row 0). We again use the TextWidth() function to estimate the appropriate width of each grid column.

```
Private Sub SetupGrid()
    Dim WideString As String
    Dim C As Integer, GridWidth As Integer
    WideString = String$(35, "X")
    grdQuery.ColWidth(0) = TextWidth(WideString)
    WideString = String$(24, "X")
    grdQuery.ColWidth(1) = TextWidth(WideString)
    WideString = String$(14, "X")
    grdQuery.ColWidth(2) = TextWidth(WideString)
    For C = 0 To 2
        GridWidth = GridWidth + grdQuery.ColWidth(C)
    Next C
    grdQuery.Width = GridWidth
    grdQuery.TextMatrix(0, 0) = "Title"
    grdQuery.TextMatrix(0, 1) = "Author"
    grdQuery.TextMatrix(0, 2) = "ISBN"
End Sub
```

Procedure FillGrid fills the grid with the data from the recordset. This procedure processes the recordset one record at a time until it encounters the end of file (EOF). For each record, it assembles a string consisting of the field values separated by tab characters. Then the grid's AddItem method is used to insert this string into the grid as a new row.

```
Private Sub FillGrid()
    Dim NewRow As String
    Do Until datQuery.Recordset.EOF = True
        NewRow = datQuery.Recordset("Title") & vbTab & datQuery.Recordset("Author") & _
            vbTab & datQuery.Recordset("ISBN")
        grdQuery.AddItem NewRow
        datQuery.Recordset.MoveNext
    Loop
End Sub
```

Observe that at design time we gave the grid just two rows (in Figure 8.40 we specified the grid's Rows property setting as 2). Each time the AddItem method is executed, VB automatically increments the Rows property before it inserts the new row into the grid.

Finally, the user is certain to notice the order in which records appear in the grid. In Figure 8.41 the records appear to be ordered by ISBN. It is usually difficult to predict the record order that will result from an SQL query. The record order may be unsatisfactory to the user. A useful and easy extension to the SQL statement is the *Order By clause*, **which you can add to the end of the SQL query to specify the desired order of the records in the recordset.** To modify the preceding code to produce a recordset ordered by Title, use the following:

```
SQLQuery = "Select Authors.Author, Titles.Title, Titles.ISBN " & _
    "From Authors, [Title Author], Titles " & _
    "Where (Authors.Au_ID = [Title Author].Au_ID) " & _
        "And ([Title Author].ISBN = Titles.ISBN) " & _
    "Order By Titles.Title"
```

EXERCISE 8.8

As Figure 8.41 shows, the application displays the first record of the recordset in row 2 of the grid, and leaves row 1 blank. Modify the application so that it displays the first record in row 1 instead of row 2. *Hint*: The AddItem method allows an optional argument, *index*, which you can use to specify the location of the new row in the grid. See online help for details.

EXERCISE 8.9

Modify the application so that it sets the column widths *after* it places the records in the grid. The application should determine the width of the longest value in a column and then use this information to set the column width accurately. (Note that the application currently uses the simple-minded strategy of setting the widths of columns 0, 1, and 2 equal to the widths of 35, 24, and 14 "X" characters, respectively.)

8.6 The DBGrid Control

The **DBGrid** (data-bound grid) control is designed to be used with database recordsets. Simply setting a DBGrid's DataSource property to a Data control causes the DBGrid to automatically process the associated recordset and display the records in a spreadsheet-like fashion. This includes automatic placement of the field names into first row of the grid.

Unlike the FlexGrid, where the user is restricted to browsing through the records of a recordset, the DBGrid permits the user to edit fields, and to add or delete records directly from the grid. These additional capabilities are programmable, so the programmer can control whether they are available to the user.

Appearance and Use

Visually the DBGrid looks very similar to the FlexGrid. The main difference is an added column on the left side of the grid that is used to indicate either the "current" record (a right arrow is placed next to the current record) or an "empty" record (an asterisk is placed next to the empty record). Figure 8.42 identifies the DBGrid tool and shows a DBGrid control on the form at design time.

FIGURE 8.42

DBGrid tool and control

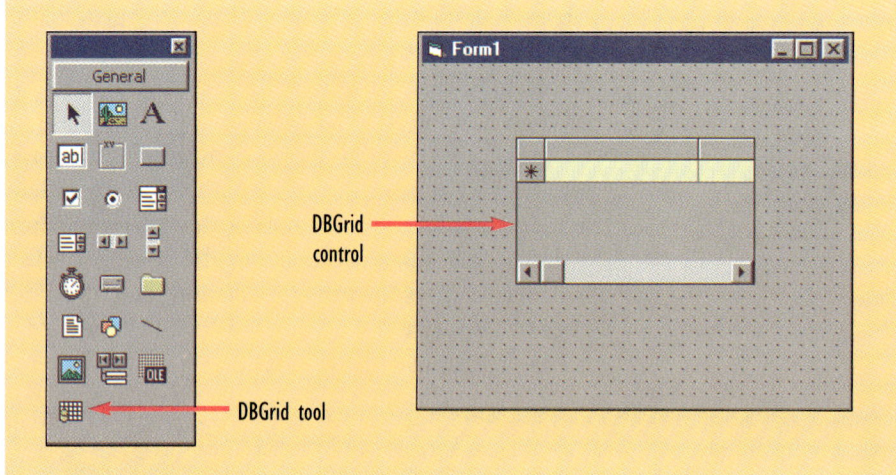

Like the FlexGrid, any project that uses a DBGrid control must include the DBGrid tool by selecting Components… from the Project menu. The DBGrid tool is called the Microsoft Data Bound Grid Control in the Components dialog box.

When first created, the DBGrid control has two columns and one empty row. An additional left-hand column contains an asterisk indicating that the row is empty. At run time the actual number of rows and columns is determined by the DBGrid control when it is bound to the recordset.

Properties

The DBGrid is a custom control created for VB by Apex Software Corporation. In addition to the usual access to properties through the Properties window, custom controls provide a customized properties dialog box. Clicking on the ellipses in the (Custom) Property setting causes a Property Pages dialog box to be displayed as shown in Figure 8.43.

The meaning of many of the property settings on the General tab shown in Figure 8.43 is obvious. The three "Allow…" properties enable or disable user

FIGURE 8.43

The DBGrid's Property Pages dialog box

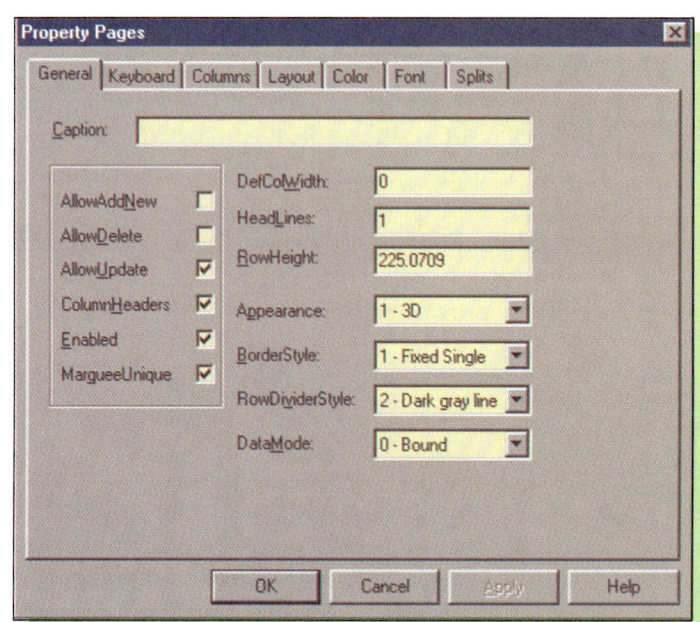

editing of the recordset. Placing check marks in these boxes allows the user to add new records, delete existing records, and update (edit) existing records.

The DefColWidth property (default column width) should be set to zero if you want the DBGrid to automatically adjust the column widths according to the data in the recordset. The DataMode property should be set to "0 - Bound" if you are going to bind the DBGrid to a Data control.

The remaining tabs on the Property Pages dialog box are generally only used in advanced applications. See online help (search phrase "DBGrid") for details of the properties on these pages.

As with any other bound control, you must have a Data control on your form that is bound to a database and a recordset. The DBGrid's DataSource property must be associated with a Data control in order for it to work properly. However, unlike a text box or label, the DBGrid does not have a DataField property. The grid displays all the fields of the associated recordset.

> **Convention** Use the prefix "dbgrd" for the names of DBGrid controls.

Events

There are over 50 events associated with the DBGrid. Some are familiar, like the Click, KeyPress, and LostFocus events. Others, like the BeforeColEdit, AfterColEdit, and RowColChange events, are designed to detect changes in the grid and can be used for data validation and correction. These additional events are beyond the scope of this text. If you are interested in investigating them, as well as other events and uses of the DBGrid, the creator of the control, Apex, provides documentation, including an excellent tutorial, on its web site (http://www.apexsc.com).

The examples that follow demonstrate how easy it is to use the DBGrid for routine tasks. The database used in the examples is named EmpDept.mdb and is shown in Figure 8.44 (as Microsoft Access tables).

Example 8.7 Using the DBGrid Control with a Single Table

In this example, we use the DBGrid to display the contents of the Employee table. The form and code are shown in Figure 8.45. The grid's AllowUpdates property is set to True, so the user will be able to edit existing records, but the AllowAddNew and AllowDelete properties are both set to False so the user will be unable to add or delete records. The only code for the example is the Form_Load event procedure, which sets the database name and the record source for the Data control.

The project is shown at run time in Figure 8.46. In this figure the user is in the middle of changing employee number 100's phone number (notice the pencil icon in the left column).

FIGURE 8.44

Tables in the EmpDept.mdb database used in Examples 8.7 and 8.8

Employee Table

EmpNo	EmpName	EmpPhone	DeptCode
100	Alice	324-5494	act
110	Ann	234-5423	prod
120	Carlos	324-9855	prod
130	Kim	234-9812	mktg
140	Yong	324-6649	act
150	Bill	324-5924	prod

Department Table

DeptCode	DeptName
act	Accounting
mktg	Marketing
prod	Production

FIGURE 8.45

The form at design time and code for Example 8.7

FIGURE 8.46

Example 8.7 at run time

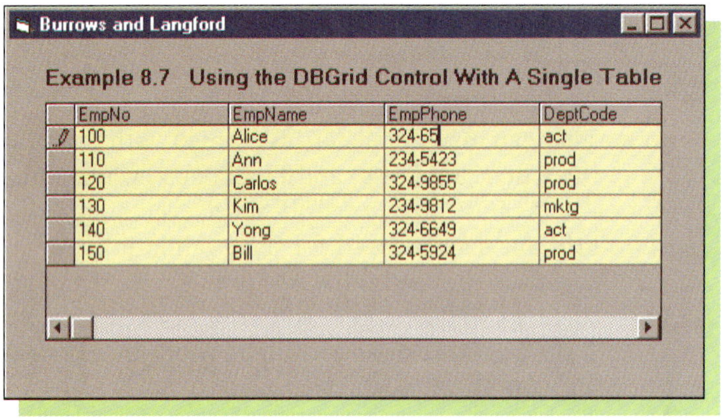

FIGURE 8.47

Example 8.7 with the AllowAddNew and AllowDelete properties set to True

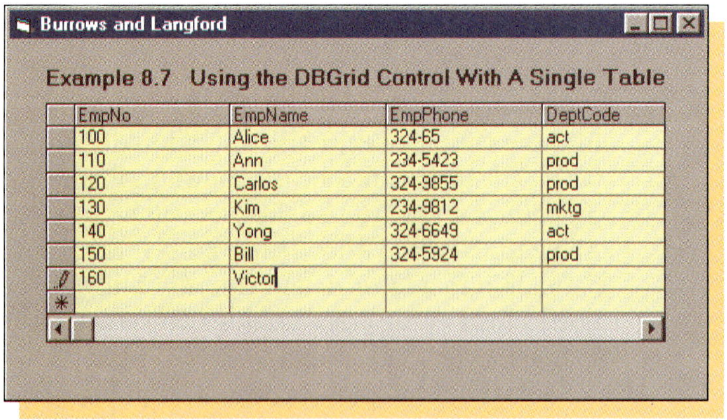

Returning to design mode, we change the AllowAddNew and AllowDelete property settings to True. Figure 8.47 shows the project at run time after this modification. Here, the user is entering a new employee (employee number 160). Notice the asterisk in the last row indicating a new record can be added to it.

To delete an existing record the user clicks on the left-most column of the desired row and presses the DELETE key. Be aware, however, that there is no automatic "undo" of this delete. Providing such an undo feature requires writing code; this is an example of a task for which some of the DBGrid's advanced events are useful.

FIGURE 8.48

Code for Example 8.8 and form at design time

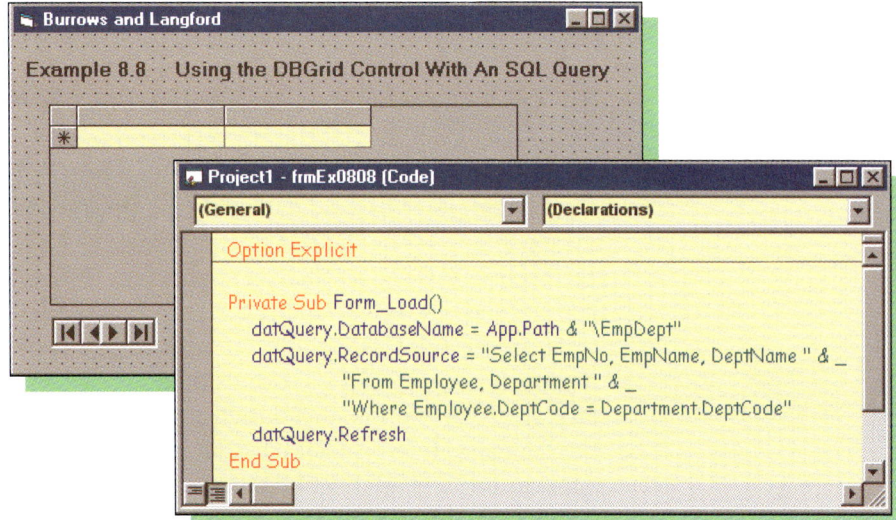

FIGURE 8.49

Example 8.8 at run time

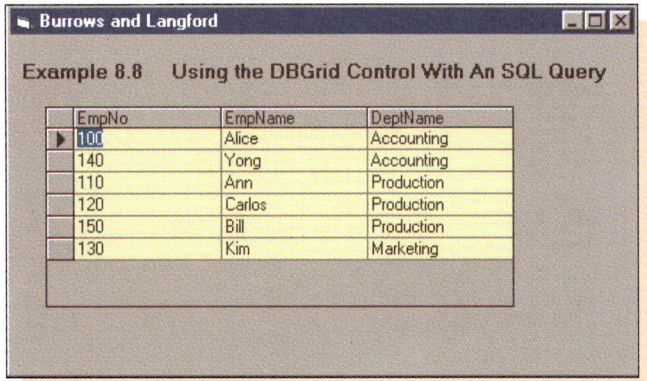

Example 8.8 **Using the DBGrid Control With An SQL Query**

In this example, we combine the records from the two tables using an SQL Select query. The form at design time and code are shown in Figure 8.48. The DBGrid's DataSource property was set to "datQuery" at design time. That's all that is needed to make the project work.

The project at run time is shown in Figure 8.49. In this example, the AllowUpdate, AllowAddNew, and AllowDelete properties were all set to True. Notice, however, that there is no empty row at the bottom for adding a new record. When a DBGrid is associated with a multitable SQL query, it does not allow the user to modify the records in any way, regardless of the "Allow…" property settings.

8.7 Project 12: Real Estate Listings Database Application

Many database applications provide support for a company's operations. In this project we describe a database application that a real estate agent might use to access information on listings (properties and homes available for sale). This realistic example not only demonstrates database principles discussed in this chapter, but it also employs many of the controls and techniques covered in earlier chapters.

Description of the Application

◆ ◆ ◆

Real estate agents require access to a large amount of data to perform their daily tasks. They often need to access this information from different locations—their office, their home, or the properties they are showing to clients. A laptop computer with moderate to high power makes it possible for them to carry a computer-based database. What they need is an application that makes it easy to access the data in various ways.

Figure 8.50 shows such an application. It displays information about each listing (address, price, square feet, etc.) on the left side of the form. The controls on the right side allow the user to browse through the entire database record by record; display listings based on selected criteria; perform elementary database maintenance functions such as adding or deleting listings from the database; find a specific listing based on the listing number; and quit the application. The application also makes it easy for the real estate agent to provide clients with an estimate of the monthly mortgage payments on a property. Figure 8.51 shows the calculator that is displayed when the user clicks the Compute Monthly Payments button.

FIGURE 8.50

Real estate listings application at run time

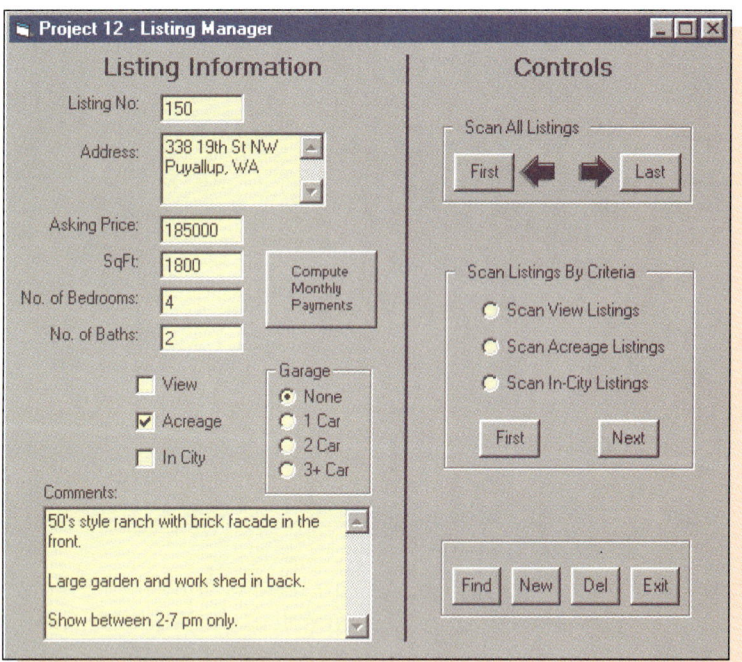

FIGURE 8.51

Real estate Payment Calculator at run time

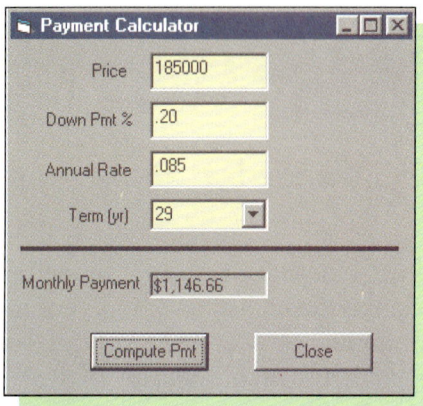

Design of the Application

The application is built around a single-table database created with Microsoft Access. This database is called Listings.mdb and the single table is called Listings. Table 8.8 shows the fields in the Listings table. The main form for the application has a Data control associated with the Listings.mdb database and the Listings table. At run time you cannot see the Data control because its Visible property is set to False. All the data except the garage information are presented via bound controls. The check boxes (View, Acreage, and In City) are bound to fields that are type Yes/No in the Microsoft Access database. The values Yes and No in Access are the same as the Boolean values True and False in VB.

The database contains a field named NoCarGarg. This is an integer field that stores the number of cars the garage holds. If the house has a two-car garage, then this field equals 2. On our form, this value is presented via option buttons. Because option buttons cannot be bound to a Data control, associating the number of cars field and the option buttons is a bit tricky.

There is a Label control on the application's form that you cannot see because its Visible property is set to False. This label is bound to the database field NoCarGarg, and the value in this label's Caption property is used to set the appropriate one of the four option buttons. Specifically, when the user moves from one record to another, the value in the label associated with the NoCarGarg database field will change. You can compose an event procedure for the label to detect that change and update the option buttons accordingly.

Also, when entering a new listing or changing a current listing, the user might set or change an option button. If so, the application must update the database field NoCarGarg, too. This is easy to do. When the user clicks an option button, have this event change the value in the invisible Label control's Caption property. That is, clicking on the 2 Car option button should cause the caption of the invisible label to be set to 2. Since the Label control is bound, its new value will be saved in the database when the user moves to another record.

TABLE 8.8 Fields in real estate Listings table

Database Field	Type	Description
ListNo	Text	Listing number
Addr	Text	Address
Price	Currency	Asking price
SqFt	Integer	Number of square feet
NoBed	Integer	Number of bedrooms
NoBath	Single	Number of bathrooms
NoCarGarg	Integer	Garage space for cars
View	Yes/No	Is there a view
Acreage	Yes/No	Is there acreage
InCity	Yes/No	Is house in the city
Comments	Text	Misc. comments

Let us now turn our attention to the command buttons on the right side of the form.

1. Navigation Controls – Scan All Listings. These controls move through the records of the database as indicated by the button captions and arrow images. Since they contain Move methods, they automatically cause the current record to be updated if it has been changed and the user moves to another record. We choose to accept this behavior.

- **First**: Moves the record pointer to the first record in the recordset. Any values stored in the payment calculator from a previous record should be cleared. Remember that the controls on the payment calculator are on a different form than the one that contains the First button.

- **Last**: Moves the record pointer to the last record in the recordset. Any values still in the payment calculator from a previous record should be cleared.

- **Next**: Advances the record pointer one position in the recordset. If this causes the record pointer to move beyond the EOF mark, the user should be informed that he or she is at the end of the listings. Any values stored in the payment calculator from a previous record should be cleared.

- **Previous**: Moves the record pointer back one position in the recordset. If this causes the record pointer to move before the BOF mark, the user should be informed that he or she is at the beginning of the listings. Any values stored in the payment calculator from a previous record should be cleared.

2. Record Manipulation Buttons – Find, New, Del, and Exit. These buttons support general database maintenance functions. They perform subtle but important tasks. For example, they update the database if the user has modified a field.

- **Delete Listing (Del)**: After verifying that the user really wants to make this change, the existing record should be deleted. When the record is deleted, the record pointer should be moved to the next record in the recordset. *Hint:* You already have a procedure (defined earlier) for moving to the next record.

- **Exit**: Closes the recordset (using the Close method) and terminates program execution. The user may have changed a value in the current record just prior to clicking the Exit button, and closing the recordset will save this change in the database.

- **Find Listing**: Gets a listing number from the user and uses the FindNext method to locate the record with this listing number. Use the greater-than-or-equal operator (>=) in the FindNext criterion so that if the listing number does not exist, the first listing after that will be located. You must enclose the listing number in single quote marks for the Find to work. This is because the ListNo field is a text field in the database. To put quotes around the user-specified listing number, use something like the following (note the single quotes between double quotes).

Target = "ListNo >= " & "'" & UserSpecifiedListingNo & "'"

If the variable UserSpecifiedListingNo holds the value 150, then after this statement is executed, Target will hold the string

ListNo >= '150'

You can then use the variable *Target* as the criterion in your FindNext.[10]

♦ **New Listing**: Executes the recordset's AddNew method to prepare a new record. Note that this automatically clears the controls on the form that are bound to the database. Also, set the focus to the Listing Number text box so the user starts with that field. As the user fills in fields that are bound to the database, VB automatically fills the copy buffer.

3. Scan Listings by Criteria Buttons. These two buttons support movement through the database based on one of three prespecified criteria. Be sure to handle possible "no match" conditions in both these buttons.

♦ **First**: Tests the option buttons to see which one is selected (Value property True), then finds the first record matching the corresponding criterion. Since the relevant fields in the database are Yes/No field types, the code for this operation is a bit odd-looking. Access's Yes/No is the same as VB's True/False, so you can find the first record with View equal to Yes with the following statement

```
datFoo.Recordset.FindFirst "View = True"
```

where datFoo is the name of your Data control.

♦ **Next**: Like the code for the First button except it uses FindNext instead of FindFirst.

In addition to the main form, you should create a second form that enables the user to calculate the monthly payments for a hypothetical loan (see Figure 8.51). The Price field should be taken from the Asking Price text box on the main form. That is, the Text property of the Price text box should automatically be set when this form is activated. Recall from Chapter 3 that to access a control on another form you must qualify the control name with the name of the form on which it resides. For example, if you are writing code for frmA and it needs to access txtExample that is on frmB, then you would specify this text box as follows:

```
frmB!txtExample
```

The Close button hides the form. The Compute button takes the purchase price, down payment percentage, annual interest rate, and the term from the text boxes and dropdown combo box, then computes and displays the monthly payment. Compute the loan amount by subtracting the down payment from the purchase price. Then use VB's Pmt() function to compute the monthly payment.

```
-Pmt(MonthlyRate, NoOfMonths, LoanAmt, 0, 0)
```

The Term combo box should include the values 10, 15, 20, 25, 29, and 30.

Construction of the Application

♦ ♦ ♦

This application looks more difficult than it actually is. The Data control does a great deal of the work for you. However, it is still a good idea to proceed carefully, and to incrementally add, test, and save controls as you go.

---

[10] There is a potential problem here. If the actual listing numbers in the database are 150, 200, 250, and 300, and the user enters the listing number 1000, the FindNext will find listing number 150. This is because the comparison is a string comparison, not a numeric comparison. Thanks to Krishnamurthy Balaji, a civil engineer for the California Department of Transportation (and a student taking a VB course) for pointing this out.

Start by creating the Data control and connecting it to the database and table. The database, Listings.mdb, is stored in directory C08/Proj12 in the code package for this text. Leave the Data control's Visible property True for now so you can use it to test your application before you create and program your own navigation controls. Next add a few of the bound text boxes like the ones for the listing number and address. Set their DataSource and DataField properties to bind them to the Data control and database. Then run the application. You should be able to use the Data control to move from record to record.

When you get the first few bound controls up and working, add a few more and get them working. Continue by setting up the remainder of the controls that are bound directly to the database.

Work on the Garage controls next. Create a frame and draw four option buttons in it. Name them and set their captions as appropriate. Then create a label and bind it to the Data control and the NoCarGarg field. This is the label that will eventually be invisible but will link the database to the option buttons. Run your project again and confirm that the label is showing different numbers as you move from record to record. You should not expect to see the option buttons work yet.

Notice that the content of the label changes each time you move to a new record. You can take advantage of this by placing code in the label's Change event procedure. This code should set the appropriate option button's Value property to True based on the label's Caption property value.[11]

After writing the code for the Change event, test it. You should now see the option buttons change as you move through the records in the database. However, at this point, if you change the selected option button for a listing, the change won't get into the database. This is because the label, not the option button, is bound to the database. Thus, you need to write code that changes the value in the label's caption when the user clicks an option button. For example, if you click on the 1 Car option button, then the label's Caption property should be set to 1.

This should complete the controls needed to display the contents of a record from the database. Now turn your attention to the controls on the right side of the form. Again, add one button (the First button in the Scan All Listings section would be a good place to start), then code and test it. Continue, one button at a time, to add and test. Use the descriptions provided earlier to guide you in writing the code.

Remember, limit what you do at each step and thoroughly test what you've done before you proceed. The strategy of doing a little coding and then testing limits the number and complexity of the problems you encounter. It also increases the chances you'll be able to correct the problem quickly.

EXERCISE The text points out that there is a problem with the "Find Listing" function due to string comparisons. Explain the problem in more detail. Suggest a way to solve the problem (assume you have the ability to modify the database).

---

[11] Be sure to test for an empty label, that is, a label with its caption equal to the empty string. This can happen if the user navigates beyond the EOF or before the BOF. If the label caption is empty, then don't do anything in the Change event.

Chapter Summary

1. A database is an organized collection of data and relationships that describe entities of interest to a business. An entity is a thing, such as an employee, a customer, a product, or a part. Examples of relationships are (a) the parts used to assemble a product and (b) the set of customers an employee is responsible for. Databases are a very important part of most business data processing, and VB is a very important tool used by businesses to access the data in their databases.

2. An entity-relationship diagram (ERD) documents entities and their relationships. This diagram indicates cardinality—the number of one entity that can be related to another entity. For example, an ERD might indicate that a customer is related to one employee and an employee is related to many customers. This would be an example of a one-to-many relationship.

3. VB supports the relational database approach for organizing data about entities and their relationships. In a relational database, the data for each entity are stored in their own two-dimensional table. Each table includes a key field that has unique values from one record to another. Relational databases use foreign keys and correlation tables to link tables according to the relationships between the entities.

4. Database designers use a process called normalization to place data items into tables in a way that minimizes the problems of redundant data while maintaining the correct relationships between the entities. The data stored in several related tables of a relational database can be combined using an SQL (Structured Query Language) query.

5. The Data control provides a VB application with access to a database. The Data control's DatabaseName and RecordSource properties are used to link the control to a table in a database. At run time, VB uses these properties to create a recordset, which is the set of records available to the Data control. The Data control manages a record pointer that VB uses to keep track of the current record in the recordset.

6. The contents of a field in a recordset can be presented to the user by binding a control, such as a Label or a Text box control, to the Data control. The bound control's DataSource and DataField properties are used to associate (bind) it to a particular field of the recordset. The Data control has four navigation buttons that let the user change the current record to the first, the last, the next, or the previous record in the recordset; the bound control always displays the value of its field in the current record.

7. The Data control can be programmed to manage the records in a recordset. The Move methods—MoveFirst, MoveLast, MoveNext, and MovePrevious—apply to a recordset and allow the programmer to specify movement through the records of a recordset just like the Data control's navigation buttons. The programmer must be aware of two possible conditions that can arise when the program moves through the records of the recordset—the End Of File (EOF) and Beginning Of File (BOF) conditions—which can be tested in code to see whether the record pointer has moved beyond the end of the recordset (EOF) or above the first record of the recordset (BOF).

8. Several methods are used to modify the contents of the recordset. These include the following: the Delete method, which deletes the current record

from the recordset; the AddNew method, which prepares the recordset to accept a new record; the Edit method, which prepares the current record for editing; and the Update method, which causes a new or edited record to be placed into the recordset (i.e., saved in the database).

9. The Find methods—FindFirst, FindLast, FindNext, and FindPrevious—are used to find records based on a specified criterion. For example, we might want to find a customer record whose customer number field is equal to a specific value. When using these methods, the recordset's NoMatch property indicates whether the find was successful.

10. VB's SQL Select query allows you to specify a recordset that combines records from multiple database tables. This ability is very important when working with relational databases, since the data needed by the user are often stored in multiple tables. VB examines the specifications in the SQL query and automatically uses the foreign keys and correlation tables in the database to combine records from the specified tables. The SQL query includes three required parts which must be supplied by the programmer. The first part specifies the fields to extract from the database tables. These fields become the fields of the recordset. The second part specifies the tables in the database from which the fields will be extracted. The third part is a condition that specifies how the tables will be combined. An optional fourth part of the SQL query allows you to specify the desired order of the records in the recordset.

11. The FlexGrid control allows the programmer to display information on the user interface in a two-dimensional, table-like manner. A grid is organized as a table with rows and columns. The rows and columns are numbered beginning with row 0 and column 0. Some of the rows at the top of the grid and some of the columns on the left of the grid can be fixed, which means that they do not scroll with the other rows or columns.

The intersection of a row and column is called a cell. The Row and Col properties together specify the currently selected cell, and the grid's Text property is used to reference the value in the selected cell. The FlexGrid control does not allow the user to type data directly into a cell—the programmer must provide code to create this functionality. Loops are commonly used in code which fills the cells of a grid.

An important use of the grid is to display the contents of a recordset. Since a recordset is a collection of records and fields, it is natural to display its contents in a grid with rows and columns. The user can then browse the recordset by scrolling through the grid.

12. The DBGrid (data-bound grid) is a custom control designed to work directly with recordsets. Simply associating a DBGrid with a Data control using the grid's DataSource property causes the grid to automatically set up the correct number of columns to display the rows of the recordset.

If the grid is bound to a recordset that represents a single table in a database, then the user can both browse and edit the records in the recordset. By setting the AllowAddNew, AllowDelete, and AllowUpdate properties, the programmer can control whether the user is able to modify the recordset using the grid.

If a grid is bound to a recordset that is the result of a multitable SQL query, then the user can only browse the recordset using the grid.

Key Terms

AddItem method	database management	normalization
AddNew method	system (DBMS)	NoMatch property
App object	DBGrid (data-bound	Order By clause
associative object	grid)	record pointer
Beginning Of File (BOF)	End Of File (EOF)	RecordCount property
bound control	entity	recordset
browsing	entity-relationship	Refresh method
cardinality	diagram (ERD)	relational database
cell	Find methods	relationship
compound key	FlexGrid control	Select query
copy buffer	foreign key	structured query
correlation table	intersection table	language (SQL)
current record	key field	TextWidth() function
Data control	Move methods	third normal form
database	navigating	Update method

End-of-Chapter Problems

1. Define the term "entity". Give several examples of entities.

2. A database stores both information on entities and information on relationships. What does this statement mean?

3. What are foreign keys and how are they used in relational databases?

4. How are many-to-many relationships implemented in relational databases?

5. Assume you have the following fields in a database table: Part Number, Part Description, Order Number, Order Date, Customer Number, and Customer Name. Assume that the key field is a compound key that includes the Part Number and Order Number. What's wrong with this table? How would a database designer correct the problem?

6. What are bound controls? How are they used in the context of database applications?

7. How does the MoveNext method differ from the FindNext method?

8. How are the NoMatch and the EOF properties similar?

9. What is a recordset? How is a recordset potentially different from a database table?

10. Assume you have the database tables shown at the top of page 436. Compose SQL Select queries to create recordsets that contain the following fields:
    a. SupplierNo, Name, ProductNo, and Cost
    b. ProductNo, Desc, and Cost
    c. Name, Desc, Cost, and Price

11. Explain the difference between the Row and Rows properties for FlexGrid controls. Also explain the difference between the Col and Cols properties.

12. Using the tables in problem 10, assume you created an SQL query that produced a recordset consisting of the SupplierNo, Name, and Desc fields.

Supplier Table

SupplierNo	Name	PhoneNo

Product Table

ProductNo	Desc	Price

SupplierProduct Table

SupplierNo	ProductNo	Cost

Also assume that the recordset was ordered by the SupplierNo. What would you have to modify to get the records to be ordered by the Name field? What would the modification look like?

Programming Problems

1. You have a database named ProdInfo.mdb that contains the two tables shown here. This database is stored in the subdirectory C08\PrgProbs in the code package for this text. All the fields are text fields except the Price field (currency) and the UnitsSold field (integer).

   ProdInfo.mdb Database

   Product Table

ProductNo	Price
100	$15.00
150	$10.00
200	$1.50
250	$5.95

   Trans Table

ProductNo	InvoiceNo	UnitsSold
100	2000	10
100	4000	100
150	3000	20
150	4000	25
200	2000	25
200	4000	10
250	4000	1
250	5000	10

   Create a VB project that uses this database to compute and display the extended price (units sold times price) for each record in the Trans table. Display the results via a FlexGrid. A sample output follows.

   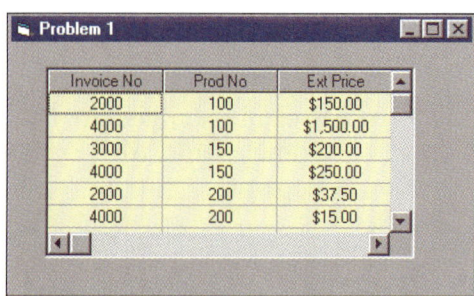

2. You have a single-table database called Comp.mdb. It contains a table named Company, which is shown here. The Comp.mdb database is stored in the subdirectory C08\PrgProbs in the code package for this text. All the fields are text fields.

Company Table

CompanyId	Name	Address	PhoneNo
1243	Glo Cleaners	3461 6th South	242-9600
3243	Farwest Paint	1605 116th NE, Suite 2143	443-6980
3456	Dova Controls	15015 NE 36th Street	632-6116
4654	MODA Ltd	453 NW Gilman Blvd.	324-9737
6534	Jaroslava	5423 Ballard Ave NW	244-4417
6732	Skyline Steel	1913 Fairview East	823-4103
7828	Quality Marble Care	2201 6th	441-0409
8330	Tubs	1012 Western Ave	323-7700
8799	Fidalgo's	5621 168th Place SE	622-6463
9765	Diamond Palace	512 N 85th	525-2121

Write a program that reads one record at a time from the database and displays the field values. An example form is shown here. Be sure to handle potential error conditions.

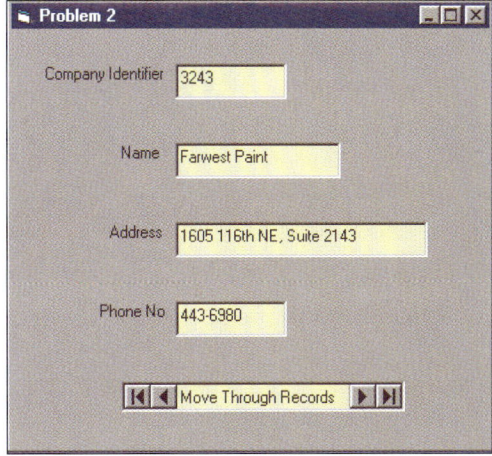

3. You have a database named Cust.mdb. This database contains one table named Customer. The Cust.mdb database is stored in the subdirectory C08\PrgProbs in the code package for this text. All fields are text fields.

Customer Table

CustomerNo	Name	Address	Zip
1346	Hagedorn	1508 E. Yesler	98125
3243	Lewine	3908 Corliss N.	98112
3589	Hagburg	2536 14th NE	98371
4265	Garman	3899 Brooklyn NE	98195
4354	Burrows	15123 Macadam Road	98125
5237	Currie	2432 142nd Place NE	98454
5275	Hager	24 Valley	98370
5632	Garmon	5435 24th NE	98112
6578	Lew	6756 13th SW	98125
8734	Currey	2387 W Commodore W	98371
9898	Burroughs	21545 NE 18th Way	98125

Create a project that will find records either by customer number or by Zip Code. The basic structure of the project is shown here.

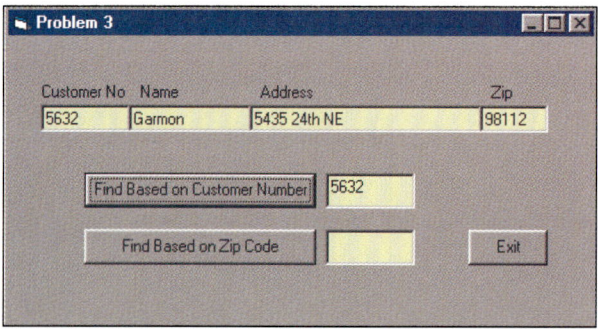

The customer number field is a text field. Remember that when you create a search criterion that includes a string value, you must enclose the string value in single quote marks (see "The Like Operator" discussion in section 8.2).

The project screen above shows the results of a search by customer number (5632). Customer numbers are unique, so you do not expect more than one match. The search by Zip Code is different because there are potentially many matches. The screen image that follows shows the beginning of a search by Zip Code.

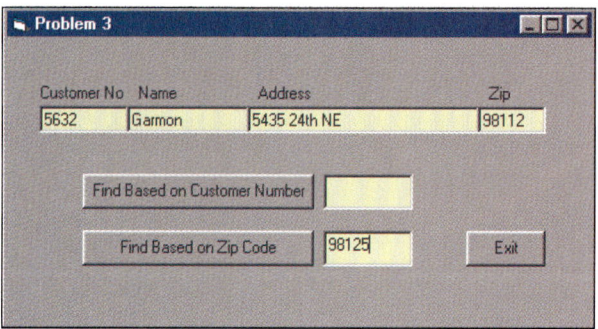

The user has entered 98125 for the Zip Code to find. Upon clicking the Find Based on Zip Code button, the search should take place and it should find the first record matching the Zip Code. However, there might be more matching records, so the Find Based on Zip Code button should change appropriately, as shown.

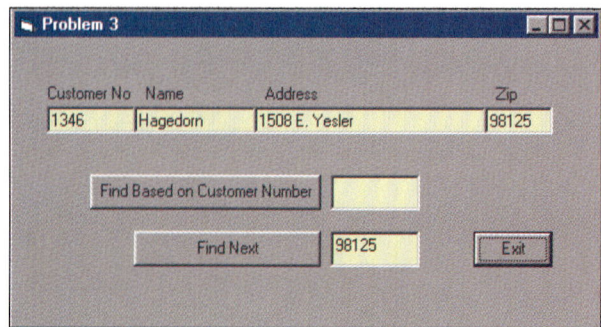

The button should return to its original state when the end of the set of matching Zip Codes is reached. You'll have to figure out a way to make this happen. (*Hint:* Don't just change the Caption property. Remember that the behavior is different in the two cases.) Be sure to handle potential error conditions.

4. Using the database described in programming problem 3, you are now asked to implement a search by name (which may not be unique). The screen image shown here gives an example.

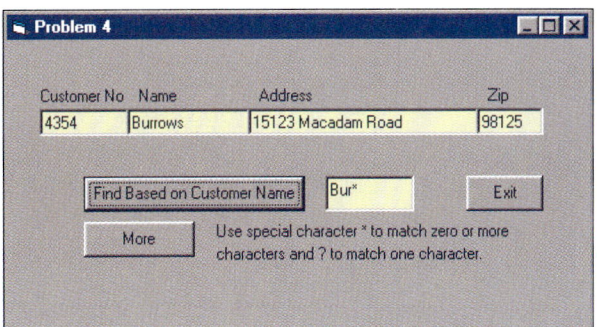

Notice that the name to find does not need to be completely spelled out: the user is allowed to use the wild card characters (* and ?). The example above with "Bur*" means that any name that starts with "Bur" will match the search criterion. This is achieved using the Like operator in the find criterion.

Remember that when you create a search criterion that includes a string value, you must enclose the string value in single quote marks (see "The Like Operator" discussion in section 8.2).

After the first match is found, additional matches are possible. The screen image shown below presents the results of the user clicking on the More button.

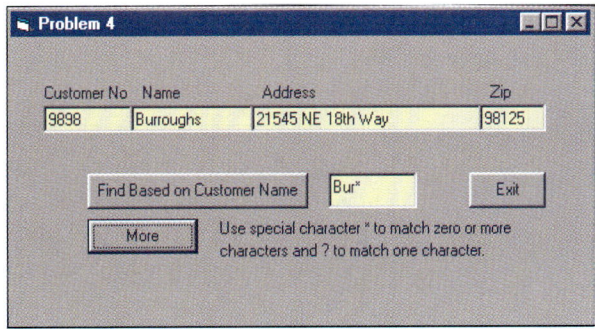

Be sure to handle potential error conditions.

5. Assume you want to maintain an address book of your friends, with their name, address, phone number, and some comments (like their birthday). You have a database named Friend.mdb that contains a table named Friends (shown at the top of page 440). The Friend.mdb database is stored in the subdirectory C08\PrgProbs in the code package for this text. All fields are text fields.

Your application should be able to navigate through all the records one at a time. You should also be able to add, delete, and modify records. Finally, you should be able to find someone by name. Use the Like operator in your search criterion. An example application is shown under the Friends table on page 440.

Friends Table

Name	Address	Phone	Comments
Lewine	3908 Corliss N.	233-5423	Owes me $5
Burrows	15123 Macadam Road	967-9543	
Garmon	5435 24th NE	981-1232	Lunch next Wednesday
Hagburg	2536 14th NE	983-3271	
Currey	2387 W Commodore W	233-8735	Birthday May 7
Lew	6756 13th SW	433-9844	Good friend of Ann
Hagedorn	1508 E. Yesler	722-9811	
Burroughs	21545 NE 18th Way	629-7639	Met at the play last week
Hager	24 Valley	988-9999	
Currie	2432 142nd Place NE	629-3487	A radiant personality
Garman	3899 Brooklyn NE	543-7746	

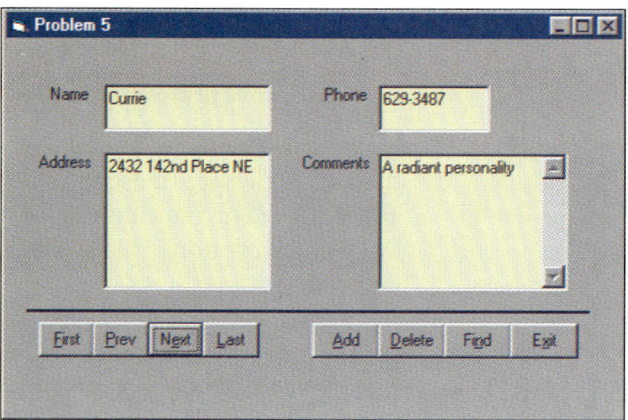

Be sure to handle potential error conditions.

6. You have a database named ProjEmp.mdb that contains three tables shown here. The database is stored in the subdirectory C08\PrgProbs in the code package for this text.

ProjEmp.mdb Database

Project Table

ProjID	ProjDesc
47Y16	Balmer Remodel
56T20	Gates Remodel
59R13	Langford Remodel

Employee Table

EmplNo	Empname
100	Brown
200	Smith
300	Chou
400	Santos

Assignment Table

EmplNo	ProjId	Percent
100	47Y16	50
100	56T20	50
200	47Y16	25
200	56T20	25
200	59R13	50
300	56T20	100
400	56T20	50
400	59R13	50

Create a VB project that combines the records in these tables and displays the EmplNo, EmpName, ProjDesc, and Percent fields. Provide the user with the ability to request that the records be sorted either by ProjDesc or by EmplNo. A sample solution is shown below (with records sorted by ProjDesc).

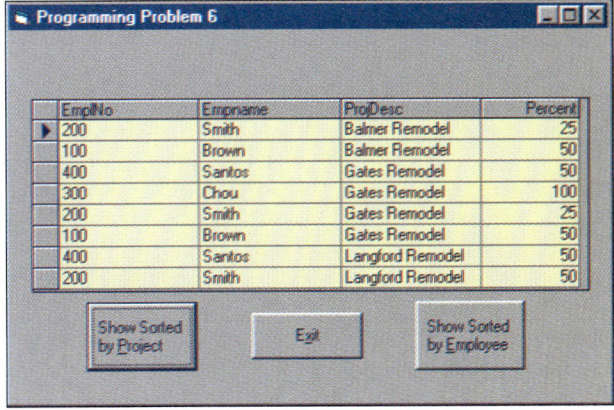

Use a DBGrid control to display the records.

chapter NINE

Handling Lists of Data

Arrays

Imagine a mail order company that sells products to customers from all 50 states in the United States. This company is required to charge sales tax on sales to customers in many states, and the sales tax rate varies from state to state. How do we represent these sales tax rates in a program? If we store them in variables of the kind we have seen so far, we will need 50 variables with names like NYTaxRate, NJTaxRate, and CATaxRate. Then the program will require a Select…Case or If…Then…Else statement to identify a customer's state of residence and determine the corresponding tax rate variable to use in the calculation of the sales tax. Because of the large number of variables, this statement will be very long.

Storing a set of related values, such as 50 sales tax rates, in separate variables is tedious at best. However, such situations are common. To resolve this problem, the VB programming language provides another kind of variable called an array. **An *array* is a variable with a single symbolic name that represents many different data items.** This chapter describes how to declare arrays and how to use them to solve some common processing tasks such as sorting data, selecting values from a table, and searching for a specific value.

Most programming languages provide arrays of data items, but VB extends the array concept to include controls as well. By providing control arrays VB enables the programmer to write a single event procedure that dictates the behavior of many controls. This chapter discusses how to create and use control arrays.

Objectives

After studying this chapter you should be able to
- Construct an array to store multiple related data values.
- Design loops to process data stored in arrays.
- Understand common processing tasks using arrays (table lookup, sequential search, binary search, and simple sorting).
- Construct a control array to allow related controls to share event procedures.

9.1 Solving Problems with Arrays

Since we are now introducing arrays, we need a term to describe the ordinary variables we have used prior to this point. We will use the term *simple variable* **to mean a variable that can store only one value.** We first examine a problem whose solution is very inefficient when we use simple variables. We then show how arrays improve our solution. As we solve the problem, we introduce the structure of arrays.

The Problem

A financial analyst has calculated last year's rate of return[1] for ten different companies and would like a program to display the names of those companies whose rate of return exceeded the average of the group. What processing steps must we perform to display this information?

The Solution Using Simple Variables

Using the programming techniques we've employed in earlier programs, we might begin to solve this problem by writing the following pseudocode.

> *Compute the average rate of return for the group of ten companies*
> *Display the names of companies whose rate of return exceeds the average*

We first have to compute the average. This requires accessing each individual company's rate of return and adding it to a cumulative total. We can refine the pseudocode for this step as follows:

> *For each company*
>   *get a rate of return and a company name*
>   *add the rate of return to the sum*
> *Next company*
> *Compute the average by dividing the sum by the number of companies*

Once we have the average, we must go back through the rates of return, comparing each to the average. If a rate of return exceeds the average, we display the company name. The pseudocode for this step might be

> *For each company*
>   *If the company's rate of return is greater than the average Then*
>   *display the company's name*
>   *End If*
> *Next company*

This problem requires two passes through the data: one pass to compute the average and a second to compare the average with each rate of return. There is no other way to solve this problem.

Now think about how you would convert this pseudocode to actual code. You would have to store each rate of return in a variable because each is used twice: first to compute the sum, then later to compare to the average. If the company names are input into the program at the same time as the rate of return values, then the company names will also have to be stored in variables. Thus, if we had ten companies, we'd need twenty variables.

---

[1] *Rate of return* is a measure of profitability.

Let's look at some code, assuming that we have only three companies instead of ten. The following code might be found in a Click event procedure for a command button captioned "Find Best Companies".

```
Private Sub cmdFindBestCompanies_Click()
    Dim CompAReturn As Currency, CompAName As String
    Dim CompBReturn As Currency, CompBName As String
    Dim CompCReturn As Currency, CompCName As String
    Dim Average As Currency
    Dim Sum As Currency
    CompAReturn = InputBox("Enter Rate of Return for Company A")
    CompAName = InputBox("Enter Company A Name")
    Sum = Sum + CompAReturn
    CompBReturn = InputBox("Enter Rate of Return for Company B")
    CompBName = InputBox("Enter Company B Name")
    Sum = Sum + CompBReturn
    CompCReturn = InputBox("Enter Rate of Return for Company C")
    CompCName = InputBox("Enter Company C Name")
    Sum = Sum + CompCReturn
    Average = Sum / 3
    If CompAReturn > Average Then
        MsgBox CompAName & " exceeds the average rate of return"
    End If
    If CompBReturn > Average Then
        MsgBox CompBName & " exceeds the average rate of return"
    End If
    If CompCReturn > Average Then
        MsgBox CompCName & " exceeds the average rate of return"
    End If
End Sub
```

This solution approach works, but it is not a good *general* solution. Imagine if you had 30, or 300, or 30,000 companies. You would be writing code for the rest of your life. There must be a better way.

You can spot two places in the code where statement blocks are "nearly repeated" three times. We would like to use loops but are prevented from doing so because each value is stored in a different variable and each variable has a different name. For example, we'd like to have something like the following loop:

```
For K = 1 To 3
    CompAReturn = InputBox("Enter Rate of Return for Company A")
    CompAName = InputBox("Enter Company A Name")
    Sum = Sum + CompAReturn
Next K
```

Although the sum would be computed correctly, the problem with this loop is that there is no way to store and preserve the individual rate of return and name for each company. Each iteration of the loop updates the value in CompAReturn, destroying the previous rate of return as it obtains the next value needed to accumulate the sum.

The Structure of an Array

♦ ♦ ♦

What we need is a different kind of variable—one that has a single name but can store more than a single value. This new kind of variable is known as an *array*. Figure 9.1 depicts an array named RateOfReturn that stores five values. **Each**

FIGURE 9.1

An array

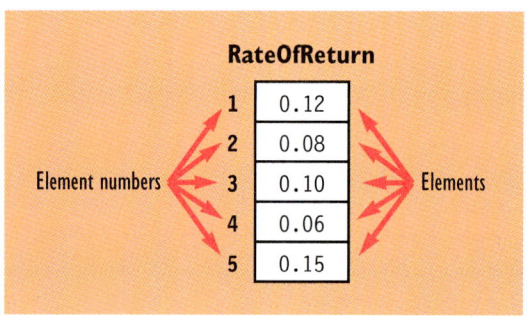

element of an array is like a simple variable. We can store a different company's rate of return in each element. The entire set of elements shares the name RateOfReturn.

The elements in an array are numbered, as shown in Figure 9.1. To access an individual element, we append its number to the array name. For example, in the array depicted in Figure 9.1, the third element is referred to as RateOfReturn(3), and it currently holds the value 0.10. **The element number is called the** *subscript*. For this reason, **another term that is sometimes used for an array is** *subscripted variable*. The array depicted in Figure 9.1 is a *one-dimensional array* **because each element is referenced using a single subscript value.** You can also create **two-, three-, and higher-dimensional arrays, called** *multidimensional arrays*.

The syntax for referencing a specific element in a one-dimensional array is

ArrayName(SubscriptValue)

where *SubscriptValue* is a numeric expression.

The Solution Using Arrays

If we store the rates of return in an array like the one shown in Figure 9.1, we can design a better solution to the problem. A procedure can process the contents of an array element just as it processes any other variable. For example, the following statement adds the values in elements 1 and 2 of the array.

Sum = RateOfReturn(1) + RateOfReturn(2)

The result stored in the variable Sum is 0.20. However, using constants as subscripts this way is almost never done. The reason is simple: using constants as subscripts in your code is no different than using simple variables. That is, the constant fixes the reference to a specific element just as the name of a simple variable refers to a specific storage location.

If we don't use constants as subscripts, then what do we use? The answer is a numeric variable, or a numeric expression containing a variable. For example, the following statement, in which K is an Integer variable, is typical of statements that refer to array elements.

Sum = Sum + RateOfReturn(K)

Which element in the array does this refer to? You don't know unless you know the value of the subscript K. This is very important. If K holds the value 2, then the statement above refers to the second element. If K holds 5, then the very same statement refers to the fifth element. Thus, we can write a For…Next loop that processes each array element in turn by using the loop's counter variable as the array subscript, as follows:

```
For K = 1 To 5
    Sum = Sum + RateOfReturn(K)
Next K
```

Figure 9.2 illustrates the execution of this code.

If the array had 5000 elements instead of 5, what change would you have to make to this code? You would simply have to change the For statement so that it starts at 1 and ends at 5000.

```
For K = 1 To 5000
```

A drawback of our first solution to this problem was that the number of lines of code would increase proportionately if the number of companies that we needed to analyze increased. However, with the array approach shown in Figure 9.2, the number of lines of code is independent of the number of companies.

The number of lines of code you write should not have to be increased in proportion to the number of items to be processed. If you find that this is happening, you probably need to use an array instead of simple variables.

To make the loop

```
For K = 1 To 5
    Sum = Sum + RateOfReturn(K)
Next K
```

even more useful, it would be a good idea to not restrict it to processing only five elements. How can we remove this restriction? Consider the following:

```
For K = 1 To NumElements
    Sum = Sum + RateOfReturn(K)
Next K
```

Now we can control the number of elements included in the summing process simply by setting the value of the variable NumElements prior to the For statement.

Let's return to our problem of finding the average rate of return and displaying the company names that exceed the average. We'll add one more array to store the company names, as shown in Figure 9.3.

Observe that the elements of the two arrays are coordinated. That is, the rate of return in element number 1 of the RateOfReturn array corresponds to the

FIGURE 9.2

Summing the elements of an array using a For...Next loop

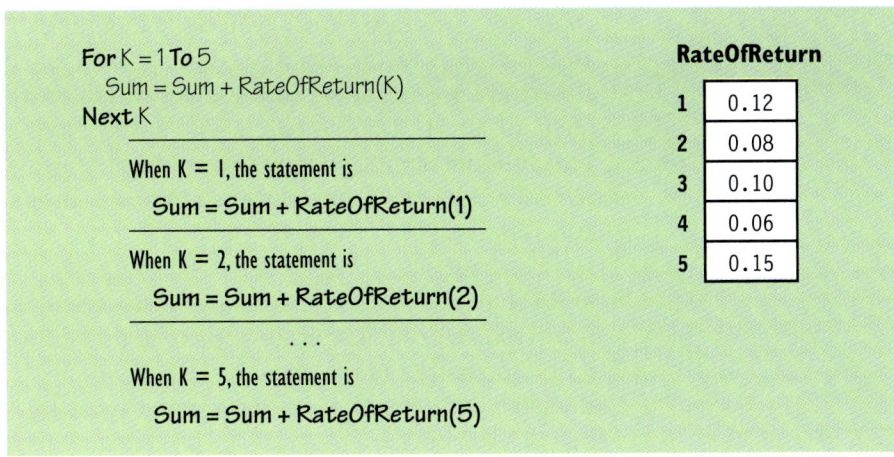

FIGURE 9.3

Arrays for rate of return problem

RateOfReturn		CompanyName	
1	0.12	1	ABC Inc
2	0.08	2	L2 Inc
3	0.10	3	XYZ Tires
4	0.06	4	Delta
5	0.15	5	FOG Inc

company name in element number 1 of the CompanyName array. This technique is often used when the data types of the two arrays are different; in the present case, RateOfReturn holds numeric data (Currency, most likely) and CompanyName holds string data. When the data types of the arrays are the same, an alternative approach is to use a two-dimensional array, which we will discuss shortly.

Consider the following code segment for the rate of return problem. It assumes that the two arrays already exist and the number of companies has already been stored in the variable NumberOfCompanies.

```
For K = 1 To NumberOfCompanies
    Sum = Sum + RateOfReturn(K)
Next K
Average = Sum / NumberOfCompanies
For K = 1 To NumberOfCompanies
    If RateOfReturn(K) > Average Then
        MsgBox CompanyName(K) & " exceeds the average"
    End If
Next K
```

Convince yourself that this solution will work for any number of companies as long as the arrays have been created and correctly initialized with values.

Storing Data in Arrays versus Databases

Could you solve this problem without arrays if the data were stored in a database? If so, what is the advantage of using arrays?

Reading the data from a database is an option. If Rate of Return and Company Name were two fields in a database table, then you could read every record from the table and compute the sum of the rates of return. You could then compute the average. Finally, you could move back to the first record of the table and read every record again to compare each rate of return to the average.

Arrays are variables and, like all variables, they exist in random access memory (RAM). Data stored in RAM are accessed quickly, typically in *nanoseconds* (billionths of a second). But storage for arrays is limited because RAM is relatively expensive and is needed for other uses such as storage of the operating system.

Databases are stored on disk. The computer must transfer database records to RAM in order to process them and, as a result, access to database records is relatively slow—it is typically measured in *milliseconds* (thousandths of a second). But storage for databases is less constrained because disk storage is considerably less expensive and a computer typically has much more disk storage than RAM storage.

When the same data items are accessed multiple times during processing, using arrays can produce a superior program. The factors that must be considered when deciding which approach to use include (1) execution speed, (2) the amount of data that needs to be processed, and (3) the clarity of the code that accomplishes the task. If the amount of data is very large (too large for RAM), then directly accessing the database would be the only feasible solution even though it might execute more slowly. If the amount of data is relatively small, then execution speed can be improved by reading the data from the database and storing it in an array for processing. The speed advantage of the array solution will be greater the more times the data are accessed during processing.

Multidimensional Arrays

The number of dimensions an array has is called its *dimensionality*. A one-dimensional array uses one subscript to refer to an element. The array Rate-OfReturn is a one-dimensional array. One-dimensional arrays are useful when the data to be stored in the array are similar to a list of numbers or a list of names.

A two-dimensional array uses two subscripts to refer to a single element and is sometimes called a *matrix* or *table*. Figure 9.4 shows a two-dimensional array. All twelve elements are collectively referred to by the single name Quantity. An individual element is identified by supplying the values of the specific row and column—the subscripts. For example, the reference Quantity(4, 2) refers to the element in row 4 and column 2 (which holds the number 62 in this case). The first value between the parentheses is always the row number and the second is always the column number. This is easy to get mixed up; for example, does Quantity(2, 3) refer to the value 13 or the value 21? It is row 2, column 3, not column 2, row 3.

The general syntax for referencing a specific element in a two-dimensional array is

ArrayName(RowSubscriptValue, ColumnSubscriptValue)

where *RowSubscriptValue* and *ColumnSubscriptValue* are numeric expressions.

For what purpose might we use a two-dimensional array like the one in Figure 9.4? Well, the rows might represent products (four products) and the columns might represent warehouses (three warehouses). Then the values stored in the array could represent the inventory count of a particular product in a particular warehouse (the quantity of product number 4 in warehouse number 2 is 62).

You are not limited to two dimensions. You can create three, four, or more (the maximum is 60). However, using subscripts slows down the execution of

FIGURE 9.4

A two-dimensional array

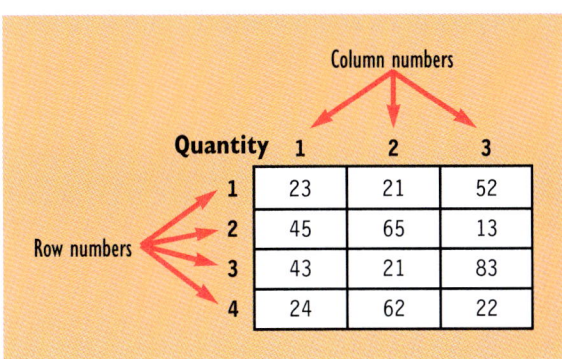

any program. The more subscripts an array has, the slower the execution, so you should always use the minimum number of subscripts necessary to solve the problem.

EXERCISE 9.1

Suppose you are writing a program that will continually retrieve and update inventory counts for four products at three warehouses. Your program contains three simple Integer variables named Stock, ProdNo, and WareNo. ProdNo currently holds a valid product number (1, 2, 3, or 4) and WareNo currently holds a valid warehouse number (1, 2, or 3).

1. Suppose you have the array depicted in Figure 9.4. Write the statement that stores in the variable Stock the inventory count of the product specified by ProdNo at the warehouse specified by WareNo.

2. Now suppose that instead of the array depicted in Figure 9.4, you have the single-table database depicted below (which contains the same data). Suppose your program has a Data control named datQty whose DatabaseName property has been set to Inventry.mdb, and whose RecordSource property has been set to Qty. Now write the statements that store in the variable Stock the inventory count of the product specified by ProdNo at the warehouse specified by WareNo.

INVENTRY.MDB

Qty Table

Product	Warehouse1	Warehouse2	Warehouse3
1	23	21	52
2	45	65	13
3	43	21	83
4	24	62	22

9.2 Declaring Arrays

Arrays can help you solve many kinds of problems like the one discussed in Section 9.1. As with simple variables, in order to use arrays in a program you must declare them. In this section we examine how to declare arrays, and we discuss subscript bounds.

Arrays can store Integers, Strings, Currency, or any other data type just as simple variables can. However, every element of an array must have the *same* data type. That is, if an array is declared as type Integer, all of its elements store integers. You cannot create an array that has some elements of type Integer and some elements of type Currency.

Use the Dim (or the Static or Public) statement to declare arrays just as you do for simple variables. But for an array, in addition to specifying the variable name and type, you must also specify the number of subscripts (number of dimensions) and their minimum and maximum values. The general syntax of the Dim statement for an array is

Dim *ArrayName(subscripts)* **As** *Type*

The *subscripts* portion of the definition has two options. The first option is simply a constant for each dimension, separated by commas if there is more than one dimension. These constants define the maximum value of each subscript. For example, you can write

> **Dim** RateOfReturn(100) **As Currency**
> **Dim** InventoryCount(3, 4) **As Integer**

to create the arrays depicted in Figure 9.5.

The first Dim statement creates a one-dimensional array with 101 elements numbered 0 through 100. The second Dim statement creates a two-dimensional array with four rows and five columns (a total of 20 elements). Notice that in this form of the Dim statement the minimum value for each subscript is zero (0). This is the default minimum value. Some people find it odd that the first element number is 0, not 1. After all, if you want to store information on 100 rates of return, it would make the most sense to start at element 1 and end at element 100, not start at element 0 and end at element 99.

Although the default minimum value for subscripts is zero, you can simply ignore element 0 if using it would make your code confusing. For the rate-of-return example in Section 9.1, we put the first company's return in element 1 and the last company's return in element 5, and we just left element 0 unused. Although this wasted one element of the array, it was a good trade-off because it made the code that used the array much easier to read, understand, and maintain.

VB has a very nice feature: it will tell you when you use a subscript value that is **outside the range**—called the *subscript bounds*—**specified by the Dim statement**. For example, suppose the RateOfReturn array is declared with maximum subscript value 100. Suppose also that K and NumberOfCompanies are simple variables of type Integer. If the value stored in NumberOfCompanies is greater than 100, executing the loop

> **For** K = 1 **To** NumberOfCompanies
>   Sum = Sum + RateOfReturn(K)
> **Next** K

will cause a **run time error**—called a *subscript out of range error*—when K equals 101. Figure 9.6 shows the message that VB displays when your program exceeds the *bounds* of an array.

You can use a second *subscript* option in the Dim statement. In this option, you specify both the lower bound and the upper bound of the subscript, separated by the keyword To, as in the following statements:

> **Dim** RateOfReturn(1 **To** 100) **As Currency**
> **Dim** DivisionEarnings(1993 **To** 1995, 1 **To** 3) **As Currency**

These two Dim statements create arrays as shown in Figure 9.7.

This second option gives you more control over the subscripts and also allows you to tie the structure of the array more closely to the real-world

FIGURE 9.5

Array dimensions

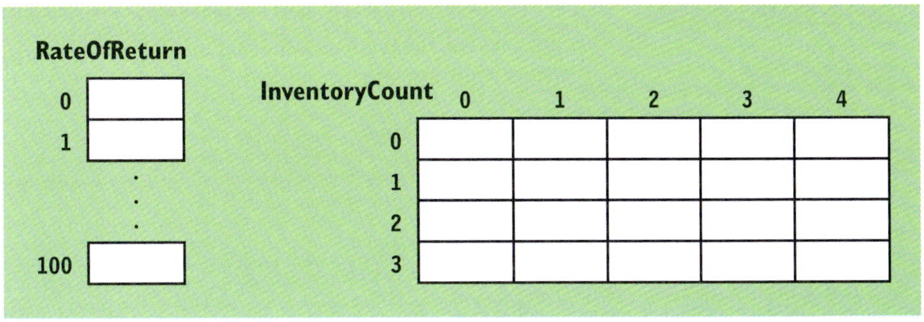

FIGURE 9.6

Error message for illegal subscript value

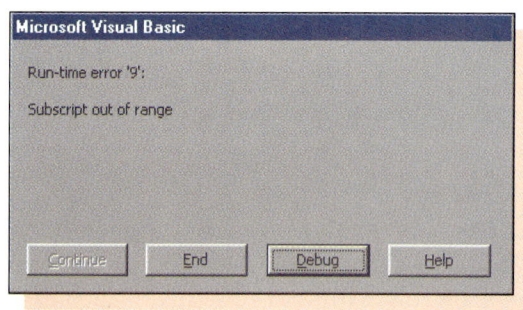

FIGURE 9.7

Specifying lower and upper bounds for array subscripts

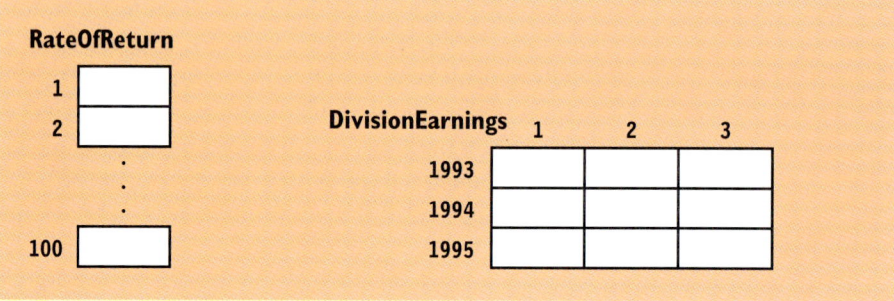

quantities that are represented by the array elements. For example, the DivisionEarnings array has one row for each year of interest (1993, 1994, and 1995) and one column for each of the three divisions. If you want to refer to the 1994 earnings for division 2, you simply use DivisionEarnings(1994, 2).

Finally, variable scope is the same for arrays as for simple variables. To create a global array, use the Public statement in the general declarations section of a code module. To create a module-level array, use the Dim statement in the general declarations section of a code module or form. To create a local array, use the Dim statement or the Static statement in the procedure or function in which you wish to use the array.

EXERCISE 9.2

For each of the following cases, write the declaration statement that creates the specified array.

1. A one-dimensional, module-level array of type String named Cities, with 500 elements and maximum subscript value 500.
2. A one-dimensional, global array of type Currency named Price, with minimum subscript value 1000 and maximum subscript value 9999.
3. A two-dimensional, module-level array of type Currency named Sales, with twenty rows and six columns. The minimum row subscript should be 1 and the minimum column subscript should be 1990.

EXERCISE 9.3

When the user clicks on the command button named cmdArrayQuiz, the following code displays three message boxes. Hand-check this code, and show the numbers that appear in each message box.

Dim A(6) **As Integer**

Private Sub cmdArrayQuiz_Click()
  Dim J **As Integer**
  A(1) = 7
  A(2) = -3

```
        A(3) = 4
        A(4) = 1
        A(5) = -4
        A(6) = 2
        DisplayArray
        A(3) = A(2)
        A(2) = A(3)
        A(6) = A(5)
        A(5) = A(4)
        DisplayArray

        For J = 2 To 6
            A(J - 1) = A(J)
        Next J
        DisplayArray
    End Sub

    Private Sub DisplayArray()
        Dim K As Integer
        Dim Message As String
        For K = 1 To 6
            Message = Message & " " & A(K)
        Next K
        MsgBox Message
    End Sub
```

9.3 Applications of Arrays

This section describes some tasks for which arrays are commonly employed. Once you understand how these tasks are coded, you can use this knowledge to solve problems in your application programs.

Populating an Array

Just like simple variables, when arrays are declared, their elements are initialized to zero (if the array is numeric) or the zero-length string (if the array is string). One of the first steps in a program that uses arrays is to store the data values to be processed into the array elements. **The process of entering data into an array is referred to as** *populating the array.* We present three examples that illustrate common approaches to this task.

Example 9.1

Populating an Array via User Input

When the amount of data is relatively small, the user can input the data to be stored in the array. Event procedure cmdPopulateArrays_Click in Figure 9.8 illustrates this approach. The arrays in this example are declared as module-level. After clicking on cmdPopulateArrays, the user first enters the number of companies, then the rate of return and company name for each company. After entering all the data, the user can review the values in the arrays by clicking on cmdReviewArrayContents.

FIGURE 9.8

Code for Example 9.1

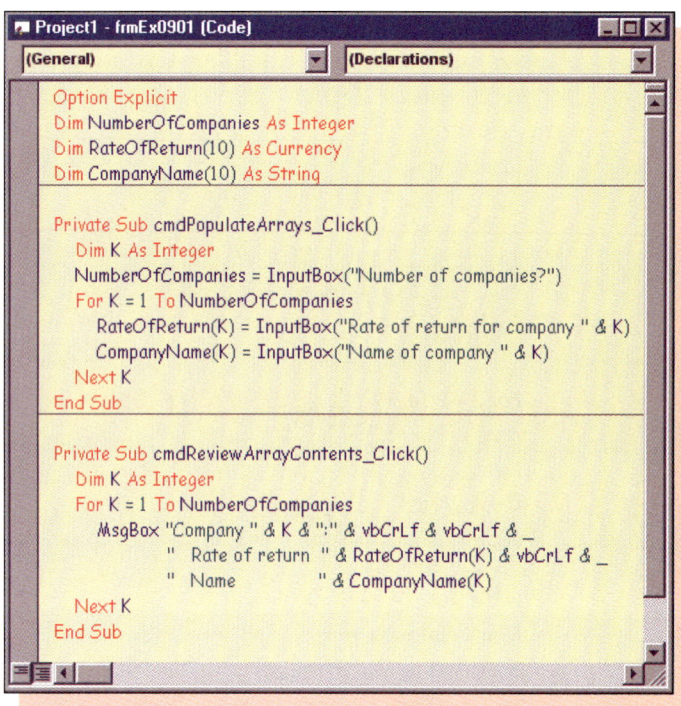

Example 9.2 Populating an Array via Another Array

Sometimes one can obtain the data to populate an array from another array that has previously been populated. This example illustrates an *array copy*, where the contents of one array are copied to a second array. The code for this example is in Figure 9.9.

FIGURE 9.9

Code for Example 9.2

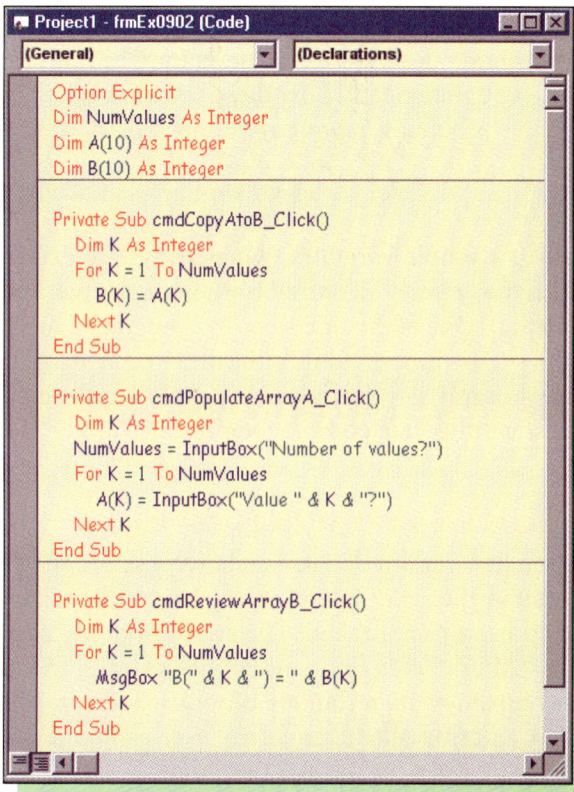

After clicking on cmdPopulateArrayA, the user first enters the number of values to be entered into the array, then enters the values. Clicking on cmdCopyAtoB will cause these values to be copied from array A to array B. Finally, the user can verify the values in array B by clicking cmdReviewArrayB.

VB does not allow you to copy all of the values from one array to another with a single assignment statement. Instead you must copy the values one element at a time. Loops are useful because you can use them to systematically specify the subscripts for the elements to be copied.

Example 9.3

Populating an Array via Database Tables

Arrays are capable of holding large quantities of data, and it is unlikely that the user will be willing (or able) to type in a large amount of data every time a program is executed. In actual business applications the data for populating an array are typically obtained from a database instead of from the user.

In this example, the Form_Load event procedure performs the task of populating two module-level arrays named CompanyName and RateOfReturn. A Data control named datComp establishes a connection to a table named CompInfo in the database named Comp.mdb. The two fields in the table are named CompName and RateOfReturn. The code for this example is in Figure 9.10. Figure 9.11 shows the user interface after the user has clicked the Review Array Contents button.

FIGURE 9.10

Code for Example 9.3

```
Option Explicit
Const MAXARRAYSIZE = 100
Dim CompanyName(1 To MAXARRAYSIZE) As String
Dim RateOfReturn(1 To MAXARRAYSIZE) As Currency
Dim NumberofCompanies As Integer

Private Sub cmdReviewArrayContents_Click()
    Dim K As Integer
    For K = 1 To NumberofCompanies
        lstComp.AddItem CompanyName(K) & ": " & _
                Format(RateOfReturn(K), "percent")
    Next K
End Sub

Private Sub Form_Load()
    Dim R As Integer
    datComp.DatabaseName = App.Path & "\Comp.MDB"
    datComp.RecordSource = "CompInfo"
    datComp.Refresh
    Do Until (datComp.Recordset.EOF = True) Or (R = MAXARRAYSIZE)
        R = R + 1
        CompanyName(R) = datComp.Recordset("CompName")
        RateOfReturn(R) = datComp.Recordset("RateOfReturn")
        datComp.Recordset.MoveNext
    Loop
    If R = MAXARRAYSIZE Then
        MsgBox "Arrays filled before EOF - some records not processed", vbInformation
    End If
    NumberofCompanies = R
End Sub
```

FIGURE 9.11

Array contents displayed when the user clicks on Review Array Contents button

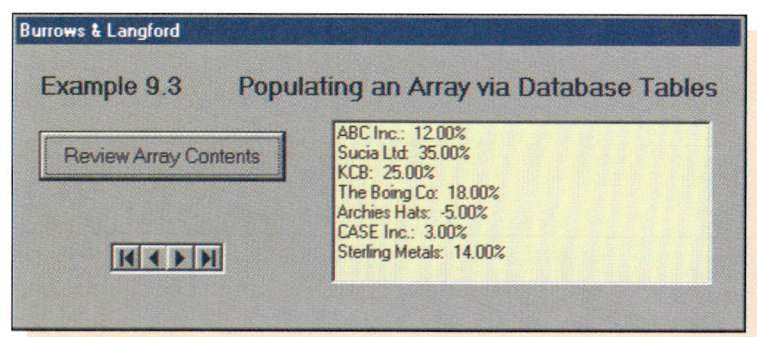

Note that the arrays have fixed upper bounds: the Dim statements fix the maximum subscript value at 100. Since the database table could conceivably have more than 100 records, in Form_Load the Do Until statement's condition checks whether the arrays are full before obtaining the next database record. The If statement following this loop notifies the user if the array did in fact become full. We will show how to overcome this fixed-size restriction later in the chapter when we introduce dynamic arrays.

EXERCISE 9.4

Write an event procedure named cmdCopyAtoBBackwards_Click to replace cmdCopyAtoB_Click in Example 9.2. This new event procedure should copy the values from array A to array B in reverse order. For example, if array A holds the values 3, 5, 7, and 9 in elements 1 through 4, respectively, clicking on cmdCopyAtoBBackwards should store the values 9, 7, 5, and 3 in elements 1 through 4, respectively, of array B.

EXERCISE 9.5

Write a Click event procedure for a command button named cmdReverseA which could be added to Example 9.2. This new event procedure should reverse the order of the values stored in the module-level array A. For example, if array A holds the values 3, 5, 7, and 9 in elements 1 through 4, respectively, clicking on cmdReverseA should rearrange the values in the array so that elements 1 through 4 hold the values 9, 7, 5, and 3, respectively. Can you write the code so that A is the only array that appears in cmdReverseA_Click?

EXERCISE 9.6

Write a Click event procedure for a command button named cmdFindBestCompanies that could be added to Example 9.3. When the user clicks this button, your code should display the names of those companies in the database whose rate of return exceeds the average of the group. Display the names of the above-average companies in the list box that is already on the form.

Performing a Table Lookup

Up to this point in the text, to solve problems involving multiple cases we have used decision-making statements (If and Select...Case). But many processing tasks require simple decisions that amount to selecting the appropriate value from a list or table of values to use in a computation. For such tasks the values can be conveniently stored in an array. If we can devise a simple way of knowing which element of the array holds the appropriate value to use in each case, the "decision" is reduced to specifying the array subscripts appropriately. This technique is called *table lookup*.

To demonstrate table lookup, we examine the task of determining how much tuition a college charges a student based on the student's class standing

TABLE 9.1 Tuition schedule for a hypothetical college

Residence Status	Class Standing		
	Undergraduate	Graduate	Professional
In State	$750	$2,300	$3,850
Out of State	$990	$3,100	$5,600

and residence status. We use the tuition schedule depicted in Table 9.1. To demonstrate the benefits of storing information in an array, we first solve the problem without an array and then compare the resulting code to a solution that uses table lookup with an array.

Suppose that the program determines via option buttons or some other method the class standing and residence status of a student. For example, assume that there is a variable ClassStanding that holds one of the values "UGrad", "Grad", or "Prof", and another variable ResStatus that holds either "InState" or "OutOfState". With this information, the following statement determines tuition:

```
Select Case ClassStanding
Case "UGrad"
   If ResStatus = "InState" Then
      Tuition = 750
   Else
      Tuition = 990
   End If
Case "Grad"
   If ResStatus = "InState" Then
      Tuition = 2300
   Else
      Tuition = 3100
   End If
Case Else
   If ResStatus = "InState" Then
      Tuition = 3850
   Else
      Tuition = 5600
   End If
End Select
```

This code works and, although it is long, is fairly easy to understand. However, if the number of class-standing or residence-status categories increases, the number of lines and the complexity of the code will increase, too. Using an array, this long compound statement can be replaced by one simple statement. Consider the table depicted in Figure 9.12. This is the same tuition schedule as in Table 9.1, but the descriptive headings have been replaced by numeric identifiers.

FIGURE 9.12

Tuition table with numeric row and column identifiers

		Class standing		
		1	2	3
Residence status	1	$750	$2,300	$3,850
	2	$990	$3,100	$5,600

If you declare a two-dimensional array with two rows and three columns, and populate this array with tuition values, then you essentially have the table depicted in Figure 9.12. Assuming you have the two numeric variables ResStatus and ClassStanding, which store a row number (1 or 2) and a column number (1, 2, or 3), respectively, you can replace the long decision-making statement with the following statement:

Tuition = TuitionTable(ResStatus, ClassStanding)

This is called a *table lookup* operation because it uses specific values of the subscripts to "look up," or find, the answer in a table.

Note in particular that if the number of residence or class categories changes, this single statement will remain unchanged. Of course, you must be sure that the values for the two subscripts ResStatus and ClassStanding remain valid. Otherwise you may try to access a nonexistent element in the array and get a run time error.

EXERCISE Suppose you have created the user interface for a project that determines tuition using the table lookup just described. Assume that it has two option buttons, named optResInState and optResOutOfState, that allow the user to specify the student's residence status. Using the information in Table 9.1 and Figure 9.12, write two complete event procedures—one for each option button—that correctly set the value of the (module-level) variable ResStatus.

Finding the Maximum and Minimum

A common array-processing task is to find the maximum or minimum value in an array. For example, if you have an array that stores the rates of return for a number of companies, then you might want to identify the company with the best (maximum) rate of return. Or suppose you have an array that contains risk coefficients for stock portfolios. If you are risk-averse, you would want to locate the portfolio with the lowest (minimum) risk.

How do humans solve this problem? For example, what's the minimum number in this list?

12   43   76   45   2   76   86   45   3   67   98   32   10   34

How did you find it? What's the maximum? Did you use the same process?

Humans appear to have the ability to see several values at a time and compare them mentally. In contrast, the best the computer can do is to compare two values at a time. Finding the maximum or minimum value in a list containing hundreds of numbers by only comparing two numbers at a time may go against your intuition, but it can be done. To see how, let's begin by solving the problem the wrong way, assuming that the list has just three numbers. Suppose we have the array shown in Figure 9.13. How can we find the maximum value? Consider the following code:

```
If List(1) > List(2) And List(1) > List(3) Then
    Max = List(1)
ElseIf List(2) > List(1) And List(2) > List(3) Then
    Max = List(2)
Else
    Max = List(3)
End If
```

FIGURE 9.13

Sample list for procedure to find maximum

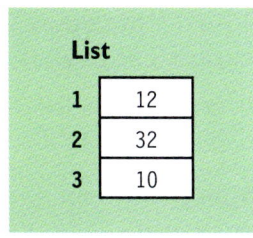

This code works—by brute force. But what if the array had 100 elements instead of just 3? Our simple approach would not be feasible. What's the solution?

The key idea is to use a loop to examine each element of the array. We compare each element, one at a time and in order from first to last, to a variable we call the BiggestSoFar. If the current element is larger than the BiggestSoFar, we update the BiggestSoFar to be equal to the value of the current element. Here is some pseudocode that describes this approach.

> *Set biggest so far equal to the value in element 1*
> *For elements 2 To the end of the list*
>   *If value of current element is greater than the biggest so far Then*
>   *set biggest so far equal to current element*
>   *End If*
> *Next element*
> *Biggest so far is the maximum*

This approach works no matter how many elements we have to scan.

Let's create a function to implement this pseudocode. We want the function to work for any one-dimensional array that stores values of type Integer. We pass the function three arguments: the array to scan, the first element number to scan, and the last element number to scan. Here is the function heading:

Public Function MaxInteger(A() **As Integer**, **ByVal** FirstElement **As Integer**, _
    ByVal LastElement **As Integer**) **As Integer**

Notice the syntax for specifying an array in the parameter list: follow the parameter name (A in this case) by an empty set of parentheses. Use the empty parentheses regardless of the number of dimensions in the array being passed to the function. Also note that VB does not allow an array parameter to be ByVal; arrays must always be passed by reference.

Here is the complete code that implements the pseudocode:

Public Function MaxInteger(A() **As Integer**, **ByVal** FirstElement **As Integer**, _
    ByVal LastElement **As Integer**) **As Integer**
  Dim BiggestSoFar **As Integer**
  Dim CurrentElement **As Integer**
  BiggestSoFar = A(FirstElement)
  For CurrentElement = FirstElement + 1 **To** LastElement
    If A(CurrentElement) > BiggestSoFar **Then**
      BiggestSoFar = A(CurrentElement)
    End If
  Next CurrentElement
  MaxInteger = BiggestSoFar
End Function

This function can be invoked from a procedure or another function as follows. Here we assume that an array named X already exists and has been populated with 1000 values.

M = MaxInteger(X(), 1, 1000)

When we invoke a function or procedure and pass it an array, we specify the array argument by giving the array name followed by an empty set of parentheses (just as we did in the function or procedure heading's parameter list).

EXERCISE 9.8 Suppose an array named X has been populated with the values

12 43 76 45 2 76 86 45 3 67 98 32 10 34

in elements 1 through 14. What values are stored in the variables L, M, and N after the following three statements are executed?

L = MaxInteger(X(), 1, 14)
M = MaxInteger(X(), 1, 0)
N = MaxInteger(X(), 5, 10)

EXERCISE 9.9 Explain what happens if we modify function MaxInteger() by changing the initialization statement

BiggestSoFar = A(FirstElement)

to

BiggestSoFar = -32768

and the For statement

For CurrentElement = FirstElement + 1 **To** LastElement

to

For CurrentElement = FirstElement **To** LastElement

Then answer Exercise 9.8 again using the modified function.

EXERCISE 9.10 Modify function MaxInteger() to find the minimum value in the list.

EXERCISE 9.11 Function MaxInteger() works properly only when it is passed a one-dimensional array. Explain why it will not work properly if it is passed a two-dimensional array.

Searching

Searching refers to the process of locating a specific value in an array. Technically, finding the maximum or minimum as we did in the previous section is a search—we searched the array to find its maximum or minimum value. However, that type of search is different from the ones we now turn to, in which we search an array for a **specific value, called a** *target*. For example, if the array stores names and addresses, we can search for a particular name, or if the array stores part numbers and prices, we can search for a specific part number.

In the examples that follow we assume that the value of the target is unique in the array. If we are searching an array containing part numbers and our target is part number 833, then the array will have at most one value equal to 833. The target may not be in the array at all, but if it is in the array, it will occur only once. We look at two different search methods here, know as sequential search and binary search.

Sequential Search

Sequential search **works by examining each element of the array individually and in turn.** The search begins at the first element, proceeds with the second element, then the third, and so on, continuing until the program finds the target or comes to the end of the array. **Sequential search is sometimes also called** *linear search.*

For our sequential search examples we use the two-dimensional array created by the following statement:

Dim PriceTable(**1 To** 5, **1 To** 2) **As Currency**

We assume that the array has been populated with the values shown in Figure 9.14. The values in the first column represent unique item numbers, and the values in the second column represent corresponding prices. Thus, we interpret the values in row 1 to mean that item number 324 has a price of $2.34.

Let us use our search procedure in the following way: given an item number, we want to know the corresponding price. The target for our search will be an item number, and once we locate the target we can easily retrieve its price.

Sequential Search of an Unordered Array

When the values in an array are in ascending (smallest to largest) or descending (largest to smallest) order, we say the array is *ordered*. Otherwise, we say the array is *unordered*. The values in Figure 9.14 are unordered.

Our sequential search uses a simple loop.

For rows 1 To the last row
    If the item number in column one of the current row equals the target Then
        we found a match; remember the row number and exit the loop
    Else
        do nothing; let loop continue with next iteration
    End If
Next row
If we reached the end of the array Then
    conclude that the item we are searching for does not exist
End If

We write our solution in the form of a general sub procedure. The procedure uses three parameters for input data: the array, the last row in the array to search, and the item number to search for (the target). The search begins in row

FIGURE 9.14

A two-dimensional array for testing search techniques

PriceTable	1	2
1	324	2.34
2	423	3.23
3	254	1.95
4	321	0.34
5	132	2.25

1 of the array. The procedure uses a fourth parameter, FoundLoc, to pass the result of the search back to the calling procedure. If it finds the target, it sets FoundLoc equal to the row number where the target is located; if it concludes that the target does not exist, it sets FoundLoc equal to zero.

```
Public Sub SeqSearch(A() As Currency, ByVal LastRow As Integer, _
        ByVal Target As Currency, FoundLoc As Integer)
    Dim Row As Integer
    For Row = 1 To LastRow
        If A(Row, 1) = Target Then
            FoundLoc = Row
            Exit Sub
        End If
    Next Row
    FoundLoc = 0           ' Target does not exist
End Sub
```

After the search is complete, the calling procedure tests the FoundLoc argument to learn the result of the search. For example, consider the following code segment:

```
Item = InputBox("Enter item number")
SeqSearch PriceTable(), 5, Item, FoundRow
If FoundRow = 0 Then
    MsgBox "The item number does not exist"
Else
    Price = PriceTable(FoundRow, 2)
    MsgBox "Price is " & Format$(Price, "Currency")
End If
```

The first statement in this code obtains the target item number from the user. The second statement invokes the sequential search procedure. The If statement uses the argument FoundRow to determine whether the search was successful and if so, in which row the target item number was found. Then the second column of this same row holds the price to be displayed to the user.

EXERCISE 9.12

Suppose that a module-level array named PriceTable has been populated with the values shown in Figure 9.14. What values are displayed by the three message boxes when the user clicks on cmdSearchTest?

```
Private Sub cmdSearchTest_Click()
    Dim FoundRow As Integer
    SeqSearch PriceTable(), 5, 321, FoundRow
    MsgBox FoundRow
    SeqSearch PriceTable(), 5, 200, FoundRow
    MsgBox FoundRow
    SeqSearch PriceTable(), 5, 423, FoundRow
    MsgBox FoundRow
End Sub
```

EXERCISE 9.13

Why is the statement FoundLoc = 0 necessary in procedure SeqSearch? Explain. Answer the question in Exercise 9.12 again, assuming the statement FoundLoc = 0 has been removed from procedure SeqSearch.

EXERCISE 9.14 Rewrite procedure SeqSearch using a Do While...Loop structure instead of a For...Next structure. Can you write the procedure without using an Exit Sub statement?

EXERCISE 9.15 In the sequential search example just given, suppose that item numbers are not equally popular; that is, some are chosen as the target more frequently than others. Can this fact be used to make the sequential search more efficient? Explain.

Sequential Search of an Ordered Array

In the sequential search of an unordered array we had to search the entire array if the target item did not exist in the array, because we could not be sure that the target value wouldn't be somewhere ahead of the element being examined. If the array is ordered, we can stop searching sooner if the target value is not in the array. Why is this the case?

In the array in Figure 9.15 the rows have been ordered so that item numbers are in ascending order. Note that this array contains the same data as the array in Figure 9.14; for example, the price of item number 324 is still $2.34.

Suppose we are searching for item number 200 (which doesn't exist). When we reach row 2, which stores item number 254, do we have to go any farther? No! If item number 200 existed, then it would have come before item 254. Thus we can terminate the search as soon as we find an item number in the array that is greater than or equal to the target. If the item number is equal to the target, then we have located the target. If it is greater than the target, then we know the target does not exist in the array. Study the following procedure:

```
Public Sub SeqSearch(A() As Currency, ByVal LastRow As Integer, _
        ByVal Target As Currency, FoundLoc As Integer)
    Dim Row As Integer
    Row = 1
    Do Until (A(Row, 1) >= Target) Or (Row = LastRow)
        Row = Row + 1
    Loop
    If A(Row, 1) = Target Then
        FoundLoc = Row
    Else
        FoundLoc = 0
    End If
End Sub
```

The Do Until loop stops when it finds an item number in the array that is greater than or equal to the target value. It also stops when the end of the array has been reached. Thus, after the loop stops, a test needs to be made to see whether the target was found (because there are two other possible reasons why the loop stopped).

FIGURE 9.15

A two-dimensional array ordered by item number

PriceTable	1	2
1	132	2.25
2	254	1.95
3	321	0.34
4	324	2.34
5	423	3.23

EXERCISE 9.16 A module-level array named A has been populated with an ordered list of letters (ascending order). The letters are stored in elements 1 through NumLetters of the array, where NumLetters is a module-level Integer variable. For example, this array might contain the following letters, in order: a, a, b, d, g, g, g, h, k, z. Note that some letters may occur more than once in the array.

Write a Click event procedure for a command button named cmdDispUniqueOrd that displays a message box showing the letters occurring in the array A, being sure to display each distinct letter only once. For example, if the array contains the preceding list of letters, the message should display a, b, d, g, h, k, z. Your procedure should work properly when the array contains *any* list of letters that is in ascending order.

Design hint: As you scan the list, "remember" the previous letter encountered.

EXERCISE 9.17 A module-level array named A has been populated with an *unordered* list of letters. The letters are stored in elements 1 through NumLetters of the array, where NumLetters is a module-level Integer variable. For example, this array might contain the following letters, in order: g, z, b, h, g, a, d, k, g, a. Note that some letters may occur more than once in the array.

Write a Click event procedure for a command button named cmdDispUniqueUnord that displays a message box showing the letters occurring in the array A, being sure to display each distinct letter only once. For example, if the array contains the preceding list of letters, the message should display a, b, d, g, h, k, z (order is not important in the display). Your procedure should work properly when the array contains *any* list of letters. Do *not* sort the list (because sorting by itself is more complicated than the direct solution to this problem).

EXERCISE 9.18 A module-level array named A has been populated with an unordered list of letters. The letters are stored in elements 1 through NumLetters of the array, where NumLetters is a module-level Integer variable. For example, this array might contain the following letters, in order: g, z, b, h, g, a, d, k, g, a. Note that some letters may occur more than once in the array.

Write a Click event procedure for a command button named cmdDispCount that counts the number of times each letter occurs in the array A and displays the count for each letter. For example, if the array contains the preceding list of letters, the procedure should display a 2, b 1, d 1, g 3, h 1, k 1, z 1 (order is not important in the display). Do *not* sort the list (because sorting by itself is more complicated than the direct solution to this problem).

Binary Search

Consider the following search process. You have an ordered list of 100 numbers and you want to determine whether a specific target number exists in that list. Your only way of proceeding is to pick one of the 100 elements in the list and see whether it is equal to the target number. If not, then you pick another one of the elements, and see if it is equal to the target, and so on, one element at a time.

If you start with the first element in the list and find that it is not equal to the target, then you have 99 more elements to search. But what if you start at the 50th element? You check the value and find that it is not equal to the target. Do you still have 99 more elements to check? Remember that your list is ordered.

Suppose the list is in ascending order. If the target value is greater than the value found at the 50th element, it doesn't make any sense to look at elements 1 through 49. You can eliminate half of the elements with this one guess, since you know that the target, if it exists, must be somewhere beyond element 50. Then your next guess should be halfway between element 51 and element 100. Using this strategy repeatedly, with each guess you either find the target or you eliminate half of the remaining elements from further consideration. For example, after your second guess you have eliminated three-fourths of the elements, after your third guess you have eliminated seven-eighths of the elements, and so on.

This search strategy is called a ***binary search* because it breaks the search area into two parts in a repetitive process**. Figure 9.16 shows the search of an 11-element array, where the target value is 76. The search proceeds by recording the *active search area*—the elements that have not yet been eliminated—at each step. The active search area is shaded in Figure 9.16 (on page 466). The lower bound marks one end of the active search area and the upper bound marks the other end. At each step the computer compares the target value to the value stored at the midpoint of the active search area. It then eliminates half of the active search area according to the outcome of the comparison.

There is a drawback and a benefit to using binary search instead of sequential search. The drawback is its complexity; it is more difficult to code a binary search than a sequential search. The benefit is the improved efficiency of programs using the binary search. Table 9.2 illustrates the improvement in efficiency.

Pseudocode for the binary search follows. Keep in mind that the array must be ordered for the binary search to work.

Set lower bound = 1
Set upper bound = n (element number of the last element to be searched)
Do While lower bound <= upper bound
    Set mid = (lower bound + upper bound) \ 2
    If target = value in element "mid" Then
        Search successful with "mid" being the location of the target
        Exit Sub
    ElseIf target > value in element "mid" Then
        Set lower bound = mid + 1
    Else
        Set upper bound = mid – 1
    End If
Loop
If the loop terminates and we get to this step (i.e., we didn't execute Exit Sub
  above), then target does not exist in the array

TABLE 9.2 Number of elements searched in binary versus sequential search

Size of Array	Sequential Search		Binary Search	
	Average	Worst Case	Average	Worst Case
1,000	500	1,000	9	10
100,000	50,000	100,000	16	17
1,000,000	500,000	1,000,000	19	20

FIGURE 9.16

Binary search with a target value of 76

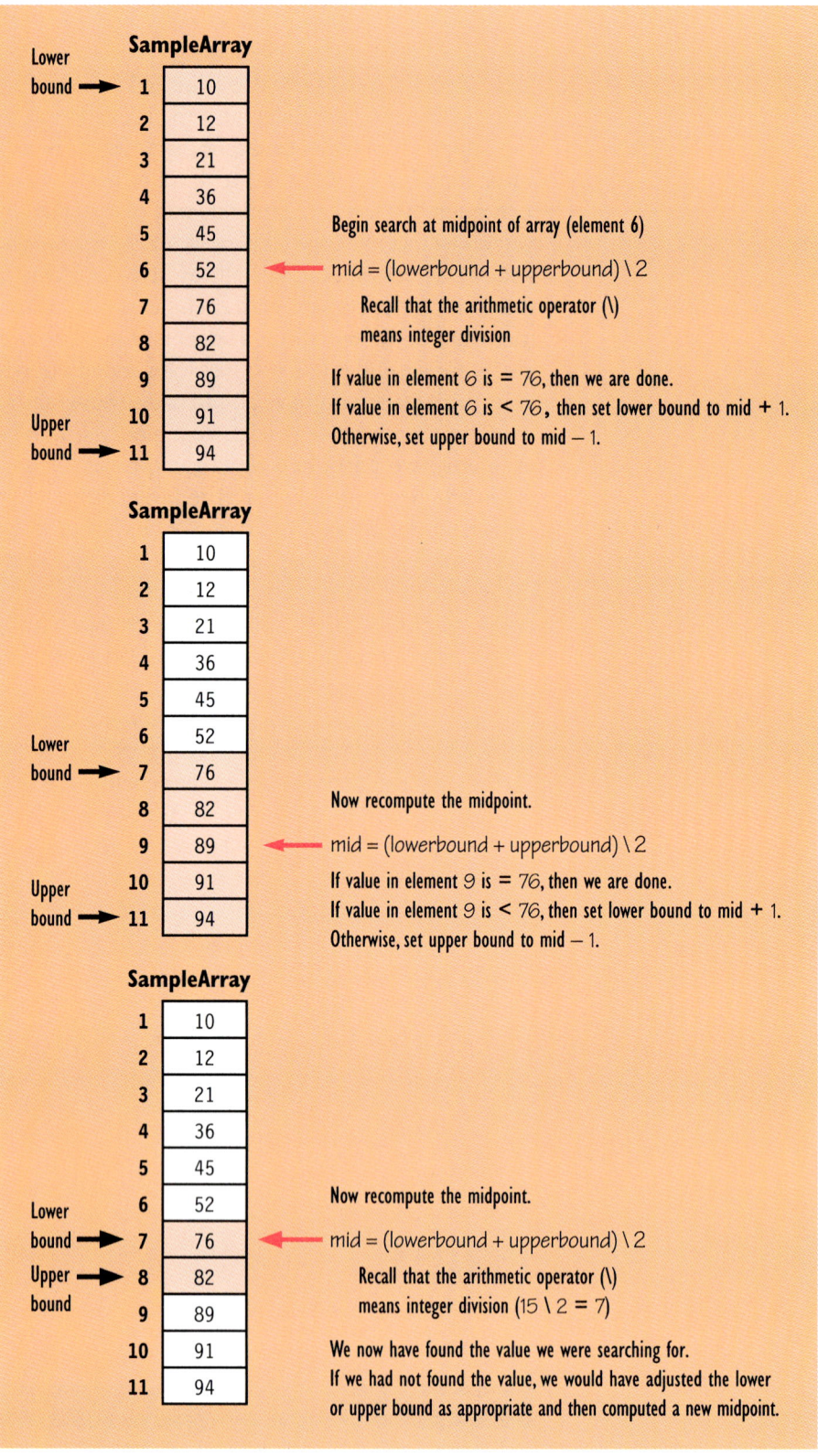

The following procedure implements the binary search. It is designed to search the same array that was used in the sequential search example (see Figure 9.15).

```
Public Sub BiSearch(A() As Currency, ByVal LastRow As Integer, _
            ByVal Target As Currency, FoundLoc As Integer)
    Dim LowerBound As Integer, UpperBound As Integer
    Dim MidPoint As Integer
    LowerBound = 1
    UpperBound = LastRow
    Do While LowerBound <= UpperBound
        MidPoint = (LowerBound + UpperBound) \ 2
        If Target = A(MidPoint, 1) Then
            FoundLoc = MidPoint
            Exit Sub
        ElseIf Target > A(MidPoint, 1) Then
            LowerBound = MidPoint + 1
        Else
            UpperBound = MidPoint - 1
        End If
    Loop
    FoundLoc = 0           ' Never found a match
End Sub
```

Again, the procedure is invoked in the same way as the previous search procedures were. This code is repeated here.

```
Item = InputBox("Enter item number")
BiSearch PriceTable(), 5, Item, FoundRow
If FoundRow = 0 Then
    MsgBox "The item number does not exist"
Else
    Price = PriceTable(FoundRow, 2)
    MsgBox "Price is " & Format$(Price, "Currency")
End If
```

It is important to test the binary search procedure carefully because it is easy to make a logic error when writing the code. In addition to the standard tests to verify correct operation when searching for existing and nonexisting values, be sure to test the procedure as follows: with a target value that is less than the value in row 1, and also with a target value that is greater than the value in the final row of the array. It is important as well to test the procedure with a target value equal to the value in row 1 and also with a target value equal to the value in the final row of the array. This is called *testing at the extremes*. Procedures that work for routine values in the array often fail at the beginning or the end. If you don't test for these "extreme" conditions you may not detect coding errors that the user will eventually encounter during normal use of the application.

Sorting

The operation of two of our search procedures required data to be ordered. In addition, many other business applications require data to be ordered. **Sorting refers to the process of rearranging the values in an array to make it ordered.** There are many sorting techniques that programmers use to order data, and many computer scientists devote their energy to creating and evaluating new and improved techniques.

In this section we introduce sorting by presenting one of the simplest techniques: the bubble sort, also called the standard exchange sort. This technique is relatively inefficient, but it will demonstrate how a sort can be coded and give you more exposure to the uses of arrays.

Bubble (Standard Exchange) Sort

In the *bubble sort,* **adjacent elements in the array are compared and, if out of order, exchanged.** Suppose we want to sort a list of data into ascending order. We start at the beginning of the array and compare the values in elements 1 and 2. If the value in element 1 is greater than the value in element 2, then we exchange the contents of the two elements. We then compare the values in elements 2 and 3. If the value in element 2 is greater than the value in element 3, then we exchange the contents of the two elements. We continue this process until we reach the end of the list. This sequence of operations constitutes one *pass* through the list. The key actions in this sort are

- *Comparison*—comparing the values in two adjacent elements.
- *Exchange*—exchanging the contents of the two elements.
- *Pass*—comparing pairs of adjacent elements starting at element 1 and going to the end of the array.

Figure 9.17a shows one pass through an array that initially contains the unsorted list of numbers 27, 35, 12, 50, 18, and 45. After completing the first pass, we start a second pass. The steps in the second pass are the same as the steps for the first, except we can stop at the second to last element because the first pass moved the largest value in the list to the last element (the shaded element in Figure 9.17a). Since the goal is to put the list in ascending order, the largest value is now in its proper position.

Figure 9.17b shows the second pass, which stops at element number 5. At the end of the second pass, the largest two values are both in their proper positions (shaded in the figure). We continue making passes until one of two conditions is met. First, if we perform a pass and make no exchanges, then we know the data are in order. Second, if the length of the pass is reduced to just two elements (with each successive pass, the length of the pass is reduced by one element), then it will be the last pass and the array is in order.

Figure 9.17c shows the third pass, which stops at element 4. The fourth pass stops at element 3. You can see that the contents of elements 1 through 3 are already in the proper order, so the fourth pass makes no exchanges. Thus, the sort terminates at the end of the fourth pass.

Example 9.4

Performing a Bubble Sort

Let's create a general sub procedure that performs a bubble sort. To test the sort, we'll create a command button that generates and stores 20 random numbers in an array, and then asks the sort procedure to sort them. When the sort is finished, we'll display the 20 numbers on the form using the Print method for the form. This technique of printing directly to the form is useful for testing and debugging. You wouldn't want to display information this way in a finished user interface, but it's great for debugging.

The form we create and its output are shown in Figure 9.18, which also shows the code for the Sort button's Click event procedure. This code uses two methods we have not seen before. Both are methods associated with the

FIGURE 9.17

Passes of a bubble sort

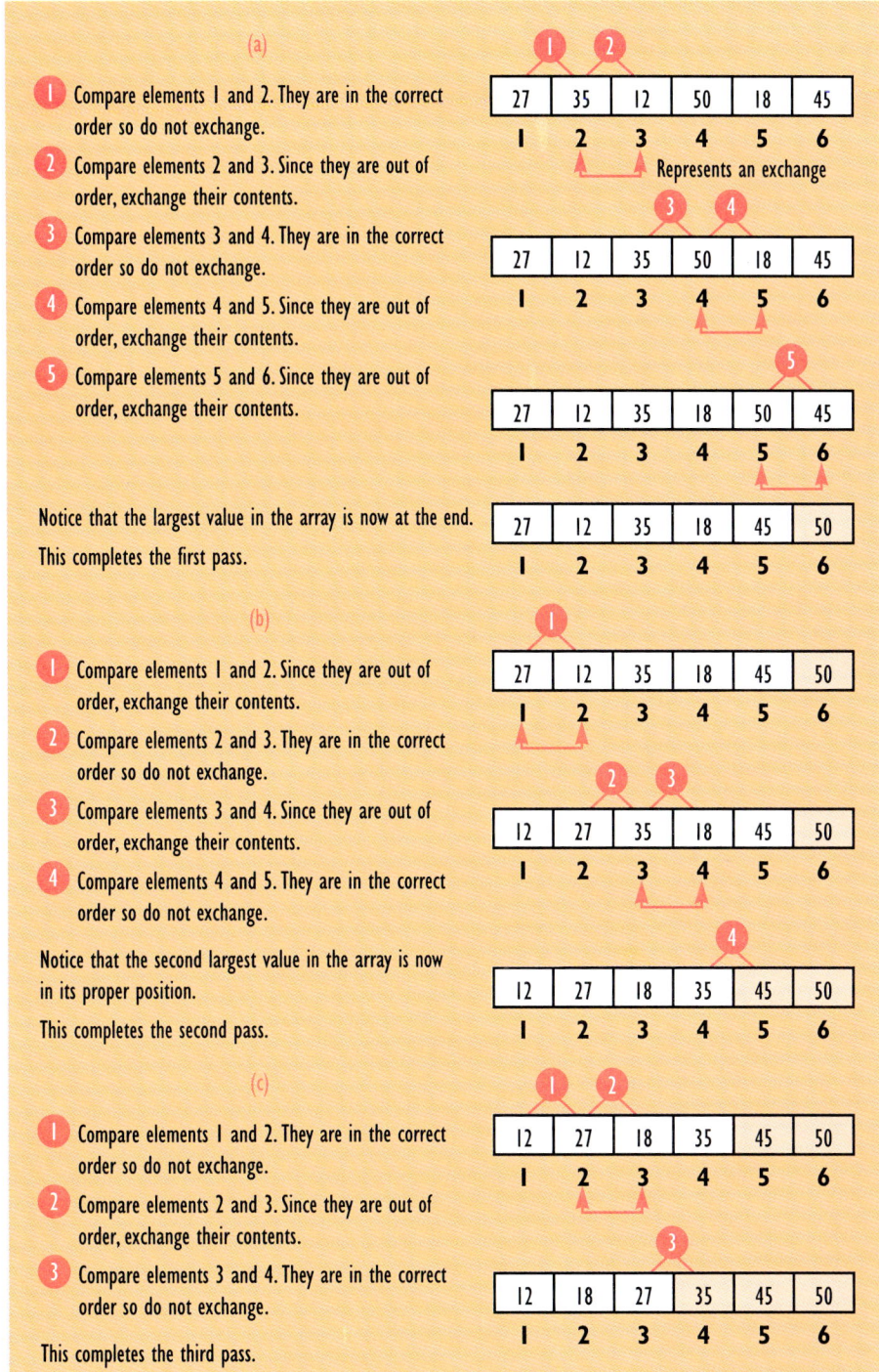

form (which in this example is named frmEx0904). The Print method displays text directly on the form, and the Cls method clears the form of any previously printed text.

Figure 9.19 shows the code for the bubble sort procedure. The statements inside the outer loop (Do Until) perform a pass. This outer loop forces the procedure to continue performing passes as long as at least one exchange has been made during the previous pass. At the start of each pass the variable NoExchangeInPass is set to True, and as the pass proceeds NoExchangeInPass is set to

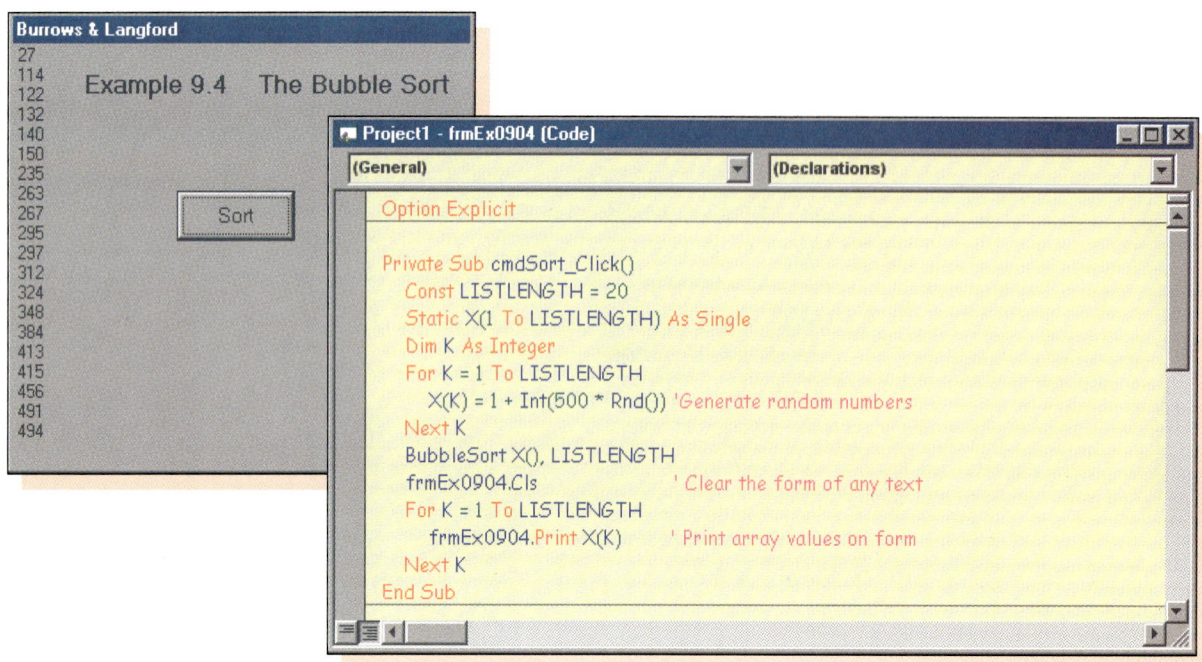

FIGURE 9.18 Sample output and partial code for Example 9.4

FIGURE 9.19

Bubble sort procedure

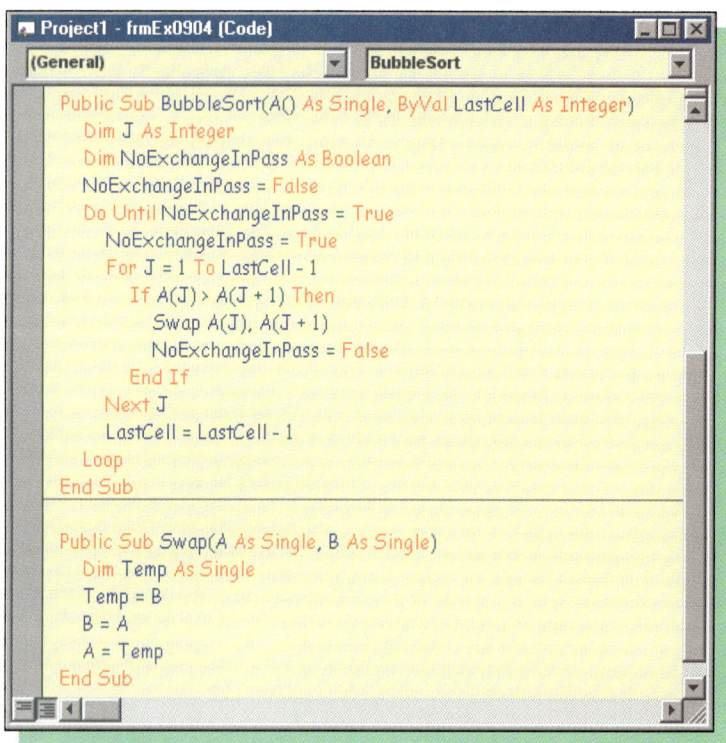

False when an exchange (a swap) is made. After a pass is complete, the outer loop examines the NoExchangeInPass variable to see if an exchange was made.

The variable NoExchangeInPass is called a *flag variable*, which is the general term for any variable used by a programmer to indicate whether a particular condition has occurred (in our case, an exchange). The use of flag variables is a common strategy in code design.

The inner loop (For J) controls a single pass through the array. Notice that the loop counter variable J starts out at 1 and stops at one less than the last element (if the last element is 10, the loop stops at 9). Why is this? Because the comparison inside this loop compares elements J and J+1. So when J is 9, the comparison is of elements 9 and 10. Also note that the variable LastCell is decreased by 1 each time a pass is completed (LastCell = LastCell - 1) because each pass places the current largest number in its final location.

The procedure calls another procedure named Swap (also shown in Figure 9.19). This procedure exchanges the contents of the two elements, A(J) and A(J + 1), that are passed to it.

There are many other sorting techniques that are more efficient than the bubble sort, but they are also more complex and require more care to code. Sorting and searching are so common that many programmers have written procedures to solve these problems. Therefore, if you scan code libraries you are likely to find search and sort procedures that you can use or adapt to solve the problem you have at hand. Indeed, you may often find highly efficient procedures that you can insert into your program with little effort.

EXERCISE 9.19 What happens if we modify procedure BubbleSort by changing the For statement from

> **For** J = 1 **To** LastCell - 1

to

> **For** J = 1 **To** LastCell

EXERCISE 9.20 Modify procedure BubbleSort so that it sorts the list in descending order instead of ascending order.

EXERCISE 9.21 Explain why the following procedure does not succeed in exchanging the values in the two arguments passed to it.

> **Public Sub** SwapFail(A **As** Single, B **As** Single)
>   A = B
>   B = A
> **End Sub**

Row and Column Totals

◆ ◆ ◆

A common processing task for two-dimensional arrays is computing row and column totals. We describe the procedure for computing these totals using the DivisionEarnings array introduced in Figure 9.7 and shown populated with sample data in Figure 9.20. Recall the interpretation of this data: the value in the element with row subscript 1994 and column subscript 2, for example, represents the earnings for division 2 in the year 1994.

With these data the row totals represent the total company earnings for each year, summed across all three divisions. How do we compute the row totals? Suppose that we have another array, declared as follows, for storing the row totals.

> **Dim** CompanyEarnings(1993 **To** 1995) **As Currency**

FIGURE 9.20

Sample data for row total computation

DivisionEarnings	1	2	3
1993	213	241	353
1994	123	242	276
1995	432	321	398

Then for the first row we would have

CompanyEarnings(1993) = DivisionEarnings(1993, 1) + _
  DivisionEarnings(1993, 2) + DivisionEarnings(1993, 3)

Notice that the row subscript (1993) is held constant while the column subscript goes from 1 to 2 to 3 in the expression on the right of the equal sign. If we wanted to perform this calculation for the next row, we would have the following:

CompanyEarnings(1994) = DivisionEarnings(1994, 1) + _
  DivisionEarnings(1994, 2) + DivisionEarnings(1994, 3)

This gives us a clue as to how we might write code to perform this row summing operation. We want the row subscript to be set to a value, and while it is held constant, we want the column subscript to go through its legal values. Consider the following code segment:

```
For Year = 1993 To 1995
    CompanyEarnings(Year) = 0
    For Division = 1 To 3
        CompanyEarnings(Year) = CompanyEarnings(Year) + DivisionEarnings(Year, Division)
    Next Division
Next Year
```

The outer loop (For Year) defines a value for the variable Year. While this row value is held constant, the inner loop (For Division) causes the column variable to vary from 1 to 3. This is exactly what we had intended. Study the code and convince yourself that it operates correctly.

EXERCISE 9.22 Write a code segment that computes column totals for the array in Figure 9.20. What is a good name for the array that holds the column totals?

EXERCISE 9.23 Write a code segment that computes the *grand total*—that is, the sum of *all* values in the array—for the array in Figure 9.20.

9.4 Dynamic Arrays

A problem that often arises when using arrays is deciding how large an array should be when you declare it. That is, you have to specify the number of elements it should have at design time, when you compose the Dim statement for the array, but you may not learn how many data items you need to store until run time.

This problem arose in Example 9.3, which populated arrays with company names and rates of return from a database table. To store this data we had to determine the maximum number of companies we expected the database to contain information about. The statement

    Dim CompanyName(1 **To** 100) **As String**

gives us elements to store up to 100 company names. But what if the database contains records for 130 companies? Or what if we really don't know beforehand the number of companies? The arrays we have studied so far—called *static arrays*[2]—require us to supply constants for the lower and upper bounds. Using static arrays, the only way to solve this problem is to make the array sufficiently large to hold the maximum number of values that we would ever expect to see at run time. This approach is often wasteful in terms of memory since in practice we seldom encounter the maximum number of values.

VB provides a solution to this problem: the ***dynamic array,* which can be resized at any time while the program is executing**. You declare a dynamic array using either a Public statement, the Dim statement at the module-level, or a Static or Dim statement in a procedure (if you want the array to be local). However, instead of specifying dimension information, you supply an empty dimension list. Examples are

    Public ArrayA() **As Integer**
    Dim ArrayB() **As Single**
    Static ArrayC() **As Currency**

Then, at the point in your code where the number of elements needed becomes known, **you use the *ReDim statement* to set the actual array size**. The ReDim statement can appear anywhere in a procedure.

For example, suppose a numeric variable named NumberOfItems has been assigned the value 130. Then the statement

    ReDim ArrayC(1 **To** NumberOfItems, 1 **To** 2)

creates ArrayC with 130 rows and 2 columns of type Currency. Note that no type is specified in the ReDim statement. For a dynamic array, the Dim statement specifies its type but not its size, and subsequently the ReDim statement specifies its size but not its type.

After executing one ReDim statement for a dynamic array, you can use another ReDim statement to change the lower and upper bounds of any or all of its dimensions. This change may result in the array having a different number of elements. You cannot, however, change the number of dimensions. Thus, once the first ReDim statement has defined ArrayC as a two-dimensional array, ArrayC must remain a two-dimensional array.

Each time you ReDim a dynamic array, the values currently stored in the array are lost. This may not be what you want. For example, suppose that you have a one-dimensional dynamic array called EmpList that currently has 500 elements. Assume that the array is full, but you want to add more elements (and keep the old values in elements 1 through 500). To do this, you add the keyword Preserve to the ReDim statement, as follows:

    ReDim Preserve EmpList(600)

Thus, the ***Redim Preserve statement*** **allows you to change the size of a dynamic array without losing its current values**. The only restriction on the Preserve

---

[2] This is a new use of the word "static." Do not confuse static arrays (fixed-sized arrays) with local arrays declared using the Static statement.

option is that it can be used only if you are changing the bounds for the last (rightmost) dimension of the array. If ArrayX is a two-dimensional array with ten rows, you can change only the second dimension. The following would be legal:

ReDim Preserve ArrayX(1 **To** 10, 1 **To** NewNumberOfColumns)

9.5 Control Arrays

In addition to arrays that store numeric and string values—the kinds of arrays found in all programming languages—Visual Basic allows programmers to construct arrays of controls. Control arrays help you improve the design of graphical interfaces that contain many controls (of the same type) whose event procedures are nearly identical.

Why would a user interface contain multiple controls whose event procedures are nearly identical? Typically this situation arises when the program needs to present the user with multiple instances of the same quantity or variable. For example, a user interface may present the number of units sold for ten different items using ten Text box controls. The processing of units sold for one item is identical to the processing of units sold for any other item: we find the extended price for each item by multiplying the units sold times the unit price. Consequently, the event procedures for the ten text boxes are nearly identical.

When the processing is identical for a group of controls, the program can be simplified by allowing these controls to share the same event procedures. To do this in VB you create a *control array*—**a group of controls that share the same name and the same event procedures**. For example, if we have a control array consisting of 10 text boxes named txtUnitsSold, there will be a single LostFocus event procedure named txtUnitsSold_LostFocus for this entire group of text boxes.

Every control that is a member of a control array has an Index property setting. **The *Index property* is used to distinguish the controls in a control array from one another,** just as a subscript is used to distinguish elements of an ordinary array. The Index property is an integer, and the Index setting for each control in a control array has to be unique. For example, if there are ten controls in the control array, you might set the Index property of one of them to 0, the Index property of the next one to 1, and so on, through 9.

Figure 9.21 depicts three text boxes that make up a control array, and their Index property settings. As in all control arrays, the three text boxes share the same name—txtUnitsSold. To refer to a specific text box in the control array, the programmer uses syntax similar to that for a one-dimensional array. The text box having Index setting 0 is referred to as txtUnitsSold(0), the text box having Index setting 1 as txtUnitsSold(1), and so on. By following the

FIGURE 9.21

Control array of three text boxes

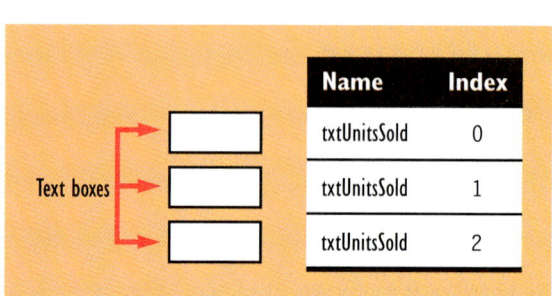

naming conventions for controls (using the txt prefix in this case), it is easy to distinguish control arrays from ordinary arrays.

All the controls in a control array share the same event procedures. When any one of the controls receives an event, the associated (shared) event procedure begins executing. VB automatically passes the control's Index property setting to the event procedure as an argument so that the event procedure can determine exactly which control generated the event.

Consider the following example, in which the form contains a label and a control array of three command buttons. The user interface is shown in Figure 9.22. Note that the caption of the first command button is "1", the caption of the second is "2", and the caption of the third is "3". When the user clicks the button captioned "1", the Label control is changed to display "1". When the user clicks the button captioned "2", the Label control is changed to display "2". And when the user clicks the button captioned "3", the Label control is changed to display "3".

It is easy to create such an application without using control arrays. But suppose there were ten command buttons instead of three. Then creating the controls and their event procedures would be tedious. A worse difficulty arises if the program's user requirements change. For example, suppose we decide to make the label display "You clicked command button 1" or "You clicked command button 2" instead of just "1" or "2". Then we would have to modify the event procedures for every command button.

Here's how we can create this simple application using a control array of command buttons.

1. Create a label on the form and name it lblButtonWithEvent.
2. Create one command button on the form, name it cmdTest, and set its Caption property to "1".
3. Copy this command button by selecting it, choosing <u>C</u>opy under the <u>E</u>dit menu (or CTRL+C) and then choosing <u>P</u>aste under the <u>E</u>dit menu (or CTRL+V). VB responds with the message "You already have a control named 'cmdTest'. Do you want to create a control array?" Figure 9.23 shows this dialog box.

FIGURE 9.22

Form with a control array of three command buttons

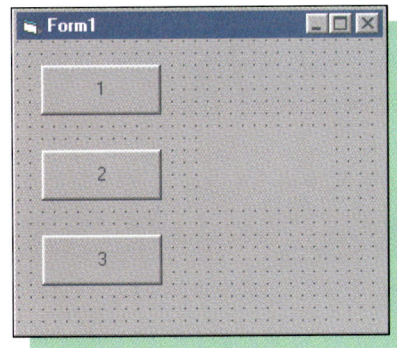

FIGURE 9.23

Dialog used to create control array

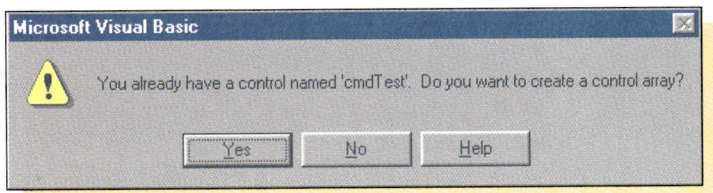

4. Click Yes. VB then places a new command button on the form. Except for the Index property, the property settings of this new command button will be identical to those of the original command button. (The first command button will have Index set to 0, the new one will have Index set to 1.) It is important to note that their Name properties will both be cmdTest.

5. Change the caption of the new command button to "2".

6. Create the third command button in the control array using Paste again. VB does not inquire whether you want to create a control array this time, since you already have one.

7. Change the third command button's caption to "3".

The final task is to create the Click event procedure.

8. Double-clicking any one of the three command buttons at design time brings up the Code window showing the event procedure template

   Private Sub cmdTest_Click(Index **As Integer**)

   End Sub

   Like the KeyPress event for a text box, an event procedure for a control array (for any type of control) has a parameter. In the current case, when the Click event occurs at run time, VB takes the Index setting of the command button the user clicked, passes it to cmdTest_Click as an argument, and then begins executing cmdTest_Click.

9. Complete the event procedure using the following code. When the user clicks the command button captioned "2", it displays "2" in the Label control because the Index property setting for this command button is 1.

   Private Sub cmdTest_Click(Index **As Integer**)
       lblButtonWithEvent.Caption = Index + 1
   End Sub

   If the user clicks the first command button, this procedure is called with Index having a value of 0; thus the label's Caption will display "1".

   Although you can create control arrays of any type of control, the most common are the command button, the text box, the label, and the check box.

The KeyPress Event for Control Arrays

◆ ◆ ◆

Control arrays are commonly used to coordinate the processing for text boxes. Frequently the KeyPress event procedure for the text boxes benefits from this coordination. Recall that the KeyPress event occurs for a text box when the text box has the focus and the user presses a key. The KeyPress event procedure has a parameter named KeyAscii, which holds the ANSI code of the key the user pressed. The KeyPress event procedure for a control array has *two* parameters: Index and KeyAscii. The heading for such an event procedure appears as follows:

Private Sub txtDemo_KeyPress(Index **As Integer**, KeyAscii **As Integer**)

As an example, the KeyPress event procedure for an array of four text boxes named txtStuff follows. This event procedure allows the user to press the ENTER key as an alternative to the TAB key to move the focus from one text box to the next. Like the tab cycle, this event procedure moves the focus cyclically from one text box to the next.

```
Private Sub txtStuff_KeyPress(Index As Integer, KeyAscii As Integer)
    Dim NextInCycle As Integer
    If KeyAscii = vbKeyReturn Then    ' the user pressed Enter
        NextInCycle = (Index + 1) Mod 4
        txtStuff(NextInCycle).SetFocus
        KeyAscii = vbEmpty
    End If
End Sub
```

This procedure examines the KeyAscii parameter to see if the key pressed by the user is the ENTER key. If it is the ENTER key, the procedure examines the Index parameter to determine which text box was active when ENTER was pressed. For example, if the first text box was active, then Index would equal 0. The variable NextInCycle is then set equal to the index of the next text box in the cycle using the expression (Index + 1) Mod 4. This expression evaluates to Index plus 1, unless Index is 3 (the last text box), in which case it evaluates to 0 (the first text box).[3] Then the variable NextInCycle is used to set the focus to the next text box in the cycle.

VB does not allow the programmer to modify the heading of an event procedure. If, for example, you attempt to delete the parameter list from the preceding event procedure, the program will fail. Similarly, if you reverse the order of the parameters, the procedure will not work properly.

VB creates the parameter list for event procedures to be consistent with its understanding of the type of control (e.g., whether or not it is a member of a control array) and the type of event (e.g., KeyPress).

Synchronized Control Arrays

Control arrays are restricted to one dimension. Therefore, if you want to create a table of controls, you have to create multiple columns. Each column can be a control array, and your program can treat them collectively as a table if you synchronize the columns.

Example 9.5 Creating Synchronized Control Arrays

This example illustrates how you can coordinate two control arrays. It uses a control array of text boxes named txtN and a control array of labels named lblSqr. Figure 9.24 shows the control arrays and their relationships. The labels have their BorderStyle set to "1 - Fixed Single".

The user gives the focus to one of the text boxes in the left-hand column (N) and enters a number. Then, when the user moves the focus to a different text box, the LostFocus event procedure computes the square root of the number and displays it in the right-hand column (Sqr(N)).

For this to work properly, we must be sure that the text box and the label next to it have the same Index number. That is, the Index settings determine

---

[3] See Example 4.3 if you wish to refresh your memory of the Mod operator and cyclic sequences.

FIGURE 9.24

Synchronized control arrays

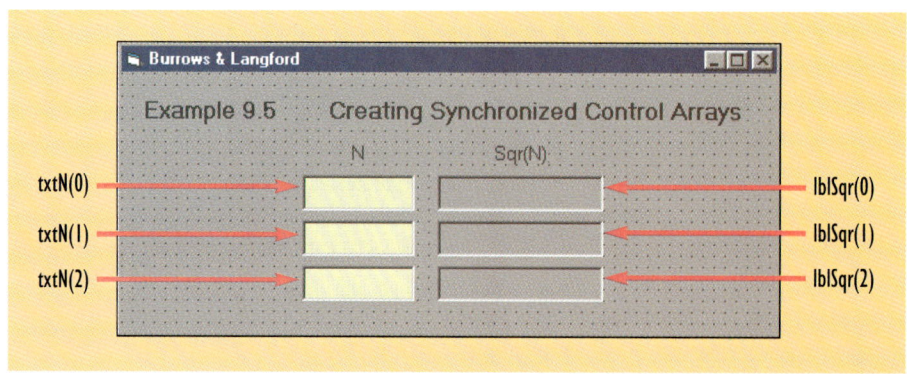

the synchronization of the text boxes and the labels. In the LostFocus event procedure in Figure 9.25, the statement

lblSqr(Index).Caption = Sqr(Val(txtN(Index).Text))

relies on this synchronization. Because the text box and the label to its right have the same Index value, the use of parameter Index for both lblSqr and txtN makes sense.

The other statements in this event procedure handle the situation when the user either types nothing in the text box (the zero-length string) or types a negative number.

Adding Controls at Run Time

Sometimes the number of controls needed in a control array is not known at design time. To handle such cases you can specify just the first control of the control array at design time and write code that creates, at run time, as many additional controls as necessary. This is called *creating controls dynamically*.

To set up a control array with just a single control you do the following: at design time create the control, set its Name property as desired, and then set its Index property to 1 (0 is also a common choice).

Use the Load statement to create new controls at run time. **The *Load statement* creates a new control, adds it to a specified control array, sets its Index property to a specified number, and sets its Visible property to False.**

FIGURE 9.25

Code for Example 9.5

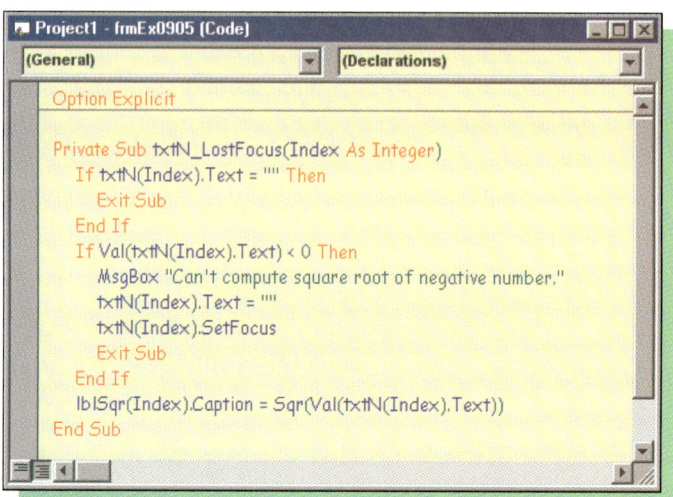

Except for the Index and Visible properties, VB automatically sets all properties of the new control to be identical to those of the original control in the array. The syntax of the Load statement is

Load *ControlArrayName(NewControlNumber)*

where *ControlArrayName* is the name of the control array to which the new control will be added, and *NewControlNumber* is a numeric expression that specifies the Index setting for the new control.

Example 9.6 Creating Controls at Run Time

This example extends our earlier example in which a label's caption changed as the user clicked on different command buttons. The modification is that the user gets to specify the number of command buttons. To do this the user first clicks on another command button named cmdCreateButtons.

Note that the Index property of the command button created at design time (i.e., the first command button in the control array) is 1, so the Index property of the first command button created at run time will be 2. Procedure cmdCreateButtons_Click (Figure 9.26) sets the Left property of new command buttons so that the command buttons will not sit right on top of one another on the form (the code aligns them in a row). Event procedure cmdRemoveButtons_Click illustrates how to **remove controls from a control array at run time using the** *Unload statement*.

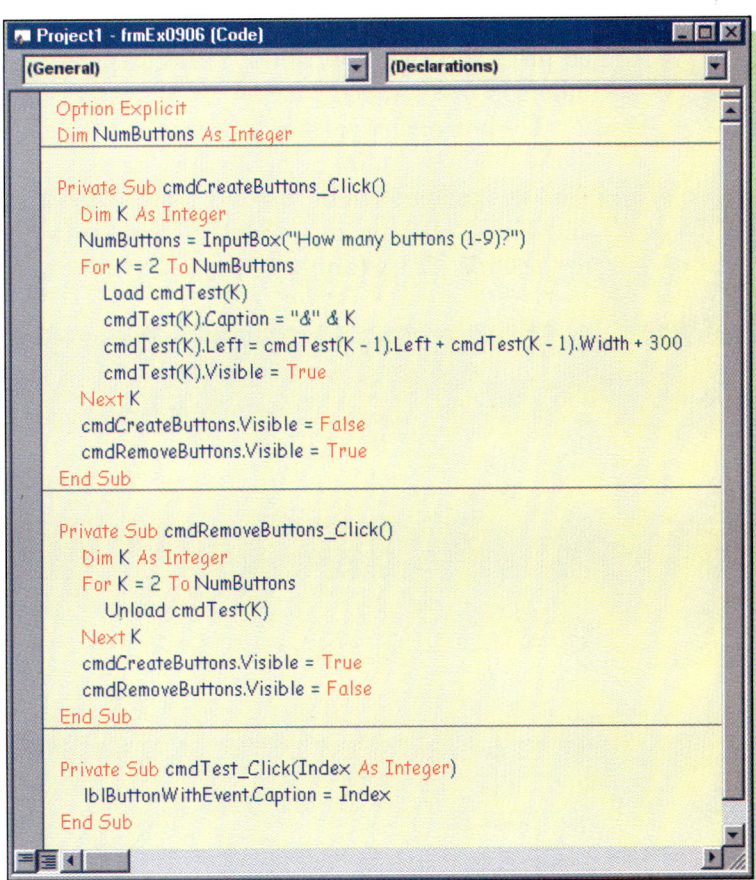

FIGURE 9.26

Code for Example 9.6

```
Option Explicit
Dim NumButtons As Integer

Private Sub cmdCreateButtons_Click()
    Dim K As Integer
    NumButtons = InputBox("How many buttons (1-9)?")
    For K = 2 To NumButtons
        Load cmdTest(K)
        cmdTest(K).Caption = "&" & K
        cmdTest(K).Left = cmdTest(K - 1).Left + cmdTest(K - 1).Width + 300
        cmdTest(K).Visible = True
    Next K
    cmdCreateButtons.Visible = False
    cmdRemoveButtons.Visible = True
End Sub

Private Sub cmdRemoveButtons_Click()
    Dim K As Integer
    For K = 2 To NumButtons
        Unload cmdTest(K)
    Next K
    cmdCreateButtons.Visible = True
    cmdRemoveButtons.Visible = False
End Sub

Private Sub cmdTest_Click(Index As Integer)
    lblButtonWithEvent.Caption = Index
End Sub
```

9.6 Project 13: Order Entry Application Prototype

Most businesses automate the process of recording orders placed by their customers. An order entry person uses an order entry application to record the customer's name, address, and phone number, and the items and quantities ordered. Ideally, this application stores the information in a database. Then other applications can access the same database to perform functions that are related to customer orders, such as billing, shipping, and inventory management.

Description of the Application

◆ ◆ ◆

In this project we build the user interface for an order entry system that accepts information about customers and the products they want to order. The program we create is a prototype. That is, the program will not be fully functional but will serve to show the user how the interface works.

Figure 9.27 shows the Order Entry screen for the prototype. The section at the top of the form records customer information. The section at the bottom contains information on the products being ordered by the customer. The order entry person fills in the customer number, information about the customer, and the order number. The program automatically fills in today's date (which the user can override).

The order entry person also fills in the information on products being ordered, starting with a product number. The program automatically fills in the product description and price, or notifies the user if the product number entered is invalid. Once a valid product number has been entered, the order entry person fills in the quantity. Then the application computes the extended price and the order total. These steps are performed for each product ordered.

The order entry person can also view a list of valid products by clicking the Show Products button. The Product List screen is shown in Figure 9.28. If the user has forgotten the product number, he or she can scroll through the list and double-click on any product to transfer the information for that product to the Order Entry form.

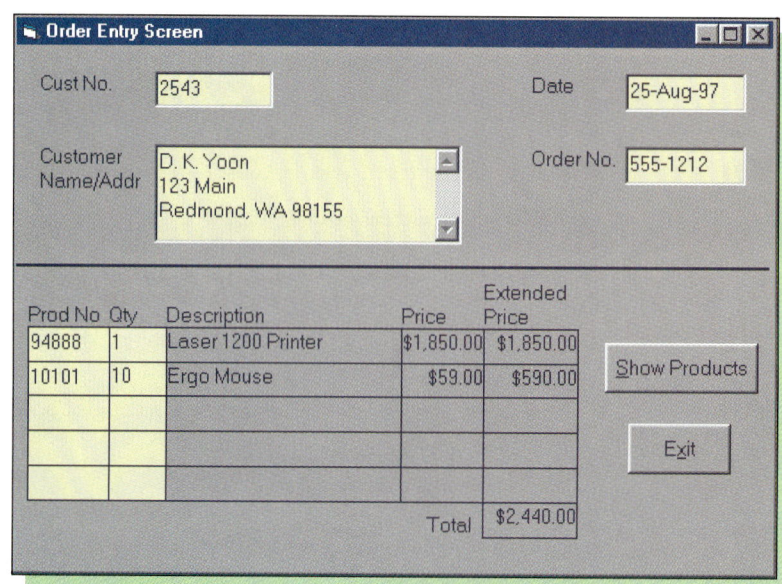

FIGURE 9.27

User interface for order entry system

FIGURE 9.28

Product List screen

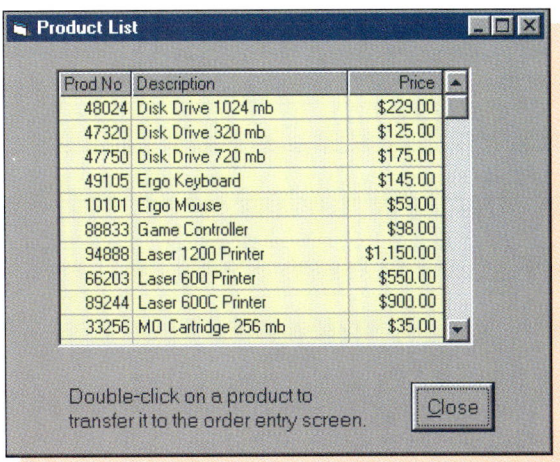

The Product List screen in Figure 9.28 is also available to the order entry person when an invalid product number is entered on the Order Entry form. Figure 9.29 shows the alert displayed to the user in that event.

This is all the processing the prototype does. It does not actually update any databases with customer or order information. The goal of the prototype is to show the user the screen design and the way the prototype handles data entry errors.

Design of the Application

The customer information section of the Order Entry form is simple. When you create this portion of the interface, use the Date$() function to obtain today's date. VB has a number of predefined date formats that you can use to specify how the date should be displayed in the text box.

The product information section presents you with some new challenges. The first challenge is designing the table for products purchased by the customer. One solution is to use a FlexGrid control. The main difficulty with this choice is that the text of a grid cell can be set only from code. That is, the user cannot simply click on a cell and enter text. Another alternative is a set of synchronized control arrays of text boxes and labels. The advantage of this choice is that the user can enter data into a text box directly (which is the natural approach). The disadvantage is that the user cannot scroll through a set of rows as he or she can with a grid.

For this prototype we will use control arrays so that the user can enter values directly into product number and quantity text boxes. As a result, our Order Entry form will limit the number of products in an order to five. However, considering the purpose of the prototype, this is not a serious disadvantage.

The synchronized set of text boxes and labels is shown in Table 9.3. Notice that the index values for each row are the same. These index values establish the synchronization among the various columns. Text boxes are used for the

FIGURE 9.29

Invalid product number alert

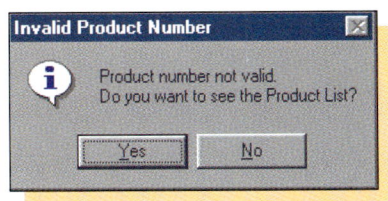

TABLE 9.3 Control arrays used in order entry application

Prod No	Qty	Description	Price	Extended Price
txtProdNo(0)	txtQty(0)	lblDesc(0)	lblPrice(0)	lblExtPrice(0)
txtProdNo(1)	txtQty(1)	lblDesc(1)	lblPrice(1)	lblExtPrice(1)
txtProdNo(2)	txtQty(2)	lblDesc(2)	lblPrice(2)	lblExtPrice(2)
txtProdNo(3)	txtQty(3)	lblDesc(3)	lblPrice(3)	lblExtPrice(3)
txtProdNo(4)	txtQty(4)	lblDesc(4)	lblPrice(4)	lblExtPrice(4)

first two control arrays because the user enters information into them. The remaining control arrays are labels (with borders) whose captions are set by program code as the product number and quantity data are supplied by the user.

The product data (product number, description, and price) are initially stored in a database table. However, these data should be transferred to arrays (ProdNo, Desc, and Price) as execution begins. This improves the program's execution speed, because access to data stored in arrays is much faster than access to data stored on disk, and there will be many searches of product numbers to find description and price. Since the product data are not modified by the application, transferring them to arrays and then using the arrays is straightforward. Figure 9.30 shows the three arrays.

Many of the procedures in the project will access the three arrays, so they should be global. When the application begins executing (during initial form loading), the database table should be read one record at a time and the data transferred one element at a time to the global arrays. The database is named Proj13.mdb and contains a single table named Product. This table contains three fields: ProdNo (5-character text), Desc (20-character text), and Price (Currency). Remember, you'll need a Data control on your form to establish the link to the database and its table; this Data control should be invisible at run time.

You should declare one additional global variable: an Integer variable to store the number of entries in your arrays. This number is the same as the number of records in the database table and serves as the upper limit of the subscript range when processing the arrays. Remember that global variables need to be declared in code modules.

The database records are ordered by product number, so if you simply transfer them directly into the arrays, the data in the arrays will be ordered by product number. However, we want the Product List screen to present the product data to the user in alphabetical order by product description, because the user will want to search this information by product description.

To get the data in the arrays ordered by description, you have two options. First, you can compose an SQL query with an appropriate "Order By" clause, which will cause the database system to perform the sort. Alternatively, you can

FIGURE 9.30

Arrays with data from database table for order entry application

ProdNo		Desc		Price	
1	10101	1	Ergo Mouse	1	59.00
2	12345	2	MultiMedia Computer	2	2200.00
3	22222	3	Scanner - 600 dpi	3	629.00
etc.		etc.		etc.	

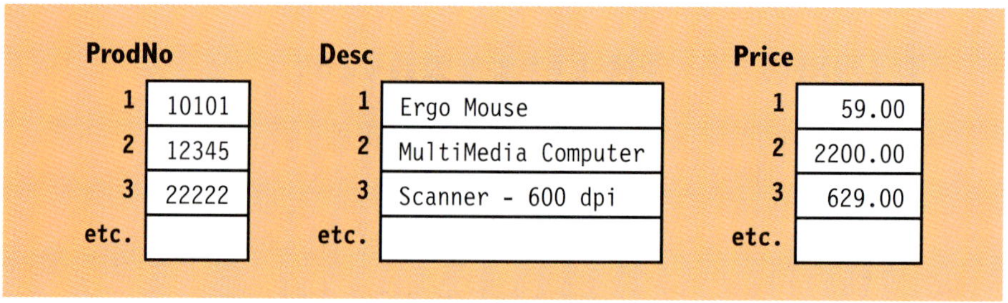

code your own sort procedure. Assuming you choose to code your own sort procedure (for the sake of gaining experience with sorting), the arrays will need to be sorted after they have been populated with data from the database. You need to perform the sort based on the Desc array; that is, the sort will compare adjacent elements[4] in the Desc array. However, when the sort swaps two elements in the Desc array, it must also swap the corresponding elements of the ProdNo and Price arrays. (If the reason for this is unclear to you, it may help you to compare Figures 9.14 and 9.15 carefully.)

Whenever the user enters a product number on the Order Entry form, the program must search the ProdNo array to see if that product number exists. If it does, the corresponding Desc and Price values must be retrieved and placed in the proper control array locations. When you design the product number search procedure, keep in mind that the arrays are ordered by product description, not by product number.

When the user clicks the Show Products button or enters an invalid product number and selects the <u>Y</u>es option from the resulting alert box (Figure 9.29), the program should display the Product List form. To display the form, use the Show method.

The Product List form should use a FlexGrid control, which must be set up and filled in with data from the three arrays. This needs to be done only once, when the form is first loaded. To set up the grid (headings, column widths, etc.), consider the following pseudocode:

1. *Set column 2's ColAlignment and FixedAlignment properties to flexAlign-Right, so that the price data and heading will be right-justified.*
2. *Set the grid's Row to 0.*
3. *Set the grid's Col to 0, then 1, then 2, and each time set the Text property to the appropriate heading text.*
4. *For each column (C = 0 to 2) (you're still in row 0)*
   4.1 *Set ColWidth to an appropriate width. Include an additional 100 twips to give a little extra room in each column.*
   4.2 *Add the new width of column C to an accumulator (W) which is accumulating the width of all columns. For example, W = W + grdProds.ColWidth(C).   ' assume grid is named grdProds*
5. *Set the grid's Width equal to the accumulator from step 4.2 plus 350. The extra 350 twips allow room for the vertical scroll bar.*
6. *Set the grid's Rows property equal to the number of products (number of records read from the database table) plus 1 (for the heading).*

A code segment that fills the grid with data from the arrays might look as follows:

```
Public Sub FillGrid()
    Dim R As Integer
    For R = 1 To NumRecords
        frmProdList!grdProds.Row = R
        frmProdList!grdProds.Col = 0
        frmProdList!grdProds.Text = ProdNo(R)
        ' Repeat last two statements for columns 1 and 2
        ' with description and price
    Next R
End Sub
```

[4] Assuming you use the bubble sort.

Once the Product List form is displayed, the user should be able to double-click on any row (product) and have its product number and description automatically transferred to the Order Entry form. The pseudocode for this double-click procedure is

1. Search the txtProdNo control array on the Order Entry form (from 0 to 4) to find the first empty text box (if any).
2. If an empty text box is found in step 1 Then
    2.1 Set the grid's Col property to zero and retrieve the current Text value from the grid. This will be the product number for the product that the user double-clicked on.
    2.2 Store the product number in the text box found in step 1.
    2.3 Set the focus to that text box (i.e., the same text box as in 2.2).
    2.4 Set the focus to the corresponding txtQty text box. This second SetFocus will cause a LostFocus event for the txtProdNo control, which will in turn cause the description and price to be looked up and displayed.
    2.5 Hide the Product List form.
   Else
       display a message stating that no new products can be added.

Finally, you must design LostFocus event procedures for the control arrays txtProdNo and txtQty. Procedure txtProdNo_LostFocus should look up and display the product description and price given the product number, and procedure txtQty_LostFocus should compute and display the extended price and grand total when the user enters a quantity. Remember that there will be only one procedure for an entire control array (one LostFocus procedure for the txtProdNo control array and one LostFocus procedure for the txtQty control array).

The pseudocode for txtProdNo_LostFocus is

1. If the text field is empty, exit the procedure.
2. Search the ProdNo array for a product number that matches the text in the txtProdNo field. Call a separate procedure to do the search.
3. If the search is successful Then
       Store the Desc and Price values from the corresponding arrays into the Caption property of the correct lblDesc and lblPrice controls. Use the Index variable to refer to the proper controls.
   Else
       Reset the text to empty, set the focus back to this text box so the user can reenter a correct product number, and display an appropriate message to the user. If the user indicates that the product list should be displayed, do so here.

The pseudocode for txtQty_LostFocus is

1. If the text field is empty, exit the procedure.
2. Compute the extended price and store it in the Caption property of the appropriate lblExtPrice control.
3. Cycle through the five rows (0 to 4) of the lblExtPrice control array accumulating the extended price.
4. Format and store this total in lblTotal's Caption property.

Note that step 3 in the pseudocode for txtQty_LostFocus suggests that you use the values stored in the lblExtPrice control array. If you have formatted these values as dollar amounts, you will need to remove the dollar signs and commas before you can sum them. One way to do this is to use Format$() with the "General Number" format specification. If you fail to do this, the text with dollar signs and commas will be concatenated instead of added.

Construction of the Application

◆ ◆ ◆

The project should have two forms and a code module. The code module contains the global variable declarations. It is also a good place to locate the various general sub procedures needed in the project. You'll need a sort procedure to sort the arrays by product description and several procedures to set up and fill the grid with product information. Depending on how you design your code, you might need one or two other general sub procedures.

Start by creating and naming the Order Entry form, and then add the controls for customer information on the top section of the form. Set the BackgroundColor of each text box to a light color that is different from the default color. Use color to signal to the user which fields can be edited and which cannot.

Add a statement to the form's Load event procedure to place today's date in the date field. Test and save the code with these controls in place. The only thing that might not work is the automatic date entry, so be sure to check it.

Next create the control arrays for the lower section of the form. Start by creating a text box and naming it txtProdNo. Now create another text box named txtQty. Then create three labels and name them lblDesc, lblPrice, and lblExtPrice. Remember that when you copy-and-paste a control to create a control array, the new controls will have the same property settings (except for Index) as the original control. Be sure to set the properties for each of the five controls you just created *before* copying them to create the control arrays; this way you will only have to set properties 5 times instead of 25 times.[5]

Set the BorderStyle of each label to "1 - Fixed Single". Set the Appearance of the two text boxes and three labels to "0 - Flat" so they look more like grid cells. Also, clear the Text and Caption properties of all five controls. Finally, change the BackgroundColor of the two text boxes (txtProdNo and txtQty) to the same color you used for the text boxes in the customer section of the form. Since the text boxes and labels all have borders, the different background colors will be the only visual cue telling the user which fields are editable.

Using Figure 9.27 and Table 9.3 as a guide, resize and arrange the five controls in a single row in the lower section of the form. Remember that you will be creating four more rows, so place this first row in such a way that the additional rows will fit.

It is now time to create the control arrays. Select txtProdNo (the left-most control). Select <u>C</u>opy and then <u>P</u>aste from the <u>E</u>dit menu. You will see a dialog box like the one in Figure 9.23. Respond by indicating that you want to create a control array. After the new text box is pasted on the form, drag it directly under the first one. Repeat these steps three more times. Now there should be five text boxes forming a column on the lower left side of the form.

---

[5] Actually, VB allows you to select multiple controls and use the Properties window to change certain property settings for all of them at once. The Properties window lists only those properties that all of the selected controls have in common.

Be careful to drag the text boxes in the correct order. The first one (with Index 0) should be at the top of the column, the second one (with Index 1) should be right below it, and so forth. If you get them mixed up, the form will not behave as you expect.

You also might find it useful to turn off the form's grid alignment while you are dragging the controls into a column. Sometimes it is impossible to get the alignment just right with the grid alignment turned on. To disable it, select Options... from the Tools menu. Then, on the General tab, turn off the Align Controls to Grid check box in the Form Grid Settings frame. You can also select Align from the Format menu and use the alignment options to help align the controls.

Repeat this process to create the control array txtQty. Start by selecting txtQty, then copy and paste it and indicate that you want to create a control array. Create and align a total of five txtQty text boxes.

Repeat these steps for each of the three labels. When you are finished, you should have a total of 25 controls aligned in 5 columns with 5 rows each. Perform these steps carefully: make sure you not only create the proper control arrays but also locate them properly.

The final step you need to perform is setting the TabIndex properties of the text boxes so that pressing the [TAB] key will move the focus from txtProdNo(0) to txtQty(0), then to txtProdNo(1), then txtQty(1), etc. This tab order is depicted in Figure 9.31.

You need three more controls on the Order Entry form: one Label control for the total price, one command button to show the Product List, and one command button to quit. Now would be a good time to create these controls.

In addition to the Order Entry form, you need to create the Product List form (see Figure 9.28). Create and name a FlexGrid control on this form. Set its properties as follows:

Property	Setting
Cols	3
FixedRows	1
FixedCols	0
HighLight	0 - flexHighlightNever
ScrollBars	2 - flexScrollBarVertical

In addition to the grid, you need to create a command button to "Close" the form, which in this case means to hide it.

FIGURE 9.31

Tab cycle within control array elements

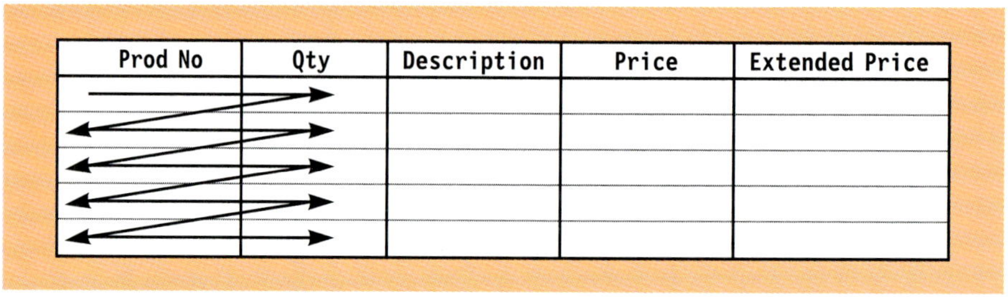

You should now have created all the graphical objects. If you haven't already done so, save the project.

The next step is programming the various controls. Review the pseudocode from the design discussion to get an idea of the code required for the various processing tasks.

After creating the code module and declaring the global variables, a logical place to start coding is the Load event for the Order Entry form. This event transfers the data from the database to the three arrays. The database, Proj13.mdb, is stored in subdirectory C09\Proj13 in the code package for this text. Form_Load also sorts the arrays in order by product description. Run the application after writing this code. Don't be surprised if you get some error messages.

After you've corrected any errors, the Order Entry form should be displayed. However, you will not be able to tell from this form whether the arrays were populated and sorted correctly. Thus, the next step might be to program the Show Products command button on the Order Entry form, and the Load event procedure for the Product List form. These procedures should display the Product List form, with the contents of the arrays in its grid, which will enable you to see if the arrays are correct.

Review the design discussion for the Load event procedure for the Product List form. Essentially, the code should set up the grid and its headings, and then cycle through the elements of the arrays, placing their contents in the appropriate rows and columns of the grid.

If the values in the grid do not look right when you run the program, the problem may be either with the arrays or with the code that fills the grid. If you are having trouble and cannot figure out where the problem originates, you may wish to add some Form.Print or Debug.Print statements (see Appendix A) to the procedure that populates the arrays. If this test demonstrates that the data are getting into the arrays correctly, then you know that your problem is with filling the grid.

Now turn your attention back to the Order Entry form and the LostFocus event for the txtProdNo control array. When one of these text boxes loses the focus, the event procedure must call a search procedure to determine whether the product number is valid. If it is valid, then the corresponding description and price need to be retrieved from the two arrays where they are stored and placed into the labels (lblDesc and lblPrice). The pseudocode in the design section outlines the steps to accomplish this. Remember that there is only one LostFocus event for the entire txtProdNo control array, so when you are finished with this procedure, all five Product Number text boxes should work.

If the product number is not valid—that is, if the search of the *ProdNo* array fails—then the user should be presented with an alert asking whether the Product List should be displayed (see Figure 9.29). Coding the LostFocus event for the txtQty control array is straightforward. Again, see the pseudocode in the design discussion.

At this point your Order Entry form should be functional. You should be able to enter a valid product number into any of the Product Number text boxes and the description and price should automatically be placed into the appropriate labels. Then, when you enter a quantity, the extended price should be displayed and the total price should be updated.

The only code left to implement is the Double-Click event for the grid. When the user double-clicks on a row of the grid, the product number for the product in that row should be placed into the first unused row in the

Order Entry form. As with the previous code requirements, you may wish to review the pseudocode for this procedure in the design discussion.

Your prototype should now be complete and ready for users to test.

Chapter Summary

1. An array is a variable that stores more than a single value. Arrays make it possible to solve many problems that cannot be solved with simple variables.

2. Like simple variables, arrays need to be declared using a Dim, Static, or Public statement. However, in addition to establishing the variable's name, type, and scope, for arrays the declaration statement also establishes the number of dimensions (the dimensionality) and the lower and upper limits on the subscript for each dimension.

3. To access an element of an array, the programmer specifies both the array name and specific subscript values. Typically, subscripts are specified using variables or more complex expressions containing variables. For example, in the reference PayRate(K) the current value of K determines which element of the array PayRate is being accessed.

4. As with simple variables, the declaration statement that creates an array initializes all of its elements to zero or the zero-length string. Thus, it is typical for a program to first store data in an array, and then use the array to process the data. Storing data in an array is referred to as populating the array. Business applications typically obtain the data to populate an array from a database. The data sometimes come from another, previously populated array. When the amount of data is small, it can be obtained from user input.

5. Programs often include decision-making steps that amount to selecting an appropriate value from a list, or table, of values. If...Then...Else and Select...Case statements are usually impractical for coding these kinds of decisions. Table lookup is an effective technique that uses arrays. In this technique, the values are stored in the elements of an array, and a specific outcome is determined by the values of the subscripts of the array.

6. A common processing task associated with arrays is finding the maximum or minimum value in the array. The basic technique uses a loop to examine each value in the array and update a separate variable, which holds the largest or smallest value found so far. When the pass through the array is complete, the separate variable holds the maximum or minimum.

7. Searching refers to the process of locating a specified value, called the target, in an array. There are several search techniques. In the simplest, known as sequential search, the search begins with the first element and proceeds to the second, third, . . . , last element. We applied one form of this search to an array that was not ordered, and another form to an array that was ordered. The two cases differ when the target does not exist in the array. When the array is unordered, it is necessary to examine every element in the array before we can conclude that the target does not exist. When the array is ordered, we can stop the search and conclude that the target does not exist as soon as we find a value in the array that exceeds the target.

Another type of search, called the binary search, is more efficient than sequential search but requires the array to be ordered. The binary search begins at the middle element of the array. If the target value is greater than the value in the middle element, the search dismisses the entire top half of the array (from the first element to the middle element), then examines the value in the element at the middle of the lower half of the array. In this way, the search homes in on the target very quickly.

8. Sorting refers to the process of rearranging the values in an array to put them in ascending or descending order. We examined the relatively simple but inefficient bubble sort technique. In this approach, adjacent elements of the array are compared and if their values are out of order, the contents of the two elements are exchanged. Performing this process repeatedly eventually results in the values being ordered.

9. A problem often encountered by programmers is determining, at design time, the actual size an array will need to be at run time. This decision is necessary because the declaration statement requires the use of constants when specifying the array bounds. The VB language includes dynamic arrays to solve this problem. Unlike static arrays, the size of a dynamic array is not specified in the declaration statement. Instead the programmer uses the ReDim statement to define the actual array size. A Dim, Static, or Public statement is still needed for a dynamic array, but all it specifies is the array name and its type. The ReDim Preserve statement allows the programmer to change the size of a dynamic array without losing the current values stored in its elements.

10. Finally, a control array is a set of controls that share the same name and the same event procedures. Since each control has the same name, controls are differentiated using an index number, which is like a subscript in a regular array. For example, to refer to the third control in a control array of text boxes named txtStudentNumber, you would specify txtStudentNumber(2).[6] Every event procedure that is shared by controls in a control array includes an integer parameter named Index that can be used by the programmer to determine which control in the control array actually generated the event.

Control arrays are limited to one dimension. To create tables of controls, the programmer can create multiple control arrays, and synchronize them by arranging controls with the same Index setting in a row on the user interface.

Control arrays provide a means of creating controls at run time. The Load statement creates a new control, and the Unload statement removes a control.

Key Terms

array	exchange	one-dimensional array
binary search	flag variable	ordered
bubble sort	Index property	pass
comparison	linear search	populating an array
control array	Load statement	ReDim statement
dimensionality	matrix	ReDim Preserve
dynamic array	multidimensional	statement
element	array	searching

[6] This assumes that the first index is 0, the second index is 1, the third index is 2, etc.

sequential search   subscript out of range   target
simple variable   error   Unload statement
sorting   subscripted variable   unordered
subscript   table
subscript bounds   table lookup

End-of-Chapter Problems

1. Is the following a legal VB statement? Explain.

   Dim Region(1 **To** NumberOfRegions)

2. A two-dimensional array named X is declared as follows:

   Static X(1 **To** 100, 1 **To** 30) **As Currency**

   Write a code segment to compute the 30 column totals for X and place them in a List box control.

3. A database named X.mdb has a single table named TableY. This table has three integer fields named FieldA, FieldB, and FieldC. Write a general sub procedure that reads the records from the table and stores their values in the module-level arrays ArrayA, ArrayB, and ArrayC. The procedure should size the arrays as necessary so that all records can be stored. Assume you do not know the actual number of records at design time.

4. Assume you have a database that contains the tax amount for a number of income categories. For example, a record in this database might have three fields—10000, 11000, and 45—which would be interpreted to mean that income between $10,000 and $11,000 would owe a tax of $45. Assume there are approximately 300 different categories (records).

   A tax program will compute tax amounts for several hundred thousand taxpayers using data stored in this database. Would it make more sense to transfer the tax information to an array, or to just access it from the database? Explain.

5. Write the correct VB statement to declare a module-level array that can store sales figures on 300 companies over the past 5 years. The array will be used to find the sales figures for specific companies and years.

   Write this declaration statement in two different ways. Is one of the two ways better than the other? Explain.

6. Assume you want to store employee information in an array or arrays. The information includes the employee number (String), name (String), pay rate (Currency), and number of dependents (Integer). Assume there are 500 employees. Write the VB declaration for one or more arrays to store this information.

7. You want to store employee information. This information includes employee number (String), name (String), number of dependents (Integer), and the first name of each dependent (String). There are 100 employees. Declare one or more arrays necessary to do this. State any assumptions you need to make. Is your solution a good "general" solution? Explain.

8. Compare the advantages and disadvantages of a control array made up of text boxes versus a FlexGrid control.

9. In a sequential search, how does having the values ordered (sorted) improve the efficiency of the search?

10. Assume you have a one-dimensional array that stores part numbers (Integer). The values in the array are already ordered from smallest to largest. Assume you want to insert a new part number into the array at its proper position (maintaining the order). Write a code segment to do this. Do not use another array. Assume there is sufficient space in the array for the new value.

Programming Problems

1. One encryption technique that is slightly more sophisticated than the Caesar cipher employs a substitution list instead of rotating letters by a specified amount. In the substitution list, element 1 holds the letter into which A should be transformed, element 2 holds the letter into which B should be transformed, and so on. For example, you might have the list shown here.

SubstitutionList

1	W
2	S
3	Q
4	D
etc.	etc.

Using this list, the word CAB would be encrypted as QWS. In addition to the 26 capital letters, the substitution list can contain an entry for the space character. This means that the space character will substitute for one of the 26 capital letters and a capital letter will substitute for a space (the result will be quite confusing to anyone trying to read the encrypted message).

Make up a substitution list such as the following:

Alphabet: A B C D E F G H I J K L M N O P Q R S T U V W X Y Z _
            ↓
Substitution List: Q A Z W S X E D C R F V T G B Y H N _ U J M I K O L P

where "_" represents the space character. Then write an event procedure named cmdEncrypt_Click that performs encryption using your substitution list. Write another event procedure named cmdDecrypt_Click that performs the reverse operation. That is, it takes encrypted text and converts it back into the original text.

Create a project that has the two command buttons. It should also have one text box for the original message and another text box for the encrypted message. Use Form_Load to populate the substitution list array. Procedure cmdEncrypt_Click should take the original text from its text box and place the encrypted text in the other text box. Procedure cmdDecrypt_Click should do just the opposite.

2. Create a program that calculates a discount price. Your program should determine the discounted price of an item depending on the item's discount category and the quantity purchased. The user selects an item (by item number) from a dropdown list and enters the quantity being purchased; the application then determines the list price, the discount price, and the total price (discount price times quantity). An example form is shown at the top of page 492.

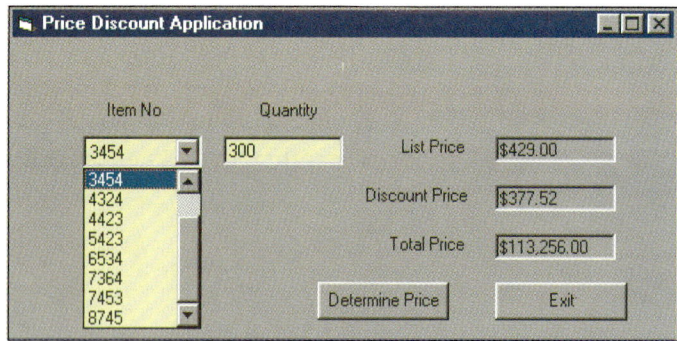

The data for this application come from a database named ItemDis.mdb, which is stored in the subdirectory C09\PrgProbs in the code package for this text. This database contains a single table, named Item, that has an ItemNo field (Text), a Price field (Currency), and a DiscountCat field (Integer). The DiscountCat field indicates in which of three discount categories the item is located. These data should be transferred from the database into module-level arrays in the program. All subsequent processing should be performed using the arrays, not the database.

The discount schedule for this application is shown below.

Discount Category	Discount Rules Qty	Discount
1	1–100	0%
	101+	10%
2	1–10	0%
	11–30	7%
	31–50	9%
	51+	12%
3	1–1,000	0%
	1,001–10,000	3%
	10,001+	5%

In your program, create a programmer-defined function to compute the discount given the discount category and the quantity.

3. A database named Inc95.mdb has a single table, named Seattle, that stores a sample of hypothetical income figures for households in the city of Seattle. The field storing the income figures is named Income and it is a Long integer field. The database is stored in the subdirectory C09\PrgProbs in the code package for this text.

Create a VB application that reads these income data, then computes the median income and displays it in a label. The *median income* is defined as the income figure that one half of the sample exceeds and the other half falls below. For example, if the income figures were $23,000, $120,000, $15,000, $49,000, and $90,000, then the median would be $49,000. Assume that the sample size (number of income records) is less than 1000.

4. Using the database in programming problem 3, create a VB application that processes these income data, then computes the modal income and displays it in a label. The *modal value* is defined as the income value that

occurs the most in the sample. For example, if the income figures were $45,000, $120,000, $15,000, $45,000, and $90,000, then the modal value would be $45,000. Assume that the sample size (number of income records) is less than 1000. Also assume that the sample has only one mode; that is, there is not a tie between two income values that occur most often.

5. You have a database named Sales95.mdb that stores sales information for a company. This database is stored in the subdirectory C09\PrgProbs in the code package for this text. The database contains one table, named SalesTrans, that has three fields. The first field is an Integer field named SalesPerNo that stores identification of the salesperson. The second field is an Integer field named Region that indicates the sales region. The final field is a Currency field named DollarSales that represents a dollar sales transaction for a specific salesperson and sales region.

The values in the SalesPerNo field range from 1 to 10. The values in the Region field range from 1 to 4. There could be thousands of records (transactions) in this table.

Write a VB application that processes this database and displays via a FlexGrid the summary information shown here.

		\multicolumn{5}{c	}{Region}
		1	2	3	4	Total
Salesperson	1					
	2					
	3					
	...					
	10					
	Total					

Each cell in the grid should contain the sum of dollar sales across transactions. For example, the cell at row 1, column 1, should show the sum of all dollar sales transactions for salesperson 1 in region 1. The "Total" cells should contain the row and column sums. That is, the total for row 1 is the total sales for salesperson 1 across all four regions.

chapter TEN

Representing Entities with Data and Behavior

Programmer-Defined Types and Object Classes

◆ ◆ ◆ ◆

To this point in our study of VB, to declare variables we have always specified standard data types like Integer, Currency, and Single. For the most part it seemed as though we could get along quite well with these data types. But in many business situations these standard types alone do not do a very good job of representing the data. This chapter extends our ability to create readable, maintainable code—first by creating data types that more closely match the data of the application, and second by creating object classes that combine variables with actions for efficiency in program design.

We have seen the versatility of arrays in solving different types of programming problems, but there is still one difficulty with arrays we have not addressed satisfactorily. All elements in an array have to be the same data type, and this is a hindrance in applications where we want to manipulate related data that have different types, such as employee names and salary amounts. We can get around this problem by synchronizing one-dimensional arrays, but this approach is unwieldy when processing large units of data composed of many elements, such as employee name, Social Security number, hourly wage, and bonus percent.

The solution is to create a new data type, called a ***programmer-defined data type,* that specifies exactly what a unit of data is**. That is, the programmer can define a compound data type consisting of elements that have different simple data types (Integer, String, etc.). For example, we can define a compound data type that represents a pair of data items: a company name (String) and a rate of return (Currency). Then we can declare an array based on this compound data type. Thus, we can have an array of 100 "pairs" of data items, instead of 2 arrays that we must keep synchronized.

Such compound data types are useful even in programs that do not use arrays. They can simplify code and improve program readability by allowing the structure of variables in the program to closely match our understanding of the real-world data items they represent.

VB also allows the programmer to define and use *object classes*, which can profoundly improve code reusability. Whereas variables represent data, objects represent both data and behavior. VB controls are examples of predefined objects; they have both data (properties) and behavior (methods and event procedures). To create and use your own kind of object, you first specify the data and behavior it should have by composing a *class definition*. Then you declare the object (much as you declare a variable). Just as a program can have many command buttons, all of which look and act similarly, you can declare many objects of your new class, all of which have the same data items and behavior.

We discuss two types of object classes. The first is an application object, like an employee object, that does not appear on the user interface but is still manipulated by the program. Businesses typically need to create many different application objects. The second is a graphical object that appears on the user interface. You have already encountered this type of object in the form of controls like text boxes and labels. With VB you can create ActiveX controls (graphical objects) which can be added to the toolbox and used just as you use ordinary controls.

Objectives

After studying this chapter you should be able to

- Create programmer-defined types to simplify the representation of related data items.
- Construct arrays of programmer-defined types to store large numbers of related data items in a simple and logical manner.
- Create and use application objects, which represent both data and behavior.
- Create and use simple ActiveX controls.
- Describe the basic concepts and benefits of object-oriented programming.

10.1 Defining and Using Your Own Data Types

We begin this section with an example of a simple programmer-defined[1] data type that has three elements, all type String. We will work through more complex examples later to demonstrate how programmer-defined data types simplify the representation and processing of related data.

Suppose that we want to represent the name of an employee in a program, and we anticipate that sometimes we'll want to refer to the entire name and other times to just the first name, last name, or middle initial. To make these references easy, **we define a new data type using VB's *Type statement* in the general**

---

[1] VB's online help, and many other programming languages, use the term "user-defined type" instead of "programmer-defined type." However, it is the programmer, not the user, who works with data types and variables.

declarations section of a form or code module. In the following statement the keyword Private specifies the scope of the new type, which we discuss shortly.

> **Private Type** FullName
>   FirstName **As String**
>   MiddleInitial **As String**
>   LastName **As String**
> **End Type**

This statement defines a type called FullName that we can use in Dim statements just as we use the standard data types (Integer, Currency, etc.). For example, the following statement declares a variable named EmpName of type FullName:

> **Dim** EmpName **As FullName**

This Dim statement creates a compound variable consisting of three individual elements. **A *compound variable* is a variable that is composed of named elements.** Figure 10.1 illustrates this idea. In program statements we can refer either to the compound variable as a whole or to its individual elements. You can see from the figure that there is a special syntax for referring to individual elements. We write the variable name, followed by a period, followed by the specific element name. This syntax is similar to the designation of a control and one of its properties. For example, suppose we have a Text box control named txtAddress. This control has many properties. We specify a particular property of the control by adding a period and the property name. Thus, txtAddress.Text refers to the Text property of the txtAddress control.

Consider the following code segment:

> **Dim** EmpName1 **As FullName**
> **Dim** EmpName2 **As FullName**
>   ...
> EmpName1.FirstName = "Art"
> EmpName1.MiddleInitial = "E"
> EmpName1.LastName = "Brown"
>   ...
> EmpName2 = EmpName1

After declaring the variables, each of the first three assignment statements accesses an individual element within the variable EmpName1. The final statement copies all three elements of EmpName1 to the corresponding three elements of EmpName2. Figure 10.2 depicts the contents of the computer's memory after this code segment is executed.

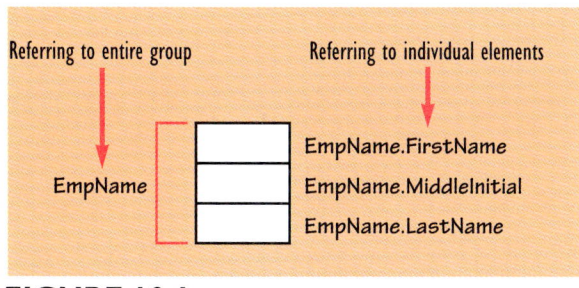

FIGURE 10.1

A variable of type FullName and its elements

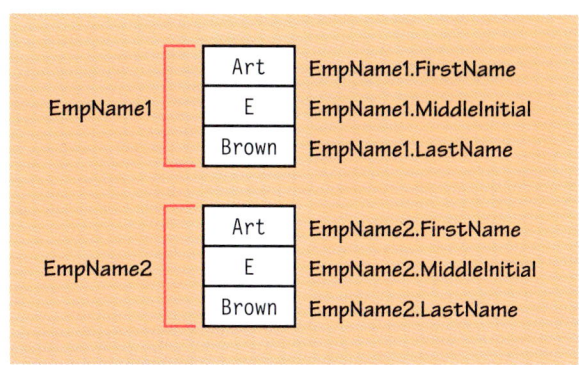

FIGURE 10.2

Data in two variables of type FullName

The Type statement must be placed in the general declarations section of a form or a code module. VB does not allow Type statements inside procedures.

Like variables and procedures, type definitions have scope. The scope of a type definition specifies where in the project the new type can be used. Type definitions are either module-level or global. A *module-level type* can be used only by variable declaration statements in the same form or code module that contains the Type statement. A *global type* can be used by variable declaration statements anywhere in the project.

To create a module-level type definition, precede the keyword Type with the keyword Private, as in the earlier example. To create a global type definition, place the Type statement in a code module, and use the keyword Public instead of Private.

Note that the scope of a programmer-defined type does not restrict the scope of variables declared using that type. For example, we can define a module-level type in a code module, and then declare a global variable using this type.

> **Design Suggestion** If you have type definitions that may be useful in multiple applications, consider creating a separate code module just for the Type statements (and making them global). This way your type definitions will always be easy to find and add to other projects.

Example 10.1 Using Programmer-Defined Types

Figure 10.3 shows a code module that defines FullName as a global type, and the code for a form that contains module-level variables of type FullName.

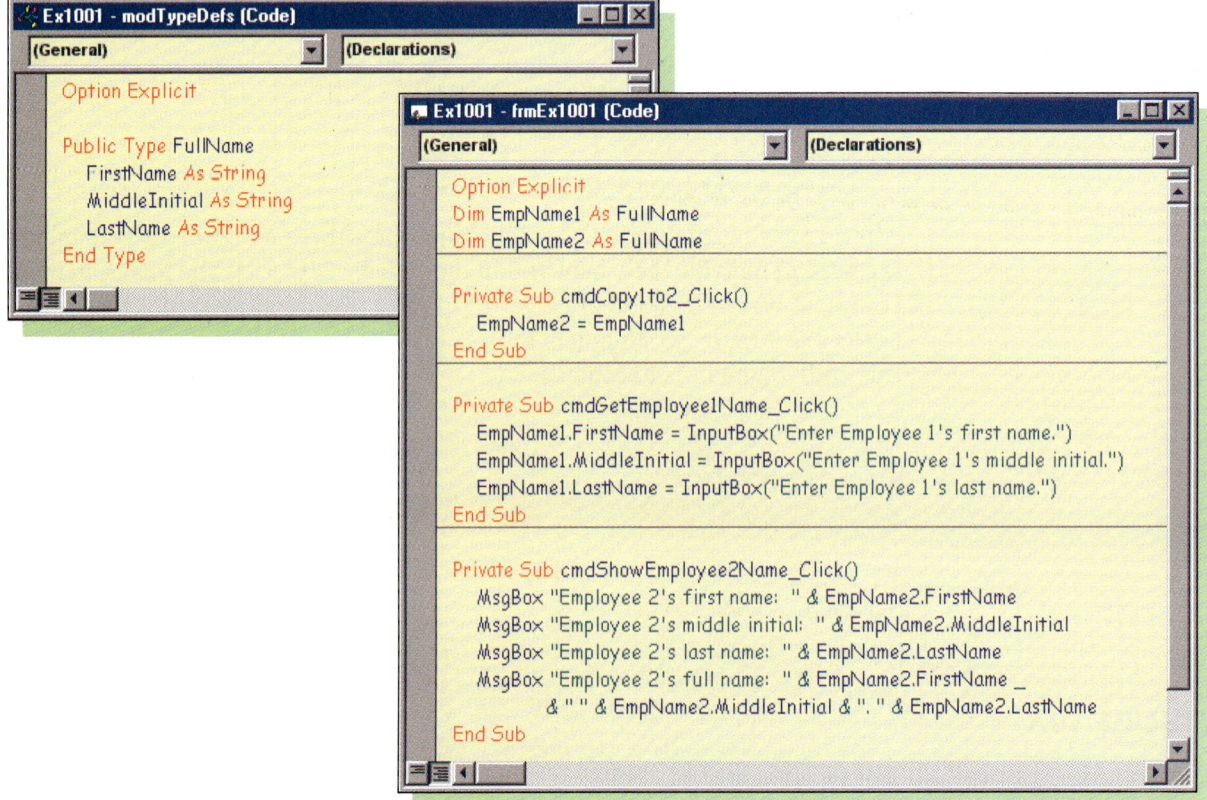

FIGURE 10.3 Code for Example 10.1

Event procedure cmdGetEmployee1Name_Click gets values from the user via the InputBox() function, and stores these values in the elements of the module-level variable EmpName1. Procedure cmdCopy1to2_Click copies all the elements of the variable EmpName1 to the variable EmpName2 using a single assignment statement. Finally, procedure cmdShowEmployee2Name_Click uses MsgBox statements to display the contents of the variable EmpName2, first one piece at a time and then in its entirety.

Defining Large Types from Small Types

A programmer-defined type can be part of the definition of another programmer-defined type. Consider the following Type statements.

```
Public Type FullName
    FirstName As String
    MiddleInitial As String
    LastName As String
End Type

Public Type Employee
    Name As FullName
    PayRate As Currency
    Age As Integer
End Type
```

In this example, the Employee type includes the element Name, which in turn includes the three elements FirstName, MiddleInitial, and LastName. The representation in memory for any variable of type Employee is shown in Figure 10.4.

Suppose we declare a variable of type Employee as follows:

Dim AccountManager **As** Employee

We can refer to the elements of the variable AccountManager in different ways. The variable name AccountManager refers to all five elements. AccountManager.Name.FirstName and AccountManager.PayRate each refer to a single element. AccountManager.Name refers to the first three elements.

For example, the following statement places the last name in lblName's caption:

lblName.Caption = AccountManager.Name.LastName

If we have another variable declared as type FullName, we can use it to assign the name to the account manager, as shown on the following page.

FIGURE 10.4

Memory representation for variable of type Employee

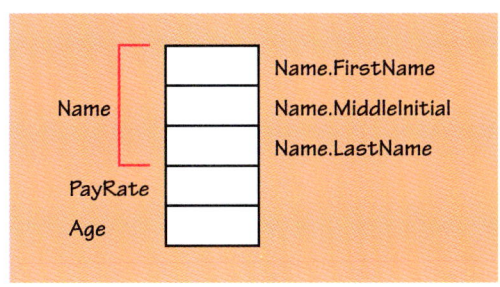

```
Dim AName As FullName
Dim AccountManager As Employee
    ...
AName.FirstName = "Alice"
AName.MiddleInitial = "N"
AName.LastName = "Wunderlund"
    ...
AccountManager.Name = AName
AccountManager.PayRate = 12.50
AccountManager.Age = 28
```

To reference a specific element, it is necessary to include all the parts of the variable from the variable name down to the specific element name. This precision in naming is required because two different programmer-defined data types can use identical element names, and these element names can be used in a third programmer-defined data type. In the code that follows, notice that within the Advisor type there are two Name elements—one for the faculty member and another for the student.

```
Public Type FacultyType
    FacultyNo As Integer
    Name As String
End Type

Public Type StudentType
    StudentNo As Integer
    Name As String
End Type

Public Type Advisor
    Faculty As FacultyType
    Student As StudentType
End Type
```

Suppose we then declare a variable of type Advisor.

```
Dim AnAdvisor As Advisor
```

Later in the code, to refer to the faculty member's name we would write AnAdvisor.Faculty.Name and to refer to the student's name we would write AnAdvisor.Student.Name. You can see that simply writing AnAdvisor.Name would be ambiguous.

EXERCISE 10.1 Write the Type statement for a new data type that represents both the name and the population of a city. Then write a Dim statement that declares a variable named StateCapital of this new type. Finally, write the assignment statements that store "Olympia" in the name element of StateCapital, and 33000 in its population element.

EXERCISE 10.2 Write the Type statement for a new data type that represents the name, title, and phone number of a key client. Then write the Type statement for a new data type that represents the name, address, and key client of a company. This Type statement should use your data type for the key client. Assume the address can be represented as a simple string value.

10.2 Programmer-Defined Types and Arrays

Programmer-defined data types and arrays can work together in two ways. First, we can define a new type that includes an array as an element. Second, we can declare an array of a programmer-defined type. As a result, the fact that all elements in an array must have the same data type is no longer a hindrance.

As an illustration of the first way we can use arrays and programmer-defined types, consider the following example. Suppose we need a programmer-defined type that defines the data for an employee, and this type must provide the ability to store the names and ages of up to eight dependents. The following type definitions meet this requirement:

Public Type NameAge
    Name **As String** * 18
    Age **As Integer**
End Type

Public Type Employee
    SSN **As String**
    Name **As String**
    NumberOfDependents **As Integer**
    Dependent(1 **To** 8) **As** NameAge
End Type

If we now declare a variable named AnEmployee of type Employee, the actual elements that are created will be as shown in Figure 10.5. Note that all references to the variable must begin with AnEmployee. Thus, the following are legal variable references:

AnEmployee.SSN
AnEmployee.Dependent(3).Name
AnEmployee.Name

The first and third variable references here refer to the employee's Social Security number and name. The second variable reference refers to the name of the employee's third dependent.

FIGURE 10.5

Memory representation for variable of type Employee

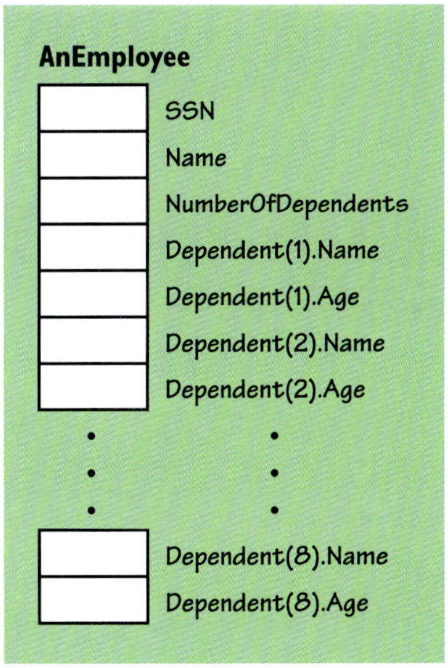

AnEmployee

☐	SSN
☐	Name
☐	NumberOfDependents
☐	Dependent(1).Name
☐	Dependent(1).Age
☐	Dependent(2).Name
☐	Dependent(2).Age
⋮	⋮
☐	Dependent(8).Name
☐	Dependent(8).Age

Now let's look at the second way we can use arrays and programmer-defined data types. Suppose we want to store and process information on 100 employees. How would we declare an array to do this and how would we reference each employee? The following declaration statement creates the desired array:

Dim EmployeeList(1 **To** 100) **As** Employee

Each element of the array EmployeeList is a compound variable that has the structure shown in Figure 10.5. That is, EmployeeList consists of 100 compound variables. The following are legal variable references:

EmployeeList(10).Name
EmployeeList(50).Dependent(2).Age

The first variable reference here refers to the name of the employee stored in element 10 of the array. The second variable reference refers to the age of the second dependent for the employee stored in element 50 of the array.

As an example application of the array EmployeeList, suppose that we want to compute the average age of the dependents of all employees at a company. Assume that array EmployeeList has been populated with valid data. Figure 10.6 depicts possible data in elements 1 and 2 of the array. Note that the number of dependents is different for each employee: the first employee has two dependents and the second employee has one dependent. How can we compute the average age of all dependents? The following pseudocode accomplishes this task:

For each employee in the list
    Determine the number of dependents for the employee
    Add the number of dependents to the count
    For each dependent
        Add the dependent's age to the sum
    Next dependent
Next employee
Compute average as sum / count

FIGURE 10.6

Sample employee data

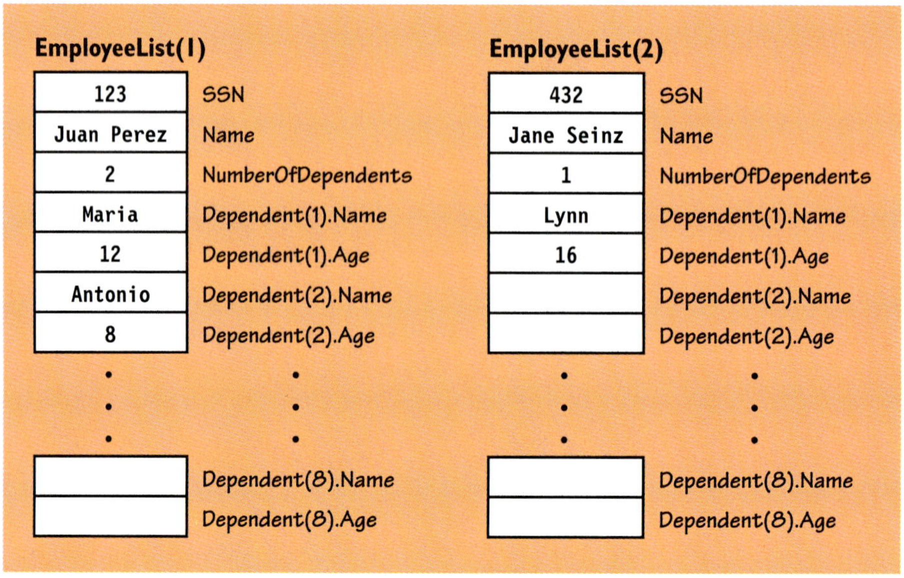

EmployeeList(1)		EmployeeList(2)	
123	SSN	432	SSN
Juan Perez	Name	Jane Seinz	Name
2	NumberOfDependents	1	NumberOfDependents
Maria	Dependent(1).Name	Lynn	Dependent(1).Name
12	Dependent(1).Age	16	Dependent(1).Age
Antonio	Dependent(2).Name		Dependent(2).Name
8	Dependent(2).Age		Dependent(2).Age
⋮	⋮	⋮	⋮
	Dependent(8).Name		Dependent(8).Name
	Dependent(8).Age		Dependent(8).Age

Let us write the code as a programmer-defined function that returns the average age. The function takes two parameters: the array and an integer variable that indicates the number of employees in the array.

```
Public Function AverageDependentAge(EmpList() As Employee, _
            ByVal NumberOfEmps As Integer) As Single
    Dim Sum As Integer, Count As Integer
    Dim E As Integer, D As Integer
    Dim NumberOfDeps As Integer
    For E = 1 To NumberOfEmps
        NumberOfDeps = EmpList(E).NumberOfDependents
        Count = Count + NumberOfDeps
        For D = 1 To NumberOfDeps
            Sum = Sum + EmpList(E).Dependent(D).Age
        Next D
    Next E
    AverageDependentAge = Sum / Count
End Function
```

Notice that even though the array's data type is a programmer-defined type, the array appears in the function's parameter list just like any other array. Likewise, to invoke the function, you pass the array just as you would any other array, as in the following statement:

```
AvgDepAge = AverageDependentAge(EmployeeList(), NumOfEmployees)
```

EXERCISE 10.3 Write a general sub procedure to compute the average age of each employee's dependents. The procedure should be similar to function AverageDependentAge(), but instead of returning a single average it should include an additional parameter that is an array of averages. Each array element will store the average age for one employee's dependents. Be sure to avoid the "divide by zero" error for employees who have no dependents.

EXERCISE 10.4 Modify the bubble sort procedure from Chapter 9 so that it sorts the array EmployeeList by Social Security number.

EXERCISE 10.5 Suppose that the general declarations section of a form contains the following statements:

```
Private Type City
    Name As String
    Population As Long
End Type

Dim Cities(1 To 1000) As City
Dim NumCities As Integer
```

Suppose also that the form already has a Load event procedure that populates array Cities and stores the number of cities in variable NumCities. Write a Click event procedure for a command button named cmdFindMaxCity that will scan the array to find the city with the largest population, and then display this city's name and population.

EXERCISE Suppose that the general declarations section of a form contains the following statements:

```
Private Type City
    Name As String
    Population As Long
End Type

Private Type Country
    Name As String
    Continent As String
    MajorCities(1 To 5) As City
End Type

Dim Countries(1 To 1000) As Country
Dim NumCountries As Integer
```

Suppose also that the form already has a Load event procedure that populates array Countries and stores the number of countries in variable NumCountries. Assume that for each country in the array, the MajorCities element contains data on the five largest cities in the country. Write a Click event procedure for a command button named cmdFindLargestCity that will scan the array Countries to find the city with the largest population, and then display this city's name, the country and continent in which it is located, and its population.

EXERCISE Using the information in Exercise 10.6, write a general sub procedure named FindMaxCityOnContinent that takes as input the name of a continent, then scans the array Countries to find the largest city on that continent, and returns as output this city's name, population, and the country in which it is located. The heading for your general sub procedure should be as follows:

```
Public Sub FindMaxCityOnContinent(ByVal TargetContinent As String, _
    CityName As String, CityPopulation As Long, CountryName As String)
```

If your procedure is correctly written, then after the following procedure call is executed, the variables MaxCityName, MaxCityPop, and MaxCityCntry should hold the name, population, and country of the largest city in Africa.

```
FindMaxCityOnContinent "Africa", MaxCityName, MaxCityPop, MaxCityCntry
```

10.3 Project 14: Student Grade Reporting

Included in any university's database is information about its students, present and past, and the courses they've taken and grades received. This information is used to generate transcripts. Various university administrators, academic counselors, potential employers, and others want rapid access to transcripts for specific students.

Description of the Application

This application generates a list of courses with grades and credits earned for a specific student at a college or university. Figure 10.7 shows the application while it is executing. To produce a transcript, the user enters a student number in the appropriate text box and then clicks the Find Student button. If

FIGURE 10.7

Student Grade Reporting application at run time

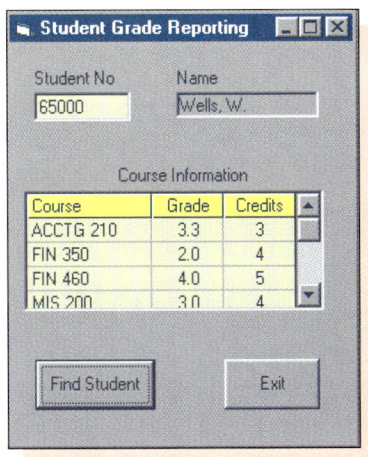

the student number is valid, the program displays in a grid the courses completed by that student.

We have limited the amount of information displayed in this application to make it easier to complete. An actual transcript would include the date the course was completed and additional information about the student. However, incorporating these additional data would not increase the complexity of the application—it would just increase the time needed to create it.

Design of the Application

The data for the application come from a database named StudInfo.mdb. The structure of its three tables is shown in Figure 10.8. The fields StNo, Name, and Desc are type String. The Grade field is Currency and the Credits field is Integer.

These data should be transferred to an array when the form is loaded. Subsequently, the data should be obtained from the array, not the database. Since we anticipate repeated retrievals of student information, using the array makes the application faster than retrieving information from the database. Of course, the decision to move the data into an array in memory assumes that the data set is not so large as to exceed memory limits.

The array is a programmer-defined type of moderate complexity. It needs to store information about the student as well as information on the courses taken by the student. Each student may complete a different number of courses, and the design of the data type must take this into account. The following statements define an appropriate data structure:

    Private Type CourseInfo
        CourseDesc **As String** * 20
        Credits **As Integer**
        Grade **As Currency**
    End Type

continues

FIGURE 10.8

Tables in the StudInfo.mdb database

Student Table		Trans Table			Course Table	
StNo	Name	StNo	Desc	Grade	Desc	Credits

```
Private Type StudentCourses
    StudentNo As String * 5
    Name As String * 30
    CourseCount As Integer
    CourseList(1 To 100) As CourseInfo
End Type
```

Most of the elements in these type definitions are straightforward. The CourseCount element represents how many courses the student has taken. Its value indicates the number of elements in the CourseList array that contain information on courses. For example, if CourseCount equals 4, then elements 1, 2, 3, and 4 of the CourseList array have course information stored in them.

We need to declare an array of type StudentCourses with 100 elements to hold the data from the database. The data presented by the application (Figure 10.7) come from all three database tables. Thus, it is necessary to use an SQL query to obtain the data.

```
Select Student.StNo, Student.Name, Trans.Desc, Trans.Grade, Course.Credits
    From Student, Trans, Course
    Where Student.StNo = Trans.StNo And Trans.Desc = Course.Desc
    Order By Trans.StNo, Trans.Desc
```

This query creates a recordset consisting of one row for each course taken by a student. Each row includes the student number, student name, course description, grade, and credits earned. The records are ordered by student number, and the records for a single student are ordered by course description.

This recordset has to be processed to populate the array. Consider the following pseudocode for this task:

1. Move the record pointer to the first record.
2. Set the count of students to 1.
3. Set the count of courses (CourseCount element) for the first student to 1.
4. Store the information of the first record into appropriate parts of the array. This includes the student number and name. It also includes the first course the student has taken (the three CourseList elements).
5. Record the student number of the first student. Call it PrevStudent.
6. Move to the next record in the recordset.
7. Repeat the following steps as long as records remain in the recordset.
   If student number in current record is not equal to PrevStudent Then
       Add 1 to count of students.   ' new student
       Set count of courses for this student to 1.   ' first course for new student
       Store the information of the current record as outlined in Step 4.
       Set PrevStudent to current student number.
   Else (student number in current record equals PrevStudent)
       Add 1 to the count of courses for this student.   ' next course for student
       Store course information into array.
   End If
   Move to the next record in the recordset.

Finally, when the user enters a student number and clicks the Find Student button, the code needs to search the array for a match in the student number element. Remember that the data loaded into the array come from a recordset that is ordered by student number. Therefore, the elements of the array will also be ordered by student number. If the student number is found in the array, then the values from the corresponding elements of the array need to be placed in the Name text box and the FlexGrid controls. If the student number is not found, then the program should display an appropriate message to the user. When the user enters a new student number, any information left over from the previous search should be removed from the form.

Construction of the Application
◆ ◆ ◆

This application requires one form. If you anticipated creating other applications that process the same data, you would use a code module to hold the Type statements, and you would make the type definitions global (by using the keyword Public instead of Private).

The Type statements and the array declaration statement should be located in the form's general declarations section. You'll also need a variable to indicate the number of elements used in the array. This value should equal the number of students in the database. Note that the number of records in the recordset will be greater than the number of students because most students complete several courses.

In addition to the controls you see on the form in Figure 10.7, you need a Data control to implement access to the database. The database file, StudInfo.mdb, is stored in the subdirectory C10\Proj14 in the code package for this text. When the form loads, code should be executed to create a recordset using the SQL query and to populate the array using the data in the recordset (see the preceding pseudocode).

To verify that the data are being correctly transferred to the array elements, you may wish to put some debugging statements in your code (see Appendix A).

The code that performs the search for the Find Student command button should be in a general sub procedure. Remember that the contents of the array are ordered by student number. Your search will be more efficient because the data are ordered.

Finally, when the user enters any character into the Student Number text box, the program should clear the Student Name label and the grid (which may contain information from a previous student). You do not want the user to see prior information while seeking information for a new student. If you don't clear the label and grid, you might give the user the impression that the residual information is associated with the new student number.

Clearing the Student Name label is easy. Clearing the grid is a bit more difficult. One strategy is to set the grid's Rows property to 1. This setting removes all rows from the grid except its heading. However, depending on how you add data to the grid, before you display course information for a new student you may need to reset the Rows property to make room for the courses. Also, when you set Rows to 1, the fixed row is lost (because Rows must always be at least 1 greater than FixedRows). So in addition to setting Rows appropriately, you also need to set FixedRows back to 1. Alternatively, you can use the FlexGrid's Clear method. This method clears the contents of all cells including the text in the fixed rows and columns. Thus, if you use this approach, you will need to restore the column headings after clearing the grid.

10.4 Programmer-Defined Classes and Object-Oriented Programming

To facilitate the creation, use, and maintenance of reusable software, VB provides the capability to construct units within a program that combine data and instructions. These units are called *objects,* **software components that include both data elements and behavior.** As a VB programmer, you have been using objects on a regular basis: controls are in fact predefined objects. Each control has a set of properties (data elements) and methods (behavior). As soon as you learned the properties and methods of the Command button control, it became easy for you to use command buttons in any application.

Designing objects can be complex, but the basic steps can be explained simply. The goal of this section is to introduce you to objects and object-oriented programming—an area of programming you might pursue in future studies. Object-oriented programming uses a special vocabulary, and we begin by presenting this vocabulary as background. Then we discuss how to design, create, and use objects.

Object Terminology

Since controls are objects, and we are already familiar with controls, let's begin by examining the terminology of objects, using a Text box control as an example.

Text Boxes as Objects

A text box includes data elements that describe it. In VB these data elements are called properties. Text box properties include Alignment, BorderStyle, Name, Text, and Visible. Each property has a value, or setting; for example, Visible may be True or False. So the properties possessed by a control and the allowable values for each of its properties define the control's data elements.

Text boxes also exhibit behavior. Some of this behavior is built into VB and some is the result of your programming efforts. For example, you might write the statement txtX.SetFocus to cause VB to make txtX the active control. VB endowed the Text box control with the SetFocus method for this purpose. So we can say that VB's methods are the first factor that defines a control's behavior.

You can also write your own code to define behavior. For example, you can program the text box's KeyPress event to specify how characters are to be processed as the user enters them into the text box. Event procedures are the second factor that defines a control's behavior.

The Toolbox contains an icon for the Text box control. When you click on this icon—the Text box tool—and then draw a new text box on a form, that text box will have the same properties and methods as all other text boxes, and its property settings will be given default initial values. The Text box tool is like a rubber stamp in that it creates a new text box whenever you want, and each new text box has exactly the same properties and behaviors. You can think of the Text box tool as a template for the actual text box that you create on the form. This template defines the data and behavior of text boxes.

As a programmer, you know that a text box has certain properties and that it can perform certain functions in your program. The advantage of objects is that they are self-contained units that always perform in the same general way, yet can be easily manipulated in specific ways by the programmer.

Characteristics of All Objects

We can generalize this discussion of the Text box control to introduce a new term: *class*. **A** *class* **is a** *template:* **it defines the data and behavior of the objects that belong to it.** An object is a specific instance (member) of a class. In the case of text boxes, the Toolbox's Text box tool is the class, and a specific text box on a form is the object. Figure 10.9 shows this relationship.

An object is referred to as an *instance* of its class. **When an object is created, we say that we** *instantiate* **the object (or that the object is instantiated).** **An** *instance variable* **is a variable associated with a specific instance of a class, that is, with a specific object.** Thus, in general object terminology a text box's properties are called instance variables. Note in Figure 10.9 that the two text boxes have different values for their Text properties. One has the value Text1 and the other has the value Text2. So in this case, each instance of the class has a different value for its Text instance variable.

Now let's consider a different class called Employee. This class was defined by a programmer. Figure 10.10 depicts the class and shows a key to the symbols used in the figure. The entire rounded rectangle is the class. Note that this is a template: it defines data (four instance variables) and behavior (one method).

Figure 10.11 shows two Employee objects (instances of the Employee class). These objects each have four instance variables, in accordance with the class definition in Figure 10.10, and they also have distinct values for their instance variables. Also note in Figure 10.10 that the class definition includes a behavior called ComputeGrossPay. **Behaviors are called** *methods* **in general object terminology.** (Methods will be discussed in detail later on.) Both objects in Figure 10.11 include this method. That is, each Employee object knows how to compute its own gross pay.

A text box and its tool differ from an Employee object and its class only in that the former is a *graphical object*—that is, one seen by the user—and the latter is an object that can only be manipulated by program statements. An *application object*, like the Employee object, **does not appear on the user interface.** In VB you can define new graphical objects as well as application

FIGURE 10.9

Classes versus objects

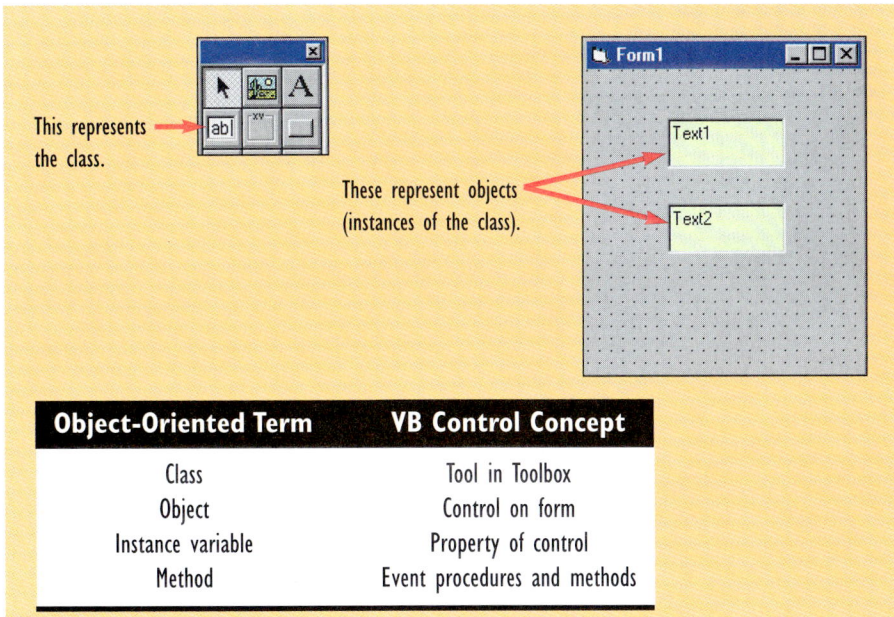

FIGURE 10.10

Employee class

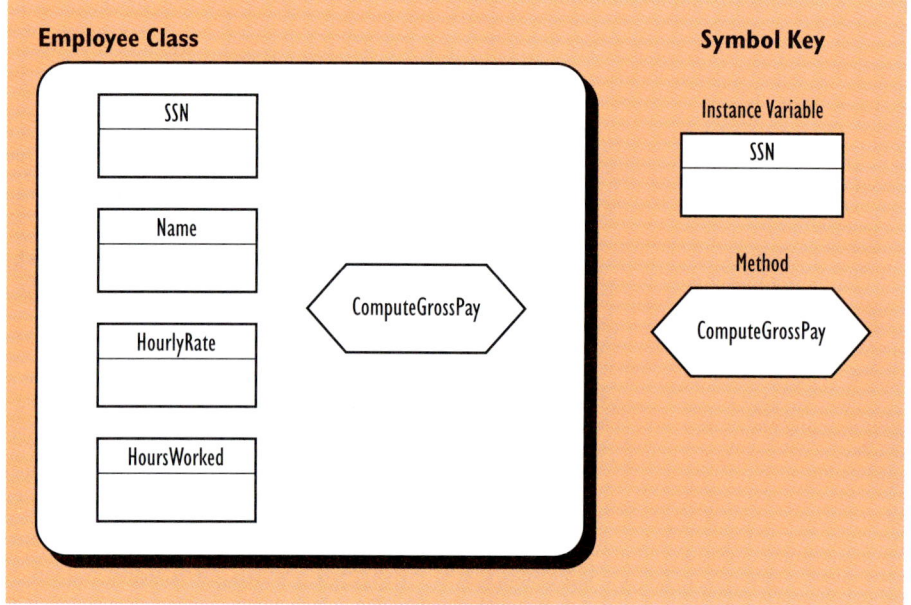

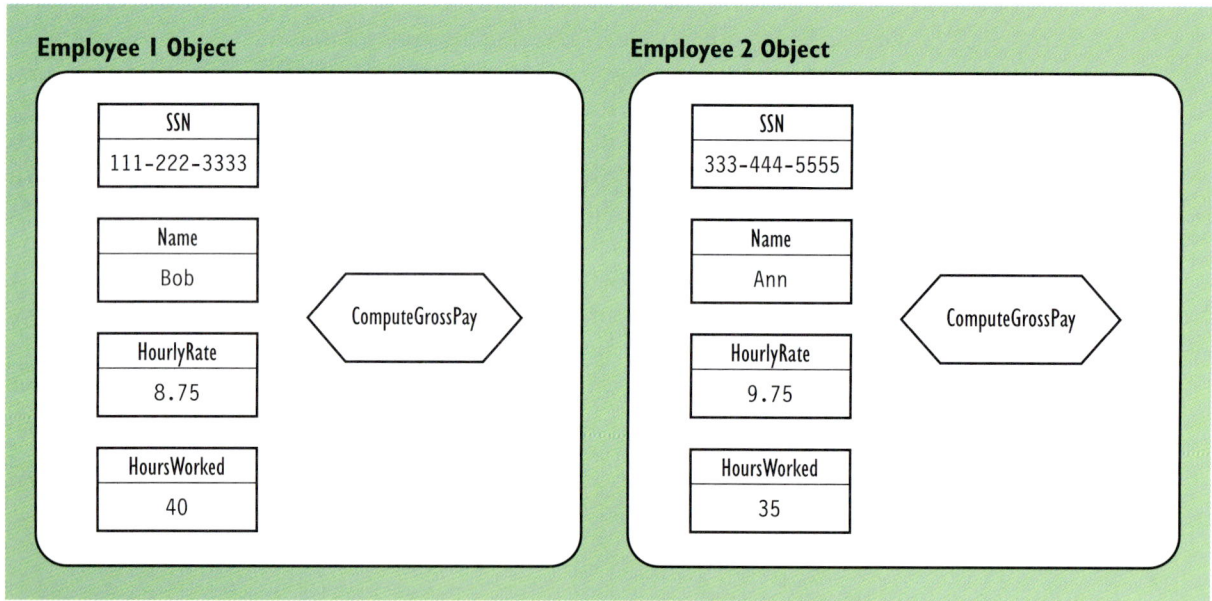

FIGURE 10.11 Two objects generated from Employee class

objects. We address application objects in this section and graphical objects in Section 10.5. While there are many similarities between the two types of objects, there are also some differences.

Defining a Class

Let us illustrate the process of defining a class by defining a very simple Hourly Employee class. Figure 10.12 shows this class with its instance variables and methods.

VB provides a **special type of module**, called a *class module*, **for creating class definitions**. A class module is similar to a code module in that it contains only code—it has no form. Unlike a code module, a class module can only be used to define the instance variables and methods for a class. Each class must be defined in its own class module.

FIGURE 10.12

Hourly Employee class

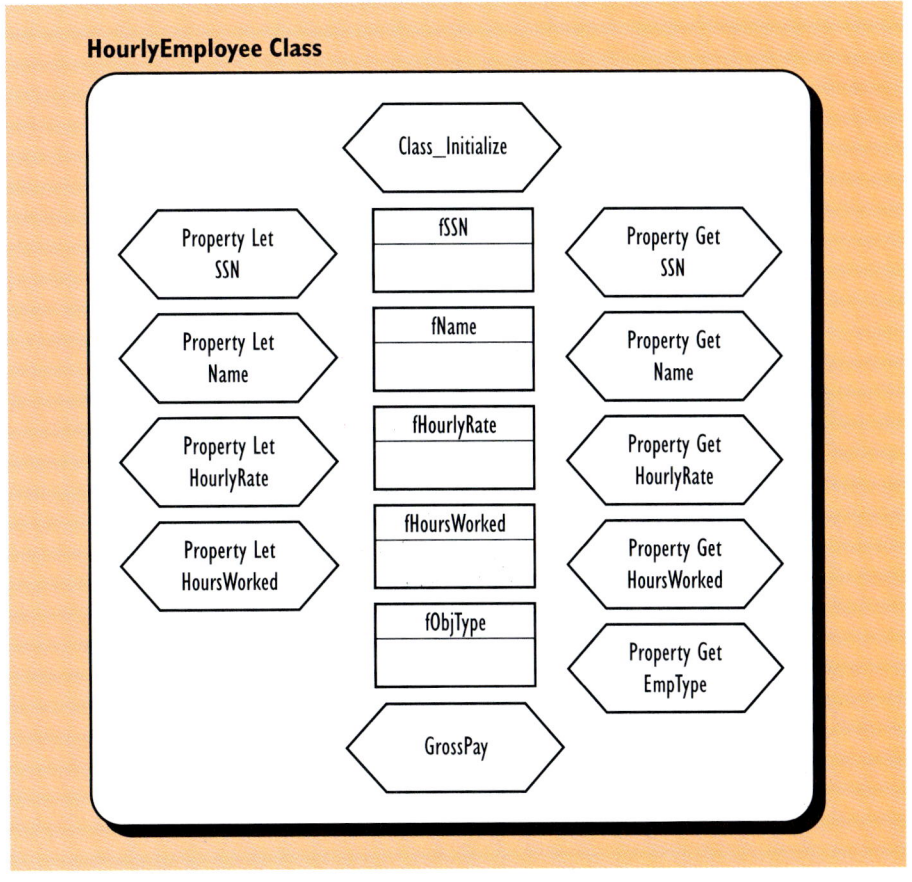

To add a new class module to a project, select Add Class Module from VB's Project menu. In the ensuing Add Class Module dialog box, click on the Class Module icon and then click on Open. VB displays a Code window for the new class, to which VB gives the default name Class1. Before proceeding further, you should use the Properties window to change the Name property to the descriptive name you wish to give the class. Figure 10.13 shows the Properties window for a class module, with the Name property changed to HourlyEmployee. We can now proceed to define the instance variables and methods for the new class.

Instance Variables

The next step in defining a class is to enter the instance variable declarations into the general declarations section of the Code window. The following statements declare the instance variables for our HourlyEmployee class. Note in Figure 10.12 that we have used a naming convention for instance variables: we start their names with a lowercase "f". This convention, which originated in object-oriented programming on the Macintosh computer, helps us quickly identify instance variables in our code.

```
Private fSSN As String
Private fName As String
Private fHourlyRate As Currency
Private fHoursWorked As Integer
Private fObjType As String
```

FIGURE 10.13

Naming the class module

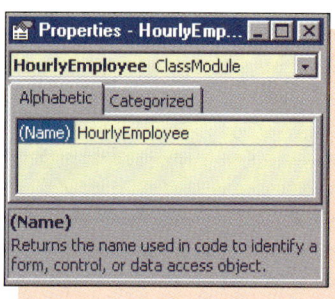

These are just like Dim statements. The keyword Private limits the scope of the instance variables to the class module. Thus, these instance variables are module-level variables that can be accessed only by procedures inside the class module. Limiting access to an object's instance variables like this is an important object-oriented design goal. Declarations like these are all that is needed to define the instance variables.

Methods

We now turn our attention to the methods for this class. *Methods* are similar to procedures and functions—they can have parameters and can return values. In fact, to create a method you compose a special type of procedure or function in the class module. The difference between methods (defined in class modules) and procedures and functions (defined in form or code modules) has to do with the way they are invoked. There are three different kinds of methods, each of which is invoked in a different way. The three kinds of methods are

1. *Accessor* methods
2. *Class initialization* (and *termination*) methods
3. *Behavior* methods

We will discuss each of these in turn.

Accessor Methods

Because instance variables are private to the objects of the class, they are known only to the methods of the class. That is, their scope is limited to the methods of the class. Thus, special methods are needed to store values in and retrieve values from instance variables. These special methods are often called *accessor methods* **because they provide access to the instance variables.** By making the accessor methods public, procedures anywhere in the project can set or retrieve the value of an instance variable by invoking the appropriate accessor method.

Conceptually, you can think of an object as a capsule that has a distinct inner portion. The only way to enter the capsule is to use methods. This is known as *encapsulation* in object-oriented terminology. For example, if you want the code that uses the object to be able to set the fName instance variable you must create an accessor method for this purpose. The code that uses the object passes a value to that accessor method, which takes the value and stores it in the instance variable. Figure 10.14 shows this behavior.

To create accessor methods for an instance variable, select Add Procedure... under VB's Tools menu to display the Insert Procedure dialog box. Select the Property option for the procedure type, enter the name you want the accessor methods to have in the Name text box, and then click OK. VB responds

FIGURE 10.14

Setting the value of an instance variable using an accessor method

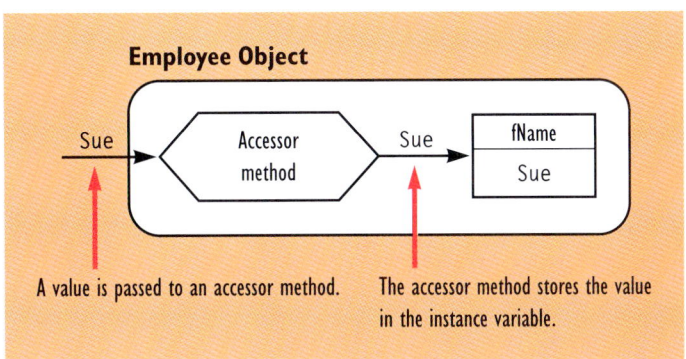

by creating two empty procedure templates in the Code window: one for **retrieving the value of the instance variable, called** *Property Get,* and one for **setting the value of the instance variable, called** *Property Let.*

Suppose we want to create accessor methods for the instance variable fName in our HourlyEmployee class. A good name for these accessor methods is Name. After the Insert Procedure operation, the following empty procedure templates appear in the Code window. Observe that the Property Get heading looks similar to a function heading (with return type Variant) and the Property Let heading looks similar to a general sub procedure heading (with one parameter of type Variant).

Public Property Get Name() **As Variant**

End Property

Public Property Let Name(**ByVal** vNewValue **As Variant**)

End Property

We will discuss the Property Let procedure first and then the Property Get procedure.

The words "Property Let" make sense if you think about them. Remember that VB calls instance variables "properties" (the data that describe an object). The word "Let" is an optional keyword[2] that can be used in an assignment statement. That is, Let X = 10 is equivalent to X = 10. Thus, you can interpret "Property Let" as "assign a value to (Let) an instance variable (Property)."

The complete Property Let procedure for setting the fName instance variable follows:

Public Property Let Name(**ByVal** NewValue **As String**)
    fName = NewValue
End Property

This procedure, called Name, has a parameter named NewValue. Note that we changed the type of NewValue from Variant to String. This is consistent with the type of the instance variable fName and is also more efficient from VB's perspective. Thus, any procedure invoking this Property Let procedure must pass an argument to it. Inside the Property Let procedure, the value of the parameter

---

[2] The original BASIC language used the keyword LET for all assignment statements, as in LET X = 10. Although this keyword has now become optional, some programmers still refer to the assignment statement as the "LET statement."

FIGURE 10.15

Executing the Property Let Name procedure

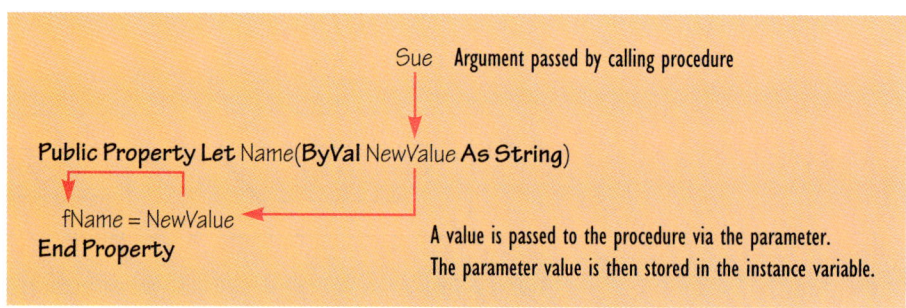

(NewValue) is stored in the instance variable (fName) as depicted in Figure 10.15. We postpone briefly our explanation of how this procedure is invoked.

In our HourlyEmployee class, Property Let procedures are also needed for the instance variables fSSN, fHourlyRate, and fHoursWorked. The code for these procedures is as follows:

```
Public Property Let SSN(ByVal NewValue As String)
    fSSN = NewValue
End Property

Public Property Let HourlyRate(ByVal NewValue As Currency)
    fHourlyRate = NewValue
End Property

Public Property Let HoursWorked(ByVal NewValue As Integer)
    fHoursWorked = NewValue
End Property
```

The Property Get procedure retrieves the value of an instance variable. Property Get is actually a function, not a procedure. Remember that functions return values in the function name. Thus, the Property Get function returns (Gets) the value of an instance variable (Property).

Let's examine in detail the Property Get function for the fName instance variable. Remember that this function returns the current value of the instance variable. The code for the function is

```
Public Property Get Name() As String
    Name = fName
End Property
```

Like all functions, this function has a type. VB initially specifies the Variant type when it creates the Property Get function. You should change this to the type that's appropriate for the specific instance variable. In this case, the type is String because the fName instance variable is type String. Also, like all functions, the function name (Name) is assigned a value inside the function. In this case, the value that it is assigned is the value of the fName instance variable.

We need a Property Get function for each instance variable whose value we might want to retrieve. For our HourlyEmployee class, we want access to all instance variables. The additional Property Get functions that follow provide this access:

```
Public Property Get SSN() As String
    SSN = fSSN
End Property
```

```
Public Property Get HourlyRate() As Currency
    HourlyRate = fHourlyRate
End Property

Public Property Get HoursWorked() As Integer
    HoursWorked = fHoursWorked
End Property

Public Property Get EmpType() As String
    EmpType = fObjType
End Property
```

Class Initialization Methods

We will use the instance variable fObjType to store a string value that identifies the type of object. We do this because we anticipate having more than one type of object in the program, and we may need to distinguish the types of individual objects (we will see examples of this later). For this class, we want to automatically set fObjType to the string "Hourly".

VB provides two special procedures for class definitions: Class_Initialize and Class_Terminate. **The *class initialization method* is invoked automatically each time an instance of the class is created and is typically used to provide default initial values for instance variables.** The *class termination method* is invoked automatically each time an instance of the class is destroyed.[3]

VB places an empty template for the Class_Initialize procedure in the Code window (under the Class object) when the class module is first created. The complete Class_Initialize procedure for our HourlyEmployee class is

```
Private Sub Class_Initialize()
    fSSN = "999-99-9999"
    fName = "None"
    fHourlyRate = 0
    fHoursWorked = 0
    fObjType = "Hourly"
End Sub
```

This procedure assigns initial values to the instance variables when an object of this class is created. These values are just like the default property settings that VB gives to a text box when you create the Text box control on a form.

Behavior Methods

For our HourlyEmployee class we need one final method to compute the gross pay (see Figure 10.12). This method is different from the accessor and class initialization methods. It does not set, get, or initialize instance variables. Instead, it computes and returns the gross pay (hours times rate) for the employee represented by the object. As its name implies, the ***behavior method*** defines a behavior of the object.

The method is a function that multiplies the instance variables fHourlyRate and fHoursWorked and returns the product. The code for this function is

```
Public Function GrossPay() As Currency
    GrossPay = fHourlyRate * fHoursWorked
End Function
```

[3] An object is destroyed when it "falls out of scope." For example, if the object is created inside a procedure, then it is local to that procedure, and is destroyed when the procedure's End Sub is encountered.

Technically, this function is not necessary. An alternative available to the calling procedure is to invoke the functions Property Get HourlyRate and Property Get HoursWorked, and then multiply the returned values to compute the gross pay. However, when we design classes, we want them to control their own behavior. We'll see why this is important later.

Figure 10.16 shows the code in the completed HourlyEmployee class module. It defines the instance variables, the accessor methods, the initialization method, and the behavior method. Every time we create an object from this class, that object will include its own instance variables and all the methods, as specified in this definition.

Figure 10.17 provides a graphical summary of the HourlyEmployee class. In this figure, the arrows show the direction of data flowing into, out of, and within the object. The methods that manage each data flow are shown at the beginning or end of the flow. A solid black arrow indicates an argument being passed to a method, a gray arrow indicates a method returning a value, and a dashed arrow indicates a data flow internal to the object.

Declaring and Using Objects

In object-oriented programming there is a strict separation of the code that defines a class and the code that creates and uses objects based on a class. In

FIGURE 10.16 *Completed HourlyEmployee class module*

FIGURE 10.17

Summary of HourlyEmployee class

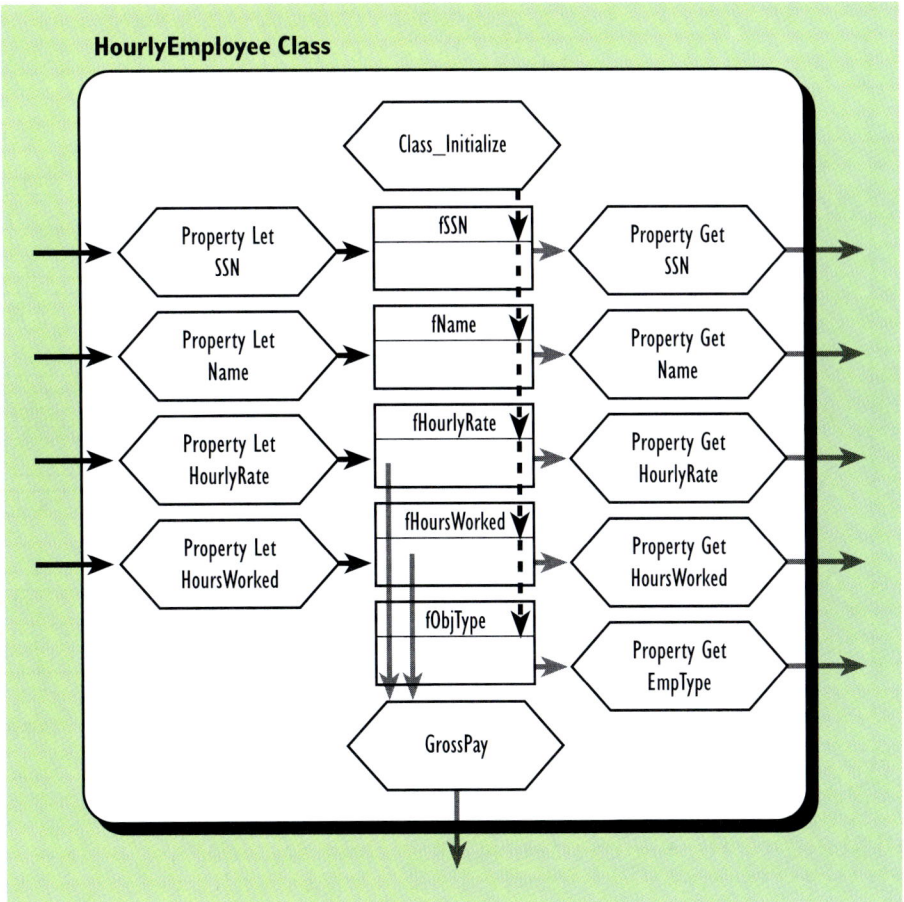

VB, code that defines a class must be placed in a class module, whereas the code that actually creates and uses objects must be placed in form and code modules.

The class module is reusable. For example, once we have completed our HourlyEmployee class module, other programmers who wish to create and use HourlyEmployee objects only need to include the HourlyEmployee class module in their projects. In this section we discuss the code that creates and uses objects. Thus, the statements we now turn to can only be used in forms and code modules.

To create an object from a class we use the Dim, Public, or Static statement to declare an *object variable,* **which is created from the template defined in the class module specified in the declaration statement.** The class module must be included in the project.

There is a slight difference in the declaration statement when it is used to declare object variables: the keyword As is changed to As New, and a class name is specified instead of a data type. The statements

Dim Emp1 **As New** HourlyEmployee
Dim Emp2 **As New** HourlyEmployee

create two object variables named Emp1 and Emp2. These object variables refer to objects that are created from the HourlyEmployee class. Thus they each have instance variables fSSN, fName, fHourlyRate, fHoursWorked, and fObjType, and they each possess the methods defined for the class. Figure 10.18 shows the two objects referred to by the object variables Emp1 and Emp2. When VB executes the

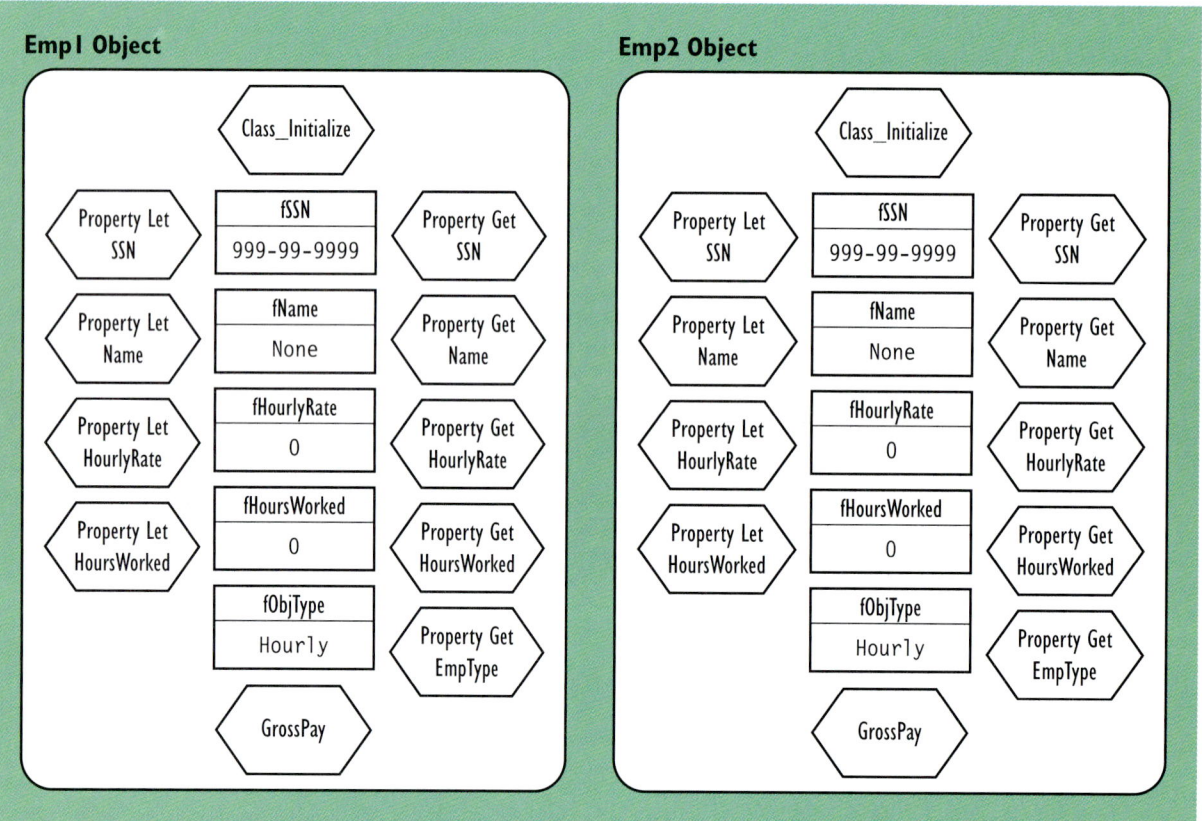

FIGURE 10.18 Two objects from the HourlyEmployee class

Dim statements, it creates the objects and executes the Class_Initialize procedures. This is why the instance variables have the values you see in the figure.

We use the phrase "object variables refer to the objects." Since an object is a complex entity that includes both data and behavior, it is not the same as a regular variable that stores only data. Thus, we use slightly different terminology with the variables that identify them. This is a subtle point and not too important at the level of detail we need for the objects created in this example; however, if you study object-oriented programming in greater depth, this distinction becomes more important. Programmers often drop the word "variable" from the phrase "object variable" and just say "object." Using this convention, we say that Emp1 and Emp2 are objects. However, technically, they *refer* to objects.

After an object variable has been created, its accessor and behavior methods can be executed. The syntax for executing these methods is consistent with what we have been doing all along with VB controls. For example, if we want to refer to the Text property of a text box named txtX, we say txtX.Text. That is, we give the object name, then a period, and finally the property name. Let us now look in more detail at how accessor and behavior methods are invoked for application objects, and discuss some examples.

Invoking Accessor Methods

Recall that accessor methods are used to set and retrieve the values of instance variables. Methods defined with the Property Let procedure store a value in an instance variable, and methods defined with the Property Get function retrieve a value from an instance variable.

To use methods defined with Property Let procedures, specify *Object-Name.method* on the left-hand side of an assignment statement. The following statement illustrates this:

Emp1.Name = "Sally"

This syntax is the same as for a graphical object, such as txtX.Text = "XYZ".

Suppose that the following code segment is executed:

Emp1.SSN = "123-45-6789"
Emp1.Name = "Sally"
Emp1.HourlyRate = 10.75
Emp1.HoursWorked = 40

Figure 10.19 shows how executing this code affects the Emp1 object.

To use methods defined with Property Get functions, specify *Object-Name.method* in an expression. Again, this syntax is the same as for graphical objects. The following statement displays the Emp1 object's fName instance variable in a message box:

MsgBox Emp1.Name

Figure 10.20 depicts how this line of code works.

Let's pause to review our discussion so far. We created a class definition called HourlyEmployee. We declared two object variables that refer to objects created from the HourlyEmployee class template. We then used Property Let and Property Get procedures to access the instance variables that are associated with each object variable.

FIGURE 10.19

Storing values in instance variables

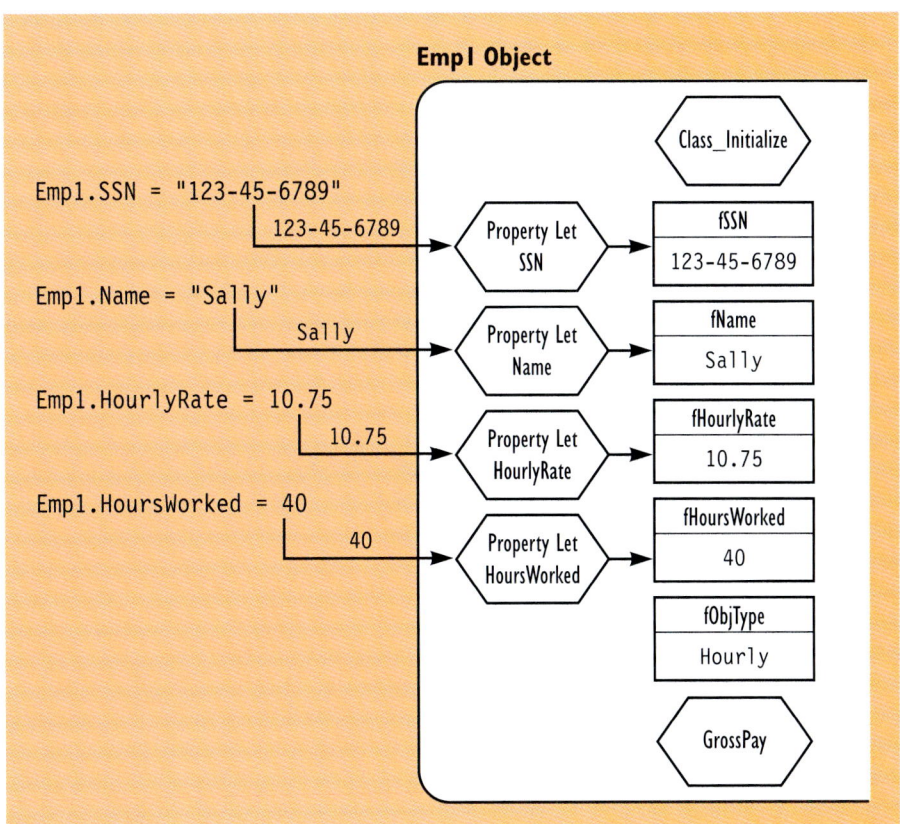

FIGURE 10.20

Retrieving the value of an instance variable

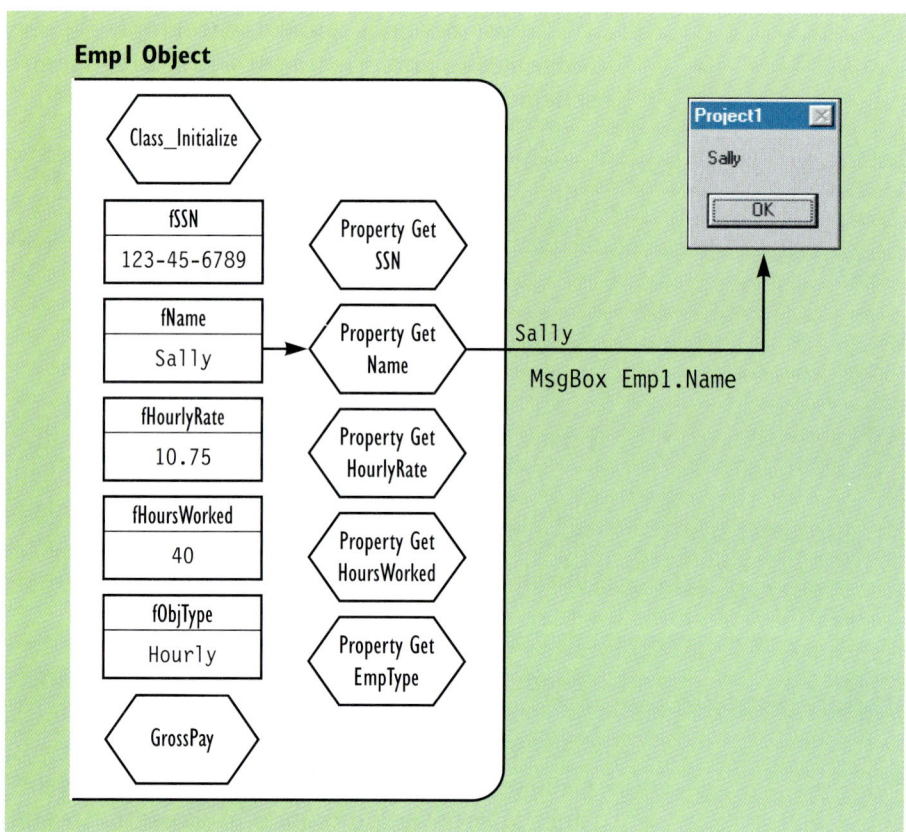

Note that the only programmers who are ever concerned with the actual instance variable names are the programmers who write the class definition. We refer to them as "authors" of the class. The code that creates and uses objects does not refer to the actual instance variables. Thus, the programmer who writes statements like

```
Emp1.SSN = "123-45-6789"
MsgBox Emp1.Name
```

does not need to know the names of the instance variables, but needs to know only the names of the Property Let and Property Get procedures (i.e., the names of the methods). In fact, this programmer can think of SSN and Name simply as properties of the Emp1 object, in the same way that Text is a property of a text box. This is one benefit of object-oriented programming: once the class definition has been written, it is very easy to write and maintain code that uses objects based on the class.

Now consider the following two lines of code:

```
Emp1.Name = "Robert"
MsgBox Emp1.Name
```

The first line of code invokes the Property Let Name procedure because it assigns a value to the instance variable. The second line invokes the Property Get Name function because it retrieves the value of the instance variable. Both statements use the syntax .Name because both the Property Let and Property Get procedures were named Name. When writing class definitions, it is very important to use the same name for Property Let and Property Get procedures that refer to the same instance variable. Otherwise, code that uses the object will be hard to understand. For example, if you defined the Property Let procedure like this

Public Property Let EmpName(**ByVal** NewValue **As String**)
   fName = NewValue
End Property

but kept the original definition of the Property Get procedure, then the two lines of code would read

Emp1.EmpName = "Robert"
MsgBox Emp1.Name

This is because the procedure names in the class module are used as the method names in the code that uses the object. It would not be apparent to someone reading this code that Emp1.EmpName and Emp1.Name actually work with the same instance variable.

Invoking Behavior Methods

Now that we've seen how to use accessor methods, understanding how to use behavior methods is straightforward. Consider the following statement, which invokes the function that returns the gross pay:

MsgBox Emp1.GrossPay

This syntax looks as if it invokes a Property Get function to retrieve the value from an instance variable that holds the employee's gross pay. We know that this is not the case because we have seen the GrossPay function's code. However, if the class had been defined by other programmers, and we were just using the class, not defining it, we really wouldn't care about how the internal details were carried out. Our only concern would be that the correct result is returned. This is another benefit of object-oriented programming: to use objects, you do not need to know the details of how their behavior is defined.

We now turn our attention to two examples that demonstrate the use of objects in short programs.

Example 10.2

Using Objects

Let us use the HourlyEmployee class to create, display, and modify an employee object. The user interface for this application is shown in Figure 10.21. As

FIGURE 10.21

Example 10.2 at run time

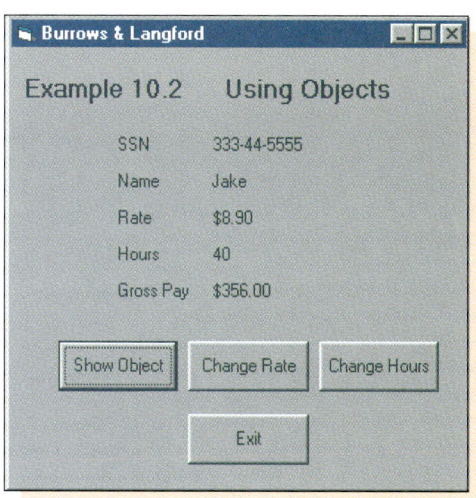

you can see, this application displays the instance variables of an hourly employee object. In addition, the user can change the hours worked or the hourly rate. After doing so, if the user clicks Show Object again, a revised gross pay amount is automatically computed and displayed.

This application uses a single form and a class module. The Project Explorer window is shown in Figure 10.22. The class module, HourlyEmployee, is the same module whose code is shown in Figure 10.16. The object variable for this application is declared in the form's general declarations section, and has module-level scope. The instance variables are set to values for a specific employee in the form's Load event procedure. Figure 10.23 shows this code, along with the event procedures for the form's command buttons.

Notice that when the user clicks on cmdChangeHours, the Property Let HoursWorked procedure is called to set the appropriate instance variable. A similar action takes place when the user clicks on cmdChangeRate. The

FIGURE 10.22

Project Explorer window for Example 10.2

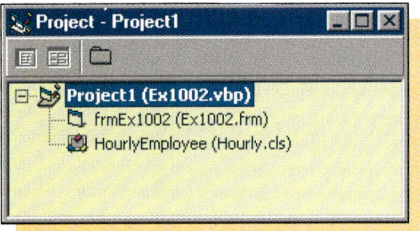

FIGURE 10.23

Code for form in Example 10.2

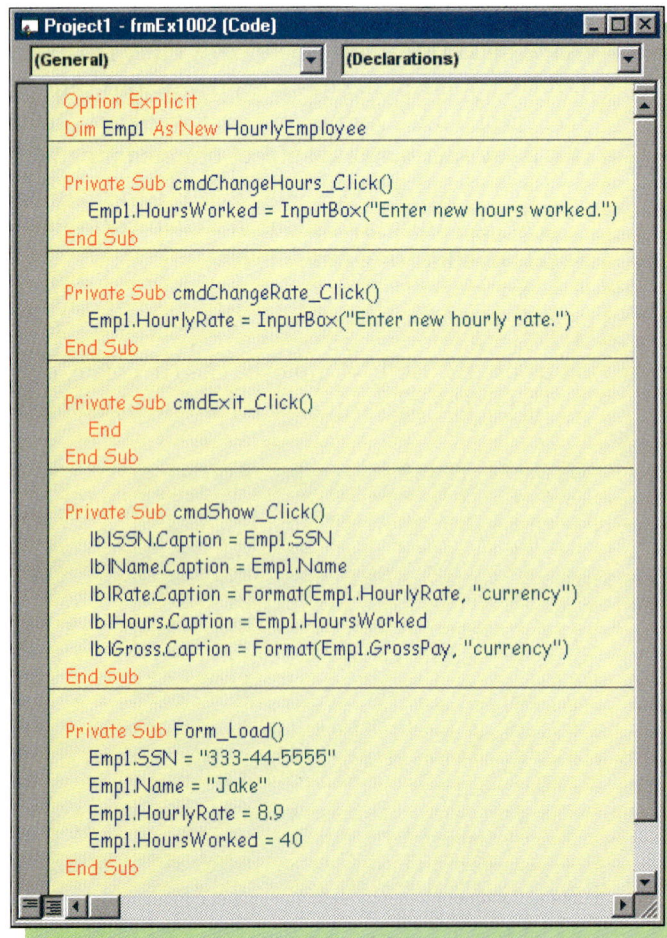

cmdShow_Click procedure uses the various Property Get functions to access the instance variables, and the GrossPay function to obtain the product of hours worked and hourly rate.

The code in Figure 10.23 does not show explicit references to the Property Let and Property Get procedures. In fact, someone reading the code who did not know about objects might think that the various references, such as Emp1.SSN and Emp1.GrossPay, refer to text boxes or labels. This similarity occurs because both a text box and the object variable Emp1 are objects—one is a graphical object and the other is an application object.

Example 10.3

Working with Similar Classes and Class Hierarchies

In this example we define two classes and create one object from each class. This example highlights a limitation in the support VB provides for classes as compared with other languages that emphasize object-oriented programming.

The two classes for this example are the hourly employee class from Example 10.2 and a new salaried employee class. Table 10.1 shows the instance variables and methods for these two classes. Notice that these two classes have more similarities than differences.

The application has a single form and two class modules. Remember that a class module can define only a single class. The class module for the HourlyEmployee class is the same as in Figure 10.16. Figure 10.24 shows the class module for the SalariedEmployee class. Note that the GrossPay function for the salaried employee simply returns the value of the fSalary instance variable divided by 24. The fSalary instance variable is used to hold the employee's gross annual salary, and the employee is paid twice each month (24 times each year).

The application displays selected instance variables of objects created from either of the two classes. The user selects which object to display. The user interface is shown in Figure 10.25. As in the previous example, object variables are

TABLE 10.1 Hourly and salaried employee classes

	HourlyEmployee Class	SalariedEmployee Class
Instance Variables	fSSN	fSSN
	fName	fName
	fHourlyRate	fSalary
	fHoursWorked	
	fObjType	fObjType
Methods	Sub Class_Initialize	Sub Class_Initialize
	Property Let SSN	Property Let SSN
	Property Get SSN	Property Get SSN
	Property Let Name	Property Let Name
	Property Get Name	Property Get Name
	Property Let HourlyRate	Property Let Salary
	Property Get HourlyRate	Property Get Salary
	Property Let HoursWorked	
	Property Get HoursWorked	
	Property Get EmpType	Property Get EmpType
	Function GrossPay	Function GrossPay

Note: Instance variables and methods that are common to the two classes are shown in green type while those that are unique to each class are shown in black type.

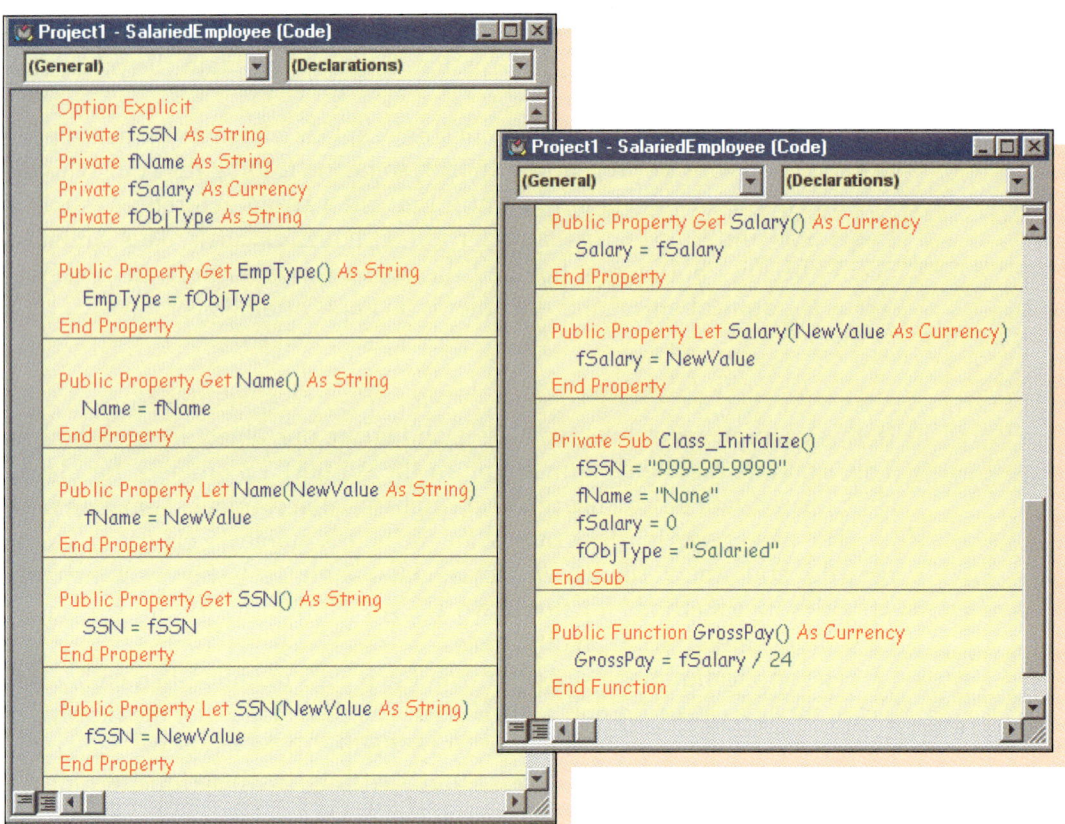

FIGURE 10.24 Code for the SalariedEmployee class module

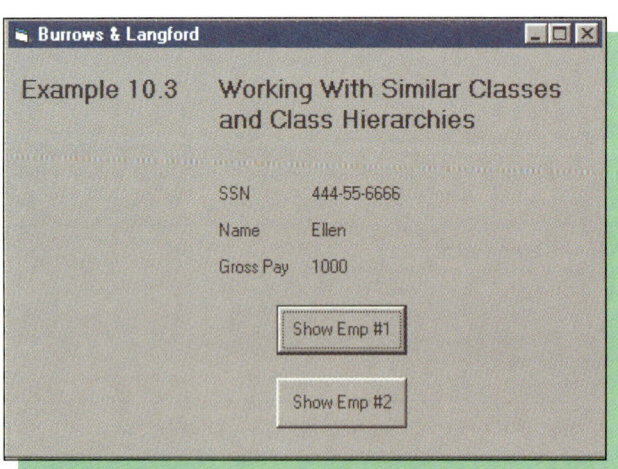

FIGURE 10.25

Example 10.3 after user clicks on Show Emp #1

declared in the form's general declarations section. In this example, two object variables are created—one for an hourly employee and one for a salaried employee. These two objects are initialized with class default values when they are created. Then, in the form's Load procedure, the instance variables are set to values for specific employees. The code for the form is shown in Figure 10.26.

Now let's compare the two class definitions HourlyEmployee and SalariedEmployee. Look at Table 10.1 and notice that three of the instance variables are the same in the two classes. In addition, six of the methods are identical or very similar. A true object-oriented language allows the programmer who defines the classes to use these similarities to great advantage.

FIGURE 10.26

Code for form in Example 10.3

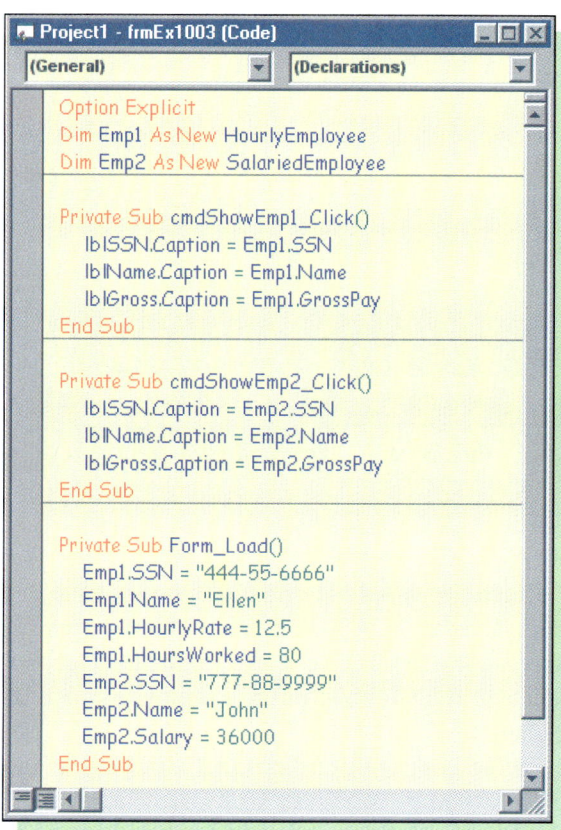

True object-oriented languages support *class hierarchies*. An example of a class hierarchy is depicted in Figure 10.27. This figure shows a class named Employee and two *subclasses* named HourlyEmployee and SalariedEmployee. The class named Employee is called a *superclass*. The subclasses are *descendants* of the superclass.

Class hierarchies permit subclasses to *inherit* instance variables and methods from their superclass. That is, any instance variable defined in the superclass automatically exists in the subclass as well. If the programmer designs class hierarchies properly, the amount of work necessary to create a new subclass is minimal.

Let's apply class hierarchies to our example. We start by defining the instance variables that are common to both hourly and salaried employees at the employee superclass level, so that both subclasses will inherit these instance variables. Then we need to define only the instance variables that are unique to each subclass at the lower level. Our class hierarchy with instance variables identified is shown in Figure 10.28. Both the hourly and salaried employee classes include (inherit) the three instance variables from the Employee superclass, and they also have their own separate instance variables.

FIGURE 10.27

Sample class hierarchy

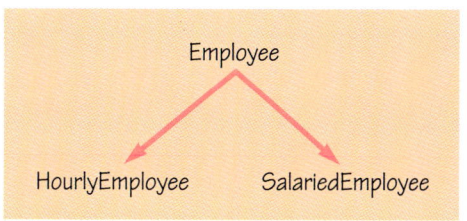

FIGURE 10.28

Class hierarchy and instance variables

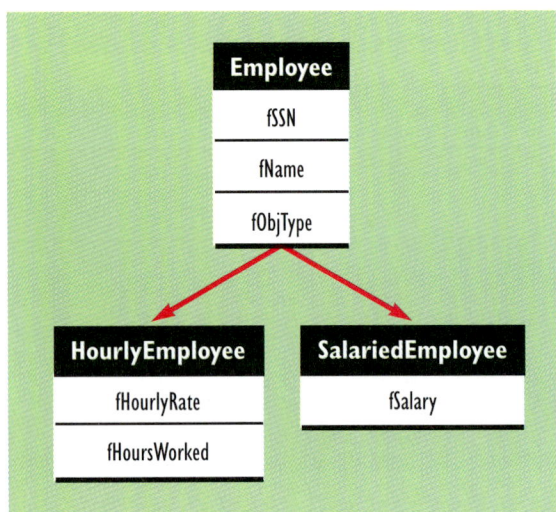

Inheritance applies to methods as well as to instance variables. Any method that is shared by subclasses can be defined once in the superclass and then inherited by all the subclasses. For example, the Get and Let procedures for SSN and Name could be defined in the Employee superclass and inherited by the two subclasses.

To see how useful inheritance can be, imagine a company with the class hierarchy shown in Figure 10.28. Now suppose the company wants to add a new type of employee called an intern. The company can easily add this class as a third subclass to the Employee class. This new subclass would inherit the fSSN, fName, and fObjType instance variables. It may or may not add some instance variables of its own. It would also inherit any methods that were defined for the superclass. Because existing instance variables and methods are inherited by the new subclass, the programmer now has to add code only for the data and behaviors that are unique to the new subclass. This reduces both the time and expense associated with modifying a program that uses objects.

Unfortunately, Visual Basic does not support class hierarchies and inheritance as described above. There is a utility called the Class Builder that provides assistance in creating class hierarchies. However, this utility just duplicates code from superclasses into the subclasses instead of supporting the code in just one place (the superclass). This fact makes later modifications difficult and prone to errors. This lack of true inheritance prevents VB from being considered a fully object-oriented language and to some extent limits the power of its programmer-defined classes.

Collections

VB provides a special object called a *collection* that can store a group of individual objects and treat this group as a single unit. The members of the collection need not be the same type. That is, a single collection can store different types of objects, such as both hourly and salaried employees.

Each object in a collection is called an *item*. Figure 10.29 depicts a hypothetical collection named EmployeeGroup that contains three employee objects. Each item in a collection has a position referred to as its *index*. In the figure, the Emp1 object has an index of 1, and the Emp3 object has an index of 3.

FIGURE 10.29

Hypothetical collection and its members

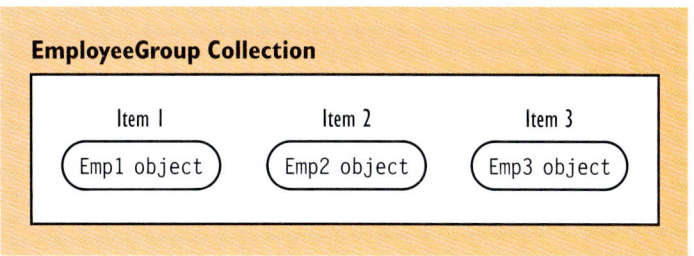

A collection is declared with a Dim, Public, or Static statement just like any other object variable. The syntax using the Dim statement is as follows:

Dim CollectionName **As New Collection**

The programmer supplies a meaningful CollectionName.

The collection object has just one property: Count. At run time VB automatically updates the value of this property to be equal to the number of items in the collection. For the example in Figure 10.29, the Count property is equal to 3.

The collection object has three methods: Add, Remove, and Item. The Add method adds an item to the collection. For example, assuming the collection shown in Figure 10.29 is named EmployeeGroup, it could have been populated using the following three statements:

```
EmployeeGroup.Add Emp1
EmployeeGroup.Add Emp2
EmployeeGroup.Add Emp3
```

The Remove method removes an item according to its index in the collection. Thus, executing the following statement would remove the second item from the collection in Figure 10.29.

```
EmployeeGroup.Remove 2
```

The Item method accesses a specific member from the collection. Like the Remove method, the Item method uses the item's index to specify which item to access. For example, to display the names of the employees in the collection one at a time we can use code like the following:

```
For K = 1 To EmployeeGroup.Count
    MsgBox EmployeeGroup.Item(K).Name
Next K
```

In this example we are assuming that all of the objects in the collection possess a Property Get Name procedure (which would be the case if they were all members of the employee classes we have defined). The reference to the collection in the MsgBox statement specifies Item(K). Thus, EmployeeGroup.Item(K).Name references the Name method of the item at position "K" in the EmployeeGroup collection.

Example 10.4

Using Collections

This example uses the same two classes, HourlyEmployee and SalariedEmployee, as in Example 10.3. When it runs, it creates eight object variables—some are hourly employees and others are salaried employees—and adds these objects to a collection object. The user can then view selected instance variables in a grid. Figure 10.30 shows the application as it is executing.

FIGURE 10.30

Example 10.4 at run time

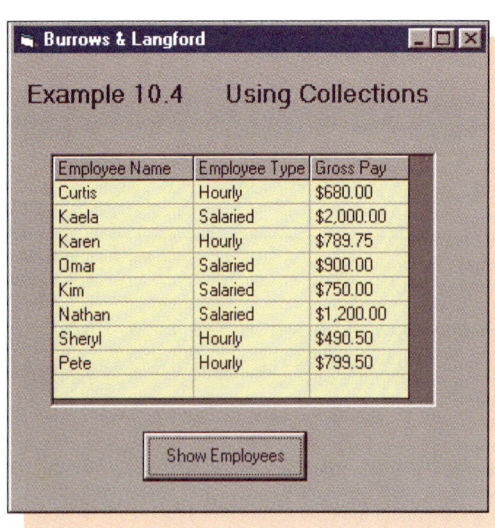

As in the previous two examples, the object variables are declared in the form's general declarations section. The collection object is also declared there. The Form_Load procedure sets the objects' instance variables to values for specific employees and adds the objects to the collection. Figure 10.31 shows the code for the form.

This code illustrates a significant advantage of object-oriented programming. Remember that the collection object references both hourly and salaried employee objects. These objects are interspersed in the collection in no particular order. That is, the first item might be an hourly employee and the next one might be a salaried employee, and there is no way of knowing beforehand which items represent which type of employee. Now consider the reference that causes the gross pay to be computed:

Employees.Item(K).GrossPay

When we invoke a method, such as GrossPay, the method works on whatever type of employee turns up as item "K" in the collection, even though the calculation of gross pay is different for the two types of employees. We don't need an If statement in this situation. If we use a nonobject solution, a decision-making statement is necessary, like that in the following pseudocode:

If the object referred to by item "K" is an hourly employee Then
  Use the function for hourly employees to compute gross pay
Else
  Use the function for salaried employees to compute gross pay
End If

In object-oriented programming, **the ability of different objects to respond differently to the same method is called *polymorphism*.** We say that the collection supports polymorphic behavior because the objects stored in the collection react in different ways to the GrossPay method. This may not seem very important, but consider what happens to our code if we add a third type of employee—for example, a commissioned employee. In the nonobject solution, we will have to modify the If statement to handle three cases instead of just two. In fact, we will need to modify the code *everywhere* in our application where we differentiate the type of employee. By contrast, in the object-based program we simply define the new employee class (which includes a method

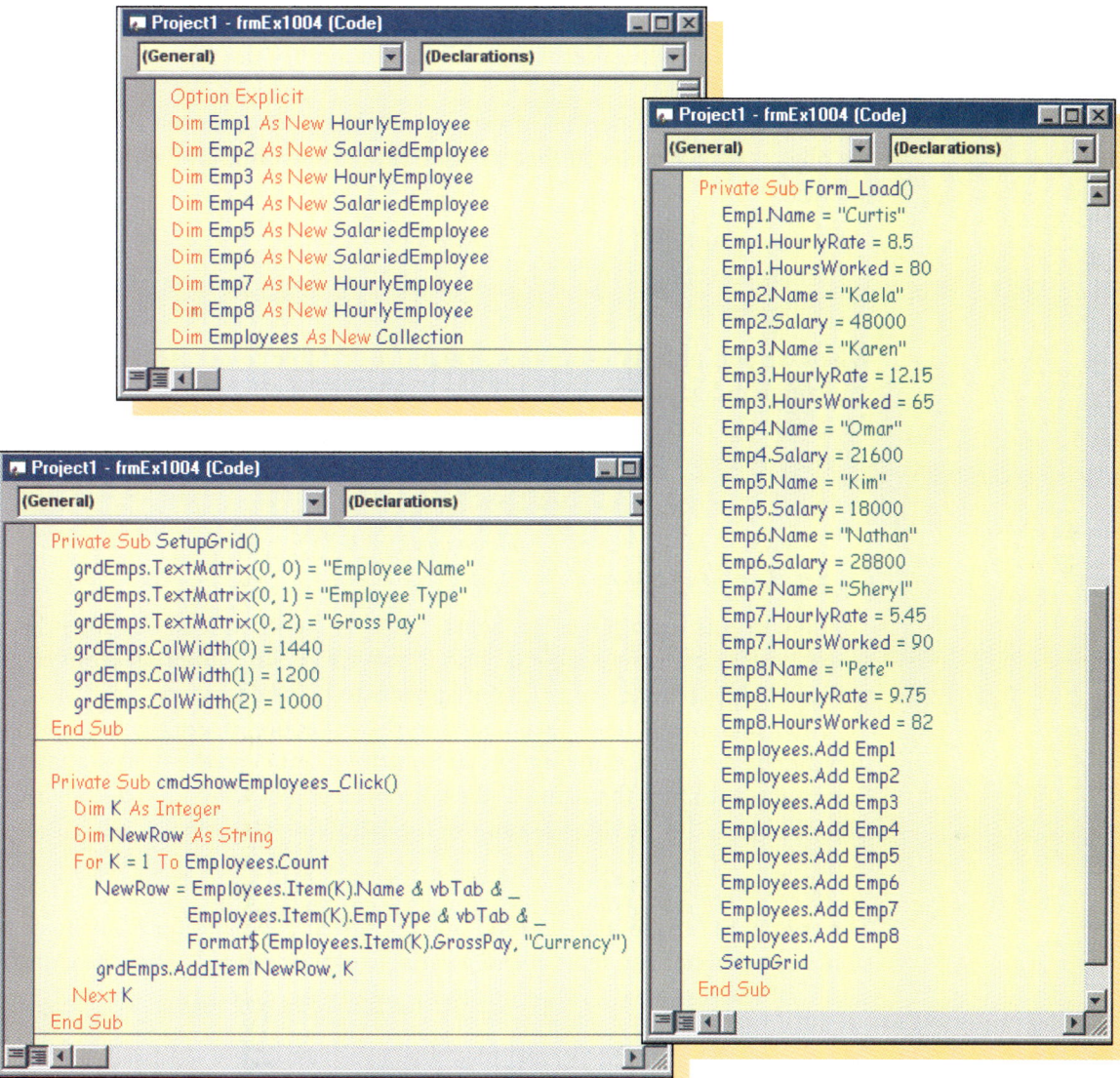

FIGURE 10.31 Code for form in Example 10.4

for computing gross pay) for commissioned employees. We can then create new objects of this class, add them to our collection, and that's it. We don't have to modify any other aspects of the code in Figure 10.31.

Although the preceding simple example illustrates the usefulness of polymorphism, it does not illustrate the full extent of its power. Because VB does not support inheritance in the standard way, it also does not support polymorphism in the same way as true object-oriented languages. VB's online help states that "Visual Basic doesn't use inheritance to provide polymorphism. Visual Basic provides polymorphism through multiple *interfaces*." A discussion of interfaces is beyond the scope of this text.

Accessing Collections by a Key

In Example 10.4 we used a collection object to store and retrieve object references. We used the Item method to access items, specifying the item number as an index. VB provides an alternative method of accessing items that uses a key value instead of an item index. This allows us to find a specific object directly by using a key, without having to search through the entire collection. To use this alternative we need to modify the way we add objects to the collection.

Let's revisit Example 10.4 to see what modifications are necessary to access the objects by a key. Recall that we used the Add method in Example 10.4 as follows:

```
Employees.Add Emp1
Employees.Add Emp2
Employees.Add Emp3
```

When we add objects using this syntax we are able to access them only by using item index numbers (1, 2, 3, etc.). Suppose we want to be able to access the objects by Social Security number (SSN). To make this possible we use a different syntax for the Add method, as follows:

```
Employees.Add Item:=Emp1, Key:=CStr(Emp1.SSN)
Employees.Add Item:=Emp2, Key:=CStr(Emp2.SSN)
Employees.Add Item:=Emp3, Key:=CStr(Emp3.SSN)
```

The key in this example is the Social Security number. The key must be a string expression, so it is a good habit to use VB's CStr() function (convert to string) as shown here, even when it appears to be unnecessary.

After the objects have been added to the collection using the key option, they can be retrieved using the Social Security number as the Item argument. For example, to find the name of the employee object which has Social Security number 123-45-6789, we can use the following statement:

```
EmpName = Employees.Item("123-45-6789").Name
```

The argument for the Item method must be a string expression (a string constant as shown here or, more likely, a variable of type String). Also, the expression's value must exist in the collection; otherwise, a run time error occurs.

Summary of Classes and Objects

♦ ♦ ♦

Although the objects we worked with in this section were relatively simple, they demonstrated several of the benefits of object-oriented programming. Once a class has been defined, it is easy for programmers to write and maintain application code that creates and uses objects of that class. Maintaining class definitions is simplified by the use of class hierarchies. A company can build class hierarchies and easily add new subclasses with much of the work inherited by the subclass. Through polymorphism, objects from new classes can be added without having to make extensive changes to the application code; thus, it is easier to write and maintain applications because much of the effort can be reused (inherited) from already existing classes.

EXERCISE 10.8 Create a class module that defines a Student class. The class's instance variables should include student number, name, cumulative credits, and cumulative grade points. The class should include accessor methods to set and retrieve the values of the instance variables. The class should also include a method called GPA that returns the student's current grade point average (computed by dividing cumulative grade points by cumulative credits).

You may wish to create a form to test your class definition. The form should create a module-level object variable for a student, allow the user to enter values for this object's instance variables, and allow the user to view these values as well as the student's GPA.

EXERCISE 10.9 Modify Example 10.4 so that instead of showing all employees, it shows only salaried or only hourly employees. The user interface should provide the user with option buttons to select which group to display.

Hint: Remember that both of the class definitions include a method named EmpType.

10.5 ActiveX Controls

We now turn our attention to the creation of graphical objects—objects that are visible on the graphical user interface. To do this, we will examine how to create ActiveX controls. **An *ActiveX control* is a control that can be added to VB's Toolbox and used like any other control**, e.g., a text box or a label control. We have already seen some ActiveX controls: the FlexGrid and DBGrid are two examples. Be aware that our discussion is limited; the topic of ActiveX controls is very broad and could fill a book itself. In this section we provide an overview, walk through the creation of an example ActiveX control, and discuss some features of ActiveX controls and how they differ from the application objects that we covered in Section 10.4.

Our example ActiveX control is the future value component shown in Figure 10.32. This control, which comprises everything you see on the form except the command button, was added to the form just as one adds a text box. As you will see, the command button's Click event invokes the Future Value control's "Calculate" method.

Terminology
◆ ◆ ◆

As discussed in Section 10.4, there is a difference between an object class and the objects instantiated from the class. This is also true with ActiveX controls. **The *control class* defines a template—the instance variables, methods, events, and graphical components that make up the class.** From this control class template, *control instances*—specific controls the programmer places on the form—are created.

FIGURE 10.32

The Future Value ActiveX control in an application

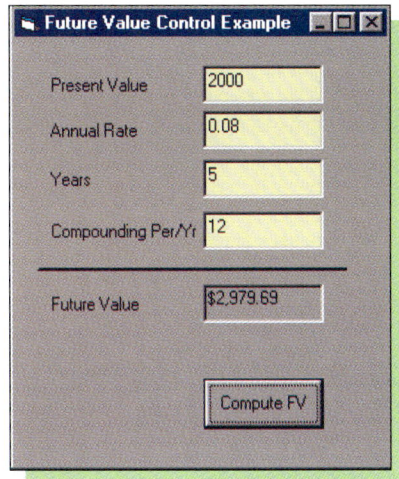

A control class is composed of three parts:

- *Appearance*—what the user sees and interacts with.
- *Interface*—a set of properties, methods, and events.
- *Implementation*—code that makes the control work.

Both the appearance and interface are public. That is, both the programmer and the user see the control. In addition, programmers who use the control while creating an application need to know about its interface. For example, as programmer, in order to use a FlexGrid control that you've placed on a form you need to know about properties such as ColAlignment(), methods such as AddItem, and events such as DoubleClick.

Implementation is private. Neither the programmer using the control nor the user know exactly how the control does what it does. For example, do you know how the FlexGrid actually performs the AddItem method? Have you seen the code? Unless you work for Microsoft, your answer is probably no. Nevertheless, even though you don't know this private implementation detail, you can still use the control effectively. Moreover, if Microsoft released an update to VB that included a more efficient implementation of the AddItem method, you could still use your projects without change.

Differences between Application Objects and Graphical Objects

While there are many similarities between application objects and graphical objects, there are also some significant differences. The first difference relates to how you create an ActiveX control. You do so by defining a UserControl class (and not a class module as is done for application objects). **A *UserControl* class is a special class with its own visual designer (very similar to the Form Designer window) as well as its own code modules.** Figure 10.33 shows a UserControl visual designer and its Properties window. Note how similar Figure 10.33 is to a form and the Properties window in an ordinary project.

Section 10.4 introduced the concept of instance variables—data items associated with a specific instance of an object. In that section, we saw an analogy between an instance variable and a property of a control (such as the

FIGURE 10.33

UserControl visual designer and its Properties window

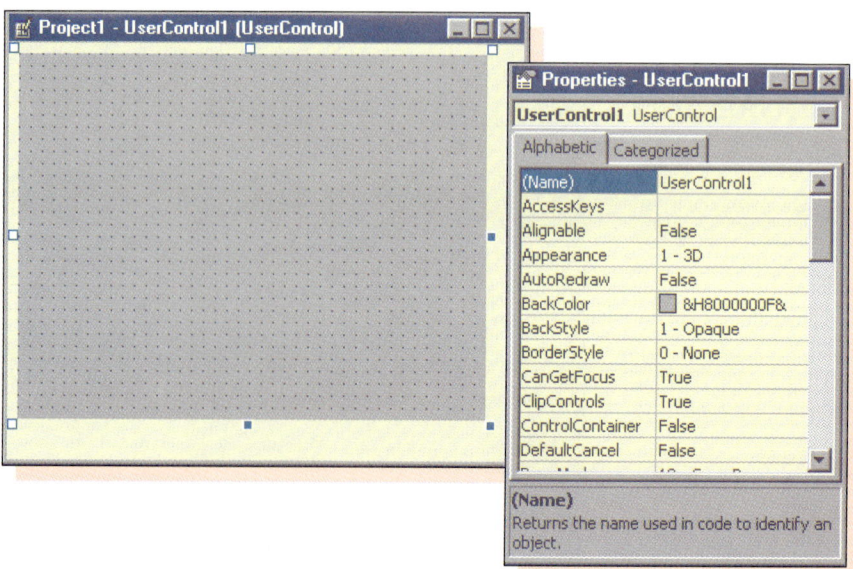

Text property of a Text box control). The instance variables were accessed (written to and read from) using the Property Let and Property Get methods. UserControl classes also have properties and also use the Property Let and Property Get methods to store and retrieve their values. However, there are two very important differences between properties for a UserControl object and properties for the type of objects discussed in Section 10.4.

- When a UserControl is placed on a form, its properties and their settings are accessible through the Properties window. These values can be viewed and edited directly in the Properties window (if you, as the designer of the UserControl, want this capability).

- A UserControl's property settings are saved when the project that includes the control is saved, and the property settings are retrieved and restored when the project is subsequently opened.

Figure 10.34 emphasizes these points by displaying the Properties window for the Future Value control. Note the four "Financial" properties shown in the figure. You can change their settings at design time, and the new settings will remain in effect if you save the project and then open it at a later time.

Another feature that differentiates a UserControl class from other types of classes is the ability to include other graphical components in addition to properties. For example, the Future Value control in Figure 10.32 includes four Text box controls, six Label controls, and a Line control.

The final difference is very important as well as enlightening. Both application objects and UserControl objects are instantiated at run time, but UserControl objects are also instantiated at design time. **When a programmer places a control on a form at design time, an actual instance of the control class is created**—the *design-time instance*. This instance is actually executing. Think about the Data control from Chapter 8. After you placed a Data control on a form and set the DatabaseName property, recall that if you then pulled down the dropdown list for the RecordSource property, all the tables in the database were displayed. How did the Data control know the names of the tables in the database? It must have been executing and performed some preliminary processing of the database.

When you switch from design mode to run mode, the design-time instance of the object is destroyed and a *run time instance* is created. This run time instance is destroyed and a new design-time instance is created when your application terminates and goes back to design mode.

FIGURE 10.34

Properties window for the Future Value control

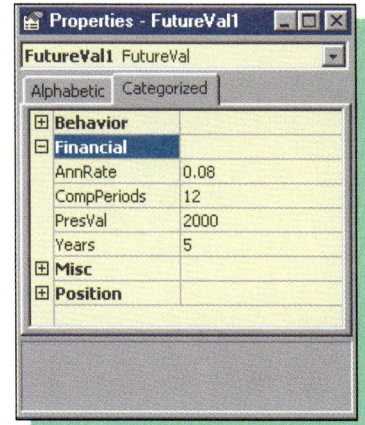

When you save the form, information about the design-time instance is saved along with other information about the form. When you open the project later in VB, the information previously saved is used to create new design-time instances of each control. These ideas are summarized in Figure 10.35. You will see later why it is important to understand that there are both design-time and run time instances of a control.

Creating a UserControl Class

We now turn our attention to the process of creating a new user control. We will construct the Future Value control shown in Figure 10.32. As mentioned at the beginning of this section, we will not cover everything there is to know about the UserControl object. An excellent source for additional information is Chapter 9 of the *Visual Basic Component Tools Guide*.

Creating a UserControl Class and a Project Group

To this point in the text we have been creating "Standard EXE" projects. A UserControl class must be created using a different type of project—the "ActiveX Control" project type. Each ActiveX Control project can define one or more UserControl classes. However, a UserControl class cannot execute within the ActiveX Control project; that is, the ActiveX Control project allows you to define the class, but not to create or execute the object. The UserControl must be added to a form in a Standard EXE project in order to execute. This might seem to make construction and testing difficult, but VB helps simplify these tasks by providing project groups. **A *project group* consists of one or more VB projects.** The .vbg file extension is used to identify project groups. The project group for our example consists of one Standard EXE project and one ActiveX Control project. Only one of the projects can be active at any given time, but you can easily switch between the two.

Figure 10.36 shows the New Project dialog box with the ActiveX Control project type selected. Clicking OK causes VB to create a new ActiveX Control project with a single UserControl class; the result appears as shown in Figure 10.33.

At this point we add a single label and text box (named txtPV) to the UserControl. We do this the same way one adds a label and text box to a form in a Standard EXE project. The UserControl now appears as shown in Figure 10.37.

FIGURE 10.35

Design-time and Run-time instances of UserControls

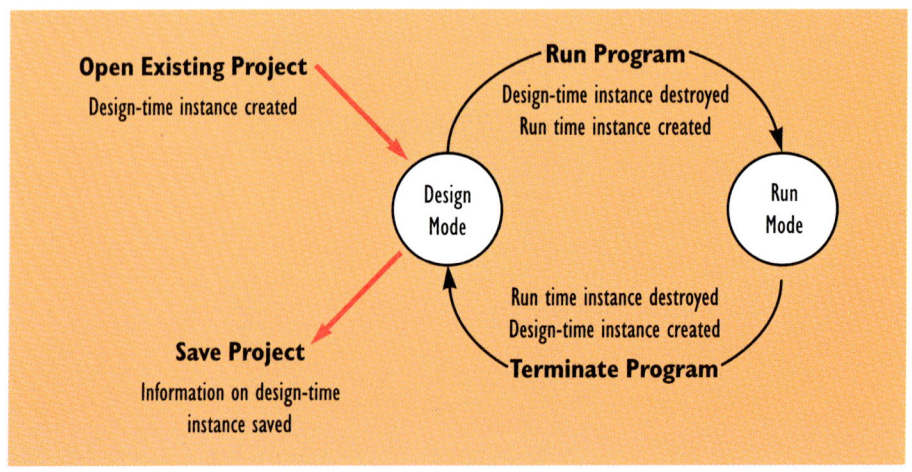

FIGURE 10.36

Selecting the ActiveX Control project type

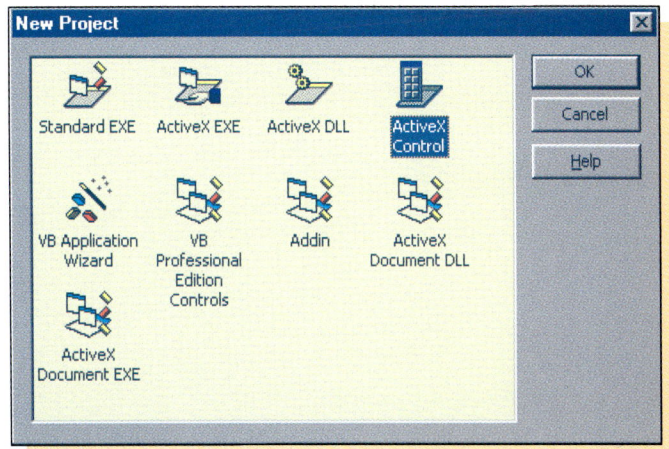

FIGURE 10.37

The UserControl after adding a label and text box control

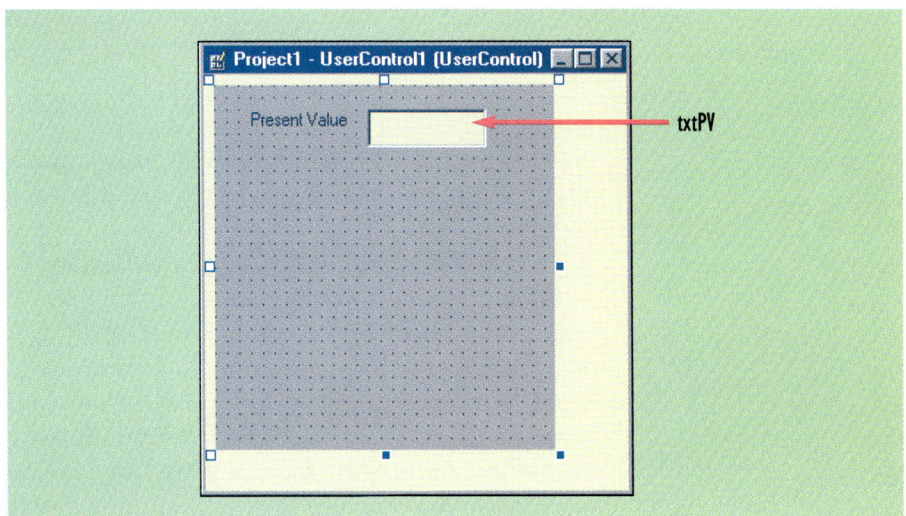

Before adding any more components to the UserControl, let's add a Standard EXE project to form a project group. This second project will let us test our control. To add the Standard EXE project, we select A_d_d Project… from the _F_ile menu (not _N_ew Project…, which would close our ActiveX Control project). After selecting A_d_d Project…, the New Project dialog box (Figure 10.36) is displayed. We select the Standard EXE project type and click on Open. This adds a new project to our project group, and the Project Explorer window now appears as shown in Figure 10.38.

Before we save the project group, we need to set some ActiveX Control project properties. We click on Project1 in the Project Explorer window and then select Project1 Prop_e_rties… from the _P_roject menu, which causes VB to display the Project Properties dialog box shown in Figure 10.39. We fill in the Project

FIGURE 10.38

The Project Explorer window after adding the new project

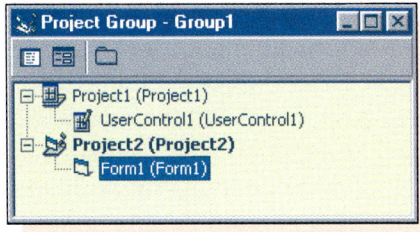

FIGURE 10.39

The UserControl Project Properties dialog box

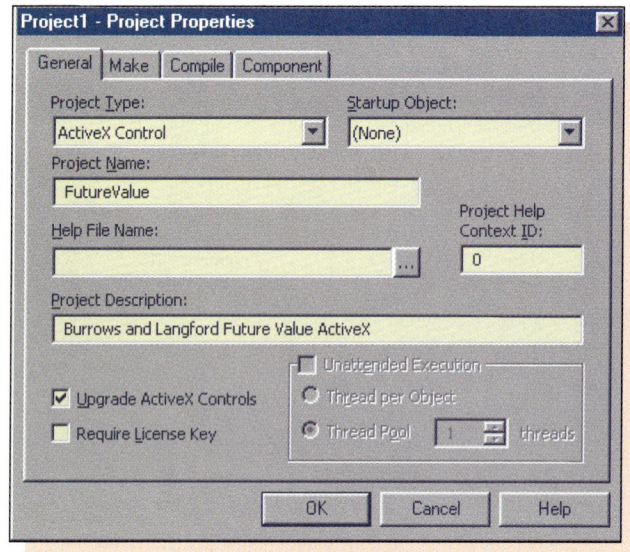

Name and Project Description text boxes as shown. The project name will simply identify the ActiveX project in the Project Explorer window, while the project description will be displayed to programmers who add the control to their projects.

Next, double-clicking on UserControl1 in the Project Explorer window activates the UserControl visual designer, which lets us construct and modify our UserControl. Before proceeding, we use the Properties window to change our control's (Name) property setting to FutureVal.

We now have a project group that includes a partially complete UserControl class definition plus a Standard EXE project to test the UserControl. It's time to save the project group. Selecting Save Project Group from the File menu saves both projects plus the project group file (which is like a project file but includes information on both projects within the group). VB prompts for names for five different files—the UserControl file (.ctl), the UserControl project (.vbp), the test form (.frm), the test project (.vbp), and finally the project group (.vbg).

Now that we have set up and saved the project group, it might make sense to test it (although there is very little functionality). *To test the UserControl, it is necessary to close the UserControl designer window.* This step is critical. If the designer window is open, the control cannot be tested. Recall that a design-time instance of the control is created when you place the control on a form. With the designer window open, VB will not create this design-time instance. To close the designer window, double-click on its name (FutureVal) in the Project Explorer window to make it active, then click the designer window's close box (the X in its upper right corner). When the designer window is closed, VB adds a new tool to the Toolbox for the test project. Figure 10.40 shows the generic UserControl tool icon in the Toolbox.

If you make the form for this test project active and then double-click on the UserControl tool, the new control will be added to the test project. Figure 10.41 shows the test form after adding the new UserControl.

At this point, the Object box of the Properties window for the test form lists two objects: the form (Form1) and the FutureVal control (FutureVal1). If we select the FutureVal control, we will see that it has a (Name) property but it does not have a "Present Value" property. We'll need to create properties for the control later.

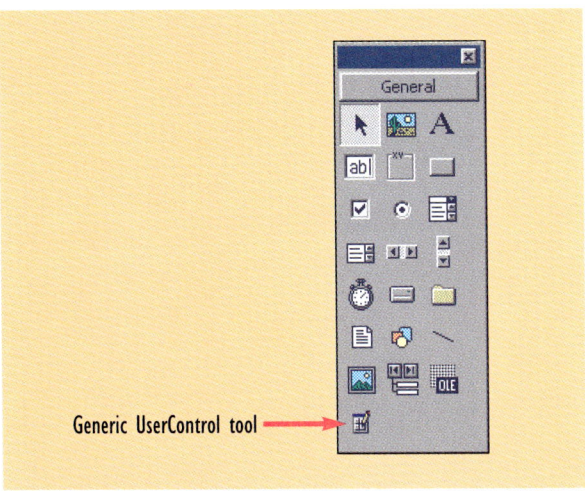

FIGURE 10.40

Generic UserControl tool in the Toolbox

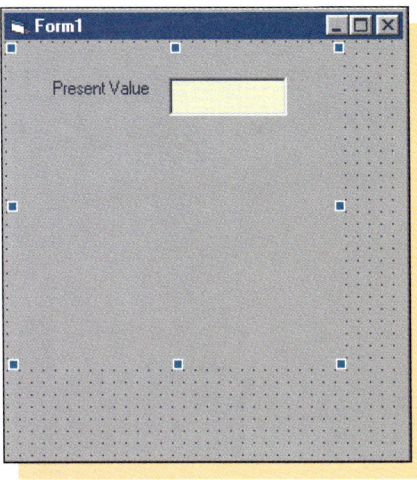

FIGURE 10.41

Future Value UserControl added to the test project

To switch back to UserControl design mode, double-click on the UserControl entry in the Project Explorer window. As you do this, the design-time instance of the UserControl terminates. You can verify this by looking at the test form. As shown in Figure 10.42, the UserControl on the test form is displayed with cross-hatches indicating that the design-time instance is not active. Switching between UserControl design mode and test mode is accomplished by simply closing and opening the designer window. These modes are illustrated in Figure 10.43. Note that test mode is the same as the ordinary design and run modes that we have been using all along; here, we are using them to test our UserControl.

Adding Properties to a UserControl

As you are aware, all controls in VB's Toolbox have properties you can set at design time and/or run time. This capability is also available for UserControl objects. Also, as pointed out earlier, the properties of a UserControl can be displayed in the Properties window and their settings are saved and retrieved

FIGURE 10.42

An inactive UserControl on the test form

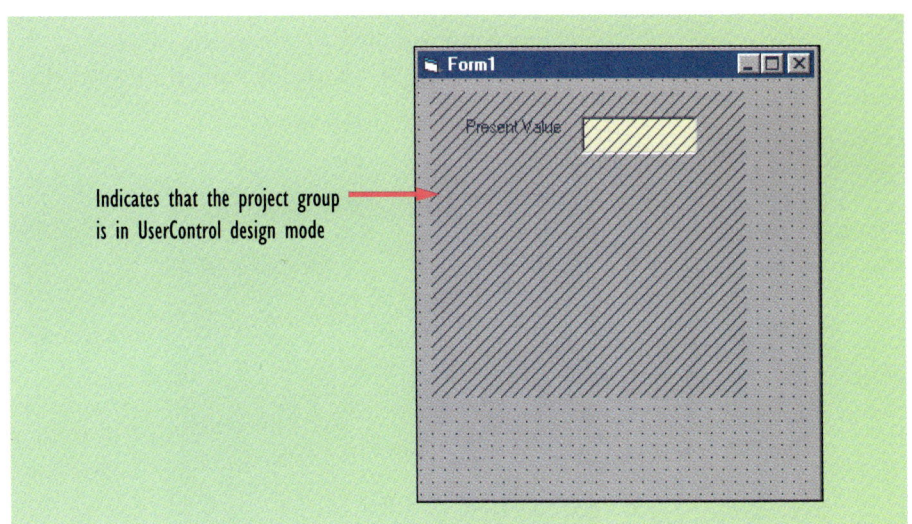

FIGURE 10.43

Switching between UserControl design mode and test mode

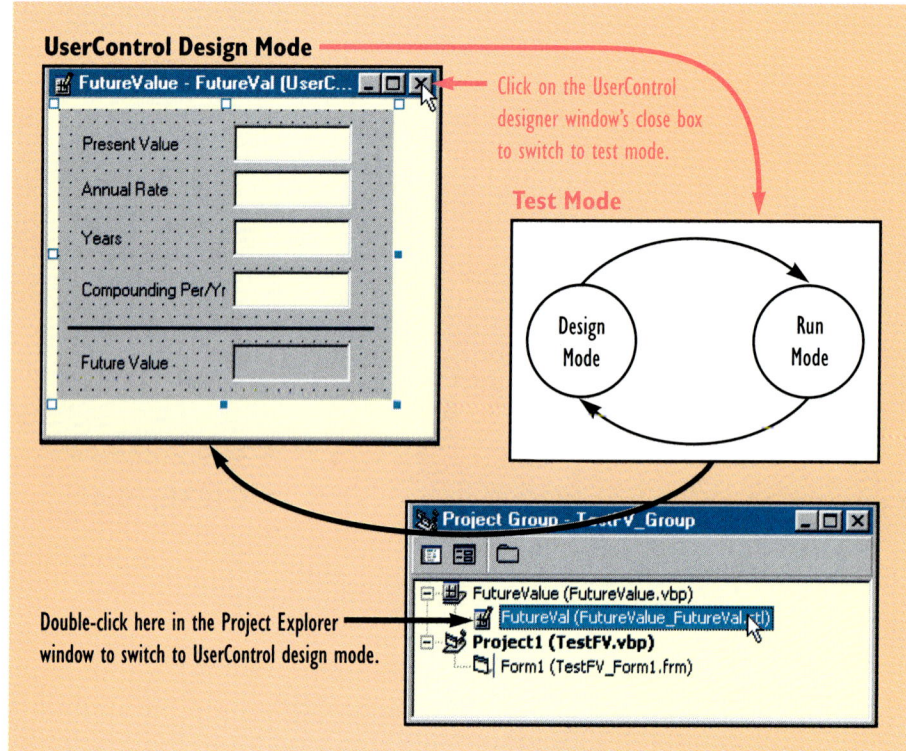

as you start and stop the VB project that contains them. Fortunately, most of this activity is handled by VB, and the designer of the control need only complete a few simple steps.

Let us create a Present Value property for our UserControl. We begin by verifying that we are in UserControl design mode (by double-clicking on the UserControl in the Project Explorer window), and then we open the Code window for the UserControl. Next, we select Add Procedure... from the Tools menu to bring up the Add Procedure dialog box. We enter PresVal for the Name, select the Property option in the Type box, and select the Public option in the Scope box, as shown in Figure 10.44.

Clicking OK causes VB to create the Property Get and Property Let procedures as shown in Figure 10.45. These two procedures are just like the Property Get and Property Let procedures discussed in Section 10.4. The Property Get procedure is called whenever the value of the property needs to be retrieved. For example, if the control is named FutureVal1, the statement

    MsgBox FutureVal1.PresVal

FIGURE 10.44

Adding a new property to the UserControl

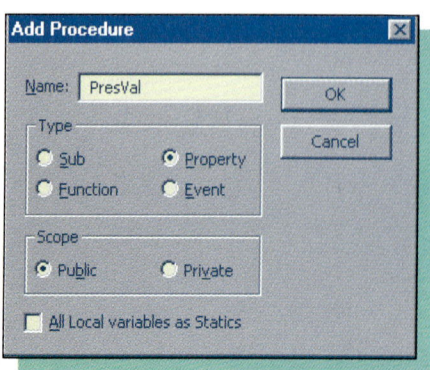

FIGURE 10.45

Property Get and Property Let procedures for the PresVal property

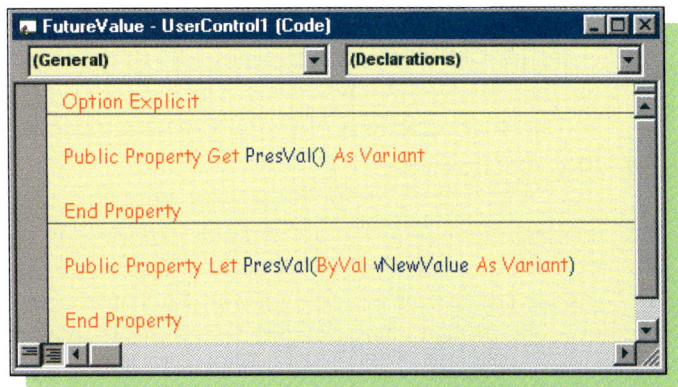

would cause the Property Get procedure to be executed. The Property Let procedure is executed whenever the value of the property needs to be changed. For example, the statement

FutureVal1.PresVal = 1000

would cause the Property Let procedure to be executed.

In Section 10.4 we declared explicit instance variables in the class module's general declarations section to store values. In a UserControl we could also use this approach. However, since there are visual components on the UserControl (text boxes and labels), we can use them to store the current value of the property.

In Figure 10.46 you can clearly see that the Present Value text box (txtPV) is being used to store the value of the Present Value property. When the value of the property is needed, the Property Get PresVal procedure is executed, and the value from the text box is retrieved and then returned via the procedure name (PresVal). When the value of the Present Value property needs to be changed, the Property Let PresVal procedure is executed, and the parameter vNewValue provides the new value that is stored in the text box. But there is a second statement in the Property Let procedure.

PropertyChanged "PresVal"

PropertyChanged is a built-in VB procedure that informs the UserControl object that a property's setting has changed. This causes the UserControl to automatically update the Properties window with the new setting. The property to be updated is specified as the argument in the procedure call (PresVal in this case). The procedure also signals the UserControl that the new property value needs to be saved.

FIGURE 10.46

Complete Property Get and Property Let procedures for the PresVal property

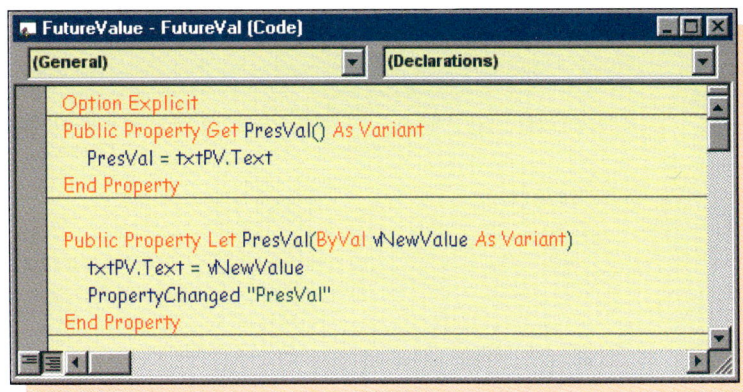

To complete the code for the PresVal property we need to write three more event procedures. These procedures are for the InitProperties, ReadProperties, and WriteProperties events. These three events are concerned with creating and preserving values of properties as a project is opened and closed. The InitProperties event occurs when the programmer first creates the UserControl (by placing it on the form). We will use it here to provide a default value for the PresVal property. The ReadProperties event is like the InitProperties event except it occurs when the second and subsequent instances of the UserControl are created. (Recall that instances of controls are destroyed and created each time the project changes from design mode to run mode, and vice-versa.) We will use the ReadProperties event to retrieve the saved value of the PresVal property. Finally, the WriteProperties event occurs when a design-time instance of the UserControl is destroyed. We will use this event to save the current value of the PresVal property. Note that this event only happens when the project switches from design mode to run mode. If it also occurred when the run time instance was destroyed (that is, when the project went from run mode to design mode), then any new value of PresVal that the user entered during run time would be saved as the current property value. You know from experience that this is not what you expect to happen in your applications. The timing of these events is summarized in Figure 10.47.

Important events associated with the UserControl object are summarized in Table 10.2.

The InitProperties, ReadProperties, and WriteProperties event procedures for our UserControl class are shown in Figure 10.48. To create these event procedures, we select UserControl in the Code window's Object box and the

TABLE 10.2 Key UserControl events

Event	Behavior
Initialize	*This event occurs every time an instance of a UserControl object is created. This includes both design-time instances and run time instances. This is the first event that occurs for an object.*
InitProperties	*This event only occurs once—when the UserControl object is first placed on a form. Generally used to establish initial values for properties.*
ReadProperties	*This event occurs the second and subsequent times an instance of a UserControl object is created. Generally used to read property values from the PropertyBag object.*
Resize	*This event occurs every time a UserControl object is re-created or resized (at both design time and run time). Generally used to resize the components that make up the control as appropriate.*
WriteProperties	*This event occurs whenever a design-time instance of a UserControl object is destroyed and one or more properties have been changed. Generally used to write the current property values to the PropertyBag object.*
Terminate	*This event occurs whenever a UserControl object is destroyed. Generally used to perform any activities (other than saving property values) associated with a UserControl object as it is being destroyed.*

FIGURE 10.47

Timing of the InitProperties, ReadProperties, and WriteProperties events

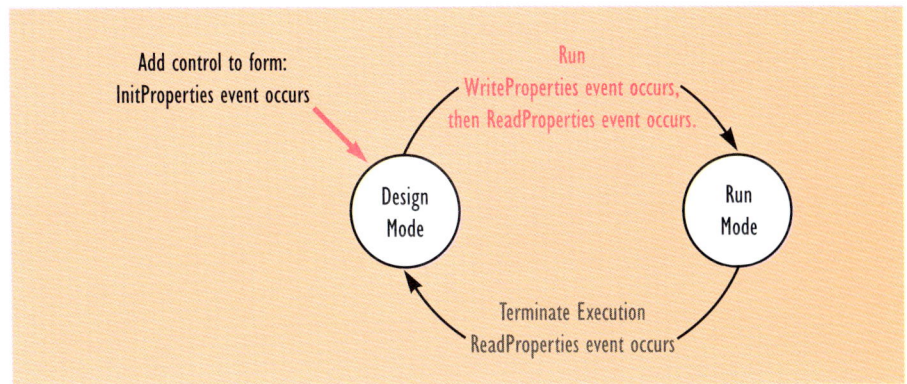

desired event in the Procedures/Events box, then type the statement in the procedure template that VB creates.

Before proceeding with the construction process, let us pause to go step-by-step through each event procedure in Figure 10.48 and examine what is happening. It is really not very difficult, but each single statement causes a chain of processing steps to occur.

The UserControl_InitProperties Event

The following actions occur when the programmer first places a UserControl on the form at design time:

1. The InitProperties event occurs.
2. The statement PresVal = 1000 is executed.
3. The assignment statement in step 2 causes the Property Let procedure to be executed with the value 1000 being passed as an argument.
4. The parameter vNewValue holds the value 1000, which is stored in the Text property of the txtPV Text box (see Figure 10.46).
5. The PropertyChanged procedure is called, which causes two things to happen. First, the value 1000 is placed in the Properties window for the PresVal property. Second, the WriteProperties event procedure is executed. Details of this event are discussed below.

You can see that one simple statement (PresVal = 1000) produces a lot of activity.

FIGURE 10.48

InitProperties, Read-Properties, and WriteProperties events for Future Value UserControl

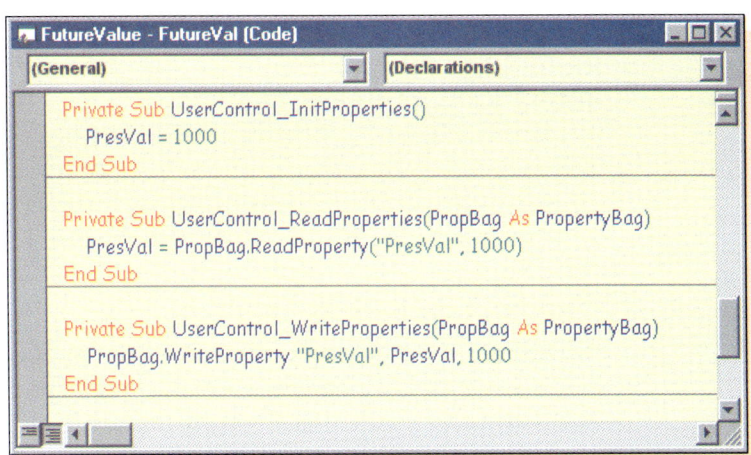

The UserControl_ReadProperties Event

The PropertyBag object holds information about the run time and design-time instances of a UserControl as they are destroyed and created. The ReadProperty method associated with the PropertyBag object retrieves saved values, and the WriteProperty method associated with the PropertyBag object saves values.

The following steps take place when the ReadProperties event occurs.

1. The ReadProperty method of the PropertyBag object is executed. The first argument is the name of the property stored in the PropertyBag object ("PresVal" in this case). The second argument is a default value to use if the property is not found in the PropertyBag.
2. Either the retrieved value or the default value is then stored in the PresVal property.
3. As a result of step 2, the property's Property Let method is executed. As discussed above, this causes the text box (txtPV) to be updated, and the property in the Properties window is updated.

The UserControl_WriteProperties Event

The following steps take place when the WriteProperties event occurs:

1. The PropertyBag's WriteProperty method is executed. The name of the property ("PresVal") is the first argument, the current value of the property is the second argument, and a default value is the third argument. This causes a property value to be written to the PropertyBag object.
2. The second argument in the WriteProperty method refers to the property (PresVal). This reference causes the property's Property Get procedure to be executed. The Property Get procedure retrieves the current value from the text box (txtPV), and this value is written to the PropertyBag.

Placing Properties into Categories

One final step completes the definition of a property. Recall that you can view the properties in the Properties window either alphabetically or by categories (using the Alphabetic or Categorized tabs). A property of a new UserControl will be categorized in the "Misc" category unless you change its category. Since the function of the Future Value UserControl is related to Finance, we will create a new property category named "Financial" and group the UserControl's properties in that category.

With the control's designer window active, selecting Procedure Attributes from the Tools menu causes the Procedure Attributes dialog box to be displayed, and then clicking its Advanced>> button causes more options to be displayed. Figure 10.49 shows this dialog box. With the PresVal property selected in the Name dropdown list box, we replace the text "(None)" in the Property Category combo box by typing "Financial". Clicking the Apply button then places the PresVal property in the new Financial category.

Testing the UserControl

Now that we have completely defined one property, it's a good time to test our UserControl. We should expect the PresVal property to appear in the Properties window (both alphabetically and under the Financial category). We should also be able to change the setting of the property in the Properties window and see the new setting show up in the control. Finally, we should be

FIGURE 10.49

Procedure Attributes dialog used to place properties in specific categories

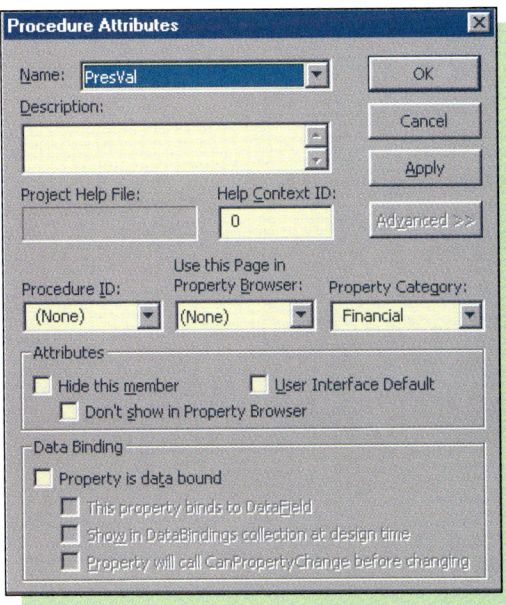

able to run the test project and directly edit the property value in the text box. However, when we stop the application, the setting of the PresVal property should revert back to its design-time value in the Properties window.

To test the UserControl, we first close the designer window by clicking on the close box. This removes the crosshatch pattern on the test form, indicating that the design-time instance of the object now exists on the form. The form and its Properties window now look like the ones in Figure 10.50.

Figure 10.51 shows that when we view the properties by category, the PresVal property appears in the Financial category as expected.

When we change the setting of the PresVal property in the Properties window to 2000, the new value automatically appears on the UserControl as shown in Figure 10.52. Note that VB automatically initiates the set of events that cause

FIGURE 10.50

Test form and Properties window with Future Value UserControl selected

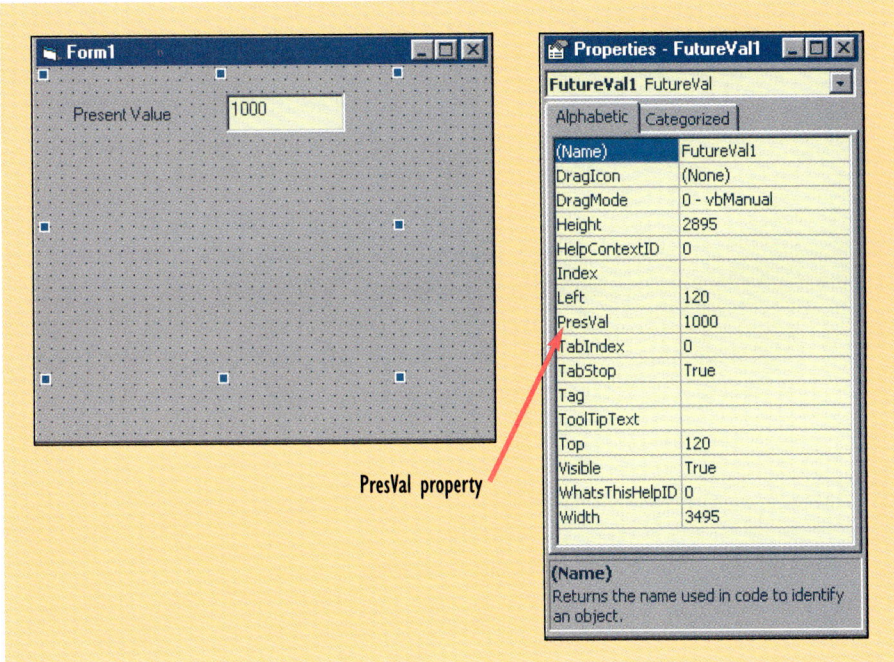

FIGURE 10.51

PresVal property shown under the Financial category

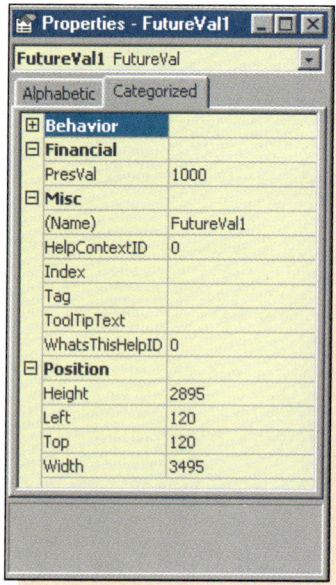

FIGURE 10.52

Changing the value of the PresVal property in the Properties window causes the value in the text box to change accordingly

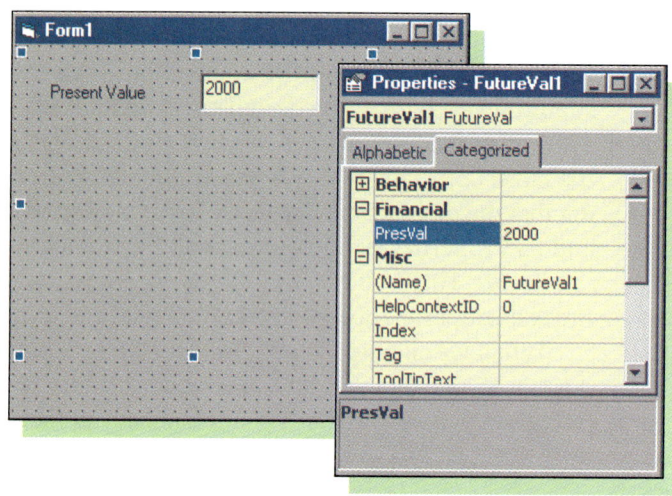

the UserControl to be updated whenever it detects a change in the Properties window. The first procedure that is executed is the Property Let procedure for the PresVal property, and this starts the series of events described previously.

Finish Adding Properties

The remaining three properties are added to the UserControl by following the steps previously described. The complete UserControl design window is shown in Figure 10.53, and the code defining all four properties is shown in Figure 10.54.

As you can see, all the properties are handled the same way within the code. That is, each property needs Property Get and Property Let procedures that store and retrieve values from appropriate text boxes, each property needs to be initialized, and each property needs to be saved and retrieved from the control's PropertyBag object.

Adding Behavior

The final step in defining this UserControl class is to add a method that calculates and displays the future value. To do this we follow the same process as

FIGURE 10.53

Complete design window for Future Value UserControl

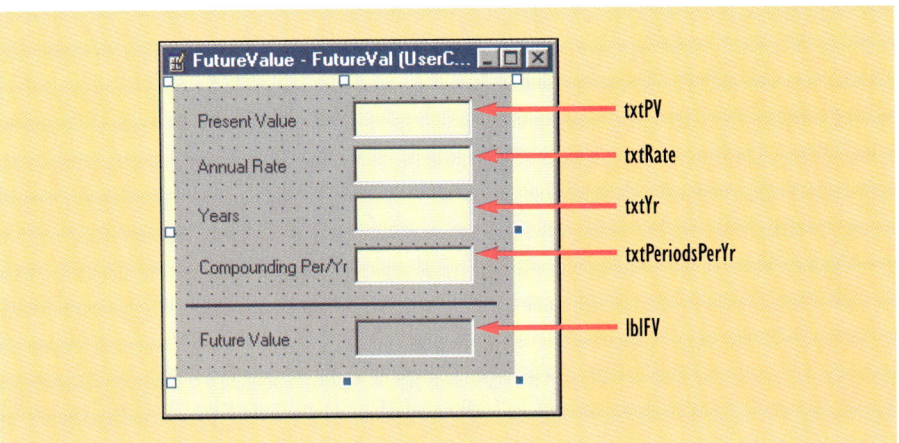

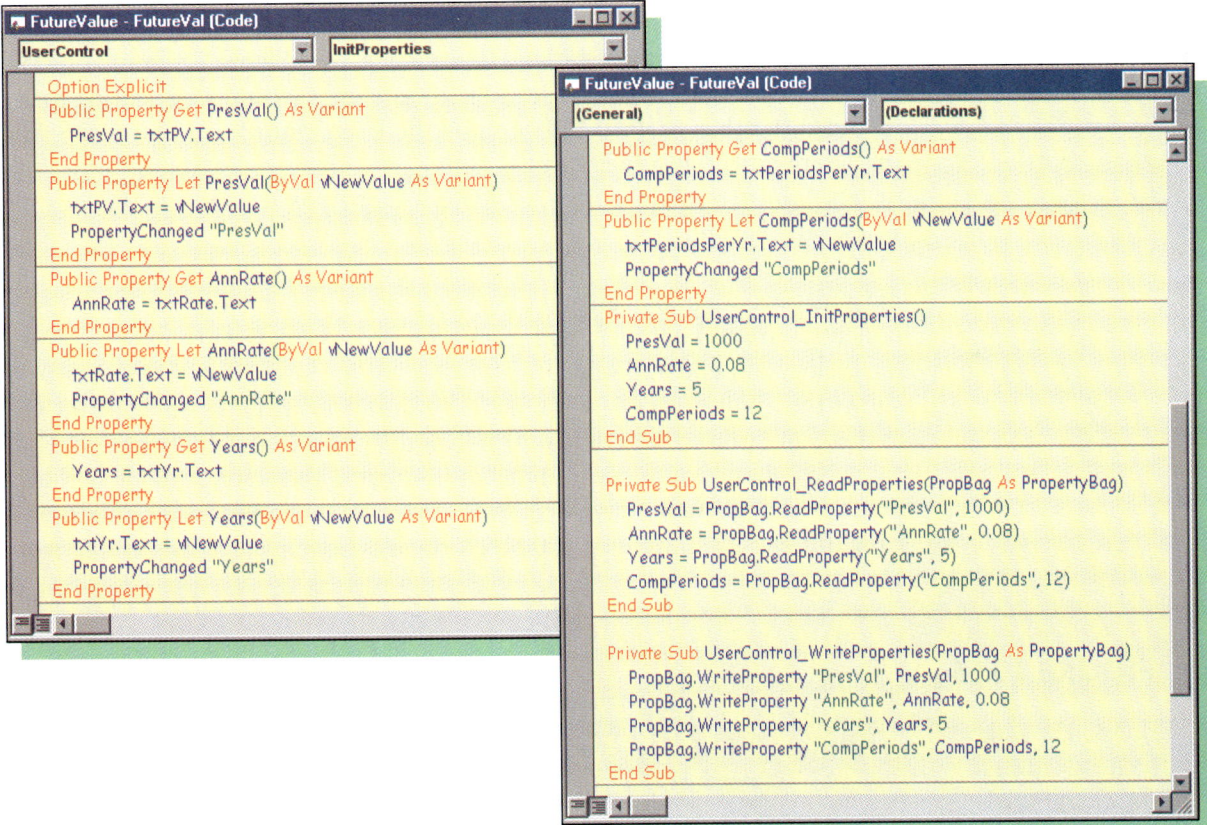

FIGURE 10.54 Code defining properties for the Future Value UserControl

we did with application objects in Section 10.4; that is, we simply add a public procedure to our UserControl object. Figure 10.55 shows this procedure.

Note that the formula that computes the future value uses all four properties. Each time a property is referenced in this way, the property's Property Get procedure is executed (which in this case gets the value from the text box). As a more efficient alternative, the procedure could have referred to the text boxes directly. However, the code as shown in Figure 10.55 is easier to read and understand, and thus is probably the best approach. It also continues to work properly even if, for some reason, the author decides to store the property values somewhere other than the text boxes.

FIGURE 10.55

Code for the UserControl's Calculate event procedure

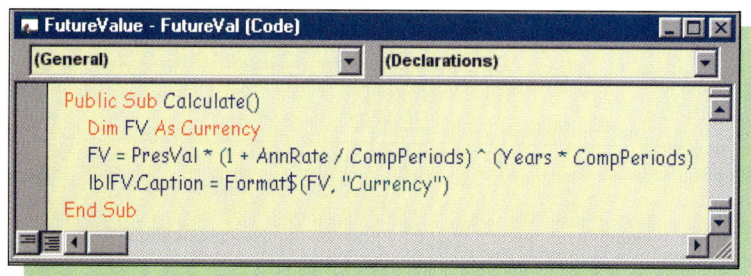

To test this code, we need to add a command button to the test form. The code for this button, shown in Figure 10.56, simply executes the UserControl's Calculate method.

Making an Independent ActiveX Control

After creating and testing our UserControl, we save the project group one last time and then compile the UserControl into an .ocx file so it can be easily included in other projects. To compile the UserControl, we first make sure the UserControl designer form is active, and then select Ma_k_e FutureValue.ocx... from the _F_ile menu. A File Save dialog box lets us save the .ocx file wherever we want.

Now we can add the UserControl to the Toolbox of any VB project. To illustrate this, we first open a new Standard EXE project. Next, we select C_o_mponents... from the _P_roject menu, then click the Browse button on the ensuing dialog, and find and select the .ocx file for the UserControl. Figure 10.57 shows the resulting dialog with the UserControl we just created. Clicking OK at this point causes the UserControl icon to appear in the Toolbox.

As mentioned at the beginning of this section, there are many more things that can be done with ActiveX controls. If you are interested in these additional capabilities, you may wish to check the *VB Component Tools Guide* from Microsoft.

FIGURE 10.56

Code on test form that executes the UserControl's Calculate method

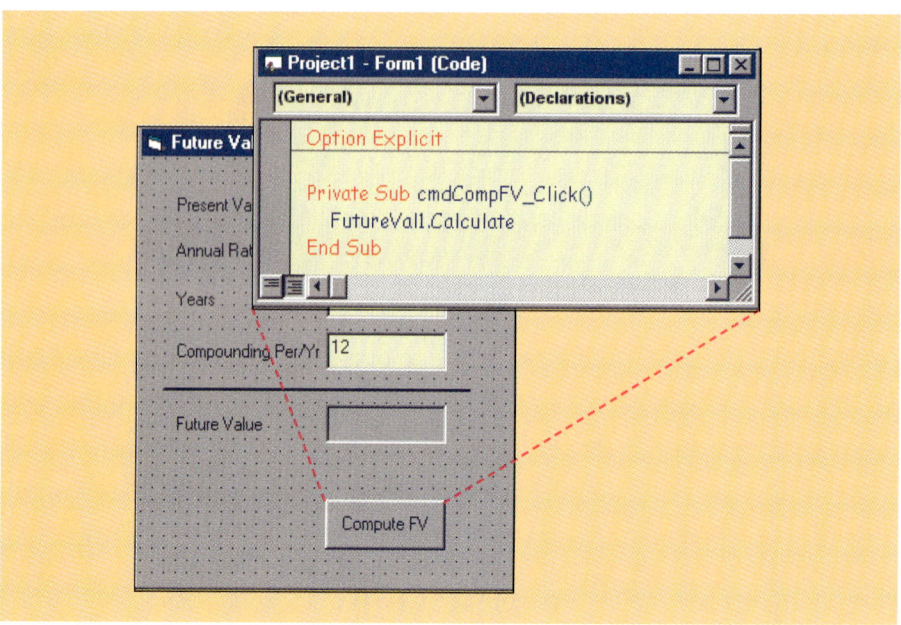

FIGURE 10.57

Adding the UserControl to a project's toolbox

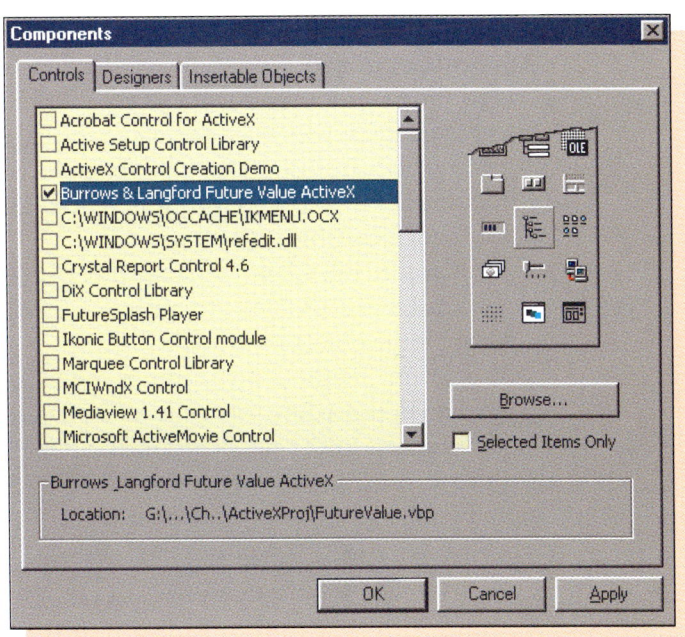

Chapter Summary

1. Programmer-defined data types more accurately match the data of the application, which improves program readability. Likewise, objects—software components that combine variables with their actions—can improve the efficiency of program design and maintenance.

2. Programmer-defined data types are compound data types. Using VB's Type statement, the programmer defines a new data type that consists of individually named elements. Each element has its own data type that can be one of VB's standard data types or a previously defined programmer-defined data type. Elements can be simple variables or they can be arrays.

3. Type definitions must be placed in the general declarations sections of forms or code modules. After defining a programmer-defined type, the programmer can declare variables of that type using the Dim, Static, or Public statements just as with any other variable. Likewise, the programmer can declare arrays of the new type.

4. Referencing a variable declared as a programmer-defined data type requires specifying the variable name and the specific element name. The syntax for this is the variable name, followed by a period, followed by the element name. If the variable or its element is an array, then a subscript must also be specified.

5. Objects are software components that include both data and behavior. In object-oriented programming, a class is a template that defines the variables (data) and methods (behavior) of members of the class. A member of a class is an object. An object is also referred to as an instance of a class.

6. A class is defined in VB using a class module. A class module is similar to a code module in that it contains only code. However, a class module can be used only to define the instance variables and methods of a class.

    Instance variables are declared as private, module-level variables in the class module. Methods are written as procedures and functions. There are three general types of methods for a class: accessor methods, initialization and termination methods, and behavior methods.

The purpose of accessor methods is to provide access to the object's instance variables, which are private to the object (hence, not known outside the object). In VB we use the Property Let procedure to store a value in an instance variable, and the Property Get function to retrieve the value of an instance variable.

VB provides the Class_Initialize procedure to store default initial values into instance variables. An object's Class_Initialize procedure is executed when the object is created.

A behavior method is written in the class definition as an ordinary VB function or procedure. Since the method is defined within the class module, it has access to the class's instance variables. Behavior methods define the basic actions that an object can perform (such as an employee object computing its gross pay or an invoice object determining its amount due).

7. Object variables are declared and used in forms and code modules. The project must include the class module that contains the definition of the class. An object is created using a variation of the declaration statements we have used all along. The syntax using a Dim statement is as follows:

Dim *ObjectVar* **As New** *ClassName*

Each object variable represents an instance of the class, has its own set of instance variables, and possesses the methods defined by the class.

Methods are invoked by specifying the object variable name, a period, and a method name. For example, to set an Employee object's name to "H. Tamura", we might use the statement

Employee1.Name = "H. Tamura"

and to display the employee's gross pay, we might use the statement

MsgBox Employee1.GrossPay

In the foregoing statement, Employee1 could be a salaried, an hourly, or a commissioned Employee object. The object possesses a method for determining its gross pay, and the methods are likely different for each object class. However, this message box statement works regardless of the type of Employee object. The ability of different objects to correctly respond to the same method (GrossPay in this case) is called polymorphism.

8. A collection is a special object that can store a group of individual objects. The objects in a collection are called items. A collection has only one property: the Count property indicates the number of items currently in the collection.

A collection object has three methods: Add, Remove, and Item. The Add method adds an object to the collection, the Remove method deletes an object from the collection, and the Item method accesses a specific object from the collection.

The objects in a collection are numbered, starting with 1. An object's number is referred to as its index. The index is used with both the Remove and Item methods to specify which item to remove or access from the collection.

As an alternative to accessing items in a collection by index number, we can also access them by a key. To use this alternative, we must supply additional information when adding an item to the collection. Specifically, it is necessary to include the Item and Key clauses with the Add method, as in the following statement:

ProductCollection.Add Item:=NewProd, Key:=CStr(NewProd.ProdNo)

The following statement illustrates how one might find and display the current inventory of product number 3344:

MsgBox ProductCollection.Item("3344").ProdInvLevel

9. Class hierarchies facilitate the definition of new classes. Subclasses are able to inherit the instance variables and methods of their superclass, reducing the amount of effort needed to define a new class. Unfortunately, VB does not support class hierarchies via inheritance.

10. ActiveX controls provide a way for programmers to develop their own controls for inclusion in the toolbox. ActiveX controls can include other graphical controls such as text boxes and labels and have properties that can be edited using the Properties window. ActiveX controls include a public appearance and interface definition as well as a private implementation definition.

    Unlike application objects, which are defined using class modules, ActiveX controls are defined using UserControl classes. A UserControl class includes a visual designer (that looks like a Form Designer window) as well as a set of properties.

    Design-time and run time instances of ActiveX controls are created and destroyed as a project switches between design and run mode. As instances are destroyed and recreated, the properties of the control must be saved and restored. VB accomplishes this using the PropertyBag object and its ReadProperty and WriteProperty methods. The UserControl object used to implement an ActiveX control responds to its ReadProperties and WriteProperties events to store and retrieve property values using the PropertyBag object.

Key Terms

accessor method
ActiveX control
application object
behavior method
class
class initialization method
class module
collection
compound variable
control class
control class appearance
control class implementation
control class instance
control class interface
design-time instance
graphical object
instance variable
instantiate
method
objects
object variable
polymorphism
programmer-defined data type
project group
Property Get
Property Let
run time instance
template
Type statement
UserControl class

End-of-Chapter Problems

1. How are programmer-defined types and "synchronized" one-dimensional arrays similar?

2. Define a programmer-defined type to represent the following information about an inventory item: an item number (Integer), description (String), quantity (Integer), and location code (String).

3. Write code that declares an inventory variable of the type you defined in problem 2 and stores values in each of its elements.

4. Define a programmer-defined type that includes a warehouse identifier (String), an address (String), and up to 1000 inventory items (as defined in problem 2). Then declare a variable of this type and write the statements to store the warehouse identifier, address, and two inventory items.

5. Assume you want to store the following information on employees: employee number (String), name (String), number of dependents (Integer), and the first name of each dependent (String). Define the data type necessary to do this. State any assumptions you need to make. Is your solution a good "general" solution? Explain.

   Now assume you need to store data for 100 employees. Declare a variable to support this requirement.

6. Assume you have the following type definition:

   Public Type PartInventory
       PartNo **As String**
       Desc **As String**
       PartCode **As Integer**
       QuantityOnHand **As Integer**
   End Type

   Declare a variable that can store up to 1000 PartInventory records. Now assume this array has been populated with data for 500 parts, and write a code segment to find the total QuantityOnHand of parts with a specific PartCode. Allow the user to specify the PartCode value via an input box.

7. How are programmer-defined data types and objects similar? How are they different?

8. What is the difference between a class and an object?

9. Define a class to represent information on an inventory item that includes an item number (Integer), description (String), quantity (Integer), price (Currency), and location code (String). Include methods to set and retrieve the values of the instance variables. Also include a method to return the current inventory value of an item (price times quantity).

10. When is an object's Class_Initialize method executed?

11. How are variables and object references similar? How are they different?

12. Is it possible for the object references in the following two statements to be referring to the same instance variable? Explain.

    Student.Name = "Sue"
    MsgBox Student.StudentName

13. How can inheritance enhance a programmer's productivity?

14. How are arrays and collections similar? How are they different?

15. Explain the term "polymorphism." How does polymorphism enhance a programmer's productivity?

16. Explain the difference and similarities between an ActiveX control and an application object.

17. What is the UserControl design mode and how does it differ from design in the test mode?

18. What does the PropertyChanged procedure do?

19. What function does the PropertyBag object perform in the context of an ActiveX control?

Programming Problems

1. A database named ProdPart.mdb stores information on parts that are used to assemble products. Manufacturers call such a list of parts the product's *bill of materials*. This database is stored in the subdirectory C10\PrgProbs in the code package for this text.

The database consists of three tables. The first table is named Part and includes two fields: PartNo (5-character text) and PartDesc (30-character text). The second table is named Product and also includes two fields: ProdNo (5-character text) and ProdDesc (30-character text). The final table stores the many-to-many relationship between products and parts and is the actual bill of materials. This table is named BOM and has three fields: ProdNo, PartNo, and Qty (Integer). The Qty (quantity) field shows how many of a specific part is used in a product (e.g., two wheels for a bicycle).

Create an application that displays the bill of materials for a specified product. Your program should accept a product number from the user and then display the parts used to assemble that product. An example user interface is shown here. In this figure the grid shows a portion of the parts used to assemble product number 92000, a wagon.

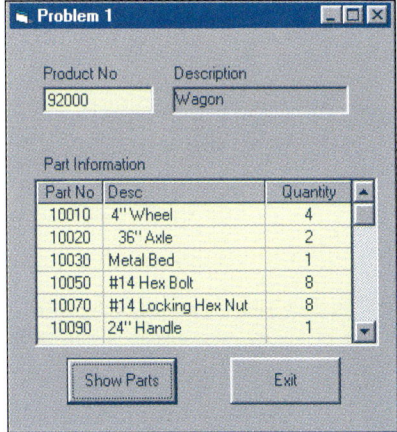

Your program will require an appropriate SQL Select query to create the recordset. When execution begins, your program should transfer this data into an array of a programmer-defined data type (see Project 14). All subsequent data retrieval should be performed using the array.

2. You are to create two class definitions, called Undergrad and Graduate, that represent students. The instance variables for each class are listed here.

Undergrad	Graduate
fStNo	fStNo
fName	fName
fCredits	fCredits
fObjType	fObjType

Each class should define methods to set and report instance variable values. Each class should also define a method that returns the tuition amount. The two classes calculate their tuition differently, as shown in these tuition schedules.

Undergrad Credits	Tuition
1-9	$75/credit
10-15	$875
16+	$875 + $75/credit over 15

Graduate Credits	Tuition
1-6	$125/credit
7-12	$1,575
13+	$1,575 + $125/credit over 12

Your program should create four to six object variables from each class. It should set the instance variables of each object with values you make up. Once the object variables have been created and values have been stored in their instance variables, add the objects to a collection.

The user interface for your application should include a grid to display the instance variable and tuition values for the objects in the collection. A sample user interface for the application is shown here.

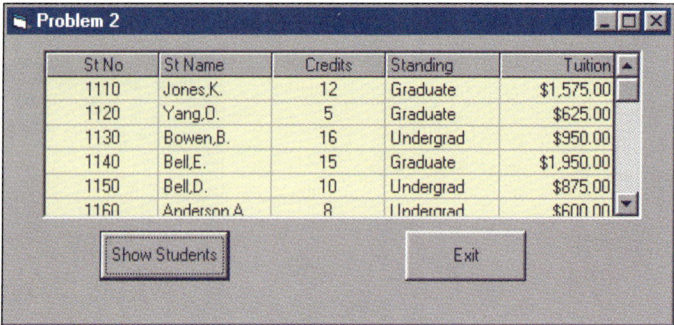

3. Create two classes and objects from the classes as described in programming problem 2. Then add the object references to a collection in such a way as to allow retrieval of object references via the value of the Student Number instance variable (fStNo).

The application should use an input box to get a student number from the user. It should then use this student number to directly retrieve the appropriate object reference and display the values of its instance variables on the form. The figure here shows the application after the user has requested to see information on the student whose student number is 1110.

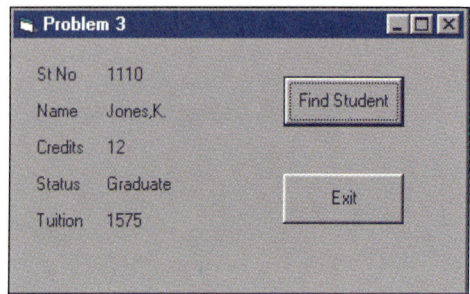

4. A database named DeptEmp.mdb stores information on departments and the employees in each department (a one-to-many relationship). This database is stored in the subdirectory C10\PrgProbs in the code package for this text. The database contains two tables. The first table is named Dept and includes a DeptNo field (4-character text) and a DeptName field (30-character text). The second table is named Employee and includes an EmplNo field (4-character text), an EmplName field (20-character text), a Title field (20-character text), and a DeptNo field (4-character text).

Create an application that accepts a department number from the user and then displays the employees associated with that department. An example user interface is shown below. The figure shows a portion of the employees associated with Department 10000 (Accounting).

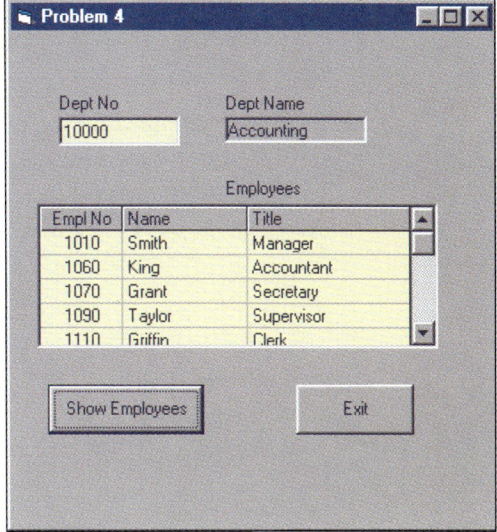

Your program will require an appropriate SQL Select query to create the recordset. When execution begins, your program should transfer this data into an array of a programmer-defined data type (see Project 14). All subsequent data retrieval should be performed using the array.

5. Create an ActiveX control that computes the monthly payment amount for a loan. A sample user interface is shown here.

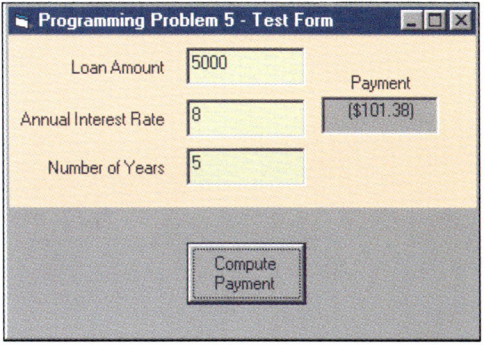

The ActiveX control is in the upper part of the test form. The properties of the control should be placed into a single category. The Properties window for the sample is shown at the top of page 554.

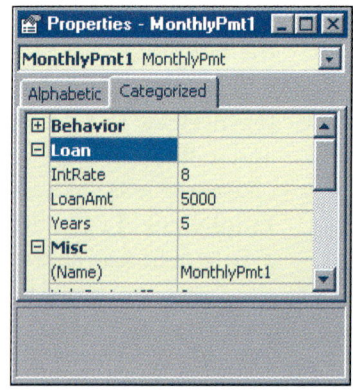

The ActiveX control should have a Calculate method. For example, the Compute Payment button on the test form includes the following statement:

MonthlyPmt1.Calculate

The Calculate method defined for the ActiveX control should use VB's Pmt() function (see online help, search phrase "Pmt function"). Be aware that this function requires the interest rate to be in decimal form, i.e., 10 percent must be represented as .10 when used in the Pmt() function.

appendix A

Debugging

In the process of coding computer applications you will inevitably make mistakes. Some will be readily apparent, as when VB halts execution of the running application and displays an error message. Others may go unnoticed for a long time until a processing problem occurs. When you do discover a mistake—a *bug* in a program—your task will be to locate its source and fix it. This task is known as *debugging*.

We begin this appendix by categorizing programming errors. We then discuss the strategies and tools for locating the source of problems and fixing them. Finally, we discuss the debugging tools provided by VB.

Categories of Errors

There are three categories of errors that can arise in programs: compile errors, run time errors, and logic errors. The category of the error is determined by the type of mistake you make and the way you find out that a problem exists. Knowing which category an error belongs to helps you determine how to begin your attack on the problem (that is, finding and fixing the error).

Compile Errors

Compile errors are also called *syntax errors* because they occur when you violate syntax rules; for example, you misspell a keyword or use a valid statement in the wrong context.

Compile errors are not hard to discover: VB informs you of them by displaying an error message either when you type the statement or when you run your code. In fact, the program will not execute until you have fixed all compile errors.

A compile error can occur as you type a statement. VB checks each new line of code for correct syntax when you enter it in the Code window. Figure A.1 shows this kind of error message.

A compile error can also occur when you run the program. VB cannot detect these errors until it scans the entire code. For example, because you are not required to enter statements in any particular order, the error in Figure A.2 cannot be detected until after you click on the Run tool, which signals the system that you have entered all the statements you intend to enter.

Fixing a compile error generally requires reviewing the correct syntax for the statement, confirming that you have correctly spelled variable names, control names, or property names, and checking that you have not omitted statements altogether.

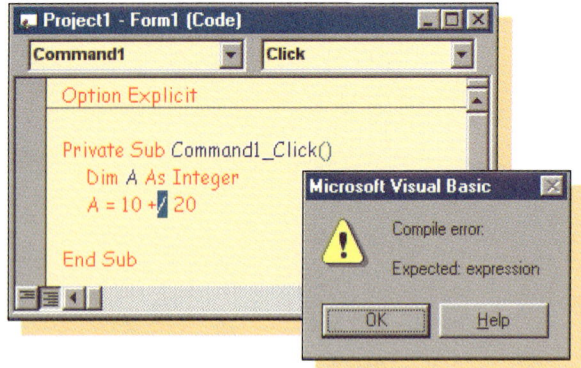

FIGURE A.1

An example syntax error

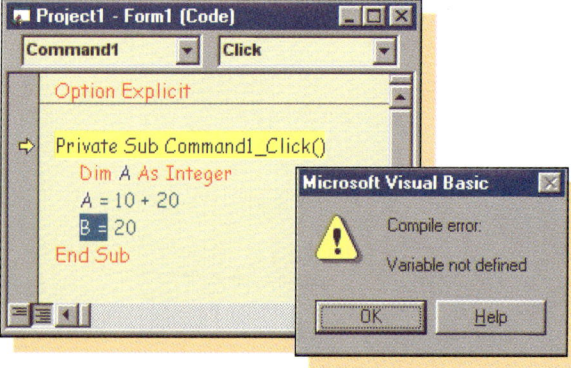

FIGURE A.2

A compile error found when the event procedure is executed

Run Time Errors

As the name suggests, *run time errors* occur while the program is running. They occur when the computer attempts to execute a statement and finds that it is unable to because a situation has arisen that prevents the statement from performing properly. Run time errors can result when the programmer fails to anticipate certain situations that may arise at run time, overlooks important details of how statements work, or has produced a flawed design for the application.

When a run time error occurs, the user cannot miss it: VB halts execution of the program and displays an error message dialog box.

As an example, suppose you have the following statement in a procedure.

Average = Sum / Count

If the variable Count is equal to zero when this statement is executed, a run time error occurs. VB halts execution of the program, then displays the error message dialog box shown in Figure A.3.

If you click on the Debug button in the error message dialog box, VB displays the Code window with the statement that failed to execute highlighted, as shown in Figure A.4. Given the error message in Figure A.3 and the highlighted statement in Figure A.4, there are two possible sources of this run time error. First, there may be a mistake in the code that arrived at the value (0) that is stored in the variable Count. This would be a *logic error*, a category of errors that we will discuss shortly. Second, the fact that Count holds 0 may

FIGURE A.3

An example run time error

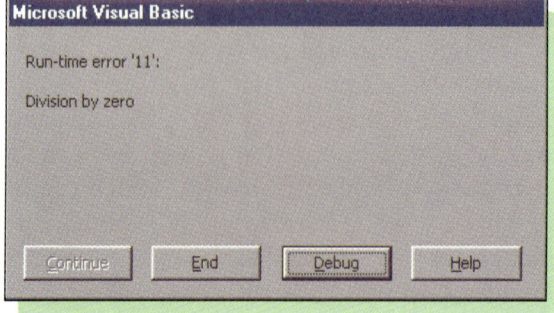

not be a mistake at all. That is, there may be legitimate reasons for the variable Count to equal zero. In this second case, the code needs to be modified to handle this situation. For example, one might write

```
If Count > 0 Then
    Average = Sum / Count
Else
    MsgBox "Unable to compute average"
    Average = 0
End If
```

The programmer could also create an *error handler* to handle this kind of run time error. We discuss error handlers in Appendix F.

End users don't like run time errors. One reason is that they cause execution of the program to terminate. Another is that when the user restarts the program, he or she will probably have to redo some of the work done before the run time error occurred. Not surprisingly, software development companies find they cannot sell programs that frequently terminate with run time errors.

A program may be used successfully for a long time before any run time errors occur. For example, sometimes only a rare combination of input data values causes the expression in the denominator of a division to equal zero. For this reason programmers expect that even programs that have been used successfully for years still have within them any number of bugs that have not yet been discovered.

Logic Errors

The last type of mistake is the *logic error*, which is a flaw in the program design. If the programmer is lucky, a logic error will cause a run time error to occur, which serves as a clue that something is wrong with the program. If the programmer is unlucky, the program will appear to run successfully but will produce incorrect results. For example, if the program miscalculates the total charge on an invoice, the customer will be paying either too much or too little. When this mistake is discovered, someone will be unhappy about it.

Logic errors are generally the most difficult to deal with because the computer does not find them and notify the programmer as it does with compile and run time errors. Instead, the programmer must attempt to discover any logic errors by thoroughly testing the program.

FIGURE A.4

Code window with offending statement highlighted

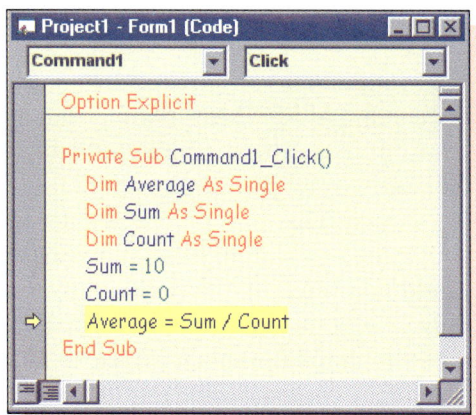

Correcting Mistakes

If a program aborts or runs incorrectly, the world hasn't come to an end. You can view a problem as a challenge. With a good attitude, a strategy to tackle the problem, and debugging tools, you have the ability to locate the error and correct it.

Attitude

The first, and some say most important, aspect of debugging is approaching the task with the right attitude. Debugging can be tedious and frustrating. Not knowing why the computer is rejecting your syntax or not being able to find a logic error can upset the best of programmers. However, by using a good strategy and the right tools, and by adopting a "detective" attitude, you can actually enjoy the process of debugging. After all, there can be a great deal of satisfaction in solving a difficult puzzle.

Think of a problem in your code as a mystery novel. Your task is to determine "who done it." You will be given a number of obvious clues such as error messages or incorrect results. You will also have to find some rather subtle clues that can be investigated with the help of VB's debugging tools. At times you will follow a clue that is deceptive and is no help at all. After some practice, you might become quite accomplished at debugging.

Strategy

Programmers use many different approaches to debug code. The following sections discuss approaches that we have found helpful.

Debug in Small Increments

Do not write the code for the entire application before attempting to run it the first time. Instead, write a small amount of code, run it, and debug it. When you get that code "clean" (no apparent bugs), then write a little more code, run it again, and debug it again.

VB naturally segments your code into small event procedures. Take advantage of this fact and debug each event procedure as you code it. Of course, there will be times when you cannot debug one procedure until another one is working. However, with a little forethought you can often choose wisely the order in which to create procedures: first create those procedures that are needed by the largest number of other procedures. This will help make it possible to debug small segments of code rather than large ones.

Carefully Select Test Cases

When a program appears to run successfully, you cannot just assume that it produces correct results. Always bear in mind that a program may contain logic errors that cause it to produce incorrect results while appearing to run successfully. The only way to gain confidence that the program is producing correct results is to test it. That is, you need to enter *test data* into your application and determine if the application is handling these data correctly.

How should you select the data to use in testing? First, select data that would typically be expected for the application. For example, if your application computes monthly mortgage payments, enter 30 years and an interest rate of 8.7 percent. Manually compute some results and check to see if your application produces the same answers.

In addition to using typical test data, you should also use unexpected values. Users often do unexpected things when they interact with an application, and your application needs to be able to handle these things. For example, what does your application do if the user enters 8.7 for the interest rate when you expected .087? Try to imagine every possible variation of input values and test each one.

As another example, suppose that your code searches a list of employee numbers to find a target value entered by the user. To test the search code, you should enter an employee number that exists and another employee number that does not exist. These should clearly result in different behaviors by your application. If the employee numbers are ordered from smallest to largest in your list, then try to find the first one and then the last one. Also try to find an employee number that is smaller than the first one and another that is larger than the last one. Called "testing at the extremes," this process often identifies places where code fails.

Peer Examination

A final strategy is to show your code to someone else. How many times have you written a term paper and proofread it carefully, only to have your instructor circle spelling and grammar errors? Errors creep in because we see what we think is there, not what is actually there. You are likely to encounter this same problem when you write code. When you are debugging, you see what you intended to write, not what you actually wrote. Someone else reading your code will often find the error quickly because he or she reads literally what is there.

It is also helpful to explain your code to another person. As you do this, you often start to explain a line of code only to ask yourself why you wrote it.

Tools

Most sophisticated programming environments, including VB, provide debugging tools that make it easy to suspend execution of code at any statement so that you can look at the values stored in variables. As an example of the value of such tools, consider the following. As programmer you know the intended effect of each procedure in your project. By examining the values of variables right before a procedure call, then executing the procedure, and then examining the values of variables again, you can check whether the procedure affects the variables as you intended. This provides a quick way of uncovering clues to the source of problems.

VB's Debugging Tools

In the remainder of this appendix we describe VB's debugging environment, discuss the various tools it provides, and give examples of how the tools are used in the debugging process.

Modes

Recall that at any given time, a VB project exists in one of three modes: design mode, run mode, or break mode. In design mode, your application is not running, and you can create controls and write code. In run mode, your application is controlling the system, and so you are interacting with your application, not directly with VB. Break mode is when your application is running but "suspended." VB's debugging tools work in break mode. Many debugging tools "look into" your code and tell you what is going on in memory.

It is easy to tell which mode you are in by looking at VB's Title bar. Figure A.5 shows the three different modes as indicated by the Title bar. The tools on the Toolbar that are shown in Figure A.6 allow you to change modes.

There is another way to enter break mode while your program is running: the [CTRL]+[BREAK] keystroke (press and hold the [CTRL] key and then press the [BREAK] key). The only way to interrupt an infinite loop (in which your program executes a number of statements repeatedly, forever) is to use the [CTRL]+[BREAK] key combination.

Debugging Tools on the Toolbar

VB has a number of debugging tools that are helpful for finding and diagnosing logic errors in your code. These tools can be accessed either by using the Debug menu or the Debug toolbar. To show the Debug toolbar, select Toolbars from the View Menu or right-click on the Toolbar and select Debug from the ensuing popup menu. The Debug toolbar is shown in Figure A.7. We'll describe the tools in the Debug toolbar now and discuss them in more detail later on.

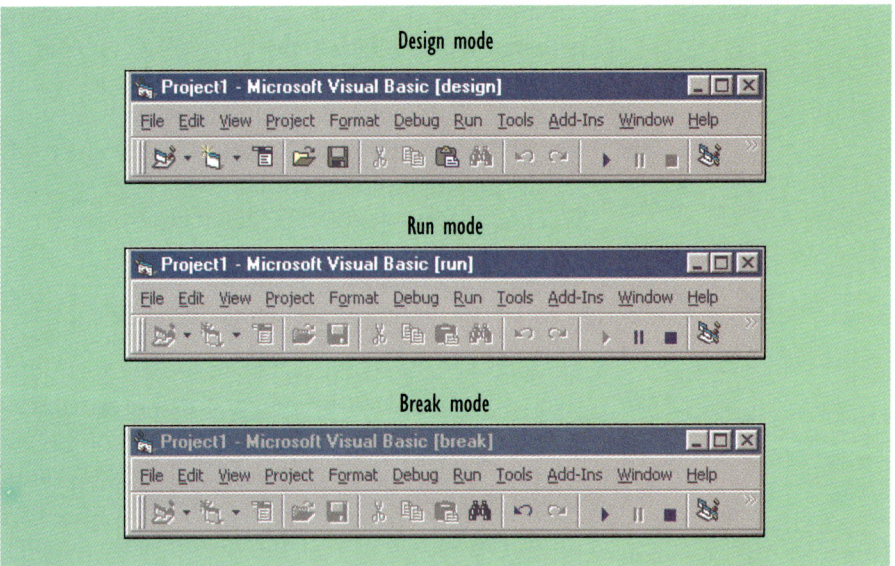

FIGURE A.5

The three modes as shown on the Title bar

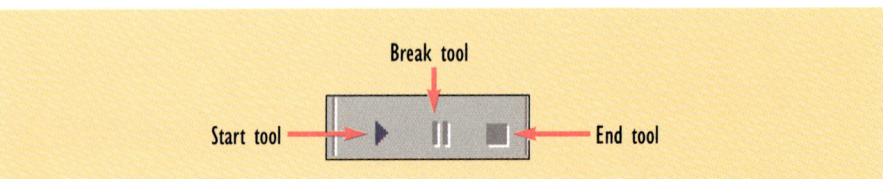

FIGURE A.6

The tools used to change modes

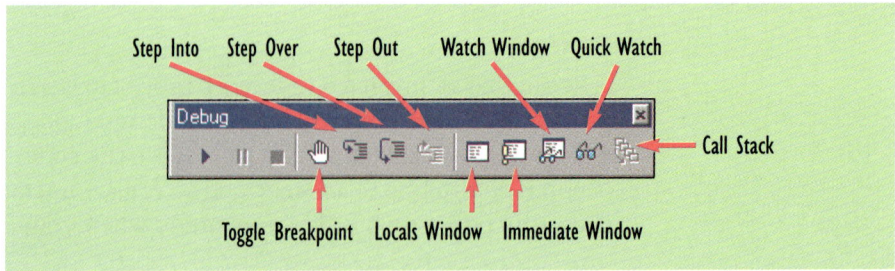

FIGURE A.7

Debugging tools

Toggle Breakpoint tool	Specifies a line or lines of code where you want VB to suspend execution and go into break mode.
Quick Watch tool	Shows the current value of an expression while the application is in break mode.
Call Stack tool	Presents a dialog box showing all the procedures that have been called but not yet run to completion; this dialog box is shown while in break mode.
Step Into/Over/Out tools	Cause code to be executed one statement at a time. Step Into will show execution of individual statements inside procedures that are called, whereas Step Over treats a procedure call as a single statement (it does not show execution of the statements inside the called procedure). Step Out causes the remainder of the statements in a procedure to execute without pausing after individual statements.
Locals Window tool	Automatically displays all of the declared variables in the current procedure and their values.
Immediate Window tool	Provides a place where any statement can be executed immediately. You type in a statement and VB executes it.
Watch Window tool	Shows the values of expressions defined using the Quick Watch tool.

Breakpoints

Breakpoints cause a program to pause and go into break mode. You can set any statement to be a breakpoint. VB suspends execution right before it executes such a statement. You can then use the Immediate window to print values of variables, view the Call Stack window, and check on the values in the Watch Window.

Since the Code window's Margin Indicator Bar is helpful during debugging, we recommend that you turn it on before setting breakpoints. To turn it on or off, select Options... from the Tools menu, then select the Editor Format tab, and click the Margin Indicator Bar checkbox.

To set a breakpoint, click on the line of code where you want the breakpoint to be placed, then click the Toggle Breakpoint tool. Alternatively, you can click in the Margin Indicator Bar next to the statement where you want the breakpoint to be placed. A round "breakpoint" indicator will be placed there to indicate that the statement is a breakpoint, and VB will highlight the statement. Figure A.8 shows the result of setting a breakpoint. To turn the breakpoint off, click on the line of code again and then click the Breakpoint tool, or click on the breakpoint indicator in the Margin Indicator Bar. (This toggles the breakpoint on and off. Each time you click on the tool or breakpoint indicator, the line of code changes to its opposite state: if it was a breakpoint before the click, it will not be after the click, and if it was not a breakpoint before the click, it will be after the click.)

During program execution, when VB encounters a breakpoint it suspends execution and shows the Code window with a yellow "current statement" indicator pointing at the breakpoint statement (Figure A.9). At this point the program is in break mode. You can click the Run tool to resume execution at this statement, or click the End tool to stop execution. Alternatively, you can use the debugging tools.

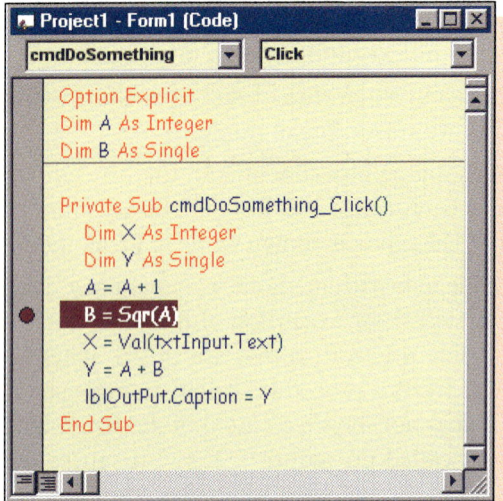

FIGURE A.8

Line of code set as a breakpoint

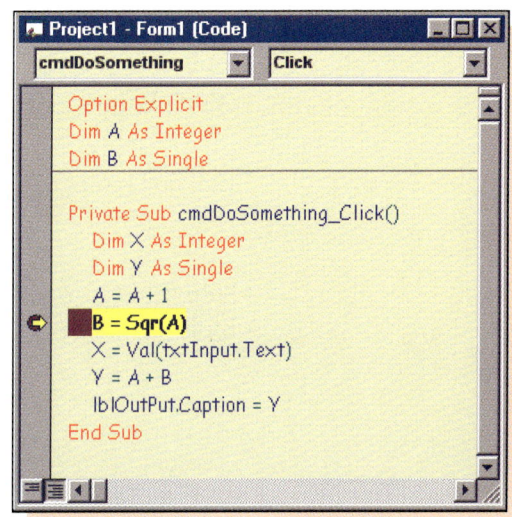

FIGURE A.9

Program code with execution suspended at a breakpoint

Let's suppose you want to see the values of some variables at this point. You can do this in three ways. First, you can simply position the cursor over any variable. VB will display the current value of the variable next to the cursor, as illustrated in Figure A.10. Second, you can click on the Locals Window tool to show the current values of all local variables. Third, you can click on the Immediate Window tool and then enter Print statements to display any variables that are defined at this point in the program. This is helpful for variables that are not visible in the current Code window, and is illustrated in Figure A.11. As a shortcut, you can replace the word Print with a question mark (?).

If you know that the final value of a series of calculations in your program is incorrect, you can set breakpoints at the statements that perform the

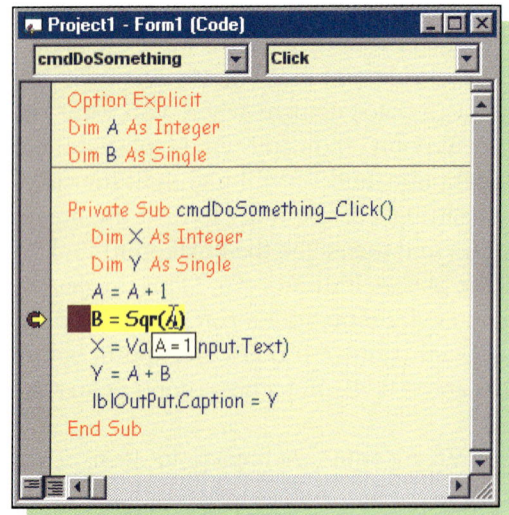

FIGURE A.10

VB displaying the current value of a variable

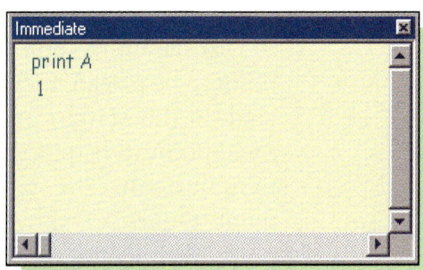

FIGURE A.11

Using the Immediate window to print the value of a variable

intermediate calculations, and check the intermediate values to see where the error is taking place.

Another way to see the values of variables in the Immediate window is to use the Debug.Print statement in your code. This causes the output from the Print statement to appear in the Immediate window. Figure A.12 shows the code with two Debug.Print statements, and the Immediate window.

You can do more in the Immediate window than just print the values of variables. In Figure A.13 the programmer typed the command "error 58" in the Immediate window, which caused an error message dialog box to be displayed. Figure A.14 shows how to print the values of control properties.

Watch Expressions and Quick Watch

A *watch expression* is an expression in your code that you want to monitor as the program executes. For example, suppose you want to monitor the expression Sqr(A) in the code shown in Figure A.15. Notice that the programmer has highlighted this expression.

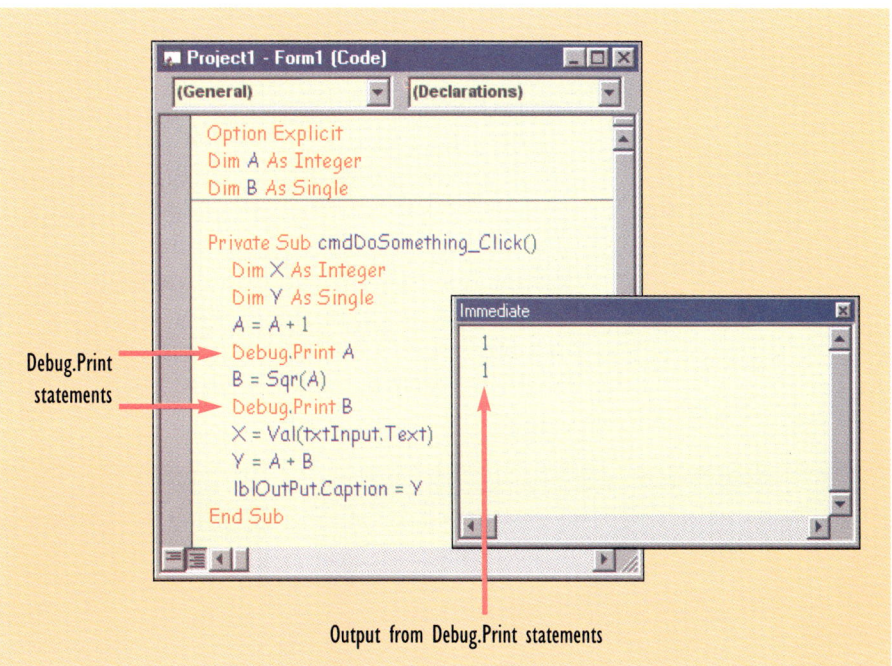

FIGURE A.12

Using Debug.Print statements

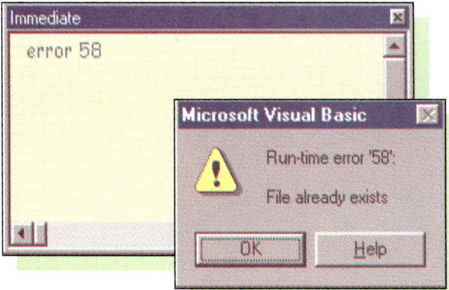

FIGURE A.13

Displaying an error message

FIGURE A.14

Displaying values of control properties

FIGURE A.15

Code with a highlighted expression

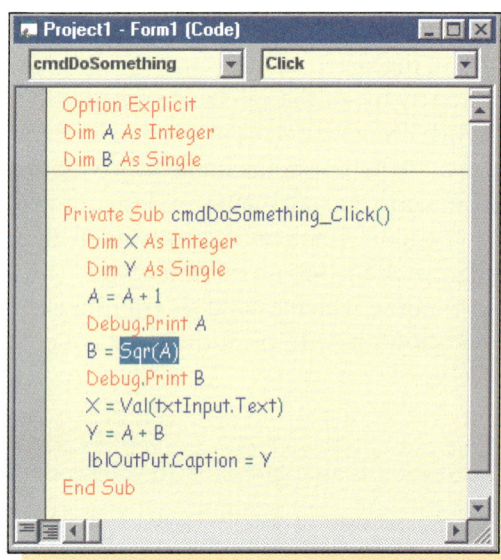

To make this expression a watch expression, select the Add Watch… command from the Debug menu. Figure A.16 shows the Add Watch dialog box. Note that VB automatically places the highlighted expression in the Expression text box.

The Watch Type options at the bottom of the dialog box let you specify the type of watch. In Figure A.16, the Break When Value Changes option has been selected. This means that the program goes into break mode whenever the value of the expression Sqr(A) changes. Figure A.17 shows the Watches window the first time the expression value changes.[1]

The Watch Expression option just *watches* the expression: you have to set a breakpoint or otherwise place the program into break mode yourself, but whenever break mode is entered, the value of the expression is displayed.

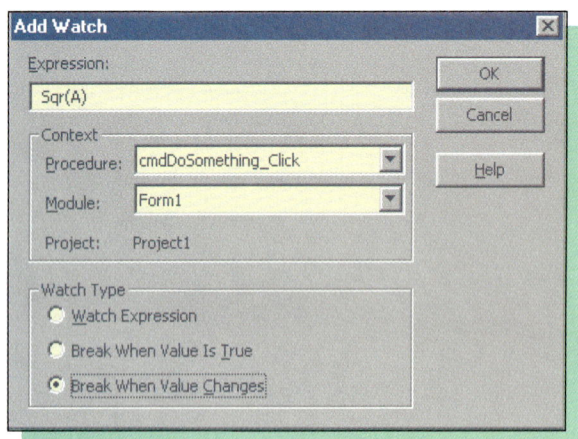

FIGURE A.16

The Add Watch dialog box

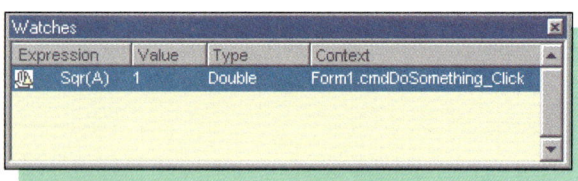

FIGURE A.17

The Watches window in break mode

[1] If you have been viewing the Locals window, the Immediate window, and the Watches window during your debug session, you will note that VB combines all three into one multipane window. You can drag the wide bar separating each pane to change its shape.

You can also use the Quick Watch tool to set a watch expression. When a program is in break mode, you can highlight an expression and then click on the Quick Watch tool. This causes the Quick Watch dialog box to be displayed. Figure A.18 shows the dialog box after selecting the expression A + 1 (while in break mode) and clicking on the Quick Watch tool.

After viewing the value, you can click the Add button to add this expression to the list of expressions in the Watches window. Otherwise, just click Cancel to close the dialog box.

Calls

When your program reaches a breakpoint, it is often useful to see which procedures are active; that is, which procedures have started executing but have not yet completed (general sub procedures and procedure calls are discussed in Chapter 6).

Figure A.19 shows a simple code example with a breakpoint set inside the programmer-defined function FindSqr(). This function is called by procedure cmdDoSomething_Click. Assume this program has started executing and the user has clicked the cmdDoSomething button. When this happens, the code inside that procedure starts to execute. When the FindSqr() function call is encountered, execution of procedure cmdDoSomething_Click is temporarily set aside, and execution passes to the FindSqr() function. Then, a breakpoint is encountered in FindSqr(), program execution is suspended, and the system is placed in break mode.

In break mode, there are two ways to display the Call Stack dialog box. You can either click the Call Stack tool in the Debug toolbar or select Call Stac_k_... from the _V_iew menu. Figure A.20 shows the resulting Call Stack dialog box. This dialog box shows that two procedures are active (have started but not yet completed). If several procedures are active, they are ordered in the list box with the earliest one at the bottom of the list and the most recent one (the one

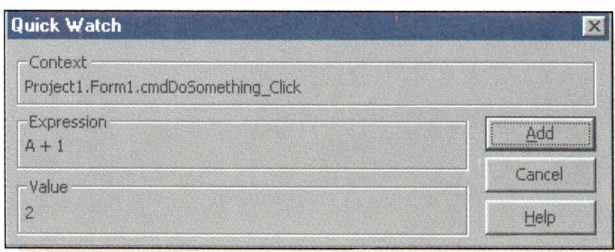

FIGURE A.18

The Quick Watch dialog box

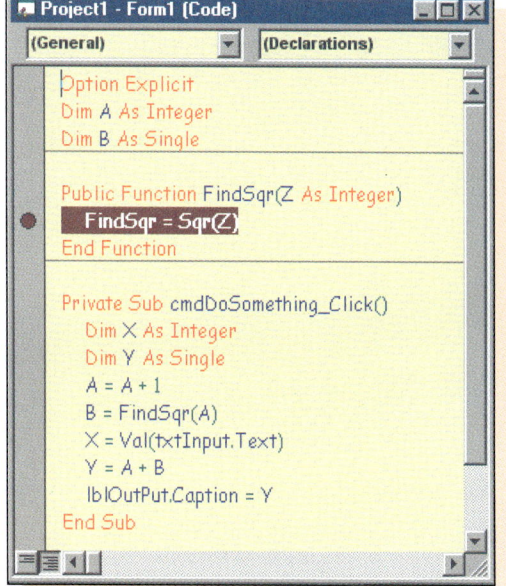

FIGURE A.19

A breakpoint set inside the FindSqr() function

FIGURE A.20

The Call Stack dialog box

being executed when break mode was entered) at the top. In Figure A.20, Project1.Form1.FindSqr was being executed when the breakpoint was encountered and Project1.Form1.cmdDoSomething_Click called it.

Using the Call Stack dialog box, it is possible to trace the execution of complex code and discover the exact sequence of procedure calls that brought execution to the breakpoint.

Step Into

Programmers use the term "stepping" to describe the step-by-step execution of program statements. When you "step through" your code, VB executes one statement and then returns the program back to break mode. You can then use any of the debugging tools to see the effects of that statement. Stepping can be very helpful in determining what is happening in your code.

Stepping "into" means that procedure calls are not treated as meta statements. That is, when a procedure invokes another procedure, VB steps "into" the called procedure to allow you to step through its statements. Figures A.21 through A.25 demonstrate the Step Into process. Figure A.21 shows a breakpoint set in the code. After the program starts to execute and the user clicks the cmdDoSomething button, the breakpoint is encountered. Figure A.22 shows the program in break mode, with the breakpoint outlined.

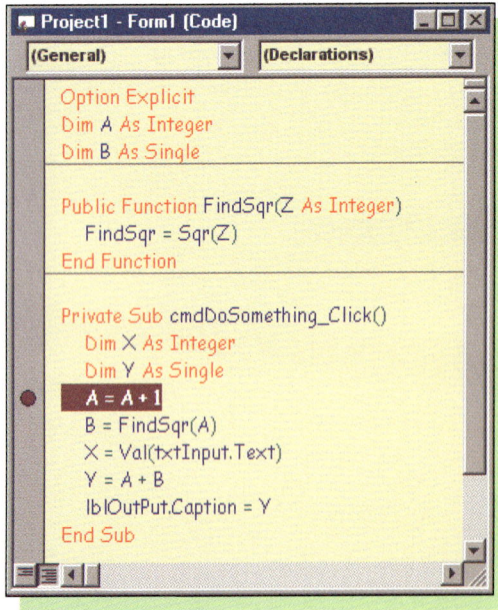

FIGURE A.21

The initial breakpoint set in code

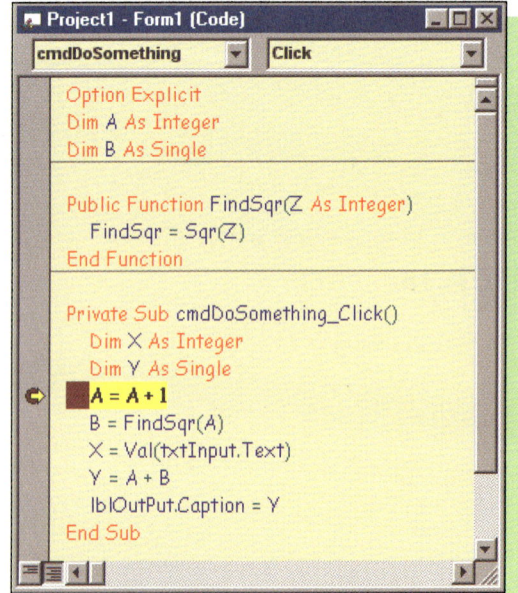

FIGURE A.22

The program in break mode at the initial breakpoint

At this point, the programmer clicks the Step Into tool, which causes the current statement to be executed. After executing the statement, the application immediately goes back into break mode. Figure A.23 shows the code at this stage. Again, the programmer clicks the Step Into tool. Execution now steps into the function. You can see this clearly in Figure A.24.

Figure A.25 shows what happens after the programmer clicks the Step Into tool again. The programmer can continue stepping through the code. To stop the program at any time, the programmer can click the End tool. Clicking the Run tool causes normal execution to resume (stepping stops).

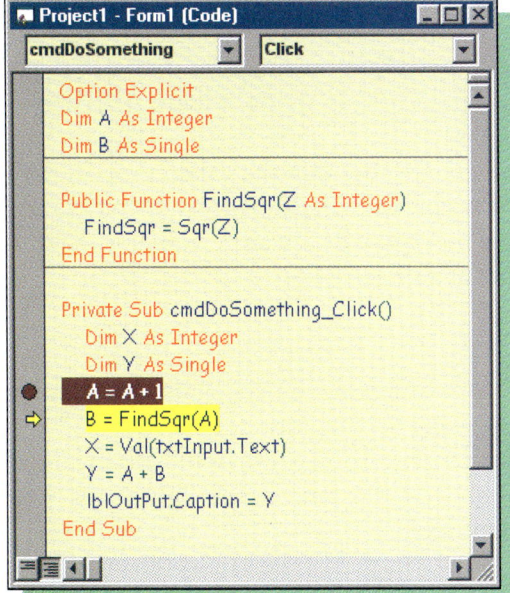

FIGURE A.23

Stepping to the next statement

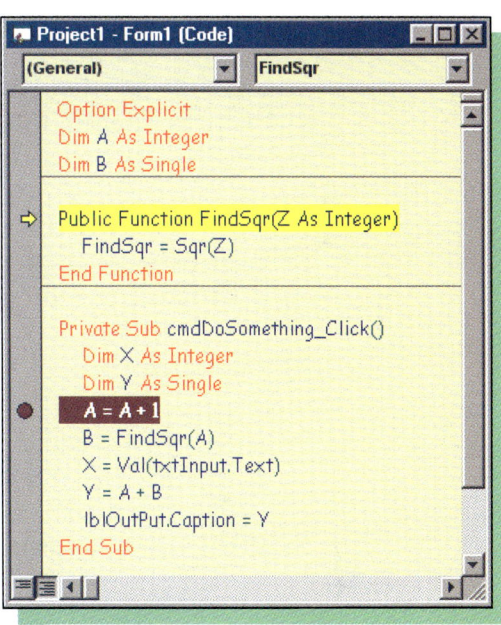

FIGURE A.24

Stepping into the function

FIGURE A.25

Continuing to step through the code

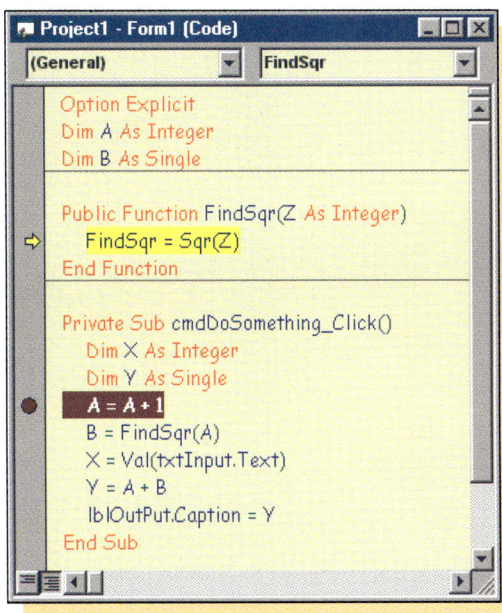

Step Over

Step Over steps through the code one line at a time just as Step Into does, except that procedure calls are treated like meta statements. That is, when it encounters a procedure call, VB executes all the statements in the procedure without stopping and suspends execution when the procedure is complete. Figures A.26 through A.28 show this process.

Figure A.26 shows the code halted at the initial breakpoint. At this point, the programmer clicks the Step Over tool. The statement outlined in Figure A.26 is executed, and the program halts as shown in Figure A.27.

Again, the programmer clicks the Step Over tool. Now the function is executed to completion. That is, all the statements inside the function are executed as if you were not stepping. (Thus, you are executing and "stepping over" the function.) Stepping over a procedure or function does not mean that it is skipped; it is just not executed in step mode. Figure A.28 shows where execution halts in our example.

You might use Step Over when you are sure that the called procedure or function either contains no bugs or is not related to the problem you are trying to diagnose. By stepping over the procedure or function, you don't have to waste time going through it one line at a time.

Step Out

If you have stepped into a procedure or function, you can continue stepping within that procedure or function by using the Step Into tool. However, if you then decide to go through the remainder of the procedure or function without stepping, but to start stepping again as soon as the procedure or function is completed, then you can use the Step Out tool.

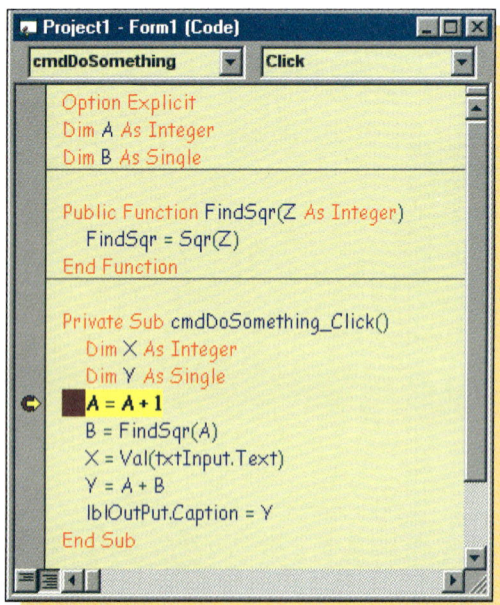

FIGURE A.26

Code in break mode at the initial breakpoint

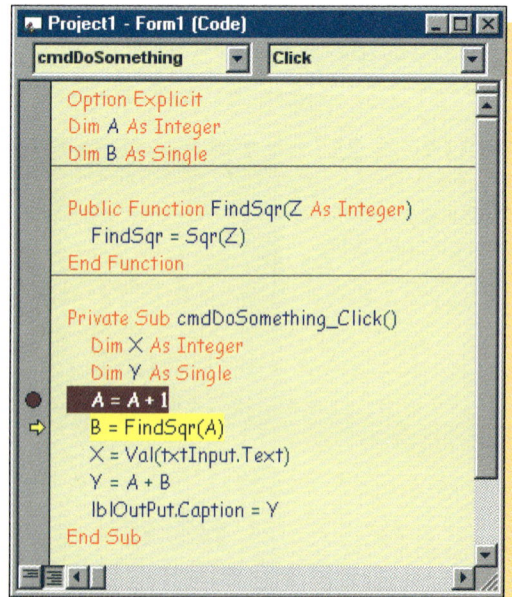

FIGURE A.27

Execution suspended at next statement

FIGURE A.28

Execution suspended after execution of the function

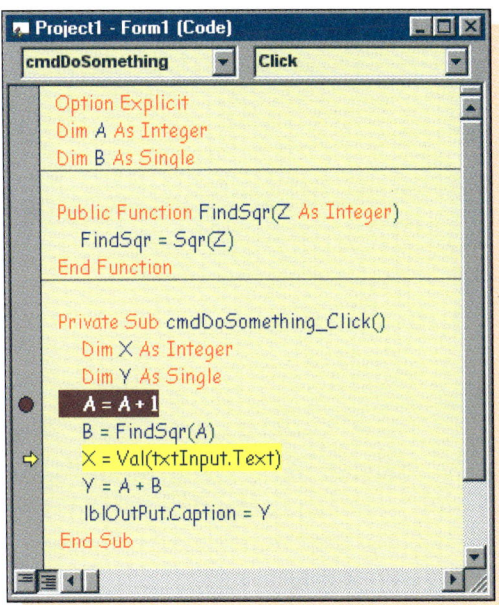

With Step Out, you stay in "step" mode but temporarily suspend this mode for the remainder of the procedure or function. In contrast, if you clicked the Run tool, then step mode would be cancelled and the program would continue to execute normally.

appendix B

The Menu Control

Menu controls function like a hierarchically organized set of command buttons. Grouping commands together in menus helps make a program user-friendly by making large numbers of commands available to the user in an organized fashion. The user simply clicks an item on the Menu bar and a list of choices appears as the menu drops down. In a project with multiple forms, each form can have its own menu.

Appearance and Use

Menus that you create in your VB projects appear just like menus in any Windows application. The Menu Editor dialog box, shown in Figure B.1, is used to create them. There is no Menu tool in the Toolbox.

To create a menu, first make active the form that is to contain the menu—an important first step in a project with multiple forms and code modules. Then bring up the Menu Editor dialog box by selecting Menu Editor... from the Tools menu or clicking the Menu Editor button on the Toolbar. Note that the Menu Editor is available only when a form (not a code module) is the active window.

For each item that you want to appear in the menu, you create and position a Menu control using the Menu Editor. The list box at the bottom of the

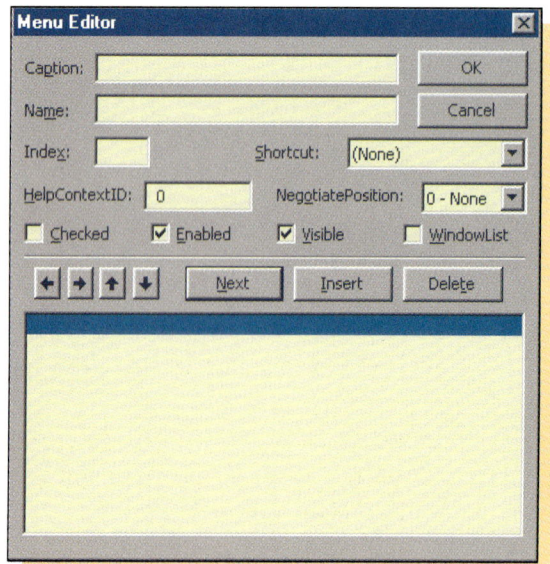

FIGURE B.1

The Menu Editor dialog box

Menu Editor dialog box will list the Menu controls and show their position in the hierarchical menu structure.

When you have created the Menu controls for every item in your menu, exit the Menu Editor by clicking its OK button. Then, to specify what a menu item does when the user selects it, you write an ordinary Click event procedure for its Menu control.

At run time, a Menu bar will appear at the top of your form. The user selects a menu item by clicking it with the mouse, or by using an access key or a shortcut key (discussed later).

Properties

Table B.1 lists some commonly used properties of the Menu control. Note that you cannot use the Properties window to set Menu control properties—you must use the Menu Editor dialog box instead.

> **Convention** Use the prefix "mnu" for the names of Menu controls.

Events

The only event for a Menu control is the Click event. It occurs when the user selects the menu item. Writing code for a Menu control is just like writing code for the Click event of other controls.

Constructing a Menu

Let us demonstrate the creation of menus by stepping through the construction of the GUI for a hypothetical application. The menus and submenus for this form are shown in Figure B.2. The File menu presents the command for exiting the application, the Edit menu presents commands for copying-and-pasting text, and the Special menu presents commands for specifying whether the interest rate is annual or monthly, and for running the application's main processing task. Notice that the Special menu has a submenu and also a

TABLE B.1 Some properties of the Menu control

Property	Specifies
Caption	*The text that the user sees for the menu item.* As with the Caption property of other controls, you can precede one letter of the caption with an ampersand (&) to define an access key.
Checked	*Whether a check mark should be displayed next to the menu item.* The check provides a visual cue to the user. For example, a check mark in a Font Size menu identifies the currently selected font size.
Enabled	*Whether the menu item is active.* When this property is set to False, the menu item appears dimmed in the menu and does not react to mouse clicks.
Shortcut	*A shortcut key for the menu item.* This property is not available at run time. An example of a shortcut is CTRL+X for the Cut item in applications with an Edit menu.
Visible	*Whether the menu item appears in the menu.* True or False.

FIGURE B.2

Menus for a hypothetical application

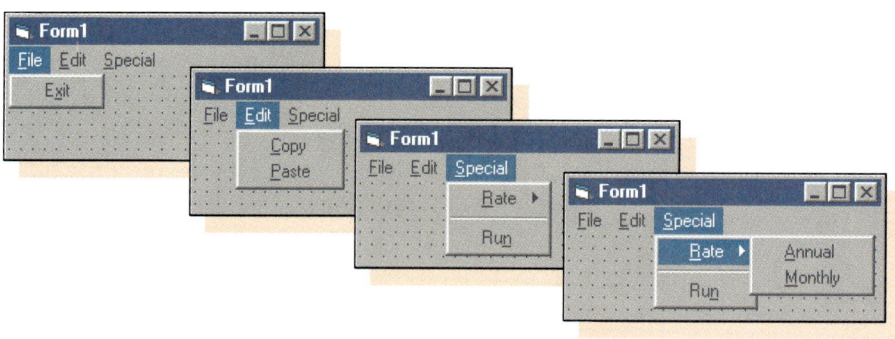

separator bar between Rate and Run. Submenus and separator bars are easy to incorporate into a menu.

The menu structure in Figure B.2 consists of 11 Menu controls: one control for each of the 10 menu items, plus one control for the separator bar. To create this menu, we use the Menu Editor to create and position the Menu controls one at a time.

To create the first Menu control—for the File item—we enter values in the Caption and Name text boxes as shown in Figure B.3. VB automatically copies the entry we make in the Caption box into the list box at the bottom of the Menu Editor.

After completing this entry we click the Next button. This moves the highlight down one position in the list box and clears the Caption and Name text boxes, which prepares the Menu Editor for creating the next Menu control.

In our application we want the second menu item to be captioned Exit, and we want it to belong to the File menu. We use the Menu Editor's indentation controls (left and right arrow buttons) to manage the hierarchical menu structure. Clicking on the right arrow indents the highlighted item in the Menu Editor's list box; the indented item then belongs to the nearest nonindented menu item above it. As we will see, *submenus* can be created by indenting items more than one level in the list box.

FIGURE B.3

Creating a File menu item

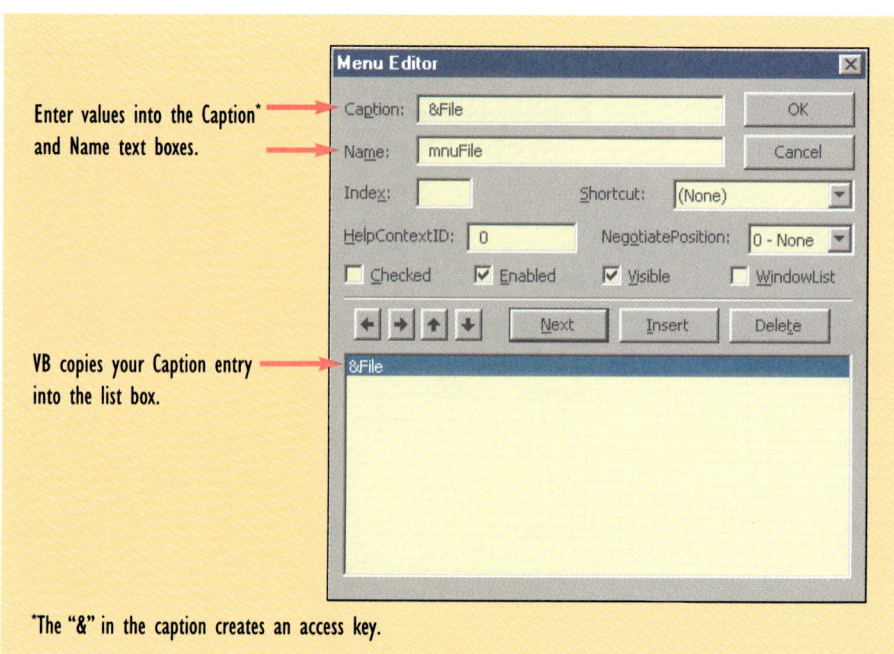

Since we want Exit to belong to the File menu, it needs to be indented one level from the File menu item. Accordingly, we click the right arrow once, then enter the Caption and Name values for the Exit menu item. Figure B.4 shows how the Menu Editor looks at this point. We say that the File menu is the *parent* of the Exit menu item.

Note the convention for naming controls in a hierarchical menu structure. For items that belong to a parent menu we name the control with both the parent menu name and its own name. Thus, the name for the Exit control under the File menu is mnuFileExit (see Figure B.4). This practice makes your programs much easier to read and therefore more maintainable.

We continue making entries as shown in Figure B.5, controlling indentation with the left and right arrow buttons.

FIGURE B.4

An Exit menu item below File

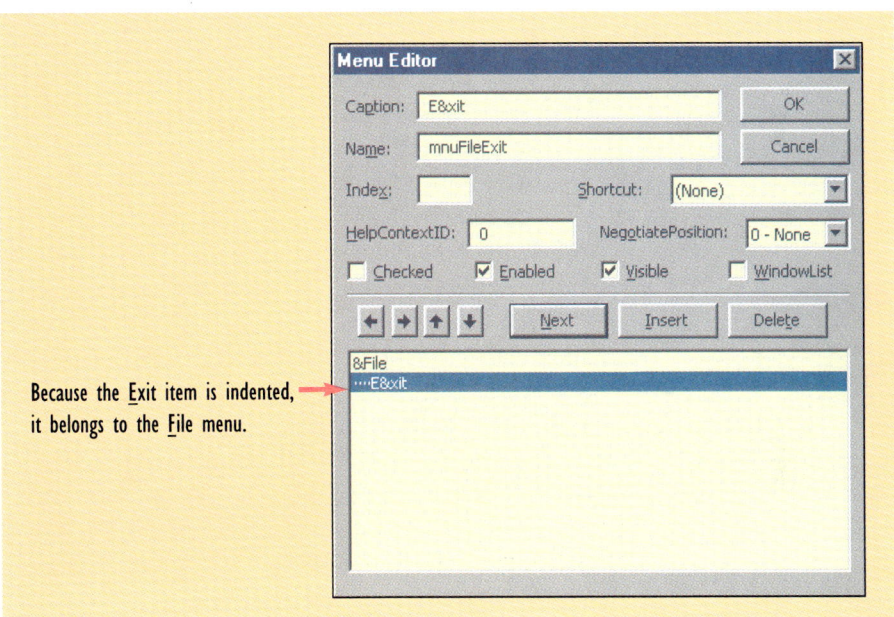

FIGURE B.5

Creating more menu items

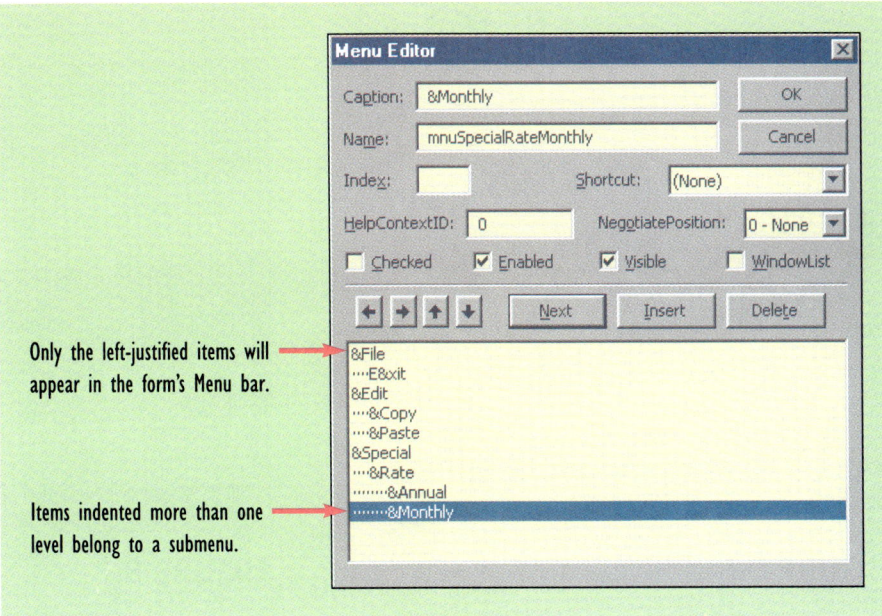

Carefully compare the list box in Figure B.5 to the menu structure in Figure B.2 and observe the following:

- Items that appear left justified in the list box—File, Edit, and Special—appear on the form's Menu bar.
- An item indented one level belongs to the nearest left-justified item above it in the list box. For example, in Figure B.2 the user had to select File in order to see Exit.
- An item indented more than one level belongs to a submenu for the prior level. For example, in Figure B.5 Annual and Monthly are both indented two levels; accordingly, in Figure B.2 Annual and Monthly belong to the Rate menu item, which in turn is a submenu of Special.

To create a separator bar, we create a Menu control and enter a hyphen as its caption. Since all Menu controls need a name, we have to provide a name for this control. This seems pointless because we will never write any code to reference the separator bar, but it is necessary anyway. A good naming convention for separator bars, which we use in Figure B.6, is mnuBar1, mnuBar2, and so forth. We indent the hyphen one level because we want it to separate the two items under the Special menu (see Figure B.2).

After we have entered all the items for our menu structure, the Menu Editor dialog box appears as shown in Figure B.7. Clicking OK closes the Menu Editor dialog box and produces the menus shown in Figure B.2.

You can reopen the Menu Editor dialog box at any time to modify the menu structure. The Insert and Delete buttons add and remove menu items. The up and down arrow buttons move the selected menu item, and the left and right arrow buttons change its indentation.

Finally, you can use the Menu Editor's Shortcut dropdown list to specify a shortcut key combination for a menu item. Similar to an access key, a *shortcut key* allows the user to select a menu item without using the mouse. The shortcut list is shown in Figure B.8. You can choose from a long list of control and function key combinations.

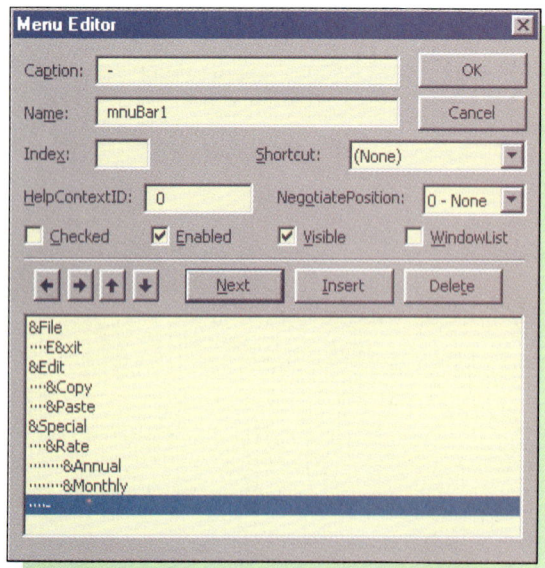

FIGURE B.6

Creating a menu separator bar

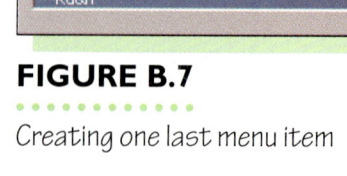

FIGURE B.7

Creating one last menu item

FIGURE B.8

The Shortcut dropdown list

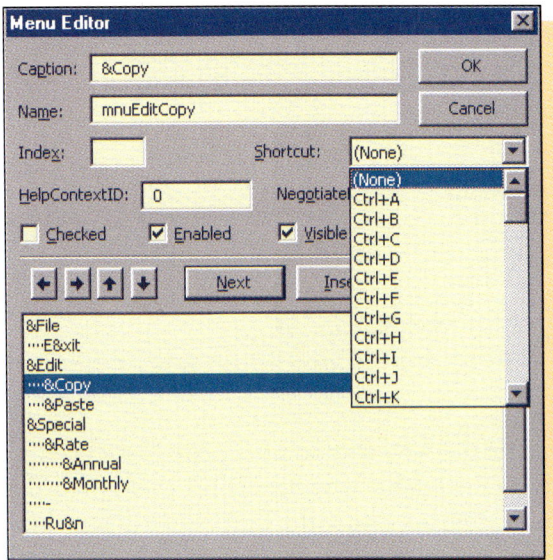

EXERCISE B.1 Use VB to create a form with the menu structure shown in Figure B.2. Then modify the menu as follows:

- Add a Cut item to the Edit menu.
- Add a Daily item to the Rate submenu.
- Add a menu called Help with an item called About.
- Define the following shortcuts:

  Cut   CTRL+X
  Copy   CTRL+C
  Paste   CTRL+V

EXERCISE B.2 Explain the difference between access keys and shortcut keys for menu items. Assuming the user is working with the form whose menu is described in Exercise B.1, how many keystrokes must the user perform in order to select the Exit menu item (under File) using access keys? How many keystrokes must the user perform in order to select the Cut menu item (under Edit) using its shortcut (CTRL+X)?

Coding a Menu Item

When the user selects a menu item, a Click event occurs for the Menu control. So you write a Click event procedure for a Menu control just as you do for a command button. Figure B.9 shows the Code window for the form in our menu example. Notice that even though there is an object for the separator bar (mnuBar1), no event will ever occur for this particular control. Also remember that the *only* event generated for a Menu control is the Click event.

As an example of an event procedure for a Menu control, suppose you want program execution to terminate when the user selects Exit from the File menu. The following event procedure accomplishes this:

    Private Sub mnuFileExit_Click()
        End
    End Sub

FIGURE B.9

The Code window for our hypothetical application

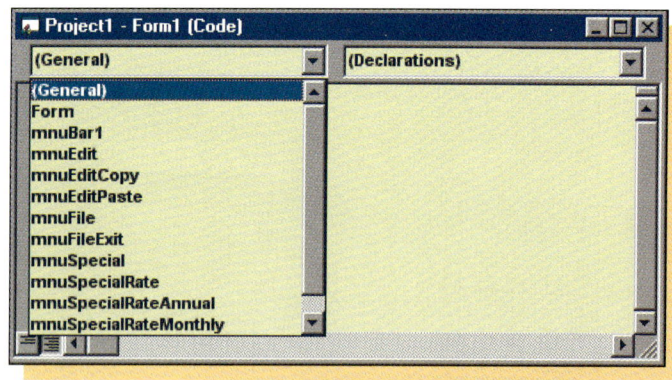

Also note that you should not create Click event procedures for parent menu items. For example, writing a Click event procedure for mnuFile will prevent the user from accessing the Exit menu item; when the user clicks on File, VB will execute mnuFile_Click instead of showing the items belonging to File.

Example B.1 Creating a Simple Text Editor

To illustrate Click event procedures for Menu controls, we create a simple text editor in this example. The text editor uses menus to allow the user to cut, copy, paste, and set the font size for text in a text box. By today's standards this application is not particularly functional; however, prior to the advent of programming environments like VB, which make it easy to construct GUIs, creating even simple menus was a challenging task.

This application uses VB's built-in *Clipboard* object, which provides an intermediate storage area for cut, copy, and paste operations. The Clipboard object has a number of methods that support these operations, including the following:

- The *Clear method* clears all text from the Clipboard.
- The *SetText method* stores text on the Clipboard.
- The *GetText method* retrieves a copy of the text from the Clipboard.

The user interface for the application is shown in Figure B.10. Aside from the Menu controls, there is only one other control on the form: a text box. The property settings for this text box are shown below.

Property	Setting
Font Size	12
MultiLine	True
Name	txtEdit
ScrollBars	2 - Vertical
Text	" "

The menu design is also shown in Figure B.10. Note that the Cut, Copy, and Paste menu items have their standard shortcut key combinations. Again, all Menu controls are named using the prefix "mnu", followed by the parent menu name (if the item has a parent), and then the name of the item itself. Thus,

FIGURE B.10

User interface and menu design for Example B.1

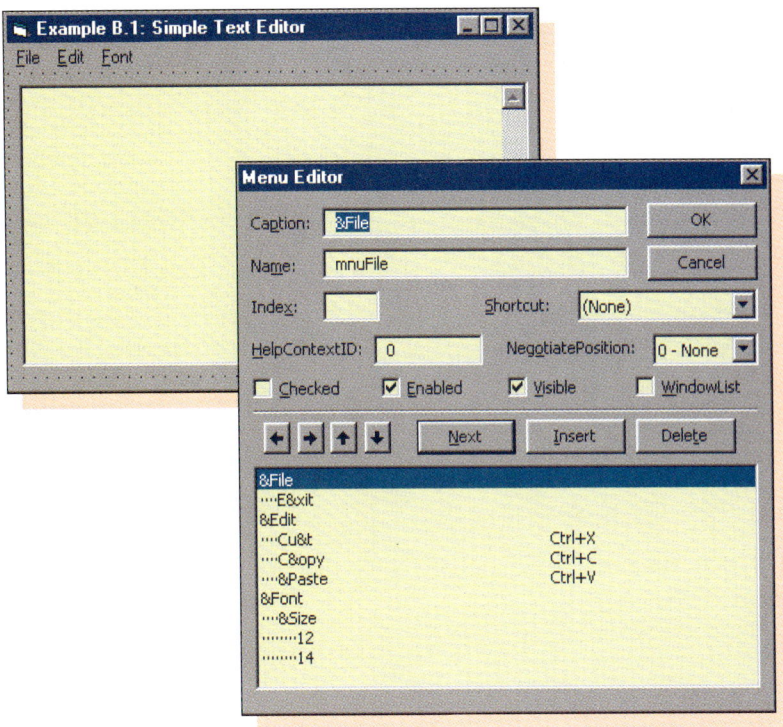

the name of the Menu control for the 12-point Font item is mnuFontSize12. This menu design generates the menus shown in Figure B.11.

The code for the menu items is straightforward. The Copy, Cut, and Paste menu items use the Clipboard object and its associated methods. They also use the SelText property of the text box to determine the text that is currently selected. The code for the File and Edit menu items is shown in Figure B.12.

The Font Size event procedures are also very simple. To implement these menu items we use the text box's run time Font Size property[1] and the menu's Checked property. The code is shown in Figure B.13.

FIGURE B.11

Menus for Example B.1

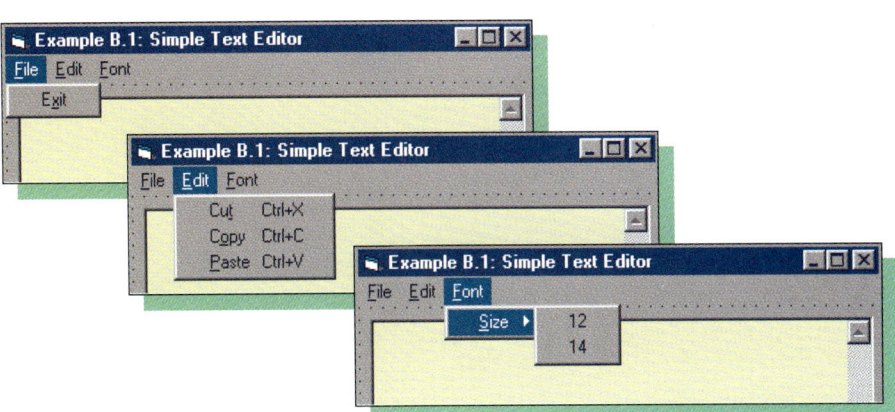

[1] The text box's Font property is actually an object (see Chapter 10), which in turn has its own properties. For example, Size and Bold are properties of the Font object, which is a property of the Text box control. The syntax for referring to the Size property of the Font property of a control is *controlName.Font.Size*.

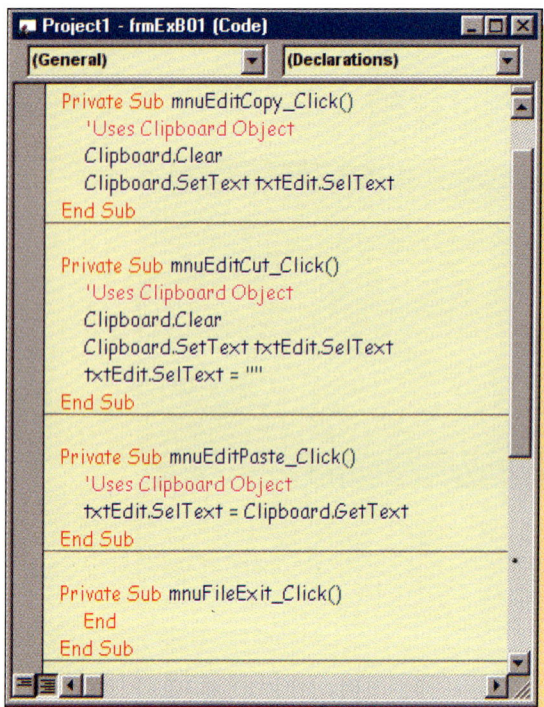

FIGURE B.12

Code for Copy, Cut, Paste, and Exit

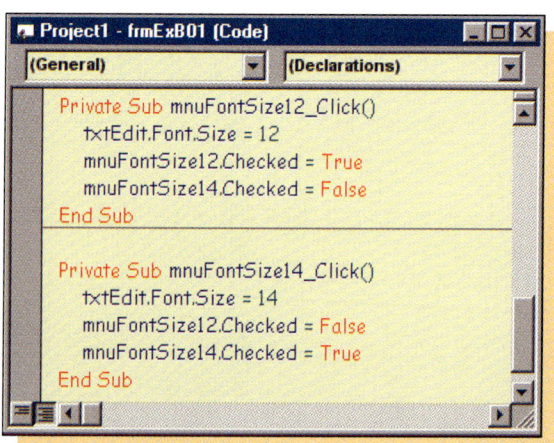

FIGURE B.13

Code for the Font Size menu items

appendix C

The Image and Picture Box Controls

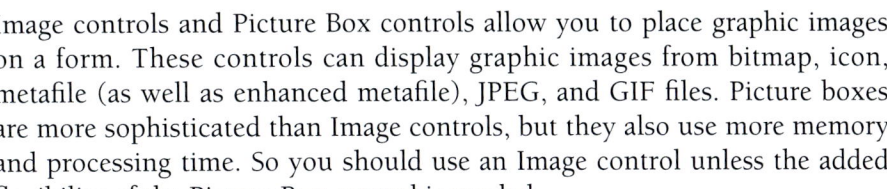

Image controls and Picture Box controls allow you to place graphic images on a form. These controls can display graphic images from bitmap, icon, metafile (as well as enhanced metafile), JPEG, and GIF files. Picture boxes are more sophisticated than Image controls, but they also use more memory and processing time. So you should use an Image control unless the added flexibility of the Picture Box control is needed.

In this appendix we show how to use each of these controls and provide examples.

The Image Control

The Image control provides a place for the programmer to place a graphical image on a form. The control has the unique ability to "stretch" an image to change its size. An Image control can be placed in any container control, such as a form or a frame, but it cannot act as a container itself (it can only hold a graphical image).

Appearance and Use

Figure C.1 identifies the Image tool and shows an Image control on the form at design time. This rectangular area can display a graphical image from a file on disk. As mentioned previously, the types of images that an Image control can display are

- Bitmaps (files with .bmp or .dib extentions)
- Icons (a 32 × 32 pixel image with a file extension of .ico)
- Enhanced metafiles (draw-type images of lines and shapes with a file extention of .wmf or .emf)
- JPEG and GIF (compressed files with .jpg and .gif extensions)

Microsoft provides a large number of graphical files of most of these types with VB.

The Image control allows the programmer to stretch the image to fit the rectangular area that identifies the boundary of the control. Figure C.2 shows the same image displayed by two Image controls. The top one is the original shape of the image and the bottom one has been "stretched" to a new shape.

Properties and Events

Some important properties of the Image control are listed in Table C.1.

FIGURE C.1

Image tool and control

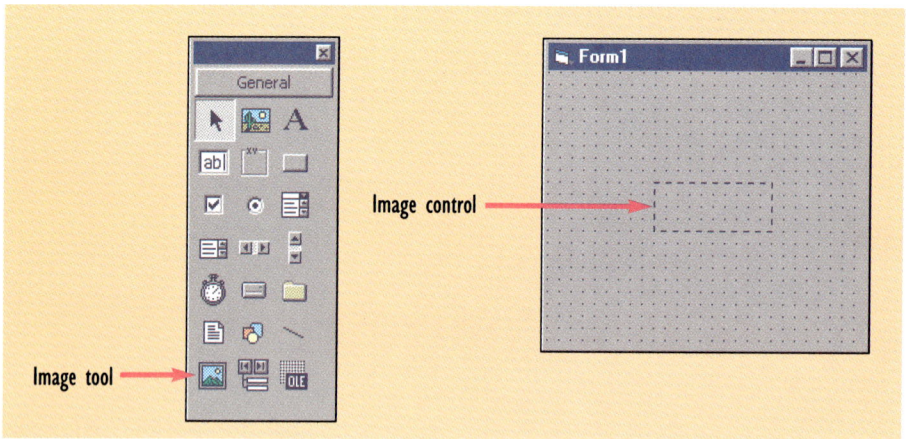

FIGURE C.2

Stretching an image to fit the Image control

TABLE C.1 Properties of the Image control

Property	Specifies
Picture	The path and file name of the file containing the graphical image to be displayed.
Stretch	Whether the image will be stretched to fit the size of the Image control set at design time. Possible values are True and False.
BorderStyle	The style of the Image control's border. Possible values are 0 - None and 1 - Fixed Single.
Enabled	Whether the Image control will respond to user actions. Possible values are True and False.
Visible	Whether the Image control is visible at run time. Possible values are True and False.
(Name)	A unique name for the control that is used by the programmer.

Convention Use the prefix "img" for names of Image controls.

The Image control can respond to a number of events, including Click, DblClick, DragDrop, DragOver, MouseDown, MouseMove, and MouseUp. The Image control can be used as a command button by assigning an appropriate image to it and then programming the Click event procedure. The Image control and code in Figure C.3 demonstrate this use.

FIGURE C.3

An Image control used as a command button and its code

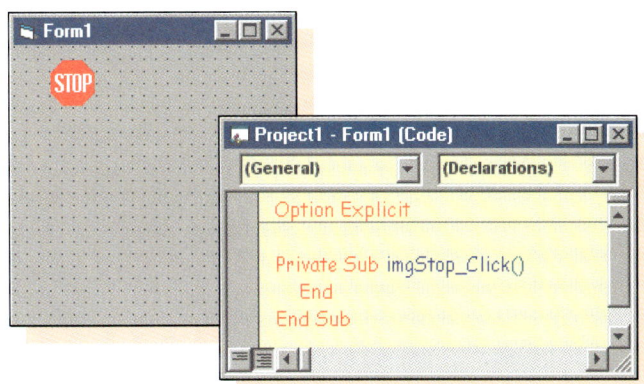

The Picture Box Control

Like the Image control, the Picture box control allows you to place pictures on a form. Compared to the Image control, picture boxes have more properties and methods, and also more capabilities, such the ability to group other controls (which can help you create Toolbars for your applications).

Appearance and Use

Figure C.4 shows the Picture box tool and a Picture box control on a form at design time.

Properties

Some important properties of the Picture box control are listed in Table C.2. In addition to pictures, the Picture box control can display text; thus it also has Font properties, which are not listed in Table C.2.

> **Convention** Use the prefix "pic" for the names of Picture box controls.

You can load a picture into a Picture box control at design time by setting the Picture property to the specific file that you want displayed when the program starts to run.

To load a picture at run time you use the *LoadPicture()* function. The syntax of this function is

LoadPicture(*filename*)

FIGURE C.4

Picture box tool and control

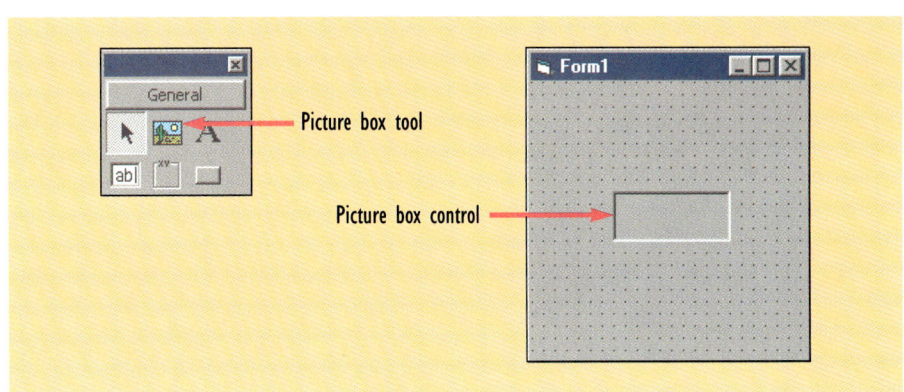

TABLE C.2 Some properties of the Picture box control

Property	Specifies
Align	Whether the picture box should be automatically positioned at the top, bottom, left, or right of the form. If so, its width or height will also be adjusted to fit the width or height of the form. This property is useful when the picture box is being used to create a Toolbar.
AutoSize	Whether the size of the Picture box control will be adjusted to fit the size of the picture it displays. Possible values are True and False.
BackColor	The background color of the picture box.
BorderStyle	The style of the picture box's border. Possible values are 0 - None and 1 - Fixed Single.
Enabled	Whether the picture box will respond to user actions. Possible values are True and False.
Picture	The path and file name of the picture to be displayed.
Visible	Whether the picture box will be visible at run time. Possible values are True and False.
(Name)	A unique name for the control that is used by the programmer.

where *filename* is the name of the picture file (including the path). The LoadPicture() function will clear a picture box if its argument is the zero-length string, that is, LoadPicture(""). To set the Picture property, you might use a statement such as the following:

    picCar.Picture = LoadPicture("a:\Ford.bmp")

Events

The Picture box control can respond to a number of events, including Click, DblClick, Change, and KeyPress. It can have the focus, so it can also respond to GotFocus and LostFocus events.

Example C.1   Creating Simple Animations

The picture box can be used to create simple animations, such as the hourglass in Windows, that act as visual cues that processing is taking place. This example demonstrates simple animation using a picture box and some icons that Microsoft provides with VB. Figure C.5 shows the form, which has a single picture box and a label.

FIGURE C.5

User interface for Example C.1

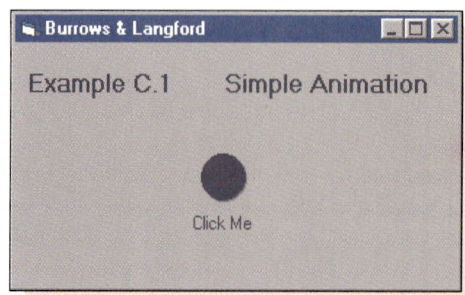

FIGURE C.6

The eight different moon icons provided with VB

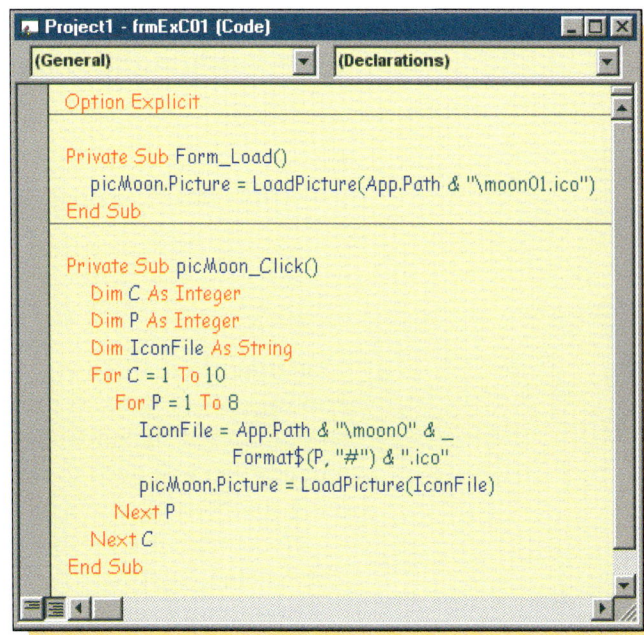

FIGURE C.7

Code for Example C.1

The picture box has its AutoSize property set to True and its BorderStyle property set to "0 - None". Its Picture property has been set equal to an icon file that comes with VB named Moon01.ico. VB provides a total of eight moon icons, which are shown in Figure C.6; each depicts a different phase of the moon. If we rapidly replace each picture of the moon with the next one in the cycle of the moon's phases, the visual effect is that of a spinning ball.

The event procedure in Figure C.7 causes the "moon" to cycle through its phases a total of ten times. The inner loop causes the moon to go through its eight phases. The integer variable P is converted to a single character and used to access the specific moon icon (moon01.ico, moon02.ico, ..., moon08.ico).

Printing to a Picture Box

In addition to displaying images, a picture box can display text information via the Print method. Traditional BASIC programmers use the Print statement all the time to display output to the user. But as you've seen, VB provides a variety of controls for presenting information to the user. As a result, in VB, the Print statement is generally used only when a program actually has to generate a long printed report.

One exception is when the application needs to inform the user of non-critical special conditions. An example of this can be seen in Project H.1, which can be found in Appendix H. In that application, the user expects to see a picture in the picture box. However, if no picture is available, then the words "No picture on file" are displayed in the picture box. This message is displayed using the Print method.

The full syntax of the Print method has many options. Consult online help if you are interested in all the options. For our purposes the basic syntax shown here will suffice.

picName.**Print** *StringExpression*

The *StringExpression* is any valid string expression: a string constant, variable, or more complex expression. An example is the following:

picCar.Print "This car is fast"

Every statement that uses the Print method this way generates a new line in the picture box. Consider the following code segment:

picCar.Print "This car is fast"
picCar.Print "This car is sleek"
picCar.Print "This car is mine"

Executing these three statements produces three lines in the picture box. Printing always starts at the upper left corner. There are ways of making the output of each statement appear on the same line (see online help), but it is unlikely you will need to do this because you will seldom need to print anything complicated into a picture box.

You can remove the displayed text from a picture box with the Cls method. The syntax is simply

picName.**Cls**

Any text that existed in the picture box prior to execution of the Cls method will be cleared, and subsequent printing will start back at the top of the picture box.

EXERCISE C.1

Create an application that has a single picture box, a text box, and a command button. The user should enter a picture file name (full path) into the text box and then click the command button, and your application should display the picture in the picture box.

Example C.2

Using a Picture Box to Create a Simple Toolbar

A picture box is classified along with forms and frames as a "container" control. This means that it can contain (hold) other controls. One useful application of this is to place command buttons inside a picture box to create a Toolbar at the top of the form. Figure C.8 shows such a Toolbar.

The "clock" tool on the left side of our Toolbar causes the time of day to be displayed on the form, the "form" tool causes a second form to be shown, and the "information" tool causes some lines of text to be displayed on the form. When the mouse is over the form, its X- and Y-coordinates are displayed in the right corner of the toolbar.

FIGURE C.8

The form for Example C.2 at run time

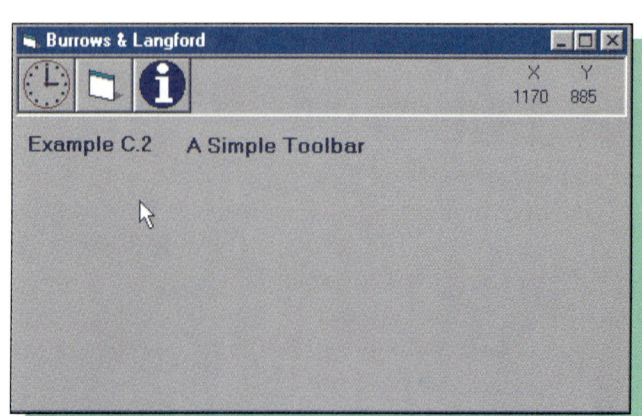

Figure C.9 shows the form at design time and identifies the important controls. The picture box (picToolBar) has its Alignment property set to "1 - Align Top". This setting automatically brings the picture box up to the top of the form. The command buttons and labels in the picture box were drawn in the picture box so that they would be contained by it. (That is, they were not created on the form and then dragged into the picture box, because in that case they would be just "sitting on top" of, and not actually contained by, the picture box.) The command buttons have their Style properties set to "1 - Graphical", and their Picture properties set to produce the appearance shown in the figure.

The code for this example is very simple, and is shown in Figure C.10. The statement

   lblY.Caption = Y – 600

in the Form_MouseMove event procedure takes the actual Y-coordinate of the mouse pointer and adjusts it to account for the height of the picture box.

FIGURE C.9

Important controls used in Example C.2

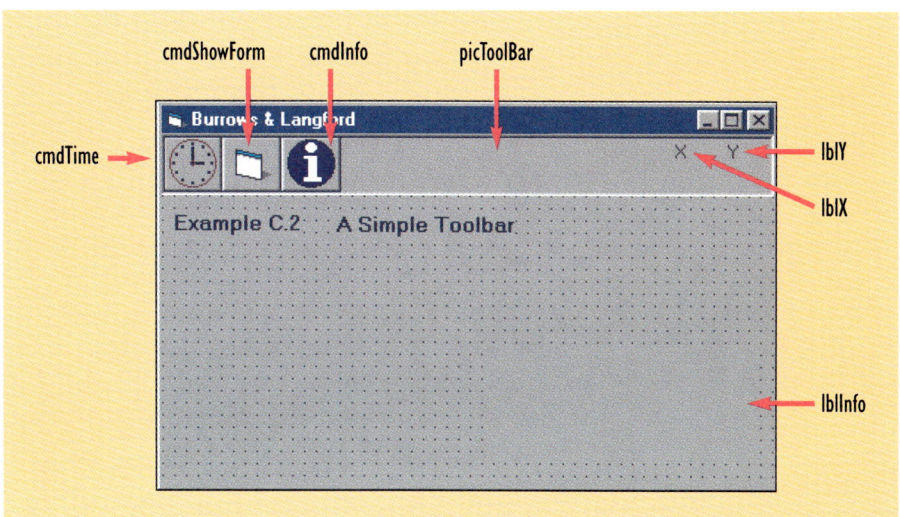

FIGURE C.10

Code for Example C.

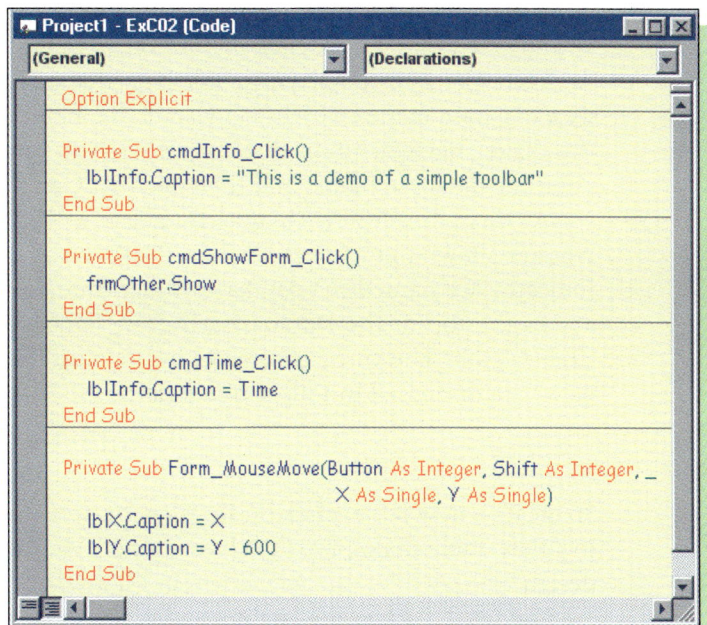

appendix D

Using Microsoft Access to Create a Database

VB has extensive database capabilities, some of which were described in Chapter 8. However, creating a new database and defining its tables and their fields is easier to do with a data management tool, such as Microsoft Access.

This appendix describes how to use Microsoft Access 97 to

- Create a database
- Add a table to the database
- Add fields to the table
- Enter data into records of the table and edit them

This appendix assumes that you are familiar with relational database terminology (see Chapter 8) and also that you have Access 97 installed on your machine (or available via a network). We step through the creation of a simple student information database which will contain one table, with student number, name, and GPA fields.

Creating a Database Using Access 97

To create a new database, select <u>N</u>ew Database... from the <u>F</u>ile menu. In the ensuing New dialog box, click on the "Blank Database" icon and then click OK. Access responds by displaying a File New Database dialog box for you to specify a database name (which will also be the name of the database file). Using this dialog, navigate to the directory where you want the database to be stored, enter the database name, and then click on <u>C</u>reate.

At this point a new (blank) Database will be created, and the database window shown in Figure D.1 will be displayed. As the Title bar in this window indicates, we named the database StudentInfo. You can see a number of tabs across the top of the Database window. This appendix addresses only the "Tables" tab. The three command buttons on the right (<u>O</u>pen, <u>D</u>esign, and <u>N</u>ew) are discussed in following sections.

Adding a Table and its Fields to a Database

To create a new table, click on the <u>N</u>ew button (see Figure D.1). In the ensuing New Table dialog box, click on Design View and then click OK. A Table design window like the one shown in Figure D.2 will be displayed.

You need to enter field names and types for each field. For field names, follow the same syntax rules as for VB variable names. Types can be selected

FIGURE D.1

The main Database window for the StudentInfo database

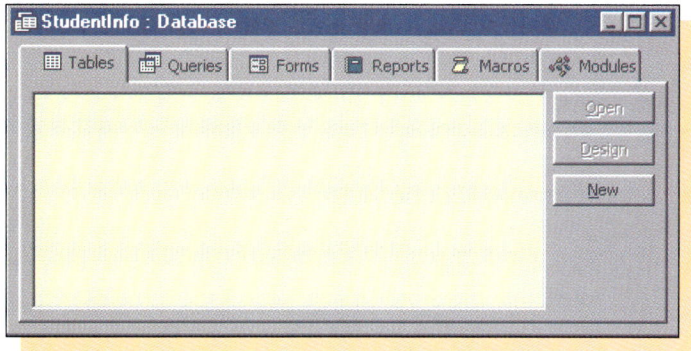

FIGURE D.2

The Table design window

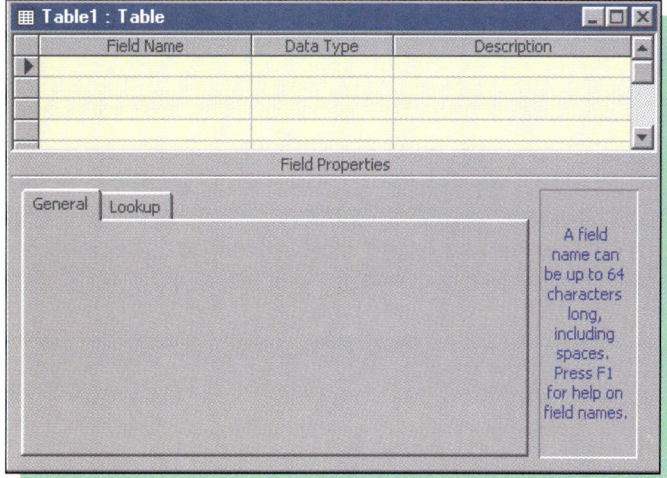

from a dropdown combo box. Figure D.3 shows this combo box with the "Number" data type chosen for the StudNo field.

Although the combo box shows only one Number type and one Text type, as in VB there are several different Number types, and you can specify the number of characters in fixed-length string fields. The Field Size item on the General tab allows you to choose a specific numeric type or string length. To enter this information, click in the Field Size text box and then either enter a

FIGURE D.3

Specifying the field type

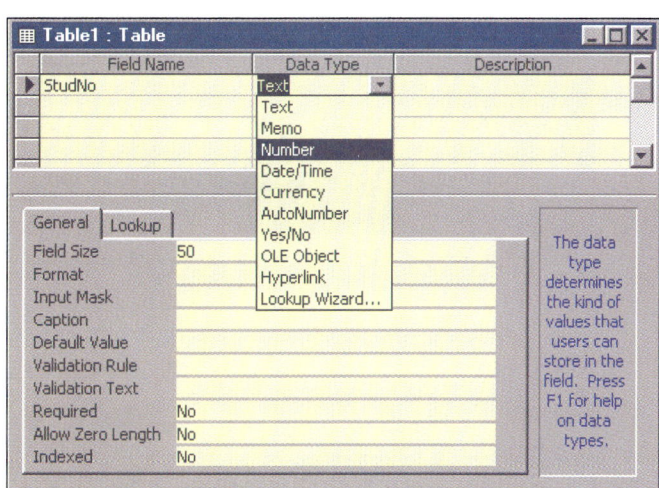

value or use the dropdown list if one is provided. Figure D.4 shows the dropdown box that is provided for the Number data types.

For our student information database, we need to add two more fields to the table. One is named "StudName", which is a Text data type with 30 characters as its field size. The other is named "HSGPA", which is a Number data type with "Single" selected as its field size.

Finally, you should specify one or more fields to represent the primary key. The value in this field should be unique in every record of the table. For our table the StudNo field serves this purpose. To make a field the primary key, click on the field name, then select Primary Key from the Edit menu. A small "key icon" will appear in the left margin of the Table design window as shown in Figure D.5.

Note that many additional field properties appear on the General tab of the Table design window. The meaning of many of these properties (such as the Required property) is not difficult to understand. Use the Access Help system to learn more about them.

The final step in the design of a table is saving the table definition in the database. When you select Save from the File menu, you are prompted for a table name. For our table, we entered the name Student. Be aware that saving

FIGURE D.4

Selecting a field size for a Number data type

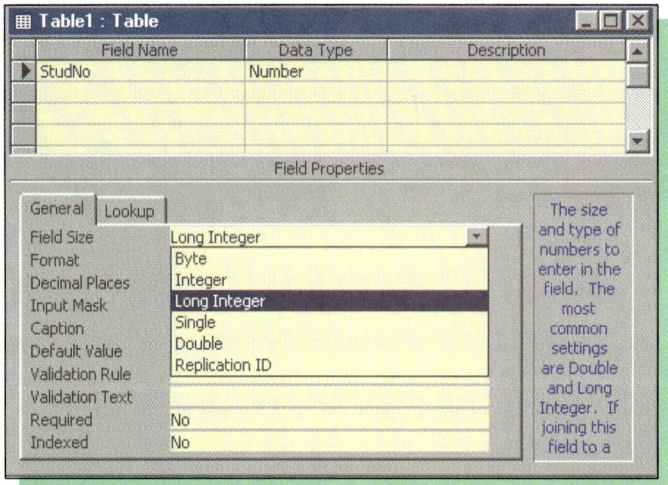

FIGURE D.5

The final table design

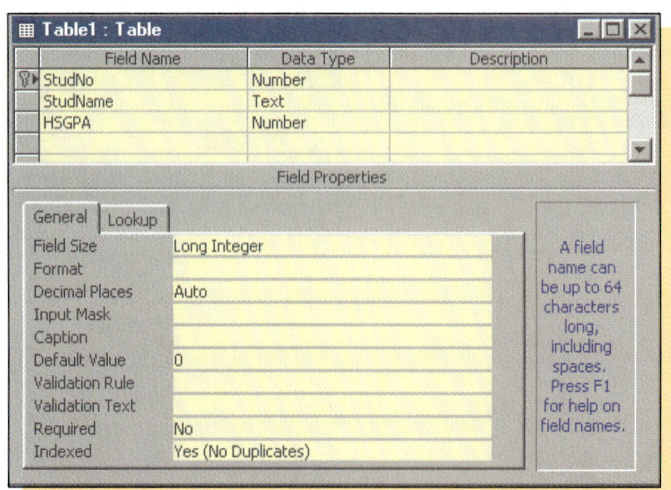

a table definition does not create a new file. The table definition becomes part of the database and is stored in the database file.

Entering and Editing Records in a Table

After the table definition has been created and saved, you can enter data into the table by switching to the datasheet view. There are several ways to do this. If the Table design window is active, you can select Data<u>s</u>heet View from the <u>V</u>iew menu, or right-click on the Table design window's Title bar and select Data<u>s</u>heet View from the pop-up menu, or you can click on the View tool on the Toolbar and select Data<u>s</u>heet View. If the main Database window (see Figure D.1) is active, you can also click on the Open command button to select the datasheet view. Any one of these methods should result in the Table window shown in Figure D.6. To enter information, simply select the appropriate field and type the data. You can either tab between fields or use the [ENTER] key to move to a new record.

Figure D.7 shows the Student table after entering information on five students.

To change any information, simply click on the value to highlight it and then make your correction. Be aware that you do not need to explicitly save the table. As you enter new records, Access automatically saves them in the database. Unlike other applications, the main function of a database is to store records. Thus, it saves them routinely without requiring you to choose a Save command.

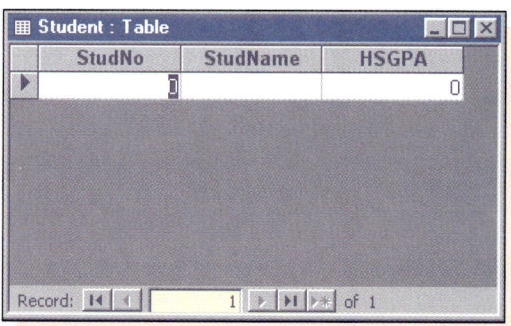

FIGURE D.6

The Table window in datasheet view mode

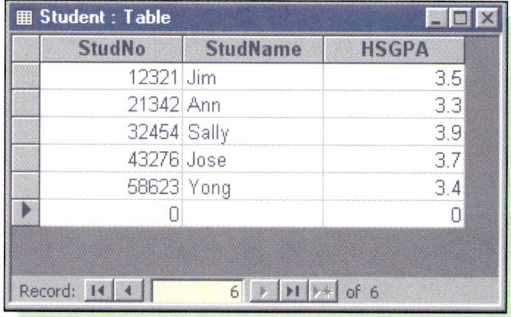

FIGURE D.7

The Student table after entering information on 5 students

appendix E

File Processing

As discussed in the introduction to Chapter 8, databases provide a powerful and convenient means of saving and retrieving most business data. However, there are situations in which programs must work with data stored in nondatabase files on disk. For example, when only a small amount of data needs to be stored, a database will consume much more disk space than a nondatabase file, and the sophisticated functionality of databases may be unnecessary. As another example, many older, "legacy" systems that were implemented before the advent of database technology were designed to use nondatabase files and are still in use today.

We begin this appendix by briefly discussing the differences between file processing and database processing. Then we introduce the basic steps common to all file processing code, and file access modes. The remainder of the appendix examines how to make your programs create, store data in, and read data from files. This discussion is structured around the following common approaches for organizing data in files: unstructured data (text), sequential access of data with fixed-width fields, sequential access of data with delimited fields, and random access.

File Processing versus Database Processing

In this section we introduce the basic concepts of file processing and make some comparisons to database processing. You may wish to read the introduction to Chapter 8, if you have not already done so, for a quick introduction to databases.

Data files, like databases, are stored on disk separate from the programs that use them. And a data file, like a database, may be used by any program that is able to interpret its contents correctly. Being able to "interpret its contents" means being able to determine the identity, location, and data type of each data item in the file.

The programmer must code the interpretation of a data file's contents into every program that uses the file. This is one of the disadvantages of using data files instead of databases, because Database Management Systems (DBMSs) automatically perform the bulk of the interpretation tasks.

DBMSs also incorporate sophisticated mechanisms, such as indexes, to speed the process of locating, retrieving, and storing individual data items. Providing indexes requires storing additional information (beyond the data itself), which is partly responsible for databases' greater consumption of disk storage. The term *flat file* refers to a data file that does not provide such mechanisms. Flat files contain very little beyond the data itself.

You should be aware that there are data files that do provide mechanisms for quick retrieval (indexed files and hashed files are two examples). Such files are in some respects intermediate between flat files and databases. In this appendix we discuss only flat files.

The Three Phases of File Processing

File processing code always follows the sequence of three phases given below.

- Open the file. *Opening a file* establishes a connection between the running program and the file on disk. VB provides the Open statement for this.

- Perform input and/or output (I/O). In the *I/O phase*, data is transferred from disk into program variables (input) or from program variables to disk (output). VB statements for input include Input, Line Input, and Get, and VB statements for output include Print, Write, and Put. The I/O phase often involves a loop, with small amounts of data being repeatedly input and then processed (or repeatedly processed and then output).

- Close the file. *Closing the file* terminates the connection between the running program and the file on disk. VB provides the Close statement for this.

A running program may have many *open files* (files that have been opened but not yet closed) at any given time. However, in most situations, a given file can be open in only one program at a time. Closing a file makes it available to other programs.

The File Pointer and File Processing Modes

When a file is opened, VB creates a *file pointer*, which is an internal variable that it uses to keep track of the location of the current data item within the file. By current data item we mean the next data item to be input from the file (or output to the file).

File processing statements reposition the file pointer. For example, the Open statement always moves the file pointer to the top (beginning) of the file, making the first data item in the file the current data item. The Input statement retrieves the current data item and moves the file pointer down to the location of the next data item. The Get statement moves the file pointer to a specified location in the file and retrieves the data item at that location.

When designing a program that will process a file, it is necessary to consider the patterns of data retrieval and storage that the program will likely follow. The two basic patterns of file processing are sequential and random.

- In *sequential processing*, data items are retrieved from (or stored in) the file in order from top to bottom (first to last). In other words, the file pointer is moved only one data item at a time, in order from top to bottom. There is no "jumping around" in the file.

- In *random processing*, data items are retrieved (or stored) in whatever order is best for the application at hand. In other words, the programmer writes code that moves the file pointer up or down in the file as appropriate for the processing task.

To understand the practical difference between these processing modes, consider the following two applications. As you read each scenario, try to answer this question: should the application employ sequential processing or random processing, and why?

The first application is a payroll application that is executed once every two weeks. It processes a file that contains the number of hours worked and hourly pay rate for each employee at a company. The program reads the data from the file and produces one paycheck for each employee.

The second application is a bank account balance program that executes continuously throughout the day. It processes a file that contains the account balance for each customer. Every time a bank customer performs a transaction that changes his or her account balance, the program retrieves the customer's current balance from the file, increases or decreases the balance by the amount of the transaction, and then saves the new balance back in the file.

It is most likely that the payroll program would use sequential processing. Since the program must process all the data in the file, processing it in top-to-bottom order should work fine. It's the simplest method, and jumping around in the file would offer no advantage. The pseudocode below demonstrates sequential access.

Do Until all employees have been processed
 Input the data for the next employee
 Compute the net pay for this employee
 Print a paycheck for this employee
Loop

In contrast, it is most likely that the bank account balance application would employ random processing. To process a transaction for a customer, the program need only access the account balance data for that customer. If the file contained data for 100,000 customers, for example, it would take a long time to retrieve the data for one specific customer by starting at the top and reading through the file one customer at a time. It would be much quicker to move the file pointer directly to the data for the desired customer, and retrieve only that data. The pseudocode below demonstrates random processing.

Input the account data for the customer performing the transaction
Compute the new balance
Ouput the revised balance for the customer

The chief difficulty associated with random processing is how to find the desired data within the file. Indexes are an example of a mechanism for solving this problem.

VB's File Access Modes

In the Open statement for a file, the programmer must specify an access mode. In VB, the *access mode* determines whether processing is restricted to sequential only, whether input or output (or both) is allowed, and also the data types to be used in interpreting the file's contents. VB provides four access modes, which it calls *input, output, append,* and *random*.[1]

If input, output, or append is specified as the access mode, then only sequential processing is allowed with the file. In these cases, at any given time the file is open either for input or for output, but not for both. When open for input, data can be retrieved from but not written to the file, and when open for

---

[1] Actually, VB provides a fifth file access mode, called *binary*. Binary access is used only in relatively specialized circumstances, and we omit it for simplicity. See online help (search phrase "Open statement") for further information.

output, data can be output to but not retrieved from the file. Opening an existing file for output erases its contents; the append mode allows the program to output data to the end of an existing file without erasing its contents. It is not possible to modify a data item in the middle of a sequential access file.[2] Finally, when input, output, or append is specified as the access mode, the data in the file are always interpreted as type String; that is, the program always interprets the data as a sequence of ANSI codes.

In contrast, if random is specified as the access mode, then both random processing and sequential processing are allowed. In this case, the programmer can freely alternate input and output operations, and can modify data items at any location in the file. When a file is opened for random access, the programmer must specify the data types to be used for each data item in the file; that is, the program will interpret the data according to the programmer's specification. For example, the programmer may choose to store dollar amounts as type Currency, names and addresses as type String, and ages as type Integer.

In the remainder of this appendix we examine common ways of organizing data in flat files and how to process them. We begin with examples that use sequential access and build up our understanding using them, then finish with an extensive example that uses random access. We suggest that you read through the examples in sequence.

To fully appreciate their operation we suggest you do the following before executing any of the examples. Using Windows, go inside the Codepack folder, then inside the AppE folder, and then inside the DatFiles folder. If there are any files inside the DatFiles folder, delete them. Be sure not to delete or rename the DatFiles folder itself.

Unstructured Data: Text

By unstructured data, we mean data that (1) consist of a sequence of characters, and (2) are not guaranteed to have any further structure. By this definition, a variable of type String can hold unstructured data. An e-mail message (specifically the text part of an e-mail message) is a good example of unstructured data.

We use unstructured data as a simple starting point for discussing file processing statements because the program's interpretation of the data is minimal. All the program does is accept characters from the user and save them as a sequence of ANSI codes on disk, or read them from disk and present them to the user. These tasks represent much of the file processing capabilities of text editing programs (such as the Windows accessory called Notepad), and are illustrated by Examples E.1 and E.2.

Example E.1 Writing Unstructured Data to a File Using Sequential Access

This example illustrates how to make your VB program create and output data to a sequential access file. It introduces the Open, Print, and Close statements. The form for this example contains a text box, named txtMemo, and a command button, named cmdOutputToTextFile. The user types text into

---

[2] If you want to do this, input the contents of the file into a string variable, modify the contents of the variable, and then output the modified contents to a new file. This is, for example, how a text editing program works (in addition, a text editing program deletes the original file and gives the new file the same name as the original file).

the text box and then clicks the command button, which then creates a file named Memo.txt and stores the contents of the text box in it. The Command button's event procedure is shown in Figure E.1.

The syntax of the Open statement that opens a sequential access file for output is

Open *filename* **For Output As** #*filenumber*

Filename specifies the path (location) and the name of the file on disk. *Filenumber* is any integer between 1 and 511, inclusive; whatever value you specify will be used in subsequent statements to refer to the file.

If *filename* specifies a file that does not already exist, then executing the Open statement creates a new, empty file; if *filename* specifies a file that does already exist, then executing the Open statement erases the contents of the existing file (i.e., it starts fresh). As an example, if you have a file folder named MyFiles on your C: drive, then the statement

Open "C:\MyFiles\Memo.txt" For Output As #1

creates an empty file named Memo.txt inside the MyFiles folder. (Note that if you do not have a file folder named MyFiles on your C: drive, executing the above statement causes a run time error.)

The *filename* specified in Figure E.1 is somewhat more complicated than the above because we (as authors) want you to execute the example, which will actually create a new file, and we do not want to clutter up your hard drive with new files. In the *filename* expression

App.Path & "\DatFiles\Memo.txt"

"App" is a built-in VB object that provides information about the currently executing project itself; its Path property specifies the location of the project on disk. For example, if this project (ExE01.Vbp) is located on your C: drive in a file folder named AppE, which is in a file folder named "Codepack", then the *filename* expression will evaluate to

C:\Codepack\AppE\DatFiles\Memo.txt

This is useful because it allows the code to execute properly regardless of whether you have placed the "Codepack" folder directly on your C: drive, or within another folder on your C: drive, or on another drive altogether.

After executing the Open statement, the Print statement

Print #1, txtMemo.Text

takes the contents of the text box and outputs it to file #1 (which, according to our Open statement, refers to the new Memo.txt file).

FIGURE E.1

Code for Example E.1

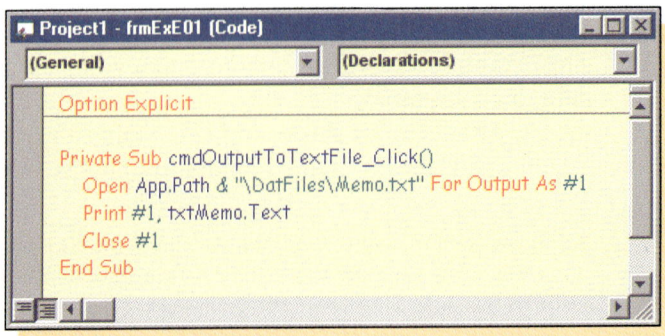

Finally, the Close statement

Close #1

closes the file, making it available for other programs to use.

If you have not already done so, execute the example. In the text box, type one or two long sentences (long enough to cause the text box to wrap the words) without pressing the ENTER key, then press ENTER, and type your name. Then click the command button to save this data.

Finally, using Windows, find the DatFiles folder and view its contents. You should see the new Memo.txt file. Double-clicking on its icon will, most likely, show its contents in the Notepad accessory. By convention, the *filename extension ".txt"* is used for files that contain only ANSI characters, and such files are referred to as *text files*. Thus, the terms "sequential access file" and "text file" are synonyms. On Windows machines the Notepad accessory is usually the default application for working with text files.

The next example will retrieve the contents from our new text file.

Example E.2 Reading Unstructured Data from a File Using Sequential Access

This example illustrates how to make your VB program input data from an existing sequential access file. It introduces the LOF() and Input() functions. The form for this example contains a combo box, named cboFiles, and a text box, named txtData. The combo box lets the user choose from three files, one of which is the Memo.txt file created in Example E.1. When the user selects a file, the combo box's Click event procedure opens the file, inputs its contents into the text box, and closes the file. The code for this example is shown in Figure E.2.

The Form_Load event procedure adds the paths and names of three files to cboFiles, then selects the first file (Memo.txt) by setting cboFiles.ListIndex to 0. This, in turn, sets cboFiles.Text equal to the path and name of the Memo.txt file, and causes a Click event for the combo box. (The Click event

FIGURE E.2

Code for Example E.2

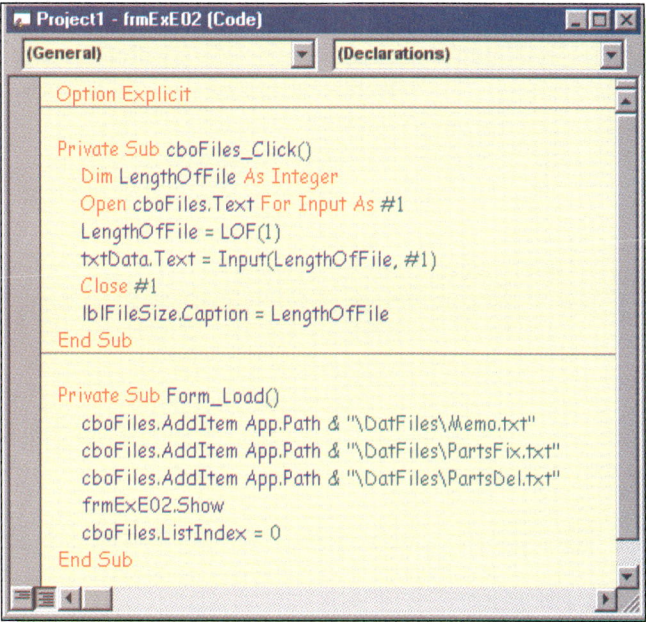

```
Option Explicit

Private Sub cboFiles_Click()
    Dim LengthOfFile As Integer
    Open cboFiles.Text For Input As #1
    LengthOfFile = LOF(1)
    txtData.Text = Input(LengthOfFile, #1)
    Close #1
    lblFileSize.Caption = LengthOfFile
End Sub

Private Sub Form_Load()
    cboFiles.AddItem App.Path & "\DatFiles\Memo.txt"
    cboFiles.AddItem App.Path & "\DatFiles\PartsFix.txt"
    cboFiles.AddItem App.Path & "\DatFiles\PartsDel.txt"
    frmExE02.Show
    cboFiles.ListIndex = 0
End Sub
```

would not have occurred if we had not executed the Show method for the form prior to setting the ListIndex property.)

The Click event procedure uses cboFiles.Text as the file name for the Open statement. The syntax of the Open statement that opens a sequential access file for input is

Open *filename* **For Input As** *#filenumber*

As in the previous example, we chose to use the number 1 for the file number, although you can use a different number for the same file in different programs; a program uses the file number as a shorthand way of referring to a file only while the file is open.

Executing the Open statement sets the file pointer to the top of the file. The next statement employs VB's built-in LOF() function to find the length of the file in bytes.[3] The argument of this function is the file number for the open file (1 in this case, since the file was opened as file #1). The LOF() function does not move the file pointer.

The next statement employs VB's Input() function. The syntax of this function is

Input(*numberOfBytes, #filenumber*)

The *numberOfBytes* argument is a numeric expression indicating the number of characters to input from the file. The Input() function reads the specified number of characters from the file (starting at the current position of the file pointer), returns the characters, and advances the file pointer by the number of characters read. Thus, the statement

txtData.Text = Input(LengthOfFile, #1)

reads the entire contents of the file and stores the characters in txtData.Text.

The final two statements close the file and display the number of characters input. When you run this example, it should display the same data you entered when you ran Example E.1. Selecting either of the other two files in the combo box at this point will cause a run time error, because these files do not yet exist; we will create them in subsequent examples.

As mentioned earlier, the file pointer is an internal variable used by VB. Although this variable cannot be directly accessed in code, it is useful for the programmer to be able to visualize the file pointer and how open, input, and output operations cause it to move within a file.

As an example, suppose that the user of the program in Example E.1 entered "abcdefghij" as the text. The file Memo.txt would then contain these characters followed by a carriage return (*cr*) character and a line feed (*lf*) character. VB automatically appends these two characters when it creates the file, and they are invisible to the user. If the user then uses Example E.2 to examine the contents of Memo.txt, he or she will see only "abcdefghij" in the text box (10 characters), but the label will report that the size of the file in bytes is 12 (10 visible characters plus *cr* and *lf*).[4] Figure E.3 illustrates what happens in this case when the function Input(LengthOfFile, #1) executes.

[3] Recall that with string data, each character occupies one byte. Thus, the number of characters in the file is the same as the number of bytes in the file.

[4] Actually, an astute user who gives the focus to the text box and moves the cursor around may notice that there are *two* lines in the text box—the bottom line is blank.

FIGURE E.3

File pointer movement as Example E.2 executes

Starting Position of File Pointer	Value returned by Input(LengthOfFile, #1)	Ending Position of File Pointer
⇓ a b c d e f g h i j cr lf	a b c d e f g h i j cr lf	a b c d e f g h i j cr lf ⇓

The following code provides a more detailed illustration of how the file pointer is manipulated by the Input() function. It uses VB's built-in EOF() function to determine when the file pointer reaches the end of the file (i.e., when all the data have been input). The argument of the EOF() function is the file number of the open file, and its return value is Boolean: it returns True if the file pointer has reached the end of the file, and False if it has not.

```
Private Sub cmdThreeAtATime_Click()
    Dim NextThree As String
    Open App.Path & "\DatFiles\Memo.txt" For Input As #1
    Do Until EOF(1) = True
        NextThree = Input(3, #1)
        MsgBox NextThree & "," & EOF(1)
    Loop
    Close #1
End Sub
```

Figure E.4 depicts the movement of the file pointer as event procedure cmdThreeAtATime_Click executes. After the fourth iteration, the EOF() function returns True because the file pointer has reached the end of the file, and the loop terminates.

The operation of cmdThreeAtATime_Click provides a good example of sequential processing. If we consider a data item to be a group of three contiguous characters, then we see that data items are input in sequence from the beginning to the end of the file.

An unfortunate feature of the loop in procedure cmdThreeAtATime_Click is that it terminates properly only when the number of characters in the file (counting the *cr* and *lf* characters) is exactly divisible by the number of characters input at each iteration. If it is not, a run time error occurs ("Input past

FIGURE E.4

File pointer movement as event procedure cmdThreeAtATime_Click executes

Iteration	Starting Position of File Pointer	Value Returned by EOF(1)	Value Returned by Input(3,#1)	Ending Position of File Pointer
1	⇓ a b c d e f g h i j cr lf	False	abc	⇓ a b c d e f g h i j cr lf
2	⇓ a b c d e f g h i j cr lf	False	def	⇓ a b c d e f g h i j cr lf
3	⇓ a b c d e f g h i j cr lf	False	ghi	⇓ a b c d e f g h i j cr lf
4	⇓ a b c d e f g h i j cr lf	False	j cr lf	⇓ a b c d e f g h i j cr lf
5	⇓ a b c d e f g h i j cr lf	True		

end of file").[5] As we shall see, business data typically have a structure that allows each input or output operation to transfer one "line" or "record" at a time, instead of some number of characters, and our resulting programs are not vulnerable to this problem. The remainder of this appendix deals with such structured data.

Structured Data: Records

Most data files have a simple structure. In particular, they are usually organized so that the data can be thought of as a table with rows and columns. Consider the file of inventory data depicted in Figure E.5, which is organized as a table with three rows and three columns. The columns are often referred to as *fields*. In Figure E.5, each row contains a part number field, a description field, and a price field for a single part. The top row, for example, contains data for a bolt whose part number is 3300 and whose price is $2.34. It's easy to imagine displaying the contents of such a file in a list box or a FlexGrid control.

When such data are stored in a sequential access file, it is customary for each "row" to reside on a separate line of the file. Carriage return and line feed characters delimit the lines (i.e., separate one line from the next). The fields in a single row may be *fixed-width*, meaning that each field occupies a pre-specified number of characters, or *delimited*, meaning that the fields are separated by commas (or some other agreed-upon character). In a sequential access file the rows may be called *records* or simply *lines*.

When such data are stored in a random access file, each row consists of a specified number of bytes. In particular, there are no carriage return and line feed characters to separate the rows. In a random access file the rows are called *records*.

The remainder of the appendix examines code for processing files containing structured data.

Sequential Access of Data in Fixed-Width Fields

When the inventory data shown in Figure E.5 are represented in a sequential access file using fixed-width fields, they appear as shown in Figure E.6. Here, the creator of the file decided to allot four characters to the part number field, ten characters to the description field, and six characters to the price field. Equivalently, we could say that within each line of this file, characters 1–4

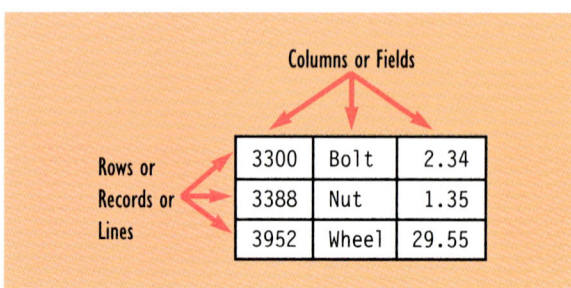

FIGURE E.5

Example of structured data

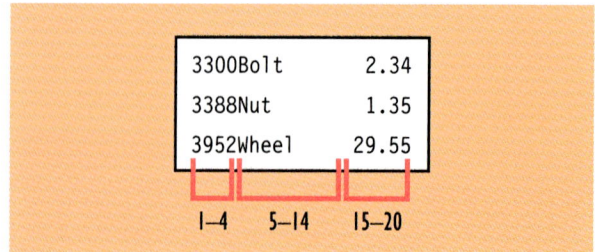

FIGURE E.6

Inventory data in a sequential access file with fixed-width fields

[5] This situation is easily handled by writing error-handling code. The topic of error-handling is addressed in Appendix F.

represent the part number, characters 5–14 represent the description, and characters 15–20 represent the price.

The creator of the file chose the number of characters for each field to be great enough to hold the largest anticipated value for the field. The programs that process this file need to know which fields occupy which character positions. What happens if, at some time in the future, it becomes necessary to store a part whose description is 12 characters long? The easiest thing to do would be to truncate the description for the new part—i.e., store only its first ten characters and throw away the last two. The alternative would be to "redesign" the file to allot 12 characters to the description field. This would require 1) modifying the file to lengthen all the existing descriptions, and 2) modifying all the existing programs that process the file to use character positions 5–16 for the description field and 17–22 for the price field. This points up a major drawback to using files instead of a database. With a database management system, this kind of change can be made to the database without requiring modifications to programs that use the database.

Example E.3

Using Fixed-Width Fields with Sequential Access

Figure E.7 shows the user interface and code for this example, which allows the user to create a part file and save part data in it, and then to review its contents. When program execution begins, the file is not open and the Part Data frame is invisible. If the user clicks the Open Output File button, the file will be opened for output; the user can then type data in the text boxes and click the Save Part button to add a new part to the file. If the user clicks the Open Input File button, the file will be opened for input, and the user can browse the file contents by clicking the Get Next Part button.

The procedures that open the file for Input or Output use VB's built-in FreeFile() function to obtain a file number that is not in use. As in previous examples, we could have arbitrarily used file number 1: it is only necessary to use the same file number consistently, and to not use the same file number for two different files that are open at the same time. Because this program uses only one file, this is not a matter of great concern. However, in programs that process several files, it becomes difficult (and tedious) for the programmer to choose a file number that is guaranteed to not be in use for another open file. The FreeFile() function returns an integer number which is guaranteed not to be in use by any open file in the program.

Procedure cmdSavePart_Click copies the values input by the user into fixed-length string variables, then uses VB's Print # statement to output the three values to the text file. The syntax of the Print # statement is

> **Print** #*filenumber, outputlist*

where *outputlist* is a list of expressions, separated by semicolons, to be saved as a single line in the file.[6] In our statement

> Print #Filenumber, PartNumber; Description; Price

the variables PartNumber, Description, and Price are fixed-length string variables with four, ten, and six characters, respectively, and so the corresponding fields in the file will also have four, ten, and six characters.

---

[6] This is an abbreviated discussion of the Print # statement. See online help (search phrase "Print # statement") for information on additional capabilities.

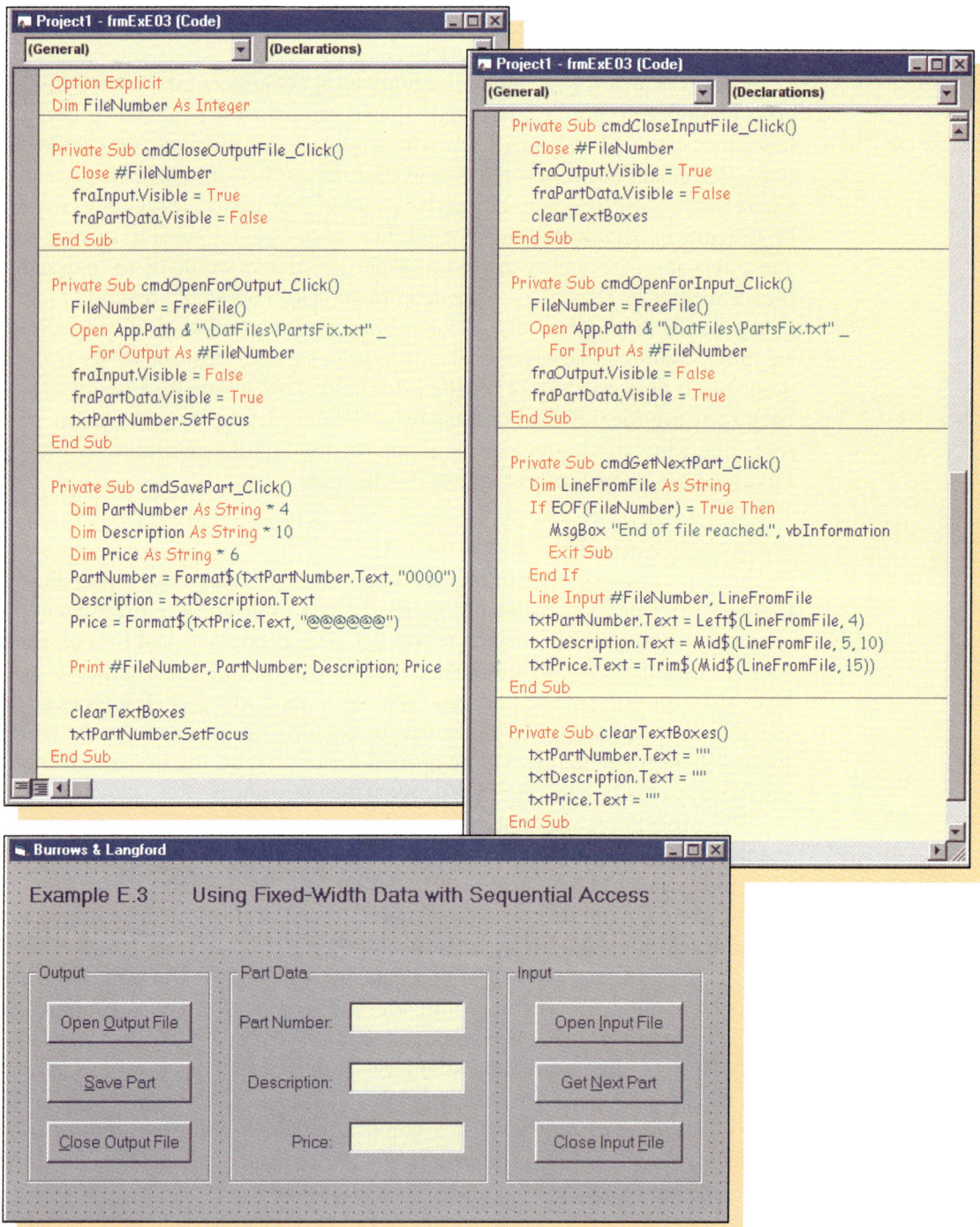

FIGURE E.7 User interface and code for Example E.3

Procedure cmdGetNextPart_Click first checks whether the file pointer has reached the end of the file and if it has not, inputs one line from the file into the string variable LineFromFile using VB's Line Input # statement. The syntax of the Line Input # statement is

Line Input #*filenumber, variable*

where *variable* is any variable of type String. The procedure then uses the Left$() and Mid$() functions to extract the substrings consisting of characters

1–4, 5–14, and 15–20 from the value in LineFromFile, and displays these substrings in the three text boxes.

If you haven't already done so, try executing the program and saving the data shown in Figure E.5 in the file. Begin by clicking the Open Output File button. Then type the data for the first row of Figure E.5 in the text boxes, and click the Save Part button; repeat this operation for the second and third rows of Figure E.5. Then click the Close Output File button.

Finally, browse the file contents by first clicking on the Open Input File button, then clicking the Get Next Part button repeatedly. Note that if you wish to browse the file again, you must click the Open Input File button again to move the file pointer back to the top of the file.

Example E.4 Reading Lines from a File Using Sequential Access

Figure E.8 shows the user interface and code for this example, which allows the user to select a file, and then inputs the contents of the file one line at a time and displays the lines in a list box. It uses the EOF() function to determine when the file pointer reaches the end of the file, i.e., when all lines have been input.

When you execute this program, select the file PartsFix.txt you created in Example E.3, and then the file Memo.txt you created in Example E.1. You may wish to try executing Example E.2 again, and view the contents of these same two files. The contents of file Memo.txt may have a different appearance in each of the two programs, because the text box in Example E.2 wraps long lines, whereas the list box in Example E.4 does not.

FIGURE E.8

User interface and code for Example E.4

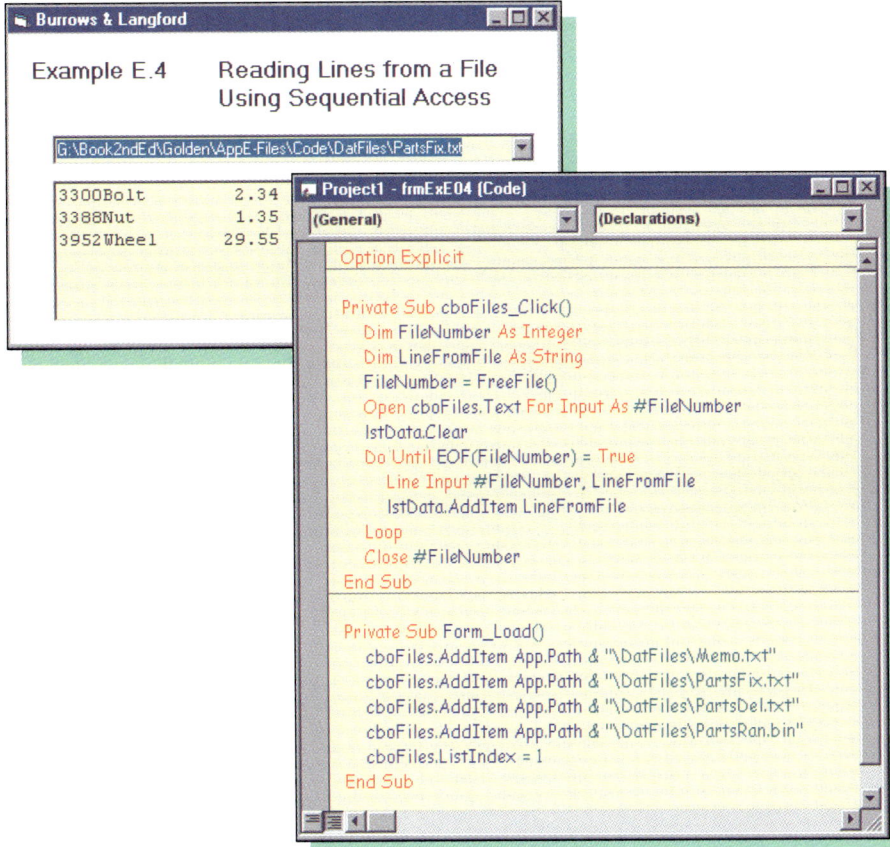

Figure E.9 shows the characters in the file PartsFix.txt, assuming that you entered the data from Figure E.5 when you created the file. Note that the carriage return and line feed characters were automatically inserted by the Print # statement as it output each line to the file. (The arrow in this figure indicates the position of the file pointer right after the file is opened for input.)

The Line Input # statement uses the carriage return and line feed characters to determine how much data to input. Each time it is executed, the Line Input # statement obtains all the characters from the current position of the file pointer up to the next carriage return and line feed characters, and then advances the file pointer. Figure E.10 depicts the movement of the file pointer as event procedure cboFiles_Click, in Example E.4, executes. After the third iteration, the EOF() function returns True because the file pointer has reached the end of the file, and the loop terminates.

Sequential Access of Data in Delimited Fields

When the inventory data shown in Figure E.5 are represented in a sequential access file using delimited fields, they appear as shown in Figure E.11.

One advantage of delimited data is that there is no limitation on the number of characters in the data values stored in each field. For example, the file can hold part descriptions of any length, without requiring modification to either the design of the file or to the programs that use it. In addition, when working with sequential access files, the code for delimited data is simpler than the code for fixed-width data, thanks to somewhat more sophisticated input and output statements provided by VB.

Example E.5 — Using Delimited Fields with Sequential Access

The user interface for this example is identical to that for Example E.4, and allows the user to do the same thing. The difference is that the data are stored

FIGURE E.9

Characters and file pointer in PartsFix.txt file

⇓
3300Bolt   2.34*crlf*3388Nut   1.35*crlf*3952Wheel   29.55*crlf*

FIGURE E.10

File pointer movement as event procedure cboFiles_Click executes

Iteration	Position of file pointer after Line Input # statement executes
1	3300Bolt 2.34*crlf*⇓3388Nut 1.35*crlf*3952Wheel 29.55*crlf*
2	3300Bolt 2.34*crlf*3388Nut 1.35*crlf*⇓3952Wheel 29.55*crlf*
3	3300Bolt 2.34*crlf*3388Nut 1.35*crlf*3952Wheel 29.55*crlf*⇓

FIGURE E.11

Inventory data in a sequential access file with delimited fields

```
3300,"Bolt",2.34
3388,"Nut",1.35
3952,"Wheel",29.55
```

in a file using delimited fields instead of fixed-width fields. The code for Example E.5 is shown in Figure E.12.

Procedure cmdSavePart_Click copies the values input by the user into variables, then uses VB's Write # statement to output the three values to the text file. The syntax of the Write # statement is

> Write #*filenumber, outputlist*

where *outputlist* is a list of expressions, separated by commas, to be saved as a single line in the file. In our statement

> Write #Filenumber, PartNumber, Description, Price

the variable PartNumber is type Integer, the variable Description is type String, and the variable Price is type Currency. When this statement executes, VB converts the three values to type String, places the value from the string variable in quotes, and writes the three values out to the file, separating them by commas and adding the carriage return and line feed characters to mark the end of the line.

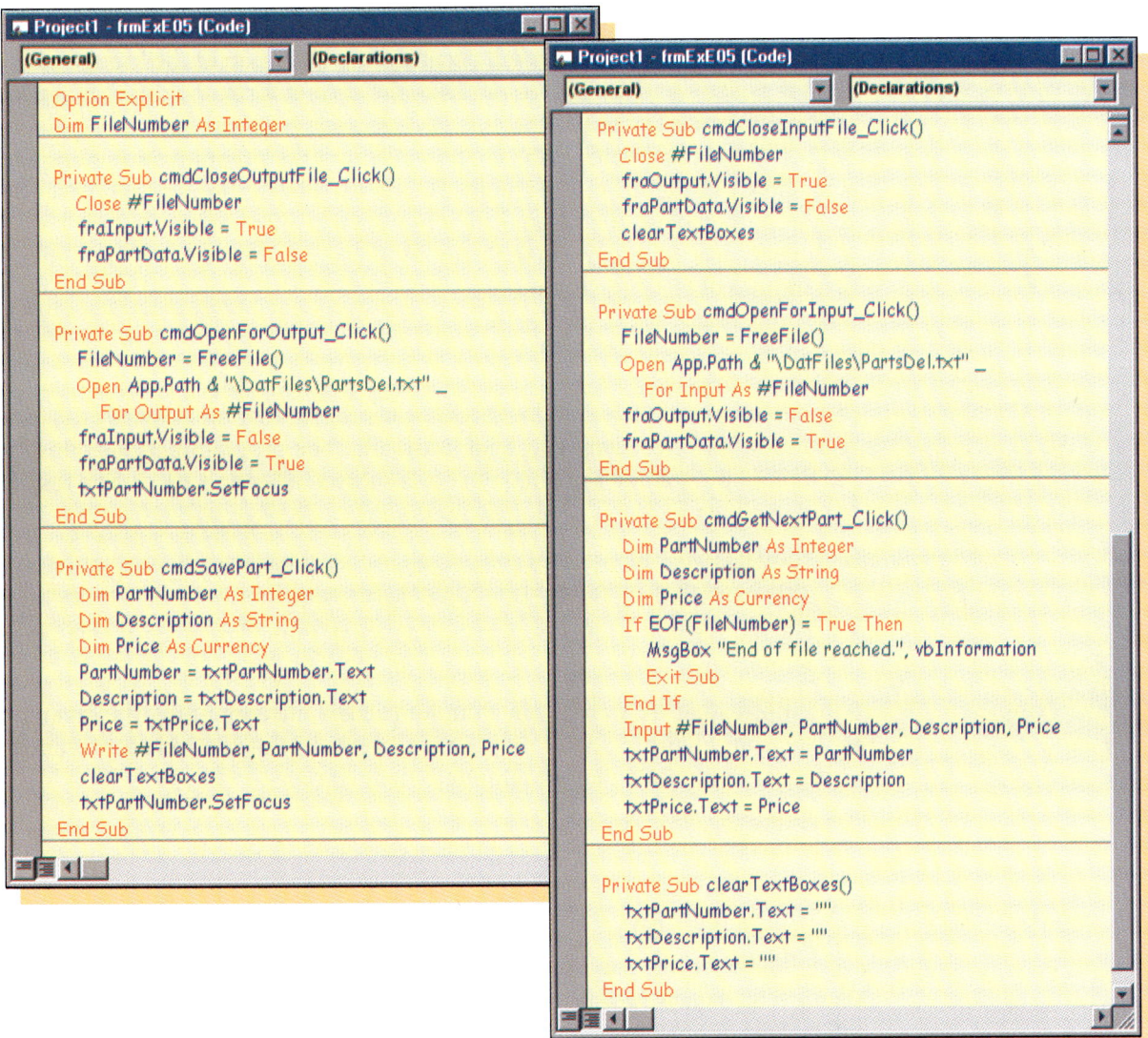

FIGURE E.12 Code for Example E.5

Procedure cmdGetNextPart_Click first checks whether the file pointer has reached the end of the file and, if not, inputs one line from the file into the variables PartNumber, Description, and Price using VB's Input # statement. The syntax of the Input # statement is

Input #*filenumber, variablelist*

where *variablelist* is a list of variables separated by commas. The number of variables provided in *variablelist* should be the same as the number of data items appearing in the line to be input from the file. When the Input # statement executes, VB reads a line from the file, then *parses* the line (breaks it into separate data items using the delimiters (commas) as a guide) then stores the separate data items in the variables specified in *variablelist*.

For example, suppose that the first line in the file is

3300,"Bolt",2.34

Then the first time the statement

Input #Filenumber, PartNumber, Description, Price

is executed, the value 3300 will be stored in the variable PartNumber, "Bolt" will be stored in Description, and 2.34 will be stored in Price. As you would expect, a type mismatch error will occur during execution of the Input # statement if a data item which does not have the correct form of a number is read into a numeric variable.

If you haven't already done so, try executing the program and saving the data shown in Figure E.5 in the file. Open the file for output, and save the data in it; then close the file and then browse its contents.

Finally, use the programs in Examples E.2 and E.4 to view the contents of this file and observe the delimiters.

Random Access

In order to open a file for random access, the programmer must specify the data types to be used for each data item in the file. The programmer does this by providing a programmer-defined type (the subject of Section 10.1). The resulting file will *not* be a text file for two reasons.

1. The data in the file will not consist solely of ANSI characters, since the specified types may include types other than String.
2. The records in the file will consist of a predetermined number of bytes, and are not separated by carriage return and line feed characters.

Suppose that we were given a random access file containing the inventory data from Figure E.5, and that the data items in this file were represented according to the following programmer-defined type.

Private Type PartRecord
    PartNumber **As Integer**
    Description **As String** * 10
    Price **As Currency**
End Type

Figure E.13 depicts how the data would appear in this file. Each box in this figure represents one byte in the file. The records are numbered, starting at 1, and each record consists of three fields.

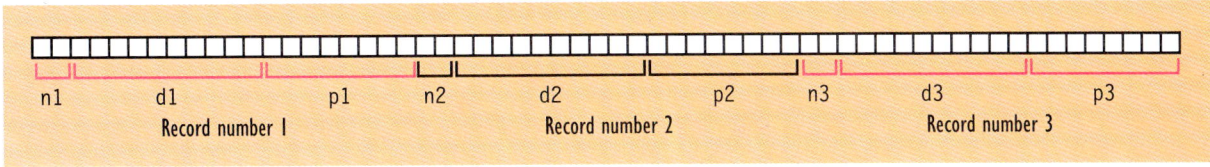

FIGURE E.13 Inventory data in a random access file

The fields in each record appear in the order specified by the type definition statement. Thus, the first field of the first record (labeled n1 in the figure) is a part number stored as type Integer. Because values of type Integer occupy two bytes of storage (see Table 4.1), field n1 occupies two bytes. The second field of the first record (labeled d1 in the figure) is a description stored as a ten-character string, and thus occupies ten bytes. The third field of the first record (p1) is a price stored as type Currency. Since values of type Currency occupy eight bytes of storage (again from Table 4.1), field p1 occupies 8 bytes. Thus, the first record occupies a total of 20 bytes (2 + 10 + 8). The second and third records have the same structure as the first, so the entire file consists of 60 bytes.

Recall from our discussion of VB's file access modes that records can be retrieved in any order from a random access file. The following procedure makes this possible: if you wish to retrieve the third record from the part file above, then VB can perform a simple calculation to determine that it must read the forty-first through sixtieth bytes from the file. In general, if you wish to retrieve record number n from this file, then the bytes to be retrieved from the file are those in positions $20*(n-1) + 1$ through $20*n$.

Conversely, data items can be retrieved only in top to bottom order from sequential access files because this simple calculation is not possible. For example, to retrieve the third record from an equivalent sequential access file, VB has to find the second pair of carriage return and line feed characters (which separates the second and third lines of the file). But VB cannot calculate where the carriage return and line feed characters are because there may be a different number of characters in each line of a sequential access file; VB's only way of finding them is to search starting from the top of the file.

Example E.6   Using Random Access

This relatively long example examines a simple application that allows the user to create a random access file, add part records to it, edit existing records, and retrieve the records in order from top to bottom, in reverse order, or individually (by specifying the number of the desired record).

Figure E.14 shows the user interface for this example, which contains two forms. The main form is similar to the forms for Examples E.3 and E.5. Note that there is only one button for opening the file, and one button for closing it. Opening the random access file opens it for both input and output (that is, the program can freely alternate input and output operations). The second form enables the user to enter values for a new record or edit values for an existing record. While not strictly necessary, the second form simplifies user interaction by making it clear to the user when he or she is in the middle of an edit operation.

The code for this example is shown in Figure E.15. Note first the module-level variables in the main form. The variable CurrentRecord, of type PartRecord, is used throughout the code to transfer records between the program and the

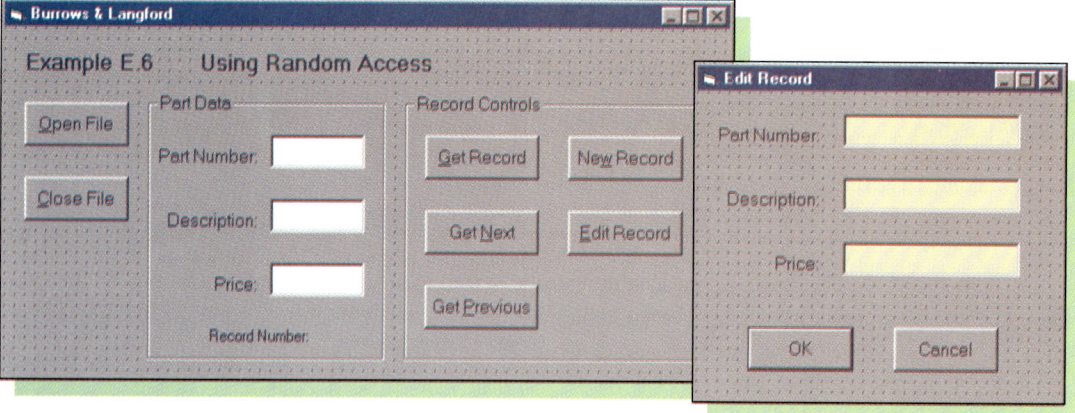

FIGURE E.14 User interface for Example E.6

```
Option Explicit
Private Type PartRecord
    PartNumber As Integer
    Description As String * 10
    Price As Currency
End Type
Dim FileNumber As Integer
Dim CurrentRecord As PartRecord
Dim RecordPointer As Integer
Dim RecordCount As Integer

Private Sub cmdOpenFile_Click()
    FileNumber = FreeFile()
    Open App.Path & "\DatFiles\PartsRan.bin" _
        For Random As #FileNumber Len = Len(CurrentRecord)
    RecordPointer = 0
    RecordCount = LOF(FileNumber) / Len(CurrentRecord)
    fraRecordButtons.Visible = True
End Sub

Private Sub cmdCloseFile_Click()
    Close #FileNumber
    clearLabels
    fraRecordButtons.Visible = False
End Sub

Private Sub cmdGetRecord_Click()
    Dim Response As String
    Response = InputBox("Enter position of record you " & _
                "wish to get (1 to " & RecordCount & ").")
    If validRecordNumber(Response) = False Then
        Exit Sub
    End If
    RecordPointer = Val(Response)
    Get #FileNumber, RecordPointer, CurrentRecord
    copyCurrentRecordToLabels
End Sub
```

```
Private Sub cmdGetNextRecord_Click()
    If RecordPointer >= RecordCount Then
        MsgBox "End of file reached.", vbInformation
        Exit Sub
    End If
    RecordPointer = RecordPointer + 1
    Get #FileNumber, RecordPointer, CurrentRecord
    copyCurrentRecordToLabels
End Sub

Private Sub cmdGetPreviousRecord_Click()
    If RecordPointer <= 1 Then
        MsgBox "Beginning of file reached.", vbInformation
        Exit Sub
    End If
    RecordPointer = RecordPointer - 1
    Get #FileNumber, RecordPointer, CurrentRecord
    copyCurrentRecordToLabels
End Sub

Private Sub cmdNewRecord_Click()
    frmEdit.Caption = "New Record"
    clearLabels
    copyFieldsFromLabelsToEditForm
    frmEdit.Show vbModal
    If frmEdit.ActionCancelled = True Then
        Exit Sub
    End If
    copyFieldsFromEditFormToLabels
    ' Make recordPointer equal to one more than
    ' old number of records in the file.
    ' This will write the new record at the bottom of the file.
    RecordCount = RecordCount + 1
    RecordPointer = RecordCount
    copyLabelsToCurrentRecord
    Put #FileNumber, RecordPointer, CurrentRecord
End Sub
```

FIGURE E.15 Code for main form in Example E.6 (Part 1)

file. The variable RecordPointer is used to keep track of the record number of the most recently retrieved (or written) record. The variable RecordCount is used to keep track of the number of records in the file (which is necessary if the user wants to add a new record).

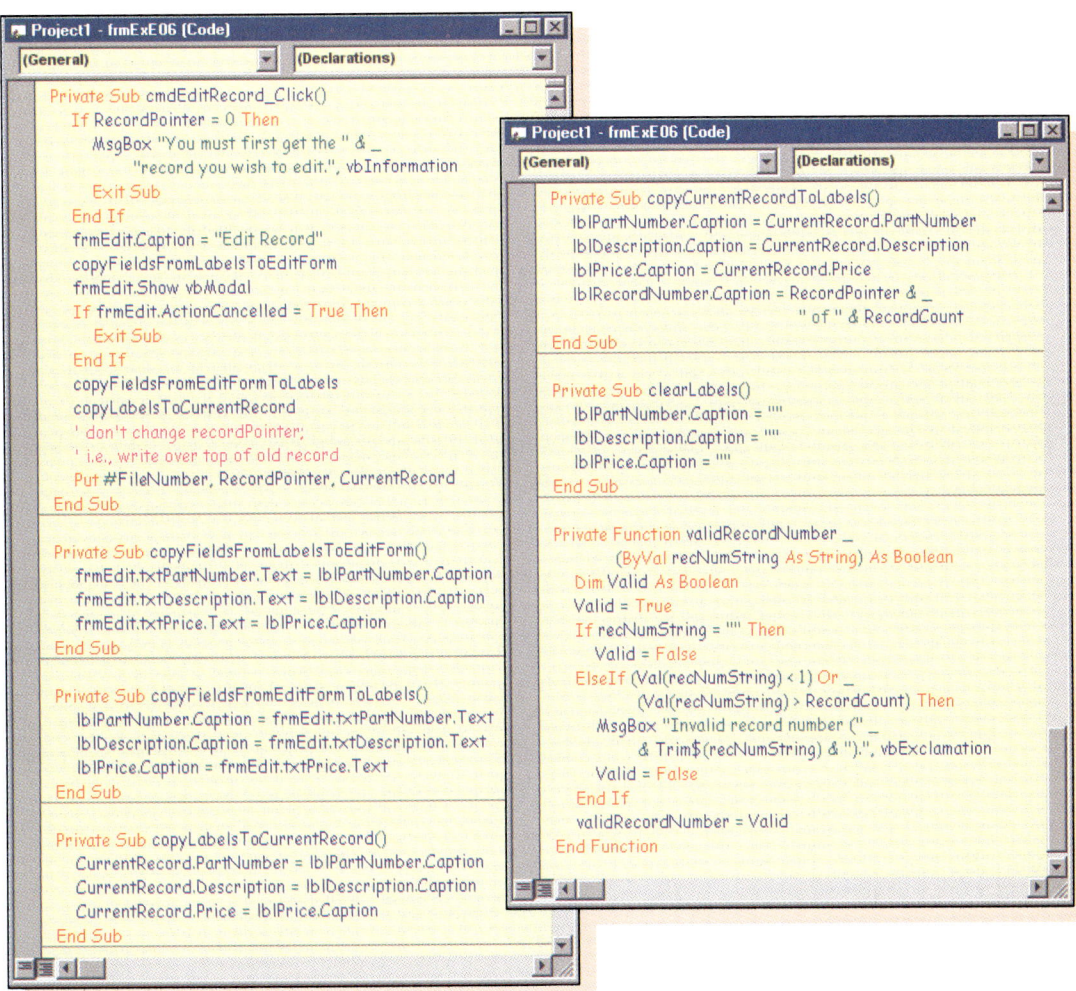

FIGURE E.15 Code for main form in Example E.6 (Part 2)

When the user clicks the button cmdOpenFile, VB executes the Open statement. The syntax of the Open statement that opens a file for random access is

Open *filename* **For Random As File** *#filenumber*, **Len** = *recordLength*

This statement contains two new elements: the keywords For Random (instead of For Input or For Output) and the record length specification. The *recordLength* is a numeric expression specifying the number of bytes in each record. You can compute this value yourself by adding up the number of bytes in each field of the type definition statement; or you can use VB's built-in Len() function, which returns the number of bytes occupied by the variable provided as its argument. After opening the file, the event procedure initializes RecordPointer to 0 and RecordCount to the number of records in the file (computed by dividing the file size by the record size).

When the user clicks the New Record button, VB executes procedure cmdNewRecord_Click. This procedure begins by setting the caption of frmEdit, then clearing the labels on the main form, to make sure that the user knows that an edit operation is in progress. The next statement calls procedure copyFieldsFromLabelsToEditForm, which simply copies the values from the labels on the main form to the text boxes on the edit form (which, in this case, clears them). The next statement shows frmEdit as a modal form, meaning that execution of cmdNewRecord_Click is suspended until the user hides frmEdit. When the user sees frmEdit, he or she enters the data items for the new record, and then clicks either OK or Cancel, which sets the variable ActionCancelled to True or False as appropriate and hides frmEdit (see Figure E.16). Execution then resumes in cmdNewRecord_Click. If the user clicked OK, then the next statement calls procedure copyFieldsFromEditFormToLabels, which copies the values from the text boxes on the edit form back to the labels on the main form. Then, in preparation for adding the new record to the file, the variable RecordCount is incremented, and the variable RecordPointer is set equal to RecordCount. (At this moment, RecordPointer is one greater than the actual number of records in the file). The next statement calls procedure copyLabelsToCurrentRecord, which copies the values from the labels on the main form into the fields of the variable CurrentRecord. Finally, the statement

> Put #FileNumber, RecordPointer, CurrentRecord

writes the values from the variable CurrentRecord into the file at position RecordPointer; this results in the new record being positioned at the end of the file.

The code for the Edit Record button is similar to that for the New Record button. The significant difference is that the Put statement writes the values from the variable CurrentRecord into the file over an existing record, instead of at the end of the file. Analyzing the code for the three "Get" buttons is left as an exercise for you.

FIGURE E.16

Code for edit form in Example E.6

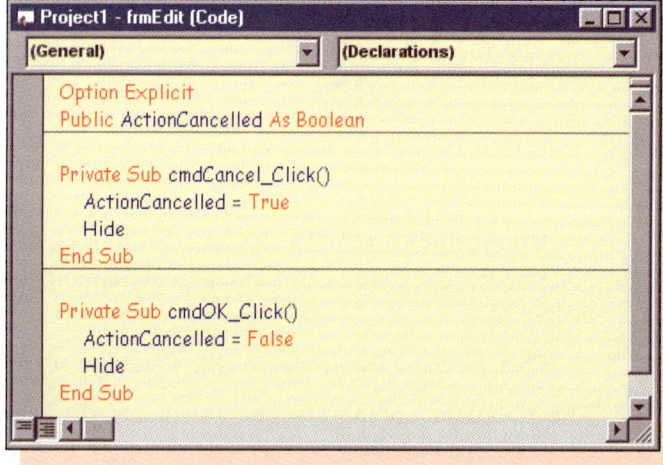

appendix F

The Common Dialog Control and Error Handling

The *Common Dialog control* provides an easy way to incorporate six standard dialog boxes in your applications. These include dialog boxes that you are familiar with from your experience with Windows applications: the File Open and Save dialog boxes, the Font dialog box, the Printer dialog box, the Color dialog box, and the Help system. You do not need a separate Common Dialog control for each different standard dialog you want to display; the same control can display an Open dialog box at one point in the program and a Font dialog box at another point in the program.

Since users can and often do make mistakes when interacting with dialog boxes, we also examine the topic of error handling in this appendix. As an example, the user may enter an invalid file name in an Open dialog box. In order to prevent program execution from ending when this happens, the programmer composes error-handling code (discussed in detail later), that responds to the error and causes execution to resume appropriately.

Appearance and Use

Figure F.1 shows the Common Dialog tool and a Common Dialog control on a form at design time. This is a custom control that Microsoft provides with VB, so you may need to add its tool to the Toolbox (by selecting Components...

FIGURE F.1

Common Dialog tool and control

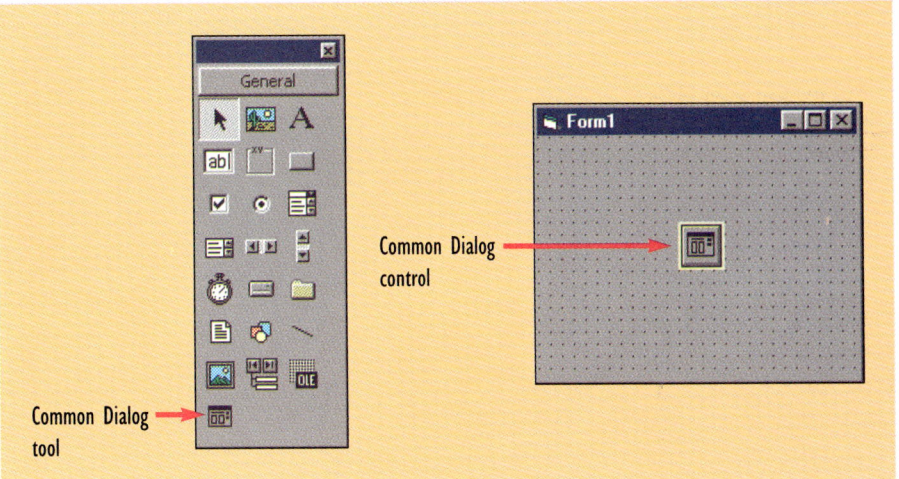

under the Project menu, then checking the box captioned Microsoft Common Dialog Control).

At run time the Common Dialog control itself is invisible to the user. The following sequence of steps describes how it is used:

1. An appropriate method is executed, which causes the Common Dialog control to display a specific dialog box. The dialog box is just a modal form.

2. The user interacts with the dialog box, which sets properties of the Common Dialog control, and then clicks OK or Cancel, which hides the dialog box.

3. Subsequent program statements access the Common Dialog control's properties to determine what the user specified during the dialog (i.e., during step 2).

Figure F.2 shows a typical File Open dialog box and Figure F.3 a typical Font dialog box. Note that these dialog boxes are what the user sees at run time. In this appendix we present examples that use these two types of dialog boxes, demonstrating the Common Dialog control and the way the dialog boxes differ. You can use Online Help to learn about the other kinds of dialog boxes.

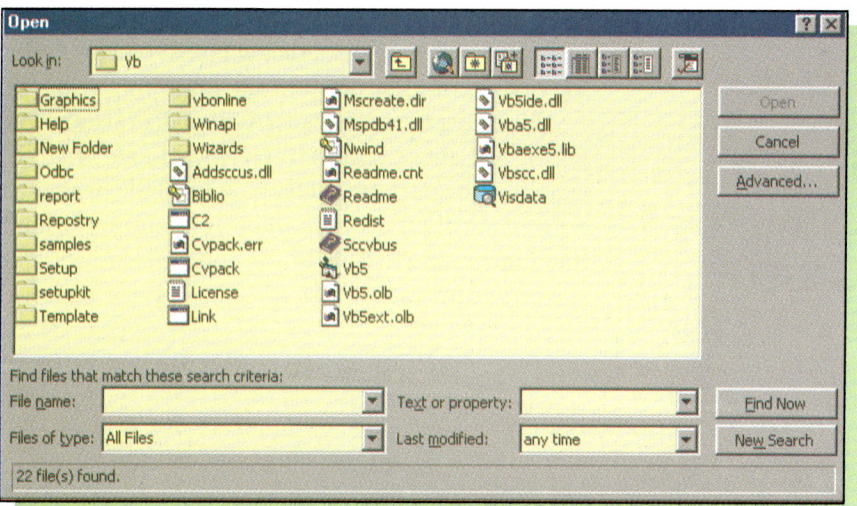

FIGURE F.2

A File Open dialog box

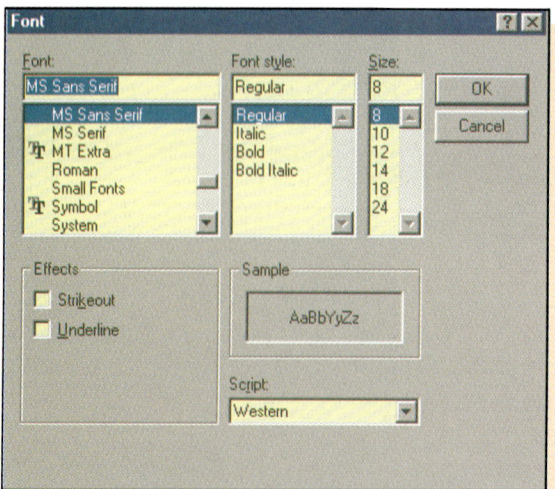

FIGURE F.3

A Font dialog box

Properties

At any point in a program, only a subset of a Common Dialog control's properties are valid. Which properties are valid depends on which kind of dialog box is displayed. Table F.1 shows the valid properties for the File Open dialog box, and Table F.2 shows the valid properties for the Font dialog box. As you can see, the properties for the Common Dialog control are moderately complex. We will demonstrate them with examples shortly.

> **Convention** Use the prefix "cdl" for the names of Common Dialog controls.

Methods

The Common Dialog control has one method for each type of dialog box it can display. Table F.3 lists the valid methods and the dialog box that each produces.

Example F.1

Using the Common Dialog Control

This example illustrates the basic use of the Common Dialog control. The application asks the user to select a file (via a File Open dialog box), then displays the name of the selected file and its size in bytes. The form contains a Common Dialog control (cdlTest), two labels (lblName and lblSize), and a command button (cmdSizeOfFile). The code for this example is shown in Figure F.4.

When the user clicks the command button, the event procedure first sets the value of the Common Dialog control's Filter property to "All Files (*.*)|*.*". This value of Filter specifies that when the Common Dialog control displays a File Open dialog box, it lists files of all types (i.e., all files).

TABLE F.1 Properties relevant to the File Open dialog box

Property	Specifies
FileName	*The complete path of the file the user has specified.* The value of this property is set when the user selects the file in the Open dialog box.
Filter	*The extensions for the types of files that will be displayed in the dialog window's File list box.* For example, if the program expects the user to specify a text file, this property should be set to Text (*.txt)	*.txt. The portion before the vertical bar, Text (*.txt), simply becomes an item in the "Files of type" dropdown list box. The portion after the vertical bar actually controls which files are displayed in the File list box. That is, this pair of values specifies both the item the user sees in the "Files of type" dropdown list, and the type of the files that will be displayed in the File list box when the user selects it. To add more than one type of file to the "Files of type" dropdown list box, list the pairs in Filter, separating them with vertical bars. For example, "Text (*.txt)|*.txt|Database (*.mdb)|*.mdb" will show both text and Microsoft Access database files.
FilterIndex	*Which Filter option will be set as the default type.* For example, if two file types are provided in the Filter, then setting FilterIndex to 1 will make the first type the default and setting it to 2 will make the second type the default.

TABLE F.2 Properties relevant to the Font dialog box

Property	Specifies
Color	*The color the user selected on the Font dialog box. The color option appears on the Font dialog box only if the Flags property setting specifies the color effect.*
Flags	*The options shown on the Font dialog box.* VB provides predefined constants for setting this property. For example, setting Flags to the constant cdlCFScreenFonts causes only screen fonts to be displayed; setting it to cdlCFPrinterFonts causes only printer fonts to be displayed; and setting it to cdlCFBoth causes both screen and printer fonts to be displayed. Setting Flags to cdlCFEffects enables the Strikeout, Underline, and Color options. Add these constants to produce their combined effects. The setting for Flags must include the value for cdlCFScreenFonts, cdlCFPrinterFonts, or cdlCFBoth; otherwise, the run time error "There are no fonts installed" results.
FontBold	*Whether the user selected Bold on the Font dialog box. True or False.*
FontItalic	*Whether the user selected Italic on the Font dialog box. True or False.*
FontName	*The font name the user selected on the Font dialog box.*
FontSize	*The font size the user selected on the Font dialog box.*
FontStrikethru	*Whether the user selected Strikeout on the Font dialog box. True or False. This option appears on the Font dialog box only if the Flags property setting specifies the strikethru effect.*
FontUnderline	*Whether the user selected Underline on the Font dialog box. True or False. This option appears on the Font dialog box only if the Flags property setting specifies the underline effect.*

TABLE F.3 Valid methods for the Common Dialog control

Method	Dialog Displayed
ShowOpen	File Open
ShowSave	Save As
ShowColor	Color
ShowFont	Font
ShowPrinter	Print
ShowHelp	Windows Help

The next statement is the ShowOpen method for the Common Dialog control, which causes the control to display a File Open dialog box (as in Figure F.2). The dialog box is a modal form, which means that execution of the event procedure is suspended until the user hides the dialog box. The user selects a file using the dialog box, and VB automatically sets the Common Dialog control's FileName property to be equal to the file name (including the path) of the file the user selects. The user then clicks either OK or Cancel, which hides the dialog box.

FIGURE F.4

Code for Example F.1

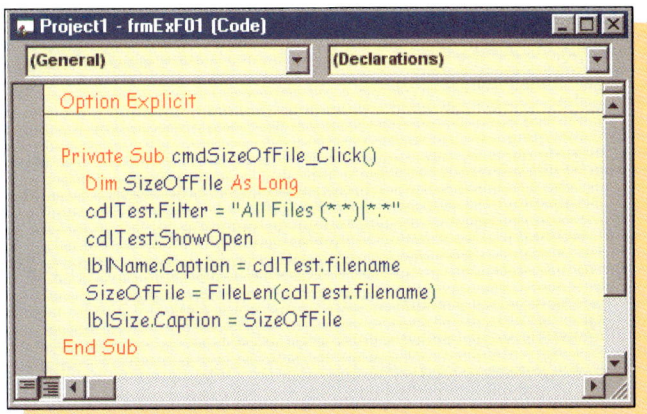

Execution of the event procedure then continues, and the next statement uses the value of the Common Dialog control's FileName property to display the name of the selected file. The statement after that finds the size of this file, in bytes, using VB's built-in FileLen() function. The final statement displays the file size. You can use this program to find the size of any file on your disk.

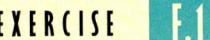

In Example F.1, what happens if the user types an invalid file name in the File Open dialog box's File Name box, then clicks OK? For example, suppose the user types "foo" in the File Name box, and there is no file named "foo" on the disk. Run the program to find out.

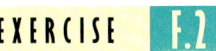

In Example F.1, what happens if the user clicks Cancel instead of OK on the File Open dialog box? Run the program to find out.

Error Handling

Because users can enter invalid data in standard dialog boxes, programs that use the Common Dialog control should contain code to *trap* (detect and respond to) the errors. The code that executes when a run time error occurs is called an *error handler*. As a programmer, you compose this code to "handle," or resolve appropriately, the errors that you anticipate may occur at run time.

For example, if the program requires the user to select a file using a File Open dialog box, you should anticipate that the user may enter an invalid file name. If this does occur, the appropriate action for the error handler to take includes politely informing the user of the mistake, then perhaps displaying the File Open dialog box again. Error-handling code can also respond to many types of run time errors besides those that occur with standard dialog boxes.

Writing an Error Handler

Because VB's full error-handling capabilities are extensive, we present just the basics here. Use online help (search phrase "Error handling") to explore further.

First, each procedure can have its own error handler, which will handle only those run time errors that occur when statements within the procedure are executed. (It is possible for procedures to "share" error handlers, but we don't discuss such sharing here.)

Traditionally, programmers place the error handler at the bottom of the procedure, out of the way of the code that does the main work of the procedure. *An Exit Sub statement must always precede the error handler, because the error handler should be executed only when an error occurs.* The Exit Sub statement prevents the error handler from being executed as part of the ordinary, top-to-bottom execution of statements.

The first statement of the error handler is a *statement label*, which is simply a descriptive name followed by a colon. This label is necessary because a procedure can have more than one error handler (they might handle errors occurring in different portions of the procedure), and VB must be able to distinguish among them. The statement label must be left justified in the Code window. A descriptive statement label for our purposes is "ErrHandler:". Place the code that handles the errors you anticipate immediately below the statement label.

Finally, near the top of the procedure (typically right below the Dim statements) you must compose an *On Error GoTo statement* to inform VB that the procedure has an error handler. The syntax is

On Error GoTo *StatementLabel*

where *StatementLabel* is the first statement of your error handler. Do not include the colon after *StatementLabel* in the On Error GoTo statement. Our next example demonstrates the structure of error handlers.

Example F.2 Error Handling

This example is a simple application that computes the square root of numbers entered by the user. The form has a label for displaying the result (lblResult), and four command buttons that perform the calculation but have different error handlers. Figure F.5 shows the event procedure for the first command button, which has no error handler. What run time errors, if any, do you anticipate may occur when this event procedure executes?

A run time error will occur if the user enters a negative number. If the user enters "–4", VB displays the following error message, then terminates program execution.

Run time error '5':

Invalid procedure call

Since there is no error handler in this procedure, VB handles the error using its built-in error handler, which displays the error message and terminates execution. Observe that VB uses numeric error codes to identify different run time errors. The code for an invalid procedure call is 5.

One way to avoid this particular error is to use an If statement to check whether X is negative before computing its square root. Another is to use an error

FIGURE F.5

Code for the first command button in Example F.2

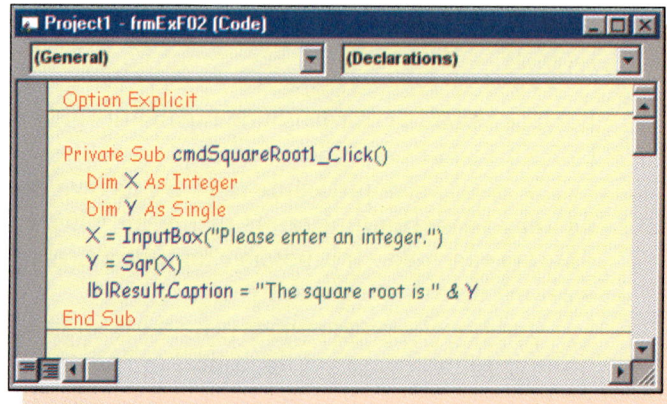

handler, as in the code for the second command button, shown in Figure F.6. This is a minimal error handler. When a run time error occurs in this procedure, its own error handler will execute instead of VB's error handler. This procedure's error handler just exits the procedure. This error handler succeeds in preventing execution from terminating, but it has a couple of shortcomings. It does not inform the user of any mistakes. Also, it does not clear the label; if the user enters "9" the first time after clicking the command button, the label will display "The square root is 3", and if the user enters "–4" the second time, the label will still display "The square root is 3", which is misleading.

You may wonder why the Exit Sub statement is necessary in the error handler. An error handler should not be thought of as part of the code for the procedure's primary processing task; conceptually, an error handler should "redirect" execution in a manner appropriate for the errors it handles. Statements used to redirect execution include Exit Sub, Exit Function, End, Resume, and Resume Next.[1] The End Sub statement is not considered to redirect execution.

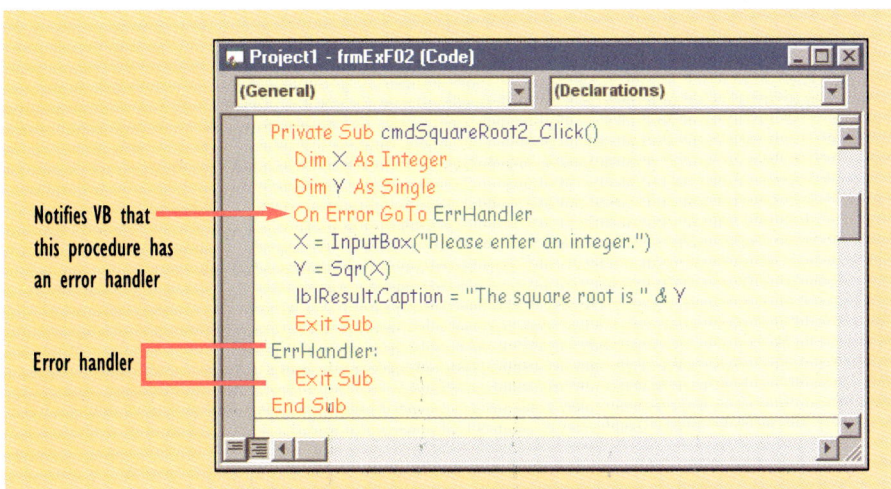

FIGURE F.6

Code for the second command button in Example F.2

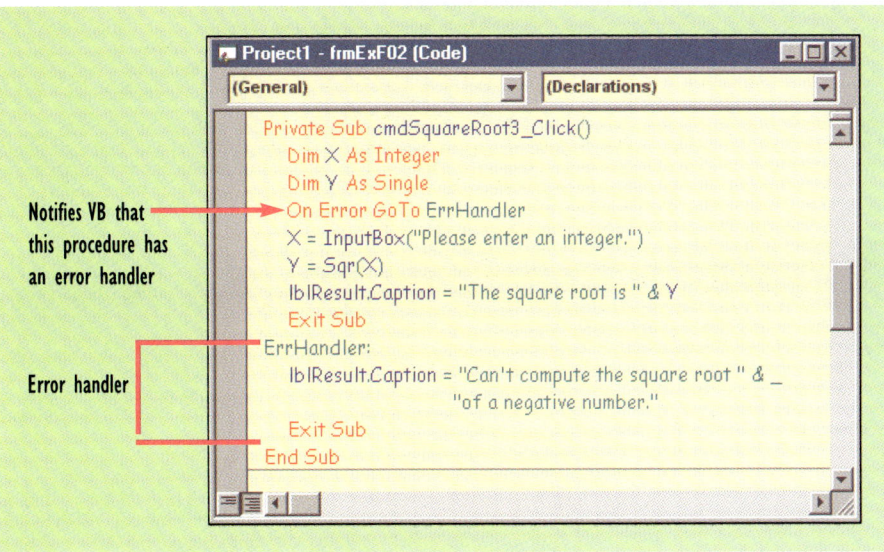

FIGURE F.7

Code for the third command button in Example F.2

[1] The Resume statement causes execution to continue with the same statement that caused the error, and Resume Next causes execution to continue with the statement following the one that caused the error. See online help (search phrase "Resume statement").

The error handler in the event procedure shown in Figure F.7 is an improvement over the one shown in Figure F.6 because it informs the user of the mistake and does not leave a residual answer that may be confusing. However, what happens if the user enters the number 40000 in response to the input box? An overflow error occurs, because X is type Integer, and the largest value it can hold is 32767. But event procedure cmdSquareRoot3_Click handles it the same way it handles all errors, by displaying "Can't compute the square root of a negative number." This message will mislead the user.

When VB (not your error handler) handles an overflow error, it displays the following error message:

Run time error '6':

Overflow

Note that the error number for an overflow error is 6. You can find the error codes for all run time errors by searching online help with the phrase "Trappable errors".

The error handler in Figure F.8 distinguishes between the square root of a negative number and overflow errors, and responds appropriately for each. Also, when any unanticipated error occurs, it responds by beeping, displaying an error message, and terminating execution. To distinguish different errors it uses VB's built-in Err object. When a run time error occurs, before it starts executing your error handler, VB automatically sets the Number property of the Err object equal to the numeric code of the error that occurred.

Some form of decision-making code is typically used in error handlers to distinguish which run time error occurred. As you can see from the sequence of error handlers in this example, programmers expend a great deal of energy perfecting error handlers for refined applications.

FIGURE F.8

Code for the fourth command button in Example F.2

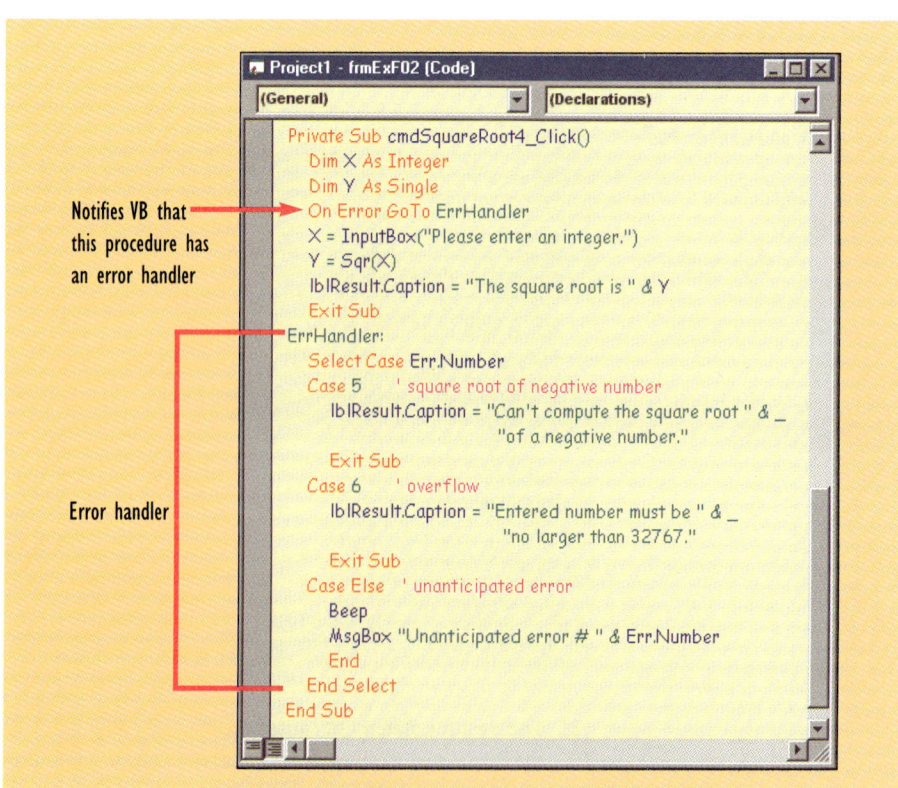

Example F.3 — Handling File Open Dialog Errors

This example revisits the application in Example F.1, which displays the name of any selected file and its size in bytes. The code is repeated in Figure F.9. If the user runs this program, clicks on cmdSizeOfFile, then clicks the Cancel button or enters a file name that does not exist, a "File not found" run time error occurs. In both cases the run time error occurs when the FileLen() function is invoked, because the function cannot find the specified file. The following error message is displayed:

> Run time error '53':
>
> File not found

Clearly, VB's built-in error handler does not provide an appropriate response to either of these user actions. We can trap the invalid file name using an error handler that checks for error number 53. The Common Dialog control has a property, CancelError, which also enables us to handle the "Cancel" situation using an error handler. If you set its CancelError property to True, the Common Dialog control generates a run time error (number 32755) when the user clicks on a dialog's Cancel button. A revised version of the event procedure that solves these problems is shown in Figure F.10.

EXERCISE F.3 In Example F.2, how does the behavior of cmdSquareRoot3_Click change if we remove the Exit Sub statement that precedes the error handler? Explain.

EXERCISE F.4 In Example F.2, event procedure cmdSquareRoot4_Click, what happens if the user enters "A" in response to the input box? Modify the error handler so that it handles this error in addition to those it already handles.

EXERCISE F.5 Modify event procedure cmdSquareRoot3_Click in Example F.2 by changing its error-handling statements from

> lblResult.Caption = "Can't compute the square root " & _
>   "of a negative number."
>
> **Exit Sub**

to

> MsgBox "Can't compute the square root of a negative number."
>
> **Resume**

FIGURE F.9

Code from Example F.1

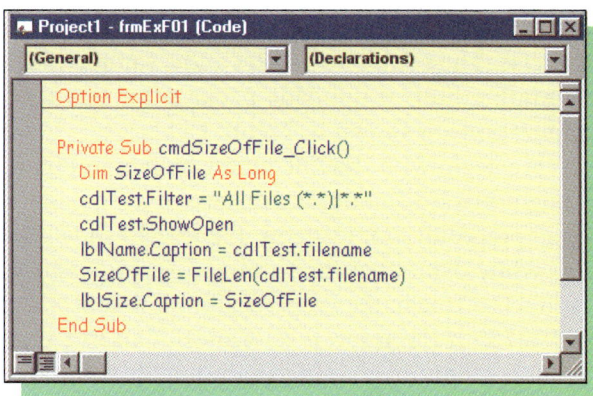

FIGURE F.10

Code for Example F.3

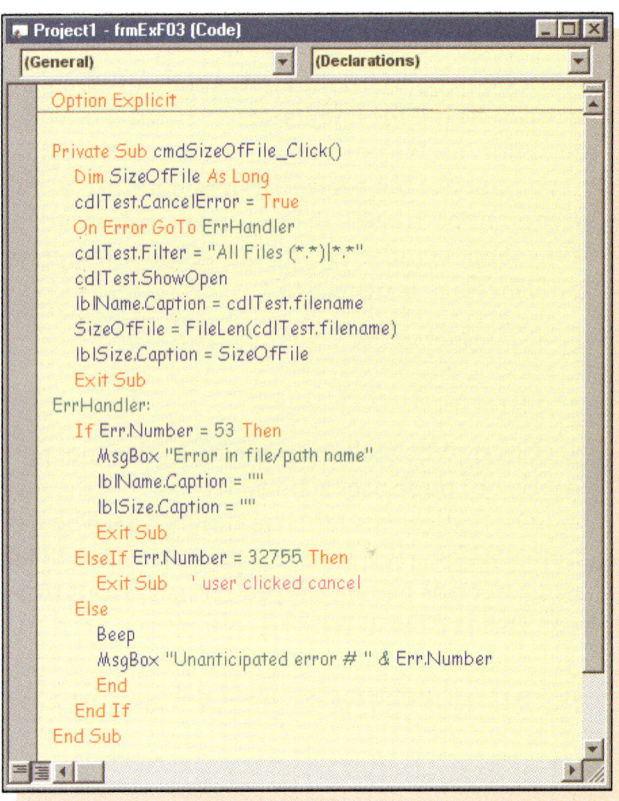

Then execute the event procedure and enter the number –4 in response to the input box. What happens? Explain. Replace Resume with Resume Next, and answer the same question.

Hint: Look up the Resume statement in online help.

Suppose that a particular run time error occurs at a statement inside a loop, and the appropriate response is to ignore the error and continue executing the loop. How would the error handler differ from those in the preceding examples? Explain.

Hint: Look up the Resume statement in online help.

Example Application: Expanding the Text Editor

This application extends the capabilities of the text editor in Example B.1 (Appendix B). It adds the ability to save or retrieve the text from a sequential access file (Appendix E), and it enables the user to fully specify the font characteristics of the displayed text. Saving the font changes in the file is left as an exercise. The complete project and a sample file are stored in the subdirectory AppF\Editor in the code package for this text. The controls used in this application are shown in Figure F.11.

We begin with the File menu, shown in Figure F.12. Creating the menu is straightforward (menus are discussed in Appendix B), so we turn to the Click event procedures for its items. Figure F.13 shows the mnuFileOpen_Click event procedure. Note that the Common Dialog control's CancelError property has been set to True in the Properties window, so it will generate run time error number 32755 if the user clicks Cancel. Observe that the error handler resolves the user actions of entering an invalid file name and clicking the Cancel button.

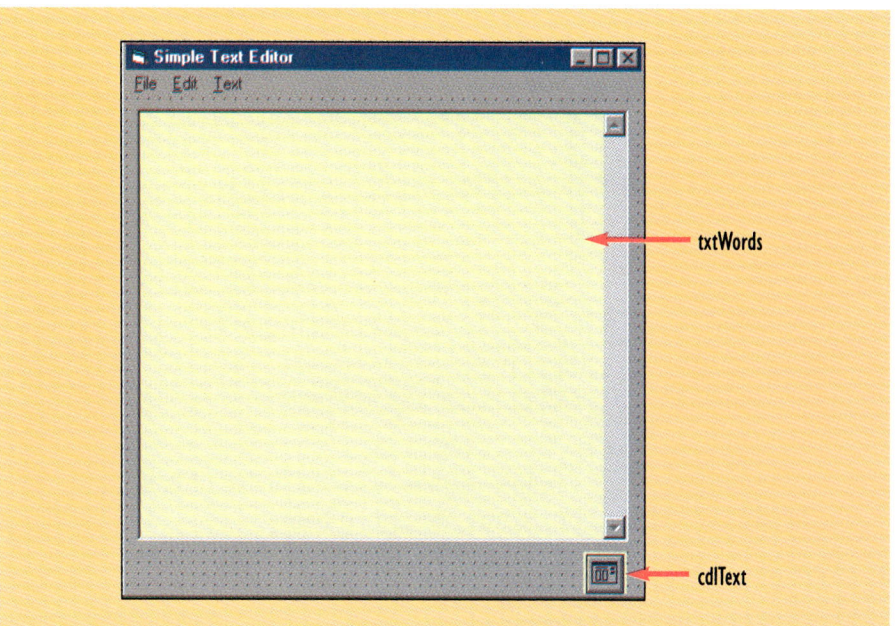

FIGURE F.11

Controls used in the text editor application

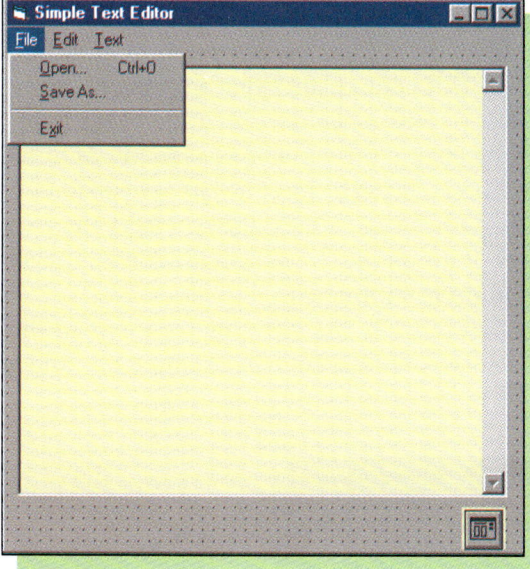

FIGURE F.12

The File menu

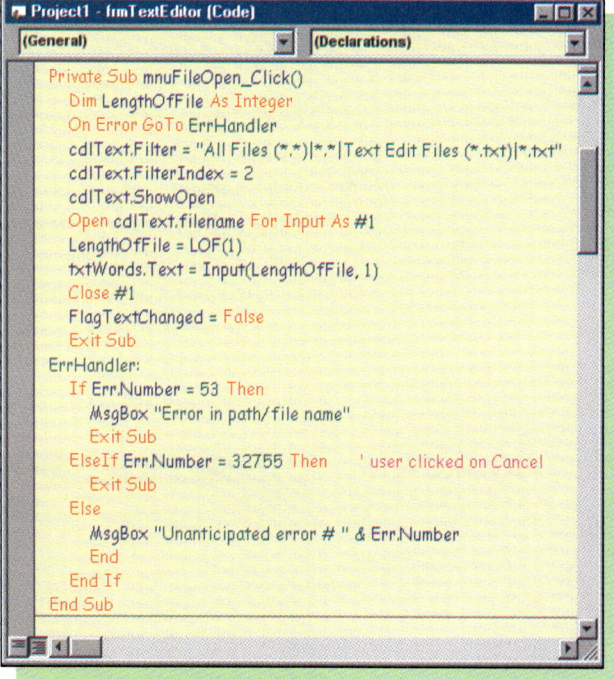

FIGURE F.13

Code for the File Open menu item

Since we are using a sequential access file to store the text, the Common Dialog control's Filter and FilterIndex properties are set to make *.txt the default file type. The ShowOpen method then displays the standard File Open dialog box shown in Figure F.14.

When the user is finished with the dialog box, the value of the FileName property is used to open the selected file for input. The code then determines the length of the file in bytes, inputs the contents of the file and stores it in txtWords.Text, and closes the file. Finally, it sets the value of the module-level

FIGURE F.14

The File Open dialog box

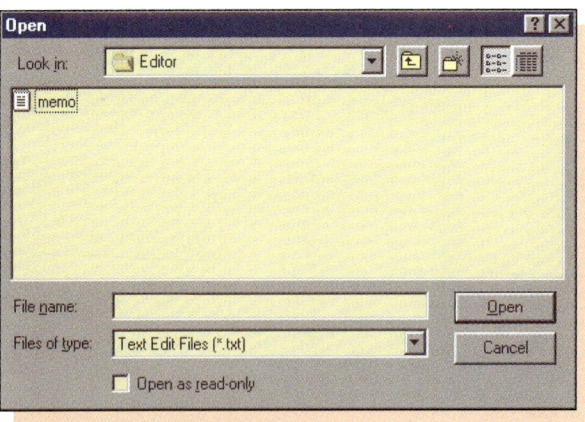

variable *FlagTextChanged* to False; this is a flag variable that is used in the Exit procedure, described below.

Figure F.15 shows the mnuFileSaveAs_Click procedure. It uses the ShowSave method to display a Save As dialog, then uses the Common Dialog control's FileName property to open the specified file for output. The remaining code writes the contents of the text box into the file, then closes the file and sets *FlagTextChanged* to False.

The other item under the File menu is Exit. Event procedure mnuFile-Exit_ Click is shown in Figure F.16. This code ensures that any changes made to the text box are saved, if the user so wishes, before execution of the application is terminated. It starts out by testing the variable *FlagTextChanged* to see if the contents of the text box have been changed since the last save operation. If not, then the application ends. Otherwise, a message box asks the user whether or not to save the changes. If the answer is yes, mnuFileSaveAs_Click is called to save the file and execution is terminated.

The Edit menu is shown in Figure F.17. The code for the items in this menu is basically the same as the corresponding code in Example B.1, and is shown in Figure F.18.

FIGURE F.15

Code for the File Save As menu item

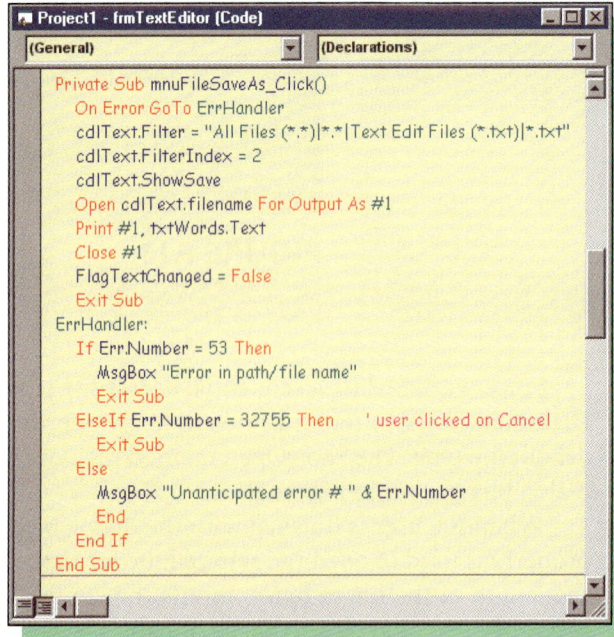

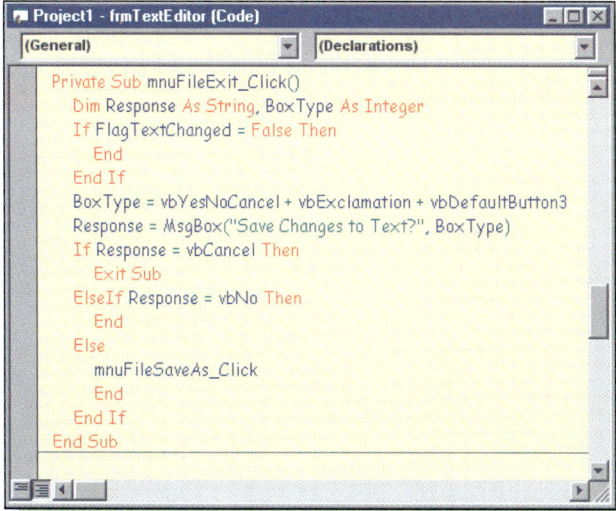

FIGURE F.16

Code for the File Exit menu item

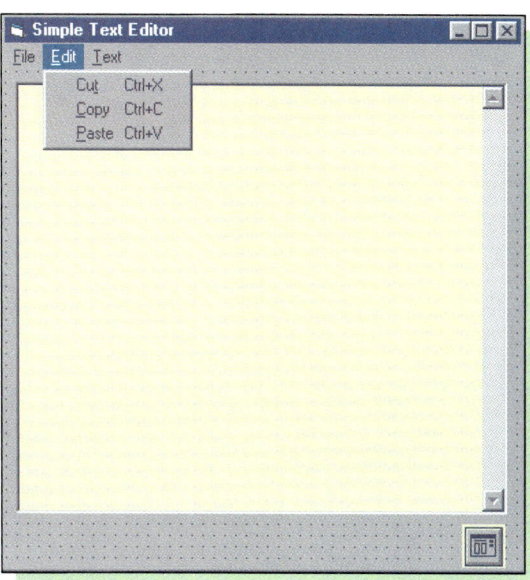

FIGURE F.17

The Edit menu

Finally, the Text menu is shown in Figure F.19. It has only one item, Font. The code for the Font item, shown in Figure F.20, includes instructions to display the standard Font dialog box. The logic of this procedure is to set the Flags property, show the dialog box, and then use the various Font properties set by the user to modify the Font properties of the text box that displays the text. The Font dialog box displayed to the user is shown in Figure F.21.

Note that the font changes affect the text box, not the text itself. That is, the text itself does not change as a result of changing the text box Font properties. Thus, when the text is saved in the file, font changes are not saved. If

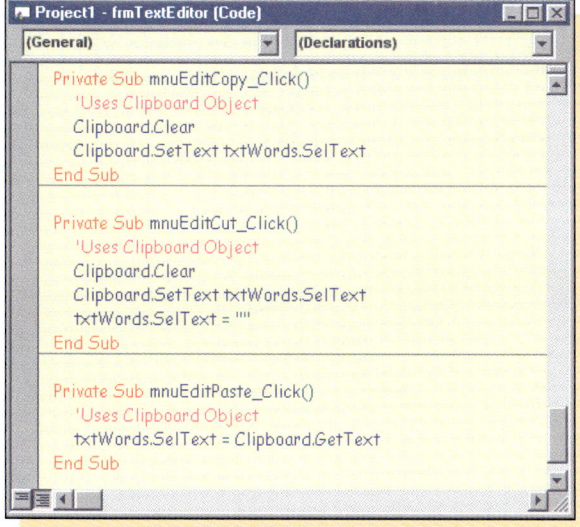

FIGURE F.18

Code for the Edit menu item

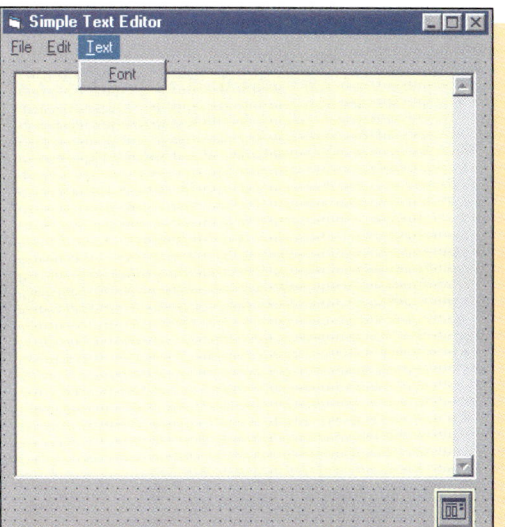

FIGURE F.19

The Text menu

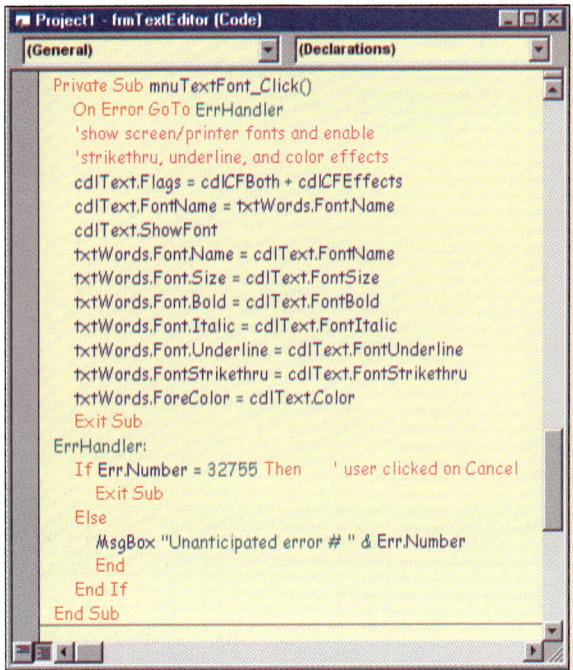

FIGURE F.20

Code for the Text Font menu item

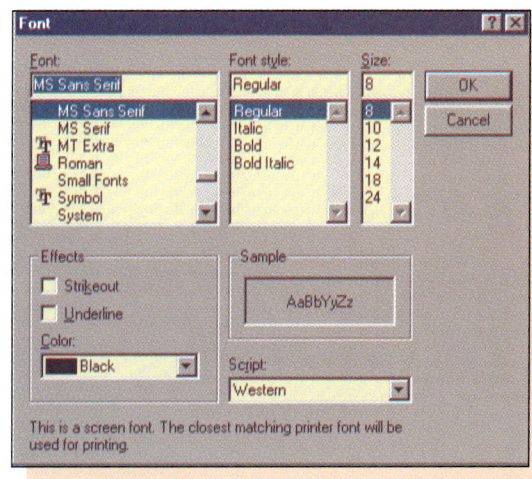

FIGURE F.21

The Font dialog box

you modify the font, save the text, and then open the file again, you will not see the font changes.

EXERCISE F.7

The simple text editor does not save font information in the file. The font changes are applied to the text box that displays the text, but not to the text itself. One way to make the font changes permanent is to include this information in the file in addition to the text. If it is stored as the first few words in the text, the application can read it when the file is opened and use it to set the text box Font properties. The application can also remove this information from the text so that the user cannot see it. Then, when the file is saved, the application can reinsert the font information at the beginning of the text.

Modify the application so that it saves the FontName and FontSize property settings in the file along with the text, and uses this information to restore the font information when the file is opened.

appendix G

The Tabbed Dialog Control

The *Tabbed Dialog control* functions like a series of tabbed notebook pages. Each tabbed page provides the user with a different set of controls (text boxes, labels, option buttons, etc.) organized around a specific function. Having a set of "pages" contained on the same dialog box allows the user to access a large number of settings and options without returning to the menu bar repeatedly. Most Windows applications (including VB) make extensive use of the tabbed dialog concept. Figure G.1 shows VB's Options tabbed dialog box.

The Tabbed Dialog control can also be used as an alternative to option buttons—each tab can represent a different option. For example, in a depreciation application that supports several depreciation methods, each tab can display the depreciation schedule for one of the methods.

Appearance and Use

The Tabbed Dialog tool can be added to the Toolbox by selecting Components... from the Project menu, then checking the box captioned Microsoft Tabbed Dialog Control 5.0. (Note that the Components dialog box is itself a tabbed dialog box.) Figure G.2 shows the Tabbed Dialog tool and the control at design time.

FIGURE G.1

An example of a tabbed dialog box that uses a Tabbed Dialog control

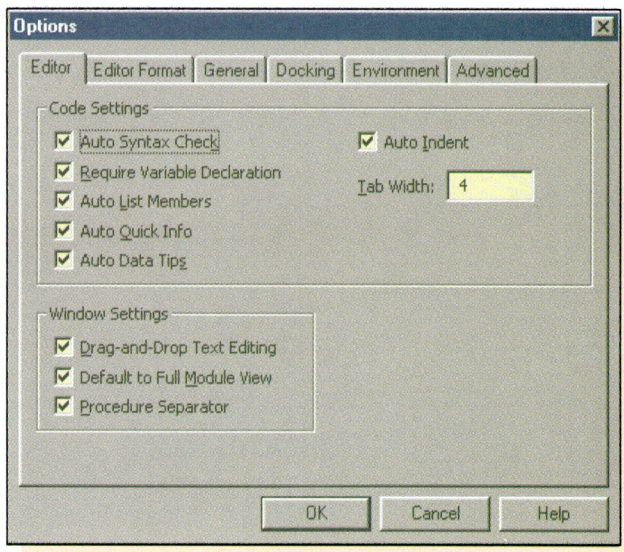

FIGURE G.2

Tabbed Dialog tool and control at design time

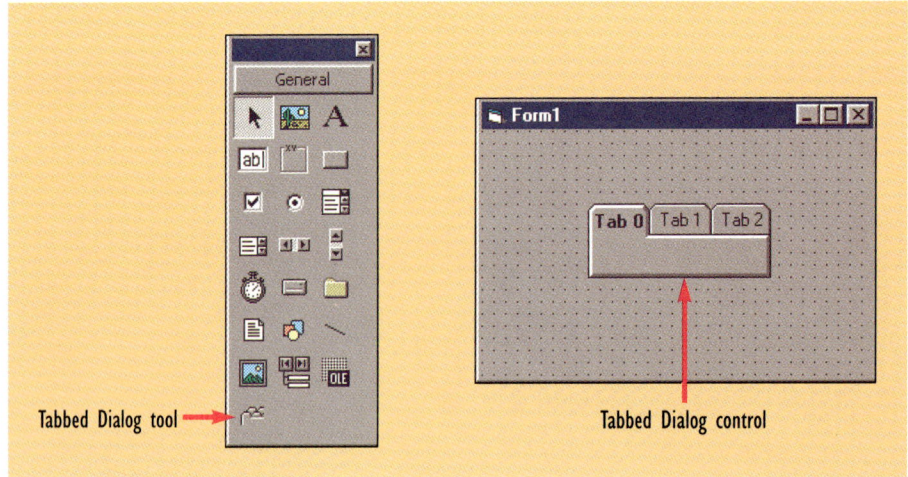

When using the Tabbed Dialog control to create a tabbed dialog box, the convention is to size the control and underlying form as shown in Figure G.3. Note that the control is centered and has equal amounts of space at the left, top, and right sides. Another convention that is generally followed is to place OK and Cancel buttons at the bottom right of the form. Sometimes a Help button is added, at the far right, in addition to the OK and Cancel buttons.

Properties

Because the Tabbed Dialog control is a custom control, it includes a custom Property Pages dialog box that provides access to most of the control properties. Figure G.4 shows this dialog box.

Use the Tab Cou<u>n</u>t property to define the number of tabs. If there are many tabs (more than can fit in one row), use the TabsPe<u>r</u>Row property to indicate how many tabs will be on each row. Use the <u>C</u>urrent Tab and <u>T</u>abCaption

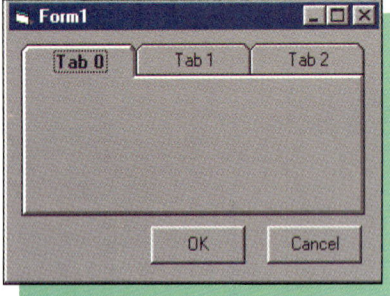

FIGURE G.3

Layout of the Tabbed Dialog control on a form to create a tabbed dialog box

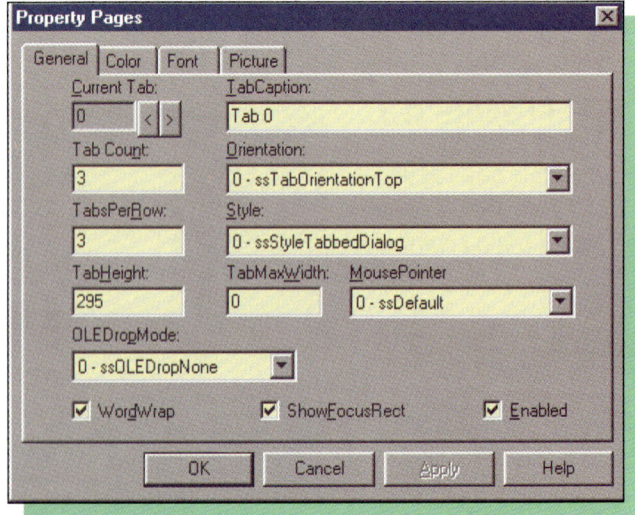

FIGURE G.4

The Tabbed Dialog control's custom Property Pages dialog box properties to create individual captions for each tab. Note that tabs are numbered beginning with zero.

The Orientation and Style properties are a bit more complex. The Orientation property determines where the tabs are located. The valid options are top, bottom, left, and right (ssTabOrientationTop, ssTabOrientationBottom, ssTabOrientationLeft, ssTabOrientationRight). Figure G.5 shows the top and bottom orientation options. To use the left and right orientations, the font for the Tabbed Dialog control must be a TrueType font. Figure G.4 shows the Font tab that can be used to select a TrueType font.

There are two styles, the ssStyleTabbedDialog and ssStylePropertyPage style. Figure G.5 shows examples of the "TabbedDialog" style. Notice that with this style, the text of the selected tab is shown in bold. Figure G.6 shows an example of the "PropertyPage" style. This style has somewhat squarer tabs, and the text of the selected tab is not bold. The two VB Tabbed Dialog controls in Figures G.1 and G.4 use this style.

When using the Tabbed Dialog control to create a tabbed dialog box, a final convention is to set the Form control's BorderStyle property to "3 - Fixed Dialog". This gives the dialog box a standard appearance, as shown in Figure G.7.

> **Convention** Use the prefix "tab" for the names of Tabbed Dialog controls.

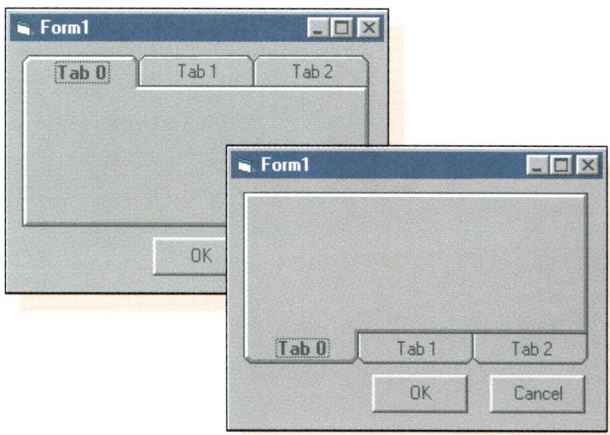

FIGURE G.5

Tabbed Dialog controls with orientation set to top and bottom

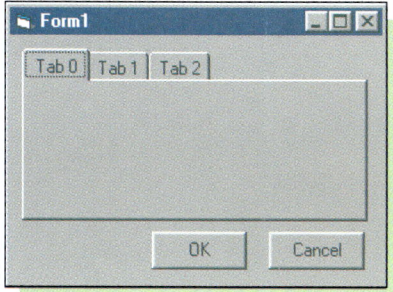

FIGURE G.6

A Tabbed Dialog control with the PropertyPage style

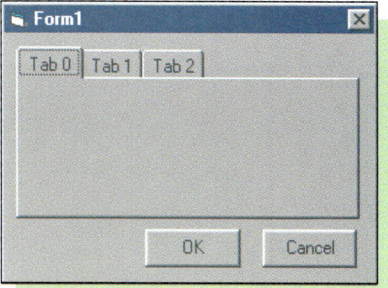

FIGURE G.7

Tabbed Dialog box with the form's BorderStyle property set to "3 - Fixed Dialog"

Events

When a Tabbed Dialog control is used to create a tabbed dialog box, the control generally does not react to any events. Instead, all processing is activated when the OK button is clicked.

When the Tabbed Dialog control is used for other purposes (for example, as an alternative to option buttons), the Click event is often used to initiate a processing step. The control has a Tab property that is automatically set equal to the number of the current tab (where the first tab is numbered 0). The Click event's procedure heading is

Private Sub SSTab1_Click(PreviousTab **As Integer**)

where the PreviousTab parameter indicates the number of the tab page that was active right before the user clicked on the present tab.

Adding Controls to Tabs

Each tab on a Tabbed Dialog control is a separate container. That is, each tab can hold (contain) its own set of controls. A Frame control (see Chapter 5) is another example of a container control. As with the Frame control, if you want a control to be contained on a tab page you must draw it directly on the tab page. To do this, first select the control's tool with a single click, then click-and-drag the control on the appropriate tab page. Do not use the double-click method on a tool in the Toolbox—this will place the control on the form and it will not be contained by the tab page.

Figure G.8 shows two tabs of a Tabbed Dialog control. Each tab has a single Label control with different text in the label captions. When the user clicks on a tab, that tab's control becomes visible.

If you create a control on the form and then drag it onto a Tabbed Dialog control, it will not be contained by any page of the tabbed control. Instead, it will appear to "float" over the control, and the user will think it's on every tab. This effect can be put to good use. Example G.1 takes advantage of this characteristic.

Example G.1 Using the Tabbed Dialog Control to Select Options

To illustrate the use of a Tabbed Dialog control to select options, we create a depreciation calculator application. Figure G.9 shows the application at run time.

When the user clicks on either the "Straight Line" or the "SYD" tab, the application automatically updates the FlexGrid control with the appropriate depreciation calculations.

FIGURE G.8

Label controls contained by tabs of a Tabbed Dialog control

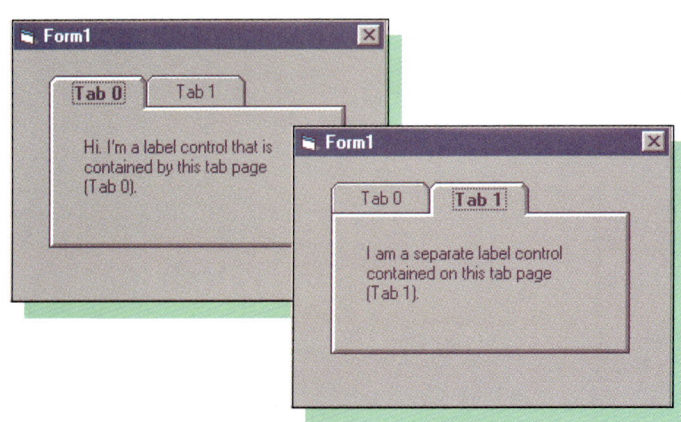

FIGURE G.9

Example G.1 at run time

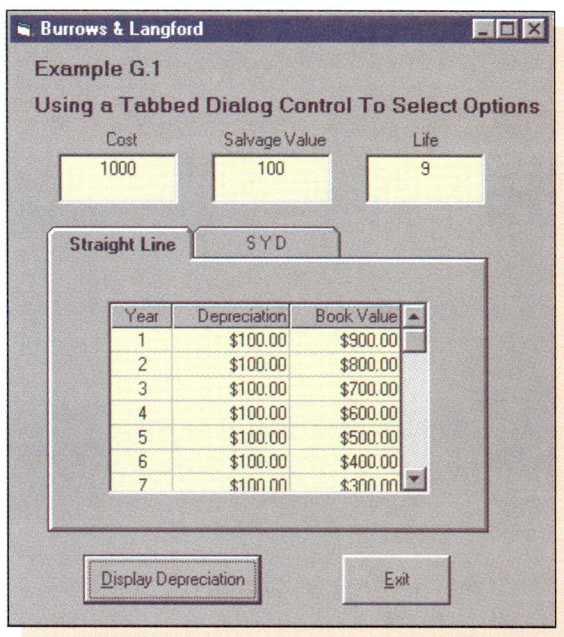

There is only one FlexGrid control and it is not contained by either page of the Tabbed Dialog control. Instead, it floats over the control and appears to be on both pages. This makes sense here because it is easiest to maintain and update just one grid, not two.

Figure G.10 shows the code for the "Display Depreciation" click event.

FIGURE G.10

Code for Example G.1's "Display Depreciation" click event

```
Private Sub cmdDisDep_Click()
    Dim Life As Integer
    Dim Cost As Currency
    Dim SalVal As Currency
    Dim Y As Integer
    Dim Dep As Currency, BookVal As Currency
    'Verify all parameters are present
    If txtLife.Text = "" Or txtCost.Text = "" Or txtSalVal.Text = "" Then
        MsgBox "You must supply values for all parameters", vbInformation
        Exit Sub
    End If
    Life = txtLife.Text
    Cost = txtCost.Text
    SalVal = txtSalVal.Text
    BookVal = Cost
    grdDep.Rows = Life + 1
    grdDep.Visible = True
    For Y = 1 To Life
        If tabDep.Tab = 0 Then
            Dep = SLN(Cost, SalVal, Life)
        Else
            Dep = SYD(Cost, SalVal, Life, Y)
        End If
        BookVal = BookVal - Dep
        grdDep.TextMatrix(Y, 0) = Format$(Y, "##")
        grdDep.TextMatrix(Y, 1) = Format$(Dep, "Currency")
        grdDep.TextMatrix(Y, 2) = Format$(BookVal, "Currency")
    Next Y
End Sub
```

FIGURE G.11

Tabbed Dialog control's Click event for Example G.1

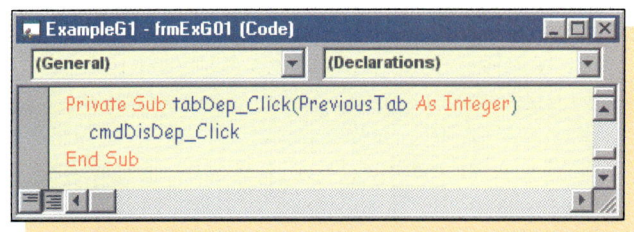

The critical code in this event procedure is the If statement in the For...Next loop:

```
If tabDep.Tab = 0 Then
    Dep = SLN(Cost, SalVal, Life)
Else
    Dep = SYD(Cost, SalVal, Life, Y)
End If
```

This code tests the Tab property of the Tabbed Dialog control (tabDep) to see which tab is active. This information is then used to determine which depreciation method to use. The remainder of the code is the same regardless of the depreciation method.

The application also needs to update the schedule when the user clicks on either tab. This is handled with the Click event for the Tabbed control. Figure G.11 shows this code. This procedure simply calls the Click event procedure for the Display Depreciation command button, which tests the Tab property to determine which depreciation method to use.

The remaining code in Figure G.10 provides data validation and sets up the grid. See Chapter 8 for details on using a FlexGrid contol.

Creating a Tabbed Dialog Box

This example demonstrates the use of the Tabbed Dialog control to create a tabbed dialog box. The application and its tabbed dialog box are shown in Figure G.12.

FIGURE G.12

Example G.2 at run time

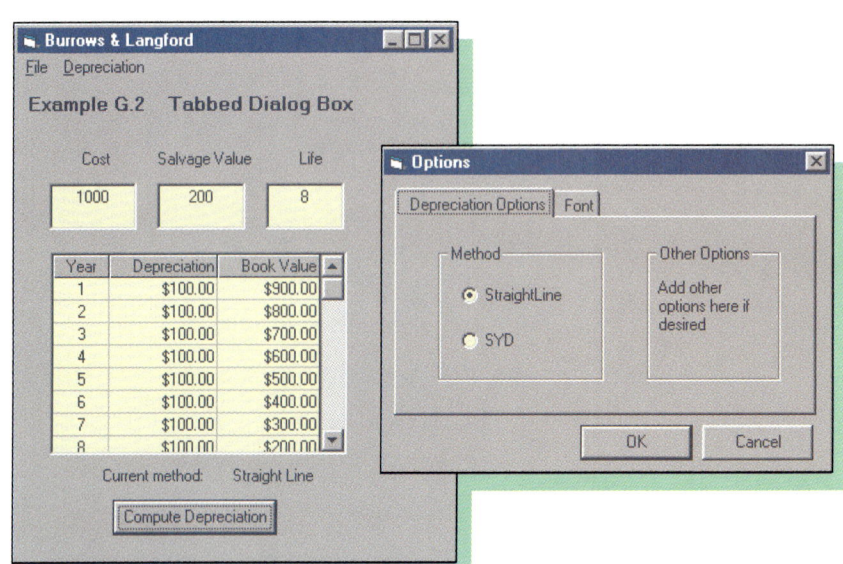

The example uses two forms. The main form shows a depreciation schedule in a FlexGrid control and is similar to Example G.1. The second form is an "Options" tabbed dialog box that allows the user to choose the depreciation method and to select some font options for the grid. This second form has a Tabbed Dialog control with two tabs. Each tab contains its own set of controls that were placed in the tabs by drawing them on the page. Figure G.13 shows both tabs with their controls.

The general processing philosophy regarding dialog boxes is to let the user change or select options and then, when the user clicks on OK, to apply the new options to the form. However, if the user makes changes and then clicks on Cancel, no changes should take place. This means that the actual processing for the dialog box is associated with the OK button's Click event procedure. Figure G.14 shows the Click event for the tabbed dialog box's OK button.

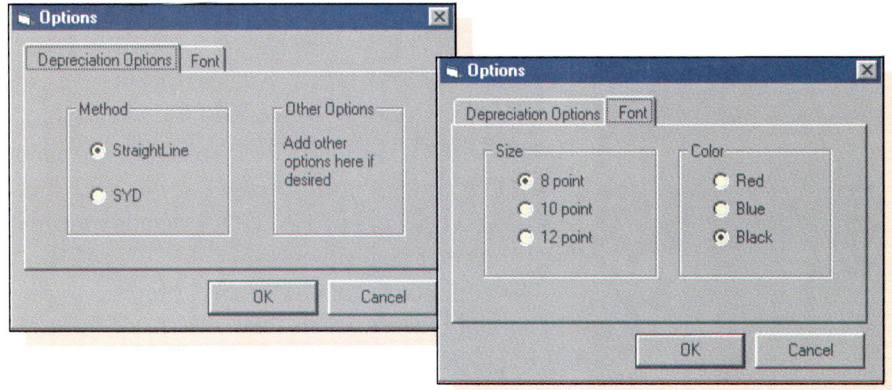

FIGURE G.13

Controls on the two tabs of the Tabbed Dialog control

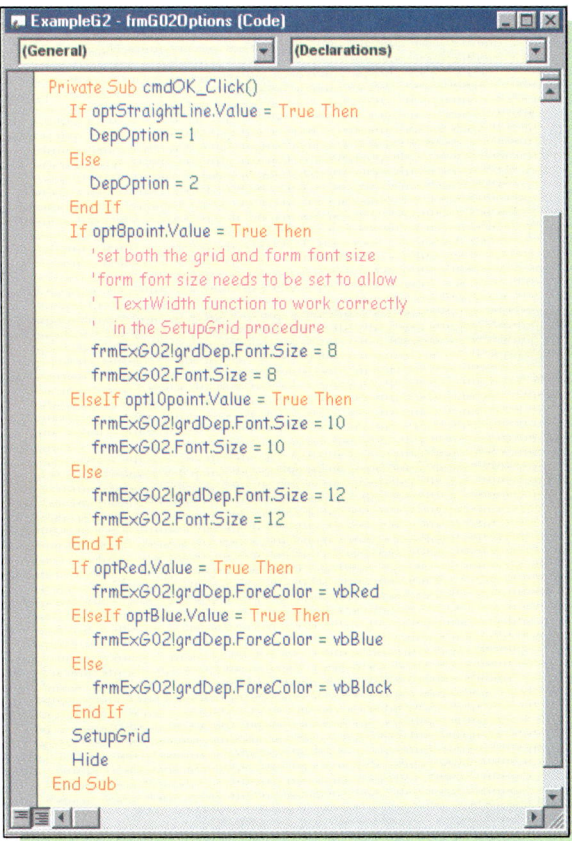

FIGURE G.14

Code for the OK button on Example G.2's tabbed dialog box

This code employs two strategies to accomplish its task. First, it uses the global variable DepOption to record the depreciation option chosen by the user, so that it is available for subsequent retrieval by the Compute Depreciation button's Click event. Second, it makes changes to some of the controls on the main form, frmExG02. (See Chapter 3 for details on working with multiple forms.) Here, the changes apply the font preferences specified by the user. The procedure SetupGrid is called at the end of the procedure to handle potential font changes and subsequent grid size considerations.

When the font size is changed, both the grid's font and the main form's font (frmExG02) have to be changed. This is because the TextWidth method, used in the SetupGrid procedure, uses the form's font characteristics to compute the width of the text it is passed.

The code for the Cancel button on the tabbed dialog box is very simple. All it does is hide the dialog box without making any changes.

```
Private Sub cmdCancel_Click()
    Hide
End Sub
```

The SetupGrid procedure is stored in a separate code module because it is invoked by code in both forms. The code for this procedure is shown in Figure G.15 (see Chapters 3 and 6 for details on code modules and Chapter 8 for details on the FlexGrid control).

The code for the main form's Compute Depreciation command button is very similar to the code in Example G.1 (Figure G.10). The main difference is in the approach used to determine which depreciation method should be used. The code related to this task is

```
If DepOption = 1 Then
    Dep = SLN(Cost, SalVal, Life)
    lblMethod.Caption = "Straight Line"
Else
    Dep = SYD(Cost, SalVal, Life, Y)
    lblMethod.Caption = "SYD"
End If
```

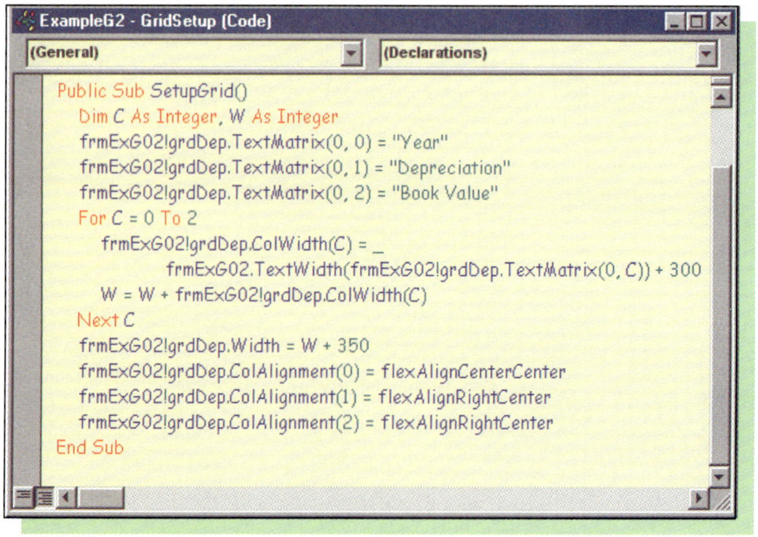

FIGURE G.15

Code for the SetupGrid Procedure in Example G.2

```
Public Sub SetupGrid()
    Dim C As Integer, W As Integer
    frmExG02!grdDep.TextMatrix(0, 0) = "Year"
    frmExG02!grdDep.TextMatrix(0, 1) = "Depreciation"
    frmExG02!grdDep.TextMatrix(0, 2) = "Book Value"
    For C = 0 To 2
        frmExG02!grdDep.ColWidth(C) = _
                frmExG02.TextWidth(frmExG02!grdDep.TextMatrix(0, C)) + 300
        W = W + frmExG02!grdDep.ColWidth(C)
    Next C
    frmExG02!grdDep.Width = W + 350
    frmExG02!grdDep.ColAlignment(0) = flexAlignCenterCenter
    frmExG02!grdDep.ColAlignment(1) = flexAlignRightCenter
    frmExG02!grdDep.ColAlignment(2) = flexAlignRightCenter
End Sub
```

FIGURE G.16

Menu used to display the tabbed dialog bo

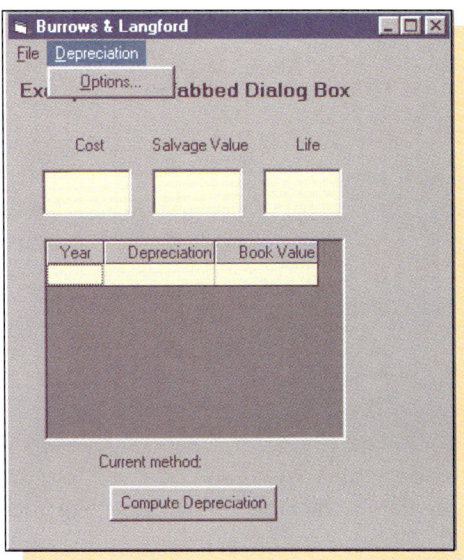

The If statement uses the same DepOption global variable used by the tabbed dialog box's OK button (see Figure G.14).

Finally, the example uses a menu (see Appendix B) to display the tabbed dialog box. Figure G.16 shows the menu that displays the dialog box.

appendix H

Additional Projects

This appendix presents two projects that are somewhat more complex than the projects in Chapters 2 through 10. They are intended to provide additional challenges for those who want to test their understanding of VB.

Project H.1: Real Estate Application Revisited

In Project 12 (Chapter 8) we presented a real estate application that helped agents find information on their firm's listings (property and homes available for sale). This project extends that application.

Description of the Application

This project extends Project 12 in two ways. First, a picture of the house is included along with the details of each listing. Second, a menu replaces some of the original command buttons. Figure H.1 shows the revised application while it is executing.

To implement these changes, the underlying database must be modified slightly to store the information about the picture. We choose not to store the picture itself in the database; instead, we store the name of the file containing

FIGURE H.1

Revised real estate application at run time

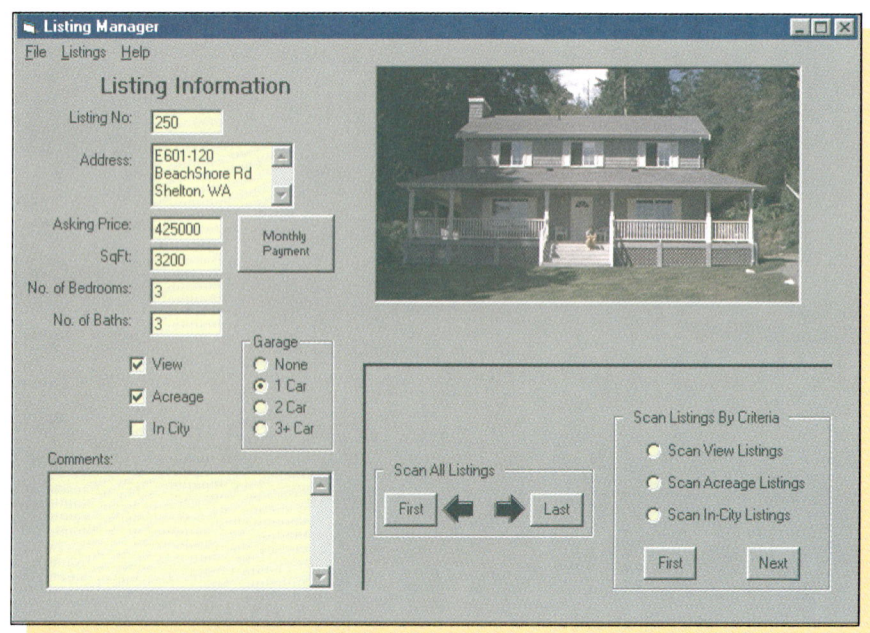

the actual picture. Other than these changes, the application's functionality remains the same as the original application in Project 12.

Design of the Application

Let's first examine how to display a picture for each listing. We modify the underlying database (Houses.mdb) by adding a new text field (PicFileName) to the table (Listings) definition. This field will contain either the name of the file that stores the actual picture or, if no picture is available, the word "none". Assume that the picture files will be stored in the same directory as the application, so only the file name itself needs to be stored in the database. Separating the actual file from the database and storing only the file name makes it possible to replace the picture file without changing the database.

A Picture box control (see Appendix C) must be added to the form to display the picture. We require a Picture box control instead of an Image control because we want to print the text "No picture on file." in the picture box if no picture file is available, and an Image control cannot print text. Figure H.2 shows a listing that has no picture file.

To link the Picture box control to the picture, we use a Label control as an intermediary. This label should be bound to the new database field (PicFileName) and should have its Visible property set to False. The program should use this label to determine the name of the picture file, if one exists. A change in the value of this label signals that the contents of the picture box must be updated. The pseudocode for displaying the picture follows:

1. Get the file name from the label's caption.
2. If the file name is empty or equals "none" Then
    Clear any text from the picture box (Cls)
    Use the LoadPicture("") function to clear an image if one exists
    Print "No picture on file." into the picture box
   Else
    Concatenate the application's path and the file name
    Use the LoadPicture() function to set the Picture property

FIGURE H.2

Listing with no picture available

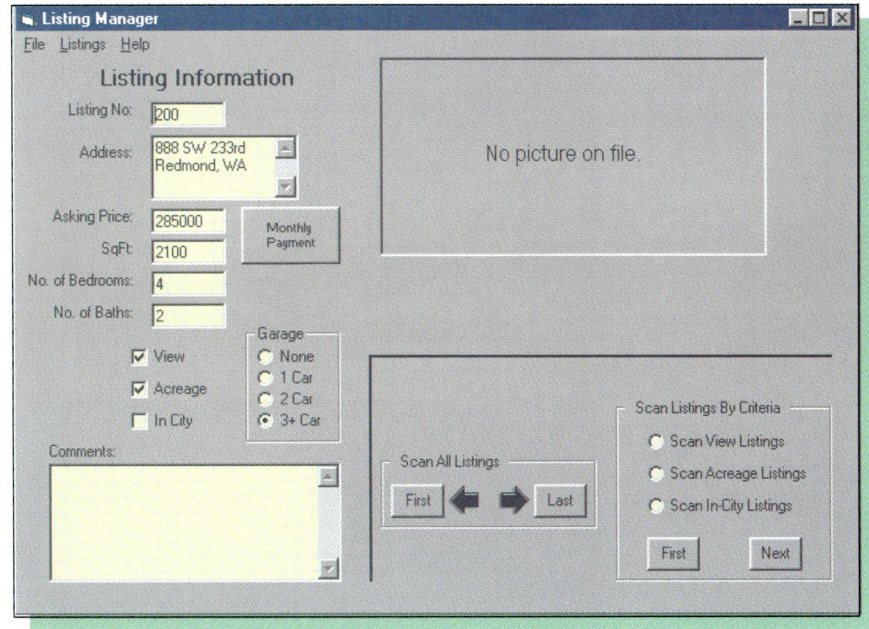

The final task associated with the picture is to ensure that the first record is displayed properly when execution of the application begins. This task requires attention because a control will not respond to an event such as Change until the form where it resides is shown. To get around this problem, the Form_Load procedure needs to execute the Show method for the form and then set the label for the picture file name equal to the value in the first record of the database. This action causes the label to change and, consequently, the pseudocode just presented to be executed.

We now turn our attention to the menu (see Appendix B). Figure H.3 shows the menu structure in the Menu Editor window. The Click event procedures for mnuListingsDelete and mnuListingsFind are identical to those for the Delete and Find buttons from Project 12. The procedure for mnuListingsNew is similar to that for the New button of Project 12; however, it needs to be modified so that it asks the user for the name of a picture file if one exists. Figure H.4 shows the input box asking for this information.

The procedure for mnuListingsAddPicture is new to this project. It first asks the user for a file name (similar to Figure H.4), and then stores this value in the file name's Label caption. Remember that if the user clicks the Cancel button of an input box, the returned value will be the zero-length string. The procedure for mnuFileExit closes the database and ends the application.

The Help menu has an About item that shows a form briefly describing the application. Figure H.5 shows an example About box for this application. The picture of a house and car comes from one of the icon files supplied with VB (Graphics\Icons\Misc\House.ico). The Close button on this form simply hides the form.

FIGURE H.3

Menu structure of real estate application

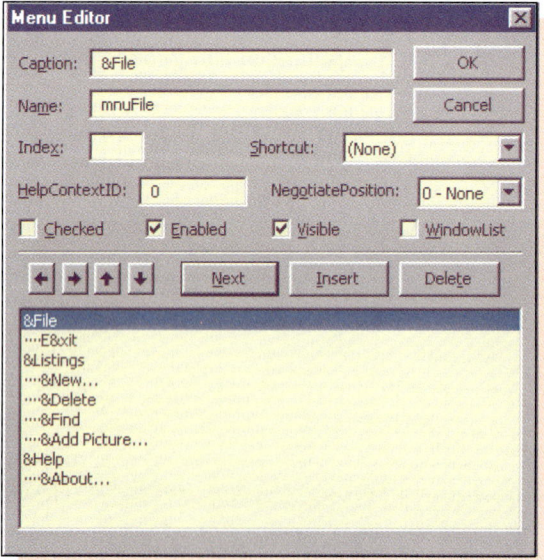

FIGURE H.4

Input box asking for a picture file name

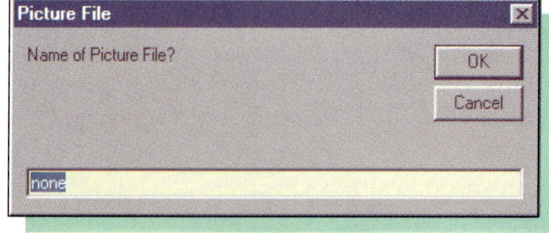

FIGURE H.5

An example About box

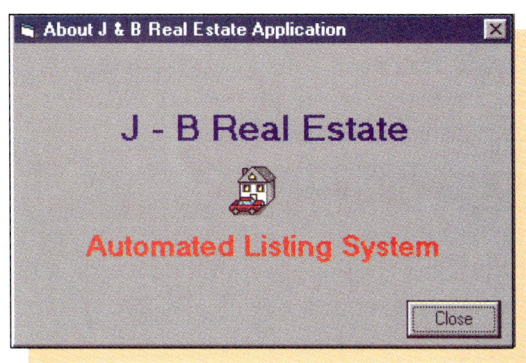

Construction of the Application

The approach you will use to construct this application depends upon whether you are modifying the forms and code from Project 12 or starting from scratch. If you are starting from scratch, first review the "Construction of the Application" discussion from Project 12. The main differences between this project and Project 12 are (1) the use of menus instead of the four command buttons at the lower right of Project 12's Listing form, and (2) the inclusion of the Picture box control.

If you are modifying Project 12, start by changing the properties for the Data control to use the modified database. The modified database, Houses.mdb, is stored in the subdirectory AppH\ProjH1 in the code package for this text. Note that a number of picture files are also stored in this subdirectory.

Now add the menus using the Menu Editor (this task should be straightforward). Then you can start programming the Click event procedures for the various menu items. Most of the code is already written, but it is associated with the existing command buttons; you can just copy-and-paste the code to its new location. For example, you can copy the code that currently exists in the Exit, Find, and Del command buttons and paste it directly to the mnuFileExit, mnuListingsFind, and mnuListingsDelete procedures, respectively. You might wonder why we suggest that you copy-and-paste, not cut-and-paste. After all, the code won't be needed in the command buttons anymore. The reason for using copy and not cut is to protect yourself from mistakes. With copy, the original (working) code is still there, and you can go back to it if you mess up the new code. With cut, you don't have this option.

You should be able to test these menu items at this point. After verifying that they work properly, go back and delete the old Exit, Find, and Del command buttons (and their event procedures).

You can also copy-and-paste the code from the existing New command button to the new mnuListingsNew procedure. However, you'll need to modify it as described in the preceding design discussion.

Next, you might want to add the label for the picture file name from the database. You can put it anywhere since it will not be visible. Name it, and bind it to the database and the PicFileName field in the database table.

Now rearrange the controls so they are similar to the user interface shown in Figure H.1. You will probably have to increase the size of the form. Allow enough room on the form for the picture box, then place one on the form, name it, and set its AutoSize property to True.

You should be ready to return to coding. Code the Click event procedure for the mnuListingsAddPicture menu item. The logic of this procedure was described in the design discussion. You also need to program the Change event for the label just created. This event displays either the picture or the "No picture…" message in the picture box. The logic of this procedure was also described in the design discussion.

Create a new form for the About box, add labels and images as you like, and then add a command button to close it. Remember that you close the form by hiding it. Then write the code for mnuHelpAbout to show your About box.

At this point your application may work, although probably not perfectly. You still need to code a Form_Load procedure for the main listing form, as described in the design discussion, to ensure that the picture for the first listing is displayed properly.

Project H.2: Order Entry Application Prototype Revisited

In Project 13 (Chapter 9) we presented a prototype user interface for an order entry system that accepted information about customers and the products they wanted to order. The program was not fully functional but served to help both the designers and users better understand how the final solution should be designed.

In this project we extend the functionality of the prototype to gain additional knowledge about the design of the final application.

Description of the Application

This project extends Project 13 by focusing on the entry of customer information. In Project 13 the main focus was on the entry of product information, and the customer number and customer address information was simply entered into text boxes (see Figure 9.27).

Figure H.6 shows the revised Order Entry Screen. One obvious change from Figure 9.27 is that the customer information has been broken down into more detail. The customer's name and address have been separated, and the

FIGURE H.6

Project H.2 at run time

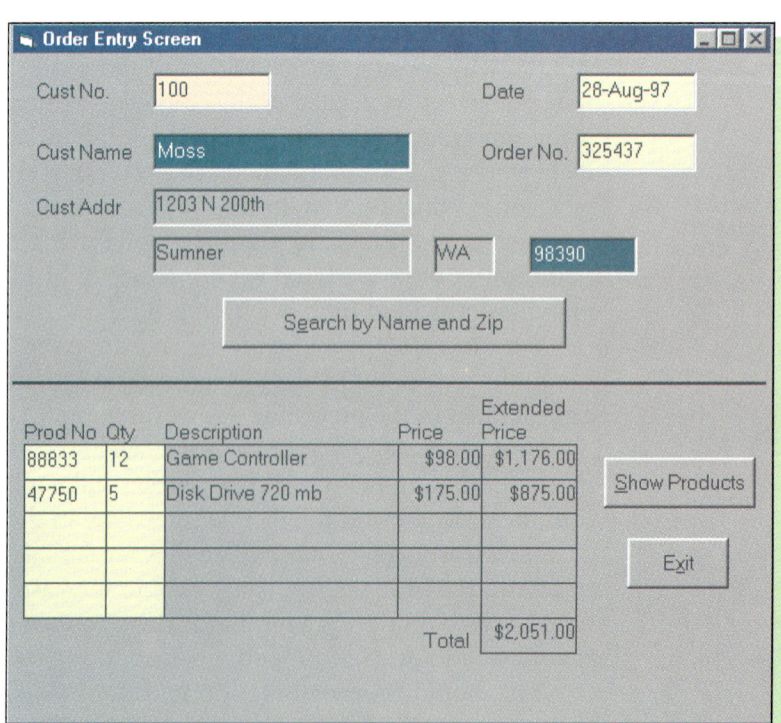

address has been broken down into street, city, state, and zip code detail. A second change, which is not obvious from the Order Entry Screen, is that the customer information is coming from a database.

This application provides two ways to enter customer information. First, the customer number can be typed into the Customer Number text box. Then, when the user moves the focus from this text box, the system searches the customer database to find information on the customer. If the database search is successful, the customer information is placed on the form as shown. If the search fails, the user is notified of this via a message box.

The second way to enter customer information helps the user—for example, an order entry person who is taking a telephone order—when the customer does not know his or her customer number. In this case, the user enters the customer's name and zip code into the appropriate fields on the form, and then clicks the Search by Name and Zip button; this causes the application to search the database for all matches. The matches are then displayed in a dialog box like the one in Figure H.7. The user can then ask the customer for more information to help determine which entry in the search table is the correct customer. Double-clicking on the correct entry transfers its information to the Order Entry form.

The customer information portion of the prototype has one limitation: it does not allow the user to add new customers or edit customer information directly on the Order Entry form. The application could be extended to do this without much trouble, but we assume that this capability is not essential to obtaining the desired design feedback.

Design of the Application

Review Project 13 for design details on the "Product" portion of the Order Entry Screen. The discussion that follows deals only with the customer information portion of the Order Entry form, and the database where this information is stored.

The database is named Customers.mdb and is stored in the subdirectory AppH\ProjH2 in the code package for this text. The database has a single table named Cust, shown in Figure H.8. The characteristics of the fields in the Cust table are shown in Table H.1.

FIGURE H.7

Result of searching the database for customer name "Kim" and zip code "98337"

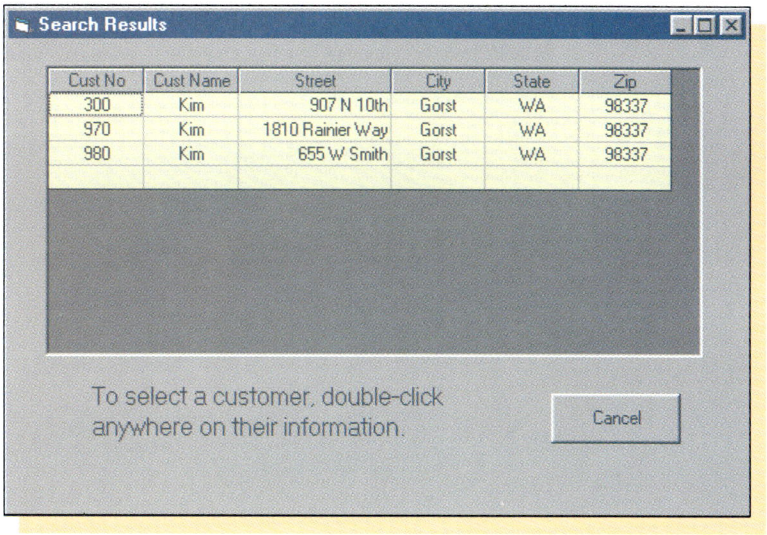

Cust No	Cust Name	Street	City	State	Zip
300	Kim	907 N 10th	Gorst	WA	98337
970	Kim	1810 Rainier Way	Gorst	WA	98337
980	Kim	655 W Smith	Gorst	WA	98337

To select a customer, double-click anywhere on their information.

FIGURE H.8

The Cust table from the Customers.mdb database

CustNo	CustName	AddrStreet	AddrCity	AddrState	AddrZip
100	Moss	1203 N 200th	Sumner	WA	98390
200	Weber	1571 8th S	Sumner	WA	98390
300	Kim	907 N 10th	Gorst	WA	98337
400	Halabi	1706 S 320th St	Shelton	WA	98584
500	Chow	14322 3rd SW	Srquim	WA	98382
600	Thomas	125 Front Street	Humptilips	WA	98552
700	Palmer	2400 N 45th St	Ephrata	WA	98823
800	Selinski	1002 Harvey Road	George	WA	98824
900	Tanaka	3255 California SW	Zillah	WA	98953
910	Powers	325 19th St	Carbonado	WA	98323
920	Dawson	550 16th Ave SE	Omak	WA	98841
930	Bryant	9200 Roosevelt Way	Walla Walla	WA	99362
940	Fidler	1001 Broadway	Home	WA	98349
950	Grav	1800 116th NE	Gorst	WA	98337
960	Chavez	1229 Madison E	Gorst	WA	98337
970	Kim	1810 Rainier Way	Gorst	WA	98337
980	Kim	655 W Smith	Gorst	WA	98337
990	Johnson	17331 143rd Ave S	Prescott	WA	99348

TABLE H.1 Cust table fields and their types

Field Name	Field Type
CustNo	Long Integer
CustName	20-character text
AddrStreet	20-character text
AddrCity	20-character text
AddrState	20-character text
AddrZip	5-character text

The important new controls for the customer portion of the form are identified in Figure H.9. Text boxes are used for the customer number, name, and zip code because the user will need to enter data in one or more of these text boxes in order to initiate a search of the database. The controls address, city, and state are labels (with borders) since the user will never enter data in these controls.

FIGURE H.9

Important controls for customer information in Example H.2

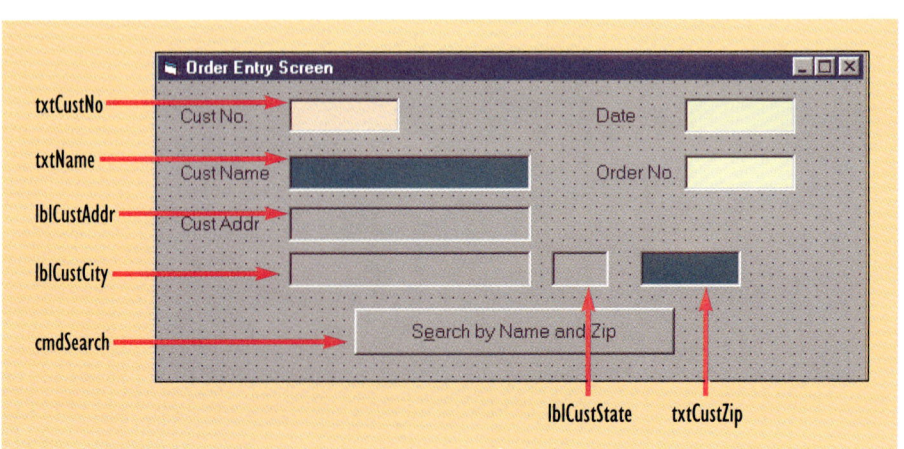

In addition to the controls identified in Figure H.9, a data control must also be added to the form to provide access to the new database and its table.

In the following sections we examine the functionality of the Customer Number text box, the Search command button, and the Search Results form.

txtCustNo

You need to write at least two event procedures for this control. First, you need to make sure that the user can only enter numbers (0 through 9) and a BACKSPACE in the text box. You also should allow the user to press the ENTER key to move the focus to the text box for the order number.

Second, you need to initiate a search of the database when the focus is moved away from the text box. This search uses the value in the text box to search the database for a matching customer number. If a match is found, then the fields for the matching record should be copied into the appropriate text boxes and labels. If the search fails, then a message box should be displayed to inform the user.

Your code should check that the user has entered something into the text box before it tries to search the database. Also, it should clear the text boxes and labels before beginning the search. Otherwise, if the search fails, the values that existed before the search will still be displayed and will confuse the user.

In formulating your search you may wish to review Chapter 8 and the Find methods associated with a recordset. Also review Chapter 8 to recall how to copy database fields to text boxes or labels. Be aware that the text boxes and labels are not bound to the data control in this application.

cmdSearch

This control searches the database for records that match the name and zip code in the txtCustName and txtCustZip controls. There may be zero or more matches. Records that match should be displayed in a grid located on a separate form (see Figure H.7). To review the use of the FlexGrid control see Chapter 9, and to review how to work with multiple forms see Chapter 3.

Pseudocode for this control's Click event procedure follows:

1. *If one or both text boxes are empty, exit the procedure.*
2. *Try to find the first record matching the name and zip code from the text boxes. (Since both of these fields are type String the values must be surrounded by single quotes; see Chapter 8). If this search fails, inform the user and exit the procedure.*
3. *Clear the grid located on the Search Results form (see Chapter 9).*
4. *Set up the grid's headings.*
5. *While there are more records matching the search criterion,*
   a. *Copy the field values from the current record to the appropriate row in the grid.*
   b. *Find the next record in the database that matches the search criterion.*
6. *Show the Search Results form and its grid.*

The Search Results Form

The Search Results form displays the result of the name/zip code search (Figure H.7) and can also be used to transfer the information for a specific customer to the Order Entry form. There are many ways to accomplish this, and one good way is to take advantage of code that already exists.

When the user double-clicks on a customer name in the grid, use the grid's Row property (and the fact that the customer number is in column zero) to determine the customer number for that customer. Use this customer number to place the Customer Number in the text box (txtCustNo) back on the Order Entry form. Finally, set the focus to txtCustNo, and then set the focus to the "Order No." text box. This sequence of steps causes the txtCustNo_LostFocus event procedure to be executed (which is already programmed to search the database by customer number and enter the resulting information into the Order Entry form).

Construction of the Application

The approach you use to construct this application will depend on whether you are modifying the forms and code from Project 13 or starting from scratch. If you are starting from scratch, first review the "Construction of the Application" discussion from Project 13. The main differences between this project and Project 13 are: (1) the additional controls for customer information; (2) the additional Data control which provides access to the Customers database; (3) the additional form with its grid that is used to display customers who match the name/zip code search; and (4) code to implement the searching.

You should first add a new Data control to your form and connect it to the database and table. You might want to place a temporary label on the Order Entry form and bind it to the CustNo field. You can then use the Data control's navigation buttons to verify that the Data control is functioning correctly.

Next, place the txtCustNo text box on the form. Write a KeyPress event procedure to limit input to numbers and the [BACKSPACE] key, then test this procedure. Now add code so that when the user presses the [ENTER] key, the focus moves to the "Order No." text box. Test this procedure, too.

Now add the remainder of the text boxes and labels for the customer information. Using the txtCustNo_LostFocus event, write the code to search the database for a record that matches the value in the txtCustNo text box (see the foregoing Design discussion).

When you get the search by customer number to work, add a new form to the project (the Search Results form). Place a FlexGrid control on the form and set its properties as appropriate. After this form is set up, place the cmdSearch command button on the Order Entry form and program its Click event as outlined in the pseudocode in the Design section.

After verifying that the grid on the Search Results form is being filled with the correct records, program the grid's double-click event to copy the fields from the record that was the target of the double-click to the Order Entry form.

Finally, you should set the new Data control's Visible property to False.

appendix I

Answers to Selected Exercises

Chapter 2

Exercise 2.3

Clicking on the command button named Command9.

Exercise 2.5

It is probably just as well to leave these controls with the names VB provided, because their names never appear in code. If a control's name doesn't appear in code, then its properties can be changed only by using the Properties window at design time. The lack of a descriptive name will not hinder the programmer much in this task.

Exercise 2.7

The opportunity cost of accepting an order is the (possibly higher) offer associated with another order that might arrive during processing of the accepted order. The opportunity cost of ignoring an order is the offer of the ignored order.

Exercise 2.9

One simple improvement would be to have the application compute and display the ratio (offer/processing time). This would make it much easier to decide which orders to accept.

Exercise 2.11

It is possible, if the user is quick with the mouse. To see how, let's call the order with the processing time of 1.1 seconds Order A, and the next order to arrive Order B. Order B arrives 2 seconds after Order A arrived, but processing of Order A completes only 1.1 seconds after Order A was accepted. If the user accepts Order A right after it arrives, then there will be a gap of a little less than 0.9 seconds between the time when the processing of Order A completes and the time that Order B arrives. During this gap, Order A remains on the screen, and the user can select it again.

It is possible to modify the application to prevent this. The problem is that cmdAcceptOrder should not be reenabled until *both* the order processing time has elapsed *and* a new order has arrived. This can be accomplished by a carefully placed decision-making statement (or two). Decision-making statements are the subject of Chapter 5.

There is a simple way to prevent the user from benefitting from selecting the same order twice. Just add statements at the bottom of cmdAcceptOrder_Click that set lblOffer.Caption and lblProcessingTime.Caption to zero.

Chapter 3

Exercise 3.1

Const NUMBEROFDAYSINJANUARY = 31

Exercise 3.3

Minimum#—The pound sign (#) is not allowed in variable names.

Item Price—Spaces are not allowed in variable names.

Sub—This is a reserved word.

3rdAlternate—Variable names must begin with a letter (not a digit).

Exercise 3.5

Assuming that I need to represent the user's height only to the nearest centimeter, I would use type Integer. Certainly a person will not be taller than 32,767 centimeters (which is more than 1000 feet). However, if I need to represent fractions of centimeters in the user's height (e.g., 180.5 cm), then the two best options would be types Currency and Single. I would prefer to use type Currency because I tend not to think of a person's height in scientific notation (does 1.805E2 cm seem sensible?). However, if computer memory were at a premium I would use type Single because it takes fewer bytes than Currency (4 bytes versus 8).

Exercise 3.9

Prior to the change, many U.S. businesses used fixed-length string variables, five characters long, to store zip codes in their applications (e.g., **Dim** ZIPCode **As String** * 5). The change to nine-digit zip codes forced these businesses to locate and change to String * 9 every variable used to store zip codes in every one of their programs. They also had to change statements that displayed or printed zip codes.

Exercise 3.11

The variable table after the computer has executed the two statements is as follows.

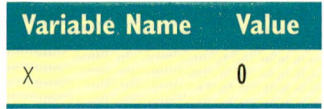

The statement X = X has no net effect (except perhaps to waste a small amount of the computer's time).

Exercise 3.13

00000X00X0

Exercise 3.15

Change the last statement to include a space as follows:

FullName = FirstName & " " & LastName

Exercise 3.17

The sequence of statements

```
Z = X
X = Y
Y = Z
```

will do it. This sequence is said to "exchange" the values in variables X and Y. (Note that variable Z was declared along with X and Y in the event procedure.)

Exercise 3.19

The values displayed by lblC, lblD, and lblE after the user clicks on cmdA are 6, 9, and 4, respectively. After the user clicks on cmdB they are 3, 0, and 3.

Exercise 3.21

The first time cmdStaticLifetimeTest is clicked, lblX will display 0. The second time it will display 1, and the third time it will display 2. As with all numeric variables, when X is first created, it is initialized to the value 0. Each time the button is clicked, the procedure retrieves the value from X and displays it in the label, then increments the value in X. Since the variable X is declared as Static, it retains its value from one execution of the event procedure to the next.

Exercise 3.23

Suppose you name the controls tmrCount and lblCount. At design time, set lblCount's Caption property to 0. Use the Form_Load event procedure to give tmrCount's Interval property a random initial setting as follows:

```
Private Sub Form_Load()
    tmrCount.Interval = 500 + (2500 * Rnd())
End Sub
```

The Timer event procedure for tmrCount should increment the count, display it, and give tmrCount a new random Interval setting, as follows:

```
Private Sub tmrCount_Timer()
    Static Count As Integer
    Count = Count + 1
    lblCount.Caption = Count
    tmrCount.Interval = 500 + (2500 * Rnd())
End Sub
```

Exercise 3.25

Since the number of calculations to verify is small, you can easily do the calculations by hand and compare your results against the results of the summary form. You should probably calculate by hand the numbers on both of the employee forms first, then add them to arrive at the values for the summary form. That is, don't take it for granted that the numbers displayed by the employee forms are correct.

Exercise 3.27

Suppose the project is divided up by assigning each team a different set of forms to create. Since global variables are shared by multiple forms, it may be that two or more teams will be writing code that uses the same global variables. It will help them immensely to agree in advance (in the design stage) on the names for these global variables. Otherwise, the teams may choose different names for the same variable, possibly causing a lot of confusion when they combine their forms to test the project.

It could also be that two or more teams are assigned to create different event procedures for the same form. In this case, it will be advantageous for them to agree in advance on the names of module-level variables for the form, because these names will occur in more than one event procedure.

Chapter 4

Exercise 4.1

X will hold 5, Y will hold 9, and Z will hold 6.

Exercise 4.3

MsgBox "Watch out!", vbExclamation, "Uh oh!"

Exercise 4.5

(3 + 5) * 10

Exercise 4.7

The values displayed by the event procedure are, in order: 4.5, 4, 2.

Exercise 4.9

There is no space between the first and last names displayed by the second message box. One way to correct this is to modify the MsgBox statement to

MsgBox "Hello, " & FirstName & " " & LastName

Note that there is a single space between the quotes in the string constant (" ").

Exercise 4.11

Private Sub cmdNibbleAtFront_Click()
    lblTest.Caption = Right$(lblTest.Caption, Len(lblTest.Caption) - 1)
End Sub

A more concise expression can be written using the Mid$() function with only two arguments, as follows:

Private Sub cmdNibbleAtFrontB_Click()
    lblTest.Caption = Mid$(lblTest.Caption, 2)
End Sub

Exercise 4.15

The symbols X, Y, and Z are transformed into the symbols [, \, and], respectively.

Exercise 4.17

Depending on your solution to Exercise 4.16, the amount of work needed to make the modification may be a little or a lot. Here is one solution.

```
Private Sub cmdCaesarCipher_Click()
    Dim Letter As String
    Dim PositionInAlphabet As Integer
    Dim RotatedPosition As Integer
    Dim RotatedLetter As String
    Letter = InputBox("Next letter?")
    lblPlaintext.Caption = lblPlaintext.Caption & Letter
    PositionInAlphabet = Asc(Letter) - 65
    RotatedPosition = (PositionInAlphabet + SHIFTAMOUNT) Mod 26
    RotatedLetter = Chr$(65 + RotatedPosition)
    lblCiphertext.Caption = lblCiphertext.Caption & RotatedLetter
End Sub
```

Exercise 4.19

The value displayed in lblCost will be $0.00. This happens because $4.55 does not have the correct form of a numeric value—numeric data items cannot contain $ symbols. Thus, the Val() function converts $4.55 to the number 0, and the calculated cost is 0.

Exercise 4.23

Y = X

Exercise 4.25

True   False   −1

Exercise 4.27

False

Exercise 4.29

```
Qualified = ((YearsExperience > 5) And (NumberOfLanguages >= 3)) _
    Or (NumberOfLanguages >= 6)
```

Exercise 4.31

```
Private Sub cmdRangeCheck_Click()
    Dim Age As Integer
    Dim BetweenTenAndTwenty As String
    Age = InputBox("How old are you?")
    BetweenTenAndTwenty = IIf((10 <= Age) And (Age <= 20), "Yes", "No")
    MsgBox "Between ten and twenty? " & BetweenTenAndTwenty
End Sub
```

Exercise 4.33

Set cmdBuy.Enabled to False inside cmdBuy_Click, and set cmdBuy.Enabled to True inside tmrAsk_Timer. This will disable the Buy button when the user clicks it, and the Buy button will be re-enabled only when a new asking price appears. (Make the analogous changes to cmdSell_Click and tmrBid_Timer.) It would still be a good idea to clear the asking price and number of units labels, however, so the user can see when there is no outstanding offer (better yet, make these labels turn gray instead of clearing them).

This approach is better than the original approach of just setting the AskPrice and AskUnits variables to zero and clearing the corresponding labels. The problem with the original approach is that it still allows the user to click the Buy button multiple times; the user gains nothing by doing this, and in fact is still charged the transaction fee. (Let the buyer beware!) Disabling the buttons prevents the user from needlessly losing the transaction fee.

Chapter 5

Exercise 5.1

A new random target is generated each time the user clicks on cmdGuessMe, so the user is guessing at a "moving target." As a result, neither strategy A nor B is better than the other. Of course, whatever numbers the user enters should be integers between 1 and 6.

Exercise 5.3

Here's one solution:

```
Private Sub cmdGuessMe_Click()
    Dim Target As Integer
    Dim Guess As Integer
    Static NumGuesses As Integer
    Static NumCorrect As Integer
    Target = 1 + Int(6 * Rnd())
    Guess = InputBox("Enter a guess between 1 and 6, inclusive.")
    NumGuesses = NumGuesses + 1
    If Guess = Target Then
        NumCorrect = NumCorrect + 1
        Beep
        MsgBox "Correct — congratulations!"
    Else
        MsgBox "Incorrect — bummer!"
    End If
    MsgBox "No. Guesses = " & NumGuesses & ", No. Correct = " & NumCorrect
End Sub
```

Exercise 5.5

```
Private Sub cmdProcessPayment_Click()
    Dim AmountPaid As Currency
    Dim AmountDue As Currency
    AmountPaid = InputBox("Enter the amount paid.")
    Balance = Balance - AmountPaid
    If Balance >= 0 Then
        AmountDue = IIf(Balance < Premium / 6, Balance, Premium / 6)
        lblBalance.Caption = Format$(Balance, "Currency")
        lblAmountDue.Caption = Format$(AmountDue, "Currency")
    Else
        AmountDue = 0
        lblBalance.Caption = Format$(Abs(Balance), "Currency") & " CR"
        lblAmountDue.Caption = Format$(AmountDue, "Currency")
    End If
End Sub
```

Exercise 5.7

The following statement block will work. A meta statement that describes the action of this statement block is "If X is greater than Y, then exchange the values in X and Y." Note that the event procedure included three Dim statements, one for variable Z.

```
If X > Y Then
    Z = X
    X = Y
    Y = Z
End If
```

Exercise 5.9

The user of the given event procedure should not include spaces, because spaces show up regularly in ordinary text and the event procedure shifts them to a nonalphabetic character in the ciphertext. This will make it easy for an eavesdropper looking at the ciphertext to break the code.

For example, suppose you are the eavesdropper, and the ciphertext you are looking at is as follows: PHHW#PH#DW#WKH#SDVN. You quickly realize that the regularly occuring # symbol must represent spaces in the plaintext. Then, by looking in the ANSI table, you see that the number of positions between the # and space characters is 3, so the shift amount must be 3. Now it's easy to decipher the ciphertext.

The following event procedure does not shift nonalphabetic characters in the plaintext; thus, spaces in the plaintext remain spaces in the ciphertext.

```
Private Sub cmdCaesarCipher_Click()
    Dim Character As String
    Character = InputBox("Next character?")
    lblPlaintext.Caption = lblPlaintext.Caption & Character
    If ((Character >= "A") And (Character <= "Z")) Or _
        ((Character >= "a") And (Character <= "z")) Then
        lblCiphertext.Caption = lblCiphertext.Caption & Chr$(Asc(Character) + 3)
    Else
        lblCiphertext.Caption = lblCiphertext.Caption & Character
    End If
End Sub
```

Exercise 5.11

Here is one solution.

```
Private Sub tmrAutoTrade_Timer()
    If (AskPrice > 0) And (AskPrice < THRESHOLDBUYPRICE) Then
        Cash = Cash - TRANSACTIONFEE - AskPrice * AskUnits
        Inventory = Inventory + AskUnits
        lblCash.Caption = Format$(Cash, "Currency")
        lblInventory.Caption = Inventory
        AskPrice = 0
        AskUnits = 0
        lblAskPrice.Caption = ""
        lblAskUnits.Caption = ""
    End If
```

continues

```
        If (BidPrice > 0) And (BidPrice > THRESHOLDSELLPRICE) Then
            Cash = Cash - TRANSACTIONFEE + BidPrice * BidUnits
            Inventory = Inventory - BidUnits
            lblCash.Caption = Format$(Cash, "Currency")
            lblInventory.Caption = Inventory
            BidPrice = 0
            BidUnits = 0
            lblBidPrice.Caption = ""
            lblBidUnits.Caption = ""
        End If
    End Sub
```

Exercise 5.13

If the user enters "male" instead of "Male" in response to the first input box, the code will use the risk rate for females. This happens because the condition Sex = "Male" will be False, so the computer executes the statement block following Else.

One possible way to improve the code is to change the condition of the If statement as follows:

```
If (Sex = "Male") Or (Sex = "male") Then
```

But this solution does not handle the case where the user enters "MALE". A better solution is to use VB's UCase$() function, which returns an uppercase version of its argument, as follows:

```
If UCase$(Sex) = "MALE" Then
```

Exercise 5.15

```
Private Sub cmdMinimumAmountDue_Click()
    Const MINTHRESHOLD = 20
    Const MINFRACTION = 0.02
    Dim Balance As Currency
    Dim MinimumDue As Currency
    Balance = InputBox("Enter the customer's balance.")
    If Balance < 0 Then
        MinimumDue = 0
    ElseIf Balance <= MINTHRESHOLD Then
        MinimumDue = Balance
    Else
        MinimumDue = IIf(MINTHRESHOLD > MINFRACTION * Balance, _
            MINTHRESHOLD, MINFRACTION * Balance)
    End If
    MsgBox "The minimum amount due is " & Format$(MinimumDue, "Currency")
End Sub
```

Exercise 5.17

You can include access keys for the option buttons to give the user a keyboard alternative to positioning and clicking the mouse. This should be better than using a text box, which opens up the possibility of typographical errors.

Exercise 5.19

Total A = 5

Total X = 20

Exercise 5.25

One way to do this is to place the last message box statement inside its own If statement, so that this message is displayed only if the value of DaysIn-Month is greater than 0.

    If DaysInMonth > 0 **Then**
        MsgBox MonthAbbr & " has " & DaysInMonth & " days."
    End If

However, there is a better way to do this, which is discussed in Section 5.10.

Exercise 5.27

Experienced programmers, who are used to working with ranges that use the keyword Is and that overlap, find the following Select Case statement more readable. The redundant data in the Select Case statement in Figure 5.34 set off alarms for an experienced programmer, who knows to be wary of gaps between the ranges (and looking for such gaps is tedious).

    Select Case Rnd()
    Case Is < 0.2
        Target = 1
    Case Is <= 0.3
        Target = 2
    Case Is <= 0.6
        Target = 3
    Case Is <= 0.75
        Target = 4
    Case Is <= 0.9
        Target = 5
    Case Else
        Target = 6
    End Select

Exercise 5.31

Private Sub cmdSquareRoot_Click()
    Dim X **As Single**
    Dim Y **As Single**
    Dim EnteredValue **As String**
    EnteredValue = InputBox("Enter a number.")
    If EnteredValue = "" **Then**
        Exit Sub
    End If
    X = EnteredValue
    Y = Sqr(X)
    MsgBox "The square root of " & X & " is " & Y
End Sub

Chapter 6

Exercise 6.1

There is an advantage to using a general sub procedure for the statements that are currently in optFSMarriedJoint_Click: giving the general sub procedure a descriptive name will make the code easier to understand. Of course, since optFSMarriedJoint_Click is currently the only event procedure that needs to use these statements, it won't shorten the program.

Exercise 6.3

The code displays four message boxes, which contain the following values:

```
7  2  5
4  4
9 -1  3
9  2  5
```

Exercise 6.7

```
Option Explicit
Dim MonthAbbr As String
Dim DaysInMonth As Integer

Private Sub FindNumDaysInMonth()
    Select Case MonthAbbr
    Case "JAN", "MAR", "MAY", "JUL", "AUG", "OCT", "DEC"
        DaysInMonth = 31
    Case "APR", "JUN", "SEP", "NOV"
        DaysInMonth = 30
    Case "FEB"
        DaysInMonth = 28
    Case Else
        MsgBox MonthAbbr & " is not a valid month abbreviation."
        DaysInMonth = 0
    End Select
End Sub

Private Sub cmdMonthDays_Click()
    MonthAbbr = InputBox("Enter 3-letter month abbreviation.")
    FindNumDaysInMonth
    MsgBox MonthAbbr & " has " & DaysInMonth & " days."
End Sub
```

Exercise 6.9

The message displayed by cmdParameterQuiz1_Click is "From short words emerges a short sentence."

Exercise 6.11

If we remove the function UCase$() and the user enters a lowercase letter, procedure Rotate will change the letter to uppercase and rotate it, but not by three positions. For example, if the user enters "a", the result will be "J", "b" will be transformed to "K", etc., and "u" will be transformed to "A".

Exercise 6.13

If we make the change suggested, the message boxes will contain the messages A = 4, B = 5, and C = 1.5.

If you studied the action of procedure SimpleCalculations carefully after doing Exercise 6.12, then you were probably able to figure out the answer to this exercise without having to hand-check the code again. The net effect of procedure SimpleCalculations is to increase its first argument by 1 (it changed B from 4 to 5), double its second argument (it changed A from 2 to 4), and change its third argument to be the sum of the new values of the first two arguments divided by the sum of the old values of the first two arguments $((5 + 4) / (4 + 2) = 1.5)$.

Exercise 6.15

The message boxes will contain "maga", "zine", "bins", and "uses".

Exercise 6.17

The message boxes will display the values 2.25, 5, and 6. As the discussion following the hand-check of the code in Figure 6.34 suggests, the action of procedure TryByValue is to change the second argument to the sum of the original values of the first two arguments divided by the second argument (in this case, $(5 + 4) / 4 = 2.25$). The first and third arguments are unchanged.

Exercise 6.19

Private Sub FindNumDaysInMonth(DaysInMonth **As Integer**, **ByVal** MonthAbbr **As String**)
   Select Case MonthAbbr
   Case "JAN", "MAR", "MAY", "JUL", "AUG", "OCT", "DEC"
      DaysInMonth = 31
   Case "APR", "JUN", "SEP", "NOV"
      DaysInMonth = 30
   Case "FEB"
      DaysInMonth = 28
   Case Else
      MsgBox MonthAbbr & " is not a valid month abbreviation."
      DaysInMonth = 0
   End Select
End Sub

Private Sub cmdMonthDays_Click()
   Dim MonthAbbr **As String**
   Dim DaysInMonth **As Integer**
   MonthAbbr = InputBox("Enter 3-letter month abbreviation.")
   FindNumDaysInMonth DaysInMonth, MonthAbbr
   MsgBox MonthAbbr & " has " & DaysInMonth & " days."
End Sub

Exercise 6.21

The easiest solution doesn't require any coding at all: simply set the text box's MaxLength property to 9.

Exercise 6.23

```
Private Sub txtSSN_LostFocus()
    If Len(txtSSN.Text) < 9 Then
        Beep
        MsgBox "Social Security Number must have 9 digits.", vbInformation
        txtSSN.SetFocus
    End If
End Sub
```

Chapter 7

Exercise 7.1

The following displays the numbers 1 through 10:

```
Private Sub cmdDoWhileTest_Click()
    Dim X As Integer
    Do While X < 10
        X = X + 1
        MsgBox X
    Loop
End Sub
```

The following code displays the even numbers from 2 through 20:

```
Private Sub cmdDoWhileTest_Click()
    Dim X As Integer
    Do While X < 20
        X = X + 2
        MsgBox X
    Loop
End Sub
```

Exercise 7.3

In Example 7.5 the user is trying to guess a "moving target"; a reasonable guessing strategy is to guess the same number (between 1 and 6, of course) every time. If we move the statement Target = 1 + Int(6 * Rnd()) from just after Do to just before Do, then the user will be trying to guess a "fixed target"; in this case, the user should not guess the same number twice.

Exercise 7.5

```
Private Sub cmdRunningSum_Click()
    Dim N As Single
    Dim Count As Integer
    Dim Sum As Single
    Do
        N = InputBox("Enter a number.")
        Count = Count + 1
        Sum = Sum + N
    Loop Until (Sum < -10) Or (Sum > 10)
    MsgBox "You entered " & Count & " numbers"
    MsgBox "The sum is " & Sum
End Sub
```

Exercise 7.7

The following will display the numbers 50 through 60, inclusive:

```
Private Sub cmdDoWhileTest_Click()
    Dim X As Integer
    X = 49
    Do While X < 60
        X = X + 1
        MsgBox X
    Loop
End Sub
```

The following solution is somewhat easier to understand:

```
Private Sub cmdDoWhileTest_Click()
    Dim X As Integer
    X = 50
    Do While X <= 60
        MsgBox X
        X = X + 1
    Loop
End Sub
```

Exercise 7.9

The solution to Exercise 7.5 should use a variation of the Do...Loop structure, because the number of times the loop will iterate is not known at the time the loop starts to execute. The number of iterations depends on what values the user enters, and the statement that obtains values from the user is inside the loop.

Exercise 7.11

The following will display the even numbers from 2 to 20, inclusive:

```
Private Sub cmdForNextTest_Click()
    Dim X As Integer
    For X = 2 To 20 Step 2
        MsgBox X
    Next X
End Sub
```

The following will display the even numbers from 20 down to 2, inclusive:

```
Private Sub cmdForNextTest_Click()
    Dim X As Integer
    For X = 20 To 2 Step -2
        MsgBox X
    Next X
End Sub
```

Exercise 7.13

The following pair of LostFocus event procedures will accomplish the task:

```
Private Sub lstTestA_LostFocus()
    lstTestA.ListIndex = -1
End Sub

Private Sub lstTestB_LostFocus()
    lstTestB.ListIndex = -1
End Sub
```

An interesting extension to the problem is to add the requirement that when the focus returns to a list box, the list box should rehighlight the same item that was selected, if any, when it last lost the focus.

Exercise 7.15

Here is one solution for the programmer-defined function. Note that it uses the format character "@" (see online help, search phrase "user-defined formats", and select "user-defined string formats" in the topic list that results).

```
Private Function NewLine(ByVal Month As Integer, ByVal Payment As Currency, _
                ByVal Balance As Currency, ByVal Principle As Currency, _
                ByVal Interest As Currency) As String
    Const MAXMONTHCHARS = 3
    Const MAXPAYMENTCHARS = 14
    Const MAXBALANCECHARS = 18
    Const MAXPRINCIPLECHARS = 14
    Const MAXINTERESTCHARS = 14
    Dim FormattedMonth As String
    Dim FormattedPayment As String
    Dim FormattedBalance As String
    Dim FormattedPrinciple As String
    Dim FormattedInterest As String
    Dim AssemblyLine As String
    FormattedMonth = Format$(Month)
    FormattedPayment = Format$(Payment, "Currency")
    FormattedBalance = Format$(Balance, "Currency")
    FormattedPrinciple = Format$(Principle, "Currency")
    FormattedInterest = Format$(Interest, "Currency")
    AssemblyLine = Format$(FormattedMonth, String$(MAXMONTHCHARS, "@"))
    AssemblyLine = AssemblyLine & _
            Format$(FormattedPayment, String$(MAXPAYMENTCHARS, "@"))
    AssemblyLine = AssemblyLine & _
            Format$(FormattedBalance, String$(MAXBALANCECHARS, "@"))
    AssemblyLine = AssemblyLine & _
            Format$(FormattedPrinciple, String$(MAXPRINCIPLECHARS, "@"))
    AssemblyLine = AssemblyLine & _
            Format$(FormattedInterest, String$(MAXINTERESTCHARS, "@"))
    NewLine = AssemblyLine
End Function
```

Chapter 8

Exercise 8.3

To save the changes, the user must reposition the record pointer by clicking on any of the four navigation controls (the First or Last buttons, or the left or right arrow buttons). To give the user the option of saving changes and ending execution, we can modify cmdExit_Click by replacing the If statement

```
If Response = vbYes Then
    End
Else
    Exit Sub
End If
```

with something like the following:

```
Select Case Response
   Case vbYes
      End
   Case vbNo
      BoxType = vbOKCancel + vbQuestion
      Response = MsgBox("Save and Exit?", BoxType)
      If Response = vbOK Then
         datPeople.Recordset.Close
         End
      Else
         Exit Sub
      End If
   Case Else           ' user clicked Cancel
      Exit Sub
End Select
```

Exercise 8.5

Add two more Text box controls to the form (txtYear and txtISBN, say). Then modify the Form_Load procedure as follows. Note that the Titles table has a field named "Year Published"; MS Access, like many DBMSs, allows spaces in field names. In an SQL query, to specify a field whose name contains a space, you must surround the field name with brackets as shown here.

```
Private Sub Form_Load()
   Dim SQLQ As String
   SQLQ = "Select Titles.Title, Titles.[Year Published], " & _
      "Titles.ISBN, Publishers.Name " & _
      "From Titles, Publishers " & _
      "Where Titles.PubID = Publishers.PubID"
   datSQLExample.RecordSource = SQLQ
   datSQLExample.Refresh
   txtTitle.DataField = "Title"
   txtName.DataField = "Name"
   txtYear.DataField = "Year Published"
   txtISBN.DataField = "ISBN"
End Sub
```

Exercise 8.7

Set the grid's Rows property to 15, Cols property to 10, and ScrollBars property to "3 - Both". In Form_Load, change the constant 4, which appears in two For statements, to 9 (this change would have been easier if a symbolic constant had been used). And in cmdComputeFV_Click, change the constant 0.1 in the outer For statement to 0.15, and the constant 5 in the inner For statement to 10.

Exercise 8.9

A good way to do this is to remove the statements that set column widths from procedure SetupGrid, create another general sub procedure, say, SetColWidths, and invoke this procedure from Form_Load (at its bottom, i.e., after the grid has been filled).

Following is the code for SetColWidths. Note that it assumes that the records are displayed in the grid starting in row 1, not row 2, as suggested in Exercise 8.8. It also uses a programmer-defined function to find the width of the widest value in a column of the grid.

```
Private Sub SetColWidths()
    Dim C As Integer
    For C = 0 To 2
        grdQuery.ColWidth(C) = WidestCell(C)
    Next C
End Sub

Private Function WidestCell(ByVal C As Integer) As Integer
    Dim R As Integer
    Dim CellWidth As Integer
    Dim WidestSoFar As Integer
    grdQuery.Col = C
    grdQuery.Row = 1
    WidestSoFar = TextWidth(grdQuery.Text)
    For R = 2 To datQuery.Recordset.RecordCount
        grdQuery.Row = R
        CellWidth = TextWidth(grdQuery.Text)
        If CellWidth > WidestSoFar Then
            WidestSoFar = CellWidth
        End If
    Next R
    WidestCell = WidestSoFar
End Sub
```

Chapter 9

Exercise 9.1

1. Stock = Quantity(ProdNo, WareNo)

2.
```
datQty.RecordSet.FindFirst "Product = " & ProdNo
Select Case WareNo
    Case 1
        Stock = datQty.Recordset("Warehouse1")
    Case 2
        Stock = datQty.Recordset("Warehouse2")
    Case Else
        Stock = datQty.Recordset("Warehouse3")
End Select
```

The Select Case statement is not actually necessary, because VB provides an alternate syntax for accessing fields of a recordset: you can specify a field number, instead of the field name, in the parentheses following Recordset. The fields are numbered beginning with 0. So the following is an alternative solution to 2:

```
datQty.RecordSet.FindFirst "Product = " & ProdNo
Stock = datQty.Recordset(WareNo - 1)
```

Exercise 9.3

When program execution begins, the Dim statement in the general declarations section is executed. This creates the module-level array A, and initializes its elements with zeros. Then when the user clicks on cmdArrayQuiz, event procedure cmdArrayQuiz_Click begins executing. Its Dim statement creates the local variable J and initializes it to zero. The next six statements are assignment statements, which store values in array elements 1 through 6. At this point, the hand-check appears as follows:

A(0)	A(1)	A(2)	A(3)	A(4)	A(5)	A(6)
0	~~0~~	~~0~~	~~0~~	~~0~~	~~0~~	~~0~~
	7	–3	4	1	–4	2

✓ **Dim** A(6) **As Integer**
✓ **Private Sub** cmdArrayQuiz_Click()
✓ **Dim** J **As Integer**
✓ A(1) = 7
✓ A(2) = -3
✓ A(3) = 4
✓ A(4) = 1
✓ A(5) = -4
✓ A(6) = 2
   DisplayArray
   ...

J
0

The next statement is the procedure call. Procedure DisplayArray now begins executing. Its Dim statements create local variables K and Message, and initialize them to zero and the zero-length string. The For loop successively concatenates the array elements from 1 to 6 to the variable Message. At this point the hand-check work for procedure DisplayArray appears as follows.

✓ **Private Sub** DisplayArray()
✓ **Dim** K **As Integer**
✓ **Dim** Message **As String**
...✓✓ **For** K = 1 **To** 6
...✓✓   Message = Message & " " & A(K)
...✓✓ **Next** K
   MsgBox Message
   End Sub

K	Message
~~0~~	" "
~~1~~	7
~~2~~	~~7 –3~~
~~3~~	~~7 –3 4~~
~~4~~	~~7 –3 4 1~~
~~5~~	~~7 –3 4 1 –4~~
~~6~~	7 –3 4 1 –4 2
7	

The final statement of procedure DisplayArray displays the numbers 7 –3 4 1 –4 2 in a message box. The net effect of executing procedure DisplayArray is to display the numbers stored in elements 1 through 6 of the array A.

We now resume execution of cmdArrayQuiz_Click. After the next four assignment statements are executed, our hand-check appears as follows:

A(0)	A(1)	A(2)	A(3)	A(4)	A(5)	A(6)
~~0~~	~~0~~	~~0~~	~~0~~	~~0~~	~~0~~	~~0~~
	7	~~–3~~	~~4~~	1	~~–4~~	~~2~~
		–3	–3		1	–4

```
✓ Dim A(6) As Integer
✓ Private Sub cmdArrayQuiz_Click()
✓     Dim J As Integer                              J
✓     A(1) = 7                                      0
✓     A(2) = -3
✓     A(3) = 4
✓     A(4) = 1
✓     A(5) = -4
✓     A(6) = 2
✓     DisplayArray
✓     A(3) = A(2)
✓     A(2) = A(3)
✓     A(6) = A(5)
✓     A(5) = A(4)
      DisplayArray
      ...
```

Now executing the procedure call displays a message box containing the values 7 –3 –3 1 1 –4. When we resume executing cmdArrayQuiz_Click, the next statement to execute is the For...Next loop. In the hand-check below, we have rewritten the statement in the loop body for each iteration of the loop.

A(0)	A(1)	A(2)	A(3)	A(4)	A(5)	A(6)
0	0̶	0̶	0̶	0̶	0̶	0̶
	7̶	–3̶	4̶	1̶	–4̶	2̶
	–3	–3̶	–3̶	1	1̶	–4
		–3	1		–4	

```
✓ Dim A(6) As Integer                               J
✓ Private Sub cmdArrayQuiz_Click()                  0̶
✓     Dim J As Integer                              2̶
✓     A(1) = 7                                      3̶
✓     A(2) = -3                                     4̶
✓     A(3) = 4                                      5̶
✓     A(4) = 1                                      6̶
✓     A(5) = -4                                     7
✓     A(6) = 2
✓     DisplayArray
✓     A(3) = A(2)
✓     A(2) = A(3)
✓     A(6) = A(5)
✓     A(5) = A(4)
✓     DisplayArray

                                                    ✓ A(1) = A(2)
...✓✓   For J = 2 To 6                              ✓ A(2) = A(3)
        A(J - 1) = A(J)                             ✓ A(3) = A(4)
...✓✓   Next J                                      ✓ A(4) = A(5)
        DisplayArray                                ✓ A(5) = A(6)
      End Sub
```

Finally, executing the procedure call displays a message box containing the values –3 –3 1 1 –4 –4. Summarizing, the values displayed in the three message boxes were

```
7  -3   4   1  -4   2
7  -3  -3   1   1  -4
-3 -3   1   1  -4  -4
```

Exercise 9.5

Private Sub cmdReverseA_Click()
  Dim J **As Integer**
  For J = 1 **To** NumValues \ 2
    A(J) = A(NumValues - J + 1)
  Next J
End Sub

Exercise 9.7

Private Sub optResInState_Click()
  ResStatus = 1
End Sub

Private Sub optResOutOfState_Click()
  ResStatus = 2
End Sub

Exercise 9.9

The array is type Integer, and –32768 is the smallest value that can be stored in a variable of type Integer. Thus, if the range of elements to be scanned has at least one element in it (i.e., if FirstElement is no greater than LastElement), then the function will behave identically to how it behaved before the change. However, if the range of elements to be scanned is empty (i.e., if FirstElement is greater than LastElement), then the function will now return the value –32768, whereas before it returned the value in element FirstElement of the array. The variable L will hold 98, M will hold –32768, and N will hold 86.

Exercise 9.11

The array references in statements inside the procedure, for example, in

    BiggestSoFar = A(FirstElement)

provide only one subscript. The number of subscripts must be the same as the dimensionality of the array. Thus, the above statement will cause a run time error if the array is not one-dimensional.

Exercise 9.13

The statement is necessary because a procedure may invoke SeqSearch many times, passing it the same argument for the FoundLoc parameter each time, and the search may sometimes be unsuccessful. If we do not include the statement FoundLoc = 0, then when the target does not exist, SeqSearch will not modify the value in FoundLoc; the argument in the calling procedure would have the same value after the call that it had before the call. That is, the calling procedure would be unaware that the target was not found.

If we remove the statement FoundLoc = 0, and then answer the question in Exercise 9.12 again, the message boxes will display 4, 4, and 2, instead of 4, 0, and 2.

Exercise 9.15

If we are able to identify the more popular item numbers, and if we are able to reorder the values in the array, then we can improve the efficiency of the search. We simply position the more popular items near the front of the list. Since the sequential search begins at the front of the list, it will frequently find the target very quickly.

Exercise 9.17

```
Private Sub cmdDispUniqueUnord_Click()
    Dim K As Integer
    Dim UniqueLetters As String
    If NumLetters = 0 Then
        Exit Sub
    End If
    UniqueLetters = A(1)
    For K = 2 To NumLetters
        If InStr(UniqueLetters, A(K)) = 0 Then
            UniqueLetters = UniqueLetters & ", " & A(K)
        End If
    Next K
    MsgBox UniqueLetters
End Sub
```

There are many other possible solutions. For example, one straightforward strategy is to build on the solution to Exercise 9.18 (display a letter if its count is greater than zero).

Exercise 9.19

This change may cause a problem at the end of the first pass. When J is equal to LastCell, the If statement inside the loop will compare A(LastCell) to A(LastCell + 1). But A(LastCell + 1) should not be involved in the sort; referencing element LastCell + 1 may bring into the sort a value that does not belong there. This may even cause a "Subscript out of range" run time error.

Exercise 9.21

When the assignment statement A = B is executed, the value that was in A is lost. In particular, after A = B is executed, both variables A and B hold the same value (and there is no point in executing the subsequent statement B = A).

Exercise 9.23

```
Dim TotalEarnings As Currency
For Year = 1993 To 1995
    For Division = 1 To 3
        TotalEarnings = TotalEarnings + DivisionEarnings(Year, Division)
    Next Division
Next Year
```

Chapter 10

Exercise 10.1

```
Type City
    Name As String
    Population As Long
End Type

Dim StateCapital As City
StateCapital.Name = "Olympia"
StateCapital.Population = 33000
```

Exercise 10.3

```
Public Sub AverageDependentAges(EmpList() As Employee, _
            ByVal NumberOfEmps As Integer, AvgDepAgeList() As Single)
    Dim Sum As Integer
    Dim E As Integer, D As Integer, NumberOfDeps As Integer
    For E = 1 To NumberOfEmps
        NumberOfDeps = EmpList(E).NumberOfDependents
        Sum = 0
        For D = 1 To NumberOfDeps
            Sum = Sum + EmpList(E).Dependent(D).Age
        Next D
        AvgDepAgeList(E) = IIf(NumberOfDeps > 0, Sum / NumberOfDeps, 0)
    Next E
End Sub
```

Exercise 10.5

```
Private Sub cmdFindMaxCity_Click()
    Dim MaxPopSoFar As Long
    Dim SubscriptOfMax As Integer
    Dim C As Integer
    For C = 1 To NumCities
        If Cities(C).Population > MaxPopSoFar Then
            MaxPopSoFar = Cities(C).Population
            SubscriptOfMax = C
        End If
    Next C
    MsgBox "The largest city is " & Cities(SubscriptOfMax).Name & _
            ", with population " & Cities(SubscriptOfMax).Population
End Sub
```

Exercise 10.7

```
Public Sub FindMaxCityOnContinent(ByVal TargetContinent As String, _
            CityName As String, CityPopulation As Long, CountryName As String)
    Dim MaxPopSoFar As Long
    Dim N As Integer, Nmax As Integer
    Dim C As Integer, Cmax As Integer
    Dim ContinentFound As Boolean
    ContinentFound = False
    For N = 1 To NumCountries
        If Countries(N).Continent = TargetContinent Then
            ContinentFound = True
            For C = 1 To 5
                If Countries(N).MajorCities(C).Population > MaxPopSoFar Then
```

continues

```
                    MaxPopSoFar = Countries(N).MajorCities(C).Population
                    Nmax = N
                    Cmax = C
                End If
            Next C
        End If
    Next N
    If ContinentFound Then
        CityName = Countries(Nmax).MajorCities(Cmax).Name
        CityPopulation = Countries(Nmax).MajorCities(Cmax).Population
        CountryName = Countries(Nmax).Country
    Else
        CityName = ""
        CityPopulation = 0
        CountryName = ""
    End If
End Sub
```

Exercise 10.9

Here is the modified code for the command button cmdShowEmployees, as well as code for the two option buttons. It assumes the option buttons are named optHourly and optSalaried, and requires an additional module-level variable of type String named SelectedClass. Observe that if neither of the option buttons are selected when the user clicks on cmdShowEmployee, nothing will be displayed in the grid.

```
Dim SelectedClass As String

Private Sub optHourly_Click()
    SelectedClass = "Hourly"
End Sub

Private Sub optSalaried_Click()
    SelectedClass = "Salaried"
End Sub

Private Sub cmdShowEmployees_Click()
    Dim J As Integer, K As Integer
    Dim NewRow As String
    For K = 1 To Employees.Count
        If Employees.Item(K).EmpType = SelectedClass Then
            NewRow = Employees.Item(K).Name & vbTab & _
                Employees.Item(K).EmpType & vbTab & _
                Format$(Employees.Item(K).GrossPay, "Currency")
            J = J + 1
            grdEmps.AddItem NewRow, J
        End If
    Next K
End Sub
```

index

Note: A "t" appended to a page reference indicates a table. An "n" indicates a footnote.

A

Abs() function, 149, 162
Access key, 198, 316, 508
Accessor methods, 512–515, 518–521
Actions, and decision making, 212–213
Activate event, 112
Active form, 111–112
Active search area, 465
ActiveX controls, 531–546
Add File, 138–139
Add Form, 8, 42
AddItem method, 358, 420
AddNew method, 394t, 399
Align property, 582t
Alignment property, 28t, 181t, 231t
AllowUserResizing property, 414t
[ALT] key, 198, 316
Alternative courses of action, 211–212
Ambiguous field error, 410
American National Standards Institute (ANSI), 175. *See also* ANSI code
American Standard Code for Information Interchange (ASCII), 176
Ampersand, 100, 169
And operator, 192–195, 218–219
Animation, 582
ANSI (American National Standards Institute), 175
ANSI code, 175–178, 188, 291–293, 311–313
Apex Software Corporation, 424
App object, 396
Appearance, control class, 532
Application objects, 509, 532–534
Applications, 2, 5, 12–13. *See also* Projects

Appropriate actions, 212–213
Argument not optional error, 301
Argument type mismatch, 301–302
Arguments, 149, 289, 302–303
Arithmetic calculation speed, 88
Arithmetic expressions, 145, 158–168, 183–187
Arithmetic functions, 162–164
Arithmetic operators, 148
Arrays, 443–488
    applications of, 444–448, 453–472
    control, 474–479
    declaring of, 450–452
    dynamic, 472–474
    multidimensional, 446, 449–450
    one-dimensional, 446
    programmer-defined types and, 501–504
Asc() function, 174–178
ASCII (American Standard Code for Information Interchange), 176
Assignment operator, 189
Assignment statement, 92–103, 189–190
Associative object, 385
Asterisk, 404
Attributes, 382
Auto Quick Info, 40, 300n
Autosave, 28
AutoSize property, 28t, 582t

B

BackColor property, 111t, 582t
Backslash symbol, 161
[BACKSPACE] key, 182, 313
Backup copies, 52. *See also* Saving of projects
Base string argument, 173
BASIC, 9. *See also* Visual Basic

Beautify controls, 23t
Beginning Of File (BOF), 393
Behavior methods, 515–516, 521
Behaviors, 509
Binary operators, 148
Binary search, 464–467
BOF (Beginning Of File), 393
Boolean data type, 189–192
BorderStyle property, 28t, 137, 181t, 580t, 582t
BorderWidth property, 137
Bound controls, 389–392
Break button, 41
Break mode, 20, 333, 559–560
Breakpoints, 561–563
Browsing, 388
Bubble sort, 468–471
Business applications, 5, 11–12. *See also* Projects
Business operations simulation, 63–68
Bytes, in standard data types, 87
ByVal keyword, 296–299, 308

C

Caesar cipher, 178, 289
CancelError property, 617
Cancel property, 325
Caption property, 22, 25, 26t, 28t, 111t, 167–168, 231t, 235t, 388t, 571t
Cardinality, 381
Carriage return, 176
Case, 82, 86, 172, 174, 189
Case Else, 246, 247, 250
Case sensitivity, 174
Cell, grid, 412
CellAlignment property, 414t
Change event, 182
Check box control, 23t, 238–240, 389

Checked property, 571t
Choices. *See* Decision-making process
Chr$() function, 174–178
CInt() function, 163
Ciphertext, 178, 289–293
Class Builder, 526
Class hierarchies, 525–526
Class initialization methods, 515
Class modules, 20–21, 42, 510–511
Class termination method, 515
Classes, 508–530
Clear method, 360
Click event, 22, 198
Close method, 394t
Codd, Edgar F., 385n
Code, 61
    hand-checking of, 287–289
    for loop body, 336–337
    pseudo-, 216–217
    reusable, 268, 310
Code modules, 42, 125, 268, 309–310. *See also* Forms
    in project structure, 20–21, 129, 280–281
Code package, xv, 94
Code sharing. *See* Data sharing; Reusable code
Code windows, 39–40
    for forms, 113–114
    for general sub procedures and general declarations section, 276–277
Col property, 413, 414t
ColAlignment() property, 414t
Collating sequence, 188
Collection object, 526–530
Colors, 237–238
Cols property, 413, 415t
Column totals, 471–472
ColWidth() property, 415t
Combo box control, 23t, 367–369, 389
Command button control, 23t, 24–26, 59–60
Command button tool, 8
Comments, 161–162
Common dialog control, 23t
Comparison, in sorting, 468
Comparison operators, 187–192, 402
Compile errors, 555
Complexity, reduction of, 267–268
Compound key, 382

Compound statements, 215–216
Compound variable, 497
Concatenation operator, 100, 169–170
Conditions, 212–213, 241
    SQL Select query and, 406, 407
Conjunction, 193t
Constant (Const) definition statement, 82. *See also* Public Const statement
Constant scope, 133
Constants, 80. *See also* Literal constants; Symbolic constants
Construction process, 13, 18–19. *See also* Projects
Container control, 110. *See also* Form control; Forms
Control arrays, 474–479
Control class, user, 531–532
Control instances, 531
Control.method, 117
Control.property, 102–103, 117, 126–127
Controls, 17, 21–24, 35–36. *See also specific controls*
    color of, 237–238
    copying of, 136–137
    form modality and, 317
    naming of, 59–62
Copy buffer, 399
Copying, 52, 136–137. *See also* Saving of projects
Correlation tables, 384–385
Counter, loop, 345–346, 350, 353–354
Country format, 80n
CTRL+BREAK keys, 333
Currency data type, 87
Current record, 387–388
Current Tab property, 624–625
Cursor, 180
Custom controls, 36
Custom functions. *See* Programmer-defined functions
Customization, 4–5
Cyclic sequences, 161–162

D

Data, 77. *See also* Constants; Variables
Data access controls, 23t
Data-Bound Combo (DBCombo) control, 389
Data-Bound Grid (DBGrid) control, 389

Data-Bound List box (DBList) control, 389
Data control, 23t, 387–405
Data lists. *See* Arrays
Data redundancy, 103–104, 379, 385
Data sharing, 283–285. *See also* Parameter passing; Reusable code
Data types, 78–79, 86–89, 189
    programmer-defined, 495–507
    type mismatch and, 101–102, 154, 190
Database management system (DBMS), 5, 380
DatabaseName property, 388t, 393
Databases, 5, 448–449. *See also* Data control; File processing; Microsoft Access
    entities in, 379, 380–381
    normalized, 385–386
    queries to, 386–387
    relational, 382–385
    relationships in, 379, 380–381, 384
DataMode property, 425
DataSource property, 425
DBCombo control, 23t
DBGrid control, 23t, 420, 423–427
DblClick event, 358, 361–362
DBlist control, 23t
DBMS (database management system), 5, 380
Debugging, 20, 165, 555–569
Decision-making process, 212–213, 247
Decision tree, 241–242
Declarations section, general, 21, 108, 121
Decryption, 364
Default property, 325
Default settings, 35
DefColWidth property, 425
Delete method, 394t, 399–400
Delete warning, 400
Descendants, 525
Description pane, 38
Deselection, 238
Design choices, 55–62
Design mode, 19, 533, 559
Design stage, 13. *See also* Projects
Design time, 20
Design-time instance, 533
Development procedure, 12–13. *See also* Projects
Dialog box, 152

Dim statement, 89–92, 450, 451. *See also* Public statement
Dimensionality, 449
Directory list box control, 23t
Disjunction, 193t
Division, integer, 160–162
Do…Loop structure, 331, 332–344, 347–349, 354–356
Do…Loop Until structure, 339–342
Do…Loop While structure, 338–339
Do Until…Loop structure, 339–342
Do While…Loop structure, 334–338, 354–356
Docked tools, 30–34
Dollar sign, 170
Double data type, 87–88
Double-quotes, 47
DownPicture property, 231t
Drive list box control, 23t
Dummy variables, 86
Dynamic arrays, 472–474

E

e (Euler's number), 163
Edit method, 394t
Elements, array, 446
Else. *See* If…Then…Else statement
ElseIf, 223–224
Embedded If statements, 222–227, 251
Embedded loops, 354–357
Enabled property, 25, 26t, 29t, 181t, 235t, 571t, 580t, 582t
Encryption, 177–178, 289–293, 349
End button, 41
End expression in For…Next, 345, 352–353
End If, 213–214
End Of File (EOF), 393
End statement, 50
Engineering application, 4
[ENTER] key, 153, 313–314, 476–477
Entities, in databases, 379, 381–382
Entity-relationship diagram (ERD), 381, 406
Environment, VB. *See* Visual Basic
EOF (End Of File), 393
Equal to operator, 188t
Equality comparison operator, 189
Eqv operator, 192
ERD (entity-relationship diagram), 381, 406

Error handling, 557, 609–622
Errors. *See also specific errors*
 arithmetic, 164–168
 correction of, 59, 60–62
 design vs. run time and, 20
 in For…Next loop structure, 352–354
 in parameter passing, 301–304
 SQL, 409–411
[ESC] key, 153
Euler's number (e), 163
Evaluation, of expressions, 148
Event-driven programs, 45–51
Event procedures, 21, 22–23, 46–47
 code and, 39–40
 compared to general sub procedures, 271, 304
 scope of, 277
Events, 22. *See also specific events*
Exchange, in sorting, 468
Executable files, 19, 51n
Exit Do statement, 354
Exit For statement, 354
Exit Function statement, 307
Exit Sub statement, 251–254
Exiting the loop, 334
Exp() function, 163
Expert system, 240–245
Exponentiation, 158, 163
Expressions, 92, 145–151, 300. *See also specific types of expressions*

F

Fields, 382, 384, 385, 401
 SQL and, 406, 410, 411
File extensions, 52
File list box control, 23t
File processing, 590–608
Files
 adding of, 138–139
 names of, 53
 organization of, 52
Files, data
 flat, 590
 fixed-length fields, 598
 delimited fields, 602
Find methods, 401–405
Fix() function, 163
Fixed-length string variables, 90
Fixed-width fonts, 363
FixedAlignment() property, 415t
FixedCols property, 415t
FixedRows property, 415t
Flag variable, 470
FlexGrid control, 23t, 389, 412–424

Floating-point data types, 88, 165
Focus, 180, 315–316
Font property, 25, 26t, 28t
Fonts, width of, 363
For…Next loop structure, 332, 344–354
 nested loops in, 356–357
Foreign key, 384
Form control, 23t, 110–114
Form Designer window, 34–35
Form file, 53
Form Layout window, 42
Form modality, 268
Form window, 34–35
Format characters, 171
Format specification, 171
Format$() function, 171
Formatting, 79
Forms, 8. *See also* Code modules
 active, 111–112
 adding of, 138–139
 code windows for, 113–114
 communication between, 114–119
 copying of, 138
 list of, 42
 modality of, 317–319
 multiple, 114–119, 278–279
 names of, 115
 printing images of, 55
 in project structure, 20–21
 resizing of, 34
 saving of, 138
 sequence of, 319
 startup, 115
Frame control, 23t, 234–238
Full Module View button, 39
Functionality, 13
Functions, 146, 148–149. *See also specific functions*
 arithmetic, 162–164
 logical, 195–196
 programmer-defined, 268, 305–309
 string, 170–179
FV() function, 376

G

Game application, 4
General declarations section, 21, 108, 121
General object, 277
General sub procedures, 267–268, 269–283
 compared to event procedures, 271, 304

General sub procedures, *continued*
  compared to programmer-defined functions, 306, 308–309
  generic, 285
  in project structure, 21, 276–282
Generic procedures, 285
Global scope, 127–129, 133
Global variables, 124–130
  drawbacks of, 284, 288
  lifetime of, 131–132
GotFocus event, 268, 315–316
Graphical objects, 509, 531–546
Graphical user interface (GUI), 5–7, 13, 24
  choices designed into, 227–240
  for loops and List box and Combo box controls, 357–369
Greater than operator, 188t
Greater than or equal to operator, 188t
GridLines property, 415t
Grids. *See* DBGrid control; FlexGrid control
GUI. *See* Graphical user interface

H

Hand-checking, 287–289
Heading, of event procedures, 46–47
Help, online, 43–44
Hierarchy, in project structure, 20–23
Hypertext links, 27

I

I/O (Input/Output), 591
Icon Library, 25n
If...Then statement, 219–220
If...Then...Else statement, 211, 212, 213–222
  embedded If statements and, 222–227, 251
IIf() function, 195–196
Image control, 23t, 389, 579–580
Immediate If function, 195–196
Imp operator, 192
Implementation, user control class, 532
Increment expression, in loops, 345–346, 350, 352–353
Index property, 474, 478
Indexes, for database tables, 399

Infinite loops, 333
Inheritance, 525, 526
Inhouse development, 3
Initial values, 48
Initializations, 112
  in Do...Loop structure, 342–344
  in For...Next loop structure, 352–353
Input controls, 23t
InputBox() function, 152–156
Insertion point, 180
Installation, of Visual Basic, 25n
Instance variables, 509, 511–512, 513
Instantiated object, 509
InStr() function, 173–174
Int() function, 163
Integer data type, 87
Integer division operator, 160–162
Integrate controls, 23t
Interface, 532. *See also* Graphical user interface
Intersection tables, 384–385
Interval property, 29, 203
Inventory replenishment, 254–260
Invoice application, 55–62
Invoking, of procedures, 271
IsNumeric() function, 195
Iteration, of a loop, 335, 345

K

Key field, 382, 384, 385
KeyAscii parameter, 311–312
KeyPress event, 268, 310–314, 476–477
Keys, for accessing collections, 529–530
Keywords, 82

L

Label control, 23t, 26–27, 389–392
Label tool, 8
LCase$() function, 172
Left$() function, 172
Len() function, 173
Less than operator, 187, 188t
Less than or equal to operator, 188t
Library, of code modules, 310
Lifetime, of variables, 130–133
Like operator, 404–405
Line-continuation character, 146n, 155
Line control, 23t, 137
Line feed, 176

Linear search, 461
List box control, 23t, 357–367, 389
List property, 359t
ListCount property, 359t
ListIndex property, 359t
Literal constants, 80–81, 84
Load event, 112
LoadPicture() function, 582
Load statement, 478
Local scope, 119, 127–129, 133
Local variables, 119–121, 123–124
  in general sub procedures, 272–276
  lifetime of, 130–131
  parameter passing and, 288
Log() function, 163
Logic errors, 557
Logical expressions, 145–146, 187–196, 218–219
Logical functions, 195–196
Logical operators, 187, 192–195
Long data type, 87
Loop body, coding of, 336–337
Loop counter, 345–346, 350, 353–354
Loop structure, 331–332. *See also* Do...Loop structure; For...Next loop structure
  FlexGrid control and, 416–419
  list boxes and, 363–364
  nested loops in, 354–357
LostFocus event, 268, 315–316
LTrim$() function, 172

M

Machine language, 19n
Many-to-many relationships, 384–385
Margin Indicator bar, 40
Matrix, 449
Maximum value, 458–460
MaxLength property, 181t
MDI (Multiple Document Interface), 35n
Mellor, Stephen J., 384n
Memory, and forms, 112
Menu bar, 34
Menu control, 23t, 25n, 570–578
Message box. *See* MsgBox statement; MsgBox() function
Meta statements, 215–216, 267
Methods, 21, 117, 509, 512–521. *See also specific methods*
Microsoft Access, 380, 405, 429, 586–589

Microsoft Data Bound Grid Control (DBGrid), 424
Microsoft FlexGrid Control 5.0, 412
Mid$() function, 172
Minimum value, 458
Missing spaces error, 409
Mod operator, 160–162
Modal forms, 317–319
Modeless forms, 317–319
Module-level scope, 121, 127–129, 133
Module-level variables, 121–124
 drawbacks of, 284, 288
 lifetime of, 131–132
Modules. *See* Code modules
MouseMove event, 22, 25, 26
MousePointer property, 231t, 235t
Move methods, 393–401
MsgBox statement, 152, 156–158
MsgBox() function, 227–229
MSVBVM50.DLL file, 51
Multidimensional arrays, 446, 449–450
MultiLine property, 181t
Multiple Document Interface (MDI), 35n
MultiSelect property, 359t, 364–366

N

Name property, 25, 26t, 28t, 29t, 111t, 580t, 582t
Names
 of arrays, 450
 of controls, 59–62, 118–119, 126–127, 235, 239
 of event procedures, 46–47
 of files, 53
 of forms, 115
 of general sub procedures, 267, 283
 of local variables, 303–304
 manipulation of people's names, 174
 in parameter list, 289
 of parameters, 303–304
 of procedures, 279
 for SQL Select query, 406–407, 411
 of symbolic constants, 81–82
 of variables, 85–86, 107–108
Navigating, 388
Negation, 159, 193t. *See also* Not operator
Nested If statements, 222–227, 251
Nested loops, 354–357
Next. *See* For...Next loop structure
NoMatch property, 401–402
Nonprintable characters, 176
Normalization, 385
Normalized databases, 385–386
Not equal to operator, 188t
Not operator, 192–195. *See also* Negation
Numeric data, 78–79, 86–88, 167–168, 171
Numeric variables, 86–88, 94–96

O

Object box, 36–37, 39
Object-oriented programming, 508–530
Object variable, 517
Objects, 508–530
Off-the-shelf programs, 2
One-dimensional arrays, 446
One-to-many relationships, 384
Online help, 43–44
Operating system, 2
Operator precedence rule, 159
Operators, 146, 148, 159–160. *See also specific operators*
Option button control, 23t, 229–233
Option Explicit statement, 108–110
Or operator, 192–195
Oracle, 380
Order
 alphabetical, 188
 of arguments, 302–303
 of operators, 159–160
 of records, 423
 sorting and, 467–471
 of statements within a loop, 337
Order By clause, 423
Order processing, 5–8, 63–68, 480–488, 636–640
Ordered array, 461
Organize controls, 23t
Orientation property, 625
Output controls, 23t
Outsourcing, 3
Overflow, 164
Overflow errors, 164–165
Overwritten value, 97

P

Padding, 363
Parameter list, 285–286, 289–290
Parameter passing, 268, 283, 285–289, 297–304
Parentheses, 160
Pass, in sorting, 468
Passing by reference, 297
Passing by value, 296–299
PasswordChar property, 324
Path, 53n, 396
Payment schedule, 369–371
Payroll applications, 4, 5, 133–139
Picture box control, 23t, 581–585
Picture property, 25, 26t, 231t, 580t, 582t
Plaintext, 178
Planning, 13
Pmt() function, 370–371
Pointer, file, 591
Pointer, record, 388, 393
Polymorphism, 528–529
Populating an array, 453–456
Pound symbol, 405
Precedence, of operators, 159–160
Precision, of standard data types, 87, 166
Predefined symbolic constants, 85
Printing, 51–52, 55
 to a picture box, 583
Private procedures, 277–279, 282
Problem solving, 216–218
Procedure calls, 271, 272–274, 286–287, 565–566. *See also* Parameter passing
Procedure View button, 39
Procedures. *See also* Event procedures; General sub procedures
 event vs. general sub, 271, 304
 private vs. public, 277–279, 282
 scope of, 277–278, 282
Procedures/Events box, 39
Processing scripts, 9–10, 13
Program, definition of, 2
Programmer-defined classes, 508–530
Programmer-defined data types, 495–507. *See also* ActiveX controls; Objects
Programmer-defined functions, 268, 305–309
Programmers, 3, 4–5
 comments by, 161–162
Programming environment, 7. *See also* Visual Basic (VB)
Programming language, 7, 9–11
Programming tools, 7–8, 30–34. *See also specific tools*
Project Explorer window, 42–43

Project files, 19, 52
Project group, 534
Projects, 17
    1: event-driven programming, 45–51
    2: design considerations, 55–62
    3: business simulation, 63–68
    4: multiple forms, 114–119
    5: payroll, 133–139
    6: present value calculator, 183–187
    7: stock trading simulation, 196–203
    8: expert system, 240–245
    9: inventory replenishment simulation, 254–260
    10: user authorization, 319–325
    11: monthly payment schedule, 369–371
    12: real estate listings database, 427–432
    13: order entry application prototype, 480–488
    14: student grade reporting, 504–507
    H.1: real estate application revisited, 632–636
    H.2: order entry application prototype revisited, 636–640
    modes in, 18–20
    saving of, 19, 51–55, 58
    structure of, 20–23, 129, 276–282
Prompt, in dialog box, 152
Properties, 21, 22, 38, 117. *See also* Scope; *and names of specific properties*
Properties window, 8, 36–38
Property Get, 513–515, 538–539
Property Let, 513–514, 538–539
Property list, 37–38
PropertyChanged, 539
Proportional fonts, 363
Pseudocode, 64, 216–217
Public Const statement, 133
Public procedures, 277–280, 282
Public statement, 124, 450. *See also* Dim statement

Q

Qualified control name, 118–119, 126–127
Queries, to databases, 386–387. *See also* Find methods; Structured query language

Question mark, 405
Quick Info box, 40, 300n
Quick Watch, 565
Quote marks, in strings, 81, 404

R

Random numbers, 163–164
Random processing, 591
Range, 87, 248–250
Rapaport, Matthew H., 385n
Real estate listings database, 427–432, 632–636
RecordCount property, 393t, 397
Records, 382, 387–388, 393–405
Recordset property, 388t, 393
Recordsets, 406, 408–409, 412, 419–423
RecordSource property, 388t, 393
ReDim Preserve statement, 473
ReDim statement, 473
Redundancy, 103–104, 379, 385
Reference, passing by, 297
Refresh method, 393
Refreshing the recordset, 408–409
Relational databases, 382–385. *See also* Structured query language
Relationships, between entities, 379, 381–382, 384
Remarks, comments for, 161–162
RemoveItem method, 358, 360
Repeat character function, 173
Repetition of tasks, 331–332
Reserved words, 82
Resizing, 31–33, 34
Resource files, 20–21, 42
RETURN key, 176
Return value, of a function, 149
Reusable code, 268, 310. *See also* Data sharing
Right$() function, 172
Rnd() function, 163–164
Roundoff, 165–166
Row property, 413, 415t
Row totals, 471–472
RowHeight() property, 415t
Rows property, 413, 415t
RTrim$() function, 172
Run mode, 19–20, 533, 559
Run time, 20
Run time errors, 102, 451, 556–557
Run time instance, 533

S

Save Form As, 138
Saving of projects, 19, 51–55, 58

Scientific notation, 81, 88
Scope, 77
    constant, 133
    procedure, 277–278, 282
    variable, 119–130
Scripts. *See* Event procedures; Processing scripts
Scroll bar control, 23t
ScrollBars property, 181t, 415t
SDI (Single Document Interface), 35
Search phrase, 44
Searching, 460–467
Select Case statement, 211, 212, 246–251
Select query, SQL, 405–411, 427
Selected property, 359t, 364–366
SelLength, SelStart, SelText properties, 208
Sequential processing, 591
Sequential search, 461–464
SetFocus method, 313–314
Setup program and icon library, 25n
Sgn() function, 162
Shape control, 23t, 235
Shape property, 235
Shells, expert system, 241
Shlaer, Sally, 384n
Shortcut property, 571t
ShowFont, 612t
Show method, 117, 318
ShowOpen, 612t
Shrink-wrap software, 2
Significant digits, 166–167
Simple variable, 444, 446
Single data type, 87–88
Single Document Interface (SDI), 35
Slash symbol, 161
SLN() function, 376
Sorted property, 359t
Sorting, 467–471
SQL Select query, 405–411, 427. *See also* Structured query language
Sqr() function, 149
SSTab control, 23t
Standard data types, 86–88, 189
Standard exchange sort, 468–471
Start button, 40–41
Start expression in For...Next, 345, 352–353
Startup form, 115
Statement block, 213, 215
Statement label, 614

Statements, 46. *See also specific statements*
    actions specified by, 147
    expressions in, 146, 151
    meta, 215–216, 267
Static statements, 450
Static variables, 132–133
Step amount, 350–352
Stepping, 566–569
Stock trading simulation, 196–203
Storage, and forms, 112
Str$() function, 171
Stretch property, 580t
String concatenation operator, 100, 169–170
String data, 78–79, 167–168, 171, 188–189
String expressions, 145, 169–179, 183–187
String functions, 170–179
String literal constants, 81
String operators, 169–170
String search operation, 173–174
String variables, 86, 90, 99–101
String$() function, 173
Structure, project, 20–23, 129, 276–282
Structured query language (SQL), 386, 405–411, 423, 427
Student grade reporting, 504–507
Style property, 25, 26t, 231t, 359t, 367, 625
Sub Main, 309, 310
Sub procedures, 46. *See also General sub procedures*
Subclasses, 525
Subscript, 446
Subscript bounds, 451
Subscript out of range error, 451
Subscripted variable, 446
Substrings, 172
Subtasks, 267. *See also General sub procedures*
Superclass, 525
SYD() function, 376
Symbolic constants, 80, 81–85, 133, 312
Synchronized control arrays, 477–478
Syntax, 92
Syntax errors, 555

T

Tab Count property, 624
TAB key, 180, 313
Tabbed Dialog control, 623–631

TabCaption property, 624–625
TabIndex property, 181t, 231t, 313
Table lookup, 456–458
Tables. *See also Recordsets*
    for arrays, 449, 455–458
    for databases, 382–386, 406–409, 455–456
TabsPerRow property, 624
TabStop property, 181t, 231t, 313
Target, search, 460
Templates, 509, 531
Termination, of a loop, 334, 337–338, 342–344
Testing, 13, 40–41
Testing at the extremes, 467
Text box control, 23t, 179–183, 389, 392
    KeyPress event for, 311–314
Text boxes, 316, 508
Text property, 180–182, 359t, 413, 415t
TextMatrix() property, 413, 415t
TextWidth() function, 417, 422
Then. *See If...Then...Else statement*
Third normal form, 385
Timer control, 23t, 27–29, 203
Timer event, 29
Title bar, 33
Toggle, 238
Toolbar, 8, 40–42
    creating using a picture box, 584
Toolbox, 8, 35–36
Tools, programming, 7–8, 30–34. *See also specific tools*
Trigger controls, 23t
Trim$() function, 172
Type mismatch, 101–102, 190
    InputBox() function and, 154
    IsNumeric() function and, 195
    in parameter passing, 301–302
Type statement, 496–498
Typographical errors, 103, 107–108

U

UCase$() function, 172
Unary operators, 148
Underscore symbol, 146n, 155
Undocked tools, 32–34
Unload statement, 479
Unordered array, 461
Until, in Do...Loop structure, 339–342
Update method, 394t, 399
User authorization, 319–325
User control class, 531–532

User-defined formats, 371
User requirements, 13
UserControl class, 533, 534–546
Users, 3, 13
    needs of, 12
    types of, 4–5
Utilities, 2

V

Val() function, 167–168, 171
Value, passing by, 296–299
Value property, 231t, 232
Values, 146
Variable declaration statement, 89. *See also Dim statement*
Variable-length string variables, 90
Variables, 85–110. *See also specific variable types*
    arrays as. *See Arrays*
    compared to control properties, 102
    lifetime of, 130–133
    scope of, 119–130
VB. *See Visual Basic*
vbCrLf constant, 176–177
vbKey constants, 322t
Visible property, 25, 26t, 28t, 478, 571t, 580t, 582t
Visual Basic (VB), 1, 7
    default settings in, 35
    environment of, 29–44
    layout of, 29–34
    modes of, 18–20, 559–560
    projects for. *See Projects*
    setup program of icon library, 25n
    starting, 29–34
    strengths of, 10–11
    tools in, 34–44

W

Watch expressions, 563–565
While, in Do...Loop structure, 334–339
Wild card characters, 404–405
Windows. *See names of specific windows*
WindowState property, 111t
Word processing application, 4

X

Xor operator, 192

Z

Zero-length string, 47, 84

CD-ROM at Back Cover